April 9–13, 2018
Berlin, Germany

**Association for
Computing Machinery**

Advancing Computing as a Science & Profession

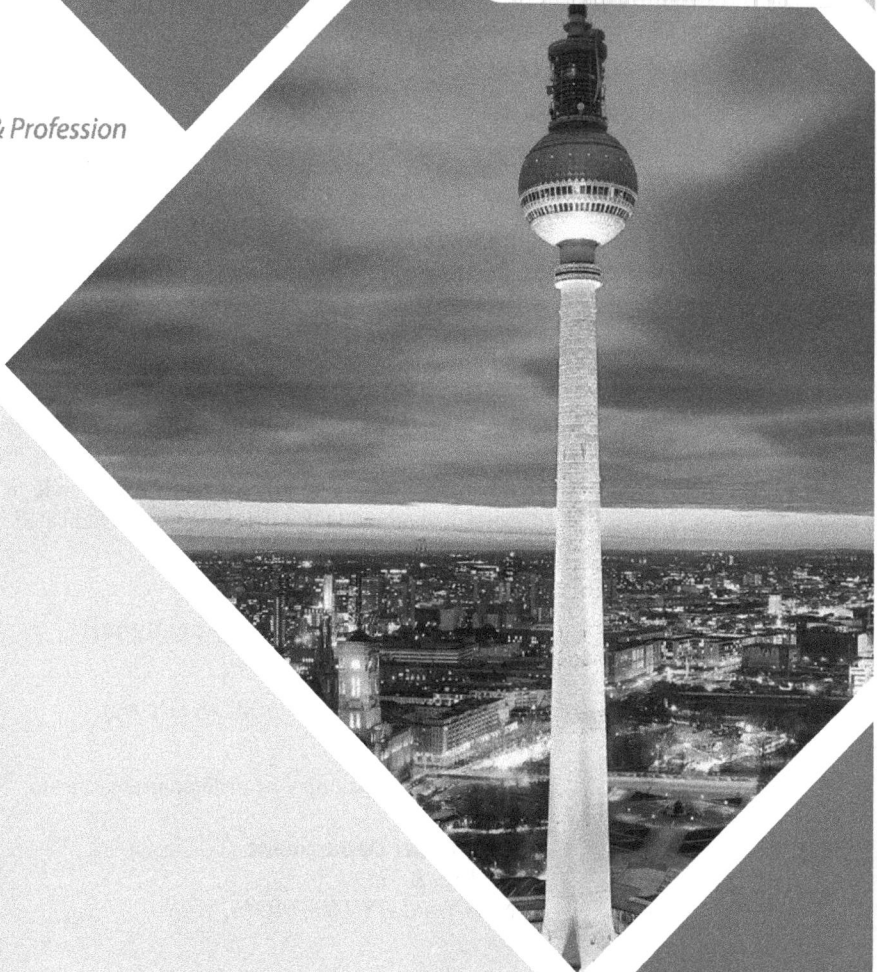

ICPE '18

Proceedings of the 2018 ACM/SPEC International Conference on
Performance Engineering

Sponsored by:
ACM SIGMETRICS, ACM SIGSOFT & SPEC
Supported by:
**Deutsche Forschungsgemeinschaft (DFG), NovaTec
& Freie Universität zu Berlin**

Association for
Computing Machinery

Advancing Computing as a Science & Profession

The Association for Computing Machinery
2 Penn Plaza, Suite 701
New York, New York 10121-0701

ISBN: 978-1-4503-5095-2 (Digital)

ISBN: 978-1-4503-5882-8 (Print)

Additional copies may be ordered prepaid from:

ACM Order Department
PO Box 30777
New York, NY 10087-0777, USA

Phone: 1-800-342-6626 (USA and Canada)
+1-212-626-0500 (Global)
Fax: +1-212-944-1318
E-mail: acmhelp@acm.org
Hours of Operation: 8:30 am – 4:30 pm ET

Printed in the USA.

ICPE 2018 General Chairs' Welcome

We are delighted to welcome you to the *9th ACM/SPEC International Conference on Performance Engineering – ICPE 2018*, which is being held in Berlin, Germany from 9-13 April 2018. ICPE was born in 2010 out of the merger of the ACM Workshop on Software Performance (WOSP) and the SPEC International Performance Engineering Workshop (SIPEW), and has grown in strength ever since. It is now established as one of the premier forums for the integration of the theory and practice of performance engineering, with a reputation for attracting high-quality contributions and bringing together researchers and practitioners from both academia and industry.

As we celebrate 20 years since the founding of WOSP and 10 years since the founding of SIPEW, this year's conference reflects the nature of performance engineering as a forward-looking discipline that supports the rapid evolution of computer science and its related disciplines. Topics covered include advanced profiling, modelling and optimisation techniques, and energy-aware resource management strategies for complex multicore IT systems. Application domains include traditional areas such as HPC, cloud and other virtualized environments, and emerging areas such as big data analytics, deep learning, IoT, microservices and blockchains. We hope you will enjoy the depth and diversity of the technical program as well as the social events, especially the conference banquet in the atmospheric environs of the Spiegelsaal in the Clärchens Balhaus.

A conference on the scale of ICPE can only be realised through the dedicated efforts of a large team. We would like to begin by thanking the Research Program Committee, led by program co-chairs André van Hoorn and Manoj Nambiar, for putting together an exciting research track. Likewise, thank you to the Industrial Program Committee, led by Heiko Koziolek, for selecting a range of high-quality industrial research papers. The conference program is enriched by a number of other activities. New for this year is the Artifact Evaluation track, which has been overseen with great skill by Wilhelm Hasselbring and Petr Tuma. The workshop chairs, Eva Kalyvianaki, and Yao-Min Chen, have done great work in putting together a stimulating mix of six workshops for participants to enjoy. These are accompanied by three high-quality tutorials, courtesy of the fine efforts of Tutorial Co-chairs Alma Dimnaku (Riska), and Andrea Marin, as well as a range of exciting posters and demos, expertly curated by Poster and Demos Chair Marco Paolieri. We were delighted to attract three first-class keynote speakers: Peter Braam, Michael Lyu and Aad van Moorsel.

Many others have made invaluable contributions. Lydia Chen and John Murphy have excelled in their sroles as Awards Chairs. Matt Forshaw has kept a watchful eye on the conference budgets in his role as Finance Chair. Proceedings Chair Vladimir Stankovic has masterfully coordinated the conference proceedings. Publicity Chairs Juan Perez and Huaming Wu have been tireless in their promotion of the conference across a broad range of channels, while Website Chair Thomas Düllmann has done a great job in creating and updating the conference website. Registration Chair Zhihao Shang and his team are to thank for the smooth processing of conference participants.

Our sincere thanks go to SPEC and ACM (especially SIGMETRICS and SIGSOFT) for their continuous support throughout. Finally, we are grateful for the generosity of our other sponsors, which include the Deutsche Forschungsgemeinschaft (DFG), the Einstein Foundation and NovaTec.

Katinka Wolter
ICPE 2018 General Co-Chair
Freie Universität zu Berlin, Germany

William Knottenbelt
ICPE 2018 General Co-Chair
Imperial College London, UK

ICPE 2018 Program Chairs' Welcome

It is our great pleasure to welcome you to the 9th ACM/SPEC International Conference on Performance Engineering (ICPE 2018), being held in Berlin, Germany from April 9 to 13, 2018. The goal of the ACM/SPEC International Conference on Performance Engineering (ICPE) is to integrate theory and practice in the field of performance engineering by providing a forum for sharing ideas and experiences between industry and academia.

The call for contributions solicited submissions for several tracks, namely for research papers, industry/experience papers, work-in-progress/vision papers, artifacts (for accepted full papers), posters and demonstrations, tutorials, and workshops.

In the research track, 14 out of 59 papers were accepted as full papers. Hence, the full paper acceptance rate is 24 %. Two full papers received an ACM artifact badge after the subsequent review process in the newly introduced artifact evaluation track. Seven submissions were accepted as short research papers. In the industry/experience track, four out of 16 papers were accepted as full papers. Six submissions were accepted as short papers. The awards chairs selected three papers from the research track and two papers from the industry/experience track as candidates for the best paper award. The winner for both tracks will be announced during the banquet, after the candidates have presented their work during the conference. In the work-in-progress/vision track, ten out of 23 papers were accepted.

The technical program features the following three invited keynotes:

- Peter Braam: Performance Engineering for the SKA Telescope

- Michael R. Lyu: AI Techniques in Software Engineering Paradigm

- Aad van Moorsel: Benchmarks and Models for Blockchain

In addition, the technical program includes three tutorials, the presentation of the SPEC Distinguished Dissertation Award, a poster and demonstration session, as well as six workshops on Performance Analysis of Big data Systems (PABS), Hot Topics in Cloud Computing Performance (HotCloudPerf), Challenges in Performance Methods for Software Development (WOSP-C), Load Testing and Benchmarking of Software Systems (LTB), Energy-aware Simulation and Modelling (ENERGY-SIM), and Quality-Aware DevOps (QUDOS).

The program covers traditional ICPE topics such as performance modeling, prediction, optimization, monitoring, profiling, load testing, benchmarking, and runtime adaptation for fields such as cloud and high performance computing, big data, energy, and enterprise applications.

We thank all authors who submitted their innovative work to ICPE this year. In addition, we thank all members of the research and industry/experience program committees, the chairs and reviewers of the artifact evaluation track, and the co-chairs and co-organizers of the several tracks and co-located events for volunteering their time for the benefit of the ICPE community and their hard work in setting up an exciting program for ICPE 2018. Finally, we thank all participants of ICPE, as we rely on you to make this event interactive, engaging, and thought-provoking for everyone involved.

André van Hoorn
Technical Program Chair
Univ. of Stuttgart, Germany

Manoj Nambiar
Technical Program Chair
Tata Consultancy Services, India

Heiko Koziolek
Industry Program Chair
ABB, Germany

Table of Contents

Cloud Computing

Enterprise Applications

Modeling, Prediction, and Optimization

Load Testing and Benchmarking

ICPE 2018 Conference Organization

General Chairs:	Katinka Wolter *(Free University of Berlin, Germany)*
	Will Knottenbelt *(Imperial College London, UK)*
Program Chairs:	André van Hoorn *(University of Stuttgart, Germany)*
	Manoj Nambiar *(Tata Consultancy Services, India)*
Industry Program Chair:	Heiko Koziolek *(ABB, Germany)*
Artifact Evaluation Chairs:	Wilhelm Hasselbring *(Kiel University, Germany)*
	Petr Tuma *(Charles University, Czech Republic)*
Workshop Chairs:	Eva Kalyvianaki *(University of Cambridge, UK)*
	Yao-Min Chen *(Oracle, USA)*
Tutorials Chairs:	Alma Dimnaku (Riska) *(Network Appliances, USA)*
	Andrea Marin *(University of Venice, Italy)*
Posters and Demos Chair:	Marco Paolieri *(University of Southern California, USA)*
Awards Chairs:	Lydia Chen *(IBM Zurich, Switzerland)*
	John Murphy *(University College Dublin, Ireland)*
Finance Chair:	Matt Forshaw *(Newcastle University, UK)*
Proceedings Chair:	Vladimir Stankovic *(City, University of London, UK)*
Publicity Chairs:	Juan F. Perez *(Universidad del Rosario, Colombia)*
	Huaming Wu *(Tianjin University, China)*
Website Chair:	Thomas F. Düllmann *(University of Stuttgart, Germany)*
Registrations Chair:	Zhihao Shang *(Free University of Berlin, Germany)*
Steering Committee:	Andre B. Bondi, Co-Chair *(Software Performance and Scalability Consulting LLC, USA)*
	Samuel Kounev, Co-Chair *(University of Würzburg, Germany)*
	Meikel Poess, Secretary *(Oracle Corporation, USA)*
	J. Nelson Amaral *(University of Alberta, Canada)*
	Vittorio Cortellessa *(University of L'Acquila, Italy)*
	Klaus-Dieter Lange *(Hewlett-Packard Enterprise, USA)*
	Catalina M. Lladó *(Universitat de les Illes Balears, Spain)*
	Raffaela Mirandola *(Politecnico di Milano, Italy)*
	Jerry Rolia *(Amazon, UK)*
	Alexandru Iosup *(Delft University of Technology, the Netherlands)*
	Bran Selic *(Malina Software Corp., Canada)*

Steering Committee (continued):	Petr Tůma *(Charles University, Czech Republic)*
	Murray Woodside *(Carleton University, Canada)*
Program Committee	J. Nelson Amaral *(University of Alberta, Canada)*
(Research Track, and	Varsha Apte *(IIT Bombay, India)*
Work-in-Progress & Vision Track):	Alberto Avritzer *(independent, USA)*
	Steffen Becker *(University of Stuttgart, Germany)*
	Umesh Bellur *(IIT Bombay, India)*
	Cor-Paul Bezemer *(Queen's University, Canada)*
	Andre B. Bondi *(Software Performance and Scalability Consulting LLC, USA)*
	Giuliano Casale *(Imperial College London, UK)*
	Lucy Cherkasova *(HyTrust, USA)*
	Vittorio Cortellessa *(Universita' dell'Aquila, Italy)*
	Vittoria de Nitto Personè *(Università di Roma Tor Vergata, Italy)*
	Tadashi Dohi *(Hiroshima University, Japan)*
	Wilhelm Hasselbring *(Kiel University, Germany)*
	Evangelia Kalyvianaki *(University of Cambridge, UK)*
	Samuel Kounev *(University of Wuerzburg, Germany)*
	Anne Koziolek *(Karlsruhe Institute of Technology Germany)*
	Patrick Lee *(The Chinese University of Hong Kong, Hong Kong)*
	Marin Litoiu *(York University, Canada)*
	Catalina M. Lladó *(Universitat Illes Balears, Spain)*
	Philipp Leitner *(University of Zurich, Switzerland)*
	Paulo R. M. Maciel *(Federal University of Pernambuco, Brazil)*
	Martina Maggio *(Lund University, Sweden)*
	Andrea Marin *(University of Venice, Italy)*
	Daniel Menasce *(George Mason University, USA)*
	José Merseguer *(Universidad de Zaragoza, Spain)*
	Ningfang Mi *(Northeastern University, USA)*
	Raffaela Mirandola *(Politecnico di Milano, Italy)*
	Juan F. Perez *(Universidad del Rosario, Colombia)*
	Dorina Petriu *(Carleton University, Canada)*
	Alma Riska *(Network Appliances, USA)*
	Evgenia Smirni *(College of William and Mary, USA)*
	Nigel Thomas *(Newcastle University, UK)*
	Mirco Tribastone *(IMT Institute for Advanced Studies, Italy)*
	Catia Trubiani *(Gran Sasso Science Institute, Italy)*
	Petr Tuma *(Charles University, Czech Republic)*
	Ana Lucia Varbanescu *(University of Amsterdam, the Netherlands)*
	Enrico Vicario *(University of Florence, Italy)*
	Murray Woodside *(Carleton University, Canada)*
	Huaming Wu *(Tianjin University, China)*
	Feng Yan *(University of Nevada-Reno, USA)*
	Xiaoyun Zhu *(Futurewei Technologies Inc., USA)*

ICPE 2018 Sponsors & Supporters

Sponsors:

Supporters:

Institutional supporters:

Performance Engineering for the SKA Telescope

Dr. Peter J. Braam

Peter.braam@peterbraam.org

ABSTRACT

The SKA radio telescope will be a massive world class scientific instrument, currently under design by a worldwide consortium, to progress to full operation in South Africa and Australia in the mid 2020's. The capabilities of the telescope are expected to enable major scientific breakthroughs. At the center of its data processing sits the Science Data Processor, a large HPC system with specialized software. In this lecture we will give a high level overview of the project and progress to the computing and data related architecture. Then we will discuss the work of the SDP design consortium to understand and achieve the many performance requirements leveraging hardware and algorithms. Among these is a requirement for memory bandwidth exceeding 100 PB/sec.

BIO

Peter Braam is a scientist and entrepreneur focused on large scale computing. After obtaining a PhD in mathematics under Michael Atiyah at Oxford, he was an academic at several universities including Oxford, CMU and Cambridge. Peter created the Lustre file system, which has become a key product for large scale HPC. From 2013, Peter has been contributing to architecture for data processing in the SKA telescope, and is researching and designing other solutions for data intensive computing.

AI Techniques in Software Engineering Paradigm

Michael R. Lyu
Department of Computer Science and Engineering,
The Chinese University of Hong Kong
Hong Kong
lyu@cse.cuhk.edu.hk

ABSTRACT

In the next decade, Artificial Intelligent (AI) techniques can see wide adoption in our daily life to release human burden. In our recent Software Engineering research, we investigated on the design of novel AI methods to facilitate all three major phases in software engineering: development, operation, and analysis. In this talk, I will first introduce the AI techniques we employed, including machine learning framework, classification, clustering, matrix factorization, topic modeling, deep learning, and parallel computing platform. Then I will explain the challenges in each phase and describe our recently proposed methodologies. First in development phase, we suggested an automated code completion technique via deep learning. Our technique learns the code style from lots of existing code bases, and recommends the most suitable token based on the trained deep learning model and current coding context. Besides, to help developers in conducting effective logging, we designed a tool named LogAdvisor, which tells developers whether they should write a logging statement in the current code block or not. Secondly, in operation phase, we implemented a continuous and passive authentication method for mobile phones based on user touch biometrics. Different from the traditional password authentication scheme, our method can recognize malicious attackers based on abnormal user behaviors. Moreover, we developed PAID, which automatically prioritizes app issues by mining user reviews. Finally, in analysis phase, we designed systematic data analytics techniques for software reliability prediction. Besides, to make full use of the crucial runtime information, we proposed effective methods for every step in log analysis, including log parsing, feature extraction, and log mining. Furthermore, we developed a CNN-based defect prediction method to help developers find the buggy code. In the end, we expect to establish a comprehensive framework for systematic employment of AI techniques in the Software Engineering paradigm.

CCS CONCEPTS

• **Software and its engineering**;

KEYWORDS

Artificial intelligence, software engineering

ICPE '18, April 9–13, 2018, Berlin, Germany
© 2018 Copyright held by the owner/author(s).
ACM ISBN 978-1-4503-5095-2/18/04.
https://doi.org/10.1145/3184407.3184440

ACM Reference Format:
Michael R. Lyu. 2018. AI Techniques in Software Engineering Paradigm. In *ICPE '18: ACM/SPEC International Conference on Performance Engineering, April 9–13, 2018, Berlin, Germany.* ACM, New York, NY, USA, 1 page. https://doi.org/10.1145/3184407.3184440

BIO

Michael Rung-Tsong Lyu is a Professor and Chairman of Computer Science and Engineering Department at The Chinese University of Hong Kong. He worked at the Jet Propulsion Laboratory, the University of Iowa, Bellcore, and Bell Laboratories. His research interests include software reliability engineering, distributed systems, fault-tolerant computing, service computing, multimedia information retrieval, and machine learning. He has published 500 refereed journal and conference papers in these areas, which recorded 26,500 Google Scholar citations and h-index of 79. He served as an Associate Editor of IEEE Transactions on Reliability, IEEE Transactions on Knowledge and Data Engineering, and Journal of Information Science and Engineering. He is currently on the editorial boards of IEEE Transactions on Service Computing and Software Testing, Verification and Reliability Journal. He was elected to IEEE Fellow (2004), AAAS Fellow (2007), Croucher Senior Research Fellow (2008), IEEE Reliability Society Engineer of the Year (2010), and ACM Fellow (2015). Prof. Lyu received his B.Sc. from National Taiwan University, his M.Sc. from University of California, Santa Barbara, and his Ph.D. in Computer Science from University of California, Los Angeles.

Benchmarks and Models for Blockchain

Aad van Moorsel
School of Computing
Newcastle University, UK
aad.vanmoorsel@newcastle.ac.uk

ABSTRACT

Blockchain is a highly popular paradigm for non-centralized applications, especially in finance and trade. Performance is a major challenge for blockchains, since consensus approaches are known not to scale. In this presentation we address blockchain performance, from the perspective of model-based prediction as well as benchmark-based assessment. We present research results about smart contracts in the Ethereum blockchain and discuss the requirements for generic benchmarks for blockchain performance.

Benchmarking is a common approach to compare industry-class systems. As blockchain technologies mature, the role of reliable benchmarks will become increasingly important. However, definitions of benchmarks for blockchains are still in their infancy. We argue that there is a clear need for benchmarks, and that benchmarks should be based on the sound scientific principles of metrology [1]. A variety of important performance issues should be addressed, including the performance of the proof (be it work, stake, or other), transaction processing and block creation. Moreover, in all these situations, establishing energy consumption benchmarks is critical in determining if incentives are in place for miners to operate the blockchain system.

A particularly interesting element in some blockchains is the mechanism of smart contracts. For instance, in Ethereum, the fees associated with executing contracts depend on the benchmarked performance of the operation code. In [2] it was demonstrated that uncertainty with respect to the correctness of the anticipated execution time impacts the decisions miners will take. We will discuss improved benchmarking approaches for operational code.

Acknowledgements.

Thanks to Amjad Aldweesh and Maher Alharby, on whose research the ICPE conference keynote is based.

CCS Concepts/ACM Classifiers

• General and reference ~ Measurement • General and reference ~ Performance

Author Keywords

Blockchain; benchmark; performance; performance modeling

BIOGRAPHY

Aad van Moorsel is a Professor at the School of Computing in Newcastle University and was its Head of School from 2012-2017. He worked in industry from 1996 until 2003, first as a researcher at Bell Labs/Lucent Technologies in Murray Hill and then as a research manager at Hewlett-Packard Labs in Palo Alto, both in the United States. He got his PhD in computer science from Universiteit Twente in The Netherlands and has a Masters in mathematics from Universiteit Leiden, also in The Netherlands. After finishing his PhD he was a postdoc at the University of Illinois at Urbana-Champaign, Illinois, USA, for two years. He is the author of over 100 peer-reviewed research papers, and holds three US patents. His research group at Newcastle University conducts research in security, privacy and trust, with applications in payment, blockchain and smart systems. The group's research all contains elements of quantification, be it through system measurement, predictive modelling or on-line adaptation.

REFERENCES

[1] A. Bondavalli, A. Ceccarelli, L. Falai and M. Vadursi, Foundations of Metrology in the Observation of Critical Systems, Chapter 10 in *Resilience Assessment and Evaluation of Computing Systems*, Springer Verlag, 2012.

[2] M. Alharby and A. van Moorsel, The Impact of Profit Uncertainty on Miner Decisions in Blockchain Systems, *UK Performance Engineering Workshop, 2018*

FOX: Cost-Awareness for Autonomic Resource Management in Public Clouds

Veronika Lesch
University of Würzburg
Würzburg, Germany
veronika.lesch@uni-wuerzburg.de

André Bauer
University of Würzburg
Würzburg, Germany
andre.bauer@uni-wuerzburg.de

Nikolas Herbst
University of Würzburg
Würzburg, Germany
nikolas.herbst@uni-wuerzburg.de

Samuel Kounev
University of Würzburg
Würzburg, Germany
samuel.kounev@uni-wuerzburg.de

ABSTRACT

Nowadays, to keep track with the fast changing requirements of internet applications, auto-scaling is an essential mechanism for adapting the number of provisioned resources to the resource demand. In the context of public clouds, there exist different natures of cost-models for charging resources. However, the accounted resource units and charged resource units may differ significantly due to the applied cost model. This can lead to a significant increase of charged costs when using an auto-scaler as it tries to match the demand of the application as close as possible. In the literature, several auto-scalers exist that support cost-aware scaling decisions but they introduce inherent drawbacks.

In this work, this lack of existing cost-aware mechanisms is addressed by introducing a mediator between an application and the auto-scaler. This cost-aware mechanism is called FOX. It leverages knowledge of the charging model of the public cloud and reviews the scaling decisions found by the auto-scaler to reduce the charged costs to a minimum. More precisely, FOX delays or omits releases of resources to avoid additional charging costs if the resource is required in the future. Hereby, FOX is not restricted to use one specific auto-scaler but offers interfaces to use any auto-scaler.

For an evalation under controlled conditions, FOX scales a multi-tier application deployed in a private cloud that is stressed with two real world workloads: BibSonomy and IBM CICS. As FOX provides an interface for auto-scalers, we evaluate the cost-aware mechanism with three state of the art auto-scalers: React, Adapt, and Reg. The experiments show that FOX is able to reduce the charged costs by 34% at maximum for the Amazon EC2 charging model. According to the cost model, FOX provisions more resources than required. This results in a decreased SLO violation rate from 28% to 2% at maximum. The accounted instance time increases at max. by 30%.

CCS CONCEPTS

• **General and reference** → **Cross-computing tools and techniques**; • **Networks** → **Cloud computing**; • **Computer systems organization** → **Self-organizing autonomic computing**; • **Software and its engineering** → **Virtual machines**;

KEYWORDS

Cloud Computing, Public Cloud, Auto-Scaling, Cost-Awareness, Charging Model

ACM Reference Format:
Veronika Lesch, André Bauer, Nikolas Herbst, and Samuel Kounev. 2018. FOX: Cost-Awareness for Autonomic Resource Management in Public Clouds. In *ICPE '18: ACM/SPEC International Conference on Performance Engineering, April 9–13, 2018, Berlin, Germany.* ACM, New York, NY, USA, 12 pages. https://doi.org/10.1145/3184407.3184415

1 INTRODUCTION

In order to face the dynamic behavior respectively requirements of internet applications, cloud computing emerged as computing model that allows fast access to resources and has a high level of scalability. Due to these benefits, the usage of auto-scalers arose in cloud computing. The developed mechanisms try on the one hand to adapt the supplied resources as close as possible to the demanded resources; on the other hand they try to consider the predefined service level objectives. When using auto-scalers in public clouds, the desired effect of adapting the number of resources can lead to high costs as the accounted costs and the charged costs can deviate depending on the cloud. For example, if a virtual machine (VM) is charged hourly, the hour has to be paid although the accounted time is less than one hour. In order to minimize the charged costs, a cost-aware mechanism is required. While taking the future demand into account, the cost-aware mechanism modifies the auto-scaling decisions.

In this work, a cost-aware mechanism, called FOX, is proposed. FOX serves as mediator between an application deployed in a public cloud and an auto-scaler. The working principle of FOX bases on the MAPE-K control loop [16] and has additional knowledge of the cost-models. The main idea is to proactively plan the resource allocation and release. In order to reduce the charged cost, FOX modifies the found scaling decisions of the auto-scaler. If the resource is already charged and will be required in the future, FOX does not stop the VM to avoid additional charging intervals. The design of FOX provides an interface for auto-scalers, i.e., FOX is able to add cost-aware functionality to any auto-scaler using this interface. Additionally, there is also an interface for a forecasting mechanism that allows to add different existing forecasters.

We evaluate FOX using a multi-tier application deployed under controlled conditions in a private cloud. The application is stressed using two real-world workloads: BibSonomy and IBM CICS. To show that FOX can add cost-awareness to multiple auto-scalers, three auto-scaling mechanisms are selected and evaluated: React [8], Adapt [2], and Reg [13].

The results of the experiments with the Amazon EC2 cost model show that FOX is able to decrease the charged costs, the cost you have to pay, for all auto-scalers by 34% at maximum. In addition to the cost reduction, the accounted instance time is increased which results in 26% less SLO violation at maximum. The elasticity metrics consider how well the supply curve fits the demand. FOX actively decides not to stop resources if they will be required, thus SLO improvements are achieved in trade for a slightly worse auto-scaling performance considering the elasticity metrics.

In order to investigate the impact of cost-aware mechanism for auto-scaling, we pose ourselves the following research questions: RQ1 *What kind of cost models exist and what are the popular ones?*, RQ2 *How can we modify the scaling decisions so that the charged costs are reduced?*, and finally, RQ3 *How well does FOX perform in the context of auto-scaling?*

The contributions of this paper align with the three addressed research questions and structure the paper as follows: in Section 2, we survey existing cost models, i.e., we answer RQ1. In Section 3, we address RQ2 by introducing the approach of FOX. Afterwards, the used tools are introduced in Section 4. Section 5 discusses the results of the experiments and addresses RQ3. In Section 6, we summarize related work before concluding the paper.

2 PUBLIC CLOUD COST MODELS

Multiple public infrastructure cloud provider exist each offering their own charging model. However, a classification into three groups can be found: hourly charging, two phase charging and minute-by-minute charging.

HOURLY-BASED CHARGING. The first group, hourly charging, charges for every started hour regardless of stopped instances before the full hour is over. By this rough granularity, a huge charging overhead can occur, e.g., Amazon EC2[1], ORACLE Cloud[2], IBM Bluemix[3], Digital Ocean[4], and OHV[5] charge on an hourly basis.

TWO-PHASE CHARGING. The Google Cloud Platform[6] is a representative providing the two phase charging model. The first phase consists of a fixed interval of ten minutes, which has to be paid regardless of a shorter runtime. Afterwards, the model switches to the second phase, where a minute-by-minute charging is applied. This cost model introduces overheads for the first ten minutes

of a virtual machine but afterwards they do not introduce large overheads.

MINUTE-BASED CHARGING. The third group of public cloud providers charge the used resources minute-by-minute. So, all instance times are rounded to the next minute. This introduces a small overhead that is negligible when looking at the minute price. Example public cloud providers that charge on this basis are the Open Telekom Cloud[7], Microsoft Azure[8], and 1&1[9].

In this work, FOX considers the cost models of the first two categories: hourly charging and two phase charging. For the hourly charging, we expect that the costs can be lowered by a significant amount when using FOX, as there is a large overhead when rounding runtimes to the next full hour. For the second group, the two phase cost models, we expect that the cost savings are not as significant as they are for the hourly charging, as the overhead by rounding to the next full minute is very small.

RELATION TO SPOT MARKETS. In addition to these groups where instances can be provisioned and released on demand, Amazon Web Services offer a Spot Market[10]. Here, the prices of instances vary dependent on supply and demand. The customer can specify a maximum price he wants to pay for an instance. If the price for an instance drops below this maximum, the instance is provisioned for this customer. The instance is released if the price rises above the maximum price the customer defined or if the customer stops the instance by himself. The cost-aware mechanism of FOX also supports a deployment with spot instances, as the logic how scaling decisions are modified to save costs is not affected. The deployment with spot instances introduces the risk that instances may not be provisioned on demand or are terminated by the platform if the actual price is higher than the bid. Thus, optimal bid placing could be the responsibility of another independent component and is not considered as a feature of FOX. To ensure reproducible results, the scenario using spot instances is omitted in the evaluation of FOX.

In this section, we address the research question RQ1: *What kind of cost models exist and what are the popular ones?* Among public cloud environments available, multiple cost models exist that can be classified into three groups: hourly charging, two phase charging and minute-by-minute charging. Example cloud providers for these cost models are Amazon EC2, Google Cloud Platform and Open Telekom Cloud. In this paper, we consider only the first two groups as the third group does not introduce large overheads that can be optimized by a cost-aware mechanism.

3 APPROACH

The main idea of FOX is that it operates as mediator between the auto-scaling mechanism and the application for adapting the associated scaling decisions based on a predefined cost-model. To this end, FOX contains a knowledge base, a forecast component and the interface for the auto-scaler. The knowledge base holds all found

---

[1]https://aws.amazon.com/de/ec2/pricing/on-demand/
[2]https://cloud.oracle.com/infrastructure/pricing
[3]https://www.ibm.com/cloud-computing/bluemix/de/pricing?lnk=hm
[4]https://www.digitalocean.com/pricing/#faq
[5]https://www.ovh.de/g677.informationen_zur_dedicated_cloud_abrechnung
[6]https://cloud.google.com/compute/pricing#machinetype

[7]https://cloud.telekom.de/fileadmin/CMS/Information/Kundenflyer/
Open-Telekom-Cloud_Pricing-Models.pdf
[8]https://azure.microsoft.com/pricing/details/virtual-machines/linux
[9]https://hosting.1und1.de/cloud-computing
[10]https://aws.amazon.com/ec2/spot/pricing/

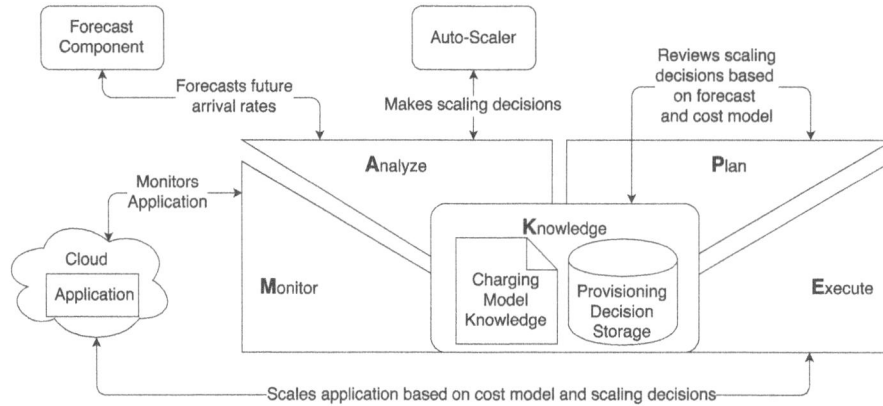

Figure 1: MAPE-K model of the Cost-Component.

scaling decisions from the auto-scaler, the predicted future arrival rates, and the knowledge about the cost model of the cloud platform provider. An overview of existing cost models are explained in Section 2. In our experiments, a simplistic forecaster returns the arrival rates of the last observerd day as forecast for the current day. As auto-scalers React, Adapt, and Reg are used (see Section 4). The auto-scaler and the forecast component can be replaced with other mechanisms. An example forecasting tool developed for auto-scaling contexts in cloud computing is the hybrid, decomposition-based approach called Telescope [28].

3.1 MAPE-K Adaptation

The approach of FOX is based on the MAPE-K control loop [16] as depicted in Figure 1. In the first phase called *Monitor*, FOX monitors the application and gathers information such as arrival rates and saves them into the knowledge base. As most of the existing auto-scalers in the literature are designed for homogeneous requests, i.e. single class case, FOX also holds this assumption. The monitoring interval is set to two minutes. Then, during the *Analyze* phase FOX fetches forecast values for the next 30 minutes from the forecast component. Based on these forecasts, the auto-scaler makes scaling decisions for all tiers for the next 15 intervals and saves them also in the knowledge base. While the application can consist of different resources, the resource types in each tier are assumed to be homogeneous. In the *Plan* phase, FOX reviews the scaling decisions based on the decisions found for the future forecasts and changes them according to the cost model. That is, for instance, that some scaling down decisions are delayed or cancelled according to the charging interval. Finally, in the *Execute* phase, FOX scales the application based on the adapted scaling decisions. The *Analyze*, *Plan* and *Execute* phases are described in more detail below.

Analyze: In the *Analyze* phase, FOX sends the observed arrival rate history to the forecaster component and receives the forecast values for the next 30 minutes, i.e., 15 forecast values. This is done every 15 minutes so that an overlap in forecasts exists. This overlap is required since FOX evaluates future events to adapt the scaling decisions. For each forecast value and each tier, the auto-scaler is called for making scaling decisions. The auto-scaler receives the

forecast value via the interface, the amount of running VMs and the request rate that a single VM can handle at the specific tier. The amount of running VMs for the first forecast value is the amount of current running VMs. For the following forecast values, the planned amount from previous decisions are used. Based on this information, scaling decisions for each forecast value are made per tier and added to the knowledge base. From the second forecaster call on, the overlap of the decisions appears. As the new decisions have more recent information, the old decisions are omitted and replaced by the new ones.

Plan: For our experiments, FOX takes two common cost models into account: First, the Amazon EC2 model with an hourly charging, and secondly, the Google Cloud Platform model where the first ten minutes are charged fix and then the charging switches to a minutely basis, see Section 2 for a more detailed explanation of the cost models. The idea of FOX is to modify the current scaling decisions based on planned decisions for the future. Hereby, a down-scaling should be avoided when a VM will be required again in the near future. In case an up-scaling should be processed, the decision will not be modified. The decision logic how FOX changes the decisions is depicted in Figure 2 and summarized in Algorithm 1. First, FOX checks whether the current decision triggers a down-scaling (Algorithm 1, L. 1). If this holds (r.t. two lower cases in Fig. 2), all future decisions are fetched that are planned during the next charging interval (Algorithm 1, L. 2), i.e., one hour for Amazon EC2 and ten minutes for Google Cloud Platform. Then, FOX iterates over all future decisions (Algorithm 1, L. 3) and checks whether the amount of the future decision is higher than the amount of the current decision (Algorithm 1, L. 4), i.e., whether a down-scaling should be processed even if the VM will be required in the future. If this holds, the amount of the current decision is changed to the number of running VMs or the amount of the future decision, depending on which one is smaller (Algorithm 1, L. 5). In case the amount of the future decision is smaller than the amount of the current decision, the current decision is not modified. Finally, the revised decision is returned.

Execute: The *Execute* phase is responsible for scaling the application according to the found scaling decisions that are reviewed

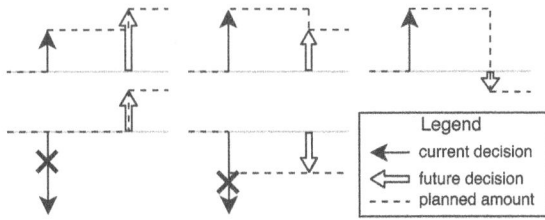

Figure 2: Decision logic for comparison to future decisions.

Algorithm 1: Revising auto-scaler decisions

Input: Decision current, runningVms run, chargInterval ci
Result: revisedDecision
/* if running VMs > amount of cur. decision, revise (acc. to Fig. 2) */
1 **if** *run > current.amount* **then**
2   futures = getFutureDecisionsInInterval(ci);
3   **foreach** *next in futures* **do**
4   **if** *next.amount > current.amount* **then**
5   current.amount = min(run, next.amount);
6 **return** *current*

---

by the cost component. In this phase, the cost component is important, again, as it can decide which VMs should be stopped in case of down-scaling to minimize financial loss. The procedure of this phase works as follows. First, the decisions for the current time are given to the execution component. In case of an up-scaling decision, the component provisions the required VMs. In case of a down-scaling decision, the execution component requests the VMs that introduce minimum financial loss if stopped from the cost component. To determine the VMs that should be stopped, the cost component takes the charging model into account. For the Amazon EC2 charging model, the runtime of all VMs are gathered. Then, the VMs that are closest to the next charging interval, i.e. one hour, are selected for down-scaling. For the Google Cloud Engine, the VMs are sorted descending by their overall runtime so that the VM which ran longest is at the beginning of the list. Then, the down-scaling amount of VMs is selected from the beginning of the list. So, the VMs with longest overall runtime are selected.

3.2 Discussion

In this section, we address the research question RQ2: *How can we modify the scaling decisions so that the charged costs are reduced?* FOX is designed according to the MAPE-K control loop. Here, the *Plan* phase consists the cost-aware mechanism where the knowledge of the cost model is used to review the existing scaling decisions from the auto-scaler to minimize costs. This mechanism is two-fold: First, the mechanism reviews all down-scaling decisions whether they are meaningful. That is, if a future decision defines that the instances that should be stopped will be required in a few minutes, the down-scaling is not executed or reduced executed. Second, in case of a reviewed down-scaling decision that should be executed, the VMs are stopped that reduce the lowest financial

loss, i.e., the instances that are closest to the next charging interval are stopped in case of Amazon EC2. For the Google Cloud Platform cost model the VMs with the longest runtime are stopped.

4 TOOLS

The following section introduces three categories of tools that are used in this work: forecaster, auto-scaler and elasticity benchmarking framework.

4.1 Forecaster

The forecast component of FOX is able to access multiple different forecaster. In this work a simple forecaster is used where the values of the last day are returned as forecast values for the next day. So, the forecast value for the next interval is the observed value 24 hours earlier. Though, different forecasting approaches can be used. Telescope, e.g., is a hybrid forecasting tool that is designed to perform multi-step-ahead forecasts for univariate time series, while maintaining a short runtime [28]. Besides Telescope, tBATS [9] or ARIMA [1] can be used as forecaster as well.

4.2 Auto-Scalers

For the evaluation of FOX, we selected a subset of the most cited and public available auto-scalers proposed in the survey of T. Lorido-Botran et al. [17].

REACT: In 2009, Chieu et al. [8] present a reactive scaling algorithm for horizontal scaling.

React provisions VM resources based on a threshold or scaling indicator of the web application. The indicators consist of the number of concurrent users, the number of active connections, the number of requests per second, and the average response time per request. React gathers these indicators for each VM and calculates the moving average. Afterwards, the current web application VMs with active sessions above or below the given threshold are determined. Then, if all VMs have active sessions above the threshold, new web application instances are provisioned. If there are VMs with active sessions below the threshold and with at least one VM that has no active session, idle instances are removed.

ADAPT: In 2012, A. Ali-Eldin et al. [2] propose a proactive auto-scaler that supports horizontal scaling. It contains a model of each service of the cloud based on a closed loop control system. Adapt models the infrastructure using queueing theory as G/G/n stable queue with variable number of servers n. Using this model the authors build two adaptive controllers that are parameter independent. Any performance metric can be used as controlled parameter. Adapt estimates the future service capacity using a gain parameter that determines the estimated change in the workload in the future. The two controllers are built by using two different gain parameters: the periodical rate of change of the system load and the ratio between the change in the load and the average system service rate over time.

REG: In 2011, W. Iqbal et al. [13], introduce their proactive auto-scaler that uses response times to find scaling decisions to remove bottlenecks. A reactive model checks if the capacity is less than the load, and makes a scale-up decision. For down-scaling, a proactive mechanism decides when and how much to deprovision. Therefore, a regression model is used to predict the number of VMs required at each time. This model is updated every time a new observation is added. The reactive mechanism feeds these observations to the proactive mechanism at every observation interval. Then, the model is recalculated using the complete history of the workload. If the current load is lower than the capacity, the model determines the required amount of VMs that can fulfill this load.

4.3 Elasticity Benchmarking Framework

In order to evaluate the two approaches, we use the BUNGEE Cloud Elasticity Benchmark controller [11]. The working principle is depicted in Figure 3. On the left side, the system under test (SUT) is depicted. It contains the IaaS cloud that hosts the multi-tier application and the scaling controller. On the right side, the experiment controller (BUNGEE) with its four phases is illustrated. First, in the System Analysis, the controller constructs a discrete mapping function for the SUT that determines the associated minimum amount of resources required to meet the SLOs (Service Level Objectives) for each load intensity. Then, the second phase, called *Benchmark Calibration*, uses the mapping from step one to generate identical changes in the curve of the demanded resource units on every platform under comparison. Based on this mapping and a predefined workload profile, the *Measurement* phase stresses the SUT while BUNGEE monitors the supplied VMs. Finally, in the *Elasticity Evaluation* phase, the elasticity and user-oriented metrics based on the collected monitoring data are calculated.

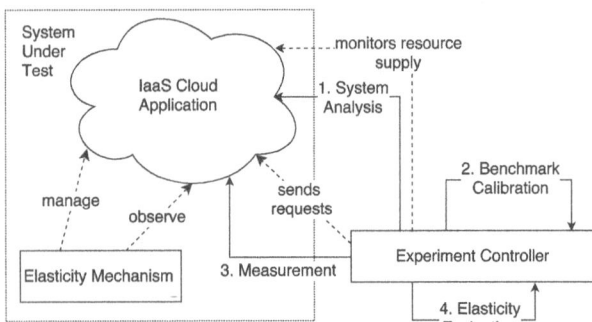

Figure 3: Elasticity Benchmarking Framework.

5 EVALUATION AND EXPERIMENT DESCRIPTION

The evaluation is split into multiple parts. First, we explain the elasticity metrics we use for evaluating the performance of the auto-scaling mechanism. Second, we introduce the cost metrics. We use these metrics to evaluate FOX and its cost saving potential. Third, we describe the experiment environment. Fourth, we explain the plots made for evaluating the scaling behavior of the auto-scaling mechanism without and with FOX in the methodology section. Fifth, we present the evaluation that contains detailed results for the experiments using React on the BibSonomy trace. Due to space limitations, we summarize the experiments for Adapt and Reg using BibSonomy in a table and omit the plots. Afterwards, we present the results of the experiment using React on the IBM workload using a detailed metric evaluation. Finally, we summarize the assumptions and limitations of the experiments and discuss whether the results can be generalized.

5.1 Elasticity Metrics

We use system-oriented elasticity metrics endorsed by the Research Group of the Standard Performance Evaluation Corporation (SPEC) [12] for quantifying the performance of FOX in context of auto-scaling. In particular, we use the provisioning accuracy and the wrong provision time share.

For the following equations, we define:

- T as the experiment duration and time $t \in [0, T]$
- s_t as the resource supply at time t
- d_t as the demanded resource units at time t
- n as the number of tiers

The demanded resource units d_t are the minimal amount of VMs required to meet the SLOs under the load intensity at time t. Δt denotes the time interval between the last and the current change either in demand d or supply s. The curve of demanded resource units d over time T is derived by BUNGEE, see Section 4. The resource supply s_t is the monitored number of running VMs at time t.

PROVISIONING ACCURACY θ_U AND θ_O: The provisioning accuracy describes the relative amount of resources that are under-provisioned, respectively, over-provisioned during the measurement interval. In other words, the *under-provisioning accuracy* θ_U is the amount of missing resources normalized by the current demanded resource units that are required to meet the SLOs normalized by the experiment time. Similarly, the *over-provisioning accuracy* θ_O is the amount of resources that the auto-scaler supplies in excess. The range of this metric is the interval $[0, \infty)$, where 0 is the best value and indicates that the supply curve lays on the demand curve during the entire measurement interval.

$$\theta_U[\%] := \frac{100}{T} \cdot \sum_{t=1}^{T} \frac{max(d_t - s_t, 0)}{d_t} \Delta t$$

$$\theta_O[\%] := \frac{100}{T} \cdot \sum_{t=1}^{T} \frac{max(s_t - d_t, 0)}{d_t} \Delta t$$

WRONG PROVISIONING TIME SHARE τ_U AND τ_O: The wrong provisioning time share captures the time in which the system is in an under-provisioned, respectively over-provisioned, state during the experiment interval, i.e., the *under-provisioning time share* τ_U is the time relative to the measurement duration, in which the system is under-provisioned. Similarly, the *over-provisioning time share* τ_O is the time relative to the measurement duration in which the system is over-provisioned. The range of this metric is the interval $[0, 100]$. The best value 0 is achieved, when the system has during the measurement no over- or under-provisioning.

$$\tau_U[\%] := \frac{100}{T} \cdot \sum_{t=1}^{T} max(sgn(d_t - s_t), 0)\Delta t$$

$$\tau_O[\%] := \frac{100}{T} \cdot \sum_{t=1}^{T} max(sgn(s_t - d_t), 0)\Delta t$$

MULTI-TIER AUTO-SCALING DEVIATION σ_n: In order to evaluate the performance of FOX according the introduced system oriented elasticity metrics, we propose to calculate the deviation of the scaling behavior across each tier compared to the theoretically optimal auto-scaler. The theoretically optimal auto-scaler is assumed to know the future load. Therefore, it knows when and how much the demanded resources change. For calculating the auto-scaling deviation, the aforementioned metrics provisioning accuracy (θ_U, θ_O) and wrong provisioning time share (τ_U, and τ_O) are considered. As these metrics calculate the deviation of the supplied resources to the demanded, the vector of the theoretical optimal auto-scaler is assumed to be the zero vector. For the determination of the deviation, we use the Minkowski distance with these vectors. If FOX is compared to the theoretically optimal auto-scaler, the L_p-norm can be used as the Minkowski distance between a vector and the zero vector is equal to the norm. We set p to the value 4 as we have four dimensions. Thus, we define the *multi-tier auto-scaling deviation* σ_n as follows, where n is the number of tiers:

$$\sigma_n[\%] = \left(\sum_{i=1}^{n} \left(\theta_{U,i}^4 + \theta_{O,i}^4 + \tau_{U,i}^4 + \tau_{O,i}^4 \right)^{\frac{n}{4}} \right)^{\frac{1}{n}}$$

SLO VIOLATION RATE ϕ: In addition to the system oriented metrics provisioning accuracy and wrong provisioning time share, the Service Level Objective (SLO) violation rate is taken into account. This metric shows how many requests the application has handled within the specified SLOs. Therefore, the requests violating the SLO are divided by the amount of sent requests during the experiment. In this work, the SLOs are specified using the response time: 95% of all requests have to be handled within two seconds.

5.2 Cost Metrics

As FOX is a cost-aware mechanism, cost metrics are also taken into account for the evaluation. To this end, we consider the instance time, however, we have to distinguish between two different instance times: *accounted instance time* and *charged instance time*. The accounted instance time is the total runtime of all VMs of all tiers. The charged instance time is the runtime, the public cloud provider charges. Figure 4 shows both instance times for the Amazon EC2 pricing model. The red blocks represent the charged instance time and the green blocks the accounted instance time. Resource instance 1 has on the left an accounted instance time of 1.25 and is charged for two hours as all started hours are charged full no matter if the resource is stopped earlier. On the right the accounted instance time matches the charged instance time of one hour. The second resource instance is started three times and runs only for a few minutes each time. However, it is charged for three full hours, even if the previous charging interval is still running. The third resource instance runs for a bit more than two hours but is charged for three hours. So, all started hours are rounded to a full hour charged instance time. In addition, each start of the same instance is considered to be a completely new instance without recognition of previous and still running charging intervals.

COST SAVING RATE Π: For a quantification of the cost savings FOX can provide, we introduce the cost saving rate metric Π. This metric compares the instance times of the auto-scaler (cost$_{AS}$) to the

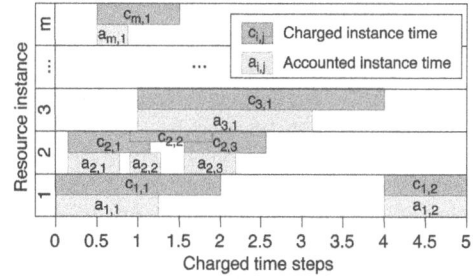

Figure 4: This example shows which instance times are accounted and which instance times are charged.

instance times of a naive approach (cost$_{Naive}$). The naive approach is assumed to provision all available resources at the start of the experiment and does not have any auto-scaling mechanisms, i.e., all available resources are running throughout the experiment. Both types of instance times are considered and a cost saving rate for accounted instance times (Π_a), respectively, charged instance time Π_c is calculated. The range of this metric is in the interval $(-1, \infty)$. If the value is negative, costs are saved. The lower the value is in the negative range the more costs are saved. If the value is greater or equals zero, the mechanism spends more or equal cost than the naive approach.

$$\Pi_x[\%] = 100 \cdot \left(\frac{\text{cost}_{AS}}{\text{cost}_{Naive}} - 1 \right)$$

5.3 Experimental Description

For the experimental evaluation, we designed a multi-tier application. It consist of three tiers with a standard workflow: The presentation tier (pt) receives requests and sends them to the business tier. An instance of the presentation tier has a processing rate of 17 requests per second. The business tier (bt) processes the forwarded requests but has a predefined number of serving units. This introduces a limitation of the number of parallel executions per instance to ten requests per second. Afterwards, the results are sent to the database tier (dt), that persists the results. The number of parallel database accesses per instance is limited to 25 per second. Finally, the results are sent back to the presentation tier that sends the response to the client. The tiers of the application are configured individually. There are different amounts of VM instances that can be provisioned per tier. At the presentation tier, 15 VMs can be provisioned. The business tier can be scaled to 25 VMs and the database tier can have 10 VMs. This configuration is made due to hardware limitations of the servers of our private cloud environment. Based on the request rates that can be served per tier and VM, 17 (pt), 10 (bt) and 25 (dt), the maximum arrival rate the application can handle with all VMs provisioned is 250 per second.

In order to stress the application with authentic workloads with time-varying behavior, we choose two real world traces: (i) BibSonomy and (ii) IBM. The *BibSonomy* represents HTTP requests to servers of the social bookmarking system BibSonomy (see the paper of Benz et al. [4]) during April 2017. The *IBM* Customer Information Control System (CICS) transactions trace captures four weeks of recorded transactions on a z10 mainframe CICS installation. Each trace was sampled in 15 minute intervals, i.e., one day consists of 96 data points. For our experiments, we accelerate each trace by the factor of 7.5. That is, one data point for each two minutes. For having an internal repetition, we select two days for each trace.

The experiments are conducted in our private cloud infrastructure. The cloud consists of eleven homogeneous, virtualized Xen-Server hosts. Eight of them are managed by Apache CloudStack[11]. The distributed application is deployed on the CloudStack environment. The last three servers are not part of the CloudStack environment and are used for hosting (i) the load-balancer (Citrix Netscaler[12]) and the cloud management for CloudStack, (ii) the auto-scaling mechanisms and FOX, and (iii) the load driver and the experiment controller. The specification of each physical machine and worker VM can be found in Table 1.

Table 1: Specification of the Servers.

Criteria	Server	Worker VMs
Model	HP DL160 Gen9	–
Operating System	Xen-Server	Ubuntu 16.06
CPU	8 cores	1 vcore
Memory	32 GB	2 GB

5.4 Methodology

All shown figures in the following have the same structure: a demand versus supply graph for each tier at the top and a request evaluation at the bottom. All graphs have the experiment duration of about 385 minutes at the x-axis. The y-axis shows the number of VMs for the demand supply plot, and the requests per second for the request evaluation. The demand and supply graph shows the demand as black dashed line and the supply as a blue solid line. If the supply line falls below the demand line there are too less VMs provisioned. In case the supply line exceeds the demand line, too many VMs are instantiated. So, the optimal auto-scaler would result in a supply line matching the demand line during the experiment. The request evaluation graph shows the sent requests as a black dashed line, the requests processed conform to the SLO as green solid line and the requests that violate the SLOs as red dashed and dotted line. The sum of the SLO conform and SLO violation lines result in the sent request line. That is, if the green line matches the black line and the red line is zero during the experiment all requests have been served within the SLO. If the red line is not equal to zero and the green line drops below the black line, more SLO violations occured. An user-oriented auto-scaler tries to configure the application so that all requests can be served within the SLO and therefore, the green line should match the black line.

5.5 Experiment Results

As mentioned earlier, the evaluation of FOX is based on two different workload traces: BibSonomy and IBM. In addition, three different auto-scalers are used to show that FOX can improve the behavior of multiple auto-scalers. Due to space limitations, detailed

[11]Apache CloudStack: https://cloudstack.apache.org/
[12]Citrix Netscaler: https://www.citrix.de/products/netscaler-adc/

evaluations are presented only for React without and with FOX for both workload traces. Additionally, for the BibSonomy workload trace plots are shown where the scaling behavior with and without FOX can be observed. Due to space limitations, the evaluation for the other auto-scalers is limited to the BibSonomy workload and the results are shown in summary in Table 3.

React on the BibSonomy workload: The scaling behaviors of React without, respectively with FOX are shown in Figure 5, respectively Figure 6. Figure 5 shows that React performs many adaptations to match the current demand. In some up-scaling cases, React starts the instances too late and under-provisioning occurs that results in increasing SLO violation rates at the bottom of the figure. However, React matches the current demand most of the time. Figure 6 shows the behavior of React with FOX using the Amazon EC2 cost model. At the top three plots, the unstable behavior of React is smoothed when using FOX. The supply curve tends to over-provision the amount of VMs. That is, the supply curve stays above the demand curve most of the time. However, some scaling actions are performed to reduce the amount of unused VMs if meaningful. As the supply curve lies above the demand curve most of the time, the SLO violations are reduced to a minimum as can be seen at the bottom of the figure. This is the behavior, we expected, as FOX performs down-scaling only if the instances that should be released will not be used in the future.

Table 2: Elasticity metrics results for React on the BibSonomy trace.

Tier	Metric	React	FOX_A	FOX_G
1	θ_U	2.65%	0.45%	0.62%
1	θ_O	33.29%	66.08%	57.91%
1	τ_U	16.48%	3.04%	3.92%
1	τ_O	68.05%	93.57%	91.01%
2	θ_U	6.10%	0.99%	1.53%
2	θ_O	20.80%	54.79%	47.25%
2	τ_U	35.34%	6.67%	8.17%
2	τ_O	52.18%	88.54%	85.45%
3	θ_U	2.22%	0.15%	0.47%
3	θ_O	27.93%	82.97%	62.66%
3	τ_U	13.45%	1.12%	2.65%
3	τ_O	57.97%	96.03%	91.71%
overall	ϕ	12%	3%	3%
overall	σ_3	89%	144%	134%

The evaluation of the elasticity metrics show the same results as observed in the figures. Table 2 shows the elasticity metrics for React without and with FOX for Amazon EC2 and Google Cloud Platform cost model on the BibSonomy workload. At the first tier, the provisioning accuracy for under-provisioning of React is about 2% while the provisioning accuracy for the experiments with FOX is about 0.5%, so the under-provisioning at the first tier is reduced by 75%. However, the over-provisioning accuracy for React is about 33% and for the experiments with FOX it is 66%, respectively 58% for Amazon EC2, respectively, Google Cloud Platform cost model. In addition, the under-provisioning time share of React without

FOX is 16% and for the experiments with FOX it is reduced to 3% and 4%. The over-provisioning time share for React is 68% and for the experiments with FOX larger than 90%. The scaling behavior at the other tiers is comparable to the one at the first tier. The SLO violation rate of React is 12% and for the experiments with FOX the violation rate is 3%. So, the SLO violation rate is reduced by 75% when using FOX. However, the auto-scaling deviation for React is 89% and for the experiments with FOX the deviation is larger than 100%. For comparison, the auto-scaling deviation for the Naive approach is 221%. So, a trade-off between SLO violation rate and auto-scaling deviation can be accessed. This is the expected behavior of FOX. It reduces under-provisioning phases by delaying or cancelling scaling down actions if future decisions state that the instances will be required. Hereby, the auto-scaler performance becomes worse in trade for a reduced SLO violation rate.

The evaluation based on the cost aspects is summarized in Table 3. For the BibSonomy workload all three auto-scalers are evaluated. First, the results of React are discussed. The cost saving rate for charged costs (Π_c) compares the charged instance time of the auto-scaler run with the naive scenario. The value of -5% shows that the charged costs are reduced by 5% when using React without FOX for the Amazon EC2 cost model. FOX is able to reduce the costs by 26% for the Amazon EC2 cost model. So, FOX saves 21% more costs than the experiment without FOX. This gain is caused by the down-scaling logic of FOX, as a down-scaling is only executed if the instances are not required in the near future. In the run without FOX, many instances are stopped due to the actual request rate but are again provisioned when the load increases. This introduces additional charging intervals to start with the Amazon EC2 cost model as described earlier. This behavior is reduced when using FOX and the charged costs are lowered. The cost saving rate for accounted instance times (Π_a) compares the accounted instance times to the naive approach where all instances run throughout the experiment. The value -45% for React with the Amazon EC2 cost model shows that the accounted instance time is reduced by 45% when using React in comparison to the naive approach. When using FOX the accounted instance time is only reduced by 28%, i.e., FOX supplies more instance time than React without FOX. This also results in a significantly reduced SLO violation rate from 12% when using React to 3% when using FOX for the Amazon EC2 cost model. However, this can only be achieved in trade for a worse auto-scaling performance in terms of elasticity metrics. In summary, for the Amazon EC2 cost model, the costs can be reduced by FOX while the accounted instance time is increased. When comparing React without FOX to React with FOX for the Google Cloud Platform cost model, it can be seen that the charged costs saving rate matches the accounted cost saving rate. So, there is no significant cost savings when using the Google Cloud Platform cost model for FOX. This can be explained by the cost model, as every minute is charged separately and there is no rounding to the next full hour as seen for the Amazon EC2 cost model.

ADAPT ON THE BIBSONOMY WORKLOAD: During the evaluation of Adapt with the BibSonomy workload the results show similar behavior as seen for React. When looking at the values of Adapt without FOX for the Amazon EC2 cost model, it can be seen that the SLO violation rate is 28% and the auto-scaling deviation is 86%. The

accounted costs are reduced by 57% compared to the naive approach and the charged costs are only reduced by 40%. In comparison to the run with FOX, the SLO violation shows a significant decrease to 2% but with a doubled auto-scaling deviation. When looking at the cost saving rates, the accounted costs are reduced less, so FOX manages to supply more accounted instance time. In addition, the charged costs are reduced by 43%. The increased amount of accounted instance time results in a significant decrease of SLO violation rate from 28% to 2% in trade for auto-scaling performance. The run with the Google Cloud Platform cost model shows similar behavior. The SLO violation rate is reduced significantly from 28% to 3% when comparing Adapt without and with FOX. However, the auto-scaling deviation is doubled. The accounted instance time is reduced by 57% for the run of Adapt without FOX and the charged costs are reduced by 56%. The evaluation with FOX shows that the accounted instance time and charged costs are reduced only slightly but the SLO violation rate is reduced by a significant amount.

REG ON THE BIBSONOMY WORKLOAD: The third auto-scaler we evaluated is called Reg. The experiment using Reg without FOX shows specific characteristics of Reg. At random points of the experiment, drops in the supply curve can be detected, where all VMs are stopped and immediately provisioned in the next interval. The plots of the experiment using Reg with FOX show that these drops in the supply curve are removed by FOX. The results for elasticity metrics and cost saving rates are summarized in Table 3. The run of Reg without FOX for the Amazon EC2 cost model shows a SLO violation rate of 22% and an auto-scaling deviation of 77%. The accounted instance time is reduced by 54% in comparison to the naive approach and the charged costs are reduced by 5%. When using FOX, the SLO violation rate is reduced to 4% but the auto-scaling deviation increases. The accounted saving rate is 35%, so more accounted instance time is supplied in comparison to the run of React without FOX. The charged cost saving rate is 35% that is 30% higher than without FOX. So, for the Amazon EC2 cost model, FOX is able to supply more accounted instance time while reducing the charged costs. This also results in a significant lower SLO violation rate of only 4%. The evaluation of React without and with FOX using the Google Cloud Platform cost model shows that React without FOX has a SLO violation rate of 22% while the run with FOX has a reduced SLO violation rate of only 11%. The auto-scaling deviation of the run without FOX is 77% and slightly increased for the run with FOX. The accounted cost saving rate is 53% for the run without FOX and 39% for the run with FOX. The charged cost saving rate is reduced by React by 54% and for the run with FOX by 39%. So, FOX supplies more accounted instance time that results in a significant lower SLO violation rate.

REACT ON THE IBM WORKLOAD: In order to evaluate FOX with different workloads, the IBM workload is selected in addition to the BibSonomy trace. Due to space limitations, only the evaluation of React using the elasticity metrics in Table 4 and the cost saving rates summarized in Table 3 are presented and the plots are omitted. First, the elasticity metrics are discussed. The under-provisioning accuracy is reduced for the first tier from about 2% to 1% with FOX. The over-provisioning accuracy is slightly increased from 86% to 91%, respectively 89%. The under-provisioning time share at the

Table 3: Cost metrics results for the BibSonomy trace.

	BibSonomy												IBM			
	React				Adapt				Reg				React			
Metric	$React_A$	FOX_A	$React_G$	FOX_G	$Adapt_A$	FOX_A	$Adapt_G$	FOX_G	Reg_A	FOX_A	Reg_G	FOX_G	$React_A$	FOX_A	$React_G$	FOX_G
ϕ	12%	3%	12%	3%	28%	2%	28%	3%	22%	4%	22%	11%	12%	4%	12%	5%
σ_3	89%	144%	89%	134%	86%	209%	86%	187%	77%	121%	77%	100%	143%	168%	143%	156%
Π_a	-45%	-28%	-45%	-32%	-57%	-43%	-57%	-11%	-54%	-35%	-53%	-39%	-59%	-51%	-59%	-53%
Π_c	-5%	-26%	-44%	-32%	-40%	-43%	-56%	-10%	-5%	-35%	-54%	-39%	-42%	-51%	-59%	-53%

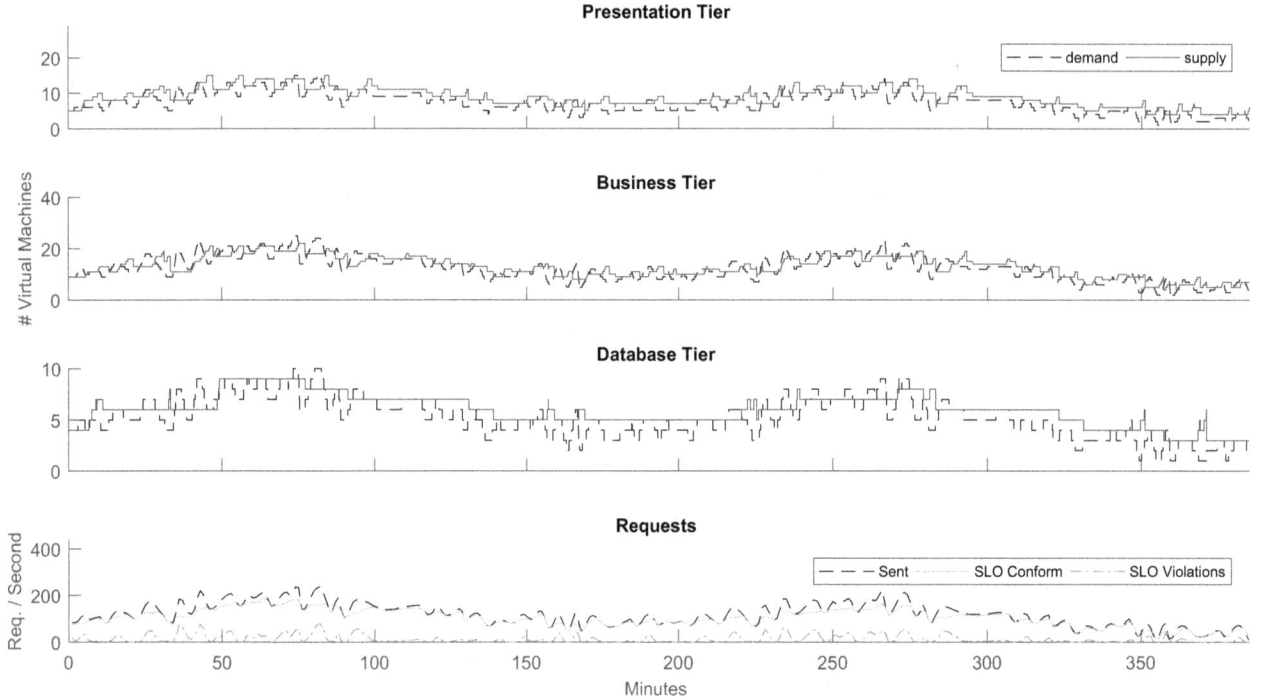

Figure 5: Scaling behavior of React without FOX on the BibSonomy trace with Amazon EC2 cost model.

first tier is reduced when using FOX from about 8% to 5%. The over-provisioning time share is increased from 86% to 90%, respectively 89%. A similar behavior for the other tiers can be derived from the metrics in the table. The SLO violation rate of React is 12% while the rate for the experiments using FOX is reduced significantly to 4%, respectively 5%. The auto-scaling deviation shows a slight increase when using FOX. So, FOX focuses on a trade-off between auto-scaler performance and SLO violation rate.

The cost saving rates shown in Table 3 show for the run with Amazon EC2 cost model that React reduces the charged instance times by 42% compared to the naive approach. When using FOX the charged costs are reduced by 51%. The accounted instance time for React without FOX is reduced by 59% in comparison to the naive approach. FOX only reduces the accounted instance times by 51%. So, FOX supplies more accounted instance time while reducing the costs in comparison to the run of React without FOX. This increased accounted instance time results in a reduction from 12% to 4% SLO violations. However, this can only be achieved in trade for a worse

auto-scaling performance in terms of elasticity metrics. When comparing the charged costs for the Google Cloud Platform charging model, For the Google Cloud Platform, the results show, that FOX supplies more accounted instance time, as the saving rate is lower as in the run without FOX, while the charged costs remain stable when using FOX. This can be explained by the charging interval of one minute, as the rounding overheads to the next charging intervals are very small. Though, the SLO violation rate is reduced from 12% to 5% when using FOX. Again, the auto-scaling deviation is increased when using FOX.

5.6 Threats to Validity

In order to perform the above discussed measurements several assumptions had to be made. These assumptions may reduce the expressiveness of the results. All assumptions and their effect on the results are discussed in the following. First, the set of experiments is run in a private cloud environment under controlled conditions for reproducible performance-related results. The cost and

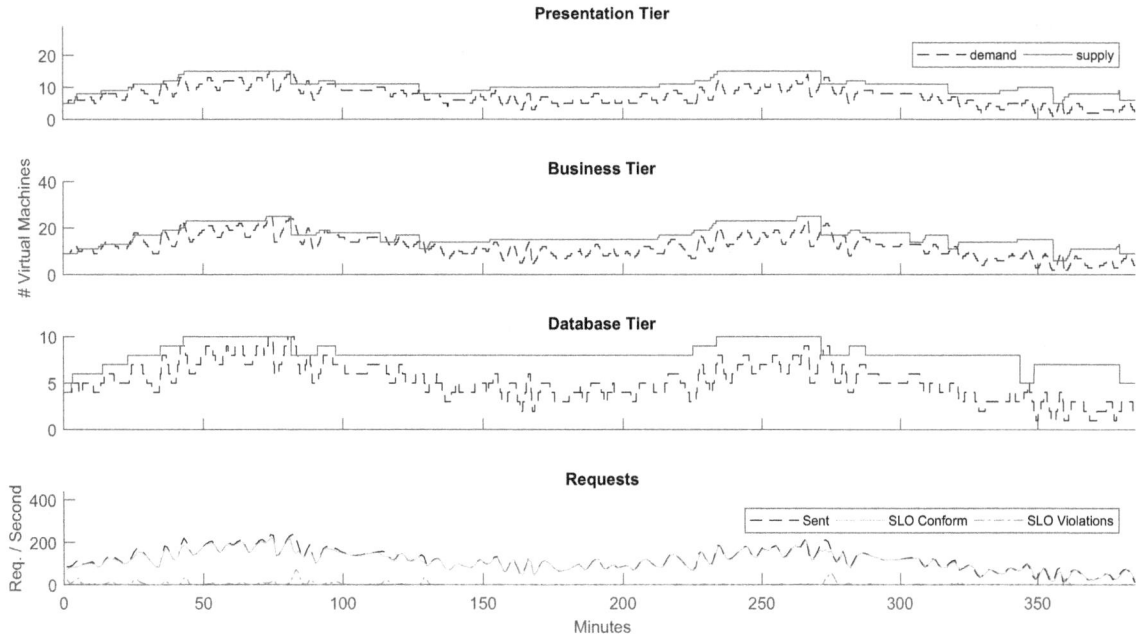

Figure 6: Scaling behavior of React with FOX on the BibSonomy trace with Amazon EC2 cost model.

Table 4: Elasticity metrics results for React on the IBM trace.

Tier	Metric	React	FOX$_A$	FOX$_G$
1	θ_U	1.93%	1.11%	1.02%
1	θ_O	86.31%	90.91%	88.61%
1	τ_U	8.33%	5.59%	5.32%
1	τ_O	85.87%	90.11%	88.86%
2	θ_U	4.76%	2.07%	1.91%
2	θ_O	66.11%	112.59%	80.56%
2	τ_U	16.43%	8.29%	9.08%
2	τ_O	78.67%	88.62%	87.41%
3	θ_U	5.82%	0.97%	0.75%
3	θ_O	96.04%	105.07%	103.92%
3	τ_U	13.61%	3.97%	2.94%
3	τ_O	79.49%	93.62%	93.36%
overall	ψ	12%	4%	5%
overall	σ_3	143%	168%	156%

elasticity-related mechanisms work independent of an experienced performance variability of a public environment. Thus, the obtained results shall be meaningful for the public cloud environments. Second, the results are strongly dependent on the used auto-scaling mechanism. Therefore, three different auto-scalers that are introduced in the literature are used and compared. However, several other auto-scaler exist and the experiments could be expanded to include more auto-scalers. However, this work does not focus on optimal auto-scaling decisions. Third, the results of the cost-aware mechanism FOX depend on the quality of the forecast approach

that is used. We used a simple forecasting method that returns the values of the last day as forecast. We proposed multiple alternative forecaster that could be included in the experiments to reduce variations in the results. Fourth, the experiments are conducted using one multi-tier application with homogeneous request types per tier. Other applications could behave in a different way and the results would be changed. Finally, only two workloads, BibSonomy and IBM are used to stress the application. The experiments should be expanded to use multiple other real world workload traces to show that FOX has similar results on many workloads. The results proposed in this paper cannot be generalized as there are too many assumptions and restrictions made for the experiments. However, the results have shown that FOX behaves as desired and is able to reduce the charged costs while increasing the accounted instance time and hereby reducing the SLO violation rate in the public cloud scenario.

5.7 Discussion

In this section, we address the research question RQ3: *How well does FOX perform in the context of auto-scaling?* The results of the evaluation show that FOX is able to decrease the charged costs significantly while increasing the accounted instance time for the Amazon EC2 cost model compared to the plain auto-salers. This results in reduced SLO violation rates but higher values for the metrics reflecting over-provisioning. However, this can only be achieved in trade for a higher auto-scaling deviation. For the Google Cloud Platform cost model, smaller improvements are measured. This can be explained by the nature of this cost model. All results are summarized in the following.

REACT ON BIBSONOMY WORKLOAD.

- React performs many scaling operations to match the demand as close as possible.
- With FOX, the supply curve is smoothed, tends to over-provision, and the oscillations are removed.
- FOX reduces the charged costs by 21% for the Amazon EC2 cost model.
- FOX provisions 17% more accounted instance time for the Amazon EC2 cost model and the SLO violation rate is reduced from 12% to 3% for the Amazon EC2 cost model.
- The auto-scaling deviation increases in trade for lowered costs for the Amazon EC2 cost model.
- The costs are not lowered for the Google Cloud Platform cost model.
- The accounted instance time is increased for the Google Cloud Platform cost model and the SLO violation rate is reduced.

ADAPT AND REG ON BIBSONOMY WORKLOAD.

- When using FOX the charged costs are reduced by 3% for Adapt, respectively 30% for Reg with the Amazon EC2 cost model.
- The accounted instance times are increased by 14%, respectively 19%. This results in a decrease in the SLO violation rates of 26%, respectively 18% for the Amazon EC2 cost model.
- The results for the auto-scaling deviation for the Amazon EC2 cost model and the evaluation for the Google Cloud Platform cost model are similar to the results of React.

REACT ON IBM WORKLOAD.

- The charged costs can be reduced by 9% for the Amazon EC2 cost model, respectively 6% for the Google Cloud Platform cost model, when using FOX.
- The accounted instance time is increased when using FOX by 8%, respectively 6%. This results in a significant decrease of SLO violation rate from 12% without FOX to 4%, respectively 5% with FOX.

6 RELATED WORK

The survey of T. Lorido-Botran et al. [17] gives a broad overview of existing auto-scalers and a classification into five groups with example implementations are proposed: (i) threshold-based rules [8, 10], (ii) queueing theory [23, 26], (iii) control theory [2, 15], (iv) reinforcement learning [19, 22], and (v) time series analysis [7, 13].

In the literature, many auto-scalers exist that can be assigned to the groups mentioned above. However, only a few auto-scalers support cost-aware scaling. The cost-awareness of the existing auto-scalers can be classified into three groups: (i) general cost optimization by using heterogeneous VM image sizes, (ii) limiting costs by defining a budget or run-time constraint, and (iii) optimization of the scaling logic with knowledge of the charging models.

The first group consists of auto-scalers that find scaling decisions and select the heterogeneous VM image size combination that introduces lowest cost while still fulfilling the specified SLAs. Example auto-scalers for this group are AutoMAP [3] and the one from Sharma et al. [21]. AutoMAP calculates the required amount

of resources to satisfy the SLAs and then searches for a heterogeneous configuration. This configuration should have low costs for the end user while still fulfilling the desired average response time. The auto-scaler introduced by Sharma et al. greedily searches for a configuration with low costs that has a high utilization. Therefore, first a homogeneous configuration is calculated and then, this configuration is translated into a heterogeneous solution. In the paper of Brataas et al. [5], a systematic search over vertically and horizontally scaled deployments is conducted to find cost-optimal configurations. This information could be leveraged by an auto-scaling mechanism to better support heterogeneous resources for distributed applications.

The auto-scalers of the second group have budget or runtime constraints that are specified by the user. Example auto-scalers of this group are introduced by Vaquero et al. [24], Jiang et al. [14], Xiong et al. [25], and Zhu and Agrawal [27]. The auto-scaler of Vaquero et al. requires a specified maximum runtime of all VMs. If this runtime is exceeded the application is no more scaled. The one from Jiang et al. requires a predefined budget constraint and SLA. It performs a trade off between cost and SLA satisfaction to find a minimum amount of resources while still satisfying the SLAs. Xiong et al. introduced an auto-scaler for a multi-tier application. It first determines the required amount of resources to satisfy the SLA on an overall basis and then it splits the new provisioned resources based on the budget constraints to the tiers. The auto-scaler of Zhu and Agrawal have predefined time-limit and resource budget constraints. Within these constraints, the Quality of Service (QoS) is optimized using control theory.

The auto-scalers of the third group have knowledge about the charging models of the public cloud where the application is deployed. The approach presented in this paper can be assigned to this group. Example auto-scalers for this group are the ones from Cardellini et al. [6], Naskos et al. [18], and Roy et al. [20]. The auto-scaler introduced by Cardellini et al. has knowledge about the costs per VM instance per time interval, here the charging interval, e.g. 60 minutes for the Amazon EC2 cloud, is used. With this knowledge the VMs are shut down immediately before the next charging interval starts. In case a new VM should be allocated at this time, the interval of the already running VM is renewed so that it is not stopped and runs for another charging interval. Naskos et al. introduce an auto-scaler for noSQL databases that is aware of the VM charging model and knows the runtimes of all VMs. In case of downscaling, it stops the VMs that are closest to the next charging interval. The auto-scaler introduced by Roy et al. handles a multi-dimensional cost-function. Besides the leasing costs of the VMs, it includes the distance between the estimated response time and the SLA and the reconfiguration costs. Different weights can be assigned to the three components that may result in different scaling decisions. The auto-scaler optimizes this function and finds the optimum strategy with minimum costs.

FOX belongs to the third group of the cost-aware auto-scaling classification. It combines and extends the approaches of the example auto-scalers of this category: First, it supports more complex charging models like the two-phased one as applied at the Google Cloud Platform, instead of one charging interval as presented in the paper from Cardellini et al. Second, FOX has knowledge of all running VMs and their runtimes. With this information and the knowledge of the charging models, the VM that is nearest to the next charging interval can be selected in case of downscaling. A similar mechanism is presented in the paper of Roy et al. Third, FOX finds proactive decisions for the future. Based on these future decisions and the knowledge of the charging model, a decision logic is presented when a downscaling is meaningful and when the already running VMs should stay running. None of the mentioned auto-scalers support future decisions and reviews the actual decision using them and the knowledge of the charging model.

7 CONCLUSION

In this paper, we examine the problem of increasing costs when using an auto-scaling mechanism in the public cloud environment. Our approach, called FOX, operates as a mediator between the application and the cloud to reduce the charged costs while still satisfying the specified SLOs. Therefore, FOX is based on the MAPE-K control loop: It monitors the application and analyzes future arrival rates using a forecaster. Based on these forecasts, the future configurations of the application are determined using the auto-scaling mechanism. Afterwards, the cost-aware mechanism reviews all found scaling decisions and modifies them to reduce the costs. Finally, the modified decisions are executed. FOX has a knowledge base, where observed and future arrival rates, as well as, the scaling decisions are stored. The cost-aware mechanism has knowledge about two different charging strategies: Amazon EC2, where a hourly charging is defined, and Google Cloud Platform, where the first ten minutes are charged fix and then, the charging switches to a minute-by-minute charging.

The evaluation of FOX is based on a multi-tier application deployed in the private cloud environment. This application is stressed using two real world workloads: BibSonomy and IBM CICS trace. To show that FOX can handle multiple auto-scaling mechanisms, three auto-scalers from the literature are used for evaluation: React, Adapt, and Reg. The results of all experiments show, that FOX is able to reduce the charged costs significantly, while increasing the accounted instance time for the Amazon EC2 charging model. This results in a significant decrease of SLO violation rate in trade for a slightly worse auto-scaling performance. For the Google Cloud Platform charging model, smaller (6%) cost savings are achieved. This can be explained due to the nature of the charging model, as there are no rounding overheads charged as for the Amazon EC2 charging model.

In the future, we plan to evaluate FOX with more real world workload traces and for different applications. In addition, other forecasting mechanisms like Telescope [28] will be integrated. Moreover, the experiments of all considered auto-scalers will be expanded to evaluate all of them at all workloads. For the future, it is planned to publish FOX as a tool on our website[13].

ACKNOWLEDGEMENTS

This work was funded by the German Research Foundation (DFG) under grant No. KO 3445/11-1. This research has been supported by the Research Group[14] of the Standard Performance Evaluation Corporation (SPEC).

---

[13]http://descartes.tools/
[14]SPEC Research: http://research.spec.org

REFERENCES

[1] R. Adhikari and R. Agrawal. 2013. An introductory study on time series modeling and forecasting. *arXiv preprint arXiv:1302.6613* (2013).
[2] A. Ali-Eldin, J. Tordsson, and E. Elmroth. [n. d.]. An Adaptive Hybrid Elasticity Controller for Cloud Infrastructures. In *IEEE NOMS 2012*. IEEE, 204–212.
[3] M. Beltrán. 2015. Automatic provisioning of multi-tier applications in cloud computing environments. *The Journal of Supercomputing* 71, 6 (2015), 2221–2250.
[4] D. Benz and more. 2010. The social bookmark and publication management system BibSonomy. *VLDB* 19, 6 (2010), 849–875.
[5] G. Brataas, N. Herbst, S. Ivansek, and J. Polutnik. 2017. Scalability Analysis of Cloud Software Services. In *Companion Proceedings of the 14th IEEE ICAC 2017, Self Organizing Self Managing Clouds Workshop (SOSeMC 2017)*. IEEE.
[6] V. Cardellini, E. Casalicchio, F. Presti, and L. Silvestri. 2011. Sla-aware resource management for application service providers in the cloud. In *First International Symposium on Network Cloud Computing and Applications (NCCA)*. IEEE, 20–27.
[7] G. Chen and more. 2008. Energy-Aware Server Provisioning and Load Dispatching for Connection-Intensive Internet Services.. In *NSDI*, Vol. 8. 337–350.
[8] T. C Chieu, A. Mohindra, A. A Karve, and A. Segal. 2009. Dynamic scaling of web applications in a virtualized cloud computing environment. In *E-Business Engineering, 2009. ICEBE'09. IEEE International Conference on*. IEEE, 281–286.
[9] A. De Livera, R. Hyndman, and R. Snyder. 2011. Forecasting time series with complex seasonal patterns using exponential smoothing. *J. Amer. Statist. Assoc.* 106, 496 (2011), 1513–1527.
[10] R. Han and more. 2012. Lightweight Resource Scaling for Cloud Applications. In *IEEE/ACM CCGrid 2012*. IEEE, 644–651.
[11] N. Herbst, S. Kounev, A. Weber, and H. Groenda. 2015. BUNGEE: An Elasticity Benchmark for Self-Adaptive IaaS Cloud Environments. In *SEAMS 2015*. IEEE Press, 46–56.
[12] N. Herbst and more. 2016. Ready for Rain? A View from SPEC Research on the Future of Cloud Metrics. *CoRR* abs/1604.03470 (2016).
[13] W. Iqbal, M. Dailey, D. Carrera, and P. Janecek. 2011. Adaptive Resource Provisioning for Read Intensive Multi-tier Applications in the Cloud. *Future Generation Computer Systems* 27, 6 (2011), 871–879.
[14] J. Jiang, J. Lu, G. Zhang, and G. Long. 2013. Optimal cloud resource auto-scaling for web applications. In *13th IEEE/ACM International Symposium on Cluster, Cloud and Grid Computing (CCGrid), 2013*. IEEE, 58–65.
[15] E. Kalyvianaki, T. Charalambous, and S. Hand. 2009. Self-adaptive and Self-configured CPU Resource Provisioning for Virtualized Servers Using Kalman Filters. In *ACM ICAC 2009*. ACM, 117–126.
[16] J. O. Kephart and D. M. Chess. 2003. The Vision of Autonomic Computing. *Computer* 36, 1 (Jan. 2003), 41–50. https://doi.org/10.1109/MC.2003.1160055
[17] T. Lorido-Botran, J. Miguel-Alonso, and J. Lozano. 2014. A Review of Auto-scaling Techniques for Elastic Applications in Cloud Environments. *Journal of Grid Computing* 12, 4 (2014), 559–592.
[18] A. Naskos, A. Gounaris, and P. Katsaros. 2017. Cost-aware horizontal scaling of NoSQL databases using probabilistic model checking. *Cluster Computing* (2017), 1–15.
[19] J. Rao and more. [n. d.]. VCONF: a Reinforcement Learning Approach to Virtual Machines Auto-configuration. In *ACM ICAC 2009*. ACM, 137–146.
[20] N. Roy, A. Dubey, and A. Gokhale. 2011. Efficient autoscaling in the cloud using predictive models for workload forecasting. In *IEEE International Conference on Cloud Computing (CLOUD), 2011*. IEEE, 500–507.
[21] U. Sharma, P. Shenoy, and D. Towsley. 2012. Provisioning multi-tier cloud applications using statistical bounds on sojourn time. In *Proceedings of the 9th international conference on Autonomic computing*. ACM, 43–52.
[22] G. Tesauro, N. K Jong, R. Das, and M. Bennani. 2006. A Hybrid Reinforcement Learning Approach to Autonomic Resource Allocation. In *IEEE ICAC 2006*. 65–73.
[23] B. Urgaonkar and more. 2008. Agile Dynamic Provisioning of Multi-tier Internet Applications. *ACM TAAS* 3, 1 (2008), 1.
[24] L. Vaquero, D. Morán, F. Galán, and J. Alcaraz-Calero. 2012. Towards runtime reconfiguration of application control policies in the cloud. *Journal of Network and Systems Management* 20, 4 (2012), 489–512.
[25] P. Xiong and more. 2011. Economical and robust provisioning of n-tier cloud workloads: A multi-level control approach. In *31st International Conference on Distributed Computing Systems (ICDCS), 2011*. IEEE, 571–580.
[26] Q. Zhang, L. Cherkasova, and E. Smirni. 2007. A Regression-based Analytic Model for Dynamic Resource Provisioning of Multi-tier Applications. In *IEEE ICAC 2007*. IEEE, 27–27.
[27] Q. Zhu and G. Agrawal. 2010. Resource provisioning with budget constraints for adaptive applications in cloud environments. In *Proceedings of the 19th ACM International Symposium on High Performance Distributed Computing*. ACM, 304–307.
[28] M. Züfle and more. 2017. Telescope: A Hybrid Forecast Method for Univariate Time Series. In *Proceedings of the International work-conference on Time Series (ITISE 2017)*.

Adaptive Performance Optimization under Power Constraint in Multi-thread Applications with Diverse Scalability

Stefano Conoci*
DIAG – Sapienza, University of Rome
Rome, Italy
conoci@diag.uniroma1.it
conoci@lockless.it

Pierangelo Di Sanzo*
DIAG – Sapienza, University of Rome
Rome, Italy
disanzo@diag.uniroma1.it
disanzo@lockless.it

Bruno Ciciani*
DIAG – Sapienza, University of Rome
Rome, Italy
ciciani@diag.uniroma1.it
ciciani@lockless.it

Francesco Quaglia*
DICII – University of Rome Tor Vergata
Rome, Italy
francesco.quaglia@uniroma2.it
quaglia@lockless.it

ABSTRACT

Energy consumption has become a core concern in computing systems. In this context, power capping is an approach that aims at ensuring that the power consumption of a system does not overcome a predefined threshold. Although various power capping techniques exist in the literature, they do not fit well the nature of multi-threaded workloads with shared data accesses and non-minimal thread-level concurrency. For these workloads, scalability may be limited by thread contention on hardware resources and/or data, to the point that performance may even decrease while increasing the thread-level parallelism, indicating scarce ability to exploit the actual computing power available in highly parallel hardware. In this paper, we consider the problem of maximizing the performance of multi-thread applications under a power cap by dynamically tuning the thread-level parallelism and the power state of CPU-cores in combination. Based on experimental observations, we design a technique that adaptively identifies, in linear time within a bi-dimensional space, the optimal parallelism and power state setting. We evaluated the proposed technique with different benchmark applications, and using different methods for synchronizing threads when accessing shared data, and we compared it with other state-of-the-art power capping techniques.

CCS CONCEPTS

• **Hardware** → **Chip-level power issues**; *Enterprise level and data centers power issues*; • **Computer systems organization** → *Multicore architectures*; • **Software and its engineering** → *Software performance*;

*Also with Lockless s.r.l.

KEYWORDS

Power cap; Multi-threaded workload; Performance optimization; Power efficiency

ACM Reference Format:
Stefano Conoci, Pierangelo Di Sanzo[1], Bruno Ciciani[1], and Francesco Quaglia[1]. 2018. Adaptive Performance Optimization under Power Constraint in Multi-thread Applications with Diverse Scalability. In *ICPE '18: ACM/SPEC International Conference on Performance Engineering, April 9–13, 2018, Berlin, Germany*. ACM, New York, NY, USA, 12 pages. https://doi.org/10.1145/3184407.3184419

1 INTRODUCTION

Multi-core architectures are nowadays dominating the computer system market. Thanks to hardware parallelism, they offer powerful environments allowing to effectively speed-up the execution of multi-threaded workloads. These kinds of workloads span a wide range of application domains, including Web applications, transactional applications and HPC ones [15, 25]. However, one disadvantage of multi-core architectures is that powering many cores requires more energy, and power demand of computing systems raised up even more as a core concern to cope with.

Over the last years, computer system manufacturers introduced some hardware mechanisms to control power consumption and, consequently, to enable improvements in the energy efficiency. Examples include Dynamic Voltage and Frequency Scaling (DVFS), which allows lowering the voltage and the frequency (hence the power consumption) of a processor/core in a controlled manner, and Clock Gating, which disables some processor/core circuitry during idle periods. Contextually, today's Operating Systems offer power management tools—like Linux CPUFreq Governor [16]—which expose interfaces to dynamically change the power state of CPU-cores via DVFS, thus allowing to tune the performance of cores and their power consumption according to the end-users' needs.

The approach of limiting the power consumption of a system is generally known as *power capping*. In this context, an interesting challenge is the one of regulating the usage of resources, thus including power, of applications based on multi-threading technology and share data accesses. More specifically, we consider the objective of maximizing the application performance under a power constraint—the *power cap*—in scenarios where the applications themselves may exhibit different degrees of scalability. This is due to different synchronization schemes that can be used for regulating the accesses to shared data (e.g. lock-based vs. speculative ones), as well as to different incidence of conflicting accesses along the application lifetime. Overall, in these applications, part of the computing power needs to be devoted to manage synchronization (including hardware level one) which is reflected on both performance and energy consumption in non-trivial manner, as already demonstrated by a few results, e.g. [20].

In the literature various power capping techniques have been proposed (e.g. [4, 10, 14, 18, 19, 21, 24, 24]). However, most of them are application-agnostic, i.e. they enforce the power cap at the level of a server machine, without accounting for workload features (e.g. scalability) of running applications. As for the specific case of multi-threaded workloads, the problem of controlling resource usage, in terms of number of used cores and core frequency, has been addressed in some literature contributions, such as [1, 19, 26]. However, the proposed approaches suffer from some limitations. In more detail, some of them still do not account for the diverse scalability profiles of multi-threaded workloads. Other approaches rely on strategies that do not always find the best-performing configuration in terms of thread-level parallelism and frequency/voltage of used cores.

Overall, to select the right combination of thread parallelism and core power state which ensures the best performance under a power cap, it looks mandatory to take into account the (possible) limited scalability of the application, as it manifests at run-time due to synchronization dynamics. Further, it is necessary to be able to react to variations of the workload since the scalability profile of an application may change depending on the workload profile.

To cope with this problem, we propose an adaptive technique that uses a novel on-line exploration-based tuning strategy. We devised our technique exploiting empirical observations of the effects on both performance and power consumption associated with the combined variation of thread-level parallelism and CPU-core power state. Specifically, by the results of an experimental study, we show that some scalability features of multi-threaded workloads, even in the presence of non-negligible incidence of synchronization, remain invariant with respect to the variation of the power state of CPU-cores. Based on this, we defined an optimized tuning strategy where the exploration moves along specific directions that depend on the power cap value and on the intrinsic scalability of the application. Remarkably, we prove that the proposed technique finds the optimal configuration of concurrent threads and CPU frequency/voltage—the configuration that provides the highest performance among the configurations with power consumption lower than the power cap—in linear time. Also, we present a refinement of our technique that exploits fluctuations between configurations—in terms of thread-level parallelism and CPU-core power state—to further improve the application performance and reduce the possibility and the incidence of power cap violations.

We demonstrate the advantages of our proposal via an experimental study based on various application contexts, including various benchmarks that use different thread synchronization methods. This allows us to robustly assess our technique via disparate test cases where contention among threads affects the application scalability in significantly different ways.

The remainder of this article is structured as follows. In Section 2 we discuss related work. Section 3 defines our target problem and presents the results of the preliminary analysis. Section 4 illustrates the proposed optimization technique, proves that the selected configuration is optimal, analyzes the time complexity of the exploration procedure and finally presents the strategy based on fluctuations. Section 5 describes the most relevant implementation details of a software architecture embedding our optimizer, and presents the experimental results.

2 RELATED WORK

As discussed, various power capping techniques have been devised, which are aimed at limiting the overall power consumption of a single (server) machine. Most of them are based on application-agnostic approaches, thus not representing fully exhaustive solutions. Less work has been carried out targeting the reduction (or the optimization) of power consumption depending on the workload features of running applications. In the following, we focus on this kind of techniques and we discuss the differences compared to our proposal.

A work specifically focused on optimizing the power efficiency of applications with multi-threaded workloads is presented in [19]. The proposed technique, called Pack and Cap, aims at selecting the best configuration, in terms of number of CPU-cores to be assigned to an application and the related CPU-core frequency, which ensures a given power cap. Based on experimental measurements of the performance and power consumption obtained running benchmarks from the Parsec suite, the authors conclude that the configuration that provides the highest performance at a given level of power consumption always assigns to the application the highest possible number of CPU-cores. However, as shown in our experimental analysis through a direct comparison with our proposed technique, this selection strategy is not optimal for multi-thread applications with sub-linear scalability.

The work in [26] considers the problem of maximizing performance under a power cap while also taking into account the effects of thread contention on scalability. This solution defines an ordered set of power knobs that are progressively tuned by performing a binary search on the respective domain, selecting the setting that provides the highest performance for the considered power knob while operating within the power cap. Specifically, it first selects the optimal number of CPU-cores that should be assigned to an application. Subsequently, once fixed this number, it progressively increases the frequency/voltage of the CPU-cores until the power consumption is below the power cap. However, this approach may not find the configuration ensuring the best performance. Indeed, there may be some other configuration with, e.g., a lower number of threads and a higher frequency/voltage, providing higher performance still within the power cap. In our experimental analysis (see Section 5), we present data that compare this approach with our technique.

The paper by Portfield et al. [17] presents a technique that reduces the energy consumption of OpenMP programs by throttling concurrency when both power and memory bandwidth usage is high. Throttled threads are put in a low-power mode by modifying the duty cycle of individual CPU-cores. This is a lightweight approach, but achieves low power reduction compared to thread pausing or modifying the frequency/voltage of CPU-cores. Nevertheless, the proposed technique does not tune the power state of the CPU-cores running non-throttled threads and does not consider power constraints.

Different literature contributions rely on Intel RAPL [4, 9] as a building block to enforce power capping at hardware level for different subsystems (e.g. CPU package or memory). They estimate the power consumption by observing different low-level hardware events, and then select the optimal CPU frequency and voltage such that the average power consumption of a specific subsystem is lower than the power cap. In our technique, we do not exploit the power capping capability offered by RAPL, although we exploit RAPL exclusively as a power measuring tool. This choice is motivated by the fact that RAPL cannot enforce power capping for whichever subset of CPU-cores. Thus, it is not adequate for application-oriented power capping, i.e. for tuning the power consumption of a specific subset of CPU-cores used by a given application, according to the fact that such number of cores well matches the scalability level of the application. Also, RAPL is a proprietary technology only supported by recent Intel x86 processors. Conversely, our technique directly controls the power state of CPU-cores via the abstraction of *P-state*, which is a standard supported by various processors from different manufacturers, also with different instruction sets.

Exploiting RAPL, Gholkar et al. [7] propose a 2-level hierarchical technique that uses an exploration-based approach to optimize the performance of a cluster under power constraints. This technique partitions the power budget of the cluster between different jobs. Then, for each job, it determines the set of nodes for assigning the job, and sets the node power level via RAPL. Differently from our proposal, this technique operates at cluster-level and does not deal with thread-level parallelism. The work presented in [1] proposes an exploration-based technique that improves the performance under a power cap for OpenMP applications. For each parallel region, it selects the appropriate number of threads, scheduling policy and chunk size using the Nelder-Mead search algorithm [6]. The search is performed at a fixed RAPL power-cap setting. Given that the search space may be large, it searches within a restricted space (e.g. 2, 4, 8 or 16 threads), which is a-priori determined to reduce the computation time. Obviously, this approach does not guarantee to find the optimal solution.

Other works in literature investigate the problem of improving the application performance under power constraints considering different power management variables. FastCap [13] defines an approach for optimizing performance under a system-wide power cap considering both CPU and memory DVFS. It defines a non-linear optimization problem solved through a queuing model that considers the interaction between CPU-cores and memory banks communicating over a shared bus. Unfortunately, although memory DVFS has not been proposed recently [3, 5], it is not yet available in commercial systems.

Kanduri et al. propose to use approximation in computation as another knob that can be used in power capping, combined with DVFS and concurrency throttling, to offer a trade-off between performance and accuracy of the results [11]. Obviously, this approach

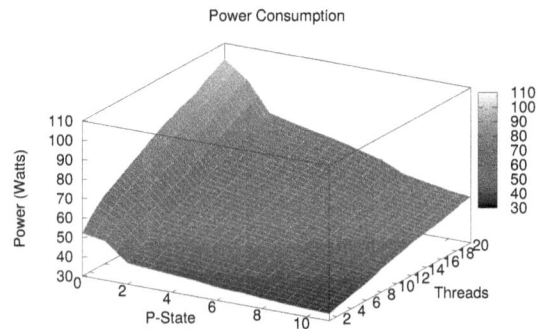

Figure 1: Throughput vs. number of concurrent threads and *P-state*

is applicable only to applications where approximation is tolerated. Another drawback is that applications require multiple implementations to allow to dynamically switch between different levels of accuracy. PPEP [24] is an online prediction framework that, based on hardware performance events and on-chip temperature measurements, estimates the performance, power consumption and energy efficiency for each different CPU *P-state*. Therefore, it allows the definition of a power capping technique that can meet power targets in a single step without requiring any exploration. However, it does not consider the possibility of altering the number of CPU-core assigned to an application, thus it would provide sub-optimal performance for multi-thread applications with limited scalability.

3 PROBLEM STATEMENT AND PRELIMINARY ANALYSIS

As discussed, we consider the problem of maximizing the performance under a power cap for applications with multi-threaded workload that may show diverse scalability profiles. We consider two tuning parameters, the number of concurrent threads and the power state of the CPU cores. We also note that tuning the number of threads implies that the application is designed in such a way to permit such a change without damages to the correctness of its execution. In particular, we focus on CPU/memory bound applications based on the working thread pool paradigm which is adopted by wide-spread real-world applications such as commodity multi-threaded application servers or modern scientific computing platforms [15, 25].

We assume that the power state of CPU-cores can be changed via DVFS. We adhere to the ACPI standard notation, where *P0* identifies the CPU core state with maximum power and performance, and progressively *P1*, *P2*, ... identify states with less power and performance. When a CPU-core has no instructions to execute (e.g. when there is no candidate thread to be executed on that core), it can be transited from the full operating state, denoted with *C0*, to some of the available idle state, progressively denoted with *C1*, *C2*, ... When residing in one of these states, the core power consumption is highly reduced. Accordingly, when the number of running threads of the application is below the number of available CPU-cores, the transition of unused cores to some idle states is favored, thus reducing the overall power consumption.

To illustrate the effects on power consumption associated with the variation of *P-state* and the number of concurrent threads, we show in Figure 1 the results of an experiment where we run Intruder, which is one of the applications included in STAMP benchmark suite [2]. This suite offers various applications with multi-threaded workloads for performance analysis of in-memory transactional multiprocessing systems [22]. Intruder emulates a signature-based network intrusion detection system where network packets are processed in parallel by a tunable number of concurrent threads. We executed different runs of this application while changing *P-state* and the number of concurrent threads up to the number of available CPU-cores in the underlying machine. We used a machine with two Intel Xeon E5, 20 physical cores total, 256 ECC DDR4 memory, with core clock frequency ranging from 1.2 GHz (whose *P-state* is denoted as P11) to 2.2 GHz (denoted as P1), and TurboBoost from 2.2 GHz to 3.1 GHz (denoted as P0). Since we focus on the effects of the joint variation of the power state of CPU-cores and the thread-level parallelism, we consider power consumption relative to the CPU and memory subsystems, which we measured via the Intel RAPL interface [9]. The plot shows that the power consumption always increases while incrementing the number of concurrent threads or while decrementing *P-state*. We observed this behaviour also with all the other benchmark applications that we used in our study (as shown in Section 5). After all, this is not a surprising result. Indeed, adding more threads leads to keeping more CPU-cores in the operating state, thus increasing the overall power consumption, and decreasing *P-state* leads to use more power per core. Accordingly, we reasonably assume that this holds true with any workload.

We denote a system configuration with the couple (p, t), where p denotes the *P-state* and t is the number of threads. Given a power cap value C, if S is the set of all possible configurations, we denote as $S_{ac} \subseteq S$ the subset of all acceptable configurations, that is the configurations for which the power cap value is not violated. Denoting with $pwr(p, t)$ the power consumption with configuration (p, t), then $pwr(p, t) \leq C$ for each $(p, t) \in S_{ac}$. Based on our experimental observations, $pwr(p, t)$ is a monotonically increasing function with respect to both p and t. Thus, the subsets of acceptable and unacceptable configurations are separated by a frontier line. In Figure 2 we show an example of frontier line for the Intruder test case with $C = 50$ Watts.

Our goal is to find the configuration $(p, t)^* \in S_{ac}$ for which the performance of the application is maximized. Without loss of generality, we consider the application throughput as the performance metric. In any case, a different performance metric could be used, such as the response time. We denote as $thr(p, t)$ the application throughput with the configuration (p, t).

In Figure 3, we report the results of an experimental study we conducted to analyse the throughput curve $thr(p, t)$ while varying p and t. We used four multi-thread applications (still taken from STAMP), namely Intruder, Genome, Vacation and Ssca2. We selected these applications since they show very different behaviour in terms of scalability. Also, to carry out a more in-depth study on how contention and synchronization scenarios materialize, in our experiments we used two different implementations of each application. They are based on two different approaches to synchronize the access of threads to shared data. The first implementation uses a coarse-grained locking approach, where shared data accesses are

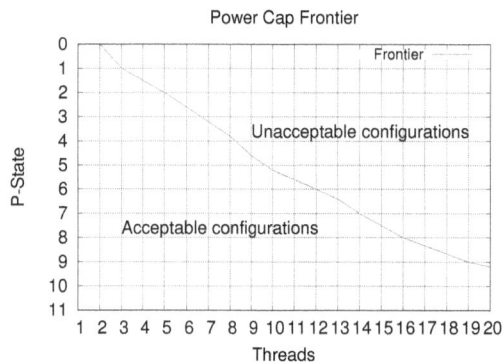

Figure 2: Frontier line between accepted and unaccepted configurations with C=50 watts

implemented as critical sections protected by a single global lock. The second one uses a fine-grained approach, relying on Software Transactional Memory [8], where shared data accesses are executed as (concurrent) transactions. This allowed us to analyze the scalability for antithetical synchronization techniques, spanning from pessimistic lock-based techniques to optimistic/speculative ones.

All plots in Figure 3 confirm our observations on the profile of the throughput curve. Indeed, in some cases, it shows an initial ascending part followed by a descending part. In other cases, the ascending part or the descending part do not exist. Also, the plots show that, when changing the application and/or the synchronization approach, the shape of the throughput curves may change. Particularly, the number of threads that provides the highest throughput may be different. In our experiments, it ranges from 1 (in the case of workloads with very limited scalability, such as for Intruder Lock-based, Vacation Lock-based and Ssca2 Lock-based) to 20 (in the case of scalable workloads as Genome Transaction-based or Vacation Transaction-based). Notably, in some cases it is in the middle (as for Intruder Transaction-based, Genome Lock-based or Ssca2 Transaction-based).

Another observation that comes out from the plots in Figure 3 is that, fixed the application and the synchronization approach, the throughput curves preserve the shape when varying p. The different curves appear translated, but the number of threads for which each curve reaches the maximum value (i.e. the highest throughput) does not change, unless for small and unpredictable variations generated by the measurement noise. Finally, the plots show that, keeping fixed the number of threads, the throughput value increases when decreasing p. We exploit these experimental findings to optimize our exploration-based technique that we presents in the next section.

4 THE ADAPTIVE POWER CAPPING TECHNIQUE

The adaptive power capping technique we propose is based on an on-line tuning strategy that periodically performs an exploration procedure. This procedure finds the optimal configuration $(p, t)^*$, which is actuated and kept until the exploration procedure restarts

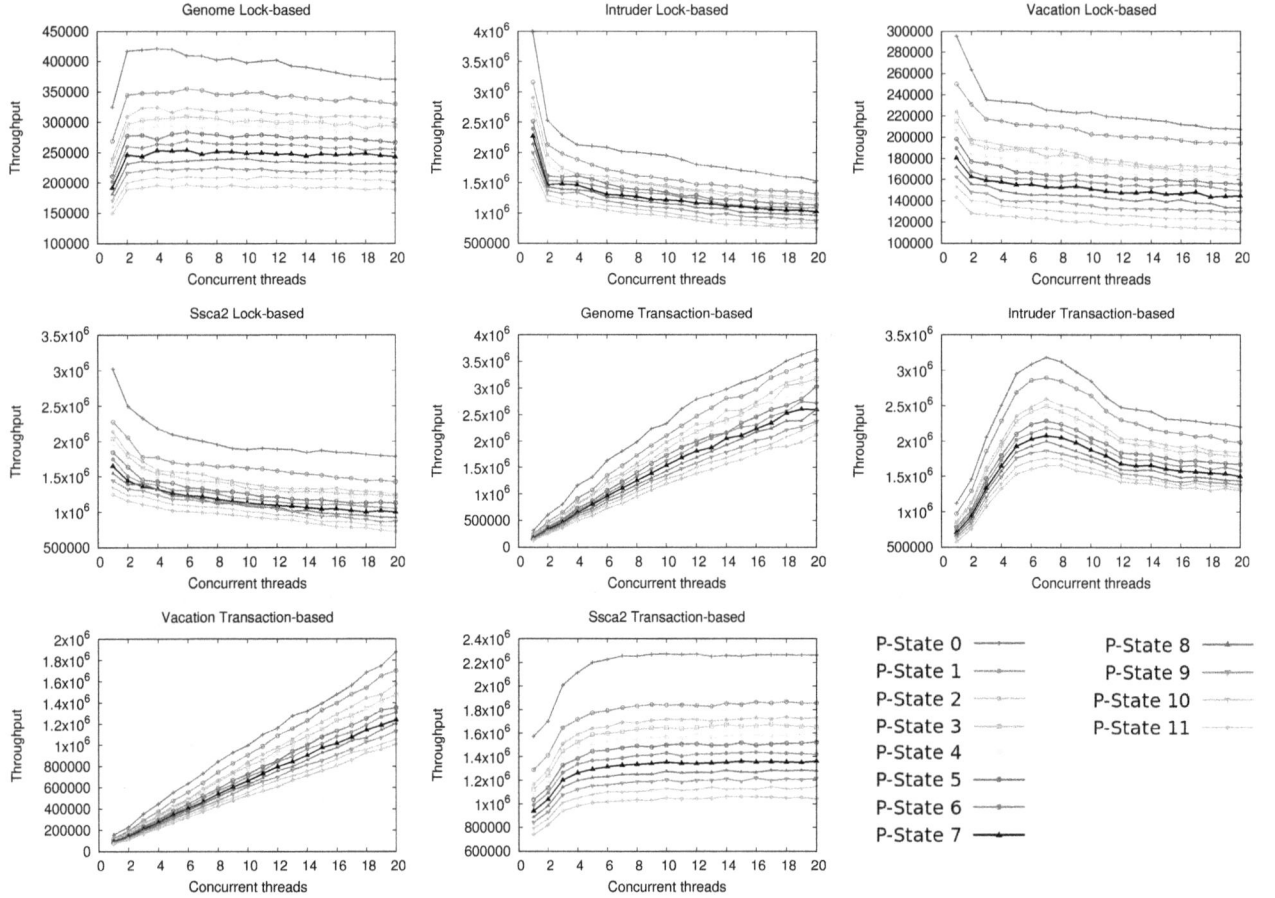

Figure 3: Throughput vs. number of concurrent threads

after a pre-established period. This allows to capture possible variations of the workload profile along time, which may lead to a different optimal configuration.

In short, the exploration procedure records the measures of the power consumption and the throughput of the application while moving along configurations within a specific path. At the end of the exploration, the one with the highest throughput is selected. The procedure is able to identify the optimal configuration by exploring only a subset of all possible configurations. We note that the full set of configurations may be very large, particularly when a large number of CPU-cores and/or p-states are available. Thus, reducing the exploration space is fundamental for an on-line exploration-based strategy.

4.1 The Exploration Procedure

The exploration procedure takes as input a starting configuration (p^s, t^s) and a power cap value C and returns $(p, t)^*$. For the first execution of the procedure, the starting configuration can be arbitrarily selected, while in subsequent executions it starts from the output configuration of the previous one. We note that the shapes of the throughput curves and the observations that we made in our preliminary analysis allow to exclude some configurations from

the exploration, thus reducing the configuration exploration space. Specifically, if during the exploration:

(1) a configuration (p^j, t^k) such that $thr(p^j, t^k) \leq thr(p^j, t^k - 1)$ is found then all configurations (p, t) where $t \geq t^k$, for whichever p, can be excluded (since we are in the descending part of the throughput curve and since the throughput curves preserve the shape while varying P-state).

(2) a configuration (p^j, t^k) such that $pwr(p^j, t^k) \leq C$ is found then all configurations (p, t^k) with $p > p^k$ can be excluded (since increasing P-state reduces the application throughput).

(3) a configuration (p^j, t^k) such that $pwr(p^j, t^k) > C$ is found then all configurations (p, t) where $t \geq t^k$ and $p \leq p^k$ can be excluded (since decreasing P-state or increasing the number of concurrent threads increments the power consumption).

Based on the above observations, we built an exploration procedure articulated in 3 phases, plus a final selection phase. The phases are described below. To help the reader while reading the description, a graphical example is shown in Figure 4, which refers to a test case where the number of concurrent threads providing the highest throughput is equal to 15.

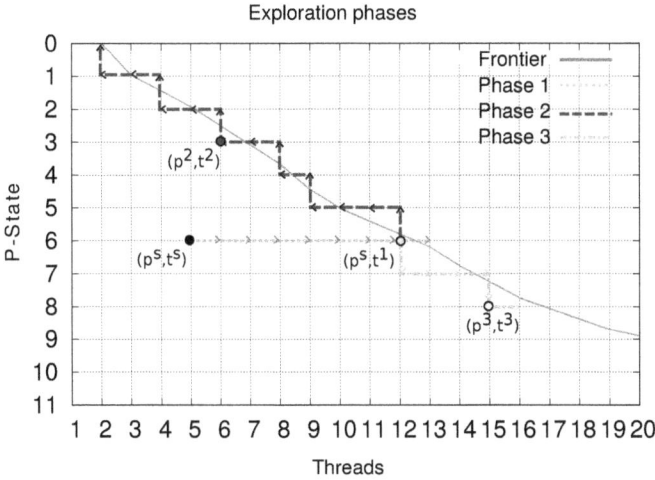

Figure 4: Example of exploration phases performed by the basic strategy

Phase 1. This phase starts from the initial configuration (p^s, t^s), and aims at finding, keeping fixed p^s, the number of threads providing the highest throughput without violating the power cap. We denote as (p^s, t^1) the configuration returned by this phase. It performs a search inspired by the hill-climbing technique [23]. Specifically, it starts incrementing by one the number of threads, and continues if the throughput increases and the power cap is not violated (if the throughput increases it means that it is moving along the ascending part of the throughput curve). It stops when the throughput starts decreasing, when the power cap is violated or when the maximum number of threads (which optionally can be pre-established by the user) has been reached. Finally, it returns the configuration for which it measured the highest throughput and which is within the power cap. If the throughput does not grow after the first increment, or the power cap is violated, it starts decreasing the number of threads (since it is moving along the descending part of the throughput curve, or the power consumption must be reduced) until the throughput starts decreasing. Then, it returns the configuration with the highest throughput if it does not violate the power cap. Otherwise, if all the explored configurations violate the power cap, or if the exploration reaches a number of threads equal to 1, it returns $(p^s, 1)$. In the example in Figure 4, the exploration during phase 1 is represented by the green line. It starts with $(p^s, t^s) = (6, 5)$, then increases the number of threads and terminates when it reaches configuration $(6, 13)$ since it violates the power cap. It returns $(p^s, t^1) = (6, 12)$, which is within the power cap.

Phase 2. This phase starts from the configuration (p^s, t^1) returned by phase 1 and is executed only if this configuration does not violate the power cap (otherwise we jump to the next phase). The goal of phase 2 is to continue the exploration along lower values of P-state (we remark that increasing the value of P-state leads to both higher core performance and higher power consumption). Specifically, it moves from the current configuration (p, t) to configuration $(p - 1, t)$. If the latter configuration does not violate the power cap, it continues to reduce the value of P-state. If a configuration such that

$pwr(p, t) > C$ is reached, it starts reducing the number of threads, thus moving to configuration $(p, t-1)$, then $(p, t-2)$ and so on (since decreasing the number of concurrent threads reduces the power consumption) until the power cap is not violated. After, it restarts the exploration by decreasing the value of P-state. The exploration terminates when p reaches 0 and the current configuration does not violate the power cap, when it reaches configuration $(0, 1)$, or when a configuration with $t = 1$ violates the power cap. Then, among the explored configurations, Phase 2 returns the configuration (that we denote as (p^2, t^2)) with the highest throughput within the power cap, or $(0, 1)$ if none of the explored configurations is within the power cap. In Figure 4, the exploration of Phase 2 is shown by the blue line. It starts from $(p^s, t^1) = (6, 12)$, and then explores up to configuration $(0, 1)$. It returns $(p^2, t^2) = (3, 6)$.

Phase 3. This phase starts again from the configuration returned by Phase 1, i.e. (p^s, t^1), and aims at continuing the exploration for higher values of P-state. If the configuration returned by Phase 1 is such that t^1 is the number of threads providing the highest throughput and is within the power cap, Phase 3 is not executed (since decrementing the value of P-state leads to lower throughput). If not, it increments by one the value of P-state and starts increasing the number of concurrent threads until the power cap is violated or the throughput decreases. In the former case, if the maximum value of P-state has not been reached, it increments by one the value of P-state and starts again incrementing the number of threads. In all the other cases the exploration terminates. Then, phase 3 returns the explored configuration (that we denote as (p^3, t^3)) with the highest throughput within the power cap, or it returns (p_{max}, t^1) (where p_{max} is the maximum value of P-state) if all the explored configurations are within the power cap. In Figure 4, the exploration of Phase 3 is represented by the yellow line. It starts from $(p^s, t^1) = (6, 12)$, then explores up to configuration $(8, 16)$, where it stops since the throughput decreases (we remark that in the example the number of concurrent threads providing the highest throughput is equal to 15). It returns $(p^3, t^3) = (8, 15)$.

Final phase: this phase selects the configuration with the highest throughput between the configurations (p^s, t^1), (p^2, t^2) and (p^3, t^3), which does not violate the power cap, or returns *null* if none of them is within the power cap.

4.2 Proof of Optimality

In this section we prove that the proposed exploration procedure finds the optimal configuration in the bi-dimensional space of configurations defined by all combinations of active threads and CPU P-state. We note that solving this problem in linear time is not trivial, since the approach of finding the optimal solution for each dimension independently—which might be trivial with some hill-climbing approach under Assumption 1—does not compose to the bi-dimensional optimum. We initially present the set of assumptions our proof relies on. We recall that all these assumptions originate from the experimental results we discussed in Section 3.

Assumption 1. Fixed P-state and increasing t from 0 to t_{max}, the throughput curve behaves as follows:
  (1) initially increases, reaches its maximum value, then decreases, otherwise
  (2) monotonically increases, otherwise

(3) monotonically decreases.

Assumption 2. If $thr(p^j, t^k) > thr(p^j, t^k + 1)$ then for each p we have $thr(p, t^k) > thr(p, t^k + 1)$. Also, if $thr(p^j, t^k) > thr(p^j, t^k-1)$ then for each p we have $thr(p, t^k) > thr(p, t^k - 1)$. In other words, if for some *P-state* and t^k threads the throughput decreases (increases) when adding (removing) one thread, then this holds true for whichever *P-state*. Overall, the ordering relations on the throughput values when changing the number of threads are not effected by *P-state*.

Assumption 3. if $p^j < p^k$ then $thr(p^j, t) > thr(p^k, t)$ for whichever t. In other words, when decreasing the value of *P-state* the throughput always increases for whichever number of threads;

Assumption 4. If $p^j < p^k$ then $pwr(p^j, t) > pwr(p^k, t)$, and if $t^j > t^k$ then $pwr(p, t^j) > pwr(p, t^k)$. In other words, the power consumption increases when decreasing *P-state* or when increasing the number of threads.

STATEMENT. The exploration procedure presented in Section 4.1 is guaranteed to find the optimal configuration of CPU *P-state* and thread-level parallelism.

PROOF. We partition the search space into three disjoint sub-spaces, based on the value of *P-state* of the initial configuration, i.e. p^s. Specifically:

- S_1 is the sub-space of configurations such that $p = p^s$;
- S_2 is the sub-space of configurations such that $p < p^s$;
- S_3 is the sub-space of configurations such that $p > p^s$.

We show that Phases 1, Phase 2 and Phase 3 find the optimal configuration for sub-spaces S_1, S_2 and S_3, respectively. This is sufficient to prove that the overall optimal configuration is found, since Final phase simply selects the optimal one among them.

Outcome by Phase 1. Phase 1 explores configurations within S1. Specifically, it keeps fixed p^s and explores while varying only the number of threads t. Phase 1 uses the hill-climbing search. By Assumption 1, the function $thr(p^s, t)$ has only one local maximum, thus it corresponds to the global maximum. Accordingly, the hill-climbing search trivially can find the maximum [23], which is the optimal configuration in S_1. The only exception is when the configuration with the global maximum violates the power cap. In this case, the exploration terminates as soon as the configuration with the highest number of threads which is within the power cap is found. Also in this case, it is the optimal configuration in S_1.

Outcome by Phase 2. We recall that Phase 2 starts exploring from the configuration returned by Phase 1, denoted as (p^s, t^1), which is the optimal one with *P-state* equal to p^s, unless none of the configurations with *P-state* equal to p^s is within the power cap. In the latter case, Phase 1 returns $(p^s, 1)$. Also, we recall that Phase 2 explores moving towards lower *P-states* and a lower number of threads. For Assumption 2, the number of threads that provides the maximum throughput does not change when decreasing *P-state*. Accordingly, if (p^s, t^1) is the optimal configuration fixed p^s, then the optimal configuration for the sub-space S_2 must have a number of threads less than or equal to t^1. Specifically, if $pwr(p^s - 1, t^1) < C$ then the optimal configuration with *P-state* equal to $p^s - 1$ has still t^1 threads. Otherwise, if the power cap is violated, the number

of threads has to be reduced to stay within the power cap. Also, this mean that reducing the number of threads leads to reduce the throughput, since the above situation can arise only if we are in the ascending part of the throughput curve. Accordingly, in this case the optimal configuration is the first one that is within the power cap while reducing the threads. Phase 2 follows exactly this behaviour, i.e. it first moves to *P-state* equal to $p^s - 1$, and if $pwr(p^s - 1, t^1) > C$ then it reduces the number of threads until it finds a configuration that does not violate the power cap. Thus, Phase 2 finds the optimal configuration for *P-state* equal to $p^s - 1$, unless none of them is within the power cap. We remark that Phase 2 performs this search for each *P-state* such that $p \in [0, p^s - 1]$. Thus, it finds the optimal configuration for each *P-state* in the sub-space S_2. Finally, it selects the optimal one of them, thus finding the optimal configuration in the sub-space S_2.

Outcome by Phase 3. We remark that Phase 3 starts exploring from the configuration returned by Phase 1, and explores moving towards higher *P-states* and a higher number of threads. Also, we remark that Phase 3 is not executed if the configuration returned by Phase 1 is such that t^1 is the number of threads that provides the highest throughput and is within the power cap. Indeed, in this case, the throughput for any configuration with a number of threads higher than t^1 and any higher *P-state* is lower for Assumption 2. Hence, Phase 3 is executed only if the number of threads that provides the highest throughput is higher than t^1, but it violates the power cap with *P-state* equal to p^1. This means that t^1 is along the ascending part of the throughput curve due to Assumption 1. Also, this holds true for any *P-state* higher than p^1 for Assumption 2. Accordingly, the throughput with any configuration in the sub-space S_3 with a number of threads less than t^1 is lower. Consequently, the optimal configuration for *P-state* equal to $p^s + 1$ must have a number of threads higher than t^1. Phase 3 first moves to *P-state* equal to $p^s + 1$, then it starts increasing the number of threads and stops when the power cap is violated or the throughput decreases. Accordingly, it finds the optimal configuration for *P-state* equal to $p^s + 1$. After, Phase 3 performs this search for each *P-state* such that $p \in [p^s + 1, p_{max}]$. Thus, it finds the optimal configuration for each *P-state* in the sub-space S_3. Finally, it selects the optimal one of them, thus finding the optimal configuration in the sub-space S_3. □

4.3 Time Complexity Analysis

We estimate the time complexity of the exploration procedure as the number of exploration steps required to return the optimal configuration. We evaluate the time complexity of each exploration phase separately:

- **Phase 1.** Each configuration with a different number of concurrent threads and $p = p^s$ is explored at most once, thus the time complexity is $O(t_{max})$;
- **Phase 2.** Starting from a configuration (p, t), Phase 2 either reduces the value of p or reduces t. Starting from the configuration returned by Phase 1, it can reduce p at most p_{max} times, and can reduce t at most t_{max} times. Thus, the time complexity of Phase 2 is $O(p_{max} + t_{max})$;
- **Phase 3.** Starting from a configuration (p, t), Phase 3 either increments the value of p or increments t. Thus, for the same

reasoning used in Phase 2, the time complexity of Phase 3 is $O(p_{max} + t_{max})$.

Therefore, the overall time complexity of the exploration procedure is $O(p_{max} + t_{max})$.

4.4 The Enhanced Tuning Strategy

In this section, we present an improvement of our tuning strategy that allows to further improve performance and reduce the probability to violate the power cap. It takes advantage of two practical factors:

(1) The power consumption with the optimal configuration $(p, t)^*$ may be lower than the power cap, thus $C - pwr(p, t)^* > 0$. This is a consequence of the discrete set of power consumption values resulting from the discrete domain of *P-states*. Statistically, the greater the difference of power consumption between adjacent configurations, the larger the difference between C and $pwr(p, t)^*$.

(2) The power consumption with the optimal configuration $(p, t)^*$ may change along the time interval in-between two subsequent exploration procedures due to possible variations of the workload profile. Thus, $pwr(p, t)^*$ could increase over the power cap. Similarly, the application power profile might change such that some configuration with both higher performance and power consumption than $(p, t)^*$ might enter the set of acceptable configurations.

Our enhanced tuning strategy performs fluctuations between different configurations to mimic a continuous domain of power consumption values, while also accounting for possible variations of the application power profile. It relies on the same exploration technique used by the basic strategy—without introducing any further step in the exploration—but in addition to $pwr(p, t)^*$ it also selects two other configurations:

- $(p, t)^H$ the explored configuration with highest throughput such that $pwr(p, t)^H < C * (1 + h)$, and
- $(p, t)^L$ the explored configuration with highest throughput such that $pwr(p, t)^L < C * (1 - h)$.

The parameter h defines the ideal distance between the power consumption of $(p, t)^H$ and $(p, t)^L$ with respect to the power cap. We note that $thr(p, t)^L \leq thr(p, t)^* \leq thr(p, t)^H$. In the time interval between the end of the exploration procedure and the start of the next one, the enhanced strategy performs fluctuations between $(p, t)^H$, $pwr(p, t)^*$ and $pwr(p, t)^L$ to maximize the performance over a window w, while keeping the average power consumption along the window lower than C. When $pwr(p, t)^* < C$, the strategy moves between $(p, t)^*$ and $(p, t)^H$, selecting the former whenever the average power consumption along the window is above the power cap, while selecting the latter in the opposite case. The result of this fluctuation can provide a performance increase over $thr(p, t)^*$. Differently, if $pwr(p, t)^* > C$ the variation of configurations is performed between $(p, t)^*$ and $(p, t)^L$, using the latter to reduce the average power consumption over the window. In this scenario, the enhanced strategy can provide a reduction in the power cap violation compared to the static exploitation of $(p, t)^*$. To limit the fluctuation frequency, an upper and a lower tolerance threshold like $C + l$ and $C - l$ can be used. Temporary power cap

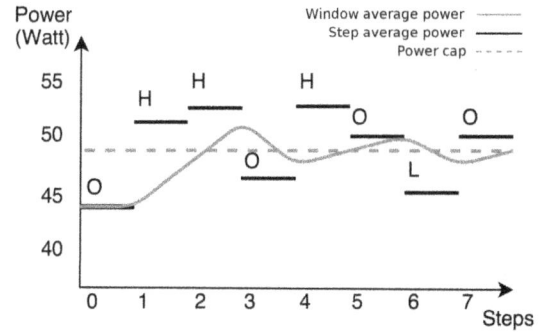

Figure 5: Example of fluctuations of configurations performed by the enhanced strategy in-between different exploration procedures. Window size is set to 8. O denotes the configuration $(p, t)^*$, H the configuration $(p, t)^H$ and L the configuration $(p, t)^L$. These configurations are fixed along each window but their power consumption could change.

violations of a few milliseconds are not relevant as power consumption is generally computed as an average value at the granularity of seconds.

To adapt to workload variations, at the end of each window, if $pwr(p, t)^L > C$ the P-state of $(p, t)^*$ is shifted up by one in order to reduce its power consumption. Moreover, $(p, t)^H$ and $(p, t)^L$ are also set to different configurations such that they have the same number of threads as $(p, t)^*$ but with P-state decremented or incremented by one respectively. This lowers the overall power consumption of the configurations, thus allowing to promptly adapt to the increase in the application power profile. Otherwise, if $pwr(p, t)^H < C$, the same modifications are applied except that the P-state of $(p, t)^*$ is shifted down by one instead of up. The possibility of increasing the power consumption of the configurations creates the opportunity for further performance gains. In both situations, we only modify the P-state and set for all configurations the number of threads equal to the configuration $(p, t)^*$ as modifying the P-state always provides either an increase or a decrease in both performance and power consumption while changing the number of threads might provide different performance results based on the workload characteristics.

A pseudo-code representation of the algorithm implemented by the enhanced strategy is presented below.

Figure 5 shows the fluctuations performed by the enhanced strategy along a window with $w = 8$. From step 0 to step 4 the strategy fluctuates between $(p, t)^*$ and $(p, t)^H$, allowing increased performance compared to the basic strategy. In step 5, to decrease the average power consumption along the window, the configuration $(p, t)^*$ is selected. However, its power consumption has increased since its last exploitation and has become higher than the power cap. In step 6, the enhanced strategy selects $(p, t)^L$ to reduce power cap violations compared to the basic strategy which would have been static to configuration $(p, t)^*$ until the next exploration procedure. Configuration $(p, t)^*$ is selected in step 7 to conclude the window. Despite no configuration shows a power consumption similar to the power cap, the average power during the window converges to its value.

Algorithm 1 Fluctuation algorithm used in the enhanced strategy

> **procedure** FLUCTUATE
> **Require:** Power cap C
> **Require:** Configuration O, T and H with attributes *(pstate, threads, power)*
> **Require:** Power cap threshold l
> **Require:** Window size w
>> $step \leftarrow 0$
>> $windowPower \leftarrow 0$
>> $windowTime \leftarrow 0$
>> $selectedConfig \leftarrow O$
>> **while** $step < w$ **do**
>>> $currentPower, time \leftarrow getMeasurements(selectedConfig)$
>>> set *power* of the measured configuration to *currentPower*
>>> $windowPower \leftarrow (windowPower * windowTime +$
>>> $currentPower * time)/(time + currentTime)$
>>> $windowTime \leftarrow windowTime + time$
>>> $slot \leftarrow slot + 1$
>>> **if** $windowPower < C * (1 - l)$ **then**
>>>> $selectedConfig \leftarrow H$
>>> **else if** $windowPower > C * (1 + l)$ **then**
>>>> **if** $O.power < C$ **then**
>>>>> $selectedConfig \leftarrow O$
>>>> **else**
>>>>> $selectedConfig \leftarrow L$
>>> **else** ▷ window power consumption close to power cap
>>>> **if** $H.power < C$ **then**
>>>>> $selectedConfig \leftarrow H$
>>>> **else if** $O.power < C$ **then**
>>>>> $selectedConfig \leftarrow O$
>>>> **else**
>>>>> $selectedConfig \leftarrow L$
>> **if** $H.power < C$ or $L.power > C$ **then**
>>> **if** $H.power < C$ **then**   ▷ can increase the power consumption
>>>> $O.pstate \leftarrow O.pstate - 1$
>>> **else**   ▷ should reduce power consumption
>>>> $O.pstate \leftarrow O.pstate + 1$
>>> $H.threads \leftarrow O.threads$
>>> $L.threads \leftarrow O.threads$
>>> $H.pstate \leftarrow O.pstate - 1$
>>> $L.pstate \leftarrow O.pstate + 1$

---

5 EXPERIMENTAL RESULTS

In this section, we present the results of an experimental study we conducted to assess the proposed power capping technique. As in previous studies on power capping (e.g. [12, 19]), we consider two evaluation metrics, the application performance and the average power cap error. The latter is the average difference between the power consumption and the power cap value along time intervals where the power cap is violated. When assessing performance and power cap errors, we also include measurements gathered along the exploration procedure. We run experiments for all application scenarios that we considered in our preliminary study (see Section 3). Thus we use Intruder, Genome, Vacation and Ssca2 as benchmark applications from STAMP, with either locks or transactions as the synchronization method. As hinted, these applications (and the different instances of the synchronization support) were specifically selected to cover a wide range of different scalability scenarios. We compared our technique with:

(1) a reference power capping technique, referred to as baseline, that selects the configuration with the lowest *P-state* from the set of configurations such that the number of threads is the highest among the configurations with power consumption lower than the power cap. It implements the selection strategy proposed in [19];

(2) a technique, referred to as dual-phase, that initially tunes the number of threads starting from the lowest *P-state*, and subsequently tunes the CPU *P-state* keeping the number of threads fixed. The initial phase is equivalent to phase 1 of the proposed exploration procedure. The selection strategy of this technique is similar to the one presented in [26].

The comparison of our proposal with the technique in point (1) allows to quantify the performance benefits achievable by properly allocating the power budget taking into account the scalability level of the specific multi-threaded workload. Additionally, the inclusion of the dual-phase technique listed in point (2) in the evaluation allows quantifying the possible performance benefits achievable by exploring the whole bi-dimensional space of configurations—as we do in our approach—over two distinct mono-dimensional explorations, which might not find the optimal configuration. We should note that, despite exploring a larger set of configurations, the technique we propose has the same time complexity of the dual-phase technique.

5.1 Implementation Details

We developed a controller module that implements our technique and the baseline technique.[1] All software of our experimental study, including benchmark applications, is developed in C language for Linux. The controller module alters the number of concurrent threads exploiting the *pause()* system call and thread-specific signals for reactivation. The CPU *P-state* is regulated through the *cpufreq* Linux sub-system, while energy readings are obtained from the *powercap* sub-system. Both these sub-systems are included by default in recent versions of the Linux kernel and expose their respective interface through the */sys* virtual file system.

At each step, the exploration procedure relies on statistical results of a previous step, such as average power consumption and throughput, to define the subsequent configuration to explore. Each step of statistics collection is determined by a fixed amount of units of work processed. We cannot rely on application independent metrics, such as the number of CPU retired operation, since it would also consider instructions related to spin-locking or aborted transactions that do not provide execution progress. For applications based on locks we defined the unit of work as the execution of one critical section guarded by a global lock. Differently, for transactions we define the unit of work as one commit. The statistics are collected in a round-robin fashion by all the active threads to reduce execution overhead and provide NUMA-aware results in modern multi-package systems.

---

[1]See github.com/HPDCS/EPADS

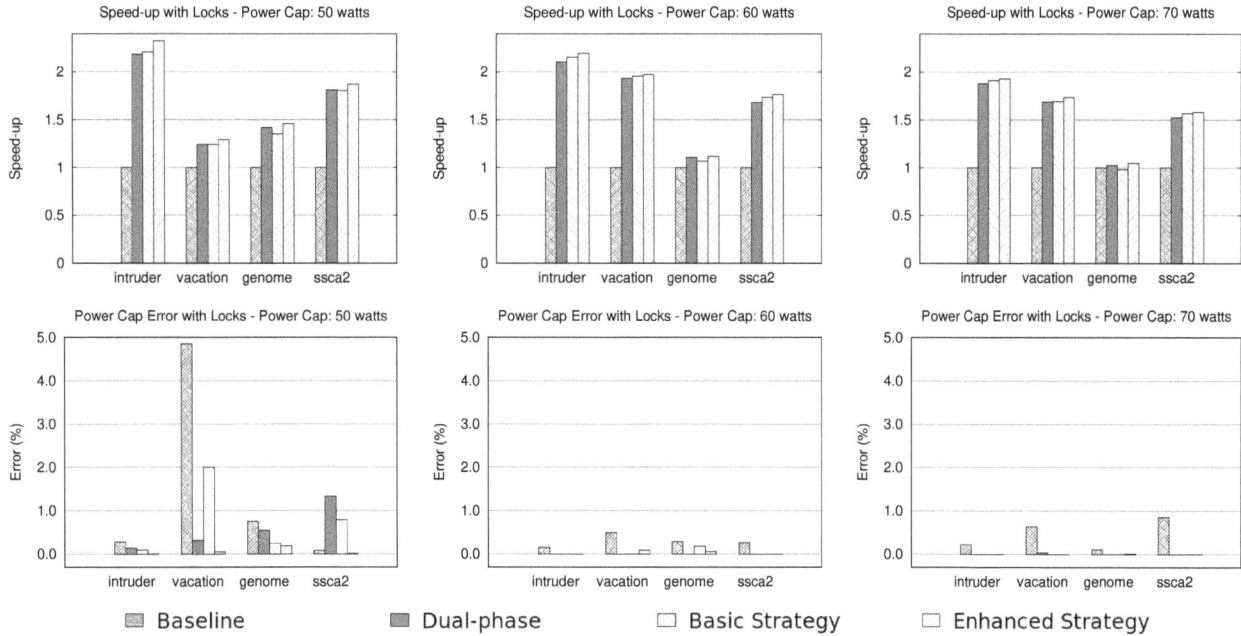

Figure 6: Speed-up and power cap error with locks

For the executions presented in the experimental results, we set the units of work per step to 5000, resulting in tens of milliseconds per step for all the considered applications and synchronization methods. In addition, we set to 150 the number of steps required to restart the exploration procedure after the conclusion of the previous exploration. Regarding the parameters of the enhanced strategy, we set the window size (w) to 10, the maximum power consumption for $(p, t)^H$ and $(p, t)^L$ to respectively the 10% higher or lower than the power cap(h) and the fluctuation threshold (l) to 1%. We always used the same parameters for all applications and synchronization techniques. Autonomic tuning of these parameters at run-time—possibly leading to increased performance benefits—will be explored in a future work. With the tested parameters, the overheads of changing configuration—dominated by *P-state* switching—and the cost of performance and power measurements are lower than 2% for all the considered executions.

5.2 Experimental Results

We consider both the tuning strategies of our technique referred to as basic strategy and enhanced strategy. We analyze the performance results of our strategies in terms of speed-up with respect to the throughput of the baseline technique. As anticipated, we also compare the average power cap error. For each test case, we present the results with three different power cap values, i.e. 50, 60 and 70 watts.

Results for the case of lock-based synchronization are reported in Figure 6. Overall, the results show an evident performance improvement with both strategies of our technique with respect to the baseline technique. Only for the case of Genome the performance is comparable. In the best cases, i.e. with Intruder, the performance improvement reaches 2.2x (2.32x) and 2.15x (2.19x) for the basic

(enhanced) strategy when the power cap is equal to 50 and 60 watts respectively, and it is close to 1.9x for both the proposed strategies with power cap set to 70 watts. The enhanced strategy further improves performance compared to the baseline technique by up to 12.5% in Intruder at 50 watts, and by 5.3% on average. For lock-based synchronization, the results of the dual-phase technique are similar to those achieved by the baseline technique.

As for the power cap error, with both the strategies of our technique and the dual-phase technique, it is clearly reduced compared to the baseline. Also, the results show that with the enhanced strategy in many cases there is a reduction of the power cap error compared to the basic strategy. Indeed, except for the case of Vacation with power cap set to 60 watts, where it is increased by less than 0.1%, the error with the enhanced strategy is lower. In the best case it is about 0.1%, while it is about 2% and 4.8% with the basic strategy and the baseline technique, respectively.

Results for the case of transaction-based synchronization are reported in Figure 7. Overall, the performance results confirm the advantage of our technique compared to the baseline technique. However, with transactions the speed-up is generally slightly lower than with locks. In the best cases, it reaches about 1.9x. Also, there is one case (with Genome and power cap = 50 watts) where it is slightly less that 1 with both the strategies. As for the power cap error, it increases with the basic strategy compared to the case with locks, overcoming the error of the baseline technique in most of the cases. However, it does not overcome 2% in all cases. The error is considerably reduced with the enhanced strategy. Particularly, it is clearly lower than the baseline technique with all applications when the power cap is equal to 50 watts and with Intruder when the power cap is equals to 60 watts, while the results are similar for the other power cap values. In addition, the enhanced strategy can

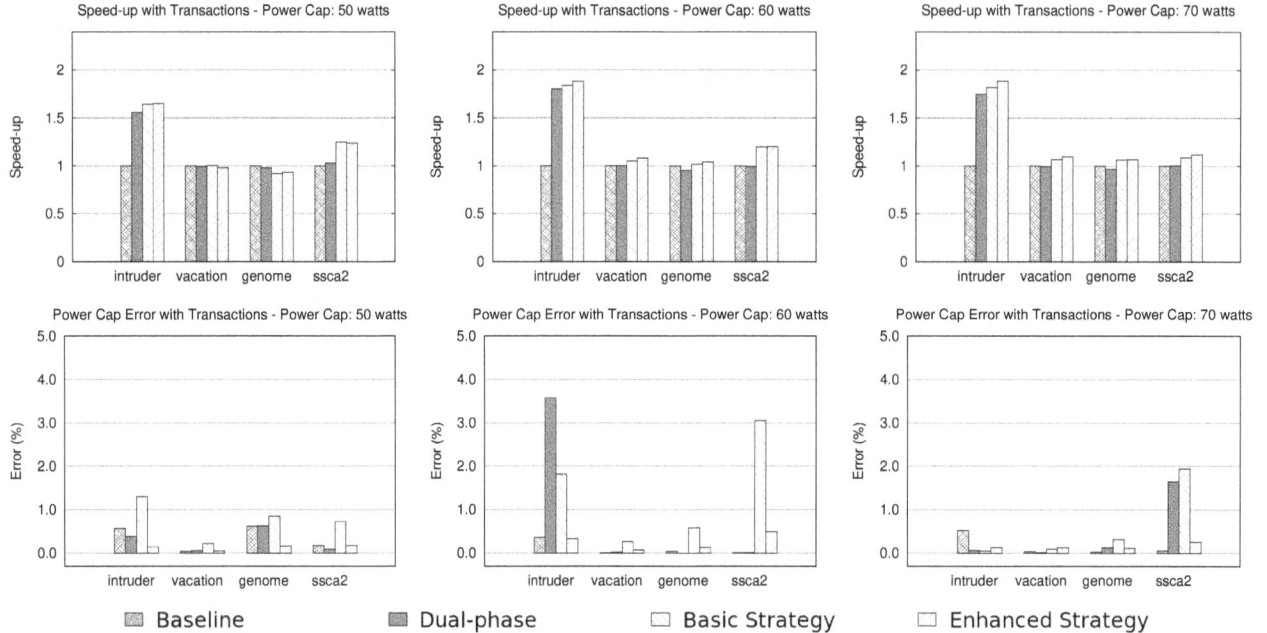

Figure 7: Speed-up and power cap error with transactions

further increase performance by up to to 8% (Vacation with power cap set to 50 watts) and by 3.5% on average. Differently from the lock-based case, both strategies of the proposed technique show an higher speed-up compared to the dual-phase technique by up to 21% (ssca2 with power cap set to 50), and by 7.7% and 10.7% on average for the basic strategy and the enhanced strategy respectively.

5.3 Analysis of the Results

As a first observation, the results show that in various cases with locks, the error of our technique and of the dual-phase technique is very close to zero. This is due to the fact that, in our study, the scalability is limited for all applications when using locks. In these scenarios, the number of concurrent threads providing higher throughput (that is selected by our technique and by the dual-phase technique) is low, thus the value of *P-state* can be changed up to 0 while the power cap frontier is still far. This keeps the error very close to 0 since it is unlikely that the power cap is violated during the exploration procedure or due to workload variations.

The error is generally reduced with the enhanced strategy compared to the basic strategy, while also improving performance. This arises since the former is able to react along the time between two consecutive exploration procedures to the possible variations of the power consumption of the selected configurations, as discussed at the end of Section 4.4.

The speed-up with our technique is less than 1 only in one case, i.e. for Genome with transactions when the power cap value is equal to 50 watts. We note that Genome with transactions is highly scalable (see Figure 3). This leads both the baseline technique and our technique to select 20 as the number of concurrent threads. As shown by the plot in Figure 3, the throughput of Genome with transactions is subject to noise when close to 20 threads . Also, we

remark that our technique is able to react to workload variations also in terms of scalability. In this scenario, these factors cause lower performance with our technique due to noise, which sometimes (wrongly) leads to temporarily selecting a less than optimal number of concurrent threads.

As expected, for lock-based synchronization the proposed technique shows similar results to the dual-phase technique since both techniques return the same configuration when the ascending part of the throughput curve is missing. For transaction-based synchronization, the best speed-up improvements over the dual-phase technique are obtained for Ssca2 and Genome which show a less than linear ascending part of the throughput curve for each fixed *P-state* (Figure 3). As the most significant example, in Ssca2 the throughput slightly increases when increasing the number of threads from 6 to 15 which makes the dual-phase technique select a configuration with 15 threads. Differently, the proposed technique allocates the power budget more efficiently by selecting a configuration with a lower number of threads at an increased frequency. We should note that the benefits of the proposed technique over the dual-phase technique are not limited to applications that rely on transactional-based synchronization. Effectively, performance benefits should be obtained for any application with a throughput function that shows an ascending part followed by a descending one, or only an ascending part that is less than linear.

Overall, the results of our experiments study show that it is possible to achieve significant performance benefits by appropriately selecting the number of concurrent threads and CPU *P-state* taking into consideration the scalability of the specific multi-threaded workload. As expected, compared to the baseline technique, the proposed solutions achieve the best results with poorly scalable applications, i.e. where contention is not minimal. Compared to the dual-phase technique, the exploration of the whole bi-dimensional space of configurations performed by the proposed technique can provide an appreciable improvement in performance for some applications, while achieving the same results for others. Finally, the enhanced strategy manages to further improve performance and reduce the power cap error over the basic strategy.

6 CONCLUSIONS

In this paper, we have proposed a novel power capping technique for dynamic tuning the number of concurrent threads and core power states for the case of multi-thread applications that materialize diverse scalability levels, also depending on the specific support for synchronizing the accesses to shared data. The technique is able to find the optimal configuration in linear time, ensuring the maximum performance achievable within the power cap. We also present an improvement of the technique that induces fluctuations between different configurations to efficiently exploit the full power budget, resulting in both increased performance and reduced power cap errors. We have shown that, compared to the baseline technique, our strategy provides an average speed-up of 1.48x, with individual test cases reaching up to 2.32x. Furthermore, we have shown that, by exploring the overall bi-dimensional space of configurations, the proposed technique can improve performance by up to 21% compared to techniques that tune the number of threads and the CPU performance state independently.

REFERENCES

[1] Md Abdullah Shahneous Bari, Nicholas Chaimov, Abid M. Malik, Kevin A. Huck, Barbara Chapman, Allen D. Malony, and Osman Sarood. 2016. ARCS: Adaptive runtime configuration selection for power-constrained OpenMP applications. *Proceedings - IEEE International Conference on Cluster Computing, ICCC* (2016), 461–470. https://doi.org/10.1109/CLUSTER.2016.39

[2] Chi Cao Minh, JaeWoong Chung, Christos Kozyrakis, and Kunle Olukotun. 2008. STAMP: Stanford Transactional Applications for Multi-Processing. *4th International Symposium on Workload Characterization*, 35–46. https://doi.org/10.1109/IISWC.2008.4636089

[3] Howard David, Chris Fallin, Eugene Gorbatov, Ulf R Hanebutte, and Onur Mutlu. 2011. Memory Power Management via Dynamic Voltage/Frequency Scaling. *Proceedings of the 8th ACM International Conference on Autonomic Computing* (2011), 31–40. https://doi.org/10.1145/1998582.1998590

[4] Howard David, Eugene Gorbatov, Ulf R. Hanebutte, Rahul Khanna, and Christian Le. 2010. RAPL: Memory power estimation and capping. *Low-Power Electronics and Design (ISLPED), 2010 ACM/IEEE International Symposium on* (2010), 189–194. https://doi.org/10.1145/1840845.1840883

[5] Qingyuan Deng, Luiz Ramos, Ricardo Bianchini, David Meisner, and Thomas Wenisch. 2012. Active low-power modes for main memory with memScale. *IEEE Micro* 32, 3 (2012), 60–69. https://doi.org/10.1109/MM.2012.21

[6] JE Dennis and Daniel J Woods. 1987. Optimization on microcomputers: The Nelder-Mead simplex algorithm. *New computing environments: microcomputers in large-scale computing* 11 (1987), 6–122.

[7] Neha Gholkar, Frank Mueller, and Barry Rountree. 2016. Power Tuning HPC Jobs on Power-Constrained Systems. *Proceedings of the 2016 International Conference on Parallel Architectures and Compilation - PACT '16* (2016), 179–191. https://doi.org/10.1145/2967938.2967961

[8] Tim Harris, James Larus, and Ravi Rajwar. 2010. *Transactional Memory, 2nd Edition* (2nd ed.). Morgan and Claypool Publishers.

[9] Intel. 2011. Intel 64 and IA-32 Architectures Software Developer Manual, Volume 3C: System Programming Guide, Part 3. (2011).

[10] Canturk Isci, Alper Buyuktosunoglu, Chen Yong Cher, Pradip Bose, and Margaret Martonosi. 2006. An analysis of efficient multi-core global power management policies: Maximizing performance for a given power budget. *Proceedings of the Annual International Symposium on Microarchitecture, MICRO* (2006), 347–358. https://doi.org/10.1109/MICRO.2006.8

[11] Anil Kanduri, Mohammad-Hashem Haghbayan, Amir M. Rahmani, Pasi Liljeberg, Axel Jantsch, Nikil Dutt, and Hannu Tenhunen. 2016. Approximation knob: power capping meets energy efficiency. *Proceedings of the 35th International Conference on Computer-Aided Design - ICCAD '16* (2016), 1–8. https://doi.org/10.1145/2966986.2967002

[12] Charles Lefurgy, Xiaorui Wang, and Malcolm Ware. 2008. Power Capping: A Prelude to Power Shifting. *Cluster Computing* 11, 2 (June 2008), 183–195. https://doi.org/10.1007/s10586-007-0045-4

[13] Yanpei Liu, Guilherme Cox, Qingyuan Deng, Stark C. Draper, and Ricardo Bianchini. 2016. FastCap: An efficient and fair algorithm for power capping in many-core systems. *ISPASS 2016 - International Symposium on Performance Analysis of Systems and Software* 3 (2016), 57–68. https://doi.org/10.1109/ISPASS.2016.7482074

[14] Thannirmalai Somu Muthukaruppan, Mihai Pricopi, Vanchinathan Venkataramani, Tulika Mitra, and Sanjay Vishin. 2013. Hierarchical power management for asymmetric multi-core in dark silicon era. *Proceedings of the 50th Annual Design Automation Conference on - DAC '13* (2013), 1. https://doi.org/10.1145/2463209.2488949

[15] Oracle. 2017. Plug into the Cloud with Oracle Database 12C (wite paper). http://www.oracle.com/technetwork/database/plug-into-cloud-wp-12c-1896100.pdf. (2017).

[16] Venkatesh Pallipadi and Alexey Starikovskiy. 2006. The ondemand governor: past, present and future. In *Proceedings of Linux Symposium, vol. 2, pp. 223-238.* https://doi.org/pub/linux/kernel/people/lenb/acpi/doc/OLS2006-ondemand-paper.pdf

[17] Allan K. Porterfield, Stephen L. Olivier, Sridutt Bhalachandra, and Jan F. Prins. 2013. Power measurement and concurrency throttling for energy reduction in OpenMP programs. *Proceedings - IEEE 27th International Parallel and Distributed Processing Symposium Workshops and PhD Forum, IPDPSW 2013* (2013), 884–891. https://doi.org/10.1109/IPDPSW.2013.15

[18] Ramya Raghavendra, Parthasarathy Ranganathan, Vanish Talwar, Zhikui Wang, and Xiaoyun Zhu. 2008. No âĂİJ Power âĂİ Struggles : Coordinated Multi-level Power Management for the Data Center. *Solutions* 36 (2008), 48–59. https://doi.org/10.1145/1346281.1346289

[19] Sherief Reda, Ryan Cochran, and Ayse Coskun. 2012. Adaptive Power Capping for Servers with Multithreaded Workloads. *IEEE Micro* 32, 5 (Sept. 2012), 64–75. https://doi.org/10.1109/MM.2012.59

[20] D. Rughetti, P. Di Sanzo, and A. Pellegrini. 2014. Adaptive Transactional Memories: Performance and Energy Consumption Tradeoffs. In *Network Cloud Computing and Applications (NCCA), 2014 IEEE 3rd Symposium on*. IEEE Computer Society, 105–112. https://doi.org/10.1109/NCCA.2014.25

[21] Osman Sarood, Akhil Langer, Laxmikant Kale, Barry Rountree, and Bronis De Supinski. 2013. Optimizing power allocation to CPU and memory subsystems in overprovisioned HPC systems. In *Proceedings - IEEE International Conference on Cluster Computing, ICCC*. https://doi.org/10.1109/CLUSTER.2013.6702684

[22] Nir Shavit and Dan Touitou. 1995. Software transactional memory. In *Proc. 14th ACM Symposium on Principles of Distributed Computing*. ACM, 204–213.

[23] Steven S. Skiena. 2008. *The Algorithm Design Manual* (2nd ed.). Springer Publishing Company, Incorporated. https://doi.org/10.1007/978-1-84800-070-4

[24] Bo Su, Junli Gu, Li Shen, Wei Huang, Joseph L. Greathouse, and Zhiying Wang. 2014. PPEP: Online Performance, Power, and Energy Prediction Framework and DVFS Space Exploration. *2014 47th Annual IEEE/ACM International Symposium on Microarchitecture* (2014), 445–457. https://doi.org/10.1109/MICRO.2014.17

[25] Roberto Vitali, Alessandro Pellegrini, and Francesco Quaglia. 2012. Load Sharing for Optimistic Parallel Simulations on Multi Core Machines. *SIGMETRICS Perform. Eval. Rev.* 40, 3 (Jan. 2012), 2–11. https://doi.org/10.1145/2425248.2425250

[26] Huazhe Zhang and Henry Hoffmann. 2016. Maximizing Performance Under a Power Cap: A Comparison of Hardware, Software, and Hybrid Techniques. *SIGPLAN Not.* 51, 4 (March 2016), 545–559. https://doi.org/10.1145/2954679.2872375

Optimising Dynamic Binary Modification Across ARM Microarchitectures

Cosmin Gorgovan
School of Computer Science
The University of Manchester
cosmin.gorgovan@manchester.ac.uk

Amanieu d'Antras
School of Computer Science
The University of Manchester
amanieu@amanieusystems.com

Mikel Luján
School of Computer Science
The University of Manchester
mikel.lujan@manchester.ac.uk

ABSTRACT

Dynamic Binary Modification (DBM) is a technique for modifying applications transparently while they are executed, working at the level of native code. However, DBM introduces a performance overhead, which in some cases can dominate execution time, making many uses impractical.

The ARM hardware ecosystem poses unique challenges for high performance DBM systems because of the large number and wide range of capabilities of the commercially available implementations: from single issue, in order cores up to 6-issue out-of-order cores and including less traditional implementations. These variations raise the question of whether it is possible to develop DBM optimisations which either improve or, at the very least, do not affect performance on all available systems and microarchitectures. To answer this question, the performance of three new optimisations for the MAMBO DBM system has been evaluated on five systems using different microarchitectures. For comparison, the overhead of DynamoRIO, a high performance DBM system which was recently ported to the ARM architecture, is also evaluated.

KEYWORDS

Dynamic Binary Modification; Dynamic Binary Instrumentation

ACM Reference Format:
Cosmin Gorgovan, Amanieu d'Antras, and Mikel Luján. 2018. Optimising Dynamic Binary Modification Across ARM Microarchitectures. In *ICPE '18: ACM/SPEC International Conference on Performance Engineering, April 9–13, 2018, Berlin, Germany*. ACM, New York, NY, USA, 12 pages. https://doi.org/10.1145/3184407.3184425

1 INTRODUCTION

Dynamic Binary Modification (DBM) is a technique for modifying applications transparently while they are executed, working at the level of native code. DBM has numerous applications, some

This work was supported by UK EPSRC grant PAMELA EP/K008730/1. Mikel Luján is supported by a Royal Society University Research Fellowship.

of the more common being dynamic instrumentation [23, 27], program analysis [26, 30], virtualisation [1, 28] and Dynamic Binary Translation (DBT) [8, 9, 13].

The ARM hardware ecosystem poses unique challenges for high performance DBM systems because of the large number and wide range of capabilities of the commercially available implementations: from single issue, in-order cores (Cortex-A5), up to out-of-order cores (Cortex-A17 or Applied Micro X-Gene).

These challenges are exacerbated by the wide adoption of single-ISA heterogeneous multicores (such as *big.LITTLE* [3]), which use different microarchitectures (e.g. a cluster of energy efficient in-order cores and a cluster of high performance out-of-order cores) in the same System on Chip (SoC) and allow the migration of active applications from one type of core to another. This raises the question of whether it is possible to develop DBM optimisations which either improve or, at the very least, do not affect performance on all ARM systems and microarchitectures.

MAMBO [17] is an open source [16], DBM framework for the ARM architecture. To further reduce its overhead, three optimisations are proposed and evaluated in this paper. The performance of these new optimisations and of the baseline MAMBO system has been measured on five ARM systems which use different microarchitectures.

The overhead of the baseline MAMBO system is partly caused by microarchitectural inefficiencies, for example by a high number of instruction cache misses [17]. Therefore, the optimisations presented in this paper aim to address this limitation by improving performance at the microarchitectural level (e.g. by reducing the number of cache misses) rather than at the architectural level (e.g. by reducing the number of executed instructions).

The contributions of this paper include:

- a trace system for MAMBO which reduces its overhead by improving code cache locality and eliminating some of the branches on the hot code path, while avoiding software branch target prediction for poorly predictable branches;
- a novel scheme to enable hardware return address prediction in a code cache without use of a software return address stack (Hardware-assisted return address prediction);
- a software indirect branch prediction scheme which allows effective prediction for polymorphic indirect branches (Adaptive Indirect Branch Inlining);
- evaluating the effectiveness of these optimisations when running on a wide range of microarchitectures, including a comparison against the state of the art; and
- reducing the geometric mean overhead of the MAMBO DBM system running SPEC CPU2006 by 27% - 54% on the five evaluation systems.

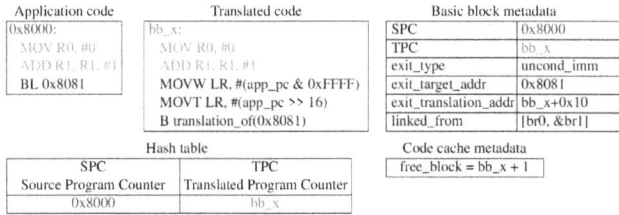

Figure 1: Example basic block and associated data structures.

The rest of the paper is organised as follows. Section 2 is a short description of the baseline MAMBO system. Section 3 describes the newly introduced trace system. Section 4 describes the new optimisations for indirect branches. Section 5 is the performance evaluation and Section 6 draws the final conclusions.

2 BASELINE SYSTEM OVERVIEW

The baseline MAMBO system was described by Gorgovan et al. [17]. MAMBO, like most other DBM tools, runs in the same process with the application it modifies and controls its execution by scanning, translating and optionally modifying all code before execution. The process of code discovery, translation and modification is done at the level of *Basic Blocks* (BBs), which are single-entry, single-exit units of code. To amortise the cost of this process, the result is stored in a *code cache* and reused for future executions. MAMBO uses thread-private code caches (and associated data structures), which allow multithreaded code scanning and execution with minimal synchronisation. A hash table is used to map application addresses (Source Program Counters - *SPCs*) to their translation in the code cache (Translated Program Counters - *TPCs*). To minimise the cost of handing over execution from one basic block to another, basic blocks which end with a direct branch are linked directly (using direct branches inside the code cache). Additionally, indirect branches are translated to inline hash table lookups, which perform a lookup of the TPC corresponding to each SPC used by the application, with minimal spilling and restoring of application registers, as opposed to a full context switch to the DBM system.

Figure 1 shows an example basic block and a simplified view of the associated data structures. The application code, at address 0x8000, contains two data processing instructions and a branch with link (procedure call) to another location. The translation in the code cache, in basic block bb_x, contains the unmodified data processing instructions (grey) and the translation of the branch with link instruction (black). The translated branch with link hides that the code is running from a code cache, at a different location than expected, by explicitly setting the value of the Link Register (LR) to the correct value and then executing a regular branch (without link) to the translation of the target address. Some of the metadata created for the example BB is shown in the right hand column: its SPC, TPC, the location, type of branch and its target (for direct branches) in a structure specific to each BB; the space used by the translation in the code cache is marked as used (in the *code cache metadata*); and an entry is added to the thread-private hash table to map the SPC to the TPC. Branches between basic blocks are tracked by maintaining a linked list of *incoming* branches for each basic block (the linked_from metadata field).

3 TRACES

The baseline code cache, organised in basic blocks, creates and stores the basic blocks in the order they are first executed. However, the basic blocks in the software code cache have high fragmentation, making inefficient use of the hardware code cache. Furthermore, the two paths of conditional branches are translated in two separate basic blocks in the software code cache, increasing the number of executed branches (by executing a branch in the translated code even when the source conditional branch is not taken). To avoid these limitations, this paper introduces traces (also known as *superblocks*) to MAMBO, which are single-entry, multiple-exit units built by merging together the basic blocks on the hot code path. The single-entry, single-exit units which make up a trace are called *trace fragments*.

Because creating a trace has a non-trivial cost (both in terms of code cache space, and execution time spent creating the trace instead of running the application), it is important to only create traces for hot code, which is expected to execute many times in the future and amortise its creation cost. On the other hand, to get the best performance, it is preferred to create traces for all of the hot code in an application and as early as possible. The challenge is in 1) quickly identifying the hot code in an application and 2) in profiling the hot execution paths through this code with low overhead. MAMBO builds traces using an improvement of the Next Executing Tail (NET) online profiling scheme [15]. The NET algorithm is summarised in Table 1. It is designed to minimise the profiling overhead. Towards that end, NET initially maintains an execution counter only for the basic blocks which are the potential start of a hot path. These instrumented basic blocks are called *trace heads*. The insight is that the hot execution path must consist of cycles, therefore NET uses the targets of backwards branches (both direct and indirect) as trace heads. Once the execution counter for a particular trace head reaches a certain threshold, then the trace is considered hot and NET records the full execution path following the trace head, until a backwards branch is encountered (which *terminates* the trace). This recorded path is then used as the predicted path, based on the rationale that the *trace tail* following a hot trace head is also likely to be part of the hot execution path. For example, let us consider the Control Flow Graph (CFG) depicted in Figure 2, where each box represents a basic block and block *A* ends with a conditional direct branch, blocks *B, D, E, F, G, H* and *I* end with unconditional direct branches, while block *C* ends with an unconditional indirect branch. Using the NET trace head selection algorithm, the trace heads in this example would be the two blocks which are the target of backwards branches: *A* and *C*. If, for example, the execution count threshold would then be reached for the trace head A and then the blocks *CEH* would execute, the

Hot code profiling	execution counter for *trace heads*
Trace head selection	the targets of backward branches
Trace path	the path taken across forward direct and indirect branches, after the execution counter of a trace head reached a certain threshold
Trace termination	a backward branch is encountered

Table 1: Overview of the NET algorithm.

29

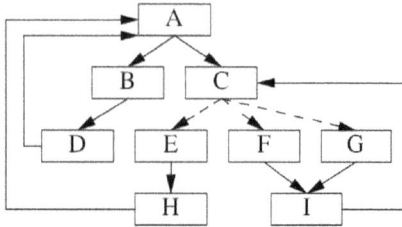

Figure 2: Example control flow graph. Each box represents a basic block. Block A, the entry point, contains a conditional direct branch, block C contains an unconditional indirect branch and all other blocks contain unconditional direct branches.

trace would consist of the blocks *ACEH*, ending with a branch back to the beginning of the trace.

An important property of NET is that it builds traces across indirect branches, statically predicting their target address to be the same as observed in the path recording phase. In the previous example involving the trace *ACEH*, the target of the indirect branch from block *C* is block *E* in the path recording stage, therefore NET builds the trace predicting that the target of block *C* is always *E*. However, analysis of the SPEC CPU benchmarks showed that most indirect branches are polymorphic and poorly predicted by a static target predictor, as used by NET. Furthermore, a static indirect branch predictor adds overhead in the case when the prediction is incorrect. This analysis is available in Section 4.2, which also presents AIBI, a more accurate indirect branch prediction scheme, which has been implemented in MAMBO. To avoid this limitation, the MAMBO trace building scheme terminates on indirect branches, which avoids static target prediction and instead allows their SPC-to-TPC lookup to be implemented using an inline hash table lookup, optionally with Adaptive Indirect Branch Inlining (Section 4.2). However, this change to NET has a number of side-effects which must be managed to maintain good performance, as discussed in the following subsections.

3.1 Trace head selection

The new trace termination condition described in Section 3 avoids adding the targets of an indirect branch to a trace tail, by terminating the trace. However, one or more of these targets are likely part of the hot execution path, therefore all targets of indirect branches should then have execution counters (i.e. become trace heads) to allow the creation of traces. Nevertheless, the NET trace head selection algorithm only instruments the targets of backwards branches and would generally fail to instrument many of these targets. If, for example, block *C* in the CFG shown in Figure 2 is on the hot code path and its indirect branch has a 70% bias toward block *E*, 30% toward block *F* and never branches to block *G*, then both the *E* and *F* blocks are also on the hot code path. If these blocks would be trace heads, then the traces *EH...* and *FI...* would be created. Nevertheless, the unmodified trace head selection of NET does not allow this and instead the blocks *E*, *H*, *F* and *I* could not be trace heads, nor would they be included in trace tails because of the additional termination condition used by MAMBO.

NET also presents an implementation challenge for DBM systems: if a basic block is first reached using a forward branch, then it will be created without an execution counter. However, if it is later reached using a backward branch, then an execution counter has to be added to the existing block or, otherwise a second version of the basic block has to be created. Both options make inefficient use of the code cache space and increase fragmentation. For example, in the control flow graph depicted in Figure 2, the first execution of block *C* would necessarily be a result of the branch from block *A*, therefore not creating a trace. If block *I* would execute at a later time, then the backwards branch to *C* would be discovered and an execution counter would have to be added to the existing block *C*.

Both of these issues are addressed in MAMBO by a single change to the trace head selection algorithm: whether a basic block is a trace head is decided at the time it is scanned, depending on whether it ends with a direct branch (then it is a trace head) or an indirect branch (then it is a regular basic block). Basic blocks containing an indirect branch are not allowed as trace heads because they would be terminated immediately and would therefore create traces containing a single fragment. This algorithm also allows the targets of indirect branches to be trace heads and avoids ulterior transformation of existing basic blocks into trace heads, by removing the reachability of basic blocks as an input to the trace head selection algorithm. Instead, it relies exclusively on the contents of the basic block itself, which are known at the time it is scanned. In the example CFG in Figure 2, all basic blocks apart from block C (which contains an indirect branch) would be trace heads.

Changing the trace head selection algorithm compared to NET results in more basic blocks becoming trace heads and incurring the overhead of updating the execution counter. However, this overhead is limited: the counter is updated by calling a shared procedure, which is implemented using only ten instructions. Additionally, the execution count threshold for trace creation is low, typically in the order of tens or hundreds, which strongly limits the maximum overhead that can be introduced by each trace head. Compared to scanning the trace head and translating it in the code cache, repeatdly incrementing the execution counter up to its threshold is relatively fast.

In MAMBO, a trace head is implemented as a basic block with a header (shown in Listing 1) which: 1) pushes to the stack the contents of 3 scratch registers and of the Link Register, 2) sets the id of the trace head in R0 and 3) calls a shared procedure which then decrements the execution counter of the trace head by one and returns, until it reaches zero. When zero is reached, trace creation is started, using the id passed to the shared procedure to identify the trace head. The rest of the trace building process is described in Section 3.2.

```
PUSH {R0-R2, LR}
MOVW R0, #(trace_head_id & 0xFFFF)
MOVT R0, #(trace_head_id >> 0xFFFF)
BL increment_exec_counter
```

Listing 1: The code added to trace heads.

	NET	MAMBO traces
Hot code profiling	execution counter for *trace heads*	same as NET
Trace head selection	the targets of backward branches	basic blocks exiting with a direct branch
Trace path	the path taken across forward direct and indirect branches, after the execution counter of a trace head reached a certain threshold	the path taken across direct branches, after the execution counter of a trace head reached a certain threshold
Trace termination	a backward branch is encountered	an indirect branch is encountered OR a direct branch to an existing trace is encountered OR the maximum number of fragments has been reached and a backward direct branch is encountered

Table 2: Comparison of MAMBO traces and NET.

3.2 Trace building

Trace building works similarly to NET: when a trace is first created, the SPC of the trace head is used to create the first fragment in the trace. Then this fragment is executed and its selected target is appended to the trace. This process continues iteratively until a termination condition is met. The first such condition is the execution of an indirect branch, as previously discussed. An additional condition is the execution of a direct branch to the entry point of an existing trace (including itself), which is intended to limit *tail duplication* between different traces. If a branch to the entry point of an existing trace is encountered, then a direct branch to that trace is inserted and the partial trace is terminated. For example if a trace was created from block *A* in Figure 2, then the trace would initially contain the fragment *A*. After the fragment *A* would execute, its target would be appended to the trace. If this target was *B*, then the partial trace would contain the fragments *AB*. Since *B* contains a branch to *D*, this fragment would also be added to the trace, which would then contain *ABD*. Finally, the target of the *D* fragment is *A*, for which a trace would already exist (the partial trace itself). The *ABD* trace would be terminated and linked directly to its own entry point.

Additionally, when a trace is created, the SPC-TPC hash table is updated to the TPC of the trace. All direct branches from other basic blocks and traces to the trace head are replaced by branches to the new trace, essentially making the trace head unreachable. In the previous example, the hash table entry for the SPC of *A* would be changed from the address of the *trace head A* to the address of the new *partial trace A...*. Similarly, any branches to *trace head A* would be replaced with branches to the partial trace.

3.3 Trace size limits

Some code duplication is allowed inside each trace, to encourage partial unrolling of short loops. However, excessive code duplication is undesirable, therefore the maximum number of fragments in each trace is limited. If this configurable limit is reached, the trace is terminated on its next backwards branch. For example in the CFG shown in Figure 2, the blocks *CFI* form a loop. If this loop would execute while the trace *ACFICFICFI...* was built, then this would result in an increasingly large trace, which would eventually fill the trace code cache. However, because the maximum number of fragments in a trace is limited, the trace would be terminated on the backward branch from *I* to *C* after a limited number of iterations.

3.4 Summary

Using a software code cache based on basic blocks contributes to the overhead of DBM systems by introducing fragmentation and by executing numerous branch instructions to transfer control between any two basic blocks. These issues are mitigated by traces, which are single-entry and multiple-exit units which group together the basic blocks likely to execute sequentially on the hot code path. The main challenges related to traces are in 1) identifying the hot code with minimal delay and 2) profiling this code to obtain the hot execution paths. The NET online profiling algorithm is commonly used to build traces in DBM systems, however it relies on static target prediction for indirect branches. Nevertheless, indirect branches are shown to generally be polymorphic and poorly predicted by a static target predictor. In this context, several changes to NET are proposed, as summarised in Table 2, which eliminate static indirect branch prediction while managing the undesired side-effects.

4 INDIRECT BRANCHES

Indirect branches are control flow instructions with a target not known at translation time. Looking up TPC for the SPC of indirect branches at runtime is the major source of overhead for DBM systems [21]. We classify indirect branches in three types:

- function returns, for which we introduce *hardware-assisted return address prediction* in Section 4.1; and
- generic indirect branches, handled in MAMBO using inline hash table lookups, for which we introduce the optional *adaptive inlining* - Section 4.2; and
- table branches, handled in MAMBO using the *space-efficient shadow branch table linking* [17].

Figure 3 shows the steps involved in an inline hash table lookup, which is the mechanism used for handling indirect branches in the baseline MAMBO: 1) first, if required and depending on the type of indirect branch, the values of up to three registers are pushed onto the stack to enable their use as scratch registers; then, 2) the SPC

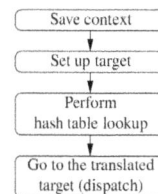

Figure 3: Inline hash table lookup.

is copied or generated in one of the scratch registers; 3) the hash table lookup is performed, with the TPC being loaded; and 4) finally the values of the scratch registers are restored and a branch to the TPC is performed. The *hardware-assisted return address prediction* and *adaptive indirect branch inlining* optimisations are both an extension to inline hash table lookups.

4.1 Hardware-assisted return address prediction

Return instructions are the instructions which execute at the end of a procedure (the callee) to return control back to the caller. More specifically, returns target the instruction immediately following the call instruction. Therefore, at the time a call is executed, the target of the first return to execute can be accurately predicted to be the address of the instruction following the call. If nested calls execute, then all predicted addresses can be recorded in a Last In, First Out (LIFO) structure for later use. These properties are used for return address prediction in virtually all modern microprocessors, including by most ARM implementations, which maintain a Return Address Stack (RAS) which is not exposed architecturally [2, 4–6]. However, the translated code generated by a DBM system does not generally maintain these properties because

(a) The original function call.

(b) The translated function call without hardware return prediction.

(c) The translated function call with hardware return prediction.

Figure 4: Example of a typical function call.

call instructions are translated to regular branches while returns are translated to regular indirect branches. Consequently, hardware return address prediction is not used. Instead, return instructions are predicted by the hardware using the generic indirect branch prediction mechanisms, which are both less accurate and also limited in the number of indirect branches which can be tracked and predicted simultaneously. Since fast return handling is critical for achieving low overhead in DBM systems [21], this limitation is an important contributor to the total overhead.

Figure 4(a) shows a typical function call in ARM code. A *caller* function contains a call (implemented using a Branch-and-Link - BL - instruction) to the entry address of the *callee*. The callee preserves the return address from the Link Register (LR), executes, and then returns to it using a return instruction (a Branch-and-eXchange - BX - instruction using the address in the LR, in this example). Because the target address of the return is in a register, this return instruction is an indirect branch.

Hardware return address prediction on ARM works thus: when a call (either a BL or a Branch-with-Link-and-eXchange - BLX - instruction) is executed, an entry, containing the address of the next instruction after the call, is automatically pushed by the core on the hardware RAS. Then, when the matching return instruction is executed, its target address is predicted by automatically popping the first value from the top of the RAS. Since the ARM architecture does not have explicit return instructions, certain types of indirect branches (*return-type instructions*) are treated by the branch predictor as returns, typically: *BX LR*, a *POP* containing the PC in the register list, a SP-relative load into PC, and *MOV PC, LR*.

The naive translation of BL and BLX instructions (from the native code in Figure 4(a) to Figure 4(b)) emulates the call instruction by setting the value of the LR explicitly to the SPC of the instruction following the call and then branches to the translation of the target using a regular (i.e. without link) branch. Similarly, return instructions are translated to an inline hash table lookup (represented by the IHL() pseudocode) followed by a regular branch (BX) to the TPC of the return address. Therefore, the naive translation of calls and returns is not compatible with the hardware return address predictor, which increases branch mispredictions by 1) translating call-type instructions to regular branch instructions, which do not cause a push on the RAS and by 2) translating return-type instructions to generic indirect branches, which are predicted using the less accurate indirect branch predictor, while also increasing the pressure on the indirect branch predictor. We propose *hardware-assisted return address prediction* to solve these issues, by modifying the translations as shown in Figure 4(c): first, it translates call-type instructions to a sequence which ends with a call-type instruction (BB #1), which allows the hardware predictor to push an entry to the RAS. Next, it inserts the translation of the following instructions, i.e. the predicted return (BB #2) immediately after the call, as expected by the predictor. Finally, it modifies the translation of return-type instructions to use a return-type instruction, which will allow the hardware predictor to pop the predicted address from the RAS (BX LR in BB #3).

For return prediction to work correctly, a single translation of each call-type instruction must exist in the code cache, otherwise multiple translations of the predicted return would be generated, which cannot be registered in the hash table mapping the SPC-TPC

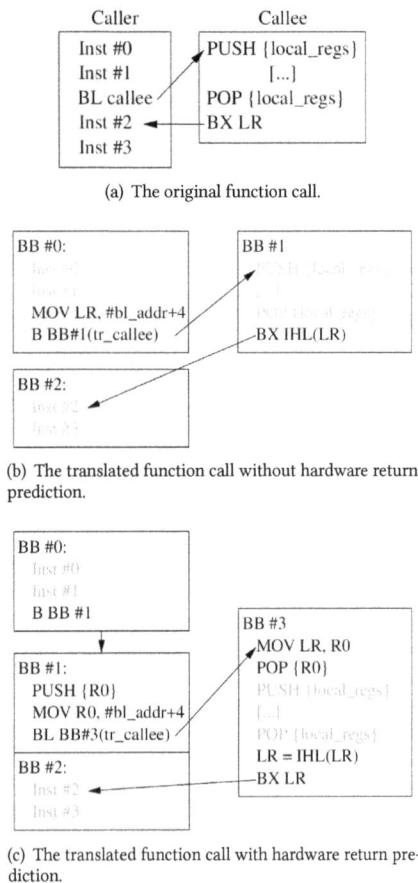

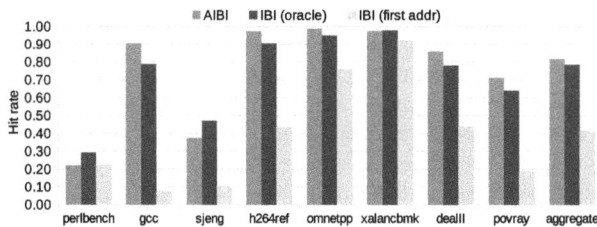

Figure 5: Comparison of hit rates on a selection of SPEC CPU2006 benchmarks for indirect branch predictors.

relationships. This is a potential issue because different entry points into a single linear code area which contain a call-type instruction would normally lead to the creation of multiple basic blocks, each one containing a translation of the call-type instruction. To avoid this issue, if a call-type instruction is scanned without being the first instruction in a basic block, a new basic block is created with the call-type instruction as the entry point, if it does not exist yet. The original basic block is then directly linked to the translation of the call-type instruction. This ensures that when a call-type instruction is scanned, its SPC-TPC mapping will be recorded. Then, if the same call-type instruction is encountered in multiple BBs by the code scanner, all are linked to the unique translation.

As an additional optimisation, when a call-type instruction is not the first one in a basic block and its translation does not exist yet, the separate basic block generated for the call-type instruction will be stored in the code cache area immediately following the first basic block, allowing the eliding of the direct branch. For the example in Figure 4(c), BB #1 would be stored immediately after BB #0, allowing the elimination of the B BB#1 instruction from BB #0.

4.2   Adaptive indirect branch inlining

Indirect branches have dynamic targets, which are not known at translation time. Due to their nature, the translated indirect branches must perform a SPC to TPC lookup every time they execute. This lookup represents a major source of overhead for DBM systems [19, 21]. The baseline version of MAMBO and other DBM systems such as DynamoRIO [10] attempt to reduce this overhead by generating a highly optimised inlined hash table lookup routine for each translated indirect branch. This approach allows the hardware branch predictors to handle separately each translated indirect branch (improving hardware branch prediction rates) and minimises the length of the critical path compared to a shared routine by taking advantage of the available dead registers, on a case-by-case basis. However, the hash table lookup operation inherently requires a number of additional instructions, including memory loads and conditional branches. Other DBM systems, such as Pin for ARM [18], use Indirect Branch Inlining (IBI) [7], which consists of a compare-and-branch chain which compares the current target address against a configurable number of previous targets, using only the code path (i.e. by using immediates). However, previous attempts to use this prediction scheme in MAMBO have failed to improve performance, due to the high overhead associated with updating the predicted target, the poor hit rate due to the polymorphic nature of indirect branches and the high penalty

of hardware branch mispredictions triggered in the relatively common case when one or more predictions at the top of the chain miss. We designed the *Adaptive Indirect Branch Inlining* (AIBI) scheme to allow quick updating of the predicted address after every misprediction, while still having a shorter critical path than the inline hash table lookup. This is similar to the way indirect branch target prediction works in most hardware implementations.

Figure 5 compares the hit rates for three indirect branch predictions schemes: *AIBI*, which always predicts the address of the most recent target; *IBI (common)*, which is a static predictor which predicts the most common target for each branch using post-mortem information; and *IBI (first)* which predicts the address of the first target seen for each branch. The selected benchmarks are those which execute a relatively high number of generic indirect branches. The *aggregate* bars show the hit rates when considering together all indirect branch executions from the selected benchmarks. IBI (common) shows the upper bound for a static predictor and since the information to choose the most common target is not available at runtime, practical IBI implementations will almost always have lower hit rates. The IBI (first) hit rate is more relevant for practical IBI implementations, which can either predict the target of the n-th execution of an indirect branch, or, alternatively, can profile the first few executions of the branch and predict the most common target among those samples. It can be observed that the hit rate for AIBI is generally similar to that of the IBI (common) predictor and for most benchmarks and overall, slightly better. On the other hand, the hit rate for IBI (first) is generally much lower, which indicates that practical IBI implementations will tend to have lower hit rates than AIBI.

A major difference of AIBI compared to IBI is that the prediction is updated for every miss, which is achieved by falling back to the inline hash table lookup and unconditionally overwriting the prediction on this execution path. Since this can occur for a large percentage of the executions of a branch, this operation must be implemented very efficiently to minimise the overhead of prediction misses. Using immediates on the code path to generate the predicted address (similar to IBI) was ruled out because ARM uses a modified Harvard architecture, which requires expensive cache flushing and invalidation via system calls to update code. Therefore, the predicted target address and its matching code cache address are accessed as data words, which is the second major difference from IBI. The addition of two unconditional store instructions with no read-after-write dependencies on the fallback execution path appears to have a minimal performance impact on most hardware implementations.

The diagram in Figure 6 shows how AIBI works, where the boxes with a solid border show the additional steps added specifically for AIBI, while the boxes with a dashed border show the unmodified steps which are part of the inline hash table lookup routine (which is shown separately in Figure 3). Listing 2 shows the implementation of AIBI. With AIBI, after the target address has been generated or loaded in a register, the predicted SPC is loaded using a single PC-relative load instruction and then two addresses are compared, as shown in the check_pred procedure. The comparison is implemented using a subtract instruction (SUB) and a Compare and Branch on NonZero (CBNZ) instruction to preserve the flags in the ARM Program Status Register (PSR). In case of a match, the

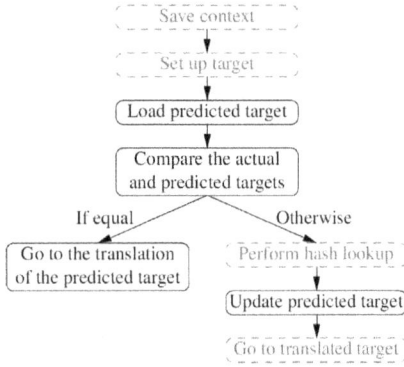

Figure 6: Adaptive indirect branch inlining.

```
check_pred:
    LDR Rs0, [PC, #16]
    SUB Rs0, Rs0, Rtarget
    CBNZ fallback
b_pred:
    POP {Rs0, ..., Rsn}
    LDR PC, [PC, #4]
pred_spc: .word
pred_tpc: .word
fallback:
    ; the fallback inline hash table lookup
    SUB Rs0, PC, offset_to_pred_spc
    STR Rtarget, [Rs0, #0]
    ; the TPC is loaded from the hash table in Rtarget,
    ; overwriting the SPC
    STR Rtarget, [Rs0, #4]
    ...
```

Listing 2: The implementation of AIBI. Rs0 to Rsn are scratch registers, while Rtarget is the register which initially contains the target address (SPC).

context is restored and execution branches to the predicted TPC using a second PC-relative load, as shown in the b_pred procedure. Otherwise, in case of a miss, the regular inline hash table lookup proceeds, with the difference that after the hash table lookup has been performed, but before branching to the destination, the predicted SPC and TPC are updated, as shown in the fallback procedure. PC-relative stores are not allowed in the Thumb mode, therefore the address where the predicted SPC and TPC are stored is first generated using a subtract instruction.

AIBI is similar in predicting the address of the most recent target to the MRU IBI prediction scheme proposed by Dhanasekaran and Hazelwood [14]. However, while the MRU scheme is used in *addition* to IBI, AIBI is an alternative to IBI. When the MRU prediction misses, it falls back to IBI, while AIBI falls back to an inline hash table lookup. MRU updates the predicted address from the IBI target fragments, while AIBI updates the predicted address in the inline hash table lookup. Furthermore, AIBI as implemented in MAMBO is effective in reducing the overhead on all systems used in the evaluation (Section 5), while MRU as prototyped for Pin failed to improve performance on average [14]. Unfortunately, insufficient information is available to determine why. The MRU publication explains that its dynamic instruction count was higher than that of standard IBI despite the increased prediction hit rate.

However, on ARM platforms we have observed that the hardware branch prediction rate and other microarchitectural events often have a stronger effect than relatively small changes in the number of executed instructions. For example, when we have implemented IBI in MAMBO, the dynamic instruction count was significantly reduced, however the overhead was increased because of the hardware branch mispredictions introduced by the IBI chain. This could indicate that 1) existing x86 implementations can predict IBI chains better than ARM implementations or, less likely, 2) that branch mispredictions are relatively cheaper on x86 implementations than on ARM implementations. Another possible explanation is that the performance of MRU was affected by the mechanism used to update the predicted address, which it duplicates across every target fragment linked by the IBI chain and whose details are not presented in the publication.

5 EVALUATION

5.1 Experimental setup

Table 3 describes the microarchitectures of the five different systems used for evaluation. All systems use a modified Harvard architecture, with separate 32 KiB L1 data caches and 32 KiB L1 instruction caches, and separate data and instruction L1 TLBs as described in Table 3. Higher level caches and TLBs are unified. The *IB predictor* row describes the hardware indirect branch prediction scheme: *previous* means that the address of the previous target of the instruction is predicted, while *adaptive* means that multiple target addresses can be predicted for each branch instruction.

All systems are running Ubuntu 14.04 LTS with the Linux kernel version supported by the manufacturer: 3.8 for ODROID-X2, 3.10 for ODROID-XU3, Tronsmart R28, Jetson TK1, and 4.2 for APM X-C1. SPEC CPU2006 has been compiled with GCC 4.6.3, configured to generate Thumb-2 code (the default configuration) for the *armhf* architecture using the *-O2* optimisation level and the executables were statically linked. Power management features such as DVFS and core offlining were disabled. The ODROID-XU3 system uses a heterogeneous *big.LITTLE* [3] configuration, with a *LITTLE* Cortex-A7 cluster, which was used for this evaluation and a *big* Cortex-A15 cluster which was not benchmarked because the same ARM core is used on the Jetson TK1 system.

The libquantum benchmark from the SPEC CPU2006 suite has been disabled because it fails to complete, both when executed natively and under MAMBO. All other CPU2006 benchmarks are enabled and produce the expected output. All SPEC CPU2006 results were obtained using the *ref* data set.

Multiple MAMBO *configurations* have been benchmarked. A configuration is a build of MAMBO with a specific set of enabled optimisations. The configuration with an empty set of optional optimisations enabled is called the *baseline* configuration. This is similar to the MAMBO configuration used by Gorgovan *et al.* [17], with the exception that the *low overhead return address prediction*, which is a return address prediction scheme based on a software RAS, has been disabled because it is incompatible with traces and therefore it is never used in this evaluation. *Hardware-assisted return address prediction*, introduced in this publication, serves a similar role while maintaining full transparency. All other configurations are named *+<name of optimisation 0> ... +<name of optimisation n>*,

System	ODROID-XU3[a]	ODROID-X2	Tronsmart R28	Jetson TK1	APM X-C1
SoC	Exynos 5422	Exynos 4412 Prime	Rockchip RK3288	NVIDIA T124	APM883208
Core	Cortex-A7	Cortex-A9	Cortex-A17	Cortex-A15	X-Gene 1
Frequency	1.4 GHz	1.7 GHz	1.6 GHz	2.3 GHz	2.4 GHz
L2 cache size	512 KiB	1 MiB	1 MiB	2 MiB	256 KiB
L3 cache size	N/A	N/A	N/A	N/A	8 MiB
L1i line length	32	32	64	64	64
L1d line length	64	32	64	64	64
L2 line length	64	32	64	64	64
L1d TLB	10	32	32	32(R) + 32(W)	20
L1i TLB	10	32	32	32	10
L2 TLB	256	132	1024	512	1024
IB predictor	previous[b]	previous	previous	adaptive	adaptive
OOO	N	Y, 2-issue	Y, 2-issue	Y, 3-issue	Y, 4-issue
Pipeline len	8	8-11	10-12	15	15

Table 3: Overview of the systems used for evaluation.

[a]The specifications for ODROID-XU3 apply to the *LITTLE* cluster only. The *big* cluster was not used for this evaluation because it uses the same microarchitecture as the Jetson TK1 system.

[b]Cortex-A7 is documented not to predict the target for branches implemented as loads or data processing operations with PC as the destination, which are used by MAMBO in the translation of most indirect branches.

for example the configuration with *hw_ras* and *traces* enabled is named +*hw_ras* +*traces*. The following optional optimisations have been evaluated:

- *traces* - code cache traces;
- *hw_ras* - hardware-assisted return address prediction; and
- *aibi* - adaptive indirect branch inlining.

As described in Section 3, traces are created when a trace head reaches a predefined execution count threshold. Our experiments on the SPEC CPU2006 benchmarks have shown that the performance of longer running tasks is not affected by setting a relatively high threshold. However, significant trace cache space savings can be obtained. Therefore, the trace creation threshold for this evaluation was set to 256, the maximum allowed by the implementation.

For comparison, we have also evaluated DynamoRIO [10], the only other maintained and publicly available low overhead DBM system for ARM. We used the git commit *38950ce2* from 19th of January, 2017. Note that DynamoRIO does not implement the hot code tracing optimisation for 32-bit ARM, the architecture used in this evaluation.

5.2 Overall performance

Table 4 summarises the overall performance of the baseline, +*traces*, the optimal MAMBO configuration and of DynamoRIO for each system (when running SPEC CPU2006), while Figures 7 to 11 show the detailed results for each benchmark. The values reported in the table are the geometric mean of execution time relative to native execution for each set of benchmarks. It can be observed that between the five test systems, two unique MAMBO configurations are needed to achieve the lowest possible overhead. This hints that, as expected, some of the optimisations have varying effectiveness depending on the microarchitecture. Another related observation is that the spread of the average overhead between the microarchitectures is quite high: from only 12% on APM X-C1, up to 21% on Jetson TK1, which further underlines the impact of microarchitecture on the performance of DBM systems. The SPECint benchmarks run

Hardware platform	DBM system	SPEC suite		
		int	fp	CPU
ODROID-XU3 (LITTLE)	baseline	1.55	1.11	1.26
in-order Cortex-A7	+traces	1.41	1.10	1.21
	+hw_ras +traces	1.36	1.09	1.19
	DynamoRIO	1.68	1.21	1.38
ODROID-X2	baseline	1.61	1.13	1.30
OOO Cortex-A9	+traces	1.33	1.07	1.17
	+aibi + traces	1.31	1.06	1.15
	DynamoRIO	1.65	1.16	1.34
Tronsmart R28	baseline	1.60	1.12	1.29
OOO Cortex-A17	+traces	1.31	1.09	1.17
	+aibi +traces	1.29	1.08	1.16
	DynamoRIO	1.71	1.26	1.42
Jetson TK1	baseline	1.71	1.16	1.35
OOO Cortex-A15	+traces	1.44	1.11	1.23
	+hw_ras +traces	1.38	1.11	1.21
	DynamoRIO	1.67	1.22	1.38
APM X-C1	baseline	1.59	1.09	1.26
OOO X-Gene1	+traces	1.34	1.07	1.17
	+hw_ras +traces	1.23	1.05	1.12
	DynamoRIO	1.64	1.18	1.34

Table 4: The slowdown of MAMBO baseline, +*traces*, the configuration with the lowest overhead and DynamoRIO for SPEC CPU2006 on each system.

with higher overhead than the SPECfp benchmarks because they tend to be control (as opposed to data) bound.

The *traces* optimisation has by far the largest overall effect. This is the expected result, as improved software code cache locality and a reduced number of executed branches reduce the overhead 1) for most benchmarks and 2) on all microarchitectures. While the geometric mean overhead is generally reduced only by a few points for the other optimisations, this is in large part due to these optimisations targeting only specific types of workloads. For example, the *hw_ras* optimisation reduces the overhead of *xalancbmk* on APM X-C1 from 96% to 66%, however, because only a few benchmarks gain a speed-up, the geometric mean overhead is only decreasing from 17% to 12%. By running the optimal configuration on each system, the geometric mean overhead is reduced compared to the

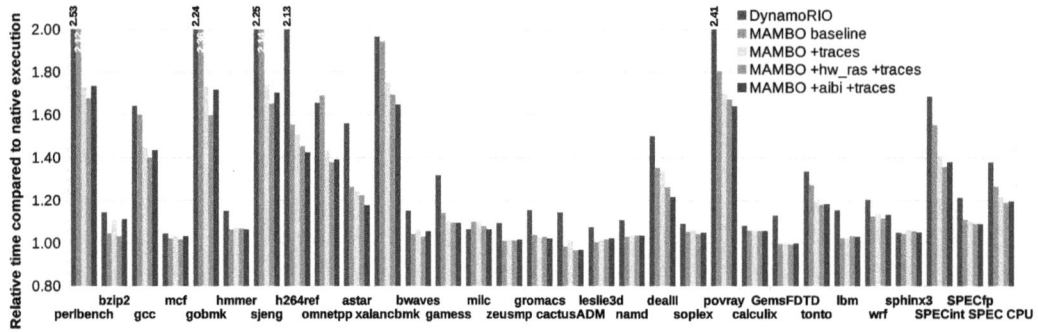

Figure 7: Relative execution time for SPEC CPU2006 on ODROID-XU3 (Cortex A7 in-order).

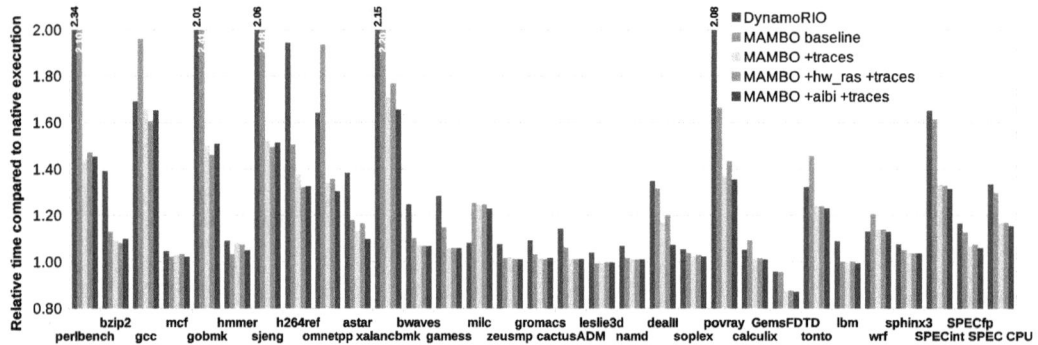

Figure 8: Relative execution time for SPEC CPU2006 on ODROID-X2 (Cortex A9 out-of-order).

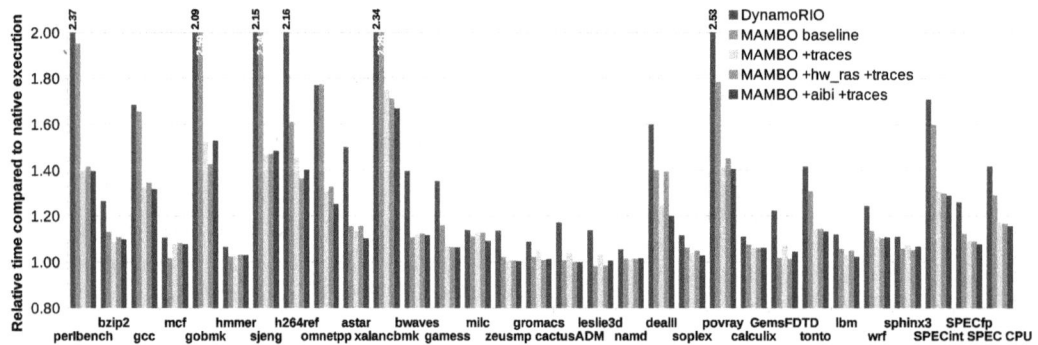

Figure 9: Relative execution time for SPEC CPU2006 on Tronsmart R28 (Cortex A17 out-of-order).

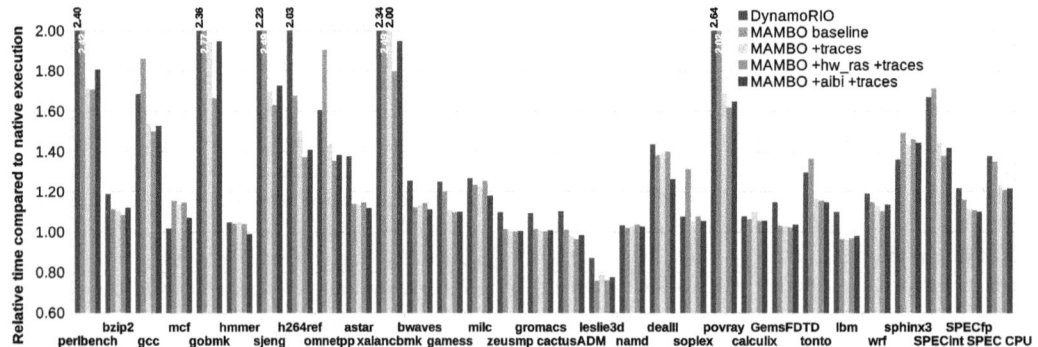

Figure 10: Relative execution time for SPEC CPU2006 on Jetson TK1 (Cortex A15 out-of-order).

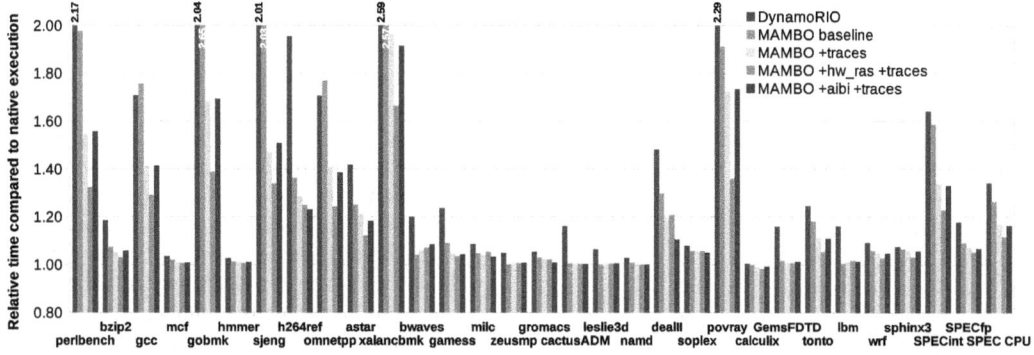

Figure 11: Relative execution time for SPEC CPU2006 on APM X-C1 (X-Gene1 out-of-order).

Config	Benchmark	ODROID-XU3		ODROID-X2		Tronsmart R28		Jetson TK1		APM X-C1	
		IPC_r	Time	IPC_r	Time	IPC_r	Time	IPC_r	Time	IPC_r	Time
Baseline	perlbench	0.73	2.12	0.76	2.10	0.79	1.95	0.64	2.42	0.73	1.98
	gobmk	0.59	2.36	0.58	2.41	0.53	2.59	0.50	2.77	0.59	2.65
	sjeng	0.70	2.14	0.66	2.18	0.62	2.34	0.59	2.49	0.70	2.03
	xalancbmk	0.93	1.94	0.91	2.20	0.73	2.28	0.73	2.49	0.93	2.57
+traces	perlbench	0.88	1.73	1.01	1.44	1.08	1.40	0.89	1.71	0.88	1.54
	gobmk	0.78	1.73	0.86	1.50	0.89	1.52	0.70	1.94	0.78	1.68
	sjeng	0.84	1.74	0.93	1.52	0.99	1.47	0.86	1.70	0.84	1.47
	xalancbmk	0.93	1.75	1.07	1.71	1.00	1.75	0.88	2.00	1.01	1.96
+hw_ras (+)	perlbench	0.93+	1.68+	1.00*	1.45*	1.09	1.40*	0.92+	1.71+	0.93+	1.32+
or	gobmk	0.87+	1.60+	0.90+	1.46+	0.97+	1.43+	0.84+	1.67+	0.87+	1.39+
+aibi (*)	sjeng	0.90+	1.65+	0.94+	1.49+	1.00+	1.47+	0.91+	1.63+	0.90+	1.34+
+traces	xalancbmk	0.97*	1.65*	1.00*	1.66*	0.96*	1.67*	1.02+	1.80+	1.07+	1.66+

Table 5: Relative IPC and slowdown for the benchmarks with the highest relative IPC

baseline configuration by 27% on ODROID-XU3, 41% on Jetson TK1, 45% on Tronsmart R28, 50% on ODROID-X2 and 54% on APM X-C1.

5.3 Performance counter analysis

Using the *perf* Linux tool, which monitors architectural and microarchitectural events using the hardware performance counters, we can gain an insight into 1) the performance differences between the various microarchitectures and 2) the effects of each optimisation introduced in this paper. The following events were counted on each system[1] for native execution and each MAMBO configuration, using the benchmarks with significant overhead: cycles, retired instructions, L1 data, L1 instruction and L2 unified cache accesses and misses, L1 data and instruction TLB misses, architecturally executed branches, mispredicted or not predicted branches speculatively executed.

5.3.1 Predicting speed-up: instructions per cycle. Increasing the dynamic instruction count is an expected effect of DBM. However, by designing the generated code to avoid pipeline stalls (i.e. by avoiding cache misses, branch mispredictions, etc.) the performance overhead should be disproportionately low (i.e. DBM execution should have an equal or higher Instructions Per Cycle − IPC − rate than native execution). Therefore, the relative IPC ($IPC_r = IPC_{DBM}/IPC_{native}$) can be used to identify the workloads which are the least efficient at a microarchitecture level when executed under a given DBM system, and which can be expected

to benefit the most from the optimisations presented in this paper. Table 5 shows the IPC_r and relative execution time under the baseline, *+traces* and optimal MAMBO configurations, for the benchmarks with the lowest IPC_r. The results in this table show that the microarchitectural optimisations are effective in reducing the overhead of the benchmarks with a low IPC_r, as intended. For example, looking at the last two columns, we can see that *gobmk* on APM X-C1 has a slowdown of 2.65x under baseline MAMBO, with a IPC_r of 0.59. When traces and then hardware-assisted return address prediction are enabled, the slowdown is reduced to 1.68x with an IPC_r of 0.78 and 1.39x with an IPC_r of 0.87 respectively.

5.3.2 The indirect branch optimisations. The two indirect branch optimisations (*hardware-assisted return address prediction* and *AIBI*) have a varying degree of effectiveness between each benchmark and each system. As a case study, we analysed *xalancbmk*. Compared to the *+traces* configuration, the performance on this benchmark was improved by *AIBI* on all systems and by *hardware-assisted return address prediction* on all systems except on ODROID-X2. *Hardware-assisted return address prediction* has better performance than *AIBI* on Jetson TK1 and APM X-C1. On this benchmark, *hw_ras* increases the number of retired instructions by around 3%, while *AIBI* reduces it by around 9%, therefore the performance difference is not determined by microarchitectural effects alone. The significant performance counter changes, relative to the *+traces* configuration, are summarised in Table 6.

We can observe that *hw_ras* is more effective than *AIBI* at reducing the number of branch mispredictions, L1 instructions cache misses and L2 cache loads. *AIBI* tends to introduce additional L1

---

[1]with several exceptions due to unsupported events: L1 instructions loads, L2 loads and L2 misses on ODROID-X2 and branch mispredictions on APM X-C1

Opt.	System	Positive effects	Negative effects	Speedup
hw_ras	ODROID-XU3	-14% icache misses -7% L2 loads	+8% icache loads +8% dTLB misses	3.3%
	ODROID-X2	-24% icache misses -13% iTLB misses	+25% branch mis-predictions	-3.5%
	Tronsmart R28	-29% branch mispre-dictions -26% icache misses -20% iTLB misses -14% L2 loads	-	2.2%
	Jetson TK1	-48% branch mispre-dictions -41% iTLB misses -24% icache misses -16% L2 loads -9% icache loads	-	11.4%
	APM X-C1	-22% icache misses -14% L2 loads -6% icache loads	-	18.0%
AIBI	ODROID-XU3	-15% icache loads -10% dcache loads -10% icache misses -9% dTLB misses -7% iTLB misses	+15% branch mis-predictions	6.1%
	ODROID-X2	-8% branch mispre-dictions -7% dcache loads	+14% iTLB misses +9% dcache misses +7% dTLB misses	3.7%
	Tronsmart R28	-18% icache loads -13% icache misses -13% branch mispre-dictions	+14% iTLB misses +12% dTLB misses +10% dcache misses	6.9%
	Jetson TK1	-13% icache loads -9% branch mispre-dictions	+20% dTLB misses +12% iTLB misses +12% dcache loads	8.4%
	APM X-C1	-16% L2 loads -11% icache loads -10% icache misses -7% dcache loads	+11% dcache misses	2.5%

Table 6: Performance counter changes for *xalancbmk* compared to the *+traces* MAMBO configuration

data cache misses, caused by accessing the predicted SPC and TPC. However, on the microarchitectures with no or less advanced out-of-order executing capabilities (Cortex-A7, Cortex-A9 and Cortex-A17), the reduced dynamic instruction count of *AIBI* allows it to achieve better performance.

The performance degradation caused by *hw_ras* on ODROID-X2 appears to be caused by an increased number of branch mispredictions. Unfortunately, the return address predictors are not documented in enough detail to determine why this is happening or the relevant differences between the return address predictors of these microarchitectures. A possible explanation is that the return address predictor of Cortex-A9 compares the predicted address and the actual address early during execution, causing it to sometimes use the SPC before it has been replaced by the TPC, however we have not been able to verify this hypothesis.

5.3.3   The effect of traces. The *traces* optimisation proved to be very effective and almost always improved or did not significantly affect performance. However, in three cases (*bzip2* on ODROID-XU3, *hmmer* on ODROID-X2 and *mcf* on Tronsmart R28) execution was measurably slowed down (by around 6% for all three). In the case of *bzip2* on ODROID-XU3, two of the events we monitor show a change which is potentially relevant: an increase in the rate of branch mispredictions (from 9.2 to 9.5 per 1000 instructions) and

L2 cache misses (from 5.0 to 5.5 per 1000 instructions). This is likely caused by the increased code size. However, because both of these changes are relatively small, there is a strong possibility that there are other microarchitectural effects contributing to the slower execution speed, which are not captured by the performance counter events we have monitored. For *hmmer* on ODROID-X2, only the number of branch mispredictions is significantly increased (by around 460 million). However, on its own, the penalty of the additional branch mispredictions cannot account for the additional 167 billion execution cycles. For *mcf* on Tronsmart R28, there was no significant change in the number of any of the monitored performance counter events. Therefore, it appears that the main cause of this rare performance regression caused by the *traces* optimisation is not captured by the performance counter events we have monitored.

6   RELATED WORK

DBT and DBM are a popular research area, with a number of available tools [8, 10, 20, 22, 24, 25]. The strength of MAMBO is in prioritising the performance of a DBM implementation for ARM.

IBI is a common software target prediction scheme for indirect branches [7, 10, 19, 22, 25, 29]. However, IBI is limited by the high misprediction rate and the high penalty for mispredictions. Kim and Smith go as far as calling this technique a *performance limiter* [21]. This paper introduces AIBI as a replacement for IBI, which improves the prediction rate by allowing the predicted address to be updated after every miss, with low overhead. AIBI is similar in concept to the MRU algorithm introduced by Dhanasekaran and Hazelwood [14], however AIBI is a replacement for IBI, while MRU is used in *addition* to IBI. Furthermore, IBI handles prediction misses differently from MRU, which likely contributes to its better performance. AIBI and MRU are compared in detail in Section 4.2.

Dynamically building traces of the hot code path was first enabled by the NET [15] profiling algorithm. NETPlus [12] was later proposed as an improvement, which allows building longer traces by working across backwards branches. However, both of these algorithms create traces across indirect branches, using static software target prediction in the form of IBI. Because of the previously discussed limitations of IBI, this paper proposes an improvement of NET, which avoids software target prediction in traces altogether.

Efficient translation of return instructions is critical for achieving low overhead in DBM systems [21]. Some of the proposed solutions for optimising returns include: modifying the ISA to allow explicit manipulation of the hardware RAS [21], however this change has not been implemented on general purpose architectures such as x86 or ARM; maintaining a software RAS [18], however this is only beneficial on modern microarchitectures if certain transparency guarantees are relaxed [17], or in the case of DBT when the target architecture provides additional registers which can be directly used as a RAS pointer [11]. In this context, this paper introduces hardware-assisted return address prediction, which was developed to allow use of the hardware mechanisms for return address prediction, while forgoing the use of a software RAS.

7 SUMMARY AND CONCLUSIONS

MAMBO is an open source implementation of a DBM framework for the ARM architecture. In this paper, we have introduced three optimisations to address some of its performance limitations: *traces* increase the code cache locality by grouping together basic blocks which are likely to execute sequentially; *hardware-assisted return address prediction* is a technique which enables use of the hardware return address prediction without maintaining a software return address stack; and *adaptive indirect branch inlining* is a software indirect branch prediction scheme which allows quick and frequent updates of the predicted address. By using the right combination of these optimisations on each system, the geometric mean overhead of MAMBO is reduced by at least 27% (on ODROID-XU3) and by as much as 54% (on APM X-C1) compared to the *baseline* MAMBO configuration.

The performance of the various optimisations is analysed on five different ARM platforms, which allows us to show that 1) whether an optimisation for a DBM system is effective or not depends on multiple factors, including the microarchitecture of the processor on which it is running and the type of workload, and that 2) the optimal combination of optimisations can be different between multiple systems.

We have shown that some optimisations can improve performance on one system and decrease performance on other systems while running the same workload. For example, *hardware return address prediction* reduced the overhead of MAMBO on the *perlbench* benchmark on ODROID-XU3 and APM X-C1 and increased it on Tronsmart R28. These results are due to the wide range of ARM microarchitectures commercially available. Therefore, we recommend that future evaluations of DBM overhead use a similar wide range of hardware platforms. Furthermore, this shows that runtime or deployment time selection of optimisations can be desirable to achieve consistent performance.

With regards to the three optimisations presented in this paper, we recommend that the *traces* optimisation is always used for SPEC CPU type workloads. *Hardware return address prediction* appears to be most effective on high performance cores (APM X-Gene) or cores with limited prediction support for generic indirect branches (Cortex-A7) because it trades off a higher dynamic instruction count for improved hardware branch prediction. The effectiveness of *AIBI* is dependent on the workload. For microarchitectures with shorter pipelines and low hardware branch misprediction penalties, AIBI appears to be more effective for translating returns than *hardware return address prediction*, as long as hardware indirect branch prediction is supported, because it reduces the dynamic instruction count.

REFERENCES

[1] Keith Adams and Ole Agesen. 2006. A comparison of software and hardware techniques for x86 virtualization. *ACM Sigplan Notices* 41, 11 (2006), 2–13.
[2] ARM. 2013. *ARM® Cortex®-A15 MPCore™ Processor Technical Reference Manual, Revision r4p0.*
[3] ARM. 2013. big.LITTLE Technology: The Future of Mobile. (2013). https://www.arm.com/files/pdf/big_LITTLE_Technology_the_Futue_of_Mobile.pdf (Visited on 13/07/2016).
[4] ARM. 2013. *Cortex™-A7 MPCore™ Technical Reference Manual, Revision r0p5.*
[5] ARM. 2014. *ARM® Cortex®-A17 MPCore Processor Technical Reference Manual, Revision r1p1.*
[6] ARM. 2016. *ARM® Cortex®-A57 MPCore Processor Technical Reference Manual, Revision r1p3.*
[7] Vasanth Bala, Evelyn Duesterwald, and Sanjeev Banerjia. 2000. Dynamo: a transparent dynamic optimization system. In *ACM SIGPLAN Notices*, Vol. 35. ACM, 1–12.
[8] Fabrice Bellard. 2005. QEMU, a Fast and Portable Dynamic Translator.. In *USENIX Annual Technical Conference, FREENIX Track.* 41–46.
[9] Darrell Boggs, Gary Brown, Nathan Tuck, and K Venkatraman. 2015. Denver: NVIDIA's First 64-bit ARM Processor. (2015).
[10] Derek Lane Bruening. 2004. *Efficient, transparent, and comprehensive runtime code manipulation.* Ph.D. Dissertation. Massachusetts Institute of Technology.
[11] Amanieu d'Antras, Cosmin Gorgovan, Jim Garside, and Mikel Luján. 2016. Optimizing indirect branches in dynamic binary translators. *ACM Transactions on Architecture and Code Optimization (TACO)* 13, 1 (2016), 7.
[12] Derek Davis and Kim Hazelwood. 2011. Improving region selection through loop completion. In *ASPLOS Workshop on Runtime Environments/Systems, Layering, and Virtualized Environments (RESoLVE).*
[13] James C Dehnert, Brian K Grant, John P Banning, Richard Johnson, Thomas Kistler, Alexander Klaiber, and Jim Mattson. 2003. The Transmeta Code Morphing™ Software: using speculation, recovery, and adaptive retranslation to address real-life challenges. In *Proceedings of the international symposium on Code generation and optimization: feedback-directed and runtime optimization.* IEEE Computer Society, 15–24.
[14] Balaji Dhanasekaran and Kim Hazelwood. 2011. Improving indirect branch translation in dynamic binary translators. In *Proceedings of the ASPLOS Workshop on Runtime Environments, Systems, Layering, and Virtualized Environments.* 11–18.
[15] Evelyn Duesterwald and Vasanth Bala. 2000. Software Profiling for Hot Path Prediction: Less is More. *SIGPLAN Not.* 35, 11 (Nov. 2000), 202–211. https://doi.org/10.1145/356989.357008
[16] Cosmin Gorgovan. 2016. MAMBO: A Low-Overhead Dynamic Binary Modification Tool for ARM. (2016). https://github.com/beehive-lab/mambo.
[17] Cosmin Gorgovan, Amanieu d'Antras, and Mikel Luján. 2016. MAMBO: A Low-Overhead Dynamic Binary Modification Tool for ARM. *ACM Trans. Archit. Code Optim.* 13, 1, Article 14 (April 2016), 26 pages. https://doi.org/10.1145/2896451
[18] Kim Hazelwood and Artur Klauser. 2006. A dynamic binary instrumentation engine for the ARM architecture. In *Proceedings of the 2006 international conference on Compilers, architecture and synthesis for embedded systems.* ACM, 261–270.
[19] Jason D Hiser, Daniel Williams, Wei Hu, Jack W Davidson, Jason Mars, and Bruce R Childers. 2007. Evaluating indirect branch handling mechanisms in software dynamic translation systems. In *Proceedings of the International Symposium on Code Generation and Optimization.* IEEE Computer Society, 61–73.
[20] Jeffrey K Hollingsworth, Barton Paul Miller, and Jon Cargille. 1994. Dynamic program instrumentation for scalable performance tools. In *Scalable High-Performance Computing Conference, 1994., Proceedings of the.* IEEE, 841–850.
[21] Ho-Seop Kim and James E Smith. 2003. Hardware support for control transfers in code caches. In *Proceedings of the 36th annual IEEE/ACM International Symposium on Microarchitecture.* IEEE Computer Society, 253.
[22] Chi-Keung Luk, Robert Cohn, Robert Muth, Harish Patil, Artur Klauser, Geoff Lowney, Steven Wallace, Vijay Janapa Reddi, and Kim Hazelwood. 2005. Pin: building customized program analysis tools with dynamic instrumentation. In *Acm Sigplan Notices*, Vol. 40. ACM, 190–200.
[23] Tipp Moseley, Daniel A Connors, Dirk Grunwald, and Ramesh Peri. 2007. Identifying potential parallelism via loop-centric profiling. In *Proceedings of the 4th international conference on Computing frontiers.* ACM, 143–152.
[24] Nicholas Nethercote and Julian Seward. 2007. Valgrind: a framework for heavyweight dynamic binary instrumentation. In *ACM Sigplan Notices*, Vol. 42. ACM, 89–100.
[25] Mathias Payer and Thomas R Gross. 2010. Generating low-overhead dynamic binary translators. In *Proceedings of the 3rd Annual Haifa Experimental Systems Conference.* ACM, 22.
[26] Yukinori Sato, Yasushi Inoguchi, and Tadao Nakamura. 2011. On-the-fly detection of precise loop nests across procedures on a dynamic binary translation system. In *Proceedings of the 8th ACM International Conference on Computing Frontiers.* ACM, 25.
[27] Julian Seward and Nicholas Nethercote. 2005. Using Valgrind to Detect Undefined Value Errors with Bit-Precision.. In *USENIX Annual Technical Conference, General Track.* 17–30.
[28] Jon Watson. 2008. Virtualbox: bits and bytes masquerading as machines. *Linux Journal* 2008, 166 (2008), 1.
[29] Emmett Witchel and Mendel Rosenblum. 1996. Embra: Fast and Flexible Machine Simulation. In *Proceedings of the 1996 ACM SIGMETRICS International Conference on Measurement and Modeling of Computer Systems (SIGMETRICS '96).* ACM, New York, NY, USA, 68–79. https://doi.org/10.1145/233013.233025
[30] Qin Zhao, David Koh, Syed Raza, Derek Bruening, Weng-Fai Wong, and Saman Amarasinghe. 2011. Dynamic cache contention detection in multi-threaded applications. In *ACM SIGPLAN Notices*, Vol. 46. ACM, 27–38.

TESS: Automated Performance Evaluation of Self-Healing and Self-Adaptive Distributed Software Systems

Jason Porter
Computer Science Department
jporte10@gmu.edu

Daniel A. Menascé
Computer Science Department
menasce@gmu.edu

Hassan Gomaa
Computer Science Department
hgomaa@gmu.edu

Emad Albassam
Computer Science Department
ealbassa@gmu.edu

ABSTRACT

This paper deals with the problem of evaluating and testing recovery and adaptation frameworks (RAF) for distributed software systems. We present TESS, a testbed for automatically generating distributed software architectures and their corresponding runtime applications, deploying them to the nodes of a cluster, running many different types of experiments involving failures and adaptation, and collecting in a database the values of a variety of failure recovery and adaptation metrics. Using the collected data, TESS automatically performs a thorough and scientific analysis of the efficiency and/or effectiveness of a RAF. This paper presents a case study on the use of TESS to evaluate DARE, a RAF developed by our group.

CCS CONCEPTS

• **General and reference** → **Empirical studies**; **Measurement**; **Metrics**; **Performance**; • **Computer systems organization** → **Distributed architectures**; • **Software and its engineering** → **Software architectures**; *Software performance*; *Software reliability*;

KEYWORDS

automated experimentation testbed; distributed component-based software systems; experimental design; self-healing software; self-adaptive software; software architecture.

ACM Reference Format:
Jason Porter, Daniel A. Menascé, Hassan Gomaa, and Emad Albassam. 2018. TESS: Automated Performance Evaluation of Self-Healing and Self-Adaptive Distributed Software Systems. In *Proceedings of ACM/SPEC International Conference on Performance Engineering (ICPE'18)*. ACM, New York, NY, USA, Article 4, 8 pages. https://doi.org/10.1145/3184407.3184408

1 INTRODUCTION

Evaluating the performance of distributed software systems in the presence of failures and adaptation is very challenging. This challenge is exarcerbated by the lack of global state knowledge, by the possibility of multiple concurrent failures of networks and nodes, and by message delays. This paper focusses on the performance evaluation of self-healing and self-adaptation frameworks that detect failures of distributed software systems, analyze their root causes, devise plans to recover from these failures, and execute these plans, according to the MAPE-K (Monitor, Analyze, Plan, and Execute based on Knowledge) model for autonomic computing [7]. Self-healing is the capability of a software system to automatically detect failures, recover to a consistent state, and resume normal execution. Self-adaptation is the capability of the software system to automatically adapt its architecture by adding, removing, or replacing components seamlessly at run-time in response to changes in operational environment or user requirements (see e.g. [10]). This paper deals with the complex problem of performance testing and measurement of distributed recovery and adaptation frameworks for distributed software systems.

The work reported here was developed in the context of the Resilient Autonomic Software Systems (RASS) project (www.cs.-gmu.edu/~menasce/rass/) aimed at designing, developing, and evaluating a framework to support highly decentralized component-based software systems. As part of the RASS project, we developed DARE (Distributed Adaptation and REcovery middleware), an architecture-based, decentralized middleware that provides self-configuration and self-healing properties to large and highly dynamic component-based software architectures [3]. We previously described DARE using an emergency response system application as an example. In that process we felt the need for a testbed that would *automatically* generate distributed architectures and applications, deploy them in the nodes of a cluster, run many different types of experiments, and collect the values of a variety of metrics in a database. The data collected could then be used to automatically perform a thorough and scientific analysis of the efficiency and/or effectiveness of a recovery and adaptation framework (RAF), such as DARE.

We designed and implemented such a testbed, called TESS, a Testbed for Evaluation of Self-Healing and Self-Adaptive Distributed Software Systems. TESS was designed and developed so that it can be used by other recovery and adaptation frameworks (RAF) besides DARE. The focus of this paper is TESS, a testbed to automatically and thoroughly evaluate autonomic systems such as DARE and similar RAFs. Thus, TESS is complimentary to DARE and DARE is used here as a case study for demonstrating TESS' capabilities.

The specific and unique contributions of this paper are: (1) design and implementation of TESS, (2) metrics to evaluate recovery and adaptation frameworks for distributed software systems, and (3) discussion of the results of using TESS for the evaluation of DARE.

This paper is organized as follows. Section 2 discusses the functionalities of RAFs and their interaction with TESS. Section 3 describes the design of TESS. Section 4 describes the DARE framework and Section 5 describes the experimental procedure used to evaluate DARE using TESS and the results of these experiments. Section 6 discusses related work and Section 7 provides concluding remarks.

2 RECOVERY AND ADAPTATION FRAMEWORK

TESS is designed to work with RAFs that provide the services described in this section and interface with TESS through two metric logs (see Fig. 1). The first log, called Core Events Log, stores data on (1) component and node failure events and (2) recovery and adaptations events. TESS reads these event data from this log in order to analyze and generate reports as described in Section 3.

The second log, called RAF-specific Events Log, records information about events specific to the RAF. Some examples of RAF-specific metrics may include the number of messages sent and received by the RAF to achieve its functionality as well as the time taken to perform specific tasks related to failure recovery and adaptation. To enable TESS to have access to the RAF-specific log, a RAF uses a file to be read by TESS to register the set of RAF-specific events and the format of this log. TESS processes and enters the information contained in the two logs into its Metrics DB, which is later used by TESS to provide detailed analysis of the experiments.

Entries in both logs have the same common prefix: timestamp, event type, event parameters. The core event types can be one of {component failure (CF), node failure (NF), component recovery (CR), node recovery (NR), adaptation start (AS), adaptation completion (AC)} and they have parameters associated with them that depend on the event type as illustrated in Table 1. For example, a component failure event has as parameters the id of the component that failed and the id of the node in which the component was running. Note that it is possible for a component to fail without the node on which it is running to fail. A node failure event generates

Table 1: Example of parameters for core recovery and adaptation events.

Event type	Parameters
Component Failure (CF)	Component Id, Node Id
Node Failure (NF)	Node Id
Component Recovery (CR)	ComponentId, Node Id
Node Recovery (NR)	Node Id
Adaptation Start (AS)	AdaptationId, AdaptationGoal
Adaptation End (AE)	AdaptationId

one component failure event for each component running on the failed node in addition to the node failure event. All CF events generated by a NF event have the same timestamp. A component recovery event is generated by a RAF when a component is recovered and instantiated on the same node, if the node did not fail, or on another node, in case the node failed. The node id parameter for the component recovery event indicates the node where the failed component was re-instantiated after recovery. The adaptation start event requires the RAF to generate a unique number to be used as an adaptation id as well as the *adaptation goal*, which consists of a set of one or more components and their interconnections that need to be replaced by a set of one or more interconnected components. Finally, the adaptation end event indicates when a previously started adaptation ended.

All the events recorded by a RAF in the two logs are timestamped so that they can be properly merged by TESS and stored into its Metrics DB. As indicated in Fig. 1, TESS also keeps an Architecture DB that stores all the architectures to be used during an experiment.

Table 2 illustrates a few entries of the Core Events Log: (a) Component C1 failed at node N2 at time t=101 and recovered at N2 at t=120. (b) Node N4 failed at t=130 and components C2 and C3 running at that node also failed. (c) Component C2 recovered at t=135 at node N5 and C3 recovered at node N6 at t=137. (d) Node N4 recovered at t=152.

A RAF is assumed to exhibit the following functionalities: (a) *Recovery from component failures*: creates a new instance of a failed component and logs event data on component failure detection and recovery events in the Core Metrics Log. (b) *Recovery from node*

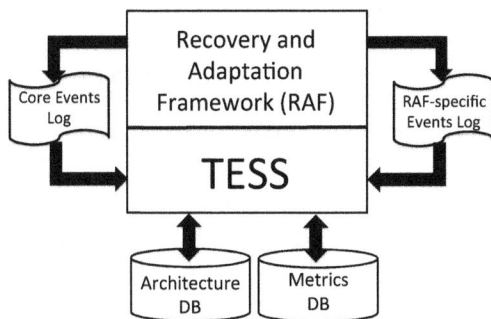

Figure 1: RAF Architecture and Interaction with TESS

Table 2: Example of a Core Events Log.

timestamp	Event type	Event Parameters
101	CF	C1 N2
120	CR	C1 N2
...	...	....
130	NF	N4
130	CF	C2 N4
130	CF	C3 N4
...	...	....
135	CR	C2 N5
137	CR	C3 N6
...	...	....
152	NR	N4

failures: creates a new instance of each component that was executing on the failed node on a new node and logs event data on node failure detection and corresponding recovery events in the Core Events Log. (c) *Adaptation*: adapts the software architecture by replacing one or more interconnected components with one or more interconnected components. Adaptation typically includes quiescing components to be disconnected from the application, removing these components, adding new components and interconnecting them with existing components [8].

To start a set of experiments a user must launch the *Start* script that interacts with the user to request (1) an id for the RAF (2) the name of a configuration file used by TESS to drive the process of generating architectures and conducting experiments (see Section 3), (3) the name of the file that contains the Core Metrics Log, and (4) the name of the file that contains the RAF-specific Metrics Log. TESS starts the experiments upon receiving these parameters.

3 DESIGN OF TESS

Figure 2 depicts the design of TESS, which consists of three stages: architecture generation, application generation, and application execution and data collection. During the first stage, TESS automatically generates a user-specified number of software architectures, which are stored in a database (step 1). Users can also add user-defined software architectures to the architecture database through a user interface. Each architecture consists of a number of components and connectors that interconnect components. Each generated architecture specifies a set of static attributes for the components. These attributes are used at run-time to determine the behavior of components as explained later. For example, these attributes determine if a component is enabled to send and/or receive messages and of which type (synchronous or asynchronous). These attributes also specify the probability that the component sends a message of a given type at set points during its execution as well as the probability that a component fails at run-time.

The application generation step (step 2) uses a *universal component template*, discussed in Section 3.3, and the static attributes of the components generated in step 1 to generate the application to be tested. The component template provides a probabilistic profile for the runtime behavior of components. The generated application is then deployed according to a deployment configuration map that indicates how software components are mapped to nodes of a distributed system (see step 3).

The third stage of TESS monitors the execution of the distributed application (step 4), collects the values of a variety of metrics related to failures and their recovery, as well as adaptation, and stores these values in a relational database (step 5). This database is analyzed during this stage and produces results based on all applications executed during the experiment but also for specific clusters of architectures based on their complexity (step 6). So, after metrics are collected in step 5 for one of the architectures, TESS checks if other applications need to be generated. In the affirmative case, TESS goes back to step 2. After all experiments are run for the generated architectures, TESS proceeds to step 6 to perform a complete statistical analysis of the results.

3.1 Architecture Generation

The architecture generation stage of TESS involves the dynamic generation of random architectures represented as labeled directed graphs [13]. Nodes are associated with component types; edges correspond to connectors and indicate the types of communication patterns between components. We consider three types of communication patterns: (1) Component A sends a synchronous (SY) message to another component and blocks while waiting for a reply. (2) A sends an asynchronous (AS) message to a single destination (SD) and can continue processing because no reply is expected. (3) A sends an asynchronous (AS) message to multiple destinations (MD); component A can continue processing after sending these messages and no reply is expected from any of the recipients. Thus, the three possible labels for an edge are: (SY, SD), (AS, SD), and (AS, MD). The architecture generation algorithm enforces the folowing constraints: (1) the architecture graph must be connected, (2) multicast messages can only be asynchronous, and (3) a component type can only send a multicast message in response to a message.

The generated architectures are stored in the Architecture DB described next.

3.2 The Architecture DB

The Architecture DB consists of two tables: *Architecture* (contains information for the generated architectures) and *Components* (contains information for the individual components of each architecture).

The *Architecture* table has the following columns:

- *ArchitectureId*: unique id for the architecture (primary key).
- *NumComponents*: number of components.
- *NumEdges*: number of edges (connections).
- *NumSyncMessages*: total number of synchronous connections.
- *NumAsyncMessages*: total number of asynchronous connections
- *NumUnicastMessages*: total number of unicast message interfaces.
- *NumMulticastMessages*: total number of multicast message interfaces.
- *ArchComplexity*: architecture complexity, inspired by the cyclomatic complexity for computer programs [9]:

$$
\begin{aligned}
\text{Complexity} \quad = \quad & \text{\# components} + \text{\# edges} + \\
& \text{\# edges/\# components} + \\
& \text{\# synchronous messages/\# edges} + \\
& \text{\# multicast messages/\# edges}.
\end{aligned}
$$

We consider component-type as opposed to component-instance architectures and cluster them into simple, moderate, and complex using k-means clustering [6].

- *ClusterId*: id of the cluster for this architecture.

The columns of the *Component* table are:

- *ComponentId*: unique id of a component (primary key).
- *Type*: type of component (e.g., sender, receiver, sender-receiver, receiver-sender).
- *ArchitectureId*: unique id of the architecture (foreign key).
- *FailureProbability*: probability that a component fails after receiving a message.

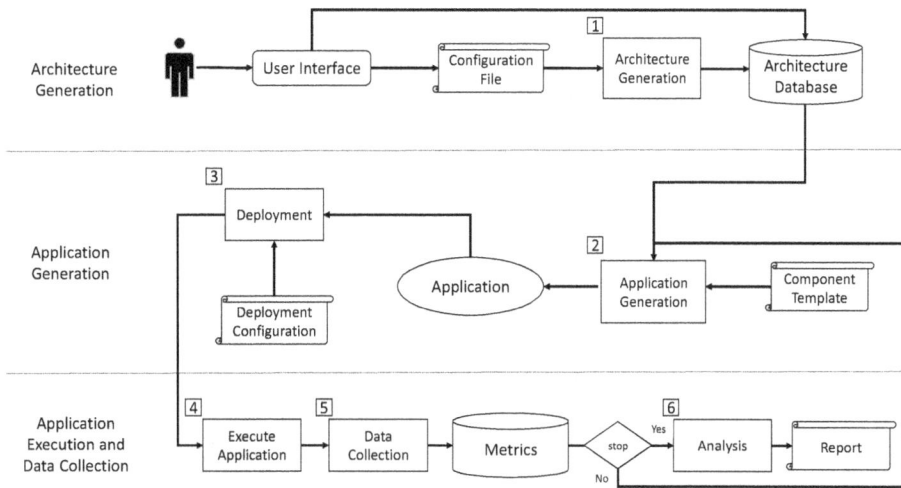

Figure 2: TESS Design

- *AvgMessageProcessingTime*: average time between a component receiving a message and sending a reply.
- *ProbSendSyncMessage*: probability that a message sent by a component is synchronous.
- *ProbSendAsyncMessage*: probability that a message sent by a component is asynchronous.
- *SendSync*: Flag indicating if a component sends synchronous messages.
- *SendAsync*: Flag indicating if a component sends asynchronous messages.
- *RecSync*: Flag indicating if a component receives synchronous messages.
- *ProbSendUnicastMessage*: probability that a message sent by a component is unicast.
- *ProbSendMulticastMessage*: probability that a message sent by a component is multicast.

3.3 Application Generation

The application generation phase of TESS uses a *universal component template* to drive the runtime behavior of the components of the architecture. The universal template component is instantiated at runtime in many different and random ways based on the static and probabilistic attributes of the component for a given architecture stored in the Architecture DB (see Section 3.2). For example, based on the static *Type* attribute, a component can be classified as a *sender*, *receiver*, *sender-receiver*, or *receiver-sender*. As an example of a probabilistic attribute, the *FailureProbability* attribute of a component determines if it fails after receiving a message.

We now describe the universal component template from the point of view of a component S that receives a message m from component C.

If a component is a *sender*, it sends an asynchronous message with probability *ProbSendAsyncMessage* and/or a synchronous message with probability *ProbSendSyncMessage*.

If component S is a *receiver*, it receives message m and fails with probability *FailureProbability* for that component as determined in the Architecture DB. If the component does not fail, it waits for a uniformly distributed time with average *AvgMessageProcessing Time*, specified for component S in the Architecture DB, to simulate the time taken by the component to process the message and act on it. If message m is synchronous, S replies to component C.

If component S is a *sender-receiver*, it sends an asynchronous message with probability *ProbSendAsyncMessage*, sends a synchronous message with probability *ProbSendSyncMessage*, receives message m and fails with probability *FailureProbability*. If S does not fail, it processes message m, and replies to it if m is a synchronous message.

Finally, if S is a *receiver-sender*, it receives message m and fails with probability *FailureProbability*. If S does not fail, it processes the received message, sends an asynchronous message with probability *ProbSendAsyncMessage*, sends a synchronous message with probability *ProbSendSyncMessage*, processes the received message m, and replies to it if m is a synchronous message.

The mechanism for potentially sending an asynchronous message works as follows. A uniformly distributed random number p between 0 and 1 is generated. If this number is less than or equal to the probability that the component sends an asynchronous message, then the component will either send a unicast message or a multicast message.

When sending an asynchronous message, component S sends a unicast message with probability *ProbSendUnicastMessage* or a multicast message with probability *ProbSendMulticastMessage*. In the unicast case, a message is sent to a randomly chosen component consistent with the generated architecture. Multicast messages are sent to the multicast group prescribed by the architecure.

Therefore, different components behave differently from each other because they have different static attributes generated during the architecture generation phase and because of the random values of the probability attributes generated at run-time.

3.4 Application Execution and Data Collection

The various components of the generated application are deployed to the various nodes of a distributed system (a computer cluster in our experiments). Once the application starts to execute, the RAF records core events and RAF-specific events in the logs described above. These logs are then merged at the end of each experiment into a single log at a master node that controls the experiments and stores the master log into the databases used by TESS. From this merged log, metrics are gathered and stored in the Metrics DB for later analysis.

As mentioned before, metrics are classified into core metrics and RAF-specific metrics. The core metrics gathered during experimentation include: (a) Component Recovery Time: time elapsed since a component failure was detected until it recovered. (b) Node Recovery Time: time elapsed since a node failure was detected until the components running at that node are recovered to a new node. (c) Adaptation Time: time elapsed from start to finish of an adaptation procedure.

The Metrics DB consists of a single table, called *Experiment*, which contains the values of the metrics gathered from each run of an experiment. The columns of this table are:

- *ExperimentId*: unique id of the experiment (primary key).
- *ArchitectureId*: unique id for the architecture (foreign key).
- *StartTime*: start time of the experiment.
- *Duration*: duration of the experiment.
- *ComponentRecoveryTime*: average component recovery time.
- *NodeRecoveryTime*: average node recovery time.
- *AdaptationTime*: adaptation time.
- *NumCompFailures*: number of component failures.
- *NumNodeFailures*: number of node failures.
- *NumAdaptations*: number of adaptation events.

The *Architecture* table has a single entry for each generated architecture and the *Components* table has a single entry for each component of a particular architecture. The *Experiments* table has multiple entries for metrics associated with a given architecture. In other words, for each architecture, multiple experiments are conducted and numerous values for each type of metric are collected and stored for later analysis. Because an architecture is associated with an experiment by its ArchitectureId, one may run queries to obtain metrics (e.g., average, coefficient of variation, range and other statistical measures) for either a specific architecture or for all architectures of a specific type.

4 THE DARE MIDDLEWARE

DARE is based on a decentralized version of the MAPE-K loop model. Every node in the distributed system runs an identical instance of the DARE middleware, which is responsible for:

- Keeping track of the current configuration map of the software system, including the mapping of components to nodes and maintaining the current configuration map of the software system.
- Automatically discovering the current architecture of the software system and rediscovering the architecture after dynamic adaptation. DARE relies on gossiping and message tracing techniques for discovering and disseminating the current software architecture (consisting of components and connectors) in a decentralized fashion [13].

- Monitoring and detecting node failures.
- Analyzing the cause of node failures.
- Planning for dynamically adapting the architecture and recovery of failed nodes.
- Executing a reconfiguration template consisting of reconfiguration commands that handle instantiating components on healthy nodes and establishing the connections between application components.
- Adapting and recovering components after run-time node and/or component failures.
- Communicating with recovery and adaptation connectors (RACs) that handle the recovery of failed transactions and steer application components to a quiescent state in order to carry out dynamic adaptation [1] [2].

5 EXPERIMENTAL PROCESS

Figure 3 depicts the deployment of TESS in a computer cluster that consists of a master node, which acts as a gateway and is connected to the other nodes. The master node hosts the main components of the testbed: a MySQL database for TESS databases, the architecture and application generation modules and the data collection module. Additionally, the master node stores the merged log used to collate all the events from the event logs for all experiments. All other nodes host the RAF and components of the distributed application generated by the application generation module, and local copies of the core and RAF-specific events logs.

We conducted detailed experiments on the use of TESS to automatically evaluate DARE. TESS, which was implemeted in Java, generated 100 random architectures and clustered them according to complexity as complex, moderate, and simple. The experiments were then conducted on 10, 15, and 20 nodes of a computer cluster, where for complex architectures each node hosted approximately three components, for moderate architectures each node hosted approximately two components and for simple architectures each node hosted a single component. Connectors were hosted on separate nodes.

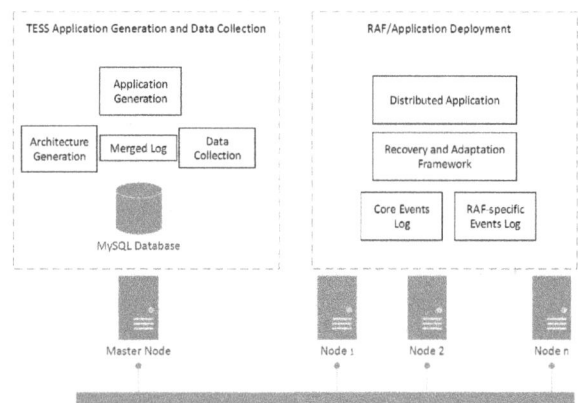

Figure 3: TESS Deployment on a Cluster

We conducted self-healing (component and node failures) and self-adaptation experiments. For component failures, each component randomly fails during execution according to its failure probability, specified in the *Components* table. With regards to node failures, a random node was selected and then taken down accordingly [3]. Component recovery is done by the RAC instantiating the failed component at another node and replaying the messages (stored in the RAC's message queues) that were in transit to/from that component. The self-adaptation experiments involved removing a randomly selected component and replacing it with a load balancing architectural pattern. This entailed adding a load balancing component along with 2 or more replicas of the original component. See [3] for more details on DARE's approach to failure recovery and adaptation.

5.1 Experimental Results

The experiments reported in this section are related to the core metrics (component recovery time, node recovery time, and component adaptation time). TESS gathered 30 observations of each metric for each architecture complexity type (complex, moderate, and simple) for three node counts (10, 15, and 20). This data was then used by TESS to calculate the mean and 95% confidence intervals (CI) for these metrics. Also, for each metric a two-factor statistical ANOVA procedure [6] was conducted. The factors are architecture complexity with three levels (simple, moderate, and complex) and node count with three levels (10, 15, and 20 nodes). The hypotheses for the ANOVA experiments are:

H_0: (a) the architecture complexity has no impact on the given metric (i.e., the metric average is the same for all complexity levels), (b) node count has no impact on the given metric (i.e., the metric average is the same for all node counts), and (c) there is no interaction between architecture complexity and node count.

H_1: (a) the architecture complexity has an impact on the given metric (i.e, the metric average is not the same for all complexity levels), (b) node count has an impact on the given metric (i.e., the metric average is not the same for all node counts), and (c) there is interaction between architecture complexity and node count.

Tables 3 and 4 show statistics (average, 95% Confidence Interval (CI), and range) for the number of components and number of connections between components for each architecture complexity type. The values in these tables help explain the observed behavior when we analyze the metrics described in what follows.

Table 3: Mean, 95% CIs and Range for No. of Components

complexity	mean	1/2 CI	range
complex	26.2	± 0.88	21-30
moderate	20.9	± 0.69	17-25
simple	13.8	± 0.91	10-20

5.2 Core Metrics

The metrics reported here are: component recovery time, node recovery time, and component adaptation time.

Table 4: Mean, 95% CIs and Range for No. of Connections

complexity	mean	1/2 CI	range
complex	109.9	± 4.1	94-151
moderate	83.5	± 2.6	69-95
simple	50.3	± 3.5	32-65

5.2.1 Component Recovery Time. This experiment assessed the impact of both architecture complexity and different node counts on component recovery time. Tables 5, 6 and 7 show the mean and 95% confidence intervals for component recovery time for each architecture complexity for 10, 15 and 20 nodes, respectively. Table 8 shows the results of the two-factor ANOVA for architecture complexity and node count for component recovery time. For architecture complexity, $F > F_{crit}$ results in the rejection of the null hypothesis and acceptance of the alternative hypothesis that the average component recovery time is impacted by architecture complexity. This happens because as architecture complexity increases, a component will communicate with a larger number of neighboring components, resulting in a larger number of reconnections required after recovery. For node count, $F > F_{crit}$ results in the rejection of the null hypothesis and acceptance of the alternative hypothesis that the number of nodes impacts the average component recovery time. This is due to the fact that for smaller node counts, more components would be hosted per node for the same architectures than for a larger node count. As a consequence, there would be more recovery overhead per node for smaller node counts. For factor interaction, $F < F_{crit}$ results in a failure to reject the null hypothesis that there is no interaction between the two factors. In other words, we fail to prove the alternative hypothesis that there is interaction between architecture complexity and node count.

Table 5: Component Recovery Time (10 Nodes)

complexity	mean (sec)	1/2 CI (sec)
complex	31.2	± 2.83
moderate	28.9	± 4.30
simple	23.0	± 2.39

Table 6: Component Recovery Time (15 Nodes)

complexity	mean (sec)	1/2 CI (sec)
complex	22.0	± 1.32
moderate	21.2	± 1.13
simple	18.5	± 1.05

Table 7: Component Recovery Time (20 Nodes)

complexity	mean (sec)	1/2 CI (sec)
complex	18.0	± 0.91
moderate	16.9	± 0.95
simple	15.2	± 0.98

Table 8: Two-Factor ANOVA for Component Recovery Time

Source of Variation	F	P-value	F crit
Architecture Complexity	16.702	1.49E-07	3.030
Node Count	82.306	1.93E-28	3.030
Interaction	2.065	0.0858	2.406

5.2.2 Node Recovery Time. This experiment assessed the impact of architecture complexity and node count on node recovery time. Tables 9, 10 and 11 show the mean and 95% confidence intervals for node recovery time for each architecture complexity for 10, 15 and 20 nodes, respectively. Table 12 shows the results of the two-factor ANOVA for architecture complexity and node count for node recovery time. For architecture complexity, $F > F_{crit}$ results in the rejection of the null hypothesis and acceptance of the alternative hypothesis that architecture complexity impacts the average node recovery time. This is due to the fact that more complex architectures consist of a higher number of components (see Table 3) being hosted per node resulting in larger node recovery times. For node count, $F > F_{crit}$ results in the rejection of the null hypothesis and acceptance of the alternative hypothesis that the number of nodes impacts the average node recovery time. As mentioned in the previous experiment, smaller node counts host more components per node than larger node counts for the same architectures. This is due to fact that if the number of components within an architecture is fixed, but the number of nodes used to host the architecture is reduced, more components will have to be hosted per node to enable the reduced node count. This in effect results in longer recovery times for smaller node counts. For factor interaction, $F > F_{crit}$ results in the rejection of the null hypothesis and acceptance of the alternative hypothesis that there is interaction between architecture complexity and node count. This is due to the fact that: (a) more (less) complex architectures implies more (less) components hosted per node for the same node count and (b) a larger (smaller) node count implies less (more) components hosted at a node for the same architectural complexity.

Table 9: Node Recovery Time (10 Nodes)

complexity	mean (min)	1/2 CI (min)
complex	6.4	± 0.85
moderate	4.9	± 0.59
simple	2.9	± 0.45

Table 10: Node Recovery Time (15 Nodes)

complexity	mean (min)	1/2 CI (min)
complex	3.5	± 0.22
moderate	2.6	± 0.32
simple	1.6	± 0.20

Table 11: Node Recovery Time (20 Nodes)

complexity	mean (min)	1/2 CI (min)
complex	1.7	± 0.18
moderate	1.3	± 0.09
simple	0.8	± 0.09

Table 12: Two-Factor ANOVA for Node Recovery Time

Source of Variation	F	P-value	F crit
Architecture Complexity	74.0	3.48E-26	3.030
Node Count	214.642	7.56E-56	3.030
Interaction	11.256	1.93E-08	2.406

5.2.3 Component Adaptation Time. This experiment assessed the impact of architecture complexity and node count on component adaptation time. Tables 13, 14 and 15 show the mean and 95% confidence intervals for component adaptation time for each architecture complexity for 10, 15 and 20 nodes, respectively. Table 16 shows the results of the two-factor ANOVA for architecture complexity and node count for component adaptation time. For architecture complexity, $F > F_{crit}$ results in the rejection of the null hypothesis and acceptance of the alternative hypothesis that architecture complexity impacts average component adaptation time. This is a consequence of the fact that a component that has a higher number of interactions with other components will take longer to complete these interactions and then transition to the quiescent state [8], thereby allowing it to be removed and replaced. For node count, $F < F_{crit}$ results in a failure to reject the null hypothesis that node count does not impact component adaptation time. In other words, we failed to prove the alternative hypothesis that node count impacts the average adaptation time. From Tables 13 and 14 it can be seen that an increase in node count from 10 to 15 nodes results in an increase in component adaptation time, and from 15 to 20 nodes there is a decrease in component adaptation time (see Tables 14 and 15). However, these differences are not statistically significant because the F value for node count (2.438) is less than F_{crit} (3.030) (see Table 16). For factor interaction, $F < F_{crit}$ results in a failure to reject the null hypothesis that there is no interaction between the two factors. In other words, we failed to prove the alternative hypothesis that there is interaction between architecture complexity and node count.

Table 13: Component Adaptation Time (10 Nodes)

complexity	mean (min)	1/2 CI (min)
complex	4.5	± 1.31
moderate	3.7	± 0.78
simple	2.6	± 0.61

6 RELATED WORK

There are two main areas related to our work. The first is the performance evaluation of distributed systems. In [11] Mohamed et

Table 14: Component Adaptation Time (15 Nodes)

complexity	mean (min)	1/2 CI (min)
complex	5.1	± 1.07
moderate	4.1	± 0.80
simple	3.4	± 0.71

Table 15: Component Adaptation Time (20 Nodes)

complexity	mean (min)	1/2 CI (min)
complex	3.9	± 2.31
moderate	3.1	± 0.69
simple	2.5	± 0.71

Table 16: Two-Factor ANOVA for Component Adaptation Time

Source of Variation	F	P-value	F crit
Architecture Complexity	6.194	0.0024	3.030
Node Count	2.438	0.0893	3.030
Interaction	0.085	0.987	2.406

al. describe the performance evaluation of distributed event-based systems. Sachs et al. [15] describe the performance evaluation of distributed message-oriented middleware.

Also related to our work is the performance evaluation of self-adaptive systems and self-healing systems. Becker et al. [4] describe an approach to the performance evaluation of self-adaptive systems while Pereira et al. [12] describe the performance evaluation of self-healing systems.

In contrast to the previous works, TESS focuses on both self-healing and self-adaptation frameworks for distributed software systems. To the best our knowledge there does not exist another **testbed** that provides an automated approach to the performance evaluation of both self-adaptive and self-healing distributed software systems.

7 CONCLUDING REMARKS

Several recovery and adaptation frameworks have been proposed for self-healing and self-adaptation of distributed software systems. In most cases, these frameworks are evaluated with one or two distributed system application examples and in many cases little or no quantitative evaluation is conducted [5]. For that reason, we decided to design and implement TESS, described above and in more detail in [14], to assist in the quantitative evaluation of recovery and adaptation frameworks. TESS was designed and implemented as a tool that can be used to evaluate a variety of self-adaptive and self-healing frameworks such as DARE. Thus, TESS is complimentary to DARE, which was used as a case study to demonstrate and evaluate TESS.

TESS follows well-known principles of experimental design [6] by generating random architectures that are clustered into complex, medium, and simple architectures, and running experiments where node and component failures and component adaptations occur

randomly. The metrics gathered by TESS are stored in a database and stored procedures are used to generate a variety of metrics such as averages, confidence intervals, and statistical procedures such as ANOVA [6]. TESS can also be used to evaluate a RAF on a user-define architecture.

Our use of TESS to evaluate DARE illustrates how TESS can be used for detailed experimental evaluation of recovery and adaptation frameworks. TESS could be extended to automatically track and report on detailed elements of the recovery and/or adaptation times as long as that information is available in the logs generated by RAFs. This would allow users to obtain a better understanding of the major sources of delay in each case. Additionally, it is possible to extend TESS to consider additional core metrics such as the ones proposed in [5] for adaptation.

ACKNOWLEDGEMENTS

This work was partially supported by the AFOSR grant FA9550-16-1-0030 and the Office of Research Computing at George Mason University.

REFERENCES

[1] Emad Albassam, Hassan Gomaa, and Daniel Menascé. 2016. Model-based Recovery Connectors for Self-adaptation and Self-healing. In *Proc. 11th Intl. Joint Conf. Software Technologies*.

[2] Emad Albassam, Hassan Gomaa, and Daniel Menascé. 2017. Model-Based Recovery and Adaptation Connectors: Design and Experimentation. *Software Technologies* (2017).

[3] Emad Albassam, Jason Porter, Hassan Gomaa, and Daniel Menascé. 2017. DARE: A Distributed Adaptation and Failure Recovery Framework for Software Systems. In *the 14th IEEE International Conference on Autonomic Computing (ICAC)*.

[4] Matthias Becker, Markus Luckey, and Steffen Becker. 2012. Model-driven performance engineering of self-adaptive systems: a survey. In *Proceedings of the 8th international ACM SIGSOFT conference on Quality of Software Architectures*. ACM, 117–122.

[5] Lachlana Birdsey, Claudia Szabo, and Katrina Falkner. 2017. Identifying Self-Organization and Adaptability in Complex Adaptive Systems. In *11th IEEE International Conference on Self-Adaptive and Self-Organizing Systems*.

[6] Raj Jain. 1991. *The Art of Computer Systems Performance Analysis: Techniques for Experimental Design, Measurement, Simulation, and Modeling*. Wiley-Interscience.

[7] Jeffrey O Kephart and David M Chess. 2003. The vision of autonomic computing. *Computer* 36, 1 (2003), 41–50.

[8] Jeff Kramer and Jeff Magee. 1990. The evolving philosophers problem: Dynamic change management. *IEEE Tr. Software Engineering* 16, 11 (1990), 1293–1306.

[9] T. J. McCabe. 1976. A Complexity Measure. *IEEE Trans. Softw. Eng.* 2, 4 (July 1976), 308–320. https://doi.org/10.1109/TSE.1976.233837

[10] Daniel Menascé, Hassan Gomaa, Joao Sousa, and Sam Malek. 2011. SASSY: A framework for self-architecting service-oriented systems. *IEEE Software* 28, 6 (2011), 78–85.

[11] Saleh Mohamed, Matthew Forshaw, Nigel Thomas, and Andrew Dinn. 2017. Performance and Dependability Evaluation of Distributed Event-based Systems: A Dynamic Code-injection Approach. In *Proceedings of the 8th ACM/SPEC on International Conference on Performance Engineering*. ACM, 349–352.

[12] E Grishikashvili Pereira, Rubem Pereira, and A Taleb-Bendiab. 2006. Performance evaluation for self-healing distributed services and fault detection mechanisms. *J. Comput. System Sci.* 72, 7 (2006), 1172–1182.

[13] Jason Porter, Daniel Menascé, and Hassan Gomaa. 2016. DeSARM: A Decentralized Mechanism for Discovering Software Architecture Models at Runtime in Distributed Systems. In *11th Intl. Workshop on Models@run.time*.

[14] Jason Porter, Daniel Menascé, Hassan Gomaa, and Emad Albassam. 2017. Design and Experimentation of an Automated Performance Evaluation Testbed for Self-Healing and Self-Adaptive Distributed Software Systems. In *Technical Report GMU-CS-TR-2017-2*. Department of Computer Science, George Mason University.

[15] Kai Sachs, Samuel Kounev, Jean Bacon, and Alejandro Buchmann. 2009. Performance evaluation of message-oriented middleware using the SPECjms2007 benchmark. *Performance Evaluation* 66, 8 (2009), 410–434.

To Adapt or Not to Adapt? Technical Debt and Learning Driven Self-Adaptation for Managing Runtime Performance

Tao Chen
Department of Computing and
Technology, Nottingham Trent
University, UK;
CERCIA, School of Computer Science,
University of Birmingham, UK
t.chen@cs.bham.ac.uk

Rami Bahsoon, Shuo Wang
CERCIA, School of Computer Science,
University of Birmingham, UK
{r.bahsoon,s.wang}@cs.bham.ac.uk

Xin Yao
Department of Computer Science and
Engineering, Southern University of
Science and Technology, China;
CERCIA, School of Computer Science,
University of Birmingham, UK
x.yao@cs.bham.ac.uk

ABSTRACT

Self-adaptive system (SAS) can adapt itself to optimize various key performance indicators in response to the dynamics and uncertainty in environment. In this paper, we present Debt Learning Driven Adaptation (DLDA), an framework that dynamically determines when and whether to adapt the SAS at runtime. DLDA leverages the temporal adaptation debt, a notion derived from the technical debt metaphor, to quantify the time-varying money that the SAS carries in relation to its performance and Service Level Agreements. We designed a temporal net debt driven labeling to label whether it is economically healthier to adapt the SAS (or not) in a circumstance, based on which an online machine learning classifier learns the correlation, and then predicts whether to adapt under the future circumstances. We conducted comprehensive experiments to evaluate DLDA with two different planners, using 5 online machine learning classifiers, and in comparison to 4 state-of-the-art debt-oblivious triggering approaches. The results reveal the effectiveness and superiority of DLDA according to different metrics.

CCS CONCEPTS

• Software and its engineering → Software performance;

KEYWORDS

Self-adaptive systems, performance, technical debt, learning

ACM Reference Format:
Tao Chen, Rami Bahsoon, Shuo Wang, and Xin Yao. 2018. To Adapt or Not to Adapt? Technical Debt and Learning Driven Self-Adaptation for Managing Runtime Performance. In ICPE '18: ACM/SPEC International Conference on Performance Engineering, April 9–13, 2018, Berlin, Germany. ACM, New York, NY, USA, 8 pages. https://doi.org/10.1145/3184407.3184413

1 INTRODUCTION

Self-adaptive system (SAS) is capable of planning and adapting itself at runtime, through a set of known control features (e.g.,

thread pool size and cache size, *etc*), to continually optimize for different key performance indicators, e.g., response time and energy consumption, under changing environment such as dynamic workload [16] [31]. SAS often operate under formally negotiated legal binding [33][18], e.g., Service Level Agreements (SLA) [3], especially in paradigms such as services and cloud computing. This binding allows us to translate the performance of SAS into a more intuitive monetary way, e.g., instead of saying the SAS's response time is 2s in average, we are able to state the SAS creates a total of $54 profit (or debt) for the owner. The real money that the SAS carries (either as profit or debt) determines its economic health.

While majority of SAS research has focused on the runtime *planning* phase of the SAS that determines *what and how to adapt* (e.g., rule-based [7], search-based [11][29][12] or control theoretic planners [32]), there is little research that explicitly tackles the challenge of *when and whether to adapt* the SAS, i.e., how to design the trigger [31]. We argue that deciding on when adaptation should be triggered is also non-trivial [31], because the effectiveness of the diverse planners can vary with the changing *circumstances*, i.e., SAS's status and environment conditions. Even if we assume perfect planning, it still comes with cost, e.g., planning delay and extra resource/energy consumptions, etc. The key problem, which we address in this paper, is how to make a binary decision at each point in time: *whether to adapt* the SAS, considering dynamic and uncertain monetary cost-benefit of adapting the SAS or not.

Existing work on SAS falls into one of the two categories when dealing with the trigger: either adapt periodically [29][21] or adapt upon some observed or predicted events[1] (e.g., violation of requirement thresholds) at certain level of significance [18][13][36]. Adapting periodically is grounded on the principle that *we constantly adapt the SAS with the best possible adaptation solution, regardless whether the SAS breaks (e.g., violate performance requirements)*. However, the problem with this method is obvious: since the adaptation may not significantly improve the performance under all circumstances, adapting when it is better not to adapt would generate unnecessary pressure, resulting additional costs and/or even degradation in performance, especially when the problem is difficult to solve, e.g., under heavy workload. Conversely, not adapting when it is needed would reduce the ability of the SAS to react to the changing environment. In contrast, adaptation upon the events relies on the principle that *if the SAS works (e.g., no requirements violation), do not change it; otherwise trigger adaptation*. Yet, adaptation upon

---

[1]The occurrence of event is indicated by the observation (or prediction) of the case when some fixed thresholds are hit.

Table 1: The elements of technical debt and net debt in the context of software development and SAS

			Software Development (asset is the software)		Running SAS (asset is the SAS itself)	
			If to improve software	*If not to improve software*	*If to adapt SAS*	*If not to adapt SAS*
Net Debt	Technical Debt	Principal	The case dependent cost for changing the software, e.g., extra money paid to employee for extra person/month.	N/A	The case dependent cost of adaptation, e.g., the rate per unit in SLA × the delay and extra resource/energy consumption of planning, etc.	N/A
		Interest	Cost, e.g., money paid for work, penalty of bad software quality, etc, incurred by old/new defects in the software as a result of wrongly spent efforts, flawed planning and bad code, etc.	Cost, e.g., penalty of bad software quality, etc, due to defects in the software.	Penalty (e.g., rate per unit from SLA × the units of violation) due to ineffective, flawed, sub-optimal or delayed planning and adaptation, etc, or too difficult environment, e.g., heavy and spiked workload.	Penalty (e.g., rate per unit from SLA × the units of violation) due to inability to react to the changing environment.
		Revenue	Bonus, e.g., more users are paying for the software, from the improved software as a result of wisely spent efforts, optimized code, etc.	Bonus, e.g., more users are paying for the software, from the software as a result of quick release, the expectation is met or exceeded, e.g., no defects reported.	Reward (e.g., reward per unit from SLA × the units above expectation) as a result of effective/optimized planning and adaptation.	Reward (e.g., reward per unit from SLA × the units above expectation) for performing as expected or better than requirements without adaptation.

the events may still cause extra pressure on the software system, providing little reward and/or worsening the performance, becuase the dynamic and uncertain cost-benefit of planning, in terms of real money, was not modelled explicitly.

In this paper, we propose the Debt Learning Driven Adaptation (DLDA), an automated framework that combines technical debt [15] and online learning [30] to determine when and whether to adapt a running SAS. The principle of DLDA is that *we adapt the SAS, if and only if, it can make the SAS economically healthier (less debt) than that of not adapting it*. Particularly, our contributions include: (i) We propose the *temporal adaptation debt* to quantify the **net debt** of SAS, which expresses the extent to which the SAS can repay its debt, if any, and create net profit from its decision (adapt or not). (ii) The labeling data is then used to train a binary and online classifier, which continuously classifies a re-emergent or unforeseen circumstances into the class label (i.e., to adapt or not) that can bring less debt, then inform the planner of SAS. (iii) DLDA is independent to the online learning classifier and planner for adaptation, in which DLDA also learns the effectiveness of a planner.

We evaluated DLDA on a complex SAS which contains the RUBiS [35] and a stack of software, under the FIFA98 trace [6] with different conditions, and in comparison to existing approaches. The results confirm the effectiveness and superiority of DLDA.

This paper is structured as follows. A high level mapping of technical debt analogy in SAS is presented in Section 2. Section 3 provides an overview of DLDA. The temporal adaptation debt and the related labeling are discussed in Section 4. Section 5 presents the combination of labeling and classification process. In Section 6, DLDA is extensively evaluated using a real-world SAS. Sections 7 and 8 discuss related work and conclude the paper, respectively.

2 THE TECHNICAL DEBT ANALOGY IN SAS

Technical debt for software engineering was coined by Cunningham [15], to help deciding whether to improve the software considering the costs and benefits of improvement versus that of not improving it. Like financial debt in the economic context, technical debt and its net value are associated with three elements:

- **Principal:** an one-off investment to an asset, e.g., a software.
- **Interest:** the extra cost of the asset accumulated over time.
- **Revenue:** the benefit of the asset accumulated over time.

While technical debt equals to *Principal + Interest*, its net value (**net debt**) is calculated as *Principal + Interest − Revenue*. Note that

the net debt can be smaller than zero, i.e., it represents net profit. Those concepts in software development bear many similarities with the problem of *when and whether to adapt* in SAS, but with different meanings of asset, principal, interest and revenue. A high level mapping of the analogy to the contexts is shown in Table 1. In both contexts, the aim is to minimize the net debt.

Generally in the software development, the debt is calculated based on real money, e.g., the salary for employing engineers to do extra work and the monetary loss/profit generated by the software. In SAS context, the debt is viewed from the monetary terms of SAS and their interplay with the runtime performance. This can be achieved by extracting the monetary rate per unit from SLA, which is a formal legal binding negotiated between the software company and the end users before the SAS is deployed [33][18]. For example, suppose the SLA states that the rate for the cost of adaptation is \$0.345 per CPU second and an adaptation utilized 2s, then the principal would be \$0.69. Similarly, the SLA may contain a penalty rate of mean response time violation as \$0.043/s for a requirement of 2s, and if there is a mean response time of 2.5s for a period, then the penalty for it would be $(2.5 - 2) \times 0.043 = \$0.0215$. All those results can be combined to form the net debt, which represents the real money related to the SAS. The SLA negotiation can be achieved using many well-established methods form the literature [37][3], thus in this work, we assume that the SLA and its performance related elements have been instrumented before using DLDA.

```
<wsag:GuaranteeTerm Name="ResponseTime">
  <wsag:ServiceScope ServiceName="SAS"/>
  <wsag:QualifyingCondition>
    {"function" : "AVG EVERY 120s"}
  </wsag:QualifyingCondition>
  <wsag:ServiceLevelObjective>
    <wsag:KPITarget>
      <wsag:KPIName>MeanTime</wsag:KPIName>
      <wsag:CustomServiceLevel>
        {"constraint" : "MeanTime LESS THAN 0.05s"}
      </wsag:CustomServiceLevel>
    </wsag:KPITarget>
  </wsag:ServiceLevelObjective>
  <wsag:BusinessValueList>
    <wsag:Penalty>
      <wsag:AssessmentInterval>
        <wsag:TimeInterval>120s</wsag:TimeInterval>
      </wsag:AssessmentInterval>
      <wsag:ValueUnit>USD_PER_SECOND</wsag:ValueUnit>
      <wsag:ValueExpression>3.5</wsag:ValueExpression>
    </wsag:Penalty>
    <wsag:Reward>
      <wsag:AssessmentInterval>
        <wsag:TimeInterval>120s</wsag:TimeInterval>
      </wsag:AssessmentInterval>
      <wsag:ValueUnit>USD_PER_SECOND</wsag:ValueUnit>
      <wsag:ValueExpression>3.5</wsag:ValueExpression>
    </wsag:Reward>
  </wsag:BusinessValueList>
</wsag:GuaranteeTerm>

<wsag:GuaranteeTerm
    Name="PlanningCPUTime">
  <wsag:ServiceScope
    ServiceName="SAS-Engine"/>
  <wsag:ServiceLevelObjective>
    <wsag:KPITarget>
      <wsag:KPIName>
        CPUTime
      </wsag:KPIName>
      <wsag:CustomServiceLevel>
        {"constraint" :
          "CPUTime LESS THAN 0s"}
      </wsag:CustomServiceLevel>
    </wsag:KPITarget>
  </wsag:ServiceLevelObjective>
  <wsag:BusinessValueList>
    <wsag:Penalty>
      <wsag:AssessmentInterval>
        <wsag:Count>1</wsag:Count>
      </wsag:AssessmentInterval>
      <wsag:ValueUnit>
        USD_PER_SECOND
      </wsag:ValueUnit>
      <wsag:ValueExpression>
        0.01
      </wsag:ValueExpression>
    </wsag:Penalty>
  </wsag:BusinessValueList>
</wsag:GuaranteeTerm>
```

Figure 1: Example SLA fragment of a SAS

An example fragment of the possible SLA for SAS, derived from the well-known WS-Agreement [3], is shown in Figure 1.

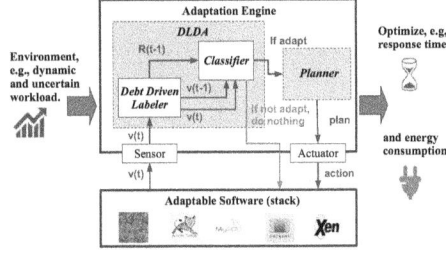

Figure 2: Overview of the DLDA framework on SAS.

3 DLDA OVERVIEW

As in Figure 2, a SAS generally has a feedback loop, with an adaptable software (e.g., a stack) that being managed at runtime, and an engine that controls the adaptation. DLDA runs in the adaptation engine and it has two components: *Debt Driven Labeler* and *Classifier*. While DLDA works within any feedback controller, it could be best placed in the *Analysis* phase of the MAPE-K loop [16].

The *Debt Driven Labeler* firstly analyzes the net debt for the past interval using the data vector from the most recent time points, i.e., $\mathbf{v}(t)$ and $\mathbf{v}(t-1)$, and the predefined SLA terms, it then produces a result, $R(t-1)$, labeling whether 'to adapt' or 'not to adapt' under the circumstance at time *t-1* can lead to less net debt (see Section 4).

In *Classifier*, the class label from the *Debt Driven Labeler*, together with the past status of SAS and the environmental factors in a vector ($\mathbf{v}(t-1)$, i.e., the circumstance), are used to train an online learning classifier (see Section 5). The decision of whether to adapt or not under the circumstance at the current point in time is then predicted by the updated classifier using the current vector of information, i.e., $\mathbf{v}(t)$. As such, DLDA can be used as an independent filter before any planner, which decides *what and how to adapt* [12][29].

4 TEMPORAL ADAPTATION DEBT MODEL

We propose the temporal adaptation debt to quantify the net debt for triggering the SAS at runtime. Like technical debt, adaptation debt equals to *Principal + Interest*, and its net debt is *Principal + Interest − Revenue*, i.e., how much money a SAS earns or costs.

Since the problem of *when and whether to adapt* SAS is a decision to be made at every point in time that could exhibit different circumstances (i.e., SAS status and environment), at the low level, temporal adaptation debt models the *newly incurred net debt*, including its one-off principal, accumulated interests and revenue *over a time interval*. This net debt expresses how the SAS performs, in terms of monetary value ($), over that time interval. The idea is that, if DLDA can predict whether adapt (or not) at each point in time can lead to less net debt, and react accordingly, then globally the net debt related to the SAS can be minimized. To this end, considering temporal notion is important as our purpose is to correlate the past circumstance of a given point in time to the class label (adapt or not) that can lead to less net debt, which in turn, will serve as a data sample to guide the learning classifier.

In the following, we transpose the high level notions from Table 1 into the low level, particularly in regards to the temporal notion.

4.1 Temporal Principal

At the low level, *we use the temporal principal to describe the temporally invested cost of planning and adaptation at a unit of time*. Intuitively, to influence the SAS for the interval between time *t-1* and *t*, the principal of adaptation invested at time *t-1* is:

$$Principal(t-1) = C_{unit} \times U(t-1) \tag{1}$$

where $U(t-1)$ is the utilized units of certain adaptation effort (given by the engineers) measured at runtime, e.g., the delay of planning, the extra resource/energy consumption for planning, etc; and C_{unit} is the monetary rate per unit extracted from the SLA.

4.2 Subtracting Temporal Interest and Revenue

At the low level, the subtraction of temporal interest and revenue observed at time t is the subtraction of accumulated interest and revenue between *t-1* and *t*, representing the temporal result of two mutually exclusive cases: *(i) the SAS did adapted at t-1; or (ii) the SAS did not adapt at t-1.* Formally, the subtraction is:

$$S(t) = Interest(t) - Revenue(t) = \sum_{i=1}^{n}(\Delta Q_i \times M_i) \tag{2}$$

$$\Delta Q_i = \begin{cases} Q_i(t, t-1) - T_i & if\ minimize\ Q_i \\ T_i - Q_i(t, t-1) & if\ maximize\ Q_i \end{cases}$$

whereby $Q_i(t, t-1)$ is the given accumulated function, from the SLA, that returns the performance of the ith performance indicator that accumulated over the time interval between *t-1* and *t*, e.g., mean, total, maximum or definite integral function, etc. Such functions monitor the actual performance of SAS at runtime. T_i is the corresponding requirement constraint for the accumulated performance over a time interval from the SLA and n is the total number of indicators. M_i is the given monetary penalty (if violating requirement) or reward (if outperforming requirement) per unit for the related indicator over a time interval in the SLA . We assume that the reward and penalty share the same unit rate, but the formula can be easily changed to handle different rates. Note that we do not need to distinguish the interest and revenue, as what we care is the subtraction of their accumulated results, which is collectively reflected by the accumulated SAS performance.

4.3 Temporal Net Debt Driven Labeling

Suppose now we are at time t, the labeling process labels whether the SAS should adapt or not for the past circumstance at time *t-1* by comparing the net debt associated with "*to adapt*" and "*not to adapt*". Beside the formal discussion below, an intuitive illustration of the different cases in the labeling process is shown in Figure 3.

1) True Class: the temporal net debt for the class of '*the SAS should adapt under the circumstance at t-1*' , $D_{adapt}(t-1)$, is:

$$D_{adapt}(t-1) = \begin{cases} Principal(t-1) + S(t) & if\ adapted\ at\ t\text{-}1 \\ 0 & otherwise \end{cases} \tag{3}$$

Now, in practice, there are two further cases to consider:

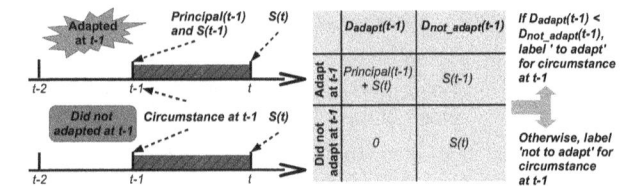

Figure 3: Different cases in the labeling process (now at *t*).

—(i) the SAS did adapted at *t-1*. If there was indeed an adaptation at time *t-1*, $D_{adapt}(t-1)$ can be computed directly because the related $S(t)$, which represents the subtraction of accumulated interest and revenue between *t-1* and *t* caused by the adaptation made at *t-1*, is observable. In this case, adding the $S(t)$ immediately after adaptation to the invested principal is revealing, because adaptation may not lead to positive effects under some circumstances. If $S(t) < 0$, then $D_{adapt}(t-1)$ would be rewarded for the positive effects of adaptation on the performance of the SAS over the time interval. Conversely, if $S(t) > 0$, then $D_{adapt}(t-1)$ would be penalized as the adaptation causes marginal change or degradation on the SAS's performance over the interval.

—(ii) the SAS did not adapted at *t-1*. If there was no adaptation at time *t-1*, $D_{adapt}(t-1)$ becomes incomputable as we cannot observe the $S(t)$ resulted from adaptation. Thus, we set $D_{adapt}(t-1) = 0$ since it is difficult to reason about the $S(t)$ related to an adaptation that has not been triggered.

2) False Class: the temporal net debt for the class 'the SAS should not adapt under the circumstance at *t-1*', $D_{not\_adapt}(t-1)$, is:

$$D_{not\_adapt}(t-1) = \begin{cases} S(t-1) & \text{if adapted at t-1} \\ S(t) & \text{otherwise} \end{cases} \quad (4)$$

Again, in practice, there are two further cases to consider:

—(i) the SAS did adapted at *t-1*. On contrary to $D_{adapt}(t-1)$, $D_{not\_adapt}(t-1)$ is only computable when there was no adaptation at time *t-1* as this is the only case that the related $S(t)$, which represents the subtraction of accumulated interest and revenue between *t-1* and *t* as a result of not adapting at *t-1*, is observable. if there was indeed an adaptation at time *t-1*, we assume that the accumulated performance of the indicators between *t-1* and *t* is similar to that between *t-2* and *t-1*, as a result of not adapting the SAS at *t-1*; in other words, we assume $D_{not\_adapt}(t-1) = S(t-1)$. This assumption is reasonable because the sampling interval of SAS can be tuned, as what we have done in this work, such that the local environment changes for two adjacent intervals are similar.

—(ii) the SAS did not adapted at *t-1*. In this case, $D_{not\_adapt}(t-1)$ can be computed via $S(t)$ directly.

When the $D_{not\_adapt}(t-1)$ (or $D_{adapt}(t-1)$) is smaller than zero, it means that the SAS did not adapt (or the SAS adapted) at *t-1* creates net profit over the time interval.

Finally, we produce a class label $R(t-1)$, indicating whether it was economically healthier to adapt (or not to adapt) the SAS under the past circumstance at time *t-1*:

$$R(t-1) = \begin{cases} true, \text{ (to adapt)} & \text{if } D_{adapt}(t-1) < D_{not\_adapt}(t-1) \\ false, \text{ (not to adapt)} & \text{otherwise} \end{cases}$$
$$(5)$$

Overall, the adaptation debt model is able to quantify the temporal debt increment related to the decision of "*to adapt*" or "*not*", and can help to label which decision tends to have less debt on a past circumstance. Net debt is the most intuitive and important criteria for the practitioners of SAS, as it shows how much money the SAS earns or costs. Further, it fully exploits the domain knowledge embedded in the SLA and it is highly interpretable; this is the benefit of analytical model over other black-box ones, e.g., regression model, which ignore existing knowledge and is hard to understand.

5 DEBT AWARE LEARNING AND PREDICTION TO TRIGGER ADAPTATION

Next, to predict whether we should adapt the SAS at the current and possibly unforeseen circumstance, we feed the information of past circumstances, i.e., SAS's status and environment (as features), together with their class labels from the *Debt Driven Labeler*, into an classifier (in *Classifier*) for learning the correlation between the circumstance and the class (to adapt or not) that leads to less net debt. As such, given the current unforeseen circumstance, the classifier decides whether to adapt in favor of less net debt.

5.1 Features of Circumstance As Training Data

Features represent the characteristics of a circumstance. Note that these features should not be confused with the functionality of software; they are quantifiable properties of the SAS in machine learning. Here, we have used the status of SAS (i.e., control features and requirement features) and environmental features as training data to describe the circumstance when training the classifier:

Control Features: This refers to different control knobs that can be adjusted to affect the SAS, e.g, number of threads.

Environmental Features: This refers to the uncontrollable yet important stimuli that cause dynamics and uncertainties. Examples include the workload, order of requests, size of incoming jobs, etc.

Requirement Features: This calculates the extents to which a requirement is violated or its satisfaction is outperformed for each performance indicator i.e., $-\Delta Q_i$ in Eq. (2).

5.2 Online Machine Learning Classifiers

In DLDA, we train the classifiers following standard online learning paradigm [26]: instead of completely retraining a classifier when a new sample becomes available, we update the existing classifier with the new sample, after which the sample is discarded. Online learning is particularly fit for SAS: it eliminates the need to store data samples and significantly shortens training time without much degradation on accuracy [30]. In this work, we perform updates for every new sample, i.e., only one sample to learn each time. It is worth noting that Eq. (2) has aggregated all performance indicators into a single formula, thereby the classification is only concerned with a binary decision based on that formula, which is scalable and SAS agnostic. This design, together with the fact that only one sample to learn for the classifier, has provided wide applicability and great efficiency for the classifier to make decision at SAS runtime.

As for initial training, the classifier can be trained at design time using any readily available data, or it can be directly constructed at runtime. In both cases, it will gradually improve its accuracy using the most up-to-date data. This follows the standard online learning approach [30]. Specifically, since DLDA works with a wide range of classifiers, in this work, we have combined our temporal net debt driven labeling and 5 widely used classifiers from the literature with setups tailored to our subject SAS (see Table 2).

Table 2: The studied online learning classifiers

Classifier	Setting
Hoeffding Tree (HT) [17]	N/A
Naive Bayes (NB) [24]	N/A
Stochastic Gradient Descent (SGD) [9]	N/A
k-Nearest Neighbors (kNN) [1]	$k = 3$
Multi-Layer Perceptron (MLP) [23]	Sigmoid function and 3 layers

Table 3: The inputs and SLA terms for the subject SAS

Input	Setting	Description
Control features	N/A	10 control knobs, e.g., $maxThread$ and $Memory$ etc.
Environmental features	N/A	The workload (number of requests) for each of the 26 services in RUBiS (i.e., 26 environmental features) under the FIFA98 trace [6].
Performance indicators and functions in Eq. (2)	N/A	Functions and sensors that return accumulated mean response time and energy consumption between time t and $t\text{-}1$. The response time is the time between a request and the response [11] while energy consumption is measured by PowerAPI [10].
Adaptation effort	N/A	The measured utilized CPU time of planning. This can be replaced by other types of effort, e.g., energy used by planning, etc.
C_{unit} in Eq. (1), from the SLA	\$0.01	Monetary rate per second of the CPU time utilized by planning.
T_1 in Eq. (2), from the SLA	0.05s	Requirement of mean response time of an interval.
M_1 in Eq. (2), from the SLA	\$3.5	Monetary rate of penalty/reward per second differences between mean response time and T_1.
T_2 in Eq. (2), from the SLA	5watt	Requirement of mean energy consumption of an interval.
M_2 in Eq. (2), from the SLA	\$0.5	Monetary rate of penalty/reward per watt differences between mean energy consumption and T_2.

5.3 Training and Prediction Procedure

As shown in Figure 4, at time t, once the temporal net debt driven labeling is completed (step 1-2), we use the vector of features measured at time $t\text{-}1$, e.g., $F(t-1) = \langle Workload\_of\_search = 19\ req/s, cacheMode = off, ...\rangle$, as inputs and the class label $R(t-1)$ (via (5) from the *Debt Driven Labeler*) as output to update the classifier (step 3-4). Therefore, the class label is reasoned and corrected by the labeling process in favor of less debt. While a deep discussion of training classifiers online is beyond the scope of this paper, interested readers can refer to [26][30] for details. Next, the vector of features at the current time t, e.g., $F(t) = \langle Workload\_of\_search = 54\ req/s, cacheMode = off, ...\rangle$, are entered into the classifier for prediction—the classifier outputs a decision as to adapt or not (step 5-6). Following online learning paradigm, it is easy to see that the classifier predicts once it is updated by the new data. The classifier is reinforced and thus it can be continually consolidated.

6 EXPERIMENTAL EVALUATION

We run comprehensive experiments to evaluate DLDA variants with all classifiers (or simply called DLDA) and to compare them with state-of-the-art triggering approaches under different metrics.[2]

1) Experiments Settings and Verifiability: The subject SAS has a complex software stack that contains RUBiS [35], which is a well-known software benchmark for SAS, and a set of real-world software including Tomcat [19], MySQL [14] and Ehcache [20] running on an adaptable guest virtual machine. To emulate a realistic workload within the capacity of our testbed, we vary the number of clients according to the compressed FIFA98 workload [6] (from June to July), which can dynamically generate up to 600 parallel read-write requests. The SAS provides 10 important control features that influence its performance[3], which are complex since the

variability of SAS is around 1.3×10^{16} alternatives. The SAS would adapt those control features, as the workload changes, to optimize for its response time and energy consumption.

To separate the adaptation engine and the adaptable software, we used Xen [27] to create a virtualized environment on a dedicated server. We have implemented DLDA using Java, and it is deployed on the Dom0 of Xen. The SLA terms of experiments are given in Table 3, which are fair settings tailored to fit with the subject SAS. In Section 6.4, we will discuss the critical parameters of DLDA.

To evaluate the generality of DLDA, we use it with two planners from the literature: one is the Multi-Objective Optimizer (MOO) that exploits pareto-dominance based, keen-point driven optimization to SAS at runtime [12][28][11]; the other relies on an equally weighted Single Objective Optimizer (SOO), in which we use equal weights to aggregate all objectives [29][21]. The objective functions are created using ensemble learning [11]. These planners are chosen as they are widely-adopted and capable to make effective, black-box planning under highly-variable SAS as the one we consider. Under each planner, we run DLDA with each of the 5 classifiers mentioned in Section 5 using their implementations in WEKA [22] and MOA [8]; we have used default settings unless otherwise stated. For all experiments, the sampling interval of the SAS is 120s for a total of 102 time points, which leads to around 5 system running hours per experiment run including end-users' thinking time.

2) Triggering Approaches in SAS: We compare DLDA with the following state-of-the-arts and debt-oblivious triggering approaches:

—**Event-driven** (*Event*). This is a typical category of approaches (e.g., in [18][4][7]) where adaptation is triggered upon certain event. In this work, we have used the SLA requirement violation as the event, which is the most commonly used setup (as in Table 3).

—**Prediction-based** (*Pred*). This category represents the work, e.g., in [5][36][2], that predicts the occurrence of an event, i.e., violation of performance requirement. The prediction results is then further analyzed by statistical inference; thus only the significant, reliable and persistent violations would trigger adaptation.

—**High-frequency** (*High-f*). This category represents the work (e.g., in [29][21]) that adapts the SAS based on high frequency, i.e., it triggers adaptation at every time point.

—**Low-frequency** (*Low-f*). This is similar to *High-f* but with low frequency, i.e., one adaptation every 10 time point.

—**Ground Truth** (*GT*). To determine whether it is indeed better to adapt (or not) at every time point under each planner, for each time point, we manually collected the decision (adapt or not) that leads to the smaller net debt by the end of the interval. Finally, the results of all those data points and their decisions together serve as an *approximate ground truth* in our evaluation.

---

[2]All code and data can be accessed at GitHub: https://github.com/taochen/ssase
[3]The control features are, e.g., $maxThread$, $Memory$, etc. A complete specification can be found at https://github.com/taochen/ssase/blob/master/misc/DLDA-SAS.pdf

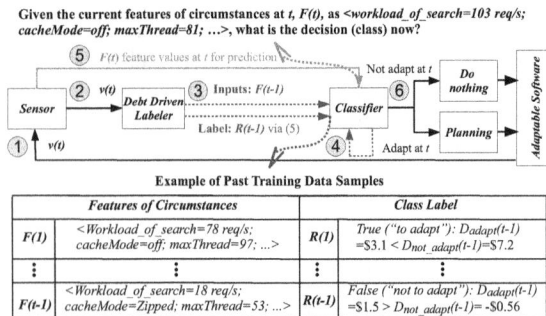

Figure 4: Combining labeling and online classification.

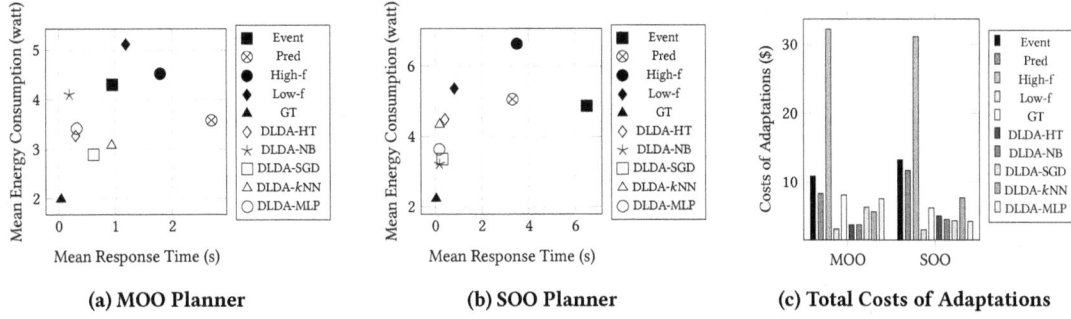

(a) MOO Planner   **(b) SOO Planner**   **(c) Total Costs of Adaptations**

Figure 5: Comparing the overall performance and total costs of adaptations between DLDA and other state-of-the-art triggering approaches using MOO and SOO in the planning over 102 timesteps.

3) Metrics: The metrics we considered in the experiments are:

—**Accuracy.** The accuracy of the labels produced by labeling and the prediction against the actual classes from ground truth. In online learning, accuracy is often calculated as c/n: c is the number of correctly labeled/classified sample when there are n samples.

—**Performance.** The measured mean value of each performance indicator over time. While DLDA works with any quantifiable indicators, we used response time and energy consumption as the performance indicators for simplicity of exposition.

—**Total costs of adaptations.** This is the total principal in order to achieve the measured performance level of SAS. Recall from Section 4, the total cost is calculated as $\sum_{t=2}^{n} Principal(t-1) = \sum_{t=2}^{n} C_{unit} \times U(t-1)$. The more adaptations, the higher total cost.

—**Total net debt.** We report on the total net debt incurred throughout the experiment run, in which the temporal net debt between *t-1* and *t* is calculated as $Principal(t-1) + S(t)$ where $Principal(t-1) = 0$ if no adaptation at *t-1*; the total net debt is simply $\sum_{t=2}^{n} Principal(t-1) + S(t)$, as explained in Section 4.

—**SLA compliance.** The average values of performance of each indicator exceeding its SLA threshold over all intervals.

—**Overshoot.** The worst value of a performance indicator exceeding the SLA threshold during the transient.

—**Overhead.** The average training and prediction time of DLDA.

6.1 Accuracy

To evaluate accuracy, we compare the results of the labels produced by temporal net debt driven labeling and the predictions of classifiers against the actual classes in ground truth (see Section 6). As from Table 4, in general, both the labeling and prediction processes in DLDA exhibit high accuracy under both MOO and SOO planners. The results, range from 75% to 90%, clearly beat a random guess, which is likely to produce an accuracy around 50% for binary classification. Notably, DLDA-NB exhibits the best accuracy for both prediction and the labeling process that guides the learning.

We will examine, in contrast to the other triggering approaches, if the good accuracy can help DLDA to improve self-adaptation.

Table 4: The accuracy of DLDA with different classifiers against the ground truth over 102 timesteps (best is in bold)

	HT	NB	SGD	*k*NN	MLP
(MOO) Labeling	83%	**88%**	86%	87%	83%
(MOO) Prediction	**89%**	**89%**	81%	79%	77%
(SOO) Labeling	84%	**90%**	87%	80%	82%
(SOO) Prediction	81%	**88%**	84%	75%	**88%**

6.2 Performance and Adaptation Costs

We now report on the mean performance values of all approaches over all time points, together with the total costs of adaptation. To validate statistical significance of the performance comparisons, we applied Wilcoxon Signed-Rank test (two-tailed) when comparing DLDA variants with the others. The results have confirmed statistical significance ($p < 0.05$) on at least one performance indicator with non-trivial effect sizes following the guidance in [25] .

As we can see from Figure 5a and 5b, under both planners, DLDA of all classifiers dominates *Event*, *Pred*, *High-f* and *Low-f* on both performance indicators. The only exception is that DLDA-NB tends to have slightly higher energy consumption than *Pred* when using MOO planner, which we have found to be statistically insignificant. As for the total costs of adaptations in Figure 5c, we note that DLDA with all classifiers and both planners achieve the superior performance by using remarkably smaller costs of adaptations, as when compared with *Event*, *Pred* and *High-f*. DLDA's costs however, as expected, is higher than that of *Low-f*. When comparing DLDA with the ground truth (*GT*) under both planners, there is still room for DLDA to improve on both performance indicators, but it is clearly closer to the performance of ground truth than the state-of-the-art triggering approaches. Further, its costs of adaptations (on all classifiers and planners) is similar to that of *GT*. These results also reveal that our temporal debt model is effective in guiding the classifiers, as DLDA significantly outperforms the others on performance and adaptation costs regardless the classifier used.

When comparing the DLDA variants on both planners from Figure 5, although DLDA-NB has higher energy consumption on the MOO planner, it generally has the best performance overall with relatively lower costs of adaptations, which can be attributed to the facts that it has the best prediction accuracy and the labeling process generates the most accurate labels to guide the classifier. However, the differences between DLDA variants are marginal.

6.3 Net Debt, SLA Compliance, Overshoot and Overhead

Next, we compare DLDA with the others on the total net debts, SLA compliance and overshoot. We have also illustrate the overhead of DLDA under different classifiers. The comparisons between DLDA and others under all metrics have been validated using Wilcoxon Signed-Rank test (two-tailed); the results have revealed statistical significance ($p < 0.05$) with non-trivial effect sizes.

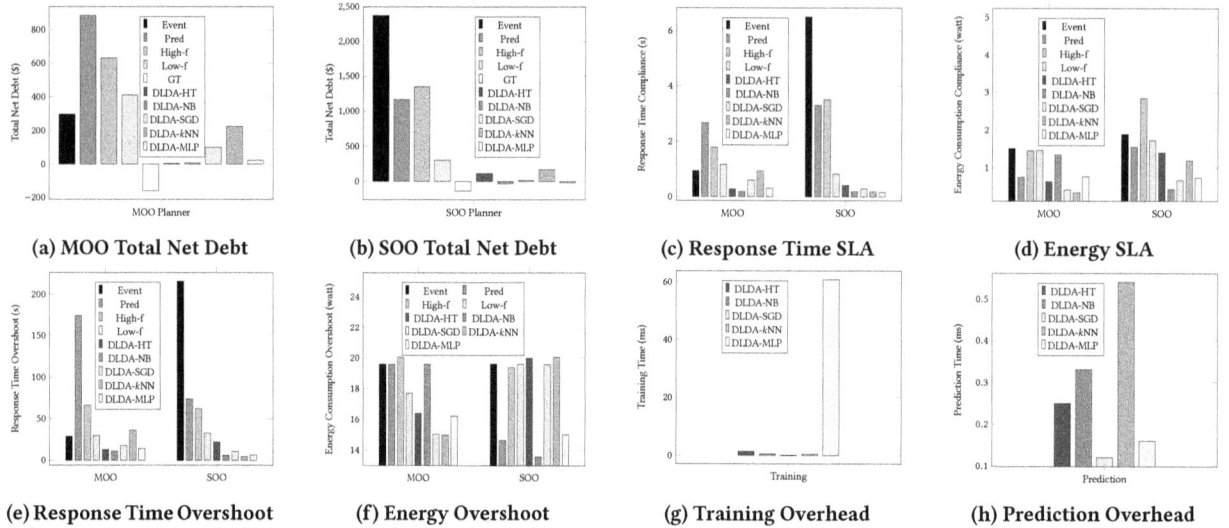

(a) MOO Total Net Debt (b) SOO Total Net Debt (c) Response Time SLA (d) Energy SLA

(e) Response Time Overshoot (f) Energy Overshoot (g) Training Overhead (h) Prediction Overhead

Figure 6: Comparing total net debt, SLA compliance, overshoot and overhead over 102 timesteps.

Figures 6a and 6b show the total net debt of the approaches. We can see that, under both planners, DLDA with different classifier produces much less net debts than that of the state-of-the-art triggering approaches, and remarkably, up to three orders of magnitude less under the SOO planner. In particular, the total net debt of DLDA-NB and DLDA-MLP are smaller than zero under SOO planner, which means that they have created some net profit overall.

As shown in Figures 6c and 6d , under both planners, DLDA variants generally outperform state-of-the-art triggering approaches on the SLA compliance for both performance indicators. In particular, when comparing with the others, DLDA's improvements for the SLA compliance on response time is much greater than that of the energy consumption (DLDA-HT and DLDA-MLP is even worse than *Pred*). This is because the two performance indicators are conflicting, and DLDA has learned that favoring response time more would help to better reduce the total net debt, as evident in Figures 6a and 6b. Similarly, in Figures 6e and 6f, the overshoot of response time in DLDA is much smaller than that of the others. However, in general, its superiority on the overshoot of energy consumption is less obvious due to the same reason stated above.

The temporal net debt driven labeling in DLDA has negligible running time of less than 0.1ms and thus we focus on the training and prediction time required for the classification. As we can see in Figures 6g and 6h, most of the DLDA variants are very efficient in training, generating an overhead less than 3ms only. The only exception is DLDA-MLP, which requires 60ms, as the complex MLP needs more computation to converge to a good training error. In general, the high efficiency is enabled by the online learning paradigm where the data samples are learned one by one as they become available, thus the overhead is not sensitive to the size of training samples. As for prediction, DLDA has negligible overhead.

6.4 Discussion on the DLDA Parameters

As shown, DLDA can be affected by the settings of the requirement thresholds and rates per unit in the SLA. In this work, the settings in Table 3 are tuned w.r.t. to our testbed to create reasonable and fair comparisons. In particular, as in most of the practical scenarios,

the requirement thresholds were reasonably tailored according to the SAS studied, i.e., they are neither too strong nor too relax. In contrast, the rates per unit on planning, reward and penalty in DLDA are more subjective, as they can be in any scales depending on the business purpose. Given an effective planner, those rates can influence the trade-off between adaptivity and stability of the SAS, i.e., increase the penalty rate implies more intensive adaptivity while increase the planning rate and/or reward rate favor stability.

In general, as mentioned in Section 2, these parameters can be tailored using many well-established methods form the literature [37][3] during the normal SLA negotiation process.

7 RELATED WORK

Existing work often fall into one of the two categories on designing trigger of SAS: either adapt periodically or adapt upon the events (e.g., violation of requirement thresholds). Adapting the SAS periodically has been the default method for many planning mechanisms from the literature. The PLATO [29] framework is one example that adapts the SAS on every point in time, within which it relies on genetic algorithm to search for the optimal (or near-optimal) adaptation solution. Other examples that rely on the same trigger include FEMOSAA [12] and VAIKYRIE [21], etc. These approaches often do not require predefined requirement thresholds, instead, they intend to optimize the SAS at every circumstances without considering net debt. In contrast, DLDA triggers adaptation only when it tends be economically healthier than not adapting.

Control theory is also another popular paradigm for engineering SAS [32]. However, most control theoretic approaches focus on the planning problem, i.e., *what and how to adapt*, and they adapt the SAS at predefined frequency of signaling cycle. In contrast, DLDA tackles explicitly *when and whether to adapt*, creating greater benefit over the others. Further, DLDA works with, e.g., rule-based [7], search-based [11][29][12] and control theoretic [32] planner, etc.

Event-based triggers are vast, e.g., Prometheus [4] and FUSION [18] are frameworks that trigger adaptation when they detect requirements violation. Other types of event also exists [7][34]: for example, Bencomo *et al.* [7] triggered adaptation based on the violation of design *claim*, e.g., the claim of *Redundancy prevents networks partitions* is invalid if two or more network links fail simultaneously. Note that the utility functions in the defined events from above work is different from DLDA as they do not declare monetary value, i.e., there is no model about the profit/debt that the SAS generates.

While an event is often used in a reactive manner, proactive and event driven adaptation can be achieved by using limited prediction [36][5][2]. For example, Wang and Pazat [36] adapted the SAS when it is predicted that there is a violation of requirements, and such violation is indeed significant after it is verified by an online learning classifier. However, adaptations are still triggered by the detected/predicted occurrences of predefined events and it is not related to the monetary cost-benefit of adapting and not adapting.

8 CONCLUSION AND FUTURE WORK

This paper presents DLDA, a novel framework that combines technical debt and online learning, to determine *when and whether to adapt* the SAS at runtime. We proposed a temporal adaptation debt model to quantify the net debt for the decision of adapting and not adapting the SAS, based on which we design a temporal net debt driven labeling that labels whichever leads to less net debt for a given circumstance. By formulating the problem of *when and whether to adapt* as a binary classification problem, we combine the labeling process and online learning classifier in DLDA to determine whether to adapt or not upon unforeseen circumstances, in favor of reducing net debt. We conducted comprehensive evaluations on DLDA with 5 classifiers and in comparison to 4 state-of-the-art debt-oblivious triggering approaches. The results reveal that DLDA is effective and better than the other on various SAS metrics.

Our future work includes investigating the possibility of predicting for the long-term adaptation triggers, and how short-/long-term prediction could affect the trigger of adaptation. We also plan to apply DLDA on extreme domains of SAS, e.g., mobile environment.

ACKNOWLEDGMENT

This work is supported by the DAASE Programme Grant from the EPSRC (Grant No. EP/J017515/1).

REFERENCES

[1] Naomi S Altman. 1992. An introduction to kernel and nearest-neighbor nonparametric regression. *The American Statistician* 46, 3 (1992), 175–185.
[2] Ayman Amin, Alan Colman, and Lars Grunske. 2012. Statistical detection of qos violations based on cusum control charts. In *Proceedings of the 3rd ACM/SPEC International Conference on Performance Engineering*. ACM, 97–108.
[3] Alain Andrieux, Karl Czajkowski, Asit Dan, Kate Keahey, Heiko Ludwig, Toshiyuki Nakata, Jim Pruyne, John Rofrano, Steve Tuecke, and Ming Xu. 2007. Web services agreement specification. In *Open grid forum*, Vol. 128. 216.
[4] Konstantinos Angelopoulos, Fatma Başak Aydemir, Paolo Giorgini, and John Mylopoulos. 2016. Solving the next adaptation problem with prometheus. In *Research Challenges in Information Science, International Conference on*. 1–10.
[5] Konstantinos Angelopoulos, Alessandro V Papadopoulos, Vítor E Silva Souza, and John Mylopoulos. 2016. Model predictive control for software systems with CobRA. In *Proceedings of the 11th International Symposium on Software Engineering for Adaptive and Self-Managing Systems*. ACM, 35–46.
[6] Martin Arlitt and Tai Jin. 2000. A workload characterization study of the 1998 world cup web site. *IEEE network* 14, 3 (2000), 30–37.
[7] Nelly Bencomo, Amel Belaggoun, and Valerie Issarny. 2013. Dynamic Decision Networks for Decision-making in Self-adaptive Systems: A Case Study. In *Proceedings of the 8th International Symposium on Software Engineering for Adaptive and Self-Managing Systems*. 113–122.
[8] Albert Bifet, Geoff Holmes, Richard Kirkby, and Bernhard Pfahringer. 2010. Moa: Massive online analysis. *Journal of Machine Learning Research* 11 (2010), 1601–1604.

[9] Léon Bottou. 1998. Online Algorithms and Stochastic Approximations. In *Online Learning and Neural Networks*, David Saad (Ed.). Cambridge University Press, Cambridge, UK. http://leon.bottou.org/papers/bottou-98x revised, oct 2012.
[10] Aurélien Bourdon, Adel Noureddine, Romain Rouvoy, and Lionel Seinturier. 2013. PowerAPI: A Software Library to Monitor the Energy Consumed at the Process-Level. *ERCIM News* 92 (Jan. 2013), 43–44.
[11] Tao Chen and Rami Bahsoon. 2017. Self-Adaptive Trade-off Decision Making for Autoscaling Cloud-Based Services. *IEEE Transactions on Services Computing* 10, 4 (July 2017), 618–632.
[12] Tao Chen, Ke Li, Rami Bahsoon, and Xin Yao. 2018. FEMOSAA: Feature Guided and Knee Driven Multi-Objective Optimization for Self-Adaptive Software. *ACM Transactions on Software Engineering and Methodology* (2018). in press.
[13] Shang-Wen Cheng, Vahe V. Poladian, David Garlan, and Bradley Schmerl. 2009. Improving Architecture-Based Self-Adaptation Through Resource Prediction, in Software Engineering for Self-Adaptive Systems. Springer-Verlag, 71–88.
[14] Oracle Corporation. 1995. MySQL. https://www.mysql.com/. (1995).
[15] Ward Cunningham. 1993. The WyCash portfolio management system. *ACM SIGPLAN OOPS Messenger* 4, 2 (1993), 29–30.
[16] Rogério de Lemos et al. 2013. *Software Engineering for Self-Adaptive Systems: A Second Research Roadmap*. Springer Berlin Heidelberg, Berlin, Heidelberg, 1–32.
[17] Pedro Domingos and Geoff Hulten. 2000. Mining High-speed Data Streams. In *Proceedings of the Sixth ACM SIGKDD International Conference on Knowledge Discovery and Data Mining (KDD '00)*. ACM, New York, NY, USA, 71–80.
[18] Naeem Esfahani, Ahmed Elkhodary, and Sam Malek. 2013. A learning-based framework for engineering feature-oriented self-adaptive software systems. *IEEE transactions on software engineering* 39, 11 (2013), 1467–1493.
[19] Apache Software Foundation. 1999. Tomcat. http://tomcat.apache.org/. (1999).
[20] Apache Software Foundation. 2003. Ehcache. http://www.ehcache.org/. (2003).
[21] Erik M. Fredericks. 2016. Automatically Hardening a Self-adaptive System Against Uncertainty. In *Proceedings of the 11th International Symposium on Software Engineering for Adaptive and Self-Managing Systems*. 16–27.
[22] Mark Hall, Eibe Frank, Geoffrey Holmes, Bernhard Pfahringer, Peter Reutemann, and Ian H. Witten. 2009. The WEKA Data Mining Software: An Update. *SIGKDD Explor. Newsl.* 11, 1 (Nov. 2009), 10–18.
[23] Simon S Haykin. 2001. *Neural networks: a comprehensive foundation*. Tsinghua University Press.
[24] George H. John and Pat Langley. 1995. Estimating Continuous Distributions in Bayesian Classifiers. In *Proceedings of the Eleventh Conference on Uncertainty in Artificial Intelligence (UAI'95)*. 338–345.
[25] Vigdis By Kampenes, Tore Dybå, Jo E Hannay, and Dag IK Sjøberg. 2007. A systematic review of effect size in software engineering experiments. *Information and Software Technology* 49, 11-12 (2007), 1073–1086.
[26] Leandro L Minku and Xin Yao. 2012. DDD: A new ensemble approach for dealing with concept drift. *IEEE transactions on knowledge and data engineering* 24, 4 (2012), 619–633.
[27] University of Cambridge Computer Laboratory. 2013. Xen: a virtual machine monitor. http://www.xenproject.org/. (2013).
[28] Gustavo G. Pascual, Roberto E. Lopez-Herrejon, MÄŞnica Pinto, Lidia Fuentes, and Alexander Egyed. 2015. Applying multiobjective evolutionary algorithms to dynamic software product lines for reconfiguring mobile applications. *Journal of Systems and Software* 103 (2015), 392 – 411.
[29] Andres J. Ramirez, David B. Knoester, Betty H. C. Cheng, and Philip K. McKinley. 2011. Plato: a genetic algorithm approach to run-time reconfiguration inäautonomic computing systems. *Cluster Computing* 14, 3 (2011), 229–244.
[30] Jesse Read, Albert Bifet, Bernhard Pfahringer, and Geoff Holmes. 2012. Batch-incremental versus instance-incremental learning in dynamic and evolving data. In *International Symposium on Intelligent Data Analysis*. Springer, 313–323.
[31] Mazeiar Salehie and Ladan Tahvildari. 2009. Self-adaptive Software: Landscape and Research Challenges. *ACM Trans. Auton. Adapt. Syst.* 4, 2 (2009), 14:1–14:42.
[32] Stepan Shevtsov and Danny Weyns. 2016. Keep it SIMPLEX: Satisfying multiple goals with guarantees in control-based self-adaptive systems. In *Proceedings of the 24th International Symposium on Foundations of Software Engineering*. 229–241.
[33] James Skene, Franco Raimondi, and Wolfgang Emmerich. 2010. Service-level agreements for electronic services. *IEEE Transactions on Software Engineering* 36, 2 (2010), 288–304.
[34] C. Stier and A. Koziolek. 2016. Considering Transient Effects of Self-Adaptations in Model-Driven Performance Analyses. In *2016 12th International ACM SIGSOFT Conference on Quality of Software Architectures (QoSA)*. 80–89.
[35] Rice University. 2009. RUBiS. http://rubis.ow2.org/. (2009).
[36] Chen Wang and Jean-Louis Pazat. 2012. A Two-Phase Online Prediction Approach for Accurate and Timely Adaptation Decision. In *Proceedings of the 2012 IEEE Ninth International Conference on Services Computing*. 218–225.
[37] Farhana H Zulkernine and Patrick Martin. 2011. An adaptive and intelligent SLA negotiation system for web services. *IEEE Transactions on Services Computing* 4, 1 (2011), 31–43.

Involving CPUs into Multi-GPU Deep Learning

Tung D. Le
IBM Research - Tokyo
Tokyo, Japan
tung@jp.ibm.com

Taro Sekiyama
IBM Research - Tokyo
Tokyo, Japan
sekiym@jp.ibm.com

Yasushi Negishi
IBM Research - Tokyo
Tokyo, Japan
negishi@jp.ibm.com

Haruki Imai
IBM Research - Tokyo
Tokyo, Japan
imaihal@jp.ibm.com

Kiyokuni Kawachiya
IBM Research - Tokyo
Tokyo, Japan
kawatiya@jp.ibm.com

ABSTRACT

The most important part of deep learning, training the neural network, often requires the processing of a large amount of data and can takes days to complete. Data parallelism is widely used for training deep neural networks on multiple GPUs in a single machine thanks to its simplicity. However, its scalability is bound by the number of data transfers, mainly for exchanging and accumulating gradients among the GPUs. In this paper, we present a novel approach to data parallel training called *CPU-GPU data parallel (CGDP) training* that utilizes free CPU time on the host to speed up the training in the GPUs. We also present a cost model for analyzing and comparing the performances of both the typical data parallel training and the CPU-GPU data parallel training. Using the cost model, we formally show why our approach is better than the typical one and clarify the remaining issues. Finally, we explain how we optimized CPU-GPU data parallel training by introducing chunks of layers and present a runtime algorithm that automatically finds a good configuration for the training. The algorithm is effective for very deep neural networks, which are the current trend in deep learning. Experimental results showed that we achieved speedups of 1.21, 1.04, 1.21 and 1.07 for four state-of-the-art neural networks: AlexNet, GoogLeNet-v1, VGGNet-16, and ResNet-152, respectively. Weak scaling efficiency greater than 90% was achieved for all networks across four GPUs.

KEYWORDS

Deep learning; data parallelism; GPUs; CPUs

ACM Reference Format:
Tung D. Le, Taro Sekiyama, Yasushi Negishi, Haruki Imai, and Kiyokuni Kawachiya. 2018. Involving CPUs into Multi-GPU Deep Learning. In *ICPE '18: ACM/SPEC International Conference on Performance Engineering, April 9–13, 2018, Berlin, Germany.* ACM, New York, NY, USA, 12 pages. https://doi.org/10.1145/3184407.3184424

1 INTRODUCTION

Deep learning is an effective tool for solving complex signal processing problems such as ones in computer vision, speech recognition, and natural language processing. In 2012, a deep convolutional neural network called AlexNet [17] achieved outstanding image classification results in the ILSVRC-2012 competition with a top-5 test error rate of 15.3%. In 2015, rectifier neural networks surpassed human-level performance on image classification with a top-5 test error rate of 4.94% [12]. Various the deep neural networks for image recognition have been used for detecting pulmonary nodules in the analysis of lung cancer [4]. Long short-term memory (LSTM) networks have reached a major milestone: a 5.5% word error rate in conversational speech recognition [21].

A deep neural network is a combination of many layers (the deepest network up to date is the 1001-layer ResNet network [13]) and is trained using a large dataset. Training a neural network is mainly based on matrix multiplications and is therefore often accelerated by using GPUs. To fully utilize multiple GPUs for training, data parallelism is often used because 1) it is simple to adapt and extend existing single-GPU training to multiple-GPUs training and 2) it fully utilizes the GPU-aware optimized training in a single GPU. In data parallel training, the same neural network is used for each GPU, but the training is done using different inputs for each GPU. Once the GPUs have finished the forward and backward phases of each training iteration, a *server* GPU accumulates the partial gradients from the other GPUs and updates the learnable parameters. The server GPU then broadcasts the updated parameters to the other GPUs at the beginning of the next training iteration to ensure that every GPU has the same parameters.

However, the scalability of data parallel training is limited by the accumulation and broadcasting of gradients. The greater the number of GPUs that are used, the greater the amount of data that are exchanged among GPUs. A simple yet effective solution is using a tree layout of GPUs so that some communications are done in parallel; this is the approach used in the BVLC/Caffe [15] and Torch [2] deep learning frameworks. Another approach is using topology-aware communication libraries such as the NVIDIA Collective Communications Library (NCCL) [3]. The TensorFlow framework [5] does both gradient accumulation and parameter update synchronously on CPUs on the host at the end of the backward phase. This approach provides the flexibility needed for distributed training but is slow for training on a single machine. The MXNet [6] deep learning framework provides a mix of the above approaches:

gradient accumulation is done on the CPUs while parameter updating is done on the GPUs.

In this paper, we first present a novel approach to data parallel training called *CPU-GPU data parallel (CGDP) training* that utilizes free CPU time on the host to speed up the training of deep neural networks on the GPUs. In this approach, gradients are collected and accumulated on the host layer-by-layer during the backward phase. Once a partial gradient for a layer is available in a GPU, it is sent to the host. Gradient accumulation is done by the CPUs while the GPU moves on to computing the partial gradients for the other layers. The accumulated gradients on the host are then sent back to the GPU for updating of the learnable parameters. This approach is particularly effective for convolutional neural networks, which are widely used in image processing. Such networks usually start with convolutional layers having a small number of parameters and end with fully connected layers having a large number of parameters. Since backward computations are performed from the ending layer to the starting layer, collection and accumulation of the gradients of the ending layers will have been completed by the end of the backward phase even though they might take a substantial amount of time. Furthermore, since collecting and accumulating the gradients of the starting layers take less time, they are completed immediately after the backward phase with a very low overhead.

Next, we present a cost model for analyzing the performance of data parallel training on multiple GPUs. The model takes into account not only the costs for computation and communication, but also the cost for synchronization among GPU streams, which is important for GPU applications. Using this model, we show a condition under which the CGDP training is better than the typical training. To the best of our knowledge, this is the first time a cost model for data parallel training on multiple GPUs has been proposed.

Finally, we extend the CGDP training by using chunks of layers to deal with very deep and "flat" neural networks in which the number of parameters for a layer is small and roughly equals the number for the other layers. For such networks, the cost model shows that the synchronization among GPU streams is a bottleneck and slows the training down. In such cases, the layers are grouped into chunks, and synchronizations are done for each chunk. We present a runtime algorithm for automatically determining the synchronization points so that the running time is optimized.

We implemented these ideas in the BVLC/Caffe [15] deep learning framework, which is widely used in deep learning communities. Experiments were done with the ImageNet dataset [20] on an IBM POWER8 machine coupled with four NVIDIA Tesla P100 GPUs [1]. Speedups of 1.21, 1.04, and 1.21 were achieved for three neural networks: AlexNet [17], GoogLeNet-v1 [24], and 16-layer VGGNet (model D) (VGGNet-16 hereafter) [22], respectively, corresponding to more than 90% weak scaling efficiency for all three networks. For a very deep neural network, the 152-layer ResNet network [11] (ResNet-152 hereafter), while the naive CGDP training was slower than the typical data parallel training, using chunks and the runtime algorithm made it 1.07 times faster than the typical data parallel training.

The rest of the paper is organized as follows. Section 2 reviews data parallelism for deep learning. Section 3 describes in detail our CPU-GPU data parallel training on a single machine coupled with multiple GPUs. Our cost model is also presented in the section. Section 4 presents a variant of the CGDP training that uses chunks of layers in training and a runtime algorithm that automatically optimizes the CGDP training with chunks for very deep neural networks. Section 5 presents the experiment results for a real dataset, ImageNet [20]. Section 6 discusses related work. Section 7 summarizes the key points and mentions future work.

2 DATA PARALLELISM FOR DEEP LEARNING

This section briefly reviews the training phase of a neural network using the back-propagation algorithm [10] and data parallelism.

2.1 Training Deep Neural Networks

We first give an overview of training deep neural networks using *feed-forward neural networks* (FFNs), which are a fundamental architecture for convolutional neural networks.

The goal of an FFN is to approximate a function f^*; i.e., $y^* = f^*(x)$ maps an input x (a tensor) to a category y^* (a scalar value). In general, an FFN defines a mapping $y = f_\theta(x)$ where the parameter θ is learnt to produce the best function approximation for f^*. If y^* is given in training, we have supervised training, otherwise, unsupervised training. In this paper, we focus on supervised training. A *cost function*, also often called a *loss function*, defines how well f_θ approximates f^*. For example, the *mean squared error* (MSE) loss function is defined on the whole training set $\mathbb{X}$ of N elements as

$$J_\theta = \frac{1}{N} \sum_{x \in \mathbb{X}} (y^* - f_\theta(x))^2.$$

Feed-forward neural networks are represented by a composition of many functions; i.e., $f(x) = f^3(f^2(f^1(x)))$, where f^i is the i-th layer of the network. Generally speaking, an l-layer FFN is represented as

$$f_\theta(x) = f_{\theta_l}^l (f_{\theta_{l-1}}^{l-1} (\cdots (f_{\theta_1}^1(x)) \cdots)),$$

where θ is the set of the layer parameters $\{\theta_1, \theta_2, \ldots, \theta_l\}$.

A layer k is often defined by an activation function to make the neural network nonlinear. Let y_{k-1} be an input vector of the layer k (the output of the previous layer); an output vector y_k of the layer k is computed as

$$y_k = f_{\theta_k}^k = \sigma(x_k)$$
$$x_k = w_k^T y_{k-1} + b_k,$$

where σ is an activation function (e.g., the *rectified linear unit* defined by $\sigma(z) = \max\{0, z\}$) and w_k^T is the transpose matrix of the *weight matrix* w_k. Let m be the size of y_{k-1} and n be the size of y_k. Then, the size of matrix w_k is $m \times n$. Vector b_k is the *bias vector* of the layer k and has the size of n. In summary, a layer is parameterized by using two learnable parameters: the weight matrix w and the bias vector b. In other words, $\theta_k = \{w_k, b_k\}$. Note that, although the equation for x_k is actually for a fully connected layer, the definition of such a layer can be applied to other kinds of layers, such as convolutional layers.

Training FFNs is almost always based on using gradients with respect to learnable parameters to decrease the loss function. In general, the training consists of three phases: *forward*, *backward* and *update*. Given an l-layer FFN with learnable parameters $\theta =$

$\{\theta_1, \theta_2, \ldots, \theta_l\}$, the forward phase computes a scalar value J_θ. The backward phase computes the gradients of the loss function with respect to the learnable parameters, which are $\nabla_{\theta_1} J, \nabla_{\theta_2} J, \ldots, \nabla_{\theta_l} J$. Actually, we need to compute two gradients $\nabla_{w_k} J$ and $\nabla_{b_k} J$ for a layer k. The update phase updates the learnable parameters using their gradients in the direction that minimizes the value of the loss function; for example,

$$w_k = w_k - \eta \nabla_{w_k} J; \; b_k = b_k - \eta \nabla_{b_k} J,$$

where η is a given learning rate.

To train an FFN using a large training dataset, a minibatch stochastic gradient decent (SGD) algorithm is used. The training is performed iteratively, in which, for each iteration, a minibatch (subset) of examples extracted from the training dataset is used as input.

2.2 Back-propagation Algorithm Used to Compute Gradients

Next, we briefly review the back-propagation algorithm for gradient computation in the backward phase. The back-propagation is based on the chain rule of calculus that is used to compute the derivatives of composite functions by propagating the derivative information from the loss function back through the composite functions. The back-propagation algorithm has five steps:

Step B-1: Compute the gradient for the output layer:

$$\nabla_{y_l} J = \nabla_f J_\theta(y^*, f)$$

Step B-2: Compute the gradient of the activation for the l-th layer:

$$\nabla_{x_l} J = \left(\frac{\partial y_l}{\partial x_l} \right)^T \nabla_{y_l} J$$

Step B-3: Compute the gradients of the learnable parameters (weights and biases):

$$\nabla_{w_l} J = \left(\frac{\partial x_l}{\partial w_l} \right)^T \nabla_{x_l} J; \; \nabla_{b_l} J = \left(\frac{\partial x_l}{\partial b_l} \right)^T \nabla_{x_l} J$$

Step B-4: Propagate the gradients with respect to the activations of the lower-level layers (e.g., layers with smaller indices):

$$\nabla_{y_{l-1}} J = \left(\frac{\partial x_l}{\partial y_{l-1}} \right)^T \nabla_{x_l} J.$$

Step B-5: Continue steps B-2 to B-4 until l reaches 1.

The $\left(\frac{\partial y}{\partial x} \right)$ denotes the $m \times n$ Jacobian matrix of a function g for $y = g(x)$, m is the size of vector y and n is the size of vector x.

2.3 Typical Data Parallel Training

In this paper, we focus on data parallel training on a single machine coupled with multiple GPUs. Let G be the number of GPUs in the machine. For data parallel training, the GPUs use the same neural network and train the network with different minibatches. Each iteration of data parallel training comprises five steps:

Step T-1: Each GPU reads one minibatch and performs the forward phase.

Step T-2: Each GPU performs the back-propagation to compute the gradients with respect to its learnable parameters. Let $\nabla_{w_k}^j J$ and $\nabla_{b_k}^j J$ be the gradients with respect to the learnable parameters $\{w_k, b_k\}$ for a layer k computed by GPU j.

Step T-3: GPU 0 collects the gradients from the other GPUs and computes their mean value:

$$\nabla_{w_k}^0 J = \frac{1}{G} \sum_{j=0}^{G-1} (\nabla_{w_k}^j J); \; \nabla_{b_k}^0 J = \frac{1}{G} \sum_{j=0}^{G-1} (\nabla_{b_k}^j J)$$

Step T-4: GPU 0 updates its learnable parameters by using the computed gradients.

Step T-5: GPU 0 broadcasts the values of its learnable parameters to the other GPUs. The other GPUs set the values of their learnable parameters to those values.

In this training, GPU 0 plays the role of a parameter server, collecting gradients and updating the learnable parameters. The backward phase consists of Steps T-2, T-3, and T-5. The training actually begins with Step T-5 to ensure that the neural networks are trained using the same parameters.

3 CPU-GPU DATA PARALLEL TRAINING

The drawback of the typical data parallel training lies in the communication steps (Steps T-3 and T-5 (Section 2.3)), leading to a poor scalability. The two steps depend on the communication pattern among GPUs. Our goal for optimizing data parallel training is to reduce as much as possible the effect of the communication steps on the running time of one training iteration.

3.1 Algorithm

Our algorithm is based on two observations. The first is that the gradients for one layer once computed will remain unchanged during the backward phase. Hence, there is no need to postpone gradient accumulation until the end of the backward phase. The second observation is that gradient accumulation can be performed with the support of CPUs on the host. We thus make Steps T-3 (gradient accumulation) and T-5 (parameter broadcast) overlapped with Step T-2 (back-propagation). We refer to our algorithm as *CPU-GPU data parallel (CGDP) training*.

To attain overlap of computation and communication in our algorithm, GPU streams are used. In GPU-CUDA programming, operations in the same stream are executed sequentially, while operations in different streams are executed in parallel. If a stream is not specified specified for an operation, the default stream is used. Three streams are maintained in our algorithm. The first stream, the *default stream*, is used to compute the loss function in the forward phase and the gradients in the backward phases; it is also used to update the parameters. The second stream, the *D2H stream*, is used to send local gradients to the host and then call a callback function on the host to accumulate the gradients. The third stream, *H2D stream*, is used to broadcast the global gradients back to the GPUs. Note that, even if more streams are used, the data transfers are not done in parallel because only one transfer in one direction is allowed at a time.

Each iteration in our CGDP training consists of three steps:

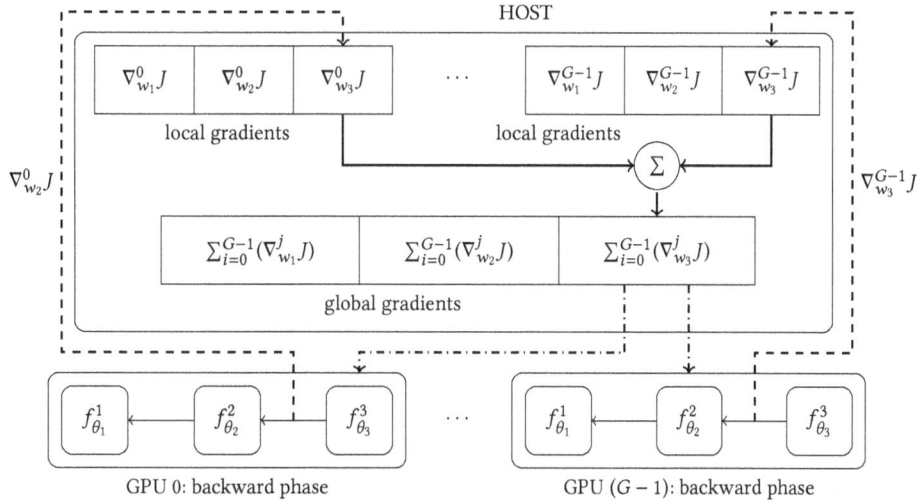

Figure 1: Communication pattern between host and GPUs during backward phase in CGDP training.

Step P-1: Each GPU reads one minibatch and performs the forward phase.

Step P-2: Each GPU performs the backward phase (explained below).

Step P-3: Each GPU performs the update phase to update its learnable parameters.

During the backward phase (Step P-2), gradients accumulations are performed on the host, and the accumulated gradients are broadcasted to all GPUs. Hence, at the end of the backward phase, all GPUs have the same accumulated gradients, and they update their learnable parameters in parallel. This is different from the typical data parallel training in which only the GPU 0 has the accumulated gradients and does the update phase. In other words, there is no parameter server in the CGDP training.

Step P-2 is an extension of the original back-propagation algorithm (Section 2.2). Five steps are added: Steps B-4-1, B-4-2, and B-4-3 after Step B-4; and Steps B-5-1 and B-5-2 after Step B-5. Let Q be a queue to store the layers for which backward computation has been completed. If a layer is in Q, its gradient has been sending to the host or accumulated into the global gradient on the host. Step P-2 for each GPU is as follows (the GPU stream is shown in parentheses):

Step B-1 (Default stream): Compute the gradient for the output layer:

$$\nabla_{y_l} J = \nabla_f J_\theta(y^*, f)$$

Step B-2 (Default stream): Compute the gradient of the activation for the l-th layer:

$$\nabla_{x_l} J = \left(\frac{\partial y_l}{\partial x_l}\right)^T \nabla_{y_l} J$$

Step B-3 (Default stream): Compute the gradients of the learnable parameters (weights and biases):

$$\nabla_{w_l} J = \left(\frac{\partial x_l}{\partial w_l}\right)^T \nabla_{x_l} J; \; \nabla_{b_l} J = \left(\frac{\partial x_l}{\partial b_l}\right)^T \nabla_{x_l} J$$

Step B-4 (Default stream): Propagate the gradients with respect to the activations of the lower-level layers (e.g., layers with smaller indices):

$$\nabla_{y_{l-1}} J = \left(\frac{\partial x_l}{\partial y_{l-1}}\right)^T \nabla_{x_l} J.$$

Step B-4-1 (Host): Synchronize the default stream with respect to the host.

Step B-4-2 (D2H stream): Send local gradients $\nabla_{\theta_l}^j J$ to the host, and call the callback function to accumulate the local gradients into the global gradient on the host. Push l to Q.

Step B-4-3 (H2D stream): For each layer k in Q, if all local gradients $\nabla_{\theta_k}^j J$, $j = 0, \ldots, (G-1)$ have been accumulated into the global gradient, broadcast the global gradient to all GPUs and remove k from Q.

Step B-5: Continue steps B-2 to B-4-3 until l reaches 1.

Step B-5-1 (H2D stream): For each layer k in Q, if all local gradients $\nabla_{\theta_k}^j J$, $j = 0, \ldots, (G-1)$ have been accumulated into the global gradient, broadcast the global gradient to all GPUs and remove k from Q. Repeat this step until Q is empty.

Step B-5-2 (Default stream): Synchronize the H2D stream with respect to the host.

The global gradient of a layer is the gradient accumulated from all local gradients of that layer from all GPUs. The synchronization step (Step B-4-1) is particularly important because it ensures that the local gradient of a layer is sent to the host after the gradient computation has finished.

Figure 1 illustrates the communication pattern between the host and GPUs during the backward phase of one iteration. On the host, for each GPU, there is a concurrent vector of the local gradients produced by the layers. There is also a concurrent vector of global gradients accumulated from the local gradients. The GPUs communicate directly with the CPUs to send gradients to the CPUs. Once a layer has computed its gradients with respect to its learnable parameters, the gradients are sent to the host, where they are accumulated into the global gradients (Step B-4-2). Gradient accumulation on the host is done in parallel using the OpenMP API. Once this gradient accumulation has been completed (by checking the existence of the layer in the queue Q), the global gradients are broadcasted back to all GPUs (Step B-4-3). At the same time, the next layer computes the other gradients (Steps B-2, B-3, B-4). Note that, once all layers have finished their computations, the completion of gradient accumulation for the last layer (or maybe the few last layers) has not finished yet. Hence, we need another step at the end of the backward phase to check for the completion by all layers and then broadcast the remaining global gradient(s) to the GPUs (Step B-5-1). Step B-5-2 ensures that all accumulated gradients are available in the GPUs before performing the update phase.

3.2 Cost model

We designed a cost model for the CGDP training and analyzed its performance. Without loss of generality, we assume that every GPU trains the same neural network in parallel at the same pace. In other words, the same layers in each network finish its computation at the same time. This means that it is sufficient to consider only the training for one GPU. Furthermore, we consider only the backward phase because we do not change the forward and update phases.

Given an l-layer FFN where f^i is its i-th layer, let t_{bp}^i be the time on the GPU for the layer's back-propagation (Steps B-1, B-2, B-3, B-4), and t_a^i be the time on the host for gradient accumulation, where t_a^i includes the synchronization time t_{as}^i (Step B-4-1) and accumulation time t_{aa}^i (Step B-4-2). Let t_{bc}^i be the time for broadcasting the accumulated gradient from the host to the GPUs (Step B-4-3).

In CGDP training, t_{aa}^i and t_{bc}^i overlap the next t_{bp}^j(s), $l \geq j > i$. In addition, t_{aa}^i and t_{aa}^j, $i \neq j$, overlap because they are handled by different processes in parallel.

Definition 3.1. The back-propagation time on a GPU for an l-layer FFN, T_{BP}, is defined by:

$$T_{BP} = \sum_{i=l}^{1} (t_{bp}^i)$$

Definition 3.2. The *total processing time* for a layer i in an l-layer FFN is defined by:

$$T_{BP}^i = \sum_{l}^{i} (t_{bp}^i + t_{as}^i) + t_{aa}^i + t_{bc}^i$$

Intuitively, the total processing time for a layer is the time from *the beginning of the backward phase* to the point where the layer's accumulated gradient is available in the GPU. Note that the definition of T_{BP}^i does not guarantee that, for $i < j$, the layer j will finish before the layer i during the backward phase.

Definition 3.3. The running time of the backward phase using CGDP training, T, is computed as

$$T = \max_{i=1,\dots,l} (T_{BP}^i).$$

Intuitively, the running time of the backward phase depends on the slowest layer (the one with the longest total processing time).

Definition 3.4. The running time of the backward phase in the typical data parallel training, T', is computed as follows (in this case, there is no synchronization as only one stream, the default stream, is used; i.e., $t_{as} = 0$):

$$T' = T_{BP} + \sum_{i=l}^{1} (t_{aa}^i + t_{bc}^i).$$

Note that t_{bc} in T is the time for broadcasting the gradients from the host to every GPU, while t_{bc} in T' is the time for broadcasting the parameters from the server GPU to the other GPUs. For each layer, the numbers of the gradients and parameters are the same. Hence, we assume that these t_{bc}(s) are the same though they might be different due to different connection topologies among CPUs and GPUs. In addition, t_{aa} in T is performed by CPUs while the one in T' is performed by GPUs.

Overhead time is defined as the additional time for accumulating and exchanging gradients among GPUs in the backward phase. For the typical data parallel training, overhead time is computed as

$$T_O' = T' - T_{BP} = \sum_{i=l}^{1} (t_{aa}^i + t_{bc}^i)$$

. For the CGDP training, overhead time is non-trivial to compute. However, simplification by assuming that t_{aa} and t_{bc} of layers $l, l-1, \dots, 2$ perfectly overlap the next t_{bp}(s) makes $T = T_{BP}^1$. The overhead time is then computed as

$$T_O = T - T_{BP} = \sum_{i=l}^{1} (t_{as}^i) + t_{aa}^1 + t_{bc}^1$$

The CGDP training is faster than the typical data parallel training if $T_O < T_O'$. If the layer 1 has a small number of parameters, then t_{aa} in T_O is approximately equal to t_{aa} in T_O'. Hence, $T_O < T_O'$ holds if $\sum_{i=l}^{1} (t_{as}^i) < \sum_{i=l}^{2} (t_{aa}^i + t_{bc}^i)$. This condition is easy to meet for several practical neural networks such as AlexNet, GoogLeNet-v1, and VGGNet-16.

4 CHUNK-SIZE OPTIMIZATION

As mentioned in the Introduction, we extend CGDP training by using chunks of layers to deal with very deep and "flat" neural networks in which the number of parameters for a layer is small and roughly equals the number for the other layers.

In the naive CGDP training, the gradients are sent to the host layer-by-layer, which is triggered by a synchronization using the default stream with respect to the host. In other words, the D2H stream waits for the computation of a layer in the default stream to finish. For neural networks that have many layers, e.g., ResNet-152 with 152 layers, there are many synchronizations in the CGDP training, which slows down the backward phase.

We first describe how the naive CGDP training is extended by using chunks to reduce the effect of synchronizations on the performance of the backward phase and then present a runtime algorithm for automatically finding a good setting for the CGDP training with chunks.

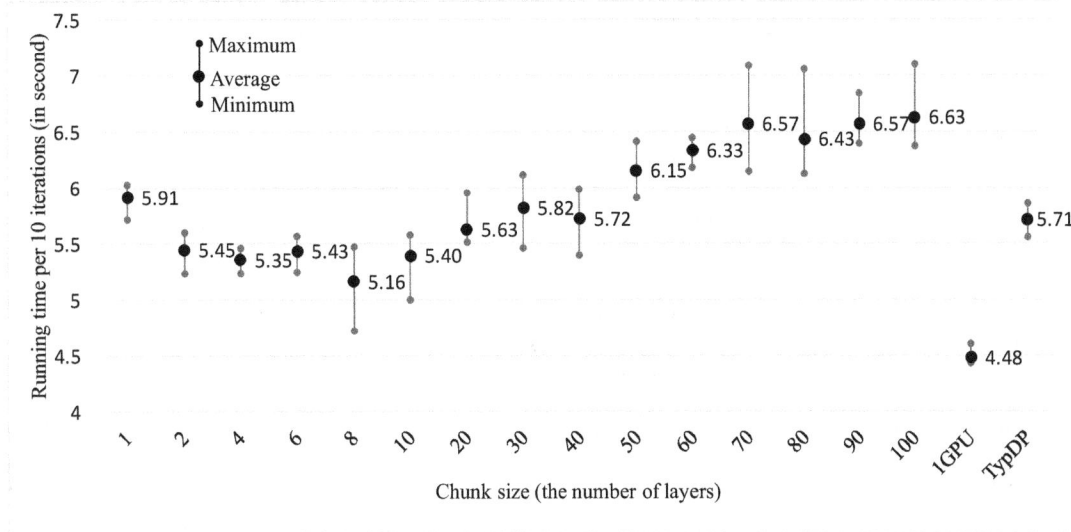

Figure 2: Running time for ten iterations of training ResNet-152 (minibatch size 16, 4 GPUs, no validation) for various chunk sizes. "TypDP" means using the typical data parallel training. The maximum, minimum, and average values were calculated for every ten iterations.

4.1 CGDP training using chunks

Because stream synchronization slows down the performance of the backward phase, it is better to perform synchronization after several layers have finished rather than after each layer has finished. In particular, it is best to optimize the $(\sum_{i=1}^{l}(t_{as}^i) + t_{aa}^i + t_{bc}^i))$ part of T.

We call a group of layers for which the gradients are sent to the host together *a chunk of layers*, and denote it by {}. Given a neural network, we can use multiple chunks with varying numbers of layers for CGDP training. For example, if a neural network has six layers $(f_{\theta_1}^1, f_{\theta_2}^2, f_{\theta_3}^3, f_{\theta_4}^4, f_{\theta_5}^5, f_{\theta_6}^6)$, we could use three chunks $\{f_{\theta_1}^1\}$, $\{f_{\theta_2}^2, f_{\theta_3}^3\}$, and $\{f_{\theta_4}^4, f_{\theta_5}^5, f_{\theta_6}^6\}$. The backward phase of the CGDP training using three chunks is performed as follows: compute gradients for the layers of chunk $\{f_{\theta_4}^4, f_{\theta_5}^5, f_{\theta_6}^6\}$ using the default stream, synchronize with the D2H stream to send the gradients of these layers to the host, compute the gradients for the layers of the chunk $\{f_{\theta_2}^2, f_{\theta_3}^3\}$ using the default stream, synchronize with the D2H stream to send the gradients of these layers to the host, compute the gradients for the layers of the chunk $\{f_{\theta_1}^1\}$, synchronize with the D2H stream to send the gradients of these layers to the host, and wait for all gradients to be available on the GPUs. In this example, only three synchronizations are needed using chunks while six synchronizations are needed without chunks.

There is a tradeoff between the number of synchronizations and the number of layers in a chunk. It is obvious that CGDP training with chunks reduces the number of synchronizations because $\sum_{i=1}^{l}(t_{as}^i)$ becomes $\sum_{j=1}^{c}(t_{as}^j)$, where c is the number of chunks. Nevertheless, using chunks potentially produces more overhead since we have postponed gradients accumulations for the layers in a chunk until the last layer in the chunk finishes its back-propagation. In other words, $(t_{aa}^i + t_{bc}^i)$ for a layer i becomes the sum of $(t_{aa}^j + t_{bc}^j)$

for all layers j in the chunk to which layer i belongs. This makes it more difficult to optimize CGDP training.

PROPOSITION 4.1. *Given an l-layer FFN, there are $\sum_{k=1}^{l-1}\binom{l-1}{k}$ ways to group layers by chunks for CGDP training with chunks.*

PROOF. The proof is completed by counting the total number of ways to insert k delimiters, $k = 1, 2, \ldots, (l-1)$, into the spaces between two consecutive characters in the sequence "$f_1 f_2 \ldots f_l$" so that there is no more than one delimiter in the same space. □

4.2 Heuristic algorithm for finding chunks

Here we present a runtime algorithm for finding the chunk size that minimizes the running time for the backward phase. It is run for the first few training iterations to determine a good chunk size for reducing the running time for training. Two heuristic rules are used for determining how to expand the search space and how to stop the algorithm.

To limit the search space, here we consider only the case in which chunks have the same size except for the few last layers of the backward phase. Assume that we train an l-layer FFN using the CGDP training with chunks of the same size, k. If $(l \bmod k = 0)$, there are $(\frac{l}{k} - 1)$ chunks with size k, including layers from l to $(k + 1)$, and there are k chunks with size 1, including the remaining layers from k to 1. If $(l \bmod k \neq 0)$, there are $\lfloor \frac{l}{k} \rfloor$ chunks with size k, including layers from l to $(l - k * \lfloor \frac{l}{k} \rfloor + 1)$, and there are $(l - k * \lfloor \frac{l}{k} \rfloor)$ chunks with size 1, including the remaining layers from $(l - k * \lfloor \frac{l}{k} \rfloor)$ to 1. The few last layers have a chunk size of 1 in order to reduce the effect of t_{aa}^i and t_{bc}^i on training overhead.

Figure 2 shows the running time for training ResNet-152 for chunk sizes from 1 to 100. It also shows the running times for single-GPU training and the typical data parallel training to illustrate the overhead of the CGDP training. The naive CGDP training (with chunks of size 1) was slower than the typical data parallel training. This is because ResNet-152 has many small layers (the number of parameters is small). Hence, the overhead of synchronizations is high, which results in the total overhead being high. Increasing the chunk size (chunk sizes 2, 4, 6, 8), gradually improved the results. However, using a large chunk size is not good due to the overhead of gradient accumulation. Compared to the running time for single-GPU training, the overhead time for multiple GPU training was very high, so there is potentially room for improvement.

Algorithm 1 shows our algorithm for finding a good chunk size for CGDP training with chunks. Assume that we train a neural network using N iterations. There are two user-defined parameters in the algorithm: step and range. The step parameter is used to heuristically determine how to expand the search space for chunk size and how to stop the algorithm. The range parameter is used to determine how to stop the algorithm and it is used together with the parameter step. Variable chunk is used to store the chunk size for the current iteration. It is the variable to be optimized. It is continually updated during the execution of the algorithm and is set to the value of variable best_chunk upon completion. Variable best_chunk holds the chunk size that results in the minimum running time, which is stored in a variable lapse_min. Variable lapse is the running time of the last interval iterations. At the beginning of training, variables chunk, best_chunk, and lapse_min are set to 1, 1, and $+\infty$, respectively (Line 1).

Our heuristic algorithm for finding a good chunk (Lines 7–25 in Algorithm 1) runs as follows. After each interval iteration, the algorithm is triggered. Although the value of interval can be changed, we use a fixed value of 10 here. The algorithm measures the running time for the interval iterations, and stores it in variable lapse (Line 13). If lapse < lapse_min, the values of best_chunk and lapse_min are updated to the current values (Lines 14–16). As mentioned, there are two heuristic rules in the algorithm. The first rule is used to expand the search space of the chunk size: chunk := (chunk < step)?(chunk+1) : (chunk + step) (Lines 18–22). The rule says that, at the beginning of the algorithm, if chunk < step, the value of the chunk size is gradually increased by 1. Otherwise, the chunk size is increased by step. This rule flexibly adjusts the search space of the algorithm. If step is large and close to the number of layers, most of the values for the chunk size are aggressively scanned. If it is small, big jumps in chunk size are made, and some values are ignored, which speeds up completion. The second rule is used to determine when to stop the algorithm; that is, chunk ≥ best_chunk + step * range (Lines 8–10). Intuitively, once a best_chunk is found, the algorithm runs another range times. If there is no a better chunk size, the algorithm stops. Note that, if best_chunk < step, the algorithm runs another (step − best_chunk + range) times before determining whether to stop.

5 EXPERIMENTAL RESULTS

5.1 Configurations

Experiments were run on an IBM POWER8 NUMA-based machine [1] equipped with two 4GHz 10-core POWER8 processors, eight simultaneous multi-threads (SMTs) per core and 256 MB RAM

Algorithm 1 Runtime algorithm for finding a good chunk size

1: **procedure** CGDP(N, $step$, $range$)
2:     $chunk \leftarrow 1$; $best\_chunk \leftarrow 1$; $lapse\_min \leftarrow FLOAT\_MAX$
3:     $iter \leftarrow 1$; $interval \leftarrow 10$; $done \leftarrow FALSE$
4:     $start\_time \leftarrow$ SYSTEM.CURRENTTIMEMILLIS()
5:     **while** $iter \leq N$ **do**   ▷ Training for N iterations
6:         CGDPTRAINBYCHUNK($chunk$)   ▷ See Section 4.1
7:         **if** ($iter$ mod $interval = 0$) **and** ($done \neq TRUE$) **then**
8:             **if** $chunk \geq best\_chunk + step * range$ **then**
9:                 $chunk \leftarrow best\_chunk$
10:                 $done \leftarrow TRUE$
11:             **else**
12:                 $end\_time \leftarrow$ SYS.CURRENTTIMEMILLIS()
13:                 $lapse \leftarrow (end\_time - start\_time)$
14:                 **if** $lapse < lapse\_min$ **then**
15:                     $lapse\_min \leftarrow lapse$
16:                     $best\_chunk \leftarrow chunk$
17:                 **end if**
18:                 **if** $chunk < step$ **then**
19:                     $chunk \leftarrow chunk + 1$
20:                 **else**
21:                     $chunk \leftarrow chunk + step$
22:                 **end if**
23:                 $start\_time \leftarrow$ SYS.CURRENTTIMEMILLIS()
24:             **end if**
25:         **end if**
26:         $iter \leftarrow iter + 1$
27:     **end while**
28:     **return**
29: **end procedure**

Table 1: Neural networks and experimental settings.

Network	Layers	Parameters (million)	Minibatch size per GPU
AlexNet	8	60	256
GoogLeNet-v1	22	7	64
VGGNet-16	16	138	32
ResNet-152	152	49	12

per processor, four NVIDIA Tesla P100 GPUs (each with 16 GB memory), and NVLinks among the GPUs and CPUs (one 80 GB/s duplex link between GPUs 0 and 1, one 80 GB/s duplex link between GPUs 2 and 3, two 80 GB/s duplex links from CPU 0 to GPUs 0 and 1, and two 80 GB/s duplex links from CPU 1 to GPUs 2 and 3). It was also equipped with CUDA Toolkit v8.0.44 and cuDNN 5.1.5 state-of-the-art library for primitives used in deep neural networks, which was developed by NVIDIA developers and is highly optimized for GPUs.

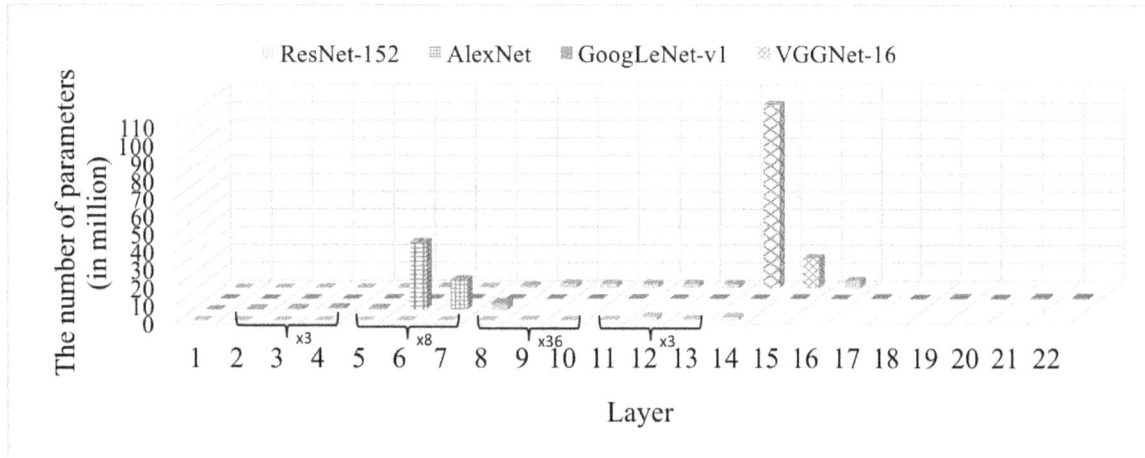

Figure 3: Number of parameters per layer for AlexNet, GoogLeNet-v1, VGGNet-16 and ResNet-152. Strings "x3", "x8", "x36", "x3" are used to indicate the number of blocks of layers for ResNet-152 only, e.g., there are three blocks of layers 2, 3, and 4.

We used four neural networks that are widely used in computer vision: AlexNet[1] [17], GoogLeNet-v1[2] (Inception-v1) [24], VGGNet-16[3] (model D) [22], and ResNet-152[4] [11]. Table 1 shows the basic information for these networks and the size of the minibatch (number of images processed by *one* GPU in one training iteration) used for training them. The distributions of parameters in the layers of these networks are shown in Figure 3. The layers in GoogLeNet-v1 and ResNet-152 have relatively the same size, and they are small, while the last few layers in AlexNet and VGGNet-16 are quite large compared to the other layers. The dataset used for training was a subset of the ImageNet ILSVRC2012 [20] database, which contains 1.2 million images classified into 1000 categories.

We implemented our optimization in the BVLC/Caffe deep learning framework [15] developed by UC Berkeley researchers. The vanilla BVLC/Caffe v1.0.0-rc3 (hereafter, BVLC/Caffe) used the standard data parallel training with a tree pattern for communication among GPUs. We refer to our optimization in BVLC/Caffe as TRL/Caffe. To obtain exact results, for each training session, we ran the program ten times and calculated the average running time. Each training session comprised 1000 training iterations. The running time for an iteration was averaged on the basis of 1000 iterations.

5.2 Results for CGDP training

5.2.1 *Running time for training.* The scalability of CGDP training compared to the typical training was determined by analyzing the running time for training. Table 2 shows the running times for one training iteration with one, two, and four GPUs for AlexNet, GoogLeNet-v1, and VGGNet-16. The results for ResNet-152 are analyzed in detail in Section 5.3. The results in Table 2 indicated that

[1]AlexNet's network definition:
  https://github.com/BVLC/caffe/tree/master/models/bvlc_alexnet
[2]GoogLeNet-v1's network definition:
  https://github.com/BVLC/caffe/tree/master/models/bvlc_googlenet
[3]VGGNet-16's network definition:
  https://gist.github.com/ksimonyan/211839e770f7b538e2d8
[4]ResNet-152's network definition:
  https://github.com/KaimingHe/deep-residual-networks

TRL/Caffe is more scalable than BVLC/Caffe. When the number of GPUs was one, the running times for both frameworks were almost the same for each network. When the number of GPUs was four, TRL/Caffe was the fastest for all networks—in particular, it was 1.21, 1.04, and 1.21 times faster than BVLC/Caffe for AlexNet, GoogLeNet-v1, and VGGNet-16, respectively. This shows that TRL/Caffe consistently had a high efficiency ($\geq$ 90%). Our approach was the least effective for GoogLeNet-v1 and the most effective for VGGNet-16. This is because the effectiveness of our approach depends on the number of parameters for the network: it makes the training of networks with more parameters faster because it distributes the computation for collecting and accumulating gradients, the number of which is the same as the number of parameters for any minibatch size. The number of parameters in GoogLeNet-v1 and VGGNet-16 are the least and the most, respectively, so we obtained corresponding results.

5.2.2 *Communication overhead.* Reducing communication overhead is our objective, and Table 3 shows the running time for every phase in training AlexNet on four GPUs. We see that, for BVLC/Caffe, the broadcast at the beginning took 20 ms and that the collection and accumulation of gradients at the end of the backward phase took 23 ms. For TRL/Caffe, these computations were hidden behind the backward phase, and the communication overhead was for only the ending layer of the backward phase. These computations took only 21.8μs in AlexNet. However, the time for backward propagation in TRL/Caffe was longer than that in BVLC/Caffe. This is reasonable because TRL/Caffe needs to do work to invoke data copy functions and callback functions between two consecutive layers during the backward phase. As for GoogLeNet-v1 and VGGNet-16, the communication overheads of TRL/Caffe were the same as the one for AlexNet ($\approx$ 21.8μs). We thus do not show them here.

5.2.3 *Time for accumulation on host.* It is important to determine whether the accumulation on the host can be overlapped with

Table 2: Running time for one training iteration (ms).

	AlexNet			GoogLeNet-v1			VGGNet-16		
no. of GPUs	1	2	4	1	2	4	1	2	4
BVLC/Caffe	157.2	174.3	202.7	140.0	151.7	163.4	345.6	383.7	445.6
TRL/Caffe	157.4	163.6	167.1	140.9	151.9	156.7	345.2	361.5	369.1

Table 3: Running time for phases in one iteration for AlexNet with four GPUs (in ms).

	broadcast	forward	backward	broadcast remaining gradients from CPUs	grad-acc	update-param	total time
BVLC/Caffe	20	50.6	104	N/A	23	5.1	202.7
TRL/Caffe	N/A	51.0	111	$21.8\mu s$	N/A	5.1	167.1

Table 4: Communication time between GPUs and CPUs, and accumulation time on CPUs for AlexNet with four GPUs.

	Layer 8	Layer 7	Layer 6	Layer 5	Layer 4	Layer 3	Layer 2	Layer 1
no. of parameters (million)	4	16.8	37.8	0.4	0.7	0.9	0.3	0.03
GPU-to-CPU copy (ms)	0.760	3.156	12.146	0.133	0.174	0.275	0.066	0.014
accumulation time on CPUs (ms)	1.263	4.441	13.074	0.285	0.465	0.578	0.155	0.018
CPU-to-GPU copy (ms)	1.786	2.568	5.538	0.064	0.095	0.123	0.041	0.007

Table 5: Memory consumption in GPUs (in MB).

	AlexNet	GoogLeNet-v1	VGGNet-16
BVLC/Caffe	6863	6095	7274
TRL/Caffe	6359	5991	6191

the computations on the GPUs. Table 4 shows the time for accumulation on the CPUs for each layers during the backward phase and the communication time between the GPUs and the CPUs for TRL/Caffe with AlexNet when using four GPUs. The communication and accumulation overlapped the backward phase. Note that in the backward phase, processing is from the top layer (layer 8) to the bottom layer (layer 1). It is clear that the accumulation time was much shorter than the time for the backward phase. Furthermore, because the ending layer in the backward phase, layer 1, had a small number of parameters, the overhead for sending the gradients of this layer to the GPUs was very small ($\approx 7\mu s$).

5.2.4 Memory consumption. By offloading gradient accumulation onto the host, we can reduce memory consumption in the GPUs, which facilitates training with a larger batch size. Table 5 shows the maximum sizes of the memories allocated on the GPUs during training. Note that the allocated memory size on the GPUs depends on the size of the minibatch used for training, not the number of iterations. The maximum size per GPU needed by TRL/Caffe was smaller than that needed by BVLC/Caffe. This is because BVLC/Caffe allocates memory on the GPUs to collect and accumulate gradients from different GPUs while TRL/Caffe does not need such memory

since the gradients are collected and accumulated on the host. Accordingly, TRL/Caffe consumed more memory on the host. This is not a big problem because memory on host is generally cheaper and easier to increase than that on the GPUs. As a result, we were able to train VGGNet-16 with 103 images per minibatch per GPU instead of 94, increasing the chance to adjust the hyperparameters for the solver algorithms.

5.2.5 Long-term runs. We conducted experiments using long-term runs to evaluate the effectiveness of our approach for long-term runs. The objective was to train AlexNet to achieve 50% accuracy using four GPUs. TRL/Caffe took 62 minutes while BVLC/Caffe took 79 minutes (Fig. 4a). Both versions reached 50% accuracy at around iteration 20,000 (21,000 iterations in total) and had the same convergence curve (Fig. 4b). Note that this training included a testing phase, in which the testing iteration was simply a forward computation using validation data (50,000 images) to verify network accuracy. After 1000 training iterations, there was one test comprising 1000 testing iterations. Hence, there were 21 tests in total, and each test took about 14.7 seconds.

5.3 Effectiveness of runtime algorithm

To test the runtime algorithm (Algorithm 1) we used ResNet-152 instead of Resnet-1001, which is too large to fit in our GPU memory, we used Resnet-152 instead. We trained ResNet-152 for 1000 iterations using four GPUs with a real world setting in which the validation phase was included. The maximum minibatch size we were able to run for ResNet-152 was 12 (16 without the validation phase). We set the value of interval to 10 to stabilize the elapsed time stable. The effectiveness of each parameter in the runtime algorithm was examined.

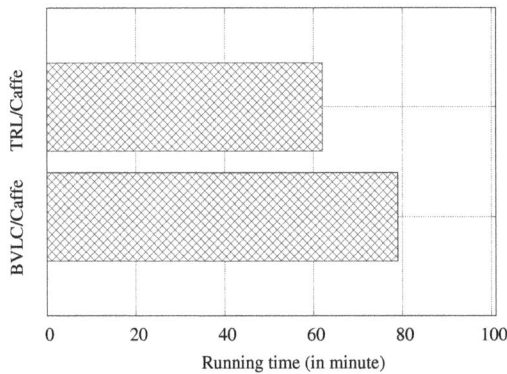

(a) Time to achieve 50% accuracy in AlexNet training.

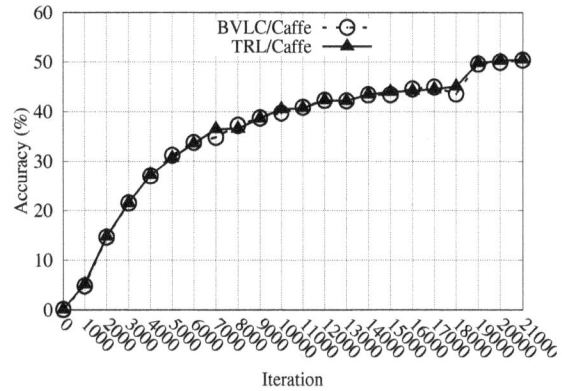

(b) Accuracy per iteration in AlexNet training.

Figure 4: Long-term run for AlexNet training (21, 000 iterations).

We first fixed the value of range to 5 and varied the value of step. Figure 5a shows the result. First, for a chunk size of 1 (OrigCGDP), CGDP training was slower than the typical data parallel training. We then changed the value of step because different values might lead to a different best chunk size. However, once the runtime algorithm finished, the trainings with different best chunk sizes looked working similarly and ran faster than the typical data parallel training. Let's analyze in detail the configuration "step = 10, range = 5". CGDP training had the best performance at iteration 90, where the chunk size had a value of 9. After that, a better running time could not be attained. Hence, the runtime algorithm stopped at iteration 150 (it ran six more times after the iteration 90), and used a chunk size of 9 for the later iterations. Finally, we included the result of single-GPU training. Although there was still overhead for CGDP training with chunks, with a simple heuristics, it was much lower than that for typical data parallel training and close to that for single-GPU training.

Figure 5b shows the results of extending the search space for a fixed value of step by increasing the value of range. A larger value for the chunk size was found: 20, when range was 10. Nevertheless, training with a chunk size of 20 had the same performance as the ones with other best chunk sizes (3, 6, or 9). In all cases, the runtime algorithm finished in at most 21 iterations, which shows that the runtime overhead of the algorithm was small because the whole training often had hundreds of thousands of iterations. Overall, CGDP training was about 1.07 times faster than the typical data parallel training for ResNet-152. For AlexNet, VGGNet-16, and GoogLeNet-v1, the runtime algorithm could not find a chunk (> 1) that produced a better result. This is because these neural networks have a small number of layers, so the effect of synchronization is small.

6 RELATED WORK

There are several ways to accelerate deep learning: data parallelism, model parallelism, and pipeline parallelism. Data parallelism is implemented in many frameworks such as Google's TensorFlow [5], Torch [8], and Microsoft's CNTK [25]. It is mainly used for deep convolutional neural networks. Model parallelism has been used

for large-scale unsupervised learning [18]. Many distributed frameworks, such as MXNet [6], Mariana [28], the COTS HPC system [7], and the DistBelief software framework [9], support both data parallelism and model parallelism so that users can use either one. For single-machine training, both TensorFlow and MXNet support gradient accumulation on the host, but the accumulation is performed at the end of the back-propagation computation instead of layer-by-layer as in our CGDP training. Krizhevsky proposed a hybrid parallelism [16], in which model parallelism is applied to layers with a large number of learnable parameters (e.g., fully connected layers), and data parallelism is applied to the ones with a small number of learnable parameters (e.g., convolutional layers). This hybrid parallelism scales better than model and data parallelism when applied to modern convolutional neural networks. In pipeline parallelism, each layer of a neural network is executed on a different GPU and communicates its activations to the next GPU [23]. Pipeline optimization is used in Mariana [28]: a three-stage pipeline, consisting of data reading, data processing, and neural network training, is used for training. Our mechanism should also be effective for hybrid parallelism and pipeline parallelism because both require collection and accumulation of gradients on different GPUs.

A closer approach to ours is Poseidon [26], a distributed deep learning framework, in which there is overlap between backward computation and communication among distributed machines. Because communication overhead is very high in a distributed environment, it is difficult to hide communication overhead behind the backward phase. It can be done with our approach because our target is training on a single machine coupled with multiple GPUs. Another approach that is close to ours is one developed at Google [19] in which a method learns to predict a set of device placements for layers in a neural network. It is targeted at heterogeneous distributed environments with a mix of hardware devices such as CPUs, and GPUs. In our CGDP training, the layers are always computed in the GPUs, so device placement is not needed.

Another approach to accelerating deep neural network training is to parallelize the solver algorithm, such as the SGD algorithm. BVLC/Caffe implements the synchronous SGD algorithm so that parameters are updated when *all* gradients have been collected

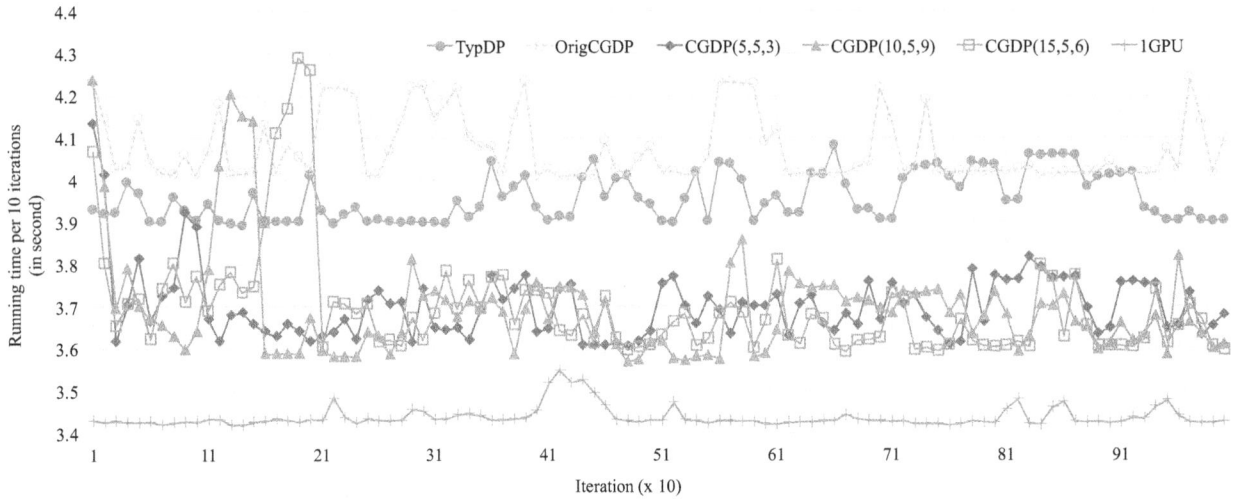

(a) step ∈ {5, 10, 15}, range = 5.

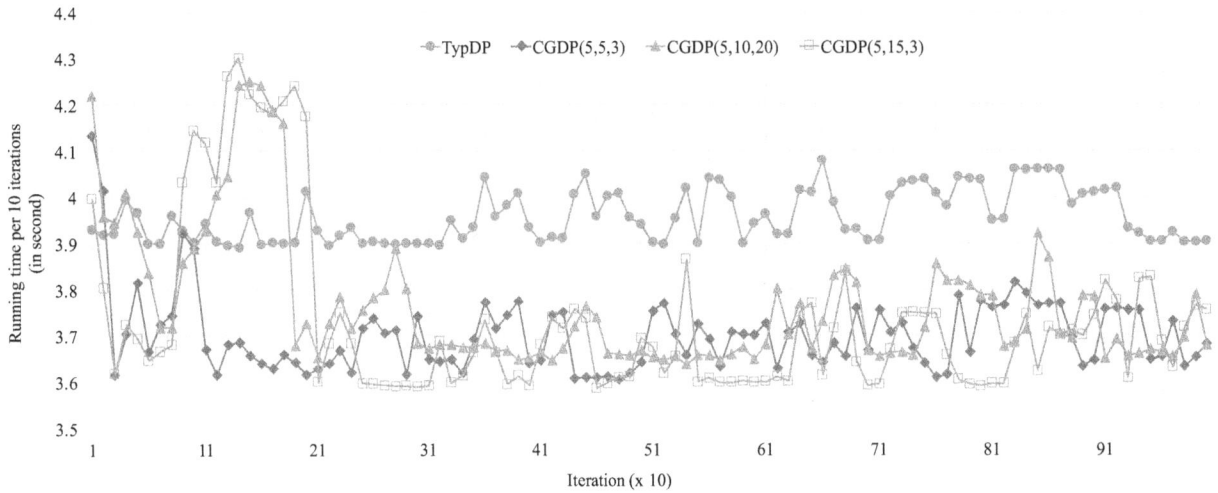

(b) step = 5, range ∈ {5, 10, 15}.

Figure 5: Effectiveness of parameters in runtime algorithm for ResNet-152 with minibatch size of 12 per GPU. Plotted are CGDP values for (step, range, best_chunk), where best_chunk is the best chunk size found by the algorithm. "TypDP" refers to the typical data parallel training. "OrigCGDP" refers to the naive CGDP training with the chunk size of 1.

from *all* GPUs [15]. Asynchronous SGD is a parallelized variant of SGD in which the parameters are updated after a certain number of gradients have been collected from a certain number of GPUs. It is very effective in a distributed environment where different machines run at different speeds [14, 27], but it changes the learning accuracy, and it is sometimes difficult to exactly reproduce the result. Therefore, the asynchronous SGD is not our target.

7 CONCLUSION AND FUTURE WORK

Deep learning is an emerging tool for signal processing and is mainly sped up by accelerators such as GPUs. This means that powerful CPUs are redundant in deep learning. Some frameworks, such

as TensorFlow and MXNet, have been utilizing CPUs for gradient accumulation, but the objective is to make the frameworks flexible instead of improving performance. We have shown here for the first time to our knowledge that utilizing free CPUs on a host accelerates GPU-based data parallel training of deep neural networks on a single machine. In our CGDP training approach, CPUs collect, accumulate, and broadcast gradients produced during the backward phase. The key idea is that those operations can be performed in parallel with the backward phase, resulting in a reduction in time for each training iteration. We also presented a cost model for data parallel training of neural networks and demonstrate its power by using it to identify a bottleneck in training very deep neural networks. Finally, we presented a runtime algorithm using simple heuristics to optimize one of the deepest neural networks, ResNet-152. Future work includes extending the CGDP training to support recurrent neural networks, which consist of cyclic links among layers. An additional mechanism is needed for such networks to determine which layer gradients are kept in the GPUs for the cyclic links, and when to send them to the host. Additionally, it is open to investigate what kind of computation is suitable for being offloaded onto the host.

REFERENCES

[1] 2016. IBM Power System S822LC for High Performance Computing. (Oct. 2016). http://www-03.ibm.com/systems/power/hardware/s822lc-hpc/.
[2] 2016. Torch. (Oct. 2016). http://torch.ch/.
[3] 2017. NVIDIA NCCL. (2017). https://developer.nvidia.com/nccl.
[4] 2017. Torch. (2017). https://luna16.grand-challenge.org.
[5] Martín Abadi, Ashish Agarwal, Paul Barham, Eugene Brevdo, Zhifeng Chen, Craig Citro, Greg S. Corrado, Andy Davis, Jeffrey Dean, Matthieu Devin, Sanjay Ghemawat, Ian Goodfellow, Andrew Harp, Geoffrey Irving, Michael Isard, Yangqing Jia, Rafal Jozefowicz, Lukasz Kaiser, Manjunath Kudlur, Josh Levenberg, Dan Mané, Rajat Monga, Sherry Moore, Derek Murray, Chris Olah, Mike Schuster, Jonathon Shlens, Benoit Steiner, Ilya Sutskever, Kunal Talwar, Paul Tucker, Vincent Vanhoucke, Vijay Vasudevan, Fernanda Viégas, Oriol Vinyals, Pete Warden, Martin Wattenberg, Martin Wicke, Yuan Yu, and Xiaoqiang Zheng. 2015. TensorFlow: Large-Scale Machine Learning on Heterogeneous Systems. (2015). http://tensorflow.org/ Software available from tensorflow.org.
[6] Tianqi Chen, Mu Li, Yutian Li, Min Lin, Naiyan Wang, Minjie Wang, Tianjun Xiao, Bing Xu, Chiyuan Zhang, and Zheng Zhang. 2015. Mxnet: A Flexible and Efficient Machine Learning Library for Heterogeneous Distributed Systems. arXiv preprint arXiv:1512.01274 (2015).
[7] Adam Coates, Brody Huval, Tao Wang, David Wu, Bryan Catanzaro, and Ng Andrew. 2013. Deep Learning with COTS HPC Systems. In International Conference on Machine Learning, Vol. 28. JMLR Workshop and Conference Proceedings, 1337–1345.
[8] Ronan Collobert, Koray Kavukcuoglu, and Clément Farabet. 2011. Torch7: A Matlab-like Environment for Machine Learning. In BigLearn, NIPS Workshop.
[9] Jeffrey Dean, Greg S. Corrado, Rajat Monga, Kai Chen, Matthieu Devin, Quoc V. Le, Mark Z. Mao, MarcÁfAurelio Ranzato, Andrew Senior, Paul Tucker, Ke Yang, and Andrew Y. Ng. 2012. Large Scale Distributed Deep Networks. In International Conference on Neural Information Processing Systems. 1232–1240.
[10] Ian Goodfellow, Yoshua Bengio, and Aaron Courville. 2016. Deep Learning. MIT Press. http://www.deeplearningbook.org.
[11] Kaiming He, Xiangyu Zhang, Shaoqing Ren, and Jian Sun. 2015. Deep Residual Learning for Image Recognition. CoRR abs/1512.03385 (2015). http://arxiv.org/abs/1512.03385
[12] Kaiming He, Xiangyu Zhang, Shaoqing Ren, and Jian Sun. 2015. Delving Deep into Rectifiers: Surpassing Human-Level Performance on ImageNet Classification. CoRR abs/1502.01852 (2015).
[13] Kaiming He, Xiangyu Zhang, Shaoqing Ren, and Jian Sun. 2016. Identity Mappings in Deep Residual Networks. Springer International Publishing, 630–645.
[14] Qirong Ho, James Cipar, Henggang Cui, Seunghak Lee, Jin Kyu Kim, Phillip B. Gibbons, Garth A Gibson, Greg Ganger, and Eric P Xing. 2013. More Effective Distributed ML via a Stale Synchronous Parallel Parameter Server. In International Conference on Neural Information Processing Systems. 1223–1231.
[15] Yangqing Jia, Evan Shelhamer, Jeff Donahue, Sergey Karayev, Jonathan Long, Ross Girshick, Sergio Guadarrama, and Trevor Darrell. 2014. Caffe: Convolutional Architecture for Fast Feature Embedding. arXiv preprint arXiv:1408.5093 (2014).
[16] Alex Krizhevsky. 2014. One Weird Trick for Parallelizing Convolutional Neural Networks. arXiv preprint arXiv:1404.5997v2 (2014).
[17] Alex Krizhevsky, Ilya Sutskever, and Geoffrey E. Hinton. 2012. ImageNet Classification with Deep Convolutional Neural Networks. In International Conference on Neural Information Processing Systems. 1097–1105.
[18] Quoc Le, Marc'Aurelio Ranzato, Rajat Monga, Matthieu Devin, Kai Chen, Greg Corrado, Jeff Dean, and Andrew Ng. 2012. Building High-Level Features Using Large Scale Unsupervised Learning. In International Conference in Machine Learning.
[19] Azalia Mirhoseini, Hieu Pham, Quoc Le, Mohammad Norouzi, Samy Bengio, Benoit Steiner, Yuefeng Zhou, Naveen Kumar, Rasmus Larsen, and Jeff Dean. 2017. Device Placement Optimization with Reinforcement Learning. https://arxiv.org/abs/1706.04972
[20] Olga Russakovsky, Jia Deng, Hao Su, Jonathan Krause, Sanjeev Satheesh, Sean Ma, Zhiheng Huang, Andrej Karpathy, Aditya Khosla, Michael Bernstein, Alexander C. Berg, and Li Fei-Fei. 2015. ImageNet Large Scale Visual Recognition Challenge. International Journal of Computer Vision 115, 3 (2015), 211–252. https://doi.org/10.1007/s11263-015-0816-y
[21] George Saon, Gakuto Kurata, Tom Sercu, Kartik Audhkhasi, Samuel Thomas, Dimitrios Dimitriadis, Xiaodong Cui, Bhuvana Ramabhadran, Michael Picheny, Lynn-Li Lim, Bergul Roomi, and Phil Hall. 2017. English Conversational Telephone Speech Recognition by Humans and Machines. CoRR abs/1703.02136 (2017).
[22] Karen Simonyan and Andrew Zisserman. 2014. Very Deep Convolutional Networks for Large-Scale Image Recognition. arXiv preprint arXiv:1409.1556 (2014).
[23] Ilya Sutskever, Oriol Vinyals, and Quoc V. Le. 2014. Sequence to Sequence Learning with Neural Networks. In International Conference on Neural Information Processing Systems. 3104–3112.
[24] Christian Szegedy, Wei Liu, Yangqing Jia, Pierre Sermanet, Scott E. Reed, Dragomir Anguelov, Dumitru Erhan, Vincent Vanhoucke, and Andrew Rabinovich. 2015. Going Deeper with Convolutions. In IEEE Conference on Computer Vision and Pattern Recognition. 1–9.
[25] Dong Yu, Adam Eversole, Mike Seltzer, Kaisheng Yao, Oleksii Kuchaiev, Yu Zhang, Frank Seide, Zhiheng Huang, Brian Guenter, Huaming Wang, Jasha Droppo, Geoffrey Zweig, Chris Rossbach, Jie Gao, Andreas Stolcke, Jon Currey, Malcolm Slaney, Guoguo Chen, Amit Agarwal, Chris Basoglu, Marko Padmilac, Alexey Kamenev, Vladimir Ivanov, Scott Cypher, Hari Parthasarathi, Bhaskar Mitra, Baolin Peng, and Xuedong Huang. 2014. An Introduction to Computational Networks and the Computational Network Toolkit. Technical Report.
[26] Hao Zhang, Zhiting Hu, Jinliang Wei, Pengtao Xie, Gunhee Kim, Qirong Ho, and Eric Xing. 2015. Poseidon: A System Architecture for Efficient GPU-based Deep Learning on Multiple Machines. arXiv preprint arXiv:1512.06216 (2015).
[27] Wei Zhang, Suyog Gupta, Xiangru Lian, and Ji Liu. 2016. Staleness-aware async-SGD for Distributed Deep Learning. In Proceedings of the Twenty-Fifth International Joint Conference on Artificial Intelligence (IJCAI'16). AAAI Press, 2350–2356.
[28] Yongqiang Zou, Xing Jin, Yi Li, Zhimao Guo, Eryu Wang, and Bin Xiao. 2014. Mariana: Tencent Deep Learning Platform and Its Applications. Proceedings of VLDB Endow. 7, 13 (Aug. 2014), 1772–1777.

Measuring Network Latency Variation Impacts to High Performance Computing Application Performance

Robert Underwood
Clemson University
Clemson, South Carolina
robertu@clemson.edu

Jason Anderson
Clemson University
Clemson, South Carolina
jwa2@clemson.edu

Amy Apon
Clemson University
Clemson, South Carolina
aapon@clemson.edu

ABSTRACT

In this paper, we study the impacts of latency variation versus latency mean on application runtime, library performance, and packet delivery. Our contributions include the design and implementation of a network latency injector that is suitable for most QLogic and Mellanox InfiniBand cards. We fit statistical distributions of latency mean and variation to varying levels of network contention for a range of parallel application workloads. We use the statistical distributions to characterize the latency variation impacts to application degradation. The level of application degradation caused by variation in network latency depends on application characteristics, and can be significant. Observed degradation varies from no degradation for applications without communicating processes to 3.5 times slower for communication-intensive parallel applications. We support our results with statistical analysis of our experimental observations. For communication-intensive high performance computing applications, we show statistically significant evidence that changes in performance are more highly correlated with changes of variation in network latency than with changes of mean network latency alone.

CCS CONCEPTS

• **Networks** → **Network experimentation**; **Network performance analysis**; **Network measurement**; • **Hardware** → **Testing with distributed and parallel systems**;

KEYWORDS

Network Latency Variation; Low Latency Networks; Parallel Application Performance; Network Load Injector; Statistical Analysis

ACM Reference Format:
Robert Underwood, Jason Anderson, and Amy Apon. 2018. Measuring Network Latency Variation Impacts to High Performance Computing Application Performance. In *ICPE '18: ACM/SPEC International Conference on Performance Engineering, April 9–13, 2018, Berlin, Germany.* ACM, New York, NY, USA, 12 pages. https://doi.org/10.1145/3184407.3184427

1 INTRODUCTION

High performance computing (HPC) depends on the performance of the underlying network. Indeed, there has been extensive research on the development of low-latency, highly performing networks for HPC [7, 8, 28], and research has demonstrated the considerable effect of average network latency on the performance of HPC applications [14, 31]. Because compute nodes are increasingly capable, with larger numbers and types of cores and memory, network resources are under increased contention creating competition for these resources and increasing the variation in network communication time. In this paper, we demonstrate that network latency variation by itself can have a significant effect on HPC workload runtime. That is, with equal mean latency, a higher variation in the network latency can result in significantly lower HPC application performance.

This paper focuses on the effects of network latency variation on HPC performance degradation. We present the design and implementation of a network latency injector that is suitable for most QLogic and Mellanox InfiniBand cards. We execute sets of experiments at the packet, library, and application levels to measure and model the latency distributions. We then synthetically produce latency using our developed latency injector in a controlled experimental environment and measure these effects.

Our developed tool and approach confirm prior research that has focused on the packet and library level. At the packet level, increasing of mean network latency affects performance, but point-to-point communication is less affected by the variation in network latency. At the library level, latency variation affects the runtime of collective operations, particular those that involve most or all nodes in the computation [12, 13].

We present new results at the application level. First, we characterize the negative impact that latency variation has to the performance of classes of communication-intensive applications. The decrease in performance ranges up to 3.5 times slower for LU Decomposition [3], for example. Next, we show that for communication-intensive HPC applications, changes in performance are more highly correlated with changes of variation in network latency than with changes of mean network latency alone. These results have implications for the design of HPC applications that must execute in a highly shared environment, say, using commercial cloud resources or in a multi-tenant environment, and suggest that implementation of mechanisms to control network variation latency may lead to better overall application and system performance than efforts to reduce average network latency alone. Our main contributions are:

- the design and implementation of a configurable latency injector for many Mellanox and QLogic InfiniBand cards,

- characterizing the distributions of network latency for an InfiniBand network in an HPC environment,
- an experimental methodology using synthetically generated latency to demonstrate the effects of latency variation on HPC workloads, and
- statistically significant evidence that latency variation is more highly correlated with HPC application performance than latency mean alone.

The remainder of this paper is organized as follows. We present background information on network latency sources and low-latency networking in Section 2. We describe our design choices and implementation tradeoffs of the latency injector in Section 3. We provide our overall experimental methodology in Section 4, and describe our workload characterization in Section 5. We show how latency variation apart from congestion can cause performance degradation in Section 6. We demonstrate that latency variation can be more highly correlated with application degradation than latency mean in Section 7. We present an overview of other works studying latency variation in Section 8. Finally, we provide conclusions and future work in Section 9.

2 BACKGROUND

Prior research has shown that congestion-induced latency variation can have significant effects on application performance [5]. This is straightforward to observe; for example, in the MPI_Barrier routine, no process can continue until all of the processes entering the barrier have completed the synchronization step. Thus, the time to complete the barrier call is determined by the process that takes the longest time to enter and complete the barrier [13]. In networks with high latency variation, the time to synchronize to a barrier can be considerable [9].

2.1 Sources of Latency Variation

The causes of latency variation in an HPC environment can include single node hardware and software, operating system policies, and resource contention. Features of a single compute node that can be a source of variation of the network latency include differences in cores and changes in the assignment of tasks to cores during execution that affect CPU rate or cache locality [25], and proximity of the network interface card to cores [29].

Operating system resource management policies can affect performance. An example is task scheduling that switches an actively communicating task, in which case the context switch can take an order of magnitude more time than sending a message using user-level networking [32]. The problem is exacerbated in virtual machine-based multi-tenant environments because the entire virtual machine may be switched [22]. Other factors include contention for system resources such as operating system locks, library/interprocess locks, device access locks, bus access, and network interface buffers [20].

Variation in the hardware can be a source of variation in network latency, such as when a CPU disables some cores in order to conserve power when not in use [21]. Factors that affect compute nodes can also affect intermediate nodes or network devices such as routers and switches in which buffers used during the routing of packets can be a source of contention [18]. Network stalls, where a packet is dropped due to a busy receiver or full buffer, have been evidentially identified as an important predictor in parallel application performance [6].

2.2 Low-latency Networking

Efforts to reduce the mean latency in HPC networks have resulted in a lengthy history of research and developed products such as Myrinet and InfiniBand. In this section, we provide background on InfiniBand and describe features that reduce both the mean and variation of network latency.

InfiniBand is the dominant low-latency network fabric for HPC. There are several factors that make it well suited for low latency networking. First, InfiniBand utilizes a zero-copy protocol. Traditional network stacks such as Ethernet are implemented such that multiple copies of each packet are made into and out of intermediate buffers. For example, to send the contents of a buffer from a user-space application, it is first copied to a kernel buffer, then to a network interface buffer, transmitted across the network, copied into a kernel buffer on the destination machine, then copied from the kernel buffer to a user-space buffer on the destination machine. With zero-copy protocols, the application allocates memory on the source and destination network interfaces. It then writes the information directly to the network interface, transmits it across the network, then reads it directly from the network interface card. Since there are fewer copies and buffers involved, the messages can be transmitted more quickly and with less variation that a traditional network can provide.

Performance is improved by the kernel bypass feature of InfiniBand. In an Ethernet stack, the operating system kernel maintains locks and controls for the network interface. This requires a trap into the kernel whenever a packet is to be sent. This trap introduces overhead and provides the kernel an opportunity to call schedule() or otherwise change contexts. These context switches can be expensive since registers and other process state must be saved prior to the trap. In comparison, InfiniBand allows the user to control the transmission in user-space using a special driver design that moves all privileged (kernel-mode) operations to the setup and tear down phases of the card for the process. This allows the user to write to a memory-mapped register on the card to send a packet. This is often accomplished by a thin-wrapper library called libibverbs which delegates to a device specific driver library using a macro to ensure in-lining of the functions. These optimizations allow for more efficient transmission of packets because variable length traps are not required.

Finally, InfiniBand performs network-offloading. Once the user writes to the register that posts a particular message, the network interface takes ownership of the task to send the message, and the CPU can continue to process other instructions. This allows for the computer to enqueue messages quickly and consistently rather than waiting for the variable length messages to be sent.

While InfiniBand and similar low-latency networking technologies remove sources of latency variation that can be attributed to the OS kernel, contention for the network device by competing processes introduces nondeterministic access delays that can result in long-tailed latency distributions in packet delivery.

3 DESIGN AND IMPLEMENTATION OF THE LATENCY INJECTOR

A key contribution of this paper is the design and implementation of the latency injector that we use in our experiments. This injector allows us to introduce delay to outgoing packets so that we can observe the effects on higher level applications. Most importantly, the delay added to each packet is sampled from a random variable, the parameters of which can model patterns observed in a real system.

We implemented the latency injector for InfiniBand cards that use the ipath and mlx4 drivers. However, the design is reasonably portable to any libibverbs compatible driver. The injector is programmed with four design goals. The injector should:

- avoid unnecessary performance impact to applications,
- support custom latency distributions,
- allow changing distribution parameters without recompiling the library, and
- not require changes to or recompilation of applications.

3.1 Injection Method

The injector consists of hooks on two methods, init and post_send. The names for these methods vary in InfiniBand implementations, but are responsible for initializing the user-space driver and posting a packet to the dispatch queue, respectively.

Hooking init. There are three key facets of the hooking init method, shown in Algorithm 1. First, we only load the distribution file into static memory at library initialization to avoid the overhead of kernel operations in later calls. This also allows us to easily customize the latency distribution for each experiment without recompilation. Secondly, we also load a seed file. This allows us to obtain consistent random results between runs of the experiments. Third, we disable the library if we fail to load the distribution or the seed file. This allows for easily alternating between injected and non-injected experiments.

Algorithm 1 init

$enabled \leftarrow exists(dist\_file) \&\& exists(seed\_file)$
if *enabled* **then**
   $dist\_table \leftarrow load\_table(dist\_file)$
   $seed \leftarrow load\_seed(seed\_file)$
else
   $warn\_user()$
end if

The distribution file contains 512 lines of eight space-separated integers. The entries in this file correspond to amounts of delay in units to add to each request. This design is consistent with the tc component of the netem command which provides similar behavior for Ethernet networks. The seed file contains a single integer corresponding to the random seed to be loaded.

Hooking post_send. Despite the name of the method, post_send does not occur after a send occurs, but rather before. It is called to add an RDMA instruction to the queue of instructions to be processed.

Algorithm 2 post_send

---
if enabled **then**
   $index \leftarrow random\_index()$
   $delay \leftarrow dist\_table[index]$
   $i \leftarrow 0$
   while $i < delay$ **do**
      $i \leftarrow i + 1$
   end while
end if

There are several key facets to the post_send function, shown in Algorithm 2. First, we do not simply use sleep() or pselect() + SIGALRM to implement a micro-second sleep. This is due to the implementation in the Linux kernel of sleep and select. Both of these calls trigger a trap into the kernel, defeating the purpose of user-space InfiniBand networking. Additionally, even if the trap overhead is insignificant, the kernel calls schedule() during both of these calls. These operations result in unpredictable sleep times when events are measured in the microsecond range of InfiniBand latency. Instead, we implement a busy wait, incrementing a static volatile variable to ensure that operations to the index are never optimized. This results in a user-space sleep operation over which we have reasonably precise control.

Secondly, instead of using a kernel-based source of randomness we utilize a constant time linear congruential pseudo-random generator. This is to avoid a trap into the kernel for entropy, but also to ensure a consistent length operation. Linear congruential generators also have the nice property of requiring little state, thus leaving the cache clean for other variables.

We then use the lower 12 bits to index into the distribution table, letting us avoid an expensive division operation. This also allows us to customize the distribution of latency without having to compute values from this distribution at runtime.

We generate distribution files off-line using a Python application and SciPy distributions [17]. This gives access to a variety of high quality distribution sampling routines for various distributions.

We choose to add the latency to the top of the post_send method for two reasons. First, the lock for interacting with the RDMA memory is not grabbed until later in the function. This allows for multiple threads to use RDMA without waiting on a locked thread that is busy waiting. Secondly, this happens after our timing instrumentation occurs so that the time spent in the busy wait is included in the measurements of the InfiniBand verb latency.

3.2 Validation

To verify that the latency injector works as intended, we collected measurements of synthetic background load as described in Section 4, fitted both uniform and log-normal distributions to each collected dataset, generated distribution tables according to the fit parameters, and then performed the same measurement while substituting injected latency for background load. The mean injected latency closely emulates the measured characteristics of each background load pattern.

3.3 Applicability to Other Networks and Hardware

One possible alternative design is to instrument `libibverbs`. All InfiniBand implementations use the `libibverbs` abstraction to have a common interface to the user-space drivers. However, the `post_send` method is implemented as a macro, which means that applications would need to be recompiled in order to be able to use our version of the library. Since many InfiniBand applications have closed source components, we did not choose this option.

One other possible design is to simply use a longer cable to create higher latency. We did not choose this alternative for the obvious inconvenience of requiring more than 40 different cables for our experimental suite. In addition, the various required lengths of cable required are not available as commercial–off–the–shelf products, and cables do not allow us to artificially inject latency variation that is needed for our final suite of experiments.

One question that arises is how much effort is required to port these changes to other InfiniBand libraries. We ported our library to Mellanox cards that use the `mlx4` driver. This case required finding the names of the `init` and `post_send` methods, adding the instrumentation code to the library, and recompiling.

4 ENVIRONMENT AND METHODOLOGY

In this section we describe the methodology used to create a controlled test environment for later experiments. Measurements of low-latency networks are fine-grained and sensitive to perturbations by other systems. Our goal is to minimize or eliminate noise in our testbed and to collect high quality measurements to ensure that relationships between independent and dependent variables are correctly characterized.

4.1 Experimentation Environment

4.1.1 Hardware Configuration. We ran our experiments on Cloudlab c8220 nodes [30], which were equipped as outlined in Table 1. This particular hardware was chosen to provide enough cores to support our MPI experiment configurations with one core per process, and adequate memory per process for each benchmark. To allow addition of an artificial latency generator in the network device driver, we chose hardware with QLogic InfiniBand cards that have an open source user-space driver.

We additionally validated our experiments on Cloudlab c6320 nodes. These nodes share the characteristics we identify as ideal for our experiments, and are equipped as outlined in Table 2. Results were similar and produced identical conclusions between the two hardware types, so the c6320 results have been omitted for brevity.

Cloudlab provides a means of specifying a desired network topology that it constructs using software defined networking (SDN). However, at the time of writing the Cloudlab InfiniBand experimental network is not managed by SDN. We accounted for any variation in the InfiniBand network by ensuring that all nodes were connected to the same InfiniBand switch. The Cloudlab control network, using 1Gb/s Ethernet, uses top-of-rack switches that may introduce artifacts in non-Infiniband communication in certain conditions, such as nodes being in different racks. We accounted for this variation by testing the latency between all nodes. If a node was found to have statistically higher latency than its neighbors

Table 1: Cloudlab c8220 Nodes

Hardware	Description
CPU	Two Intel E5-2660 v2 10-core CPUs at 2.20 GHz (Ivy Bridge)
RAM	256GB ECC Memory (16x 16 GB DDR4 1600MT/s dual rank RDIMMs
Disk	Two 1 TB 7.2K RPM 3G SATA HDDs
NIC	Dual-port Intel 10Gbe NIC (PCIe v3.0, 8 lanes)
NIC	QLogic QLE 7340 40 Gb/s InfiniBand HCA (PCIe v3.0, 8 lanes)

Table 2: Cloudlab c6320 Nodes

Hardware	Description
CPU	Two Intel E5-2683 v3 14-core CPUs at 2.00 GHz (Haswell)
RAM	256GB ECC Memory
Disk	Two 1 TB 7.2K RPM 3G SATA HDDs
NIC	Dual-port Intel 10Gbe NIC (X520)
NIC	QLogic QLE 7340 40 Gb/s InfiniBand HCA (PCIe v3.0, 8 lanes)

(to the level of $\alpha = 0.05$), that node was removed from testing and another was selected.

4.1.2 Software stack. Given the sensitive nature of latency measurements below $10\mu s$ and awareness of the impact of OS noise on parallel computer performance [27], the software configuration was carefully tuned to minimize noise and eliminate extraneous variables. To avoid introducing traffic over the processor interconnect in a dual-socket system, we designed our experiments to use the cores of a single CPU package with the shortest electrical distance to the network interface over the PCIe bus. We also required that core "0" was not used for experiment processes, as the operating system always assigns certain critical tasks to that core. As our MPI experiments required 8 processes per node, the hardware was required to have more than 8 physical cores per CPU package.

We ran the experiments on a patched Ubuntu 16.04. To prevent OS scheduling of tasks on the same cores as our experiment processes, we controlled the CPU affinity of tasks by isolating physical cores 2-9 on CPU 0 of each node with the kernel flag `isolcpus=4-27`, and then forcing MPI to distribute processes only among those cores. This required a minor change to the Linux kernel to prevent scheduling kernel tasks on the isolated cores, a known issue that is detailed in [10].

Other OS configurations included disabling hyperthreading and disabling CPU low power states to prevent clock speed throttling. We achieved this using the kernel commandline options `processor.max_cstate=1` and `intel_idle.max_cstate=0`.

We compiled our experimental codes using gcc version 5.4.0. When flags were not provided by the benchmark code, we used the flags `-O3 -march=native`. When build flags were provided, we used the provided flags.

We chose OpenMPI 1.10.2 from the Ubuntu repositories as our MPI implementation because of its performance on InfiniBand interconnects. At the application level we chose the NASA Advanced Supercomputing (NAS) Parallel Benchmarks (NPB) version 3.3.1 [3].

We also modified the ipathverbs user-space driver version 1.3 to introduce a latency injector. More information on these modifications can be found in Section 3.

The entire environment was deployed and managed using Ansible [11]. The playbooks and helper scripts are available at [34].

4.2 Common Methodology

Packet level. We conducted experiments to measure the performance of the network interfaces with a minimal amount of overhead. We chose codes from the perftest package from the Open Fabrics Enterprise Distribution (OFED) [2], which is well–established for testing InfiniBand performance at the packet level. In particular, we used ib_write_lat with Reliable Connection (RC) transport protocol. This tool uses raw InfiniBand commands (called *verbs*) to measure the time to send remote write commands with delivery confirmation, and forms a low level pingpong test.

We did not consider other tests from OFED such as atomic or send operations because they introduce additional operations above and beyond that of ib_write_lat, and have higher latency and latency variation because they require additional CPU assistance to complete. Our preliminary experiments indicated use of a software MTU of 2048 bytes as the most efficient configuration without message fragmentation.

Library level. The purpose of these tests is to capture the performance in a more realistic scenario where a well–established abstraction such as MPI is used. We used two codes: ping-pong, which times a sequence of MPI_Send and MPI_Recv calls between two processes, and barrier, which tests the efficiency of collective communications by calling MPI_Barrier on eight nodes. In each of tests, the time to complete a single operation was considered the runtime.

Application level. The NPB consist of a suite of codes designed to test many features of a high performance computing cluster, including its network, based on problems seen in computational fluid dynamics. It consists of five benchmarks: Integer Sort (IS), Embarrassingly Parallel (EP), Conjugate Gradiant (CG), MultiGrid (MG), and 3D Fast Fourier Transform (FT). Of these benchmarks, three of them have high communication volume: CG, MG, and FT [3]. The NPB also include three pseudo applications: a block tri-diagonal solver (BT), a scalar penta-diagonal solver (SP), and a lower-upper Gauss-Seidel solver (LU). These tests stress the network interconnect and provide a model of latency variation similar to real-world network conditions.

Table 3: NAS Parallel Benchmarks Tests

Name		size	procs	nodes	Mpkts	GB
Conjugate Gradient	CG	C	64	8	9.30	3.92
3D fast Fourier Transform	FT	C	64	8	22.34	9.76
Integer Sort	IS	C	64	8	2.77	1.22
Lower-Upper Gause-Seidel	LU	B	64	8	4.75	0.62
Multi-Grid	MG	C	64	8	1.47	0.55

To examine the effects of increased latency variation on real applications, we executed the NAS Parallel Benchmarks across the eight nodes in our cluster. We ran five of the eight included tests, detailed in Table 3. NPB problem sizes were chosen to ensure a long enough runtime for repeatable results, and the number of processors was chosen to fit each test's particular requirements while being evenly divisible by our eight nodes. In Table 3, size corresponds to the NPB problem size (e.g., A-F, where C is a "medium" size) we configured for our cluster, procs corresponds to the number of processes used at that size, nodes is the number of compute nodes the processes were divided between, Mpackets corresponds to the number of millions of packets sent across the network, and GB corresponds to the number of gigabytes of traffic generated during the experiment.

5 WORKLOAD CHARACTERIZATION

In this section we describe our methodology for simulating and characterizing the effects of network resource contention (i.e., congestion). Our goal is to measure the effect of network device contention on latency at the packet level, so that we can create a latency model for controlled emulation of congested network resources. This model allows us to configure our latency injector to match various levels of congestion without introducing other effects of real congestion such as high CPU or memory usage.

5.1 Characterization Procedure

To simulate network congestion, we created an MPI-based network load generator to send data between pairs of compute nodes, saturating the one-way bandwidth between the network interfaces. We then controlled the level of congestion by altering the proportion of time that the sending node was transmitting. By having each node run the application twice in both sending and receiving mode, we were able to saturate a fraction of the node's maximum transmission rate. For each measurement of congested performance, we ran the load generator on all involved nodes, as illustrated in Figure 1.

The sending application, detailed in Algorithm 3, is based on the "leaky bucket" rate control mechanism first described in [33]. To simulate the transmission characteristics of applications competing for network resources, we sampled the delays between messages from an exponential distribution, which models the long-tailed and highly variable inter-message gaps in large flow background traffic observed in [1]. Samples were provided by a Mersenne Twister

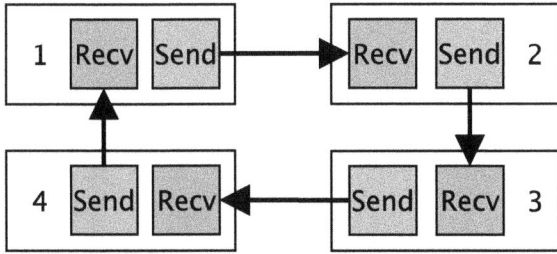

Figure 1: Send/receive pairs of background load generating processes on four compute nodes. Each pair saturates a controllable fraction of the one-way bandwidth between two compute nodes.

19937 pseudo-random number generator, which provides high quality entropy for its performance [23].

Algorithm 3 Congestion Simulator

```
clock_gettime(CLOCK_MONOTONIC, &last_time);
nsec_delay ← 0;
while !stopping do
    if nsec_bucket ≥ nsec_delay then
        MPI_Send(. . . )
        nsec_bucket -= nsec_delay;
        nsec_delay = random_from_exponential();
    end if
    clock_gettime(CLOCK_MONOTONIC, &cur_time);
    diff_time ← cur_time - last_time;
    last_time ← cur_time;
    nsec_bucket += diff_time
end while
```

A key feature to observe from Algorithm 3 is that we used the POSIX interface `clock_gettime` to measure time. It has two important characteristics: `clock_gettime` is the highest performing and most precise clock available on most POSIX systems, and it does not require a trap into the kernel to measure the time as `gettimeofday` and other interfaces do. On the x86_64 hardware that we used, it is implemented using a read of a timing register on the processor.

5.2 Characterization Results

Figures 2 and 3 illustrate the effects of background load on network packet latency for our topology, expressed as a percentage of the network interface's bandwidth. As the simulated network load increases from 0% to 100%, latency mean and variation increase as the sending applications compete for the network device queues.

There are two conditions to notice about the characterization results. First, for congestion above 80%, the latency mean and standard deviation become highly chaotic. For that reason we restrict the remainder of the measurement studies to simulated congestions below 80%. We leave studies of the higher region for future work. Secondly, we observe that our results of increasing mean and standard deviation of latency are consistent with the existing work on congestion. While the particular distribution collected is hardware

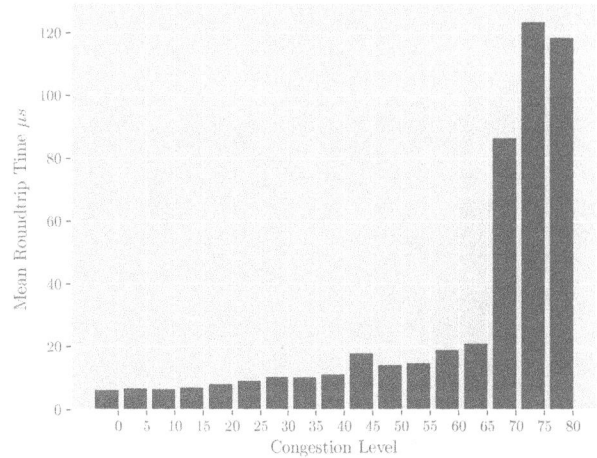

Figure 2: Mean round trip time in a congested environment. As congestion increases, so does the mean latency.

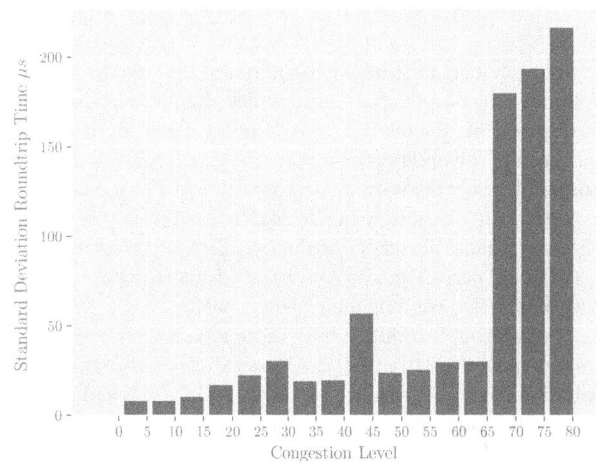

Figure 3: Round trip time standard deviation in a congested environment. As congestion increases, so does the standard deviation.

and software dependent, the general shape center, and spread are consistent across hardware.

5.3 Modeling the Existing Distribution

To create synthetic latency that models the observations of workload congestion, we fit statistical distributions to the measured latency at each workload level. For an example distribution without background congestion, refer to Figure 4. We observe that the distribution is skew-right. Preliminary curve fitting showed that it is best modeled by a log–normal function, which is intuitive because of the unique property of the log–normal distribution to model a combination of many random variables. The dominant mode is at approximately $6.1\mu s$ with a minor mode of $7.2\mu s$. When plotted against cumulative packet count, the higher latency values are correlated with harmonics of the CPU and PCIe bus frequencies occurring approximately every 45 to $50\mu s$.

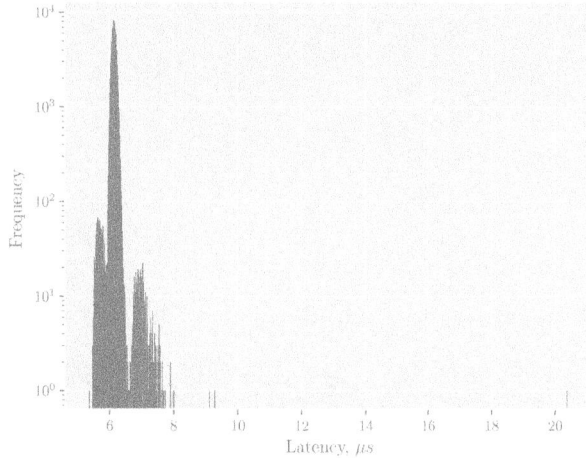

Figure 4: Distribution of latency of packets is tight, and highly skew right in an environment with no background congestion. Note the outlier observation above 20μs.

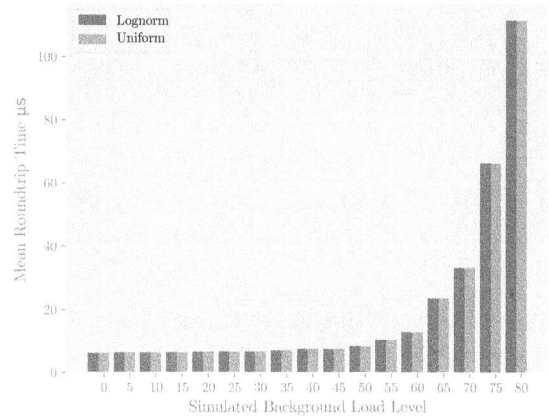

Figure 5: Mean observed latency of InfiniBand packets with injected delay. The distributions have equivalent means at each level of simulated latency. This validates the choice of distributions from the workload classification.

For each level of synthetic background load, we fit five distributions to the observed network latency: a lognormal distribution that closely fits the observations, a uniform distribution that fits the mean of the observations (note that this is equivalent to a lognormal distribution with zero variance), and three intermediate lognormal distributions with altered shape and scale that retain the observed mean. This set of distributions allow us to test the hypothesis that an increase in latency variance is more highly correlated with application runtime than latency mean.

The uniform distribution only has one parameter, mean, which was computed directly from the observations. The lognormal distribution has three parameters: shape, scale, and location. We estimated the parameters by using SciPy's `lognormal.fit` method for the corresponding level of congestion [17]. For intermediate distributions, we varied the scale parameter to values at 25%, 50%, and 75% of the observed scale, and then used binary search to identify a shape parameter that resulted in a mean equivalent to the observations.

Finally, we wrote a generator that uses the distributions from the statistical functions included in SciPy 0.16.1 to generate the distribution files for use with the latency injector. The distribution files generated along with the distribution file generator are included with the source code distribution [34].

6 EXPERIMENTAL SUITE 1: LATENCY VARIATION, APART FROM CONGESTION, CAUSES APPLICATION DEGRADATION

In this section, we use the results of our workload characterization to show that even without congestion or contention, latency variation is sufficient to cause application degradation. We accomplish this by simulating latencies along the distributions caused by congestion and contention. By injecting the latencies, no network resources are constrained during these tests.

We use the same tests that we utilized in workload characterization, except that instead of running a background process to induce

load, we use the latency injector. Ideally, we would just increase the standard deviation of the distribution. However, by virtue of increasing the standard deviation of a distribution with a strong lower bound, we would also raise its mean. Therefore, we must also consider a distribution where we just increase the mean but leave the spread unperturbed.

We consider two distributions: 1) one where we increase only the mean (Uniform), and 2) one where we increase the mean and standard deviation (Lognorm). The means of these distributions were chosen to correspond to the means of the distributions caused by synthetic workload congestion.

Packet level. At the packet level, we have results that are as expected. In Figure 5 we observe that the two distributions have very similar mean values. That is, mean latency of network packets is the same mean (Uniform) as compared to when latency is injected to increase the mean and variance (Lognorm). This validates the calculation of distributions from the measured congestion distributions and also validates the functionality of the latency injector.

We also observe in Figure 6 some of the differences between these distributions. Here we see that the median latency is significantly higher for the uniform distribution at higher load levels than the lognorm distribution. This suggests as we observe that there are a few very large latencies that were measured in the lognorm distribution that were not present in the uniform distribution. We finally observe that there is little difference between the uniform distribution mean and median.

When we examined the results from the packet and library levels, we determined that their runtime distributions were not normally distributed. We confirmed our suspicions using the Kolmogorov–Smirnov test for Normality [26] (p=0.0, $\alpha = .05$)[1]. With non–normal distributions we cannot use parametric statistical methods for evaluation. Instead, we rely on the nonparametric Mann–Whitney U

---

[1]due to limited precision of the hardware the result rounds to 0

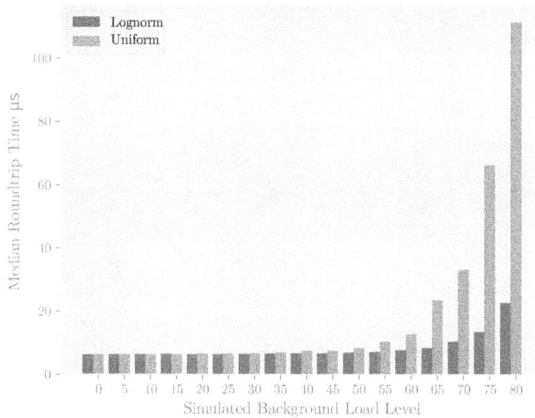

Figure 6: Median observed latency of InfiniBand packets with injected delay. Observe that lognorm has a lower median at higher simulated latencies, but matched mean. This indicates there are a small number of large latencies at higher simulated latency levels.

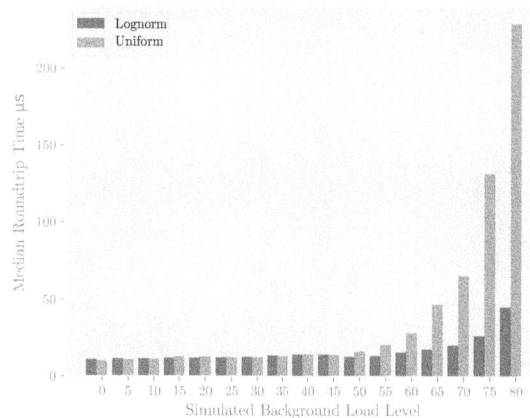

Figure 8: Median round trip time of MPI ping pong. Again, the results at the packet level carry over to the library level. The lower median time of lognorm compared to the mean indicates higher variance.

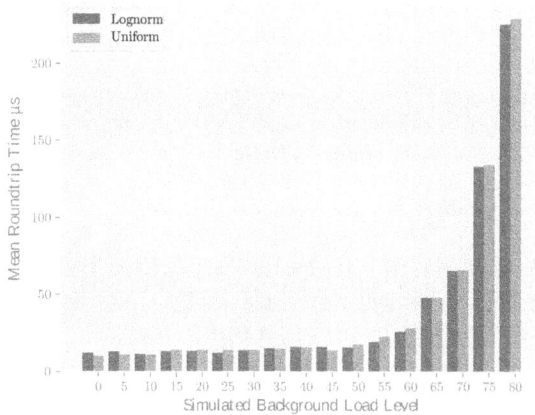

Figure 7: Mean round trip time of MPI ping pong, similar to the results from the packet level. The mean is slightly higher than the packet level tests which represents overhead at the library level.

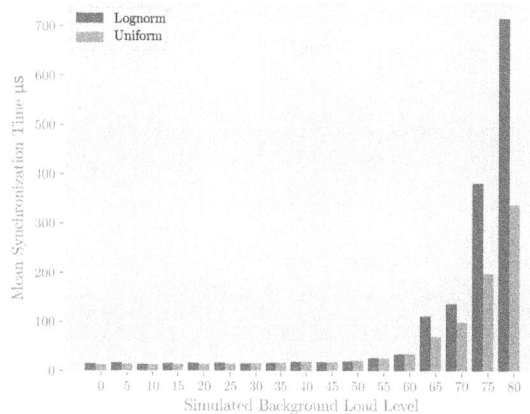

Figure 9: Mean time to synchronize in an MPI barrier. Unlike the packet level test, the means diverge. This is to be expected as synchronization time is determined by the slowest member.

test, in which the null hypothesis states that neither sample stochastically dominates the other. Nonparametric tests do not require the values to be sampled from a normal distribution.

Library level. At the MPI library level, we see a slightly more interesting picture. First, we consider the results from the MPI pingpong test. We observe in Figures 7 and 8 that the MPI results have the same shape, centers, and spreads as the packet level results, with a slightly higher latency. This is consistent with a small amount of constant overhead introduced by the MPI framework.

Secondly, we consider the results from the MPI barrier test. As opposed to the packet level test, we see in Figure 9 that the mean latencies diverge at higher synthetic latencies (Note the higher range on the y-axis). We also observe that the lognorm distribution results in higher mean values of latency. This is to be expected as the

lognorm distribution produces a small number of extremely large latencies. The mean, being sensitive to these extremes, is pulled to the largest values. The median displays a shape and spread that is similar to that of the pingpong test (Figure 10). This is consistent with the robustness of the median to a few extreme values. The vast majority of the latencies in the lognormal are shorter than the mean, resulting in a smaller median latency than uniform distribution.

Application level. Unlike the packet and library level, the application runtimes follow normal distributions. As such we are justified in using traditional statistical parametric methods to evaluate these results. We show only the results for the mean; there are no substantive differences between the mean and median for these results. This can be explained in part by the central limit theorem [19] which states that the sum of independent random variables tends towards normality when the sample is suitably large. Secondly,

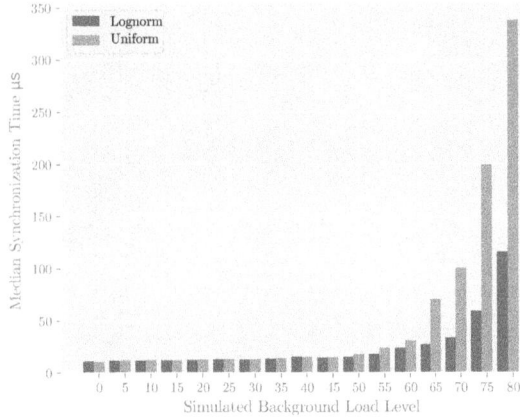

Figure 10: Median time to synchronize in an MPI barrier, where the results are similar to ping pong with slightly higher latency. This is consistent with the medians robustness to extreme values.

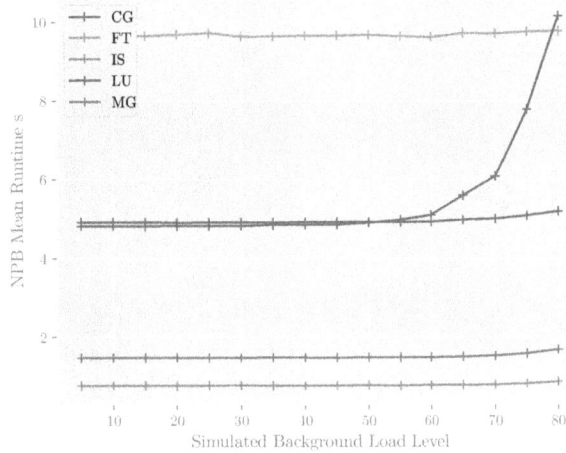

Figure 11: NPB runtimes with a uniform distribution of injected latency. The increased mean results in noticeably higher runtimes in LU only.

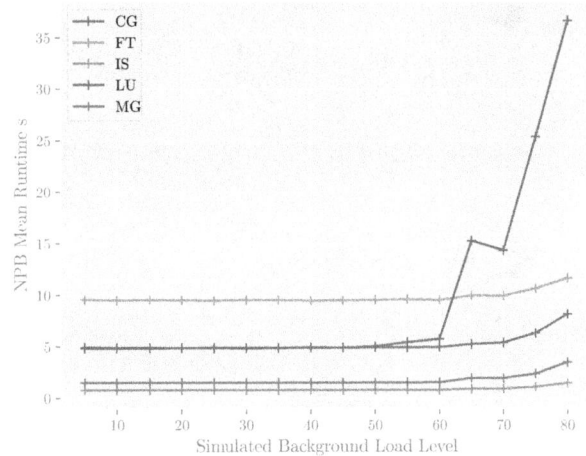

Figure 12: NPB runtimes with a lognormal distribution of injected latency. The increased spread results in significantly greater runtime for LU, but also greater run times for the communication intensive CG, FT, and MG.

the latency variation has a significant effect on the runtime of applications beyond that of mean latency.

In Experimental Suite I we have demonstrated that increased latency variation is sufficient to cause application degradation. We have traced these effects from the packet level up to the application level, and have shown that this phenomenon is reproducible even without other effects of contention or congestion.

7 EXPERIMENTAL SUITE 2: LATENCY VARIATION IS MORE HIGHLY CORRELATED WITH APPLICATION DEGRADATION THAN LATENCY MEAN

In this section we examine the claim that latency variation better explains application degradation than latency mean. We analyze the results from the previous section, focusing on the application layer – NPB tests. For each test from the NPB, we plot its application runtime against latency mean for the injected distribution. We assess the strength of a linear relationship between runtime and mean using Pearson's Coefficient of Correlation [19]. Similarly, for each test from the NPB, we plot its application runtime against latency standard deviation for the injected distribution. Again, we assess the strength of a linear relationship between runtime and standard deviation using Pearson's Coefficient of Correlation. We carefully choose the underlying distributions to inject so as to hold the mean constant for subset of experiments that correspond to a given simulated congestion level. We vary the standard deviation of the latency in each subset of experiments by adjusting the scale parameter of the injected distribution.

Figure 13 shows the relationship between the mean latency and application runtimes. We observe that a linear relationship is a plausible model for explaining application runtimes with respect to latency mean. Similarly, Figure 14 shows the relationship between the latency standard deviation and application runtimes. Again, a linear relationship is a plausible model for explaining application

unlike the previous levels, we are measuring total application run time as opposed to a particular message delivery time. Both of these factors drive the overall distribution towards normality and, in effect, the mean towards the median.

There are some interesting results at this level. First, observe in Figure 11 that the majority of the applications are relatively unaffected by the increases in latency mean at higher synthetic latencies. The principal exception is the LU solver code runtime which roughly doubles at higher latency values. This can be explained by the communication–intensive nature of the LU solver.

Then, observe in Figure 12 that several of the applications increase run times at higher levels of variation in synthetic latency. The LU code roughly increases its runtime by a factor of 3.5. The communication intensive CG, FT, and MG codes also show increases in runtime that are not apparent in Figure 11. This suggests that

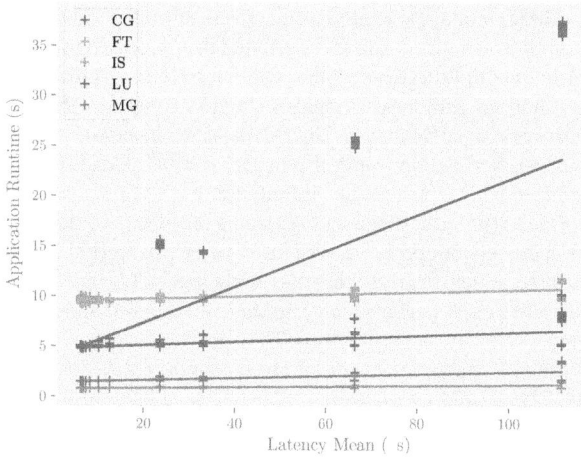

Figure 13: Mean runtime of NPB tests vs. increased mean latency. Random scatter above and below the line of best fit indicates the suitability of a linear model. High and low spreads about the line of best fit correspond to different standard deviations.

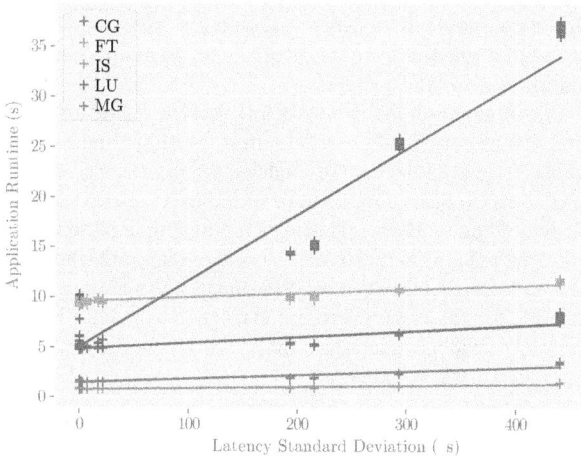

Figure 14: Mean runtime of NPB tests vs. increased latency variation. Tight fitting about the line of best fit indicates the strength of the model. Unlike the mean, variations above and below the line are not correlated with different means.

runtimes with respect to latency standard deviation. We further observe that of the five applications tested, the performance of the LU Decomposition application suffers the most radical effects of changes in latency. In the worst case in with a latency standard deviation above $400\mu s$, the application runs 3.5 times slower than when the standard deviation near zero.

To access the strength of the relationship between latency mean and latency standard deviation vs. runtime, we Pearson's correlation coefficient for each test. These results are summarized in Table 4. A sample correlation coefficient (usually labeled r) above 0.7 is evidence of a linear relation, and a correlation coefficient above 0.9 is evidence of a strong linear relationship [19]. As shown in

Table 4: Correlation Results Rounded to the Nearest.01

Test	r_{mean}	r_{std}	Significant?
FT	0.70	.89	$p = 7.89 \times 10^{-33}$
CG	0.73	.91	$p = 4.94 \times 10^{-39}$
IS	0.76	.93	$p = 8.89 \times 10^{-50}$
MG	0.73	.95	$p = 1.31 \times 10^{-93}$
LU	0.76	.97	$p = 5.24 \times 10^{-148}$

Table 4, the correlation coefficient, r_{mean}, that tests the strength of the linear relationship between the FT application runtimes and latency mean is $r_{mean} = 0.70$. The correlation coefficient, r_{std}, that tests the strength of the linear relationship between the FT application runtimes and latency standard deviation is $r_{std} = 0.89$. The correlation coefficients for four other NPB applications are also shown in Table 4.

The values in the column labeled "Significant?" are calculated using the Fisher z transform[19], derived as:

$$\frac{1}{\sqrt{2\pi}} \int_{-\infty}^{z} e^{\frac{-t^2}{2}} dt$$

where,

$$z = \frac{arctanh(r_{mean}) - arctanh(r_{std})}{\sqrt{\frac{2}{n-3}}}$$

The very small values (close to zero) in the column labeled "Significant?" indicate that the difference between r_{mean} and r_{std} is highly statistically significant (to the level of $\alpha = 0.05$) for all applications tested, meaning that the network latency variation is more highly correlated with application runtimes than network latency mean values. Pearson's coefficient is not considered to be robust to outliers; however, as illustrated in Figure 14, the residuals between the line of best fit and observed values are sufficiently small. Thus, outliers are not a primary factor in the correlation coefficients.

Finally, we examine the performance impact of latency variation on application runtime. We examine two sets of experiments. In each set the mean network latency is fixed and there are several values for the network latency variation. We chose experiment sets with network mean latency that correspond to a congestion level of 20% and a congestion level of 70%, which are typically-observed means in cluster networks. In Figure 15, we see that for a fixed mean corresponding to a congestion of 20%, changes in the standard deviation of network latency have a limited effect. However, in Figure 16, we see that for a fixed mean corresponding to a network congestion of 70%, increases in standard deviation cause a substantial increase to application runtimes. In particular, LU shows a nearly 25% increase in runtime with the larger latency variation, while CG and MG show more modest increases in runtime of 5% to 10%. Together, these charts suggests future work to study at which level of latency mean that latency variation begins to have a substantial effect on application runtime.

Based on the results of Experimental Suite II, we conclude that the mean latency is strictly less correlated with application runtime than latency standard deviation for all tests we considered. We

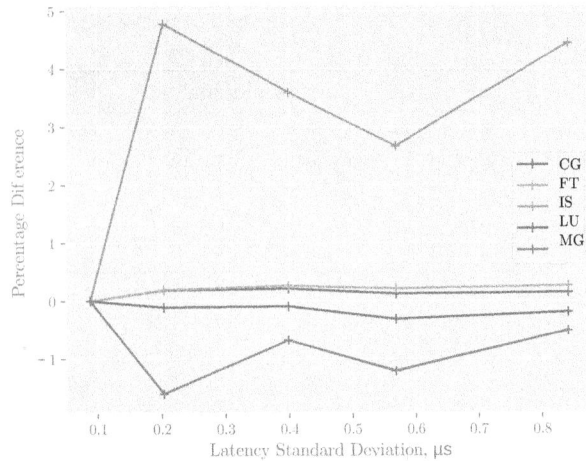

Figure 15: Difference in mean NPB runtime relative to zero injected latency. At the 20% level of network congestion, increases in standard deviation have a limited effect to application runtimes.

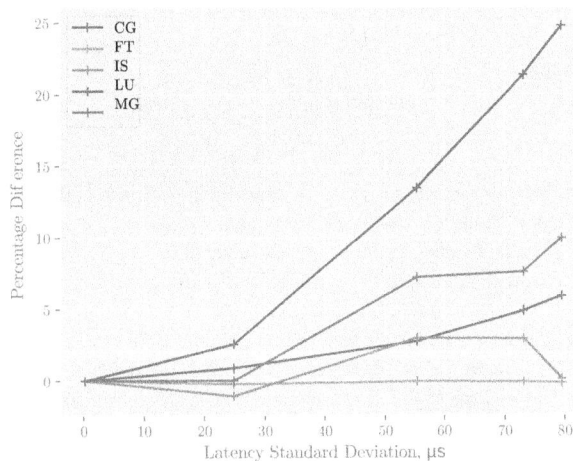

Figure 16: Difference in mean NPB runtime relative to zero injected latency. At the 70% level of network congestion, increases in standard deviation correspond to significant increases in application runtime.

calculated the significance of the difference in the correlation coefficient results using Fisher's Z transformation. We find the results to be statistically significant (to the level of $\alpha = 0.05$), indicating that measurements that are this different are unlikely to occur by chance. The key result is that latency variation is more highly correlated with application runtime than latency mean.

8 RELATED WORK

Network latency is a fundamental concern in HPC system design, and there exists a large body of knowledge on its role in application performance. In this section, we highlight the work that complements this paper, and clarify our specific contributions.

Alizadeh et al [1] explored the effects of high bandwidth consumption on network latency, and found that increased competition for buffers in Ethernet switches could lead to long-tailed latency distributions with measurements as high as 1000 times the median. Our work is partly inspired by theirs, as we questioned whether the latency variation would also impact HPC workloads using MPI and zero-copy networks like InfiniBand.

One of the earliest papers to examine the effects of latency variation on network protocols was the done by Zhang et al in [36]. In their work, they observed that the throughput of TCP streams could degrade if ACK packets were significantly delayed and triggered congestion control mechanisms. They proposed some adjustments to the TCP congestion control protocol to reduce the effects of ACK clustering. Unlike their work on the effects of latency on network control algorithms, our work focuses on the impact of this variation on applications supported by the network.

There have been many studies of the effect of congestion on network latency. [4, 5, 15] and [16] observed that increased bandwidth contention on links between nodes in a large cluster resulted in larger mean latencies and significant impact on HPC workloads. These studies essentially show that congestion introduces additional latency, and that latency variation increases when congestion is present as there is additional contention for the hardware. Our work asserts that latency variation can have negative effects in and of itself, and the impacts of latency variation can be more significant than mean latency.

One other aspect that our work intersects is tooling for synthetic load. Our approach induces CPU spin at the InfiniBand driver level, similar to [35]. However, we modeled the interface on the traffic control (tc) tool, a component of which uses a distribution input file for adding randomized latency on outgoing IP packets passing through the Linux kernel packet scheduler. Our work complements tc by allowing latency control on a subset of QLogic and Mellanox InfiniBand cards at sub-microsecond resolution, and builds on prior work by providing an interface and support tools that enable future work with artificial latency.

9 CONCLUSIONS AND FUTURE WORK

In this paper we have presented the design and implementation of a configurable latency injector for many Mellanox and QLogic InfiniBand cards. The latency injector offers features not found in prior similar work, and can be extended to include network cards beyond the original implementations. We have presented measurement and workload characterization studies of the distributions of latency in network performance for an InfiniBand network in an HPC environment. These distributions are utilized directly in two experimental suites. We have presented an experimental methodology using synthetically-generated latency to demonstrate the effects of latency variation on HPC workloads. In the worst case, we measured that the LU application runs 3.5 times slower for high variation than when the standard deviation is near zero.

We found statistically significant evidence that latency variation is more highly correlated with HPC application performance than latency mean alone. This result is somewhat surprising, since studies that focus on mean latency alone have shown the strong impacts of low message latency to applications in an HPC environment.

We believe that these results may be important to consider in the design of scalable HPC systems and applications. As multitenancy becomes increasingly common in dedicated HPC systems and as HPC applications are more commonly run on cloud architectures, competition for network resources could lead to increased levels of network latency variation. We have demonstrated that serious degradation of application performance can result from high variation in latency.

Future work is to consider how to manage variation in latency in HPC networks that implement low latency protocols, and to consider the impacts and management of latency variation in enterprise or cloud environments where low latency protocols are not implemented, but where high variation in latency can occur due to sharing of network resources across user applications. The ultimate control over these factors that affect the variation of latency is to move to a real-time operating system and application environment. We do not advocate that here, since the slowdown imposed by the real-time constraints may impact performance more than network latency variation alone. Investigation of which factors have the most impact and systematically evaluating the resolution of the factors are aspects of future work.

ACKNOWLEDGMENTS

Funding for this research was provided by the National Science Foundation under award numbers 1642542 and 1633608. We utilized Cloudlab hardware for these experiments[30]. We utilized Pandas and SciPy extensively for statistical analysis [17, 24].

REFERENCES

[1] Mohammad Alizadeh, Albert Greenberg, David A Maltz, Jitendra Padhye, Parveen Patel, Balaji Prabhakar, Sudipta Sengupta, and Murari Sridharan. 2010. Data center TCP (DCTCP). In *ACM SIGCOMM Computer Communication Review*, Vol. 40. ACM, 63–74.

[2] OpenFabrics Alliance. 2012. Openfabrics Enterprise Distribution. (2012). https://www.openfabrics.org/index.php/openfabrics-software.html

[3] David H Bailey, Eric Barszcz, John T Barton, David S Browning, Robert L Carter, Leonardo Dagum, Rod A Fatoohi, Paul O Frederickson, Thomas A Lasinski, Rob S Schreiber, et al. 1991. The NAS parallel benchmarks. *The International Journal of Supercomputing Applications* 5, 3 (1991), 63–73.

[4] Abhinav Bhatelé and Laxmikant V Kalé. 2009. Quantifying network contention on large parallel machines. *Parallel Processing Letters* 19, 04 (2009), 553–572.

[5] Abhinav Bhatelé, Kathryn Mohror, Steven H Langer, and Katherine E Isaacs. 2013. There goes the neighborhood: performance degradation due to nearby jobs. In *Proceedings of the International Conference on High Performance Computing, Networking, Storage and Analysis*. ACM, 41.

[6] Abhinav Bhatelé, Andrew R Titus, Jayaraman J Thiagarajan, Nikhil Jain, Todd Gamblin, Peer-Timo Bremer, Martin Schulz, and Laxmikant V Kalé. 2015. Identifying the culprits behind network congestion. In *Parallel and Distributed Processing Symposium (IPDPS), 2015 IEEE International*. IEEE, 113–122.

[7] Mark S Birrittella, Mark Debbage, Ram Huggahalli, James Kunz, Tom Lovett, Todd Rimmer, Keith D Underwood, and Robert C Zak. 2015. Intel® Omni-path architecture: Enabling scalable, high performance fabrics. In *High-Performance Interconnects (HOTI), 2015 IEEE 23rd Annual Symposium on*. IEEE, 1–9.

[8] Nanette J Boden, Danny Cohen, Robert E Felderman, Alan E. Kulawik, Charles L Seitz, Jakov N Seizovic, and Wen-King Su. 1995. Myrinet: A gigabit-per-second local area network. *IEEE Micro* 15, 1 (1995), 29–36.

[9] David Culler, Richard Karp, David Patterson, Abhijit Sahay, Klaus Erik Schauser, Eunice Santos, Ramesh Subramonian, and Thorsten Von Eicken. 1993. LogP: Towards a realistic model of parallel computation. In *ACM Sigplan Notices*, Vol. 28. ACM, 1–12.

[10] Daniel Bristot de Oliveira. 2015. [RFC] workqueue: avoiding unbounded wq on isolated CPUs by default. (2015). https://lists.gt.net/linux/kernel/2218495

[11] Michael DeHaan. 2012. Ansible. (2012). https://www.github.com/ansible/ansible [Online].

[12] Corbin Higgs and Jason Anderson. 2016. Narrowing the Gap: Effects of Latency with Docker in IP Networks. In *The International Conference for High Performance Computing, Networking, Storage and Analysis, Student Poster*.

[13] Torsten Hoefler, Lavinio Cerquetti, Torsten Mehlan, Frank Mietke, and Wolfgang Rehm. 2005. A practical approach to the rating of barrier algorithms using the LogP model and Open MPI. In *Parallel Processing, 2005. ICPP 2005 Workshops. International Conference Workshops on*. IEEE, 562–569.

[14] Keith R Jackson, Lavanya Ramakrishnan, Krishna Muriki, Shane Canon, Shreyas Cholia, John Shalf, Harvey J Wasserman, and Nicholas J Wright. 2010. Performance analysis of high performance computing applications on the Amazon Web Services cloud. In *Cloud Computing Technology and Science (CloudCom), 2010 IEEE Second International Conference on*. IEEE, 159–168.

[15] Van Jacobson. 1988. Congestion avoidance and control. In *ACM SIGCOMM Computer Communication Review*, Vol. 18. ACM, 314–329.

[16] Ana Jokanovic, Jose Carlos Sancho, German Rodriguez, Alejandro Lucero, Cyriel Minkenberg, and Jesus Labarta. 2015. Quiet neighborhoods: Key to protect job performance predictability. In *Parallel and Distributed Processing Symposium (IPDPS), 2015 IEEE International*. IEEE, 449–459.

[17] Eric Jones, Travis Oliphant, Pearu Peterson, et al. 2001–. SciPy: Open source scientific tools for Python. (2001–). http://www.scipy.org/ [Online].

[18] Mark Karol, Michael Hluchyj, and Samuel Morgan. 1987. Input versus output queueing on a space-division packet switch. *IEEE Transactions on Communications* 35, 12 (1987), 1347–1356.

[19] G. Maurice Kendall. 1948. *The Advanced Theory Of Statistics*. Vol. 1. Charles Griffin and Company Limited, 42 Drury Lane, London.

[20] Richard B Langley. 1997. GPS receiver system noise. *GPS World* 8, 6 (1997), 40–45.

[21] Jacob Leverich, Matteo Monchiero, Vanish Talwar, Parthasarathy Ranganathan, and Christos Kozyrakis. 2009. Power management of datacenter workloads using per-core power gating. *IEEE Computer Architecture Letters* 8, 2 (2009), 48–51.

[22] J Martin, V Rajasekaran, and James Westall. 2005. Virtual machine effects on network traffic dynamics. In *Performance, Computing, and Communications Conference, 2005. IPCCC 2005. 24th IEEE International*. IEEE, 233–238.

[23] Makoto Matsumoto and Takuji Nishimura. 1998. Mersenne Twister: a 623-dimensionally equidistributed uniform pseudo-random number generator. *ACM Transactions on Modeling and Computer Simulation (TOMACS)* 8, 1 (1998), 3–30.

[24] Wes McKinney. 2010. Data Structures for Statistical Computing in Python. In *Proceedings of the 9th Python in Science Conference*, Stéfan van der Walt and Jarrod Millman (Eds.). 51 – 56.

[25] Daniel Molka, Daniel Hackenberg, Robert Schone, and Matthias S Muller. 2009. Memory performance and cache coherency effects on an Intel Nehalem multiprocessor system. In *Parallel Architectures and Compilation Techniques, 2009. PACT'09. 18th International Conference on*. IEEE, 261–270.

[26] Gottfried E. Noether. 1967. *Elements of Nonparametric Statistics*. John Wiley and Sons, Inc., New York.

[27] Fabrizio Petrini, Darren J Kerbyson, and Scott Pakin. 2003. The case of the missing supercomputer performance: achieving optimal performance on the 8,192 processors of ASCI Q. In *Supercomputing, 2003 ACM/IEEE Conference*. IEEE, 55–55.

[28] Gregory F Pfister. 2001. An introduction to the Infiniband architecture. *High Performance Mass Storage and Parallel I/O* 42 (2001), 617–632.

[29] Rolf Rabenseifner, Georg Hager, and Gabriele Jost. 2009. Hybrid MPI/OpenMP parallel programming on clusters of multi-core SMP nodes. In *Parallel, Distributed and Network-based Processing, 2009 17th Euromicro International Conference on*. IEEE, 427–436.

[30] Robert Ricci, Eric Eide, and the CloudLab Team. 2014. Introducing CloudLab: scientific infrastructure for advancing cloud architectures and applications. *;login:* 39, 6 (Dec. 2014), 36–38. https://www.usenix.org/publications/login/dec14/ricci

[31] Stephen M Rumble, Diego Ongaro, Ryan Stutsman, Mendel Rosenblum, and John K Ousterhout. 2011. It's time for low latency. In *HotOS*, Vol. 13. 11–11.

[32] Piyush Shivam, Pete Wyckoff, and Dhabaleswar Panda. 2001. EMP: zero-copy OS-bypass NIC-driven gigabit ethernet message passing. In *Supercomputing, ACM/IEEE 2001 Conference*. IEEE, 49–49.

[33] Jonathan Turner. 1986. New directions in communications (or which way to the information age?). *IEEE communications Magazine* 24, 10 (1986), 8–15.

[34] Robert Underwood, Jason Anderson, and Amy Apon. 2018. ICPE 2018 Artifact - Measuring Network Latency Variation Impacts to High Performance Computing Application Performance. (Jan 2018). https://doi.org/10.5281/zenodo.1145911

[35] Qi Wang, Ludmila Cherkasova, Jun Li, and Haris Volos. 2016. Interconnect emulator for aiding performance analysis of distributed memory applications. In *Proceedings of the 7th ACM/SPEC on International Conference on Performance Engineering*. ACM, 75–83.

[36] Lixia Zhang, Scott Shenker, and Daivd D Clark. 1991. Observations on the dynamics of a congestion control algorithm: The effects of two-way traffic. *ACM SIGCOMM Computer Communication Review* 21, 4 (1991), 133–147.

Pattern-based Modeling of Multiresilience Solutions for High-Performance Computing

Rizwan A. Ashraf, Saurabh Hukerikar, and Christian Engelmann

[ashrafra,hukerikarsr,engelmannc]@ornl.gov

Computer Science and Mathematics Division,

Oak Ridge National Laboratory,

Oak Ridge, Tennessee 37831, USA

ABSTRACT

Resiliency is the ability of large-scale high-performance computing (HPC) applications to gracefully handle errors, and recover from failures. In this paper, we propose a pattern-based approach to constructing resilience solutions that handle multiple error modes. Using resilience patterns, we evaluate the performance and reliability characteristics of detection, containment and mitigation techniques for transient errors that cause silent data corruptions and techniques for fail-stop errors that result in process failures. We demonstrate the design and implementation of the multiresilience solution based on patterns instantiated across multiple layers of the system stack. The patterns are integrated to work together to achieve resiliency to different error types in a performance-efficient manner.

CCS CONCEPTS

• **Software and its engineering** → **Software fault tolerance**;

KEYWORDS

Resilience; Solver; Soft Errors; Process Failures; Checkpoint/Restart

ACM Reference Format:

Rizwan A. Ashraf, Saurabh Hukerikar, and Christian Engelmann. 2018. Pattern-based Modeling of Multiresilience Solutions for High-Performance Computing. In *Proceedings of ACM/SPEC International Conference on Performance Engineering, Berlin, Germany, April 9–13, 2018 (ICPE '18),* 8 pages. https://doi.org/10.1145/3184407.3184421

1 INTRODUCTION

Resiliency solutions provide capabilities for high-performance computing (HPC) applications to deal with the effects of different types of errors, and recover from failures. Resiliency is becoming an increasingly important attribute for HPC systems and their applications, as systems of unprecedented scale and complexity are designed and deployed for running advanced scientific simulation, modeling, big-data analysis and machine learning applications. The continuous occurrence of faults is typical on the fastest supercomputing systems today due to reduction in reliability of individual system components caused by shrinking process technology, and operation at low voltage. As a consequence of these disturbing trends, and the growing complexity of the architectures and the software environment of HPC systems, future extreme-scale systems are projected to encounter frequent, persistent and erratic errors of different types [4]. Therefore, the development of comprehensive resiliency solutions is critical to deliver sustained high performance for scientific applications.

Many of the resilience solutions in use today are designed to support a specific fault model. However, fault analyses indicate that modern HPC systems experience multiple types of error events with different levels of severity in terms of the application's ability to produce a correct solution and their impact on performance. Transient errors that cause silent data corruptions in the application state may result in outcomes ranging from loss in precision to wildly incorrect results. Unrecoverable errors often result in fail-stop behavior, which is fatal for the application program. Therefore, HPC applications require multiresilience solutions that provide comprehensive protection against multiple modes of errors. These solutions must be constructed systematically through integration of various techniques to detect and gracefully handle the error events without sacrificing application performance.

In this paper, we demonstrate a performance-oriented approach to the design and implementation of software-based multiresilience solutions. We leverage resilience design patterns, which we developed in previous work [11], to identify and evaluate techniques for detection, containment and mitigation for specific error modes. We explore an implementation of the complete multiresilience solution, in which patterns are instantiated across multiple layers of the system stack and work together to achieve required levels of performance and resiliency. The pattern-based approach also enables global optimization of the solution, avoiding costly over-protection and emphasizing end-to-end application performance. With this approach, we make the following significant contributions:

- We demonstrate a novel approach based on resilience design patterns that systematically explores techniques with different performance and reliability characteristics, and enables the design of comprehensive multiresilience solutions through composition of patterns.

This manuscript has been authored by UT-Battelle, LLC under Contract No. DE-AC05-00OR22725 with the U.S. Department of Energy. The United States Government retains and the publisher, by accepting the article for publication, acknowledges that the United States Government retains a non-exclusive, paid-up, irrevocable, worldwide license to publish or reproduce the published form of this manuscript, or allow others to do so, for United States Government purposes. The Department of Energy will provide public access to these results of federally sponsored research in accordance with the DOE Public Access Plan (http://energy.gov/downloads/doe-public-access-plan).

- We design a cross-layer multiresilience solution from conception to implementation using patterns for linear solver methods. The solution is implemented by instantiating algorithmic patterns to work in concert with patterns incorporated in the message-passing layer of a parallel application.
- We present a detailed experimental evaluation of our pattern-based solution that assesses the interdependencies between patterns for hard and soft errors, and characterizes the performance of the complete multiresilience solution.

2 BACKGROUND: DESIGN PATTERNS FOR RESILIENCE

Design patterns describe a generalizable solution to a recurring problem that occurs within a well-defined context. Many of the HPC resilience solutions in use today are based on a fixed set of techniques that are repeatedly found in various solutions. We mined existing solutions, which have been used in HPC environments to confront faults, errors and failures, to discover patterns [11].

Each resilience design pattern consists of a set of activation and response interfaces, and a behavior specification, which describes the semantics of how the pattern handles a fault event and its consequences. While the patterns are not finished designs that can be transformed into code, they outline the strategies for detecting a fault, error, or a failure, limiting its propagation, and mitigating its impact through recovery or masking. Therefore, discrete implementations of the same pattern may have different levels of performance and reliability characteristics. We presented the resilience design patterns in a catalog [10], which organizes the patterns in a layered hierarchy. Based on the insight that HPC resilience has two important aspects, namely the forward progress of an application and the consistency and fidelity of an application's data, the catalog broadly categorizes patterns into state and behavioral patterns.

2.1 State Patterns

The state patterns describe the protection domain of a resilience solution. These patterns encapsulate the particular aspects of an application's state. The careful scoping of the protection domain enables defining the resilience behavior in a modular fashion for the specific domain captured by the state pattern. The selection of the state pattern also helps define the containment scope, i.e., the scope of how far a fault or error event propagates. The state patterns have been classified into: (1) *Static State* pattern, which encapsulates the application data that is computed once in the initialization phase and is unchanged thereafter, (2) *Dynamic State* pattern, which describes the changing application state as the application progresses, (3) *Environment State* pattern, which includes the state necessary to perform the computation, i.e., program code, environment variables, libraries, etc, and (4) *Stateless* pattern, which defines null state, enabling designers to create solutions that define behavior without predefined scope.

2.2 Behavioral Patterns

The behavioral patterns identify common detection, containment, mitigation techniques that enable an application or the system that instantiates and implements these patterns to cope with the presence of fault, error, or failure events. These patterns have been classified hierarchically describing solutions from abstract to concrete. The categories include: (1) *Strategy* patterns, which describe high-level solutions for fault treatment, error or failure recovery and compensation. (2) *Architecture* patterns, which convey specific methods necessary for the construction of a resilience solution. These patterns are a sub-class to the strategy patterns. Both the architecture and strategy patterns are organized by the types of event (fault, error or failure) they handle and the specific actions taken to handle an event. (3) *Structural* patterns, which provide concrete description of a solution that is intended to guide the implementation of the resilience solution. These patterns describe specific solutions for fault monitoring and prediction, the forward and backward checkpoint recovery, and patterns that describe the specific ways of applying the redundancy approaches.

3 PATTERN-BASED MODELING OF MULTIRESILIENCE SOLUTIONS

Among the difficult challenges that face HPC application developers and system designers is the emergence of different types of errors caused by intermittent or permanent faults, gradual degradation and system aging related effects. Naïvely stacking multiple resilience solutions often leads to overprotection, and is exorbitantly expensive in terms of the overhead to application performance, since each solution for each fault types imposes its own overhead. In order for applications to harness the capabilities of modern extreme-scale HPC systems, comprehensive resilience solutions must be designed and implemented thoughtfully and methodically.

In this section, we explore the construction of multiresilience solutions for HPC applications using the resilience design patterns to guide the selection of techniques for detection, containment and mitigation, and for optimization of the protection domain and overall application performance. As a case study, we choose an iterative linear solver since such solver methods are at the heart of most scientific simulation and modeling applications. Our design of a multiresilience solution aims to address two of the most prevalent fault models in modern HPC systems, including transient errors that result in silent data corruptions (SDCs) and unrecoverable errors, which in the context of parallel applications based on communicating processes tends to be fatal causing failure of the entire application. The scope of this work is limited to faults which affect application correctness or completion, and does not include faults which explicitly affect performance, such as due to a slow parallel file system, a congested network, a code bug during application development, etc.

The patterns in our catalog [10] each have significantly different performance efficiency and complexity characteristics. Therefore, we quantitatively evaluate their viability for our context. The complete design of the multiresilience solution entails combining the selected patterns and optimizing their interactions to ensure complete protection to both error types while delivering greater end-to-end application performance.

3.1 Patterns for Soft Error (SE) Detection and Mitigation

Soft errors that cause SDCs affect the convergence properties of a linear solver method. A typical linear solver method solves a system of equations of the form $Ax = b$, in which the matrix A and right hand side vector b are known, and we solve to determine vector x. When affected by SDCs during the solution phase, the corruption may cause unbounded numerical errors in the outcome, slower convergence to solution, or the premature termination of the solver. However, application specific knowledge about the data structures and the algorithm used is required to detect SDCs in the solver and mitigate their effects.

State Patterns for SE resilience: In the linear solver, the operand matrix A and right hand side vector b are initialized during the setup and remain unchanged throughout the computation. Therefore, variables A and b are encapsulated in *static* state patterns. The solution vector x is updated as the solver makes progress, until the linear solver converges. The remainder of the variables, which includes matrix index structures, pointers, loop counters, etc, are included in an *environment* state pattern. The separation of the linear solver state into these distinct state patterns enables the exploration of different behavioral patterns for detection and recovery that leverage the properties of each state pattern.

SE Detection Patterns: For detecting the presence of SDCs in application state encapsulated by the *static* state patterns, the behavioral patterns may take advantage of the invariance property of this state from initialization until the solver converges. Between the behavioral strategy patterns that offer *recovery* and *compensation*, the latter is more suitable based on the insight that the protection domain is contained in a static pattern, and therefore the redundant information required for detection is also computed at initialization. In contrast, the *recovery* behavioral pattern incurs the overhead of preserving a checkpoint of its protection domain at periodic intervals, which in the case of a static state pattern is unnecessary.

For the solver's protection domain contained in the *dynamic* state pattern, the detection of SDCs requires insight into the changing nature of the dynamic state, which is a capability supported by the *diagnosis* pattern, and specifically the *monitoring* pattern. This pattern uses cause-effect analysis to infer the presence of faults or errors. For the linear solver application employing an iterative algorithm, the residual error in the solution indicates how close the solver is from a correct solution.

An alternative pattern for detection of SDC that we considered is the *compensation* pattern, which is realized as a *n-modular* pattern. However, SDC detection using this pattern requires at least 2x computation and consumes additional communication bandwidth at large-scale resulting in high performance overheads.

SE Mitigation Patterns: The patterns for mitigating the impact of SDCs on the linear solver application seek to ensure that the solver converges to a correct solution despite SDCs. For the protection domain scope in the *static* state pattern, we apply a *compensation* strategy pattern, which is realized using a *redundancy* architectural pattern. Rather than implement this as a *n-modular redundancy* pattern, we select the *forward error correction* pattern to leverage the structure of the matrix and vector variables.

For the variable state in the *dynamic* state pattern, i.e., the solution vector, we must select the *recovery* pattern; any *compensation* strategy pattern is not viable due to the dynamic nature of the protected state and the exorbitant cost of instantiating modular redundancy pattern. The rollback recovery pattern derivative structural pattern is suitable for this context. This solution entails periodically

preserving the *dynamic* state pattern to persistent storage, which incurs an overhead to the application. However, by limiting the scope of the protection domain to the *dynamic* state pattern, the *recovery* pattern is applied to the solver computation only.

3.2 Patterns for Hard Error (HE) Detection and Recovery

Parallel implementation of linear solver uses distributed memory model with message passing to distribute the problem over multiple processes that run on a number of compute nodes of a HPC system. In the utilized message passing interface (MPI), a communicator is a logical collection of processes that can send messages to each other. The processes use point-to-point or collective primitives to distribute data, exchange partial results and synchronize. The occurrence of an unrecoverable error causes MPI calls made by any process in the communicator to block indefinitely. Most MPI library implementations cannot stabilize after the failure of any one process in the communicator, causing the remaining processes to deadlock, which renders the parallel application incapable of forward progress.

State Patterns for HE resilience: To enable an MPI-based application to survive the occurrence of a hard error, the MPI library implementation must guarantee that it will stabilize the communicator itself following the process failure caused by the hard error, and the application must resolve the loss of partial application state that was resident on the failed process. Therefore, in defining the scope of the protection domain, we encapsulate the MPI library and its runtime into an *environment* state pattern. Much of the variable state associated with linear solver is distributed by partitioning the data in a block manner, i.e., row-wise chunks of matrices and vectors are distributed to processes. When a process failure occurs, all the variable state associated with process is lost. Accordingly, we encapsulate the state of each process in the MPI communicator into *dynamic* state patterns. In this case, there is no advantage to encapsulating the individual variables into different state patterns. Based on such scoping of the MPI-based application's global state, the behavioral patterns for resolving the deadlock in the MPI communicator following a process failure may be applied separately from the behavioral patterns that resolve the loss of part of the solver's operands, i.e., the solution matrix and vector state.

HE Detection Patterns: For the protection domain scope contained by the *environment* state pattern, i.e., the MPI communicator, the detection pattern must determine which processes within a communicator have failed. The *dynamic* state does not require an explicit detection pattern, since any unrecoverable error in the process state propagates to the environment state pattern.

The failure detection pattern for the the *environment* state pattern must be robust, and may take a proactive or a reactive approach. Typical detection techniques use periodic signaling to detect the liveliness of neighboring processes, or by building consensus between the processes alive. For scalability, failure detection may also be local, where failure detection is initiated only among the neighbors of a process. To accomplish detection, we select a *consensus* structural pattern, which is a derivative of the *decentralized detection* strategy pattern. For its implementation, if an application requires timely notification of failure to all processes, then a proactive approach may involve strategic placement of collective operations inside the code, such that a failure is detected early on and costly re-computation is avoided. However, this can lead to high synchronization overheads, especially if there are no failures. Another approach is to wait for error notification by a collective operation in the code, i.e., a reactive approach.

The implementation of the pattern is realizable using the failure detection primitives offered by the User-Level Failure Mitigation (ULFM) [3] implementation of an extended MPI. ULFM provides primitives such as MPI_COMM_AGREE, MPI_COMM_REVOKE, MPI_COMM_FAILURE_ACK, and MPI_COMM_FAILURE_GET_ACKED to facilitate detection. Whereas, notification of failures to other processes is propagated through constructs such as MPI_ERR_REVOKED and MPI_ERR_PROC_FAILED. It should be pointed that use of ULFM constructs require that MPI application changes the default error handler MPI_ERRORS_ARE_FATAL.

HE Recovery Patterns: The mitigation of a parallel application must be concerned with the *environment* and *dynamic* state patterns. The mitigation of the *environment* entails stabilizing the MPI communicator following the detection of a process failure. While the *dynamic* state pattern doesn't explicitly use a pattern for detection, its mitigation is critical since it encapsulates part of the parallel application's state, which is lost upon occurrence of a failure.

To recreate the failed MPI communicator, the *recovery* strategy pattern instantiated as a *reconfiguration* architectural pattern is suitable. This pattern may be instantiated using the *rejuvenation* or *reinitialization* structural pattern. An implementation of this pattern using the ULFM extensions to MPI would use MPI_COMM_SHRINK primitive to isolate a failed process from the MPI communicator used by the application. The key benefit of applying this pattern is that it offers the opportunity to resume the application without the need to resubmit the job to the scheduler in an HPC system.

The hard error mitigation for the *environment* state pattern may also be accomplished by applying the *compensation* strategy pattern. The instantiation of this pattern substitutes the failed process with another from a pool of spare processes. The use of this pattern as opposed to rejuvenation pattern eliminates the need to redistribute the workload among surviving processes which can be time-consuming and strongly application dependent. Besides, some HPC applications have strict requirements on the number of processes due to problem decomposition restrictions or memory pressure on nodes restricting additional workload.

The compensation pattern can be implemented by spawning processes at runtime called cold spares or allocating spare processes during initialization called hot or warm spares depending on how they are used. Hot spares perform active concurrent execution, whereas warm spares are initialized and do nothing until a failure takes place. Warm spares do not maintain any dynamic or static state until they are put into service. There is also no need to have a spare for every process, if only a few failures are expected during the execution of the application. On the other hand, a hot spare is required for every process in the application to sustain arbitrary process failures. This is analogous to redundant computation and does not require the checkpoint pattern for state recovery. However, processes lost over time result in loss of redundancy. Thus, use of hot spares can lead to significantly higher overheads and the inability to sustain failures of lost redundant processes as compared

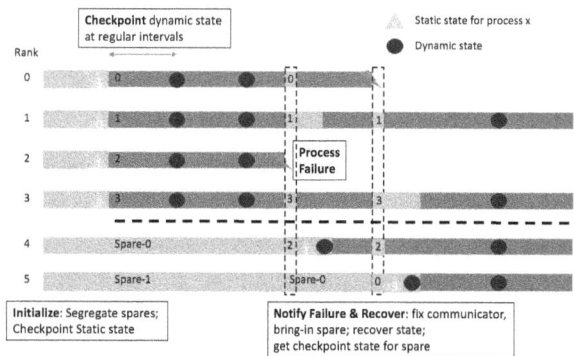

Figure 1: Checkpoint restart pattern using warm spares.

to an approach based on warm or cold spares. In general, spares are useful for applications which perform compute-intensive data distribution plan at the start of the application.

When applying either the rejuvenation or compensation pattern for mitigation of the *environment* state pattern, the *dynamic* state pattern of the failed process must also be mitigated. Since the complete process state is lost in the event of a failure, a *recovery* pattern is appropriate, specifically the *checkpoint restart* pattern. We use in-memory checkpointing on a neighbor process to implement the checkpoint restart pattern, which efficiently leverages point-to-point communication between compute nodes rather than commit the checkpoint to a parallel file system [15]. The in-memory checkpointing is feasible because we have carefully defined the scope of the state patterns thereby limiting the memory overhead required for the checkpoints. The use of *checkpoint restart* pattern with warm spares strategy to mitigate process failures is illustrated in Figure 1.

4 IMPLEMENTATION OF PATTERN-BASED MULTIRESILIENCE FOR LINEAR SOLVER

To demonstrate the design of multiresilience solution for a linear solver application encompassing soft and hard error resilience patterns, we consider the Generalized minimal residual (GMRES) method as a case study. We enumerate the design patterns for defining the protection domain, detection and mitigation patterns for each error class, and subsequently justify our selections. The suitability of patterns working in combination to provide a holistic multiresilience solution is an important consideration.

The GMRES method, which underlies many scientific computing applications, is a Krylov subspace method for the iterative solution of large sparse non-symmetric linear systems [17]. The *flexible* GMRES extends this solver to permit the pre-conditioner to be changed every iteration [16] using inner-outer iterations; the "inner" solve step preconditions the "outer" flexible iteration. The inner-outer solver structure was leveraged to design Fault Tolerant GMRES (FT-GMRES) [8] which provides robustness in the presence of unbounded errors. The FT-GMRES algorithm is designed to reach eventual convergence in the presence of soft errors, i.e., the solver produces a correct outcome at the cost of needing additional iterations to arrive at the right answer. It divides the computation into reliable and unreliable phases, i.e., *selective reliability*. There is

Table 1: Design Summary for Multiresilient FT-GMRES solver.

Fault Model	Pattern Class	Choices	Selection	Reason
Soft Error	State	Dynamic, static, environment	Dynamic	Static state corruption is detectable, environment corruption transforms to process failure
	Detection	Monotonicity, bounded compute, checksums	Bounded compute	About 14 times lower overhead compared to monotonicity pattern
	Recovery	*Solver state:* restart inner, abort inner & restart outer	Restart inner	Low detection latency
		Variable state: checkpoint, checksums	Checkpoint	Less computational overhead
Hard Error	State	Dynamic, static, environment	Dynamic, static, environment	Process failures are fatal for application
	Detection	Proactive, reactive	Proactive	Low overhead & collective in every iteration
	Recovery	*Solver state:* restart inner, abort inner & restart outer	Abort inner & restart outer	Checkpoint state of outer
		MPI environment: cold/warm spares, rejuvenate	Warm spares	Workload distribution
		Variable state: checkpoint-restart, diskless checkpoint, interpolation	Checkpoint-restart	Less computational overhead

no assumption of reliability in the inner solver, i.e., it may return incorrect results as long as the solution is completed in finite time. On the other hand, the outer solver needs to be reliable, which is feasible since most of the time is spent in the inner solver. The outer solver can also detect invalid values within the solution vector and replace them with arbitrary values for forward progress of the solver. The flexible inner-outer iterations have the property that the dimension of the Krylov subspace grows at each outer iteration, which guarantees eventual convergence.

Implementation of SDC Detection and Recovery Patterns
We resolved to applying the monitoring structural pattern for detection of SDCs. The pattern implementation entails defining bounds on values produced during critical computational phases of GMRES. Specifically, an orthogonalization process based on the Arnoldi method is utilized to find orthonormal basis of the Krylov subspace [17]. The basis is used to approximate the solution at each iteration of the solver. The projections produced during this critical computational phase are bounded by the upper bound of Frobenius norm of the input matrix. In a parallel implementation, the comparison of the projection length with the Frobenius norm is performed locally. This pattern implementation is referred to as the *bounded compute* pattern. An alternate algorithmic implementation of this pattern is possible using a monotonicity violation check. This implementation uses sparse matrix-vector multiplication (SpMVM) for calculating residue. While more generally applicable, it incurs as much as 14 times higher overhead in comparison to the implementation based on bounded compute pattern.

For implementing the recovery pattern for SDCs, we use an instantiation of the *rollback* pattern. When applying this pattern, we leverage the inner-outer solver structure that expects high reliability from only the outer solver phases by scoping the rollback recovery pattern to exclude the inner solver phase. Our implementation creates local in-memory checkpoints.

Implementation of HE Detection and Mitigation Patterns
Hard errors in an MPI-based implementation of the GMRES solver causes failure of the affected MPI process. For implementing the process failure detection and mitigation patterns, we embed ULFM primitives in the GMRES solver implementation.

For detection of process failure within the MPI communicator, we leverage the collective SpMVM operations performed in every iteration of the GMRES solver. Detection is done using the returned error codes from MPI collective operations, which are caught by

the error handler for the MPI communicator. Since no additional application code is required, the overhead of the detection pattern's implementation is negligible. For the mitigation of process failures, we implement a compensation strategy pattern, which instantiates a redundancy pattern. The implementation entails the creation of a pool of spare processes, which replace the failed ranks in the communicator; this implementation avoids the need to redistribute workload. For the recovery of the dynamic application state after a failure, we consider an algorithm-based compensation pattern that uses linear interpolation of known correct values to mitigate the affected state. While this method has no overhead during error-free operation, it causes slower convergence of the solver. Therefore, in our solution we apply the rollback recovery pattern for the static and dynamic state recovery after process failures. Its implementation creates in-memory checkpoints on neighboring processes.

Implementing Multiresilience Solution for FT-GMRES Table 1 summarizes our design choices for supporting multiresilience in FT-GMRES solver, describing the various resilience patterns considered for each fault model, the patterns selected for our multiresilience solution as well as the justification for their selection. Based on our empirical evaluation, we select algorithm-based instantiations of the patterns for SDC detection and recovery since they incur low performance overheads. However, the coverage of these pattern instances risks the possibility of prolonged execution on account of additional solver iterations. The selection of rollback pattern for state recovery while handling process failures unintentionally causes the SDC detection pattern to be invoked more often than intended by the application programmer during re-execution after rollback. However, interaction of the rollback pattern with the SDC detection pattern limits propagation of SDC by preventing incorrect state from being captured during checkpointing.

5   EXPERIMENTAL SETUP AND EVALUATION

The FT-GMRES is implemented using the Trilinos 12.6.4 framework [7] and uses the Tpetra package for parallel linear algebra operations such as SpMVM, vector dot products, etc. We use ULFM release 1.1, which is derived from Open MPI-1.7.1, for process failure detection, notification, and rebuilding failed communicators.

Test problem and configuration: We solve a linear problem generated by discretizing a regular 3-D mesh using the Intrepid package [1] in Trilinos framework. The generated sparse matrix has 6,967,871

---
[1]https://trilinos.org/packages/intrepid/

rows and 186,169,411 non-zero elements. We use the same problem size while scaling the number of processes, which causes the size of per-process checkpoint to shrink with increasing process counts. We fix the number of iterations of the inner solver of the FT-GMRES to 25, and number of iterations of the outer solver to 20 for a maximum iteration count of 500.

Evaluation platform: We use a Linux cluster with 40 compute nodes interconnected with a dual-bonded 1 Gbps Ethernet. Each compute node has two AMD Opteron processors (a total of 24 cores) and 64 GB memory, for a total of 960 processor cores. The switches support fully non-blocking point-to-point bandwidth of 215 MB/s. We perform our fault injection experiments with 32, 64, 128, 256, and 512 processes, which are distributed across nodes of the cluster. The spare processes created by hard error recovery pattern instance are mapped to the last physical node. We maintain the same process mapping for all experiments to prevent application performance variability due to mapping.

Soft error injection: The errors are injected at fixed intervals after every 10, 20, or 30 SpMVM operations. We randomly corrupt data elements produced after the completion of a SpMVM operation. These fault rates are chosen to understand the interaction with process failure resilience patterns; injecting a soft error after every 10 SpMVM operations means that the checkpointed dynamic state is affected more often than the injection after every 30 SpMVMs.

Process failure injection: To simulate hard errors and for reproducibility of results, the rank positions of MPI processes to be terminated are pre-selected. We also guarantee that the failed processes are on different physical nodes than the ones on which spare processes are mapped, and that sufficient spares are always available. Following these constraints, the processes are terminated randomly based on an exponential distribution with an average failure rate corresponding to time to complete at least 75 iterations. Under this assumption and based on Young's formulation, the checkpoint of dynamic state is performed at every iteration of the outer solver or after 25 iterations. While other analytical models for estimating the checkpoint interval are available based on failure distributions [1], we found our assumptions to be adequate for this work based on observed failure trends in current HPC systems.

6 RESULTS

The experiments are designed to analyze the reliability and performance characteristics of individual patterns. We therefore evaluate the performance overheads of the patterns with different error rates and process counts. In each case, enough experiments are performed such that standard deviation is low. For instance, the coefficient of variation for all cases range between 0.01 and 0.15.

The main motivation for these experiments is to assess the accuracy with which we can estimate the performance overhead for multiresilience solution from stand-alone soft error and hard error resilience experiments. This provides feasibility and constraints of various combination of patterns by analyzing their performance and resilience impact on the application.

6.1 Soft Error (SE) Resilience

The performance impact with three different soft error injection rates is quantified in Figure 2. The y-axis shows the overhead on

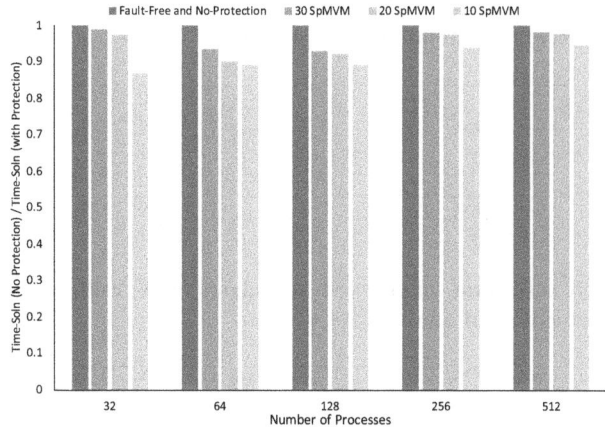

Figure 2: Overheads of SE resilience with error injection after every 30 SpMVM, 20 SpMVM, and 10 SpMVM operations.

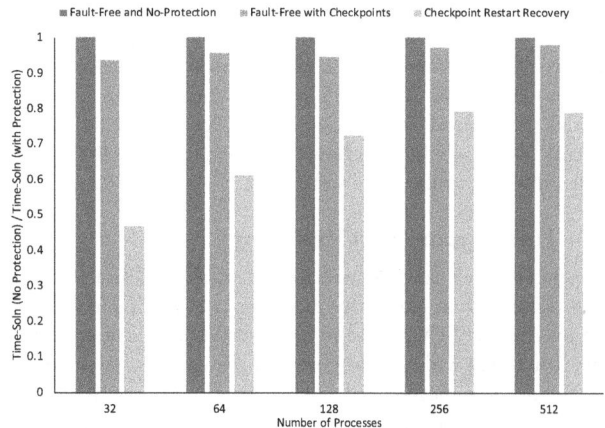

Figure 3: Overheads of PF resilience with up to four process failures using checkpoint restart pattern and warm spares.

time-to-solution of providing resilience to errors, which includes the overheads of including detection and recovery patterns. In all cases, solver converged to a correct solution in the allotted time.

The soft error rates are chosen such that every inner solve operation is corrupted multiple times (10 SpMVM) or once (20 SpMVM), or after every other inner solve operation (30 SpMVM). Results indicate that high SDC rate leads to higher overheads across all processor counts. The prime factor is the slower convergence of the solver in presence of more errors. The breakdown of overheads with two extreme error rates is listed in Table 2. The average number of extra iterations, represented as N_{extra}, consumed with error rate of 10 SpMVM is always higher than at 30 SpMVM. Mostly, the overhead due to extra computation is higher than the combined overheads of detection and recovery, which are represented as t_{SDC-d} and t_{SDC-r}, respectively. On the other hand, the SDC detection and recovery overheads tend to decrease with scale.

Table 2: Breakdown of overheads related to SE resilience as a percentage of total time to solution.

Processes	$t_{SDC-d} + t_{SDC-r}$		N_{extra} [max]	
	30 SpMVM	10 SpMVM	30 SpMVM	10 SpMVM
32	2.06%	8.91%	30.1 [75]	35.5 [150]
64	6.45%	4.75%	26.9 [50]	33.7 [75]
128	8.10%	8.75%	25 [25]	32.5 [125]
256	1.07%	1.94%	32 [50]	35.6 [125]
512	0.69%	0.72%	28.3 [50]	34.6 [100]

Table 3: Breakdown of overheads related to PF resilience as a percentage of total time to solution.

Processes	t_{PF-x}	t_{PF-r}	t_{check} [% dynamic]	$t_{recompute}$
32	0.02%	17.1%	28.1% [25.6%]	10.9%
64	0.03%	9.4%	18.5% [22.9%]	13.4%
128	0.04%	5.4%	12.9% [14.7%]	12.9%
256	0.02%	1.9%	7.5% [16.7%]	13.5%
512	0.05%	1.2%	5.1% [12.2%]	16.2%

The results indicate a tradeoff between SDC detection overhead and the extra computation overhead. The use of monotonicity violation for SDC detection causes high overhead, but the number of extra iterations needed for convergence tends to decrease in comparison to detection based on the bounded computation pattern. Overall, the utilized combination of SDC detection and recovery patterns results in minimum time to solution for FT-GMRES solver while providing resilience to soft errors.

6.2 Hard Error (HE) Resilience

The performance impact of process failure resilience through checkpoint restart pattern and spare processes is quantified in Figure 3. The overheads of checkpointing application state are indicative from 'Fault-Free with Checkpoints' bar in Figure 3, where no process failures are injected. This includes the overheads to perform initial checkpoint of static state and multiple checkpoints of dynamic state. These overheads tend to decrease with increasing number of processes, since the problem size is kept constant. On average, the overheads range between 6.28% to 1.98%.

The overheads of providing mitigation to process failures are indicated from 'Checkpoint Restart Recovery' bar in Figure 3, where up to four independent process failures are injected based on the selected failure rate. Significant overheads are notable at lower processor counts, while overheads tend to decrease at higher processor counts. These overheads include the following components: re-computation time, $t_{recompute}$, time to recover dynamic and static states using checkpoints, t_{PF-r}, time to fix MPI environment and include spares, t_{PF-x}, and the time to perform checkpoint of dynamic and static states, t_{check}.

Our analysis indicates that time to fix the distributed environment tends to be negligible, e.g., it varies between 0.02% to 0.05% of the total time to solution at our scale of experiments. The dominant overheads are due to the following: t_{PF-r}, t_{check} and $t_{recompute}$. These overheads tend to be additive with the number of failures, whereas t_{check} can be controlled via selection of checkpoint interval. The average values of these parameters are listed in Table 3. The checkpoint related overheads tend to decrease with scale from as high as 45% at 32 processes to as low as 6% at 512 processes, since

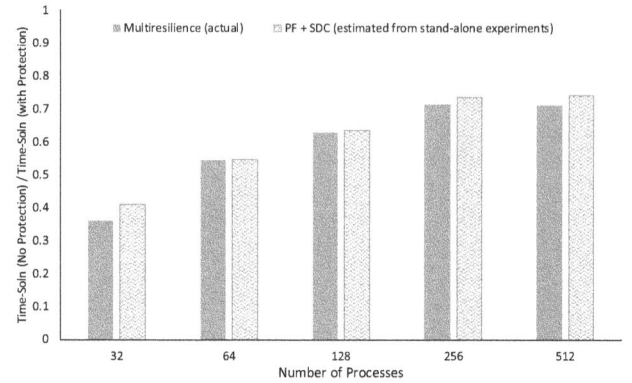

Figure 4: Comparison of normalized times in case of multiresilience solution with estimated times from stand-alone PF resilience and SE resilience experiments.

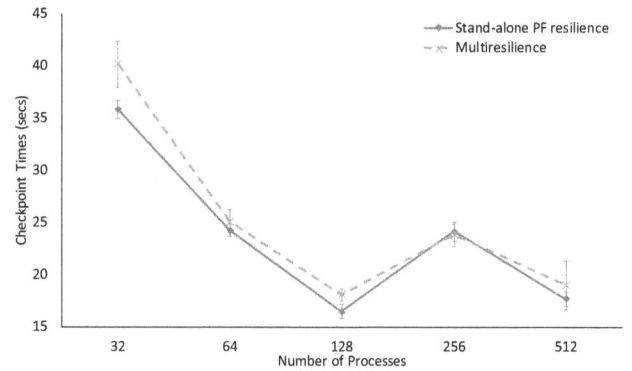

Figure 5: Comparison of average checkpoint times between PF resilience and multiresilience solutions.

the workload is kept constant. The recovery overhead is mostly consumed by the time to deliver application state to the spare process which is put in service, i.e., communication of the spare with the neighbor of the failed process (see Figure 1). Further investigation shows that significantly more time is spent in restoring static state as compared to dynamic state, which emphasizes the need to carefully scope the static and dynamic state patterns.

6.3 Multiresilience Solution

The performance impact of using the proposed multiresilience solution is quantified in Figure 4. In this figure, we also plot an estimate of the time-to-solution (patterned bars) obtained via results from standalone SE and PF resilience experiments. The overheads for multiresilience solution tend to decrease with scale in line with the results obtained from PF experiments. The observed minute discrepancies between estimated and actual times is due to the interaction between PF and SE resilience patterns which is not captured in stand-alone PF experiments. Results in Figure 5 indicate higher average and standard deviation of checkpoint times in multiresilience experiments as compared to stand-alone PF experiments. The higher checkpoint times are primarily due to extra iterations in multiresilience experiments as a result of SDCs (see Table 2) causing more checkpoints to be performed.

In our experiments, we are able to achieve decent overall performance estimates for multiresilience solution using stand-alone experiments for two reasons: 1) the cost of performing extra checkpoints of dynamic state due to SDCs is significantly low (see % dynamic state in checkpoint overhead from Table 3), 2) the additional time to converge to a solution in presence of SDCs is less than the expected time of process failure, preventing accumulation of additional overheads as a result of process failure. This demonstrates that the careful selection of resilience patterns can alleviate some of the complications associated with design of multiresilience solutions for HPC applications. However, in general, it is important to consider the interactions between different resilience patterns.

7 RELATED WORK

There have been numerous proposals for resilience solutions that attempt to solve the challenge at different layers of the system stack. To deal with memory errors, HPC systems use memory modules with error correcting codes (ECC). Algorithm specific schemes, such as algorithm-based fault tolerance (ABFT) apply row and column checksum encoding on dense matrix structures [9], or use the diagonal, banded diagonal, block diagonal structures of sparse problems [18] for application-level detection and correction of errors. The design of solutions that combine capabilities across different layers of the system stack has also been previously explored, but using ad-hoc methods. For example, using the ABFT technique to protect application data structures permits different ECC mechanisms for different page frames in memory [13]. To deal with fail-stop and silent errors simultaneously, recent work has proposed combining ABFT methods with system-based checkpointing [2], in which each computational phase is followed by ABFT verification for SDCs and an in-memory checkpoint. This approach has also been shown to facilitate roll-forward recovery for conjugate gradient solvers [5].

Design patterns have been extensively used in software engineering, particularly in the context of object-oriented (OO) programming [6]. Patterns in this context define class interfaces and inheritance hierarchies, and help establish key relationships among the classes. For parallel software design, there have been efforts to codify the various parallel computation and communication structures into a pattern catalog [14]. The Our Pattern Language (OPL) [12] supports the design and implementation of a parallel algorithm by linking the various parallel design patterns. To the best of our knowledge, this work is the first demonstration of applying resilience design patterns for modeling and implementation of multiresilience solutions.

8 CONCLUSION

A pattern-oriented approach to the design and implementation of a multiresilience solution is described in this paper. We leveraged resilience design patterns to systematically identify and evaluate the appropriate detection and mitigation techniques for two very different fault models: soft errors that cause silent data corruptions and fail-stop failures. We demonstrated the development of a multiresilience solution and presented the experimental evaluation for an iterative linear solver application using algorithm-based pattern instances together with patterns realized using ULFM extensions to MPI. The broader impact of this work is two fold: it demonstrates a structured model-based approach to identifying alternative patterns for detection, containment and mitigation of specific types of errors, and it facilitates the development of roadmaps for architecting multiresilience solutions by composing patterns from multiple layers of the system stack and iteratively refining the pattern relationships to optimize end-to-end application performance.

ACKNOWLEDGMENTS

This material is based upon work supported by the U.S. Department of Energy, Office of Science, Office of Advanced Scientific Computing Research, program manager Lucy Nowell, under contract number DE-AC05-00OR22725. The authors would like to thank James Elliot from Sandia National Laboratories for his help with the FT-GMRES code.

REFERENCES

[1] N. Bajunaid and D. A. Menasce. 2017. Analytic Models of Checkpointing for Concurrent Component-Based Software Systems. In *Proceedings of the 8th ACM/SPEC on International Conference on Performance Engineering (ICPE '17)*.

[2] A. Benoit, A. Cavelan, Y. Robert, and H. Sun. 2015. *Optimal resilience patterns to cope with fail-stop and silent errors*. Research Report RR-8786. LIP - ENS Lyon.

[3] W. Bland, A. Bouteiller, T. Herault, G. Bosilca, and J. Dongarra. 2013. Post-failure recovery of MPI communication capability. *The International Journal of High Performance Computing Applications* 27, 3 (2013), 244–254.

[4] J. Daly et al. 2012. *Inter-Agency Workshop on HPC Resilience at Extreme Scale*. Technical Report. Advanced Computing Systems, National Security Agency.

[5] M. Fasi, Y. Robert, and B. Uçar. 2015. *Combining algorithm-based fault tolerance and checkpointing for iterative solvers*. Research Report RR-8675. INRIA Grenoble - Rhône-Alpes ; INRIA.

[6] E. Gamma, R. Helm, R. Johnson, and J. Vlissides. 1995. *Design Patterns: Elements of Reusable Object-oriented Software*. Addison-Wesley Longman Pub. Co., Inc.

[7] M. A. Heroux et al. 2005. An overview of the Trilinos project. *ACM Trans. Math. Softw.* 31, 3 (2005), 397–423.

[8] M. Hoemmen and M. Heroux. 2011. Fault-Tolerant Iterative Methods via Selective Reliability. In *Proceedings of the International Conference for High Performance Computing, Networking, Storage and Analysis (SC '11)*. 12.

[9] K.-H. Huang and J. A. Abraham. 1984. Algorithm-Based Fault Tolerance for Matrix Operations. *IEEE Trans. Comput.* C-33, 6 (June 1984), 518–528.

[10] S. Hukerikar and C. Engelmann. 2016. *Resilience Design Patterns: A Structured Approach to Resilience at Extreme Scale (Version 1.1)*. Technical Report ORNL/TM-2016/767. Oak Ridge National Laboratory, Oak Ridge, TN, USA.

[11] S. Hukerikar and C. Engelmann. 2017. Resilience Design Patterns: A Structured Approach to Resilience at Extreme Scale. *Supercomputing Frontiers and Innovations* 4, 3 (2017), 1–38.

[12] K. Keutzer and T. Mattson. 2009. Our Pattern Language (OPL): A design pattern language for engineering (parallel) software. In *ParaPLoP Workshop on Parallel Programming Patterns*.

[13] D. Li, Z. Chen, P. Wu, and J. S. Vetter. 2013. Rethinking algorithm-based fault tolerance with a cooperative software-hardware approach. In *International Conference for High Performance Computing, Networking, Storage and Analysis (SC)*.

[14] T. Mattson, B. Sanders, and B. Massingill. 2004. *Patterns for Parallel Programming* (first ed.). Addison-Wesley Professional.

[15] A. Moody, G. Bronevetsky, K. Mohror, and B. R. de Supinski. 2010. Design, Modeling, and Evaluation of a Scalable Multi-level Checkpointing System. In *2010 ACM/IEEE International Conference for High Performance Computing, Networking, Storage and Analysis (SC)*. 1–11.

[16] Y. Saad. 1993. A Flexible Inner-outer Preconditioned GMRES Algorithm. *SIAM J. Sci. Comput.* 14, 2 (March 1993), 461–469.

[17] Y. Saad and M. H Schultz. 1986. GMRES: A Generalized Minimal Residual Algorithm for Solving Nonsymmetric Linear Systems. *SIAM J. Sci. Statist. Comput.* 7, 3 (July 1986), 856–869. https://doi.org/10.1137/0907058

[18] J. Sloan, R. Kumar, and G. Bronevetsky. 2012. Algorithmic approaches to low overhead fault detection for sparse linear algebra. In *Dependable Systems and Networks (DSN), 2012 42nd Annual IEEE/IFIP International Conference on*. 1–12.

Energy and Performance Analysis of Parallel Particle Solvers from the ScaFaCoS Library

Michael Hofmann, Robert Kiesel, Gudula Rünger

Department of Computer Science, Chemnitz University of Technology

{michael.hofmann,robert.kiesel,ruenger}@cs.tu-chemnitz.de

ABSTRACT

Performance analysis in high performance computing (HPC) has traditionally focused on improving application programs, for example, by decreasing the overall runtime or increasing the throughput of floating point operations. However, the same approaches might also be used to influence the energy behavior. Since the increasing energy consumption of HPC platforms is gaining more and more attention, the identification of applications and platforms for which energy and performance measurement lead to differing results is of great importance. In this article, we analyze the energy and performance behavior of particle solvers from the ScaFaCoS library. Four different criteria are investigated with respect to their influence on the energy consumption and achieved performance. These criteria are the solution method chosen, the parameters of the solution method, the degree of parallelism, and the parameters of the hardware platform.

KEYWORDS

particle simulations; energy consumption; performance analysis

ACM Reference Format:

Michael Hofmann, Robert Kiesel, Gudula Rünger. 2018. Energy and Performance Analysis of Parallel Particle Solvers from the ScaFaCoS Library. In *ICPE '18: ACM/SPEC International Conference on Performance Engineering, April 9–13, 2018, Berlin, Germany.* ACM, New York, NY, USA, 8 pages. https://doi.org/10.1145/3184407.3184409

1 INTRODUCTION

The ever increasing usage of computer systems in almost all areas of modern life goes along with increasing operational costs. An important part of these costs is caused by the energy requirements, both directly as a consumable resource as well as indirectly, for example, for power supply infrastructures or cooling facilities. Besides hardware properties, also software-based decisions such as the utilized algorithms and their parameters [12], the exploited degree of parallelism [18], and adjustable hardware parameters such as the processor frequency [10] or the mapping of workloads to processors [16] have an influence on the energy consumption. However, these decisions also affect the achievable performance of applications and their implementation. A joint analysis of energy and performance characteristics is therefore highly required.

Investigations of energy requirements on high performance computing (HPC) platforms are often performed with regard to applications in scientific computing [7]. For these kinds of applications, it is usually more important to determine the solution of a specific problem instead of utilizing a specific hardware or software. This allows for various optimizations where time-to-solution and energy-to-solution can be seen as competing goals. Particle simulations are widely used in different areas of computational scientific, such as biology, chemistry, and astrophysics. A major computational part of the simulations is spent for determining long-range particle interactions such as Coulomb or gravitational interactions. Several efficient methods with individual parameters exist for the computation of these interactions, thus providing various opportunities for investigating their energy and performance behavior.

In this article, we analyze the energy consumption and the performance of different parallel particle solvers from the ScaFaCoS library[1]. The library contains, for example, hierarchical methods such as the Fast Multipole Method (FMM) and the Barnes-Hut algorithm or mesh-based methods such as Particle-Particle-Particle-Mesh (P^3M) and Particle-Particle NFFT (P^2NFFT). All solvers are utilized through a common programming interface and compute the same particle interactions in parallel. Thus, the library allows to solve a single problem with several methods that might expose different energy and performance behaviors. Four different aspects are investigated to analyze the behavior of the particle solvers:

    I. varying the utilized solver method,
    II. varying parameters of the solver method,
    III. varying the degree of parallelism, and
    IV. varying the hardware platform.

The energy consumption and the performance of the solvers are determined experimentally using particle systems of different size and hardware platforms with different processor microarchitectures. The analyses investigate whether there are situations in which the energy behavior deviates from the performance behavior. Identifying such situations is a necessary requirement for improvements where either an optimal (i. e., lowest) energy consumption or an optimal (i. e., highest) performance is preferred.

The rest of this article is organized as follows: Section 2 introduces the ScaFaCoS library and the different variation approaches. Section 3 describes the hardware and software environment and the particle solvers. Section 4 presents the experimental results. Section 5 discusses related work and Section 6 concludes the article.

[1] http://www.scafacos.de

2 ENERGY AND PERFORMANCE INFLUENCES ON PARTICLE SOLVERS

Particle solvers for Coulomb interactions are compute and data intensive program parts of particle simulations. In the following, the ScaFaCoS library with different solver methods and the different variation approaches for influencing the energy and performance behavior of the computations are described.

2.1 Scalable Fast Coulomb Solvers (ScaFaCoS)

The ScaFaCoS library is a numerical software library that contains various methods for the calculation of long-range particle interactions, i. e. Coulomb or gravitational interactions. The provided solver methods include tree-based methods, such as the Fast Multipole Method (FMM) [11] or the Barnes-Hut algorithm [5], as well as mesh-based methods, such as Particle-Particle-Particle-Mesh (P^3M) [3] or fast summations based on nonequispaced fast Fourier transforms (P^2NFFT) [15]. Parallelization is implemented using the Message Passing Interface (MPI). The library provides a common programming interface for invoking the different solver methods. Thus, alternative solver methods can be employed without additional programming efforts. However, additional solver-specific parameters can be set individually for each solver method. Additional information about the solver methods of the library and a comparison of their capabilities is presented in [4].

After building the ScaFaCoS library, the utilization within an application program proceeds in the following steps:

- Initialization of a solver method.
- Setting of particle system properties.
- Setting of solver-specific parameters.
- Tuning of the solver method.
- Computation of particle interactions.
- Termination of the solver method.

These steps have to be executed in parallel by all participating MPI processes. The input data describing the particle system consists of the three-dimensional position and the charge value of each particle. The user of the library is responsible for distributing the particle data initially among the processes such that each process contributes its local share of the overall particle system. Computing the particle interactions represents the step with the main computational effort. This step might also be executed repeatedly, for example, with slightly changing particle positions in a particle dynamics simulation.

2.2 Variation approaches for energy and performance behaviors

Applications in scientific computing are usually focused on the solution of a specific problem (e. g., with numerical simulations) instead of utilizing a specific hardware platform or software implementation. This might allow to vary several aspects of the calculations and computations as long as the determined results are the acceptable, for example, in terms of correctness or accuracy. To analyze the energy and performance behavior of the particle solver methods, the following four variation approaches are investigated:

I. **Variation of the solver method:** For many computational problems, there exist several alternative approaches or algorithms. Their different program codes lead to a different utilization of the hardware platform, for example, due to the employed operations or memory access patterns. Thus, depending on the executed program code, individual energy and performance behaviors might be expose. The ScaFaCoS library contains several alternative algorithms for computing Coulomb interactions of particle systems. All solver methods are able to compute the same results, even though they might differ in terms of the achieved accuracy. However, in general it is possible to choose the specific solver method as part of an optimization towards energy or performance.

II. **Variation of solver parameters:** Algorithms and implementations usually have parameters that control their computational behavior. The resulting different kinds of computations lead to the execution of different parts of the program codes which might expose different performance and energy behaviors. Important parameters of the solver methods of the ScaFaCoS library are, for example, the tree depths for the tree-based methods or the mesh sizes for the for mesh-based methods. These parameters determine the separation of the overall computations into near-field computations (i. e., direct computations of pairwise particle interactions) and far-field computation (i. e., approximations of interactions of groups of particles). Since both kinds of computations represent different parts of the program codes, shifting the computational load between them can be adapted as part of an optimization towards energy or performance.

III. **Variation of the degree of parallelism:** The degree of parallelism of a parallel program code is controlled by specifying its number of processes or threads. Increasing the parallelism can lead to lower runtimes and a higher computational performance. Decreasing the parallelism can lead to idle compute units, such as cores of multi-core processors or processors of multi-processor systems. Placing these units in a standby mode might reduce the energy consumption. All solver methods of the ScaFaCoS library are parallelized with MPI. Thus, the number of utilized compute units can be adapted as part of an optimization towards energy or performance by specifying the number of MPI processes.

IV. **Variation of the hardware platform:** The utilized hardware platform has a strong influence on the resulting energy and performance behaviors. Furthermore, modern hardware platforms allow to control parameters, such as the frequency of processor cores, which directly influence the power consumption. Especially, for data-intensive applications, whose computational performance is limited by memory accesses or data exchanges instead of the amount of operations, it might be advantageous to operate with a lower processor core frequency. Even though this can lead to a higher runtime, a lower energy consumption can be achieved if the reduced power consumption outweighs the runtime increase. Computing particle interaction with the ScaFaCoS library is a data-intensive part of particle simulations and, thus, it can be beneficial to adapt the hardware platform parameters as part of an optimization towards energy or performance.

3 EXPERIMENTAL SETUP

The variation approaches described in the previous section are used to analyze the energy and performance behavior of the ScaFaCoS library. In the following, the solver methods and their parameters as well as the hardware and software environment are described.

3.1 Particle solver methods

The energy and performance measurements are performed with a generic test program that can invoke any solver method of the ScaFaCoS library. The test program is part of the library package and was mainly developed for the verification and comparison of the different solver methods. The measurements include only the computation of the particle interactions while all other library functions (e. g., initialization, parameter setup, tuning) are not considered. A benchmark particle system (called cloud-wall) is used for the experimental analysis. The three-dimensional base system contains 300 particles, whereas 100 particles are distributed randomly (cloud) and 200 particles are distributed on a regular grid (wall). Larger systems with $300 \times 8, \ldots, 300 \times 8^5$ particles are created by repeating the base system several times in each dimension. All parameters of the solver methods either have default values or are tuned automatically. Unless otherwise stated, these values are used.

The experimental analysis uses the following solver methods:

Direct: The Direct solver computes the particle interactions by a direct summation of the contributions of all pairs of particles. With n particles, the method has a runtime of $O(n^2)$. Periodic boundary conditions are computed by placing a layer of copies of the given particles around the original particle system. Thus, the method is only appropriate for small particle systems. The method has no parameters that can influence the behavior of the computations.

Ewald: The Ewald solver computes the particle interactions using the Ewald summation [3]. The approach separates the contributions of the particle interactions into two parts: The k-space part (i. e., far-field computations) is calculated with a reciprocal lattice. The real-space part (i. e., near-field computations) is calculated directly between particles within a given cutoff range. Both the maximum number of k-space vectors and the cutoff range are parameters of the method that influence the computational demands and the accuracy of the results.

P³M: The P³M solver is a parallel implementation of the Particle-Particle-Particle-Mesh algorithm [3]. The algorithm uses a grid-based approach to accelerate the time-consuming k-space part of the Ewald summation using Fast Fourier Transforms (FFT). Similar to the Ewald solver, the computational demands of the far-field computations depend on the size of the FFT grid and the computational demands of the near-field computations depend on the cutoff range. Both can be controlled by parameters.

P²NFFT: The Particle-Particle NFFT (P²NFFT) solver performs fast Ewald summations based on nonequispaced fast Fourier transforms (NFFT) [15]. The P²NFFT solver represents a general framework for particle mesh algorithms and supports periodic and nonperiodic boundary conditions. Similar to

the Ewald solver and the P³M solver, the computational demands of the far-field and near-field computations can be controlled by parameters that specify the size of the FFT grid and the cutoff range.

FMM: The FMM solver is a parallel implementation of the Fast Multipole Method [11]. This tree-based algorithm uses a recursive subdivision of the particle system into smaller boxes. Contributions from interactions between particles inside each box and between neighboring boxes belong to the near-field and are calculated directly. All other contributions belong to the far-field and are approximated with multipole expansions. Using these expansions allows for a hierarchical grouping of the contributions and enables efficient operations for calculating interactions between entire boxes of particles at once. The level up to which the subdivision into boxes is performed can be set by a parameter that controls the computational costs of the near-field and far-field computations.

3.2 Hardware platforms

The experimental analysis uses three hardware platforms with different processor microarchitectures as shown in Table 1. The platforms comprise of two Intel Xeon server systems and one Intel Core desktop system. The server systems have dual sockets, a high number of cores, and large L3 caches, but only a narrow range of frequencies with a low maximum frequency. In contrast, the desktop system has only a single socket, a low number of cores, and a smaller L3 cache. However, the range of processor frequencies is wider and includes a significantly higher maximum frequency.

3.3 Software environment

The utilized hardware platforms use the Debian GNU/Linux 8.6 operating system with kernel version 4.7. The processor frequencies are controlled manually through the CPUFreq kernel interface using the userspace governor. Energy measurements are performed with the Running Average Power Limit (RAPL) interface by accessing model specific registers of the processor. Instead of reading the appropriate results directly from the registers, the Performance Application Programming Interface (PAPI)[2] is used. A dedicated RAPL component allows for transparent power and energy readings for Intel Sandy Bridge processors and its successors [23]. The PAPI library of version 5.5.1 was used for the measurements.

Table 1: Overview of the utilized hardware platforms.

Name	Sandybridge	Haswell	Skylake
Processor	Xeon E5-2650	Xeon E5-2683 v3	Core i7-6700
Cores	2×8	2×14	1×4
Frequency	1.2–2.0 GHz	1.2–2.0 GHz	0.8–3.4 GHz
L3 cache	20 MB	35 MB	8 MB
Memory	32 GB	128 GB	16 GB

[2]http://icl.utk.edu/papi

3.4 Measurement methodology

The measurements were conducted by performing *multiple consecutive trials* [1]. For a specific configuration of the settings and parameters to be varied, ten consecutive trials are executed and measured. This process is repeated for the trials of the next configurations to be investigated. Average values of the consecutive trials are used for the analyses. The hardware platforms were used exclusively, i. e. no other users or processes except from the operating system have utilized the platform at the same time.

The PAPI library provides a uniform interface for starting, stopping, and querying performance-relevant measurements for the execution of program codes at runtime [6]. Measuring the energy consumption of the processors is performed using the hardware counters `rapl:::PACKAGE_ENERGY:PACKAGE0` (first socket) and `rapl:::PACKAGE_ENERGY:PACKAGE1` (second socket if present). The program code for the measurements is integrated into the library function that performs the step for computing the particle interactions (see Sect. 2.1). However, since this library function is executed in parallel with MPI, only a single process per compute node performs the measurements and determines the energy consumption of all processors of the compute node. The overall execution of the library and its solver methods is performed with a generic test program that is part of the ScaFaCoS library.

4 ENERGY AND PERFORMANCE ANALYSES

The energy and performance behavior of the different solvers of the ScaFaCoS library is analyzed experimentally as described in the previous section. In the following, the results of the four variation approaches from Sect. 2.2 are shown and the findings are discussed.

4.1 Variation of the solver method

To investigate the influence of the specific particle solver method, the five methods Direct, Ewald, P^3M, P^2NFFT, and FMM are compared. Figure 1 shows the runtime (left), the energy consumption (middle), and the power consumption (right) depending on the number of particles for the different methods. All methods are executed sequentially on the Haswell platform. The runtimes of all solvers increase strongly for increasing numbers of particles. However, especially the Direct method and the Ewald method show a very steep increase and their runtimes are even for the smallest number of particles at least one order of magnitude higher than the other methods. Both methods represent reference methods which are not designed for efficient computations and thus, results with larger numbers of particles are omitted. The fast methods P^3M, P^2NFFT, and FMM show a very similar runtime with the FMM method being slightly slower and the P^3M being slightly faster. The runtime of the P^2NFFT method varies between them.

The behavior of the energy consumption of all methods corresponds to their runtimes. This indicates that the operations performed by the different methods lead to almost the same utilization of the hardware. Even though the methods are based on different mathematical and computational approaches, neither of them provides a significant increase or reduction of the energy consumption during the course of the computations. However, the power consumption shows a more different behavior. All methods are within

a range of about $58.5\,\mathrm{J\,s^{-1}}\pm5\,\%$, but the lowest power consumption is now achieved with the P^2NFFT method. Furthermore, also the two reference methods Direct and Ewald are able to achieve a lower power consumption than the two fast methods P^3M and FMM. However, in general these differences occur mainly for short computations with small numbers of particles, while during longer running computations the power consumption of all methods approaches similar values of $58\,\mathrm{J\,s^{-1}}$ to $59\,\mathrm{J\,s^{-1}}$.

4.2 Variation of solver parameters

To investigate the influence of method parameters, the separation of the computations into near-field computations and far-field computation is varied for the methods P^2NFFT and FMM. For the P^2NFFT method, an increase of the far-field computations is achieved by increasing the grid size parameter. At the same time, the near-field computations are reduced by reducing the utilized cutoff radius as far possible while still achieving a specific accuracy of the results. For the FMM method, the far-field computations are increased and the near-field computations are decreased by using a larger tree depth for the subdivision into boxes. The methods are executed sequentially on the Haswell platform using particle systems of size 300×8^2 and 300×8^5. Total results as well as separate results for the near-field and far-field computations of the methods are shown.

Figure 2 shows the sequential runtime (left) and the energy consumption (right) of the P^2NFFT method depending on the grid size. It can be observed that the grid size has a significant influence on the runtime of the P^2NFFT method. This behavior is caused by the near-field and far-field computations whose runtimes behave as expected. The minimum of the total runtime is achieved with a grid size of 32 for 300×8^2 particles and with a grid size of 448 for 300×8^5 particles. The energy consumption reflects the general behavior observed for the runtime. For 300×8^2 particles, the minimum of the total energy is achieved with the same grid size that also leads to the minimum of the total runtime (i. e., 32). Choosing slightly lower or higher grid sizes leads to an increase of both the runtime and the energy consumption. For 300×8^5 particles, the minimum of the total energy is achieved with a grid size of 384. The corresponding runtime is about $5\,\%$ higher than the runtime minimum. However, using the optimal grid size of the runtime (i. e., 384) leads to an increase of the energy consumption of only about $1\,\%$. Even though the potential savings in runtime or energy are relatively small, the results indicate a difference between the energy and runtime requirements of the two computational parts of the P^2NFFT method.

Figure 3 shows the sequential runtime (left) and the energy consumption (right) of the FMM method depending on the maximum tree depth. It can be observed that the tree depth has a significant influence on the runtime of the FMM method. However, the parameter controls only the maximum tree depth while the actual tree depth is determined automatically by the specific FMM solver [9]. Thus, using a larger maximum tree depth (i. e., larger than 3 for 300×8^2 particles and larger than 6 for 300×8^5 particles) do not lead to further differences. The minimum of the total runtime is achieved when the runtimes of the near-field and far-field computations are about the same. The same behavior is observed for the energy consumption. The minimum of the total runtime and the total energy is achieved with the same maximum tree depth.

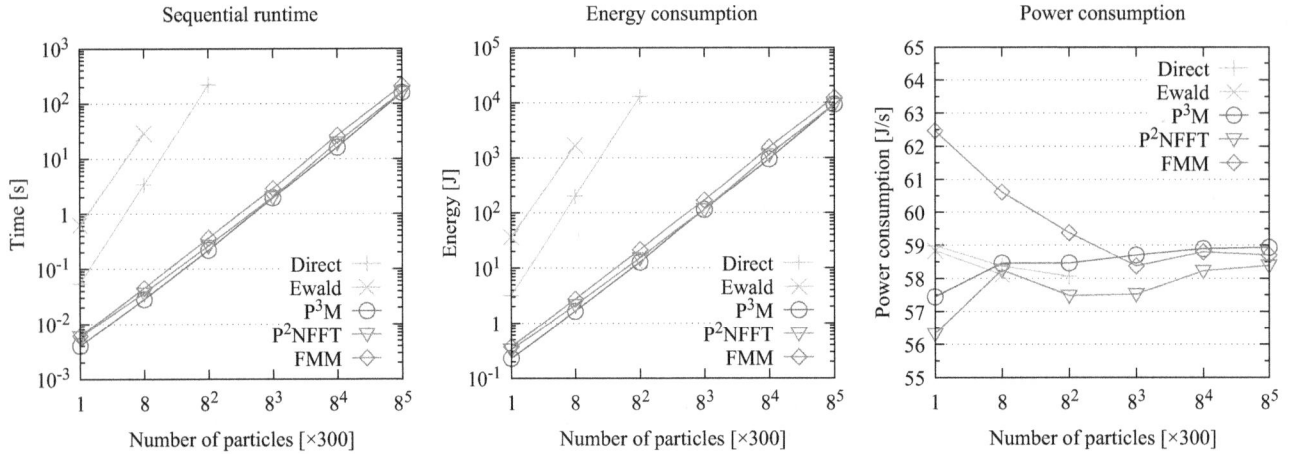

Figure 1: Sequential runtime (left), energy consumption (middle), and power consumption (right) depending on the number of particles for different particle solver methods.

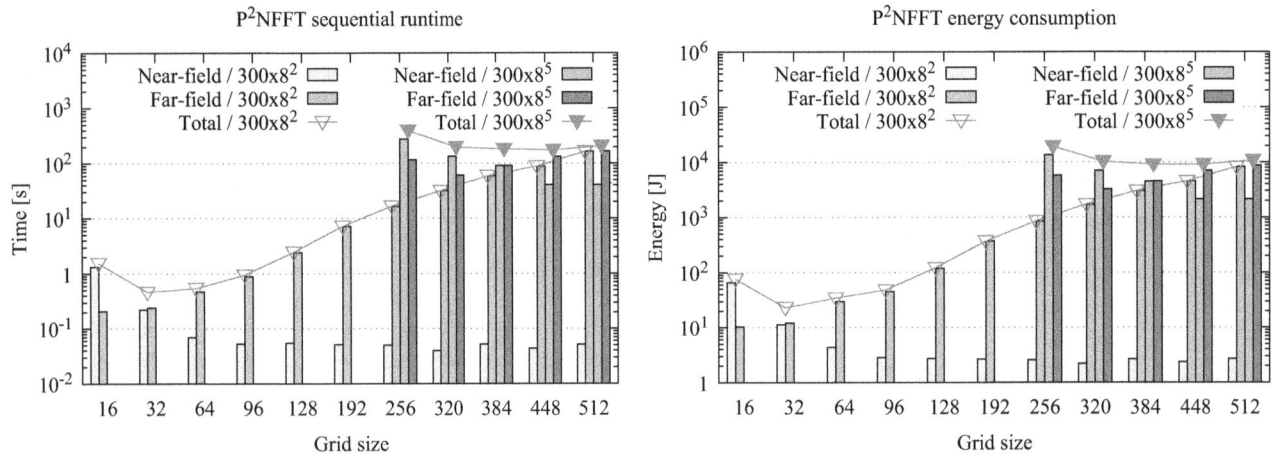

Figure 2: Sequential runtime (left) and energy consumption (right) of the P^2NFFT method depending on the grid size.

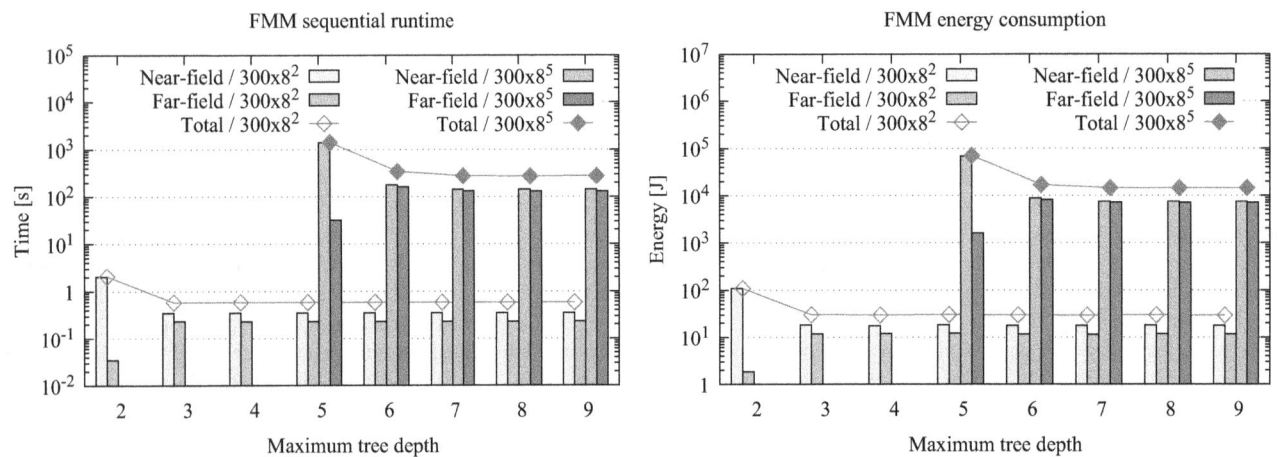

Figure 3: Sequential runtime (left) and energy consumption (right) of the FMM method depending on the maximum tree depth.

4.3 Variation of the degree of parallelism

To investigate the parallel behavior of the particle solver methods, the degree of parallelism represented by the number of utilized MPI processes is varied. The two methods P^2NFFT and FMM are considered. The methods are executed on the Haswell platform using particle systems of size 300×8^2 and 300×8^5.

Figure 4 shows the parallel runtime (left), the parallel speedup (middle), and the energy consumption (right) depending on the number of MPI processes. The results show that the parallel runtimes of all solver methods decrease for increasing numbers of MPI processes. However, for 300×8^2 particles, this runtime improvement deteriorates when using more than 14 MPI processes (i. e., more than the number of cores of one processor). For the larger number of particles, the runtime improvement becomes less significant when using more than 28 MPI processes (i. e., more than the total number of physical cores of both processors). Nevertheless, the P^2NFFT method still achieves a reduction of the parallel runtime when using the Hyper-Threading capabilities of processors (i. e., with 56 MPI processes). The runtime results are reflected by achieved parallel speedups. While with the smaller number of particles, a maximum speedup of about 8 is achieved, the larger number of particles lead to a maximum speedup close to the total number of physical cores available. Only for the P^2NFFT method, a further increase of the parallel speedup is achieved using Hyper-Threading.

The energy consumption corresponds to the general runtime behavior. However, there are quantitative differences, especially for high numbers of MPI processes. When using Hyper-Threading for the P^2NFFT method, the resulting reduction of the energy consumption of about 6 % to 7 % is smaller than the runtime reduction of about 14 % to 34 % occurring at the same time. Furthermore, for larger numbers of MPI processes (i. e., 28 and 56), the parallel runtime of the FMM method increases only slightly while the increase of the energy consumption is stronger at the same time. Nevertheless, these results do not indicate significant differences between optimal energy and performance behaviors. The number of MPI processes with the smallest parallel runtime leads also to the smallest energy consumption for the considered measurements.

4.4 Variation of the hardware platform

To investigate the influence of parameters of the hardware platform on the energy and performance behavior, the utilized hardware platform as well as the processor frequency is varied. The two methods P^2NFFT and FMM and the particle system of size 300×8^5 are considered. All methods are executed by using one MPI process per physical processor core of the specific hardware platform, i. e., 16 MPI processes for Sandybridge, 28 MPI processes for Haswell, and 4 MPI processes for Skylake (see Table 1).

Figure 5 shows the parallel runtime (left) and the energy consumption (right) depending on the processor frequency. The results show that the processor frequency has a significant influence on the parallel runtime of the solver methods. For the two server platforms (i. e., Sandybridge and Haswell), the rather small range of supported processor frequencies of 1.2 GHz to 2.0 GHz leads to a reduction of the parallel runtime by a factor of about 1.6. For the Skylake desktop platform, the larger range of 0.8 GHz to 3.4 GHz leads to a runtime reduction by a factor of about 4. This corresponds to an almost linear improvement for both solver methods, thus showing that their performance behavior is mainly determined by the computational speed of the processors. Furthermore, even for equal processor frequencies, there is a strong difference between the hardware platforms resulting from the different numbers of processor cores available. The minimum of the parallel runtime is achieved by choosing the maximum processor frequency on each platform as well as the Haswell platform among the three available platforms.

The energy consumption shows a very different behavior than the parallel runtime. For all measurements, there occurs a U-shape where the energy consumption first decreases and later increases for increasing processor frequencies. Thus, the minimum of the energy consumption is achieved by choosing an intermediate processor frequency of about 1.6 GHz to 1.7 GHz. The optimal choice of the processor frequency is almost the same for the two solver methods and the three hardware platforms. In comparison to using the maximum frequency (i. e., with the minimum parallel runtime), the optimal frequency with respect to the energy consumption leads to an increase of the parallel runtime of about 22 % to 23 % for the Sandybridge and Haswell platform and 90 % to 98 % for the Skylake platform. At the same time, the achieved reduction of the energy consumption is only up to 6 % for the Sandybridge and Haswell platform but up to 46 % for the Skylake platform. The results demonstrate that optimizations towards energy or performance require differing approaches. Even though the loss of performance observed is larger than the energy improvement obtained, a significant reduction of the energy consumption can still be achieved especially for platforms with large ranges of processor frequencies.

4.5 Discussion

The measurements indicate that all variation approaches investigated in the previous subsections have a significant influence on the energy and performance behavior. However, varying the solution methods or their parameters often requires additional programming efforts and a deep knowledge of the specific solution methods. The common programming interface of the ScaFaCoS library and the parameterized implementations of their solvers lower the required efforts for these kinds of investigations significantly, thus demonstrating that this library design is very advantageous for subsequent analyses and optimization approaches. Varying the degree of parallelism or the processor frequency is already common practice and can be performed without significant efforts. However, the findings have shown that especially the achievable reduction of the energy consumption with an optimal processor frequency depends strongly on the range of frequencies supported by the processor. The desktop platform was much more affected by this effect, thus showing that the priorities of the analyses might have to incorporate, for example, differences between desktop and server platforms or the direction of future hardware platform developments.

So far, the analysis has considered only selected configurations of particle solver methods, parameters, and input data. However, an investigation encompassing the entire space of possible configurations leads to large amounts of measurement results that would be very time consuming to obtain and to analyze. This would require a generalization of the approach, for example, with consecutive iterations parameter spaces and automated detection of

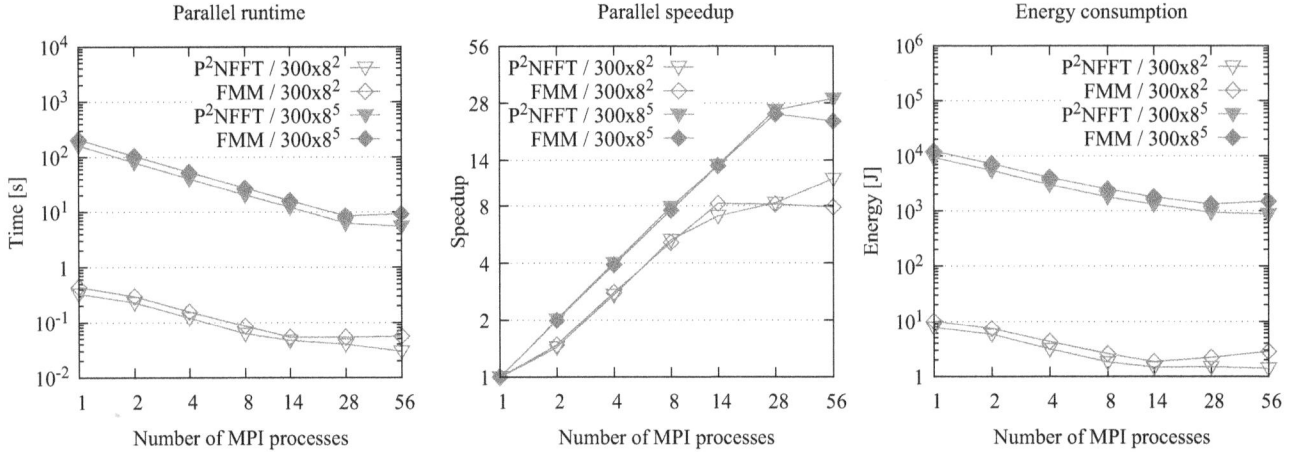

Figure 4: Parallel runtime (left), parallel speedup (middle), and energy consumption (right) depending on the number of MPI processes for different particle solver methods.

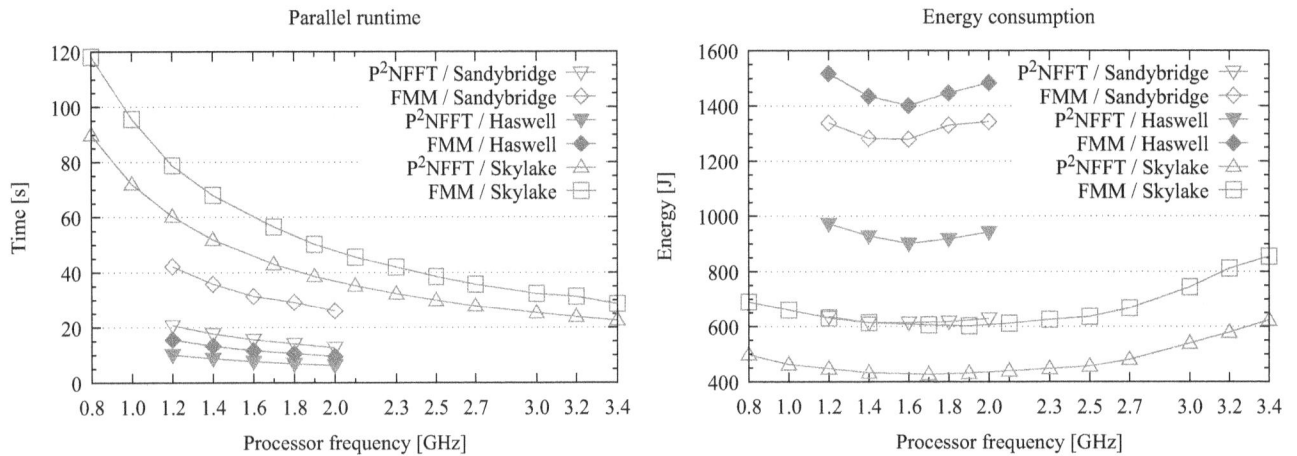

Figure 5: Parallel runtime (left) and energy consumption (right) depending on the processor frequency for different particle solver methods and hardware platforms.

optimal energy and performance behaviors. The analysis based on the four considered variation approaches is independent from the considered library of particle solver methods and can be applied to other libraries as well. However, single investigations might not be applicable to all kinds of libraries, for example, a variation of the solution method can only be exploited if there are several alternative methods available for solving a single problem. Furthermore, the overall approach is not limit to software libraries at all, but can be generalized to other computational problems where different algorithms or implementations are available.

5 RELATED WORK

In the past, studies about the energy and power consumption in scientific computing have focused on linear algebra operations [21] as well as on general benchmarks, such as NPB and PARSEC [22]. However, only few investigate specifically the differences between

energy/power and performance [2, 13]. Commonly analyzed influences on the energy requirements include code optimizations, dynamic concurrency throttling (DCT), and dynamic voltage and frequency scaling (DVFS). The overall results show large variations in the achieved improvements of the energy requirements, thus demonstrating that dedicated analyses for individual applications and their various influences are necessary. This article provides a dedicated analysis of solver methods for particle simulations, which represent an important class of applications that have not been investigated in detail so far. Furthermore, we have extended the analysis to include novel influences, such as the usage of alternative solution methods and the selection of method-specific parameters.

For an older version of the FMM solver method, an autotuning approach for its method parameters, such as the utilized tree depth, was developed [9]. The presented results showed the significant influence of the method parameters on the performance of the

FMM method. While the optimization approach was also based on experimental measurements, it did not consider the parallelization or the energy consumption. An analysis of the energy behavior of the FMM with DVFS is presented in [8]. The work focuses on the the prediction of energy-efficient settings using a system-on-chip platform. The results showed that due to a large percentage of energy consumed by constant power of the platform, a maximum frequency setting minimized both the execution time and the energy consumption. For the hardware platforms and measurements presented in this article, the minimum of the energy consumption is achieved with an intermediate processor frequency.

Several approaches were developed to measure, model, and predict the energy behavior of parallel hardware platforms. Various benchmark suites were used to include a representative set of applications codes into the studies. For example, the ASC Sequoia benchmark suite and the multi-zone version of the NAS Parallel Benchmarks were used to analyze the effects of DCT and DVFS in hybrid MPI/OpenMP applications [14]. In [20], the SPEC CPU2006 benchmark suite is used to compare the measurements obtained with external power-meters and with internal hardware counters on multi-core platforms. Benchmark suites, such as SPLASH-2 or PARSEC, also include particle solver methods. These benchmark suites are used, for example, to investigate different power and energy models with respect to their prediction capabilities [19] or to quantify the amount of energy required for shared memory programming of an energy-efficient system-on-chip many-core system [17]. The results presented in these works also include energy measurements of particle solver methods. However, a dedicated analysis of these methods is not included as they represent only a small part of the utilized applications. The analysis provided in this article, focuses solely on particle solver methods and investigates especially the relation between energy and performance behaviors.

6 CONCLUSIONS

In this article, we have analyzed the energy and performance behavior of different particle solver methods from the ScaFaCoS library. Four different aspects were presented to systematically vary the computations used to solve a specific problem. The results showed that the energy consumption and the required runtime often exhibit the same general behavior. Small deviations occurred for the power consumption when varying the particle solver method as well as for the energy consumption when varying the grid size parameter of the P^2NFFT solver method. However, much larger differences between the energy and the parallel behavior were observed for varying the processor frequency. While the minimum of the parallel runtime is always achieved with the maximum processor frequency, the minimum of the energy consumption requires to use significantly smaller processor frequencies. The findings indicate that there can be situations in which the energy behavior deviates from the performance behavior. Due to the large number of potential influences for particle solvers, the presented grouping allows to identify specific aspects that might be used for further analyses or optimizations. Furthermore, the implementation of the particle solvers as a library has demonstrated to be of great advantage for the analyses, because all investigated variations of the solvers could be performed without additional programming efforts.

ACKNOWLEDGMENTS

This work was supported by the German Ministry of Science and Education (BMBF) under Grant No. 01IH16012B.

REFERENCES

[1] A. Abedi and T. Brecht. 2017. Conducting repeatable experiments in highly variable cloud computing environments. In *Int. Conf. on Performance Engineering (ICPE'17)*. ACM, 287–292.

[2] J.I. Aliaga, M. Barreda, M.F. Dolz, and E.S. Quintana-Ortí. 2015. Are our dense linear algebra libraries energy-friendly? *Computer Science-Research and Development* 30, 2 (2015), 187–196.

[3] A. Arnold. 2011. Fourier transformed-based methods for long-range interactions: Ewald, P^3M and more. In *Fast Methods for Long-Range Interactions in Complex Systems*. IAS Series, Vol. 6. Forschungszentrum Jülich, 39–64.

[4] A. Arnold, F. Fahrenberger, C. Holm, O. Lenz, M. Bolten, H. Dachsel, R. Halver, I. Kabadshow, F. Gähler, F. Heber, J. Iseringhausen, M. Hofmann, M. Pippig, D. Potts, and G. Sutmann. 2013. Comparison of scalable fast methods for long-range interactions. *Physical Review E* 88 (2013), 063308. Issue 6.

[5] J. Barnes and P. Hut. 1986. A hierarchical $O(N \log N)$ force-calculation algorithm. *Nature* 324, 6096 (1986), 446–449.

[6] S. Browne, J. Dongarra, N. Garner, G. Ho, and P. Mucci. 2000. A portable programming interface for performance evaluation on modern processors. *Int. J. of High Performance Computing Applications* 14, 3 (2000), 189–204.

[7] J. Carretero, S. Distefano, D. Petcu, D. Pop, T. Rauber, G. Rünger, and D.E. Singh. 2015. Energy-efficient algorithms for ultrascale systems. *Supercomputing Frontiers and Innovations* 2, 2 (2015), 77–104.

[8] J.W. Choi and R.W. Vuduc. 2016. Analyzing the energy efficiency of the fast multipole method in a DVFS-aware energy model. In *Int. Parallel and Distributed Processing Symposium Workshops (IPDPSW'16)*. IEEE, 79–88.

[9] H. Dachsel, M. Hofmann, J. Lang, and G. Rünger. 2012. Automatic tuning of the fast multipole method based on integrated performance prediction. In *Int. Conf. on High Performance Computing and Communication (HPCC'12)*. IEEE, 617–624.

[10] M. Etinski, J. Corbalán, J. Labarta, and M. Valero. 2012. Understanding the future of energy-performance trade-off via DVFS in HPC environments. *J. of Parallel and Distributed Computing* 72, 4 (2012), 579–590.

[11] L. Greengard and V. Rokhlin. 1987. A fast algorithm for particle simulations. *J. of Computational Physics* 73 (1987), 325–348.

[12] T. Jakobs, J. Lang, G. Rünger, and P. Stöcker. 2017. Tuning linear algebra for energy efficiency on multicore machines by adapting the ATLAS library. *Future Generation Computer Systems* (2017). (to appear).

[13] E.A. León, I. Karlin, R.E. Grant, and M. Dosanjh. 2016. Program optimizations: The interplay between power, performance, and energy. *Parallel Comput.* 58 (2016), 56–75.

[14] D. Li, B.R. de Supinski, M. Schulz, K. Cameron, and D.S. Nikolopoulos. 2010. Hybrid MPI/OpenMP power-aware computing. In *Int. Symposium on Parallel Distributed Processing (IPDPS 2010)*. IEEE, 1–12.

[15] M. Pippig and D. Potts. 2013. Parallel three-dimensional nonequispaced fast Fourier transforms and their application to particle simulation. *SIAM J. on Scientific Computing* 35, 4 (2013), C411–C437.

[16] A. Podzimek, L. Bulej, L.Y. Chen, W. Binder, and P. Tuma. 2015. Analyzing the impact of CPU pinning and partial CPU loads on performance and energy efficiency. In *Int. Symposium on Cluster, Cloud and Grid Computing (CCGrid'15)*. IEEE, 1–10.

[17] M. Puzović, S. Manne, S. GalOn, and M. Ono. 2016. Quantifying energy use in dense shared memory HPC node. In *Int. Workshop on Energy Efficient Supercomputing (E2SC 2016)*. IEEE, 16–23.

[18] T. Rauber and G. Rünger. 2015. Modeling and analyzing the energy consumption of fork-join-based task parallel programs. *Concurrency and Computation: Practice and Experience* 27, 1 (2015), 211–236.

[19] T. Rauber, G. Rünger, and M. Schwind. 2014. Energy measurement and prediction for multi-threaded programs. In *High Performance Computing Symposium (HPC 2014)*. Society for Computer Simulation International, 20:1–20:9.

[20] T. Rauber, G. Rünger, M. Schwind, H. Xu, and S. Melzner. 2014. Energy measurement, modeling, and prediction for processors with frequency scaling. *J. of Supercomputing* 70, 3 (2014), 1451–1476.

[21] L. Tan, S. Kothapalli, L. Chen, O. Hussaini, R. Bissiri, and Z. Chen. 2014. A survey of power and energy efficient techniques for high performance numerical linear algebra operations. *Parallel Comput.* 40, 10 (2014), 559–573.

[22] S. Wang, B. Luo, W. Shi, and D. Tiwari. 2016. Application configuration selection for energy-efficient execution on multicore systems. *J. of Parallel and Distributed Computing* 87 (2016), 43–54.

[23] V.M. Weaver, D. Terpstra, H. McCraw, M. Johnson, K. Kasichayanula, J. Ralph, J. Nelson, P. Mucci, T. Mohan, and S. Moore. 2013. PAPI 5: Measuring power, energy, and the cloud. In *Int. Symposium on Performance Analysis of Systems and Software (ISPASS'13)*. IEEE, 124–125.

Characterizing the Microarchitectural Implications of a Convolutional Neural Network (CNN) Execution on GPUs

Shi Dong
Dept. of Electrical and
Computer Engineering
Northeastern University
shidong@ece.neu.edu

Xiang Gong
Dept. of Electrical and
Computer Engineering
Northeastern University
xgong@ece.neu.edu

Yifan Sun
Dept. of Electrical and
Computer Engineering
Northeastern University
yifansun@ece.neu.edu

Trinayan Baruah
Dept. of Electrical and
Computer Engineering
Northeastern University
tbaruah@ece.neu.edu

David Kaeli
Dept. of Electrical and
Computer Engineering
Northeastern University
kaeli@ece.neu.edu

ABSTRACT

GPUs have become a very popular platform for accelerating the processing involved in deep learning applications. One class of popular variants, Convolutional Neural Networks (CNNs), have been widely deployed to run on GPUs. In many application settings, a GPU has sufficient computing power and memory space to accommodate the dense matrix operations performed during CNN training. However, few characterization studies have considered how CNNs can impact microarchitectural structures in a GPU. In this paper, we perform a characterization of one selected CNN workload as run on two different NVIDIA GPUs from distinct microarchitecture families, highlighting the impact that microarchitecture plays on this important class of workload.

First, we analyze the performance implications of a CNN model using microarchitectural details on a layer-by-layer basis, and characterize the memory access behavior in the context of a typical GPU memory hierarchy, considering hardware resource utilization associated with each primitive in the CNN model. We identify major bottlenecks by considering the potential limits of using a single GPU. Additionally, we evaluate a number of optimization approaches, such as L1 cache bypassing and kernel fusion. L1 cache bypassing can achieve up to a 6.2% speedup for a single layer, but manipulating L1 cache provides very limited benefits in terms of application speedup, while kernel fusion provides an overall application speedup of 4.0%, on average.

CCS CONCEPTS

• **General and reference** → **Evaluation**; **Performance**; • **Computer systems organization** → **Neural networks**; • **Computing methodologies** → *Neural networks*;

KEYWORDS

Convolutional Neural Networks; GPU; Characterization; Performance analysis

ACM Reference Format:
Shi Dong, Xiang Gong, Yifan Sun, Trinayan Baruah, and David Kaeli. 2018. Characterizing the Microarchitectural Implications of a Convolutional Neural Network (CNN) Execution on GPUs. In *Proceedings of ACM/SPEC International Conference on Performance Engineering, Berlin, Germany, April 9–13, 2018 (ICPE '18)*, 11 pages.
https://doi.org/10.1145/3184407.3184423

1 INTRODUCTION

Deep Learning (DL) algorithms have emerged as a "celebrity" in the field of machine learning, especially given that they can leverage GPUs to accelerate their execution. Deep Learning and Artificial Neural Networks were first described many years ago, but were considered viable for learning problems until recently. With support of the state-of-the-art GPU hardware, neural networks have been deployed in a wide range of applications including artificial intelligence, natural language processing, and human-computer interfacing. A commonly cited exemplary application is autonomous vehicle guidance [8]. Using DL algorithms, a self-driving car is able to identify its surrounding environment and make corresponding movements without any human intervention. Another highly publicized AI-related application, AlphaGO, uses DL as one of its key algorithms during the training process [25]. In order to capture the rapid growth of deep learning research, a number of frameworks have been developed by both the academic and industry communities to further facilitate their development. Caffe [9], TensorFlow[1], Theano [26], CNTK [22] and MXNet [2] are a few of the well-known deep learning frameworks that provide users to design and deploy neural network models efficiently.

Convolutional Neural Network (CNN) is one popular variant of deep neural network (DNN) that leverages convolution as its major linear transformation for feature extraction. It has been demonstrated that CNN can be very effective in vision and speech classification domains [11, 13]. Similar to other models of deep neural networks, the essential computations in CNNs have been accelerated using a GPU, especially given that most computational operations involving convolution are matrix-based. Since GPUs are an effective target for accelerating matrix operations, they have been quickly developed into a key resource for accelerating CNNs. However, there has only been limited prior work with regards to the execution of this type of workload on GPUs. Given this limited knowledge, it becomes challenging to optimize GPU architectures to run this class of compute-intensive applications.

In this paper, we capture and analyze the micro-architectural information from two GPUs. The two GPUs are of different product grade, server (Tesla K40) and desktop (GTX1080), and from different microarchitecture family, kepler and pascal, respectively. After then, we study the microarchitectural implications of efficiently running CNNs. To begin this study, we have selected to study AlexNet [11], which is a popular CNN model. Even though the AlexNet is not the latest state-of-the-art CNN model, it covers most of the commonly used primitives in deep neural networks, and most importantly, its structure is simple to evaluate and its execution presents a number of challenges to current GPU designs. In terms of an implementation of AlexNet, we utilize DNNMark [7] to drive this study, providing a highly configurable and light weight infrastructure, that builds its core function using cuDNN[3] and cuBLAS[5]. These two highly optimized libraries have been used in many DNN frameworks that leverage Nvidia GPUs. Considering their performance, cuDNN and cuBLAS provide a rich software core for us to study DNN execution, working at a microarchitectural level. In our evaluation, we report on execution performance, memory behavior, and resource utilization. Furthermore, we identify some of the major limiting factors in GPU microarchitectures when executing DNN primitives.

Based on our results, we first characterize the performance trends of the workload on the two GPU platforms and identify the characteristics of each layer, and then we identify that the convolution layer are the main bottleneck during execution of the convolutional neural networks. From a microarchitectural perspective, we also identify additional limiting factors in the convolution layer, including hardware limits, bandwidth of texture cache. Other than that, we can improve the performance of CNN model with little or even no source code modification. Given challenges in the cache hit rate across all of the layers, we can optimize some layers by bypassing the L1 cache. When L1 cache bypass is enabled, the backward propagation of one convolution layer can achieve a 6.2% speedup on GTX1080. Additionally, we propose a kernel fusion method in which the kernels from the linear data transformation and non-linearity layers can be combined to reduce unnecessary memory transactions without introducing too much extra computation. We have constructed an experiment and observed that the entire DNN model execution is accelerated by 4% on GTX1080. We also discuss the results accordingly.

Although the convolution layer is the main limiting layer in convolutional neural networks, we notice a trend that as hardware advances with many optimization specifically proposed for linear transformations such as convolution, the other layers start to contribute more in execution time. Hence, a thorough characterization of each primitive should be carried out in order to understand the overall execution behavior of CNNs for future optimization.

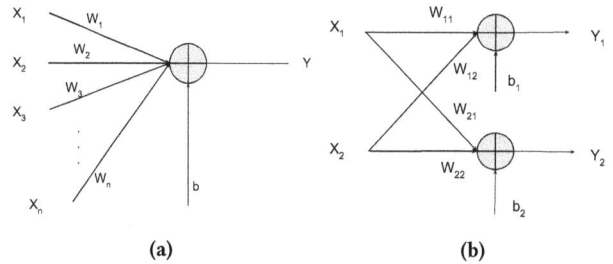

Figure 1: (a) Model of an artificial neuron. (b) A simple example of a fully-connected layer.

The rest of this paper is organized as follows. In section 2, we provide an overview of the basic elements and structure of a convolutional neural network, and review GPU architecture. In section 3, we discuss our characterization approach, the database-backed trace tracking framework and the details of the hardware used for experiments. In section 4, we present detailed analysis on both an entire model and individual primitives. In section 5 we review the contributions of this work, and in section 6 we discuss previous work on convolutional neural networks characterization, and in section 7 we conclude the paper.

2 BACKGROUND

2.1 Deep Neural Networks

The operations involved in Deep Neural Networks are basically combinations of linear and non-linear data transformations, as well as other techniques used to avoid over-fitting and improve prediction accuracy. In this paper, we mainly concentrate on Convolutional Neural Network (CNN), a variant of a DNN that applies convolutional operations. Generally, in a CNN model, the linear data transformations can be broken down into two major categories: i) fully-connected and ii) convolution. These two transformations are carried out by applying elementary operations, such as multiplications and summations, which are performed on data, trainable weights, and biases. For image processing, the data moving across the network model is usually managed in a tensor format, meaning that the data has at least 4 dimensions, N, C, H, and W, in which N is the batch size, C is the number of channels, H is the height, and W is the width. The tensor data is stored in memory as a matrix in column-major format, with the number of rows equal to $C * H * W$ and the number of columns equal to N.

2.1.1 Linear Data Transformations. In the **fully-connected layer**, the basic unit to construct is an artificial neuron, which is a simple mathematical model, as presented in Figure 1a. The neuron is composed of operations such as multiplications and summations, as expressed in Equation 1.

$$Y = \sum_{i=1}^{n} W_i * X_i + b \qquad (1)$$

The fully-connected layer is constructed of multiple artificial neural interconnects, as shown in figure 1b.

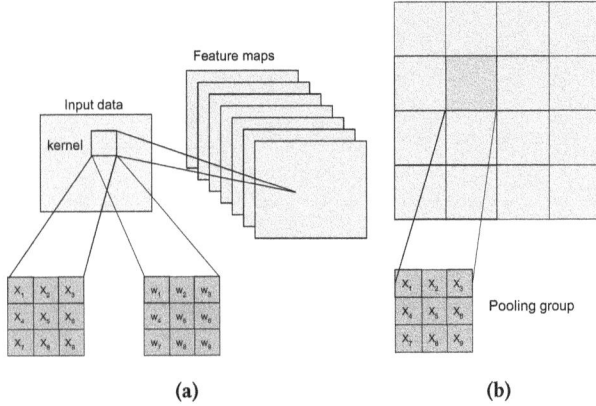

Figure 2: (a) 2-D image convolution. (b) Feature map data divided into multiple pooling groups.

Based on this model, the fully-connected layer can be interpreted using a matrix-vector multiplication, as indicated in equation 2. This example has only one set of data inputs. If there are multiple sets of data inputs, then the computation becomes a multiplication and a summation of matrices.

$$\begin{bmatrix} Y_1 \\ Y_2 \end{bmatrix} = \begin{bmatrix} W_{11} & W_{12} \\ W_{21} & W_{22} \end{bmatrix} * \begin{bmatrix} X_1 \\ X_2 \end{bmatrix} + \begin{bmatrix} b_1 \\ b_2 \end{bmatrix} \qquad (2)$$

In the **convolution layer**, the operations are performed in a different fashion. Figure 2a shows an example of a 2-D image convolution that is used in a typical CNN model.

In this figure, a convolution kernel of $3X3$ is applied to an area in the image of the same size. The input data is X_i, and the kernel weights are W_i. Using the computation shown in equation 3, we can calculate a single result for Y based on the data covered by the kernel as follows:

$$Y_{i,j} = \sum_{h=-k_h/2}^{k_h/2} \sum_{w=-k_w/2}^{k_w/2} W_{h,w} * X_{i+h,j+w} \qquad (3)$$

In the above equations, k is the kernel size. In the next step, the kernel is applied to the next data sample using a specified stride, and we repeat the same process across samples of every channel until all of the feature maps are calculated. During image convolution, the weights are shared by all of the data samples (i.e., pixels, if image data is used). Note that, as the stride grows, the calculated feature map has a narrower height and width.

There are multiple options on how best to perform 2D image convolution, including Direct, GEMM, FFT [20], and Winograd [12]. The Direct algorithm expresses the convolution as a direct convolution [3]; The GEMM method transforms the entire process into a matrix-matrix multiplication. The FFT and Winograd algorithms are fast implementations that are widely used [12], the former requires significant memory space, while the latter is memory-efficient [6].

2.1.2 Non-linearity. The non-linearity is introduced as **activation functions** to deal with linear inseparable problems. Some commonly used activation functions include the Rectified Linear Unit (ReLU), the sigmoid, and the hyperbolic tangent (tanh) [19].

The non-linear activation functions should be used together with linear transforms, meaning that every activation function follows a linear data transformation. The equations below provide mathematical descriptions of these functions.

$$y_i = \max(0, x_i) \qquad y_i = \frac{1}{1 + e^{-x_i}} \qquad y_i = \frac{e^{x_i} - e^{-x_i}}{e^{x_i} + e^{-x_i}} \qquad (4)$$

These functions are implemented as element-wise matrix operations.

2.1.3 Other Techniques. Some other techniques involved in neural networks computations include **pooling**, **local response normalization (LRN)**, and **Softmax**. Each one of these steps has a different mathematical model, and each with its own functionality and operations. Pooling is a down-sampling technique to reduce the amount of computation for the following layers, and it has been shown to be an effective approach to improve robustness in practice. As described in the Alexnet documentation [11], the pooling layer can reduce the error rate by around 0.4%. Normally, pooling groups are not overlapped, so the pooling layer can be viewed as a grid of pooling groups spaced k data samples apart [11], where k is the size of the pooling group. Figure 2b shows an example of the feature map data being divided into 16 pooling groups.

The down sampling within one pooling group can be completed either by selecting the maximum value (i.e., Max Pooling) or computing the average of the group (i.e., Average Pooling). Max Pooling is usually more widely used in CNN models, e.g. AlexNet. Max Pooling selects the most representative value from a sub-group of the feature map. By doing so, interference by neighboring pixels can be reduced significantly. Similar to convolution, pooling also needs a kernel to select the pooling group. But the kernel cannot be overlapped when it moves to next data sample. Besides, we can see that Max Pooling has no complex arithmetic operations executed, other than simple comparison and loading/storing of the data. The only computation is to identify the maximum value among the pooling groups.

In general, LRN is a normalization method that works across various feature maps or channels. Basically, normalization is done across data samples from multiple adjacent kernel maps, but at the same relative position. Equation 5 describes its computation:

$$y_i = \frac{x_i}{k + \alpha \left(\displaystyle\sum_{j=\max(0, i-n/2)}^{\min(N-1, i+n/2)} (x_j)^2 \right)^\beta} \qquad (5)$$

where k, α, β are all configurable parameters of LRN, N is the number of kernel maps, n is the window size for normalization, x_i is the input data, and y_i is the output with the same spatial location. With this algorithm, the prediction error rate can drop by 2%[11].

The computation of the Softmax function should be performed at the end of neural network model. It is the core function in the output layer, as it interprets the output data from the previous layer, and generates a set of probability-like values in the range of 0 to 1 (note, the sum of all of these values equals 1). For each value that Softmax computes, it represents the extent to which the input data should be classified into one of the predefined classes. The Softmax function is defined in equation 6:

$$Y_i = \frac{e^{x_i}}{\sum_{j=1}^{N} e^{x_j}} \qquad (6)$$

where N is both the number of outputs from the previous layer and the number of classes.

2.1.4 Training of Neural Networks. To describe the entire training process mathematically, we can treat the whole network model as a loss function, specifying inputs, outputs and model parameters as arguments. The objective is try to optimize the in-network parameters so that the overall loss can be minimized.

Training deep neural networks is an iterative and time consuming task. It usually requires more than a thousand iterations before the network parameters are properly trained. One of the most effective algorithms used to update the parameters is *Stochastic Gradient Descent* (SGD), which is an iterative algorithm that processes a mini-batch of the training data [11].

The detailed mechanism for training can be further divided into a forward and a backward propagation. The purpose for performing forward propagation during training is to calculate the loss of the overall network based on the current parameters. The ultimate goal of the backward propagation is to obtain the derivatives of the loss function, with respect to the parameters for the SGD algorithm. When computing the loss, we are able to calculate the derivatives with respect to the inputs, outputs, and parameters of each layer by applying the derivative chain rule in a backward-cascaded fashion.

2.2 Graphic Processing Units

The architecture of a Graphic Processing Unit (GPU) is designed to improve instruction throughput rather than reduce the latency of a single instruction. As such, the compute unit organization is much simpler than a CPU core design. Nevertheless, the GPU has many more cores than a CPU and is able to run thousands of threads simultaneously with support of low-overhead thread switching to hide latency. Therefore, GPUs clearly outperform CPUs in most cases where instruction throughput matters. A good example is with matrix-based computations, which are heavily used in almost every DNN variant. Thus, GPUs are well-suited to execute DNNs that are designed to run on parallel platforms.

The basic building block of an Nvidia GPU is the multi-threaded Streaming Multiprosessors (SMs). As shown in Figure 3, each SM contains a collection of computational resources that includes single precision CUDA cores, load store units, special functional units, and texture units. Each SM is also equipped with a large register file, so that threads can have their own set. Dedicated registers, assigned to each thread, means that data no longer needs to be swapped out during context switching, as adopted in CPU This can potentially reduce the corresponding overhead. With a low context switch overhead, threads can hide pipeline stalls and effectively utilize the computational resources of the GPU.

An array of SMs is connected to a hierarchical memory system. Each SM has limited memory resources that are exclusive to themselves, including the L1 cache, the shared memory and the read-only/texture cache. The shared memory is a scratchpad cache that is accessible by the programmer. In Kepler architecture, it shares a configurable on-chip memory area with the L1 cache, whereas it is a dedicated memory in Pascal. The read-only/texture

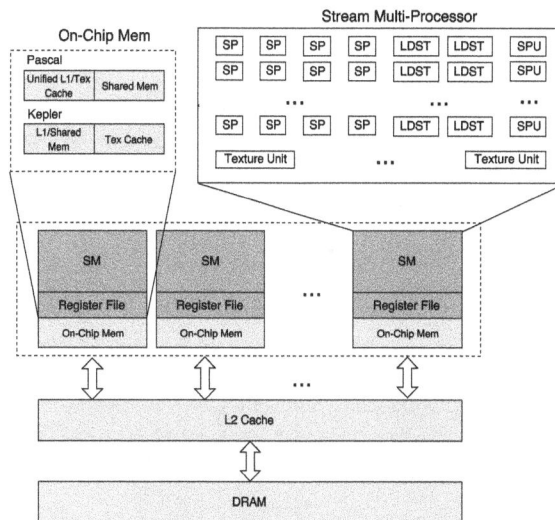

Figure 3: Diagram of a typical GPU architecture.

cache is accessible by the texture unit and the SM for general load operations. It is a dedicated memory in Kepler but shares a configurable on-chip memory area with the L1 cache in Pascal. Each SM has exclusive memory resources connected to a shared L2 cache. The L2 cache is the primary point of data unification between the SMs, servicing all general and texture memory requests, providing efficient, high speed data sharing across the GPU. The L2 cache is backed by a high bandwidth DRAM memory, which is the largest memory on a GPU that programmers can access directly.

An SM in a Pascal GPU has 128 single-precision (FP32) CUDA cores. In comparison, in the Kepler family, each SM has 192 CUDA cores. Pascal maintains the same register file size and supports similar occupancy of warps and thread blocks. However, more SMs can be accommodated in a Pascal GPU thanks to the smaller SM and better technology. Overall, the size of shared memory on the Pascal GPU is also increased due to the increased SM count, and aggregate shared memory bandwidth is effectively improved. A higher ratio of shared memory, registers, and warps per SM in Pascal GPUs allows the SM to execute code more efficiently. An SM in Pascal also features a simpler datapath organization that requires less die area and power to manage data transfers within the SM. Pascal also provides superior scheduling and overlapped load/store instructions to increase floating point utilization.

3 EVALUATION METHODOLOGY

3.1 Workload

In this paper, we select the AlexNet model to drive our characterization study. Although it is not the latest CNN model, it provides an organization that lends itself to evaluation, while including almost all of the primitives widely used in current state-of-the-art CNN models. Therefore, our microarchitectural characterization when running Alexnet can serve as a representative CNN model. Figure 4 shows the organization of AlexNet. As shown in this figure, AlexNet consists of 5 convolution layers, 3 fully-connected layers, 3 maxpooling layers, 2 LRN layers, 7 ReLU activation layers, and 1

Softmax layer. The number of operations in each layer is listed in Table 1. Note that we count every occurrence of either arithmetic or logical operations.

In terms of workload, we select cuDNNv6[3], a highly optimized DNN library specifically designed to run on Nvidia GPUs. This implementation has been used extensively by the deep learning research community, since it provides a user-friendly interface and is able to achieve high performance in terms of execution time. We use DNNMark [7], a configurable DNN benchmark suite composed of both cuDNN and cuBLAS, to construct the AlexNet model. Unlike applications found in other popular DNN frameworks, the AlexNet benchmark constructed within DNNMark is designed specifically for measuring hardware performance, essentially reducing the benchmarking effort by removing the need to develop new code. For input, we use a set of synthetic images, generated in batches, with the same dimensions as shown in the figure 4.

Table 1: Number of operations in each layer of AlexNet.

Layer	Number of Operations	Layer	Number of Operations
conv1	210M	conv4	448M
relu1	290K	relu4	65K
lrn1	4M	conv5	299M
pool1	630K	relu5	43K
conv2	896M	pool5	83K
relu2	186K	fc6	75M
lrn2	3M	relu6	4K
pool2	389K	fc7	33M
conv3	299M	relu7	4K
relu3	65K	fc8	8M
softmax	1M		

3.2 Hardware

In this paper, we select the Nvidia Tesla K40 [18] and GTX1080 [16] as the hardware platforms to run our experiments. The K40 microarchitecture was developed as part of Nvidia Kepler family of GPUs [14], while the GTX1080 is part of the Pascal family. They represents different product grades, as well. K40 is designed for servers, while the GTX1080 is designed for desktop acceleration. These two platforms have different architectures and computing capabilities, serving as good candidates to capture performance trends, while migrating the same workload from one platform to another. Table 2 provides details about each device.

3.3 Profiling Tools

Capturing and parsing the micro-architectural information of CNNs has many challenges due to the limitations of Nvidia profiler, nvprof[15]. These issues include: i) some layers invoke the same GPU kernel, but specify very different kernel template arguments, meaning that even though the kernel names are identical, they are in fact different kernels. If we want to capture the layer-specific information, using the kernel name only is not sufficient to uniquely identify the kernel; ii) some layers launch the exact same kernel based on their invocation order, according to the network model, so profiling using only the kernel name will return average results for these

Table 2: Nvidia Tesla K40 and GTX1080 configuration details.

Type	Tesla k40	Pascal GTX 1080
Number of processor cores	2880	2560
SIMD lane width	8	
Maximum threads per processor	2048	
Maximum threads per block	1024	
Number of 32-bit registers	65536	
Maximum registers per threads	255	
Shared memory	64KB shared	96KB dedicated
L1 cache	64KB shared	64KB shared
Read-only data cache	48KB dedicated	64KB shared
L2 cache	1536KB	2048KB
GPU maximum clock rate	745Mhz	1607MHz
Memory clock rate	3004Mhz	10000MHz
Memory interface	384-bit	256-bit
Memory bandwidth	208 GB/sec	320 GB/sec
Memory size	12GB	8GB

layers. Therefore, we need to take the invocation order into account so we can capture the information of each individual layer.

This imposes challenges to tie the characterized microarchitectural information to a specific layer. In order to address this challenge, we designed a database-backed trace tracking system that can capture the microarchitectural information for each layer in the CNN model. We establish a relational database to store platform-specific information, providing indices including the layer ID, kernel name, invocation order, and etc. With the help of this trace tracking system, we are able to obtain layer-specific micro-architectural information in a convenient and accurate manner. Figure 5 shows the overall workflow of the trace tracking system. We first profile the general execution information, i.e. kernel name and invocation order to create the relational database table, and then we leverage the database to profile the layer-specific microarchitectural metrics and extract the necessary information to drive our analytical tools.

3.4 Experimental Setup

Our experimental framework is designed to capture microarchitectural information at a kernel level for each layer involved in computing a single iteration during the AlexNet training process, without applying SGD. Thus, we focus on the execution of forward and backward propagation. A full evaluation of SGD during training is future work. Although hundreds of thousands iterations will be involved in a complete training, we believe the evaluation of one single iteration can be generalized given that performance metrics are measured at a kernel level, and for each iteration, the same kernels are executed. We use our database-backed trace tracking Framework to capture the information from the GPU kernels launched. We run the same experiments with various batch sizes. The number of images in one batch is 16, 64, and 128, which are typical batch-size configurations used in practice.

4 EVALUATION RESULTS

In this section, we present several key metrics that capture performance in terms of microarchitectural details. Our evaluation is done on a kernel basis. Considering that cuDNN uses a flexible

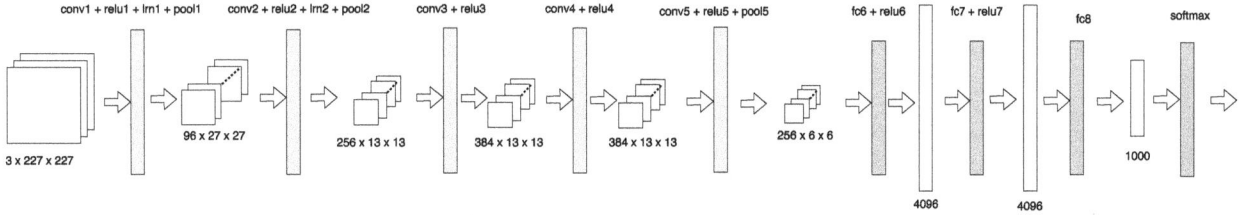

Figure 4: The organization of AlexNet.

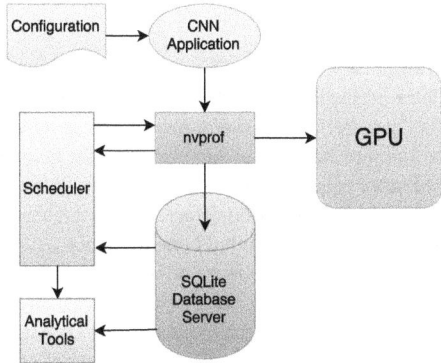

Figure 5: Database-based trace tracking system.

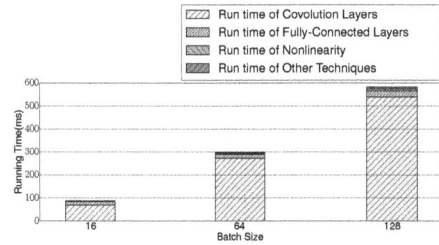

Figure 6: Runtime of AlexNet on the K40.

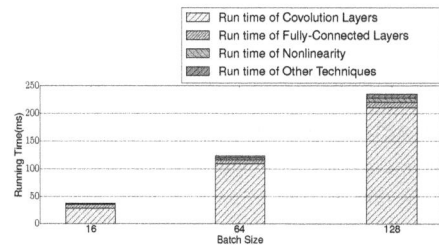

Figure 7: Runtime of AlexNet on the GTX1080.

strategy to instantiate kernels while varying template arguments for optimization purposes, we use the layer name rather than kernel name to present our evaluation results, even though the results are measured for kernels of primitives in cuDNN and cuBLAS.

4.1 Performance Analysis

First, we evaluate the runtime of each layer involved in one epoch of AlexNet, running across various batch sizes. This gives us a overview of performance for each layer, allowing us to identify the important steps during model execution. Since both the size of input image, as well as the training parameters, are fixed in the model, the batch size becomes the only variable that controls the scale of the final workload and size of the intermediate data. Figures 6 and 7 showcase the run times of AlexNet running on the K40 and GTX1080, respectively. During backward propagation, layers with trainable parameters should have at least two computations performing both data and backward propagation of weights. Bias is not considered in this paper, since the related computations are very simple.

From Figures 6 and 7, we can clearly see that the layers performing linear transformations are the major bottlenecks during the execution of the entire AlexNet model on both platforms. Convolution layers dominate performance of the linear transformations. This trend is consistent on both platforms, which shows that using a larger batch size leads to better throughput in terms of image processing, meaning that the both platforms achieve good scalability. The execution time is drastically reduced on the GTX1080, though the runtime of the other layers (other than the convolution layers) tends to become more prominent. Moreover, we noticed that the execution time of each layer is well-correlated with the

number of operations indicated in Table 1. All of the linear data transformation layers take longer to finish.

In Figure 8 we report the speedup of running AlexNet on a GTX1080, using the K40 performance as a baseline. Generally, the GTX1080 has more SMs, (although there are fewer CUDA cores in each SM) and a higher clock rate in terms of both processing cores and memory, so the speedup is expected. But it can be observed that the performance gain for each layer varies. The convolution, fully-connected and pooling layers have significantly higher speedup than the activation (ReLU) and softmax layers. The LRN layer has relatively higher speedup during backward propagation versus forward propagation. Based on this observation, we find that the more advanced hardware has varied impact on the different layers while the floating-point instruction counts are basically equal in the applications built for each platform. The floating-point instruction counts of layers in backward propagation are listed in figure 9. Note that we only present the results from backward propagation because we noticed that the metric trends for the forward and backward propagation across every layer are very similar in most cases, and backward propagation is the most critical part during the CNN training. We present results for a batch size of 128, since

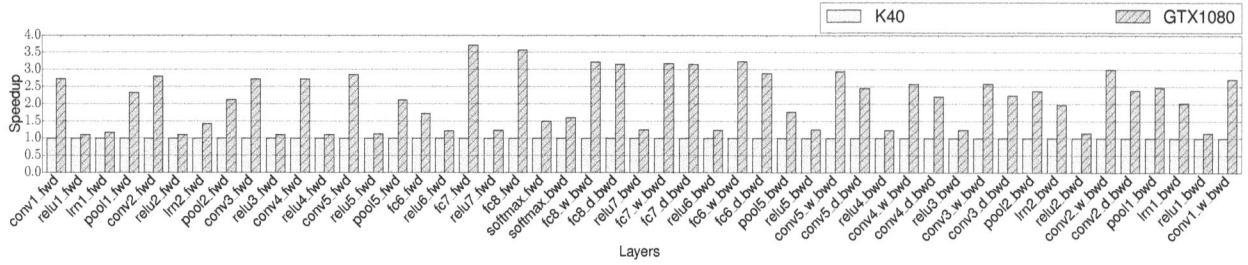

Figure 8: Speedup of running AlexNet on the GTX1080, using K40 performance as the baseline.

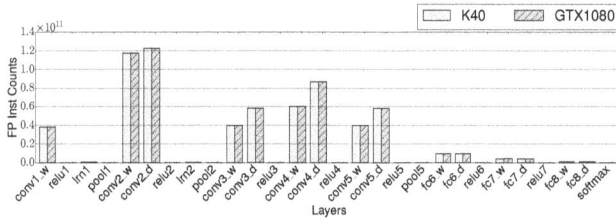

Figure 9: The floating-point instruction counts.

that this configuration can fully utilize the massive hardware of a GPU.

4.2 Characteristics Analysis of Layers

Next, we delve a step deeper into the microarchitectural details that can explain the difference in terms of performance observed across different layers. First, we highlight the reason for stalls during kernel execution on the baseline K40 platform in order to understand the characteristics of each layer. Figure 10 shows a breakdown of the stalls in each layer of AlexNet running on the K40.

Based on the stall categories chosen, we can identify the major bottleneck present in each layer, identifying the two largest contributors. We select conv2_w, relu2, lrn2, pool2, fc6_w, and softmax to represent convolution, activation, LRN, pooling, fully-connected, and softmax layer, respectively. As indicated in the figure, the two dominating stall categories for conv2_w are *stall_exec_dependency* and *stall_not_selected*. The former indicates the intrinsic program characteristics of this layer, meaning that there are many dependencies during instruction execution within a warp. The latter implies the warp is not selected to run since the scheduler selects competing warps. In other words, the SMs are always busy when warps are scheduled. Therefore, the performance of conv2_w is mainly bounded by computing. The two major stall reasons for relu2 are *stall_memory_throttle* and *stall_memory_dependency*. The meaning of these two reasons are obvious. The former is caused by memory bottlenecks, and the latter is due to program characteristics related to data dependencies on memory loads and stores. Hence, the relu2 layer is memory-bound. Due to the dominating stall reasons in lrn2, pool2, and softmax as indicated in the figure, they are all compute and memory bound. fc6_w is somewhat special in that it is partially bounded by memory and partially bounded by instruction fetch. Even though there is little public documentation describing how does instruction fetch works on Nvidia GPUs, we believe it should

be related to the performance of the warp scheduler, and will be explained later according to the results of the GTX1080.

Given the characteristics of the representative layers/ primitives, it is expected that performance gain varies on the given hardware. Generally, a higher processor clock rate and more SMs should benefit compute-intensive applications more, while increasing the memory clock rate only creates limited benefits. Since data load/write performance is not only dependent on the memory clock rates, but also the demands and bandwidth of the different memory components in the memory hierarchy, our performance gains, due to using a faster memory clock rate, can to some extent remove memory bottlenecks. But this is only true for for more memory-bound applications. Alternatively, higher processor clock rates and higher number of SMs have a direct impact on the FLOP rate. Hence, this explains variations in performance gains as we migrate AlexNet from the K40 to the GTX1080, which has more SMs, and higher processor and memory speeds.

In Figure 11, we present the stall breakdown when running AlexNet on the GTX1080. We can now see how the distribution of stalls change when running with a higher clock rate and with more SMs. One obvious finding is that the reason *stall_memory_throttle* is gone for all layers, meaning that the GTX1080 provides a faster data-path for moving data between processors and memory. For relu2, the major reason for stalls is tied to program characteristics that are highly dependent on memory operations. Increasing the memory frequency should lead to limited performance benefits, given that relu2 is a stream-like application with little temporal locality. The breakdown of stalls in conv2_w does not change much. Given that we see that the scheduler is choosing to run other warps, this layer still has headroom to improve if a higher GPU core clock rate is used, or SMs are added. The lrn2, pool2, and softmax layers become memory-bound on GTX1080, because the compute performance of the GTX1080 over the K40 has improved more versus the memory performance of the two systems. The fc6_w layer is both memory and compute bound. Since we see the same warp scheduling issues we encountered for conv2_w, there is headroom to improve performance for fc6_w. The new scheduler design in the Pascal architecture significantly alleviates the problems experienced with instruction fetching on the K40, so the new scheduler is able to handle more warps [17].

Finally, we list the CUDA cores ALU utilization for both platforms, considering that this metric reflects, to a great extent, how well the available hardware can be exploited. Figure 12 shows the ALU utilization while running AlexNet. As shown in the figure,

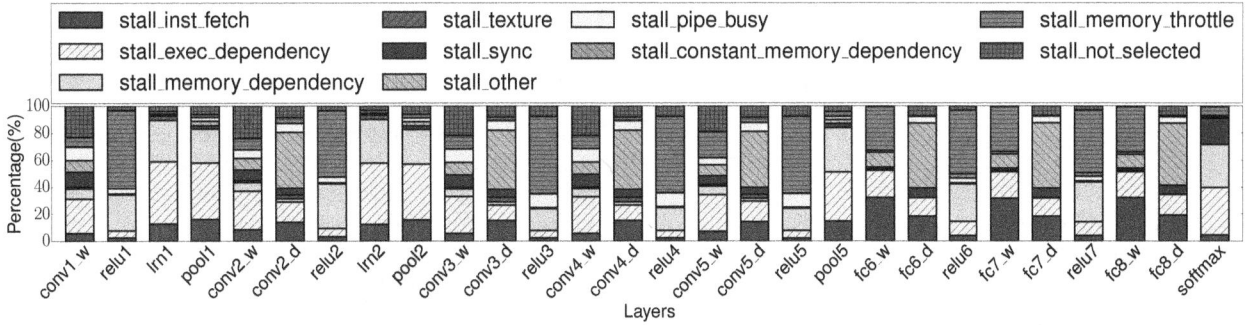

Figure 10: Stall breakdown for AlexNet running backward propagation on the K40.

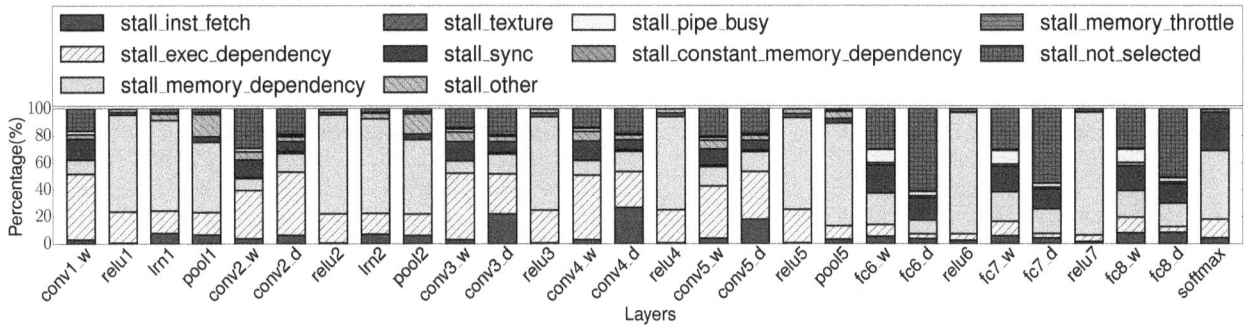

Figure 11: Stall breakdown for AlexNet, running backward propagation on the GTX1080.

almost all of the layers involved in linear transformations have higher ALU utilization levels on the GTX1080. There is one case in lrn1, where the utilization level on GTX1080 is lower. This is because the LRN layer becomes memory-bound on the GTX1080, due to the increased computing capability, requiring more data to be accessed. This results in more processing core idle time.

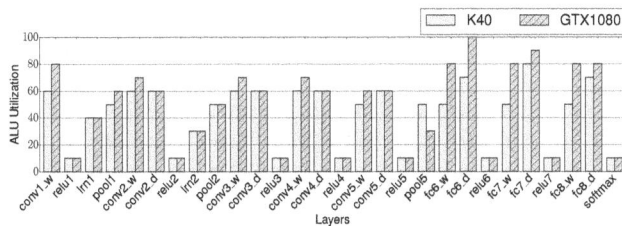

Figure 12: Compute unit utilization levels.

4.3 Memory Access Behavior

In this section, we focus on characterizing the memory behavior of each layer in AlexNet. Generally, in a discrete GPU, other than the main memory, the other critical memory component is the cache. The design of cache takes advantage of the locality present in applications, both in time and space, reducing the latency between instruction processing and memory access. In the GPU models we use, there are three different types of cache working together to support the streaming multiprocessors: i) an L2 cache, ii) a texture

cache, and iii) an L1 cache, as shown in figure 3. Other than that, there is also an on-chip fast scratch-pad memory, shared memory, for the programmer to directly utilize in order to achieve better performance. Depending on the memory space specified by the CUDA programmer, the processor will initially request the data from either the L1, shared memory, or the texture cache. If not present in any of the three locations, the data will be requested from higher levels in the memory hierarchy.

Given that the K40 and GTX1080 have different on-chip memory arrangements, as observed in Table 2, we showcase the cache hit rate on both platforms. In this section, we only present a subset of layers in backward propagation, using a batch size of 128 for simplicity, because the layers of the same type have very similar characteristics, as discussed earlier in our stall analysis and in our utilization evaluation. Likewise, we select conv2_w/d, relu2, lrn2, pool2, fc6_w/d, and softmax to represent convolution, activation, LRN, pooling, fully-connected, and softmax layer, respectively. We also only present backward propagation with a batch size of 128 for the same reasons as in our earlier discussion. Figures 13 and 14 present the cache hit rates of all caching components.

From the cache hit rates shown for the K40 in Figure 13, we notice that layers of the linear data transformation make good use of the texture cache. This can be explained since the computations in both the convolution and fully-connected layers exhibit a high degree of spatial locality. The texture cache is designed in such a way as to take advantage of spatial locality. The L1 cache is a bit too limited in terms of space to handle this data. As a result, we see no L1 activities. In terms of the L2 hit rate, we can see cache accesses exist

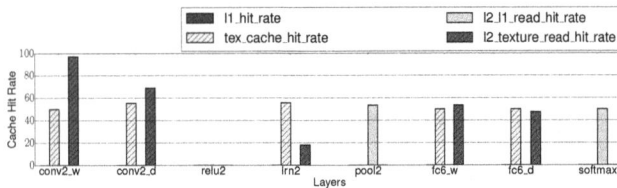

Figure 13: Cache hit rate for backward propagation of selected layers on the K40.

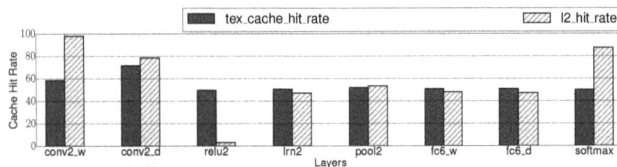

Figure 14: Cache hit rate for backward propagation of selected layers on the GTX1080.

in almost every layer except the activation layers. This is caused by the element-wise operations present, so the activation layer acts as a streaming application with no temporal locality. Likewise, the texture cache is heavily utilized as well on the GTX1080. Even the activation layer, which has no temporal locality, also makes use of the texture cache to exploit spatial locality. In order make a fair comparison, we enable the usage of L1 cache on the GTX1080 by toggling the corresponding compile flag [4]. However, the L1 cache is unified with the texture cache, so it is difficult to observe any L1 cache activities merely through the texture cache hit rate. To address this issue, we compare the texture cache hit rate between the two cases where L1 cache is enabled, and then disabled. The results show no change in the texture cache hit rate, meaning that there is basically no L1 activities as well.

Next, we analyze the number of memory transactions and memory throughput for each level within the GPU memory hierarchy. Besides the improvements in memory throughput at every memory level (thanks to the increased clock rate), we also notice an increase in the number of memory transactions handled by the memory components on the GTX1080 with higher capacity, such as shared memory and L2 cache. In contrast, the number of memory transactions issued to the DRAM is reduced significantly. This means that the larger L2 cache can better exploit locality, storing data closer to the processor and reducing DRAM request. Similarly, a larger shared memory provides more opportunity to store data structures that will be re-used frequently.

Although there are many differences in memory performance between the two platforms, the trend in these metrics for the two platforms is still very similar in most cases. To provide a better view from both the processing core side and DRAM side, we split the metrics into two parts, each of which represents the memory components closer to the processor or closer to the DRAM, respectively. Figures 15- 16 shows the number of memory transaction and the memory throughput in various memory components. Note that we only present results from the GTX1080 because the trends are very similar.

From Figure 15a, we can see that the linear data transformation layers rely heavily on shared memory and the texture cache. As indicated in the cache hit rate figures, both the convolution and fully-connected layers possess high temporal and spatial locality, given that data accessed within a region is repeatedly accessed. As a result, there are a large number of memory transactions issued to these two memory levels, especially read requests. This means that some shared memory data is heavily reused during the computation. On the contrary, for other layers, the utilization of shared memory and texture cache is very limited. Even for the pooling and LRN layers, the data reuse rate is very low. Figure 15b supports the previous statement. For the other layers, including pooling, LRN, activation, and Softmax, the number of memory transactions does not vary significantly across the memory hierarchy.

With regards to memory throughput, In figure 16a, we can see that shared memory throughput was almost 4x higher than on the texture cache, even though the number of memory transactions in these two components is similar in the convolution layers. This indicates that shared memory has much higher bandwidth than the texture cache. For instance, shared memory usually takes 38 cycles to read, while the texture cache takes 436-443 cycles [29]. The latest hardware has shortened the performance gap between those two, but the gap is still significantly wide. Therefore, the bandwidth of texture cache is a limiting factor for the convolution layers.

Note that increasing the bandwidth of texture memory without taking other associated memory components into account, could result in limited benefits. For example, if the texture cache becomes much faster than the L2 cache, execution will bottleneck at the L2. Increasing the bandwidth of the texture cache further would not benefit performance.

From Figure 16b, we can see that the throughput of DRAM in the activation layers is higher than that for the other layers. This is because the memory access pattern in the activation layers is more regular, meaning that memory requests can be coalesced, resulting in a better ratio between the size of useful data to number of memory transactions. Given that throughput is computed using the size of the requested data, divided by the time between the first and last memory transaction, a higher ratio leads to higher throughput.

We evaluate the utilization of the memory hierarchy in Figure 17. We show how each layer utilizes individual memory levels in the hierarchy. We find that the convolution layers can leverage shared memory and the texture cache, while activation layers utilize the DRAM heavily during the execution.

4.4 Potential Optimization

From our analysis, we propose a number of design changes that can benefit CNN execution on GPUs, especially the GTX1080. First, we begin with the major bottleneck which are present in the convolution layer, as indicated in figures 6 and 7. Stalls during convolution are due both to intrinsic program characteristics, and the limits of the hardware (even on the GTX1080). A simple solution is to add more SMs. Increasing the DRAM bandwidth on the GTX1080 will not benefit the CNN throughput very much. Instead, if we increase the bandwidth of the texture cache, we should see much better performance. As discussed earlier, a significant number of memory

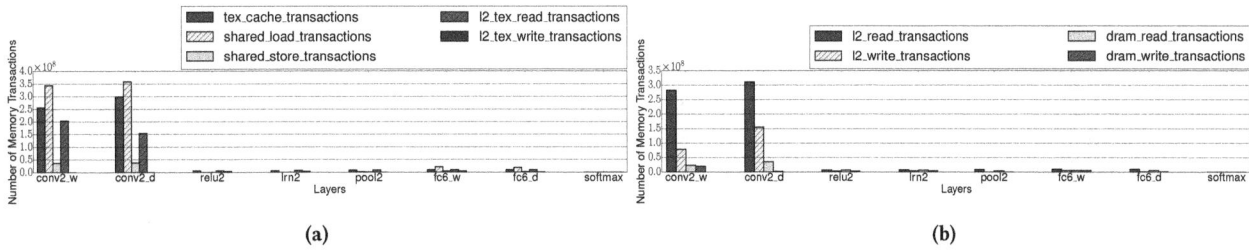

(a)

(b)

Figure 15: (a) Number of memory transactions in memory components closer to processor. (b) Number of memory transactions in memory components closer to DRAM.

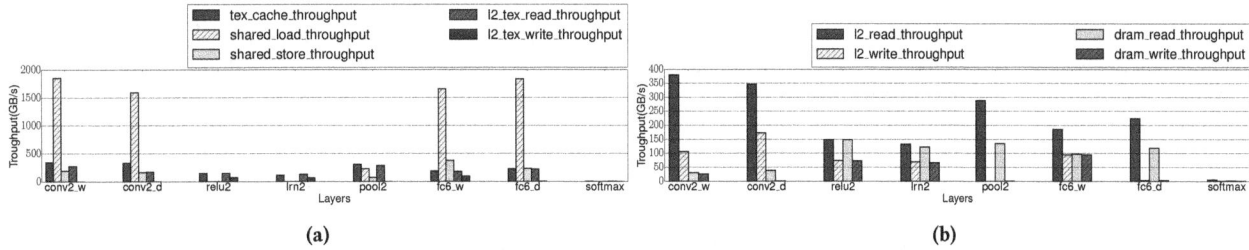

(a)

(b)

Figure 16: (a) Memory throughput of memory components closer to processor. (b) Memory throughput of memory components closer to DRAM.

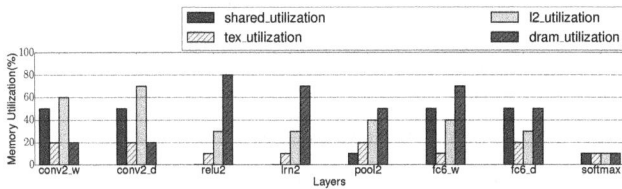

Figure 17: Memory components utilization of selected layers on the GTX1080.

transactions occur in the texture cache, but given its meager bandwidth, low throughput results. Thus, increasing the bandwidth of texture cache is beneficial in terms of reducing the read latency from the texture cache.

Next, we find that L1 cache is essentially unused in most of the layers. The main reason is that the L1 cache is too small to hold data that has a strided access pattern. Based on this observation, we can enable L1 cache bypassing[27] for selected layers to avoid unnecessary data requests to the L1 cache. When we re-run our application with the L1 cache disabled for both reads and writes, we observe a speedup in some layers for both forward and backward propagation. From these results, we find that a single layer used in backward propagation (calculating the convolution layer weights) can achieve a 6.2% speedup on the GTX1080. However, this approach is limited in terms of achieving better overall application throughput. One issue is that some layers exhibit temporal locality, so L1 cache bypassing needs to be applied selectively by these layers. If we focus on optimizations that only benefit a subset of layers, the overall performance gains will be limited.

Another optimization we explore is to apply kernel fusion[28] for the linear data transformation layers and the non-linear activation layers. As indicated in the results from the utilization breakdown, the activation layers place little pressure on compute resources due to its simple, element-wise, operations. The idea is to combine the linear data transformation and non-linearity. By doing so, we can eliminate all activation layers in the neural network model, leading to a significant reduction in the number of memory transactions, with only a small amount of computation added in the linear data transformation layers. Although the run time of the activation layers is insignificant, we can still save the time spent on running the driver and kernel launch, improving power efficiency as well. Given that cuDNN is not an open-source library, we are not able to further explore kernel fusion. So in order to evaluate the potential benefits of kernel fusion, we directly removed activation layers, assuming that the additional computation in the linear data transformation layers can be ignored. In this experiment, we measure the overall runtime, not just the kernel execution time. We are able to produce a speedup of 4% on average. As the activation layers only take 3% of the overall execution time, we save approximately 1% the time spent on driver and kernel launch.

5 DISCUSSION

Convolutional neural networks are quickly becoming very important applications in a number of domains. CNN computations have a set of applications with distinct characteristics both in computing and memory access. Given the diversity of CNN applications, exploring characteristics of the basic primitives in CNN is a prerequisite to accelerating this class of applications in general. Some researchers have explored using FPGAs for application-specific solutions [23]. However, the GPU is still preferred in most cases, given that it provides a more flexible parallel programming framework and large memory space for storing massive amount of training data. Our evaluation in this paper focused on the microarchitectural demands associated with CNNs when mapped to two Nvidia GPUs. We evaluated how the same workload scales on platforms with different computing capabilities. We also analyzed microarchitectural metrics across different layers, considering the pressure placed on both compute units and memory components. We also proposed optimization methods based on the observed bottlenecks and insights. Through our experiments, we find there is still further room for improvements from perspective of both hardware and software optimizations.

As a further step, rather than reducing the execution time, we will focus on power efficiency. Considering that each layer has different needs in terms of computing resources and main memory, the GPU architecture can be argumented with big-little core techniques, so that heavy layers that hunger for compute resources can be scheduled on big cores, while lightweight layers can run on the smaller cores. Another approach is to design a dynamic clock rate tailored for each layer. It is demonstrated that not every layer requires the same processor and memory frequency, so finding a set of clock rate configurations for each layer can achieve better power efficiency.

6 RELATED WORK

There have been a number of earlier evaluation studies that focused on Neural Networks. Shi et al. conducted a series experiments of evaluating the current state-of-the-art deep learning software tools [24]. They evaluate a number of neural network models using state-of-the-art deep learning tools on both single and multiple GPUs. They propose a general guide of leveraging proper software tools on the targeted platforms, They also point out possible optimization directions for researchers. Kim et al. also evaluate several existing deep learning frameworks and suggest possible optimization methods leveraging convolution algorithms to improve CNN efficiency [10]. They characterize existing deep learning frameworks at an application level and explore the benefits of using different convolution algorithms in order to achieve better performance. Rhu et al. measure the memory usage of DNNs and propose a virtualization method to deal with issues of memory limits of a GPU [21]. Basically, they characterize the data access and data re-use patterns to create a virtual memory management strategy for DNN applications. The first two works above only evaluate performance at an application level, and the last focuses on data usage in the memory. The work presented in this paper provides a much more comprehensive dive into CNN execution behavior from a GPU microarchitectural perspective.

7 CONCLUSION

In this paper, we characterize the demands placed on a GPU microarchitecture while running a commonly used CNN model (AlexNet). We consider performance on a layer-by-layer basis. We carefully select metrics that can characterize the execution behavior of each layer in the model, and identify the major limiting factors for each layer. From our evaluation, we find that the characteristics of each

layer vary significantly due to the distinct type of operations performed. Based on the microarchitectual demands imposed by each layer, we identify the major bottlenecks present in both an entire CNN model, and each individual layer, and suggest several optimization approaches that are able to improve the performance with only minor changes and overhead.

REFERENCES

[1] Martín Abadi et al. 2015. TensorFlow: Large-Scale Machine Learning on Heterogeneous Systems. (2015). http://tensorflow.org/
[2] Tianqi Chen, Mu Li, and et al. 2015. MXNet: A Flexible and Efficient Machine Learning Library for Heterogeneous Distributed Systems. *CoRR* (2015). http://arxiv.org/abs/1512.01274
[3] Sharan Chetlur, Cliff Woolley, Philippe Vandermersch, Jonathan Cohen, John Tran, Bryan Catanzaro, and Evan Shelhamer. 2014. cuDNN: Efficient Primitives for Deep Learning. *arXiv preprint arXiv:1410.0759* (2014).
[4] NVIDIA Corporation. 2014. CUDA C Programming Guide. (2014).
[5] NVIDIA Corporation. 2015. CuBlas library v7.5. (2015).
[6] NVIDIA Corporation. 2017. CuDNN library v6.0. (2017).
[7] Shi Dong and David Kaeli. 2017. DNNMark: A Deep Neural Network Benchmark Suite for GPUs. *GPGPU-10* (2017), 63–72. https://doi.org/10.1145/3038228.3038239
[8] Erico Guizzo. 2016. How Google's Self-Driving Car Works. (2016).
[9] Yangqing Jia, Evan Shelhamer, Jeff Donahue, Sergey Karayev, Jonathan Long, Ross Girshick, Sergio Guadarrama, and Trevor Darrell. 2014. Caffe: Convolutional Architecture for Fast Feature Embedding. *arXiv preprint arXiv:1408.5093* (2014).
[10] Heehoon Kim, Hyoungwook Nam, Wookeun Jung, and Jaejin Lee. 2017. Performance Analysis of CNN Frameworks for GPUs. *Performance Analysis of Systems and Software (ISPASS)* (2017).
[11] Alex Krizhevsky, Ilya Sutskever, and Geoffrey E Hinton. 2012. ImageNet Classification with Deep Convolutional Neural Networks. *Advances in Neural Information Processing Systems 25* (2012), 1097–1105.
[12] Andrew Lavin and Scott Gray. 2015. Fast Algorithms for Convolutional Neural Networks. *arXiv preprint arXiv:1509.09308* (2015).
[13] Yann LeCun, Yoshua Bengio, and Geoffrey Hinton. 2015. Deep learning. *Nature* (2015), 436–444. https://doi.org/10.1038/nature14539
[14] NVIDIA. 2012. NVIDIA's Next Generation CUDA™ Compute Architecture, Kepler™ GK110. (2012).
[15] NVIDIA. 2016. CUDA Toolkit Documentation. (2016).
[16] NVIDIA. 2016. NVIDIA GeForce GTX 1080. (2016).
[17] NVIDIA. 2016. NVIDIA Tesla P100. (2016).
[18] NVIDIA. 2016. TESLA GPU ACCELERATORS FOR SERVERS. (2016).
[19] Genevieve B. Orr and Klaus-Robert Mueller (Eds.). 1998. *Neural Networks : Tricks of the Trade.* Lecture Notes in Computer Science, Vol. 1524. Springer.
[20] Victor Podlozhnyuk. 2007. FFT-based 2D convolution. (2007).
[21] Minsoo Rhu, Natalia Gimelshein, Jason Clemons, Arslan Zulfiqar, and Stephen W. Keckler. 2016. vDNN: Virtualized deep neural networks for scalable, memory-efficient neural network design. *Microarchitecture (MICRO)* (2016).
[22] Frank Seide and Amit Agarwal. [n. d.]. CNTK: Microsoft's Open-Source Deep-Learning Toolkit. ACM, 2135–2135. https://doi.org/10.1145/2939672.2945397
[23] Hardik Sharma, Jongse Park, Divya Mahajan, Emmanuel Amaro, Joon Kyung Kim, Chenkai Shao, Asit Mishra, and Hadi Es. 2016. From high-level deep neural models to FPGAs. *Microarchitecture (MICRO)* (2016).
[24] Shaohuai Shi, Qiang Wang, Pengfei Xu, and Xiaowen Chu. 2016. Benchmarking State-of-the-Art Deep Learning Software Tools. *CoRR abs/1608.07249* (2016). http://arxiv.org/abs/1608.07249
[25] David Silver and Google DeepMind Demis Hassabis. 2016. AlphaGo: Mastering the ancient game of Go with Machine Learning. (2016).
[26] Theano Development Team. 2016. Theano: A Python framework for fast computation of mathematical expressions. *arXiv e-prints abs/1605.02688* (May 2016).
[27] Yingying Tian, Sooraj Puthoor, Joseph L. Greathouse, Bradford M. Beckmann, and Daniel A. Jiménez. 2015. Adaptive GPU Cache Bypassing. *Proceedings of the 8th Workshop on General Purpose Processing Using GPUs.* https://doi.org/10.1145/2716282.2716283
[28] Guibin Wang, YiSong Lin, and Wei Yi. 2010. Kernel Fusion: An Effective Method for Better Power Efficiency on Multithreaded GPU. *Proceedings of the 2010 IEEE/ACM Int'L Conference on Green Computing and Communications & Int'L Conference on Cyber, Physical and Social Computing.* https://doi.org/10.1109/GreenCom-CPSCom.2010.102
[29] Henry Wong, Misel-Myrto Papadopoulou, Maryam Sadooghi-Alvandi, and Andreas Moshovos. 2010. Demystifying GPU microarchitecture through microbenchmarking. *Performance Analysis of Systems and Software (ISPASS)* (2010).

Round-Trip Time Anomaly Detection

Daniel Brahneborg
Infoflex Connect AB
Stockholm, Sweden
firstname.lastname@infoflexconnect.se

Wasif Afzal, Adnan Čaušević,
Daniel Sundmark, Mats Björkman
Mälardalen University
Västerås, Sweden
firstname.lastname@mdh.se

ABSTRACT

Mobile text messages (SMS) are sometimes used for authentication, which requires short and reliable delivery times. The observed round-trip times when sending an SMS message provide valuable information on the quality of the connection.

In this industry paper, we propose a method for detecting round-trip time anomalies, where the exact distribution is unknown, the variance is several orders of magnitude, and there are lots of shorter spikes that should be ignored. In particular, we show that using an adaption of Double Seasonal Exponential Smoothing to reduce the content dependent variations, followed by the Remedian to find short-term and long-term medians, successfully identifies larger groups of outliers. As training data for our method we use log files from a live SMS gateway. In order to verify the effectiveness of our approach, we utilize simulated data. Our contributions are a description on how to isolate content dependent variations, and the sequence of steps to find significant anomalies in big data.

KEYWORDS

log file analysis; round-trip time; exponential smoothing

ACM Reference Format:
Daniel Brahneborg and Wasif Afzal, Adnan Čaušević, Daniel Sundmark, Mats Björkman. 2018. Round-Trip Time Anomaly Detection. In *ICPE '18: ACM/SPEC International Conference on Performance Engineering, April 9–13, 2018, Berlin, Germany*. ACM, New York, NY, USA, 8 pages. https://doi.org/10.1145/3184407.3184436

1 INTRODUCTION

Measuring and monitoring round-trip times (RTTs) of data packets in a networked environment is important for at least two reasons: (1) to maintain the negotiated service levels of quality and (2) to minimize operational costs. To better understand the importance of this monitoring, let us consider a scenario where a person wants to login to an Internet bank.

(1) The customer goes to the bank website and enters a personal, unique identification number.
(2) The bank finds this information in its customer database, and sends a verification code as an SMS message to the

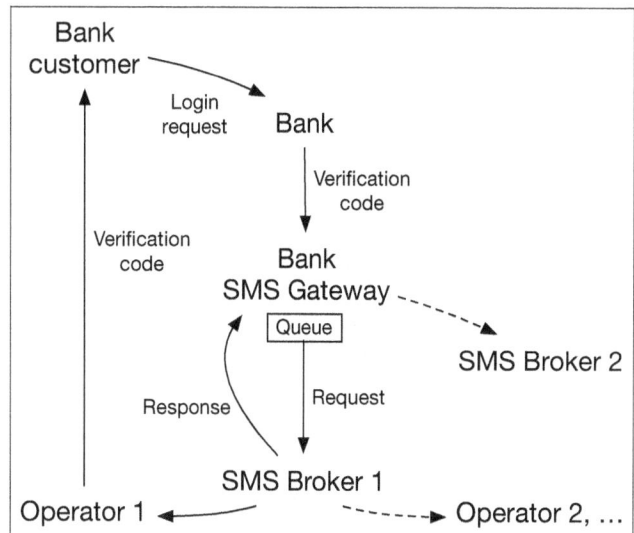

Figure 1: An example scenario emphasizing the importance of measuring and monitoring round-trip times: the bank customer, the bank, two SMS brokers and some operators.

registered mobile phone for this customer. In most cases, the SMS arrives to the mobile phone well within the negotiated, stipulated time, but in some anomaly situations, the message could be delayed for a considerable amount of time.

(3) The customer enters the verification code, completing the login procedure.

There are many mobile network operators, and as the bank does not want to maintain connections and agreements with all of them, this service is outsourced to one or more "SMS brokers". SMS brokers (SBs) manage the SMS traffic between their customers and the network operators. For increased reliability, the bank connects to two SMS brokers (Figure 1). Assuming the cost for sending messages via SB1 is lower than via SB2, by default the bank sends all messages via SB1. If the connection to SB1 is lost for some reason, the bank quickly switches to SB2 in order to avoid delays in the SMS deliveries. In the worst case it could take hours for the connection to SB1 to be fully functional again, so without this switch, the problem with SB1 would result in dissatisfied customers for the bank as the verification codes would stay in the outgoing queue in the bank's SMS Gateway. The sooner the switch to SB2 can be made, the smaller the delay seen by the bank's customers. Using SB2 all the time would not improve the situation, as SB2 could also become unreachable for any number of reasons, e.g. broken hardware, or problems at their Internet service provider.

The bank customer is the only one who knows the exact delivery time, and that is just for their own message. In order to get an overall view, from this point on we will use a simpler measurement: the RTT between the bank and the SMS broker.

In this paper we focus on detecting violations that fall somewhere between a few individual messages being slightly delayed and a fully broken connection. Let us assume the operator normally has two servers handling SMS traffic, and one of them temporarily breaks. With incoming throughput to the SMS broker being constant and outgoing throughput being halved, a queue of messages may form. To prevent this queue from growing without bounds, the SMS broker can throttle incoming traffic by delaying its responses. Clients must implement proper windowing, so these delays will cause them to delay their future requests.

The SMS system behaves much like a train of cars, in that we can draw conclusions on the situation further ahead by observing the car in front of us. If the car slows down, we can assume there is a problem with the traffic in general. Provided the slow speed persists, we might decide to choose an alternate route. Similarly, the RTT towards the SMS broker provides the client (the bank) with valuable feedback on the effective throughput of the entire chain of SMS brokers and operators.

This paper addresses the situation when the absolute values of the delivery time are not known. We know from earlier results [4] that the RTT has very few anomalies, but when they happen, we want to know as soon as possible. We have seen that there are several shorter spikes in these RTTs, so our research objective is to develop a method of automatically finding longer periods of outliers in RTTs while ignoring these short uninteresting spikes. In particular, we examine the variation of the RTTs in a production system of an SMS broker between their own system and several external operators.

Section 2 describes the context in more detail and Section 3 describes related work for RTT measurement and anomaly detection. Our approach is described in Section 4. We then describe our case study in Section 5, and the results in Section 6. Section 7 discusses these results, and the paper ends with conclusions and future work in Section 8.

2 BACKGROUND AND TERMINOLOGY

Figure 2 shows the simple base scenario of the network traffic as seen from the SMS Gateway software used by the SMS brokers. The filled arrows represent SMS messages, the unfilled arrows are responses, and A, B etc. are points in time. The SMS Gateway only knows about the times B, C, E and H. The arrow from J to K is dashed, as we do not know when this event occurs. The difference between B and C shows the processing time required for an incoming message, while the difference between E and H shows the full RTT to the operator. We will examine both these differences, as anomalies between B and C reveal problems in the local environment and anomalies between E and H reveal problems in the network or with the remote node. The difference between C and E is how long the message sits in the outgoing queue, waiting to be sent. From the bank customer's point of view, the login request starts at some point before A, and the verification code arrives to the phone at K. The delivery of the message to the mobile phone and the response sent

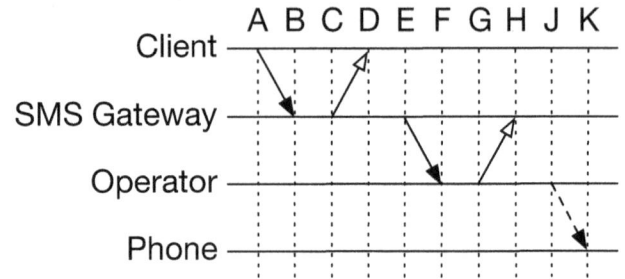

Figure 2: The network traffic between a client, an SMS Gateway, an operator and a mobile phone.

back to the SMS Gateway happens in parallel, so the relationship between H and K is undefined.

In many cases, monitoring of response times is required as a way of making sure the system works as expected. According to our industrial experience, one of two methods are commonly used for this monitoring. 1) Visualize selected measurements on a display, which is simple to implement but requires a human to look at the display. This is easily forgotten if anomalies are rare. 2) Utilize tools based on Simple Network Management Protocol (SNMP), reporting detected anomalies without requiring human interaction. A drawback is that those checks are usually trivial with static tolerance levels, e.g. whether a single RTT is longer than 1 second or whether the processing queue contains more than 1000 elements.

Once an anomaly has been detected, some fault localization technique [22] should be applied to find the root cause of the problem. This is however outside the scope of this paper.

While SMS brokers reduce the number of accounts needed, the combined network traffic becomes more difficult to analyze. Some brokers specialize in operators in a particular region, decreasing the number of accounts but increasing the number of intermediate nodes. Broker handling of messages varies, e.g. they may store the messages on disk for safety, or wait for acknowledgment from the next node before responding back to the previous. These factors incur variability in response times, even between the same nodes. We assume that if a node uses a server cluster, all these servers are homogeneous, giving consistent RTTs.

2.1 Terminology

We will now define the concepts discussed in this paper:

Node: Common term for clients, operators and SMS brokers.

Downstream/Upstream: Downstream is as ordered in Figure 2, i.e. client to SMS broker to operator to mobile phone. Upstream is, obviously, the reverse direction.

Request: A data packet containing an SMS message, including the sender, recipient and message body, or a delivery report.

Response: Acknowledgement of a received request.

PDU: Protocol Data Unit, refers to both requests and responses.

Delivery report: A data packet sent as confirmation of successful message delivery to the recipient or rejection by a node.

Round-trip time (RTT): For outgoing traffic, RTT is the interval between when the request is sent and the response comes back. For incoming traffic, RTT is the interval after receiving a request until the response is sent. In Figure 2, these are the intervals from E to H and from B to C respectively.

Throughput: The number of messages received and forwarded by a node, per some specified time unit.

Window size: The number of requests the client sends before waiting for a response.

Outlier: A single RTT measurement significantly higher than usual for a specific connection. Responses arriving earlier than usual is both very rare and typically not a problem.

Anomaly: A larger cluster of outliers. This is defined in more detail in Section 4.4.

3 RELATED WORK

Earlier studies have focused on either RTT measurement or anomaly detection, so we will describe these groups of papers separately.

3.1 RTT measurement

For RTT measurement, existing work can be structured according to what protocol they analyze. A relatively common layer for RTT measurements is TCP, as it is used for many applications and therefore enables analysis of large amounts of data. Here we find an examination of several different TCP implementations [18], and a description of the experiences using the tool Tstat [16].

TCP includes an ACK packet which, similarly to our response PDUs, provides an easy way to calculate the RTT. The RTT can then be either approximated using just the SYN/ACK pair used to initiate the connection [12] or more correctly using also the data packets and their responses [26]. Martin et al. [15] took this further by using the minimum and average values of the RTT for both the SYN and data packets to separate the physical latency from the server side processing time. The packet-pair strategy was then generalized for raw IP traffic [27].

At the application layer, which is most similar to our work, we have studies on HTTP traffic by Mosberger and Jin [17] using their tool httperf, and Halepovic et al. [9] who examined the RTTs from mobile clients to web servers. The throughput values given by httperf had an average close to the maximum, which corresponds to an average RTT being close to the minimum.

In some cases, the minimum and maximum RTT values are the most interesting [8], in which case there is no need to examine the distribution in more detail. Papers that have analyzed the data deeper, have found variances in RTT for TCP traffic between 1 millisecond and 200 seconds [2, 11]. In an analysis for Controller Area Networks, the type of network used in real-time environments, the data had a good fit with the Gamma distribution [28]. Taken together, most papers that have examined the distribution of RTT values, explicitly or implicitly describe it as exponential in some way. This is consistent with our findings.

3.2 Anomaly detection

Shanbhag and Wolf suggest using multiple anomaly detection algorithms in parallel [21], and using the combined result as the trigger. Even though we do not use multiple algorithms, we use all relevant data fields in the PDU to calculate the expected values with as much precision as possible.

E2EProf, as described by Agarwala et al. [1], is similar to our approach as it also uses time-series analysis, of which exponential smoothing is one of the methods, to analyze the performance of each subsystem of an application. They define a "spike" as a local maximum, exceeding a threshold of the mean plus three times the standard deviation. For testing, they used httperf.

Bayesian Principal Anomaly Detection (BPAD) warns for individual outliers [10], and because these occur too frequently, it does not suit our context.

Between the years 2000 and 2010, there were several papers [13, 14, 19] on using Principal Component Analysis (PCA) for anomaly detection. Even though the method worked fine, it was difficult to find the right sensitivity [5].

Wang et al. [25] stress that anomaly detection methods must in some circumstances be "lightweight", both in terms of the number of metrics they require to run (the volume of data continuously captured and used), and in terms of their runtime complexity. They suggest smoothing the data, just as we use exponential smoothing (Section 4.2), and detect anomalies using the Tukey method based on "fences" and "hinges" [24]. This method splits the data into quartiles separated at Q1, Q2 and Q3, and classifies anomalies in multiples of the difference between Q1 and Q3. While different from our method, it also uses the median instead of the mean.

4 APPROACH

In order to understand the RTT values, we first calculated the mean and standard deviation of a few collections of RTTs (Section 4.1). We then used exponential smoothing to get a mean value that gave higher importance to newer RTTs (Section 4.2). Some parts of the variance turned out to be related to specific aspects of the message data, so the exponential smoothing was further refined to isolate these as adjustment factors (Section 4.3). Finally we calculated the median of smaller and larger groups of RTTs as a way of identifying outlier clusters (Section 4.4).

4.1 Mean and standard deviation

As mentioned in Section 2.1, the time spent by a node processing a request can vary significantly, so the RTT varies from fractions of a millisecond to multiple seconds. Calculating the mean from such data does not give meaningful results.

The exact distribution of the RTTs is not known to us. However, earlier work shows that it resembles a log-normal distribution, so we calculate the mean and variance of the logarithms of the RTTs.

For efficiency, we use formulas based on those described by Finch [7]. The formula used for the incrementally calculated mean is shown in Equation 1. Here, x_n is the new value, and n is the number of values so far. We use Equation 2 to get the variance S_n, and Equation 3 for the standard deviation σ_n.

$$\mu_n = \mu_{n-1} + \frac{1}{n}(\ln x_n - \mu_{n-1}) \tag{1}$$

$$S_n = S_{n-1} + (\ln x_n - \mu_{n-1})(\ln x_n - \mu_n) \tag{2}$$

$$\sigma_n = \sqrt{S_n/n} \tag{3}$$

4.2 Exponential smoothing

Over time, the effect of new values added to Equation 1 shown in Section 4.1 will diminish. By instead using exponential smoothing, we are able to analyze an endless series of data.

We calculate the expected value E_n using the well-known Equation 4, where n is the number of observations, and V_n is the nth value. Or rather, V_n is the logarithm of the measured RTT, and E_n is the logarithm of the expected value. The new value is the sum of two terms based on the current observation and on the previously expected value, respectively. The constant α is used to select the scaling factor between them, where a lower value of α gives a more stable E_n, as the effect from individual values of V_n is smaller. We set E_1 to V_1.

$$E_n = \alpha V_n + (1 - \alpha)E_{n-1}, \; n > 1 \tag{4}$$

4.3 Adjustment factors

As the traffic between SMS brokers uses Internet, network related RTTs can vary both by time of day and day of week. While grouping the data by hour gives a lower variance and therefore improved anomaly detection, it also gives less data in each group, resulting in reduced stability. Moreover, it disregards the similarities of RTTs during consecutive hours.

Communication protocols for SMS consist of fields with key-value pairs which specify how the SMS should be handled, so we assume their values might affect the RTT. To minimize the variance, each unique combination of fields should be analyzed separately. This strategy leads to a combinatorial explosion, and requires large amounts of data for satisfactory stability of E_n. In the financial domain Double Seasonal Exponential Smoothing [23] is sometimes used, basing the result on time values, e.g. day of month and month of year. The idea is to get a single average value for the entire dataset, with a small number of adjustment factors. Similar approaches have also been used in network contexts [6]. We use a variation of this method, but with field values instead of time values.

We need one adjustment factor per field value, and use the syntax F_n^v for the nth value of the adjustment factor for field value v. The value of F_0^v is set to 0, representing the case when the RTT is identical for all values. The adjustment factor can be either additive or multiplicative, and because of the exponential nature of the RTT distribution, multiplicative adjustments seem to make the most sense. However, as the values of E_n and V_n are logarithms, the actual adjustment needs to use addition. The calculation of the effect from a specific field value is shown in Equation 5. We want the expected value E_n to be free from these variations, so Equation 4 is modified to instead use the adjusted value of V_n, as shown in Equation 6.

$$F_n^v = \alpha(V_n - E_n) + (1 - \alpha)F_{n-1}^v \tag{5}$$
$$E_n = \alpha(V_n - F_{n-1}^v) + (1 - \alpha)E_{n-1} \tag{6}$$

For the more general case, we see the difference between the expected value E_n and the measured value V_n as the sum of all adjustment factors for all fields. We can then update the adjustment factors using the same exponential smoothing as in Equation 4. This is shown in detail in Algorithm 1, lines 11 to 19. For simplicity we

use the same scaling factor α as for the expected value in Equation 4, but it is possible to use different scaling factors for each adjustment factor.

4.4 Medians

Even with α as low as 0.0001, the wide range of values in the input data renders E_n too unstable to be useful in detecting anomalies. A more reliable reference point is given by the median, in our case calculated using the Remedian [20] method. The algorithm is simple but effective, using k arrays A_i, each of length b.

(1) Store the first b values in A_0, where typically $b < 10$.
(2) Calculate the median of A_0 and append the result to A_1.
(3) Repeat steps 1 and 2 until A_1 contains b values. Calculate the median of them, and append the result to A_2.
(4) Repeat the previous steps up to A_k for all i less than some k, appending the median of A_{i-1} to A_i.

The median of A_k is now an estimate of the median of the full series of values. The number of operations required to find the median of b values is fixed for each b, giving an execution time complexity of $O(n)$ for n values. We can think of it as a software version of multiple connected Geneva drives [3].

The value we append to A_0 is E_n, the most recent measurement with all adjustment factors removed. Using arrays with $b = 5$ values each achieves a good balance between stability, which requires more values in each array, and sensitivity, which requires fewer values. This way A_0 has the median of the most recent 5 values, A_1 of 25 values, A_2 of 125, etc.

We can now define an anomaly as a cluster of outlier measurements that increase the median of A_3 above twice the median of A_5. To avoid repetitive notifications, each notification suspends further ones until the median of A_3 goes below the median of A_5. A period of large values that is long enough to affect the median of A_3 this way occurs sufficiently seldom, as shown in Section 6.3.

4.5 Summary

Algorithm 1 combines the steps described earlier in this section. The algorithm is implemented as an extension to our existing tool called ELFA (EMG Log File Analyser - initially introduced in [4]). The method described here has several benefits.

(1) All calculations are done in constant time, depending only on the number of adjustment factors. This is necessary as we need to be able to handle continuous traffic with up to 1000 measurements per second.
(2) The sensitivity is easily adjusted, even online.
(3) It is independent of the frequency of values.
(4) The expected value is calculated from all observations, not just from an artificial subset.
(5) Adjustment factors can be added and removed online as needed.
(6) For each connection we need to persist only the base value E_n and the non-zero adjustment factors F_n^v to be able to resume a paused analysis.
(7) It is self-adapting, using the most recent RTT values for each individual connection as the basis for detecting outliers.

ALGORITHM 1: Find Outlier Clusters

input : A list of data points, each one consisting of a list of key-value pairs and a measured value V_n.

output: A list of start and end points for anomalies.

```
   // Initialization.
 1 forall A do A ⟵ ∅            // Clear all Remedian arrays.
 2 haveReported ⟵ false
 3 outliers ⟵ ∅
 4 expected ⟵ 0
 5 foreach possible key do
 6 │  foreach value used by key do
 7 │  │  adjustments[key,value] ⟵ 0
 8 │  end
 9 end
10 foreach data point dp do
      // Update the expected value from measurement(dp), minus
         the current adjustment factors.
11 │  b ⟵ 0
12 │  foreach (key,value) in dp do
13 │  │  b ⟵ b + adjustments[key,value]
14 │  end
      // Normal exponential smoothing.
15 │  expected ⟵ α * (measurement(dp) − b) + (1 − α) * expected
      // Update the adjustment factors.
16 │  foreach (key,value) in dp do
      │  // Assume all other adjustment factors are correct,
      │     and calculate what is left.
17 │  │  diff ⟵
      │    measurement(dp) − (expected + b − adjustments[key,value])
      │  // Update the adjustment factor for this key-value
      │     pair.
18 │  │  adjustments[key,value] ⟵
      │    α * diff + (1 − α) * adjustments[key,value]
19 │  end
      // Update the Remedian arrays.
20 │  i ⟵ 0
21 │  Append expected to A[0]
22 │  while A[i] is full and i + 1 < 6         // We have 6 arrays
23 │  do
24 │  │  Append median(A[i]) to A[i + 1]
25 │  │  A[i] ⟵ ∅
26 │  │  i ⟵ i + 1
27 │  end
      // Find start and end points for anomalies.
28 │  if not haveReported and A[5] has been filled at least once and
      │  median(A[3]) > 2 * median(A[5]) then
29 │  │  Add ('start', timestamp(dp)) to outliers
30 │  │  haveReported ⟵ true
31 │  end
32 │  if haveReported and median(A[3]) < median(A[5]) then
33 │  │  Add ('end', timestamp(dp)) to outliers
34 │  │  haveReported ⟵ false
35 │  end
36 end
37 return outliers
```

5 CASE STUDY DESIGN

To evaluate our approach for detecting anomalies in the RTTs, we undertook an industrial case study. Specifically, we wanted to investigate and exemplify how log files generated by the production system of an SMS broker can be utilized to identify anomalies in RTTs between itself and several external operators.

5.1 Data collection

We examined data from the Enterprise Messaging Gateway (EMG), an Infoflex Connect AB product used by many SMS brokers. The data was taken from existing log files as they contained the data we needed without requiring modifications to the core product with a risk of introducing bugs. The amount of data per operator varied between 33 and 497 MB.

In this study we selected one of the most commonly used protocols for SMS traffic, SMPP (Short Message Peer to Peer). Each PDU starts with a header, comprised of the operation number, a transaction number, a status and the length of the data section. Following the header is the data section, consisting of a sequence of key-value pairs, where the keys and their order depend on the operation. As responses can arrive in an undefined order, the transaction number from the request must be exactly duplicated in the response.

The EMG log files contain information on whether each PDU was sent or received, the timestamp, which connection was used, the operation name, the transaction number, and all key-value fields from the data section.

6 CASE STUDY RESULTS

This section presents the results of the industrial case study. In particular, we first discuss how different characteristics (keys) of the data and messages sent affect the RTT (Section 6.1). Second, we discuss how using certain adjustment factors enabled higher accuracy in the outlier detection (Section 6.2). Third, we detail the results of applying the anomaly detection algorithm to a large dataset of network traffic (Section 6.3).

In the presented results, data is analyzed for three different operators, referred to as "O1", "O2" and "O3".

6.1 RTT for selected keys

To explore how individual keys affected the RTTs, we counted the number of unique values used by each key. This revealed three distinct categories.

Message specific: 11 keys, e.g. destination numbers and message bodies. We assume these values are unique for each message.

Groups: 11 keys, e.g. whether a delivery report is requested, the character encoding, and similar keys with a very limited set of values. We identified "data coding", "esm class" and "registered delivery" as having the largest effect on the RTTs.

Constants: 4 keys that are either not supported by EMG, or ignored by most recipients, and therefore always sent with the same value.

Next we describe the key "data coding" in more detail, and how its value affects the RTT. All RTT values in this section are shown with their mean and one standard deviation up and down, to give an indication of their relative positions and spread.

Table 1 shows the RTT grouped by data coding. The values in the first column have the following meaning.

0 Text message, using the GSM character encoding IA5.
8 Text message, using the character encoding UCS-2.
240 Special messages, e.g. configuration settings.
245 8 bit data, e.g. ring tones.

With the exception of the values 240 and 245 to operator "O1", the RTT distributions for different values are clearly separated. The operators seem to perform some time consuming processing of UCS-2 texts, as those RTTs are significantly longer than for IA5 texts. "N/A" means the value was not used with that operator.

Value	O1	O2	O3
0	9.3/9.7/10	8.1/8.2/8.4	440/466/493
8	23/25/28	21/24/27	651/673/697
240	3.6/3.7/3.7	3.5/3.5/3.5	N/A
245	3.2/4.9/7.7	N/A	329/358/390

Table 1: RTT in milliseconds, grouped by data coding. The three values are $\mu - \sigma$, μ and $\mu + \sigma$, respectively.

The RTTs when grouped by the "esm class" and "registered delivery" keys showed similar patterns, with a ratio of up to 3 for some values. This motivates us to show the results with a deeper analysis using the adjustment factors.

6.2 Adjustment factors

The adjustment factors for the message key values were mostly consistent with the results in Section 6.1. The "data coding" adjustment factors are shown in Table 2. As the values represent the difference in exponent, a value of 1 corresponds to a ratio between the RTTs equal to e.

For O1, whether data coding is 8 or 240 gives an RTT that varies by a factor of $e^{0.92-(-1.12)} \approx 7.69$. UCS-2 data requires twice as much space as IA5, but even if we adjust for this, there is still a remaining factor of $7.69/2 \approx 3.84$. We see a similar pattern for O2, with adjustment factors 1.30 and -0.87 for data coding 8 and 240. The "esm class" and "registered delivery" keys also showed a clear correlation between the RTTs and the adjustment factors.

Value	O1	O2	O3
0	-0.46 (9.7)	-0.13 (8.2)	-0.10 (466)
8	**0.92** (25)	1.30 (24)	0.11 (673)
240	**-1.12** (3.7)	-0.87 (3.5)	N/A
245	-0.03 (4.9)	N/A	-0.25 (358)

Table 2: Adjustment factors, by data coding. The value inside parentheses is μ from Table 1.

6.3 Anomaly frequencies

Figure 3 uses blue circles to show the RTTs for 288,515 outgoing requests to O1, over a period of approximately two months. Most measurements are around 10 milliseconds (1e+04 microseconds), but RTTs of up to several seconds are common enough that they

are not considered outliers. The black, green and red lines show the medians from A_1, A_3 and A_5, respectively, as described in Section 4.4. The black line shows the median of the $5^2 = 25$ most recent measurements. Even with the large number of measurements above 1e+06 microseconds at Index 240,000, there is still enough data with lower values to keep the median below 1e+05 microseconds. The green line shows the median of 25 values from the black line, i.e. $25^2 = 625$ measurements. It stays significantly calmer, peaking only for indices 18,000, 190,000 and around 240,000, all corresponding to wider peaks of the black line. The red line shows the median yet another factor of 25 up, for $25^3 = 15,625$ measurements. Although some noise remains, the values shown by the red line (A_5) can be used for comparisons with those shown by the green line (A_3).

The intervals that satisfy our condition for anomalies, i.e. when the median of A_3 is more than twice the median of A_5 as described in Section 4.4, are marked with red lines at the bottom of the graph, surrounded by grey dotted rectangles. These lines perfectly mark the sections with many slow responses.

Despite the large variance shown in Section 6.1, using adjustment factors and medians provides a base level that is relatively stable. The area containing outliers for O2 is shown in Figure 4(b), where the blue dots have been removed for clarity. The end point of the marked area is quite far away from the starting point, indicating low precision of our method. This is the trade-off for high recall and avoiding multiple adjacent groups of outliers. There are no round-trips at 196,000 shorter than 5000 microseconds, causing A_3 (shown by the green line) to increase from 4267 microseconds to 8229. This makes A_3 more than twice the value of A_5 (shown by the red line), i.e. $8229 > 2 * 3964$, satisfying our condition for outliers.

The effect of the adjustment factors is illustrated in Figure 4(a) and Figure 4(b). Both figures show the same data, without and with adjustment factors, respectively. The black and green lines in Figure 4(b) are more stable, reporting one anomaly instead of three.

The algorithm detected no anomalies in the traffic towards O3.

For validation, we created simulated log files. The RTTs were randomized with a log normal distribution and a minimum value of 1000 microseconds. After at least 20,000 roundtrips, a group of up to 4095 entries with up to half a second slower responses was added. The results from the analysis on one such file are shown in Figure 5. There were three groups with slow responses, one at 48,515 with 2488 entries, one at 82,120 with 1222 entries, and one at 9133 with 192 entries, corresponding to the three blue peaks. Given there must be at least $625/2 = 313$ entries for our algorithm to report an anomaly, only the first two peaks are reported.

The red line is almost perfectly flat, showing the Remedian [20] is stable.

7 VALIDITY THREATS

Below we discuss the threats to the validity of our study.

Internal: We see two possible internal validity threats. First, although the 8 option keys we discarded in Section 6.1 showed no significance in the RTTs in our preliminary results, a more advanced analysis might show an effect. Second, any implementation errors were mitigated by carefully examining the program output, manually comparing it with the raw data in the log files.

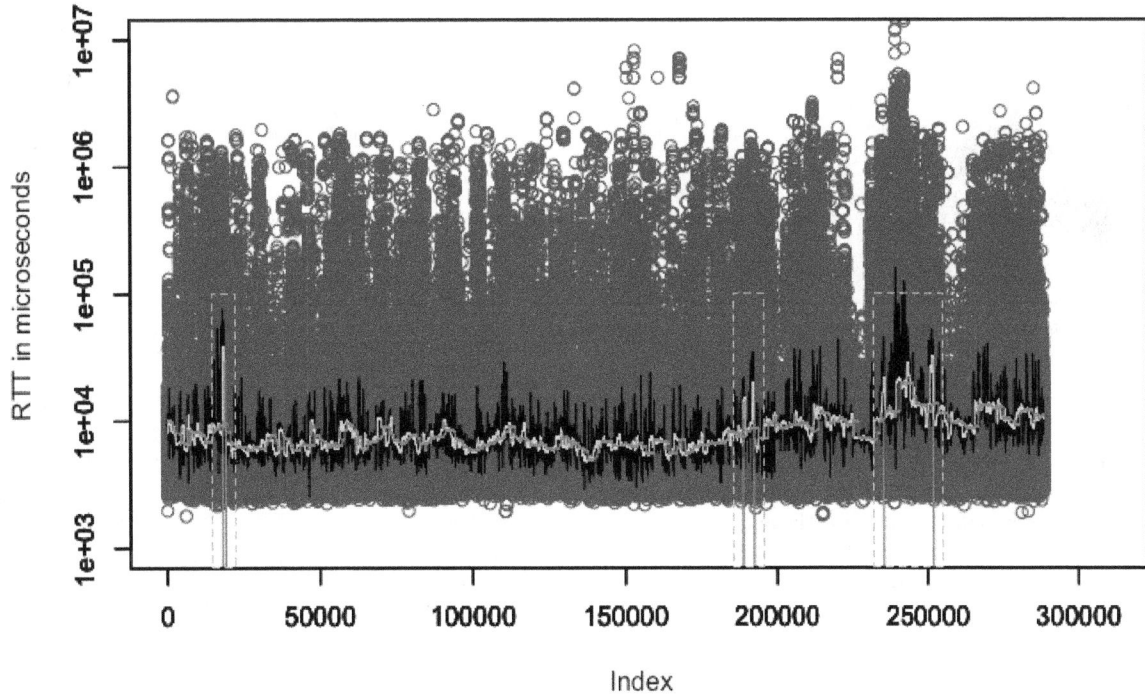

Figure 3: RTT and medians for O1.

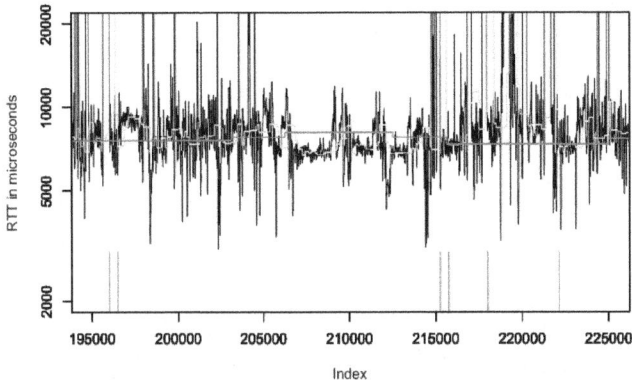

(a) RTT and medians for O2, without adjustment factors.

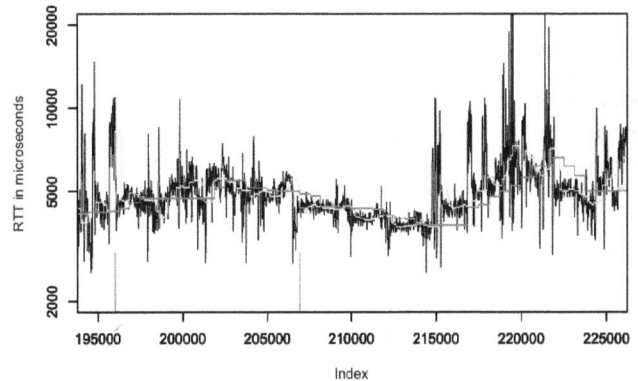

(b) RTT and medians for O2, with adjustment factors.

Figure 4: RTT and medians for O2 with and without adjustment factors.

External: The analyzed log files in this paper all contain SMS traffic over SMPP, but the approach with exponential smoothing and the equations in Section 4.2 should be usable in any system where parameter values affect which parts of the code are executed, and therefore also the response time. When calculating the median, the sensitivity can easily be changed by adjusting the array length, and selecting which arrays to compare.

Reliability: We consider the reliability threat to be small, as we have seen similar RTT distributions for connections to several operators around the world.

Construct: The system model used in this paper is somewhat simplified, abstracting the network traffic into logged "send" and "receive" events. In reality, an outgoing PDU requires multiple steps:

(1) The data structure with the information to be sent is created.
(2) The data is packed into a byte array that can be transmitted on a socket.
(3) The data in the data structure is logged.
(4) The byte array is sent to the operating system kernel.
(5) The operating system sends the byte array to the network device.
(6) The network device transmits the byte array to the network.

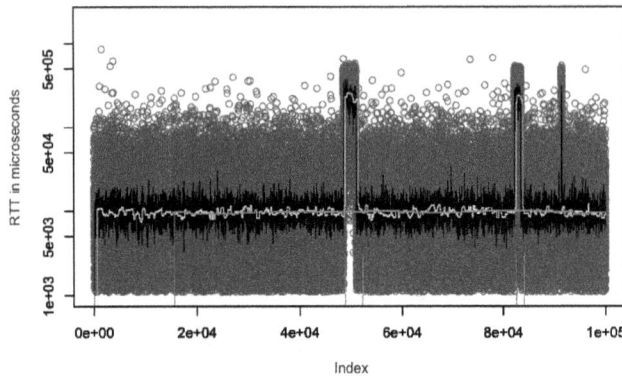

Figure 5: Simulated RTTs, with medians and outliers.

The timestamp used for the PDU comes from step 3, ignoring any delays caused by the subsequent steps. The operating system used is Unix, which does not provide a simple way to find the exact time for step 6. Instead we assume that delays are small compared to the network transmission and application processing times.

A limitation of the Remedian (described in Section 4.4) is that only value sequences that start on multiples of 5^n are considered, so the number of outliers required to trigger an anomaly notification varies. We do not consider this a problem, as the algorithm must always be adapted in order to achieve the desired sensitivity.

8 CONCLUSIONS AND FUTURE WORK

Anomaly detection in production systems is valuable for ensuring service levels towards customers. Making use of our domain knowledge, we developed an algorithm that reduces noise, enabling the detection of larger clusters of outliers. The algorithm is implemented as an extension to our tool ELFA which calculates RTTs between different communicating systems.

Even when the average RTT is within acceptable limits when analyzing data from the live production environment of an SMS broker, our approach can be used to identify conditions which have an unreasonable effect. A relevant example would be the UCS-2 handling (see Table 2, the factor when the parameter is 8) by O1 and O2. Whilst being functionally correct, it suggests the UCS-2 handling could possibly be made more efficient in those systems.

RTT anomalies may also be possible to detect by observing their side effects, such as a queue of outgoing messages being formed. The higher the throughput normally is, the longer the queue can be while maintaining an acceptable delivery time, so such an algorithm would have to take the current throughput into account. The throughput is not logged by EMG, so we could not use this method.

ACKNOWLEDGMENTS

This work was sponsored by The Knowledge Foundation industrial PhD school ITS ESS-H, 20160139 (TestMine), 20130085 (TOCSYC) and Infoflex Connect AB.

REFERENCES

[1] Sandip Agarwala, Fernando Alegre, Karsten Schwan, and Jegannathan Mehalingham. 2007. E2EProf: Automated end-to-end performance management for enterprise systems. In *Proceedings - IEEE International Conference on Dependable Systems and Networks (DSN'07)*.
[2] Jay Aikat, Jasleen Kaur, F. Donelson Smith, and Kevin Jeffay. 2003. Variability in TCP round-trip times. In *Proceedings - ACM SIGCOMM Conference on Internet Measurement (IMC'03)*.
[3] John H Bickford. 1972. *Mechanisms for intermittent motion*. Krieger Pub Co.
[4] Daniel Brahneborg, Wasif Afzal, and Adnan Čaušević. 2017. A Black-Box Approach to Latency and Throughput Analysis. In *Proceedings - IEEE International Conference on Software Quality, Reliability and Security Companion (QRS-C'17)*.
[5] Daniela Brauckhoff, Kave Salamatian, and Martin May. 2009. Applying PCA for traffic anomaly detection: Problems and solutions. In *Proceedings - IEEE International Conference on Computer Communications (INFOCOM'09)*.
[6] Jake D Brutlag. 2000. Aberrant Behavior Detection in Time Series for Network Monitoring. In *LISA*, Vol. 14. 139–146.
[7] Tony Finch. 2009. Incremental calculation of weighted mean and variance. (2009).
[8] Marina Gutiérrez, Wilfried Steiner, Radu Dobrin, and Sasikumar Punnekkat. 2015. Learning the parameters of periodic traffic based on network measurements. In *Measurements & Networking (M&N), 2015 IEEE International Workshop on*. IEEE.
[9] Emir Halepovic, Jeffrey Pang, and Oliver Spatscheck. 2012. Can you GET me now? Estimating the time-to-first-byte of HTTP transactions with passive measurements. In *Proceedings - ACM SIGCOMM conference on Internet measurement*.
[10] Anders Holst and Bjorn Bjurling. 2013. A bayesian parametric statistical anomaly detection method for finding trends and patterns in criminal behavior. In *Proceedings - European Intelligence and Security Informatics Conference*.
[11] Sharad Jaiswal, Gianluca Iannaccone, Christophe Diot, Jim Kurose, and Don Towsley. 2004. Inferring TCP Connection Characteristics Through Passive Measurements. In *Joint Conf. of IEEE Computer and Communications Societies*.
[12] Hao Jiang and Constantinos Dovrolis. 2002. Passive estimation of TCP round-trip times. *ACM SIGCOMM Computer Communication Review* 32, 3 (2002), 75–88.
[13] Anukool Lakhina, Mark Crovella, and Christophe Diot. 2005. Mining anomalies using traffic feature distributions. *ACM SIGCOMM Comp. Comm. Rev.* 35, 4 (2005).
[14] Yang Liu, Linfeng Zhang, and Yong Guan. 2010. Sketch-based streaming PCA algorithm for network-wide traffic anomaly detection. In *Proceedings - IEEE International Conference on Distributed Computing Systems (ICDCS'10)*.
[15] H Martin, A McGregor, and J Cleary. 2000. *Analysis of internet delay times*. Technical Report.
[16] A Finamore M Mellia and M Meo M M Munaf. 2011. Experiences of Internet Traffic Monitoring with Tstat. *IEEE Network* June (2011), 8–14.
[17] David Mosberger and Tai Jin. 1998. httperf - A Tool for Measuring Web Server Performance. *SIGMETRICS Performance Evaluation Review* 26, 3 (1998), 31–37.
[18] Vern Paxson. 1997. Automated packet trace analysis of TCP implementations. *ACM SIGCOMM Computer Communication Review* 27, 4 (1997), 167–179.
[19] Haakon Ringberg, Augustin Soule, Jennifer Rexford, and Christophe Diot. 2007. Sensitivity of PCA for traffic anomaly detection. *ACM SIGMETRICS Performance Evaluation Review* 35, 1 (2007).
[20] Peter J Rousseeuw and Gilbert W Bassett. 1990. The Remedian: A Robust Averaging Method for Large Data Sets. *J. Amer. Statist. Assoc.* 85, 409 (1990), 97–104.
[21] Shashank Shanbhag and Tilman Wolf. 2009. Accurate anomaly detection through parallelism. *IEEE Network* 23, 1 (2009), 22–28.
[22] Małgorzata Steinder and Adarshpal S. Sethi. 2004. A survey of fault localization techniques in computer networks. *Sci. of Comp. Prog.* 53, 2 (2004), 165–194.
[23] James W Taylor. 2003. Short-Term Electricity Demand Forecasting Using Double Seasonal Exponential Smoothing. *J. of Oper. Res. Society* 54, 8 (2003), 799–805.
[24] John W Tukey. 1977. Exploratory data analysis. (1977), 43–45.
[25] Chengwei Wang, Krishnamurthy Viswanathan, Lakshminarayan Choudur, Vanish Talwar, Wade Satterfield, and Karsten Schwan. 2011. Statistical techniques for online anomaly detection in data centers. In *IFIP/IEEE International Symposium on Integrated Network Management (IM'11) and Workshops*.
[26] Haijin Yan, Kang Li, Scott Watterson, and David Lowenthal. 2004. Improving passive estimation of TCP round-trip times using TCP timestamps. *IEEE International Workshop on IP Operations and Management* (2004), 181–185.
[27] Sebastian Zander and Grenville Armitage. 2013. Minimally-intrusive frequent round trip time measurements using synthetic packet-pairs. In *Proceedings - Conference on Local Computer Networks (LCN'13)*.
[28] Haibo Zeng, M Di Natale, Paolo Giusto, and A Sangiovanni-Vincentelli. 2010. Using Statistical Methods to Compute the Probability Distribution of Message Response Time in Controller Area Network. *IEEE Transactions on Industrial Informatics* 6, 4 (2010), 678–691.

Received October 2017; final version February 2018

User-defined Classification and Multi-level Grouping of Objects in Memory Monitoring

Markus Weninger
Institute for System Software
Christian Doppler Laboratory MEVSS
Johannes Kepler University Linz, Austria
markus.weninger@jku.at

Hanspeter Mössenböck
Institute for System Software
Johannes Kepler University Linz, Austria
hanspeter.moessenboeck@jku.at

ABSTRACT

Software becomes more and more complex. Performance degradations and anomalies can often only be understood by using monitoring approaches, e.g., for tracing the allocations and lifetimes of objects on the heap. However, this leads to huge amounts of data that have to be classified, grouped and visualized in order to be useful for developers. In this paper, we present a flexible offline memory analysis approach that allows classifying heap objects based on arbitrary criteria. A small set of predefined classification criteria such as the type and the allocation site of an object can further be extended by additional user-defined criteria. In contrast to state-of-the-art tools, which group objects based on a single criterion, our approach allows the combination of multiple criteria using multi-level grouping. The resulting classification trees allow a flexible in-depth analysis of the data and a natural hierarchical visualization of the results.

KEYWORDS

Memory, Monitoring, Analysis, Tool, Grouping, Classification

ACM Reference Format:
Markus Weninger and Hanspeter Mössenböck. 2018. User-defined Classification and Multi-level Grouping of Objects in Memory Monitoring. In *ICPE '18: ACM/SPEC International Conference on Performance Engineering, April 9–13, 2018, Berlin, Germany.* ACM, New York, NY, USA, 12 pages. https://doi.org/10.1145/3184407.3184412

1 INTRODUCTION

The increasing complexity of software systems requires tools and techniques for monitoring the behavior of large and complex applications. Many of these tools trace an application by recording events at run time and writing them to a trace file for later analysis. For example, a memory monitoring tool could record object allocations and garbage collector activity (e.g., object moves) so that the application's heap can be later reconstructed offline for various analyses.

Such monitoring tools produce huge amounts of data, which have to be classified, grouped and visualized in order to be helpful

for the user. For example, users might want to know how many objects of a certain type were allocated, at which locations they were allocated, and how long they survived. Unfortunately, many state-of-the-art tools fail to provide a flexible information retrieval technique. Most of them only support hard-coded classification criteria (often *type* is the only one) in conjunction with tabular histograms, e.g., showing the number of instances per class and the number of allocated bytes. They don't allow users to classify the data based on multiple criteria (e.g., type, allocation site and age) and miss features to organize and aggregate the resulting information hierarchically on multiple levels.

Our tool AntTracks [12, 13] is a memory monitoring tool for Java based on the Java Hotspot™ VM [21] that records object allocations and garbage collection moves. It also offers offline analysis of trace files, in which the heap can be reconstructed for any garbage collection point in time. Bitto et al. [3] showed how to reconstruct an application's heap from traces produced by AntTracks. Based on this work, Weninger et al. [25] presented first ideas on object classifiers with the goal to make the classification of memory monitoring data more general and customizable.

In this paper, we extend our work by presenting a generally applicable object classification and multi-level grouping concept. An object classifier processes an object and classifies it based on a certain criterion derived from the object's properties, e.g., classifying heap objects based on their type. Objects with the same classification result are grouped together. As already mentioned, most state-of-the-art memory monitoring tools have two major restrictions: (1) They only offer a restricted set of classification criteria, such as *Type* or *Allocation Site*, and (2) their grouping mechanism is based on just a single classification criterion, i.e., single-level grouping. Our approach eliminates both restrictions. In addition to a set of predefined object classifiers that are usable out-of-the-box, users can define custom object classifiers as small dynamically-loaded code snippets. Furthermore, the grouping is not based on a single criterion but on dynamic classification trees, i.e., on multi-level grouping based on multiple object classifiers. Such classification trees store classification results in a hierarchical manner and allow a more flexible top-down data analysis approach. The concepts of object classification, multi-level grouping and classification trees are not restricted to memory data and may therefore also be used in other domains.

Our scientific contributions are (1) a novel concept of *object classifiers*, a way to classify a collection of objects based on their properties, (2) a multi-level grouping algorithm that classifies a collection of objects based on a user-chosen set of object classifiers into a *classification tree*, (3) various classification tree data structures that differ in terms of classification throughput, memory overhead and information loss, and (4) a quantitative evaluation based on well-known benchmarks as well as a functional evaluation based on typical memory analysis use cases.

2 BACKGROUND

AntTracks consists of a virtual machine based on the Java Hotspot™ VM and a memory analysis tool. The AntTracks VM records memory events into trace files, which can then be analyzed offline with the tool. Since our object classifier approach has been integrated into this tool, it is essential to understand AntTracks's architecture and workflow.

2.1 Trace Recording

The AntTracks VM records memory events, e.g., events for object allocations and object movements executed by the garbage collector (GC), throughout an application's execution and writes them into trace files. Furthermore, it is also capable of recording pointers between objects [11]. After loading such a trace file, the AntTracks analysis tool provides overview of the memory behavior over time and can reconstruct the heap's state and layout for every garbage collection point by incrementally processing the events in the trace.

2.2 Trace Reconstruction and Data Structure

Bitto et al. [3] show that a naïve approach, in which every heap object is represented by a Java object in the analysis tool, would result in an unacceptable memory overhead. Therefore, we developed the data structure shown in Figure 1. It separates the heap into multiple spaces. For example, the *ParallelOldGC*'s heap consists of one eden space, two survivor spaces, and one old space. Each of these spaces encompasses various fields such as the starting address, the size, or the kind of the space (i.e., *eden*, *survivor* or *old*). Additionally, each space contains an address-to-LAB map. A *LAB* (local allocation buffer) represents a sequence of objects that have been processed together by the same thread (e.g., objects that have been allocated by the same thread within the same thread-local allocation buffer (TLAB)). Each entry in the LAB's object array represents one heap object and contains a pointer to a global cache of object representations, called *ObjectInfo*. ObjectInfos are cached structures that contain information which is shared by multiple objects, namely the event which created the object (e.g., an allocation by the interpreter), the object's allocation site, its type and its size. For array allocations, also the array length is stored. Using this mechanism, many different objects can be represented by the same ObjectInfo. Their addresses do not have to be explicitly stored

but can be computed from their LAB's address. In addition to the object array, each LAB contains two arrays of the same length to store pointer information. For each entry in the object array, i.e., for each heap object, the respective entry in the *pointers to* array contains the addresses of all objects that are referenced by this object. Analogously, each entry in the *pointed from* array contains the addresses of all objects that point to the respective object.

3 APPROACH

This section presents the domain-independent concepts of classification (i.e., representing an object by a classification result made up of one or more classification values) and multi-level grouping (i.e., arranging classification results in a tree structure). Examples on how these concepts can be applied in a specific domain / tool will be given in the context of Java and the classification of Java heap objects within the AntTracks memory analysis tool. If a specific heap state is shown, it has been reconstructed from a trace of a *DaCapo xalan* benchmark run.

3.1 Source Collection and Source Objects

Classification and grouping always operate on a *source collection* which consists of *source objects* of a certain type. AntTracks's source collection when classifying a heap state are the Java heap objects that have been live at the given point in time.

The source collection does not have to be represented by a single class but may be made up of multiple classes that interact with each other, see Figure 2. One of these classes must act as *the* source collection to the public. This class is required to provide functionality to iterate the contained source objects. In AntTracks, as explained in Section 2, a heap state is modeled by multiple classes (i.e., the heap itself, which further consists of multiple spaces, which further consist of multiple LABs), yet the Heap class acts as the source collection to the public.

Similarly, the properties of a source object do not have to be stored in a single object. In AntTracks, for example, they are stored in different locations: Most of them are stored in the ObjectInfo, but a heap object's pointers are stored in the LAB, and its address is calculated on demand.

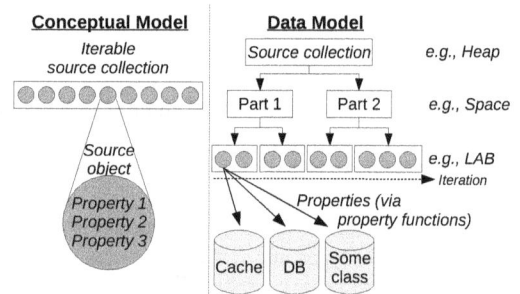

Figure 2: Basic classification concepts: Source collection, source objects and source object properties.

We distinguish the term *object* from the term *source object* because *object* is often used in the context of programming languages to describe a certain instance of a class. A source object, on the other hand, represents properties that may be stored in various places.

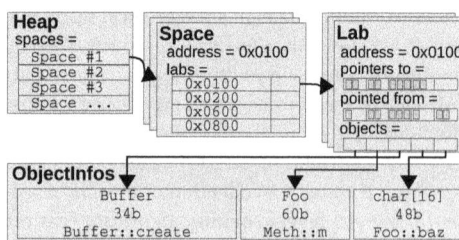

Figure 1: AntTracks's data structure to represent a heap at a certain point in time.

3.2 Source Object Properties and Source Collection Iteration

A source object is described by its m properties based on its position P within its source collection, as shown in Definition 3.1.

Definition 3.1. A source object at position P within its source collection is described by its m distributed properties:

$$so_P \quad \text{is described by} \quad (prop_1, prop_2, \ldots, prop_m)_P$$

P's format depends on the source collection. For example, in a list, source objects are identified by their index i, i.e., $P = i$. In AntTracks's heap data structure, a source object's position, i.e., the position of a heap object within the reconstructed heap, is described by (1) the space in which the object is, (2) the lab inside the object's space, and (3) the object's position within the lab, i.e., $P = (spaceIndex, labIndex, objectIndex)$.

Source collection iteration describes the task of visiting every position in the source collection and obtaining the properties of the respective source object. In AntTracks, iterating the heap means to visit every element in the `ObjectInfo` array of every LAB in every space, and collecting all properties of the currently visited heap object, e.g., calculating its address based on its containing LAB.

3.3 Object Classifiers

As soon as a source object's properties have been obtained, object classifiers can be used to classify it. Object classifiers are entities that classify a source object based on a certain criterion derived from the source object's properties. Each object classifier provides a `classify` function, which takes one parameter per source object property and returns the classification result. Additionally, every object classifier contains the following meta-data:

Name. A unique name used to identify the classifier.

Return Type. The `classify` method's return type.

Description (Optional). Useful to keep the classifier's names short while still offering additional information about the classifier's purpose.

Example (Optional). A possible classification result returned by the classifier, e.g., `java.lang.Integer` returned by AntTracks's *Type classifier*. This can be shown as a classification sample to the user in the UI.

Cardinality. Each classifier can be of one of the following three cardinalities: *One-to-one, one-to-many* or *one-to-hierarchy*. Depending on the cardinality, the classifier's classification result may be made up of a different number of classification values, see Figure 3.

In AntTracks, object classifiers are used to classify Java heap objects based on their properties such as the object's type, its allocation site and so on. Each classifier, e.g., the *Type classifier*, implements a common Java interface (most importantly the `classify` method), see Section 4.2.

3.3.1 One-to-one Classifier. A *one-to-one classifier* classifies a source object by a unique classification value as classification result (see top part in Figure 3). The returned classification value is an instance of the classifier's return type, i.e., a one-to-one `String` classifier returns a single `String` as value.

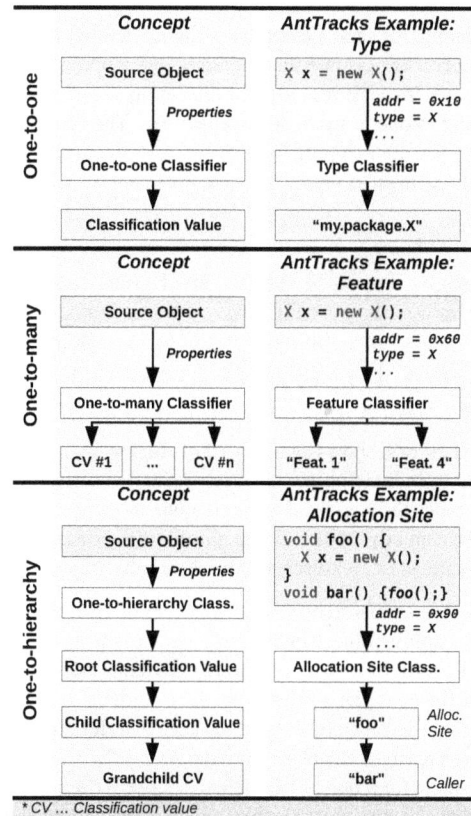

Figure 3: Object classifiers classify a source object based on its properties. The three types of classifiers vary in their classification value cardinality.

An example for a one-to-one classifier is AntTracks's predefined *Type classifier*, which classifies a Java heap object based on its type's name. Figure 4 shows a part of AntTracks's analysis view where each heap object has been classified using the *Type classifier*. Overall

Name	Objects		Bytes	
	# ▼	%	#	%
▼ Overall	11.077.848	100,0	1.061.744.056	100,0
⊕ java.nio.HeapCharBuffer	3.919.909	35,4	188.155.632	17,7
⊕ char[]	3.886.043	35,1	237.942.968	22,4
⊕ java.util.HashMap$Node	736.420	6,6	23.565.440	2,2

Figure 4: Classifying heap objects by type in AntTracks.

shows the number and byte count of the whole heap, and each child row represent a group of heap objects that have been classified by the same value, i.e., that are of the same type. Each heap object is part of exactly one group, i.e., *one-to-one* classification.

Filters. *Filters* are a special kind of *one-to-one classifiers*, which are of type `Boolean`. Filters are used in the classification process to define whether a source object should be further processed by subsequent operations.

3.3.2 One-to-many Classifier. A *one-to-many classifier* classifies a source object by multiple classification values, as can be seen in the middle part of Figure 3. The result is a set of instances of the classifier's type: If the classifier's type is `String`, a set of strings will be returned.

An example for such a classifier is the predefined *Feature classifier* in AntTracks. Assume that (possibly overlapping) code ranges represent specific features [10]. The allocation site of an object may then belong to one or more of these features. The *Feature classifier* performs a feature mapping for every Java heap object and returns the set of features to which its allocation site belongs. Figure 5,

Name	Objects			Bytes	
	#	▼	%	#	%
▼ Overall	11.077.848		100,0	1.061.744.056	100,0
⊞ java	9.025.314		81,5	478.658.200	45,1
⊞ xml	1.604.657		14,5	542.529.088	51,1
⊞ others	191.918		1,7	27.304.992	2,6

Figure 5: Classifying heap objects by feature in AntTracks.

similar to Figure 4, shows again a part of AntTracks's analysis view. This time, each heap object has been classified using the *Feature classifier*. Since the *Feature classifier* is a *one-to-many classifier*, each heap object can be part of multiple groups (if the classifier returned multiple values, i.e., features, for that heap object).

3.3.3 One-to-hierarchy Classifier. A *one-to-hierarchy classifier* classifies a source object by hierarchical classification values, as shown in the bottom part of Figure 3. Such a classifier returns objects of the classifier's return type in an ordered list. The object at index 0 is the root object, and for all $i > 0$ the object at index $i - 1$ is the parent of the object at index i.

An example for a *one-to-hierarchy classifier* is the predefined *Allocation Site classifier* in AntTracks, which classifies an object based on its allocation site and the allocation's call sites. The root object (at index 0) is the code location where the object was allocated, the object at index 1 is the code location from where the allocating method was called, and so on (i.e., the code location at index i is the callee and the code location at index $i + 1$ the caller). Figure 6

Name	Objects			Bytes	
	#	▼	%	#	%
▼ Overall	11.077.848		100,0	1.061.744.056	100,0
▼ ⊞ java.nio.CharBuffer.wrap(char[], int, int) : java.nio.Cha...	3.919.909		35,4	188.155.632	17,7
▼ ⊞ sun.nio.cs.StreamEncoder.implWrite(char[], int, int)...	3.916.234		35,4	187.979.232	17,7
▶ ⊞ sun.nio.cs.StreamEncoder.write(char[], int, int) : ...	3.916.234		35,4	187.979.232	17,7
▶ ⊞ sun.nio.cs.StreamDecoder.implRead(char[], int, i...	3.675		0,0	176.400	0,0
▼ ⊞ sun.nio.cs.StreamEncoder.write(java.lang.String, int, i...	1.725.368		15,6	44.568.696	4,2
▼ ⊞ java.io.OutputStreamWriter.write(java.lang.String, i...	1.725.368		15,6	44.568.696	4,2
▶ ⊞ java.io.Writer.write(java.lang.String) : void : 7	1.725.368		15,6	44.568.696	4,2

Figure 6: Classifying heap objects by allocation site in AntTracks.

also shows a part of AntTracks's analysis view similar to Figure 5, yet each heap object has been classified using the *Allocation Site classifier* instead. First-level children of the *Overall* group, i.e., row 2 and row 6, are allocation sites where objects have been allocated. Child relations represent the call chain, e.g., the call sites on row 3 and row 5 called the allocation site on row 2, and the call site on row 4 has been the single caller to the call site on row 3.

3.4 Multi-level Grouping

Single-level grouping splits a set of objects into multiple groups. Each group represents a distinct classification result (i.e., the classifier's return value) and contains all objects that are classified by

this result. Typical single-level grouping only supports one-to-one classifiers, i.e., each object is mapped to exactly one classification value. In addition to introducing other classifier types beside one-to-one classifiers, we present multi-level grouping to enhance the flexibility and level of analysis detail.

3.4.1 Classification. Similar to single-level grouping, multi-level grouping is an operation that groups a set of source objects. Yet, instead of applying a single classifier, a list of classifiers is applied one after the other to every source object, and the sorted list of their classification results (where each classification result may be made up of multiple classification values) make up the source object's classification.

Obj.	Classification and results in parentheses
O(1)	[Age(1) → Feat(F1, F2) → AS(add, A)]
O(2)	[Age(1) → Feat(F1, F2) → AS(add, B, D)]
O(3)	[Age(3) → Feat(F1) → AS(main, C, A)]
O(4)	[Age(3) → Feat(F1) → AS(clone, D)]
O(5)	[Age(3) → Feat(F1) → AS(main, C, A)]
O(6)	[Age(1) → Feat(F1, F2) → AS(add, A)]

Table 1: Example classification of 6 Java heap objects based on three classifiers: Age (one-to-one), feature (one-to-many) and allocation site (one-to-hierarchy).

Table 1 shows an example classification for six objects $O(1)$ to $O(6)$. The three classifiers that get applied are (1) the *Age classifier*, a one-to-one classifier categorizing heap objects based on their number of survived GCs, (2) the *Feature classifier* (see Section 3.3.2) and (3) the *Allocation Site classifier* (see Section 3.3.3). Each classification contains three classification results, one per classifier, sorted in the order in which the classifiers were applied.

3.4.2 Classification Tree. Raw information as presented in Table 1 is not very helpful for the user. Classification trees bring such classification results into a hierarchical format that allows (1) flexible processing of data, such as merging, subgrouping, counting and so on as well as (2) straightforward visualization, e.g., as a tree table view, for user-driven analysis.

Figure 7 shows the creation of a classification tree for the objects in Table 1. Rectangles (yellow) represent tree nodes containing their keys as text, and arrows point to their child nodes. Smoothed rectangles (blue) represent the data that a node is holding, i.e., the source objects assigned to the node.

The following example explains how $O(1)$ gets added to the classification tree. The algorithm starts with the root node as the *current node*. During the classification process, when looking for a child node with a certain key that does not exist yet, a new child gets created for that key.

The *Age classifier* returns *1* as the classification result for $O(1)$. For each current node (i.e., the root node), the child matching this classification becomes the new current node, i.e. the status of current node moves from the parent to the child. Then, the *Feature classifier* is applied, which returns *F1* and *F2* as its classification values for the source object $O(1)$. Both features get added as children of *1* and become the new current nodes. Finally, the *Allocation Site classifier* gets applied on the source object and returns the allocation site *add* and its caller *A*. *add* nodes are appended as children

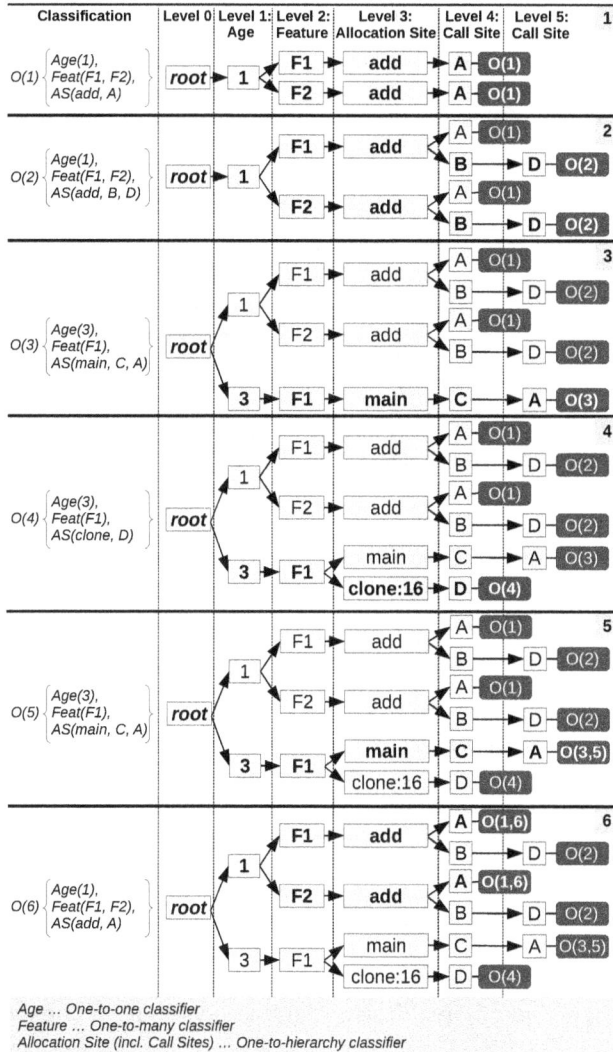

Figure 7: Step-by-step multi-level grouping of six heap objects into a classification tree based on age, feature and allocation site.

to all current nodes (i.e., to *F1* and *F2*) and *A* nodes are appended to the two *add* nodes.

Since no more classifiers have to be applied, the object is then added as a data entry at the current nodes, i.e., at both *A* nodes. This is the state that is shown in the top part of Figure 7. To reach the state at the bottom of Figure 7 the above steps are repeated for every source object *O(2)* to *O(6)*.

Figure 8 shows an example on how classification trees get visualized in AntTracks. It displays a part of AntTracks's heap state analysis view where all heap objects have first been classified by *Age*, then by *Feature*, followed by *Allocation Site*.

3.5 Data Representation in Nodes

Source objects have to be associated with certain nodes of the classification tree. Various approaches are possible, some of which sacrifice information in favor of reduced memory overhead (see Figure 9).

Figure 8: AntTracks's visualization of classification trees.

3.5.1 Lossless Approaches. Information lossless approaches allow to retrieve all properties of all source objects stored in the classification tree. This is needed if the classification tree should later be used for further complex processing.

Naïve List Approach. A naïve approach is to represent the node's data as a list of objects. A source object's properties (which are distributively stored) would have to be combined into a new object on demand (e.g., new MyObject(p1, p2, p3)).

We chose to store source object properties in a scattered way exactly because we want to *prevent* the creation of class instances, which would lead to increased memory footprint (e.g., due to object headers). Further, the more live objects reside in the heap, the less memory is available for new allocations. This results in more frequent GC invocations, which may slow down the application.

Property List Approach. Instead of storing a list of objects, this approach only stores a list of one of the source object's properties. This is possible if the object's remaining properties can be derived from this property, which is the case for nearly all use cases. In AntTracks, for example, heap objects can be identified by their address. The downside of this approach is the additional indirection when obtaining the other properties on demand.

3.5.2 Lossy Approaches. The lossless approaches retain object identity, i.e., we know exactly which source objects have been added to which tree nodes. This level of detail may be traded for less memory-consuming tree node data structures.

Mapping Approach. This approach relies on a map, where the key's type is application-dependent and the value is represented by a counter.

When adding a source object to a node, information of interest about the object gets extracted as the *object key*. This object key is

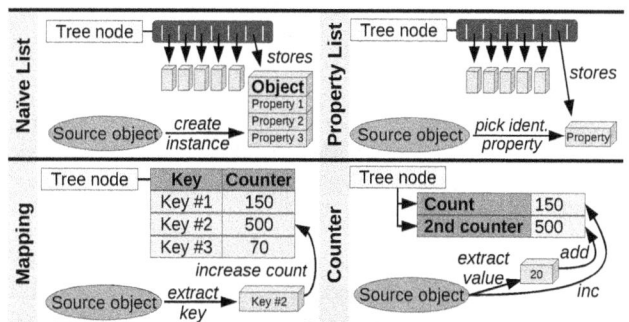

Figure 9: Two lossless list approaches and two lossy approaches based on counters to store node data.

then looked up in the node's data map and the respective counter gets incremented (or created if it does not yet exist).

It is crucial to take two aspects into account when choosing the object key: (1) What data should be reconstructed from the classification tree and (2) that many source objects should share the same object key to keep the number of entries in the map small. For example, AntTracks uses the object size (in bytes) as the object key. While this allows to only aggregate the number of objects and number of bytes represented by a certain node, it offers high memory saving potential which is discussed in more detail in Section 5. For example, if 1000 objects of only three different sizes get added to the same node, this approach just needs three key-value pairs compared to 1000 list entries as in the list approaches.

Counter Approach. This approach is designed to have the lowest memory footprint, while giving up flexibility and accepting the highest loss of information. Every time a source object gets classified at a certain node, counters stored in the node get incremented based on a fixed scheme. In AntTracks, for example, we could store two counters, one for the number of objects and one for the number of bytes classified at the given node.

This approach even loses information about specific properties. For example, it would not be possible to determine how many heap objects of a certain size have been classified, which is possible using the mapping approach.

3.6 Aggregation and Duplicate Detection

Using a one-to-many classifier may cause a source object to be added to multiple nodes. To avoid wrong results when aggregating this data, we have to detect duplicate entries in the tree and ignore them.

3.6.1 List Approaches. Since the entries in every data list are distinct, the lists can be treated as sets. The set of objects in a tree with head n can be computed recursively as the union of the objects in n and in the subtrees (Equation 1). Duplicates will be removed and the resulting set can be used for counting.

$$objects(n) = n.data \cup (\bigcup_{n.children}^{child} objects(child)) \quad (1)$$

3.6.2 Mapping Approach. By extracting a source object's object key, we lose the object identity which would be needed for duplicate detection. Therefore, we additionally have to keep track of multiple classifications. This can be done by installing a second map, i.e., the *duplicate map*, in each node.

If a source object is added to more than one subtree of a node n, a counter for the object's key is incremented in the duplication map of node n, which is later used for sifting out duplicates when the total number of objects in a tree is computed.

3.6.3 Counter Approach. Similar to the mapping approach, every node could store a duplicate counter per data counter. In all situations where a duplicate counter in the mapping approach would be incremented, the duplicate counter in the counter approach is incremented.

3.7 Advanced Classifiers

For advanced use, a special kind of classifiers are *transformers*. So far, a classifier always took a source object's properties as its input and returned one or more classification values as classification result. A transformer takes a source object and (1) transforms it

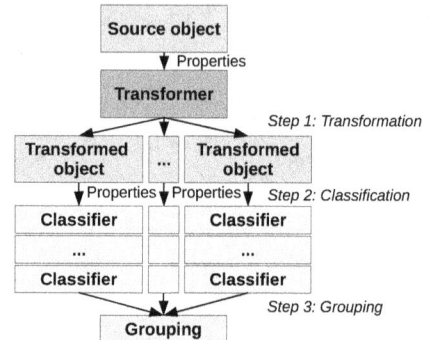

Figure 10: Transformers transform a source object into a set of other source objects, classify each of these objects and group them.

into a set of other source objects, (2) classifies each of these objects based on a selected set of object classifiers, and (3) multi-groups them based on their classification results (see Figure 10).

A use case for transformers in the domain of memory monitoring is pointer analysis. First, a heap object gets transformed into the set of all objects that are referenced by it. Second, this set of objects gets classified based on a list of other classifiers selected by the user. Finally, the classification results get multi-grouped into the resulting classification tree. For example, this can be used to analyze type-points-to-type graphs, as done by Jump and McKinley [8, 9].

4 IMPLEMENTATION

The previous section explained the domain-independent core concepts of classification and multi-level grouping based on object classifiers alongside some examples in the context of AntTracks. This section discusses some implementation details on how these concepts have been incorporated into AntTracks and its memory analysis.

Property	Additional info
address	
space	Space index, name, address, length, ...
type	Name, package, fields, ...
size	The object's size in bytes
isArray	true / false
arrayLength	-1 for non-arrays
allocationSite	Call stack, ...
pointedFrom	Addresses of all referencing objects
pointsTo	Addresses of all pointees
eventType	Allocation event (alloc. subsystem, ...)

Table 2: Source object properties for heap objects.

4.1 Source Objects: Java Heap Objects

AntTracks's source objects are Java heap objects that were alive in the monitored application at a given point in time, i.e., the heap objects that make up a certain heap state. Table 2 shows which properties make up a Java heap object in AntTracks, i.e., the source object properties. Every object classifier classifies a Java heap object based on a criterion derived from these properties.

4.2 Object Classifiers

In AntTracks, classifiers implement a common base interface. This interface defines the classify method, with its parameter signature matching the Java heap object properties.

To provide a convenient analysis environment for most use cases, AntTracks comprises multiple predefined object classifiers. These classifiers, listed in Table 3, can be used and combined freely on every heap state. An example implementation of the *Type classifier* can be seen in Listing 1.

Listing 1: Implementation of the *Type classifier* in AntTracks.

```
public class TypeClassifier implements Classifier<String> {
    // Fields modifiable by user, e.g., showPackage

    @Override public String classify(
        long address, Space space, Type type, long size,
        boolean isArray, int arrayLength, AllocationSite allocSite,
        long[] pointedFrom, long[] pointsTo, Event eventType) {
        return type.getName(showPackage);
    }
}
```

When a heap state is opened in AntTracks, a default classification (*Type classifier* followed by the *Allocation Site classifier*) gets applied. This gives a fast overview that shows which types have the most living objects, and where these objects have been allocated.

4.3 Heap Iteration

We implemented three different iteration approaches for AntTracks's heap data structure to evaluate their influence on the classification speed.

4.3.1 Java Streams. This approach has been implemented as a baseline for performance comparison. It uses the default technique for Java streams on custom data structures by implementing a Spliterator, the concurrent counterpart of an Iterator.

Java Stream Memory Overhead. The main problem with Java streams and spliterators is that they are generic classes working on Java objects of type T. Therefore, to support Java streams in AntTracks, we have to transform AntTracks's source objects (i.e., heap objects that are stored as scattered properties) into instances of an auxiliary HeapObject class. These short-living objects (which only exist while the stream is processed) may put unnecessary burden on the garbage collector, especially for large heap states.

4.3.2 Fake Spliterator. This approach relies on a custom iteration class that provides a tryAdvance and a trySplit method, similar to the Spliterator implemented for the Java stream approach. However, this *fake* spliterator does not inherit from Java's Spliterator interface, but only mimics its behavior. More specifically, the fake spliterator's tryAdvance does not match the official interface but been changed in a way that allows the fake spliterator to process a heap object's properties separately, which has the advantage of avoiding the need for auxiliary objects.

4.3.3 Integrated Iteration Functions. A basic implementation of this approach already existed in the previous versions of AntTracks. It provided sequential iteration functions on each data structure level, i.e., on the Heap, the Space, and the LAB. In our approach, we added support for parallel iteration, which significantly increased performance.

4.4 User-defined Classifiers

Classification in AntTracks is not restricted to predefined classifiers, but allows users to define new classifiers, i.e., *user-defined classifiers*, in two different ways: (1) By using Java's Service Provider Interface (SPI) concept, where new classifiers can be added to AntTracks as pre-compiled JAR files, and (2) by using in-memory on-the-fly compilation to support classifier development at run time.

4.4.1 Service Provider Interfaces (SPI). A *service provider interface* is a set of public interfaces and abstract classes that a third-party developer can implement. In AntTracks, the SPI encompasses abstract classes for classifiers, transformers, and filters. All of them define an abstract classify method which can be implemented by third-party developers in a sub-class. If a JAR containing such an implementation is detected on AntTracks's class path (using convenient SPI methods), it will be added to the list of available classifiers or filters.

4.4.2 On-the-fly Compilation. It is also possible to define new object classifiers, transformers and filters at run time. For example, whenever users have to select one of the available classifiers, they are offered to define a new one. The user then has to provide the classify method, the classifier's name, description, example and cardinality. This information gets merged into an object classifier template file which will then be compiled with a modified Java compiler that enables compilation without generating a Java class file on disk, i.e., the classifier gets compiled in-memory and on-the-fly.

This compilation relies on the JavaCompiler instance returned by ToolProvider.getSystemJavaCompiler(). This instance allows modifying the compilation process in various ways. The most important step is to provide a modified JavaFileManager. Instead of providing a stream to a file on disk, AntTracks's version returns a ByteArrayOutputStream that keeps a class's byte code stored in memory. Additionally, the file manager's class loader has been modified to not only look up classes stored on disk, but also to look up classes that are stored in memory.

5 EVALUATION

To evaluate the applicability of AntTracks's object classifiers and multi-level grouping we show how one can use the tool to detect memory leaks and how to reproduce memory classification done in related work.

Even though lossless classification tree implementations may be needed in certain situations, a lossy approach provides enough information for most use cases, including AntTracks's heap state analysis. Therefore, another goal of this evaluation is to analyze how much classification throughput can be gained as well as how much memory can be saved by accepting the information loss due to using a lossy classification tree implementation. All of these

Name	Description
Address	Classifies objects based on their address.
Type	Classifies objects based on their type's name.
Allocating Subsystem	Either *VM*, *Interpreter*, *C1-compiled code* or *C2-compiled code*.
Array Length	Classifies array objects based on their length. Non-array objects are classified as -1.
Object Kind	Either *Instance* (class instances), *Small Array* (< 255 elements), or *Big Array* (≥ 255 elements).
Space	Classifies objects based on the heap space in which they are contained.
Space Mode	Classifies objects based on the mode, i.e., a GC-dependent space info, of their containing heap space.
Space Type	Classifies objects based on the type (e.g., *Eden*) of the space in which they are contained.
Feature	Classifies objects based on a loaded feature-to-code mapping file.
Allocation Site	Classifies objects based on their allocation site (allocating method + var. number of call sites).
Pointed From	This transformer is used to classify the objects that reference a given object.
Points To	This transformer is used to classify the objects that a given object references.

Table 3: Predefined classifiers in AntTracks.

analyses have been conducted based on well-known benchmarks using three different classifier combinations: (1) Type classifier (2) Allocation Site classifier (3) Type classifier, followed by the Allocation Site classifier.

Setup. All measurements were run on an Intel® Core™ i7-4790K CPU @ 4.00GHz x 4 (8 Threads) on 64-bit with 32 GB RAM and a Samsung SSD 850, running Ubuntu 17.10 with the Kernel Linux 4.13.0-16-generic. All unnecessary services were disabled in order not to distort the experiments.

5.1 Performance Evaluation

The goal of this evaluation is to gain insight into how much the classification throughput increases when giving up object identity and if Java streams are suitable to iterate distributed source objects. Thus, we compare both implemented tree node types (i.e., the property list approach (lossless) and the mapping approach (lossy)) using three different parallel heap iteration techniques (i.e., Java stream, fake spliterator and integrated iteration).

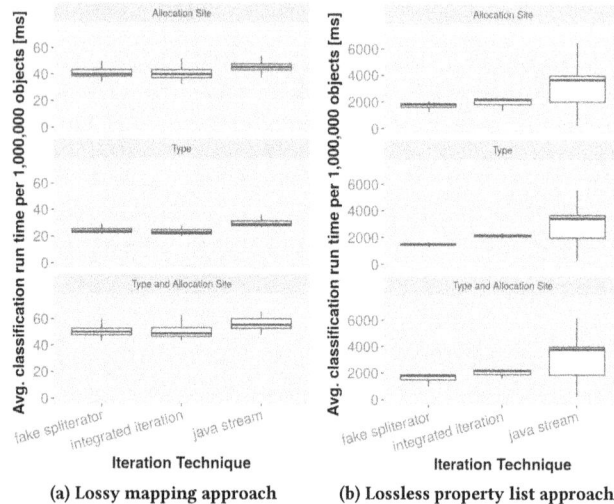

(a) Lossy mapping approach   (b) Lossless property list approach

Figure 11: Performance comparison between the mapping approach and the property list approach.

We used the DaCapo [4] and the DaCapo Scala [6] benchmark suites, in which, according to Lengauer at el. [14], h2 and factorie are the benchmarks with the largest live set. We chose to only analyze these two benchmarks since the other benchmarks from the

mentioned suites do not provide heap states in the same dimension. Both trace files (h2: 2.9 GB trace file covering 26 garbage collections with 15,800,000 objects on average per heap state; factorie: 19.5 GB trace file covering 205 GCs with 8,600,000 objects on average per heap state) have been parsed and a classification tree has been generated at every garbage collection end using every parameter combination (i.e., iteration type, classifier, tree type).

Figure 11a shows the average throughput of this classification tree generation when using the lossy mapping approach, while Figure 11b shows the throughput using the property list approach. We can see that the mapping approach is orders of magnitude faster than the property list approach due to the work that is needed to add the object's address to the sorted data list when using the property list approach. This strengthens our assumption to use the mapping approach when object-identity loss is acceptable.

Furthermore, it shows that heap iteration using Java streams is in general slower than the other two approaches. Especially for larger heap states, the streaming approach falls behind the other approaches. As hypothesized, this may be due to the temporary objects that have to be generated during the iteration. Independent of the domain this indicates that Java streams are not suitable for iterating distributively stored source objects. The fake spliterator approach is able to scale and parallelize the best, which explains its advantage when using the property list approach.

5.2 Memory Footprint

Beside providing the better classification performance, it is interesting to see how much memory can be saved when using the object-identity-losing mapping approach instead of the property list approach.

We analyzed a traced run of every DaCapo and DaCapo Scala benchmark and reconstructed the heap state after every garbage collection, if the heap state contained at least 200,000 objects. The *Type classifier* showed that the number of types of live objects at a certain point in time is approximately the same across all benchmarks (around 500 objects), independent of the number of live objects. Some of the benchmarks have few live objects with a high number of different allocation site nodes (i.e., few objects allocated at different sites) while some benchmarks with a large number of live objects only generate a small number of allocation site nodes (i.e., a lot of objects allocated at the same sites). Nevertheless, the tree never reached a critical size in terms of node count for any of the tested applications (tree size always below 20,000 nodes).

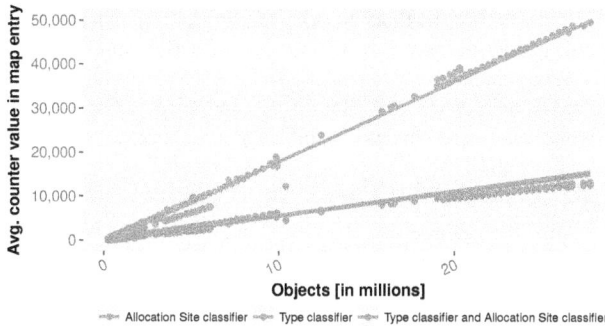

Figure 12: Average object count per data map entry using the mapping approach.

Figure 12 shows that with a rising number of classified objects, the average number of objects represented by a single data map entry in the mapping approach increases. For example, classifying about 10,000,000 objects based on the Type classifier resulted in data map entries each representing about 18,000 objects on average (see regression line in Figure 12). Assume that the property list approach is implemented using arrays and needs 8 bytes per classified object (i.e., the heap object's 64-bit address excluding memory needed by auxiliary data structures). Let's further assume that each map entry in the mapping approach points to a key (containing an int) and a value (containing a long), thus taking up $3*16$ ($3*$VM header)$+2*8$ ($2*$pointer)$+4$ (int)$+8$ (long) $= 76$ bytes. If one such data map entry represents 18,000 objects, the property list approach ($8 * 18,000$ bytes) consumes about 1900 times as much memory as the mapping approach (76 bytes).

Based on these results and those presented in Section 5.1, we decided to use classification tree generation based on fake spliterator heap iteration and the mapping approach in AntTracks.

The next section shows that the lossy mapping approach still provides enough information to detect memory leaks and allows general memory analysis.

5.3 Functional Evaluation

AntTracks's goal is to provide a general memory monitoring and analysis tool that primarily focuses on developers and their needs, for example performing memory leak detection. In addition, user-defined classifiers, their flexible combination, and multi-level grouping allows developers and also researchers to use AntTracks for more general and experimental memory analyses.

5.3.1 Memory Leak Detection. Memory leak detection is the main task developers perform when using AntTracks. To evaluate AntTracks's ability to allow memory leak detection, as well as finding the root cause, we used it on an example artificial application that uses a stack[1] for storing its data. It first pushes 1 million objects onto the stack, then pops these 1 million objects, followed by another 100,000 pushes and another 100,000 pop operations. Opening the application's trace displays the overview shown in Figure 13. We can clearly see that we miss a drop of the number of live objects after the 1 million objects got popped from

[1]https://www.codeproject.com/Articles/30593/Effective-Java; Item 6: Eliminate obsolete object references; last accessed October 17, 2017

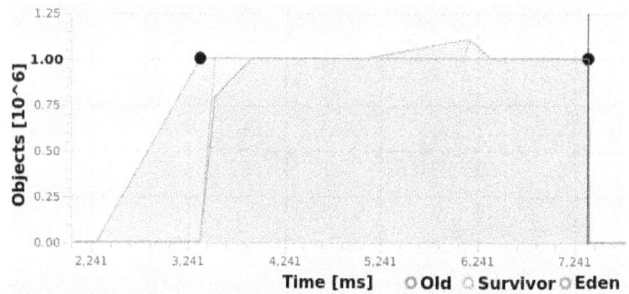

Figure 13: Object count overview of the buggy stack implementation.

the stack, as we would expect in a non-faulty implementation. To further investigate this problem, we utilized AntTracks's heap diffing functionality, which also supports object classifiers and allows to analyze heap changes over time. Figure 14 shows the application

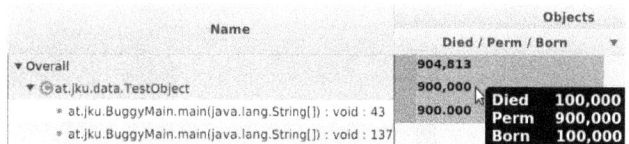

Figure 14: Heap diff of the buggy stack implementation.

of the *Type classifier* followed by the *Allocation Site classifier* on the time frame selected in Figure 13 (black dots). On the type node (2nd row, at.jku.data.TestObject), we can see that only 100.000 objects of this type were deallocated (red bar), while exactly the same amount of objects were allocated (green bar). 900,000 objects stayed alive during the whole time frame (blue bar). Looking at the indented allocation site nodes (3rd and 4th row), we see how many TestObjects that were originally allocated at these sites were born, have survived, or have died.

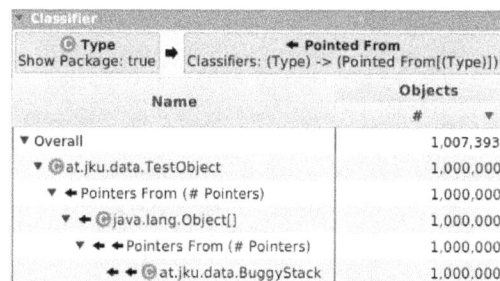

Figure 15: Pointer analysis of the buggy stack implementation.

Additionally, we would like to know which objects keep those objects alive. Figure 15 shows a rather advanced application of object classifiers: It first classifies a given object by its type, then transforms that object into its set of referencing objects, classifies them by type and then transforms them again into their sets of referencing objects, finally classifying those objects by type. It shows that the TestObject instances are referenced from the type Object[], which is again referenced by the type BuggyStack. With this information, it is easy to find the bug in the source code. BuggyStack is a faulty stack implementation that keeps references to previously stored objects even after pop operations until a subsequent push operation overwrites them.

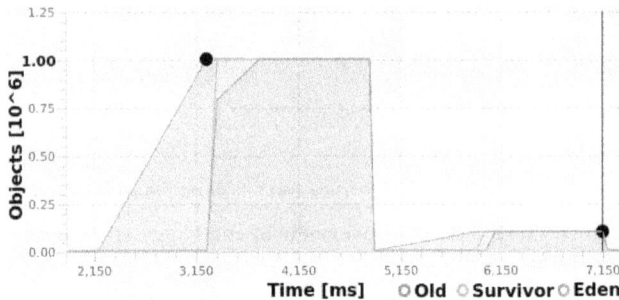

Figure 16: Object count overview of the fixed application.

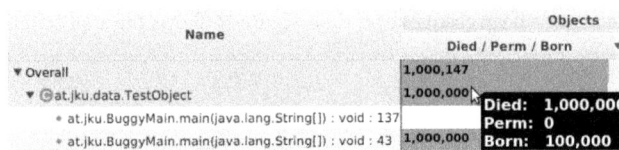

Figure 17: Heap diff of the fixed application.

Figure 16 and Figure 17 show the object counts and the heap diff results after the stack implementation was fixed.

5.3.2 Memory Analysis. Developers as well as researchers may want to classify heap objects based on a criterion not yet covered by one of the predefined classifiers, which is possible by writing a *user-defined* classifier. To showcase the implementation of *user-defined* classifiers, we searched for related work on heap object classification. For example, Mitchell and Sevitsky [17] classified heap objects in terms of *collection health* and *instance health*. Both classification criteria have been successfully implemented as *user-defined* classifiers and can be used and freely combined with other classifiers in AntTracks.

Collection Health. Collection health classifies every heap object as one of four types, depending on its use inside collections. (1) *head*, the head of a collection, e.g., HashMap, (2) *array*, array backbones, e.g., HashMap$Entry[], (3) *entry*, recursive list-style elements, e.g., HashMap$Entry, and (4) *contained*, anything else.

The classification for collection health is a typical use-case for a user-defined one-to-one object classifier. Every object gets classified by exactly one value, i.e., either *head*, *array*, *entry* or *contained*. According to Mitchell and Sevitsky, every object that is an array of a reference type gets classified as *array*. This is straightforward to check in the classifier implementation[2] since we know the object's type. If an object is not classified as *array*, it falls in the *entry* category if it is of a type T and references an object of the same type T. This check can be accomplished by following and analyzing the pointers in the object's pointer array. If the object has not been categorized as *array* or *entry*, the object's pointers are checked again. If one of them references an object that is a primitive array or is classified as *array* or *entry*, the object gets classified as *head*. Otherwise, the object gets classified as *contained*.

[2]http://ssw.jku.at/General/Staff/Weninger/AntTracks/ICPE18/
CollectionHealthClassifier.java

Instance Health. Instance health splits every heap object's bytes into four different parts: (1) *primitive*, which encompasses primitive array elements and primitive fields (2) *header*, the memory consumed by the virtual machine (3) *pointer*, memory occupied by references between objects (4) *null*, memory reserved for pointers but set to null.

The classification for instance health has been reproduced as a user-defined transformer in AntTracks[3]. The source object gets transformed into four *virtual objects*, one per instance health part, and every part gets assigned its appropriate size (i.e., byte count). The amount of bytes of the *primitive* part can be calculated by iterating the type's fields and filtering them for primitive types. The information about the *header* size (which depends on the VM architecture, as well as whether compressed oops are used) is stored in the symbols information generated alongside the trace file. Since an object's pointer array contains one entry per pointer, either with the referenced object's address or −1 if the pointer is null, the bytes made up by *pointers* and *null* can also be easily calculated.

The judgment schemes presented by Mitchell and Sevitsky, i.e., the ways how to interpret combinations of both classifiers, can now also be analyzed in AntTracks by using both classifiers at the same time. Furthermore, they can be used in combination with any other classifier that AntTracks provides.

Mitchell and Sevitsky used *"the built-in facilities of Java virtual machines (JVM) to trigger writing a snapshot to disk"* [17]. Before being able to write an analysis tool for such heap snapshots, one must obtain knowledge about the binary file format, how to parse it, and how to combine the parsed data into a convenient data structure. Depending on the use-case, results also have to be presented graphically to the user to allow user-friendly manual analysis, which also may take up a significant amount of development time. Compared to that, the implementation of the two classifiers presented above took about two hours each, including writing unit tests (by checking the correct classification of known Java classes such as HashMap). The classify methods of both classifiers cover less than 150 lines of code (LOC). Therefore, we claim that writing *user-defined classifiers* takes less work, with regard to person hours as well as LOC. Additionally, AntTracks provides convenient visualization out-of-the-box and the possibility to combine the newly developed classifier with any other available classifier.

6 RELATED WORK

Current state-of-the-art tools share one common problem. Nearly all of them represent heap states (or the change of the heap over time) only as type histograms. No free selection of classification exists, not even to mention multi-level grouping. Even basic information such as an object's allocation site is not available in many cases, since most tools rely on heap dumps that do not provide that level of detail. Still, some tools provide additional functionality such as pointer information on object level (plainly reconstructed from a heap dump).

The most basic approach supported by the Java Hotspot VM are the -XX:+PrintClassHistogramBeforeFullGC and -XX:+PrintClassHistogramAfterFullGC flags. They cause a class

[3]http://ssw.jku.at/General/Staff/Weninger/AntTracks/ICPE18/
InstanceHealthClassifier.java

histogram to be printed to the console on every full GC. *JConsole* [18] can connect to a running Java application and retrieves data from its Java Management Beans. Due to the restricted functionality of the memory bean, it can only show the current heap memory consumption separated into eden space, survivor space, and old space. *jhat* [19] can be used to analyze a Java heap dump file which has previously been generated using the *jmap* tool. It starts a webserver that hosts the heap dump results and can be accessed via a webbrowser. Beside a type histogram, also the rootset (i.e., objects that are referenced by a GC root) can be shown. *Visual VM* [23] is a general performance monitoring tool for Java applications that provides memory analysis based on heap dumps. In addition to a type histogram, it allows users to analyze individual objects of a certain type, including functionality to follow an object's pointers and go to the referencing object. It is also able to calculate the retained set of objects. The retained set of an object X is the set of objects which would be removed when X is garbage collected. In addition to that, the *Eclipse Memory Analyzer (MAT)* [7] also allows users to analyze the application's dominator tree [15]. The *Netbeans profiler* [20] is just a slimmed down version of Visual VM and is integrated into the Netbeans IDE.

Other approaches such as the one presented by Aftandilian et al. [1] or De Pauw and Wim [22] focus on visualizing a heap state's object graph. To reduce the complexity of such graphs, certain reduction operations such merging, cutting, and so on, are applied. Such approaches may work well for pointer analysis, e.g., which types references which types, yet most of them lack the flexibility to take other properties into account, e.g., heap spaces or allocation sites.

A query technique that is integrated into some of the mentioned tools is the *Object Query Language (OQL)* [2, 5]. It has been developed by the Object Data Management Group and is an SQL-like query language used to query objects from object-oriented databases. The downside of OQL is its complexity, which results in the problem that no vendor implements the whole standard. For example, the Eclipse Memory Analyzer (MAT) as well as VisualVM only allow queries in the form of SELECT `<select clause>` FROM `<from clause>` WHERE `<where clause>`. *Where clauses* can be represented in our approach using filters, while *select clauses* can be represented using an object classifier. Multi-level grouping, as supported in our approach, is neither possible in MAT nor in VisualVM.

7 FUTURE WORK

The concept of object classifiers and multi-level grouping as well as their implementation in AntTracks opened a number of interesting ideas. This section will shortly introduce these ideas and point out possible ways how to approach them.

Extended Pointer Support in AntTracks. Currently, Ant-Tracks provides only basic support for pointer analysis. For every object, it records the referencing and the referenced objects and makes them available for offline analysis. However, state-of-the-art tools [1, 16] often use advanced data structures such as dominator trees for analyzing whole pointer graphs. We plan to use similar data structures also in AntTracks to compute, for example, all objects that are reachable from a certain object (i.e., the transitive closure [24])

as well as the amount of memory that is kept alive by a specific object (i.e., the retained size).

Heap Diffing. Weninger et. al. [25] suggest heap diffing, i.e., analyzing how the heap changes over a certain time span, which is currently already supported to a certain level in AntTracks. The grouping and classification techniques that were described for heap states in this paper can partially also be applied to heap diffing. Extending classifiers with information about a source object's development over time, e.g., how a heap object's pointers changed over time, could further increase the potential application of heap diffing in combination with object classifiers.

Combined Tree Types. We showed that the memory consumption of a lossless classification tree is orders of magnitude higher than that of a lossy one. In a classification tree, often only a small subtree is of interest to the user. Since both classification tree types use node data structures inheriting from the same interface, they could be combined to only give lossless information for parts of the tree that are of higher interest to the user.

AntTracks DSL. To abstract from classifiers and their underlying programming language, the heap could also be analyzed by using a domain-specific query language. Such a language could, for example, be used to ask for the amount of objects of type T that were allocated at site S and survived at least n garbage collections. Based on our classifiers, we plan to develop such a language to provide even better support for expressing application-specific queries in a user-friendly way.

8 THREATS TO VALIDITY AND LIMITATIONS

Visualization of data in memory analysis tools is often strongly coupled with the kind of data that is collected and analyzed by those tools. Even though AntTracks collects more information about objects than most of the presented tools (e.g., only few tools collect allocation site information), the general classification principles using multi-level grouping and classification trees based on object classifiers and as well as AntTracks visualization features are not dependent on that amount of information. Only the number and the complexity of the classifiers that developers can implement is limited by the available information. The fewer source object properties are available, i.e., the less information the tool collects about heap objects, the less flexibility the developer has when it comes to writing classifiers. Assuming that AntTracks only collected type and heap space information for each object, we would still be able to provide the *Type classifier*, the *Object Kind classifier*, the *Space classifier* and so on as predefined classifiers, but due to the missing information, no *Allocation Site classifier* could be provided. Yet, all the available classifiers could still be freely combined, for example, by first classifying all objects by space and then by type, or first by object kind and then by space, or in any other possible combination. This outclasses the flexibility of the data aggregation and visualization techniques available in other tools presented in Section 6.

Similar to the limitation mentioned above, current pointer-based classifiers are restricted to adjacent objects via the from-pointer and to-pointer information. As explained in Section 7, new classifiers may become possible as soon as AntTracks provides full object graph traversal and root pointer information.

To verify that the extra flexibility simplifies memory analysis, specifically that it facilitates detecting and resolving memory-related problems such as memory leaks, a user study is planned as future work. Technical metrics such as *task completion time* or *number of found memory leaks* and subjective metrics such as *user satisfaction* can be collected during the study, based on faulty benchmark implementations or industry applications.

A limitation of our current study is that we have not yet investigated, which combinations of classifiers are best for detecting specific memory-related problems. This is another topic to be tackled by the mentioned user study.

9 CONCLUSION

In this paper, we presented the domain-independent concepts of (user-defined) object classifiers and multi-level grouping, which are novel and general concepts for classifying large amounts of objects, processing them, and arranging their classification results as a tree for later analysis. Object classifiers are entities that classify objects based on a certain criterion derived from the objects' properties. Multi-level grouping is the process of applying multiple object classifiers to a collection of objects and grouping these objects based on the classification results. In contrast to single-level grouping, which results in a key-value map, multi-level grouping results in a classification tree. Such a tree can be visualized in various ways and allows a top-down, fine-grained manual data analysis by the user.

Various lossless and lossy *classification tree* data structures were presented and analyzed with respect to their performance, their memory consumption, and their ability to retain object identity. We showed that the lossy tree structures allow a tremendous reduction of memory overhead when accepting certain information loss in the classification tree.

We integrated the concept of object classifiers and multi-level grouping into the memory monitoring tool AntTracks, a tool that primarily focuses on helping developers to detect and understand memory anomalies, thus replacing its previous rigid classification scheme. Developers benefit from AntTracks's new ability to classify heap states based on any combination of classifiers, which distinguishes our approach from existing state-of-the-art tools. Furthermore, our tool supports *user-defined* object classifiers, i.e, it allows the user to write small, dynamically loaded source code snippets to classify heap objects based on arbitrary criteria. This may also be of interest to researchers who want to perform more general and experimental memory analyses. Our memory analysis approach opens new ways how AntTracks can be used and how memory can be analyzed, and its applicability has been shown in a quantitative and a functional evaluation.

ACKNOWLEDGMENTS

This work was supported by the Christian Doppler Forschungsgesellschaft, and by Dynatrace Austria GmbH.

REFERENCES

[1] Edward E. Aftandilian, Sean Kelley, Connor Gramazio, Nathan Ricci, Sara L. Su, and Samuel Z. Guyer. 2010. Heapviz: Interactive Heap Visualization for Program Understanding and Debugging. In *Proc. of the 5th Int'l. Symposium on Software Visualization (SOFTVIS '10)*. 53–62.

[2] A. M. Alashqur, S. Y. W. Su, and H. Lam. 1989. OQL: A Query Language for Manipulating Object-oriented Databases. In *Proc. of the 15th Int'l. Conference on Very Large Data Bases (VLDB '89)*. 433–442.

[3] Verena Bitto, Philipp Lengauer, and Hanspeter Mössenböck. 2015. Efficient Rebuilding of Large Java Heaps from Event Traces. In *Proc. of the Principles and Practices of Programming on The Java Platform (PPPJ '15)*. 76–89.

[4] S. M. Blackburn, R. Garner, C. Hoffman, A. M. Khan, K. S. McKinley, R. Bentzur, A. Diwan, D. Feinberg, D. Frampton, S. Z. Guyer, M. Hirzel, A. Hosking, M. Jump, H. Lee, J. E. B. Moss, A. Phansalkar, D. Stefanović, T. VanDrunen, D. von Dincklage, and B. Wiedermann. 2006. The DaCapo Benchmarks: Java Benchmarking Development and Analysis. In *Proc. of the 21st annual ACM SIGPLAN conference on Object-Oriented Programing, Systems, Languages, and Applications (OOPSLA '06)*. 169–190.

[5] R.G.G. Cattell, Douglas K. Barry, Mark Berler, Jeff Eastman, David Jordan, Craig Russell, Olaf Schadow, Torsten Stanienda, and Fernando Velez. 2000. *The Object Data Standard: ODMG 3.0*.

[6] Technische Universität Darmstadt. 2012. DaCapoScala (last accessed October 10, 2017). http://www.benchmarks.scalabench.org/modules/scala-benchmark-suite/. (2012).

[7] Andrew Johnson and Krum Tsvetkov. 2017. MAT - Eclipse Memory Analyzer (last accessed October 10, 2017). http://www.eclipse.org/mat/. (2017).

[8] Maria Jump and Kathryn S. McKinley. 2007. Cork: Dynamic Memory Leak Detection for Garbage-collected Languages. In *Proc. of the 34th Annual ACM SIGPLAN-SIGACT Symposium on Principles of Programming Languages (POPL '07)*. 31–38.

[9] Maria Jump and Kathryn S. McKinley. 2009. Dynamic Shape Analysis via Degree Metrics. In *Proc. of the 2009 Int'l. Symposium on Memory Management (ISMM '09)*. 119–128.

[10] Philipp Lengauer, Verena Bitto, Florian Angerer, Paul Grünbacher, and Hanspeter Mössenböck. 2013. Where Has All My Memory Gone?: Determining Memory Characteristics of Product Variants Using Virtual-machine-level Monitoring. In *Proc. of the Eighth Int'l. Workshop on Variability Modelling of Software-Intensive Systems (VaMoS '14)*. Article 13, 13:1–13:8 pages.

[11] Philipp Lengauer, Verena Bitto, Stefan Fitzek, Markus Weninger, and Hanspeter Mössenböck. 2016. Efficient Memory Traces with Full Pointer Information. In *Proc. of the 13th Int'l. Conference on Principles and Practices of Programming on the Java Platform: Virtual Machines, Languages, and Tools (PPPJ '16)*.

[12] Philipp Lengauer, Verena Bitto, and Hanspeter Mössenböck. 2015. Accurate and Efficient Object Tracing for Java Applications. In *Proc. of the 6th ACM/SPEC Int'l. Conference on Performance Engineering (ICPE '15)*. 51–62.

[13] Philipp Lengauer, Verena Bitto, and Hanspeter Mössenböck. 2016. Efficient and Viable Handling of Large Object Traces. In *Proc. of the 7th ACM/SPEC on Int'l. Conference on Performance Engineering (ICPE '16)*. 249–260.

[14] Philipp Lengauer, Verena Bitto, Hanspeter Mössenböck, and Markus Weninger. 2017. A Comprehensive Java Benchmark Study on Memory and Garbage Collection Behavior of DaCapo, DaCapo Scala, and SPECjvm2008. In *Proc. of the 8th ACM/SPEC on Int'l. Conference on Performance Engineering (ICPE '17)*. 3–14.

[15] Thomas Lengauer and Robert Endre Tarjan. 1979. A Fast Algorithm for Finding Dominators in a Flowgraph. *ACM Trans. Program. Lang. Syst.* 1, 1 (Jan. 1979), 121–141.

[16] Evan K. Maxwell, Godmar Back, and Naren Ramakrishnan. 2010. Diagnosing Memory Leaks Using Graph Mining on Heap Dumps. In *Proc. of the 16th ACM SIGKDD Int'l. Conference on Knowledge Discovery and Data Mining (KDD '10)*.

[17] Nick Mitchell and Gary Sevitsky. 2007. The Causes of Bloat, the Limits of Health. In *Proc. of the 22Nd Annual ACM SIGPLAN Conference on Object-oriented Programming Systems and Applications (OOPSLA '07)*. 245–260.

[18] Oracle. 2017. JConsole (last accessed October 10, 2017). https://docs.oracle.com/javase/9/troubleshoot/diagnostic-tools.htm#JSTGD174. (2017).

[19] Oracle. 2017. jhat (last accessed October 10, 2017). https://docs.oracle.com/javase/8/docs/technotes/tools/unix/jhat.html. (2017).

[20] Oracle. 2017. Netbeans profiler (last accessed October 10, 2017). https://profiler.netbeans.org/. (2017).

[21] Oracle. 2017. OpenJDK HotSpot group (last accessed October 22, 2017). (2017).

[22] Wim De Pauw and Gary Sevitsky. 1999. Visualizing Reference Patterns for Solving Memory Leaks in Java. In *Proceedings of the 13th European Conf. on Object-Oriented Programming (ECOOP '99)*. 116–134.

[23] Jiri Sedlacek and Tomas Hurka. 2017. Visual VM - All-in-One Java Troubleshooting Tool (last accessed October 10, 2017). https://visualvm.github.io/. (2017).

[24] R. Tarjan. 1971. Depth-first search and linear graph algorithms. In *12th Annual Symposium on Switching and Automata Theory (swat 1971)*. 114–121. https://doi.org/10.1109/SWAT.1971.10

[25] Markus Weninger, Philipp Lengauer, and Hanspeter Mössenböck. 2017. User-centered Offline Analysis of Memory Monitoring Data. In *Proc. of the 8th ACM/SPEC on Int'l. Conference on Performance Engineering (ICPE '17)*. 357–360.

Log4Perf: Suggesting Logging Locations for Web-based Systems' Performance Monitoring

Kundi Yao, Guilherme B. de Pádua, Weiyi Shang
Department of Computer Science and Software
Engineering
Concordia University
Montreal, Quebec, Canada
{ku_yao,g_bicalh,shang}@encs.concordia.ca

Steve Sporea, Andrei Toma, Sarah Sajedi
ERA Environmental Management Solutions
Montreal, Quebec, Canada

ABSTRACT

Performance assurance activities are an essential step in the release cycle of software systems. Logs have become one of the most important sources of information that is used to monitor, understand and improve software performance. However, developers often face the challenge of making logging decisions, i.e., neither logging too little and logging too much is desirable. Although prior research has proposed techniques to assist in logging decisions, those automated logging guidance techniques are rather general, without considering a particular goal, such as monitoring software performance. In this paper, we present Log4Perf, an automated approach that provides suggestions of where to insert logging statement with the goal of monitoring web-based systems' software performance. In particular, our approach builds and manipulates a statistical performance model to identify the locations in the source code that statistically significantly influences software performance. To evaluate Log4Perf, we conduct case studies on open source system, i.e., CloudStore and OpenMRS, and one large-scale commercial system. Our evaluation results show that Log4Perf can build well-fit statistical performance models, indicating that such models can be leveraged to investigate the influence of locations in the source code on performance. Also, the suggested logging locations are often small and simple methods that do not have logging statements and that are not performance hotspots, making our approach an ideal complement to traditional approaches that are based on software metrics or performance hotspots. Log4Perf is integrated into the release engineering process of the commercial software to provide logging suggestions on a regular basis.

CCS CONCEPTS

• **General and reference** → **Performance**; • **Software and its engineering** → **Software performance**;

KEYWORDS

Software logs; Logging suggestion; Performance monitoring; Performance modeling; Performance Engineering

ACM Reference Format:
Kundi Yao, Guilherme B. de Pádua, Weiyi Shang and Steve Sporea, Andrei Toma, Sarah Sajedi. 2018. Log4Perf: Suggesting Logging Locations for Web-based Systems' Performance Monitoring. In *ICPE '18: ACM/SPEC International Conference on Performance Engineering, April 9–13, 2018, Berlin, Germany*. ACM, New York, NY, USA, 12 pages. https://doi.org/10.1145/3184407.3184416

1 INTRODUCTION

The rise of large-scale software systems, such as web-based system like Amazon, has imposed an impact on people's daily lives from mobile devices users to space station operators. The increasing importance and complexity of such systems make their quality a critical, yet a hard issue to address. Failures in such systems are more often associated with performance issues, rather than with feature bugs [39]. Therefore, performance assurance activities are an essential step in the release cycle of large software systems.

Monitoring performance of large systems is a crucial task of performance assurance activities. In practice, performance data is often collected either based on system-level information [17], such as collecting CPU usage, or application-level information, such as response time or throughput. In particular, Application Performance Management tools, such as Kieker [38], are widely used in practice. They collect performance data from the systems when they are running in the field environment. However, such system or application-level performance data often leads to the challenges of pinpointing the exact location in the source code that is related to performance issues.

On the other hand, the knowledge of logs has been widely identified to improve the quality of large software systems [14, 15, 24, 25, 33]. Prior research proposed and used logs to monitor and improve software performance [14, 15, 24, 33]. The success of those performance assurance techniques depends on the well-maintained logging infrastructure and the high quality of the logs. Although prior research has proposed various approaches to improve the quality of logs [21, 27, 28, 42, 43, 46, 47], all of these approaches consider logs in general, i.e., not considering the particular need of using logs for performance assurance activities. Therefore, the suggested improvement of logs may not be of interest in performance assurance activities.

In this paper, we present an approach that automatically provides logging location suggestion for web-based systems based on the particular interest in performance modeling. Our approach first automatically insert logging statements into the source code. After conducting performance tests with the system, our approach builds statistical performance models to represent the system performance (such as CPU usage) using logs that are generated by the automatically inserted logging statements in the source code. By improving and analyzing statistical performance models, our approach identifies the logging statements that are statistically significant in explaining the system performance. Such logging statements are suggested to practitioners as potential logging locations for the use of performance assurance activities.

We evaluate our approach with two open source systems, namely OpenMRS and CloudStore, and one commercial system. Our evaluation results show that we can build high-quality statistical performance models with R^2 between 26.9% and 90.2%. By studying the suggested logging locations, we find that they all have a high influence on the system performance. Also, these locations cannot be identified using code complexity metrics or detected as performance hotspots. This paper makes the following contributions:

- To the best of our knowledge, our work is the first to provide logging suggestions with the particular goal of performance monitoring.
- We propose a statistically rigorous approach to identifying source code locations that can statistically explain system performance.
- The outcome of our approach can complement the use of traditional code metrics and performance hotspots to assist performance engineers in practice.

Our approach is already adopted in an industrial environment and is integrated into a continuous deployment environment. Developers receive logging suggestions from our automated approach regularly to better monitor the system performance in the field.

The rest of this paper is organized as follows: Section 3 presents our automated approach to suggest logging locations. Section 4 and 5 present the results of evaluating our approach through answering three research questions and discuss related topics based on the results. Section 6 presents the prior research that is related to this project. Section 7 presents the threats to the validity of our study. Finally, Section 8 concludes this paper.

2 A MOTIVATING EXAMPLE

Tom is a performance engineering of an e-commerce web system. He often uses the information from web logs (e.g., page requests) to build performance models to understand system performance or to detect performance issues.

Tom finds that the performance models are often unreliable in predicting the system's performance. He examines the performance of each log entry and found that some entries have a significant variance. However, there is not enough information in the web logs to accurately pinpoint the issue for further monitoring. Hence, by knowing only which web requests were called is not enough to explain the performance of the system.

Let us consider an example (Algorithm 1) in which the function process a list of products of a given signed-in customer. The products have an expiration date and, if they are expired, the program needs to consult a different supplier. In this example, the method

LoadProductStock response time varies according to different factors, such as the number of products for that customer, and whether the products are expired or not. If the products are not expired the method might return very fast; while if the current customer has many expired products, there will be too many calls to consult suppliers, leading to the significantly long response time.

Algorithm 1 Example: Load products that has an expiration date.

1: **function** LOADPRODUCTSTOCK(c)
2:     $products \leftarrow$ product list of customer c
3:     **for each** p in $products$ **do**
4:         **if** $IsExpired(p)$ **then**
5:             $p.Stock \leftarrow StockFromSupplier(p)$
6:         **end if**
7:     **end for**
8: **end function**

Although Tom can identify and monitor some complex requests in the web logs, he finds that some complex requests may not be so useful to monitor, since they have a steady performance behavior. For those cases, the information provided by the web logs is sufficient. Nevertheless, for the requests that their performance is not steady (e.g., Algorithm 1), there exists a high degree of uncertainty. Due to this reason, Tom needs to manually go through all the web log entries to find the scenarios (e.g., particular customer and product(s)) that required further monitoring and, therefore, require more logging statements. For a large-scale system with a non-trivial workload, this manual operation is not feasible, and, consequently, Tom needs a technique to automatically suggest where the monitoring and logging are needed, without repetitive information. Such technique would significantly reduce the uncertainty of monitoring or not the right places.

In this next section of this paper, we will present an approach that seeks to suggest logging locations by examining whether the location in the source code can provide significant explanatory power to the systems' performance.

3 APPROACH

In this section, we present our approach that can automatically suggest logging locations for software performance monitoring. To reduce the performance overhead caused by introducing instrumentation into the source code, we first leverage the readily available web logs to build a statistical performance model, and we identify the web requests that are statistically significantly performance-influencing. In the second step, we only focus on the methods that are associated with the performance-influencing web requests and identify which method is statistically significantly performance-influencing. Finally, we focus on the basic block in the source code that is associated with the performance-influencing method, and we identify and suggest the code blocks that logs should be inserted.

For each step, we apply a workload on the subject system while monitoring its performance. Afterwards, we build a statistical model for the performance of the subject system using either the readily available web logs or the automatically generated logs from instrumentation during the workload. Using the statistical performance model, we identify the statistically significant performance-influencing logging statements. The overview of our approach is presented in Figure 1.

Step 1: Identifying performance-influencing web requests

In the first step, we aim to identify the source code associated with the web requests that influence system performance.

1.1 Parsing web logs

We run performance test for our subject systems and monitor their performance during the test. After the performance test, we parse the generated web logs. In particular, we keep the time stamp of the web log and the web request (e.g., a restful web request).

We then calculate log metrics based on those logs. Each value of each log metric L is the number of times that each web request executes during the period. For example, if a web request *index.jsp* is executed 10 times during a 30-second time period, the metric *index.jsp*'s value is 10 for that period.

1.2 Building statistical performance models using web logs

We follow a model building approach that is similar to the approach from prior software performance research [17, 33, 40]. We build a linear regression model [20] to model the performance of the software. We choose linear regression model because: 1) the goal of the approach is not to build a perfect model but to interpret the model easily instead, and 2) prior research used such modeling techniques to model software performance [17, 18, 40]. We use the log metrics that are generated from web logs as independent variables. The dependent variable of the model is the performance metrics that are collected during applying the load on the software system, such as CPU usage.

After building a linear regression model for the performance of the software, we examine each independent variable, i.e., log metric, to see how statistically significant it is to the model's output, i.e., performance metrics. In particular, we only consider the log metrics that have p-value ≤ 0.05. Since each log metric represents the number of times that the associated source code of each web request executes, the significance of a log metric shows whether the execution of the web log associated source code has a statistically significant influence on the software performance. Based on the list of statistically significant log metrics, we identify the performance-influencing web requests.

Step 2: Identifying performance-influencing methods

In the second step, we focus only on the performance-influencing web requests, and we aim to identify which methods in the source code are statistically significantly influencing performance. To reduce the performance overhead of the instrumentation, we note that every time we only focus on *one* performance-influencing web request. If multiple web requests are found performance-influencing, we repeat this step for every one of them.

2.1 Automatically inserting logging statements into methods

In this step, we automatically insert a logging statement into every method that is associated with the performance-influencing web requests. We use source code analysis frameworks, such as Eclipse JDT [2] and .NET Compiler Platform ("Roslyn") [5], to parse the source code and to identify the associated methods in the source code. We automatically insert a logging statement based on *Log4j2* and *Log4Net.Async* at the beginning of each method source code. Since the goal of our approach only suggests the location to insert logging statement, we only print the time stamp and the method signature using the logging statement. After re-building the systems and applying performance tests to each subject system, logs will be generated automatically.

Similar to step 1.1, we parse both the web logs and the logs that are generated by our inserted logging statement. Then we generate log metrics based on these logs.

2.2 Reducing metrics

Intuitively, methods that never execute during a workload, or the execution of the method has a constant value during the workload do not influence the performance of the system. Hence, we first remove any log metric that has constant values in the dataset. Methods may often be called together, or one method may always call another one. In such cases, not all methods need to be logged. Hence, we perform a correlation analysis on the log metrics [26]. We used the Pearson correlation coefficient among all performance metrics from one environment. We find the pair of log metrics that have a correlation value higher than 0.9. From these two log metrics, we remove the metric that has a higher average correlation with all other metrics. We repeat this step until there exists no correlation higher than 0.9.

We then perform redundancy analysis on the log metrics. The redundancy analysis would consider a log metric redundant if it can be predicted from a combination of other metrics [23]. We use each log metric as a dependent variable and use the rest of the log metrics as independent variables to build multiple regression models. We calculate the R^2 of each model and if the R^2 is larger than a threshold (0.9), the current dependent variable (i.e., log metric) is considered redundant. We then remove the performance metric with the highest R^2 and repeat the process until no log metric can be predicted with R^2 higher than the threshold. For example, if method *foo* can be linearly modeled by the rest of the performance metrics with $R^2 > 0.9$, we remove the metric for method *foo*.

2.3 Building statistical performance models using both web logs and our generated logs

In this step, we build a similar statistical model as step 1.2. As a difference, we do not include the log metrics from web logs that are found not performance influencing from step 1.2. We follow the same model building process and the same way of identifying statistically significant log metrics. The outcome of this step is the methods that are statistically significantly performance-influencing.

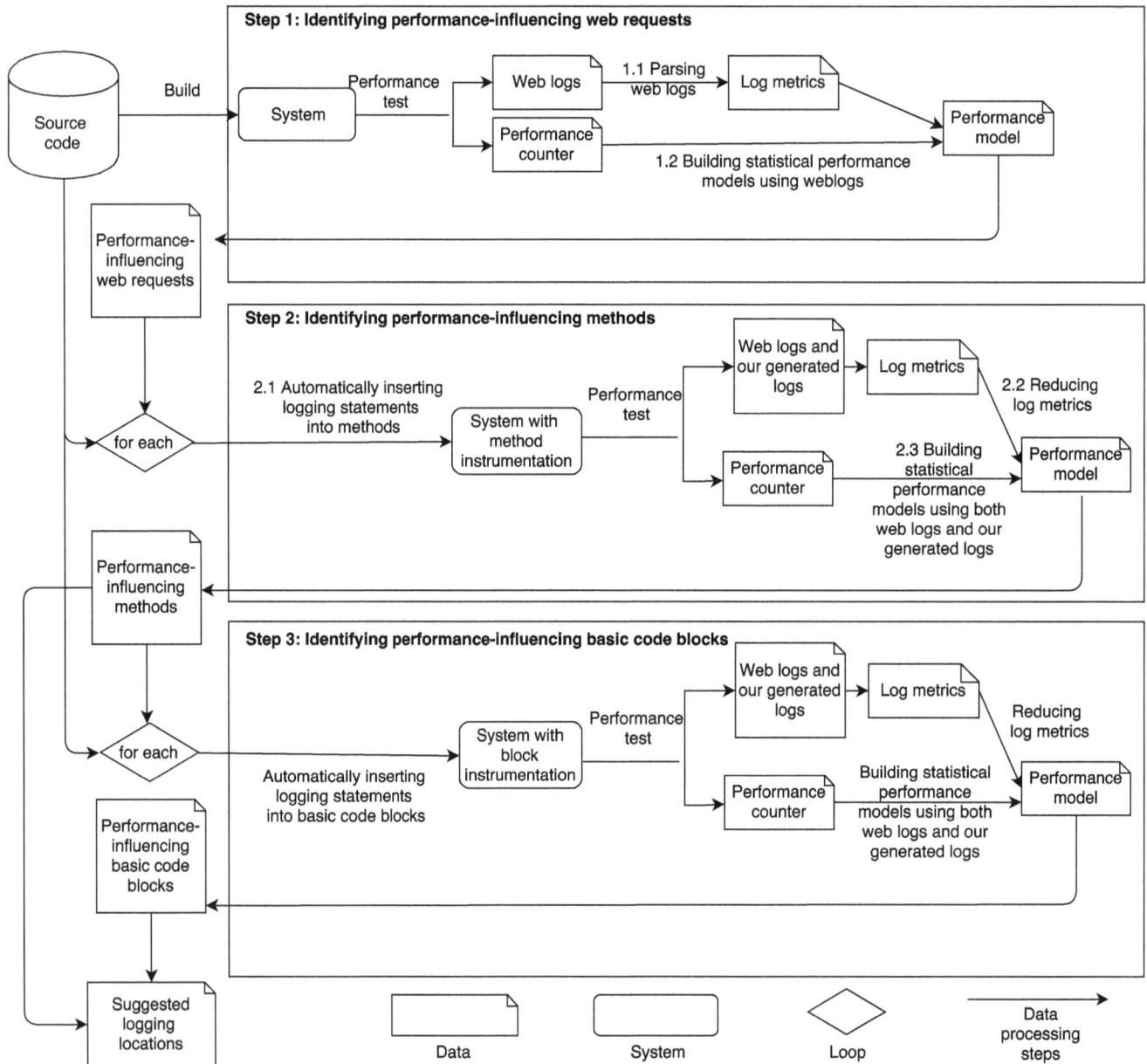

Figure 1: An overview of our approach. The numbered steps in the figure correspond to the steps in Section 3.

Step 3: Identifying performance-influencing basic code blocks

A method may be long and consist of many basic blocks. It may be the case that only a small number of basic blocks are performance-influencing. Therefore, in the final step, we focus only on the performance-influencing methods, and we aim to identify which basic code block is performance-influencing. Similarly, every time we only focus on one method. If multiple methods are found performance-influencing, we repeat this step for each method.

We use the code analysis frameworks to identify basic blocks of each performance-influencing methods. If a performance influencing method only contains one basic block, we do not proceed with this step. For the methods with multiple basic blocks, similar to step 2.1, we automatically insert logging statement into every basic block and generate log metrics by both the web logs and our generated logs. We also follow a similar approach as step 2.2 and 2.3 to identify which code block is statistically significantly influencing performance. We then automatically suggest to developers the logging statement insertions into the basic code block, to assist in performance monitoring. If none of the log metrics that are based on basic blocks are significant, we suggest to developers the direct insertion of logging statement at the beginning of the method itself.

4 EVALUATION

In this section, we first present the setup of our evaluation, including the subject systems, the workload, and the experimental environment. Then we evaluate our approach by answering three research questions. For each research question, we present the motivation for the question, the approach that we use to answer the question and finally the results.

4.1 Subject systems and their workload

We evaluate our approach with open-source software, including *OpenMRS* and *CloudStore*, and one commercial software, *ES*. The overview of the subject software is shown in Table 1.

Table 1: Overview of our subject systems.

Subjects	Version	SLOC (K)	# files	# methods
CloudStore	v2	7.7	98	995
OpenMRS	2.0.5	67.3	772	8,361
ES	2017	>2,000	>9,000	>100,000

4.1.1 OpenMRS. OpenMRS is an open-source patient-based medical record system commonly used in developing countries. *OpenMRS* is built by an open community that aims to improve healthcare delivery through a robust, scalable, user-driven, open source medical record system platform. Their application design is customizable with low programming requirements, using a core application with extendable modules. We choose *OpenMRS* since it is highly concerned with scalability and its performance has been studied in prior research [13]. *OpenMRS* provides a web-based interface and RESTFul services. We deployed the *OpenMRS* version 2.0.5 and the data used are from MySQL backup files that are provided by *OpenMRS* developers. The backup file contains data for over 5K patients and 476K observations. We use the RESTFul API test cases created by Chen et al. [13]. The tests are composed of various searches, such as: by patient, concept, encounter, and observation, and editing/adding/retrieving patient information. The tests include randomness to simulate real-world workloads better. We keep the workload running for five hours. To minimize the noise from the system warmup and cool-down periods, we do not include the data from the first and last half an hour of running the workload. In the end, we keep four hours of data from each performance test.

4.1.2 CloudStore. CloudStore is an open-source sample e-commerce web application developed to be used for the analysis of cloud characteristics of systems, such as capacity, scalability, elasticity, and efficiency. It follows the functional requirements defined by the TPC-W standard for verifiable transaction processing and database benchmarks data [7]. It was developed to validate the European Union funded project called CloudScale [1]. We choose *CloudStore* due to its importance in improving cloud systems performance and scalability. It has also been studied in prior research [13]. We deployed the *CloudStore* version v2 and the data used was generated using scripts provided by *CloudStore* developers. The generated data for CloudStore contains about 864K customers, 777K orders, and 300 items. We use the test cases created by Chen et al [13] to cover searching, browsing, adding items to shopping carts, and checking out. The tests include randomness to simulate real-world workloads better. For example, there is randomness to ensure that some customers may check out, and some may not. We run the performance tests with the same length as OpenMRS.

4.1.3 ES. ES is a commercial software that provides government-regulation related reporting services. The service is widely used as the market leader of its domain. Because of a non-disclosure agreement, we cannot reveal additional details about the system. We do note that it has over ten years of history with more than two million lines of code that are based on Microsoft .Net. We run a typical loading testing suite as the workload of the system.

4.2 Experimental environment

The experimental environment for the open-source software is set up on three separate machines. The first machine is the database server; the second is the web server in which the web application was deployed and, finally, the third machine simulates users using the JMeter load driver [11]. These machines have the same hardware configuration, which is 8G of RAM and Intel Core i5-4690 @ 3.5 GHz quad-core CPU. They all run the Linux operating system and are connected to a local network.

We use *PSUtil* [6] to monitor the performance of the software. To minimize the noise of other background processes, we only monitor the process of the subject system that is under the workload. We monitor the CPU usage during the workload for every 10 seconds. In particular, similar to prior research [10, 37], CPU percentage of the monitored process between two timestamps are calculated as the CPU usage of the corresponding workload during the period.

The experimental environment for *ES* is an internal dedicated performance testing environment, also with three machines. The testing environment is deployed with performance monitoring infrastructure. Similar to the open-source software, we monitor the CPU usage of the process of *ES* for every 10-seconds and use a logging library to generate automatically instrumented logs.

To combine the two datasets of performance metrics and logs, and to further reduce the impact of recording noises, we calculate the mean values of the performance metrics in every 30 seconds. Then, we combine the datasets of performance metrics and system throughput based on the time stamp on a per 30-seconds basis. A similar approach has been applied to address mining performance metrics challenges [19]. We use *Log4J2*'s asynchronous logging to generate the automatically instrumented logs since it is shown to have the smallest performance overhead [4].

RQ1: How well can we model system performance?

Motivation.

The success of our approach depends on the ability to build a well fit statistical models for software performance. If the models built by our approach are of low quality, we cannot use such models to understand the influence of logged source code locations (i.e., log metrics) to the software performance (i.e., performance metrics).

Additionally, the automatically inserted logging statements have an impact on software performance. If the performance is influenced by those inserted logging statements, instead of the existing source code itself, our model cannot be used to identify performance-influencing source code locations to log.

Furthermore, if we identify too many locations that are statistically significantly influencing performance, it is not practical for developers to log all locations nor can developers deeply investigate every location to ensure the need for logging. Besides, if all the identified locations are already well logged, developers may not need our approach's logging suggestion.

Approach.

We measure the model fit to assess the quality of the statistical models for software performance. In particular, we calculate the R^2 of each model to measure model fit. If the model perfectly fits the data, the R^2 of the model is 1, while a zero R^2 value indicates that the model does not explain the variability of the dependent variable (i.e., performance metric). We also count the number of logging locations that are suggested by our approach. For every suggested logging location, we manually examine whether there already exists a logging statement.

Results.

Our model can well explain system performance. Shown by Table 2, our statistical performance models have an R^2 of 26.9% and 90.2%. Such high values of the model fit confirms that our performance models can well explain system performance. By looking closely at the models, we can see that the models with our automatically inserted logging statement typically has higher R^2 than the models that are only using web logs. For example, by insert logging statements into two methods in OpenMRS, the fit of the performance model almost doubles (from 26.9% to 46.3%). However, the models that are with inserted logging statements into basic code blocks have a relatively smaller increase of R^2 in comparison to the ones with method-level logging. In the same example of OpenMRS, inserting the logs into basic code blocks only provides 1.6% increase of the R^2.

Our approach does not suggest an overwhelming amount of logging locations for performance modeling. In total, our approach suggests three, two, and four locations for CloudStore, OpenMRS, and ES respectively. We consider such an amount of suggestion as an appropriate amount for practitioners. By measuring the total number of methods in the subject systems, we only suggest to log in less than 0.5% of them. By providing such suggestions to our industrial practitioners, we also received the feedback that such an amount of suggestions is not overwhelming. Hence, practitioners can allocate resource to examine each suggestion and make the final decision of whether to insert logging statements to those locations. Moreover, by manually examining each of the logging locations, we find that **None of the suggested logging locations contain logging statements.** This implies that our approach may provide additional information about the system performance other than what is already known by developers.

> The logging locations suggested by our approach significantly improve the performance models that are with a high model fit. None of those locations initially contain a logging statement.

RQ2: How large is the performance influence by the recommended logging locations?

Motivation.

In the previous research question, we find that, with our approach, we can suggest logging locations that are statistically significant for performance modeling. Even though these logging locations are statistically significant, the effect of the logging location may still be trivial. Therefore, in this research question, we would like to examine the magnitude of the influence on system performance by our suggested logging locations.

Approach.

To understand the magnitude of the influence on system performance by our recommended logging locations, we first calculate Pearson correlation between the system performance, i.e., CPU, and with the appearance of the suggested logging locations. Higher correlation implies that the suggested logging locations may have a higher influence on the system performance.

To quantify the influence, we follow a similar approach used in prior research [31, 35]. To quantify this magnitude, we set all of the metrics in the model (each as a suggested logging location) to their mean value and record the predicted system performance. Then, to measure the effect of every logging location, we keep all of the metrics at their median value, except for the metric whose effect we wish to measure. We double the median value of that metric and re-calculate the predicted system performance. We then calculate the percentage of difference caused by doubling the value of that metric. For example, if the CPU is 60% at all metrics with median value and 90% by increasing one log metrics, the effect is 0.5, i.e., $\frac{90\% - 60\%}{60\%}$. The effect of a metric can be positive or negative. A positive effect means that a higher chance of execution the suggested logging location may increase the system performance, e.g., higher CPU usage. This approach permits us to study metrics that are of different scales, in contrast to using odds ratios analysis, which is commonly used in prior research [34].

Results.

The appearance of the suggested logging locations influences the system performance. Table 3 shows that the appearance of the suggested logging locations typically has a strong correlation to system performance. In CloudStore, all of the logging locations have a strong correlation to CPU usage, while the correlations are moderate in OpenMRS. The relative effect shows the influence of one method while controlling all other methods. `DaoImpl.getCurrentSession()` in CloudStore has the largest effect when the appearance of the method is double to its median value: the CPU usage increases 124%. Table 3 shows that even method with a small effect, e.g., `ConceptServiceImpl.getFalse-Concept()`, can increase the CPU usage by 19% if doubling its appearance.

Table 2: R^2 values of the statistical performance models built by our approach.

Cloud Store				
Steps:	Web request name	Method name/Block location	R^2	
			Original	With logging statement as a metric
Step 1: Web logs only	N/A		90.20%	N/A
Step 2: With method instrumentation	"cloudstore/ "	HomeController.getProductUrl() (No block)	78.50%	80.50%
	"cloudstore/buy"	DaoImpl.getCurrentSession()(No block)	49.40%	49.50%
	"cloudstore/search"	ItemDaoImpl.findAllByAuthor()	78.00%	81.20%
Step 3: With block instrumentation	"cloudstore/search"	ItemDaoImpl.java, line 233 to 243	81.30%	81.60%

OpenMRS				
Steps:	Web request name	Method name/Block location	R^2	
			Original	With logging statement as a metric
Step 1: Web logs only	N/A		26.90%	N/A
Step 2: With method instrumentation	concept/	ConceptServiceImpl.getAllConcepts() ConceptServiceImpl.getFalseConcept()	46.30%	47.80%
Step 3: With block instrumentation	concept/	ConceptServiceImpl.java, line 300 to 302 ConceptServiceImpl.java, line 929 to 930	47.90%	48.00%

ES				
Steps:	Web request name	Method name/Block location	R^2	
			Original	With logging statement as a metric
Step 1: Web logs only	N/A		43.80%	N/A
Step 2: With method instrumentation	Web request A	file1.m() file2.n()	75.90%	76.40%
	Web request B	(No significance)	30.00%	N/A
	Web request C	file3.o() file4.p()	42.90%	43%
Step 3: With block instrumentation	Web request A	file1, block.r file2, block.x	70.80%	70.80%
	Web request C	file3, block.y file4, block.z	76.00%	76.30%

"No block" means that the method only has one basic block in the method body.
"No significance" means that none of the methods are significant in the performance model.
We only present the class names, the method names and the file names due to the limit of space, without showing the package names and the full path of the files.

The influence on the system performance may be both positive or negative. We find that some suggested logging locations in ES may have a negative influence on the CPU usage of the system, i.e., the higher the appearance of the logging location, the lower the CPU usage. By manually examining those methods, we find that these methods are related to synchronized external dependency, i.e., the invocation of these methods will cause the system to wait, leading to lower CPU usage. By having these logs, developers can consider addressing such synchronized dependency based on how often real-life users call these methods.

> Our suggested logging locations have influences on system performance; while such influence can be both positive and negative.

RQ3: What are the characteristics of the recommended logging locations?

Motivation.

In the previous research questions, we leverage our approach to suggest logging locations to assist in performance modeling. If we can study the characteristic of these locations in the source code being performance influential, we may provide more general guidance for a developer to log similar locations in the source code.

Furthermore, prior research has proposed various techniques to provide general guidance on logging locations [21, 47] or to monitor hot methods in performance. Our approach may be of less interest if prior techniques also suggest such locations to log.

Approach.

For each of the suggested logging locations, we manually examine the surrounding source code to understand their characteristics. In particular, the size of the source code, such as lines of code, one of the factors prior study used to model logging decisions [47]. Moreover, uncertainty concerning control flow branches is also considered in logging decisions [46]. Therefore, we measure the source lines of code (SLOC) of the suggested methods and blocks and the cyclomatic complexity of the methods that are suggested to be logged.

Furthermore, we massively instrument the execution of all subject systems with JProfiler and Visual Studio Profiling tool [3, 8]. We measure both inclusive and exclusive execution time of each method and rank all the methods by their execution time. We would

Table 3: The influences of our suggested logging locations on system performance.

Cloud Store			
Suggested logging locations		Influence	
Web request name	Method name/Block location	Peason correlation	Relative effect
cloudstore/	HomeController.getProductUrl()	+0.80	+0.19
cloudstore/buy	DaoImpl.getCurrentSession()	+0.70	+1.24
cloudstore/search	ItemDaoImpl.findAllByAuthor()	+0.87	+0.60
cloudstore/search	ItemDaoImpl.java, line 233 to 243	+0.73	+0.25

OpenMRS			
Suggested logging locations		Influence	
Web request name	Method name/Block location	Peason correlation	Relative effect
concept/	ConceptServiceImpl.getFalseConcept()	+0.51	+0.19
concept/	ConceptServiceImpl.getAllConcepts()	+0.53	+0.22
concept/	ConceptServiceImpl.java, line 300 to 302	+0.56	+0.25
concept/	ConceptServiceImpl.java, line 929 to 930	+0.56	+0.22

ES			
Suggested logging locations		Influence	
Web request name	Method name/Block location	Peason correlation	Relative effect
Web request A	file1.m()	-0.27	-0.34
Web request A	file2.n()	+0.81	+1.17
Web request C	file3.o()	-0.40	-0.80
Web request C	file4.p()	+0.56	+0.49
Web request A	file1, block.r	-0.26	-0.39
Web request A	file2, block.x	+0.78	+1.11
Web request C	file3, block.y	-0.11	-0.28
Web request C	file4, block.z	+0.86	+0.88

A relative positive effect means that more appearances of the logging location may result in CPU usage increase.
We only present the class names, the method names and the file names due to the limit of space, without showing the package names and the full path of the files.

like to examine whether our suggested methods are one of the hot methods, i.e., with the highest executed time.

Results.

The suggested logging locations are not in complex methods.
By measuring the SLOC and cyclomatic complexity, we find that the suggested logging locations are in the methods with small sizes and low complexity. The methods that are suggested to be logged have a SLOC of 4, 5 and 15 in CloudStore, and methods in OpenMRS consists of only 3 and 6 SLOC. In ES, all suggested methods have a SLOC less than 35. Similarly, the values of the cyclomatic complexity of the suggested methods in CloudStore are only 1, 2 and 2; the same values are merely 1 and 2 in OpenMRS. The small sizes and the low complexity of the methods imply that practitioner may use our approach in tandem with other approaches that are based on source code metrics.

Most of the suggested logging locations are not the performance hotspot. By examining the results of detecting hotspots using both inclusive and exclusive execution time, we find that our suggested logging locations are not typical performance hotspots. In particular, only one of the logging locations (ItemDaoImpl.findAll ByAuthor()) is in the top 10 of hotspots in the source code (excluding methods in the library). We consider the reason is that our approach does not aim to identify the methods that are invoked

often, but the ones that can explain the system performance variance. Therefore, our approach may complement the detection of performance hotspots in performance assurances activities.

> The suggested logging locations are typically not in complex methods nor performance hotspots. Performance engineers can use our approach to complement those traditional measurements in performance engineering activities.

5 DISCUSSION

In this section, we discuss the related topics based on our results.

5.1 Performance influence from the inserted logging statement.

The invocation of logging statements themselves has a performance overhead. To minimize such performance overhead, we opt to reduce the instrumentation scope at every run of the system by focusing on only one web request, web page or method at each time. Moreover, we also leveraged async-logging provided by the logging library to reduce overhead. However, introducing those logging statements still brings overhead to the system.

Therefore, we measure the influence of the inserted logging statement to the fit of the model. We consider the invocation to the logging library itself as a method to monitor and create a log metric measuring the times that the logging library is called to generate logs. For every model that we built in our case study (see Table 2), we add the new log metric as an independent variable. By adding this independent variable into the model, we can study whether the log metric provides an increase of R^2, which represents the additional explanatory power of the execution of the inserted logging statement to the system performance. The increase of R^2 measures the explanatory power of the model that is provided only by the execution of the logging statements, but not the software system itself.

The automatically inserted logging statements do not contribute significantly to the performance models. We find that the log metric that measures the execution of the logging statements provides only little explanatory power to the models. In particular, the maximum of the increase of the R^2 is only 3.4% (see Table 2). Therefore, the inserted logging statement do not have a large impact to bias the explanatory power of our suggested logging locations.

5.2 Not all web requests need additional logging.

After applying our approach, inserting logging statements may not provide statistically significantly more explanation power to the model. For example, in the Web Request B of ES, after inserting logging statements into all associated method, none of them are statistically significant in the performance model. Such results imply that over-inserting logging statements into the source code may only provide repetitive information that is already available from other logs, whiling leading to more noise to practitioners [41]. By looking at the web request and the methods that do not need additional logging, we find that these cases are typically simple sequential executions with low complexity. For example, ItemDaoImpl.findAllByAuthor() in CloudStore has a loop as an extra basic block. However, our results show that inserting logging statement into the loop would not improve the performance model. That implies that the number of iterations of the loop may not influence performance significantly.

5.3 How long do we need to test performance to suggest logging locations?

Performance testing is a time-consuming task [10]. However, our approach requires multiple iterations of conducting performance tests. Even though it is straightforward to deploy the multiple performance tests in separate testing environments to reduce the time, such solution may still be resource-costly. In order to minimize the cost of the resource, we investigate whether we may shorten the duration of the performance tests and still yield similar results.

For every performance test, we take the data from the period of the first hour, the first two hours and the first three hours. We then follow the same steps as Section 3 and examine whether we can suggest the same locations to insert logging statements. We find that in 4 models, we can achieve the same logging suggestions by only running one hour, two hours and three hours of the test in four, one, and six models, respectively. We need the complete four hours only in two models. This result shows that practitioners

may be able to reduce the test duration in practice to receive the suggestion in a more timely manner.

6 RELATED WORK

In this section, we present the prior research related to this paper in three aspects: 1) software performance monitoring, 2) assisting logging decisions and 3) software performance modeling.

6.1 Software performance monitoring

There exist three typical levels of software monitoring techniques. The first, *system monitoring*, monitors the status of a running software based on the performance counters from the system. Examples of such counters include, CPU usage, memory usage and I/O traffic. Rich data from these counters are widely used to monitor system performance [17], allocate system resources and plan capacities [48] or predict system crash [16]. Despite the usefulness of such data, the lack of domain knowledge of the software running on top of the system makes the data difficult to use for improving the system in a detailed level (like improving source code).

The second type of widely used techniques are based on massive *tracing*. The tracing information records every function call that is invoked during the running of the system. Prior research leverage the tracking information to system quality and efficiency [44, 45]. In order to generate such tracing information, tools such as *JProfiler* [3] is widely used in practice and research. The challenge of leveraging such tracing information is the extra overhead from the tracing tools. Such overhead prevent the use of tracing in a large scale system or during the field running of the system, hence tracing is often used in the development environment by developers. Nevertheless, Maplesden et al. took advantage of patterns in tracing information. They built an automated tool to detect such patterns with the goal of improving the performance investigations and the systems' performance [29, 30].

To minimize the overhead from tracing, techniques are proposed to only trace a selected set of function calls, such that the tracing information from the field is possible to be monitored. For example, Application Performance Management tools [9] typically choose REST API call entry points to monitor. However, trace information is often generated automatically without the interference of developers' knowledge. The collected trace information may not all be needed for developers' particular purpose while the actual needed information may be missing.

The third type of monitoring technique is based on logging. Developers write logging statements in the source code to expose valuable information of runtime system behavior. A logging statement, e.g., *logger.info("static string"+ variable)*, typically consists of a log level (e.g., trace/debug/info/warn/error/fatal), a logged event using a static text, and variables that are related to the event context. During system runtime, the invocation of these logging statements would generate logs that are often treated as the most important, sometimes only, source of information for debugging and maintenance of large software systems. The logging information are generated based on developers' knowledge of the system, and are flexible to monitor various information in the code. Due to the extensive value in logs, prior research has proposed to leverage logging data to improve the efficiency and quality of large software systems [14, 15, 24, 33]. The advantage of using logging to monitor and analyze system performance motivates our paper. In particular, with our approach, the prior research that depends on logging may benefit from the extra information that are captured from the suggested logging statements.

6.2 Assist in logging decisions

Although logging is a significant technique for software performance monitoring, the logging practice in general is not as straight forward as one would expect. Logging involves a trade-off between the overhead it can generate and having the appropriate information. In a previous work, Zhao et al. proposed an algorithm that touches such trade-off. They increase the debugging assertiveness by automatically placing logs based on an overhead limit threshold [46]. Even if no overhead existed, there is still a need to balance between too much information and too little information [21].

Aiming to support the logging decisions, many previous works have contributed in ways to understand, automate and suggest opportunities of where to log. Fu et al. performed an empirical study on industry systems categorizing logged snippets of code. Their work also revealed the possibility of predicting where to log according to the extracted logging features [21]. Zhu et al. follow up the work and predict where to log as suggestions to developer. Similarly, a called *Errlog* presented by Yuan et al. indicated the benefits of automatically detecting logging opportunities for failure diagnosis using exception patterns and failure reports [42].

Previous research also presented other aspects to consider when taking logging decisions. Li et al. modeled which log level should be used when adding new logging statements [27]. In a different work, Li et al. studied log changes and modeled those log changes to provide a just-in-time suggestion to developers for changing logs [28]. Different previous research has presented what to log for a diverse set of concerns. Yuan et al. presented *LogEnhancer* that adds causally-related information to existing logging statements. Their focus was on software failures and software diagnosability [43]. Despite of above research effort, there exists no research focus on providing logging suggestions with the goal of monitoring system performance. In contrast with previous research, paper work focus on logging suggestion for performance.

6.3 Performance modeling

Performance modeling is a typical practice in system performance engineering. Due to the more complex nature of performance problems in distributed systems, simple raw metrics might not be enough. Therefore, Cohen et al. introduced the concept and use of *signatures* and *clustering* from logging data and system metrics to detect system states that are of significant impact in the system's performance [17]. With such data, Cohen et al. [16] used TAN (Tree-Augmented Bayesian Networks) models to model the high-level system performance states based on a small subset of metrics without *a priori* knowledge of the system. Brebner et al. have application performance management (APM) data in multiple industry projects to build performance models. However, the models that depend on APM can get very complex, and customization is needed [12]. In order to improve the quality of performance modeling and prediction. Stewart et al. [36] consider the inconsistency

of usage in enterprise and large e-commerce systems. In their work, they modeled using measurement data and *transaction mix*, and they report a better prediction quality instead of the existing scalar workload volume approach.

Since there could be too many performance metrics to be used in performance modeling, different previous researches address the issue. Xiong et al. [40] propose an automatic creation and selection of multiple models based on different metrics. They execute tests on virtual machines using standard performance benchmarks. Shang et al. [33] presented an approach to automatically group metrics in a smaller number of clusters. They used regression models on injected and real-life scenarios, and their approach outperforms traditional approaches.

Besides the use of regression models, other statistical techniques have been used to facilitate the communication of results, such as control charts [32]. Many different modeling approaches have been summarized by Gao et al. in three categories: rule-based models, data mining models and queueing models. In their work, they used the models to compare the effectiveness of load testing and provide insights on how to better do load testing [22]. Farshchi et al. [18] build correlation model between logs and operation activity's effect on system resources. Such correlation is later leveraged to detect system anomalies.

The rich usage of performance modeling supports our approach that leverages such model to suggest logging locations. We iteratively find the best logging locations that would provide most significant explanatory power to the performance of the system.

7 THREATS TO VALIDITY

This section discusses the threats to the validity of our study.

7.1 External Validity

Our evaluation is conducted on CloudStore, OpenMRS and ES. All subject systems have years of history and there are prior performance engineering research studying these systems' workload [13]. Nevertheless, more case studies on other software in other domains are needed to evaluate our approach. All our subject systems are developed based on either Java or .Net. Our approach may not be directly applicable for other programming languages, especially dynamic languages such as Python. Further work may investigate approaches to minimize the uncertainty in performance characterization of dynamic languages.

Our approach currently only focuses on web application. We leverage web logs in the first step in order to scope down the amount of source code to instrument. However, other researchers and practitioners may adapt our approach by applying our approach by starting on a few hot locations in the source code. Yet, without evaluation with such an approach, we cannot claim the usefulness of our approach on other types of systems.

7.2 Internal validity

Our approach is based on the system performance that is recorded by *Psutil*. The quality of recorded performance can impact the internal validity of our study. Similarly, the frequency of recording system performance by *Psutil* may also impact the results of our approach. Further work may further evaluate our approach by varying such frequency. Our approach depends on building statistical models. Therefore, with a smaller amount of performance data, our approach may not perform well due to the quality of the statistical model. Determining the optimal amount of performance data needed for our approach is in our plan. Although our approach builds statistical models using logs, we do not aim to predict nor claim causal relationship between the dependent variable and independent variables in the models. The only purpose of building regression models is to capture the relation between logs and system performance.

7.3 Construct validity

Our approach uses linear regression models to model system performance. Although linear regression models have been used in prior research in performance engineering [33, 40], there exist other statistical models that may model system performance more accurately. Our goal is not to accurately predict system performance but rather capture the relationship between logs and the system performance. Further work may investigate the use of other models.

We chose to design our approach in an aggressive manner when deciding potential logging locations. For example, we choose a low p-value to ensure the statistical significance of the logging location. Our approach may miss potential possible logging locations. However, our goal is to prioritize on the precision of the suggestion hence making the suggestion less intrusive to practitioners. By working with our industrial collaboration, we find that a large number of logging suggestions can be overwhelming since practitioners prefer to manually verify each logging location before having actual changes to the source code.

The overhead of the logs may influence system performance. Although we evaluate the impact of logs on system performance by examining the explanatory power of logging statements themselves, the overhead may still impact the results of our approach. Minimizing such overhead is in our further plan.

Our evaluation of our approach is based on modeling system CPU usage. There exist other performance metrics, such as memory and response time, that can be modeled by logs when evaluating our approach. Also, the performance of the subject systems is recorded while running their performance tests. If a logging location is not executed by performance tests, it cannot be identified by our approach. To address this threat, we sought to use the performance test that mimics the field workload from our industrial collaborators. However, a different workload may lead to different performance influencing locations in the source code. Therefore, when applying our approach, practitioners should always be aware of the impact from the workload (the performance tests on the system). Hence, evaluation with more performance metrics and more performance tests may lead to better understanding of the usefulness of our approach.

Although we suggest logging locations for performance assurance activities, we do not claim that they are the only relevant logging locations. Additionally, the R^2 of our models is between 26.9% and 90.2%. The R^2 shows that logs cannot explain all the variance in the system performance. The unexplained variance of performance may due to other performance influencing source code

or external influence of the system (e.g., network latency). In our future work, we plan to model other influencing factors of system performance to improve our approach.

Our approach is based on automated code analysis and code manipulation, when changing and rebuilding the software is needed. Such an approach may require extra resources to the performance infrastructure. In our future work, we plan to alter the source code adaptively during the runtime of performance testing or in the field to improve our approach.

8 CONCLUSION

Logging information is one of the most significant sources of data in performance monitoring and modeling. Due to the extensive use of logs, all too often, the success of various performance modeling and analysis techniques often rely on the availability of logs. However, existing empirical studies and automated techniques for logging decisions do not consider the particular need for system performance monitoring. In this paper, we propose an approach to automatically suggest where to insert logging statements with the goal of support performance monitoring for web-based systems. Our approach suggests inserting logging statement into the source code locations that can complement the explanation power of statistical performance models. By evaluating our approach on two open source systems (CloudStore and OpenMRS) and one commercial system (ES), we find that our approach suggests logging locations that improve the statistical performance models and those suggested logging locations have a high influence on system performance while not being traditional complex methods nor performance hotspots. Practitioners can integrate our approach into the release pipeline of their system to have logging suggestions periodically.

ACKNOWLEDGEMENT

We would like to thank ERA Environmental Management Solutions for providing access to the enterprise system used in our case study. The findings and opinions expressed in this paper are those of the authors and do not necessarily represent or reflect those of ERA Environmental Management Solutions and/or its subsidiaries and affiliates. Moreover, our results do not reflect the quality of ERA Environmental Management Solutions' products.

REFERENCES

[1] 2017. CloudScale Project. (oct 2017). Retrieved Oct 9, 2017 from http://www.cloudscale-project.eu/
[2] 2017. Eclipse Java development tools (JDT). (oct 2017). Retrieved Oct 9, 2017 from http://www.eclipse.org/jdt/
[3] 2017. JProfiler. (oct 2017). Retrieved Oct 9, 2017 from https://www.ej-technologies.com/products/jprofiler/overview.html
[4] 2017. Log4J Async. (oct 2017). Retrieved Oct 9, 2017 from https://logging.apache.org/log4j/2.x/manual/async.html
[5] 2017. .NET Compiler Platform ("Roslyn"). (oct 2017). Retrieved Oct 9, 2017 from https://github.com/dotnet/roslyn
[6] 2017. psutil. (feb 2017). Retrieved Feb 2, 2017 from https://github.com/giampaolo/psutil
[7] 2017. TPC Benchmark W (TPC-W). (oct 2017). Retrieved Oct 9, 2017 from http://www.tpc.org/tpcw/
[8] 2017. Visual Studio Profiling. (oct 2017). Retrieved Oct 9, 2017 from https://docs.microsoft.com/en-us/visualstudio/profiling
[9] Tarek M. Ahmed, Cor-Paul Bezemer, Tse-Hsun Chen, Ahmed E. Hassan, and Weiyi Shang. 2016. Studying the Effectiveness of Application Performance Management (APM) Tools for Detecting Performance Regressions for Web Applications: An Experience Report. In *Proceedings of the 13th International Conference on Mining Software Repositories (MSR '16)*. ACM, New York, NY, USA, 1–12.

[10] H. M. Alghmadi, M. D. Syer, W. Shang, and A. E. Hassan. 2016. An Automated Approach for Recommending When to Stop Performance Tests. In *2016 IEEE International Conference on Software Maintenance and Evolution (ICSME)*. 279–289.

[11] Apache. [n. d.]. Jmeter. http://jmeter.apache.org/. ([n. d.]). Accessed: 2015-06-01.

[12] Paul Charles Brebner. 2016. Automatic Performance Modelling from Application Performance Management (APM) Data: An Experience Report. In *Proceedings of the 7th ACM/SPEC on International Conference on Performance Engineering (ICPE '16)*. ACM, New York, NY, USA, 55–61.

[13] Tse-Hsun Chen, Weiyi Shang, Ahmed E. Hassan, Mohamed Nasser, and Parminder Flora. 2016. CacheOptimizer: Helping Developers Configure Caching Frameworks for Hibernate-based Database-centric Web Applications. In *Proceedings of the 2016 24th ACM SIGSOFT International Symposium on Foundations of Software Engineering (FSE 2016)*. ACM, New York, NY, USA, 666–677.

[14] Tse-Hsun Chen, Weiyi Shang, Zhen Ming Jiang, Ahmed E. Hassan, Mohamed Nasser, and Parminder Flora. 2014. Detecting Performance Anti-patterns for Applications Developed Using Object-relational Mapping. In *Proceedings of the 36th International Conference on Software Engineering (ICSE 2014)*. ACM, New York, NY, USA, 1001–1012.

[15] T. H. Chen, W. Shang, Z. M. Jiang, A. E. Hassan, M. Nasser, and P. Flora. 2016. Finding and Evaluating the Performance Impact of Redundant Data Access for Applications that are Developed Using Object-Relational Mapping Frameworks. *IEEE Transactions on Software Engineering* PP, 99 (2016), 1–1.

[16] Ira Cohen, Jeffrey S Chase, Moises Goldszmidt, Terence Kelly, and Julie Symons. 2004. Correlating Instrumentation Data to System States: A Building Block for Automated Diagnosis and Control.. In *OSDI*, Vol. 4. 16–16.

[17] Ira Cohen, Steve Zhang, Moises Goldszmidt, Julie Symons, Terence Kelly, and Armando Fox. 2005. Capturing, Indexing, Clustering, and Retrieving System History. In *Proceedings of the Twentieth ACM Symposium on Operating Systems Principles (SOSP '05)*. ACM, New York, NY, USA, 105–118.

[18] M. Farshchi, J. G. Schneider, I. Weber, and J. Grundy. 2015. Experience report: Anomaly detection of cloud application operations using log and cloud metric correlation analysis. In *2015 IEEE 26th International Symposium on Software Reliability Engineering (ISSRE)*. 24–34.

[19] King Chun Foo, Zhen Ming Jiang, Bram Adams, Ahmed E Hassan, Ying Zou, and Parminder Flora. 2010. Mining performance regression testing repositories for automated performance analysis. In *Quality Software (QSIC), 2010 10th International Conference on*. IEEE, 32–41.

[20] David A Freedman. 2009. *Statistical models: theory and practice*. cambridge university press.

[21] Qiang Fu, Jieming Zhu, Wenlu Hu, Jian-Guang Lou, Rui Ding, Qingwei Lin, Dongmei Zhang, and Tao Xie. 2014. Where Do Developers Log? An Empirical Study on Logging Practices in Industry. In *Companion Proceedings of the 36th International Conference on Software Engineering (ICSE Companion 2014)*. ACM, New York, NY, USA, 24–33.

[22] R. Gao, Z. M. Jiang, C. Barna, and M. Litoiu. 2016. A Framework to Evaluate the Effectiveness of Different Load Testing Analysis Techniques. In *2016 IEEE International Conference on Software Testing, Verification and Validation (ICST)*. 22–32.

[23] FE Harrell. 2001. Regression modeling strategies. 2001. *Nashville: Springer CrossRef Google Scholar* (2001).

[24] Zhen Ming Jiang, Ahmed E. Hassan, Gilbert Hamann, and Parminder Flora. 2009. Automated performance analysis of load tests. In *ICSM '09: 25th IEEE International Conference on Software Maintenance*.

[25] Brian W. Kernighan and Rob Pike. 1999. *The Practice of Programming*. Addison-Wesley Longman Publishing Co., Inc., Boston, MA, USA.

[26] Max Kuhn. 2008. Building Predictive Models in R Using the caret Package. *Journal of Statistical Software, Articles* 28, 5 (2008), 1–26.

[27] Heng Li, Weiyi Shang, and Ahmed E. Hassan. 2017. Which Log Level Should Developers Choose for a New Logging Statement? *Empirical Softw. Engg.* 22, 4 (Aug. 2017), 1684–1716.

[28] Heng Li, Weiyi Shang, Ying Zou, and Ahmed E. Hassan. 2017. Towards Just-in-time Suggestions for Log Changes. *Empirical Softw. Engg.* 22, 4 (Aug. 2017), 1831–1865.

[29] David Maplesden, Ewan Tempero, John Hosking, and John C. Grundy. 2015. Subsuming Methods: Finding New Optimisation Opportunities in Object-Oriented Software. In *Proceedings of the 6th ACM/SPEC International Conference on Performance Engineering (ICPE '15)*. ACM, New York, NY, USA, 175–186.

[30] David Maplesden, Karl von Randow, Ewan Tempero, John Hosking, and John Grundy. 2015. Performance Analysis Using Subsuming Methods: An Industrial Case Study. In *Proceedings of the 37th International Conference on Software Engineering - Volume 2 (ICSE '15)*. IEEE Press, Piscataway, NJ, USA, 149–158.

[31] Audris Mockus. 2010. Organizational Volatility and Its Effects on Software Defects. In *Proceedings of the Eighteenth ACM SIGSOFT International Symposium on Foundations of Software Engineering (FSE '10)*. ACM, New York, NY, USA,

117–126.

[32] Thanh H.D. Nguyen, Bram Adams, Zhen Ming Jiang, Ahmed E. Hassan, Mohamed Nasser, and Parminder Flora. 2012. Automated Detection of Performance Regressions Using Statistical Process Control Techniques. In *Proceedings of the 3rd ACM/SPEC International Conference on Performance Engineering (ICPE '12)*. ACM, New York, NY, USA, 299–310.

[33] Weiyi Shang, Ahmed E. Hassan, Mohamed Nasser, and Parminder Flora. 2015. Automated Detection of Performance Regressions Using Regression Models on Clustered Performance Counters. In *Proceedings of the 6th ACM/SPEC International Conference on Performance Engineering (ICPE '15)*. ACM, New York, NY, USA, 15–26.

[34] Emad Shihab, Zhen Ming Jiang, Walid M. Ibrahim, Bram Adams, and Ahmed E. Hassan. 2010. Understanding the Impact of Code and Process Metrics on Post-release Defects: A Case Study on the Eclipse Project. In *Proceedings of the 2010 ACM-IEEE International Symposium on Empirical Software Engineering and Measurement (ESEM '10)*. ACM, New York, NY, USA, Article 4, 10 pages.

[35] Emad Shihab, Audris Mockus, Yasutaka Kamei, Bram Adams, and Ahmed E. Hassan. 2011. High-impact Defects: A Study of Breakage and Surprise Defects. In *Proceedings of the 19th ACM SIGSOFT Symposium and the 13th European Conference on Foundations of Software Engineering (ESEC/FSE '11)*. ACM, New York, NY, USA, 300–310.

[36] Christopher Stewart, Terence Kelly, and Alex Zhang. 2007. Exploiting nonstationarity for performance prediction. In *ACM SIGOPS Operating Systems Review*, Vol. 41. ACM, 31–44.

[37] Mark D. Syer, Weiyi Shang, Zhen Ming Jiang, and Ahmed E. Hassan. 2017. Continuous validation of performance test workloads. *Automated Software Engineering* 24, 1 (2017), 189–231. https://doi.org/10.1007/s10515-016-0196-8

[38] André van Hoorn, Jan Waller, and Wilhelm Hasselbring. 2012. Kieker: A Framework for Application Performance Monitoring and Dynamic Software Analysis. In *Proceedings of the 3rd ACM/SPEC International Conference on Performance Engineering (ICPE '12)*. ACM, New York, NY, USA, 247–248.

[39] E.J. Weyuker and F.I. Vokolos. 2000. Experience with performance testing of software systems: issues, an approach, and case study. *Transactions on Software Engineering* 26, 12 (Dec 2000), 1147–1156.

[40] Pengcheng Xiong, Calton Pu, Xiaoyun Zhu, and Rean Griffith. 2013. vPerfGuard: An Automated Model-driven Framework for Application Performance Diagnosis in Consolidated Cloud Environments. In *Proceedings of the 4th ACM/SPEC International Conference on Performance Engineering (ICPE '13)*. ACM, New York, NY, USA, 271–282.

[41] Ding Yuan, Yu Luo, Xin Zhuang, Guilherme Renna Rodrigues, Xu Zhao, Yongle Zhang, Pranay U. Jain, and Michael Stumm. 2014. Simple Testing Can Prevent Most Critical Failures: An Analysis of Production Failures in Distributed Data-intensive Systems. In *Proceedings of the 11th USENIX Conference on Operating Systems Design and Implementation (OSDI'14)*. USENIX Association, Berkeley, CA, USA, 249–265.

[42] Ding Yuan, Soyeon Park, Peng Huang, Yang Liu, Michael M Lee, Xiaoming Tang, Yuanyuan Zhou, and Stefan Savage. 2012. Be Conservative: Enhancing Failure Diagnosis with Proactive Logging.. In *OSDI '12: Proceedings of the 10th USENIX conference on Operating Systems Design and Implementation*, Vol. 12. 293–306.

[43] Ding Yuan, Jing Zheng, Soyeon Park, Yuanyuan Zhou, and Stefan Savage. 2011. Improving software diagnosability via log enhancement. In *ASPLOS '11: Proc. of the 16th international conference on Architectural support for programming languages and operating systems*.

[44] Sai Zhang and Michael D. Ernst. 2014. Which Configuration Option Should I Change?. In *Proceedings of the 36th International Conference on Software Engineering (ICSE 2014)*. ACM, New York, NY, USA, 152–163.

[45] Sai Zhang and Michael D. Ernst. 2015. Proactive Detection of Inadequate Diagnostic Messages for Software Configuration Errors. In *Proceedings of the 2015 International Symposium on Software Testing and Analysis (ISSTA 2015)*. ACM, New York, NY, USA, 12–23.

[46] Xu Zhao, Kirk Rodrigues, Yu Luo, Michael Stumm, Ding Yuan, and Yuanyuan Zhou. 2017. The Game of Twenty Questions: Do You Know Where to Log?. In *Proceedings of the 16th Workshop on Hot Topics in Operating Systems (HotOS '17)*. ACM, New York, NY, USA, 125–131.

[47] Jieming Zhu, Pinjia He, Qiang Fu, Hongyu Zhang, Michael R. Lyu, and Dongmei Zhang. 2015. Learning to Log: Helping Developers Make Informed Logging Decisions. In *Proceedings of the 37th International Conference on Software Engineering - Volume 1 (ICSE '15)*. IEEE Press, Piscataway, NJ, USA, 415–425.

[48] Zhenyun Zhuang, Haricharan Ramachandra, Cuong Tran, Subbu Subramaniam, Chavdar Botev, Chaoyue Xiong, and Badri Sridharan. 2015. Capacity Planning and Headroom Analysis for Taming Database Replication Latency: Experiences with LinkedIn Internet Traffic. In *Proceedings of the 6th ACM/SPEC International Conference on Performance Engineering (ICPE '15)*. ACM, New York, NY, USA, 39–50.

ODP: An Infrastructure for On-Demand Service Profiling

John Nicol*
jnicol@linkedin.com
LinkedIn Corp

Chen Li*
cnli@linkedin.com
LinkedIn Corp

Peinan Chen*
pchen@linkedin.com
LinkedIn Corp

Tao Feng*
tofeng@linkedin.com
LinkedIn Corp

Haricharan Ramachandra
hramacha@linkedin.com
LinkedIn Corp

ABSTRACT

CPU and memory profiling of services are commonly-used methods to identify potential performance and cost optimizations. However, the tooling solutions for profiling are often nonstandard, not centralized, inconvenient for users, and costly, leading to limited adoption.

Additionally, with projects and companies employing Agile methodologies such as the microservices model, the service diversity, number, and frequency of changes can drastically increase, further limiting adoption due to scalability concerns and needs for varied profiler technologies.

To address these challenges, we present the *ODP* ("On-Demand Profiling") framework. This is a scalable, language- and platform-independent framework designed to enable on-demand CPU and memory profiling of microservices, and centralized storage, sharing, and analysis of the resulting data.

CCS CONCEPTS

• **Software and its engineering** → **Software performance**;

KEYWORDS

microservices, performance, profiling

ACM Reference Format:
John Nicol, Chen Li, Peinan Chen, Tao Feng, and Haricharan Ramachandra. 2018. ODP: An Infrastructure for On-Demand Service Profiling. In *ICPE '18: ACM/SPEC International Conference on Performance Engineering, April 9–13, 2018, Berlin, Germany*. ACM, New York, NY, USA, 7 pages. https://doi.org/10.1145/3184407.3184433

1 INTRODUCTION

Service profiling is a form of dynamic program analysis which is commonly used to aid in service optimization. Two primary analyses are CPU and memory profiling.

CPU profiling is a technique to analyze the execution time of methods of a service; this can find service "hotspots" which can be optimized. This technique has a long history; for example, the *prof* command has been implemented in Unix since the early 1970s [18].

Memory profiling can refer to analysis of whole memory (often called "core" or "heap") or to memory allocation events. These techniques are often used to find memory leaks, but also can be used to optimize memory usage. Optimization of memory can also have effects on application latency; this can be due to reduced garbage collection in managed languages, but can also be due to reduced allocation and deallocation events, copying of data, and improved paging and caching.

Although CPU and memory profiling are old techniques, there are few standards for their use, especially across platforms or languages. As a result, unless a profiler tool is supported internally, users may need to configure the tool, acquire licenses, and request installation on remote hosts before profiling. In addition, viewing the profiled results often requires manual data transfer or setting up a tunnel from the production environment to the development environment. Furthermore, sharing and comparing profiling data is difficult or effectively impossible, especially when profiling runs are captured by different users with different profiler settings, or even different profiling tools.

Additionally, companies and projects have begun to adopt Agile software architectures such as microservices, where software applications are designed as suites of independently deployable services [7]. (LinkedIn uses a microservice and continuous deployment model itself [1]. Thus for the remainder of the paper, we will use the terms "service" and "microservice" interchangeably.)

Although microservice architectures are very useful, they can drastically increase the total count of services, their diversity, and the frequency of their changes and deployments. More services and more frequent deployments of those services lead to more frequent profiling; this generates more data, thus leading to challenges in scalability. Higher diversity in services can also necessitate more varied profiler technologies. These further limit profiler adoption due to scalability concerns and needs for varied profiler technologies.

The scalability concerns for microservice profiling are not limited to hardware and software; there are user scalability concerns as well. Each microservice requires independent optimization, and versioning of dependencies becomes a significant issue. For example, if a newer version of a library is optimized, not all of the services depending upon that library will immediately choose to consume this new version; service owners will often be unaware of the optimizations, or won't prioritize the upgrades unless they're known to improve the service behavior.

---

*These authors contributed equally to the work.

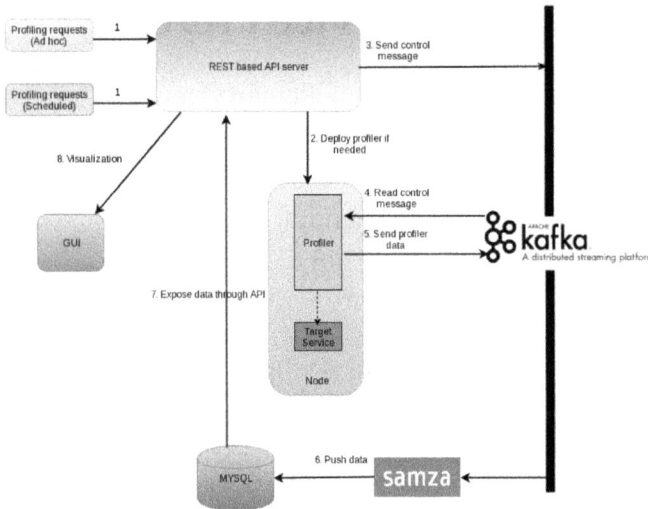

Figure 1: High-level architecture of the ODP framework

Clearly there are challenges in significant adoption of profiling in the Agile methodology. But there are huge benefits as well. Rapid changes allow for rapid optimizations; improvements to libraries, for example, can quickly be consumed by all dependers, resulting in profound optimizations from simple analyses.

We have developed the *ODP* ("On-Demand Profiling") framework to address these challenges.

The ODP framework is itself a collection of microservices. It consists of: RESTful APIs for starting and stopping profilers and for accessing reported data; profiler plugins for different profiling modes, languages, and platforms; scalable messaging and data storage; scalable data processing (including Common Issue Detection); and a GUI for users to visualize and share results.

2 ARCHITECTURE

We now present the high-level architecture of our solution (the ODP framework). As shown in Figure 1, the key components are the Profiler request, the Profiler API server, a Profiler service with profiler plugins, a messaging backbone, and a data pipeline and datastore.

A user or a scheduled job (from an arbitrary host machine) requests a specific service ("target service", also called "STP" for the Service To Profile) be profiled on a specified host machine ("target host").

The request to profile is passed to a REST-based API service. The API service deploys the Profiler service on the target host if necessary, and then signals the Profiler service on the target host to profile the STP.

The Profiler sends its data through a scalable pipeline. After post-processing, the data can be viewed via a GUI, or consumed directly via another REST-based endpoint.

2.1 Profiling requests

Profiling requests can come from both users and approved services (e.g., automated performance testing). In addition to on demand

requests, profile requests can be scheduled for regular events, such as traffic shifts. Profiling requests are simple HTTPS calls in REST style.

Requests can be made to start or stop STPs on specified hosts. Additionally, requests can be made to simply deploy or undeploy the Profiler service, without actually executing plugins. All requests and their current state are stored within the Profiler database for monitoring and analysis.

The framework requires authentications to protect services from untrusted or duplicated profile requests. Once a request is verified, the framework will take care of additional authentications in production clusters to ease developers' job.

For flexibility, the framework supports authenticated requests from all hosts in the network, and allows requests to any hosts that are approved to run the Profiler service.

2.2 REST-based API

Our REST-based API service acts as an interface for the profiling requests. The profiling requests come from CLIs (Command Line Interfaces) or GUIs, or are scheduled jobs stored within the Profiler database.

For a "deploy" request, the API service queries the target host (or the Profiler database) to determine if a Profiler service is already running, and if not, deploys the Profiler service.

For a "start" request, the API service executes a "deploy" request, and then sends a command to the target host's Profiler service via an Apache Kafka message (see Section 2.5) in order to start a profile of the STP.

For a "stop" request, the API service sends a similar Kafka message to the target host's Profiler service to stop a profile of the STP (if it is running).

For an "undeploy" request, the API service queries the target host (or the Profiler database) to determine if a Profiler service is already running. If it is, the API service can either undeploy the service immediately (thus terminating any ongoing profiles on that host), or wait until all profiler requests have finished on the target host.

2.3 Profiler Service

The Profiler is a microservice that's either deployed on-demand or is continuously running on target hosts where STPs are requested. Each language-specific CPU profiler and each language-specific memory profiler is implemented as a plugin of the Profiler.

The Profiler polls for Kafka messages from the Profiler API service. Then it verifies that those messages are authenticated, and activates itself when a message to profile a service on the given host (the STP) arrives. The Profiler verifies the existence of the requested STP on the host, and determines its characteristics (e.g., process ID, language, version, and flags).

Based on these characteristics, the Profiler executes the appropriate profiler plugin. If multiple profiling requests arrive contemporaraneously to the same host, multiple plugins (or multiple instances of the same plugin if necessary) can be invoked.

2.4 Profiler Plugins

Each Profiler plugin can profile one or more combinations of profiler mode (e.g., CPU, memory allocation tracking, heap dump), platform (e.g. Linux, MacOS, or Windows), and language (e.g., JVM, .NET, C++, or Python).

There are varied technologies and techniques that can be used to profile such as [12] and [14]. The ODP framework is agnostic to these choices.

The data generated from a profiling plugin often has high redundancy, as the stack traces or classes (for memory allocation profiling) are expected to recur frequently. To avoid the potential for network congestion, this data is periodically aggregated, which dramatically reduces the data redundancy. As aggregation will take CPU and memory resources, the aggregation frequency must be carefully balanced to ensure that the Profiler's CPU and memory footprint remain small.

This aggregate data is then sent to Kafka for later consumption by the data pipeline; see Sections 2.5 and 2.6. Some profiler plugins cannot periodically aggregate (for example, heap dumps) and can only send all of their data at profile completion. This is supported functionality, but additional care must be taken within such plugins to not overload memory or network considerations for the Profiler service.

A lightweight sampling-based JVM CPU/memory profiler is currently used at LinkedIn, which supports late attach functionality and avoids restarting service in production environment before/after profiling requests.

2.5 Messaging Backbone

We use Apache Kafka both to send command messages to the Profiler instances and to publish profiling data generated by the profiler plugins.

Kafka is a distributed streaming platform that, among other functionality, can "read and write stream data like a messaging system" [3] and "store streams of data safely in a distributed, replicated, fault-tolerant cluster" [3]. Kafka also supports authentication and SSL encryption/decryption, which resolves potential security concerns such as message spoofing.

2.6 Data Store

The profiling data sent to our Kafka topic is processed and written to a data store via Apache Samza [4]. Samza is a scalable, lossless, streaming processing framework that uses Kafka for messaging; if multiple Profiler services send data simultaneously to the Kafka topic, Samza catches up with the produced messages and pushes them to our remote data store.

We have chosen MySQL [19] for our data store. This is a very popular and well-supported database technology. It works well for our needs (simple tables, low/medium traffic, large storage). A simple sharding technique allows scaling for the storage of profiler data.

To ensure a manageable database size, we have scheduled jobs to deduplicate redundant data and delete old data.

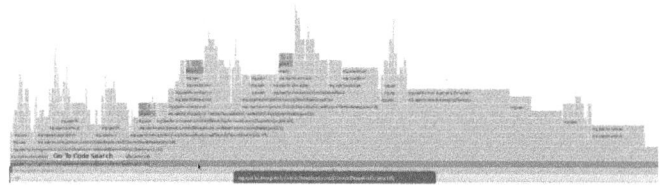

Figure 2: A Flame Graph: cell width indicates percentage of method within the graph; higher cells are child methods of lower cells. Note the clicked context menu linking to a code search tool.

Figure 3: Comparison Flamegraph: Red coloration at leaf nodes indicates an increase compared to the baseline, while blue indicates a decrease.

2.7 Visualization

The CPU and memory profiling results are visualized through an internal web application. Visualizing via a native application would also be an option, as would be a plugin to an IDE (Integrated Development Environment), but we have found the current approach to be simple and to allow easy sharing of URLs.

These profiling results and visualizations have been quite popular at LinkedIn; similar ones have also experienced success at other companies [13]. As a result, there are a great deal of open-source resources to help implement elements of this web-based visualization ([13]).

The visualization is done with Flame Graphs [13], see Figure 2. The flame graph is rendered as an interactive SVG (Scalable Vector Graphic) allowing easy zooming into and out of stack traces. Additionally there are options to filter and highlight based on regular expressions, and functionality to compare profiling results (see Figure 3). Some teams have used the comparison functionality to generate regular performance assurance reports to guard against regressions, see Section 4.

There is also a context menu associated with each cell. This menu contains contextual information for both the cell's method and the full stack trace. From this menu we have both: a link to a code-search tool, which allows us to view the source code associated with a given stack trace (internally we use [5], but there are certainly

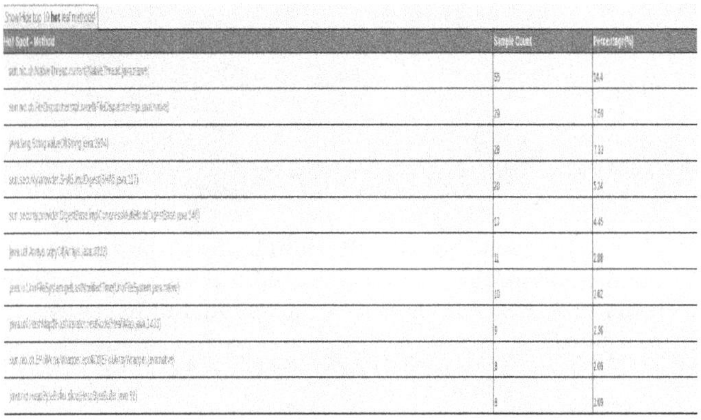

Figure 4: Hot Leaf Calls: A list of the most common "leaf" methods in a profile, linked to their occurrence within the profiled service.

Show/Hide Identified Issues

Identified Issues	Description of Issue
java.util.UUID.randomUUID	Regardless of CPU percentage, this method may affect your product. See this Foundation Newsletter for details
ForkJoinPool.awaitWork	Consider upgrading to JRE 1.8.u72+; see JDK-8080925
java.security.SecureRandom.nextBytes	SecureRandom is slow and synchronized. Consider replacing, or upgrading to JRE 1.8u121, where it is unsynchronized.
org.apache.log4j.Category	Convert to Log4J2, preferably asynchronous, for potentially significant performance benefits
java.util.Hashtable	Hashtable is slow and synchronized. Consider replacing with HashMap or ConcurrentHashMap
java.lang.Throwable.fillInStackTrace	Exception handling takes CPU resources, even for silent Exceptions. Here are some suggestions for improving this.
java.util.regex.Pattern	Regex methods are slower than handcrafted parsing. Consider optimizing this.
java.lang.StringBuffer	StringBuffer is slower than StringBuilder, and synchronized. Consider replacing

Figure 5: Common Issue Detection: A list of issues autodetected by ODP, linked to their desriptions and their occurrence within the profiled service.

others such as [11]); and a link to crowdsource known issues, see Section 3.

Additionally, we have a table-based "hot leaf call" (see Figure 4), which is often more convenient than the graphically-intensive flame graph.

3 COMMON ISSUE DETECTION

Many of the issues found during analyses of profiling results have been found to pop up repeatedly for different microservices. This can result in a great deal of repeated analyses and differing optimizations as common performance patterns (and their solutions) are rediscovered. This becomes even more noticeable for larger and decentralized groups for whom information sharing is more difficult.

We have developed a crowdsourcing technique and technology that helps alleviate this [15]. By centralizing the repeated issues and automatically detecting them, we can save valuable development resources. This technique is applied to both future profile results and to previous results, which are re-analyzed to link to newly-discovered patterns.

Additionally, these detected patterns can be sent directly to affected teams; this may be of use when, say, a profiler result is generated on a scheduled basis and a newly-detected issue is not noticed by a user. If an issue is found to occur in a library that is consumed by several teams, this auto-alerting can help prioritize a resolution to the underlying library problem.

Issue detection can be applied to aggregate stack percentages (as in Figure 5), with a customizable threshold percentage to avoid flagging low-impact issues. It can also be applied to detect when certain library versions or runtime options are used by the profiled service.

4 RESULTS

The ODP framework has gained significant traction at LinkedIn. In sixteen months, it has grown to incorporate analyses of roughly 150 of the services used in production. This represents well over 50% of the critical, expensive, or heavily-used services (e.g., those with a high number of instances, custom or particularly expensive hardware, or those services directly corresponding to user latency). This adoption rate compares quite favorably to that of other LinkedIn performance tools such as Redliner [20].

Dozens of improvements have been applied based upon analyses from ODP profile results. Most of these have been applied to common internal libraries, thus affecting many services. Some have even been applied to external open-source libraries, helping the larger software community.

The effects of these improvements are not always easy to predict; for example, some improvements based on CPU profiling may have dramatic effects on average latency, some on P99 latency, some on service throughput, and some on CPU usage. Improvements based on memory profiling may reduce overall memory usage or reduce time spent in garbage collection; these will have effects on latency, throughput, and CPU usage as well, but again those effects are often hard to predict.

The results at LinkedIn have been undeniable, however. A synchronization fix led to a roughly 40% increase in throughput of a critical service. A series of smaller improvements led to a roughly 25% increase in throughput of another critical service. Both of these improvements have enabled reductions in hardware needed to support those services, resulting in substantial cost savings for the company.

Scheduled profile results helped detect and mitigate a library regression, which if it had made it to production, would have reduced a critical service's throughput by 40% and would have likely caused cascading failures.

Other improvements have resulted in significant latency reductions in critical services: over 10% average latency reduction for one, and over 20% P99 latency reduction for another.

A key point: many of these improvements were made to internal libraries (and some to open-source external libraries). As such, there are synergistic effects to other services as well.

5 OVERHEAD

As with other profilers, ODP adds some overhead to services. The overhead varies depending on the service, but we found that the current profiler plugin in ODP generally adds 11% to 13% throughput overhead based on SPECjvm2008 benchmarks [9], and less than 5%

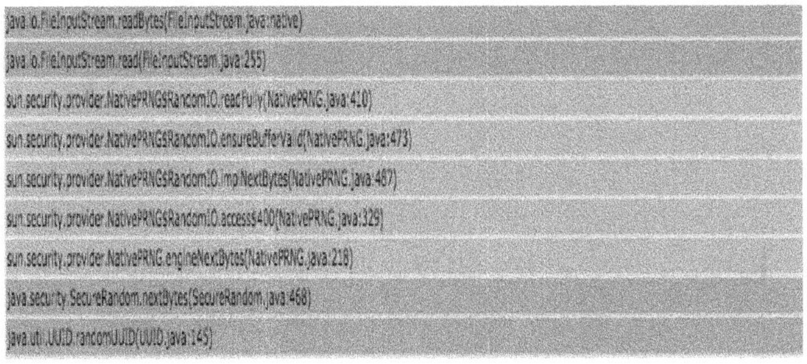

Figure 6: Case study: problematic stack traces.

latency overhead on LinkedIn servers. ODP also adds network overhead when it sends results to Kafka. To reduce this, ODP cuts and compresses results to small snapshots and sends them periodically at a configurable rate.

6 CASE STUDY

An example of how LinkedIn has used ODP is with the backend service of the People You May Know (PYMK) feature of LinkedIn. In order to diagnose why this service was experiencing high latency in production, its service owners used ODP to capture a CPU profile. Through their profile, they found that the routine shown in Figure 6 occupies more than 18% of CPU time for their service.

This routine involves using the UUID.randomUUID call to generate tracking entity IDs in a highly concurrent fashion. UUID.randomUUID internally uses NativePRNG to generate random numbers which uses randomness from /dev/urandom and has a global lock within the implNextBytes method (as shown in Figure 6).

To address this problem, we proposed that the service owners write their own UUID generation call based on another non-blocking security algorithm which we found provides comparable randomness and security with improved performance benefit. After this change, about 12% of 90% latency has been reduced based on production data.

7 RELATED WORK

Profiling and debugging services that are running in production environments is a critical requirement for projects and companies that need to resolve performance regressions.

7.1 Profiling tools

There are standalone profilers that support remote profiling [10] [8], but production clusters usually require additional authentication checks and make it difficult or impossible to use those standalone profilers directly.

7.2 Frameworks

[1]Frameworks			
Features	ODP	GWP	Vector
On demand/Always on	On demand	Always on	On demand
CPU information	Yes	Yes	No
Memory information	Yes	No	No
Machine level metrics	No	Yes	Yes
Pluggable profilers	Yes	No	No
Flexible sampling rate	Yes	No	No

Frameworks similar to ODP have been created for system and application metrics (such as Netflix's Vector [2]) as well as for daily or scheduled profiles of a sample of hosts (such as Google's Google-Wide Profiling [16]). The ODP framework differs from these as it focuses on diagnosing performance problems through on-demand requests rather than monitoring the state of systems – although it is occasionally used for that purpose. The most similar framework that could be found is Alibaba's ZProfiler and ZDebugger [6], which provides profiling and detected issue sharing features.

8 FUTURE WORK AND CONCLUSION

For certain languages and platforms, employing particularly light-weight profilers such as Linux Perf [12] would enable an "always-on" approach, which would help support continuous performance assurance. An always-on approach would significantly increase data processing and storage, but the scalability of the ODP framework allows this. Unlike similar efforts [16], we plan to allow both on-demand and always-on requests. This is a straightforward generalization: one can think of "always-on" as simply a long-running on-demand request.

Profiling of embedded devices (for example, mobile devices) represents a challenge. There exist profiling tools for devices, emulators, and simulators, but we are not currently aware of any that could be adapted as a Profiler plugin.

The technologies for virtualized or containerized services are in flux in the industry [17]. Some of these technologies would require additional permissions or additional steps to ensure the STP is visible to the Profiler service and its plugins; as such, we must stay in sync with those efforts.

In this submission we have presented the ODP framework, our solution for on-demand CPU and memory profiling of microservices. This is a scalable, language- and platform- independent framework that has been widely adopted within LinkedIn.

REFERENCES

[1] 2013. The Software Revolution Behind LinkedIn's Gushing Profits. (April 2013). https://www.wired.com/2013/04/linkedin-software-revolution/
[2] 2015. Introducing Vector: Netflix's On-Host Performance Monitoring Tool. (April 2015). https://medium.com/netflix-techblog/introducing-vector-netflixs-on-host-performance-monitoring-tool-c0d3058c3f6f
[3] 2017. Apache Kafka. (Sept. 2017). http://kafka.apache.org
[4] 2017. Apache Samza. (Sept. 2017). http://samza.apache.org
[5] 2017. JARVIS: Helping LinkedIn Navigate its Source Code. (Sept. 2017). https://engineering.linkedin.com/blog/2017/08/jarvis--helping-linkedin-navigate-its-source-code

[1]Data are based on existing paper/doc, and might not reflect the current state of the frameworks

[6] 2017. Java at Alibaba. (Sept. 2017). https://jcp.org/aboutJava/communityprocess/ec-public/materials/2017-02-14/Java_at_Alibaba.pdf

[7] 2017. Microservices: a definition of this new architectural term. (Sept. 2017). https://martinfowler.com/articles/microservices.html

[8] 2017. NetBeans. (Sept. 2017). https://profiler.netbeans.org/docs/help/5.5/attach.html

[9] 2017. SPECjvm2008 Benchmark. (Dec. 2017). https://www.spec.org/jvm2008/

[10] 2017. YourKit. (Sept. 2017). https://www.yourkit.com/docs/java/help/attach_agent.jsp

[11] Sushil Bajracharya, Trung Ngo, Erik Linstead, Yimeng Dou, Paul Rigor, Pierre Baldi, and Cristina Lopes. 2006. Sourcerer: a search engine for open source code supporting structure-based search. In *Companion to the 21st ACM SIGPLAN symposium on Object-oriented programming systems, languages, and applications.* ACM, 681–682.

[12] Arnaldo Carvalho de Melo. 2010. The new linux perf tools.

[13] Brendan Gregg. 2017. Flame Graphs. (Sept. 2017). http://www.brendangregg.com/flamegraphs.html

[14] Peter Hofer, David Gnedt, and Hanspeter Mössenböck. 2015. Lightweight Java Profiling with Partial Safepoints and Incremental Stack Tracing. In *Proceedings of the 6th ACM/SPEC International Conference on Performance Engineering (ICPE '15).* ACM, New York, NY, USA, 75–86. https://doi.org/10.1145/2668930.2688038

[15] John Nicol, Chen Li, Peinan Chen, Tao Feng, and Hari Ramachandra. 2017. Common Issue Detection for CPU Profiling. (Sept. 2017). https://engineering.linkedin.com/blog/2017/09/common-issue-detection-for-cpu-profiling

[16] Gang Ren, Eric Tune, Tipp Moseley, Yixin Shi, Silvius Rus, and Robert Hundt. 2010. Google-Wide Profiling: A Continuous Profiling Infrastructure for Data Centers. *IEEE Micro* (2010), 65–79. http://www.computer.org/portal/web/csdl/doi/10.1109/MM.2010.68

[17] Mathijs Jeroen Scheepers. 2014. Virtualization and containerization of application infrastructure: A comparison.

[18] Ken Thompson and Dennis M Ritchie. 1973. *Unix Programmer's Manual* (4 ed.). Bell Telephone Laboratories, Inc.

[19] Michael Widenius and David Axmark. 2002. *MySQL reference manual: documentation from the source.* " O'Reilly Media, Inc.".

[20] J. Xia, Z. Zhuang, A. Rao, H. Ramachandra, Y. Feng, and R. Pasumarti. 2017. RedLiner: Measuring Service Capacity with Live Production Traffic. In *2017 IEEE International Conference on Web Services (ICWS).* 628–635. https://doi.org/10.1109/ICWS.2017.75

Virtualization Techniques Compared: Performance, Resource, and Power Usage Overheads in Clouds

Selome Kostentinos Tesfatsion
Department of Computing Science
Umeå University, Sweden
selome@cs.umu.se

Cristian Klein
Department of Computing Science
Umeå University, Sweden
cklein@cs.umu.se

Johan Tordsson
Department of Computing Science
Umeå University, Sweden
tordsson@cs.umu.se

ABSTRACT

Virtualization solutions based on hypervisors or containers are enabling technologies for scalable, flexible, and cost-effective resource sharing. As the fundamental limitations of each technology are yet to be understood, they need to be regularly reevaluated to better understand the trade-off provided by latest technological advances. This paper presents an in-depth quantitative analysis of virtualization overheads in these two groups of systems and their gaps relative to native environments based on a diverse set of workloads that stress CPU, memory, storage, and networking resources. KVM and XEN are used to represent hypervisor-based virtualization, and LXC and Docker for container-based platforms. The systems were evaluated with respect to several cloud resource management dimensions including performance, isolation, resource usage, energy efficiency, start-up time, and density. Our study is useful both to practitioners to understand the current state of the technology in order to make the right decision in the selection, operation and/or design of platforms and to scholars to illustrate how these technologies evolved over time.

ACM Reference Format:

Selome Kostentinos Tesfatsion, Cristian Klein, and Johan Tordsson. 2018. Virtualization Techniques Compared: Performance, Resource, and Power Usage Overheads in Clouds. In *ICPE '18: ACM/SPEC International Conference on Performance Engineering, April 9–13, 2018, Berlin, Germany*. ACM, New York, NY, USA, 12 pages. https://doi.org/10.1145/3184407.3184414

1 INTRODUCTION

Virtualization is a fundamental technology in cloud computing. The motivations for adopting virtualization include increased flexibility, dynamic resource allocation, and improved resource utilization. Virtualization provides the ability to pack applications into fewer physical servers and thereby reduce the power consumption of both physical servers and their cooling systems. Consequently the paradigm has become attractive, leading to the emergence of different solutions over the years. These solutions can be broadly categorized into *hypervisor (H)-based* and *Operating system (OS)-based* virtualization methods.

H-based systems are the traditional virtualization systems supported by many cloud computing platforms. For example, Rackspace

and Amazon Web Services (AWS) use the XEN Hypervisor [28], which has gained tremendous popularity because of its early open source inclusion in the Linux kernel, and is one of the most mature virtualization solutions available [29]. The Kernel-based Virtual Machine (KVM) [1], a relatively new open source H-based system, has gained momentum and popularity in recent years [37]. It has found its way into more recently established clouds such as those operated by AT&T, HP, Comcast, and Orange [29]. KVM has become a natural choice for Linux VMs because it is included in the upstream Linux kernel. It is also a de facto standard for the open source cloud management platform OpenStack [15].

Hypervisor-free OS-based virtualization systems are widely used by successful cloud providers such as Google to manage their clusters, and have attracted considerable interest because they offer new possibilities for easy provisioning and fast deployment environment. Google has stated that it launches over 2 billion containers a week across all of its data centers [5]. Several OS-based systems have been released, including Linux Container (LXC) [19], Docker [16], BSD Jails [39], and Windows Containers [7]. Docker is the most widely used, whereas LXC, which is included in most Linux distributions, is used by cluster management frameworks such as Mesos [6] and YARN [8] to achieve stronger resource isolation among applications.

Significant efforts have been made to characterize the effects of virtualization on application performance [46, 49, 50]. However, less effort has been invested in the various additional resource overheads that virtualization imposes. For example, a Virtual Machine (VM) process may use other virtualization components (e.g. Dom0 in the case of the XEN, the hypervisor) to handle requests, which in turn generate additional resource overhead and application performance penalties. Moreover, there is a lack of detailed quantitative studies comparing H-based and OS-based platforms and their gaps relative to native environments across multiple resources under a diverse set of workload types. Co-located applications can cause interference problems due to the absence of strong performance and fault isolation, which is an important but under-explored concern for public multi-tenant clouds. In addition, the energy efficiency of different virtualization methods has not been well analyzed. Finally, many earlier works have focused on specific application areas [34, 49] and overlooked opportunities for optimization exposed by individual technologies, leading to under- or over-stated results.

Consequently, a comprehensive, detailed, and up-to-date comparative analysis of H- and OS-based virtualization solutions is needed to allow data center operators make the best possible decisions relating to issues such as resource allocation, admission control, and migration, to accurately bill cloud customers and to improve the overall performance and energy efficiency of their infrastructures. In addition, a better understanding of the key factors that contribute to overheads can be used to guide efforts to improve existing systems. For example, efforts such as CoreOS have significantly reduced the slow (in minutes) VM booting time to as fast as few seconds (10s). Container systems are also advancing, for instance in security, e.g. the latest 1.8 version [25] of Kubernetes provides enhanced security support.

To this end, this paper presents the results of a comprehensive investigation into the performance, power, and resource usages overhead of four virtualization technologies widely used in modern data centers (LXC, Docker, KVM, and XEN) running four different workload types (CPU–intensive, memory-intensive, network-intensive, and disk-intensive) under varying intensities. We also compare the virtualization platforms with respect to performance isolation, resource over-commitment, start-up time, and density. To the best of our knowledge, this is the first such comprehensive comparative study to be reported. The empirical results presented in this work are useful for practitioners to understand the current state of the technology so as to make a proper decision in choosing the best technology for a given situation, in making relevant trade-offs, and possibly designing systems that address the limitations. It is also useful for academia to illustrate how these technologies evolved over time and to call upon further research to uncover the underlying causes for each of these platform in the areas where they under-perform. To facilitate comparison, we developed a methodology for virtualization that automates the testing process.

In particular, our contributions are:

(1) A methodology to quantify the resource and power usage overheads of virtualized systems. We present methods for automatic and synchronized monitoring of the utilization of virtual instances, the device driver domain, the virtualization engine/hypervisor, and the physical machine along with server power usages for a diverse set of workloads.

(2) A comprehensive comparison of the selected virtualization techniques in terms of performance (throughput, and latency), resource, and power usages overheads along with analysis of the impact of co-location, scheduling techniques, resource over-commitment, start-up latency and density.

(3) Evaluation results of each platform from several dimensions demonstrates that there is no single technology that outperforms in all cases. This fact provides useful insights in how to choose the best technology for a specific scenario, how to make trade-offs in optimizing systems, or on what to do differently when designing platforms. The results also reveals that part of the limitations of each platform are technological obstacles that did/can improve over time.

2 BACKGROUND

This section introduces the core concepts of H-based and OS-based virtualization platforms, and provides brief overviews of the four state-of-the-art platforms considered in our evaluation.

2.1 H-based platforms

In H-based systems, a hypervisor or a virtual machine monitor is used to emulate the underlying physical hardware by creating virtual hardware. As such, the virtualization occurs at the hardware level. The hypervisor manages the execution of virtual machines (VMs) and the underlying physical hardware. Because hypervisors

isolate the VMs from the host system, the platform is OS-agnostic in the sense that multiple instances of many different OSes may share the virtualized hardware resources. Hypervisors are generally classified into two categories: Type-1 (native or bare-metal) hypervisors that operate directly on the host hardware (e.g. XEN), and Type-2 (hosted) hypervisors that operate on top of the host's operating system. However, the distinction between the two types of hypervisors is not always clear. For example, KVM has characteristics of both types [24]. In this paper, we focus on two H-based systems that are widely used in production systems: XEN and KVM.

2.1.1 XEN. XEN is well known for its paravirtualization (PV) implementation. In PV, the interface presented to the guest OS differs slightly from the underlying hardware and the kernel of the guest OS is modified specifically to run on the hypervisor. As guests are aware that they are running on a hypervisor, no hardware emulation is needed and overhead is reduced.

To achieve virtualization, XEN relies on special privileged VMs called Domain-0 (Dom0). The Dom0 VM provides access to the management and control interface of the hypervisor itself and manages other unprivileged VMs (DomU). Each DomU VM runs a simple device driver that communicates with Dom0 to access the real hardware devices.

2.1.2 KVM. KVM is an open source solution that allows VMs to run with unmodified guest OS. Guest VMs need not be aware that they are running in a virtualized environment. KVM is implemented as a loadable kernel module, reducing the hypervisor size significantly by reusing many Linux kernel facilities such as the memory manager and scheduler. From the host's perspective, every VM is implemented, scheduled, and managed as a regular Linux process. QEMU is used to provide emulation for devices such as the BIOS, PCI bus, USB bus, disk controllers and network cards. KVM can also be used with a standard paravirtualized framework, *VirtIO*, to increase I/O performance for network and block devices. Recently introduced processors include hardware-assisted virtualization features (such as Intel-VT and AMD-V) that KVM uses to reduce complexity and overhead.

2.2 OS-based platforms

OS-based platforms, which are also known as container-based systems, virtualize resources at the OS level. They do not achieve virtualization in the same sense as VMs, but can be used for many of the same reasons one would use VMs [34]. The OS kernel is shared among containers, with no extra OS installed in each container. The containers, which are created by encapsulating the standard OS processes and their dependencies, are collectively managed by the underlying OS kernel. More specifically, the container engine (CE) performs the same duties as the hypervisor in a traditional virtualization, managing containers and images while leveraging the underlying OS kernel for core resource management and allocation. Because containers are sandboxed environments running on the kernel, they take up fewer resources than traditional VMs, making them a light weight alternative to H-based virtualization.

OS-based platforms can further be classified as either system containers or application containers. System containers allow multiple processes to be run in a single container, as can be done in a VM. They are designed to provide a complete runtime environment but with a more lightweight design. OS-based platforms that use system containers include LXC, OpenVZ [21], and Linux VServer [17]. Application containers, on the other hand, are designed to run a single process, and are a lightweight alternative for deploying applications based on distributed microservices. Platforms that use application containers include Docker and Rocket [22]. The OS-based platforms examined in this paper are LXC and Docker.

2.2.1 LXC. LXC is an OS virtualization method for running multiple isolated containers on a host using a single Linux kernel. Each container has its own process and network space, which provides the illusion of a VM but without the overhead of having a separate kernel. Resource management is performed by the kernel *namespace* and *CGroup*. CGroup is used to partition and restrict resources amongst different process groups, and the kernel namespace is used to isolate resources from the host and any other containers.

2.2.2 Docker. Docker is an open-source platform for container deployment and management. In Docker, containers are built on top of decoupled images in a multi-layer filesystem model, usually powered by AUFS (Another Union File System). A single OS image can be used as a basis for many containers while each container can have its own overlay of modified files. The host OS launches a Docker daemon, which is responsible for managing Docker images as well as creating and monitoring containers. Docker introduces a new level of granularity in virtualization in terms of fast deployment and easy management of systems. Like LXC, Docker uses CGroups and namespaces for resource allocation and isolation.

3 BENCHMARKS, METRICS, AND MEASUREMENT METHOD

3.1 Benchmarks and performance metrics

We chose a representative set of benchmarks to address different resource consumption characteristics across applications. The benchmarks chosen for each resource type have relatively little impact on other resources, and are described below.

3.1.1 CPU-Sysbench. To investigate the effect of virtualization overhead on CPU resources, we used the CPU-bound benchmark from the SysBench [14] package to compute prime numbers from 1 to N (user-specified). The application was loaded with a maximum of 4,000,000 requests. The number of threads (and hence target CPU utilization) was changed during the course of the experiments to evaluate the behaviour of each platform under different workload intensities. The benchmarking tool reports the 95th percentile latency as well as the total number of requests and elapsed time, which are used to calculate the average throughput.

3.1.2 Memory-STREAM. Memory performance was evaluated using STREAM [2], a synthetic benchmark program that measures sustainable memory bandwidth for four vector operations (Copy, Scale, Add, and Triad). STREAM is configured to use datasets much larger than (more than 4X the size of) the available cache memory in the physical machine to ensure that only the time to access RAM is measured and not the cache access speed.

3.1.3 Disk I/O-FIO. Disk I/O performance was investigated using the Flexible I/O (FIO) [10] benchmark, which measures the file system's read and write performance. It spawns a number of processes that perform particular kinds of disk I/O operations specified by the user. We used sequential and random read/writes with different file sizes, using the default block size of 4 KiB. The value of the ioengine parameter was set to *libaio*, meaning that the benchmark

used a Linux-native asynchronous I/O library. Direct I/O mode was used to disallow prefetching and writing behind the filesystem's buffer cache. The benchmark measured disk I/O operations per second (IOPS), bandwidth (KB/s), and the 95th percentile latency.

3.1.4 Network I/O-netperf. The impact of virtualization on network performance was measured using the netperf [38] benchmark. We used the TCP STREAM (TCP_STREAM) unidirectional bulk data transfer option for throughput and the TCP request-response (TCP_RR) mode to test round-trip latency. Netperf has two components: netserver and netperf. Netserver is run on one machine, and waits for netperf client connections from another machine. The client connects to the server, does a short handshake, and then sends data to the netserver. To reduce performance variation due to network congestion or other issues, we configured both the server and the client to run in the same network. Table 1 summarizes the workloads, metrics, and load intensities used for evaluating various resource management dimensions. Refer Table 6 under Section 4.4 for additional benchmarks used for resource isolation tests.

Table 1: Benchmarks, performance metrics, and workload intensities used.

Resource	Metric	Benchmark	Workload intensity			
CPU	Throughput (reqs/s)	Sysbench	CPU(%)	1, 30, 60, 90, 99		
	Latency (ms)					
Memory	Throughput (MB/s)	Stream				
Disk	Throughput (KB/s-sequential)	Fio	Disk I/O-R/W (KB/s)	Seq	Rand	Rand-mix
	Throughput (IOPS-random)					
	Latency (us)			5, 20, 30	30	50R/50W
Network	Throughput (Mb/s)	netperf	Network I/O (KB)	0.5, 1, 4, 8, 16		
	Latency (s)					

3.2 Virtualization overhead metrics

Virtualization overhead was quantified in terms of performance, power, and resource usages overhead. The performance overhead is the performance loss relative to the baseline scenario (i.e. execution in the native environment), and is defined as:

$$Perf_{ovh} = \frac{|Perf_{virt} - Perf_{native}|}{Perf_{native}}, \tag{1}$$

where $Perf_{ovh}$ is the performance overhead, computed by dividing the performance under virtualization ($Perf_{virt}$) by that in the native ($Perf_{native}$) environment.

The power usage overhead is the extra power usage relative to running in the native environment. It is defined as:

$$Power_{ovh} = \frac{|Power_{virt} - Power_{native}|}{Power_{native}}. \tag{2}$$

For resource utilization overhead, we use a more fine-grained approach that takes into account the resource usage of different components involved in virtualization (guests, Dom0, and/or hypervisor/container engine). The resource overhead is defined as the extra resources used by the virtualization system relative to the resources used by the guest alone. More precisely, it is defined as:

$$U_{j-ovh} = \frac{|\sum U_{j-guest}^i - U_{j-virt}|}{\sum U_{j-guest}^i}, \tag{3}$$

where $\sum U_{j-guest}^i$ is the summation of the j resource (j=CPU, memory bandwidth, disk or network I/O) utilization of all instances running on a server, U_{j-virt} is the overall j resource usage of the *virt* (LXC,Docker,KVM, or XEN) virtualization system including usages for guests, Dom0, and/or hypervisor/container engine.

3.3 Measurement methods and tools

To understand the utilization overhead of multiple resources, it is important to monitor resource usage at all levels of virtualization. There are several tools that measure resource usage, but none of them can simultaneously measure every resource of interest in this work. We therefore extended a set of previously developed scripts [30] for analyzing the resource utilization of the XEN platform using one benchmark. The extended scripts can be used to analyze resource usage based on several benchmarks for each platform considered in this work (XEN, KVM, LXC, Docker, native). The scripts incorporate various tools (shown in Table 2) for different resource types, and performs automatic and synchronized measurements.

The scripts implement the following stepwise procedure for each virtualized platform:

(1) It logs into the system under test (SUT), i.e. the native or virtualized environment, and starts running a benchmark.
(2) It waits for a user-specified period X (we used a 5s warm-up interval) for the benchmark to stabilize before starting monitoring. We sampled monitoring data once per second.
(3) After running the benchmark and monitoring resource usage at multiple virtualization levels (VM/host, Dom0, H/CE/PM) for a user-specified period Y, the script triggers the termination of the benchmark and monitoring tools.
(4) The script then waits for a user-specified interval, Z, before running the next benchmark to increase the reliability of the results. The length of this interval depends on the benchmark.
(5) The test is completed after repeating the above steps for a user-specified number of times (4 repeats were used in this work).
(6) The script then summarizes the measured information into one file per VM/container and PM, and compiles these files into a single log file containing results for all used machines. Finally the results are averaged over the duration of the run.

We collected utilization data using standard tools available for the Linux OS platform (top, free, mpstat, vmstat, and ifconfig) and specialized tools provided with the tested virtualization platforms for monitoring instances: xentop (XEN), virt-top (KVM), ctop and lxc-info (LXC), and Docker stats (Docker).

Monitoring overhead: We evaluated the overhead of our chosen

Table 2: Measurement tools used for the virtualization systems under study.

		VM				DOM0				H/PM			
		CPU	Mem	I/O	Net	CPU	Mem	I/O	Net	CPU	Mem	I/O	Net
XEN	xentop	Y		Y	Y	Y		Y	Y				
	free		Y*			Y							
		VM								**H/PM**			
		CPU	Mem	I/O	Net					CPU	Mem	I/O	Net
KVM	virt-top	Y		Y	Y								
	free		Y*							Y			
		Container								**CE/PM**			
		CPU	Mem	I/O	Net					CPU	Mem	I/O	Net
LXC	ctop	Y	Y	Y									
	lxc-info				Y								
	free									Y			
		Container								**CE/PM**			
		CPU	Mem	I/O	Net					CPU	Mem	I/O	Net
Docker	Docker stats	Y	Y	Y	Y								
	free									Y			
		VM/Container								**H/CE/PM**			
										CPU	Mem	I/O	Net
All	mpstat									Y			
	vmstat											Y	
	ifconfig												Y
Power	snmp	**PM**											

*-need to run inside the VM.

resource monitoring tools, including resource and power usages, by running them alone for the four virtualization platforms. Monitoring was a light weight process in all cases (CPU and memory usage by less than 1%), and hence the results are not shown here. This reflects that virtualization overheads are essentially unaffected by the resource monitoring systems used in the benchmarks.

4 EXPERIMENTATION

4.1 Hardware setup

All the experiments were performed on physical machines with 32 cores (AMD OpteronTM6272), 12288KB of L3 cache, 56 GB of RAM, 4x500 GB SATA disks, and a 1 GB network adapter. The CPU had two sockets, each socket had 2 NUMA nodes, and each node had 8 cores. One of these machines was used to run the script for starting the benchmarks and monitoring tools. Power management for the SUT host was disabled to reduce the effects of resource scaling and to increase the comparability of the results. The physical server's power consumption was monitored using HP Intelligent Modular PDUs, which provide per-power-socket power usage data using the Simple Network Management Protocol (SNMP). These PDUs have a resolution of 0.01A (*230V = 2.3W), updated every 0.5s. The server's idle power consumption was 130W, and its cores operate at 1.7GHz. To analyze the average boot-time latency of the studied techniques, we instrumented the boot process of KVM and XEN VMs using the bootchart [9] tool, used the *systemd-analyze* tool for CoreOs-based VMs and measured instance creation times for LXC and Docker by using the Linux *time* command to determine the duration of the container-start up execution commands.

We used the Ubuntu 14.04 LTS Linux distribution for the native, VM, and container environments. We also used the same kernel version (3.19) for all systems because the use of different kernel versions could introduce experimental noise. Virtualization was achieved using LXC 1.0.9, Docker 1.12.3, QEMU with KVM 2.0.0, and Xen 4.4.2. We used the standard default installations for containers and VMs unless otherwise stated. Each instance was allocated the same amount of memory (10 GB), and CPU allocations were set on a per-instance basis depending on individual needs. The *cpuset.cpus* and *memory.limit* CGroup subsystems were used to limit specific CPUs and the amount of memory per container. We used *virsh's setvcpus* and *xm vcpu-set* to assign cores to KVM and XEN VMs respectively. The VMs were created with 50GB hard disk images. To measure the overhead imposed by the virtualization layer, we first ran all the workloads on the bare-metal OS in a PM.

We ran the different benchmarks with different intensities using single- and multi-instance (for additional overhead, isolation, and over-commitment) configurations to investigate the impact of virtualization on overall performance (throughput and latency), isolation, resource usage, power consumption, and start-up time.

4.2 Single-instance virtualization overhead

We evaluated the performance and resource/power usage overhead incurred by using single VMs/containers, and compared them to results obtained in the native environment. This made it possible to determine the overhead imposed by virtualization and the additional overhead imposed by running multiple instances.

4.2.1 CPU. Figure 1 presents the results of the CPU-bound sysbench benchmark analysis for LXC, Docker, KVM and XEN at different levels of CPU load. We normalized the result of each test against the native performance. The results presented in Figures 1a and 1b for throughput and latency, respectively, show that OS-based systems achieved similar performance to the native environment. Howerver, some correlation between performance and input size is apparent for KVM and XEN: their performance decreases slightly as the CPU load increases (a maximum overhead of 4.6% for XEN at full utilization). This aside, the H-based systems do not impose a greater performance penalty than the OS-based platforms when only a single instance is being run in the system.

The resource and power usage associated with the results shown in Figure 1 are presented in Figure 2. We only present CPU utilization data, shown in Figure 2a, because the benchmark had minimal effects on other resources for any instance or virtualization layer. CPU usage overhead was negligible in all cases. The power usage data, shown in Figure 2b also reveal no large or interesting differences between the virtualization platforms. One platform may consume less power for a lightly loaded CPU workload while it may consume higher if the intensity of workload increases (e.g. Docker). All of the tested platforms incur only a small power overhead when compared to the native environment (avg. overhead of 1.5%). Another observation is the lack of energy proportionality (EP) in the system, i.e., the energy consumed does not decrease linearly with load. At lower loads, power usage is primarily dominated by idle power consumption. In the idle scenario, KVM and XEN use 1.46% more power than the native environment (due to issues such as the cost of supporting a complete guest OS). Interestingly, the dynamic power usage (i.e. the power usage after discounting idle power) of the virtualized systems is far greater than would be expected at low utilizations. Figure 2c shows the percentage of the dynamic peak power usage. Although Docker makes the system more EP than the rest, on all the tested systems the average power usage is about 43% of their peak power at very low utilization (1% CPU load).

Summary: For the CPU-bound benchmark, the overhead of both H-based and OS-based virtualization platforms are rather insignificant when running a single VM/container. At low workload levels, the systems draw far more power than expected, making them less EP. The insight can be used by system designers to make power-aware workload placement decisions.

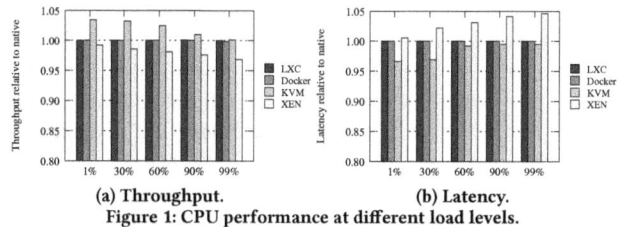

(a) Throughput.   (b) Latency.
Figure 1: CPU performance at different load levels.

4.2.2 Memory: The STREAM benchmark supports four vector kernels (Copy, Scale, Add and Triad). We only present results for the Triad operation here because it is most practically relevant to large systems [4].

As shown in Table 3, H-based systems had poorer memory throughput than OS-based systems: KVM has a 11% performance overhead, while XEN achieved the worst performance, with an overhead of 22% relative to the native environment. The memory performance of the OS-based platforms was comparable to that of the native environment.

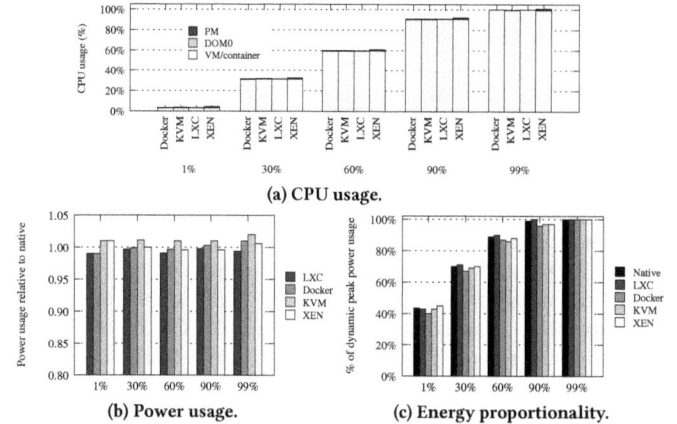

(a) CPU usage.

(b) Power usage.   (c) Energy proportionality.
Figure 2: Resource utilization at different level of CPU load.

As the main determinant of performance is the bandwidth to the main memory, the benchmark is less dependent on the total amount of memory or other resources [32]. We therefore do not discuss resource usage across the execution environments. Note that the benchmark was run using default and non-tuned memory configurations, allowing the tested systems to use any NUMA node. Performance could be improved by ensuring execution was done using a single NUMA node. A more detailed analysis of the effect of NUMA is left for future work.

Summary: H-based virtualization imposes a much higher memory access overhead than OS-based virtualization.

Table 3: Throughput of Triad operation using STREAM benchmark.

	Native	LXC	Docker	KVM	XEN
(MB/s)	4384	4389	4289	3882	3419

4.2.3 Disk I/O. For KVM and XEN, the file system is mounted inside the VMs and both use raw file formats. LXC uses the default directory backing store as file system. We tested Docker with two file stores, *AUFS* and *volume*. We first show the results for AUFS, the default storage driver for managing images and layers and later for volumes that are suited for write-heavy workloads. We measure the performance of Disk I/O when reading and writing files of 5GB to 30GB using sequential and random access modes. Figure 3

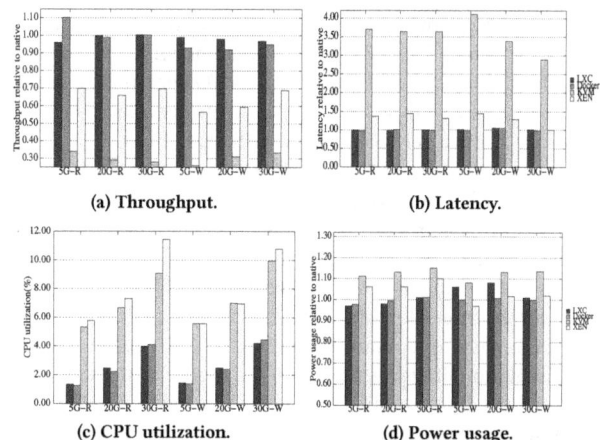

(a) Throughput.   (b) Latency.

(c) CPU utilization.   (d) Power usage.
Figure 3: Performance, CPU and power usage for sequential operations.

shows the sequential read and write throughput, latency, CPU, and

Table 4: Average CPU and disk I/O usage for read and write operations.

		VM/container	Hypervisor/PM	Dom0
CPU (%)	LXC	2.2	0.3	
	Docker	2.8	0.2	
	KVM	6.9	0.23	
	XEN	4.2	1.16	2.5
Disk I/O (KB/s)	XEN	73371	87932	0

power usage for the tested systems during the I/O benchmarking experiments. LXC and Docker achieved native-like performance, but KVM and XEN were slower. As shown in Figure 3a, the average throughput overhead of KVM and XEN were 69% and 35% respectively. The latency overhead for disk I/O using KVM was much more severe – 256%, as shown in Figure 3b. This is mostly due to the greater overhead (buffering, copying, and synchronization) involved in pushing filesystem activities from the guest VM via the Dom0/hypervisor to the disk device. Each guest I/O operation must go through the paravirtualized VirtIO drivers, which cannot yet match the performance of OS-based systems.

Figures 3c and 3d show the measured CPU and power usage values. While the CPU usage never rose above 12% during the disk-intensive benchmarks, KVM and XEN exhibited larger increases in CPU usage, and therefore used more power (8% more, on average). As shown in Table 4, the extra CPU overhead imposed by virtualization with XEN (46%) was greater than that for the other tested platforms due to the CPU utilization of Dom0 and the hypervisor. XEN also imposes extra disk I/O overhead on the H/PM; the magnitude of this extra overhead is equal to (for read) or greater than (for write) than that for the VM's I/O. The remaining techniques do not impose extra I/O utilization on the H/PM. Therefore, we do not show any corresponding results for these platforms.

We investigated the KVM disk I/O process in more detail to identify possible pitfalls in its performance, focusing on the impact of cache settings, image formats, and disk controllers. Experiments were performed using different KVM caching policies: no caching, write-through (read-only cache), and the default write-back (read and write cache). The *write-back* technique outperformed the read-only and write-only options by 40% for write operations and/or 20% for read operations. We also changed the disk controller from the *VirtIO* to the *IDE* driver, but found that this caused a performance loss of around 66%. These results indicate that using VirtIO produces a much lower virtualization overhead than regular emulated devices. We also compared the raw file format to the copy-on-write (*QCOW2*) format. While QCOW2 is well known for its snapshot support, the overhead associated with its I/O operations is greater than that for raw storage. In our experiments, it achieved only 80% of the raw-storage performance for write operations.

To quantify the disk I/O performance of using different file stores other than AUFS for Docker, we tested the use of *volumes*, which mounts a file system in the container, and *direct device mapping* that exposes the host directory to the container. The test involved reading and writing 30 GB on an existing file. Table 5 shows the results for the three file stores. AUFS exhibited significant overhead due to the *copy up* operation it performs in its image layering implementation: it copies the entire file even if only a small part of the file is being modified. If the file is being modified for the first time, the entire file is copied up from the underlying image to the container's top writable layer, producing the worst possible write performance (0.552 bytes/s). Subsequent reads and writes

are faster, however, because the operations are performed on the file copy that is already available in the container's top layer. The use of Docker volumes confers a noticeable performance increase over AUFS, and direct device mapping offers a smaller increase. Hence, the performance penalty of AUFS must be balanced against its advantages in terms of fast start-up times and efficient use of storage and memory. The magnitude of the penalty depends on the size of the file being manipulated, the number of image layers, and/or the depth of the directory tree.

Table 5: Docker sequential disk I/O performance with AUFS, volumes, and direct device mapping.

Operation		AUFS	Volume	Direct mapping
Write-30G (KB/s)	First	0.55	161793	128407
	Second	84251		
	Subsequent	153378		
Read-30G(KB/s)		172493	319754	184458

Figure 4 presents measured IOPS results relative to native for random read, write, and mixed (50% read/50% write) operations on 30 GB files. The OS-based systems achieved similar performance as native, followed by KVM. XEN showed worst performance (40% overhead) on random read operation. However, it performs better than the rest on random write operations, calling for more investigation on possible optimization available in the platform.

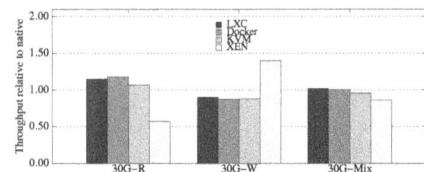

Figure 4: Disk performance for random operations.

Summary: Virtualization technology should be selected with extra care in case of disk intensive workloads due to variations in performance and resource usage.

4.2.4 Network. LXC, KVM and XEN use bridged networks for public IP addresses, whereas Docker uses the default docker0 bridge. Figure 5 shows the throughput and latency for Netperf benchmark. Figure 5a shows the unidirectional bulk transfer throughput for outgoing communication. For packet sizes of 4K bytes and above, LXC, Docker and XEN all achieved the maximum possible throughput and equaled the performance of the native environment, showing that bulk data transfer can be handled efficiently by both H- and OS-based systems. KVM achieved the worst throughput, showing that H-based systems still suffer from a significant performance gap. Smaller packet sizes (512B and 1K) require more CPU resources and power (as shown in Figure 6). Figure 5b shows the results obtained from Netperf request and response (TCP_RR) test. KVM increased the round trip latency and has an overhead of 250% overhead, while the latency overhead for LXC, Docker, and XEN were 7%, 12% and 58%, respectively.

Making use of the host's networking instead of bridged network allows Docker containers to achieve near-native performance. Figure 7 shows the impact of this approach relative to the default network setting. Bridged networking achieves worse performance in terms of both throughput and latency for smaller message sizes, as shown in Figures 7a and 7b, respectively. Although host networking gives direct access to the host network stack and improves performance, it removes the benefits of network namespaces and isolation between the host machine and containers.

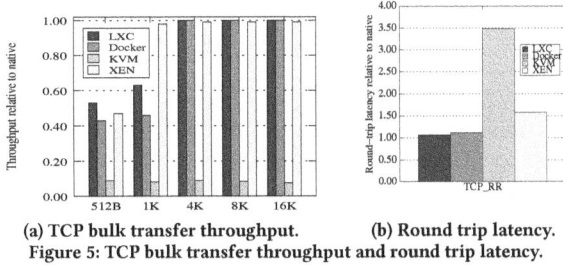

(a) TCP bulk transfer throughput.　　(b) Round trip latency.
Figure 5: TCP bulk transfer throughput and round trip latency.

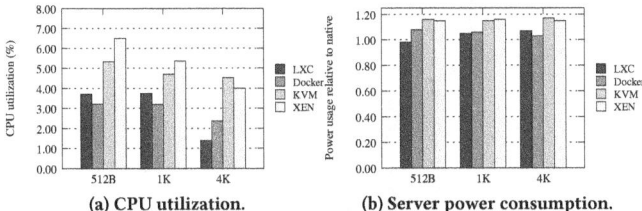

(a) CPU utilization.　　(b) Server power consumption.
Figure 6: CPU utilization and server power usage for TCP bulk transfer.

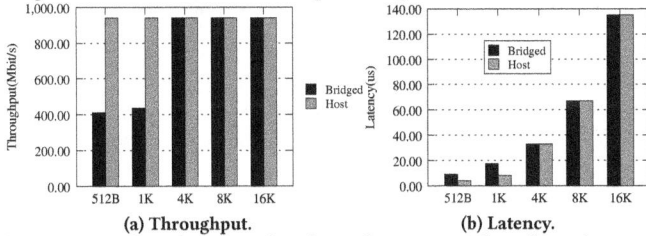

(a) Throughput.　　(b) Latency.
Figure 7: Network performance of Docker under two network configurations.

4.3 Multi-instance virtualization overhead

We conducted another set of experiments to study how virtualization overhead for the selected platforms is affected by co-location. The intent here is to quantify the change in overhead and hence not show the observations similar to single instance run. Figure 8 shows the performance, and CPU/power usage for compute-, network-, and disk intensive workloads run on a PM hosting four concurrent instances. In all cases, the load was distributed equally across the instances to match the baseline single instance test.

Figure 8a shows the sums of the measured throughout, CPU and power usage for the compute-bound benchmark over four instances. The workload run on each individual instance is equal to 25% of that used in the single instance tests. The results clearly show that co-locating CPU-bound instances (in the absence of resource contention) does not impose any significant overhead on throughput, CPU usage, or power consumption for any platform.

Figure 8b shows the total bandwidth, CPU, and power usage for the network-bound benchmark based on a test in which each instance sends a 512 byte packet (the corresponding single instance test used 2k byte packages). XEN achieved similar bandwidth to the baseline value, whereas LXC, Docker and KVM exhibited 1.1x, 1.45x, and 7x bandwidth improvements, respectively. The use of multiple instances had no appreciable effect on CPU or power usage for Docker. However, LXC, KVM and XEN exhibited CPU usage increases of 40%, 426%,and 100%, respectively, and power usage increases of 4.7%, 79%, and 38%, respectively. The increased CPU usage was attributed to increases in the CPU usage of individual instances and the virtualization layers in order to serve the workload. Figure 9a shows the distribution of CPU usage for both OS- and H-based systems. In general, instance CPU usage increased for all

techniques. While the Docker and LXC container engines exhibit minimal increments, the KVM hypervisor and XEN Dom0 incur more overhead when running multiple VM instances (increment of 270% and 111%, respectively, compared to single VMs). This could significantly affect the performance of applications with high CPU requirements in oversubscribed systems.

Figure 8c shows the total disk I/O performance, CPU and power usage for instances reading/writing 5GB of files. Every platform performed better (particularly on read operations) in the multi-instance test but had higher CPU usage. KVM exhibited the largest increase in CPU usage (234%) for read and write operations, and offered smaller performance gains due to scaling. Figure 9b shows the distribution of CPU usage for read operations on each platform. While the increase in CPU usage for KVM is due to an increase in the CPU usage of the VMs themselves, much of the extra CPU usage under XEN is due to DOM0 and the hypervisor for the co-located guest VMs (224% and 109%, respectively). The throughputs of the individual instances in our multi-instance memory-bandwidth experiment were similar to those for the single instance test. Therefore, results for the memory benchmark are not shown.

Summary: H-based systems use more resources in co-located environments, particularly on disk- and network-intensive workloads.

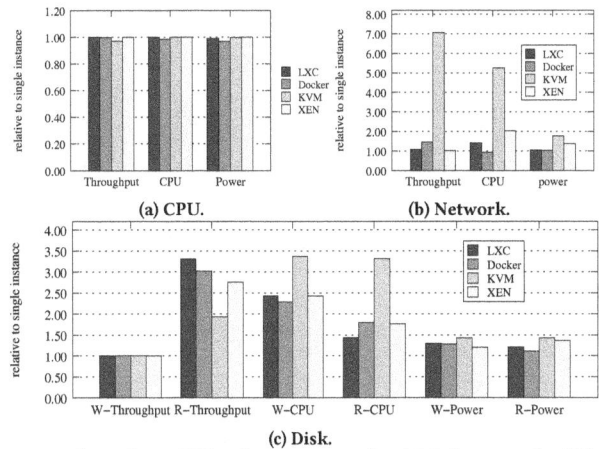

(a) CPU.　　(b) Network.

(c) Disk.
Figure 8: Throughput, CPU and power usage of multiple instances for different benchmarks.

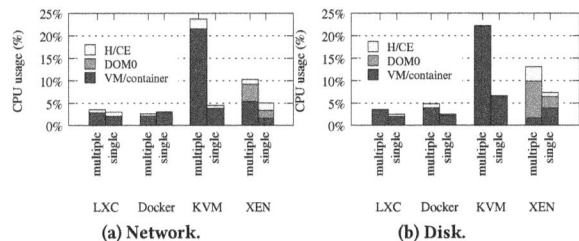

(a) Network.　　(b) Disk.
Figure 9: CPU usage for network bandwidth- and disk-intensive workloads.

4.4 Resource isolation

So far, we have discussed the virtualization overhead in terms of performance, resource usage, and power consumption for physical machines running single and multiple instances for *each* benchmark described in Table 1. Our focus now is to highlight the interference caused by deploying a *diverse* range of co-located applications on shared hardware resources as commonly done in a cloud. To this end, we performed isolation tests using the four environments, with two guests running on the same host machine.

We first ran a baseline application in one guest and used the obtained data to compare to the results obtained when running the same application side-by-side with another application. The second application was chosen to complement the baseline application, compete with it, or have an adversarial impact. The summary of experimentation performed based on Table 6 is shown in Figure 10. The sections below present analysis of the results obtained in terms of CPU, memory, disk, and network resources.

Table 6: Benchmarks used for isolation tests.

	CPU	Memory	Disk	Network	adversarial
CPU *Sysbench*	lookbusy [18]	Memtester [20]	FIO	Netperf	ForkBomb [12]
Memory *Blogbench [11]*	lookbusy	Blogbench	FIO	Netperf	MallocBomb [13]
Disk *Fio*	lookbusy	Memtester	FIO	Netperf	Bonnie++ [3]
Network *Neperf*	lookbusy	Memtester	FIO	Netperf	TCP SYN

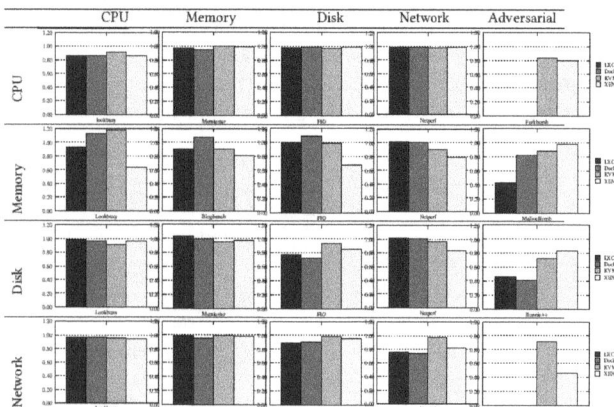

Figure 10: Performance of applications when co-located with instances running different workload types.

4.4.1 CPU isolation. The top row of Figure 10 shows how the performance of Sysbench was affected by the different co-located applications. All the virtualization systems performed within a reasonable range of their baseline performance for complementary workloads. When co-located with the adversarial fork-bomb workload – a classic test that loops to create new child processes until there are no resources available, KVM and XEN achieved 83% and 80% of their stand-alone performance. On the other hand, LXC and Docker were unable to complete the benchmark: the container that ran Sysbench was starved of resources and thus unable to serve its requests. Although it is possible to prevent the forkbomb effect by using the *pids cgroup* in LXC or the *nproc cgroup* in Docker to limit the number of processes allowed, preventing this type of extreme starvation generally requires careful accounting for, and control over, every physical and kernel operation [43].

In the competing workload experiments, LXC, Docker and XEN achieved 85% of the performance observed in the absence of co-location, but KVM performed better, achieving 91%. It is noteworthy that all of the available physical CPU cores were shared between the guests on all the platforms.

CPU pinning: To demonstrate the impact of CPU pinning on CPU interference, we performed an experiment in which each VM/container was assigned to specific physical CPU cores while

using the same amount of CPU resources as in the previous case. For this purpose, we used CGroup methods to assign CPU affinity for LXC and Docker, and the vCPU affinity technique for KVM and XEN. Figure 11 shows the performance achieved with and without pinning. For both H- and OS-based systems, the unpinned configuration outperformed the pinned configuration when the VM/container was running in isolation, showing that the default scheduler does work well in the absence of resource competition [48]. However as competition increased (i.e. when the baseline application was co-located with a competing or adversarial VM/container), the pinned configuration outperforms that without pinning (by up to 19%).

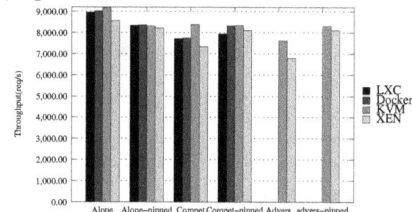

Figure 11: Impact of pinning on throughput of a CPU-bound instance when co-located with competing and adversarial instances.

Scheduling technique: CPU schedulers can support work-conserving (WC) and/or non work-conserving (NWC) scheduling modes [31], with the former usually being the default choice. In WC mode, CPU resources are allocated in proportion to the number of shares (weights) that VMs have been assigned. For example, given two VMs with equal weights, each VM would be allowed to use at least 50% of CPU and could potentially consume the entire CPU if the other VM is idle. Conversely, NWC mode defines a hard bound or ceiling enforcement on CPU resources, i.e. each instance owns a specific fraction of the CPU. In the above example, each VM would be allocated up to, but no more than, 50% of the CPU resources even if the other VM was completely idle.

Figure 12 shows the performance of the compute-bound Sysbench benchmark when co-located with the background lookbusy instance under WC and NWC modes. XEN uses the *weight* and *cap* functionality of the credit scheduler to specify WC and NWC behaviors, respectively. LXC, Docker, and KVM use the standard Linux control group scheduling interfaces, *CGroup-quota* (WC) and *CGroup-sharing* (NWC) in the Completely Fair Scheduler (CFS). The same CPU resources were allocated in both the WC and NWC cases — 50% of total CPU cycles. There are three notable aspects of Figure 12. First, the WC technique exploits all available CPU cycles to achieve better performance at lower background loads. As the background load increases, its performance decreases (with an average reduction of 44% when increasing from 1% to 100% load), reducing each application's performance isolation. On the other hand, NWC only permits each instance to use resources up to a predefined threshold, resulting in consistent performance. Second, the performance of WC is higher than that of NWC, even at higher loads, on all platforms. This is because it exploits any underutilized CPU resource in the system. This is particularly important for applications that have strict performance requirements or when high system utilization is desired. Third, the XEN WC method achieves higher throughput than the others (except at full load). This presumably occurs because the XEN credit scheduler tends to over-allocate CPU share to guest VMs [31, 51].

Summary: H-based systems provide stronger isolation than OS-based systems that use shared host OS kernels, which can potentially lead to denial of service. CPU allocations can be optimized by using CPU pinning and scheduling to manage resource contention.

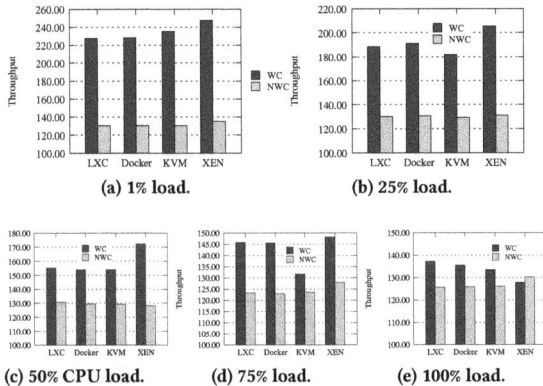

Figure 12: Performance impact of using WC and NWC scheduling modes at varying level of background CPU loads.

4.4.2 Memory Isolation. The second row of Figure 10 shows the normalized read performance of the baseline application, Blogbench (high memory- and low disk-intensive application). LXC achieves only 42% of the standalone performance when faced with the adversarial workload, while the other platforms achieve at least 80% of the standalone performance. Though not shown in the table, Docker achieved lower write scores (70% of the standalone value, on average) with a competitive workload. All of the platforms achieved write scores of at least 93% with an adversarial workload except Docker, which achieved only 83%.

4.4.3 Disk Isolation. The results of disk isolation tests (shown in the third row of Figure 10) show that LXC and Docker achieved 77% and 72% of the standalone performance when co-located with the competitive workload, but only 45% and 41%, respectively, when co-located with the adversarial Bonnie++ workload (Bonnie++ was set to continuously read and write to the hard disk). XEN achieved consistent performance for these two workload types, with an average of 83% of the standalone value. KVM performed slightly worse when co-located with the adversarial workload, achieving 71% of the stand-alone performance.

4.4.4 Network Isolation. To measure adversarial interference, we used the *hping3* tool to create and send a large number of TCP SYN packets to a target system. We configured the co-located guest to serve as the victim of the attack, and the attack emulator was run on another machine in the same local area network. The last row of Figure 10 shows the impact of co-location on the network-bound application's throughput. KVM performed better than the other platforms for all workload types, while XEN performed particularly badly with the adversarial workload, exhibiting 54% degradation compared to standalone. LXC and Docker could not complete the benchmark when co-located with the adversarial workloads, but achieved 76% and 74% of their standalone performance when co-located with competitive workloads. Similar results were obtained for latency, and are hence not shown.

Summary: While isolation is better managed by H-based systems, no platform achieves perfect performance isolation. Except for CPU which can properly be isolated by tuning the CPU allocation, other resources such as cache, memory bandwidth, and disk

I/O are difficult to isolate. Our findings may be of interest for designers of interference-aware resource allocation systems that aim to predict expected performance by grouping applications based on workload characteristics.

4.5 Over-commitment

In cloud data centers, it is often observed that all requested capacity is not fully utilized; utilization can be as low as 20% [33]. This creates an opportunity to employ resource over-commitment—allocating more virtualized resources than are available in the physical infrastructure [47]. In this work, we use instances running at 50% utilization to represent a fairly utilized datacenter.

We analyze and quantify the level of overcommitment for each virtualized system in relation to its impact on performance, CPU usage, and power consumption using the compute-intensive sysbench benchmark. The virtualization platforms accommodate CPU-overcommitment by multiplexing the virtual CPUs onto the actual physical cores. The results obtained are shown in Figure 13. For all environments, the throughput (Figure 13a) increases sub-linearly for higher OC ratios (vCPU to pCPU ratios). LXC and Docker show higher throughput rates at higher OC ratios than KVM and XEN. However, as shown in Figure 13b, unlike throughput, the latency for KVM and XEN starts to increase quickly with the OC ratio, rising by as much as 8.6% and 7.5%, respectively, at an OC ratio of 1. With an OC of 1.5, the latency for LXC and Docker reaches a maximum, whereas for the H-based platforms latency increases even further. Consequently, if latency (a crucial metric for many workloads) is particularly important, it is advisable not to use over-commit ratios above 1.5, even if there is more room for increased throughput. This illustrates the need to monitor the right performance metrics to determine the level of over-commitment that can be achieved with minimal impact on performance. Increasing the OC level also increases CPU and power usage as shown in Figures 13c and 13d.

Memory over-commitment is more challenging than CPU over-commitment as it requires careful analysis of the memory needs of all instances. It is generally outside the scope of the virtualization management framework and is therefore left for future work.

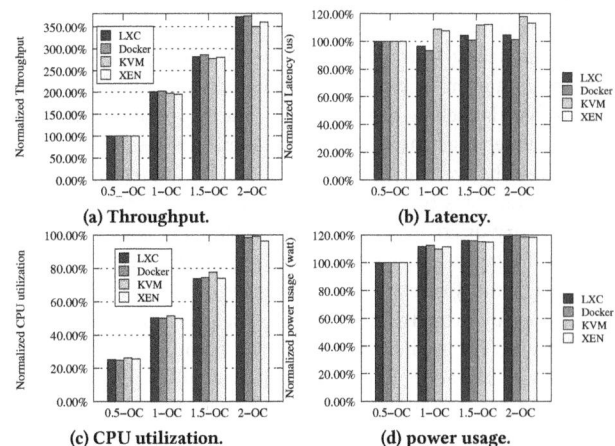

Figure 13: Impact of CPU over-commit on performance and resource usage.

4.6 Start-up latency and density

Start-up latency and density—the number of instances that can be supported per physical machine are two important characteristics of highly flexible resource management systems. A low start-up latency and the ability to support many instances per PM makes it possible to achieve better placement, dynamic scaling, consolidation, and/or recovery in case of failures.

Containers inherently have lower start-up latencies due to their lightweight nature while VMs are considered to take longer to start. To highlight the difference in start-up performance and show how technological advancement is changing the start-up cost, particularly for VMs, we performed experiments on the four virtualization platforms. For H-based systems, booting times were tested both using an Ubuntu 14.0 OS image image with a basic configurations and CoreOS—a container Linux image designed for minimal operational overhead. For both H- and OS-based systems, provisioning time is taken without considering benchmark start-up time. Figure 14 summarizes the start-up times and energy usage values for each platform. Docker offered the fastest provisioning time (0.5s), followed by LXC (4s) (shown in Figure 14a). While Docker needs only bring up the container process, LXC must start system-level processes like systemd, dhclient and sshd, XEN and KVM have booting times of 48s and 55s, respectively when using the Ubuntu image, with the corresponding high energy usage (shown in Figure 14b). In general, the H-based systems must boot a separate full OS with its own device drivers, daemons, and so on. But with CoreOS the booting times for KVM and XEN are reduced to 10s and 11.4s, respectively. This is an interesting direction for H-based systems which commonly are considered to start-up slowly.

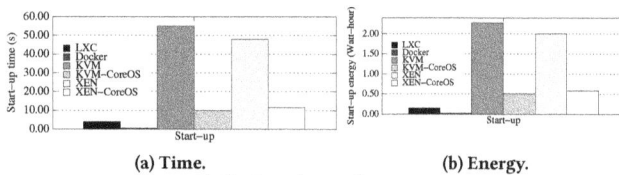

(a) Time.   (b) Energy.
Figure 14: Start-up time and energy usage.

Summary: OS-based platforms have lower start-up latencies (achieving average improvements of 91% and 15% over the "default" image of H-based systems in boot-time and power usage, respectively). Optimized measurements, such as the use of CoreOS, have significantly reduced VM start-up time (avg. 10.7s), making H-based systems better suited for rapid deployment.

Once in steady-state, our density test measured the impact of increasing numbers of instances on a shared physical machine. The test involved launching guest instances one by one and monitoring their resource usage. Memory costs constitute the biggest difference in overhead between containers and VMs [27] when it comes to consolidation density, hence we focus on this resource. We evaluated memory usage by summing the Resident set size (RSS) [23] values of each process of the instance held in RAM. The rest of the occupied memory exists in the swap space or file system. RSS values were easily extracted from CGroup pseudo-files. KVM was the only H-based system included in this test because it uses CGroup for resource allocation. KVM was evaluated with and without the Kernel Same Page Merging (KSM) feature. KSM works by removing duplicate copies and merging identical memory pages from multiple guests into a single memory region.

We created VMs with 1 vCPU and 1 GB memory. Figure 15 shows the average results of running 1-20 simultaneous instances. The results show that KVM without KSM (KVM-WKSM) used in average 213 MB memory per VM, 1.9x more than KVM with KSM

(KVM-KSM). The LXC system container used 6 MB of RAM, while the memory usage of Docker container was mainly 1 MB, 6x and 109x lower than the corresponding values for LXC and KVM-KSM, respectively. RSS values reflect the total of the shared libraries used by the process, even though a shared library is only loaded into memory once. Hence, the actual memory footprint difference can be even larger between H-based and OS-based systems.

Summary: Containers provide a smaller memory footprint (avg. 31x smaller) than KVM, even when the later is used with KSM. KSM enables a more efficient use of available memory for certain workload types (up to 2x improvement) and can potentially be used to achieve a high level of memory overcommitment.

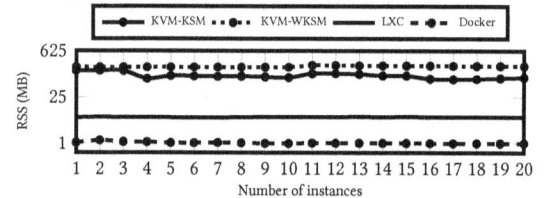

Figure 15: Memory footprints for KVM, LXC and Docker.

4.7 Power efficiency considerations

As the evaluated virtualization techniques differ in resource usage, we performed additional experiments to illustrate the impact of resource usage (CPU, memory, network, and disk) on power consumption to further guide data center operators.

Resource and power usage relationship: The processor is considered as one of the largest power consumers in modern servers [36].

To evaluate this and the dynamic power contribution by CPU, memory, network activity, and disks, we ran workloads that stress each resource (Lookbusy, Memtester, Netperf and FIO respectively) at varying intensities and monitored their power consumption. Figure 16 shows the utilization of each resource normalized against the peak usage and the respective power usage over time. The workloads were generated so as to first utilize the CPU followed by the memory, the network, and finally the disk. The corresponding power usage values are shown at the top of the figure, where it is shown that CPU utilization has larger impact on power usage than memory, network, and disk. Although the contributions of individual resources to system power usage is generally dependent on the workload and hardware architecture, the CPU accounted for the lion's share - 31% of the server's total power usage. Resource allocation systems should consider differences in resource power usage to reduce power usage and datacenter energy efficiency.

Impact of CPU frequency scaling on memory bandwidth: Dynamic voltage and frequency scaling (DVFS) is a commonly-used power-management technique that reduces the processor's clock frequency to reduce the energy usage for a computation, particularly for memory-bound workloads [45]. The motivation is often that a system's main memory bandwidth is unaffected by the reduced clock frequency but power usage is reduced appreciably.

To validate this common assumption, we performed experiments using STREAM with different CPU frequencies on each run. Figure 17 shows the correlation between CPU frequency and main memory bandwidth with power usage. Figure 17a, shows the memory bandwidth normalized against the peak CPU frequency. As the CPU frequency was scaled down, the memory bandwidth also fell, showing the dependency of the latter on the former: reducing

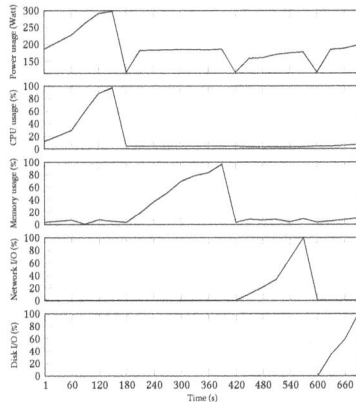

Figure 16: Impact of CPU, memory, network, and disk resources in power usage of a server.

the CPU frequency from the highest value to the lowest reduced the memory bandwidth by 23%. The power usage at different CPU frequencies is shown in Figure 17b. Similar behaviour has been observed on different micro-architectures [42].

Summary: Our analysis reveals the dependency of memory performance on CPU frequency. These results are likely to be useful in performance and power modeling, and for application developers aiming to optimize their applications.

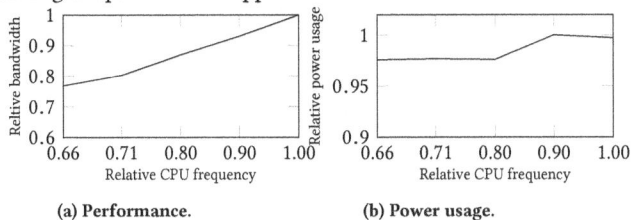

(a) Performance.	(b) Power usage.

Figure 17: Performance of a memory-bound application and power usage for varying CPU frequency.

4.8 Summary of Results

Our results for single instance tests show that all of the studied platforms impose negligible CPU usage overhead. OS-based platforms are more efficient in terms of memory performance, followed by KVM and then XEN. LXC outperformed the other platforms in terms of disk I/O, while Docker suffered from a relatively high performance penalty when used with the default AUFS file storage but was more efficient with Docker volumes. KVM exhibited the worst performance for sequential disk I/O, even when using the faster para-virtualized driver, virtIO. Also for network I/O, KVM provided the worst performance, whereas LXC and Docker (using the host's networking capabilities) operated at native speeds. Docker's default Bridge-based network introduces more overhead but provides better isolation. Our multi-instance experiments confirmed the observations from the single instance tests and focused on the extent of overhead due to co-location. With respect to resource and power usage overhead, KVM exhibited the highest usage with respect to both disk and network I/O, followed by XEN. This was attributed to increased CPU utilization (and hence power usage) by the VMs , DOM0, and/or the hypervisor.

While VMs offer better isolation and protection against noisy neighbors, containers can be adversely affected to the extent that malicious instances could cause the whole OS to fail. CPU can by fully isolated e.g., through the use of CPU pinning. The rest show poor performance isolation due to imperfect resource partitioning.

In CPU over-commit scenarios, H-based platforms perform very similarly to OS-based platforms; in both cases, the effectiveness of over-subscription depends heavily on the performance metrics of interest, the number of instances, and the types of applications that are being run. Our start-up time and density tests show that OS-based systems are more efficient and also that VMs are becoming more efficient as technology advances.

5 RELATED WORK

Many works have evaluated and compared the different aspects of H-based and/or OS-based virtualization platforms. Chen et al. [30] studied the resource utilization overhead introduced by virtualization layers by conducting experiments to characterize the relationship between the resource utilizations of virtual machines (VMs) and the virtualization layer in the Xen virtualization environment. Tafa et al. [46] compared the performance of hypervisors in terms of CPU consumption, memory utilization, total migration time, and downtime. Xavier et al. [49] conducted experiments to compare the performance of container-based systems alone. Containers have also been analyzed in high performance computing environments [26, 41, 50]. Felter et al. [35] conducted an experiment in which KVM was compared to Docker by stressing CPU, memory, networking and storage resources. The authors assumed that the two platforms provide similar performance to other platforms of the same type. Soltesz et al. [44] compared performance and relative scalability of the Linux-VServer environment to the XEN environment. Morabito et al. [40] compared the performance of hypervisor based virtualization and containers. Xavier et al. [50] compared the performance isolation of Xen to OS-based systems including Linux VServer, OpenVZ and Linux Containers (LXC). Sharma et al. [43] evaluated the effects of performance interference and overcommitment on the LXC and the KVM platforms.

All these works provide partial insight but lack comparative analysis encompassing performance, resource usage, and power consumption overheads, as well as isolation, over-commitment, start-up and density for multiple H-based and OS-based virtualization platforms using a diverse set of workloads. Hence, this paper provides an updated, thorough, and formal evaluation of different virtualization techniques to bridges gaps in previous evaluations and guide resource allocation decision.

6 CONCLUSION

H-based (hypervisor) and OS-based (container) virtualization are both used extensively in cloud data centers. Virtualization solutions need to be regularly reevaluated to better understand the trade-off provided by technological advances. This paper presents a thorough investigation of four virtualization platforms that are widely used. The analysis focuses on the most important cloud resource management dimensions, namely performance, isolation, over-commitment, efficiency of power and resource usage, provisioning times, and density to understand the current state of the technology. Our study is relevant to infrastructure providers seeking to improve resource, power usage, and/or facilitate deployment, to developers seeking to select the best solution for their needs, and to scholars to illustrate how these technologies evolved over time.

Our results show that no single system provide optimal results with respect to every criterion considered in this work, but that there are trade-offs. The higher density of OS-based virtualization makes it possible to minimize the total number of servers needed to run a given set of applications, making the system more energy efficient. However, this comes at the cost of reduced isolation and greater cross-platform challenges. Consequently, OS-based virtualization is appropriate in cases where multiple copies of specific applications are to be run. This is particularly convenient for cloud providers that run their own services and/or for applications that lack strict performance requirements (e.g. batch workloads). If the aim is to run multiple applications on servers (i.e. to operate a multi-tenancy environment) and/or to have a wide variety of OS, H-based virtualization is preferred. This is especially important when security is a major priority because VMs provide more robust isolation from untrusted co-located VMs.

Some of the shortcomings of each platform can be addressed using existing techniques. It is important to understand the capabilities and techniques available for a given platform as well as the characteristics of workloads to optimize systems. For example, it may be possible to alleviate the security issues associated with containers by extending existing security policies (e.g., anti-colocation constraints) rather than completely redesigning them and also to reduce the overhead of VMs by optimizing start-up performance and memory footprint. Overhead could be reduced by employing techniques such as CPU pinning and scheduling techniques, by sharing memory pages (KSM), by selecting appropriate image formats, by modifying storage allocations and/or network drivers. Another way to address shortfalls is to combine the best characteristics of multiple platforms into a single architecture. Hybrid systems formed in this way offer promising solutions that combine the isolation and compatibility benefits of H-based systems with the easy provisioning and deployment speed of OS-based systems.

In the near future, we hope to expand this work by including an analysis of hybrid solutions that nest containers in VMs. We also aim to extend the comparison to include unikernels, which offer greater security and efficiency than traditional operating systems. We are also hoping that our work inspires developers to further push the envelop of what is technically achievable and further reduce the gap between the two types of virtualization technologies.

REFERENCES

[1] Dec 2016. KVM [online]. (Dec 2016). https://www.linux-kvm.org/page/Main_Page.
[2] Feb 2016. STREAM Benchmark [online]. (Feb 2016). http://www.cs.virginia.edu/stream/.
[3] Feb 2017. Bonnie++ [online]. (Feb 2017). http://www.coker.com.au/bonnie++/.
[4] Jan 2015. Optimizing memory bandwidth on stream triad [online]. (Jan 2015). https://software.intel.com/en-us/articles/optimizing-memory-bandwidth-on-stream-triad.
[5] Jan 2017. Google containers [online]. (Jan 2017). https://cloudplatform.googleblog.com/2014/06/an-update-on-container-support-on-google-cloud-platform.html.
[6] June 2015. Mesos [online]. (June 2015). http://mesos.apache.org.
[7] June 2016. Window container [online]. (June 2016). https://docs.microsoft.com/en-us/virtualization/windowscontainers/index.
[8] March 2014. YARN [online]. (March 2014). https://www.ibm.com/developerworks/library/bd-yarn-intro/.
[9] March 2015. Bootchart [online]. (March 2015). http://www.bootchart.org.
[10] March 2016. Fio Benchmark [online]. (March 2016). https://github.com/axboe/fio.
[11] March 2017. Blogbench [online]. (March 2017). https://www.pureftpd.org/project/blogbench.
[12] March 2017. Isolation Benchmark Suite (IBS) [online]. (March 2017). http://web2.clarkson.edu/class/cs644/isolation.
[13] March 2017. MallocBomb [online]. (March 2017). http://web2.clarkson.edu/class/cs644/isolation/download.html.
[14] May 2015. Sysbench [online]. (May 2015). https://www.howtoforge.com/how-to-benchmark-your-system-cpu-file-io-mysql-with-sysbench.
[15] Nov 2015. Openstack [online]. (Nov 2015). https://www.openstack.org/.
[16] Nov 2016. Docker [online]. (Nov 2016). https://www.docker.com/.
[17] Nov 2016. Linux VServer [online]. (Nov 2016). http://linux-vserver.org/Welcome_to_Linux-VServer.org.
[18] Nov 2016. Lookbusy:A synthetic load generator [online]. (Nov 2016). http://www.devin.com/lookbusy/.
[19] Nov 2016. LXC [online]. (Nov 2016). https://linuxcontainers.org/.
[20] Nov 2016. Memtester:Memory-stresser benchmark [online]. (Nov 2016). https://linux.die.net/man/8/memtester.
[21] Nov 2016. OpenVZ [online]. (Nov 2016). https://openvz.org/Main_Page.
[22] Nov 2016. Rocket Container [online]. (Nov 2016). https://coreos.com/rkt.
[23] Nov 2016. RSS:Resident set size [online]. (Nov 2016). http://www.unixlore.net/articles/quick-easy-way-monitor-process-memory-usage.html.
[24] Nov 2016. Type1vsType2 [online]. (Nov 2016). http://searchservervirtualization.techtarget.com/news/2240034817/KVM-reignites-Type-1-vs-Type-2-hypervisor-debate.
[25] Sep 2017. Kubernetes 1.8 [online]. (Sep 2017). https://www.mirantis.com/blog/expect-kubernetes-1-8/.
[26] T. Adufu, J. Choi, and Y. Kim. 2015. Is container-based technology a winner for high performance scientific applications?. In *17th Asia-Pacific Network Operations and Management Symposium (APNOMS)*. 507–510.
[27] K. Agarwal, B. Jain, and D. E. Porter. 2015. Containing the hype. In *The 6th Asia-Pacific Workshop on Systems*. 8.
[28] P. Barham, B. Dragovic, K. Fraser, S. Hand, T. Harris, A. Ho, R. Neugebauer, I. Pratt, and A. Warfield. 2003. Xen and the Art of Virtualization. *SIGOPS Oper. Syst. Rev.* 37, 5 (Oct. 2003), 164–177.
[29] D. Bernstein. 2014. Containers and cloud: From LXC to Docker to kubernetes. *IEEE Cloud Computing* 1, 3 (2014), 81–84.
[30] L. Chen, S. Patel, H. Shen, and Z. Zhou. 2015. Profiling and understanding virtualization overhead in cloud. In *ICPP*. 31–40.
[31] L. Cherkasova, D. Gupta, and A. Vahdat. 2007. Comparison of the three CPU schedulers in Xen. *SIGMETRICS Perform. Eval. Rev.* 35, 2 (2007), 42–51.
[32] C. Delimitrou and C. Kozyrakis. 2013. ibench: Quantifying interference for datacenter applications. In *Workload Characterization (IISWC)*. 23–33.
[33] C. Delimitrou and C. Kozyrakis. 2014. Quasar: resource-efficient and QoS-aware cluster management. In *ACM SIGPLAN Notices*, Vol. 49. 127–144.
[34] Z. J. Estrada, Z. Stephens, C. Pham, Z. Kalbarczyk, and R. K. Iyer. 2014. A performance evaluation of sequence alignment software in virtualized environments. In *CCGrid*. 730–737.
[35] W. Felter, A. Ferreira, R. Rajamony, and J. Rubio. 2015. An updated performance comparison of virtual machines and linux containers. In *ISPASS*. 171–172.
[36] Y. Gao, H. Guan, Z. Qi, B. Wang, and L. Liu. 2013. Quality of service aware power management for virtualized data centers. *JSA* 59, 4 (2013), 245–259.
[37] C. D. Graziano. 2011. A performance analysis of Xen and KVM hypervisors for hosting the Xen Worlds Project. (2011).
[38] R. Jones et al. 1996. NetPerf: a network performance benchmark. *Information Networks Division, Hewlett-Packard Company* (1996).
[39] P.H. Kamp and R. NM. Watson. 2000. Jails: Confining the omnipotent root. In *The 2nd International SANE Conference*, Vol. 43. 116.
[40] R. Morabito, J. Kjällman, and M. Komu. 2015. Hypervisors vs. lightweight virtualization: a performance comparison. In *IC2E*. 386–393.
[41] C. Ruiz, E. Jeanvoine, and L. Nussbaum. 2015. Performance evaluation of containers for HPC. In *VHPC*. 12.
[42] R. Schöne, D. Hackenberg, and D. Molka. 2012. Memory Performance at Reduced CPU Clock Speeds: An Analysis of Current x86_64 Processors. *HotPower* 12.
[43] P. Sharma, L. Chaufournier, P. J Shenoy, and YC Tay. 2016. Containers and Virtual Machines at Scale: A Comparative Study. In *Middleware*. 1–1.
[44] S. Soltesz, H. Pötzl, M. E. Fiuczynski, A. Bavier, and L. Peterson. 2007. Container-based operating system virtualization: a scalable, high-performance alternative to hypervisors. In *ACM SIGOPS Operating Systems Review*, Vol. 41. 275–287.
[45] V. Spiliopoulos, S. Kaxiras, and G. Keramidas. 2011. Green governors: A framework for continuously adaptive DVFS. In *GCC*. 1–8.
[46] I. Tafa, E. Zanaj, E. Kajo, A. Bejleri, and A. Xhuvani. 2011. The comparison of virtual machine migration performance between xen-hvm, xen-pv, open-vz, kvm-fv, kvm-pv. *IJCSMS Int. J. Comput. Sci.: Manag. Stud* 11, 2 (2011), 65–75.
[47] S.K. Tesfatsion, L. Tomás, and J. Tordsson. 2017. OptiBook: Optimal resource booking for energy-efficient datacenters. In *IWQoS*.
[48] S.K. Tesfatsion, E. Wadbro, and J. Tordsson. 2016. Autonomic Resource Management for Optimized Power and Performance in Multi-tenant Clouds. In *ICAC*.
[49] M. G. Xavier, M. V. Neves, and C. A. F. De Rose. 2014. A performance comparison of container-based virtualization systems for mapreduce clusters. In *PDP*.
[50] M. G Xavier, M. V. Neves, F. D Rossi, T. C Ferreto, T. Lange, and C. AF De Rose. 2013. Performance evaluation of container-based virtualization for high performance computing environments. In *PDP*. IEEE, 233–240.
[51] J. Zhi. 2015. Literature Survey on Virtual Machine Performance Isolation. (2015).

Investigating Performance Metrics for Scaling Microservices in CloudIoT-Environments

Manuel Gotin
Robert Bosch GmbH
Renningen, Germany
manuel.gotin@de.bosch.com

Felix Lösch
Robert Bosch GmbH
Renningen, Germany
felix.loesch@de.bosch.com

Robert Heinrich
Karlsruhe Institute of Technology
Karlsruhe, Germany
robert.heinrich@kit.edu

Ralf Reussner
Karlsruhe Institute of Technology
Karlsruhe, Germany
ralf.reussner@kit.edu

ABSTRACT

A CloudIoT solution typically connects thousands of IoT things with cloud applications in order to store or process sensor data. In this environment, the cloud applications often consist of microservices which are connected to each other via message queues and must reliably handle a large number of messages produced by the IoT things. The state of a message queue in such a system can be a challenge if the rate of incoming messages continuously exceeds the rate of outgoing messages. This can lead to performance and reliability degradations due to overloaded queues and result in the unavailability of the cloud application.

In this paper we present a case study to investigate which performance metrics to be used by a threshold-based auto-scaler for scaling consuming microservices of a message queue in order to prevent overloaded queues and to avoid SLA violations. We evaluate the suitability of each metric for scaling I/O-intensive and compute-intensive microservices with constant and varying characteristics, such as service time. We show, that scaling decisions based on message queue metrics are much more resilient to microservice characteristics variations. In this case, relying on the CPU utilization may result in massive overprovisioning or no scaling decision at all which could lead to an overloaded queue and SLA violations. We underline the benefits of using message queue metrics for scaling decisions instead of the more traditional CPU utilization particularly for I/O-intensive microservices due to the vulnerability to variations in the microservice characteristics.

CCS CONCEPTS

• **Computer systems organization** → **Cloud computing**; • **Software and its engineering** → *Software performance*; *Software reliability*;

KEYWORDS

Cloud Computing, Internet of Things (IoT), Microservices, Message Queues, Performance Metrics, Auto-Scaler, Threshold-based rules, Performance

ACM Reference Format:
Manuel Gotin, Felix Lösch, Robert Heinrich, and Ralf Reussner. 2018. Investigating Performance Metrics for Scaling Microservices in CloudIoT-Environments. In *ICPE '18: ACM/SPEC International Conference on Performance Engineering, April 9–13, 2018, Berlin, Germany.* ACM, New York, NY, USA, 11 pages. https://doi.org/10.1145/3184407.3184430

1 INTRODUCTION

The uprising CloudIoT paradigm addresses the limitations of IoT by merging it with a cloud infrastructure to provide virtually unlimited computational and storage capabilities [4]. Bosch offers with the Bosch IoT Suite a Platform-as-a-Service (PaaS) to provide a toolbox to quickly build IoT applications and deploy them on the Bosch IoT Cloud which is based on Pivotal CloudFoundry. A common usage scenario in this environment is Sensing-as-a-Service (SaaS) which describes the process of making sensor data available to clients and applications over the cloud infrastructure [20]. Sensor data arise from a range of domains like mobility to smart home and result in a huge amount of data to be processed and stored on the cloud.

In recent years the focus in software industry has shifted from monolithic architectures to the microservice architectural style [2]. This architectural style allows to leverage the capabilities of cloud computing in terms of scalability and maintainability. Whereas traditional applications exhibit a monolithic architecture which tends to put multiple functionality into a single process the microservice architectural style separates functionalities into self-contained services. Breaking down software to loosely coupled and highly cohesive modules offers multiple benefits in terms of flexibility and evolvability [7]. By supporting scaling operations on a fine-granular level infrastructure costs can be reduced up to 70 % compared to a traditional monolithic architecture [25].

Microservices are typically connected to each other via a lightweight communication protocol, most commonly REST or message queues [9]. In this paper we focus on the communication via message queues provided by a message broker system. There are many message broker systems which differ in their mechanism and feature set and a short survey describing the most popular message broker systems can be found in [13]. The state of a message queue

ICPE '18, April 9–13, 2018, Berlin, Germany
© 2018 Association for Computing Machinery.
ACM ISBN 978-1-4503-5095-2/18/04...$15.00
https://doi.org/10.1145/3184407.3184430

can be a challenge in such a system if the rate of incoming messages continuously exceeds the rate of outgoing messages eventually resulting in performance and reliability degradations. Due to the accumulation of messages in the queue these issues can persist even after the rate of incoming and outgoing messages is in balance again. This underlines the need to reflect the message queue state in scaling decisions.

The Bosch IoT Cloud offers a built-in threshold-based auto-scaling mechanism to scale microservices in and out based on the CPU utilization, HTTP latency or HTTP throughput. In this paper we investigate the suitability of the CPU utilization for scaling microservices which are consuming messages from a message queue. Furthermore we investigate which information of the state of the message queue is suitable for scaling consuming microservices. We focus on two classes of microservices: I/O-intensive and compute-intensive. In the first class the time of processing a task is determined by waiting for I/O-operations to be completed whereas in the second class it is determined by the computation power. We investigate the suitability of each metric to cope with the challenges in this environment using a threshold-based rules auto-scaling setup. This allows us to use a single performance metric and compare it to other metrics in coping with the challenges in respect to each microservice class. Subsequently we explore the vulnerability of each metric to variations in the microservice characteristics.

The remainder of this paper is organized as follows: Section 2 describes a running example which serves as a CloudIoT application for the pre-processing and storing part of a SaaS use case. Section 3 explores the challenges in scaling consuming microservices. The case study in section 4 evaluates the suitability of each performance metric using a threshold-based auto-scaling system. Section 5 gives a brief overview of related work. Section 6 concludes the results extracted from the case study.

2 RUNNING EXAMPLE

One of the most common usage scenarios of the Bosch IoT Suite is SaaS in the areas of mobility, industry 4.0 or smart home. The main idea is to store data from things on the cloud and make it available to clients and applications.

In the running example we examine the pre-processing and storing of sensor data on the cloud. Such a system needs to cope with a high amount of data. An architecture to support this use case was proposed by Cecchinel et al. [5]. In order to allow a more fine-granular scaling we refine the proposed architecture. Instead of processing and persisting sensor data within a single service we propose a dedicated service for each of these functionalities to be more in line with the microservice architectural style. The services are connected to each other via message queues provided by a message broker system. By using message queues consuming and producing services are decoupled from each other and communication is asynchronous. Figure 1 illustrates the components in this architecture.

Components – The **Connection Service** serves as a gateway for connecting IoT things with the cloud. Typically it retrieves sensor data via a lightweight communication protocol, e. g. REST or MQTT. This sensor data is then enqueued in a message queue. As a consuming service the **Data Processing Service** retrieves messages

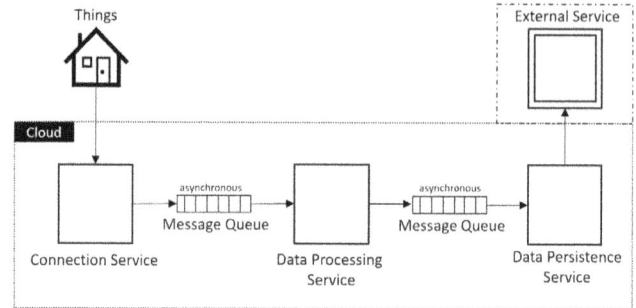

Figure 1: Illustration of the running example.

from this queue and pre-processes them. Pre-processed messages are enqueued towards the **Data Persistence Service**. This service retrieves processed messages and stores them by communicating with an **External Service**, i. e. a database management system via a RESTful API.

Constraints – Communication with the external service is synchronous. To avoid losing sensor data, a consuming service must acknowledge a message as processed before the message queue releases it. In case of a service failure an unacknowledged message can be retransmitted to a healthy service instance.

Microservice classes – We classify the **Data Processing Service** as a compute-intensive microservice, since the processing of messages is in this example a mainly CPU-bound operation. We classify the **Data Persistence Service** as an I/O-intensive microservice since the time for processing a message is determined by communicating with the external service.

Environment – We deploy the running example on the Bosch IoT Cloud which is based on Pivotal CloudFoundry. CloudFoundry abstracts the underlying infrastructure and offers an interface to deploy and manage applications with a customizable runtime environment. For this reason an application developer scales application instances instead of virtual machines. In our environment an application instance of a lightweight microservice – like these in the running example – is provisioned in less than one minute. Furthermore CloudFoundry offers self-healing capabilities by discovering runtime failures of application instances and restarting them. As a message broker system we use Pivotal RabbitMQ. It is an implementation of the AMQP protocol which was initially designed for financial transactions thus aiming for reliability and scalability. In the most common scenario RabbitMQ enqueues and dequeues messages in a first-come, first-served (FCFS) manner [1].

3 CHALLENGES IN SCALING CONSUMING MICROSERVICES

In this section we address specific challenges for scaling microservices consuming messages from message queues. The challenges are motivated by issues we experienced on the messaging middleware caused by an accumulation of messages in message queues due to underprovisioned microservices on the consuming side.

Let q be a queue, l the number of messages in the queue, p the production rate and c the consumption rate. Let the service policy of q be first-come, first-served (FCFS). This queue is illustrated in Figure 2.

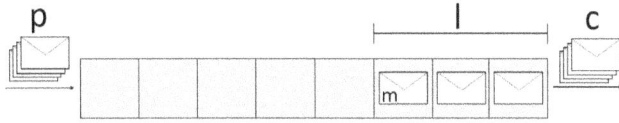

Figure 2: Illustration of a message queue.

There are three basic states for a queue q based on the growth $\Delta l = p - c$:

- **Steady**: A queue q is in a steady state if $\Delta l = 0$
- **Filling**: A queue q is in a filling state if $\Delta l > 0$
- **Draining**: A queue q is in a draining state if $\Delta l < 0$

A filling state leads to the accumulation of messages in the queue. Since the policy is FCFS they induce a delay on application-layer caused by a wait time for each message in the queue. Let $t_q(m)$ be the delay for a message m to pass through a queue q and T_{max} the maximal desired delay, e. g. derived using the applications SLA. Let L_{max} be the maximal length of a queue q the message broker system is able to cope with. We define the following conditions:

- **Congested**: A queue q is considered as congested if $t_q(m) > T_{max}$
- **Flooded**: A queue q is considered as flooded if $l > L_{max}$

A congested queue degrades the performance on application-layer since each message experiences a delay. In a flooded state a message broker system may try to stabilize the queue by blocking and unblocking the connection to keep the rate of incoming messages at a level the consumers can handle. In RabbitMQ this behavior is called **flow control mode**. On application-layer a flooded queue induces like a congested queue a delay but furthermore leads to a degradation of reliability by rejecting messages. A congested or flooded queue may remain after a queue has been stabilized from a filling state to a steady state. For this reason we identify the following challenge:

- **Challenge I** – Recover or avoid flooded or congested queues.

The underlying issue of a congested or flooded queue is based on the provisioning of consuming microservices. Underprovisioned microservices lead to a filling queue state since the consumption rate is lower than the production rate. For this reason it eventually transits to a congested or flooded state inducing a performance degradation on application-layer and may result in reliability issues such as a rejection of messages. Overprovisioned microservices have a low utilization but do not degrade the message queue state since the consumption rate exceeds the production rate. However, due to the typical pay-as-you-go cost model, each provisioned resource increases the operating costs.

Since the microservices are consuming messages from the message queue, information about the state of the message queue could be beneficial if utilized for scaling decisions. For this reason we identify the following challenges regarding microservices in respect to the message queue:

- **Challenge II** – How to utilize informations of the state of the message queue to prevent underprovisioning of consuming microservices?
- **Challenge III** – How to utilize informations of the state of the message queue to prevent overprovisioning of consuming microservices?

4 CASE STUDY

The rationale of this case study is to investigate the suitability of a set of performance metrics in a threshold-based rules auto-scaling setup for different microservices classes to cope with the challenges which were mentioned in section 3. Furthermore we investigate how vulnerable an auto-scaling system is to variations in the microservice characteristics in terms of elasticity and the message queues state in respect to each performance metric.

Threshold-based rules auto-scaling. This class of auto-scaling is one of the most common strategies to address under- and overprovisioning in cloud environments. It exhibits a widespread use in industry due to the simplicity and high availability among commercial cloud providers like Amazon EC2. Rules in this context consist of a condition and an action to be executed. Usually they define a lower and upper threshold for a performance metric. If the current value of the metric exceeds a threshold, the auto-scaling systems scales application instances in or out. The quality of scaling decisions of an auto-scaling systems can be evaluated via its elasticity. Elasticity in this context describes the degree to which a system is able to adapt to workload changes by provisioning and de-provisioning resources [12].

Performance metrics. A set of performance metrics for scaling decisions is listed in the survey [15]. The internal state of the message broker system poses a challenge in the running example. For this reason we want to compare the suitability of relying directly on message queue metrics for scaling decisions instead of the traditional CPU metric. Many message brokers such as RabbitMQ support the monitoring of queue-specific metrics like arrival rate (ingress), departure rate (egress) and queue length. In order to approximate the queueing delay we measure the end-to-end latency between message transmission and receiving in a consuming microservice. Arrival rate and departure rate are conceptually not viable for scaling decisions in a threshold-based rules auto-scaling setup. For example: the arrival rate is not influenced by scaling decision thus offers no feedback. For this reason we investigate the queue growth which includes both metrics. The following list gives an overview over the set of investigated metrics:

- **Microservice – CPU:** The average CPU utilization is a popular proxy of the current systems workload.
- **Message Queue – Length:** The queue length describes the number of enqueued messages.
- **Message Queue – Growth:** The queue growth is the difference between arrival and departure rate thus describing the current growth in the queue.
- **Message Queue - Delay:** The queueing delay describes the wait time for a message in the queue before being processed.

4.1 Research Questions

We propose the following research questions to address the suitability of performance metrics to represent the systems workloads in a manner which allows an auto-scaling system to cope with the described challenges:

- **RQ1** – What degree of elasticity achieves a threshold-based rules auto-scaling system for each performance metric and each microservice class?
- **RQ2** – How suitable is such an auto-scaling system in avoiding a congested or flooded message queue?

In a dynamic environment like CloudIoT changes or variations in the characteristics of microservices can be expected. For example: the I/O-intensive microservice exhibits a dependency to an external service, how does an already configured auto-scaling system cope with changed external service times? How well does an already configured auto-scaling system cope with variations of the compute-intensive tasks?

- **RQ3** – How vulnerable is a configured threshold to variations in the microservice characteristics for each microservice class in respect to the auto-scalers elasticity?
- **RQ4** – How vulnerable is a configured threshold to variations in the microservice characteristics for each microservice class in respect to avoiding a congested or flooded message queue?

4.2 Methodology

We use a synthetic setup with a threshold-based rules auto-scaling system to perform horizontal scaling operations based on a single performance metric for different microservice classes which are described in the running example in section 2. In this synthetic setup we can directly set the characteristics of the external service and the configuration of the internal services. In order to evaluate each metric for the specific microservice class we investigate the auto-scaling system as a whole since it relies on the metric and its thresholds to trigger actions. To answer the research questions we need to evaluate the elasticity of the auto-scaler and the state of the message queue.

Evaluate scaling decisions. In order to qualify elastic adaptations we apply the elastic speedup measure proposed by SPEC RG Cloud [11]. The elastic speedup measure reflects the difference between supplied and demanded resources within the measurement period regarding timing and accuracy aspects. Whereas the timing aspects are expressed by the share of time in an under- or overprovisioned state the accuracy describes the absolute deviation of each state in respect to the demanded resources. Both aspects are normalized over the measurement period and each aspect is aggregated to a single *accuracy* and *timeshare* metric using a custom weight for under- and overprovisioning. The elastic speedup measure is based on a speedup vector s_k for a benchmarked platform k. The speedup vector s_k is computed with the accuracy and timing aspects of the benchmarked platform k and a baseline platform *base*:

$$s_k = (\frac{accuracy_{base}}{accuracy_k}, \frac{timeshare_{base}}{timeshare_k}) = (accuracy, timeshare)$$

The elastic speedup measure for a benchmarked platform k is the geometric mean of its speedup vector s_k:

$$elasticspeedupmeasure = \sqrt{s_{k_{accuracy}} + s_{k_{timeshare}}}$$

In our test setup we weight all metrics equally. To obtain the baseline metrics we execute a configured workload on the system using no auto-scaling system. The baseline is used to compute the elastic speedup measure for each configuration of the auto-scaling system in identical workload setups. In this paper we refer to the elastic speedup measure as the elasticity score.

Evaluate queue state. In order to evaluate the suitability of avoiding a flooded or congested message queue we compare the average queue length for each setup run. A queue length aiming towards zero indicates that the auto-scaling mechanism based on the performance metric is suitable to avoid a flooded or congested queue.

Threshold optimization. Threshold-based rules auto-scaling systems rely on an upper and lower threshold for deciding scaling operations. The performance of a threshold-based auto-scaling system depends on the configured threshold. An application developer has degrees of freedom to configure the thresholds to achieve a specific goal regarding reaction speed, costs or performance. We optimize the thresholds for each metric with a heuristic algorithm using the achieved elasticity as fitness function to capture the accuracy and timing aspects of scaling decisions. By optimizing the thresholds for each performance metric we can compare them to each other. The concrete steps for the compute-intensive and I/O-intensive microservices are as follows:

(1) Configure the microservice characteristics for a specific setup.
(2) Configure the workload and execute it on the system without using an auto-scaler to define the baseline score.
(3) For each metric approximate the optimal threshold constellation. In this phase we apply differential evolution (DE) as a heuristic to find the global minima [23]. As fitness function we use the elasticity score.
(4) Compare the results of each optimal threshold metric run in order to quantify the suitability of each metric.

Variations in microservice characteristics. To address research question 3 and 4 we configure the characteristics of each microservice class. For the compute-intensive microservice we variate the computational operation to require more or less processing steps in order to simulate a change in task. For the I/O-intensive microservice we vary the service time of the external service ST_{ext} and investigate the influence of the transferred payload N_{data}.

4.2.1 Auto-Scaling system. The setup of the auto-scaling system is illustrated in Figure 3. The scaling system monitors a single microservice and uses the CPU or message queue metrics as underlying performance metrics for scaling decisions. In this setup we scale application instances in and out (horizontal scaling). After a scaling decision the system enters a cooldown-period which ends after the scaling decision has actually an impact, i. e. the scaled application instance is destroyed or ready, which occurs usually within 20-40 seconds.

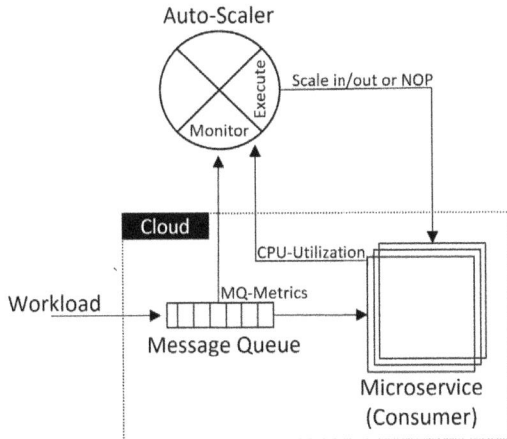

Figure 3: Illustration of the threshold-based rules auto-scaling system

Metric	Threshold	Avg. Q.-Length	Score
CPU	60 / 100 [%]	1.76 [msg]	305.94
Queue Delay	0.75 / 1.25 [sec]	3.17 [msg]	259.13
Queue Growth	0 / 1 [msgs/sec]	95.96 [msg]	247.16
Queue Length	0 / 10 [msgs]	8.41 [msg]	221.01
Baseline	- / -	-	100

Table 1: Elasticity score for each performance metric adapting the compute-intensive microservice

The workload consists of three phases to observe the systems behavior for an increasing, steady and decreasing workload intensity. We send a total of 4000 messages over a duration of 10 minutes. We configure both microservices to process a message in circa 400 ms.

4.3 Results

In the first test setup we optimize the thresholds of each performance metric for a specific microservice characteristic.

Compute-intensive microservice. Table 1 shows the ranking of each metric in respect to the elasticity score and also shows the average queue length in order to address the second research question. Figure 4 shows the adaptation behavior of each scaling system in respect to the demanded and supplied number of application instances.

The CPU-metric achieves a substantially high ranking by exhibiting a stable and accurate behavior. Message queue metrics are inferior by having a high number of adaptations which increases the non-ideal timeshare and inaccuracy. All metrics except queue growth tend to have an empty queue, indicating that they are suitable to cope with the challenges of a message broker system.

I/O-intensive Microservice. In the next setup we investigate the achieved elasticity for each performance metric to scale an I/O-intensive microservice. We define as external service time $ST_{ext} = 400ms$ and as transferred payload $N_{data} = 15kB$. Table 2 shows the ranking and Figure 5 the adaptation behavior of each metric.

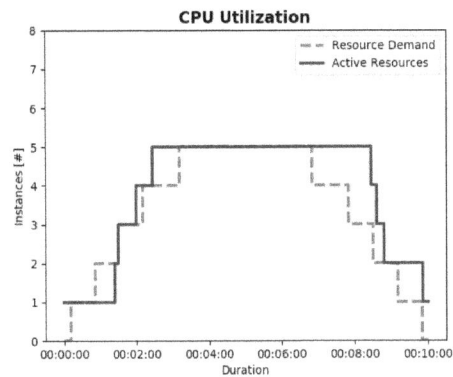

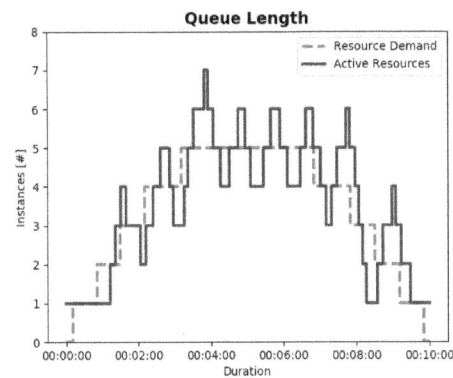

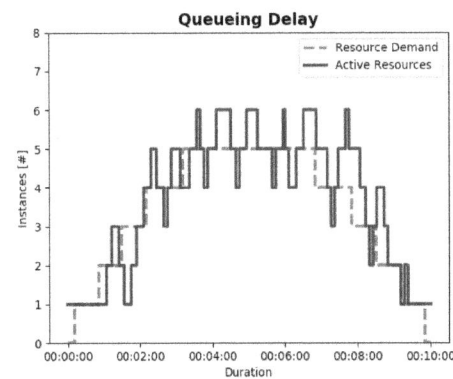

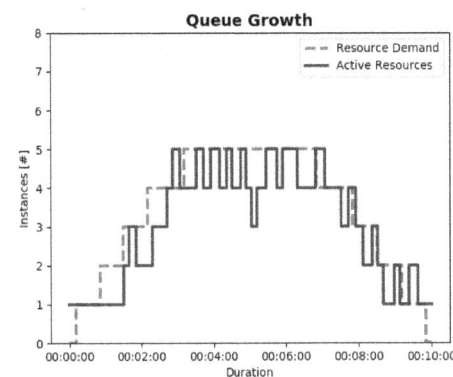

Figure 4: Adaptation behavior of a threshold-based rules auto-scaler for each performance metric in a compute-intensive microservice setup.

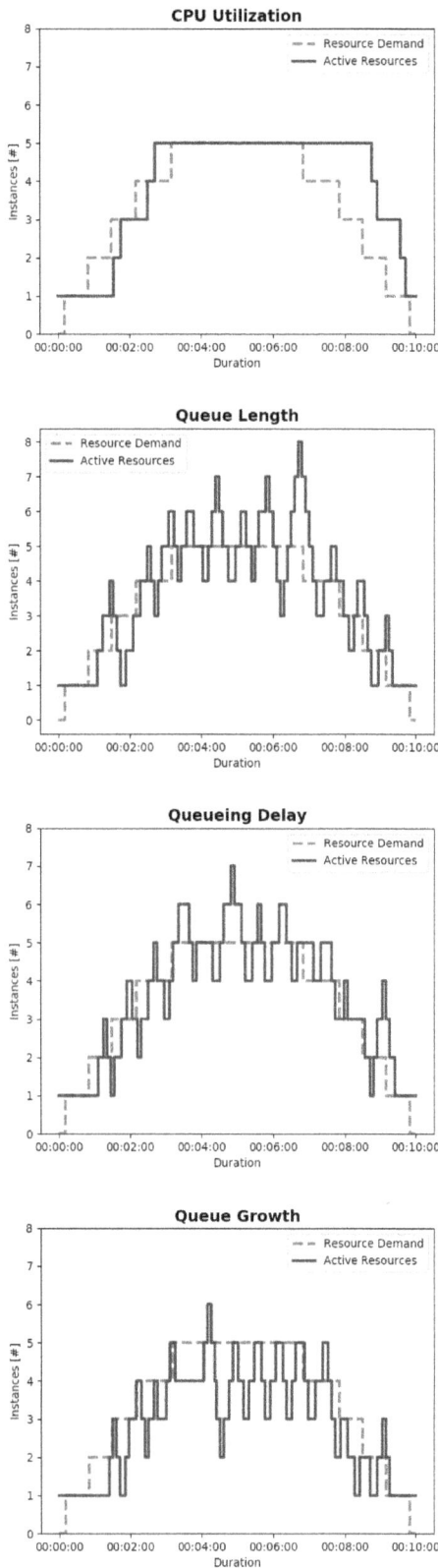

Figure 5: Adaptation behavior of a threshold-based rules auto-scaler for each performance metric in an I/O-intensive microservice setup.

Metric	Threshold	Avg. Q.-Length	Score
Queue Delay	0.75 / 1.25 [sec]	2.89 [msg]	270.78
CPU	0.4 / 0.9 [%]	3.99 [msg]	253.98
Queue Length	0 / 0 [msgs]	4.32 [msg]	228.13
Queue Growth	0 / 1 [msgs/sec]	163.87 [msg]	219.24
Baseline	- / -	-	100

Table 2: Elasticity score for each performance metric adapting the I/O-intensive microservice

The CPU-metric is in this setup a suitable metric. Its threshold is in a narrow and small area induced by waiting for the external service. This renders this metric vulnerable to background processes on the same system. Queueing delay has achieved the highest score but has as the other message queue metrics a high number of adaptations.

Discussion. If the microservices have a constant behavior all metrics are suitable for scaling decisions and exhibit a high score. However, message queue metrics suffer from oscillation which can increase the costs depending on the pricing model. CPU is a suitable proxy to represent the current work on the system in both microservice classes. Queue growth is the only metric which has a high number of messages in the queue. The queue growth metric considers the relation of arrival and departure rate thus aiming to a steady state of the queue. If the queue length is not zero and the arrival rate is zero such a system tends to scale down since it has a negative growth resulting in a slow draining of the accumulated messages in the queue.

To answer the third and fourth research question we vary the service characteristics and observe the behavior of each configured auto-scaling system.

Compute-intensive microservice. To investigate the influence of varying computational time on the performance of a configured threshold-based rules auto-scaling system we vary the computational steps required to process a message. Figure 6 shows the elasticity score and Figure 7 the average queue length.

With decreasing computation time the throughput of the microservice increases. For this reason the resource demand can be so small that no scaling operation is required and the baseline exhibits an ideal provisioning. Therefore the score of each metric is approximating the baseline score. With increasing computation time the difference between baseline – with a potentially massive underprovisioning – and scaling operations based on the performance metrics is more prominent leading to a generally higher score.

The elasticity score is heavily influenced by the computation time but is in nearly all the cases above the baseline score. The length of the message queue is stable in all cases, coping with the challenge of a flooded queue.

I/O-intensive Microservice. We address research questions 3 and 4 by varying the service time of the external service in a range of $0ms - 1200ms$. The thresholds for each metric were optimized for an external service time of $400ms$. Figure 8 shows the ranking of each metric in dependency to the external service time and Figure 9 the average queue length.

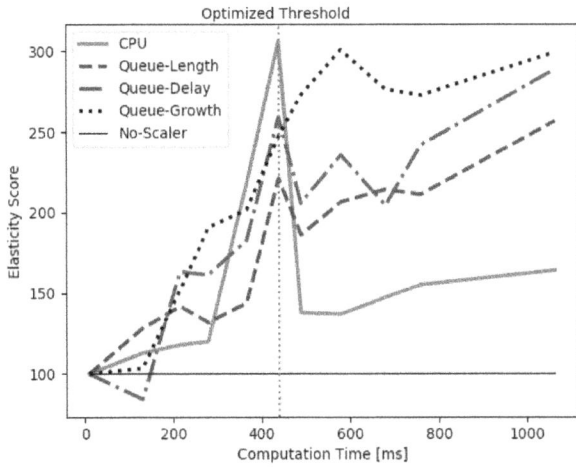

Figure 6: Elasticity for each performance metric with optimized thresholds for varying computational service time of a compute-intensive microservice.

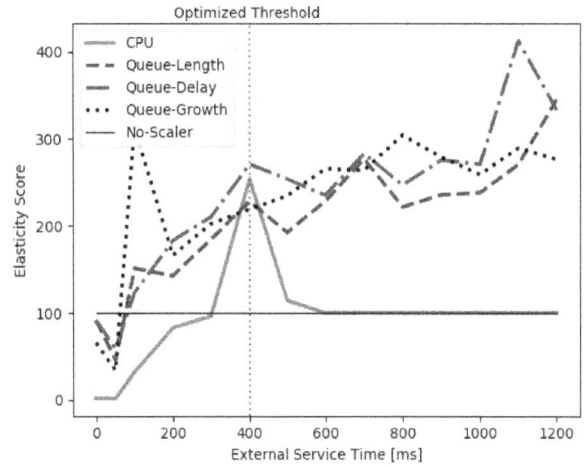

Figure 8: Elasticity for each performance metric with optimized thresholds for a specific external service time setup of an I/O-intensive microservice.

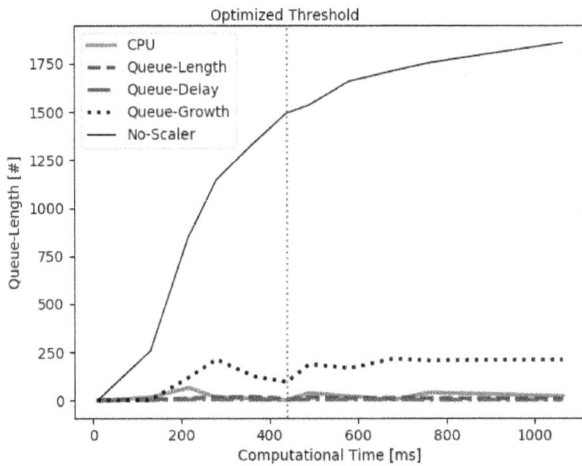

Figure 7: Average queue length for each performance metric with optimized thresholds for varying computational service time of a compute-intensive microservice.

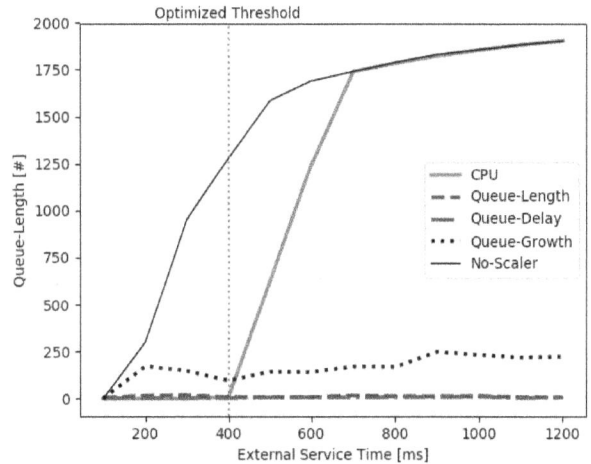

Figure 9: Average queue length for each performance metric with optimized thresholds for a specific external service time setup of an I/O-intensive microservice.

The CPU utilization is sensitive to changes of the external service time. The underlying issue is the strong influence of the external service time on the microservices CPU utilization. We observe that with an increasing external service time the CPU utilization decreases and with a decreasing external service time it increases. For this reason the auto-scaling system will scale out with a decreasing external service time even though the throughput of the microservice is increased. With an increasing external service time the auto-scaling system scales in even though the throughput of the microservice is degraded. Whereas the first case leads to high costs,

the second case leads eventually to a flooded queue thus degrading both performance and reliability.

Discussion. This set of experiments has shown that the CPU is sensitive to changes in the external service characteristics and shows a significantly worse behavior than relying on message queue metrics. Thresholds for message queue metrics are much more resistant to changes in microservice characteristics. For this reason we underline the benefits on relying on message queue metrics for I/O-intensive microservices instead of the traditional CPU metric. However, if the microservices have a constant behavior the CPU is more suitable due its capability to proxy the work on the system.

4.4 Discussion

In this section we investigate the influence of the external service time and the transferred payload on the microservices CPU utilization in order to understand the results of the previous section.

The I/O-intensive microservice of the running example communicates with the external service via the lightweight REST-protocol in a synchronous manner. The previous evaluation has already revealed an intense influence on the CPU utilization and throughput of a microservice in dependency to the characteristics of the external service. We assume that the response time for a single request is driven by the external service time ST_{ext}, the internal service time ST_{int} and the transfer time $T_{transfer}$. Thus leading to the following throughput model in a fully utilized service:

$$X = \frac{1}{ST_{ext} + ST_{int} + T_{transfer}}$$

The average CPU utilization U_{CPU} is the fraction of the CPU busy time T_{CPU} to the average response time $T_{response} = \frac{1}{X}$:

$$U_{CPU} = 100 * \frac{T_{CPU}}{T_{response}}$$

To simplify the relation between CPU and data transfer let λ be a factor of the transfer time $T_{transfer}$ to describe a linear influence on the CPU time such as $T_{CPU} = T_{BaseCPU} + \lambda * T_{transfer}$.

The transfer time $T_{transfer}$ is influenced by the transfer rate v such as $T_{transfer}(N_{data}) = \frac{N_{data}}{v}$ This leads to the final model for the throughput X and CPU utilization U_{CPU}:

$$X(ST_{ext}, N_{data}) = \frac{1}{ST_{ext} + ST_{int} + T_{transfer}(N_{data})}$$

$$U_{CPU}(ST_{ext}, N_{data}) = 100 * \frac{T_{BaseCPU} + \lambda * T_{transfer}(N_{data})}{T_{response}}$$

To parameterize this analytical model we perform two measurements with $ST_{ext} = 1ms$ and $N_{data} = [1Byte, 10MByte]$ for the sending and receiving scenario. In the first case we neglect the influence of data transfer to retrieve the base service time ST_{int} and base CPU time $T_{BaseCPU}$ per request. In the second case we calculate the transfer speed and can derive the factor λ for the CPU utilization. We solve this formula analytically to predict the CPU utilization and throughput in dependency to the external service time and the transferred payload. The measurements and prediction results for the receiving scenario are shown in Figure 10, 12 and for the sending scenario in Figure 11, 13. The dashed line shows the predicted value whereas the solid line shows the measured values.

The model has a relative error in predicting the CPU utilization of 22.0 % in the sending scenario and 21.6 % in the receiving. The relative error of the throughput is 5.2 % and 3.9 %, respectively. We assume that the relative high error of predicting the CPU utilization is caused by modeling a linear relationship between CPU utilization and transfer time since the prediction is much more precise for variations in service time.

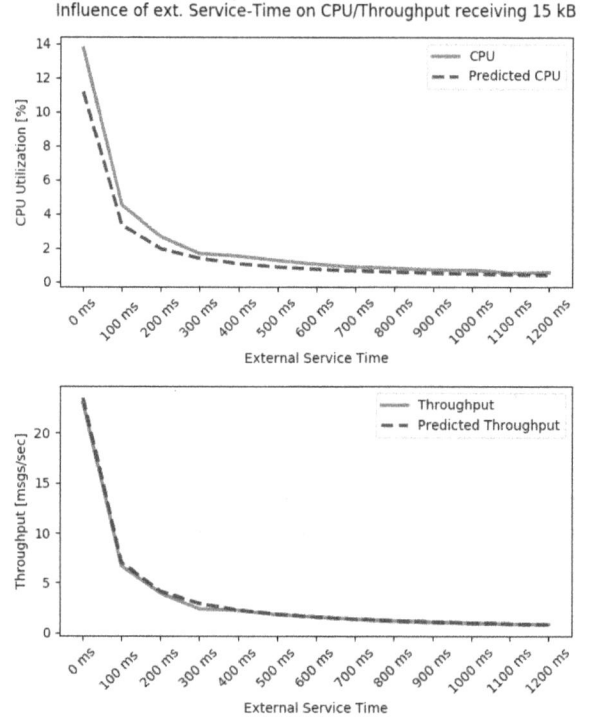

Figure 10: Influence of the external service time on the CPU utilization and throughput of the I/O-intensive microservice in a receiving scenario. With an increasing external service time the wait time increases leading to a decreased CPU utilization and throughput.

Ext. Service Time	Payload	CPU Utilization	Throughput
0 ms	1,25 MB	12.92 %	4.13
50 ms	15 kB	11.16 %	23.07

Table 3: Variations of throughput with a similar CPU utilization.

The influence of the external service time ST_{ext} is intuitive as it directly affects the throughput. However, by increasing the payload N_{data} the CPU utilization grows in a receiving and shrinks in a sending scenario. This is counter-intuitive and requires further investigation.

Some constellation of the external service characteristics can lead to fundamentally different throughput with a similar CPU utilization. Especially when using static thresholds the CPU threatens to be a false indicator of the actual performance. We measure a difference up to 600 % with a roughly equal CPU utilization in some configurations for the external service, as shown in Table 3.

Another factor is the transfer rate v, which is strongly influenced by the network bandwidth. Since many cloud environments like Amazon AWS or Microsoft Azure exhibit a varying network throughput on the same configuration [18][19] variations affect the transfer time and influence CPU and throughput.

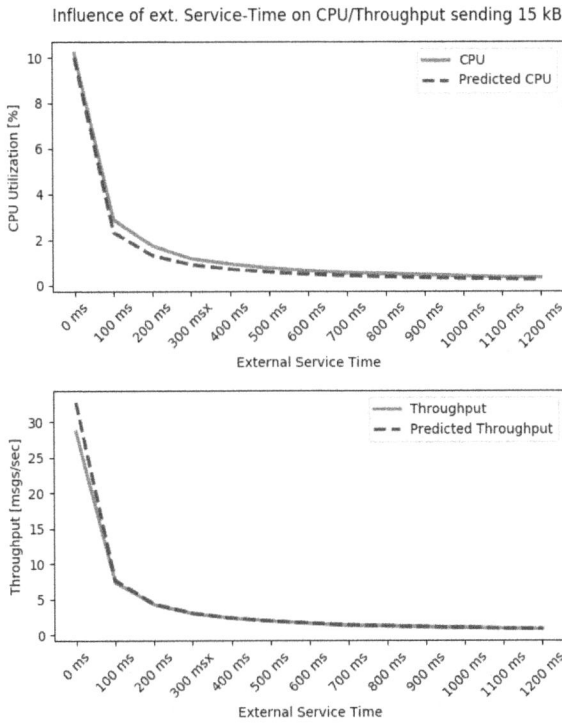

Figure 11: Influence of the external service time on the CPU utilization and throughput of the I/O-intensive microservice in a sending scenario. With an increasing external service time the wait time increases leading to a decreased CPU utilization and throughput.

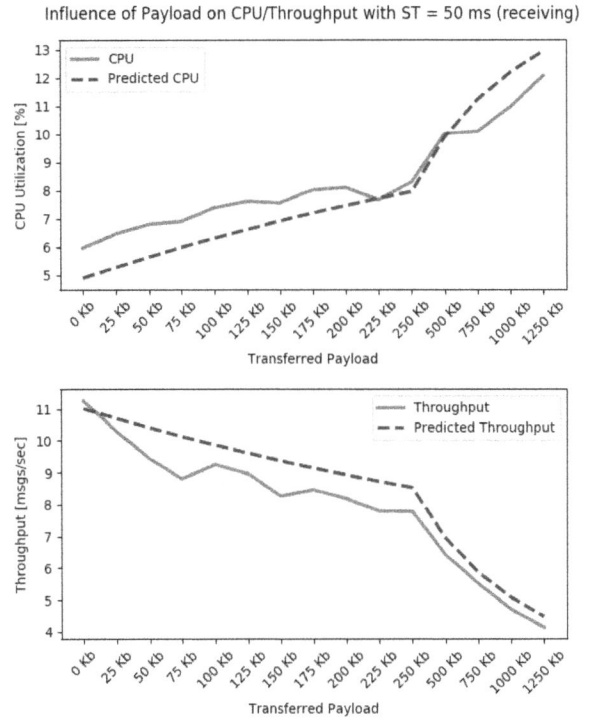

Figure 12: Influence of the transferred payload on the CPU utilization and throughput of the I/O-intensive microservice in a receiving scenario. With increasing payload the CPU utilization increases whereas the throughput decreases.

4.5 Threats to validity

In this section we consider the four classes of validity of a case study [22]:

4.5.1 Internal validity. In the running example the I/O-intensive microservice utilizes a single thread to process messages and communicate with the external service. By relying on a single blocking thread, the characteristics of the external service have a stronger influence on the microservice thus limiting the influence of other factors.

4.5.2 External validity. The running example is a simplified model of a real-world application for the SaaS use case. Nevertheless the fundamental architecture is already discussed in academia and derived of the work of [5]. For this reason we assume that it is sufficient to represent this class of cloud applications.

Message queues offers built-in benefits for the communication of microservices by supporting a loose coupling and reliability. However, often microservice communication is based on the typically synchronous REST paradigm. Relying on such a communication paradigm would abolish the challenge regarding the message queue state of a message broker system. However, the influence of the external service characteristics on a microservice in terms of CPU

utilization and throughput are still present in this case so it is possible to generalize the results for microservices which do not utilize a message queue.

4.5.3 Construct validity. Threshold-based rules auto-scaling is one of the simplest mechanisms to provision resources in a cloud environment. In this setup we identified that the quality of performance metrics for scaling decisions depends on microservice characteristics. We cannot exclude the possibility that other scaling mechanisms are more adaptive to changes in the microservice characteristics and their influence on the performance metrics. However, since we perceive threshold-based rules as one of the most common scaling strategies in industry we see validity of our investigation in real-world scenarios. By creating an analytical model of the influence of the external service characteristics on the microservices CPU utilization and throughput we emphasize the validity of the case study in an analytical manner.

In the case study we investigate the behavior based on a homogeneous workload. In practice the workload is expected to be heterogeneous, varying in size and computational requirements. However, since microservices usually deliver one functionality it mitigates the heterogeneity of workload compared to a monolithic application.

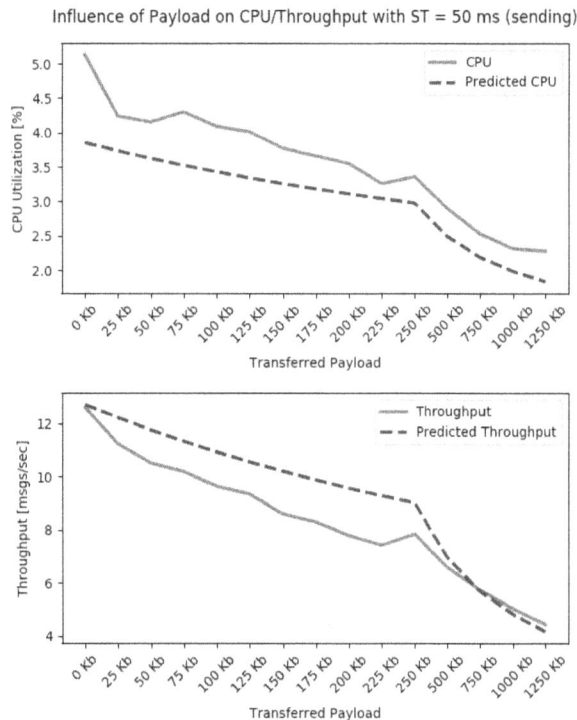

Figure 13: Influence of the transferred payload on the CPU utilization and throughput of the I/O-intensive microservice in a sending scenario. With an increasing payload the CPU utilization and the throughput decreases.

4.5.4   Reliability. By describing the concrete environment, the workload characteristics and the functionality of the microservices and the threshold-based rules auto-scaling system we strongly assume that the results are reproducible thus making it possible for another researcher to conduct the same study and obtain the same or very similar results. We see a limitation in the dynamic nature of the cloud environment which could possible change the optimal thresholds based on the time of experiment.

5   RELATED WORK

Runtime management is a well researched area in cloud computing with resource provisioning in an automatic manner as one of the main strategies. Extensive surveys can be found in [15] and [6]. An usual technique are threshold-based rules auto-scalers but there are approaches based on control theory, queueing theory, reinforcement learning or time-series analysis. More sophisticated approaches like [3] rely on workload forecasting, online resource demand estimation and performance models to improve the adaptation behavior. These techniques deeply rely on metrics which are able to represent the condition of the cloud system.

The performance of microservices is discussed in [10] and [7]. Whereas the first work addresses performance engineering for

microservices the second work discusses challenges for the performance of microservices in general and mentions reliability challenges through the message-passing mechanisms. Both works do not discuss challenges associated with using performance metrics for scaling message consuming microservices in this environment.

With the uprising microservice architectural style message broker systems gain more importance. A short survey can be found in [13]. An approach to scale message queues is proposed in [24]. Whereas it offers the possibility to mitigate the challenge of a flooded or congested queue by replicating queues it does not address the underlying challenge of a long-pending imbalance in consumption and production rate. However, it is still a suitable strategy to improve the performance by reconfiguring the middleware if the number of consumers and producers exceeds the capacity of the message broker system. In [8] an approach is presented to load balance message queues to ensure that provisioned resources are used at max capacity. Furthermore it scales message queues and consumers in case of an overload. However, this is a sophisticated approach which does not address scaling consuming microservices in a generic threshold-based auto-scaling setup.

Since message queues resemble structurally a queueing system performance modeling of this area could be transferable. Performance modeling of queueing systems is described in-depth in [16]. Furthermore simulation of queueing petri nets like [14] could be suitable to performance analyze cloud applications with message queues in order to have a fine-granular view of the message queue state at design- and run-time.

The disadvantages of relying on the CPU utilization are addressed in [21]. In this work they measured a 150 % variation in response time of an E-Commerce benchmark with an equal CPU utilization of 80 %. In [17] the disadvantages of relying on a single performance metric – like CPU utilization – is mitigated by merging heterogeneous metrics into a single representation.

To the best of our knowledge we cannot identify related work which investigates the suitability of performance metrics for scaling different microservice classes and evaluates the resilience of thresholds to changes in the microservices characteristics.

6   CONCLUSION

In this paper we investigated the suitability of a set of performance metrics in a threshold-based rules auto-scaling system for scaling a SaaS cloud application in terms of elasticity and coping with the message queue state. We have shown, that the CPU utilization is a suitable metric for scaling all classes of microservices if they exhibit constant characteristics. However, it is a vulnerable metric for changes in the microservice characteristic. Especially if the CPU utilization of an I/O-intensive microservice is used as performance metric, it can result in no scaling decisions at all, threating the application in performance and reliability. We modeled the influence of the external service time and the transferred payload on the CPU utilization and identified further factors which renders the CPU unreliable. We have shown that thresholds based on message queue metrics are much more resilient to changes in the microservice characteristics. For this reason we underline the benefits on relying on message queue metrics instead of the microservices CPU utilization in similar setups.

REFERENCES

[1] [n. d.]. RabbitMQ Queue Description. https://www.rabbitmq.com/queues.html. ([n. d.]). Accessed: 2017-09-14.

[2] Len Bass, Ingo Weber, and Liming Zhu. 2015. *DevOps: A Software Architect's Perspective*. Addison-Wesley Professional.

[3] André Bauer, Nikolas Herbst, and Samuel Kounev. 2017. Design and Evaluation of a Proactive, Application-Aware Auto-Scaler: Tutorial Paper. In *Proceedings of the 8th ACM/SPEC on International Conference on Performance Engineering*. ACM, 425–428.

[4] Alessio Botta, Walter de Donato, Valerio Persico, and Antonio Pescapé. 2016. Integration of Cloud computing and Internet of Things: A survey. *Future Generation Computer Systems* 56 (March 2016), 684–700. https://doi.org/10.1016/j.future.2015.09.021

[5] Cyril Cecchinel, Matthieu Jimenez, Sebastien Mosser, and Michel Riveill. 2014. An Architecture to Support the Collection of Big Data in the Internet of Things. IEEE, 442–449. https://doi.org/10.1109/SERVICES.2014.83

[6] You Chen, Yang Li, Xue-Qi Cheng, and Li Guo. 2006. Survey and taxonomy of feature selection algorithms in intrusion detection system. In *Information security and cryptology*. Springer, 153–167.

[7] Nicola Dragoni, Saverio Giallorenzo, Alberto Lluch Lafuente, Manuel Mazzara, Fabrizio Montesi, Ruslan Mustafin, and Larisa Safina. 2016. Microservices: yesterday, today, and tomorrow. *arXiv preprint arXiv:1606.04036* (2016).

[8] Ahmed El Rheddane, Noël De Palma, Alain Tchana, and Daniel Hagimont. 2014. Elastic message queues. In *Cloud Computing (CLOUD), 2014 IEEE 7th International Conference on*. IEEE, 17–23.

[9] Martin Fowler and James Lewis. 2014. Microservices. *ThoughtWorks*. *http://martinfowler.com/articles/microservices.html [last accessed on February 17, 2015]* (2014).

[10] Robert Heinrich, André van Hoorn, Holger Knoche, Fei Li, Lucy Ellen Lwakatare, Claus Pahl, Stefan Schulte, and Johannes Wettinger. 2017. Performance Engineering for Microservices: Research Challenges and Directions. In *Proceedings of the 8th ACM/SPEC on International Conference on Performance Engineering Companion*. ACM, 223–226.

[11] Nikolas Herbst, Rouven Krebs, Giorgos Oikonomou, George Kousiouris, Athanasia Evangelinou, Alexandru Iosup, and Samuel Kounev. 2016. Ready for Rain? A View from SPEC Research on the Future of Cloud Metrics. *arXiv preprint arXiv:1604.03470* (2016).

[12] Nikolas Roman Herbst, Samuel Kounev, and Ralf H Reussner. 2013. Elasticity in Cloud Computing: What It Is, and What It Is Not.. In *ICAC*, Vol. 13. 23–27.

[13] Vineet John and Xia Liu. 2017. A Survey of Distributed Message Broker Queues. *arXiv preprint arXiv:1704.00411* (2017).

[14] Samuel Kounev. 2006. Performance modeling and evaluation of distributed component-based systems using queueing petri nets. *IEEE Transactions on Software Engineering* 32, 7 (2006), 486–502.

[15] Tania Lorido-Botran, Jose Miguel-Alonso, and Jose A. Lozano. 2014. A Review of Auto-scaling Techniques for Elastic Applications in Cloud Environments. *Journal of Grid Computing* 12, 4 (Dec. 2014), 559–592. https://doi.org/10.1007/s10723-014-9314-7

[16] Randolph Nelson. 2013. *Probability, stochastic processes, and queueing theory: the mathematics of computer performance modeling*. Springer Science & Business Media.

[17] Valerio Persico, Domenico Grimaldi, Antonio Pescape, Alessandro Salvi, and Stefania Santini. 2017. A Fuzzy Approach Based on Heterogeneous Metrics for Scaling Out Public Clouds. *IEEE Transactions on Parallel and Distributed Systems* 28, 8 (2017), 2117–2130.

[18] Valerio Persico, Pietro Marchetta, Alessio Botta, and Antonio Pescapé. 2015. Measuring network throughput in the cloud: the case of amazon ec2. *Computer Networks* 93 (2015), 408–422.

[19] Valerio Persico, Pietro Marchetta, Alessio Botta, and Antonio Pescapé. 2015. On network throughput variability in microsoft azure cloud. In *Global Communications Conference (GLOBECOM), 2015 IEEE*. IEEE, 1–6.

[20] B. B. P. Rao, P. Saluia, N. Sharma, A. Mittal, and S. V. Sharma. 2012. Cloud computing for Internet of Things and sensing based applications. IEEE, 374–380. https://doi.org/10.1109/ICSensT.2012.6461705

[21] Jia Rao, Yudi Wei, Jiayu Gong, and Cheng-Zhong Xu. 2013. QoS guarantees and service differentiation for dynamic cloud applications. *IEEE Transactions on Network and Service Management* 10, 1 (2013), 43–55.

[22] Per Runeson, Martin Host, Austen Rainer, and Bjorn Regnell. 2012. *Case study research in software engineering: Guidelines and examples*. John Wiley & Sons.

[23] Rainer Storn and Kenneth Price. 1997. Differential evolution–a simple and efficient heuristic for global optimization over continuous spaces. *Journal of global optimization* 11, 4 (1997), 341–359.

[24] Nam-Luc Tran, Yudi Wei, Sabri Skhiri, Esteban Zim, et al. 2011. Eqs: An elastic and scalable message queue for the cloud. In *Cloud Computing Technology and Science (CloudCom), 2011 IEEE Third International Conference on*. IEEE, 391–398.

[25] Mario Villamizar, Oscar Garces, Lina Ochoa, Harold Castro, Lorena Salamanca, Mauricio Verano, Rubby Casallas, Santiago Gil, Carlos Valencia, Angee Zambrano, and Mery Lang. 2016. Infrastructure Cost Comparison of Running Web Applications in the Cloud Using AWS Lambda and Monolithic and Microservice Architectures. IEEE, 179–182. https://doi.org/10.1109/CCGrid.2016.37

Evaluating Scalability and Performance of a Security Management Solution in Large Virtualized Environments

Lishan Yang
College of William and Mary
Williamsburg, Virginia
lyang11@cs.wm.edu

Ludmila Cherkasova
HyTrust Inc
Mountain View, California
lucy.cherkasova@gmail.com

Rajeev Badgujar
HyTrust Inc
Mountain View, California
rbadgujar@hytrust.com

Jack Blancaflor
HyTrust Inc
Mountain View, California
jblancaflor@hytrust.com

Rahul Konde
HyTrust Inc
Mountain View, California
rkonde@hytrust.com

Jason Mills
HyTrust Inc
Mountain View, California
jmills@hytrust.com

Evgenia Smirni
College of William and Mary
Williamsburg, Virginia
esmirni@cs.wm.edu

ABSTRACT

Virtualized infrastructure is a key capability of modern enterprise data centers and cloud computing, enabling a more agile and dynamic IT infrastructure with fast IT provisioning, simplified, automated management, and flexible resource allocation to handle a broad set of workloads. However, at the same time, virtualization introduces new challenges, since securing virtual servers is more difficult than physical machines. HyTrust Inc. has developed an innovative security solution, called HyTrust Cloud Control (HTCC), to mitigate risks associated with virtualization and cloud technologies. HTCC is a virtual appliance deployed as a transparent proxy in front of a VMware-based virtualized environment. Since HTCC serves as a gateway to a customer virtualized environment, it is important to carefully assess its performance and scalability as well as provide its accurate resource sizing. In this work[1], we introduce a novel approach for accomplishing this goal. First, we describe a special framework, based on a *nested virtualization* technique, which enables the creation and deployment of a large-scale virtualized environment (with 30,000 VMs) using a limited number of physical servers (4 servers in our experiments). Second, we introduce a design and implementation of a novel, extensible benchmark, called *HT-vmbench*, that allows to mimic the session-based activities of different system administrators and users in virtualized environments. The benchmark is implemented using VMware Web Service SDK. By executing *HT-vmbench* in the emulated large-scale virtualized environments, we can support an efficient performance assessment of management and security solutions (such as HTCC), their overhead, and provide capacity planning rules and resource sizing recommendations.

KEYWORDS

Benchmark; scalability; performance; virtualization

ACM Reference Format:
Lishan Yang, Ludmila Cherkasova, Rajeev Badgujar, Jack Blancaflor, Rahul Konde, Jason Mills, and Evgenia Smirni. 2018. Evaluating Scalability and Performance of a Security Management Solution in Large Virtualized Environments. In *ICPE '18: ACM/SPEC International Conference on Performance Engineering, April 9–13, 2018, Berlin, Germany*. ACM, New York, NY, USA, 8 pages. https://doi.org/10.1145/3184407.3184435

1 INTRODUCTION

Many companies adopt virtualization and its ability to slice larger, underutilized physical servers into smaller, virtual ones, to get significant cost savings resulting from server consolidation. Nowadays, in the era of large multi-core servers this approach became even more economically appealing to enterprise customers. Virtualization and cloud introduce a set of new challenges for reliably secure virtual servers and supporting additional authentication procedures across a large set of virtual machines in the enterprise environments. HyTrust Inc. developed a security solution, called HyTrust CloudControl (HTCC) [1–3], to mitigate the security risks and compliance gaps that exist in virtual and cloud environments. In essence, any action issued by a privileged user is proxied, evaluated, logged, and then forwarded to a vCenter (if approved). Since HTCC serves as a gateway to a customer virtualized environment, it is important to carefully assess its performance and scalability in order to minimize the introduced overhead and provide adequate resource sizing for managing and protecting customer's large-scale virtualized environment. To accomplish this goal there are two main challenges to be addressed:

- First, to assess the scalability of the HTCC solution, we need to emulate a large scale virtualized environment with tens of thousands of virtual machines. This is a real challenge since not every company or research organization has an access to a production size virtualized environment needed for such evaluation and performance experiments.

[1] This work was mostly completed during L. Yang's summer internship in 2017 at HyTrust Inc. E. Smirni and L. Yang are partially supported by NSF grant CCF-1649087.

- Second, we need to generate a variety of typical customer workloads to drive the performance and scalability assessment of HTCC in a large-scale virtualized environment. Currently, we are not aware of any available benchmark which is representative of system administrators' actions and users' activities typically performed in virtualized environments.

In this work, we introduce our solution for solving both challenges:

- First, we describe an approach, based on a *nested virtualization* technique [18, 19], which enables us to create a large scale virtualized environment (with 30,000 VMs) using a limited number of physical servers (4 servers in our experiments). Nested virtualization is the ability to run a hypervisor inside a virtual machine. This enables a recursive-based approach for creating a high number of additional "slim" VMs inside an original virtual machine deployed on a bare metal hypervisor. This allows deploying a large-scale virtualized environment without the need to actually have a large number of dedicated physical machines.
- Second, we design and implement a novel, extensible benchmark, called *HT-vmbench*, which allows us to mimic *session-based* activities of different system administrators and users in virtualized environments. The benchmark is implemented using VMware Web Service SDK [20]. *HT-vmbench* allows issuing a set of typical operations in virtualized environments. These operations have strong interdependencies and causalities. In addition, almost all the VM operations do take seconds (i.e., they are far from being "instantaneous"), and one needs to be very careful in avoiding the possibility of introducing *race conditions*, i.e., when an operation over a VM is issued while the previous operation over the same VM is not yet finished. The proposed benchmark design and implementation carefully considers such challenges and provides means to correctly handle them.

By executing *HT-vmbench*, on an emulated large scale virtualized environment, we can measure the latency of performed operations as well as the benchmark throughput, and estimate the overhead introduced by the HTCC proxy.

This paper is organized as follows. Section 2 provides background on HTCC. Section 3 describes nested virtualization for creating large-scale virtualized environment using a limited set of physical resources. Section 4 introduces the design of *HT-vmbench* and discusses its main features. Section 5 evaluates the proposed framework by using measurement and a variety of performance experiments. Section 6 outlines related work. Section 7 summarizes our contribution and gives directions for future work. For more details on the architecture of *HT-vmbench*, we direct the interested reader to the extended version of this paper [23].

2 BACKGROUND ON HYTRUST CLOUD CONTROL SOLUTION

As companies continue to embrace virtualization and cloud by migrating from physical to virtualized environments, they are under increased pressure to secure user and corporate data and follow multiple compliance regulations (many of them are country and industry specific). With tighter control and higher penalties, the new compliance laws in US and EU [3] enforce stricter requirements for data protection of private and sensitive data.

In a traditional data center with physical servers, there is a well understood set of demarcation lines for managing different resources, e.g., server's OS and storage within one physical server is managed by a system administrator while the network is managed by a networking specialist. Similarly, many security policies rely on the separation of duties as well as physical barriers.

Virtualization and cloud have blurred these boundaries by merging many IT roles and functions during provisioning and configuration tasks over virtualized physical infrastructure. Moreover, workload consolidation results in a higher density of information assets with very different security requirements and data sensitivity levels. All these challenges reduce the ability of security administrators to adequately monitor and audit workloads for compliance and security management in virtualized environments.

HyTrust Cloud Control Solution (HTCC) was purposely designed from ground up to address the security and compliance gaps existing in virtual environments. The HTCC solution provides a powerful set of policy-based access controls as well as an automated enforcement of industry specific compliance templates. HTCC is a virtual appliance deployed as a transparent proxy in front of a VMware-based virtualized environment (vSphere) as shown in Figure 1.

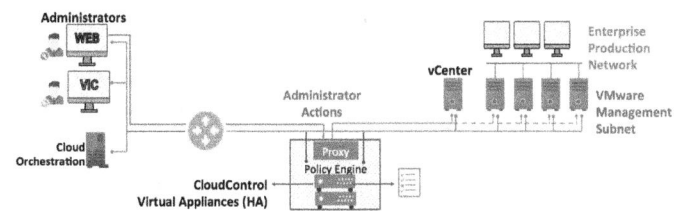

Figure 1: vSphere Architecture with HTCC Appliance.

HTCC transparent proxy allows a single-entry gateway to a protected virtual environment. It offers a non-intrusive security control to all administrators and users actions. In essence, any action issued by a privileged user (through any of VMware management tools) is proxied, evaluated against the specified access rules, logged for the audit trail, and then forwarded to vCenter (only if it was approved).

The HTCC transparent proxy acts as a central point of control: it seamlessly monitors and intercepts all the administrative requests, originated from a variety of possible access mechanisms in VMware vSphere as shown in Figure 2. The access mechanisms include vSphere Client and vSphere Web Client to vCenter, as well as the direct SSH user sessions to ESXi hosts.

The HTCC transparent proxy relies on the support of the following five key components as shown in Figure 2:

- *HTCC Policy Engine* is the main enforcement mechanism which allows to define Role Based Access Control in the organization among its privileged users.
- *HTCC Authentication Engine* supports an enhanced security layer along with the usual username and passwords.
- *HTCC Inventory Engine* supports the up to date "map" (inventory) of the protected virtual infrastructure under control. It is a critical component since VMs can be migrated, and the entire infrastructure can be changed with just a few clicks, e.g., adding a new vCenter.
- *HTCC Compliance Engine* provides and enforces the compliances templates for various industry and government standards, e.g., HIPPA, DISA, PCI-DSS.

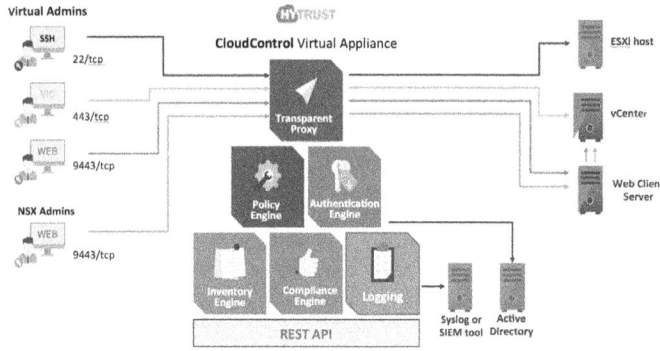

Figure 2: HyTrust CloudControl Architecture.

- *HTCC Logging Engine* supports a complete audit trail of privileged users' activities. The HTCC's logging engine also captures the attempted actions that have been denied by security policy.

Since the HTCC proxy acts as a main gateway to protected virtualized and cloud environments and it controls and intercepts all the administrative requests as shown in Figure 2, it is important to measure and evaluate the performance overhead introduced by the HTCC proxy. In order to answer the scalability questions, i.e., evaluate HTCC proxy overhead for different sizes of the protected environment, we should be able to efficiently emulate these large-scale virtualized environments. In the next section, we describe our approach for accomplishing this goal.

3 USING NESTED VIRTUALIZATION FOR EMULATING LARGE-SCALE VIRTUAL ENVIRONMENTS

Nested virtualization is a novel virtualization technique first proposed by IBM, which offers an opportunity to run a hypervisor inside a virtual machine. It has actively evolved over the last decade and is available on many virtualization platforms, such as Xen, VMware, and KVM. The general theory behind the nested virtualization, its implementation and performance characteristics are described in more detail in [7].

Applied to VMware solutions, the nested ESXi involves running ESXi on top of ESXi within a virtual machine. As shown in Figure 3, a typical deployment of ESXi and virtual machines consists of Layer 0 through Layer 2.

The hypervisor that runs on the real hardware is called Level 0 (or L0); the hypervisor that runs as a guest on L0 is called Level 1 (or L1); a guest that runs on the L1 hypervisor is called a Level 2 (or L2). In a nested ESXi deployment the third layer (Layer 3) is introduced by creating one level of recursion within the nested ESXi hypervisor at Layer 2.

With nested virtualization and its ability to run a hypervisor inside a virtual machine, we can apply a recursive-based approach for creating a high number of additional "slim" VMs inside an original virtual machine deployed on a bare metal hypervisor. Let us show how the scale of the deployed environment is defined (i.e., the numbers of deployed ESXI hosts and VMs) when we use the *traditional* approach for creating the virtual environment versus the *nested virtualization* approach. Let us consider a modern two

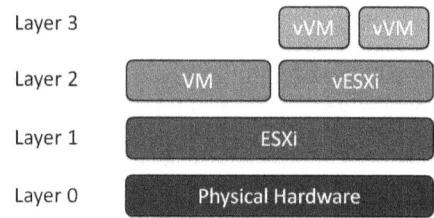

Figure 3: Nested Virtualization Approach.

socket, multi-core server (say, with 10 physical cores per socket, or 20 hyper-threaded virtual cores), with 256GB DRAM.

- Under the *traditional* approach with a ESXi hypervisor that runs on real hardware (at Layer 1), we can realistically deploy, say, 100 VMs per server at Layer 2. Therefore, if we need to create a virtual environment of 10,000 VMs, we would need to have 100 physical hosts under the *traditional* approach.
- Under the *nested virtualization* approach, we could recursively deploy inside of each VM at Layer 2, vESXi hypervisor (as shown in Figure 3). Then on top of each vESXi hypervisor, we can deploy 100 "slim" VMs at Layer 3. This way, we could get a large-scale virtual environment with 10,000 VMs deployed on a single physical host.

Following the described above logic, one can create a variety of different templates of large-scale environments for evaluating the scalability dimensions of the tested management solution under the test. Note, that similarly, we can deploy a number of vCenter appliances which manage the deployed ESXi hosts and VMs, and could be used as a gateway for created virtual environments.

4 HT-VMBENCH DESIGN AND IMPLEMENTATION

In this section, we present the design, main features, and implementation of *HT-vmbench*. First, we introduce the main terms and notations. Then we explain the idea and the formal algorithm of organizing VM operations as user sessions, and the execution of user sessions. Finally, we discuss the set of metrics reported at the end of the benchmark execution.

4.1 VM Operations and Interdependencies

A lifecycle of a VM starts with its creation and ends up with its deletion as shown in Figure 4. User can *create* a VM, then perform operations such as *clone, migrate, snapshot* before *delete* operation. In addition, *power_on* and *power_off* operations can happen on a created VM, and user can *reboot* a powered_on VM.

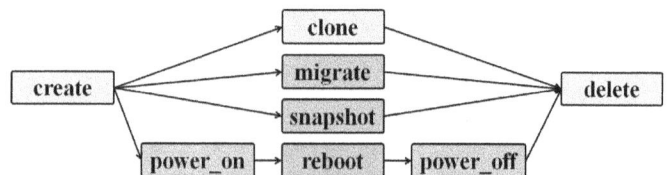

Figure 4: Lifecycle of a VM.

Some operations can be considered as *paired* operations (or *pairs,* for brevity), such as:

- (*create*, *delete*),
- (*clone*, *delete*),
- (*power_on*, *power_off*).

As operations paired together, every *delete* VM operation follows after a *create* or *clone* VM operation. Thus every *delete* VM operation has an existing VM to be performed on. Similar, for *power_on* and *power_off*, with the concept of paired operations, every *power_off* VM operation has a powered_on VM to execute on.

For the remaining operations, *snapshot*, *migrate* and *reboot*, they are regarded as *single* operations. To make things more structured, we introduce the concept of *operation units*. An operation unit is either a *single* operation or a *pair* of operations. Some operation units may require preconditions:

- The *paired* operation (*create*, *delete*) can be executed if there are enough resources available for creating a new VM;
- The *paired* operations (*clone*, *delete*), (*power_on*, *power_off*), and the *single* operations *migrate* and *snapshot* require a precondition that there is at least one VM existing in the system;
- The *reboot* operation requires a precondition that there is at least one VM powered on to execute.

All the *paired* operations change the system state. We use two counters *Num_VM* and *Num_VM_Powered_On* to represent the system state:

- *Num_VM*: the number of VMs existing in the system. *Create*, *clone* and *delete* operations change *Num_VM*;
- *Num_VM_Powered_On*: the number of powered_on VMs. It can be changed by *power_on* and *power_off* operations.

With these two counters, all these preconditions can be easily satisfied and implemented.

4.2 User Sessions

The goal of *HT-vmbench* is to simulate VM operations performed by administrators on managed virtualized environments. We introduce the concept of a *user session*, a sequence of VM operations issued by an administrator. Each user session follows a *close-loop* model, i.e., the next request is issued only when the response to the previous request is received by the user. To reflect the ordering of VM operations, we use a pseudo-timeline. The pseudo-timestamps are numbers generated randomly, for the purpose of operation ordering, i.e., for defining which VM operation should be executed before the other one.

Every user session has its own counters *Num_VM* and *Num_VM_Powered_On*. To construct a user session, *HT-vmbench* organizes VM operations as operation units, and inserts them into the user session's timeline according to the interdependencies between the operations.

4.3 Transaction Mix

A transaction mix determines the percentage and combination of operations in a single benchmark run. User sessions should follow the specified transaction mix. A *well-formed* mix should satisfy the following constraints:

- $Num\_Create + Num\_Clone = Num\_Delete$;
- $Num\_Power\_On = Num\_Power\_Off$;
- If $Num\_Reboot > 0$, then $Num\_Power\_On > 0$.

Although we define $Num\_Create + Num\_Clone = Num\_Delete$, our design still supports $Num\_Create + Num\_Clone \geq Num\_Delete$.

This relaxation of restriction allows the creation of special "test" transaction mixes, such as 100% *create* VM operations. These "test" cases are executed with an additional *clean-up* phase, implemented in the benchmark, to meet the close-loop benchmark design.

4.4 User Session Creation and Execution

This section discusses in detail the algorithm of the *user session* creation, and the execution of user sessions.

4.4.1 Priority. Every operation unit has its own priority. Priorities are assigned according to interdependencies between operations, shown in Table 1 (a smaller number means a higher priority):

Table 1: Priorities of Operation Units

Operation Unit	Priority
create & delete	1
power_on & power_off	2
clone & delete	3
migrate	4
snapshot	5
reboot	6

- The *create & delete* pair has the highest priority, since they start and end a VM's lifecycle.
- The *power_on* and *power_off* pair has the second highest priority. Note, because of the significant resource pressure introduced by *power_on* operation, we force the *power_on & power_off* pairs to be inserted as neighbours, i.e., there is no other *power_on* or *power_off* VM operations between a pair of *power_on & power_off*. By putting *power_on* and *power_off* as neighbours, the randomness of insertion is decreased. To remain as much randomness as possible, *power_on* and *power_off* pairs are given the second highest priority.
- The *clone & delete* pair has the third highest priority, because they also change counter *Num_VM*.
- The other operations such as *migrate*, *snapshot*, and *reboot* VM operations have the lowest priorities.

4.4.2 Algorithm for user session creation. Algorithm 1 below shows the pseudo-code of constructing user sessions. To explain the algorithm, consider the following example. Let the transaction mix be as shown in the second column of Table 2, with the number of operations *Num_Ops* = 24, and the number of user sessions *Num_User_Session* = 2. First, all operations in the transaction mix are evenly distributed among the specified number of user sessions (Algorithm 1, Line 2). In our example, the two specified user sessions have the same subset of operations, see the third column of Table 2.

Lines 3-6 (Algorithm 1) refer to the preprocessing process before inserting operations. For every user session, operations are paired according to the operation interdependencies, and each operation unit is assigned a priority based on Table 1. Then, we sort the operation units by priority, and get a list of operation units, as shown in Figure 5.

Next, we construct a sequence for every user session (Algorithm 1, Line 7). In our example with two user sessions, we first construct a sequence for user session A, and then in a similar way, for user session B. All operation units in user session A are inserted into the pseudo-timeline from high priority to low priority:

Algorithm 1 Construct a sequence for a user session

Input: *Transaction_Mix; Num_User_Session; Num_Ops*
Output: List of user sessions *User_Session_List*
1: **function** CREATE_USER_SESSIONS()
2: evenly distribute operations to user sessions
3: **for all** user session **do**
4:   pair the operations (*create,delete*), (*clone,delete*) and (*power_on,power_off*)
5:   assign priority to every operation unit
6:   sort operation units by priority to get *Op_Unit_List*
7:   CONSTRUCT_A_SEQUENCE()

Table 2: Example of a Transaction Mix of a Single Benchmark Run

Operation Type	Number of Operations	Number of Operations per User Session
create	6	3
delete	8	4
power_on	2	1
power_off	2	1
clone	2	1
migrate	2	1
reboot	2	1

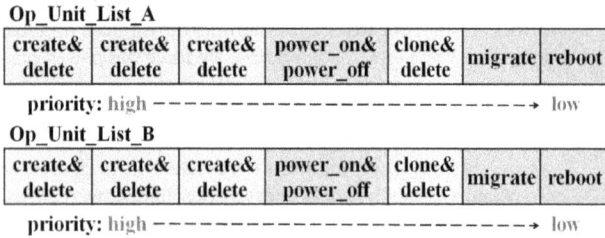

Op_Unit_List_A

create& delete	create& delete	create& delete	power_on& power_off	clone& delete	migrate	reboot

priority: high – → low

Op_Unit_List_B

create& delete	create& delete	create& delete	power_on& power_off	clone& delete	migrate	reboot

priority: high – → low

Figure 5: An Example of Operation Unit List.

- Referring to the list *Op_Unit_List_A* in Figure 5, the first operation unit is a pair of operations, *create & delete*. The *create* VM operation is given a random number representing the pseudo-time, and inserted into the timeline; then the *delete* VM operation is randomly inserted into the interval after the *create* VM operation, as shown in Figure 6(a). The counter *Num_VM* is calculated, shown in the Table below the timeline.
- Other two *create* and *delete* pairs are inserted in the same way, resulting in Figure 6(b). *Create* and *delete* pairs can be neighbours, as the ( ) pair and [ ] pair; also, *create* and *delete* pair can be nested, as the ( ) pair and { } pair. Each time when the pair is inserted, the counter *Num_VM* is refreshed.
- After inserting all *create & delete* pairs, the next step is the insertion of *power_on & power_off* pairs. The pair of *power_on & power_off* should be inserted as neighbours into the intervals, where *Num_VM* > 0 (as shown in Figure 6(c)). Counter *Num_VM_Powered_On* is calculated after each insertion.
- Figure 6(d) shows the insertion of *clone & delete* pair. First, we find some interval, where *Num_VM* is larger than 0, and

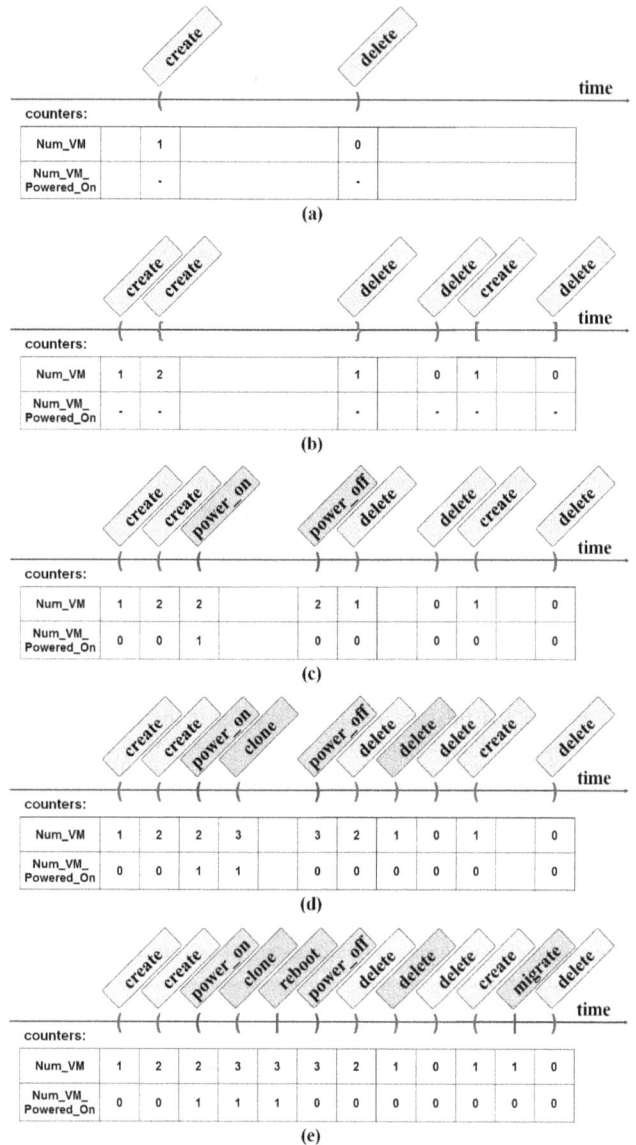

Figure 6: An Example of User Session Creation.

insert *clone* VM operation into this interval; then *delete* VM operation is randomly inserted after the *clone* into the same interval. After each insertion, the counter *Num_VM* is updated.

- After the insertion of *clone & delete* pair, all the pairs are inserted into the timeline. The remaining single operations are a *migrate* VM operation and a *reboot* VM operation. The *migrate* VM operation can be inserted into any interval, where *Num_VM* > 0; the *reboot* VM operation can only be inserted into the intervals, where *Num_VM_Powered_On* > 0, i.e., between a pair of *power_on & power_off*. In this way, we get the timeline of user session A as shown in Figure 6(e).

Table 3 (left column) shows a sequence of operations that corresponds to the constructed user session A. Similarly, we can construct a user session B, resulting in the sequence of operations shown in the right column of Table 3.

Table 3: Constructed User Sessions

User Session A	User Session B
create	create
create	delete
power_on	create
clone	clone
reboot	power_on
power_off	migrate
delete	delete
delete	reboot
delete	power_off
create	delete
migrate	create
delete	delete

The detailed pseudo-code of *Construct_a_sequence* is shown in Algorithm 2, with four basic insertion functions.

- *insert_create_delete_pair_op():* The *create & delete* pairs can be inserted randomly into any place in the sequence, with *delete* following after *create*. After insertion, the counter *Num_VM* is calculated and updated as a set of intervals *Exist_VM_Intervals_Set*, shown in the algorithm 2, Line 7.
- *insert_power_on_off_pair_op():* The *power_on & power_off* pairs are inserted to a randomly chosen interval, where the counter *Num_VM* is larger than 0 as neighbours. In other words, there is no operation between the *power_on* and *power_off* operations which come from the same pair. Similarly, counter *Num_VM_Powered_On* is refreshed after inserting *power_on & power_off* pairs.
- *insert_generic_pair_op():* This method inserts a generic pair to a proper position according to the requirement of preconditions. If the operation pair requires at least one VM powered on, the pair will be inserted to a randomly chosen interval where the counter *Num_VM_Powered_On* is larger than 0; if the operation pair requires at least one VM but not necessarily powered on, the pair will be inserted to a randomly chosen interval where the counter *Num_VM* is larger than 0; if the operation pair has no preconditions, the pair can be inserted to any position in the sequence.
- *insert_single_op():* Every single operation is inserted into a sequence according to the random number assigned under the requirements of preconditions.

Algorithm 2 takes the operation units from *Op_Unit_List*, checks the type of this operation unit, and finally calls the corresponding function to do the insertion. After inserting all the operation units, a sequence is constructed.

4.4.3 User Session Execution. After constructing all user sessions, each user session has a sequence of VM operations. Next, *HT-vmbench* starts the preparation of VM operation execution, including creating user session cache, loading vCenter information, and populating host information. Then, all user sessions are submitted to start their execution. Finally, after all the executions are finished, results are processed. There is an additional *clean-up* phase to clean up the remaining VMs created by the benchmark execution.

HT-vmbench gets the access to execute VM operations on the virtualized environment by invoking the APIs provided by *vSphere*. Every user session holds a close-loop model. Corresponding to the time spent by administrators to make decision between operations,

---

Algorithm 2 Construct a sequence for a user session

Input: List of operation units *Op_Unit_List*
Output: Sequence S

1: **function** CONSTRUCT_A_SEQUENCE()
2:     *Exist_VM_Intervals_Set = null*
3:     *Powered_On_VM_Intervals_Set = null*
4:     **for each** operation unit *op_unit* in *Op_Unit_List*, priority from high to low **do**
5:         **if** *op_unit* is *Create_Delete_Pair_Op* **then**
6:             INSERT_CREATE_DELETE_PAIR_OP()
7:             find all intervals of *Num_VM* > 0, and add to *Exist_VM_Intervals_Set*
8:         **else if** *op_unit* is *Power_On_Off_Pair_Op* **then**
9:             INSERT_POWER_ON_OFF_PAIR_OP()
10:             find all intervals of *Num_VM_Powered_On* > 0, and add to *Powered_On_VM_Intervals_Set*
11:         **else if** *op_unit* is *Generic_Pair_Op* **then**
12:             INSERT_GENERIC_PAIR_OP()
13:         **else if** *op_unit* is *Single_Op* **then**
14:             INSERT_SINGLE_OP()
15: **function** INSERT_CREATE_DELETE_PAIR_OP()
16:     insert *Create_Delete_Pair_Op* to Sequence S
17: **function** INSERT_POWER_ON_OFF_PAIR_OP()
18:     randomly choose an interval (a, b) from *Exist_VM_Intervals_Set*
19:     insert *Power_On_Off_Pair_Op* to Sequence S between a and b as neighbours
20: **function** INSERT_GENERIC_PAIR_OP()
21:     **if** *Generic_Pair_Op* requires at least one VM powered on **then**
22:         randomly choose an interval (a, b) from *Powered_On_VM_Intervals_Set*
23:         insert *Generic_Pair_Op* to Sequence S between a and b
24:     **else if** *Generic_Pair_Op* requires at least one VM existing **then**
25:         randomly choose an interval (a, b) from *Exist_VM_Intervals_Set*
26:         insert *Generic_Pair_Op* to Sequence S between a and b
27:     **else if** no precondition **then**
28:         insert *Generic_Pair_Op* to Sequence S
29: **function** INSERT_SINGLE_OP()
30:     **if** *Single_Op* requires at least one VM powered on **then**
31:         randomly choose an interval (a, b) from *Powered_On_VM_Intervals_Set*
32:         insert *Single_Op* to Sequence S between a and b
33:     **else if** *Single_Op* requires at least one VM existing **then**
34:         randomly choose an interval (a, b) from *Exist_VM_Intervals_Set*
35:         insert *Single_Op* to Sequence S between a and b
36:     **else if** no precondition **then**
37:         insert *Single_Op* to Sequence S

---

we introduce *think time* between operations in a single user session, defined as the random variable *Think_Time*. To give the system maximum pressure, we set the think time to 0 as default.

When generating user sessions, we focus on the operation types (specified by the transaction mix) rather than specifying which specific VM is going to be operated on. A VM operation may take seconds to finish, so if different user sessions submit VM operations performing on the same VM, a *race condition* occurs. To avoid these race conditions, a *blocking queue* is used to record all the VMs involved in the current state of the benchmark. When a VM operation is issued, a VM (in the required state) is dequeued from the blocking queue, and the VM operation is performed on this VM. After the operation is finished, the VM is enqueued into the blocking queue again. Note, the *create* VM operation creates a VM directly, and puts the new VM into the blocking queue; the *delete* VM operation gets a VM from the blocking queue and deletes this VM. This blocking queue ensures that there is always at most one operation performing on the same VM. This way the race conditions are avoided.

4.5 Benchmark Output and Metrics

To characterize the performance characteristics of a deployed virtualized environment as well as the performance of the HTCC proxy protecting it, the benchmark measures two sets of metrics: *latency* of performed operations (in seconds) and the overall system *throughput* in operations per second (*ops/sec*). Additionally, the benchmark collects and outputs *(i)* the detailed log of performed operations with measured latency of each operation and *(ii)* the summary output (computed from the detailed log) with the average latency per performed operation.

The execution of benchmark can be divided into three phases:

- *warm-up:* Before the slowest user session starts its execution;
- *main:* All the user sessions are executing their VM operations;
- *cool-down:* After the fastest user session finishes its execution.

The reported throughput and operation latencies are calculated in the *main* phase of the benchmark execution.

5 EVALUATION

The emulated large scale virtualized environment is deployed on four physical servers, each machine is DellC6320, with two sockets Intel Xeon E5-2640 v4, 2.4 GHz processors (Broadwell family), each processor with 10 physical cores (20 virtual processors, due to hyper-threading), i.e., 40 virtual processors per server, with 256 GB of RAM. Each server had 2 x 10Gb/s network.

We deployed (via nested virtualization) the VMware-based virtualized environment with two clusters: 10K and 20K VMs. Each cluster is configured with two vCenters. In such a way, by combining the resources of these clusters, we can perform experiments in large-scale virtualized environments having 10K, 20K, and 30K VMs.

By executing *HT-vmbench* on an emulated large scale virtualized environment, we measured the latency of performed operations. We performed a set of experiments using two types of environments:

- *virtual-original:* an emulated large scale VMware-based virtualized environment (with 10K, 20K, 30K VMs);
- *virtual-protected:* an emulated large scale VMware-based virtualized environment (with 10K, 20K, 30K VMs) protected by HTCC solution deployed as a gateway (transparent proxy) to the original virtualized environment.

We performed 500 operations for every user session during each *HT-vmbench* run, configured with the following transaction mix:

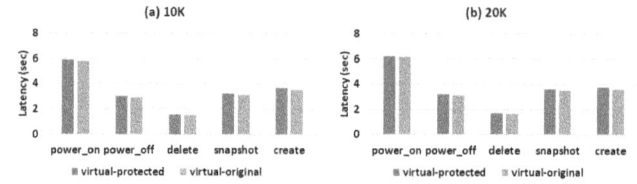

Figure 7: Average Latency of Different VM operations.

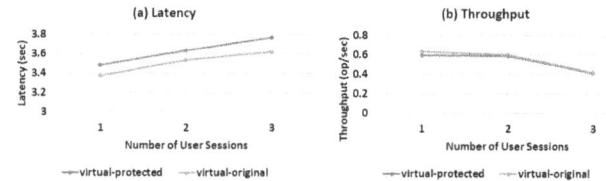

Figure 8: Average Latency and Throughput of VM operations in 10K VMs Environment.

- *create* =20%
- *delete* =20%
- *power_on* =20%
- *power_off* =20%
- *snapshot* =20%

Figure 7(a) shows the average latency of VM operations in *virtual-original* or *virtual-protected* environment of 10K object clusters with 3 user sessions. When running in *virtual-protected* environment, the execution time of operations is slightly higher than the execution time in *virtual-original* environment, due to the overhead introduced by HTCC. As results show, HTCC has a very reasonable performance overhead for most operations in virtualized environment tested by our benchmark.

Figure 7(b) shows the average latency in 20K object clusters with 3 user sessions, for both *virtual-original* and *virtual-protected* environment. These numbers are similar compared to the 10K cluster result shown in Figure 7(a). It indicates that the scale of virtualized environment does not have a significant impact on the performance overhead introduced by HTCC proxy.

Figure 8 shows the latency and throughput of VM operations as a function of the number of user sessions. As the number of user sessions grow, latency and throughput also increase. The latency is slightly higher, since the system is more crowded, and the throughput is increasing rapidly due to the paralellism.

By executing *HT-vmbench* in the emulated large-scale virtualized environments, we can support an efficient performance assessment of management and security solutions (such as HTCC), their overhead, and provide capacity planning rules and resource sizing recommendations.

6 RELATED WORK

Benchmarking Virtualized Environments: Over the last decade virtualization has gained popularity in enterprise and cloud environments as a software-based solution for creating shared hardware infrastructures. VMware released a *VMmark* benchmark [21] for quantifying the performance of virtualized environments. This benchmark aims to provide some basis for comparison of different hardware and virtualization platforms in *server consolidation* use cases, and therefore, aims to evaluate very different scenarios compared to *HT-vmbench*.

Application performance and resource consumption in virtualized environments might be quite different compared to their execution on bare metal hardware because of additional virtualization overheads, which are typically caused by I/O processing and the application interactions with the underlying virtual machine monitor (VMM). Different papers describe various VMM implementations and analyze virtualization overhead when executing specially selected microbenchmarks or macrobenchmarks (e.g., [6, 8, 12, 22]). The reported virtualization overhead greatly depends on the server hardware used in such experiments. This extensive body of previous benchmarks characterizes performance in virtualized environments from a very different angle compared to the goals and functionality of *HT-vmbench*.

Nested Virtualization Technique: During the last decade software virtualization solutions for x86 systems were broadly adopted, forcing both Intel and AMD to add virtualization extensions to their x86 platforms [5, 17]. There was a stream of efforts to incorporate nested virtualization in Xen hypervisor [4, 10]. Nested virtualization has many potential uses: e.g., platforms with hypervisors embedded in firmware might need to support other hypervisors as guest virtual machines. In the Cloud, IaaS providers might offer a user the ability to run the user-controlled hypervisor as a VM. In such a way, the user can manage his own virtual environment with with the choice of his favorite hypervisor. This might significantly simplify many management tasks, such as the live migration of their virtual machines as a single entity, e.g., for disaster recovery or load balancing. It could also be used for testing, demonstrating, benchmarking and debugging hypervisors and virtualization setups.

Nested virtualization enables new approaches to security in virtualized environments, such as honeypots capable of running hypervisor-level rootkits [14], hypervisor-level rootkit protection [13, 15], hypervisor-level intrusion detection [9, 11] for both hypervisors and operating systems. Nested virtualization is a foundation of the AERIE reference architecture [16]: it supports a set of components and services in a managed platform to reduce the level of trust required for IaaS providers. It helps to increase control and isolation and improve the system security and data protection.

In our work, we applied nested virtualization for creating a large scale virtualized environment using a limited number of physical servers to perform scalability assessment of security management solution (HTCC). This approach is of interest to many startups, small companies, and research organizations, which might not have access to a production size virtual environment needed for their scalability studies and performance experiments.

7 CONCLUSIONS

Engineering teams face many challenges when they implement new management and security solutions in large-scale virtual environment. They need to assess performance and scalability of such management solutions, analyze their performance overheads, and perform solution's capacity planning and resource sizing. In this paper, we introduce a novel approach for accomplishing these performance goals. We offer an extensible benchmark, called *HT-vmbench*, which allows users to mimic *session-based* activities of system administrators in virtualized environments. To perform scalability studies with *HT-vmbench*, the users need access to large-scale testbeds (that mimic the production virtual environments). To solve this challenge, we describe and promote an approach, based on a nested virtualization technique, which enables us to create

a large scale virtualized environment (with 30,000 VMs) using a limited number of physical servers (4 servers in our experiments).

We believe that more interesting opportunities are available for constructing specialized virtual environment using this approach. Combined with an extensible nature of *HT-vmbench*, the proposed framework offers a powerful solution for performance assessment of different management and security solutions in large-scale virtual environments.

8 ACKNOWLEDGMENT

The research presented in the paper has been partially supported by NSF grant CCF-1649087.

REFERENCES

[1] HyTrust Inc. Cloud Control Virtual and Private Cloud Security. https://www.hytrust.com/products/cloudcontrol/.
[2] HyTrust Inc. HyTrust Cloud Control: Security, Compliance and Control for Virtual Infrastructure. https://www.hytrust.com/uploads/HyTrust-CloudControl.pdf.
[3] HyTrust Inc. Protecting Sensitive Data and achieving compliance in a multi-cloud world. https://www.hytrust.com/uploads/Compliance-in-a-Multi-Cloud-World_WP.pdf.
[4] Nested Virtualization on Xen. https://wiki.xenproject.org/wiki/Nested_Virtualization_in_Xen.
[5] AMD. Secure Virtual Machine Architecture Reference Manual. https://www.mimuw.edu.pl/~vincent/lecture6/sources/amd-pacifica-specification.pdf.
[6] P. Barham, B. Dragovic, K. Fraser, S. Hand, T. Harris, A. Ho, R. Neugebauer, I. Pratt, and A. Warfield. Xen and the Art of Virtualization. In *Proceedings of the Nineteenth ACM Symposium on Operating Systems Principles*, SOSP '03, 2003.
[7] M. Ben-Yehuda, M. D. Day, Z. Dubitzky, M. Factor, N. Har'El, A. Gordon, A. Liguori, O. Wasserman, and B.-A. Yassour. The Turtles Project: Design and Implementation of Nested Virtualization. In *Proceedings of the 9th USENIX Conference on Operating Systems Design and Implementation*, OSDI'10, 2010.
[8] L. Cherkasova and R. Gardner. Measuring CPU Overhead for I/O Processing in the Xen Virtual Machine Monitor. In *Proceedings of the Annual Conference on USENIX Annual Technical Conference*, ATEC '05, 2005.
[9] T. Garfinkel and M. Rosenblum. A Virtual Machine Introspection Based Architecture for Intrusion Detection. In *Proceedings of Network and Distributed Systems Security Symposium*, 2003.
[10] Q. He. Nested Virtualization on Xen. In *Proceedings of Xen Summit Asia*, 2009.
[11] J.-C. HUANG, M. MONCHIERO, and Y. TURNER. Ally: OS-Transparent Packet Inspection Using Sequestered Cores . In *Proceedings of Seventh ACM/IEEE Symposium on Architectures for Networking and Communications Systems (ANCS)*, 2011.
[12] S. T. King, G. W. Dunlap, and P. M. Chen. Operating System Support for Virtual Machines. In *Proceedings of the Annual Conference on USENIX Annual Technical Conference*, ATEC '03, 2003.
[13] R. Riley, X. Jiang, and D. Xu. Guest-Transparent Prevention of Kernel Rootkits with VMM-Based Memory Shadowing. In *Proceedings of the 11th International Symposium on Recent Advances in Intrusion Detection*, RAID '08, 2008.
[14] J. Rutkowska. Subverting Vista Kernel for Fun and Profit. In *Proceedings of SysScan'06 and Black Hat Briefings*, Aug 2006.
[15] A. Seshadri, M. Luk, N. Qu, and A. Perrig. SecVisor: A Tiny Hypervisor to Provide Lifetime Kernel Code Integrity for Commodity OSes. In *Proceedings of Twenty-first ACM SIGOPS Symposium on Operating Systems Principles*, SOSP '07, 2007.
[16] M. Shtern, B. Simmons, M. Smit, and M. Litoiu. An Architecture for Overlaying Private Clouds on Public Providers. In *Proceedings of 8th International Conference on Network and Service Management (CNSM)*, 2012.
[17] L. Smith, A. Kagi, F. C. Martins, G. Neiger, F. Leung, D. Rodgers, A. Santoni, S. Bennett, R. Uhlig, and A. Anderson. Intel virtualization technology. *Computer*, 38, 2005.
[18] VMware. Running Nested VMs | VMware Communities. https://communities.vmware.com/docs/DOC-8970.
[19] VMware. VMware vSphere 6.5 Nested Virtualization. http://jermsmit.com/vmware-vsphere-6-5-nested-virtualization-create-and-install-esxi-6-5/.
[20] VMware. VMware vSphere Web Services SDK Documentation. https://www.vmware.com/support/developer/vc-sdk/.
[21] VMware VMmark Virtualization Benchmark, http://www.vmware.com/products/vmmark.html.
[22] T. Wood, L. Cherkasova, K. Ozonat, and P. Shenoy. Profiling and Modeling Resource Usage of Virtualized Applications. In *Proceedings of the 9th ACM/IFIP/USENIX International Conference on Middleware*, Middleware '08, 2008.
[23] L. Yang, L. Cherkasova, R. Badgujar, J. Blancaflor, R. Konde, J. Mills, and E. Smirni. Evaluating Scalability and Performance of a Security Management Solution in Large Virtualized Environments.

Runtime Performance Management for Cloud Applications with Adaptive Controllers

Cornel Barna
Dept. of El. Eng. and Comp. Sci.
York University
Toronto, Canada
cornel@cse.yorku.ca

Marin Litoiu
Dept. of El. Eng. and Comp. Sci.
York University
Toronto, Canada
mlitoiu@yorku.ca

Marios Fokaefs
Dept. of Comp. and Soft. Eng.
Polytechnique Montreal
Montreal, Canada
marios.fokaefs@polymtl.ca

Mark Shtern
Dept. of El. Eng. and Comp. Sci.
York University
Toronto, Canada
mark@cse.yorku.ca

Joe Wigglesworth
IBM Toronto Lab
IBM Canada Ltd.
Markham, Canada
wiggles@ca.ib.com

ABSTRACT

Adaptability is an expected property of modern software systems in order to cope with changes in the environment by self-adjusting their structure and behaviour. Robustness is a crucial component of adaptability and it refers to the ability of the systems to deal with uncertainty, i.e. perturbations or unmodelled system dynamics that can affect the quality of the adaptation. Cost is another important property to ensure that resources are used prudently and frugally, whenever possible. Engineering robust and cost-effective adaptive systems can be accomplished using a control theory approach. In this paper, we show how to implement a model identification adaptive controller (MIAC) using a combination of performance and control models and how such a system satisfies the goals for robustness and cost-effectiveness. The controller we employ is multi-input, meaning that it can issue a variety of commands to adapt the system and multi-output, meaning it can regulate multiple performance indicators simultaneously. We show that such a solution can account for uncertainty and modelling errors and efficiently adapt a web application with multiple tiers of functionality spanning multiple layers of deployment, software and virtual machines, on Amazon EC2, an actual cloud environment.

CCS CONCEPTS

• **Mathematics of computing** → **Kalman filters and hidden Markov models**; • **Software and its engineering** → **Cloud computing**; **Software performance**; *System administration*;

KEYWORDS

software, adaptive systems, performance modelling, performance optimization, cost, cloud computing, control theory, linear quadratic regulator

ACM Reference Format:
Cornel Barna, Marin Litoiu, Marios Fokaefs, Mark Shtern, and Joe Wigglesworth. 2018. Runtime Performance Management for Cloud Applications with Adaptive Controllers. In *ICPE '18: ACM/SPEC International Conference on Performance Engineering, April 9–13, 2018, Berlin, Germany*. ACM, New York, NY, USA, 8 pages. https://doi.org/10.1145/3184407.3184438

1 INTRODUCTION

Novel technologies, like cloud computing and resource virtualization have allowed for the better management of computation resources of software systems leading to the need for self-managing and autonomic systems [2], which eventually bore the field of self-adaptive software systems. In essence, a self-adaptive system senses the changes in the operating conditions and in the environment and adjusts its structure and behaviour to meet its goals in the presence of those changes. A reference MAPE architecture [14], which consists of Monitoring, Analysis, Planning and Execution components, allows the design and the implementation of an Autonomic Manager that regulates the performance of the software system against fluctuating incoming traffic.

While there has been major theoretical progress in the field, there are still substantial challenges in designing and implementing self-adaptive systems and eventually limited engineering solutions, which can guarantee the degree of automation and robustness expected from such an autonomic manager. Control theory has long been a popular choice for autonomous systems, especially in the domain of physical systems, including manufacturing, automotive and aerospace industries. However, it is only recently that it has been explored as an alternative for self-adaptive software systems and its popularity has not yet reached high levels. This is probably due to the complexity of designing such systems. Nevertheless, the benefits in robustness and cost-effectiveness can potentially outweigh the effort for designing control systems.

Our work aims to demonstrate and clarify the process of developing an automated controller for software applications deployed on cloud infrastructure. We discuss the key components of the controller, namely the performance model and the actual control. As far as the model is concerned, we discuss the representation of the cloud deployment as a *layered queuing network*, which very accurately captures the non-linear nature of the software performance. We use a *layered queuing model* (LQM) as the performance model and we employ Kalman filters as the parameter estimator. In contrast with the model, we opt for a simpler, yet as robust as required, linear controller. We detail the construction of this controller through the linearization of LQM. More importantly, we discuss the benefits of *multi-linearization*, which constitutes a novel contribution, at frequent intervals as the system progresses and its conditions change during runtime. The linear controller of choice is called *linear quadratic controller* (LQR). The synergy between LQM, Kalman and LQR results in a *model identification adaptive controller* (MIAC) architecture, which eventually constitutes our autonomic management system (AMS).

The remainder of the paper is organized as follows: Section 2 presents the proposed architecture and the development process. Section 3 presents the experimental results that validate our approach. Section 4 discusses the key challenges we had to overcome and the key lessons we learned in the process of developing a MIAC controller. Section 5 introduces the background and related work. The conclusions are presented in Section 6.

2 MODEL IDENTIFICATION ADAPTIVE CONTROLLER

To construct a management system based on a MIAC architecture, we need two key components; the performance model and the controller. In this section, we first describe the layered queuing model (LQM) [10] used to capture the performance of the subject software system. We present how the model is designed to operate under uncertainty so that it allows the controller to be robust against perturbations. Second, we describe the process to design a linear quadratic regulator (LQR) [2] as our controller. We discuss how LQR consumes the state of the system through the performance model, and how the latter has to first be linearized. Necessary steps are also discussed so that the controller can handle dynamic and volatile environments through an adaptive recalibration cycle.

2.1 Performance Model

We opt to use a similarly non-linear model, a *layered queuing model* (LQM) to capture the system's performance. According to LQM [10], the functional tiers of the system are represented as queues, introducing delays to the service time of the overall system, and the nested nature of the infrastructure (software, VMs) is represented as layers. The model orchestrates the layered queues to evaluate the state of the system. The state of the system can be any quality index representing its performance, e.g., CPU utilization or response time, and it is determined mathematically as a set of functions of the incoming workload (w), the topology of the system's infrastructure (u) and the demand of the service requests in terms of resources for each queue (d). Formally, the discrete time model is $y(t) = LQM(w, u, d)$, where $y(t)$ is the vector of the system's output for a given moment in time t. Assuming that the demands of the system are known (by measurement or estimation), we can use the

model to estimate the output under any combination of workload and infrastructure. It is important to note here that while u represents the topology of the system for the LQM, it also represents the input of the controller, i.e., the commands, which are also scaling actions upon the system's infrastructure.

2.1.1 Modelling under uncertainties and volatility. When an application is deployed on cloud, its performance is affected by the dynamics of the cloud infrastructure. Only certain cloud components (such as VMs) are visible to the application modeller, others, including hardware or resource management services, are not visible. However, these invisible components may be the cause for delays, which affect the application performance. Although such delays are reflected in the measured performance metrics, their source cannot always be identified [19, 20] and, thus, they are considered *uncertainties*.

There can be two types of uncertainties that may affect the accuracy of the application model in cloud and therefore the efficiency of the performance controllers we design: parametric uncertainties and unmodelled dynamics. The parametric uncertainties refer to both parameters of the model (such as service times, number or probabilities of calls between different components of the software, communication delays, etc.) or the intensity and mix of the workloads. The unmodelled dynamics refer to structural deficiencies of the model, that is missing components and queues that we have not knowledge of. The latter are very important in cloud where we do not have complete knowledge of the deployment environment.

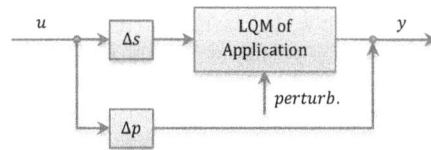

Figure 1: *Extended LQM. Includes structural uncertainties*

To account for unmodelled dynamics, we add two sub-models to extend the application model as seen in Figure 1: a serial sub-model, made of a queuing centre, Δs, and a parallel sub-model, made of another queuing centre, Δp. The serial model Δs will account for the delays in the application requests processing, due to additional proxies in the cloud. The parallel model Δp, will account for speed ups at higher loads, due to possible caching or heterogeneity of the cloud resources. The parameters of those queuing centres, such as service times and visit probabilities (for the parallel model) are unknown at design time and they will be identified at runtime together with other parameters of the model. As a result, the architecture of the LQM model will consider the model for the deployed application in the cloud, as well as these two additional queuing centres.

Parametric uncertainties can occur due to the high volatility of the application's environment, either with respect to users, e.g., changes in volume or type of incoming traffic, or the cloud deployment, e.g., changes in number or type of resources. The model is valid for a specific mix of workload and infrastructure. When the operational conditions change (a change in the topology, the workload intensity or the type of the workload), the model becomes outdated and needs to be retuned. In the case of the proposed LQM, this tuning happens with the use of Kalman filters. Prebuilding all the models at design time is infeasible because of the large number of possible changes and combinations of changes. Therefore, runtime retuning of the model is more efficient and, therefore, preferable. This gives the adaptive nature to our MIAC architecture.

2.2 Control System

Having captured the performance of the managed application as a non-linear model, we can now proceed to design the controller, which will consume said model. We opted for the feedback controller LQR, where the system is modelled as a set of linear differential equations and the goal is modelled as a quadratic function. A significant advantage of feedback controllers is that they can give an optimal, in terms of efficiency and effectiveness, set of adaptive actions both automatically and fast. Alternatively, we would have to simulate and evaluate every possible combination of states and adaptive actions, possibly over multiple dimensions, in terms of performance parameters and types of resources, before we can find the optimal adjustment.

2.2.1 Linearizing and discretizing the models. Given how LQR is specified, the first step is to linearize LQM and feed the linear models in the controller. We can extract such a linear model, if we observe the behavior of the system around an operational point (OP) $[x_{op}, y_{op}, u_{op}]$, where x generally refers to the state of the system, i.e., the monitored performance metrics, y is the observable output of the system and u is the controller's input commands, i.e., the adaptive actions. If we focus closely to the OP, we can linearly approximate the system's behavior from the non-linear model. We can take points close to the OP in discrete time k by applying the corresponding *deltas* (i.e. small differences). In the case of a cloud-deployed software system, given an OP, the process can be achieved by slightly varying the infrastructure (commands u) with respect to that of the operational point. At this point and within a small range, we can assume that the workload is constant. Thus, by taking model measurements for slightly different commands, we can generate a set of discrete points around the operational point.

Using these equations to find points close to the operational point, we can define a discrete-time linear system described by:

$$\begin{cases} x(k+1) & = Ax(k) + Bu(k) \\ y(k) & = Cx(k) + Du(k) \end{cases} \quad (1)$$

where A, B, C and D are matrices; y, u and x are vectors. When the matrices are constant in time, the system described by Equation 1 is a linear time invariant (LTI). To find the matrices A, B, C and D, which make up the linear approximation of the system, given the OP and some points around it, we use linear regression. Given that linear regression is simple and efficient, we chose it in order to create models that may be valid for points further than the OP. Other linearization techniques focus too much around the OP. In our case, we can afford to sacrifice some of the accuracy, since according to our method the linear model will at some point have to be updated around a new OP.

2.2.2 Designing the controller. After the linear model is available, the next step is to design the actual controller in terms of the

goals to be optimized. More specifically, the goals are defined as a performance index across the state and command variables in form of a quadratic function (Equation 2), with the objective of finding the command u that minimizes this quadratic function subject to the system in Equation 1. The weight, or penalty, matrices Q_x and Q_u penalize the state variations or the cost of adaptive commands, respectively. The construction of the weight matrices depends on the domain on which we apply the controller. Although the matrix Q_u refers to cost, it does not necessarily capture it directly as the monetary cost for resources, set by a provider. More precisely, it declares the preferences of the system's designer on the various commands. Nevertheless, the matrix can be derived directly from the provider's financial costs through some mathematical transformations, thus producing cost-effective adaptations. The specific design method of the penalty matrices remain out of scope for this work, although we validate the impact of choosing different penalty matrices.

$$J = \sum_0^\infty x^T Q_x x + u^T Q_u u \quad (2)$$

An optimal, feedback controller will find the u that minimizes J. Given the linear model and Equation 2 and assuming that the system is controllable, the steps to synthesize the controller [2] are summarized next. The optimization problem has the following solution:

$$u = -Kx + k_r y_r \quad (3)$$

where x is the system's state as defined earlier, y_r is the goal for the output, K is the feedback gain matrix and k_r is the steady-state factor.

The feedback gain matrix guarantees that the system will remain stable, in the form of $y = 0$, meaning that the output of the system will remain close to the operational point ($y_a(k) = y_{op}$). Since our goal is to bring, in fact, the output towards its desired state (i.e. $y = y_r$), we need another factor, which is k_r.

K is calculated with LQR as:

$$K = -Q_u^{-1} B^T Px$$

where $P \in \mathbb{R}^{n \times n}$ is a positive definite, symmetric matrix that satisfies the *Riccati equation*:

$$PA + A^T P - PBQ_u^{-1}B^T P + Q_x = 0$$

Based on K, we can calculate k_r by solving the following equation:

$$1 = C(A - BK)^{-1}Bk_r \quad (4)$$

2.3 Autonomic Management System

With the LQM performance model and the LQR controller constructed, we can move on with building the final autonomic management system for cloud applications, following the MIAC architecture as illustrated in Figure 2. This architecture has the ability to be robust in the face of uncertainty, thanks to the extended LQM performance model(which incorporates the structural uncertainties), and in spite of the dynamic nature of the software system, thanks to the recalibration and relinearization of the LQM when it becomes outdated, so that LQR has always an accurate model to operate with.

The flow of data and control is further presented in Algorithm 1. The algorithm requires as input four sets $\mathcal{W}$, $\mathcal{Y}$, $\mathcal{U}$, and $\mathcal{X}$. $\mathcal{W}$ contains the names for the workload parameters that are to be monitored. $\mathcal{Y}$ contains the outputs of the system, which will determine whether the system operates normally or not. $\mathcal{U}$ contains the set of resources or parameters, e.g. number of threads or servers, which we can change to bring the system back to a healthy state. $\mathcal{X}$ is a subset of measured or estimated performance variables that we use in linearized model Sets $\mathcal{W}$, $\mathcal{Y}$ $\mathcal{U}$ and $\mathcal{X}$ are *nominal* sets, meaning they only specify *what* is to be included, based on which the actual measurement vectors w, y, u, x are monitored or generated by the manager. Apart from these four sets, the algorithm requires as input the original (before runtime calibration) non-linear model, LQM_0.

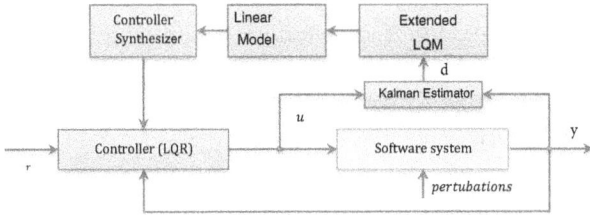

Figure 2: *Model Identification Adaptive Control Architecture.*

Algorithm 1: Model Identification Adaptive Controller (MIAC)

input: $\mathcal{W}$ – the set of workload parameters to be monitored;
$\mathcal{Y}$ – the set of system outputs;
$\mathcal{U}$ – the set of possible commands;
$\mathcal{X}$ – the set of state variables;
LQM_0 – the original non-linear performance model

1 **while** *TRUE* **do**
2 **for** *each sampling interval t* **do**
3   Measure system variables $\rightarrow [y_c, u_c, w_c]$;
4   Estimate performance parameters(Kalman) $\rightarrow [d_c]$;
5   Update Extended LQM
6   **if** *linear model not accurate– its outputs deviates from those of LQM;* **then**
7   Set $[x_{op}, y_{op}, u_{op}] = [x_c, y_c, u_c]$;
8   Linearize $LQM \rightarrow [A, B, C, D]$;
9   Synthesize LQR for linear model $\rightarrow [K, k_r]$;
10 Controller produces adaptive commands $\rightarrow \Delta u$;

In step 1 of the algorithm, and illustrated in Figure 2, it can be seen that the monitoring and control of the system by MIAC is a closed loop. Step 2 is the iteration over time. At each iteration, we maintain the model synchronized through Kalman calibration. In step 3, we measure the current state of the system, where vector y_c contains the current measurements for the system's outputs, vector u_c is the current configuration of the system, for example, its virtual resources and their topology, and vector w_c is the current state of the workload, e.g., arrival rate. In step 4, the *Kalman Estimator* estimates the new performance parameters, with which it updates the extended LQM, in step 5. In step 6, we check whether the

current linear model is still accurate, after the update of LQM. If not, then, we activate the upper loop of Figure 2. We, first, use the current state of the system, as extracted in step 3, to define a new operational point in step 7 (as discussed in Section 2.2.1), where vector x_c includes measurements for the system's current state as they come from the monitoring service. In step 8, the updated LQM is linearized, a process which is detailed later, where A, B, C, and D are the coefficient matrices for the linear model. Based on the linear model, in step 9, we design an optimal controller, as described in Section 2.2.2. The controller is now ready to operate in the lower loop of Figure 2. By monitoring the deployed system and comparing its behavior against a set of goals y_r, in step 10, the controller can issue a set of commands u to rectify any problematic situations.

Notice that the upper loop of Figure 2 is activated only when the linear model diverges too much from the actual system (step 3 of Algorithm 1). If the linear model is accurate, then only the lower loop is executed. This will ensure that the controller is always valid for the current state of the system. A second observation is that when the output of the system is the same as the goal (i.e., $y = y_r$), then the command set produced by the controller Δu is empty; this result is guaranteed by the mathematical definition of the controller.

3 EXPERIMENTAL STUDIES

To validate the MIAC manager we constructed in the previous section, we have conducted a series of experiments. For all experiments, we deployed a *bookstore* application, developed using J2EE technology, on multiple Linux (Ubuntu) virtual machines on the Amazon EC2 cloud. The application performs various SQL commands (select, insert, update). We developed an LQM model for this setting to capture the performance of the application. The efficiency of the controller was first validated on the model itself and later on an actual deployment in Amazon. Any change in the controlled system is reflected in the model. In the initial topology, the database server (MySql) was deployed on one instance, the web application server (Tomcat) was deployed on two instances, while a fourth instance was acting as a load balancer (Apache 2) to distribute the incoming web requests between the application servers.

As input to our algorithm and in order to design the controller, we need to define the set of commands $\mathcal{U}$, the set of monitored state parameters $\mathcal{X}$ and the set of controlled system outputs $\mathcal{Y}$. We define the command points for our system as $\mathcal{U} = [S_d, T_d, S_w, T_w]$, where T_d is the number of threads for database servers and T_w for web servers; S_d is the number of database servers and S_w is the number of web servers. The state vector, x, contains the response time of the web application, the same as the output vector, y (see Equation 1). For the rest of our experiments, when we refer to specific values of these vectors, we will note them with their lower case representation, i.e. u, x and y.

We construct the LQM using the OPERA tool [16] to track the behavior of the system. In every iteration, the LQM is retuned using Kalman filters to recalculate the model parameters, so that the model remains accurate.

(a) *Without re-linearization.*

(b) *With re-linearization.*

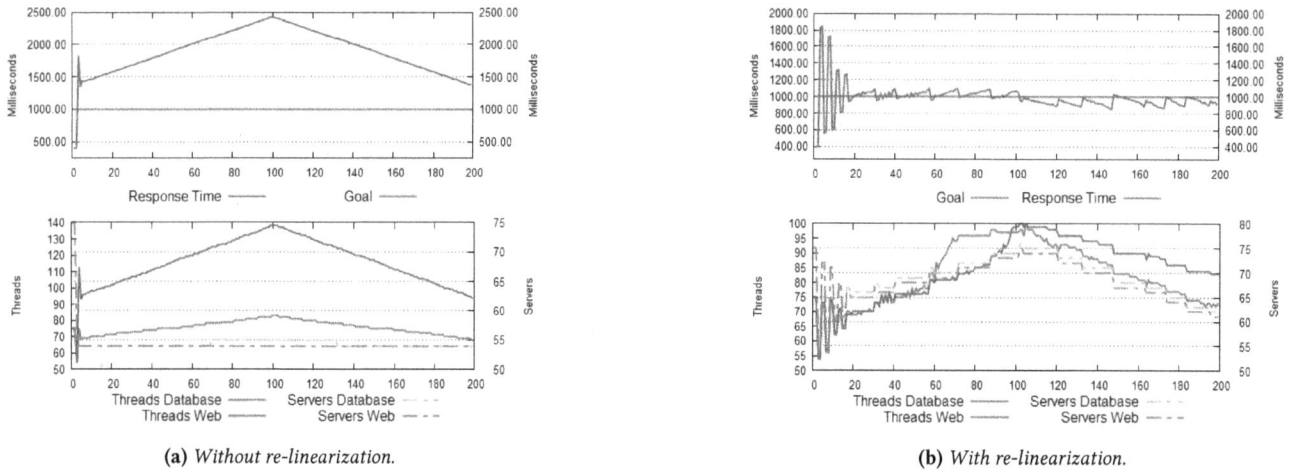

Figure 3: *Behaviour of the system when the goal for Response Time was set to 1000 ms and the workload monotonically increases / decreases.*

To linearize the LQM, we have used the `LinearRegression` function from the package `optim` [1] in Octave to calculate the matrices A and B from Equation 1.

We have also chosen $C = [1]$ and $D = 0$. The reason for this is because we picked response time to represent both the state and the output of the system. From Equation 1, we have that $y(k) = Cx(k) + Du(k)$. Given that $y = x$, it is derived that $C = [1]$ and $D = 0$.

For the LQR, we have used the implementation offered by Octave's package `control` [18]. The parameters for the `lqr` function were the matrices A and B identified during linearization and the following weight matrices Q_x and Q_u:

$$Q_x = [1]; \quad Q_u = \begin{bmatrix} 100\,000 & 0 & 0 & 0 \\ 0 & 1\,000 & 0 & 0 \\ 0 & 0 & 100\,000 & 0 \\ 0 & 0 & 0 & 1\,500 \end{bmatrix} \quad (5)$$

The `lqr` function calculated the matrix K as discussed in Section 2.2.2. To calculate k_r, we assumed that all of its four components were equal and applied the Equation 4:

$$k_r = \frac{1}{b_1 + b_2 + b_3 + b_4} \times \begin{bmatrix} 1 \\ 1 \\ 1 \\ 1 \end{bmatrix} \times (1 - (A - BK))$$

where b_i are the components of B:

$$B = \begin{bmatrix} b_1 & b_2 & b_3 & b_4 \end{bmatrix}$$

K and k_r form our controller, and allow us to calculate a command by applying Equation 3.

For the first experiment (Figure 3), we have set the goal for the response time to be 1000 ms. As for the workload, we start with 18000 users, linearly increasing up to 23000 and then linearly decreasing again down to 18000 users. Figure 3a shows the behavior of the system when using a conventional LQM, liniarized only at the beginning of the experiment, thus creating only one controller (K and k_r from Equation 3), while Figure 3b shows the behavior

when the LQM is relinearized every time its error (the difference between the measured response time and the estimated one using the linear model) exceeds the threshold of 100 ms.

The experiment shows that when we linearize often (we have built 31 linear models for the whole duration of the experiment), we manage to stabilize the system and maintain the response time close to the desired value. Also, the value of J (Equation 2) in this case was approximately 21×10^6, which is significantly smaller than the value obtained with a single linearization: 17×10^9. Considering that the goal of the controller is to minimize J, this shows that multiple linearization is a significantly better model. Figure 3a shows that the controller fails to maintain the response time close to the goal when the workload fluctuates.

Running more experiments with different goals (at 300 ms, 500 ms and 700 ms) produced similar results: the relinearization of the LQM model enabled the controller(s) to maintain a response time close to the desired goal, while doing a single linearization at the beginning of the experiment generated poor results.

In the second experiment, we wanted to evaluate the behaviour of the system in the presence of irregular workload, i.e., when the workload suddenly increases or decreases non-monotonically. The results are summarized in Figure 4. The bottom plot shows the shape of the workload. The goal for the response time in this experiment was set to 700 ms and as it can be seen in the figure, the controller is able to stabilize the system around this goal. In fact, the controller helps the system achieve an average response time of 703 ms (standard deviation of 73.37).

In order to evaluate the influence of the weight matrices Q_x and Q_u on the behaviour of the controller, we have set up an additional experiment with the following matrices:

$$Q_x = [1]; \quad Q_u = \begin{bmatrix} 1\,000 & 0 & 0 & 0 \\ 0 & 100\,000 & 0 & 0 \\ 0 & 0 & 1\,500 & 0 \\ 0 & 0 & 0 & 100\,000 \end{bmatrix} \quad (6)$$

We set the response time goal to be 700 ms, and then increased the workload linearly and then decreased it, also linearly. Figure 5a

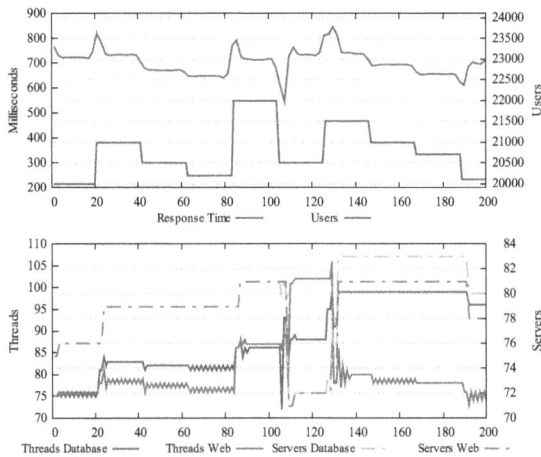

Figure 4: *Behaviour of the system when the goal for Response Time was set to 700 ms, and the workload increasing/decreasing suddenly.*

shows the behaviour of the system when the matrices from Equation 5 (prefer to add servers) are used, while Figure 5b shows the results for matrices from Equation 6 (prefer to add threads).

In both situations, the system was stable and the goal has been maintained. Using the matrices from Equation 5, the value for J (Equation 2) was approximately 27×10^7; the utilization of the weights from Equation 6 resulted in a value for J of almost half, in the range of 14×10^7. This experiment shows that the choice of the penalty matrices affects the adaptation strategies, but performance-wise LQR remains unaffected.

In the last experiment, we deployed our topology on the Amazon EC2 cloud along with the MIAC system. We used small instances (1 CPU, 2 GB RAM and 160 GB hard drive) for the web cluster and the database. We used the regular workload (linearly increasing and then decreasing) starting with 35 users reaching a maximum of about 85. We set the goal for response time at 300 ms. We bounded the number of VMs in the web cluster between 1 and 16. We consider relatively small clusters in order to keep the cost of the experiment low, given that it is conducted with an actual public cloud provider. In addition, given that our database is a single-node MySQL server, we did not consider scaling this cluster. Therefore, it was removed from the set of available commands of the controller. To simplify our experiments, we also excluded web and database threads from consideration due to this reason. Therefore, only the web cluster was scaled. We monitored the system every minute. After every scaling action, we enforced 6 minutes of scaling inactivity to allow for the elastic operation to finish and the system to stabilize itself.

As it can be seen in Figure 6, MIAC was able to maintain the response time close to the set goal even in a real deployment, further strengthening our argument for a robust controller. In fact, the average error was 3.5 ms, with a standard deviation of 84.09. Naturally, it cannot be expected for the controller to keep the response time exactly on the goal. One reason is that for small clusters, the addition or deletion of a single VM can have a great impact to the performance. Nevertheless, response time was eventually kept at the desired levels. In addition, as the figure shows for the response time, the recalculation and calibration of the LQM model resulted

in very accurate estimations, with the average error between the measured metrics (m) and the estimated ones (e) from the model to be 0.55 ms (standard deviation of 13.43).

4 LESSONS LEARNED AND CHALLENGES

In this paper, we present our process for building a controller to manage the performance parameters of software systems. The task on its own is not trivial and requires a solid background on the mathematical foundations of control theory and the performance model used by the controller. For this reason, in this paper, we also provide all the theoretical details on the LQM model and the LQR controller we built. Although the effort may seem too much compared to other less complex techniques, the benefits can possibly outweigh the extra effort [9]. More specifically, as we have shown the adaptive nature of our controller through the multilinearization process make the controller be more resilient and robust against perturbations coming from the system or its deployment environment. Additionally, thanks to the runtime adaptive mechanisms of both the model and the controller, this extra effort is required only once during the design of the controller, and afterwards the management system requires little to no maintenance, unless the system itself changes.

Another challenge in setting up a controller for software performance is understanding the nature of the inputs and their constraints. For example, in public clouds, computations resources (VMs) come in packages predefined by the provider. Therefore, resources may not be added individually, e.g., only memory or only CPU. This detail has to be carefully taken into account when designing the controller, since the impact of the adaptive action can be less fine-grained than the action seemingly is. This is the main reason behind our choosing response time to choose both the state and the output of the system. The addition of a VM may add multiple resources at the same time (CPU, memory, disk), but its exact effect will be definitely measurable on response time. If we were to model the utilization of the individual resources, the addition/removal of a VM would change all utilizations, even if the respective resources had no problem, which could actually affect the whole control process.

Another issue related to the predefined sizes of VMs is that one can add whatever resources the VM offers *at minimum*. For example, if at one point the application needs one additional CPU core to fix its response time, but we assume that the smallest VM available has 2 CPU cores, the controller cannot do anything but add a VM with 2 cores. This problematic behaviour is exacerbated by the fact that our actions are discrete (e.g., add/remove one, two, three VMs), but the command of the controller can be continuous (e.g., add 1.5 VMs). In this case, a meta-decision needs to be taken (do we round up or down?), which can depend on other factors, for example cost or minimal error compared to goal. In any case, this can cause oscillation or overshooting, as it is exemplified in Figure 6, where response time "jumps" when we add or remove a VM. We can mitigate this situation by selecting a good mix of fine-grained and coarse-grained inputs for our controller. In our experiments, the threads play the role of the fine-grained command, while the VM is the coarse-grained solution. An alternative to the coarse-grained VMs can be the use of containers, like Docker, where one

(a) *Using the Q_x and Q_u from Equation 5.*

(b) *Using the Q_x and Q_u from Equation 6.*

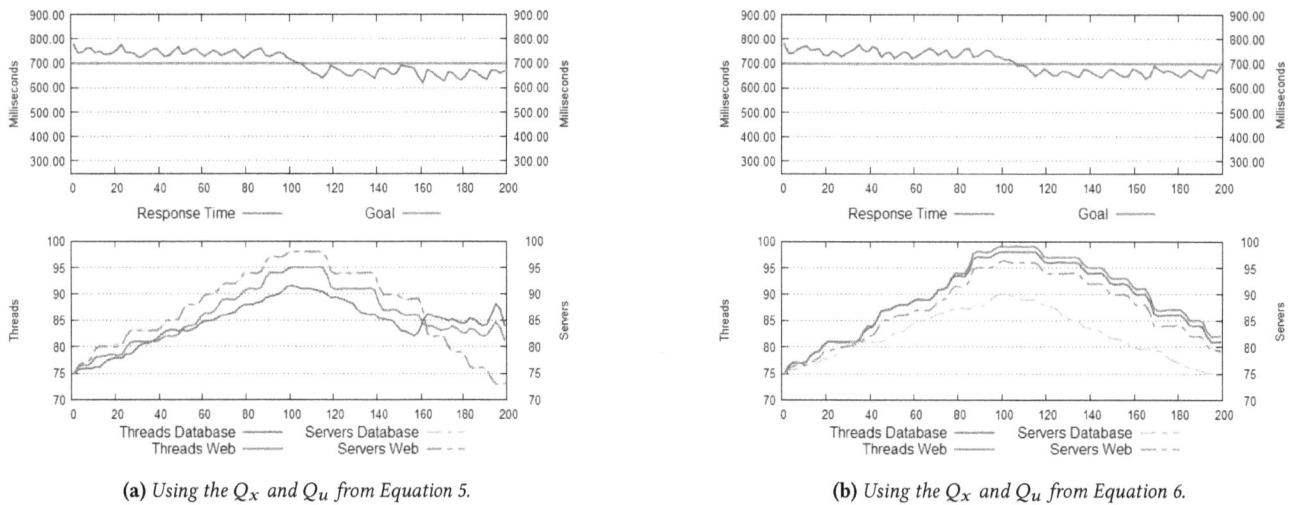

Figure 5: *The effect of the weight matrices Q_x and Q_u on the behaviour of the controller.*

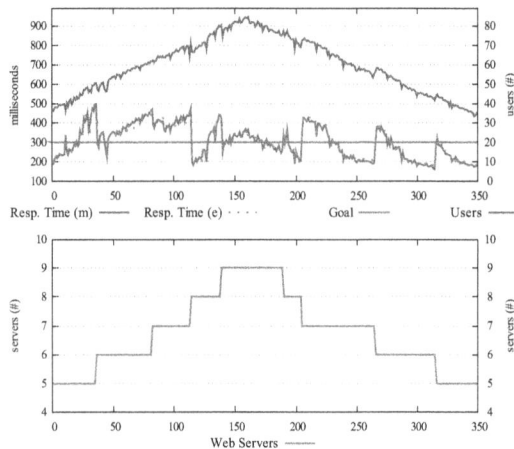

Figure 6: *Behaviour of the system with a real deployment on Amazon EC2. Regular workload was used and the goal was set at 300 ms.*

can slice the host's resources at will and create some more granular than the smallest VM available. Nevertheless, containers may pose challenges on their own like, for example, having one more layer to manage [8] or how container resources can be modelled in a layered queuing model [3].

An important conclusion we drew from the exercise of building MIAC controller is that the effectiveness of a controller implemented using this methodology relies heavily on the capabilities of the model. Resources that cannot be modelled cannot be captured by the controller. In our case, OPERA cannot capture the memory of a software system, so the controller we developed is not able to use memory as a command. In other words, even if our resources where granular enough to allow us to issue commands like increase/decrease the memory, we could not have done so, because the controller would not have been able to asses the impact of the

new memory using the model. The key lesson for practitioners here is that *the limitations of the model are transferred to the controller.*

5 BACKGROUND AND RELATED WORK

Feedback loops have been identified as important components in self-adaptive systems [5, 15]. At the conceptual level, feedback loops follow the MAPE architecture [14], but at the implementation levels there are many variations. A prevalent one is based on control theory [4] and has been used for some time. Hellerstein et al. [13] introduced several case studies, where control theory has been used for controlling the threading level, memory allocation or buffer pool sharing in commercial products such as IBM Lotus Notes and IBM DB2.

Although the performance in software is more accurately modelled with non-linear models, many authors use linear models due to their simplicity [7, 12, 13]. Because the models are linear and valid only around the linearization point, controllers designed based on linear models will most likely be valid only around that linearization point and will not be able to handle a large spectrum of perturbations. This is a well known problem in the control of non-linear systems and often control switch approaches [17] are employed to switch between many statically designed controllers. In this paper, we consider the system to be non-linear, represent it with a non-linear model and then linearize it at runtime, around multiple operational points. In this case, the system is modelled as series of linear models and one controller, which is updated multiple times at runtime.

One of the most important reasons for having a model is to study the properties of the system it models and then to design the controller. In control theory, the significant properties are *stability, controllability, observability. Stability* is probably the the main *raison d'être* of control theory. In simple terms, stability means that for bound inputs (commands), the system will produce bound state and output values. Examples of stability studies in control of software and computing systems have been presented in [13].

Observability is the property of the model that allows finding, or at least estimating, the internal state variables of a system from the output variables. This property is important from pragmatic point of view. In a real system, it is impossible, hard or impractical to measure all state variables. On the other hand, the commands and outputs are easier to measure. Examples of how to use observability and how to estimate software performance parameters for applications deployed across multi-tiers and using Kalman filters are presented in [21]. Other authors have used other techniques to estimated runtime model parameters [6] on the same assumption that the system was observable. The concept of controllability (or reachability) describes the possibility of driving the system to a desired state, i.e. to bring its internal state variables to certain values [2]. This property ensures that we can design a controller. We use the concept of observability, in our paper, when we estimate the performance model in cloud. In this aspect, we extend [21] for cloud environments. Our goal is to achieve controllability across a large design space and for any model and controller we design and to make the system stable. Although one can synthesize empirical controllers [11], we follow classic control theory to build optimal controllers [15].

6 CONCLUSIONS

In this work, we demonstrated the construction of a model identification adaptive control architecture as a management system to monitor and maintain applications on cloud environments. Our experiments have shown that the use of control theory in an Adaptive Manager for cloud applications performs exceptionally well and can produce a robust and effective controller. Additionally, the mathematical background of control theory allows us to systematically design and verify such adaptive management systems. This method is capable of operating on a multidimensional level both with respect to the goals that are to be achieved, as well as the adaptive actions. The proposed controller performs better than previous methods thanks to the concept of multilinearization, which allows the controller to readjust itself in order to better monitor the system and produce more efficient adaptive actions. Our experiments on Amazon EC2 showed that our controller is applicable and performant in real settings.

REFERENCES

[1] 2015. Octave Optim Package v1.4.1. http://octave.sourceforge.net/optim/overview.html. (2015).

[2] Karl Johan Aström and Richard M Murray. 2010. *Feedback systems: an introduction for scientists and engineers*. Princeton university press.

[3] Cornel Barna, Hamzeh Khazaei, Marios Fokaefs, and Marin Litoiu. 2017. Delivering Elastic Containerized Cloud Applications to Enable DevOps. In *Proceedings of the 12th International Symposium on Software Engineering for Adaptive and Self-Managing Systems*. ACM.

[4] Yuriy Brun, Ron Desmarais, Kurt Geihs, Marin Litoiu, Antonia Lopes, Mary Shaw, and Michael Smit. 2013. A design space for self-adaptive systems. In *Software Engineering for Self-adaptive Systems II*. Springer, 33–50.

[5] R de Lemos, H Giese, HA Müller, M Shaw, J Andersson, L Baresi, B Becker, et al. 2009. Software engineering for self-adaptive systems. In *Dagstuhl Seminar*, Vol. 10431. Springer.

[6] Antonio Filieri, Lars Grunske, and Alberto Leva. 2015. Lightweight adaptive filtering for efficient learning and updating of probabilistic models. *ICSE. IEEE* (2015).

[7] Antonio Filieri, Henry Hoffmann, and Martina Maggio. 2014. Automated Design of Self-adaptive Software with Control-theoretical Formal Guarantees. In *Proceedings of the 36th International Conference on Software Engineering (ICSE 2014)*. ACM, New York, NY, USA, 299–310. https://doi.org/10.1145/2568225.2568272

[8] Marios Fokaefs, Cornel Barna, Rodrigo Veleda, Marin Litoiu, Joe Wigglesworth, and Radu Mateescu. 2016. Enabling devops for containerized data-intensive applications: an exploratory study. In *Proceedings of the 26th Annual International Conference on Computer Science and Software Engineering*. IBM Corp., 138–148.

[9] Marios Fokaefs, Yar Rouf, Cornel Barna, and Marin Litoiu. 2017. Evaluating Adaptation Methods for Cloud Applications: An Empirical Study. In *Cloud Computing (CLOUD), 2017 IEEE 10th International Conference on*. IEEE, 632–639.

[10] Greg Franks, Tariq Al-Omari, Murray Woodside, Olivia Das, and Salem Derisavi. 2009. Enhanced modeling and solution of layered queueing networks. *IEEE Transactions on Software Engineering* 35, 2 (2009), 148–161.

[11] Hamoun Ghanbari, Marin Litoiu, Przemyslaw Pawluk, and Cornel Barna. 2014. Replica Placement in Cloud through Simple Stochastic Model Predictive Control. In *Cloud Computing (CLOUD), 2014 IEEE 7th International Conference on*. IEEE, 80–87.

[12] Hamoun Ghanbari, Bradley Simmons, Marin Litoiu, and Gabriel Iszlai. 2012. Feedback-based Optimization of a Private Cloud. *Future Generation Computer Systems* 28, 1 (January 2012), 104–111. https://doi.org/10.1016/j.future.2011.05.019

[13] Joseph L Hellerstein, Yixin Diao, Sujay Parekh, and Dawn M Tilbury. 2004. *Feedback control of computing systems*. John Wiley & Sons.

[14] IBM. 2005. *An Architectural Blueprint for Autonomic Computing*. Technical Report. IBM. http://www-03.ibm.com/autonomic/pdfs/AC%20Blueprint%20White%20Paper%20V7.pdf

[15] Rudolf Kalman. 1959. On the general theory of control systems. *IRE Transactions on Automatic Control* 4, 3 (1959), 110–110.

[16] Marin Litoiu. 2013. Optimization, Performance Evaluation and Resource Allocator (OPERA). (2013). http://www.ceraslabs.com/technologies/opera

[17] Tharindu Patikirikorala, Alan Colman, Jun Han, and Liuping Wang. 2011. A multi-model framework to implement self-managing control systems for QoS management. In *Proceedings of the 6th International Symposium on Software Engineering for Adaptive and Self-Managing Systems*. ACM, 218–227.

[18] Lukas Reichlin. 2015. Octave Control Package v2.3.8. http://octave.sourceforge.net/control/overview.html. (2015).

[19] Joerg Schad, Jens Dittrich, and Jorge-Arnulfo Quiane-Ruiz. 2010. Runtime Measurements in the Cloud: Observing, Analyzing, and Reducing Variance. *Proceedings of the VLDB Endowment* 3, 1 (2010).

[20] Michael Smit, Bradley Simmons, and Marin Litoiu. 2013. Distributed, Application-level Monitoring of Heterogeneous Clouds using Stream Processing. *Future Generation Computer Systems* 29, 8 (2013), 2103–2114.

[21] C. Murray Woodside, Tao Zheng, and Marin Litoiu. 2008. Performance Model Estimation and Tracking Using Optimal Filters. *IEEE Transactions on Software Engineering* 34, 3 (2008), 391–406. https://doi.org/10.1109/TSE.2008.30

Rapid Testing of IaaS Resource Management Algorithms via Cloud Middleware Simulation

Christian Stier
FZI Research Center for Information
Technology
Karlsruhe, Germany
stier@fzi.de

Jörg Domaschka
Institute of Information Resource
Management, Ulm University
Ulm, Germany
joerg.domaschka@uni-ulm.de

Anne Koziolek
Karlsruhe Institute of Technology
Karlsruhe, Germany
koziolek@kit.edu

Sebastian Krach
FZI Research Center for Information
Technology
Karlsruhe, Germany
krach@fzi.de

Jakub Krzywda
Department of Computing Science
Umeå University
Umeå, Sweden
jakub@cs.umu.se

Ralf Reussner
Karlsruhe Institute of Technology
Karlsruhe, Germany
reussner@kit.edu

ABSTRACT

Infrastructure as a Service (IaaS) Cloud services allow users to deploy distributed applications in a virtualized environment without having to customize their applications to a specific Platform as a Service (PaaS) stack. It is common practice to host multiple Virtual Machines (VMs) on the same server to save resources. Traditionally, IaaS data center management required manual effort for optimization, e.g., by consolidating VM placement based on changes in usage patterns. Many resource management algorithms and frameworks have been developed to automate this process. Resource management algorithms are typically tested via experimentation or using simulation. The main drawback of both approaches is the high effort required to conduct the testing. Existing Cloud or IaaS simulators require the algorithm engineer to reimplement their algorithm against the simulator's API. Furthermore, the engineer manually needs to define the workload model used for algorithm testing. We propose an approach for the simulative analysis of IaaS Cloud infrastructure that allows algorithm engineers and data center operators to evaluate optimization algorithms without investing additional effort to reimplement them in a simulation environment. By leveraging runtime monitoring data, we automatically construct the simulation models used to test the algorithms. Our validation shows that algorithm tests conducted using our IaaS Cloud simulator match the measured behavior on actual hardware.

ACM Reference Format:
Christian Stier, Jörg Domaschka, Anne Koziolek, Sebastian Krach, Jakub Krzywda, and Ralf Reussner. 2018. Rapid Testing of IaaS Resource Management Algorithms via Cloud Middleware Simulation. In *ICPE '18: ACM/SPEC International Conference on Performance Engineering, April 9–13, 2018, Berlin, Germany.* ACM, New York, NY, USA, 8 pages. https://doi.org/10.1145/3184407.3184428

1 INTRODUCTION

IaaS Cloud services allow users to deploy a distributed application in a virtualized environment without having to customize their application to a specific PaaS stack. It is common practice to host multiple VMs on the same server. The shared hosting of VMs reduces operational cost. Traditionally, IaaS data center management required manual effort for optimization, e.g. by consolidating VM placement based on changes in usage patterns. Autonomic resource management addresses this problem by automating the allocation of virtual to physical resources. Resource management frameworks continuously optimize, e.g., the mapping of VMs to servers. For this, they can leverage adaptation actions like VM migration.

However, the design and selection of autonomic resource management algorithms for IaaS data centers is a challenging task. In particular, the performance of the algorithms varies [14]. Theoretical guarantees on the performance of resource management algorithms are only valid under impractical assumptions and thus cannot directly be used for the design and selection. The selection of resource management algorithms depends on the Quality of Service (QoS) goals of an IaaS data center operator, and tenant Service Level Agreements (SLAs). The selection of an algorithm thus requires an informed trade-off between conflicting goals [14].

The experimental evaluation of algorithms, e.g. via benchmarking, requires large data center testbeds. This is both time consuming and costly. *Cloud simulators* like CloudSim [5] or GreenCloud [12] offer reproducible conditions for algorithm testing. Once defined, it is possible to use the same workload scenarios to compare different resource management algorithms and configurations.

However, existing IaaS Cloud simulators [5, 12, 18] have specialized APIs, against which resource management algorithms need to be implemented. The re-implementation of algorithms for specific simulators is a challenging task. It requires expert knowledge of the simulator execution semantics, and their correspondence to the managed elements of the runtime management algorithms. Changes made to the algorithm need to be implemented in the runtime and simulation variant of the algorithm. This induces significant effort. Non-expert users, e.g. data center operators, have to rely on the availability of an algorithm implementation for their IaaS simulator of choice.

Another difficulty of simulation-based evaluations is the acquisition of representative and accurate simulation models. The manual construction of simulation models, either in code, or graphical editors, requires significant effort. Furthermore, it requires detailed knowledge of the level of abstraction of the input model used by the simulator.

In this paper, we present an approach to integrate native resource management algorithm implementations into a data center simulation tool. The integration of native resource management algorithm implementations with the data center simulation has two main advantages. First, it removes the need to re-implement the algorithm against a simulation specific interface. This makes it easier to test resource management algorithms using simulation. Second, an evaluation of the actual algorithm implementation increases confidence that it performs as intended.

We build upon our previous work, in which we suggested a generic approach to couple run-time models and simulation models [19]. The implementation of the integration approach leverages instances of the *Adaptation Action* metamodel [20] to define reusable and composable model-to-model transformation rules.

To address the challenge of simulation model acquisition, we present an automated simulation model extraction approach in order to reduce the effort for simulation model acquisition. Our approach reconstructs IaaS workloads, including VM submission and termination requests from historical measurements. Thereby, we enable the reconstruction of complex workloads. This enables the evaluation of runtime management algorithm performance under varying load. We represent extracted VM submissions using our timeline-based modeling language. In a previous short paper [13], we introduced this language and an early evaluation of the language. Algorithm engineers and data center operators can easily modify an extracted model to evaluate alternative scenarios.

To summarize, the contributions of this paper are:

(1) An approach to integrate native resource management algorithm implementations into a data center simulation tool,
(2) A simulation model extraction approach that automatically reconstructs timeline-based, complex workload scenarios,
(3) An evaluation of (1), (2), and the timeline-based modeling language [13].

We evaluated our approach for a diverse set of IaaS workloads. We used a set of scientific computing workloads to investigate the accuracy of extracted simulation models. The workloads were constructed based on expert knowledge on typical workloads submitted at the High Performance Computing Center at Ulm University. We investigated the consistency of resource management decisions between simulation and a real world IaaS testbed deployment at Ulm University. We showed that our integrated approach accurately predicts data center utilization and power consumption metrics. Resource management decisions performed in the simulation are consistent with the behavior in the IaaS testbed. Finally, we illustrated the benefit of simulation-based testing for the selection of power management and autoscaling algorithms. The simulation based evaluation of a power management algorithm showcased significant savings in energy consumption. Simultaneously, the algorithm did not compromise the deployment of VMs. The comparison of autoscalers enabled us to evaluate which algorithm better suited the scalability requirements for the investigated workload.

This paper is organized as follows: Section 2 describes the foundations of our work. In Section 3 we illustrate an example use case of our approach. Section 4 describes how native resource management algorithm implementations can be integrated into our data center simulation tool. Section 5 describes our simulation model extraction approach. The evaluation is presented in Section 6. Section 7 compares our work to related work and Section 8 concludes.

2 FOUNDATIONS

2.1 The CACTOS Project

The CACTOS project [16] developed an approach for the autonomic management of IaaS Cloud data centers. As part of the CACTOS project, two toolkits were developed. The *CACTOS Runtime Toolkit* integrates monitoring and resource management via a variety of algorithms. The *CACTOS Prediction Toolkit* supports the systematic evaluation of alternative data center deployment scenarios. This paper focuses on the prediction toolkit.

2.1.1 CACTOS Runtime Toolkit. The CACTOS Runtime Toolkit is designed to support different IaaS Cloud platforms. The toolkit integrates with these platforms to offer enhanced resource management capabilities. As part of the project, OpenStack [15] and Flexiant Cloud Orchestrator (FCO) [8] support was developed. CACTOS uses an optimization framework, CactoOpt [1], to derive adaptation action plans. The algorithms offered by CactoOpt [1] aim for different QoS trade-offs. In order to achieve these trade-offs, the algorithms formulate adaptation actions. They span the initial placement of VMs, VM migration, server level power management, and further resource management actions. CactoOpt also offers autoscaling capabilities to horizontally scalable, multi-tier applications. Autoscaling algorithms supported by CACTOS cover *Hist*, *ConPaaS*, *Reg* and *React* [9]. The CACTOS Runtime Toolkit uses a runtime model, which was built specifically to automate the management of heterogeneous IaaS data centers. The CactoOpt algorithms derive their plans from the runtime state that is represented in the runtime model. A set of Cloud middleware components execute the adaptation actions in the data center environment.

2.1.2 CACTOS Prediction Toolkit. The development, selection and parametrization of resource management algorithms are complex tasks. The CACTOS project developed the CACTOS Prediction Toolkit to support what-if analyses for IaaS Cloud data center environments. The CACTOS Prediction Toolkit builds upon the Palladio Component Model (PCM) software performance model [3], and the self-adaptive software systems simulator SimuLizar [2]. The toolkit supports the simulation of applications modeled at different levels of details, ranging from black-box VMs to detailed application architecture models. This paper contributes extensions to the toolkit that enable data center operators and algorithm engineers to systematically investigate the effectiveness and efficiency of resource management algorithms. Our work builds upon [19, 21, 11], which we discuss in the following.

2.2 Achieving Model Consistency between Runtime and Simulation Models

The model consistency approach described in [19] leverages correspondence models and correspondence rules to synchronize runtime and simulation models. The correspondence model holds the relationship between entities in the runtime and simulation model. Correspondence rules can be subdivided in two categories. *Mapping operations* synchronize the runtime model with changes in the simulation. Example changes are updates of measurements in simulation. The updated simulation measurements need to be propagated to the runtime model. This enables runtime management mechanisms to observe and react to changes in load. *Adaptation enactment rules* enact and synchronize the effect of adaptation decisions made by autonomic resource management mechanisms. This paper applies [19] to support the evaluation of resource management algorithms in the CACTOS Prediction Toolkit.

2.3 Timeline-Based Experiment Scenarios

In order to assess the performance of IaaS data center optimization algorithms, algorithm engineers and data center operators need workload models that are representative for the intended use cases of the algorithms. Our *Experiment Scenario* [13] metamodel enables the specification of complex user interactions with data centers. Instances of the metamodel represent interactions of users with a data center as a timeline of events.

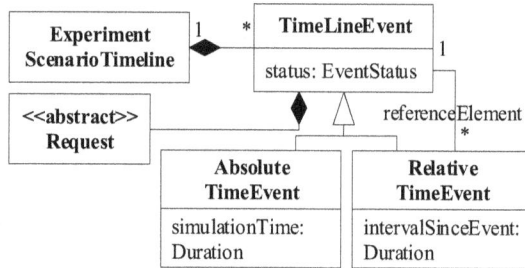

Figure 1: Excerpt from the Experiment Scenario metamodel.

Figure 1 depicts the central classes from the metamodel. The *ExperimentScenarioTimeline* consists of *TimeLineEvents*. Each event maps a *Request* model element to the timeline. There are two types of events. *AbsoluteTimeEvent* specifies an absolute point in time at which a request should be triggered. *RelativeTimeEvent* defines the request time relative to another event. An example request type is *StartApplicationRequest*. *StartApplicationRequest* models a user request to start a new individual VM or distributed application. The request references an application template that is used to assemble the application. Reconfigurations of the data center caused by manual intervention of operators can be expressed with appropriate requests. For an overview of all supported types we refer to [13].

In simulation, a dedicated event scheduler processes the *AbsoluteTimeEvents* ordered by ascending simulation time. The scheduler tracks the execution status of events in their *EventStatus*. Adaptation enactment rules trigger the execution of the requests.

Figure 2 depicts an example excerpt from an Experiment Scenario model based on one of our evaluation scenarios. It contains a start-up request for the VM *instance-1e22*. The scenario prescribes that *instance-1e22* should be started at simulation time 1747s, and terminated 1780s later. The startup request references the VM template, used VM flavor and input parameters. The terminate request references the prior *StartApplicationRequest*, as the VM to be terminated is not yet running in the initial simulation model.

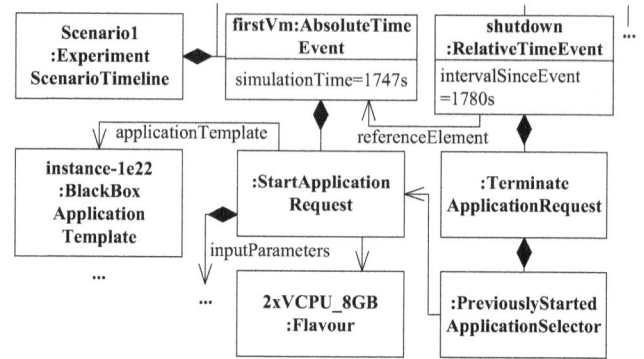

Figure 2: Excerpt from example Experiment Scenario model.

2.4 Extracting Data Center Simulation Models

Svorobej et al. [21] present an initial approach that leverages a runtime model snapshot from the CACTOS Runtime Toolkit as foundation for simulations. The runtime model lacks information on historically executed VMs and their workloads. The runtime model thus can only be used to evaluate how runtime management algorithms would perform under stable load conditions. Kistowski et al. [11] sketches an algorithm for the reconstruction of black-box resource demand functions from a series of load measurements.

This paper contributes a novel model extraction approach that supports the reconstruction of timeline-based workload models from historical measurements. It leverages [21] to gather basic infrastructure information, i.e., on the available servers. Our model extraction approach applies the algorithm from [11] to reconstruct workload models for individual VMs.

3 EXAMPLE USE

A data center operator might use our approach as follows. As a starting point, she might be interested in evaluating how the introduction of automated resource management would affect the performance and efficiency of a manually managed data center. For this, the data center operator can install the monitoring tools provided by the CACTOS Runtime Toolkit to gather monitoring data. Next, the operator applies our simulation model reconstruction methods to the data. The operator then can simulate how the application of an existing runtime resource management algorithm implementation would have affected the performance and efficiency of the data center for this scenario under investigation.

The use of existing algorithm implementations and automated model construction significantly reduces the evaluation effort for the data center operator. It rules out inconsistencies between simulation and runtime implementation variants. It thus increases confidence in the simulation results. Once she has invested the initial effort for the monitoring setup, the operator can continuously reevaluate and compare different algorithms. This enables the operator to adapt the algorithm choice and configuration to changes in the data center setup, workload and performance requirements.

4 INTEGRATING MIDDLEWARE-SPECIFIC RUNTIME MANAGEMENT ALGORITHMS WITH SIMULATION

Runtime management frameworks use *runtime models* to manage resources. Runtime management algorithms leverage information from the runtime models to plan adaptation decisions. Existing Cloud and simulation frameworks lack support for simulating these algorithms in their middleware-specific implementation. This section presents our approach for the integration of middleware-specific runtime management algorithms with an IaaS Cloud simulator. It enables algorithm engineers and data center operators to test and evaluate algorithms, while requiring minimal knowledge of the simulation API.

4.1 Information Gap between Runtime Models and Simulation Models

Software system simulators like SimuLizar [2] or CloudSim [5] naturally abstract from information that is not needed to predict the metrics which are relevant to the use cases of the simulator. The abstraction covers characteristics of the hardware and software stack. This simplifies the simulation, as well as the construction of input models for simulator users.

The level of abstraction chosen when modeling individual entities depends on the pragmatism of the simulation. Many software performance simulators do not model memory [2, 3, 12], as (i) memory accesses are difficult to predict, and (ii) their effect on QoS is considered negligible for CPU-bound applications.

Runtime models are designed to support autonomic resource management. This contrasts the pragmatism of design time performance models like PCM [3]. Design time models focus on modeling system characteristics that impact performance. Runtime models capture all characteristics which are relevant to the management of a system. In IaaS data centers, this can include user management information and detailed VM instantiation parameters. Unlike design time performance models, runtime models may not capture information on user and application behavior on a level that is detailed enough for performance simulations.

A naive approach is to transform the runtime models to performance models of the simulator. This approach, however, requires that all resource management algorithms are reimplemented against the model of the simulator. Runtime management algorithms, which consider properties that are not reflected in the simulation model, can not be simulated. We designed an approach for achieving model consistency between runtime models and simulation models. Our approach supports simulation-based analysis and testing of optimization algorithms without the need to modify or re-implement the algorithms.

4.2 Achieving Model Consistency

We achieve model consistency by implementing the approach discussed in Section 2.2 to achieve model consistency between the CACTOS runtime model and the PCM simulation model. A specialized metamodel maintains the correspondence between runtime and simulation model. In total, the metamodel distinguishes 40 correspondence types.

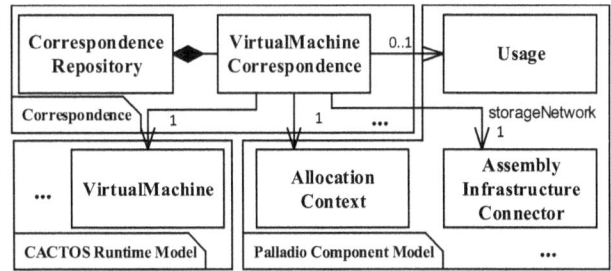

Figure 3: Excerpt from the correspondence metamodel between runtime and simulation model.

Figure 3 provides an example correspondence from this metamodel. Each *VirtualMachine* in the CACTOS runtime model corresponds to multiple entities in the simulation model, the PCM. The *AllocationContext* represents the deployment of a set of software components to a server. It can be used to represent VM allocations in PCM. However, the correspondence with allocated components fails to cover all aspects that are needed to enable meaningful simulations. The CACTOS runtime model contains detailed storage information of VMs. This includes, e.g., the location of their network attached devices. In order to reason the effects of remote storage accesses, the storage characteristics need to be mapped to PCM. Unlike the runtime model, the PCM explicitly models user interactions with the VM components. The correspondence covers this with the reference to the *Usage* model.

A model-to-model transformation from the CACTOS runtime model to PCM establishes the initial correspondence between runtime and simulation model. The mapping operations update the correspondence model during simulation. We implemented the operations as modular model-to-model transformations for the model-based simulated runtime management of SimuLizar [2, 20]. The implementation uses the Adaptation Action metamodel [20] to specify the mapping operations in a reusable manner.

4.3 Implementation of Runtime Management Integration

We integrated all runtime management algorithm types supported by the Cloud middleware of the CACTOS Runtime Toolkit with the simulation environment of the CACTOS Prediction Toolkit. This enabled us to support all algorithms of the same type. No additional effort was required to integrate specific algorithms with the simulator.

A *Placement Connector* bridges the gap between the simulated runtime management, and the placement algorithms of CactoOpt. When a new VM startup request is issued, the simulated runtime management calls the native optimization implementation via the placement connector. The model consistency mechanism discussed in Section 4.2 realizes the simulated runtime management.

We integrated data center optimization algorithms via an *Optimization Connector*. This connector couples the resource management optimization algorithms and heuristics of CactoOpt with the simulation. The Optimization Connector functions similar to the Placement Connector. Instead of a single supported decision, i.e., placement, the consistency mechanism translates a wide range of server and VM reconfiguration decisions to simulation. It uses the adaptation enactment rules for this purpose.

The *Autoscaling Connector* communicates with the native autoscaling middleware of CACTOS. The middleware manages autoscaling on a per-application basis. It uses the runtime model passed by the simulation to decide on horizontal scaling. Instead of measurements from a real world data center, the simulation runtime management exposes simulated measurements to the autoscalers. Mapping operations of the rule-based synchronization engine update the measurement representations in the runtime model, as Section 4.2 described.

5 AUTOMATED SIMULATION MODEL CONSTRUCTION

A major challenge in the application of simulations is the acquisition of simulation models. It is more attractive to reason on the performance of resource management algorithm using simulation if the models can be obtained with little effort. We implemented an approach that enables the evaluation of resource management algorithm performance using automatically constructed performance models. Our approach uses the historical information collected by the CACTOS Runtime Toolkit to construct performance models.

5.1 Black-Box Performance Models

Black-box VM workload models describe VM workloads in terms of their resource usage over time. The main benefit of black-box VM models is that they do not require insight into the applications deployed in a VM. As they only depend upon metrics and topology information available to the data center operator, they can be constructed for any VM based on its past observed behavior. We construct the black-box models from past load measurements, which were recorded in the historical database of the CACTOS Runtime Toolkit. We normalize the load levels of VMs using the processing speed of their original host to account for VM migrations.

5.2 Timeline-Based Experiment Scenarios

Data center operators and algorithm engineers can use instances of the Experiment Scenario model to evaluate complex user interaction with the simulated data centers. Section 2.3 introduced the Experiment Scenario metamodel, and provided an overview of supported user interactions, e.g., VM submissions. The manual modeling of Experiment Scenarios requires expert knowledge of potential VM submission patterns, typical VM configurations, and workloads. We realized an automated approach for the reconstruction of Experiment Scenarios from historical measurements. It enables data center operators and algorithm engineers to evaluate resource management algorithms based on past workloads and user interactions.

Our approach uses recorded VM submission and reconfiguration events to reconstruct an Experiment Scenario timeline. We link each VM submission to a black-box performance model, which is automatically constructed. In order to construct an Experiment Scenario model, the user specifies a period of time, and a subset of servers she is interested in. We translate this to a set of queries on a historical measurement database. The data from these queries

is funneled into the reconstruction of user interactions. We enrich the Experiment Scenario with VM instantiation parameters. This increases the accuracy of placement decisions in simulation. Placement algorithms [1] consider these parameters to determine if VMs can be deployed on the same server without causing resource contention.

5.3 Power Models

Power consumption decisively determines the operational cost of data centers. System-level power models [17] enable power consumption predictions of individual servers based on metrics like CPU utilization. Power models need to be trained for specific servers in order to make accurate power consumption predictions. We realized an approach that uses the historical data collected in the historical measurement database as the source of training data for statistical power model learning. For a given time frame, we query the collected measurements. We use this data as input to power model training. A non-linear regression technique trains a given power model type on the selected training data set.

5.4 Limitations

The reconstruction of black-box VM and timeline-based scenario models is well suited to evaluate the performance of resource management algorithms for workloads observed in the past. It is of limited use to explore scenarios that involve user-facing applications with varying workloads. For this, other means of performance model acquisition are more suited. The extraction of server power models from historical measurements requires that the server has run workloads which cover the utilization ranges investigated in simulation.

6 EVALUATION

In order to evaluate our approach, we compared simulation results and measurements for a set of experiments conducted in a data center testbed.

6.1 Scientific Computing

We evaluated the applicability of our approach using a case study from the scientific computing domain.

6.1.1 Scenario Description. We conducted the case study in a commodity hardware testbed. The testbed was operated using the OpenStack Cloud middleware in combination with the CACTOS Runtime Toolkit. The servers ran KVM hypervisors. The CACTOS Runtime Toolkit contributed autonomic resource management. In each of the evaluated configurations, VM placement and migration algorithms were in use. We used IPMI to collect power consumption measurements of the servers over time.

In order to evaluate the accuracy of our integration and model extraction methods, we proceeded as follows. First, we ran an experiment in an IaaS data center testbed. Second, we obtained a simulation model by applying our model extraction method. We applied our Experiment Scenario extraction to obtain models of the user interactions, and VM black-box workload models from the experiment run. Next, we conducted a simulation using the resulting input models. We used the same algorithm implementations and configurations for the simulated run as in the testbed experiment run. Finally, we compared measured and predicted results.

The following outlines the scenarios for which we conducted the experimental evaluation. Every scenario encompassed a set of scientific computing workloads. Specifically, we executed a set of Molpro [23] workloads. Molpro is a framework for quantum chemistry calculations. Molpro follows run-to-completion semantics, as is common for scientific computing applications. A compute job submission system translated each scientific compute job submission request to a VM submission request on the IaaS testbed. Per scenario, a load driver submitted the jobs over time based on a predefined submission schedule. We constructed the submission schedule to resemble a typical daily cycle of user job submissions in the High Performance Computing Center at Ulm University. The job submissions consist of a mix of long and short running jobs. The short jobs reach execution times of up to two hours. Long running jobs may span eight to ten hours.

Scenario 1. The first scenario covered 26 VM submissions to a testbed setup which consisted of eight servers. Six of these eight servers had a power meter, from which we could collect measurements. The experiment lasted just short of one and a half hours. We used consolidation algorithms for both VM placement and migration. They consolidated the VMs based on their RAM requirements.

Scenario 2. The second scenario consisted of 15 compute job submissions. It covered a run time of approximately eight and a half hours. We allocated the same eight servers as Scenario 1. We configured the Runtime Toolkit to use load balancing algorithms for both VM migrations and placement. The algorithms aim to evenly distribute the VMs on all servers based on their RAM requirements.

Scenario 3. Scenario 3 encompassed 19 compute job submissions. It covered the same basic experiment as Scenario 1, but with an extended run time of eight hours and 46 minutes. The 26 VM submissions from Scenario 1 were reduced to 19. The VMs were hosted on the same set of eight servers. We used RAM based consolidation algorithms for VM placement and migrations.

Scenario 4. The fourth scenario consisted of 37 Molpro job submissions. It covered a run time of roughly 26 hours. It used six servers from the IaaS testbed. We could collect power measurements from four of these six servers. Scenario 4 used the same migration and placement algorithms as Scenario 1 and 2.

6.1.2 Results. For Scenario 1, the algorithms placed the VMs on the same servers as in the measured experiment. In order to quantify the prediction accuracy over the duration of the experiment, we compared the predicted and measured accumulated energy consumption of all servers with power meters using the error formula $|\frac{E_{Meas}-E_{Sim}}{E_{Meas}}|$, where E is the aggregate energy consumption.

In Scenario 1 we employed a linear power model to predict the energy consumption of the servers. The linear model was trained using historical measurements from each server. We used more complex power models for the other scenarios, e.g., with exponential components. Table 1 lists the measured and predicted total energy consumption over each run. In Scenario 2, the energy consumption prediction reached a prediction error of 0.39%. Scenario 3 had the highest prediction error at 7.08%.

Table 1: Total measured and predicted energy consumption for the four evaluated scenarios, with prediction error. Duration in minutes. Energy consumption in W h, error in %.

Scenario	Duration	Measured	Predicted	Error
1	75 min	1 783 W h	1 661 W h	6.85%
2	514 min	5 443 W h	5 464 W h	0.39%
3	526 min	5 238 W h	5 609 W h	7.08%
4	1561 min	13 558 W h	12 826 W h	5.40%

We could trace back the source of the prediction error for Scenario 3 to a lack of historical measurements from one of the VMs. While the VM was running in the experiment, its measurements were not recorded due to the failure of VM internal monitoring. Thus, our tooling was unable to reconstruct a behavior model of the VM. Down the line, this led to the placement of a highly active VM on one of the servers with a power meter. This increased the predicted energy consumption.

6.2 Power Management

In order to validate that our algorithm integration approach also supports the analysis of power management algorithms, we applied an existing algorithm to the Scenario 3 workload. We configured VM migration and placement to consolidation algorithms. This enabled the power management algorithm to turn off free servers. Our simulations were able to show significant power savings, without negatively affecting the deployment of new VMs.

6.3 Autoscaling

The selection of the right autoscaling algorithm for an application is a challenging task. This section explores how we can employ our simulation-based method to compare different autoscaling policies for an enterprise web application.

6.3.1 Compared Autoscalers. We evaluated which of two autoscalers performed the best for the evaluated enterprise application. We compared the two autoscalers *React* and *Reg*.

React [6] is a rule-based autoscaler. Its algorithm increases the number of active instances of a scalable application tier if the measured user workload surpasses a specified threshold capacity. If at least two instances are under-utilized, React shuts down and decommissions one instance.

Reg [10] is an autoscaler, which scales the number of active instances based on a regression model. If the measured load falls below a specified threshold, the autoscaler reduces the number of active instances. It uses a regression model to determine the number of active instances, which should remain active. For user workload levels higher than a threshold capacity, Reg initiates the startup of additional instances.

6.3.2 Case Study System. DataPlay[1] is a horizontally scalable multi-tier enterprise web application. It is a gamified social platform for data exploration. DataPlay follows a three-tier architecture style, where the business tier can be horizontally scaled.

---

[1] https://github.com/cactos/DataPlay, last retrieved 24.10.2017.

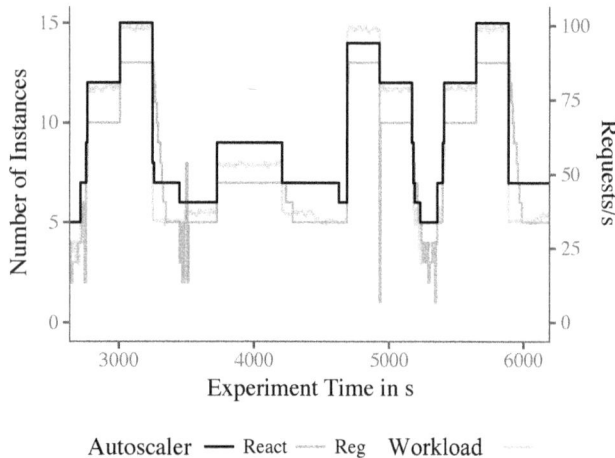

Autoscaler — React ---- Reg   Workload ······

Figure 4: Experimental dynamics of the two simulated autoscaling policies. Excerpt from the full experiment, which spanned a time frame of over 11 hours. The black line shows the workload intensity as requests per s. The grey lines represent the number of active instances over time, which the autoscalers allocate.

We obtained the input model for our simulation by enriching a runtime model snapshot of the data center. The snapshot contained a description of its server infrastructure, and an application model of DataPlay. We instantiated the application at the beginning of the simulated experiment using our Experiment Scenario model.

We used a synthetic workload that covered a wide range of workload intensities, and workload variations. The workload covered a time frame of over eleven and a half hours of simulation time. Over this period, a seasonal pattern repeated sixteen times. The workload reached approximately 100 requests per second at its peak. It contained short periods with request rates just above, or at zero. The seasonal pattern was folded with uniform noise in the interval $[-3, 2]$ requests per second.

6.3.3 Results. We look at an excerpt of the whole experiment results to discuss our findings. Figure 4 illustrates the experimental dynamics of the autoscalers and the workload. The *workload* line shows the rate at which requests arrived at the DataPlay application. The grey lines represent the total number of VMs over time, which the autoscaling algorithms suggested to keep allocated. The behavior of both algorithms differed significantly. Reg frequently triggered scale-out and scale-in decisions. Particularly, Reg overeagerly performed scale-ins once the workload started to decrease. This led to staggered scaling, e.g., at around 3500 experiment time. React over-provisioned VMs. Compared to Reg, it allocated more or an equal number of VMs most of the time. React recommended to operate 9.12 VMs on average, while Reg only proposed 7.47. Over the course of the experiment, Reg issued 2544 scale-in or scale-out actions, while React only adapted 647 times. The higher frequency of Reg led to a larger overhead for (de-)commissioning VMs.

The poor performance of Reg is in line with the experimental comparison of autoscalers by Ilyushkin et al. [9]. In their experiments, Reg also under-provisioned VMs and quickly varied the

number of active VMs. The authors only could improve the performance of Reg, once they implemented a set of improvements to the original algorithm and its implementations. React manages to match demand in most periods, or overprovisions.

In conclusion, we determined that React provides better operational stability at the cost of light overprovisioning. Thus, we consider React to be better suited as a autoscaler for DataPlay for the investigated workload patterns. We did not record performance metrics, such as response time, and average, minimum and maximum CPU utilization as part of our comparison. In future work, we plan to compare the autoscaling policies based upon these further metrics, and the metrics outlined in Ilyushkin et al. [9].

7 RELATED WORK

The simulation-based evaluation of Cloud resource management has been a topic of great interest in recent years. Sakellari and Loukas [18] provide an overview of Cloud simulators. Two popular IaaS Cloud simulators discussed by the survey are CloudSim [5] and GreenCloud [12]. Both support the evaluation of resource management algorithms. However, they require a reimplementation of the algorithms for the simulator specific APIs.

Vondra and Šedivý [22] present a Cloud simulator that has been built for the simulation-based evaluation of autoscaling algorithms. Like CloudSim and GreenCloud, their simulator requires a reimplementation of each algorithm for the simulator interface.

CDOSim [7] extends CloudSim [5] to support the evaluation of enterprise Cloud application migration scenarios. CDOSim offers an approach to extract white-box application models using static code analysis, and dynamic instruction counting. This requires source-code level access to, and extensive profiling of the evaluated Cloud application. In the context of our work, it could be applied to extract white-box application models.

Calheiros et al. [4] propose a profiling based approach to construct coarse grey-box workload models of applications. Their approach requires dedicated profiling infrastructure. It profiles the Cloud application with varying workload intensities and compute resources. This complements our black-box model extraction approach. Unlike our approach it can, however, not be applied to model arbitrary VM workloads.

Ilyushkin et al. [9] experimentally evaluate a set of seven state of the art autoscaling algorithms. The authors evaluate the algorithms for scientific computing workloads. The comparison required a complex IaaS testbed setup and extensive experiments. Our work aims to reduce the effort for testing using simulations. Indeed, we were able to evaluate two of the algorithms from [9], of which we had the implementations.

8 CONCLUSION

This paper presents an approach for rapid testing of resource management algorithms for IaaS Cloud data centers. Our approach enables algorithm engineers and data center operators to evaluate IaaS Cloud resource management algorithms using simulations. Our simulation-based approach supports the simulation of algorithms which are natively implemented for Cloud middleware. The CACTOS Prediction Toolkit implements our approach for the CACTOS Runtime Toolkit, and its supported adaptation actions. These actions include the initial placement of VMs, VM migration, power management and autoscaling. We show that our integration approach enables reasoning on the performance of diverse types of resource management algorithms.

We evaluated our approach for a diverse set of real-world workloads. We evaluated a set of resource management algorithms for scientific computing application workloads. The results from simulation have a high accuracy for energy consumption and utilization measurements. VM placement and migration decisions are consistent between the measured and simulated experiments. Our simulation enabled us to explore the effect of active power management algorithms on total consumption, and the reliability of VM placements. Thereby, the simulation-based evaluation helps avoid scenarios where power management interferes with the ability of a data center to serve all VM submission requests. We applied our approach to compare two autoscalers for an enterprise web application. Our observations on the autoscaler dynamics from simulation are consistent with published experimental evaluations [9].

Our approach enables algorithm engineers and data center operators to rapidly evaluate the performance of IaaS resource management algorithms. It requires no additional effort or in-depth knowledge of simulation models and APIs. The users of our approach can simply evaluate their existing resource management algorithm implementations. We automate the construction of simulation models. For this, we leverage existing runtime models and historical measurements.

We plan to expand our approach in two directions. First, we aim to automate the construction of detailed application models of scientific computing applications. This will reduce the effort for the construction of accurate simulation models, which consider the phases of scientific computing applications. Second, we plan to conduct case studies which investigate the prediction accuracy of application workloads with large heterogeneity between workloads, and used servers. We intend to expand the quantitative comparison of simulation and measurements of autoscaling policies to the metrics listed in Section 6.3.3.

ACKNOWLEDGMENTS

This work is funded by the European Union's Seventh Framework Programme under grant agreement 610711 (CACTOS), the Swedish Research Council (VR) project Cloud Control and the Swedish Government's strategic research project eSSENCE.

REFERENCES

[1] Ahmed Ali-Eldin, Per-Olov Östberg, Jakub Krzywda, Christopher Hauser, Jörg Domaschka, and Henning Groenda. 2017. Predictive Cloud Application Model: Project Deliverable D3.2. Tech. rep.

[2] Matthias Becker, Markus Luckey, and Steffen Becker. 2013. Performance Analysis of Self-Adaptive Systems for Requirements Validation at Design-Time. In *Proc. of the 9th ACM SigSoft Intl Conf on Quality of Software Architectures (QoSA'13)*. ACM, (June 2013).

[3] Steffen Becker, Heiko Koziolek, and Ralf Reussner. 2009. The Palladio component model for model-driven performance prediction. *Journal of Systems and Software*, 82, 1, 3–22.

[4] Rodrigo N. Calheiros, Marco A.S. Netto, César A.F. De Rose, and Rajkumar Buyya. 2013. Emusim: an integrated emulation and simulation environment for modeling, evaluation, and validation of performance of cloud computing applications. *Software: Practice and Experience*, 43, 5, 595–612.

[5] Rodrigo N. Calheiros, Rajiv Ranjan, Anton Beloglazov, César A. F. De Rose, and Rajkumar Buyya. 2011. Cloudsim: a toolkit for modeling and simulation

[6] of cloud computing environments and evaluation of resource provisioning algorithms. *Softw. Pract. Exper.*, 41, 1, (Jan. 2011), 23–50.

[7] Trieu C. Chieu, Ajay Mohindra, Alexei A. Karve, and Alla Segal. 2009. Dynamic Scaling of Web Applications in a Virtualized Cloud Computing Environment. In *Proc of the IEEE Intl Conf on e-Business Engineering* (ICEBE). IEEE CS, 281–286.

[7] F. Fittkau, S. Frey, and W. Hasselbring. 2012. CDOSim: Simulating cloud deployment options for software migration support. In *2012 IEEE 6th International Workshop on the Maintenance and Evolution of Service-Oriented and Cloud-Based Systems (MESOCA)*. (Sept. 2012), 37–46.

[8] [n. d.] Flexiant Cloud Orchestrator. Last retrieved 2017-10-26. Flexiant Ltd. https://www.flexiant.com/flexiant-cloud-orchestrator/.

[9] A. Ilyushkin, A. Ali-Eldin, N. Herbst, A. V. Papadopoulos, B. Ghit, D. Epema, and A. Iosup. 2017. An Experimental Performance Evaluation of Autoscaling Policies for Complex Workflows. In *Proc. of the 8th ACM/SPEC Intl Conf on Performance Engineering* (ICPE '17). ACM, L'Aquila, Italy, 75–86.

[10] Waheed Iqbal, Matthew N. Dailey, David Carrera, and Paul Janecek. 2011. Adaptive resource provisioning for read intensive multi-tier applications in the cloud. *Future Gener. Comput. Syst.*, 27, 6, (June 2011), 871–879.

[11] Jóakim Von Kistowski, Nikolas Herbst, Samuel Kounev, Henning Groenda, Christian Stier, and Sebastian Lehrig. 2017. Modeling and extracting load intensity profiles. *ACM Trans. Auton. Adapt. Syst.*, 11, 4, Article 23, (Jan. 2017), 23:1–23:28.

[12] D. Kliazovich, P. Bouvry, Y. Audzevich, and S.U. Khan. 2010. Greencloud: a packet-level simulator of energy-aware cloud computing data centers. In *Global Telecommunications Conference (GLOBECOM 2010), 2010 IEEE*. (Dec. 2010), 1–5.

[13] Sebastian Krach, Christian Stier, and Athanasios Tsitsipas. 2016. Modeling IaaS Usage Patterns for the Analysis of Cloud Optimization Policies. *Softwaretechnik-Trends*, 36, 4.

[14] Sunilkumar S. Manvi and Gopal Krishna Shyam. 2014. Resource management for infrastructure as a service (iaas) in cloud computing: a survey. *Journal of Network and Computer Applications*, 41, Supplement C, 424–440.

[15] [n. d.] OpenStack. Last retrieved 2017-10-26. The OpenStack Foundation. https://www.openstack.org/.

[16] P-O Östberg et al. 2014. The CACTOS Vision of Context-Aware Cloud Topology Optimization and Simulation. In *Proc. of the Sixth IEEE Intl Conf on Cloud Computing Technology and Science (CloudCom)*. IEEE CS, Singapore, 26–31.

[17] Suzanne Rivoire, Parthasarathy Ranganathan, and Christos Kozyrakis. 2008. A Comparison of High-level Full-system Power Models. In *Proceedings of the 2008 Conference on Power Aware Computing and Systems* (HotPower'08). USENIX Association, San Diego, California, 3–3.

[18] Georgia Sakellari and George Loukas. 2013. A survey of mathematical models, simulation approaches and testbeds used for research in cloud computing. *Simulation Modelling Practice and Theory*, 39, 92–103. Special Issue Energy Efficiency in Grids and Clouds.

[19] Christian Stier and Henning Groenda. 2016. Ensuring Model Continuity when Simulating Self-adaptive Software Systems. In *Proc. of the Modeling and Simulation of Complexity in Intelligent, Adaptive and Autonomous Systems 2016* (MS-CIAAS '16) Article 2. Society for Computer Simulation International, Pasadena, California, 2:1–2:8.

[20] Christian Stier and Anne Koziolek. 2016. Considering Transient Effects of Self-Adaptations in Model-Driven Performance Analyses. In *Proceedings of the 12th International ACM SIGSOFT Conference on the Quality of Software Architectures* (QoSA'16). ACM, Venice, Italy.

[21] Sergej Svorobej, James Byrne, Paul Liston, Peter J. Byrne, Christian Stier, Henning Groenda, Zafeirios C. Papazachos, and Dimitrios S. Nikolopoulos. 2015. Towards automated data-driven model creation for cloud computing simulation. In *Proceedings of the 8th International Conference on Simulation Tools and Techniques, Athens, Greece, August 24-26, 2015*, 248–255.

[22] T. Vondra and J. Šedivý. 2017. Cloud autoscaling simulation based on queueing network model. *Simulation Modelling Practice and Theory*, 70, Supplement C, 83–100.

[23] Hans-Joachim Werner, Peter J. Knowles, Gerald Knizia, Frederick R. Manby, and Martin Schütz. 2012. Molpro: a general-purpose quantum chemistry program package. *Wiley Interdisciplinary Reviews: Computational Molecular Science*, 2, 2, 242–253.

Performance Prediction of Cloud-Based Big Data Applications

Danilo Ardagna, Enrico Barbierato,
Athanasia Evangelinou, Eugenio Gianniti,
Marco Gribaudo
Dipartimento di Elettronica e Informazione
Politecnico di Milano
Milano, Italy
name.lastname@polimi.it

Túlio B. M. Pinto, Anna Guimarães,
Ana Paula Couto da Silva,
Jussara M. Almeida
Departamento de Ciência da Computação
Universidade Federal de Minas Gerais
Belo Horizonte, Brazil
tuliobraga@dcc.ufmg.br, anna@dcc.ufmg.br,
ana.coutosilva@dcc.ufmg.br, jussara@dcc.ufmg.br

ABSTRACT

Data heterogeneity and irregularity are key characteristics of big data applications that often overwhelm the existing software and hardware infrastructures. In such context, the flexibility and elasticity provided by the cloud computing paradigm offer a natural approach to cost-effectively adapting the allocated resources to the application's current needs. Yet, the same characteristics impose extra challenges to predicting the performance of cloud-based big data applications, a central step in proper management and planning. This paper explores two modeling approaches for performance prediction of cloud-based big data applications. We evaluate a queuing-based analytical model and a novel fast ad-hoc simulator in various scenarios based on different applications and infrastructure setups. Our results show that our approaches can predict average application execution times with 26% relative error in the very worst case and about 12% on average. Moreover, our simulator provides performance estimates 70 times faster than state of the art simulation tools.

KEYWORDS

Performance modeling; Big data; Spark; Approximate methods; Simulation

ACM Reference Format:
Danilo Ardagna, Enrico Barbierato, Athanasia Evangelinou, Eugenio Gianniti, Marco Gribaudo and Túlio B. M. Pinto, Anna Guimarães, Ana Paula Couto da Silva, Jussara M. Almeida . 2018. Performance Prediction of Cloud-Based Big Data Applications. In *ICPE '18: ACM/SPEC International Conference on Performance Engineering, April 9–13, 2018, Berlin, Germany*. ACM, New York, NY, USA, 8 pages. https://doi.org/10.1145/3184407.3184420

1 INTRODUCTION

Nowadays, the big data adoption has moved from experimental projects to mission-critical, enterprise-wide deployments providing

new insights, competitive advantage, and business innovation [13]. IDC estimates that the big data market grew from $3.2 billion in 2010 to $16.9 billion in 2015 with a compound annual growth rate of 39.4%, about seven times the one of the overall ICT market [2].

Key properties characterizing big data applications are high volumes of data and increasing heterogeneity and irregularity in data access patterns. Such properties impose challenges to the hardware and software infrastructure. On the other hand, the elastic nature of cloud computing systems provide a natural hosting platform to cost-effectively provision the dynamic resource requirements of big data applications. Indeed, 61% of Spark adopters ran their applications on the cloud in 2016 [1].

Yet, though flexible, the shared infrastructure that powers the cloud together with the natural irregularity of big data applications may impact the predictability of cloud-based big data jobs. Accurate performance prediction of an application is a key step to both planning and managing: it is a key component to drive the automatic system (re-)configuration so as to meet the applications' dynamic needs, avoiding Service Level Agreement (SLA) violations.

A plethora of different modeling techniques, varying from analytical approaches to simulation tools, have been proposed and applied in the past to study system performance [5, 7, 16, 19, 23, 24, 26]. Nevertheless, their efficiency to model massively parallel applications introducing thousands of parallel tasks has been shown to be an issue [3]. Thus, we here take the challenge of predicting the performance of big data applications by exploring two very different techniques, an analytical model and a simulation tool, which, as will be discussed, have complementary pros and cons in terms of prediction accuracy and efficiency. Our goal is to efficiently estimate (in a few seconds), the *average execution time* of a target application, given the available resources, in a way we can support run-time reconfiguration decisions. That is, given a target application, specified by a directed acyclic graph (DAG) representing the individual tasks and their parallelism and dependencies, the purpose is to predict how long it will take for the application to run (on average) on a given resource deployment (described in terms, e.g., of numbers of cores or nodes). We focus on applications running on Spark[1], which is a fast and general engine for large-scale data processing whose adoption has steadily increased and which probably will be the reference big data engine for the next 5–10 years [9].

Firstly, we investigate the use of an analytical queuing network (QN) model for predicting the performance of Spark applications.

---
[1] http://spark.apache.org/

The model, originally proposed in [16] for performance prediction of parallel application, extends an Approximated Mean Value Analysis (AMVA) technique by modeling the precedence relationships and parallelism between individual tasks of the same job. This model, here referred to as *Task Precedence model*, explicitly captures the overlap in execution times of different tasks of the same job to estimate the average application execution time.

We also propose and evaluate *dagSim*, a novel ad-hoc and fast discrete event simulator to model the execution of complex DAGs. The advantages of dagSim with respect to state of the art simulators and AMVA techniques are twofold. On one side, the simulation process achieved great accuracy within a shorter timescale with respect to other formalisms (e.g., Stochastic Petri Nets) or specific tools (e.g., JMT [5] or GreatSPN [7]). Furthermore, the tool provides percentile estimate, which cannot be obtained via the analytical *Task Precedence model*.

We evaluate the modeling approaches in four scenarios consisting of different virtual machine environments and applications, as well as different resource configurations. Our results indicate a good overall accuracy for both Task Precedence model and the dagSim simulator (with 26% relative error in the very worst case and about 12% on average). Both models presented similar performance, specifically dagSim performed better for interactive queries while the Task Precedence model performed better for iterative machine learning (ML) algorithms. dagSim demonstrated to be on average 70 times faster than JMT while providing the same accuracy.

The rest of this paper is organized as follows. Section 2 presents related work, while Section 3 introduces our two prediction models. Section 4 describes the experimental scenarios we explored and discusses our main results. Conclusions are offered in Section 5.

2 RELATED WORK

This paper focuses on the use of modeling techniques to enable the analysis of the viability of big data jobs. Recently, sophisticated projects have emerged in the study of Spark applications performance, such as PREDIcT [20] and RISE2016 [12]. PREDIcT is a tool including a set of prediction techniques for different areas of data analytics, while RISE2016 is a collection of scalable performance prediction techniques for big data processing in distributed multicore systems. From a more general perspective, the most relevant related work has been subdivided into two parts, specifically i) analytical queuing network methods and ii) simulation approaches.

Analytical Queuing Network Methods: Applications running in parallel systems have to share physical resources (processors, memory, bus, etc.). Competition for computational resources can occur among different applications (inter-application concurrency) or among tasks of the same application (intra-application concurrency). Given system resource limitations, performance analysis techniques are important for studying fundamental performance measures, such as mean response time, system throughput, and resource utilization. In this context, queuing networks have been successfully used for studying the impacts of the resource contention and the queuing for service in applications running on top of parallel systems [16, 19, 23, 24, 26].

The parallel execution of multiple tasks within higher level jobs is usually modeled in the QN literature with the concept of fork/join:

jobs are spawned at a fork node in multiple tasks, which are then submitted to queuing stations modeling the available servers. After all the tasks have been served, they synchronize at a join node.

The authors in [19] present a model for predicting the response time of homogeneous fork/join queuing systems. The observed system is made up of a cluster of *homogeneous* index servers, each holding portions of queriable data. The index server subsystem is modeled as a fork-join network. In this model, an incoming task is split into identical subtasks, which are sent to individual servers and executed in parallel, independently from one another. Once all subtasks have finished executing, they are joined and the task execution is completed. The average response time is determined by the slowest server.

Following the fork-join model paradigm, the authors in [26] present an analysis of closed, balanced fork-join queuing networks, in which a fixed number of identical jobs circulate. They introduce an inexpensive bounding technique, which is analogous to balanced job bounds developed for product form networks. In the same direction, [23] models a multiprocessing computer system as K homogeneous servers, each with an infinite capacity queue. The authors provide a computationally efficient algorithm for obtaining upper and lower bounds on the system expected response time.

The work in [16] also considers the issue of estimating performance metrics in parallel applications. The proposed method is computationally efficient and accurate for predicting performance of a class of parallel computations, which can be modeled as task systems with deterministic precedence relationships represented as series-parallel DAGs. Tasks are represented as nodes and edges mark precedence relationships between pairs of nodes. While the models proposed in [19, 23, 26] assume a fork-join abstraction to represent parallel behavior, here the authors focus on the precedence relationships resulting from tasks that must run sequentially, combined with those that may run in parallel. An extension of this model, capturing not only intra-job but also inter-job overlap to evaluate application response times, is presented in [24].

In our work, we apply the model proposed by the authors in [16], given that the model parameters are easily obtained (for instance, service demands and task structure) and results are obtained with low complexity cost. More model details are presented in Section 3.2.

Simulation Approaches: Several simulation tools, which are tailored to study the behavior of parallel applications through stochastic formalisms such as SPNs (Stochastic Petri Nets see [21]) have been implemented. GreatSPN supports the analysis of Generalized Stochastic Petri Nets (GSPNs) including both immediate and timed (the fire event occurs either immediately or within a stochastic time) transitions and of Stochastic Well-Formed Nets (SWNs, i.e., Petri nets where the tokens can be distinguished) [7]. SMART (Symbolic Model checking Analyzer for Reliability and Timing, [8]) includes both stochastic models and logical analysis. SHARPE (Symbolic Hierarchical Automated Reliability and Performance Evaluator) is a tool to analyze stochastic models [25], the most notable being fault trees, product form queuing networks, Markov chains, and GSPNs. It is also able to mix submodels of fork-joins and queues. JMT [5] is a suite of applications offering a framework for performance evaluation, system modeling, and capacity planning.

The problem of studying the performance prediction of individual jobs is explored in [22] through a framework consisting of a Hadoop job analyzer, while the prediction component exploits locally weighted regression methods. A similar issue is studied in [27] by using instead a hierarchical model including a precedence graph model and a queuing network model to simulate the intra-job synchronization constraints. In [6], the authors consider the problem of minimizing the cost involved in the search of the optimal resource provisioning, proposing a cost function that takes into account: i) the time cost, ii) the amount of input data, iii) the available system resources (Map and Reduce slots), and iv) the complexity of the Reduce function for the target MapReduce job. The usage of a simulator to better understand the performance of MapReduce setups is described in [28] with particular attention to i) the effect of several component inter-connect topologies, ii) data locality, and iii) software and hardware failures.

Our previous work [3] describes multiple queuing network models (simulated with JMT) and stochastic well formed nets (simulated with GreatSPN) to model MapReduce applications, highlighting the trade-offs and additional complexity required to capture system behavior to improve prediction accuracy. As a result, general purpose simulators such as GreatSPN and JMT are not suitable to study efficiently massively parallel applications introducing tens (or even hundreds) of stages and thousands of parallel tasks for each stage. A comparison between dagSim and JMT is reported in Section 4.2.

Finally, parallel and distributed processing have been investigated also by means of Process Algebra (PA, [10]). A PA is a mathematical framework describing how a system evolves by using algebraic components and providing a set of methods for their manipulation. Among the different implementations, Performance Evaluation Process Algebra (PEPA, [11] is a formal language for distributed systems, whose models correspond to continuous time Markov chains (CTMC).

3 PERFORMANCE PREDICTION MODELS

This section presents the two modeling approaches analyzed in this paper to predict the performance of cloud-based big data applications. Since our main focus is on applications running on Spark, we start by first presenting some key components of this framework, highlighting some assumptions behind its parallel execution model that may affect the performance models (Section 3.1). We then discuss the Task Precedence queuing network model (Section 3.2), and introduce the dagSim discrete event simulator (Section 3.3).

3.1 Spark Overview and Model Assumptions

Spark is a fault-tolerant cluster computing framework that provides abstractions for parallel computation across distributed nodes with multiple cores. It is a fast and general purpose engine for large-scale data processing, which was first proposed as an alternative to Hadoop MapReduce [29]. Spark is the state of the art for fault-tolerant parallel processing and it recently became popular for big data processing on the cloud [1].

The general unit of computation in Spark is an application. It can be composed of a single job, multiple jobs, or a continuous processing. A job is composed of a set of data transformations and terminates with an action requesting a value from the transformed data. Each transformation represents a specific piece of code that launches data-parallel tasks on read-only data divided into blocks of almost equal size, called partitions. This set of same class tasks is called a stage. Within a stage, a single task is launched for each data partition, thus the number of tasks inside the stage is equal to the number of partitions. During the stage run time, each core (also called CPU slot) can run only a single task at a time. Since cores are a limited resource, the tasks are assigned to CPU slots until all resources become busy. Thus, the remaining tasks are enqueued and scheduled to be executed as soon as the cores become available.

The Spark execution model is represented by a Directed Acyclic Graph (DAG). Considering a logical plan of transformations that is fired by an action, the Spark *DAGScheduler* constructs a DAG of stages and their precedence relations. The stages are submitted for execution as a set of tasks that follows FCFS policy. The *TaskScheduler* does not know the dependencies between stages. Each stage is a sequence of fully-independent tasks that can run right away based on the data that is already on the cluster [14]. Only stages have precedence relationships, which are represented by the DAG.

Our present goal is to evaluate the effectiveness of two performance prediction techniques to estimate the execution time of Spark applications. The performance prediction in parallel systems has been approached in several ways, with varying degrees of detail, cost, and accuracy. Focusing on a data-parallel framework based on a DAG execution model, one of the main concerns is to model the synchronization step that happens when a stage terminates. That is, the models for calculating performance measures have to take into account how the executions of stages overlap among themselves.

To that end, we made the following assumptions for both (analytical and simulation) models: i) the concurrent system is modeled as a closed queuing model, with a single application that splits into one or more Spark jobs, ii) jobs are sequentially scheduled and comprehend one or more stages, iii) multiple stages may run in parallel or may have some precedence relationships, iv) a stage is composed of tasks of the same class with no precedence relationship among themselves (i.e., they may run in parallel), v) the number of tasks within a stage is constant and known a priori, vi) an individual application obtains dedicated resources for its execution (i.e., VMs that are executed on a cloud cluster), vii) resources (such as memory, CPU, disk) are homogeneous (as often happens in cloud deployments, see, e.g., [18]).

3.2 Task Precedence Model

In this prediction method, the performance of a parallel application is modeled by explicitly capturing the precedence relationships between different blocks of computation. We start by presenting the main ideas behind the model, as proposed in [16], and then discuss how it was applied to Spark applications. The reader is referred to the original paper for a detailed derivation of the model.

In the original paper [16], each block of computation was called a task, and the goal was to estimate the average execution time of an application composed of multiple parallel/sequential tasks. The precedence relationships between different tasks are expressed as a series-parallel DAG, where each node is a task. Available resources (e.g., cores) are modeled as service centers in a queuing network model. By exploiting both the queuing network and the DAG, the authors modified a traditional iterative Mean Value Analysis (MVA) approach to account for delays caused by synchronization and resource constraints originated from task precedence and parallelism.

The solution uses a traditional MVA model to estimate the average execution time of each task. In order to explicitly capture the synchronization delays between parallel tasks, the model estimates an *overlap* probability between each pair of tasks based on the input task precedence DAG. This probability captures the chance that the executions of the two tasks overlap in time, and is used as an inflation factor to estimate a new set of task average execution times, according to the MVA equations. The model iterates over these computations until they converge below a given error threshold. At each iteration, the precedence graph is reduced by aggregating multiple tasks and estimating the average execution time of aggregated node. In particular, execution times of sequential tasks are added, and execution times of parallel tasks are aggregated according to a probabilistic approach that takes into account the overlap probabilities between them.

Since jobs in Spark are sequentially executed by default, we apply the model by considering each node in the input DAG as a stage of the Spark application, thus explicitly capturing the dependencies among stages. Each stage is fully described by its average execution time, which is estimated based on historic data (Spark logs of previous executions of the same application). Thus, the model takes as input the application DAG and the average execution time of each individual stage, and produces as output the average execution time of each job. To estimate the average execution time of the application, the execution times of all jobs are summed up.

As a final note, the original model assumes that the times required to process the execution times of each block of computation represented by a node in the input DAG are exponentially distributed [16]. Since we here consider each node in the DAG as a stage, the assumption is that the execution times of Spark stages are exponentially distributed. Having said that, we emphasize that this assumption may not hold in practice, possibly depending on characteristics of the application. In other words, it is a potential source of approximation error of the model. Yet, the low prediction errors we obtain in all considered scenarios, as will be shown in Section 4, indicate that the model is quite robust to such assumption.

3.3 dagSim Simulator

dagSim is a high speed discrete event simulator built to analyze DAGs corresponding to MapReduce and Spark jobs[2].

Models are described with a data driven approach defining the DAG stages and the workload they have to handle. Specifically, a DAG model is defined as a tuple:

$$\text{DAG} = (S, N_{\text{Nodes}}, N_{\text{Users}}, \mathcal{Z}), \tag{1}$$

where $N_{\text{Nodes}} \in \mathbb{N}, N_{\text{Nodes}} \geq 1$ represents the number of computational nodes $N_{\text{Users}} \in \mathbb{N}, N_{\text{Users}} \geq 1$ the number of users concurrently submitting jobs to the system, and $\mathcal{Z}$ is the "think time distribution", i.e., the time a user will wait before submitting a new job. Set $S = \left\{ s_1, \ldots, s_{N_{\text{Stages}}} \right\}$ is the set of stages that define the DAG.

Furthermore, each stage $s_i \in S$ is a tuple:

$$s_i = (\text{id}, N_{\text{Tasks}}, Pre, Post, \mathcal{T}), \tag{2}$$

where id is a symbolic constant assigning a name to the stage, $N_{\text{Tasks}} \in \mathbb{N}, N_{\text{Tasks}} \geq 1$ accounts for the tasks composing the stage, $Pre \in S$ and $Post \in S$ define respectively the stages that must have been completed for s_i to be executable, and the set of stages that will be able to run after the completion of s_i. The probability distribution $\mathcal{T}$ defines the duration of each task of the stage and is obtained from Spark logs.

The simulation engine has been written in the C language. It is based on a classic discrete event simulation algorithm and has been designed for high performance. Though dagSim is a lightweight tool compared to other commercial programs, it targets specifically DAG models. Simulation can run efficiently thanks to a proprietary scheduler library ([4]) offering data structures that perform well when a high volume of events is generated. The tool is highly portable, since it can be easily recompiled without the requirement of external tools or libraries not supplied with the source code.

In order to perform an efficient simulation of jobs, stages are characterized by a set of possible states:

- *CAN_START*: represents stages that can be executed, since all the previous stages have completed, but that have not started yet because the scheduler is still waiting for resources to be available.
- *WAITING*: identifies stages that cannot be executed since some of the previous stages have not been completed.
- *RUNNING*: Tasks belonging to the stage in this state are being executed (i.e., a stage that was in the *CAN_START* state has found the necessary resources).
- *ENDED*: all the tasks of the considered stage have been completed.

Initially, only the stages s_i that have no dependencies (i.e., such that $Pre(s_i) = \emptyset$) are in the *CAN_START* state, and all the other are in the *WAITING* state. Each stage in the *RUNNING* state exploits a variable to count the number of tasks that still need to be completed. The core idea of the simulation engine is that each time a task of stage s_k has been executed, this counter is decremented of one unit. When the counter reaches zero, the engine can determine i) that a stage has been completed and ii) which stages are now eligible to start, changing their state from *WAITING* to *CAN_START*.

By using a doubly-linked list storing the relevant information about the tasks belonging to stages in the *CAN_START* state, it is possible to determine which one can be executed without performing a full search on the complete set of tasks in the DAG. In this sense, the approach provided by dagSim's engine is original and more efficient with respect to other scheduling mechanisms implemented in general purpose tools such as JMT [5] or GreatSPN [7].

Algorithm 3.1 summarizes the procedure to simulate the execution of one job according to the given DAG. Initially (lines 2–5), for each of the N_{Users} users accessing the system, a doubly-linked list called *UJD* is populated with a set of information, notably i) the number of stages ready to be started, ii) the remaining tasks that need to be completed for each stage, iii) the state of each stage, iv) the start and end time of each stage, and v) a pointer to a list of jobs ready to start. The data structure modeling the execution nodes is

---

[2]The tool is available at https://github.com/eubr-bigsea/dagSim

initialized at line 6: it is mainly used to determine whether a node is free or working on a task.

The algorithm continues by scheduling the time at which each user submits her first job (lines 7–9) by adding a new event whose timestamp corresponds to the *think time*. Events are collected in a *CalendarEvent* data structure. Each job is characterized by a doubly-linked list *JobData*, populated by i) a user identifier, ii) a job and a stage status, and a iii) task identifier.

The most important part of the algorithm consists of the cycle repeating the simulation for all the considered jobs (lines 11–37). At line 12, the next simulation event is extracted (*pop* operation) from the *CalendarEvent* structure.

If the event represents a user requesting the launch of a new job (line 14), the function *initUserJobData* is invoked (line 15) to initialize all the job's stages to *CAN_START* or *WAITING* state depending on whether the stage has dependencies or not.

The simulator assumes that nodes are locked for a job and that they can be used by the next one only when they are no longer needed by a user. This is implemented by exploiting a lock that is set when a new job starts and reset when all its stages have been started. If there are available computational nodes and no lock has been set (line 16), the *scheduleReadyTasksOnAvailNodes* function is invoked (line 17) to i) set a lock if a new job is started and ii) schedule the waiting jobs on available nodes. If instead the job cannot be started, it is inserted into an auxiliary list (line 19).

If the event identifies the end of a task (line 21), the corresponding counter of the remaining tasks in the stage is decremented by one unit (line 22). Function *releaseNode* is invoked (line 23) in order to free the computational resources; this also removes the lock on the nodes if the following conditions are met: i) no more tasks need to be executed, ii) no other user has locked the node, and iii) there are no other stages to start.

The stage is considered to be over if there are no tasks left (line 24): in this case the stage state is updated to *ENDED* (line 25) and the *UpdateStageStatus* function is invoked to see if the completion of this stage allows other stages to change their status from *WAITING* to *CAN_START*. If another stage can start (line 27), the new tasks are scheduled (line 28); otherwise the job is considered to be completed. The job ending time (line 30) is set at the current time and the next job from the same user is submitted after another think time (lines 31-32). To allow the simulation to stop when the total number of considered jobs has been executed, the number of completed jobs is increased (line 33).

4 EXPERIMENTAL RESULTS

In this section, we present the results of a set of experiments we performed to explore and validate the Task Precedence analytical model as well as the dagSim simulator. Our evaluation considers scenarios with different types of applications: the TPC-DS industry benchmark and some reference machine learning (ML) benchmarks, namely K-Means and Logistic Regression. In other words, our tests include SQL workloads (obtained from the TPC-DS SQL queries execution plan) and iterative workloads, which characterize ML algorithms and are becoming more and more popular in the Spark community [1]. All experiments were performed on the Microsoft Azure cloud platform.

Algorithm 3.1 Simulation engine algorithm

```
 1: function SOLVE(Model M, Users U, CalendarEvent ce)
 2:     UserJobData **UJD;
 3:     for user_i ∈ Users do
 4:         UJD[i] = createUserJobData(M);
 5:     end for
 6:     NodeData *ND = initNodeData(M);
 7:     for user_i ∈ Users do
 8:         nEv = AddEvent( ce, ThinkTime);
 9:     end for
10:     int TotalJobEnded = 0;
11:     while TotalJobEnded < maxJobs(M) do
12:         event = pop(CE);
13:         Job *jd = event->data;
14:         if isNewJobStarting(event) then
15:             initUserJobData(jd->userId, M);
16:             if (ND->freeNodes > 0) AND (!lock(ND)) then
17:                 scheduleReadyTasksOnAvailNodes(ce, ND);
18:             else
19:                 addToAux(event, WAITLIST);
20:             end if
21:         else
22:             remainingTasksXStage[jd->stageId]–;
23:             releaseNode(currTime, ce, ND, UJD);
24:             if remainingTasksXStage[jd->stageId] ≤ 0 then
25:                 setstatus($s_k$, ENDED);
26:                 UpdateStageStatus(UJD, M);
27:                 if NewStageCanStart($J_i$, M) then;
28:                     scheduleReadyTasksOnAvailNodes(ce, ND);
29:                 else
30:                     SetJobEndTime(currTime);
31:                     nEv = addEvent(ce, T);
32:                     nEv->data = populateJobData();
33:                     TotalJobEnded++;
34:                 end if
35:             end if
36:         end if
37:     end while
38: end function
```

4.1 Scenarios

Our experimental scenarios cover the most widely used applications on Spark [1]. The ML benchmarks, namely K-means and Logistic Regression, are core activities in machine learning applications and represent important steps on such data processing pipelines. They are iterative algorithms. We also selected the TPC-DS Q26 and Q52 queries as examples of interactive SQL queries that are currently popular on Spark. Indeed nowadays big data applications are moving from the early days' batch processing to more interactive workloads. Note that while TPC-DS DAGs are rather simple, including up to 7 stages, ML DAGs are very complex and introduce a high level of parallelism, up to 114 stages for Logistic Regression.

We conduct our experiments on two types of virtual machine environments on the Microsoft Azure HDInsight PaaS [17], namely D12v2 and D4v2. The goal is to explore different deployments of what the provider has to offer, including general purpose, CPU, and memory optimized instances. Considering that fault-tolerant parallel systems such as Spark are built to run on commodity clusters, it is important to guarantee the stability of the methods across different resource configurations.

Two different Spark versions have also been taken in account. For what concerns the D12v2 VMs, the Spark 1.6.2 release and Ubuntu 14.04 were considered. The D4v2 VM featured Ubuntu 16.04 and Spark 2.1.0. All the scenarios had two dedicated master nodes over D12v2 VMs. In the D12v2 case, the workers' configuration

Table 1: Scenarios Description

#	Application	VM	Configuration (nodes; cores; data)
1	TPCDS Q26	D12v2	3-13; 4 cores per node; 500GB
2	TPCDS Q52	D12v2	3-13; 4 cores per node; 500GB
3	K-Means	D4v2	3 and 6; 8 per node; 8GB,48GB,96GB
4	Log. Regression	D4v2	3 and 6; 8 per node; 8GB,48GB,96GB

consisted of 12 up to 52 cores. The D4v2 deployments consisted of 24 cores and 48 cores, on three and six nodes respectively.

Table 1 describes the set of scenarios we analyze. Each TPC-DS query and ML benchmark was run 10 times for each considered configuration.

We evaluate the Task Precedence analytical model and the dagSim simulation with respect to prediction accuracy and average execution time. Prediction accuracy is estimated by the relative error ε_r, computed using the average real execution time (T_{real}), measured on the real system, and the execution time predicted by the model ($T_{predict}$), for each application:

$$\varepsilon_r = \frac{T_{real} - T_{predict}}{T_{real}}. \tag{3}$$

Note that negative values of ε_r imply overestimates, while positive values correspond to underestimates.

Execution times of the analytical model and simulator have been gathered on a Ubuntu 16.04 Virtualbox VM with eight cores running on an Intel Nehalem dual socket quad-core system with 32 GB of RAM. The virtual machine has eight physical cores dedicated with guaranteed performance and 4 GB of memory reserved. Unless otherwise stated, we report the average of 10 runs.

Before presenting our results, we first compare the execution time of dagSim against the one of the JMT tool.

4.2 Comparison with JMT

In this section, we compare the average execution time of dagSim with that of the event based QN simulator available within the JMT 1.0.2 tool suite. JMT is very popular among researchers and practitioners and since 2006 has been downloaded more than 58,000 times. The comparison focuses on the average execution time at 95% confidence level. JMT accuracy analyses are reported in our previous work [3], where we obtained an average percentage error up to 33% while the mean of its absolute value was around 14.13%. The ratio between the average simulation times of JMT and dagSim for two considered scenarios are reported in Figure 1. dagSim is clearly much faster than JMT (about 70 times on average and up to 115 times in the very worst case for the Q26 DAG, which includes a larger number of stages), also with slightly better accuracy than JMT (as will be discussed extensively in the following sections).

4.3 Results on the D12v2 VMs (Scenarios 1 & 2)

This section presents the results obtained by the Task Precedence model and the dagSim simulator in scenarios 1 and 2, over Spark 1.6.2 executed on Azure HDInsight D12v12 VMs. Real and predicted application execution times for each scenario and various configurations (i.e., numbers of nodes and cores) are shown in Table 2. In this

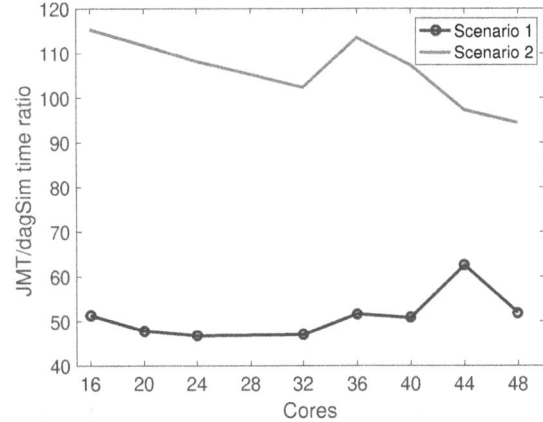

Figure 1: JMT and dagSim execution time ratio

table (as in the following ones), relative errors of each tool in each scenario/configuration are presented in parentheses, and maximum and minimum errors are shown in bold and shaded, respectively.

For scenario 1, both the Task Precedence model and the dagSim simulator showed very good estimates, with errors ranging from 4.4% to 20.7% and −0.1% to 16.2%, respectively. Similar results were also obtained in scenario 2: the errors of the Task Precedence model varied between 8.1% and 23.7%, whereas dagSim showed excellent accuracy, with errors below 1%.

Table 2: Scenarios 1 & 2: Real and predicted execution times (seconds).

Nodes (cores)	Scenario 1 (error %) Real	Task Prec.	DagSim	Scenario 2 (error %) Real	Task Prec.	DagSim
3(12)	722.2	690.2 (4.4)	682.3 (5.5)	719.9	660.8 (8.2)	716.0 (0.6)
4(16)	582.9	543.9 (6.7)	526.5 (9.7)	562.7	517.3 (8.1)	559.6 (0.6)
5(20)	515.9	469.0 (9.1)	455.3 (11.8)	471.8	412.7 (12.5)	468.3 (0.8)
6(24)	447.6	398.3 (11.0)	394.3 (11.9)	417.7	358.3 (14.2)	415.3 (0.6)
7(28)	415.7	367.2 (11.7)	**348.4 (16.2)**	364.1	304.7 (16.3)	**360.7 (0.9)**
8(32)	366.1	316.5 (13.5)	312.4 (14.7)	324.7	265.0 (18.4)	322.3 (0.7)
9(36)	306.1	256.1 (16.3)	290.3 (5.2)	306.8	247.0 (19.5)	**304.2 (0.9)**
10(40)	287.5	236.8 (17.6)	270.3 (6.0)	275.2	215.2 (21.8)	273.1 (0.8)
11(44)	259.7	209.6 (19.3)	250.6 (3.5)	258.8	200.2 (22.7)	257.0 (0.7)
12(48)	248.6	**197.2 (20.7)**	249.0 (-0.1)	250.0	**190.7 (23.7)**	248.3 (0.7)
13(52)	220.2	181.4 (17.6)	221.0 (-0.4)	226.1	179.3 (20.7)	224.2 (0.8)

Overall, taking absolute values, average errors were 13.45% and 16.92% for the Task Precedence model, and 7.73% and 0.74% for dagSim, in scenarios 1 and 2, respectively. These are very good estimates, given the complexity of the environment and workloads, especially for practical purposes of planning and managing the resource requirements. The greater errors of the analytical model are probably due to the several sources of approximations embedded in this solution (see Section 3.2 and [16]).

Table 3 reports, as an example, the quartiles of Q26 and Q52 at 16 cores. The table displays both the simulated quartiles and the ones

Table 3: Real and predicted execution time quartiles

Query	Quartile	dagSim [s]	Real [s]	ε_r [%]
Q26	Q_1	492.496	515.449	4.66
Q26	Q_2	495.077	537.436	8.56
Q26	Q_3	497.800	597.302	19.99
Q52	Q_1	509.974	509.810	0.03
Q52	Q_2	511.676	515.547	0.76
Q52	Q_3	513.454	520.582	1.39

derived from 20 sample runs on the real system. The estimated quartiles are quite accurate, with a worst case relative error of 19.99%, but at an average as low as 5.90%. Note that percentile distributions can be obtained only through simulation based approaches and cannot be provided by the Task Precedence method.

4.4 Results on the D4v2 VMs (Scenarios 3 & 4)

In scenarios 3 and 4 we executed the Task Precedence model and dagSim simulator considering Spark 2.1.0 logs for two machine learning algorithms, namely Logistic Regression and K-Means. The ML workloads are iterative algorithms and characterized by a larger number of stages than the scenarios 1 and 2. For these applications, data partitions are cached and accessed multiple times during the iterations. As noticed, these workloads present a higher variability since each iteration consists of data processing and RDD partitions re-computation in case of RDD cache eviction.

As detailed by Table 4, for both algorithms, the Task Precedence model prediction error is inversely correlated to the size of data sets, i.e., the larger the data sets, the lower the prediction error. Since processing larger data sets requires more tasks to be executed, the experiments yield a lower variance on the application response times. Analogously, a smaller number of tasks would result in higher variance across multiple runs. We also found that the model produces somewhat higher errors for larger cluster sizes. This is attributed to the accumulation of synchronization delays over a larger number of distributed tasks running in multiple cores.

We further looked into the response times measured for individual runs of each algorithm on each configuration and observed that the setup with the largest errors for the two benchmarks for Task Precedence (8 GB on 48 cores) coincides with the scenario with the highest variance across multiple runs. The large number of cores used on a relatively small dataset, which might occasionally cause resource underutilization, may explain the slightly worse performance of the model in this setup.

In contrast, dagSim did not show any error pattern and its worst-case error (−25.6%) is achieved for K-Means.

With regards to errors taken in absolute value, once again we find that both Task Precedence and dagSim provide very good prediction accuracy across the considered set of experiments, covering different platforms and configurations. Average errors for the analytical model are 9.03% and 1.62% for scenarios 3 and 4, respectively. Average errors for dagSim were somewhat higher — 16.45% and 2.42%, respectively — though still very low for practical purposes.

Table 4: Scenarios 3 & 4: Real and predicted execution times (seconds).

Nodes (cores)	Data set size (GB)	Real	Task Prec. (error %)	dagSim (error %)
Scenario 3: K-Means				
3 (24)	8	99.0	81.9 (17.3)	75.6 (23.6)
3 (24)	48	342.2	325.1 (5.0)	364.6 (-6.5)
3 (24)	96	862.1	845.9 (1.9)	788.4 (8.5)
6 (48)	8	90.3	**74 (18.1)**	70.3 (22.1)
6 (48)	48	195.0	178.8 (8.3)	219.2 (-12.4)
6 (48)	96	594.3	572.9 (3.6)	**746.2 (-25.6)**
Scenario 4: Logistic Regression				
3 (24)	8	164.6	159.5 (3.1)	156.1 (5.1)
3 (24)	48	669.4	664.4 (0.7)	671.7 (-0.3)
3 (24)	96	1418.8	1414.1 (0.3)	1404.9 (0.9)
6 (48)	8	166.5	**161.0 (3.3)**	**156.5 (6.0)**
6 (48)	48	368.2	362.5 (1.5)	362.9 (1.4)
6 (48)	96	1200.7	1192.6 (0.6)	1193.9 (0.5)

4.5 Summary of Results

In sum, we observe that the Task Precedence model achieved errors that vary from 0.8% to 20.7%, being on average 11.70% (average computed across all errors taken in absolute values). The errors achieved by dagSim, on the other hand, vary from −0.1% up to −25.6%, but with an average of only 6.06%. It is important to observe that in the performance evaluation literature, 30% errors (consistent across cluster sizes) in execution time predictions can be usually expected, especially from analytical models (see [15]). Thus, both approaches are suitable for predicting the performance of big data applications. Moreover, we notice that dagSim outperforms the Task Precedence model in the scenarios with interactive queries, whereas the latter was the best approach for the iterative ML algorithms. Figure 2 summarizes our results.

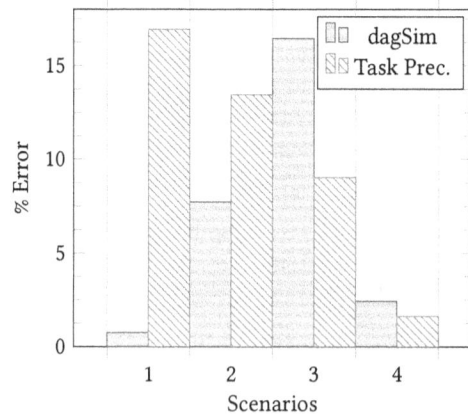

Figure 2: Prediction errors across analyzed scenarios (averages computed across errors taken in absolute values)

Moreover, both tools ran very quickly and are suitable for online predictions. The average execution times of dagSim were 3.09 seconds for scenario 1 and only 0.76 seconds for scenario 2, with very low variability across multiple runs (coefficient of variation[3] (CV) of 0.06 in both cases). Vice versa, JMT took on average 156 and 83 seconds, respectively.

For scenarios 3 and 4, despite the higher variability (CVs of 0.9 and 0.8, respectively), the average execution times were still short, 1.2 and 2.4 seconds, respectively. Note that in this latter scenario the higher variability was due to the different size of the underlying dataset (which has an impact on the number of tasks within stages and the number of simulated events).

The execution times of the analytical Task Precedence model was very short, varying from only 4.18 milliseconds (for scenario 2) to up to 40 milliseconds (for scenario 4). They were also mostly stable (i.e., low CVs) across all scenarios. The average execution times are 5.35 ms, 4.59 ms, 9.42 ms and 28.38 ms for scenarios 1 to 4, respectively, whereas the corresponding CVs are 0.12, 0.05, 0.32, and 0.29. Thus, comparing both tools, dagSim's execution times exceed those of our analytical model by some orders of magnitude: their ratio varies from around 10 to over 680. However, the Task Precedence model is limited to assess average execution time, whereas dagSim can provide also percentiles of application performance, thus enabling much finer-grained analyses.

5 CONCLUSIONS

In this paper, we analized an analytical models and proposed an ad-hoc simulator for the performance prediction of Spark applications running on cloud clusters.

Multiple cloud configurations and workloads (including SQL and iterative machine learning benchmarks) have been considered. From the results we achieved, Lundstrom and the dagSim simulator perform very well for predicting the average system response time and are effective in capturing the dynamic resource assignment implemented in Spark, achieving 11.07% and 6.06% average percentage error across all the experiments, respectively.

In our future work, we plan to extend our models to cope with scenarios where multiple applications run concurrently competing to access the resources in the same clusters. Finally, we will embed the models into a run-time optimization tool for dynamically managing cloud resources with the aim of providing application execution within an a priori fixed deadline while minimizing cloud operational costs.

ACKNOWLEDGEMENT

The authors' work has been partially funded by the EUBra-BIGSEA project by the European Commission under the Cooperation Programme (MCTI/RNP 3rd Coordinated Call), Horizon 2020 grant agreement 690116. This research was also be partially funded by CNPq and FAPEMIG, Brazil.

REFERENCES

[1] [n. d.]. Apache Spark Survey 2016 Results Now Available. ([n. d.]). https://databricks.com/blog/2016/09/27/spark-survey-2016-released.html

[2] [n. d.]. The Digital Universe in 2020. ([n. d.]). http://idcdocserv.com/1414

[3] D. Ardagna, S. Bernardi, E. Gianniti, S. Karimian Aliabadi, D. Perez-Palacin, and J. I. Requeno. 2016. Modeling Performance of Hadoop Applications: A Journey from Queueing Networks to Stochastic Well Formed Nets. In ICA3PP. 599–613. https://doi.org/10.1007/978-3-319-49583-5_47

[4] E. Barbierato. 2016. dagSim Documentation. Technical Report. Politecnico di Milano. https://github.com/eubr-bigsea/dagSim/blob/master/simlib/Documentation/scheduler/manual/1.63/manual.html

[5] M. Bertoli, G. Casale, and G. Serazzi. 2009. JMT: Performance Engineering Tools for System Modeling. ACM SIGMETRICS Performance Evaluation Review 36, 4 (2009), 10–15.

[6] K. Chen, J. Powers, S.Guo, and F. Tian. 2014. CRESP: Towards Optimal Resource Provisioning for MapReduce Computing in Public Clouds. IEEE TPDS 25, 6 (2014), 1403–1412. https://doi.org/10.1109/TPDS.2013.297

[7] G. Chiola. 1985. A Software Package for the Analysis of Generalized Stochastic Petri Net Models. In International Workshop on Timed Petri Nets. 136–143.

[8] G. Ciardo, R. L. Jones, III, A. S. Miner, and R. I. Siminiceanu. 2006. Logic and Stochastic Modeling with SMART. Perform. Eval. 63 (June 2006), 578–608. Issue 6. https://doi.org/10.1016/j.peva.2005.06.001

[9] H. Derrick. 2015. Survey Shows Huge Popularity Spike for Apache Spark. (2015). http://fortune.com/2015/09/25/apache-spark-survey

[10] W.J. Fokkinkk. 2000. Introduction to Process Algebra. Springer.

[11] J. Hillston. 1996. A Compositional Approach to Performance Modelling. Cambridge University Press, New York, NY, USA.

[12] M. Leeser J. Bhimani, N. Mi. [n. d.]. Scalable Performance Prediction Techniques for Big Data Processing in Distributed Multi-Core Systems. ([n. d.]). http://hdl.handle.net/2047/D20215315

[13] H. V. Jagadish, Johannes Gehrke, Alexandros Labrinidis, Yannis Papakonstantinou, Jignesh M. Patel, Raghu Ramakrishnan, and Cyrus Shahabi. 2014. Big Data and Its Technical Challenges. Commun. ACM 57, 7 (July 2014), 86–94.

[14] J. Laskowski. 2016. Mastering Apache Spark. (2016). https://www.gitbook.com/book/jaceklaskowski/mastering-apache-spark

[15] E. D. Lazowska, J. Zahorjan, G. S. Graham, and K. C. Sevcik. 1984. Quantitative System Performance. Prentice-Hall. http://homes.cs.washington.edu/~lazowska/qsp/

[16] V. W. Mak and S. F. Lundstrom. 1990. Predicting Performance of Parallel Computations. IEEE Trans. Parallel Distrib. Syst. 1, 3 (July 1990), 257–270. https://doi.org/10.1109/71.80155

[17] Microsoft. [n. d.]. Sizes for Windows Virtual Machines in Azure. https://docs.microsoft.com/en-us/azure/virtual-machines/windows/sizes. ([n. d.]). [Online; accessed 15-January-2017].

[18] Microsoft. 2016. What is PaaS? (2016). https://azure.microsoft.com/en-us/overview/what-is-paas/

[19] R. D. Nelson and A. N. Tantawi. 1988. Approximate Analysis of Fork/Join Synchronization in Parallel Queues. IEEE Trans. Computers 37, 6 (1988), 739–743.

[20] A. D. Popescu. 2015. Runtime Prediction for Scale-Out Data Analytics. Ph.D. Dissertation. IC, Lausanne. https://doi.org/10.5075/epfl-thesis-6629

[21] W. Reisig, G. Rozenberg, and P. S. Thiagarajan. 2013. In Memoriam: Carl Adam Petri. Springer Berlin Heidelberg, Berlin, Heidelberg, 1–5. https://doi.org/10.1007/978-3-642-38143-0_1

[22] G. Song, Z. Meng, F. Huet, F. Magoules, L. Yu, and et al. 2013. A Hadoop MapReduce Performance Prediction Method. In HPCC. 820–825.

[23] D. Towsley, J. C.S. Lui, and R. R. Muntz. 1998. Computing Performance Bounds of Fork-Join Parallel Programs under a Multiprocessing Environment. IEEE Transactions on Parallel & Distributed Systems 9, 3 (1998), 295–311. https://doi.org/10.1109/71.674321

[24] S. K. Tripathi and D. Liang. 2000. On Performance Prediction of Parallel Computations with Precedent Constraints. IEEE Transactions on Parallel & Distributed Systems 11 (2000), 491–508. https://doi.org/10.1109/71.852402

[25] K. S. Trivedi. 2002. SHARPE 2002: Symbolic Hierarchical Automated Reliability and Performance Evaluator. In DSN. IEEE Computer Society, Washington, DC, USA, 544.

[26] E. Varki and L. W. Dowdy. 1996. Analysis of Balanced Fork-join Queueing Networks. SIGMETRICS Perform. Eval. Rev. 24, 1 (May 1996), 232–241. https://doi.org/10.1145/233008.233048

[27] E. Vianna, G. Comarela, T. Pontes, J. Almeida, V. Almeida, K. Wilkinson, H. Kuno, and U. Dayal. 2013. Analytical Performance Models for MapReduce Workloads. International Journal of Parallel Programming 41, 4 (2013), 495–525. https://doi.org/10.1007/s10766-012-0227-4

[28] Gu. Wang, A. R. Butt, P. Pandey, and K. Gupta. 2009. A Simulation Approach to Evaluating Design Decisions in MapReduce Setups. In MASCOTS. IEEE Computer Society, 1–11.

[29] M. Zaharia, M. Chowdhury, M. J. Franklin, S. Shenker, and I. Stoica. 2010. Spark: Cluster Computing with Working Sets. In HotCloud. USENIX Association, Berkeley, CA, USA, 10–10. http://dl.acm.org/citation.cfm?id=1863103.1863113

---

[3]Ratio of standard deviation to mean value.

Generating Workload for ERP Applications through End-User Organization Categorization using High Level Business Operation Data

Gururaj Maddodi
Utrecht University
Utrecht, Netherlands
g.maddodi@uu.nl

Slinger Jansen
Utrecht University
Utrecht, Netherlands
slinger.jansen@uu.nl

Rolf de Jong
AFAS Software
Leusden, Netherlands
rolf.dejong@afas.nl

ABSTRACT

For software companies performance testing is an essential part of new application development. In this paper we present a performance engineering method that extracts the workload of an existing legacy ERP application with more than 1 million users and generates workload for a radically new version of the application. The workload is used to classify groups of end user organizations, i.e., enterprises whose customers are end users of the application, with unsupervised machine learning techniques. The method shows that (1) workload for new application testing and architecture validation can be generated from legacy application behavior, (2) end user organizations have significantly different usage patterns, and (3) for ERP applications, high-level operations, such as a salary calculations, provide a useful method for analyzing and generating workload, as opposed to for instance low level page views. The method is evaluated within a Dutch software company, where it is found to be accurate and effective for performance engineering.

KEYWORDS

Workload Generation; Software Usage Behavior; Unsupervised Learning; Software Performance Engineering

ACM Reference Format:
Gururaj Maddodi, Slinger Jansen, and Rolf de Jong. 2018. Generating Workload for ERP Applications through End-User Organization Categorization using High Level Business Operation Data. In *ICPE '18: ACM/SPEC International Conference on Performance Engineering, April 9–13, 2018, Berlin, Germany*. ACM, New York, NY, USA, 11 pages. https://doi.org/10.1145/3184407.3184432

1 INTRODUCTION

Performance testing of software under development is essential for the software development life-cycle, as it helps to make choices for architecture to improve performance. For accurate results in performance testing, it is essential to use realistic workload; workload that the software system is expected to handle in production use. For software under development, a similar application in a similar

domain or a predecessor can be used as a usage reference to estimate the kinds of load in production use. The usage data from an application in production can be used to detect usage patterns and to simulate realistic workloads, even if the new architecture and even some of the application's features are significantly different.

Several works have investigated workload modeling using production usage data. Many such research works use low-level application usage parameters, such as page accesses [11, 18, 22] or resource-level metrics [2, 4]. However, in a highly complicated software system such as Enterprise Resource Planning (ERP) software, using low-level concepts such as page access is too course grained, as for instance some pages might incur complex operations such as salary and pension calculations. A high-level abstraction helps to capture the features of ERP software and map them from the old application to a new application (also on different types of interfaces). We hypothesize and illustrate in this paper that with the behavior patterns and high level operations, we can create more accurate workloads for realistic usage simulation on new products.

In order to investigate the production workload of ERP systems, several aspects have to be considered. ERP applications are complicated and have several distinct domains that serve needs of different types of end-user organizations. Since these domains are distinct, different workload patterns exist and analysis needs to be performed separately for each. There is also a hierarchical structure in ERP software: for example, users receive an invoice for the order they place. The invoice contains details of one or more items that were ordered at a particular time. Processing more invoices require more resources as will more items within each invoice. These features are not captured by low-level metrics such as page access. For these reasons, high-level abstractions based on business operation metrics is proposed to get more realistic insight into usage of an ERP software and simulate workload for performance testing.

The contributions of this paper are: (1) Workload metrics are defined using High-level abstractions to identify categories of end-user organizations that help to translate workload patterns of existing application to new applications, (2) An exploratory study of the usage of an ERP application from a big software producing company is presented combining several machine learning and statistical methods, and (3) A mechanism is presented to simulate workload for an ERP application that is under development at the same company, based on patterns discovered from the older application.

The remainder of the paper is organized as follows: Section 2 describes how the work in this paper is related to and is different from similar works; with main similarity being that all the works employ some type of machine leaning technique to detect patterns in usage and use them to simulate workload while primary difference being that we use high-level abstractions for end-user organization categorization and workload simulation on new application. In Section 3, a description of the research motivation, case-study context, and research questions is presented. Section 4 describes the research method being used to address the research questions. A description of data attribute selection strategy and data collection for facilitating identification of categories of end-user organization is discussed, followed by an explanation of each step of the knowledge discovery process, and mechanism for simulating workload in new application is discussed in subsections. Section 5 shows the results from the statistical experiments applied on the application usage data. In particular, we present the identified clusters, and simulate workload on new version of the software taking examples from the discovered knowledge. Section 7 present discussion of results and the threats to validity of the study; and the section 8 concludes the paper, where we show that more accurate workload can be generated when taking behavioral aspects of customer groups into account.

2 RELATED WORKS

Workload categorization and simulation using existing usage data is studied extensively in literature. The application areas include e-commerce, cloud applications, big data applications, etc. The results of categorization has been used for performance testing, load prediction, and in some instances resource scaling. Not much research is done on ERP applications, although on-line shopping and e-commerce applications come close. In many of these works, the main theme is to categorize users of the software, generating concrete groups of users or tasks with definitive usage patterns, which helps to model the behavior accurately on a test setup. In this section, a few of the related works in the area of workload and performance testing is presented.

In Menasce et al. [15], workload characterization based on customer behavior graphs for e-commerce sites is investigated. State transition graphs called customer behavior model graphs (CBMG) are used to capture user navigation patterns. User behavior is expressed in terms of sessions, i.e. a sequence of requests users perform during on-line shopping such as browse, search, and add to cart. Metrics used are average session length, number of purchased items per customer, and visit-to-buy ratio. K-means clustering is used to categorize the customers. The CBMG associated with a specific cluster has certain characteristics in terms of session length, buy-to-visit ratio, add-to-cart-to-visit ratio, etc.

Moreno et al. [18] study Google cloud trace logs to identify patterns in user requests. The authors defined cloud workload in terms of "users" and "tasks", where user is a combination of submission rate, CPU, and memory requested while task is combination of session length, average CPU, and memory utilization. Users and tasks are clustered using k-means algorithm. From the resulting clusters workload is simulated and compared to the production load. In Elijorde et al. [4], dynamic resource allocation for virtual machines (VM) is proposed based on clustering of virtual machines according to workload patterns. The authors identify workload metrics which help to cluster workload, i,e, parameters such as CPU and memory requested and CPU and memory used are used to classify workloads. Here the users are identified on the basis of the amount of resources requested on the VMs. These works define high-level metrics in terms of customer/user of the application and session/task they produce. We were inspired by these works to use high level operations. However, our work is in a different domain and concerns workload generation for a new version of an ERP application, as opposed to simulating workload for the same application.

In Kulkarni et al. [13] a classification algorithm is proposed for categorizing cloud workloads. The classification is done to identify if the workloads are based on metrics such as their I/O, computation, or communication (network I/O) intensiveness on BigDataBench workloads on Cloudera Impala SQL query engine. The queries are classified as belonging to either of the three categories, and based on the type, infrastructure choice is made. In this work the authors know the categories of workloads that exist in the system, hence a supervised approach is sufficient while we need to discover the patterns which will help us in decision making in architecture selection.

In Mian et al. [16], workload prediction models for data intensive workloads are created. Although the authors acknowledge that the variation in tenant types (Online Transaction Processing, Online Analytical Processing, or a combination) could affect the resource, the models are built considering multi-tenant scenario. In Herbst et al. [7], proactive forecasting of resource requirement based on classification of workload in terms of intensity is proposed. The workload classes are based on intensity metrics such as burstiness and relative monotonicity. Workload classes are predetermined based on historical data and the framework dynamically forecasts workload resource requirement. This is not a problem when the types of workload is known, but without knowing the workload types building workload models is inaccurate.

In [17], an analysis of Google cloud back-end workload is presented for forecasting future workloads. The workload is defined in terms of tasks, and a task classification methodology is proposed such that ones with similar resource requirements are grouped together. The workload dimensions used for task classification are task duration, average core usage, and average memory usage. For categorization, the authors use K-means clustering algorithm. Then, the classes which are based on individual workload dimension is merged if the coefficient of variation between then are almost equal to get the final workload classes. Similarly, [19] study Google cloud workload by clustering tasks that are received based on resource required. This is used to predict resource requirement for future tasks that are predicted to belong to a specific cluster.

Aggarwal et al. [1] use clustering to find characteristics of MapReduce jobs on Apache Hadoop. For clustering, the workload metrics selected are map and reduce tasks, i.e. bytes read/written to the file system, format of the input/output files, and type of compression. In [20], Hadoop job workloads are categorized according to their data transformation patterns and running times. The parameters chosen were input size, shuffle size, output size, job duration, map task time, and reduced task time; it also used K-means clustering for workload types. Jia et al. [8] use clustering to categorize workload into different types of queries on big data workloads. The authors

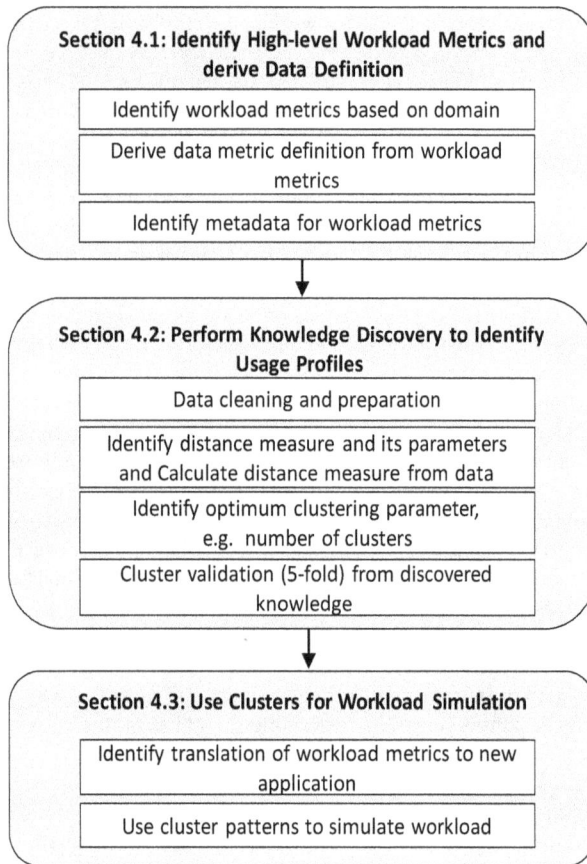

Figure 1: The research steps are modeled in a process diagram. The paper follows these steps and the Section headings are the same as the titles of the main process steps.

identified 32 different types of workloads such as sort, word count, and identified 45 metrics associated with each workload. In these works, the level of abstraction identified to categorize workloads is low and in terms of metrics on infrastructure side rather than from the user point of view.

We define high level abstraction for clustering, which makes it applicable to other enterprise applications. While in [15, 18] the authors do consider a somewhat higher level of abstraction, they are still tied to the application itself rather than to the underlying business model. In our previous work [14], we surveyed a number workload generation methods and performance testing methods available and we describe the workload and performance testing used at the case company in more detail.

3   RESEARCH CONTEXT
The research concerns a theory testing case study; our aim is to prove that high level metrics and end user organization clustering are supportive pillars for reliable workload generation in ERP.

3.1   Case-study Scenario
The research is conducted at a Dutch ERP software vendor called AFAS Software. The privately held company currently employs over 350 people, annually generates €100 million in revenue, and has been highly profitable since it was founded. The case-company currently delivers a fully integrated ERP suite called *Profit 2016*, which is used daily by more than 1.000.000 professional users from more than 10.000 End-User organizations.

From here on in this paper, we will refer to the case-company as ERPComp and their currently most successful product *Profit 2016* as ERPSoft. ERPSoft comprises of several distinct domain modules that cater to different needs of end-user organizations ranging from small businesses to huge retailers, and businesses in the domains of health care, educational institutions, retailers, accountancies, etc. The domains in ERPSoft that facilitate different types of business operations are: *Sales* which facilitates companies selling their products to buyers; *Purchasing* for companies buying raw materials from other suppliers; *human resource management (HRM)* which automates operations such as salary and leave registration.

ERPComp is developing a new version of their software, which we will call as ERPSoftNext. ERPSoftNext is a cloud-based application, developed using a model-driven development approach. Because ERPSoftNext will replace ERPSoft, it is expected to handle similar usage, even if the architectures of the products differ significantly.

The research questions that we investigate in this study are:

(1) What are the high-level metrics that can define the behavior of end-user organizations using an ERP application?
(2) what types of end-user organizations groups exist in an ERP application usage?
(3) How can usage sourced from high-level workload metrics be used for simulation in future versions of software products with different architectures?

The research follows an investigative approach into performance engineering using machine learning in the context of a case study. The research steps are modeled in Figure 1. In the next Section, we explain how the workload is extracted from the existing 'legacy' software application.

4   RESEARCH METHOD AND APPROACH
In this section, we describe the research methods of describing the data attributes, data collection strategy, and data analysis and presentation techniques.

4.1   Usage Data Extraction
4.1.1   Workload Metrics Identification and Data Attribute Derivation: In order to translate workload from ERPSoft running on different types of interfaces to ERPSoftNext, we have chosen to express the application usage in terms of high-level abstractions or workload metrics, i.e. interface and architecture independent parameters. Experts at the ERPComp were consulted to identify the metrics, which along with their definitions, enumerated below:

(1) **END-USER ORGANIZATIONS**: END-USER ORGANIZATIONS or simply ORGANIZATIONS purchase the license for the use of

the ERPSoft provided by ERPComp. The licenses vary based on requirements of the ORGANIZATION.

(2) **Roles**: ROLES indicate the personnel involved with or within an ORGANIZATION in performing business operations. Different types of ROLES have different access levels and functionality available in the application. ROLES can be distinguished into: Customer (who purchases an end product), Supplier (who supplies raw materials), and Employee.

(3) **Business-Events**: BUSINESS-EVENTS are the business operations performed by ROLES. BUSINESS-EVENTS can be classified into four types based on the domain: 1. Sales Related BUSINESS-EVENTS, are the ones where customer ROLE is involved along with one or more items, 2. Purchases Related BUSINESS-EVENTS, involve supplier and items, 3. HRM Related BUSINESS-EVENTS, involve the employees, and 4. Other BUSINESS-EVENTS that are not associated with any ROLES, such are mostly bookkeeping tasks executed by ORGANIZATIONS.

(4) **Business-Event Attributes**: BUSINESS-EVENT ATTRIBUTES are the details of items that are associated with a BUSINESS-EVENT. An example for BUSINESS-EVENT ATTRIBUTES is individual products purchased by a customer from an ORGANIZATION such as an electronic store under a sales order. The order might contain for example a monitor and mouse in which case both are BUSINESS-EVENT ATTRIBUTES under BUSINESS-EVENT sales order. Only sales and purchase domains have BUSINESS-EVENT ATTRIBUTES associated with **business-event**s as a single ROLE can have many items purchased/sold under a **business-event**, while HRM **business-event**s have only one ROLE with details such as salary slips and leave requests.

There is a hierarchical pattern that can depict the operation of an ORGANIZATION in an abstract way using the metrics described above, i.e. ORGANIZATIONS have instances of ROLES that perform BUSINESS-EVENTS which themselves have BUSINESS-EVENT ATTRIBUTES. This pattern is used in modeling on ERP application, please refer to [21] for more details.

Table 1 shows the ROLES, and associated BUSINESS-EVENTS, and if BUSINESS-EVENTS LINES are present in ERPSoft for that specific domain. We study only the BUSINESS-EVENTS associated with the *sales* domain because it is the most used part of the application.

From the chosen high-level workload metrics described above, data attributes were constructed. As in the work of [15], where the authors use ratios such as visit-to-buy ratio to represent user behavior, we use the ratio of BUSINESS-EVENTS to ROLE and BUSINESS-EVENT ATTRIBUTES to BUSINESS-EVENT to represent behavior of an ORGANIZATIONS. We call them *BE-factor* and are described in the equations 1 and 2.

$$BE - factor = \frac{No.\ of\ Business - Events}{Instance\ of\ Role} \quad (1)$$

$$BE - factor = \frac{No.\ of\ Business - Event\ Attributes}{Instance\ of\ Business - Event} \quad (2)$$

The *BE-factor*s represent the number of BUSINESS-EVENTS that are generated by an instance of ROLE and BUSINESS-EVENT ATTRIBUTES for an instance of BUSINESS-EVENT in an ORGANIZATION.

Table 1: List of Domains in ERPSoft, and Associated ROLES and BUSINESS-EVENTS and BUSINESS-EVENT ATTRIBUTES

Domain/Roles	Business-Events	Business-Event Attributes
HRM/Employee	Salary Slip generation	No
	Employee data change	
	Time Sheet filling	
	Absence Registration	
	Leave Registration	
Sales/Customers	Sales quotation creation	Yes
	Sales order creation	
	Delivery note creation	
	Invoice (sales) generation	
	Invoice (projects) generation	
	Invoice (subscriptions) generation	
Purchases/ Suppliers	Purchase quotation creation	Yes
	Purchase order creation	
	Goods received creation	
	Invoices (purchases) generation	
General/ Automated	Financial entries addition	No
	Workflow mutations	
	Time sheet (invoiced) generation	
	Cost estimation	

*BE-factor*s were chosen because of the assumption that it represents the behavior of the ROLES associated with the ORGANIZATIONS more accurately in terms of use of ERPSoft, and hence the behavior of the ORGANIZATION. This leads to identifying groups of similar ORGANIZATIONS that use the software in a similar manner. Using absolute BUSINESS-EVENT numbers will group the ORGANIZATIONS based on their sizes, as bigger ORGANIZATIONS will have more instances of ROLES (for e.g. customers), and hence more BUSINESS-EVENTS.

Since We choose to use the sales part of ERPSoft, the *BE-factor*s in the data will be related to sales domain. Sales domain includes subtypes such as: sales, projects, and subscriptions that ORGANIZATIONS sell to the ROLE of type CUSTOMER, varying in the way in which the selling process is arranged. We only consider invoices to calculate for BE-factors. This is because orders and delivery notices are highly correlated with invoices, i.e. invoices follow orders and deliveries in the process.

The distribution of *BE-factor* data most of the times shows a positive skew. In such cases a single value does not describe the distribution very well. Taking quartiles that divide the distribution into four regions or at three points captures data in finer granularity and helps to reduce error. The points that divide distribution at 25% (1qtl), 50% (med), and 75% (3qtl) are taken. Maximum and minimum points are not considered as they do not add any information (mostly 0 or 1 for min and very high value for max). An example of an attribute is the *BE-factor* is sales invoices per customer denoted as $SIpC_{1qtl}$ with 25% value denoted using a subscript. Table 2 shows the *BE-factor* data attributes with the quartiles from rows 2 to 7. The remaining rows, represents the metadata about the ORGANIZATIONS. Rows from 8 to 10 describes the type of items or goods the ORGANIZATIONS sell represented as SItem, PItem, and SuItem for sales, projects, and subscription respectively. Rows 11 to 15 represent the license or sub-functionality of ERPSoft that ORGANIZATIONS use represented by LType. In the table 2, for Boolean variables "yes" value represents that the feature is present and "no" value represents that the feature is not present.

Data was extracted from production database servers at ERP-Comp running ERPSoft. SQL queries were written such that only the active ROLES within an ORGANIZATION, i.e. ROLES having at least one BUSINESS-EVENT over the period of one year, were selected. This was due to the assumption, along with advice from experts at the ERPComp, that the ROLE instances without any BUSINESS-EVENTS for over a year can be considered not to be associated anymore with the ORGANIZATION.

4.1.2 Data Cleaning and Preparation: Initial inspection of the data showed that there were several duplicates, as all the attributes of some record pairs had identical or almost identical values. This was due to clients replicating their production database instances and using the new instance for testing purposes, which resulted in duplicate record pairs. With help from experts at ERPComp, we used specific attributes of few selected tables, i.e. the tables used were Financial Entries, Projects, and Subscriptions to identify similar databases. Based on expert suggestion, the data was collected from the mentioned tables that have at least 10,000 or more records. We calculated hash of the resulting records and compared all the database pairs. The number 10,000 was chosen based on the expert suggestion because the probability of two clients having 10,000 similar records in those tables is highly unlikely and it could be said with nearly 100% confidence that the compared databases are duplicate pairs and one them is a test instance. It was not clear which of the identified duplicate pairs was the production database and which one was the test copy. Since the duplicate pairs have similar database names in that the ORGANIZATION license number is same, but the characters representing instances were different. One convention we used was that the database instance with higher characters for instance representation as test instances.

4.2 Clustering and End User Organization Classification

In order to categorize the ORGANIZATIONS, several steps need to be followed. First, a distance or dissimilarity measure should be identified to represent dissimilarity between the data points. Second, an algorithm and its input parameters should be determined to categorize the ORGANIZATIONS. Finally, the resulting categorization should be verified for stability. In the subsections below, we describe the steps.

4.2.1 Distance Measure. Typically, clustering algorithms do not take the raw data as it is. A pair-wise measure of distance or dissimilarity matrix between data points has to be provided to the algorithm. For datasets containing a mix of different types of data (i.e. continuous or numeric, nominal etc.), a distance measure called Gower Distance [6] is popularly used. Gower Distance calculates a pair-wise dissimilarity matrix by combining distance/dissimilarity measures of each attribute of data points.

The Gower distance algorithm needs to calculate a dissimilarity matrix. Based on the dataset we have, the following specification was used: As an ORGANIZATION cannot have negative value for BUSINESS-EVENTS, for instance there cannot be negative number of

Table 2: List of Identified Metrics for Clustering ORGANIZATIONS with their Relevance and Data Type

Attribute	Relevance	Type
Org_{id}	Identifier which uniquely identifies an ORGANIZATION	-
$SIpC_{1qtl}$ $SIpC_{med}$ $SIpC_{3qtl}$	Number of sales invoices per customer with quartiles	$\mathbb{R}_{\geq 0}$
$SILpSI_{1qtl}$ $SILpSI_{med}$ $SILpSI_{3qtl}$	Number of invoice lines per sales invoice with quartiles	$\mathbb{R}_{\geq 0}$
$PIpC_{1qtl}$ $PIpC_{med}$ $PIpC_{3qtl}$	Number of project invoices per customer with quartiles	$\mathbb{R}_{\geq 0}$
$PILpPI_{1qtl}$ $PILpPI_{med}$ $PILpPI_{3qtl}$	Number of invoice lines per project invoice with quartiles	$\mathbb{R}_{\geq 0}$
$SuIpC_{1qtl}$ $SuIpC_{med}$ $SuIpC_{3qtl}$	Number of subscription invoices per customer with quartiles	$\mathbb{R}_{\geq 0}$
$SuILpSuI_{1qtl}$ $SuILpSuI_{med}$ $SuILpSuI_{3qtl}$	Number of invoice lines per subscription invoice with quartiles	$\mathbb{R}_{\geq 0}$
$SItem_{article}$ $SItem_{ToW}$ $SItem_{course}$	Indicates if an ORGANIZATION uses physical goods, uses type of work (ToW, i.e. billing based on work type and time), and/or courses in sales invoices	{yes, no}
$PItem_{article}$ $PItem_{ToW}$ $PItem_{course}$	Indicates if an ORGANIZATION uses physical goods, uses type of work (ToW, i.e. billing based on work type and time), and/or courses in project invoices	{yes, no}
$SuItem_{article}$ $SuItem_{ToW}$ $SuItem_{course}$	Indicates if an ORGANIZATION uses physical goods, uses type of work (ToW, i.e. billing based on work type and time), and/or courses in subscription invoices	{yes, no}
$LType_{SB}$	Small Business (SB) license is a limited set of functionality available for ERP and Accountancy focusing on use in smaller ORGANIZATIONS, e.g. 1 to 5 employees	{yes, no}
$LType_{ERP}$	ERP license offers functionality to automate the secondary processes in a ORGANIZATION such as bookkeeping, HRM and payrolling, order management, project administration, subscription administration and general functionality like reporting, workflow management, and BI	{yes, no}
$LType_{HRM}$	HRM/Payroll license is a limited set of ERP focusing on HRM and payrolling mostly used by bigger ORGANIZATIONS having another solution for ERP	{yes, no}
$LType_{ACC}$	Accountancy (ACC) license is a specific set of ERP focusing on administration offices such as accountants, there is some limitation of the functionality they use and also some specific functionality for this kind of ORGANIZATIONS	{yes, no}
$LType_{ASB}$	Accountancy and Small Business (ASB) license is a combination of Accountancy and Small Business features	{yes, no}

orders being created, the *BE-factors* are a ratio-scaled continuous variables [10]. For example $SIpC_{1qtl}$ (along with variables in row 2 to 7 in the table 2) are ratio-scaled continuous variables. Also, as there can be '0' values for the BE-factors, we calculate the rank scores and then treat them as interval-scaled [10]. The binary variables, such as $SItem_{article}$ (and variables from row 8 to 21 in the table 2), indicate a particular item type or license is present or not and there is no ambiguity for a 'NO' value. Hence they are treated as symmetric binary variables [10].

4.2.2 Clustering and Selection of Optimum Input Parameters. Since clustering is an exploratory approach, generally the best parameters to get the optimal clusters for a given algorithm are not known. There is a plethora of techniques to determine the input parameters to clustering algorithms and validate clustering quality. One technique commonly used is the Internal Cluster Validation techniques [12] which does not use any external information such as class memberships (as many times it is not available beforehand). One of the main parameters required for most clustering algorithms is number of clusters to be generated. There are several internal validation methods that could be used to estimate the optimal cluster number, we used a few of them as they suited the dataset that we have (for e.g. some measures only work on continuous numeric variables, and so doesn't suit the dataset):

(1) **Silhouette Width** is a measure of similarity of an data point to its own cluster compared to other clusters. The value ranges from -1 to 1. A higher value suggests better clusters.

(2) **Dunn Index** helps to identify clusters that are compact, with a small variance among the members of the clusters. A higher value indicates well separated clusters with high correlation among cluster members.

(3) **Connectivity** indicates the degree of connectedness of clusters determined by k-nearest neighbors. A lower value indicates lower correlation for cluster members to their nearest neighbors in the data space.

(4) **Davies-Bouldin (DB) Index** calculates for each cluster, ratio of within cluster distance to between cluster distance. Then over all the clusters an average value is calculated. A smaller value represents better clustering result.

We use Partitioning Around Medoid (PAM) clustering method, which is a partition-based method. PAM takes the distance or dissimilarity matrix and the number of clusters to be generated as input. It works by randomly selecting data points (equal to the specified number of clusters) as cluster centers, then iteratively assigns the remaining data points to the closest cluster centers (using median), meanwhile recalculating the cluster centers until the clusters are as far apart as possible.

In order to find out the best number of clusters, clustering should be run several number of times using the same Gower distance calculated from the dataset, but with the number of clusters to be generated varying, for e.g. 2 to 20. Then, for each experiment, the value of the internal validation metrics are calculated. By plotting the internal validation metrics, the best number of clusters can be determnined. Then, the data set can be appended with a cluster membership vector (the cluster/class to which a data point belongs) obtained by the cluster model given by the optimum cluster number.

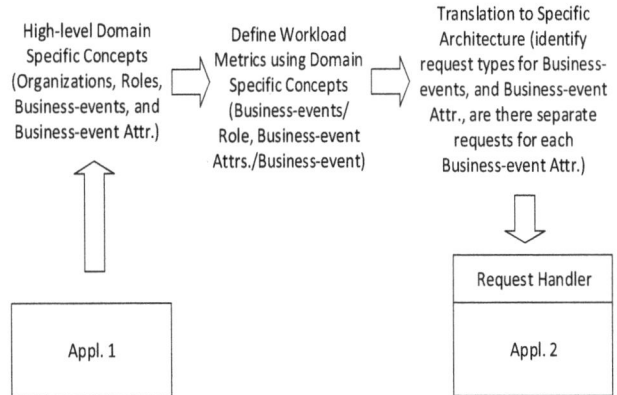

Figure 2: Translation of Workload Metrics to New Application.

4.2.3 Classification Model from Discovered Knowledge: Clusters can be validated by the knowledge discovered using supervised learning approach. This can be accomplished by building a classification model from the clusters. We built a classification model from the clusters using the cluster membership assigned to the data points as class variable. only binary variables as predictors for the classification model, as they represent the type of ORGANIZATIONS that are present in the clusters. The classification is a multi-class classification problem, since there are more than 2 clusters (or classes) in the dataset. To build a classification model, we used Randomforest classifier as it allows multiple classes. To test the hypothesis, an n-fold validation can be used by dividing the dataset into training and test sets. Then, by only using to training set to build clusters and building classification model from those clusters, the membership of data points in test set can be predicted, the stability of clusters can be calculated.

4.3 Workload Simulation

In this section, we demonstrate how we can translate the patterns from the existing application onto a new application with different architecture and workflow pattern. Figure 2 shows the translation of workload metrics to new application.

In order to translate the workload to the new system, the high-level workload metrics have to be expressed in terms of request types that the new application architecture can handle. We illustrate it here in the case-study using architecture of ERPSoftNext. ERPSoftNext runs on Command-Query Responsibility Segregation (CQRS) [9, 23] back-end architecture and Event Sourcing [5]. CQRS architecture separates actions that change the state of the system, i.e. commands, and the queries which just reads the current state of the system. The changes made by commands are propagated to the query side through events that register the changes and project them to the query side.

The workload metrics, i.e. BUSINESS-EVENTS and BUSINESS-EVENT ATTRIBUTES creation occur on the command side as they create new state of the system. Each type of BUSINESS-EVENT and BUSINESS-EVENT ATTRIBUTE translate to a particular type of command in ERPSoftNext, for example a sales invoice will translate to a sales

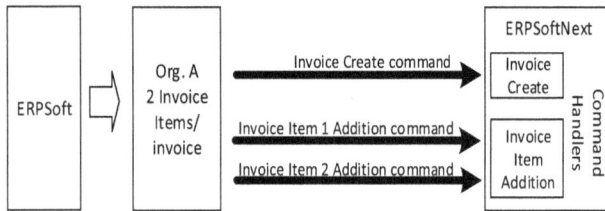

Figure 3: Illustration of Translation of Workload Metrics from ERPSoft to ERPSoftNext.

invoice creation command and adding invoice items to an invoice leads to sales invoice item addition command.

The Figure 3 shows the translation of workload metrics from ERPSoft to ERPSoftNext. Let us say that one of the cluster is ORGANIZATION with 2 invoice items per invoice, then the workload on ERPSoftNext for one invoice creation for a ROLE will have 3 commands: one for invoice creation, and 2 for addition of items to the created invoice.

The research method used is described in the algorithm 1. For the sake of simplicity, method shown applies only to sales *BE-factor* and not to project and subscription.

5 RESULTS

In this section, the tests to determine the optimum cluster number and validation of determined cluster model is presented. In order to evaluate the accuracy and stability of clustering , we used n-fold validation where we sampled 5% of the dataset as test set and the remaining 95% was used to build clusters and classification model. In order to calculate the accuracy of prediction for n-fold tests, we built a clustering and classification model on the full dataset to know the cluster memberships for the data points in 5% test dataset beforehand.

5.1 Clustering of ORGANIZATIONS for Knowledge Discovery

First step in clustering is to determine the number of clusters. We ran tests using PAM on several cluster numbers ranging from 5 to 28. We calculated the internal cluster validation measures mentioned in the section 4, i.e. silhouette width, Dunn index, connectivity index, and DB index. The results of the test are shown in the Figure 4.

Overall, it can be observed that as the cluster number increases, internal validation measures approach optimum values. It can also be observed from the plot that internal validation measures reach optimum values at cluster number 22, i.e. silhouette width is high, Dunn index is low and does not change much after 22, connectivity is low, and DB index is minimized. The internal validation measures only help determine cluster numbers which give optimum clusters, but the choice selection is based on expert knowledge. With expert opinion, we chose to 22 as the optimum cluster number to use.

Figure 5 shows the clusters obtained from the data. The clusters are plotted by extracting features using t-Distributed Stochastic Neighborhood (t-SNE) algorithm. t-SNE is a non-linear dimensionality reduction technique which extracts a small number of features that account for most of the variance in the data. t-SNE

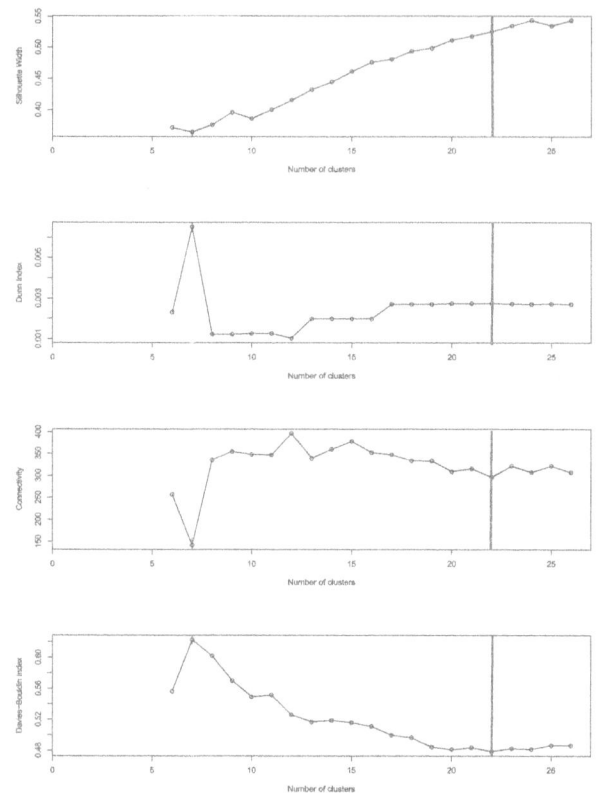

Figure 4: Plot of Internal Validation Metrics Using Calculated for Clustering Models with Clusters Numbers from from 6 to 28.

algorithm can be used to visualize localized similarities in the multidimensional data by reducing it to two or three features. The plot shows distinct clusters of ORGANIZATIONS.

5.2 Classification Validation

For each fold of the 5-fold validation, the sub dataset containing train or model building set was used to build the clustering model. Using the discovered cluster labels, we built a classification model. Then, the test set was used to predict the cluster membership from the classification model. Using the already known membership for the data points in the test set from the cluster model of full dataset, we calculated the accuracy of prediction of membership to clusters for test set data points.

The table 3 shows the prediction accuracy for 5-fold validation. An overall prediction accuracy over 5-fold validation of 93.2% was obtained from the tests. The values for folds 2 and 4 were affected because the sampling chose too many data points from a specific cluster as could be the case when there are a lot of clusters in the data and relatively small number of data points. This validation indicates that the clusters are stable.

Algorithm 1: Categorization of ORGANIZATIONS and Validation

---

1   $Data \leftarrow (Org_{id}, SIpC_{1qtl}, .., SILpSI_{1qtl}, .., PIpC_{1qtl}, .., PILpPI_{1qtl}, .., SuIpC_{1qtl}, .., SuILpSuI_{1qtl}, .., SItem_{article},$
    $SItem_{ToW}, SItem_{course}, PItem_{article}, PItem_{ToW}, PItem_{course}, SuItem_{article}, SuItem_{ToW}, SuItem_{course}, LType_{SB},$
    $LType_{ERP}, LType_{HRM}, LType_{ACC}, LType_{ASB})$

2   **for** $i \leftarrow 1$ **to** $NumOfColumns(Data)$ **do**

3   **if** $data(,i)$ *is numeric* **then**

4        $data(,i) \leftarrow rank(data(,i))$;

5   $Diss_{Gower} \leftarrow GowerDistance(Data)$;

6   **for** $j \leftarrow 2$ **to** m **do**

7      $Clusters_j \leftarrow PAM(Diss_{Gower}, j)$;

8      $SilWidth_j \leftarrow SilhouetteWidth(Clusters_j)$; $Dunn_j \leftarrow DunnIndex(Clusters_j)$; $Conn_j \leftarrow Connectivity(Clusters_j)$;
      $DB_j \leftarrow DBIndex(Clusters_j)$;

9   $Clusters_{optimum} \leftarrow optimum(SilWidth_j, Dunn_j, Conn_j, DB_j)$ where $j = 2$ to m;

10   $Data_{mem} \leftarrow Data + Clusters_{optimum}[membership]$;

11   **for** $k \leftarrow 1$ **to** n **do**

12      $TrainSet \leftarrow sample(Data_{mem})$;

13      $TestSet \leftarrow Data_{mem} - trainSet$;

14      $classificationModel \leftarrow Randonforest(TrainSet)$;

15      $Prediction \leftarrow Predict(TestSet)$;

16      $Accuracy \leftarrow TruePositives(Prediction)/Size(TestSet)$

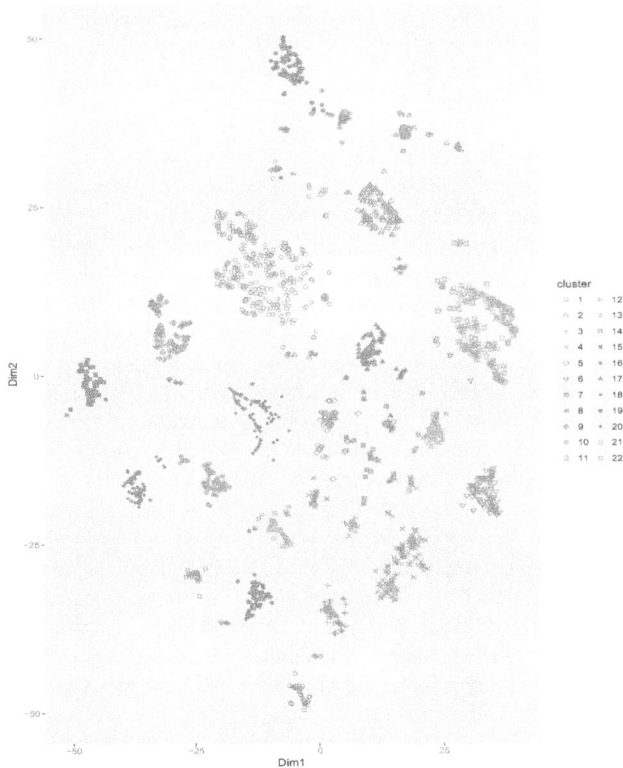

Figure 5: Plot of t-sne Reduced Dimensions Showing Clusters of organizations.

Table 3: Classification Accuracy for 5-fold Validation for Cluster Membership Prediction

Fold	Testset size	True Positives	Accuracy
1	154	148	96.1%
2	154	134	87%
3	154	147	95.45%
4	154	139	90.02%
5	154	150	97.4%

5.3 Analysis of the ORGANIZATION Clusters

In the table 4 the statistics and information about the clusters is presented. It can be seen from the table 4 that, every cluster has a specific LType or a combination and combined with type/s of items they sell categorize the ORGANIZATIONS into clusters which shows up as variations in BE-factors.

Even if the ORGANIZATIONS have similar license types between clusters, the type of invoice make a difference. For example in the table 4, clusters cl4 and cl9 both have high number of ORGANIZATIONS (more than 98%) ERP license; the difference comes from the types of invoice they have. Cluster cl4 has SItem and SuItem of type article as majority while cl9 has PItem of type article in majority.

Furthermore, not just type of invoice (sales, project, or subscription), but also the type of item makes a difference. For e.g. in table 4 clusters cl3 and cl19 are similar in terms of license type. Both have project invoices, even though cl19 also has subscription invoices. But if we see the project invoices, the item types are different. Cluster cl3 has only PItem type article, cl19 has PItem type article and ToW. This suggests that, by knowing the information about the ORGANIZATIONS, the expected workload depends on the number of ROLE instances present in the ORGANIZATION.

TABLE 4. CLUSTER STATISTICS SHOWING THE NUMBER OF BE-FACTOR FOR SALES, PROJECTS, AND SUBSCRIPTIONS ALONG WITH PERCENTAGE OF ORGANIZATIONS IN THE CLUSTER HAVING A SPECIFIC ITEM AND LICENSE TYPE

No.	BE-Factor SIpC/SILpSI	BE-Factor PIpC/PILpPI	BE-Factor SuIpC/SuILpSuI	SItem %			PItem %			SuItem %			LType %				
				article	ToW	course	article	ToW	course	article	ToW	course	SB	ERP	HRM	ACC	ASB
cl1	(1,2,3)/(1,2,3)	(0,0,0)/(0,0,0)	(0,0,0)/(0,0,0)	100	0	4	2	0.7	0	0	0.1	0	1	98	1.5	3	0
cl2	(1,2,3)/(1,2,3)	(0,0,0)/(0,0,0)	(0,0,0)/(0,0,0)	85	100	5	0	0.5	0	0	1.5	0	1.5	98	0.5	2	0
cl3	(0,0,0)/(0,0,0)	(1,1,2)/(1,1,2)	(1,2,3)/(1,1,2)	13	0	4	100	0	4	100	5	1	1	99	2	7	0
cl4	(1,2,3)/(1,2,3)	(0,0,0)/(0,0,0)	(2,3,5)/(1,1,2)	100	19.5	6.5	6.5	2.5	0	100	4	1	0.4	100	2	0.8	0
cl5	**(1,1,2)/(1,2,3)**	**(1,2,4)/(1,2,4)**	**(1,2,3)/(1,1,2)**	**97**	**80**	**16**	**88**	**94**	**1.5**	**100**	**12**	**1**	**0.6**	**100**	**1**	**0**	**0**
cl6	(0,0,0)/(0,0,0)	(1,2,4)/(1,2,3)	(0,0,0)/(0,0,0)	0	1	0	0	100	1	0.8	1	0	0.8	1	0.7	97	0
cl7	(2,3,5)/(1,1,2)	(3,6,8)/(1,2,3)	(2,5,6)/(1,1,2)	94	4	94	83	87.5	12.5	100	4	0	0	96	21	3	0
cl8	(1,1,2)/(1,2,3)	(1,2,2.5)/(1,1,3)	(0,0,0)/(0,0,0)	96.5	78	8	76	97.5	3.5	0	0	0	1	100	0	1	0
cl9	(0,0,0)/(0,0,0)	(1,1,2)/(1,1,2)	(0,0,0)/(0,0,0)	12.5	0	3.5	100	0	0.7	0	0	0	1	98	3	1.5	0
cl10	(0,0,0)/(0,0,0)	(1,2,4)/(1,3,5)	(4,6,11)/(1,1,1)	5	2	1	100	100	1	100	19	1	2	0	0	100	0
cl11	(0,0,0)/(0,0,0)	(1,2,4)/(1,1,2)	(0,0,0)/(0,0,0)	2	5	3	0	100	0.9	0	0	0	0	99.5	3	0	0
cl12	(0,0,0)/(0,0,0)	(0,0,0)/(0,0,0)	(3,6,6)/(1,1,1)	10	5	1	0	0	0	95	9	1	0	0	0	100	0
cl13	(0,0,0)/(0,0,0)	(1,2,4)/(1,1.5,3)	(2,3,5)/(1,1,1)	9	3	5	0	100	0	100	12.5	2	0	100	4	0	0
cl14	(0,0,0)/(0,0,0)	(0,0,0)/(0,0,0)	(0,0,0)/(0,0,0)	0	0	14	0	0	1	0	0	0	31.5	100	0	1.5	0
cl15	(1,2,4)/(1,1,1)	(0,0,0)/(0,0,0)	(0,0,0)/(0,0,0)	94.5	12.5	0.0	0	0	0	0	0	0	3.5	0	0	3.5	95.5
cl16	(0,0,0)/(0,0,0)	(1,2,4)/(1,1,2)	(0,0,0)/(0,0,0)	5.5	1.8	1	97	0	0	0	1	0	13	3.5	0.8	100	0
cl17	(0,0,0)/(0,0,0)	(1,2,5)/(1,2,3)	(2,4,6)/(1,1,2)	7	1.5	6	100	100	2.2	100	18.5	3	0	100	0	0.5	0
cl18	**(0,0,0)/(0,0,0)**	**(1,2,4)/ (2,4,8.5)**	**(4,6.5,11)/ (1,1,1)**	**1**	**3**	**2**	**0**	**100**	**0**	**100**	**18**	**0.0**	**2**	**2**	**2**	**100**	**0**
cl19	(0,0,0)/(0,0,0)	(1,2,5)/(1,2,4)	(0,0,0)/(0,0,0)	1	1.8	6	100	100	2.5	0	0	0	0	100	2	2	0
cl20	(0,0,0)/(0,0,0)	(0,0,0)/(0,0,0)	(1,2,3)/(1,2,2)	0	2.5	3.5	0	0	0	100	3.5	0.7	0.5	100	3.5	2.5	0
cl21	(0,0,0)/(0,0,0)	(1,1,2)/(1,1,2)	(3,4,7)/(1,1,1)	6	0	0	100	0	0	100	0	0	6	8	3	100	0
cl22	(0,0,0)/(0,0,0)	(1,2,4)/(1,2,4.5)	(0,0,0)/(0,0,0)	6	0	0	100	100	0	0	0	0	14	2	0	100	0

6 WORKLOAD SIMULATION TESTS

In this section we present simulation of workload on ERPSoftNext using the clusters discovered from the simulations the affect of different ORGANIZATION behavior patterns on resource consumption can also be analyzed. Since the temporal aspect of the workload in production is not taken into account in this work, we make few assumptions on the distribution of the workload. We assume that the workload is evenly distributed. This means that total BUSINESS-EVENTS obtained by multiplying *BE-factor* by the number of ROLES (which is for the period of a year), is distributed over each day of the year evenly. In order to demonstrate the effect of variation in BUSINESS-EVENT ATTRIBUTES on resource consumption, we take two clusters, cl5 and cl18 from the table 4, that have similar *PIpC BE-factor* but different *PILpPI BE-factor*. With the different usage pattern of the two ORGANIZATION classes, we can check the impact of difference in behavior of ORGANIZATIONS in terms of BUSINESS-EVENTS to resource consumption.

We simulate the workload on a test server running ERPSoftNext using a custom-built workload generator. Figure 6 shows the setup for workload simulation from existing system ERPSoft to the system under development ERPSoftNext. As discussed in section 4, the BUSINESS=EVENTS and BUSINESS=EVENT ATTRIBUTES translate to commands in the CQRS architecture of ERPSoftNext. For the sake of simplicity of implementation, BUSINESS=EVENT ATTRIBUTES are implemented as separate commands. Hence, the total number of BUSINESS=EVENTS corresponds to the total number of invoice

create commands and BUSINESS=EVENT ATTRIBUTES in each BUSINESS=EVENT to the total invoice attribute create commands. By using the command template for the business-event and business-event attributes, corresponding workload can be generated.

Let us assume that the number of instances of the role customer in the ORGANIZATIONS belonging to clusters cl5 and cl18 is 10,000. This leads to 22,500 project invoices for both ORGANIZATIONS in clusters cl5 and cl18. Distributing the total number of invoices over a year, makes around 62 invoices per day. The total number of attributes in invoices will then be 139 for an ORGANIZATION in cl5 taking into account the quartiles. Similarly, for the ORGANIZATION in cl18, we have 287 invoice lines. We also assume that the invoices are generated at the same time, as it helps us to record resource utilization in a convenient way. We used a custom-built workload generator for simulations. The workload generator tool contains JSON template files for specific commands that will be invoked when generating a specific type of command. The actual workload generator fills in templates with dummy data and generates JSON messages as command for the application. In the setup, we use ELK stack [3] to capture and display the resource statistics.

Figure 7[a] shows the simulation of workload for ORGANIZATION in clusters cl5 and Figure 7[b] for cl18. From Figures 7[a] and [b], the first plots show the number of commands processed. The difference in the first plots is that the total number of commands is dissimilar. This is because in ERPSoftNext the CQRS back-end system receives more commands for cl18 than cl5, as more invoice attributes are present, even though the number of invoices that is created is the

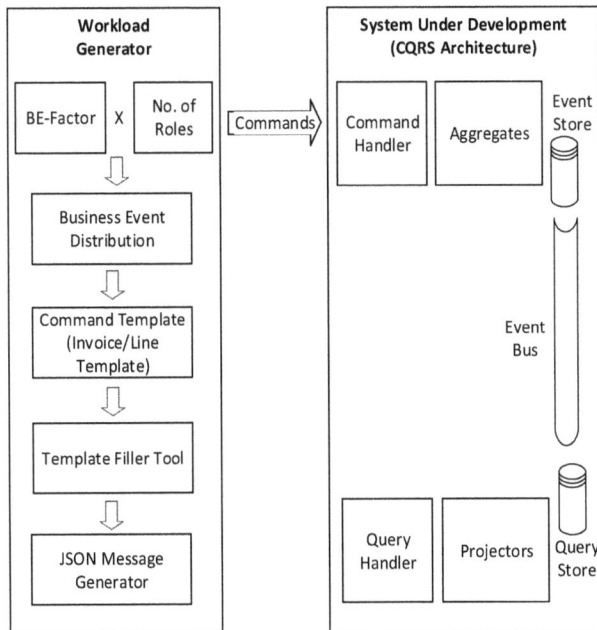

FIGURE 6. WORKLOAD SIMULATION ON SYSTEM UNDER DEVELOPMENT BY EXTRACTING PATTERNS FROM EXISTING SYSTEM.

same. The average duration for processing commands is higher on cl18, as more requests are being processed simultaneously. Also, for a similar number of invoices for the two clusters, the average CPU consumption for cl5 is around 15% while for cl18 it is around 25%. This is because of a higher number of requests processed simultaneously, as cl18 generates more invoice attributes, and hence more requests. Disk transfer is also higher in cl18 compared to cl5.

If low level metrics, such as page accesses, were used in categorization of ORGANIZATIONS, the details of the advanced business processes in ERPSoft would not have been captured in a transportable format to ERPSoftNext. In other words, only through ORGANIZATION categorization of high-level operations, we can create more accurate workloads for realistic usage simulation on new products. Furthermore, the significant workload difference between the clusters proves that clustering -USER ORGANIZATIONS is useful for performance testing.

7   DISCUSSION AND THREATS

The concepts presented in the paper are applicable to other ERP software applications, as business actions in the ERP domain are similar in other ERP software applications. Therefore, the high-level of Organizations, Roles, Business-Events, and Business-event Attributes are generalizable to most, if not all cases.

In an ERP software case, identifying representative metrics for simulating workload is essential, especially in the case if an existing application is used with a different architecture. With the chosen high-level metrics defined in terms of BUSINESS-EVENTS and ROLES in an ORGANIZATION, we show that the ORGANIZATIONS can be categorized into groups based on the usage of an application. It was shown that the items ORGANIZATIONS sell and the license for ERP software have a strong correlation to application usage. We choose

three abstract concepts to represent items sold and license types in relation to the case-study, but depending on the scenario different metrics might need to be determined.

There are validity threats in this work. One of the main threats is that the study is conducted at single case-company. This is a limitation since getting production data from ERP application is difficult to the reasons of sensitive and confidentiality. This is also why not many studies are available in literature on enterprise applications.

Additionally, simulating workload exactly similar to the load on the production server requires temporal data of ERP workload generated by the ROLES. Most ORGANIZATIONS choose to generate BUSINESS-EVENTS at a specific period of year or month or is based on behavior of ROLES. Without studying the temporal relation of the generation of BUSINESS-EVENTS, simulations will be inaccurate. We plan to study temporal aspect of ERP workload in future work. Also load generated by modify and view actions needs to be analyzed separately.

8   CONCLUSION

In this paper an extensive study at a large software company to simulate workload on an application under development is presented. We defined high-level abstractions or workload metrics in terms of business operations, BUSINESS-EVENTS, BUSINESS-EVENT ATTRIBUTES, and ROLES, which are translated to a new application with a different architecture. From the high-level abstractions, data metrics were derived that characterize the behavior of ROLES in END-USER ORGANIZATIONS. Metrics were extracted from an existing application in use by the END-USER ORGANIZATIONS and used to derive the patterns using an unsupervised learning approach. Next, a workload simulation mechanism is described by translating the high-level workload to actual workload on a an application under development using a different architecture, i.e., the CQRS framework. From the simulations we showed that for ORGANIZATIONS with similar number of BUSINESS-EVENTS but varying BUSINESS-EVENT ATTRIBUTES show significant difference in resource consumption, which prompts that more usage based performance testing is required when redesigning system.

In future work, we plan to investigate temporal behavior of OR-GANIZATIONS, for instance to analyze peak load on the servers. In addition other parts of the enterprise application could be investigated to gain overall understanding of usage. We also wish to investigate reactive architectures that self-adapt to the behavior of the ORGANIZATIONS during production usage.

ACKNOWLEDGMENTS

This is an AMUSE Paper. This research was supported by the NWO AMUSE project (628.006.001): a collaboration between Vrije Universiteit Amsterdam, Utrecht University, and AFAS Software in the Netherlands. The NEXT Platform is developed and maintained by AFAS Software. Please see amuse-project.org for more information.

REFERENCES

[1] Sonali Aggarwal, Shashank Phadke, and Milind Bhandarkar. 2010. Characterization of hadoop jobs using unsupervised learning. In *Cloud Computing Technology and Science (CloudCom), 2010 IEEE Second International Conference on.* IEEE, 748–753.

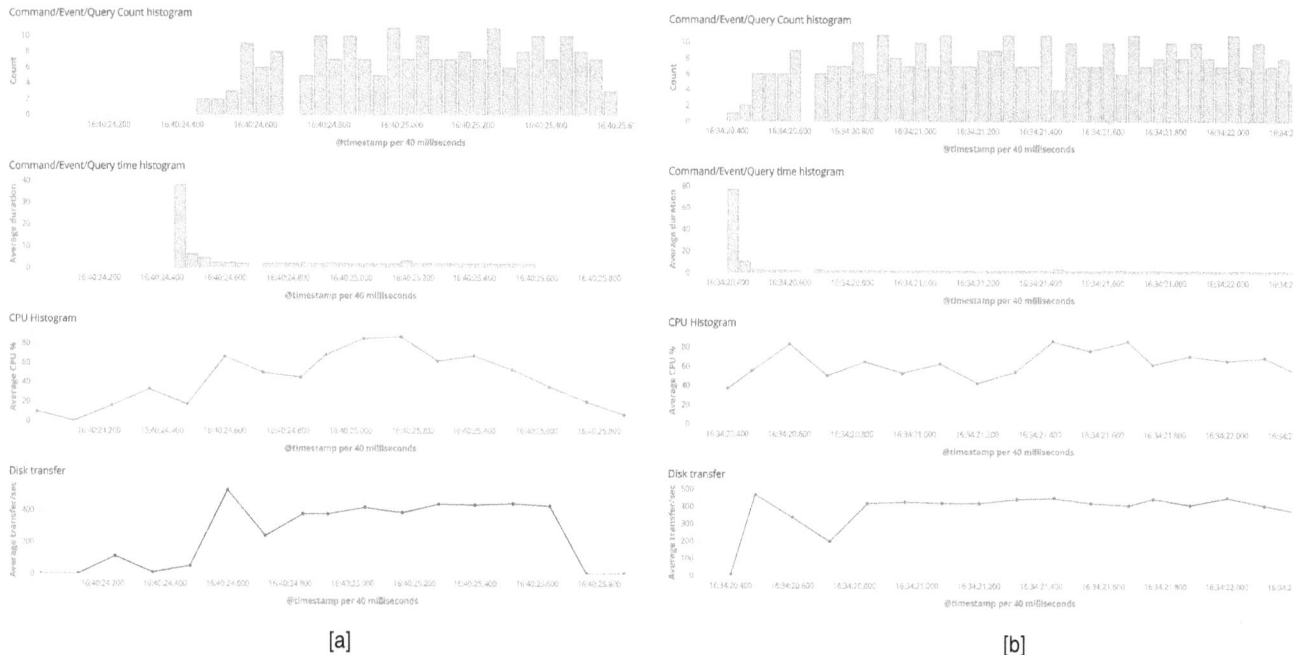

Figure 7. Kibana Dashboard for Workload Simulation for an organization in [a] cl5 and [b] cl18. We in particular note the longer ramp-up and steady drop in CPU and disk transfer at the end of the test of the organization in cl5.

[2] Claudia Canali and Riccardo Lancellotti. 2017. AGATE: Adaptive Gray Area-based TEchnique to Cluster Virtual Machines with Similar Behavior. *IEEE Transactions on Cloud Computing* (2017).

[3] Saurabh Chhajed. 2015. *Learning ELK Stack*. Packt Publishing Ltd.

[4] Frank Elijorde and Jaewan Lee. 2015. Attaining Reliability and Energy Efficiency in Cloud Data Centers Through Workload Profiling and SLA-Aware VM Assignment. *International Journal of Advances in Soft Computing & Its Applications* 7, 1 (2015).

[5] Martin Fowler. 2005. Event sourcing. *Online, Dec* (2005), 18.

[6] John C Gower. 1966. Some distance properties of latent root and vector methods used in multivariate analysis. *Biometrika* (1966), 325–338.

[7] Nikolas Roman Herbst, Nikolaus Huber, Samuel Kounev, and Erich Amrehn. 2014. Self-adaptive workload classification and forecasting for proactive resource provisioning. *Concurrency and computation: practice and experience* 26, 12 (2014), 2053–2078.

[8] Zhen Jia, Jianfeng Zhan, Lei Wang, Rui Han, Sally A McKee, Qiang Yang, Chunjie Luo, and Jingwei Li. 2014. Characterizing and subsetting big data workloads. In *Workload Characterization (IISWC), 2014 IEEE International Symposium on*. IEEE, 191–201.

[9] Jaap Kabbedijk, Slinger Jansen, and Sjaak Brinkkemper. 2012. A case study of the variability consequences of the CQRS pattern in online business software. In *Proc. of the 17th European Conference on Pattern Languages of Programs*. 2:1–2:10.

[10] Leonard Kaufman and Peter J Rousseeuw. 2009. *Finding groups in data: an introduction to cluster analysis*. Vol. 344. John Wiley & Sons.

[11] Dao-Lei Liang and Hai-Bo Chen. 2017. An Online Mall CRM Model Based on Data Mining. In *Quantitative Logic and Soft Computing 2016*. Springer, 599–606.

[12] Yanchi Liu, Zhongmou Li, Hui Xiong, Xuedong Gao, and Junjie Wu. 2010. Understanding of internal clustering validation measures. In *Data Mining (ICDM), 2010 IEEE 10th International Conference on*. IEEE, 911–916.

[13] Kunal Kulkarni Xiaoyi Lu and Dhabaleswar K DK Panda. 2016. Characterizing Cloudera Impala Workloads with BigDataBench on InfiniBand Clusters. (2016).

[14] Gururaj Maddodi, Slinger Jansen, Jan Pieter Guelen, and Rolf de Jong. 2016. The daily crash: a reflection on continuous performance testing. In *11th International Conference on Software Engineering Advances*. IARIA, 171–180.

[15] Daniel A Menascé, Virgilio AF Almeida, Rodrigo Fonseca, and Marco A Mendes. 1999. A methodology for workload characterization of e-commerce sites. In *Proceedings of the 1st ACM conference on Electronic commerce*. ACM, 119–128.

[16] Rizwan Mian, Patrick Martin, Farhana Zulkernine, and Jose Luis Vazquez-Poletti. 2013. Towards building performance models for data-intensive workloads in public clouds. In *Proceedings of the 4th ACM/SPEC International Conference on*

Performance Engineering. ACM, 259–270.

[17] Asit K Mishra, Joseph L Hellerstein, Walfredo Cirne, and Chita R Das. 2010. Towards characterizing cloud backend workloads: insights from Google compute clusters. *ACM SIGMETRICS Performance Evaluation Review* 37, 4 (2010), 34–41.

[18] Ismael Solis Moreno, Peter Garraghan, Paul Townend, and Jie Xu. 2014. Analysis, modeling and simulation of workload patterns in a large-scale utility cloud. *IEEE Transactions on Cloud Computing* 2, 2 (2014), 208–221.

[19] Jemishkumar Patel, Vasu Jindal, I-Ling Yen, Farokh Bastani, Jie Xu, and Peter Garraghan. 2015. Workload estimation for improving resource management decisions in the cloud. In *Autonomous Decentralized Systems (ISADS), 2015 IEEE Twelfth International Symposium on*. IEEE, 25–32.

[20] Kai Ren, Garth Gibson, YongChul Kwon, Magdalena Balazinska, and Bill Howe. 2012. Hadoop's Adolescence; A Comparative Workloads Analysis from Three Research Clusters.. In *Proceedings of 2012 SC Companion: High Performance Computing, Networking Storage and Analysis, SCC 2012, (Washington, DC, USA)*. 1452.

[21] Henk van der Schuur, Erik van de Ven, Rolf de Jong, Dennis M M Schunselaar, Hajo A Reijers, Michiel Overeem, Machiel de Graaf, Slinger Jansen, and Sjaak Brinkkemper. 2017. NEXT: Generating Tailored ERP Applications from Ontological Enterprise Models. In *10th IFIP WG 8.1 Working Conference on the Practice of Enterprise Modeling (POEM)*.

[22] André van Hoorn, Christian Vögele, Eike Schulz, Wilhelm Hasselbring, and Helmut Krcmar. 2014. Automatic extraction of probabilistic workload specifications for load testing session-based application systems. In *Proceedings of the 8th International Conference on Performance Evaluation Methodologies and Tools*. ICST (Institute for Computer Sciences, Social-Informatics and Telecommunications Engineering), 139–146.

[23] Greg Young. [n. d.]. CQRS and Event Sourcing. Feb. 2010. *URl: http://codebetter. com/gregy oung/2010/02/13/cqrs-and-event-sourcing* ([n. d.]).

One Size Does Not Fit All: In-Test Workload Adaptation for Performance Testing of Enterprise Applications

Vanessa Ayala-Rivera
Lero@UCD, School of Computer
Science, University College Dublin,
Ireland
vanessa.ayalarivera@ucd.ie

Maciej Kaczmarski
Lero@UCD, School of Computer
Science, University College Dublin,
Ireland
maciej.kaczmarski@ucdconnect.ie

John Murphy
Lero@UCD, School of Computer
Science, University College Dublin,
Ireland
j.murphy@ucd.ie

Amarendra Darisa
IBM Ireland, Dublin, Ireland
darisaam@ie.ibm.com

A. Omar Portillo-Dominguez
Lero@UCD, School of Computer
Science, University College Dublin,
Ireland
andres.portillodominguez@ucd.ie

ABSTRACT

The identification of workload-dependent performance issues, as well as their root causes, is a time-consuming and complex process which typically requires several iterations of tests (as this type of issues can depend on the input workloads), and heavily relies on human expert knowledge. To improve this process, this paper presents an automated approach to dynamically adapt the workload (used by a performance testing tool) during the test runs. As a result, the performance issues of the tested application can be revealed more quickly; hence, identifying them with less effort and expertise. Our experimental evaluation has assessed the accuracy of the proposed approach and the time savings that it brings to testers. The results have demonstrated the benefits of the approach by achieving a significant decrease in the time invested in performance testing (without compromising the accuracy of the test results), while introducing a low overhead in the testing environment.

CCS CONCEPTS

• **General and reference** → **Performance**; • **Software and its engineering** → Software testing and debugging;

KEYWORDS

Performance; Testing; Workload; Analysis; Automation

ACM Reference Format:
Vanessa Ayala-Rivera, Maciej Kaczmarski, John Murphy, Amarendra Darisa, and A. Omar Portillo-Dominguez. 2018. One Size Does Not Fit All: In-Test Workload Adaptation for Performance Testing of Enterprise Applications. In *ICPE '18: ACM/SPEC International Conference on Performance Engineering, April 9–13, 2018, Berlin, Germany.* ACM, New York, NY, USA, 12 pages. https://doi.org/10.1145/3184407.3184418

1 INTRODUCTION

Performance is a crucial dimension of quality and a major concern of any software project. This is especially true at the enterprise level, where system performance can play a critical role in achieving companies' goals (e.g., trading systems, airlines' websites). However, despite the efforts invested in performance engineering tasks, it is common that performance issues occur and materialise into severe problems with serious business consequences (e.g., outages on production or even cancellation of software projects). For instance, a survey conducted among information technology executives documented that half of them had experienced performance problems in more than 20% of their managed applications [12]. This situation has been exacerbated by the introduction of recent trends in information technology (e.g., Cloud Computing and Big Data) which have augmented the complexity of enterprise-level applications, complicating, even more, the performance testing of such applications [18].

A particularly complex challenge in the area is that a considerable number of performance issues, occurring at enterprise-level applications, are workload-dependent [32]. Even though existing performance testing tools (e.g., Apache JMeter [1]) can be used to detect these types of issues, this is usually ineffective because these tools use static (i.e., pre-configured) workloads. Thus, they rely on the expertise of human testers to set an adequate workload that can reveal the performance issues that might exist in the Application-Under-Test (AUT). Typically, testers use "standard" workloads (e.g., based on their own knowledge and previous experience, or based on corporate policies), which might not be sufficient in order to identify issues that may not surface even on relatively large workloads [17]. This is because it is often unclear how large is large enough for a workload to exhibit such issues (as the appropriate workload can be different for each application, or even for different versions of the same application).

An example that illustrates well the motivation of this work is the outage exhibited by the Skype network in December 2010 [6]. It lasted approximately 24 hours and affected more than 20 million users worldwide (around 90% of the Skype users at that time). The analysis performed during its fixing revealed that it was caused by an insufficient amount of performance testing [25]. In particular,

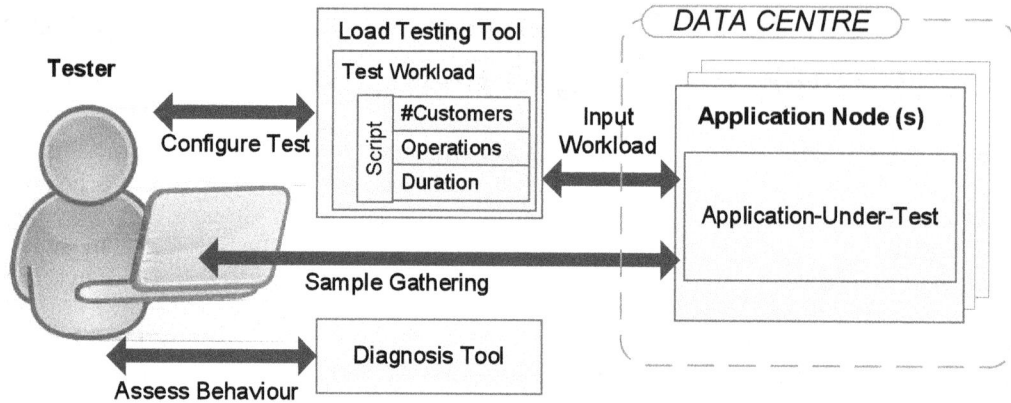

Figure 1: Performance Testing - Contextual view

an untested significantly high workload peak caused an overload of the offline messaging service, which started sending delayed responses. A specific version of the Skype clients could not process well the delayed messages and crashed. These clients included around 25% of the super-nodes (special Skype nodes that work as address books to connect the calls). Consequently, the remaining super-nodes received a traffic 100 times bigger than usual. As the super-nodes have a built-in mechanism to avoid having a huge impact on the host system, this made more super-nodes to shut down, creating a vicious cycle that ended affecting 90% of the Skype users. This scenario clearly illustrates how conducting performance testing with the right amount of workload is important to identify any performance bugs that exist on a system. Otherwise, the consequences might be very serious (like the outage experienced by Skype users). Similarly, research works have also documented the (potential) magnitude of this problem. For instance, a recent research study investigated 109 performance issues and found that 41 of them occurred due to incorrect workload assumptions [14].

Contributions. To address this challenge, our research has focused on developing techniques that improve the identification of workload-dependent performance issues, as well as their root causes, in order to increase the productivity of testers (hereinafter referred as users) by reducing the effort and expertise required in this process. In a previous work [15], we proposed an automated approach which dynamically adapts the workload used by a testing tool. However, that preliminary version was based on heuristic policies derived from the studied AUT; hence, it was not practical for real-world usage (as it was not application-independent). In this paper, we propose a new set of adaptive policies which leverage performance metrics, retrieved from the underlying AUT and evaluated in real-time, to self-configure the test workload according to the specific application behaviour. Such automated policies manage (i) when (i.e., time) and for how much (i.e., amount) the test workload needs to be modified, and (ii) to which application functionality (from the tested one) the workload will be applied. We also extend our approach to support the existing functional dependencies in the tested transactions involved, as well as to determine to which operations the workload will be more useful. As a result of the previous strategies, the need of the testers to manually configure an

appropriate test workload is eliminated. Finally, we conduct a practical validation of the approach (denominated DYNAMO) consisting of an implementation prototype and a series of experiments using three different applications. They evaluate the productivity benefits (i.e., time savings) that can be achieved by using DYNAMO, as well as the amount of overhead (i.e., computational costs) introduced to the test environment.

The rest of this paper is structured as follows: Section 2 presents the background and the related work. Section 3 explains the proposed approach, while Section 4 describes the experimental evaluation and results. Finally, Section 5 presents the conclusions and future work.

2 BACKGROUND AND RELATED WORK

Performance testing is an important type of testing which aims to assess whether or not an application (i.e., AUT) will be able to perform its business functionality under a given workload [13, 19]. As shown in Fig. 1, a performance test run typically involves the execution of a performance testing tool (e.g., Apache JMeter [1]) during a certain period of time (usually several hours, or even days, in an industrial scenario) in order to apply a desired test workload to the AUT. In this context, a test workload is traditionally composed of a number of concurrent customers (normally virtual), as well as a set of functional operations (e.g., search, buy, sell), mimicking an expected type of real usage of the AUT. In order to identify performance issues, users commonly collect performance-related counters (e.g., response time, throughput) periodically during the test execution, so that their trendings and behaviours can be analysed through time. Finally, users commonly utilise some type of diagnosis tool (e.g., IBM WAIT [8]) in order to deepen their analysis of the gathered information.

The literature on performance testing has shown a variety of approaches to improve this process from different perspectives: Some research works have centred on automating the tasks related to benchmark an application (from a performance testing perspective). For instance, the work on [26] presents a framework to automatically conduct a set of typical application-related benchmarking tasks, including a workload generator. Another solution is described

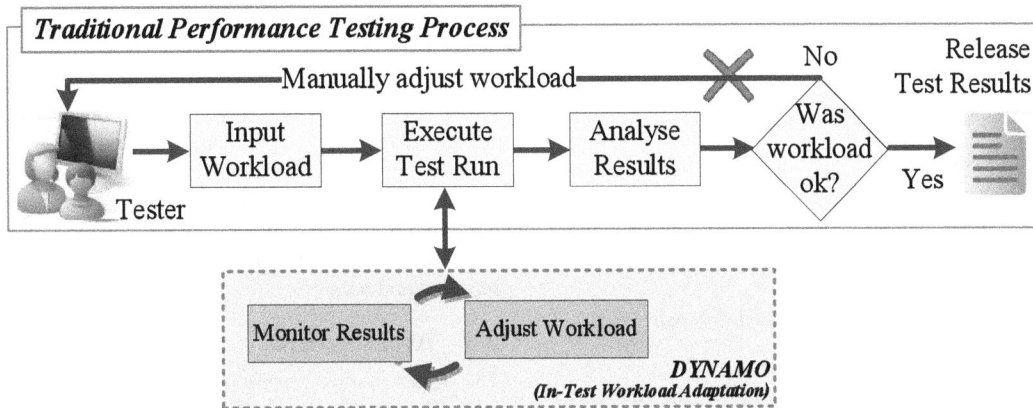

Figure 2: DYNAMO - Contextual View

in [27], which presents a cloud-based benchmark-as-a-service platform that includes a component to create traffic for the benched application. Meanwhile, the work on [29] proposes an approach to automate the extraction of workload specifications (from production logs) in order to be reused in the performance testing of session-based applications; while the work discussed in [9] aims to produce easy-to-process output (from a controlled performance testing run) in order to create a performance model of the tested application.

Meanwhile, other research works have proposed techniques to facilitate the identification of potential performance issues. For example, the authors of [16] proposed a performance test framework tailored to the particular needs of the dynamic multi-tenant cloud environments. Similarly, the work on [23] presents a technique to identify the early warning signs that typically precede a relevant performance degradation in a system. Moreover, some other works have centred on generating useful synthetic testing data [10, 11], or on providing techniques that can reduce the expertise required in order to efficiently automate the usage of the diagnosis tools in the performance testing domain [20]. In contrast to these works, which aim to improve other facets of performance testing, our solution addresses the particular need of setting a suitable test workload for a particular application; hence, successfully isolating a user from the complexities of determining such workload.

Finally, some research works have proposed the use of pre-configured workloads [28, 30] in order to simulate a real customer behaviour using Markov chains. Although these approaches can successfully mimic the desired test workload (which is based on the modelled customer behaviour), there is no guarantee that the mimicked workload is sufficient to identify any existing performance issues in the tested application. In contrast, our research work aims to address that particular challenge in the performance testing domain.

3 PROPOSED APPROACH: DYNAMO

In this section, we provide the overview of our solution and describe the processes involved, its architecture, and supporting policies.

3.1 Overview

The goal of this work was to develop an automated approach (i.e., DYNAMO) that could dynamically adjust the test workload (used in the performance testing of applications) to the specific characteristics of the underlying AUT. The aim is to shield the user from the complexities of identifying a suitable test workload, as they are normally application-dependent and can even change between versions of the same application. In this manner, users can improve their productivity as well as maximise valuable testing resources and time (as they are usually limited due to project constraints, such as budget or schedule).

As explained in Section 1, DYNAMO is motivated by the fact that current testing tools need to be manually configured with an appropriate test workload in order to avoid negative impacts on the accuracy of the test run's outputs (e.g., overlooking any relevant workload-dependant issues). This is because, if an inappropriate configuration is used, the tools might fail to obtain the desired outputs, resulting in significant time wasted. This scenario is exemplified in Fig. 3 (presented for illustrative purposes only, as the actual workload curves are application-specific), which shows how not all test workloads are typically useful to identify the workload-dependent issues existing within a system. If the workload is "too low", the issues might not surface (hence the users would overlook them). Likewise, if the workload is "too high", the test environment would get saturated. If this occurs, most of the identified issues would be caused by the environment saturation, rather than being actual application performance issues.

DYNAMO addresses these types of problems by actively adapting the workload used by a performance testing tool, so that it stresses more the application functionality which is suspicious of having a performance issue in order to have more certainty about whether or not a bug exists. This action would enhance the results obtained by a performance test run, which can be a very time-consuming activity (as discussed in Section 2). As a consequence, DYNAMO leads to a better utilisation of the available resources (in terms of workload) for a performance testing tool in order to maximise its results (e.g., identification of performance bugs or more certainty about the achieved Service Level Agreements). Internally, DYNAMO leverages policies to automatically monitor the effectiveness of the

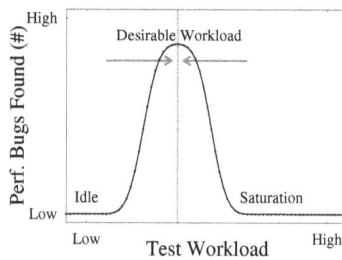

Figure 3: Bugs vs. Test Workload Trade-off

workload used by the performance diagnosis tool. Furthermore, our approach relies on a set of diagnostic metrics, which are evaluated in real-time, to determine when a workload adjustment is required for a specific transaction under test.

Figure 2 depicts the contextual view of our solution within the traditional performance testing process (discussed in Section 2). There, it can be noticed how DYNAMO enhances this process. This is achieved by proactively monitoring the intermediate test results (in real-time) in order to automatically adjust the workload (if needed) during the test run execution. Consequently, the usage of DYNAMO eliminates the need of (potentially costly) trial-and-error test cycles, which would traditionally require the intervention of the users to manually adjust the utilised test workload.

3.2 Core Process

DYNAMO performs a series of steps (i.e., core process) during the execution of the AUT. The process is depicted in Fig. 4. It starts by initialising the set of input parameters as well as the selected policies. There are two different types of policies that can be configured: (1) A diagnosis policy, which defines the criteria that will be used to decide if a transaction is suspicious of suffering a performance issue, the data sources required to perform the assessment (e.g., performance metrics), and any other specific information required to execute the policy. (2) An adjustment policy, which defines the rules to adjust (either increase or decrease) the workload whenever a change is required. These policies are described in more detail in Section 3.4.

DYNAMO requires at least one policy of each type. The encapsulation of these two types of business logic into configurable policies allows our approach to be easily extensible. The aim is that multiple policies can be developed which can be used to fulfil the requirements of different use cases. In order to fully configure DYNAMO, the tester needs to: (i) indicate how long the test run will be executed (i.e., test duration); (ii) indicate an assessment interval in order to specify how often the diagnosis policy will be evaluated to determine if a workload adjustment is needed; (iii) indicate which diagnosis and adjustment policies will be used (among the available alternatives); (iv) provide any inputs required by the chosen policies.

Once the initialisation phase finishes, the process starts the following cycle, which is performed in parallel to the performance test run execution: First, the logic awaits the configured assessment interval during which the AUT has processed a certain amount of transactions (as per an initial test workload) before any diagnosis

is carried out. Next, a new set of samples is collected (based on the data sources defined in the diagnosis policy). After the collection finishes, the process checks if any transaction is suspicious of suffering a performance issue (as dictated by the criteria defined in the selected diagnosis policy). Then, if any transaction is suspicious of suffering a performance issue, the workload gets automatically adjusted. Such adjustments are controlled by the chosen adjustment policy. This process iteratively continues until the performance test run finishes. Finally, any errors that might occur are internally reported and handled.

3.3 Architecture

The design of our approach is complemented by a component-based architecture. There are three main components that compose the core process of DYNAMO (depicted in Fig. 4): The generic component contains all the functionality which is independent of the policies (e.g., the control logic of the core process). The other two components are the *action* and *decision makers*, which encapsulate the logic related to the adjustment of the workload and the diagnosis of performance issues, respectively. This architecture was designed with the aim of minimising the code changes required to extend the approach (e.g., to support other performance test tools, such as IBM RPT [4]). Along with this line of thinking, at an architectural level, the components are only accessed through interfaces. This is exemplified in Fig. 5, which presents the high-level class hierarchy of the action and decision maker components. There, it can be seen that each package contains a main interface to expose the set of supported actions, as well as an abstract class which contains all common functionality (with respect to the tools). Then, the hierarchy is easily extendable to support specific types of policies. For instance, one decision maker can leverage common performance metrics (e.g., response time, throughput, error rate) in order to assess the health of the AUT from a customer's perspective. Alternatively, another decision maker can assess the health of the AUT from a server's perspective, by measuring the amount of consumed resources (as shown in Fig. 5).

3.4 Supported Policies

In the following paragraphs, we describe the set of diagnosis and adjustment policies that DYNAMO supports:

3.4.1 Adjustment Policies. This type of policy defines the actions to follow for modifying the test workload used by the performance testing tool (once a diagnosis policy has determined that an adjustment action is required). Among the alternative approaches to develop adjustment policies for DYNAMO, we have initially focused on the following two:

- A *full house* policy, in which any modifications made to the test workload affects all transaction types (either all types increasing or decreasing at once by the same workload amount). This approach can be useful in the scenario when a new enterprise application is about to be released to production. Since there is no historical data regarding the application's performance, its reliability remains undetermined. Therefore, it is reasonable to assume that all transactions are equally likely of experiencing workload-dependent performance issues.

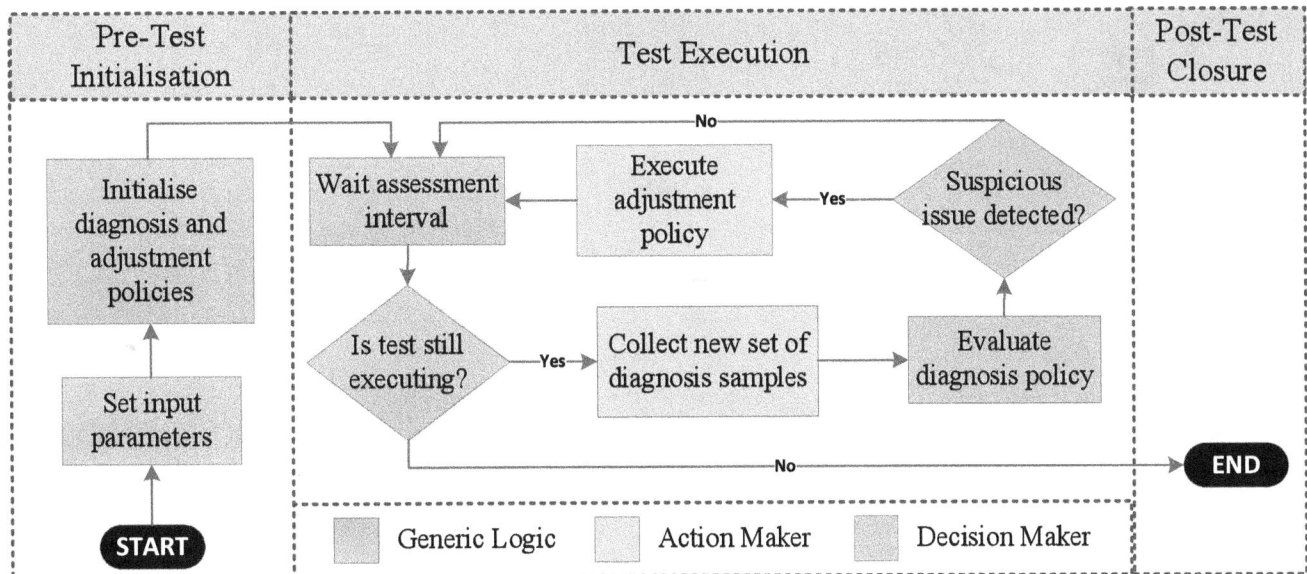

Figure 4: DYNAMO - Core Process

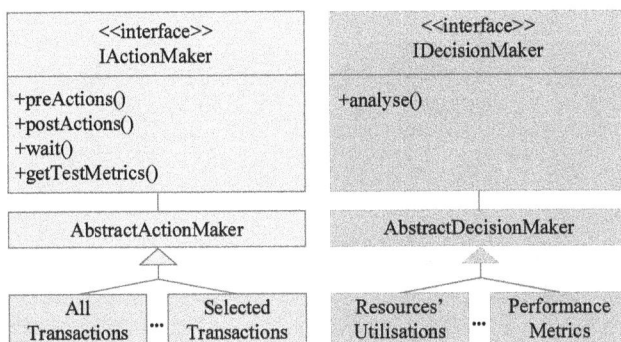

Figure 5: DYNAMO - Class Hierarchy of Decision and Action Makers

- A *mix and match* policy, in which only a subset of the tested transaction types are increased. This approach would be useful in cases when only some of the transactions are suspicious of suffering a performance issue (i.e., they are workload-dependent). It is important to remark that this policy is also responsible for preserving the functional dependencies existing among the transactions. For instance, consider that an online shopping store website is the AUT. The *"purchase"* functionality has exhibited abnormal behaviour (based on its performance indicators). Thus, it has been determined to adjust its test workload with the aim of stressing this part of the application. In this scenario, the functional dependencies of *"purchase"* can be the *"login"* and *"add to cart"* operations, as both actions need to occur before being able to buy a product. Hence, the workload of these three transaction types will be equally adjusted as they are dependent.

3.4.2 Diagnosis Policies. This type of policy is used to detect if a transaction type in the AUT is suffering a performance degradation. As a result, the test workload used by the performance testing tool might be adjusted (as specified by the adjustment policy used). Among the possible approaches to develop diagnosis policies for DYNAMO, we have initially concentrated on one policy based on the *error rate* performance metric. This policy was designed to leverage the observed behaviour that, even though it is expected that some errors may occur when processing client requests, these errors will considerably increase when the load has reached a point that exceeds the application's ability to deliver its service. The policy is also inspired by concepts of supervised machine learning, in which the test execution is divided into two phases: The first phase is exploratory, where the main goal is to identify which transactions are the most workload-sensitive; the second phase is operational, and it is mainly focused on stressing, as much as possible (and within the constraints of the test environment), those transactions that have been previously identified (in phase one) as workload-sensitive. The ultimate goal of such strategy is to maximise the number of performance issues that can be identified by a single performance test run.

This policy requires the following inputs:

(1) Phase ratio: As the policy is composed of two phases, this optional parameter indicates what percentages of the total test duration will be used for the first and second phases, respectively. If the values for this parameter are not configured, a default ratio of 20/80% will be used. This default value has been taken from the Pareto law, which states that, for many events, roughly 80% of the total effects come from 20% of the causes [24].

(2) Initial workloads: As a starting calibration point, the user needs to indicate a known low workload (e.g., 50 customers) and a relative ratio where the workload sensitivity might

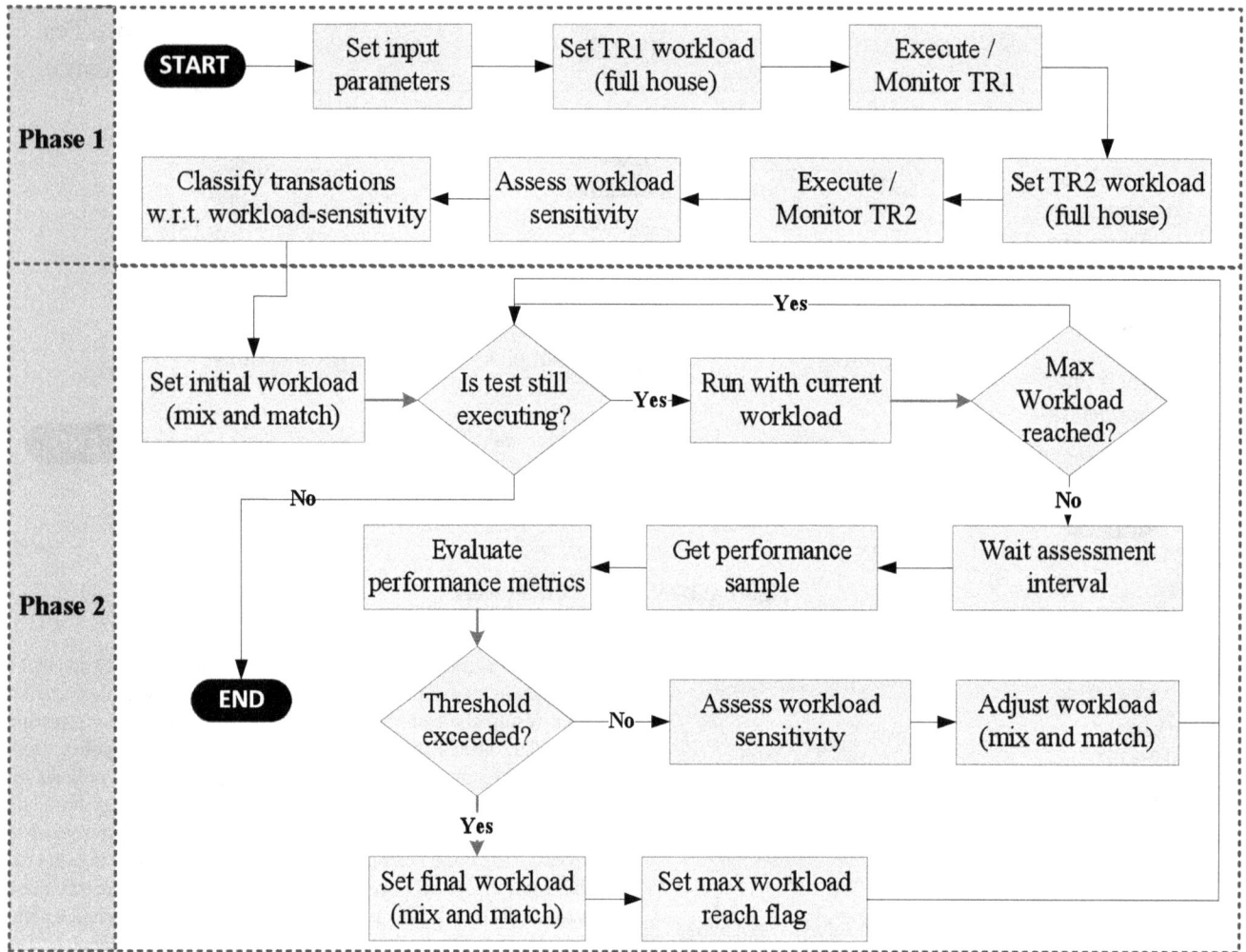

Figure 6: DYNAMO - Error rate-based Adjustment Policy

be noticeable (e.g., 10 times). Understanding that the user might not know the exact test workload, it is only assumed that s/he can still provide an educated estimation.

(3) Error rate threshold: This optional parameter defines the upper bound value that indicates that the system has become saturated. If this parameter is not configured, a default value of 90% will be used (as this is a value commonly identified as saturation point [19]).

(4) Functional dependencies: This is the set of dependency relationships that might exist between the tested transactions (e.g., a purchase cannot occur without first logging into the system). If configured, such dependencies will be considered by the policy's logic to keep the test workload consistent (by propagating the dependencies to the applicable adjustment policy).

(5) Workload-sensitivity identification strategies: This parameter defines which strategy (among the ones supported for each of the two phases) will be used to assess the workload-sensitivity of the transactions to determine if their workload

needs to be adjusted. They are explained in the following paragraphs (as part of the phases' descriptions).

The core process of the *error-based adjustment policy* is depicted in Fig. 6. Below, we explain the two main phases that compose the execution of the policy.

Phase 1: Here, the goal is to find what transactions, among the overall set of functional transactions been tested, are workload-sensitive (WkS) or workload-insensitive (WkI). First, all the elements required to properly execute the policy are initialised. Next, two initial Test Runs are conducted (TR1, TR2); each test lasts half of the time configured for phase 1. TR1 is executed using the initial test workload provided by the user (i.e., a low workload such as 50 customers), while TR2 uses an incremented test workload that results from multiplying the initial low workload by the relative ratio parameter (i.e., 500 customers, assuming a ratio of 10 and an initial workload of 50 customers). Internally, this phase leverages the *full house* adjustment policy (i.e., all transactions are equally modified at the same time). This policy is suitable for this scenario because, at this stage, it is still uncertain which transactions are workload-sensitive and which are not. During the execution of the test runs, a set of performance metrics is gathered (i.e., response time, throughput, error rate). Once TR2 finishes, the process will assess the workload-sensitivity of the transactions by comparing the differences (i.e., deltas) between the performance metrics gathered from TR1 and TR2.

Two different strategies for workload-sensitivity identification are supported: (1) *Absolute*, in which all the transactions whose delta percentage is greater than or equal to a pre-configured value (e.g., 20%) are tagged as WkS; the rest are tagged as WkI. (2) *Relative*, in which all the transactions are sorted based on their deltas and only the top *N* transactions (either using an absolute number, such as 5, or a percentage, such as 20%) are tagged WkS; the rest are tagged as WkI. It is worth mentioning that the functional dependencies among the transactions are respected. This means that, if a WkI transaction has a functional dependency with a WkS transaction, the WkI transaction will be altered to tag it as WkS in order to respect that dependency. The final output of phase 1 is the set of transactions tagged as either WkS or WkI.

Phase 2: Here, the aim is to increase the test workload of the WkS transactions as much as possible without reaching the saturation point of the system. When phase 2 starts, the transactions will use an initial workload using the *mix and match* adjustment policy. For WkI transactions, this will be half of the workload used in TR2 of phase 1, while the WkS transactions will use the full workload. These values are configurable, however, their default values have been defined with the aim of accelerating the identification of performance issues. For instance, the last workload used in TR2 of phase 1 has already proven to be effective as it was used to identify the WkS transactions. Also, since the adaptive logic of phase 2 only applies to WkS transactions, WkI transactions can use the initially configured workload during the rest of the test execution. In that manner, they do not spend resources that can be invested in the testing of WkS transactions.

Once the initial workloads are set, the following loop will be executed until the configured test duration has passed: First, the process awaits the current assessment interval, so that the test run can make use of the current test workload for some time before evaluating whether or not it is the right workload for the particular application's behaviour. Once the interval has elapsed (and assuming that the maximum suitable workload has not been reached), a sample of the performance metrics is retrieved from the test loader tool (i.e., the error rate for all WkS transactions that comprehend the most recent assessment interval). Then, the deltas for the sampled error rates are calculated for each WkS transaction (as previously explained in phase 1). These deltas are then used to determine if the workload of any individual transaction type requires being adjusted. Before doing this, DYNAMO first needs to assess if the test run has not reached the saturation point yet. In order to assess this, the average error rate is compared to the configured threshold. If the average error rate (across all tested transactions) is higher than the threshold, it means that the test environment is already saturated. In this case, a final adjustment to the test workload is done by rolling it back to the one used before the last increment (as such workload is the highest one reached before exceeding the

error rate threshold). Also, a flag is set to indicate that the maximum workload point has been reached, so that DYNAMO stops modifying the workload.

On the contrary, if the saturation point has not been reached yet, the process checks which of the WkS transaction(s) will be increased. To determine this, the policy can use three different selection strategies (inspired by the commonly-known load balancing algorithms, random and round-robin): (1) *Random:* Here, the transaction whose workload will be increased is randomly picked. This can be either a uniform or a weighted random selection. In the uniform mode, all the transactions have the same probability of being selected. In the weighted mode, the transactions are weighted so that the probability of each transaction to be selected is determined by its relative weight. For example, based on their performances, the worst performing transaction would have more chances to be chosen. (2) *Maximum:* Here, the workloads of the top *N* transactions that have the worst performance are increased. In order to avoid a "selfish" behaviour, the workload of a transaction cannot be increased in two consecutive adjustment rounds. (3) *Minimum:* Here, the workloads of the top *N* transactions that have the best performance are increased. This alternative tends to be fairer (than maximum) because it is more likely that the transaction whose workload was increased will be the worst performer in the next round. Hence, this strategy gives other transactions the chance to have their workloads increased (without the need to keep track of the adjusted transactions, as in the maximum strategy).

The loop continues until the performance test run finishes. It is worth mentioning that any exceptions are internally reported and handled. Furthermore, similarly to the previous phase, the functional dependencies that exist among the transactions are always respected. This means that, if the workload of a transaction needs to be modified (as per any of the previously discussed adjustment strategies), all its functional dependencies must also be modified accordingly.

4 EXPERIMENTAL EVALUATION

4.1 Experimental Setup

Our experiments aimed to evaluate the benefits brought by DYNAMO (e.g., its bug accuracy and time savings), as well as the costs of its usage (e.g., its computational resources). All experiments were carried out in an isolated test environment to prevent environmental noise (so the entire load was controlled). The environment was composed of two virtual machines (VMs): One acted as application node (running Apache Tomcat 6.0.35 [2], a widely used Java Application Server); while the other VM acted as load tester (running Apache JMeter 2.9 [1], a popular performance testing tool). Each VM had 4GB of RAM, 2 CPUs at 2.20GHz, Linux Ubuntu 12.04L, and OpenJDK JVM 7 with a 1.6GB heap. From a technical perspective, we built our prototype on top of the JMeter tool, developing it in Java [21]. This was done in order to make our solution highly portable, as there are Java Virtual Machines (JVM) available for most contemporary operating systems.

As AUT, we used three different applications:

(1) PetStore, an e-commerce application commonly used in the literature [19, 22]. It is composed of 11 different business operations. They are described in Table 1.

Table 1: PetStore Operations

Name	Description
Index	Welcome page.
Add user	Page to register a new user.
Login	Page to perform the login action.
Login button	Process to validate the user and password.
Search product	Search page to find particular items.
Select product	This action will display the details of the chosen product.
Update cart	Add the selected product to the shopping cart.
New order	Page displayed after the first item is added to provide general information about the order.
Add payment	Page where the payment information is captured.
Confirm order	The final step in the purchase process, where the order is confirmed.
Log out	Link to perform the logout action.

Table 2: DaCapo Programs

Name	Description
avrora	It simulates a set of programs running on a grid of microcontrollers.
batik	It processes a set of vector-based images.
eclipse	It executes a set of performance tests in an eclipse development environment.
fop	It generates PDF files based on a set of XSL-FO files that are parsed and formatted.
h2	It executes a set of banking transactions against a database-centric application.
jython	It executes a set of python scripts in Java.
luindex	It indexes a set of documents.
lusearch	It performs a set of keyword searchs over a corpus of data.
pmd	It reviews a set of Java classes, looking for bugs in their source code.
sunflow	It renders a set of images.
tomcat	It executes a set of queries against a Tomcat server.
tradebeans	It executes a set of stock transactions, via Java Beans calls.
tradesoap	It executes a set of stock transactions, via SOAP calls.
xalan	It transforms a set of XML files into HTML files.

(2) m-PetStore, a modified version of Petstore that mimics the scenario of an evolving AUT in which ten performance issues were injected (a blend of lock contention, I/O latency, and deadlock bugs) following a strategy previously used in other works [20].

(3) DaCapo, one of the Java benchmarks most widely-used in the literature, offering a wide range of 14 real-life programs from different business domains [3] (shown in Table 2). To enable the execution of any DaCapo program from within a test script, a wrapper JSP was also developed and deployed on the application node. Finally, each program execution was considered a transaction.

As evaluation criteria, we adopted the following metrics and units: Throughput (tps), response time (ms), error rate (%), CPU (%) and memory (MB) utilisations. Also, the analysed performance issues were retrieved from the outputs of IBM WAIT (popular Java diagnosis tool used due to its strong analytic capabilities to detect performance bugs [8, 31]). In order to do this, WAIT was fed with Javacores [5] (snapshots of the JVM state). They were generated with the native Linux *kill* command (i.e., no instrumentation was required to create them) and collected every 30 secs (following a sampling interval commonly used in the industry [19]). Finally, a 2-hour test duration (per test run) was used to reflect realistic test conditions. Besides, three types of test runs were performed:

(1) The first type used the traditional approach of static workloads (as per common industrial practices [7]). For this purpose, all the AUTs started with a close-to-idle scenario an ended with a saturated environment. However, since the AUTs have diverse functional behaviours, their saturation points were different. Consequently, the workload ranges (as well as the workload increments) varied per AUT. For PetStore, the workload range was [100..1800] in increments of 100; for m-PetStore, it was [100..3500] in increments of 100 (up to 2300) and then 300; and for DaCapo, it was [200..4400]

in increments of 200 (up to 3600) and then 400. These configurations exemplify the challenges typically experienced by users to select an appropriate test workload.

(2) The second type of run used the preliminary version of DYNAMO based on heuristic policies derived from PetStore (referred as h-DYNAMO [15]).

(3) The third type of run used the work proposed in this paper which adopts our new adaptive logic (DYNAMO). It involved a 5-minute assessment interval and a 20%-80% phase-ratio. The initial workload for both PetStore versions was 100 (with a ratio of 4), while for DaCapo was 800 (with a ratio of 2). Additionally, the error rate threshold was set to 8%, using the *relative* strategy for phase 1 (to homogenise DYNAMO's configuration, as the AUTs were composed of different numbers of functional transactions), and the *minimum* strategy for phase 2 (to give all WkS transactions a fair possibility of getting stressed).

4.2 Experimental Results

In this section, we present the results obtained, discussing them in terms of the relevant perspectives: bug accuracy, time savings, and computational costs. Due to space constraints, we only present the most relevant results (as this experiment involved above 140 hours of test run executions).

4.2.1 Performance Bugs Analysis. Our analysis first focused on assessing the bug accuracy of all test runs. The obtained results are presented in Figs. 7, 8 and 9, which compare the number of

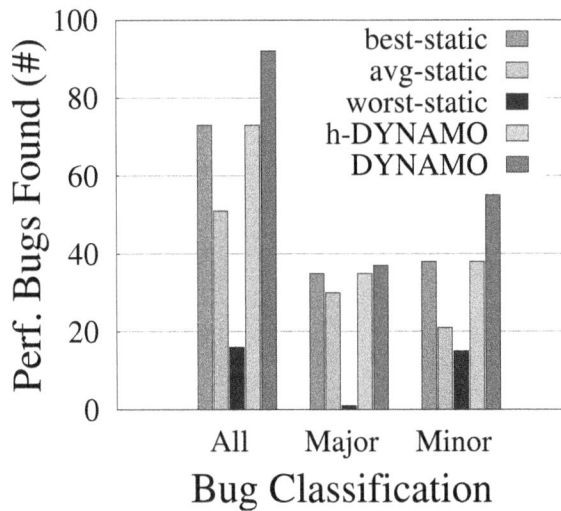

Figure 7: PetStore

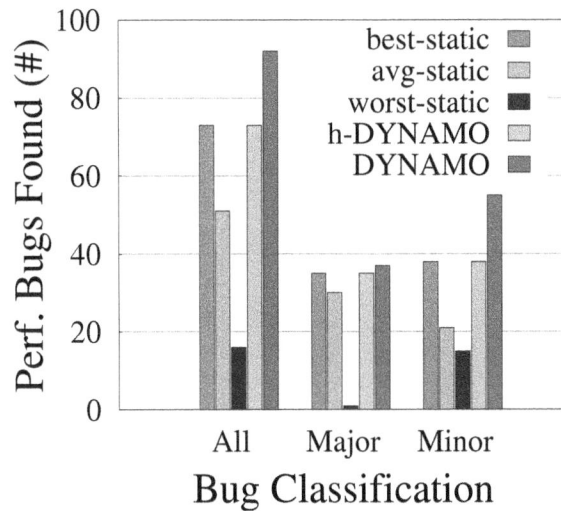

Figure 8: m-PetStore

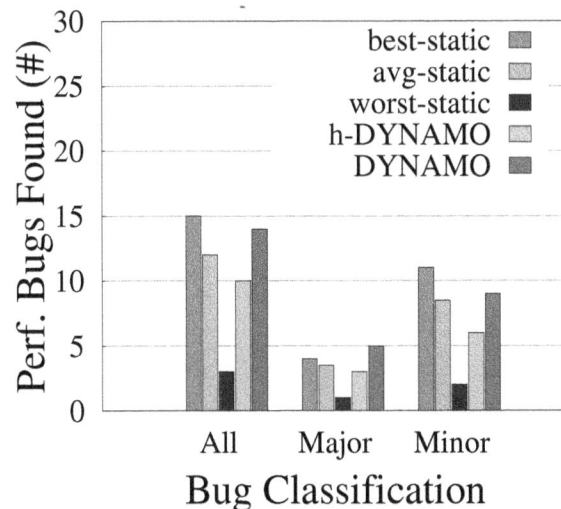

Figure 9: DaCapo

performance bugs found in each test run for the three AUTs. For the static type test run, we report the best (best-static), worst (worst-static), and average (avg-static) performing workload. It can be observed how DYNAMO worked well, as it was able to identify more bugs than all of the other test runs. The only exception was the best-static test run of DaCapo, which found one more bug than DYNAMO.

The improvements in bug identification accuracy achieved by DYNAMO were the result of increasing the test workload for those functional transactions which were the most workload-sensitive. This is because such workload adjustments provoked that the workload-sensitive transactions were considerably more frequently executed (compared to the static test runs) during DYNAMO's test run executions. These behaviours, which were captured by the sampled Javacores, allowed to better feed the diagnosis tool (i.e., WAIT), which was pushed to do a more detailed analysis of the AUTs (as those samples contained more information about the most workload-sensitive transactions, which typically are the main causes of the workload-dependent issues existing in an application). For instance, in the case of PetStore (whose results as shown in Fig. 7), DYNAMO's phase 1 identified 6 highly workload-sensitive operations (among the 11 which compose the application). This information allowed that the additional test workload (introduced during phase 2) could concentrate on those 6 operations. Thus, the workloads of those transactions were gradually increased (during the assessment intervals, based on their error rate deltas) until reaching a peak of 1300 concurrent virtual customers for the 3 transactions which were more frequently chosen for workload increase (i.e., search, select product, and add item). On the contrary, other transactions were only occasionally chosen (e.g., login), causing that the workload used to test them were relatively lower (e.g., login only reached a maximum of 700 concurrent virtual customers).

Similar trends were observed for the other two AUTs (i.e., m-PetStore and DaCapo), as comparable improvements in terms of bug accuracy were obtained (as shown in Figs. 8 and 9). However, some (expected) differences in terms of the results were obtained due to their diverse application behaviours. For example, the highest test workload reached by a transaction in m-PetStore was 1100 customers. Moreover, this test run was the only one (among those that used DYNAMO) which triggered a rollback action (i.e., decrease the test workload to the previously used amount) because the error rate threshold was exceeded at some moment of the test run. This exemplifies how even different versions of the same application can require considerably different test workloads. Finally, 4 transactions were the most workload-sensitive ones in DaCapo (i.e., avrora, batik, sunflow, and xalan), whose highest transaction-level workloads were 1400, 1400, 1700, and 1600 customers (respectively).

To offer a more comprehensive perspective of the results, we also performed a breakdown of the bugs by classifying them based on their frequency of occurrence. A bug was labelled as *major* if it occurred above 5% of the test run duration (i.e., 2 hours). Otherwise, it was considered as *minor*. This analysis confirmed the results discussed previously, as DYNAMO always outperformed worst-static, avg-static, and best-static (except in DaCapo). Regarding the best-static of DaCapo, the results showed an interesting finding: DYNAMO found more major bugs (typically the ones that matter the most from a performance perspective). Therefore, best-static of DaCapo only surpassed DYNAMO in terms of minor bugs.

Moreover, it is worth noting that DYNAMO always outmatched h-DYNAMO, even for PetStore (which is the AUT from which h-DYNAMO was derived). This was the result of two main factors: Firstly, h-DYNAMO used the same workload for all types of tested transactions. However, this strategy was not optimal because not all transactions suffered performance issues. Thus, stressing more some types of transactions (i.e., those with suspected problems), while leaving the others to use lower test workloads (like DYNA-MO did) produced better results in terms of bug accuracy. Secondly, h-DYNAMO did not adapt to the AUT's behaviour (e.g., its saturation point), but it only reused the test workload that was useful for PetStore. Not surprisingly, it was not an optimal test workload for the other AUTs. Finally, the differences between h-DYNAMO and DYNAMO were relatively small because the same test environment was used for all test runs. If an alternative (i.e., bigger) test environment were used, the differences would be far more notorious (as h-DYNAMO would not be able to escalate to the characteristics of the new test environment, while DYNAMO would do).

4.2.2 Testing Time. The second part of our analysis centred on assessing the time savings achieved with our solution. Since DYNAMO was able to adjust the workload during the test run execution, it avoided the need for costly trial-and-error test runs. More specifically, the user only required one test run (instead of the 18, 27, and 20 runs required to cover the full range of static workloads for PetStore, m-PetStore, and DaCapo, respectively). This means that DYNAMO reduced the duration of the total performance testing activities by an average of 95% across the three AUTs (as DYNAMO was able to avoid the execution of 17, 26, and 19 test runs, for PetStore, m-PetStore, and DaCapo, respectively). This is depicted in Figs. 10, 11 and 12, which compare the testing time of the static runs against DYNAMO for each AUT. h-DYNAMO is not included in the figures as it behaves similarly to DYNAMO in terms of execution time. Moreover, the differences in the total time of the static test runs across AUTs is the result of using different ranges of test workloads for each AUT (due to their diverse functional behaviours, as explained in Section 4.1).

Finally, in order to provide a more conservative analysis of these results, we have also included another series in the figures (i.e., bad static runs) in order to indicate the time invested in the static test runs where DYNAMO was better (in terms of bug accuracy). Even under this conservative analysis, significant time savings were obtained. This is because only one static test run (out of 65) obtained marginally better results than DYNAMO.

4.2.3 Cost Analysis. We also measured the computational resources required by DYNAMO in order to understand the costs of using our solution. We focused on the JMeter (load tester) node because DYNAMO resides there. The obtained results are shown in Figs. 13, 14, and 15, which depict the average CPU and memory utilisations during the test runs' executions. It can be noted how the test runs were more memory-intensive than CPU-intensive. The main factor behind the amount of consumed resources was the test workload (e.g., dictating the number of threads that are used to mimic the virtual customers' behaviours). Consequently,

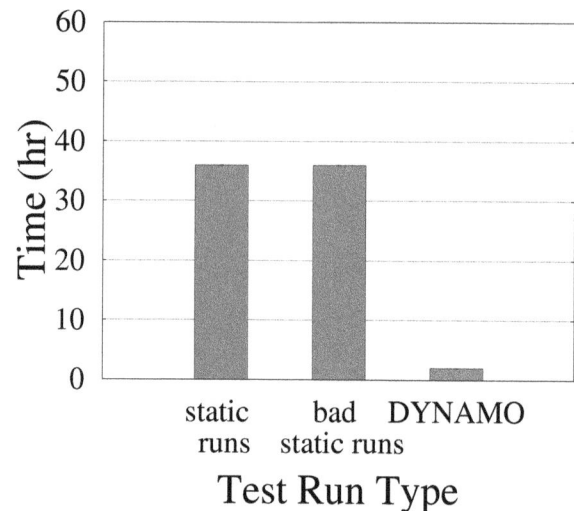

Figure 10: PetStore

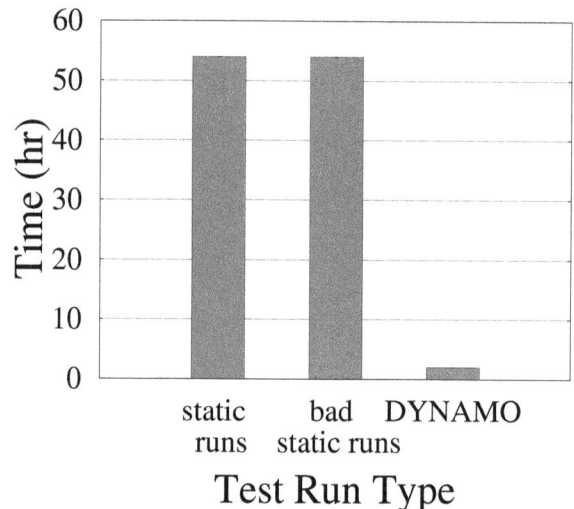

Figure 11: m-PetStore

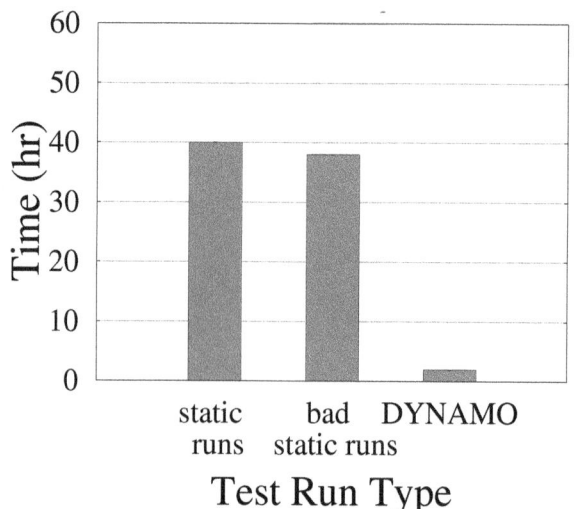

Figure 12: DaCapo

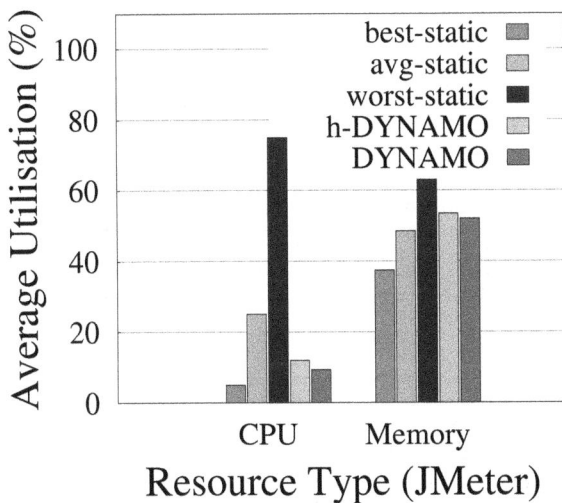

Figure 13: PetStore

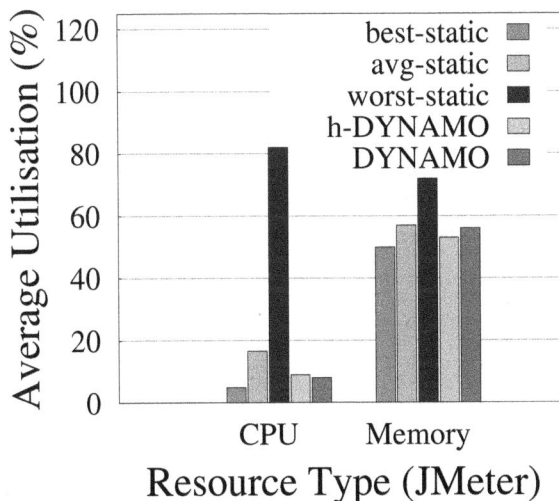

Figure 14: m-PetStore

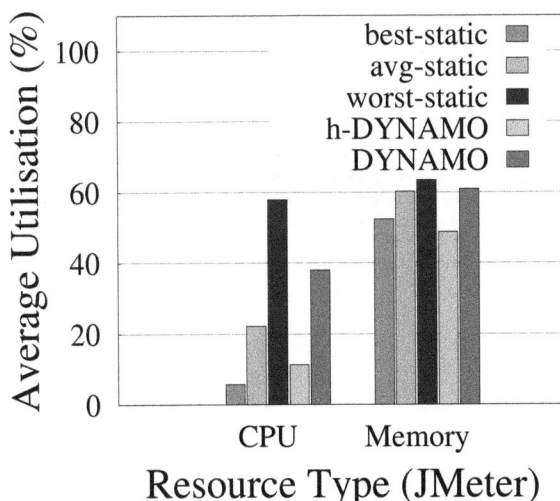

Figure 15: DaCapo

the amount of resources varied among the three AUTs (as each application reached a different optimal test workload).

In the case of both PetStore versions, since the average test workload (across all tested transactions) was relatively lower than DaCapo's (ranged between 900 and 1200 customers for PetStore and between 3000 and 3500 for DaCapo), the costs of DYNAMO were closer to the best-static (in terms of CPU) and average-static (in terms of memory). Meanwhile, for DaCapo, the costs were closer to the worst-static. It is important to highlight that the best-static was always the static test run with the lowest test workload (per AUT), which not surprisingly, derived in a poor performance in terms of bug accuracy. Finally, it can also be seen on the figures how h-DYNAMO exhibited the same computational costs across the three AUTs. This was the result of not adapting itself to the specific behaviour of each AUT.

4.2.4 Final Discussion. In our evaluation, we utilised three applications to assess, to a certain degree, the generality of the benefits and costs of DYNAMO. As the results have shown, DYNAMO offered substantial time savings across all the AUTs. Based on our in-depth analysis, it is expected that DYNAMO can yield similar results with other applications. However, additional experiments would provide more certainty about the broader applicability of our approach (e.g., the usefulness of its default values). It is also possible to conclude that similar bug accuracy results can be obtained when using other diagnosis tools, as long as they are capable of detecting the same types of performance bugs tested.

Additionally, the proposed approach assumes that the user can provide an educated estimation of a known low workload (e.g., 50 customers) and a relative ratio where the workload sensitivity might be noticeable (e.g., 10 times). We consider this is reasonable because the aim is only to identify which transactions are, relatively, more workload-sensitive than the others. Similarly, it is also assumed that the user knows the AUT well-enough to indicate the functional dependencies. For instance, that a user needs to log in before making a purchase, or that a logout cannot be done without first logging in. This is a fair input at enterprise level because that information is usually documented during the analysis phase of the software development cycle (e.g., in the requirements traceability matrix).

Regarding the strategy followed to conduct the static test runs, we explored the full spectrum of test workloads in our planned range (by gradually increasing the test workload linearly) because this is a practice commonly used in the industry [7]. Moreover, this strategy allowed us to have certainty of when the saturation point was reached (as it was application-specific). However, we understand that other test strategies might be used. For instance, instead of linearly increasing the static test workloads in a range, a user might prefer to start his/her performance test work by choosing two very different static workloads (within the planned range) and then, based on the results of those test runs, select only other workloads in the range that look most promising to reveal performance issues. Thereby, it might not be required to execute the same number of static test runs than those conducted in this paper. Hence, the results for the total testing time of the static approach (as well as the time savings achieved by DYNAMO) might be different from those obtained in our experiments. Despite those differences, from the outcome of our investigation, it is expected that the time savings gained by using DYNAMO would be still significative. This is because, even in the extreme case of only requiring 2 static test runs (which would be very unlikely to achieve, as even an experienced user might struggle to easily identify the exact test workload needed for different AUTs), DYNAMO would still be able to save 50% of the testing time (by only requiring 1 test run, instead of the 2 used by the static approach).

Finally, we understand that, even though there is a rationale behind our chosen default values in our experimental evaluation, and they have proven useful for the AUTs used, they might not be applicable to all scenarios. Thus, we plan to explore the range of possible values for each of our configuration parameters (e.g., the ratio between phases 1 and 2) in order to develop guidelines that can help practitioners in the usage of DYNAMO.

5 CONCLUSIONS AND FUTURE WORK

This paper presented an automated approach (DYNAMO) which can adapt, in real-time, the workload used by a performance testing tool during the test run execution. Thus, it eliminates the need for manually identifying a suitable test workload, as well as costly trial-and-error test runs. A prototype was built on top of the JMeter tool and a series of experiments were conducted in order to assess DYNAMO's benefits and costs. Our experimental results have proved the usefulness of the approach by significantly reducing the testing time (by an average of 95%, compared to a range of static standard workloads), without compromising the accuracy of the test results. This is demonstrated by the fact that DYNAMO achieved a high bug accuracy (as it always identified more relevant performance bugs than the best test run counterparts, among the ones using static workloads). Moreover, only a moderate overhead was introduced by DYNAMO (i.e., the average CPU utilisation, in the node where DYNAMO resides, never exceeded 40%).

In terms of future work, our research will centre on investigating how best to extend the capabilities of the approach. For instance, by assessing which other types of metrics (other than the performance ones) can be leveraged to enhance the accuracy of the approach (e.g., the outputs of a diagnosis tool), or by reducing the number of required input parameters (e.g., the need of manually providing the functional dependencies existing among the tested operations). Additionally, we plan to keep assessing the benefits and costs of DYNAMO through broader experiments with the aim of strengthening its validation. For instance, by diversifying the composition and size of the test environments, the tested applications, and the duration of the test runs. The aim is to develop guidelines to help practitioners to configure/use DYNAMO more easily. Finally, we also plan to make the tool freely available (e.g., as a web service).

6 ACKNOWLEDGMENTS

This work was supported, in part, by Science Foundation Ireland grant 13/RC/2094 and co-funded under the European Regional Development Fund through the Southern & Eastern Regional Operational Programme to Lero - the Irish Software Research Centre (www.lero.ie).

REFERENCES

[1] Apache JMeter. http://jmeter.apache.org/. Last accessed: 2018-02-01.
[2] Apache Tomcat. http://tomcat.apache.org/. Last accessed: 2018-02-01.
[3] DaCapo Benchmark. http://dacapobench.org/. Last accessed: 2018-02-01.
[4] IBM RPT. http://www-03.ibm.com/software/products/en/performance. Last accessed: 2018-02-01.
[5] Javacores. http://www-01.ibm.com/support/docview.wss?uid=swg27017906&aid=1. Last accessed: 2018-02-01.
[6] Post-mortem on the Skype outage. http://beeyeas.blogspot.mx/2014/01/cio-update-post-mortem-on-skype-outage.html. Last accessed: 2018-02-01.
[7] Performance Workload Design. Technical report, IBM, 2013.
[8] E. Altman, M. Arnold, S. Fink, and N. Mitchell. Performance analysis of idle programs. *ACM SIGPLAN Notices*, 45(10), Oct. 2010.
[9] V. Apte, T. Viswanath, D. Gawali, A. Kommireddy, and A. Gupta. Autoperf: Automated load testing and resource usage profiling of multi-tier internet applications. In *ICPE*, 2017.
[10] V. Ayala-Rivera, A. O. Portillo-Dominguez, L. Murphy, and C. Thorpe. COCOA: A synthetic data generator for testing anonymization techniques. *Privacy in Statistical Databases*, 2016.
[11] M. W. Aziz and S. A. B. Shah. Test-data generation for testing parallel real-time systems. In *ICTSS*, 2015.
[12] Compuware. *Applied Perf. Management Survey*. 2007.
[13] Z. M. Jiang. Automated analysis of load testing results. *ISSTA*, 2010.
[14] G. Jin, L. Song, X. Shi, J. Scherpelz, and S. Lu. Understanding and detecting real-world performance bugs. *ACM SIGPLAN Notices*, 47(6):77–88, 2012.
[15] M. Kaczmarski, P. Perry, J. Murphy, and A. O. Portillo-Dominguez. In-test adaptation of workload in enterprise application performance testing. In *International Conference on Performance Engineering Companion*, 2017.
[16] N. Michael, N. Ramannavar, Y. Shen, S. Patil, and J.-L. Sung. Cloudperf: A performance test framework for distributed and dynamic multi-tenant environments. In *ICPE*, 2017.
[17] I. Molyneaux. *The Art of Application Performance Testing: Help for Programmers and Quality Assurance*. " O'Reilly Media, Inc.", 2009.
[18] A. O. Portillo-Dominguez, J. Murphy, and P. O'Sullivan. Leverage of extended information to enhance the performance of JEE systems. *Information Technology and Telecommunications Conference*, 2012.
[19] A. O. Portillo-Dominguez, P. Perry, D. Magoni, and J. Murphy. PHOEBE: an automation framework for the effective usage of diagnosis tools in the performance testing of clustered systems. *Software: Practice and Experience*, 2017.
[20] A. O. Portillo-Dominguez, M. Wang, J. Murphy, and D. Magoni. Automated wait for cloud-based application testing. *International Conference in Software Testing Workshops*, 2014.
[21] A. O. Portillo-Dominguez, M. Wang, J. Murphy, and D. Magoni. Adaptive gc-aware load balancing strategy for high-assurance java distributed systems. In *International Symposium on High Assurance Systems Engineering*, 2015.
[22] A. O. Portillo-Dominguez, M. Wang, J. Murphy, D. Magoni, N. Mitchell, P. F. Sweeney, and E. Altman. Towards an automated approach to use expert systems in the performance testing of distributed systems. *Workshop on Joining AcadeMiA and Industry Contributions to Test Automation and Model-Based Testing*, 2014.
[23] R. Ramakrishnan and A. Kaur. Technique for detecting early-warning signals of performance deterioration in large scale software systems. In *ICPE*, 2017.
[24] K. T. Rosen and M. Resnick. The size distribution of cities: an examination of the pareto law and primacy. *Journal of Urban Economics*, 8(2):165–186, 1980.
[25] D. Rossi, M. Mellia, and M. Meo. Evidences behind Skype outage. In *ICC*, 2009.
[26] P. Shivam, V. Marupadi, J. S. Chase, T. Subramaniam, and S. Babu. Cutting corners: Workbench automation for server benchmarking. In *USENIX Annual Technical Conference*, 2008.
[27] A. Tchana, B. Dillenseger, N. De Palma, X. Etchevers, J.-M. Vincent, N. Salmi, and A. Harbaoui. Self-scalable benchmarking as a service with automatic saturation detection. In *ICDSP*, 2013.
[28] A. Van Hoorn, M. Rohr, and W. Hasselbring. Generating probabilistic and intensity-varying workload for web-based software systems. *ICPE*, 2008.
[29] C. Vögele, A. van Hoorn, E. Schulz, W. Hasselbring, and H. Krcmar. WESSBAS: extraction of probabilistic workload specifications for load testing and performance prediction - a model-driven approach for session-based application systems. *Software and Systems Modeling*, Oct 2016.
[30] E. Weyuker and A. Avritzer. A metric for predicting the performance of an application under a growing workload. *IBM Systems Journal*, 41(1):45–54, 2002.
[31] H. Wu, A. N. Tantawi, and T. Yu. A self-optimizing workload management solution for cloud applications. *ICWS*, 2013.
[32] E. Xiao, Xusheng. Context-Sensitive Delta Inference for Identifying Workload-Dependent Performance Bottlenecks. *ISSTA*, 2013.

Performance Improvement Barriers for SAP Enterprise Applications: An Analysis of Expert Interviews

Adrian Streitz
Technische Universität München
Garching, Germany
adrian.streitz@in.tum.de

Harald Kienegger
Technische Universität München
Garching, Germany
harald.kienegger@in.tum.de

Maximilian Barnert
Technische Universität München
Garching, Germany
maximilian.barnert@in.tum.de

Helmut Krcmar
Technische Universität München
Garching, Germany
krcmar@in.tum.de

ABSTRACT

Performance evaluation with regard to response time of software applications is a crucial task. In particular, this is essential for Enterprise Applications with high demand for time-sensitive transactional operations. Although the effects of neglecting performance considerations within the software development life cycle are known, the development process has not significantly changed over the last years. However, companies' interest in software performance is increasing. This paper identifies the barriers regarding performance improvement of software applications during early stages of the development process by focusing on SAP Enterprise Applications. In order to capture recent situations within the industry, we conducted expert interviews with both experienced SAP software developers and product managers working in different industry sectors in Germany. Our key findings show a range of different reasons for poor or missing performance improvement considerations.

KEYWORDS

Software Performance Evaluation, SAP ERP, Response Time, Performance Improvement Barriers, Software Development Life Cycle, SAP Enterprise Applications

ACM Reference Format:
Adrian Streitz, Maximilian Barnert, Harald Kienegger, and Helmut Krcmar. 2018. Performance Improvement Barriers for SAP Enterprise Applications: An Analysis of Expert Interviews. In *ICPE '18: ACM/SPEC International Conference on Performance Engineering, April 9–13, 2018, Berlin, Germany.* ACM, New York, NY, USA, 6 pages. https://doi.org/10.1145/3184407.3184434

1 INTRODUCTION

Well-defined business processes are essential for every company and form a fundamental structure to aim for a certain business goal. Moreover, the success of companies in a competitive environment associates that all its business processes run effectively

[12]. In the industry, most business processes are supported by Enterprise Resource Planning (ERP) systems. Therefore, companies are dependent on the IT infrastructure where these processes are used. Market leader for ERP systems is SAP SE with 23% market share, as stated in a report by Panorama Consulting Solutions [15]. In Germany, this share is almost twice as big - 46% [1]. Therefore, companies have to rely on stable and efficient SAP ERP solutions. Interruptions and bad performance, which cover not only response time, but also throughput and resource utilization [3], lead to financial damage due to unused working hours, forgone turnover or delays within production lines.

According to Brunnert et al. [4], there are two possibilities to ensure performance goals with regard to predefined metrics. Software performance engineering [18] describes how to achieve performance goals during system development. Application performance management [13] is the counterpart for providing stable performance during the operation phase of a software product. Both organizational units follow different paradigms for their work. While development teams aim for realizing new functionalities in a short period of time, operation teams are interested to keep the entire IT landscape in a stable state. However, they are both crucial in order to achieve the performance goals together.

From an operational point of view, performance metrics are defined to ensure service-level agreements by optimizing system parameters on infrastructure, operating system or software level and dynamic resource allocation. Instead, development teams focus on optimizing algorithms, data queries respecting database indices and quality of source code. Following the idea of Shen et al. [14], it is reasonable to put more effort in the development phase, since software changes later in the development life cycle increase overall product costs significantly. Performance tests of Enterprise Applications are one possible solution, but at the same time difficult to perform during the development phase of a software product [18].

Although there are existing tools in SAP ERP systems to test and analyze performance metrics of SAP Enterprise Applications, e.g. Single Transaction Analysis, SQL Performance Trace or ABAP Runtime Trace, which support SAP developers during implementation, 43% of SAP end-users are not satisfied with the performance of their daily in-use SAP Enterprise Applications [6]. In order to close this gap, we want to identify barriers which hinder performance improvement during the development phase of SAP Enterprise Applications.

The major goal of this paper is to show the current situation of performance evaluation procedures in companies relying on SAP ERP software and developing Enterprise Applications within this ecosystem. This includes the identification of current barriers in the applied performance evaluation process and a following discussion of approaches. The contributions of this paper are: (1) to present barriers considering performance improvements for SAP Enterprise Applications and (2) to discuss and come up with ideas to address the identified barriers in order to improve the process of performance evaluation for SAP Enterprise Applications.

The paper is structured as follows: in Section 2 we present the environment and surrounding components of an SAP Enterprise Application to highlight the main differences to other Enterprise Applications. Section 3 inspects related work in this area. Section 4 describes the applied approach, gives insights about the interview partners and summarizes the open-structured interview design. In Section 5 we outline our findings extracted from the expert interviews conducted. We follow up with a discussion in Section 6 and address ideas for future work. Section 7 summarizes and concludes the paper.

2 SAP ECOSYSTEM

In this section, we present the SAP ERP ecosystem with its programming language ABAP for which we consider all following SAP Enterprise Applications. Before ABAP is described as programming language, the concept and the background are mentioned. As the client-server-based development of business applications requires a different approach than the development of locally executable software, an overview of the SAP architecture, the modular concept and the development environment is important for the developer.

ABAP as programming language is thereby intended for dialogue-oriented database applications. The business and technological environment must provide a basis for many users working simultaneously on a shared database. These circumstances require an appropriate data security and system architecture, which is provided by SAP ERP. The SAP Business Suite complements it with some further software applications.

For legal reasons, certain data must be made available for several years or even decades. That is why SAP ensured its independence by introducing their own programming language. As one of the key values, today's ABAP interpreter are still able to process source code from early day programs. This is also the basis for an open and expandable system [11].

On the other hand, these opportunities require a modular design of the system. From a technical perspective, this results in a distribution on several servers and services. From a business perspective, different functional modules are set up and complemented by customer or industry specific solutions, e.g. banking or healthcare. Common SAP modules of ERP systems are Production Planning (PP), Material Management (MM), Sales and Distribution (SD), Human Resource Management (HRM) and many more. But even with those modules, all users work with the same data pool to avoid redundancies and isolated applications [11].

3 RELATED WORK

Compared to Enterprise Applications from other global IT players, SAP Applications are known for their long execution times. Simple tasks as handling billings from business trips or requesting planned holidays using SAP Applications end up with bad performance. This performance results even though the SAP system and the utilized applications are deployed on premise. In contrast, Amazon Online Store, as famous and known example, performs much faster, although the Enterprise Application is not deployed locally. Instead, it has to deal with additional latency issues caused by the individual internet connection of each customer.

With the intention to improve performance considerations on a theoretical basis, Tůma defined in 2014 the term Performance Awareness [16] as an act of performance observation with a follow-up procedure to reduce performance anomalies. According to Tůma [16], without the respect of Performance Awareness in early stages of the software development life cycle, a long-term balance of application performance against development effort and maintenance costs cannot be achieved.

For a component-based system, as the SAP ERP system is intended to be designed, one major factor besides the deployment platform and the dispute of resource allocation is the fact of how efficient the component has been implemented [10]. Since receiving insights on performance of Enterprise Applications gets increasingly difficult due to factors like continuous development [4], it is important to reduce the complexity of a feedback for the developer to a minimum.

As a cooperation project between Compuware Corporation and Pierre Audoin Consultants (PAC), both companies conducted a trend study on the topic of SAP Performance Management in the year 2010 [6]. The trend study was performed with 588 companies in different industry sectors employing at least 500 people and using SAP in their production environment in Belgium, France, Germany, Italy, the Netherlands, Spain, United Kingdom and the United States. The survey covered three main topics: (1) current rating of SAP Enterprise Application performance, (2) financial risks considering SAP performance problems, and (3) applied solutions for SAP Performance Management.

Although all companies run critical business processes on their SAP system landscape, almost 43% complained about bad performance of their SAP systems and 40% consider not being prepared for real-time performance identifications. 96% answered that there is a financial risk, if SAP performance problems arise and 50% of them plan to invest in software solutions to monitor performance values of SAP Enterprise Applications in order to provide the necessary service quality.

Following this purpose, Compuware developed a software product based on the information from the trend study to provide a wide-ranging performance management tool. However, it does not reach out to the developers who are in charge for creating an efficient application.

Our analysis of conducted expert interviews identifies barriers for performance improvements of SAP Enterprise Applications and offers at the same time a research roadmap presenting an approach to address the problem of complexity by reducing the provided performance information for the developer to a minimum.

4 RESEARCH DESIGN

The status quo of current literature for performance consideration in software development processes of SAP Enterprise Applications is rather scarce. Due to lack of theoretical knowledge in the field of performance evaluation for SAP Enterprise Applications, we decided to conduct interviews with experts in the field of Application Development for SAP. According to Bogner et al. [2], expert interviews are a suitable qualitative assessment method since they concern expert's perception. Moreover, it enables open questions for personal opinions and insights in current SAP development processes. In our case, we made use of this research design to discover current situations of the software development processes for the SAP ecosystem and draw parallels to existing statements.

The performed research design follows the rules of an open-structured interview. This means the interviewer has a predefined interview guide with multiple questions. However, neither the exact formulation, nor the order of questions is determined. With this strategy, we allow even additional questions fitting in the current discussion context revealing new interesting issues on the research topic. After a fixed prolog, in which the interview partner and we as interview initiator introduced ourselves, we started asking about the personal experience and the current occupation. Afterwards, no matter in which direction the interview has moved, all experts contributed to the following main questions:

- Is performance considered in current SAP development projects?
- Who is in charge for fixing performance problems of SAP Enterprise Applications?
- Does performance reflect a critical success factor for SAP Enterprise Applications?
- How do you measure performance of SAP Enterprise Applications?
- When do you discover performance issues of SAP Enterprise Applications?
- What are main barriers evaluating performance in early stages of the SAP development process?

4.1 Interview Partners

In a first step of the interview process, we had to look for a suitable target group. According to Glaeser and Laudel [8], the selection of the interview partners is an important task, since a good set of interview partners is crucial for the quality of gathered information.

Since we require knowledge about SAP Enterprise Applications, the resulting performance values and the software development process, we focused on a target group that is currently involved in the field of either IT Development or IT Operations.

To get in touch with people who were willing to share their experiences, we contacted first SAP mentors who are key partners in certain technical fields, like SAP Development, by email. Besides, we made contact with the DSAG[1] who initially created a new initiative for the topic DevOps[2]. Together, we collected six interview partners, principally SAP developers with more than fifteen years of ABAP development experience. Some of them act currently with different

Table 1: List of Interview Partners

Expert	Business Sector	Job Position	SAP ABAP Experience
A	SAP Consulting	CEO	8
B	SAP Consulting	IT Development	10
C	Automotive	IT Operations	9
D	Insurance	IT Development	7
E	Software vendor	Division Manager	4
F	Software vendor	IT Development	8

roles, e.g. as CEO, division or product manager. All available experts are listed in Table 1.

As part of the interview, all experts had to assess themselves regarding their SAP ABAP development experience on a scale from 0 to 10, where 0 means having no experience and 10 being a full ABAP expert. This information is integrated in Table 1 in the fourth column. Because most of the interview partners are spread over Germany, all interviews, except of one, have been conducted via telephone. The interviews lasted 35 minutes on average. In order to capture the interviews entirely, they were all recorded and transcribed afterwards.

5 FINDINGS

In general, all interview partners confirmed the main result statements from the trend study described in Section 3 for SAP Enterprise Applications. Although, the trend study has been conducted in the year 2010, which reflects a big time period for IT evolution with technical changes of SAP components of the ERP environment, the raised statements are still valid today. *"Until now, performance has always played a tangential role. However, it is set to be more focused in the future[3]"*. Regarding the statements of the conducted interviews, some aspects of the trend study have been described in more detail by the experts and combined with the current situation within the development divisions.

All interview participants agreed consistently that performance evaluation regarding SAP Enterprise Applications is still an important topic that should not be forgotten to be considered. However, some of them admitted that present development projects often do not consider performance evaluation at all. *"Performance or load tests are not performed at all (...). This is because from a strategical point of view, there is currently no demand from the management for it"*. According to the experts, today's software development projects focus primarily on functionality, clarified in the requirements engineering phase, or software usability due to time and budget constraints. *"First of all, the application has to run and the compliance has to fit. If there is some time left, we can look after the application performance"*. Nevertheless, almost all interview partners mentioned a trend towards higher integration of performance evaluations, especially for SAP Enterprise Applications, in the software development process for the future. The basis for that statement is the increasingly complex software and system landscape of the entire IT environment. *"In a certain part, the current trend is to put*

---

[1] German community of SAP users located in Walldorf; members are from all kind of business sectors
[2] A software engineering concept combining software development (Dev) and software operation (Ops).

[3] All interviews were conducted and transcribed in German language. For this paper statements have been translated by the author.

everything on high performing machines (...). Of course we can put a bad performing application on high performing hardware, but for a permanent solution this is very expensive (...) I am certainly convinced that machines are not able to solve problems of bad designed software applications".

Regarding the question who eventually should be responsible to fix performance problems, the opinions differ from expert to expert. Some interview partners issued the statement that performance consideration is mainly a task of an SAP Basis consultant [4]. Others however, think that SAP developers should be skilled in the topic of application performance. Concerning our proposition of an extra occupation for a specialist in performance engineering, all interview partners were clearly against it. Performance expertise should not be focused in a new job role, but rather be integrated within existing ones, e.g. software developers, administrators or project managers. *"If a software developer has no feeling and knowledge about performance criteria, he is not a real developer but rather a programmer".* Nevertheless, it is preferable to create a new taskforce which consists of software developers and system administrators. Both groups should complement each other. *"If a software developer does not succeed by himself, it is a good idea to get together with people from SAP Basis"* and exchange knowledge in order to manage the issue together. This central idea follows the aspect of bridging the gap between the organizational units of the development and operations division.

Regarding the importance of performance for SAP Enterprise Applications, the experts had the opinion that this non-functional requirement reflects a critical success factor for each single software application. In combination with direct visibility for customers, e.g. through a web application using a SAP Enterprise Portal in the background, or a SAP Enterprise Application which is used by employees of the IT support division communicating with customers, the sense of importance for performance evaluation is much higher. *"Colleagues from the support division often need information in a certain time window. (...) If a customer is on the phone, we need quick access in order to provide further information. There is no time for delays".*

By directing the focus towards performance measurement of SAP Applications in today's companies, we had to determine that performance is principally measured against a subjective feeling. *"There are no SLAs, KPIs or other objective values, which we use for evaluating our SAP Applications at the moment"* was the answer of one of our interview partners. Application users who get in touch with a new software are either happy because of the given functionality which reduces time effort of a certain task, or they complain about missing functionalities and long response times of the new application. Depending on the user's subjective acceptance, performance anomalies are either discovered or not.

Regarding the initial discovery moment of bad performing SAP Enterprise Applications, all interview partners agreed that the identification of performance problems happens too late in today's software development life cycle. *"Performance consideration during the development phase of a software product has played a tangential role in the past (...). Performance anomalies are only discovered because they occurred during functional testing." "It is possible that some*

---

[4]Special job position term for a system administrator in the context of SAP

software developers look after performance of their own programs just for fun. But in general, they do not. So it is postponed to a later point in time". Another *"big problem is that programmers are often provided from external consulting companies (...) and performance tests are performed after a certain milestone of the software project has been reached. This leads to the circumstance that the programmer of the software code is not available anymore when the problem arises".*

When we asked our experts about current barriers leading to a late consideration of performance in the life cycle of a software product, we noticed that one of the mentioned barriers was consistently the same. Almost all experts pointed out the fact that nowadays software developers have a non-existing knowledge of software performance. *"There are software developers en masse who have not been confronted with performance issues of software applications before".*

Table 2 lists further results of identified barriers from our conducted interviews ranked by number of occurrences. Each barrier will be discussed in more detail in Section 6 and enhanced by possible solutions when given by the experts.

6 DISCUSSION

In this section we want to discuss the identified barriers and possible solutions to encounter them in an appropriate way. First of all, we want to present the current situation of performance consideration and performance evaluation for SAP Enterprise Applications in a nutshell. Based on the results from the conducted expert interviews, we describe the problems and barriers in detail. The individual points that have been covered will be enriched by further comments of the experts and the ideas of how they could be resolved. Finally, we want to present a promising approach called Performance Awareness [16] with an ongoing research roadmap.

Our findings of the conducted interviews show a current lack of performance consideration of SAP Enterprise Applications. If performance evaluation is considered at all, it is often just a subjective feeling by asking end-users about their overall satisfaction with the application. This does not reflect the sense of a real performance evaluation against certain KPIs or SLAs. As a good example, those objectives should be provided with a given technical specification created in the requirements engineering part of a software life cycle process.

6.1 Problems and Barriers

The most specified barrier against performance improvements of SAP Enterprise Applications is that *"SAP software developers do not have sufficient knowledge about software performance or performance tuning".* *"We have currently a lack of performance qualification for software developers. Every software developer follows an individual programming style based and extended on personal experience, technical opportunities, trainings, trial-and-error proceedings, and much more".* However, they are not taught *"in methods to look after software performance, e.g. how do I have to construct a performance optimized program operation or SQL statement".* *"Available training sessions, performance seminars, or other qualification courses are very rare".* At this point, we could offer more opportunities in order to sensitize software developers by paying more attention to performance aspects of software applications.

Table 2: Performance Improvement Barriers for SAP Enterprise Applications

Rank	Barrier	Expert Mentions
1	Missing knowledge about software performance	A, B, C, D, E
2	Different characteristics of SAP development, evaluation and production system	A, D, E, F
3	Bad communication between IT Operations, Development and Specialist Department	C, D, E, F
4	Missing dedicated experts for software performance	C, D, E
5	Missing information about existing SAP tools to analyze software performance	A, B, C
6	Unavailable production workload on SAP development and evaluation system	C, E
7	Handling of existing performance tools complex and complicated	D

Another problem considering performance issues, as early as possible in the software development life cycle, is that applications are initially developed on another system with different characteristics than the production one. SAP propagates as best practice to establish a system landscape divided in at least three parts, providing a development, quality assurance and production system. In an optimal way, the development system represents a sandbox environment where all necessary SAP components but no data according to the target system are installed. *"It makes a huge difference conducting performance and load tests on real data sets or generated example data, which does not reflect the real world scenario afterwards"*. Therefore, it is crucial to generate or consider real data sets by not affecting the production system by itself.

The next aspect claims a bad communication between colleagues from IT Operations, Software Development and Specialist Departments, e.g. Sales, Logistics or Human Resource Management. *"Many users from the Specialist Departments adjusted to the fact that certain SAP Applications perform badly"*. So to speak, they get used to this situation step by step and *"do not report upcoming performance problems immediately when they notice them"*. Consequently, the actual *"problem stays undiscovered until the application gets used on a massive scale"*. A reasonable solution to encounter the existing communication gap is to integrate people from Specialist Departments deeper into software development projects. Hence, feedback from an end-user's perspective reaches effectively the responsible person from the software development department.

In contrast to the first aspect where software developers should be trained with topics of performance issues, e.g. being aware of memory consumptions of certain operations or iterating over a ton of data which is not necessary to end up with the needed result, there is also the idea of a *"dedicated IT expert regarding performance engineering of software applications"*. Today's *"software developers are not feasible to meet all demands with the same quality"* because of the increasing complexity of current and future software projects. This does not mean that software developers should not be aware of performance at all. In fact, they should *"have knowledge and insights of developing well performing applications"*, but at the same time be open-minded to work together with people from IT Operations or in this case with performance engineering experts.

Despite, SAP already offers existing tools to gather information about different performance and software metrics. However, the information about existing tools is not available to all SAP developers. *"There are for example SAP tools to analyze the execution plan of an SQL statement regarding its JOIN conditions (...). Using this tool, you will get information about created indices and the fact whether they are used in your certain statement or not. If not, you may continue your investigation about the root cause"*.

Even though the development system reflects the same characteristics as the production one, the production workload is still missing. The workload on the production system is essential since it affects resource allocation and response time of other applications executed at the same time. *"In addition, big companies perform a lot of batch processes. This means automatically that at a certain time during the day the number of SAP dialog work processes are reduced and SAP batch processes are added instead (...), vice versa for the daylight time"*. This behavior has to be taken into account if we are interested in reliable performance evaluation results.

As the last point, one of the interview partner referred to the fact that even when people, in particular software developers, are aware of some existing SAP performance tools, they often do not use them because of a complicated handling. The mixture of not being a performance expert on the one hand and the existing time pressure to finish the software project by a given deadline on the other hand, directs the decision of each single software developer *"to fulfill all function requirements first"*. Moreover, *"the compliance of the software application has to fit"*. Only thereafter, and with respect to the remaining time for the application development part, software developers look after the application performance.

6.2 Performance Awareness

One response to the lack of performance consideration of software applications is the concept of Performance Awareness [16]. Tůma presented the term at the ICPE 2014 as one of the keynote speakers. Performance Awareness defines the ability to observe performance, detect problems and react to them. A major part of this concept concentrates on the support of software developers providing insights on performance of application source code that is currently developed.

A number of approaches already encounter the issue of supporting software developers to increase Performance Awareness during development. The existing approaches may be classified in either measurement-based or model-driven performance engineering ones.

For the first category, Bureš et al. [5] propose an approach to formulate performance goals during the design phase, even before the software application is started to be implemented. Afterwards, their approach collects performance measurements during application runtime and presents the information to the developers. Weiss et al. [17] aim at a similar approach, where lightweight and tailored benchmarks are automatically performed in order to track the impact of source code changes. Since software is often modularized, the approach of Horký et al. [9] takes advantage of this paradigm and proposes to enhance software libraries by adding performance information to them.

The work of Danciu et al. [7] forces a model-driven approach instead. Here, a performance model is automatically derived from source code and enhanced with annotations from the developers. Based on a performance model, the approach is able to provide response time estimations for Java EE applications.

Regarding SAP Enterprise Applications, it is conceivable to develop a model-driven performance engineering approach following the example of Danciu et al. [7]. The model-driven approach is the most promising one considering both already existing performance values from a deployed SAP system and different hardware specifications of other systems of the entire landscape at the same time, e.g. of a quality assurance system. Following this strategy, it is possible to estimate response times from performance simulations paying attention to the SAP system environment where the developed SAP Enterprise Application is intended to be finally deployed.

7 CONCLUSION

Software performance improvement is relevant in order to address long-running and bad performing applications. According to a study of Compuware and PAC [6], 43% of the interviewed companies quoted being dissatisfied with the performance of their SAP systems. Moreover, it is well known that in modern development processes performance tests are conducted in late development phases after the main functionality is implemented. This phenomenon has not changed over the years, although we are aware of increasingly high costs for optimizations of late software changes.

This paper outlines barriers for performance improvement in early stages of the software development life cycle of SAP Enterprise Applications. With open-structured expert interviews we identified seven barriers that hinder performance improvement during the development phase of a software product. The key findings show that most barriers are based on missing performance skills of software developers, different technical characteristics of development and production system, and bad communication between different departments of a company.

While applying the concept of Performance Awareness [16], software developers get insights on the performance of applications they are currently developing. Following this strategy and encouraging both software developers and IT administrators to work tighter with people from the Specialist Departments together can help create more efficient SAP Enterprise Applications on lower costs. The work of integrating Performance Awareness into the SAP Development Environment is a promising task and needs to be considered for future research.

REFERENCES

[1] Martin Bayer. 2016. Kampf der ERP-Titanen. (Feb. 2016). Retrieved October 17th, 2017 from https://www.computerwoche.de/a/kampf-der-erp-titanen,3223108
[2] Alexander Bogner, Beate Littig, and Wolfgang Menz. 2009. *Interviewing Experts.* Palgrave Macmillan, London, UK.
[3] Andreas Brunnert, André van Hoorn, Felix Willnecker, Alexandru Danciu, Wilhelm Hasselbring, Christoph Heger, Nikolas Roman Herbst, Pooyan Jamshidi, Reiner Jung, Jóakim von Kistowski, Anne Koziolek, Johannes Kroß, Simon Spinner, Christian Vögele, Jürgen Walter, and Alexander Wert. 2015. *Performance-oriented DevOps: A Research Agenda.* Technical Report. http://arxiv.org/abs/1508.04752
[4] Andreas Brunnert, Christian Vögele, Alexandru Danciu, Matthias Pfaff, Manuel Mayer, and Helmut Krcmar. 2014. Performance Management Work. *Business & Information Systems Engineering* 6, 3 (Jun 2014), 177–179. https://doi.org/10.1007/s12599-014-0323-7
[5] Tomáš Bureš, Vojtěch Horký, Michał Kit, Lukáš Marek, and Petr Tůma. 2014. *Towards Performance-Aware Engineering of Autonomic Component Ensembles.* Springer Berlin Heidelberg, Berlin, Heidelberg, 131–146. https://doi.org/10.1007/978-3-662-45234-9_10
[6] Compuware Corporation and Pierre Audoin Consultants. 2010. *SAP Performance Management - A Trend Study by Compuware and PAC.* Technical Report.
[7] Alexandru Danciu, Alexander Chrusciel, Andreas Brunnert, and Helmut Krcmar. 2015. *Performance Awareness in Java EE Development Environments.* Lecture Notes in Computer Science, Vol. 9272. Springer International Publishing, Chapter 10, 146–160. https://doi.org/10.1007/978-3-319-23267-6_10
[8] Jochen Gläser and Grit Laudel. 2010. *Experteninterviews und qualitative Inhaltsanalyse.* Springer-Verlag, Wiesbaden, Germany.
[9] Vojtěch Horký, Peter Libič, Lukáš Marek, Antonin Steinhauser, and Petr Tůma. 2015. Utilizing Performance Unit Tests To Increase Performance Awareness. In *Proceedings of the 6th ACM/SPEC International Conference on Performance Engineering (ICPE '15).* ACM, New York, NY, USA, 289–300. https://doi.org/10.1145/2668930.2688051
[10] Heiko Koziolek. 2010. Performance evaluation of component-based software systems: A survey. *Performance Evaluation* 67, 8 (2010), 634–658. https://doi.org/10.1016/j.peva.2009.07.007
[11] Karl-Heinz Kühnhauser and Thorsten Franz. 2015. *Einstieg in ABAP* (4., aktualisierte und erw. aufl. ed.). Rheinwerk, Bonn, Germany. 575 pages.
[12] Kevin P. McCormack and William C. Johnson. 2001. *Business Process Orientation: Gaining the E-Business Competitive Advantage.* CRC Press.
[13] Daniel A. Menascé. 2002. Load Testing, Benchmarking, and Application Performance Management for the Web. In *Int. CMG Conference.* 271–282.
[14] V. Y. Shen, Yu Tze-jie, S. M. Thebaut, and L. R. Paulsen. 1985. Identifying Error-Prone Software: An Empirical Study. *IEEE Transactions on Software Engineering* SE-11, 4 (April 1985), 317–324. https://doi.org/10.1109/TSE.1985.232222
[15] Panorama Consulting Solutions. 2017. *2017 Top 10 ERP Systems Rankings Report.* Technical Report.
[16] Petr Tůma. 2014. Performance Awareness: Keynote Abstract. In *Proceedings of the 5th ACM/SPEC International Conference on Performance Engineering (ICPE '14).* ACM, New York, NY, USA, 135–136. https://doi.org/10.1145/2568088.2576097
[17] Christian Weiss, Dennis Westermann, Christoph Heger, and Martin Moser. 2013. Systematic Performance Evaluation Based on Tailored Benchmark Applications. In *Proceedings of the 4th ACM/SPEC International Conference on Performance Engineering (ICPE '13).* ACM, New York, NY, USA, 411–420. https://doi.org/10.1145/2479871.2479934
[18] M. Woodside, G. Franks, and D. C. Petriu. 2007. The Future of Software Performance Engineering. In *Future of Software Engineering, 2007. FOSE '07.* 171–187. https://doi.org/10.1109/FOSE.2007.32

Joint Data Compression and Caching: Approaching Optimality with Guarantees

Jian Li
College of Information and
Computer Sciences
University of Massachusetts
Amherst, MA 01003, USA
jianli@cs.umass.edu

Faheem Zafari[*]
Department of Electrical and
Electronic Engineering,
Imperial College London,
London SW72AZ, U.K.
faheem16@imperial.ac.uk

Don Towsley
College of Information and
Computer Sciences
University of Massachusetts
Amherst, MA 01003, USA
towsley@cs.umass.edu

Kin K. Leung
Department of Electrical and
Electronic Engineering,
Imperial College London,
London SW72AZ, U.K.
kin.leung@imperial.ac.uk

Ananthram Swami
U.S. Army Research Laboratory
Adelphi, MD 20783 USA
ananthram.swami.civ@mail.mil

ABSTRACT

We consider the problem of optimally compressing and caching data across a communication network. Given the data generated at edge nodes and a routing path, our goal is to determine the optimal data compression ratios and caching decisions across the network in order to minimize average latency, which can be shown to be equivalent to maximizing *the compression and caching gain* under an energy consumption constraint. We show that this problem is NP-hard in general and the hardness is caused by the caching decision subproblem, while the compression sub-problem is polynomial-time solvable. We then propose an approximation algorithm that achieves a $(1 - 1/e)$-approximation solution to the optimum in strongly polynomial time. We show that our proposed algorithm achieve the near-optimal performance in synthetic-based evaluations. In this paper, we consider a tree-structured network as an illustrative example, but our results easily extend to general network topology at the expense of more complicated notations.

ACM Reference Format:
Jian Li, Faheem Zafari, Don Towsley, Kin K. Leung, and Ananthram Swami. 2018. Joint Data Compression and Caching: Approaching Optimality with Guarantees. In *ICPE '18: ACM/SPEC International Conference on Performance Engineering, April 9–13, 2018, Berlin, Germany.* ACM, New York, NY, USA, 12 pages. https://doi.org/10.1145/3184407.3184410

1 INTRODUCTION

In recent years, with the ever increasing prevalence of edge computing enabled mobile devices and applications, such as social media, weather reports, emails notifications, etc., the demand for data communication has significantly increased. As bandwidth and the

[*]Co-primary authors with equal contribution

ICPE '18, April 9–13, 2018, Berlin, Germany
© 2018 Association for Computing Machinery.
ACM ISBN 978-1-4503-5095-2/18/04...$15.00
https://doi.org/10.1145/3184407.3184410

power supply associated with mobile devices are limited, efficient data communication is critical.

In this paper, we consider a network of nodes, each capable of compressing data and caching a constant amount of data. A set of nodes generates real time data and a sink node collects the data from these nodes through fixed paths to serve requests for these data. However, the requests need not reach nodes that generated the data, i.e. request forwarding stops upon reaching a node on the path that has cached the requested data. Upon finding the data, it is sent along the reverse path to the sink node to serve the requests.

While each node can cache data to serve future requests so as to reduce access latency and bandwidth requirement, it incurs additional caching costs [9]. Furthermore, data compression reduces the transmission cost at the expense of computation cost [4, 26]. Thus, there is an energy consumption tradeoff among data compression, transmission, and caching to reduce latency. Since bandwidth and energy required for network operation is expensive [26], it is critical to efficiently compress, transmit and cache the data to reduce latency. This raises the following question, what is the right balance between compression and caching to minimize total communication latency for limited energy consumption?

Our primary goal is to minimize average network latency (delay) due to data transfer across the network, subject to an energy consumption constraint on compression and caching of the data. This problem is naturally abstracted and motivated by many real world applications, including wireless sensor networks (WSNs) [9], peer-to-peer networks [10], content distribution networks (CDNs) [6, 13, 23], Information Centric Networks (ICNs) [18] and so on. For example, in a hierarchical WSN, the sensors generate data, which can be compressed and forwarded to the sink node through fixed paths to serve requests generated from outside the network. These requests can be served from the intermediate nodes along the path that cache the data; if, however, data are not cached on any node along the path, the request can subsequently be forwarded to the edge sensor that generates the requested data. Similarly, in an ICN, requests for data can be served locally from intermediate caches placed between the server and origin. Both applications can be mapped into the problem we consider here.

For these and many other applications, it is natural to assume that edge nodes in the network generate data which is then compressed and transmitted by all the nodes along the path to the sink node. The sink node receives and serves requests generated outside the communication network. The intermediate nodes along the path can cache data to serve requests. However, compression, transmission, and caching consume energy, while the node power supply is usually limited. To address this challenge, our main goal is to design a lightweight and efficient algorithm with provable performance guarantees that minimizes average latency. We make the following contributions:

- We propose a formal mathematical framework for joint data compression and cache optimization. Specifically, we formulate the problem of finding optimal data compression ratios and caching locations that minimize average delay in serving requests subject to an energy constraint.
- We analyze the complexity of the problem and show that it is NP-hard in general. The hardness is caused by data allocation to the caches.
- We propose polynomial time solvable algorithms for the formulated problem. Because the original optimization problem is NP-hard and non-convex, we relax the constraints and show that the relaxed problem can be transformed into an equivalent convex optimization problem that can be solved in polynomial time. We then show that combining this solution with greedy caching allocation achieves a solution with 1/2-approximation to the optimum. Moreover, we construct a polynomial-time $(1 - 1/e)$ approximation algorithm for the problem.
- We conduct extensive simulations using synthetic network topologies and compare our proposed algorithm with benchmark techniques. Our results show that the proposed algorithm achieves near-optimal performance, and significantly outperforms benchmarks Genetic Algorithm [12], Bonmin [5], and NOMAD [21] by obtaining a feasible solution in less time for various network topologies.

The rest of the paper is organized as follows: We discuss related work in Section 2 and present our mathematical formulation in Section 3. Our main results are presented in Section 4. Numerical evaluation of our algorithms against benchmarks is given in Section 5 and finally we conclude the paper in Section 6.

2 RELATED WORK

Optimizing energy consumption has been widely studied in the literature with a primary focus on clustering [33], routing [25] and MAC protocols [15]. With the proliferation of smart sensors [26], in-network data processing, such as data aggregation, has been widely used as a way to reduce system energy cost by lowering data volume for transmission. Yu et al. [35] proposed an efficient algorithm for data compression in a tree structured networks. Nazemi et al. [26] further presented a distributed algorithm to obtain the optimal compression ratio at each node in a tree structured network so as to minimize the overall energy consumption.

However, none of these works considered caching costs. As caches have been widely deployed in many modern data communication networks, they can be used to enhance system performance by making data available close to end users, which in turn reduces the communication costs [9] and latencies.

A number of authors have studied optimization problems for cache allocation [2, 3, 6, 16, 23, 27–29, 31]. Ioannidis, Li and Shanmugam et. al [16, 22, 31] showed that it is NP-hard to determine the optimal data caching location, and an $(1 - 1/e)$ approximation algorithm was obtained through the pipage rounding algorithm [1, 8]. Beyond cache placement, [13] and [17] have jointly optimized routing and caching under a single hop bipartite graph and general graph, respectively. However, none of the existing work considered data compression and the corresponding costs for caching and compression.

The recent paper by Zafari et al. [36] is closest to the problem we tackle here. The differences between our work and [36] are mainly from two perspectives. First, the mathematical formulations (objectives) are quite different. Zafari et al. [36] considered energy tradeoffs among communication, compression, and caching in communication network, while we focus on maximizing the overall compression and caching gain by characterizing the tradeoff between compression and caching costs with an overall energy consumption constraint. This difference requires different techniques to handle the problem. Second, the methodologies are different. [36] aimed to provide a solution to the non-convex mixed integer programming problem (MINLP) with an ϵ-global[1] optimality guarantee. Since MINLP is NP-hard in general, the proposed algorithm V-SBB in [36] is complex and slow to converge to an ϵ-global optimal solution. Furthermore, it is difficult to generalize V-SBB to larger network topologies as the algorithm relies on symbolically reformulating the original non-convex MINLP problem that results in extra constraints and variables. Instead, in this paper, we focus on developing an approximation algorithm to optimize the gain defined above. In doing so, we first allow the caching decision variables to be continuous, approximate the objective function and then convert the problem into a convex one. Finally, we propose a master-slave based algorithm to efficiently solve the approximated relaxed problem, and show that the rounded solutions are feasible to the original problem with performance guarantee, and our algorithm is more efficient than that in [36] and can be applied to a larger problem size.

Note that we focus on minimizing the latency and ignore throughput issues, since we do not model congestion. Combing these two issues together and proposing efficient approximation algorithms is an interesting problem, which is out of the scope of this paper.

3 MODEL

We represent the network as a directed graph $G = (V, E)$. For simplicity, we consider a tree, with $N = |V|$ nodes, as shown in Figure 1. Node $v \in V$ is capable of storing S_v amount of data. Let $\mathcal{K} \subseteq V$ with $K = |\mathcal{K}|$ be the set of leaf nodes, i.e., $\mathcal{K} = \{1, 2, \cdots, K\}$. Time is partitioned into periods of equal length $T > 0$ and data generated

---

[1] ϵ-global optimality means that the obtained solution is within ϵ tolerance of the global optimal solution i.e., achieved cost/optimal cost $\leq 1 + \epsilon$. The value of ϵ depends on the requirement of different problems. Usually it is very small such as 0.0001.

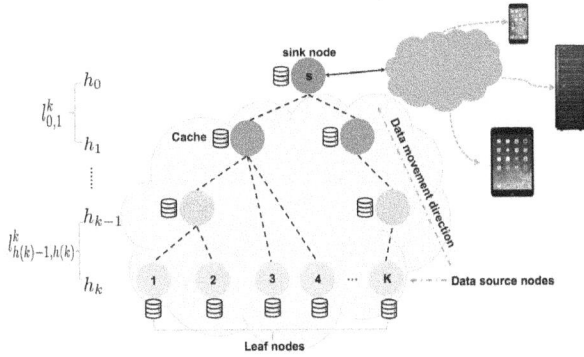

Figure 1: Tree-Structured Network Model.

Table 1: Summary of Notations

Notation	Description
$G(V, E)$	Network graph with $|V| = N$ nodes
$\mathcal{K}$	Set of leaf nodes with $|\mathcal{K}| = K$
S_v	Cache capacity at node $v \in V$
h_i^k	The i-th node on the path between leaf node k and sink node
$\delta_{k,i}$	Compression ratio for data generated by leaf node k at i^{th} node on path from $k \in \mathcal{K}$ to sink
l_{ij}	Latency of edge $(i, j) \in E$
ε_{vR}	per-bit reception cost of node $v \in V$
ε_{vT}	per-bit transmission cost of node $v \in V$
ε_{vC}	per-bit compression cost of node $v \in V$
y_k	Number of data (bits) generated at node $k \in \mathcal{K}$
$b_{k,i}$	Variable indicating whether i^{th} node on path from k to sink caches the data from leaf node $k \in \mathcal{K}$
w_{ca}	Caching power efficiency
R_k	Request rate for data from node $k \in \mathcal{K}$
W	Global Energy constraint
T	Time duration for which data are cached
δ_v	Reduction rate at node v
C_v	Set of leaf nodes that are children of node v
s.t.	Subject to

in each period are independent. Without loss of generality (w.l.o.g.), we consider one particular period in the remainder of the paper. We assume that only leaf nodes $k \in \mathcal{K}$ can generate data, and all other nodes in the tree receive and compress data from their children nodes, and transmit and/or cache the compressed data to their parent nodes during time T. In Section 3.5, we discuss how these assumptions can be relaxed. For ease of exposition, the parameters used throughout this paper are summarized in Table 1.

Our objective is to determine the optimal data compression ratio and caching locations across the network to minimize average latency under an energy constraint.

3.1 Compression and Caching Costs

Let y_k be the amount of data generated by leaf node $k \in \mathcal{K}$. Data generated at the leaf nodes are transmitted up the tree to the sink node s, which serves requests for the data generated in the network. Let $h(k)$ be the depth of node k in the tree. W.l.o.g., we assume that

the sink node is located at level $h(s) = 0$. We represent the unique path from node k to the sink node by $\mathcal{H}^k$ of length $h(k)$, a sequence $\{h_0^k, h_1^k, \cdots, h_{h(k)}^k\}$ of nodes $h_j^k \in V$ such that $(h_j^k, h_{j+1}^k) \in E$, where $h_0^k \triangleq s$ (i.e., the sink node) and $h_{h(k)}^k \triangleq k$ (i.e., the node itself).

We denote the per-bit reception, transmission, and compression costs of node $v \in V$ as $\varepsilon_{vR}, \varepsilon_{vT}$, and ε_{vC}, respectively. Each node h_i^k along the path $\mathcal{H}^k$ compresses the data generated by leaf node k at a *data reduction rate[2]* $\delta_{k,i}$, where $0 < \delta_{k,i} \leq 1$, $\forall i, k$. The higher the value of $\delta_{k,i}$, the lower the compression will be, and vice versa. The higher the degree of data compression, the larger will be the amount of energy consumed by compression (computation). Similarly, caching data closer to the sink node can reduce the transmission cost for serving the request, however, each node only has a finite storage capacity. We study the tradeoff among the energy consumed at each node for transmitting, compressing and caching data to minimize the average delay (which will be defined in (4)) in serving a request.

We consider an energy-proportional model [9] for caching, i.e., $w_{ca}\delta_v y_v T$ units of energy is consumed if the received data y_v is cached for a duration of T where w_{ca} represents the power efficiency of caching, which strongly depends on the storage hardware technology. w_{ca} is assumed to be identical for all the nodes.

Data produced by every leaf node k is received, transmitted, and possibly compressed by all nodes in the path from the leaf node k to the root node. On the first request, the energy consumed for this processing of the data from leaf node k is

$$E_k^C = \sum_{i=0}^{h(k)} y_k f(\delta_{k,i}) \prod_{m=i+1}^{h(k)} \delta_{k,m}, \tag{1}$$

where $\prod_{m=i}^{j} \delta_{k,m} := 1$ if $i \geq j$ and $f(\delta_v) = \varepsilon_{vR} + \varepsilon_{vT}\delta_v + \varepsilon_{vC}l_v(\delta_v)$ is the sum of per-bit reception, transmission and compression cost at node v per unit time. We take $l_v(\delta_v) = 1/\delta_v - 1$ which was used in [26, 36] to capture compression costs.

Let E_k^R be the total energy consumed in responding to the subsequent $(R_k - 1)$ requests for the data originally generated by leaf node k. We have

$$E_k^R = \sum_{i=0}^{h(k)} y_k (R_k - 1) \left\{ f(\delta_{k,i}) \prod_{m=i+1}^{h(k)} \delta_{k,m} \left(1 - \sum_{j=0}^{i-1} b_{k,j} \right) \right.$$
$$\left. + \left(\prod_{m=i}^{h(k)} \delta_{k,m} \right) b_{k,i} \left(\frac{w_{ca}T}{R_k - 1} + \varepsilon_k T \right) \right\}, \tag{2}$$

where $b_{k,j} = 1$ if node j caches data generated by k, otherwise $b_{k,j} = 0$. The first term captures the energy cost for reception, transmission, and compression up the tree from node $v_{k,i-1}$ to $v_{k,0}$ and the second term captures the energy cost for storage and transmission by node $v_{k,i}$. A detailed explanation of (1) and (2) with a toy example is provided in [24].

To consider data generated by all leaf nodes, the total energy consumed in the network is

$$E^{total}(\boldsymbol{\delta}, \boldsymbol{b}) \triangleq \sum_{k \in \mathcal{K}} \left(E_k^C + E_k^R \right)$$

---

[2]defined as the ratio of the volume of the output data to the volume of input data at any node

$$
\begin{aligned}
&= \sum_{k \in \mathcal{K}} \sum_{i=0}^{h(k)} y_k R_k f(\delta_{k,i}) \prod_{m=i+1}^{h(k)} \delta_{k,m} - \sum_{k \in \mathcal{K}} \sum_{i=0}^{h(k)} y_k (R_k - 1) \\
&\quad \cdot f(\delta_{k,i}) \prod_{m=i+1}^{h(k)} \delta_{k,m} \sum_{j=0}^{i-1} b_{k,j} + \sum_{k \in \mathcal{K}} \sum_{i=0}^{h(k)} y_k (R_k - 1) \\
&\quad \cdot \left(\prod_{m=i}^{h(k)} \delta_{k,m} \right) b_{k,i} \left(\frac{w_{ca} T}{R_k - 1} + \varepsilon_{kT} \right) \\
&= \sum_{k \in \mathcal{K}} \sum_{i=0}^{h(k)} y_k \Bigg\{ R_k f(\delta_{k,i}) \prod_{m=i+1}^{h(k)} \delta_{k,m} + \left(\prod_{m=i}^{h(k)} \delta_{k,m} \right) b_{k,i} (w_{ca} T + \\
&\quad (R_k - 1)\varepsilon_{kT}) \Bigg\} - \sum_{k \in \mathcal{K}} \sum_{i=0}^{h(k)} y_k (R_k - 1) f(\delta_{k,i}) \prod_{m=i+1}^{h(k)} \delta_{k,m} \sum_{j=0}^{i-1} b_{k,j} \\
&\leq \sum_{k \in \mathcal{K}} \sum_{i=0}^{h(k)} y_k \Bigg\{ R_k f(\delta_{k,i}) \prod_{m=i+1}^{h(k)} \delta_{k,m} + \left(\prod_{m=i}^{h(k)} \delta_{k,m} \right) b_{k,i} (w_{ca} T + \\
&\quad (R_k - 1)\varepsilon_{kT}) \Bigg\} \triangleq \tilde{E}^{\text{total}}(\boldsymbol{\delta}, \boldsymbol{b}),
\end{aligned} \tag{3}
$$

where $\boldsymbol{\delta} = \{\delta_{k,i}, \forall k \in \mathcal{K}, i = 0, \cdots, h(k)\}$ and $\boldsymbol{b} = \{b_{k,i}, \forall k \in \mathcal{K}, i = 0, \cdots, h(k)\}$.

Note that $\tilde{E}^{\text{total}}(\boldsymbol{\delta}, \boldsymbol{b})$ is an upper bound of $E^{\text{total}}(\boldsymbol{\delta}, \boldsymbol{b})$, which is tight when there is no caching in the network. In the following optimization, we use $\tilde{E}^{\text{total}}(\boldsymbol{\delta}, \boldsymbol{b})$ for energy constraint.

3.2 Latency Performance

W.l.o.g., we consider the path $\{h_0^k, h_1^k, \cdots, h_{h(k)}^k\}$. A request for data generated by leaf node k is forwarded along this path from the root node s until it reaches the node that has cached the requested data. Upon finding the requested data, it is propagated along the reverse direction of the path, i.e., carrying the requested data to the sink node where the request originated. To capture the average latency due to data transfer at any particular link, we associate each link with a cost $l_{i,j}$ for $(i, j) \in E$, representing the latency of transmitting the data across the link (i, j). Denote the latency associated with path $\{h_0^k, h_1^k, \cdots, h_{h(k)}^k\}$ as $\{l_{0,1}^k, l_{1,2}^k, \cdots, l_{h(k)-1, h(k)}^k\}$.

Then the overall latency for all the paths is

$$
L(\boldsymbol{\delta}, \boldsymbol{b}) = \sum_{k \in \mathcal{K}} \sum_{i=0}^{h(k)-1} \prod_{m=i+1}^{h(k)} \delta_{k,m} y_k R_k l_{i,i+1}^k \prod_{j=0}^{i} (1 - b_{k,j}). \tag{4}
$$

3.3 Optimization

Our objective is to determine the optimal compression ratio $\boldsymbol{\delta} = \{\delta_{k,i}, \forall k \in \mathcal{K}, i = 0, \cdots, h(k)\}$ and data caching location $\boldsymbol{b} = \{b_{k,i}, \forall k \in \mathcal{K}, i = 0, \cdots, h(k)\}$ to minimize the expected total latency subject to the energy constraint. That is,

$$
\min \quad L(\boldsymbol{\delta}, \boldsymbol{b}) \tag{5a}
$$

$$
\text{s.t.} \quad \sum_{k \in \mathcal{K}} \sum_{i=0}^{h(k)} y_k \Bigg\{ R_k f(\delta_{k,i}) \prod_{m=i+1}^{h(k)} \delta_{k,m} + \left(\prod_{m=i}^{h(k)} \delta_{k,m} \right) b_{k,i}
$$

$$
\cdot (w_{ca} T + (R_k - 1)\varepsilon_{kT}) \Bigg\} \leq W, \tag{5b}
$$

$$
b_{k,i} \in \{0, 1\}, \forall k \in \mathcal{K}, i = 0, \cdots, h(k), \tag{5c}
$$

$$
\sum_{k \in C_v} b_{k,h(v)} y_k \prod_{j=h(k)}^{h(v)} \delta_{k,j} \leq S_v, \forall \, v \in V, \tag{5d}
$$

$$
\sum_{i=0}^{h(k)} b_{k,i} \leq 1, \forall k \in \mathcal{K}. \tag{5e}
$$

Now suppose that there is no compression or caching, then all the requests need to be served from leaf nodes. The corresponding total latency L^u is given as

$$
L^u = \sum_{k \in \mathcal{K}} \sum_{i=0}^{h(k)-1} y_k l_{i,i+1}^k R_k. \tag{6}
$$

Clearly, L^u is an upper bound on the expected total latency.

Then the *compression and caching gain* is

$$
\begin{aligned}
G(\boldsymbol{\delta}, \boldsymbol{b}) &= L^u - L(\boldsymbol{\delta}, \boldsymbol{b}) \\
&= \sum_{k \in \mathcal{K}} \sum_{i=0}^{h(k)-1} R_k y_k l_{i,i+1}^k \left(1 - \prod_{m=i+1}^{h(k)} \delta_{k,m} \prod_{j=0}^{i} (1 - b_{k,j}) \right).
\end{aligned} \tag{7}
$$

An equivalent *optimization problem* to (5) is to maximize the above gain, given as follows

$$
\begin{aligned}
\max \quad & G(\boldsymbol{\delta}, \boldsymbol{b}) \\
\text{s.t.} \quad & \text{Constraints in (5).}
\end{aligned} \tag{8}
$$

The objective in (8) is to maximize the expected compression and caching gain. Constraint (5b) ensures that the total energy consumption in the network as given in (3) is limited. Constraint (5c) constrains our caching decision variables to be binary. Constraint (5d) ensures that each cache v stores no more than S_v amount of data. Constraint (5e) ensures that at most one copy of the generated data can be cached at any node along the path between the leaf and the sink node. Each node potentially compresses data from different leaf nodes differently; the coupling occurs due to the storage and energy constraints.

3.4 Complexity Analysis

There are two decision variables in (8), i.e., the compression ratio and the caching decision variables. In the following, we show the impact of these variables on the hardness of our problem, i.e., we consider two cases, (i) given the caching decisions variables $\boldsymbol{b}$; (ii) given the compression ratio $\boldsymbol{\delta}$.

3.4.1 Given Caching Decisions: For given caching decision variables $\boldsymbol{b}$, the optimization problem in (8) turns into a geometric programming problem over the compression ratio $\boldsymbol{\delta}$ that can be solved in polynomial time.

THEOREM 3.1. *Given fixed caching decisions $\boldsymbol{b}$, the optimization problem in (8) is polynomial-time solvable.*

PROOF. Once $\boldsymbol{b}$ is given, (8) becomes a geometric programming problem in $\boldsymbol{\delta}$; we will show in Section 4.2 that it can be transformed into a convex optimization problem, which can be solved in polynomial time. □

3.4.2 Given Compression Ratios: Given compression ratios δ, the optimization problem in (8) is only over the caching decision variables b. Hence, we obtain an integer programming problem, which is NP-hard.

THEOREM 3.2. *Given a fixed compression ratio δ, the optimization problem in (8) is NP-hard.*

PROOF. We prove the hardness by reduction from the classical job-shop problem which is NP-hard [19].

We can reduce the job-shop problem to our problem in (8) with fixed compression ratios δ as follows. Consider each node $v \in V$ in our model to be a machine M_i. Denote the set of machines as $\mathcal{M} = \{M_1, M_2 \cdots M_{|V|}\}$. The caching decision constitutes the set of jobs $\mathcal{J} = \{J_1, J_2\}$, where J_1 means that the data is cached and J_2 means otherwise. Let $\mathcal{X}$ be the set of all sequential job assignments to different machines so that every machine performs every job only once. The elements $x \in \mathcal{X}$ can be written as $2 \times |V|$ matrices, where column v order-wise lists the sequential jobs that the machine M_v will perform. There is a cost function C that captures the cost (i.e., latency) for any machine to perform a particular job. Our objective in the optimization problem (8) is to find assignments of job $x \in \mathcal{X}$ to minimize the latency or maximize the gain, which is equivalent to the classical job-shop problem. Since job-shop problem is NP-hard [19], our problem in (8) with given compression ratios δ is also NP-hard. □

Therefore, given the results in Theorems 3.1 and 3.2, we know that our optimization problem is NP-hard in general.

COROLLARY 3.3. *The optimization problem defined in (8) is NP-hard.*

3.5 Relaxation of Assumptions

We made several assumptions in the above for the sake of model simplicity. In the following, we discuss how these assumptions can be relaxed.

First, the network is assumed to be structured as a tree, however, we can easily relax this assumption by incorporating routing into our joint optimization problem. We take the tree structure as our motivating example since it is a simple and representative topology that captures the key parameters in the optimization formulation without introducing more complexity for a general network topology.

Second, while we only allow leaf nodes to generate data, our model can be extended to allow intermediate nodes to generate data at the cost of added complexity, i.e., the number of decision variables will be increased to represent the caching decision and compression ratio for the data produced at the intermediate nodes. Furthermore, rather than having a constant R_k requests for data generated at the leaf node k, we can generalize our approach to the case where R_k for various leaf nodes are drawn from a distribution such as the Zipf distribution [9].

Third, in our model, we assume that the requests for the data that are generated and valid for a time period T are known. But our solutions can be applied to an online setting with predicted user requests.

4 APPROXIMATION ALGORITHM

Since our optimization problem (8) is NP-hard, we focus on developing efficient approximation algorithms. In particular, we develop a polynomial-time solvable algorithm that produces compression ratios and cache decisions with a constant approximation of the minimum average latency. In the following, we first derive several properties that allow us to develop such an approximation algorithm. Then we discuss how to obtain a constant approximation solution in polynomial time.

4.1 Properties of the Problem Formulation

In this section, we show that (8) is a submodular maximization problem under matroid constraints. To begin, we first review the concepts of submodular functions and matroids.

Definition 4.1. (Submodular function [30]) If Ω is a finite set, a submodular function is a set function $f: 2^\Omega \to \mathbb{R}$, where 2^Ω denotes the power set of Ω, which satisfies one of the following equivalent conditions:

(1) For every $X, Y \subseteq \Omega$ with $X \subseteq Y$ and every $x \in \Omega \setminus Y$, we have $f(X \cup \{x\}) - f(X) \geq f(Y \cup \{x\}) - f(Y)$;
(2) For every $S, T \subseteq \Omega$, we have $f(S) + f(T) \geq f(S \cup T) + f(S \cap T)$;
(3) For every $X \subseteq \Omega$ and $x, y \in \Omega \setminus X$, we have $f(X \cup \{x\}) + f(X \cup \{y\}) \geq f(X \cup \{x, y\}) + f(X)$.

Definition 4.2. (Monotone sub-modular function [20]) A submodular function f is monotone if for every $T \subseteq S$, we have $f(T) \geq f(S)$.

Definition 4.3. (Matroid [32]) A finite matroid M is a pair $(E, \mathcal{I})$, where E is a finite set and $\mathcal{I}$ is a family of subsets of E (called the independent sets) with the following properties:

(1) The empty set is independent, i.e., $\emptyset \in \mathcal{I}$;
(2) Every subset of an independent set is independent, i.e., for each $A \subset B \subset E$, if $B \in \mathcal{I}$ then $A \in \mathcal{I}$;
(3) If A and B are two independent set of $\mathcal{I}$ and A has more elements than B, then there exists $x \in A \setminus B$ such that $B \cup \{x\}$ is in $\mathcal{I}$.

Given the above concepts, we easily obtain the following result

THEOREM 4.4. *The objective function in (8) is monotone and submodular, and the constraints in (8) are matroid.*

The proof is simply to verify that the objective function and constraints in (8) satisfy Definitions 4.1, 4.2 and 4.3. We skip the details due to space limitations.

COROLLARY 4.5. *Since (8) is a sub-modular maximization problem under matroid constraints, a solution with 1/2 approximation from the optimum can be constructed by a greedy algorithm[3].*

Now we are ready to develop a polynomial-time solvable approximation algorithm with improved approximation ratio when compared to the greedy algorithm. Since the optimization problem in (8) is a non-convex mixed integer non-linear programing problem (MINLP), we first relax the integer variables and transform it into a

---

[3]Start with caching all data at the leaf nodes, then compute the optimal compression ratio, and then iteratively add the data to caches by selecting feasible caching decisions at each step that leads to the largest increase in the compression and caching gain.

convex optimization problem, which can be solved in polynomial time. Then we round the achieved solutions to ones that satisfy the original integer constraints, if there are any fractional solutions.

4.2 Convex Relaxation

We first relax the integer variables $b_{k,i} \in \{0, 1\}$ to $\tilde{b}_{k,i} \in [0, 1]$ for $\forall k \in \mathcal{K}$ and $i = 0, \cdots, h(k)$, in (4), (5), (7) and (8). Let μ be the joint distribution over b, and let $\mathbb{P}_\mu(\cdot)$ and $\mathbb{E}_\mu(\cdot)$ be the corresponding probability and expectation with respect to μ, i.e.,

$$\tilde{b}_{k,i} = \mathbb{P}_\mu[b_{k,i} = 1] = \mathbb{E}_\mu[b_{k,i}]. \tag{9}$$

Then the relaxed expected latency and gain are given as

$$L(\boldsymbol{\delta}, \tilde{\boldsymbol{b}}) = \sum_{k \in \mathcal{K}} \sum_{i=0}^{h(k)-1} \prod_{m=i+1}^{h(k)} \delta_{k,m} y_k R_k l_{i,i+1}^k \prod_{j=0}^{i} (1 - \tilde{b}_{k,j}),$$

$$G(\boldsymbol{\delta}, \tilde{\boldsymbol{b}}) = L^u - L(\boldsymbol{\delta}, \tilde{\boldsymbol{b}})$$

$$= \sum_{k \in \mathcal{K}} \sum_{i=0}^{h(k)-1} R_k y_k l_{i,i+1}^k \left(1 - \prod_{m=i+1}^{h(k)} \delta_{k,m} \prod_{j=0}^{i} (1 - \tilde{b}_{k,j}) \right). \tag{10}$$

Therefore, the relaxed optimization problem is

$$\max \quad G(\boldsymbol{\delta}, \tilde{\boldsymbol{b}})$$

$$\text{s.t.} \quad \sum_{k \in \mathcal{K}} \sum_{i=0}^{h(k)} y_k \left\{ R_k f(\delta_{k,i}) \prod_{m=i+1}^{h(k)} \delta_{k,m} + \left(\prod_{m=i}^{h(k)} \delta_{k,m} \right) \tilde{b}_{k,i} \right.$$

$$\left. \cdot (w_{ca} T + (R_k - 1)\varepsilon_{kT}) \right\} \leq W,$$

$$\tilde{b}_{k,i} \in [0, 1], \forall k \in \mathcal{K}, i = 0, \cdots, h(k),$$

$$\sum_{k \in C_v} \tilde{b}_{k,h(v)} y_k \prod_{j=h(k)}^{h(v)} \delta_{k,j} \leq S_v, \forall\, v \in V,$$

$$\sum_{i=0}^{h(k)} \tilde{b}_{k,i} \leq 1, \forall k \in \mathcal{K}. \tag{11}$$

THEOREM 4.6. *Suppose that* $(\boldsymbol{\delta}^*, \boldsymbol{b}^*)$ *and* $(\tilde{\boldsymbol{\delta}}^*, \tilde{\boldsymbol{b}}^*)$ *are the optimal solutions to (8) and (11), respectively, then*

$$G(\tilde{\boldsymbol{\delta}}^*, \tilde{\boldsymbol{b}}^*) \geq G(\boldsymbol{\delta}^*, \boldsymbol{b}^*). \tag{12}$$

PROOF. The results hold since (11) maximizes the same objective function over a larger domain due to relaxation of integer variables b and energy constraint in (3). □

However, (11) is not a convex optimization problem. Since $e^x \approx 1 + x$ for $x \to 0$ and $\log(1 - x) \approx -x$ for $x \to 0$, we obtain an approximation for (10). The approximated expected total latency and *approximated compression and caching gain* are given as follows

$$L(\boldsymbol{\delta}, \tilde{\boldsymbol{b}}) = \sum_{k \in \mathcal{K}} \sum_{i=0}^{h(k)-1} \prod_{m=i+1}^{h(k)} \delta_{k,m} y_k R_k l_{i,i+1}^k \prod_{j=0}^{i} (1 - \tilde{b}_{k,j})$$

$$= \sum_{k \in \mathcal{K}} \sum_{i=0}^{h(k)-1} \prod_{m=i+1}^{h(k)} \delta_{k,m} y_k R_k l_{i,i+1}^k e^{\sum_{j=0}^{i} \log(1 - \tilde{b}_{k,j})}$$

$$\overset{(a)}{\approx} \sum_{k \in \mathcal{K}} \sum_{i=0}^{h(k)-1} \prod_{m=i+1}^{h(k)} \delta_{k,m} y_k R_k l_{i,i+1}^k \left(1 - \min \left\{ 1, \sum_{j=0}^{i} \tilde{b}_{k,j} \right\} \right)$$

$$\triangleq \tilde{L}(\boldsymbol{\delta}, \tilde{\boldsymbol{b}}),$$

$$\tilde{G}(\boldsymbol{\delta}, \tilde{\boldsymbol{b}}) = L^u - \tilde{L}(\boldsymbol{\delta}, \tilde{\boldsymbol{b}}) = \sum_{k \in \mathcal{K}} \sum_{i=0}^{h(k)-1} R_k y_k l_{i,i+1}^k \left(1 - \prod_{m=i+1}^{h(k)} \delta_{k,m} \right.$$

$$\left. \cdot \left(1 - \min \left\{ 1, \sum_{j=0}^{i} \tilde{b}_{k,j} \right\} \right) \right), \tag{13}$$

where (a) is based on the two approximate properties discussed above.

Then, the *relaxed approximated optimization problem* is given as

$$\max \quad \tilde{G}(\boldsymbol{\delta}, \tilde{\boldsymbol{b}}) \tag{14a}$$

$$\text{s.t.} \quad \sum_{k \in \mathcal{K}} \sum_{i=0}^{h(k)} y_k \left\{ R_k f(\delta_{k,i}) \prod_{m=i+1}^{h(k)} \delta_{k,m} + \left(\prod_{m=i}^{h(k)} \delta_{k,m} \right) \tilde{b}_{k,i} \right.$$

$$\left. \cdot (w_{ca} T + (R_k - 1)\varepsilon_{kT}) \right\} \leq W, \tag{14b}$$

$$\tilde{b}_{k,i} \in [0, 1], \forall k \in \mathcal{K}, i = 0, \cdots, h(k), \tag{14c}$$

$$\sum_{k \in C_v} \tilde{b}_{k,h(v)} y_k \prod_{j=h(k)}^{h(v)} \delta_{k,j} \leq S_v, \forall\, v \in V, \tag{14d}$$

$$\sum_{i=0}^{h(k)} \tilde{b}_{k,i} \leq 1, \forall k \in \mathcal{K}. \tag{14e}$$

However, $\tilde{G}(\boldsymbol{\delta}, \tilde{\boldsymbol{b}})$ is not concave. In the following, we transform it into a convex term through Boyd's method (Section 4.5 [7]) to deal with posynomial terms in (14a), (14b) and (14d).

4.2.1 Transformation of the Objective Function. Given our approximated objective function

$$\tilde{L}(\boldsymbol{\delta}, \tilde{\boldsymbol{b}}) \triangleq \sum_{k \in \mathcal{K}} \sum_{i=0}^{h(k)-1} \prod_{m=i+1}^{h(k)} \delta_{k,m} y_k R_k l_{i,i+1}^k \left(1 - \min \left\{ 1, \sum_{j=0}^{i} \tilde{b}_{k,j} \right\} \right), \tag{15}$$

we define two new variables as follows

$$\log(\tilde{b}_{k,j}) \triangleq u_{k,j}, \quad i.e., \quad \tilde{b}_{k,j} = e^{u_{k,j}},$$

$$\log \delta_{k,m} \triangleq \tau_{k,m}, \quad i.e., \quad \delta_{k,m} = e^{\tau_{k,m}}. \tag{16}$$

Then the approximated objective function can be transformed into

$$\tilde{L}(\boldsymbol{\tau}, \boldsymbol{u}) \triangleq \sum_{k \in \mathcal{K}} \sum_{i=0}^{h(k)-1} \sum_{m=i+1}^{h(k)} e^{\tau_{k,m} + \log(y_k R_k l_{i,i+1}^k)} \left(1 - \min \left\{ 1, \sum_{j=0}^{i} e^{u_{k,j}} \right\} \right). \tag{17}$$

Therefore, we can transform $\tilde{G}(\boldsymbol{\delta}, \tilde{\boldsymbol{b}})$ into

$$\tilde{G}(\boldsymbol{\tau}, \boldsymbol{u}) = L^u - \tilde{L}(\boldsymbol{\tau}, \boldsymbol{u})$$

$$= \sum_{k \in \mathcal{K}} \sum_{i=0}^{h(k)-1} e^{\log(R_k y_k l_{i,i+1}^k)} \left(1 - \sum_{m=i+1}^{h(k)} e^{\tau_{k,m}} \left(1 - \min \left\{ 1, \sum_{j=0}^{i} e^{u_{k,j}} \right\} \right) \right). \tag{18}$$

Next we need to transform the constraints following Boyd's method.

4.2.2 Transformation of the Constraints.

Constraint (14b): We take the left hand side of the constraint and transform it. To simplify, we divide the equation into multiple parts,

$$
\underbrace{\sum_{k \in \mathcal{K}} \sum_{i=0}^{h(k)} R_k y_k f(\delta_{k,i}) \prod_{m=i+1}^{h(k)} \delta_{k,m}}_{\text{Part 1}} + \underbrace{\sum_{k \in \mathcal{K}} \sum_{i=0}^{h(k)} y_k w_{ca} T \tilde{b}_{k,i} \prod_{m=i}^{h(k)} \delta_{k,m}}_{\text{Part 2}}
$$
$$
+ \underbrace{\sum_{k \in \mathcal{K}} \sum_{i=0}^{h(k)} y_k \varepsilon_{kT} (R_k - 1) \tilde{b}_{k,i} \prod_{m=i}^{h(k)} \delta_{k,m}}_{\text{Part 3}} . \tag{19}
$$

Part 1: From (16), i.e., $\tau_{k,i} = \log \delta_{k,i}$, we have

$$
\textbf{Part 1} = \sum_{k \in \mathcal{K}} \sum_{i=0}^{h(k)} R_k y_k (\varepsilon_{kR} - \varepsilon_{kC} + \delta_{k,i}\varepsilon_{kT} + \frac{\varepsilon_{kC}}{\delta_{k,i}}) \prod_{m=i+1}^{h(k)} \delta_{k,m}
$$
$$
= \sum_{k \in \mathcal{K}} \sum_{i=0}^{h(k)} R_k y_k (\varepsilon_{kR} - \varepsilon_{kC} + e^{\tau_{k,i}}\varepsilon_{kT} + \frac{\varepsilon_{kC}}{e^{\tau_{k,i}}}) \prod_{m=i+1}^{h(k)} \delta_{k,m}
$$
$$
= \sum_{k \in \mathcal{K}} \sum_{i=0}^{h(k)} R_k y_k (\varepsilon_{kR} - \varepsilon_{kc} + \varepsilon_{kT} e^{\tau_{k,i}} + \varepsilon_{kc} e^{-\tau_{k,i}}) e^{\sum_{m=i+1}^{h(k)} \tau_{k,m}} . \tag{20}
$$

Part 2: From (16), i.e., $\tilde{b}_{k,j} = e^{u_{k,j}}$, we have

$$
\textbf{Part 2} = \sum_{k \in \mathcal{K}} \sum_{i=0}^{h(k)} e^{\sum_{m=i}^{h(k)} \tau_{k,m} + \log(y_k w_{ca} T) + u_{k,i}} . \tag{21}
$$

Part 3: Similarly, we have

$$
\textbf{Part 3} = \sum_{k \in \mathcal{K}} \sum_{i=0}^{h(k)} e^{\sum_{m=i}^{h(k)} \tau_{k,m} + \log (y_k (R_k - 1) \varepsilon_{kT}) + u_{k,i}} . \tag{22}
$$

Combining (20), (21) and (22), Constraint (14b) becomes

$$
\sum_{k \in \mathcal{K}} \sum_{i=0}^{h(k)} R_k (y_k \varepsilon_{kR} - y_k \varepsilon_{kc} + y_k \varepsilon_{kT} e^{\tau_{k,i}} + y_k \varepsilon_{kc} e^{-\tau_{k,i}}) e^{\sum_{m=i+1}^{h(k)} \tau_{k,m}}
$$
$$
+ \sum_{k \in \mathcal{K}} \sum_{i=0}^{h(k)} e^{\sum_{m=i}^{h(k)} \tau_{k,m} + \log(y_k w_{ca} T) + u_{k,i}}
$$
$$
+ \sum_{k \in \mathcal{K}} \sum_{i=0}^{h(k)} e^{\sum_{m=i}^{h(k)} \tau_{k,m} + \log (y_k (R_k - 1) \varepsilon_{kT}) + u_{k,i}} \le W, \tag{23}
$$

which is convex in τ and u on the left hand side, respectively.
Constraint (14d): Similarly, we have

$$
\sum_{k \in C_v} e^{\sum_{j=h(k)}^{h(v)} \tau_{k,j} + \log y_k + u_{k,h(v)}} \le S_v, \tag{24}
$$

which is convex in τ and u on the left hand side, respectively.

4.2.3 Optimization Problem in Convex Form.
Following the transformation given in (18), (23) and (24), we obtain the convex form for the optimization problem, i.e.,

$$
\max \quad \tilde{G}(\tau, u)
$$
$$
\text{s.t.} \quad \sum_{k \in \mathcal{K}} \sum_{i=0}^{h(k)} R_k y_k (\varepsilon_{kR} - \varepsilon_{kc} + \varepsilon_{kT} e^{\tau_{k,i}} + \varepsilon_{kc} e^{-\tau_{k,i}}) e^{\sum_{m=i+1}^{h(k)} \tau_{k,m}}
$$
$$
+ \sum_{k \in \mathcal{K}} \sum_{i=0}^{h(k)} e^{\sum_{m=i}^{h(k)} \tau_{k,m} + \log(y_k w_{ca} T) + u_{k,i}}
$$
$$
+ \sum_{k \in \mathcal{K}} \sum_{i=0}^{h(k)} e^{\sum_{m=i}^{h(k)} \tau_{k,m} + \log (y_k (R_k - 1) \varepsilon_{kT}) + u_{k,i}} \le W,
$$
$$
e^{u_{k,i}} \in [0, 1], \forall k \in \mathcal{K}, i = 0, \cdots, h(k),
$$
$$
\sum_{k \in C_v} e^{\sum_{j=h(k)}^{h(v)} \tau_{k,j} + \log y_k + u_{k,h(v)}} \le S_v,
$$
$$
\sum_{i=0}^{h(k)} e^{u_{k,i}} \le 1, \forall k \in \mathcal{K}. \tag{25}
$$

THEOREM 4.7. *The optimization problem given in (25) is convex in τ and u, respectively.*

PROOF. It can be easily checked that the objective function in (25) satisfies the second order condition [7] for τ and u, respectively. We omit the details due to space constraints. □

REMARK 1. *Note that the optimization problem given in (25) is convex in τ for a given u, and vice versa. In the following, we will present an efficient master-slave algorithm to solve the convex optimization problem in τ and u, respectively.*

4.3 Efficient Algorithms

THEOREM 4.8. *The optimization problems given in (14a) and (25) are equivalent.*

PROOF. This is clear from the way we convexified the problem. □

Note that after the convex relaxation and transformation, the optimization problem in (25) is point-wise convex in τ and u. We focus on designing a polynomial-time solvable algorithm.
Algorithm: We consider the master-slave algorithm shown in Algorithm 1, i.e., given a fixed τ_0, we solve (25) to obtain u_0, and then given u_0, we solve (25) to obtain τ_1. We repeat the above process until that the values of τ and u converge[4][5]. We denote this as the optimal solution of (25) as (τ^*, u^*)[6].

Given the optimal solution to (25) as (τ^*, u^*), then from Theorem 4.8, we know there exists $(\delta^{**}, \tilde{b}^{**})$, which is the optimal

---

[4] If the difference between the current value and the previous one is within a tolerance, we say the value converges.

[5] Since our objective function is a function of the variables u and τ, once these variables converge, the value of the objective function must converge. As we are interested in the objective value, in Algorithm 1, we write the convergence criteria with respect to the objective function value, where ϵ equals to 0.001.

[6] Note that our master-slave algorithm is very efficient to solve this convex optimization problem, we can obtain a solution within one or two iterations.

Algorithm 1 Master-Slave Algorithm

Input: $R_k, y_k, W, l, \text{obj}_0$

Output: b, δ, obj_f

Step 1: Initialize u

Step 2: $\tau \longleftarrow \text{Random}(lb, ub)$ ▷ Generate random τ between lower bound lb and upper bound ub

while $\text{obj}_\chi - \text{obj}_{\chi-1} \geq \epsilon$ **do**

    Step 3: $u_\chi \longleftarrow \text{Convex}(\text{master}, \tau_\chi)$ ▷ Solve the master optimization problem for u_χ

    Step 4: $\tau_\chi \longleftarrow \text{Convex}(\text{slave}, u_\chi)$ ▷ Solve the slave optimization problem for τ_χ

    Step 5: $(b_\chi, \delta_\chi, \text{obj}_\chi) \longleftarrow \text{Rounding}(u_\chi, \tau_\chi)$ ▷ Round the values of u_χ, remap u_χ, τ_χ to b_χ and δ_χ and obtain the new objective function value

---

solution to (14a) such that $\tilde{G}(\tau^*, u^*) = \tilde{G}(\delta^{**}, \tilde{b}^{**})$ and $G(\tau^*, u^*) = G(\delta^{**}, \tilde{b}^{**})$.

THEOREM 4.9. *Denote the optimal solutions to (11) and (25) as* $(\tilde{\delta}^*, \tilde{b}^*)$ *and* (τ^*, u^*)*, respectively. Then, we have*

$$\left(1 - \frac{1}{e}\right) G(\tilde{\delta}^*, \tilde{b}^*) \leq G(\tau^*, u^*) \leq G(\tilde{\delta}^*, \tilde{b}^*). \tag{26}$$

PROOF. Consider any $(\delta, \tilde{b})$ that satisfies the constraints in (11) and (14a).

First, we show that $G(\delta, \tilde{b}) \leq \tilde{G}(\delta, \tilde{b})$, as follows

$$G(\delta, \tilde{b}) \overset{(a)}{=} \sum_{k \in \mathcal{K}} \sum_{i=0}^{h(k)-1} R_k y_k l_{i,i+1}^k \mathbb{E}\left(1 - \prod_{m=i+1}^{h(k)} \delta_{k,m} \prod_{j=0}^{i}(1 - b_{k,j})\right)$$

$$= \sum_{k \in \mathcal{K}} \sum_{i=0}^{h(k)-1} R_k y_k l_{i,i+1}^k - \sum_{k \in \mathcal{K}} \sum_{i=0}^{h(k)-1} R_k y_k l_{i,i+1}^k$$

$$\cdot \prod_{m=i+1}^{h(k)} \delta_{k,m} \mathbb{E}\left[\prod_{j=0}^{i}(1 - b_{k,j})\right]$$

$$= \sum_{k \in \mathcal{K}} \sum_{i=0}^{h(k)-1} R_k y_k l_{i,i+1}^k - \sum_{k \in \mathcal{K}} \sum_{i=0}^{h(k)-1} R_k y_k l_{i,i+1}^k$$

$$\cdot \prod_{m=i+1}^{h(k)} \delta_{k,m} \mathbb{E}\left[1 - \min\left\{1, \sum_{j=0}^{i} b_{k,j}\right\}\right]$$

$$\overset{(b)}{\leq} \sum_{k \in \mathcal{K}} \sum_{i=0}^{h(k)-1} R_k y_k l_{i,i+1}^k - \sum_{k \in \mathcal{K}} \sum_{i=0}^{h(k)-1} R_k y_k l_{i,i+1}^k$$

$$\cdot \prod_{m=i+1}^{h(k)} \delta_{k,m}\left(1 - \min\left\{1, \mathbb{E}\left[\sum_{j=0}^{i} b_{k,j}\right]\right\}\right)$$

$$= \tilde{G}(\delta, \tilde{b}), \tag{27}$$

where the expectation $\mathbb{E}$ in (a) is taken over b due to the linear relaxation, and (b) holds true due to the concavity of the min operator.

Next, we show that $G(\delta, \tilde{b}) \geq \left(1 - \frac{1}{e}\right) \tilde{G}(\delta, \tilde{b})$, as follows

$$G(\delta, \tilde{b}) = \sum_{k \in \mathcal{K}} \sum_{i=0}^{h(k)-1} R_k y_k l_{i,i+1}^k\left(1 - \prod_{m=i+1}^{h(k)} \delta_{k,m} \prod_{j=0}^{i}(1 - \tilde{b}_{k,j})\right)$$

$$\geq \sum_{k \in \mathcal{K}} \sum_{i=0}^{h(k)-1} R_k y_k l_{i,i+1}^k\left(1 - \prod_{j=0}^{i}(1 - \tilde{b}_{k,j})\right)$$

$$\overset{(a)}{\geq} \sum_{k \in \mathcal{K}} \sum_{i=0}^{h(k)-1} R_k y_k l_{i,i+1}^k\left(1 - (1 - 1/i)^i\right)\min\left\{1, \sum_{j=0}^{i} \tilde{b}_{k,j}\right\}$$

$$\overset{(b)}{\geq} \left(1 - \frac{1}{e}\right) \sum_{k \in \mathcal{K}} \sum_{i=0}^{h(k)-1} R_k y_k l_{i,i+1}^k \min\left\{1, \sum_{j=0}^{i} \tilde{b}_{k,j}\right\}, \tag{28}$$

where (a) holds true since [11, 14]

$$1 - \prod_{j=0}^{i}(1 - \tilde{b}_{k,j}) \geq \left(1 - (1 - 1/i)^i\right)\min\left\{1, \sum_{j=0}^{i} \tilde{b}_{k,j}\right\}, \tag{29}$$

and (b) holds true since $(1 - 1/i)^i \leq 1/e$. Also we have

$$\left(1 - \frac{1}{e}\right) \tilde{G}(\delta, \tilde{b}) = \left(1 - \frac{1}{e}\right) \sum_{k \in \mathcal{K}} \sum_{i=0}^{h(k)-1} R_k y_k l_{i,i+1}^k - \left(1 - \frac{1}{e}\right) \tilde{L}(\delta, \tilde{b})$$

$$= \left(1 - \frac{1}{e}\right) \sum_{k \in \mathcal{K}} \sum_{i=0}^{h(k)-1} R_k y_k l_{i,i+1}^k - \left(1 - \frac{1}{e}\right) \sum_{k \in \mathcal{K}} \sum_{i=0}^{h(k)-1}$$

$$\cdot \prod_{m=i+1}^{h(k)} \delta_{k,m} y_k R_k l_{i,i+1}^k\left(1 - \min\left\{1, \sum_{j=0}^{i} \tilde{b}_{k,j}\right\}\right)$$

$$= \left(1 - \frac{1}{e}\right) \sum_{k \in \mathcal{K}} \sum_{i=0}^{h(k)-1} R_k y_k l_{i,i+1}^k - \left(1 - \frac{1}{e}\right) \sum_{k \in \mathcal{K}} \sum_{i=0}^{h(k)-1} y_k R_k l_{i,i+1}^k$$

$$\cdot \left(1 - \min\left\{1, \sum_{j=0}^{i} \tilde{b}_{k,j}\right\}\right)$$

$$= \left(1 - \frac{1}{e}\right) \sum_{k \in \mathcal{K}} \sum_{i=0}^{h(k)-1} y_k R_k l_{i,i+1}^k \min\left\{1, \sum_{j=0}^{i} \tilde{b}_{k,j}\right\}, \tag{30}$$

then from (28) and (30), we immediately have

$$G(\delta, \tilde{b}) \geq \left(1 - \frac{1}{e}\right) \tilde{G}(\delta, \tilde{b}), \tag{31}$$

therefore, for any $(\delta, \tilde{b})$ that satisfies the constraints in (11) and (14a), we have

$$\left(1 - \frac{1}{e}\right) \tilde{G}(\delta, \tilde{b}) \leq G(\delta, \tilde{b}) \leq \tilde{G}(\delta, \tilde{b}). \tag{32}$$

Now, since $(\tilde{\delta}^*, \tilde{b}^*)$ is optimal to (11), then

$$G(\delta^{**}, \tilde{b}^{**}) \leq G(\tilde{\delta}^*, \tilde{b}^*). \tag{33}$$

Similarly, since $(\delta^{**}, \tilde{b}^{**})$ is optimal to (14a),

$$G(\tilde{\delta}^*, \tilde{b}^*) \leq \tilde{G}(\tilde{\delta}^*, \tilde{b}^*) \leq \tilde{G}(\delta^{**}, \tilde{b}^{**}) \leq \frac{e}{e-1} G(\delta^{**}, \tilde{b}^{**}), \tag{34}$$

where the first and third inequality hold due to (32).

Therefore, we have

$$\left(1 - \frac{1}{e}\right) G(\tilde{\delta}^*, \tilde{b}^*) \leq G(\delta^{**}, \tilde{b}^{**}) \leq G(\tilde{\delta}^*, \tilde{b}^*), \tag{35}$$

i.e.,

$$\left(1 - \frac{1}{e}\right) G(\tilde{\delta}^*, \tilde{b}^*) \leq G(\tau^*, u^*) \leq G(\tilde{\delta}^*, \tilde{b}^*). \tag{36}$$

$\square$

Since (25) is a convex optimization problem, (τ^*, u^*) can be obtained in strongly polynomial time.

4.4 Rounding

To provide a constant approximation solution to (8), the optimal solution $(\delta^{**}, \tilde{b}^{**})$ needs to be rounded.

Property: W.l.o.g., we consider a feasible solution $(\delta, \tilde{b})$ and assume that there are two fractional solutions $\tilde{b}_{k,j}$ and $\tilde{b}_{k,l}$. We define

$$\epsilon_1 = \min\{\tilde{b}_{k,j}, 1 - \tilde{b}_{k,l}\},$$
$$\epsilon_2 = \min\{1 - \tilde{b}_{k,j}, \tilde{b}_{k,l}\}, \tag{37}$$

and set

$$\tilde{b}'(1) = (\tilde{b}_{-(j,l)}, \tilde{b}_{k,j} - \epsilon_1, \tilde{b}_{k,l} + \epsilon_1),$$
$$\tilde{b}'(2) = (\tilde{b}_{-(j,l)}, \tilde{b}_{k,j} + \epsilon_2, \tilde{b}_{k,l} - \epsilon_2), \tag{38}$$

where $\tilde{b}_{-(j,l)}$ means all other components in $\tilde{b}$ remain the same besides $\tilde{b}_{k,j}$ and $\tilde{b}_{k,l}$. Set $\tilde{b} = \tilde{b}'(1)$, if $G(\tilde{b}'(1)) > G(\tilde{b}'(2))$, otherwise set $\tilde{b} = \tilde{b}'(2)$.

REMARK 2. *From the above rounding steps (37) and (38), it is clear that $\tilde{b}'$ has smaller number of fractional components than $\tilde{b}$. Since the number of components in $\tilde{b}$ is finite, the rounding steps terminate in a finite number of steps. Also, it is clear that $\tilde{b}'$ satisfies the second and the fourth constraints in (11) and (14a) for $\forall \epsilon \in [-\epsilon_1, \epsilon_2]$ or $\forall \epsilon \in [-\epsilon_2, \epsilon_1]$.*

Now suppose that $(\delta, \tilde{b}')$ is the rounded solution. Then following an argument similar to that in [1], we have

LEMMA 4.10. *For $k \in \mathcal{K}$, if $\sum_{j=1}^{h(k)} b_{k,j}$ is an integer, then $\sum_{j=1}^{h(k)} b'_{k,j}$ is also an integer; if $\sum_{j=1}^{h(k)} b_{k,j}$ is a fraction, then $\left\lfloor \sum_{j=1}^{h(k)} b_{k,j} \right\rfloor \leq \sum_{j=1}^{h(k)} b'_{k,j} \leq \left\lfloor \sum_{j=1}^{h(k)} b_{k,j} \right\rfloor + 1$.*

We refer the interested reader to [1] for more details.

Now since the energy constraint is integer, given that $(w_{ca}T + (R_k - 1)\epsilon_k T) \leq 1$, Lemma (4.10) implies that $(\delta, \tilde{b}')$ satisfies the constraints in (11). Therefore, after the rounding, we obtain a feasible solution obeying the constraints in (11).

THEOREM 4.11. *We consider a feasible solution $(\delta, \tilde{b})$ and assume that there are two fractional solutions $\tilde{b}_{k,j}$ and $\tilde{b}_{k,l}$. W.l.o.g., we assume that $\tilde{b}' = (\tilde{b}_{-(j,l)}, \tilde{b}_{k,j} - \epsilon, \tilde{b}_{k,l} + \epsilon)$ following rounding steps (37) and (38), then $G(\cdot)$ is convex in ϵ.*

PROOF. Recall that

$$G(\delta, \tilde{b}) = \sum_{k \in \mathcal{K}} \sum_{i=0}^{h(k)-1} R_k y_k l_{i,i+1}^k \left(1 - \prod_{m=i+1}^{h(k)} \delta_{k,m} \prod_{j=0}^{i} (1 - \tilde{b}_{k,j})\right),$$

then

$$G(\delta, \tilde{b}', \epsilon) = \sum_{k \in \mathcal{K}} \sum_{i=0}^{h(k)-1} R_k y_k l_{i,i+1}^k \left(1 - \prod_{m=i+1}^{h(k)} \delta_{k,m} \prod_{j' \neq j,l}^{i} (1 - \tilde{b}_{k,j'})\right.$$
$$\left. \cdot (1 - \tilde{b}_{k,j} + \epsilon)(1 - \tilde{b}_{k,l} - \epsilon)\right),$$

by the second order condition, it is obvious that $G(\cdot)$ is convex in ϵ. This property is called ϵ-convexity property in [1]. □

COROLLARY 4.12. *Since $G(\cdot)$ is convex in ϵ, it should achieve its maximum at the endpoint of $[-\epsilon_1, \epsilon_2]$ or $\epsilon \in [-\epsilon_2, \epsilon_1]$. Therefore, following the above rounding steps (37) and (38), we have $G(\delta, \tilde{b}') \geq G(\delta, \tilde{b})$.*

PROOF. $G(\delta, \tilde{b}') \geq G(\delta, \tilde{b})$ follows directly from the convexity of $G(\cdot)$ in ϵ and the rounding steps in (37) and (38). □

Rounding Scheme: Now for any solution $(\delta, \tilde{b})$ that satisfies the constraints in (11) and (14a), where $\tilde{b}$ contains fractional terms. There always exists a way to transfer mass between any two fractional variables $\tilde{b}_{k,j}$ and $\tilde{b}_{k,l}$ such that

- (i) at least one of them becomes 0 or 1;
- (ii) the resultant solution $(\delta, \tilde{b}')$ is feasible, i.e., $(\delta, \tilde{b}')$ satisfy the constraints in (11) and (14a);
- (iii) the gain satisfies $G(\delta, \tilde{b}') \geq G(\delta, \tilde{b})$.

Then we can obtain an integral solution with the following iterative algorithm:

(1) Given the optimal solution (τ^*, u^*) to (25), we first obtain the optimal solution $(\delta^{**}, \tilde{b}^{**})$ through the convexity mapping defined in (16).

(2) If there are fractional solutions in $\tilde{b}^{**}$, the number of fractional solutions must be at least two since the capacities are integer. W.l.o.g., consider two fractional solutions $\tilde{b}_{k,j}^{**}$ and $\tilde{b}_{k,l}^{**}$, for $j, l \in \{1, \cdots, h(k)\}$ and $j \neq l$.

(3) Following the above properties (i) (ii) and (iii) to transform at least one of them into 0 or 1 and the resultant gain G is increased.

(4) Repeat steps 2 and 3 until there are no fractional solutions in $\tilde{b}^{**}$.

Denote the resultant solution as $(\delta^{**}, \tilde{b}^{**\prime})$ which satisfies the constraints in (8). Note that each step can round at least one fractional solution to an integer one, the above iterative algorithm can terminate at most in $|\mathcal{K}| \times \sum_{k \in \mathcal{K}} |h(k)|$ steps. As each rounding step increases the gain, we have

$$G(\delta^{**}, \tilde{b}^{**\prime}) \geq G(\delta^{**}, \tilde{b}^{**}) \overset{(a)}{\geq} \left(1 - \frac{1}{e}\right) G(\tilde{\delta}^*, \tilde{b}^*)$$
$$\overset{(b)}{\geq} \left(1 - \frac{1}{e}\right) G(\delta^*, b^*), \tag{39}$$

where (a) holds from Theorem 4.9 and (b) holds from Theorem 4.6. Therefore, we have obtained a $(1 - 1/e)$-approximation solution to the original optimization problem (8).

5 PERFORMANCE EVALUATION

We evaluate the performance of our proposed algorithm against benchmarks over synthetic data-based network topologies.

5.1 Benchmarks

To compare our proposed solution technique with existing ones, we solve the original non-convex mixed integer non-linear optimization (MINLP) in (7) using conventional online solvers, including

Table 2: Characteristics of the Online Solvers

Solver	Characteristics
Bonmin [5]	A deterministic approach based on Branch-and-Cut method that solves relaxation problem with Interior Point Optimization tool (IPOPT), as well as mixed integer problem with Coin or Branch and Cut (CBC).
NOMAD [21]	A stochastic approach based on Mesh Adaptive Direct Search Algorithm (MADS) that guarantees local optimality. It can be used to solve non-convex MINLP.
GA [12]	A meta-heuristic stochastic approach that can be tuned to solve global optimization problems.

Bonmin [5], NOMAD [21] and Genetic Algorithm (GA) [12], which have all been designed to solve classes of MINLP problems. The characteristics of these solvers are given in Table 2.

Note that GA is a stochastic approach whose performance greatly varies from one simulation run to other. In order to reduce the variance, we run the algorithm 10 times and provide the average, maximum and minimum time along with objective function value obtained using GA. For sake of comparison, we also ran our algorithm 10 times. For our proposed algorithm, we use Algorithm 1 to solve the approximate relaxed convex problem and then use the rounding scheme discussed in Section 4.4 to obtain a feasible solution to the original problem. We compare the performance of our proposed algorithm with these benchmarks with respect to average latency as well as the complexity (measured in units of time).

Table 3: Parameters Used in Simulations

Parameter	Value	Parameter	Value
y_k	100	ε_{vR}	50×10^{-9} J
R_k	1000	ε_{vT}	200×10^{-9} J
w_{ca}	1.88×10^{-6}	ε_{cR}	80×10^{-9} J
T	10s	l	0.6
S_v	120	W	200

5.2 Synthetic Evaluation

5.2.1 Simulation Setting. We consider binary tree networks with 7, 15, 31 and 63 nodes, respectively. We assume that each leaf node generates $y_k = 100$ data items[7], which will be requested $R_k = 1000$ times during a time period $T = 10s$. $S_v = 120$ is the storage capacity of each node. For simplicity, we assume that the latency along each link in the network is identical and take $l = 0.6$. Our simulation parameters are provided in Table 3, which are typical values used in the literature [15, 26, 34]. We implement Bonmin, NOMAD and Algorithm 1 in Matlab using OPTI-Toolbox and Matlab's built-in GA algorithm on a Windows 7 64 bits, 3.40 GHz Intel Core-i7 Processor with 16 GB memory.

5.2.2 Evaluation Results. The performance of these algorithms with respect to the obtained value of the objective function and the time needed to obtain it, are given in Table 4.

On the one hand, we observe that neither Bonmin or NOMAD provide feasible solution with the constraint in (5e). We then further

relax this constraint for Bonmin and NOMAD. Hence, the results provided in Table 4 for Bonmin and NOMAD are solved without constraint (5e). Again, we notice that even after relaxing the constraint, Bonmin and NOMAD still exhibit poor performance, i.e. they either provide an infeasible solution or do not converge to a feasible solution. This is mainly due to the hardness of the original non-convex MINLP (7). Hence, it is important to provide an efficient approximation algorithm to solve it.

On the other hand, we observe that both our proposed algorithm and GA provide encouraging results. We run both GA and our algorithm 10 times and report their average as the obtained solutions and run time in Table 4. Tables 5 and 6 provide detailed results for the two algorithms. It is clear that our proposed algorithm significantly outperforms these conventional online solvers both in terms of run time and the obtained objective function value.

In particular, for the 63 node network, GA provides a solution faster than ours. However, GA is not robust and reliable for larger networks. We characterize the robustness of GA, as shown in Table 6, where the maximal (Max.), minimal (Min.) and average values of the objective function are presented as well as the corresponding time to obtain them for 7, 15, 31 and 63 nodes binary tree networks. We notice that for the 63 nodes network, only 4 out of 10 runs converge to a feasible solution using GA. Therefore, GA cannot always guarantee a feasible solution though it may complete in less time. Table 5 provides a detailed overview of our algorithm. The maximal, minimal and average values in terms of time, obtained solution and number of iterations are given. Our master-slave algorithm converges to a solution in small number of iterations.

Also note that our proposed approach always achieves a feasible solution within the $(1 - 1/e)$ approximation of the optimal solution[8]. Therefore, our proposed algorithm can efficiently solve the problem, i.e., provides a feasible solution in a reasonable time and is robust to network topologies changes.

We also characterize the impact of the number of requests on the caching and compression gain, shown in Figure 2. We observe that as the number of requests increases, the gain increases, as reflected in the objective function (7). Note that the objective function (7) is monotonically increasing in the number of requests R_k for all $k \in \mathcal{K}$ provided that δ and b are fixed.

REMARK 3. *Throughout the evaluations, we notice that the compression ratio at a leaf node is much smaller than the ratio at the root node. For example, in the 63 node network, the compression ratio[9] at a leaf node is 0.01 while it is 0.37 at the root node. This captures the tradeoff between the costs of compression, communication and caching in our optimization framework. Similar observations can be made in other networks and hence are omitted here.*

5.2.3 Heterogeneous Networks. In the previous section, we consider binary tree networks under homogeneous settings, i.e., the

---

[7]Note that this can be equivalently taken as 100 sensors generating data

[8]Note that the original optimization problem (7) is non-convex MINLP, which is NP-hard. Bonmin, NOMAD and GA all claim to solve MINLP with a ϵ-optimal solution. However, GA and NOMAD are stochastic approaches, they cannot guarantee ϵ-global optimality. Hence, we compare our solution with these of Bonmin, NOMAD and GA to verify the approximation ratio.

[9]Defined as the ratio of the volume of the output data to that of the input data at a node. The higher the compression ratio is, the lower is the data compression.

Table 4: Comparison Among Selected Algorithms Using Synthetic Data for Various Network Topologies

Nodes	Proposed		GA		Nomad		Bonmin	
	Obj. Value	Time(s)	Obj. Value	Time(s)	Obj. Value	Time(s)	Obj. Value	Time(s)
7	480000	3.30	479820	273.29	Infeasible	9.45	Infeasible	1.01
15	1440000	6.33	1440000	15.12	1439900	16.18	Infeasible	> 4000
31	3840000	29.28	3839000	3501.10	Non-Convergence	98.90	Non-Convergence	1232.31
63	9599900	538.17	8792100	158.56	Non-Convergence	966.16	Non-Convergence	2.04

Table 5: Detailed Results for Our Proposed Algorithm

Node	Time			Obj. Value			Iterations		
	Max.	Min.	Average	Max.	Min.	Average	Max.	Min.	Average
7	3.5848	3.12	3.30	480000	480000	480000	4	4	4
15	7.23	6.00	6.33	1440000	1440000	1440000	2	2	2
31	30.99	28.57	29.28	3840000	3839900	3840000	2	2	2
63	553.94	531.61	538.17	9600000	9599900	9599900	3	3	3

Table 6: Robustness of GA Algorithm

Node	Time (s)			Objective Value			Convergence (%)
	Max.	Min.	Average	Max.	Min.	Average	
7	369.43	161.76	273.29	479880	479750	479820	100
15	18.15	12.56	15.12	1440000	1440000	1440000	100
31	4446.70	2552.40	3501.10	3839100	3838900	3839000	100
63	413.28	24.41	158.56	9599100	8041500	8792100	40

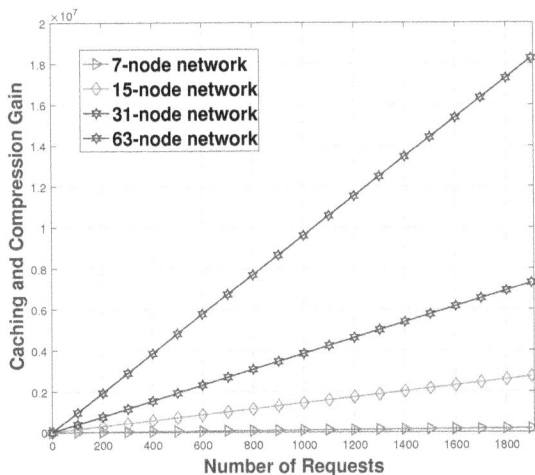

Figure 2: Impact of number of requests on performance.

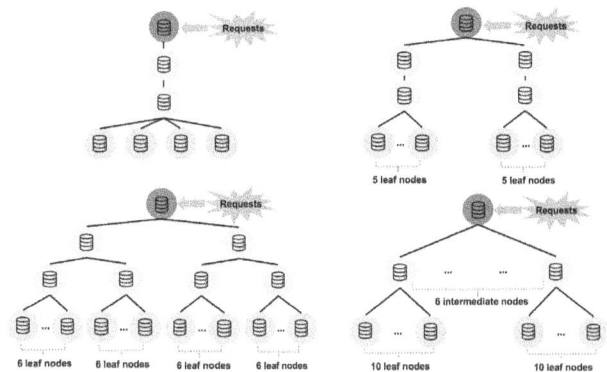

Figure 3: Heterogeneous Tree Networks used in Simulations

value of different parameters are identical for all nodes in the network, as given in Table 3. In this section, we generalize the simulation setting from two perspectives: (i) First, we consider heterogeneous parameter values across the network. For example, for the node cache capacity S_v, we assume that $S_v = 100+rand(1, 20)$, where $rand(i, j)$ assigns a random number between i and j. Similarly, we assign a random number to ε_{vR}, ε_{vT} and ε_{cR} on each node; (ii) Second, instead of considering binary tree, we consider more general network topologies with 7, 15, 31 and 67 nodes, as shown in Figure 3.

The performance of these algorithms with respect to the obtained value of the objective function and the time needed to obtain it, are given in Table 7. Again, we observe that neither Bonmin nor NOMAD can effectively solve the original problem in (7), which

shows the hardness of the problem. Hence, it is important to provide an efficient approximation algorithm to solve it.

Similarly, we also observe that both our proposed algorithm and GA provide encouraging results. We run both GA and our algorithm 10 times and report their average as the obtained solutions and run time in Table 7. We also obtain detailed results for both algorithms, where trends similar to Tables 5 and 6 are observed. These are omitted here due to space constraints, and are available in [24]. It is clear that our proposed algorithm significantly outperforms these conventional online solvers both in terms of run time and the obtained objective function value. Furthermore, again we notice that GA cannot always guarantee a feasible solution.

We also characterize the impact of the number of requests on the caching and compression gain. Similar to Figure 2, we observe that as the number of requests increases, the gain increases, hence the plot is omitted, which is available in [24].

Table 7: Comparison Among Selected Algorithms Using Synthetic Data for Various Network Topologies II

Nodes	Proposed		GA		Nomad		Bonmin	
	Obj. Value	Time(s)	Obj. Value	Time(s)	Obj. Value	Time(s)	Obj. Value	Time(s)
7	720000	5.5261	720000	6.14	720000	78.99	Infeasible	45.37
15	1799900	5.87	1800000	20.08	Non-Convergence	37.27	Infeasible	1151.05
31	4319500	33.81	4318700	66.68	Non-Convergence	179.21	Non-Convergence	32293.37
67	7197900	115.17	6531200	399.39	Non-Convergence	1037	Non-Convergence	> 40000

6 CONCLUSION

We considered the problem of optimally compressing and caching data across a communication network, with the goal of minimizing the total latency under an energy constraint. We reformulated this as a problem of maximizing compression and caching gain. This problem is NP-hard. We then proposed an efficient approximation algorithm that can achieve a $(1 - 1/e)$ approximation solution to the optimum in strongly polynomial time. Finally, we evaluated the performance of our proposed algorithm through extensive synthetic simulations, and made a comparison with benchmarks. We observed that our proposed algorithm can achieve near-optimal solution and outperform the benchmarks.

ACKNOWLEDGMENTS

This work was supported by the U.S. Army Research Laboratory and the U.K. Ministry of Defence under Agreement Number W911NF-16-3-0001. The views and conclusions contained in this document are those of the authors and should not be interpreted as representing the official policies, either expressed or implied, of the U.S. Army Research Laboratory, the U.S. Government, the U.K. Ministry of Defence or the U.K. Government. The U.S. and U.K. Governments are authorized to reproduce and distribute reprints for Government purposes notwithstanding any copy-right notation hereon. Faheem Zafari also acknowledges the financial support by EPSRC Centre for Doctoral Training in High Performance Embedded and Distributed Systems (HiPEDS, Grant Reference EP/L016796/1), and Department of Electrical and Electronics Engineering, Imperial College London.

REFERENCES

[1] Alexander A Ageev and Maxim I Sviridenko. 2004. Pipage Rounding: A New Method of Constructing Algorithms with Proven Performance Guarantee. *Journal of Combinatorial Optimization* 8, 3 (2004), 307–328.

[2] David Applegate, Aaron Archer, Vijay Gopalakrishnan, Seungjoon Lee, and KK Ramakrishnan. 2016. Optimal Content Placement for a Large-Scale VoD System. *IEEE/ACM Transactions on Networking* 24, 4 (2016), 2114–2127.

[3] Ivan Baev, Rajmohan Rajaraman, and Chaitanya Swamy. 2008. Approximation Algorithms for Data Placement Problems. *SIAM J. Comput.* 38, 4 (2008), 1411–1429.

[4] Kenneth C Barr and Krste Asanović. 2006. Energy-aware Lossless Data Compression. *ACM Transactions on Computer Systems* (2006).

[5] Pierre Bonami et al. 2008. An Algorithmic Framework for Convex Mixed Integer Nonlinear Programs. *Disc. Opt.* 5, 2 (2008), 186–204.

[6] Sem Borst, Varun Gupta, and Anwar Walid. 2010. Distributed Caching Algorithms for Content Distribution Networks. In *Proc. IEEE INFOCOM*. 1–9.

[7] Stephen Boyd and Lieven Vandenberghe. 2004. *Convex Optimization*. Cambridge University Press.

[8] Gruia Calinescu, Chandra Chekuri, Martin Pál, and Jan Vondrák. 2007. Maximizing a Submodular Set Function Subject to a Matroid Constraint. In *IPCO*, Vol. 7. Springer, 182–196.

[9] Nakjung Choi, Kyle Guan, Daniel C Kilper, and Gary Atkinson. 2012. In-network Caching Effect on Optimal Energy Consumption in Content-Centric Networking. In *Proc. IEEE ICC*.

[10] Edith Cohen and Scott Shenker. 2002. Replication Strategies in Unstructured Peer-to-Peer Networks. In *ACM SIGCOMM CCR*, Vol. 32. 177–190.

[11] G Cornnejols, M Fisher, and G Nemhauser. 1977. Location of Bank Accounts of Optimize Float: An Analytic Study of Exact and Approximate Algorithm. *Management Science* 23 (1977), 789–810.

[12] Kalyanmoy Deb, Amrit Pratap, Sameer Agarwal, and TAMT Meyarivan. 2002. A Fast and Elitist Multiobjective Genetic Algorithm: NSGA-II. *IEEE Transactions on Evolutionary Computation* 6, 2 (2002), 182–197.

[13] Mostafa Dehghan, Anand Seetharam, Bo Jiang, Ting He, Theodoros Salonidis, Jim Kurose, Don Towsley, and Ramesh Sitaraman. 2015. On the Complexity of Optimal Routing and Content Caching in Heterogeneous Networks. In *Proc. IEEE INFOCOM*. 936–944.

[14] Michel X. Goemans and David P. Williamson. 1994. NEW 3/4-APPROXIMATION ALGORITHMS FOR THE MAXIMUM SATISFIABILITY PROBLEM. *SIAM Journal on Discrete Mathematics* 7, 4 (1994).

[15] Wendi Rabiner Heinzelman, Anantha Chandrakasan, and Hari Balakrishnan. 2000. Energy-Efficient Communication Protocol for Wireless Microsensor Networks. In *System sciences*.

[16] Stratis Ioannidis and Edmund Yeh. 2016. Adaptive Caching Networks with Optimality Guarantees. In *Proc. ACM SIGMETRICS*. 113–124.

[17] Stratis Ioannidis and Edmund Yeh. 2017. Jointly Optimal Routing and Caching for Arbitrary Network Topologies. *arXiv preprint arXiv:1708.05999* (2017).

[18] Van Jacobson, Diana K Smetters, James D Thornton, Michael F Plass, Nicholas H Briggs, and Rebecca L Braynard. 2009. Networking Named Content. In *Proc. ACM CoNEXT*. 1–12.

[19] Anant Singh Jain and Sheik Meeran. 1999. Deterministic Job-Shop Scheduling: Past, Present and Future. *European journal of operational research* 113, 2 (1999).

[20] Andreas Krause and Daniel Golovin. 2014. Submodular Function Maximization. http://www.cs.cmu.edu/afs/.cs.cmu.edu/Web/People/dgolovin/papers/submodular_survey12.pdf. (2014).

[21] Sébastien Le Digabel. 2011. Algorithm 909: NOMAD: Nonlinear Optimization with the MADS Algorithm. *ACM TOMS* 37, 4 (2011), 44.

[22] Jian Li, Truong Khoa Phan, Wei Koong Chai, Daphne Tuncer, George Pavlou, David Griffin, and Miguel Rio. 2018. DR-Cache: Distributed Resilient Caching with Latency Guarantees. In *Proc. IEEE INFOCOM*.

[23] Jian Li, Srinivas Shakkottai, John C.S. Lui, and Vijay Subramanian. 2017. Accurate Learning or Fast Mixing? Dynamic Adaptability of Caching Algorithms. *arXiv preprint arXiv:1701.02214* (2017).

[24] Jian Li, Faheem Zafari, Don Towsley, Kin K. Leung, and Aanathram Swami. 2018. Joint Data Compression and Caching: Approaching Optimality with Guarantees. *Arxiv preprint arXiv:1801.02099* (2018).

[25] A. Manjeshwar and D. P. Agrawal. 2001. TEEN: a Routing Protocol for Enhanced Efficiency in Wireless Sensor Networks. In *IPDPS*.

[26] Sepideh Nazemi, Kin K Leung, and Aanathram Swami. 2016. QoI-aware Tradeoff Between Communication and Computation in Wireless Ad-hoc Networks. In *Proc. IEEE PIMRC*.

[27] Nitish K. Panigrahy, Jian Li, and Don Towsley. 2017. Hit Rate vs. Hit Probability Based Cache Utility Maximization. In *Proc. ACM MAMA*.

[28] Nitish K. Panigrahy, Jian Li, and Don Towsley. 2017. Network Cache Design under Stationary Requests: Challenges, Algorithms and Experiments. *Arxiv preprint arXiv:1712.07307* (2017).

[29] Nitish K. Panigrahy, Jian Li, Faheem Zafari, Don Towsley, and Paul Yu. 2017. What, When and Where to Cache: A Unified Optimization Approach. *Arxiv preprint arXiv:1711.03941* (2017).

[30] Alexander Schrijver. 2003. *Combinatorial Optimization: Polyhedra and Efficiency*. Vol. 24. Springer Science & Business Media.

[31] Karthikeyan Shanmugam, Negin Golrezaei, Alexandros G Dimakis, Andreas F Molisch, and Giuseppe Caire. 2013. Femtocaching: Wireless Content Delivery through Distributed Caching Helpers. *IEEE Transactions on Information Theory* 59, 12 (2013), 8402–8413.

[32] Dominic JA Welsh. 2010. *Matroid Theory*. Courier Corporation.

[33] Mao Ye, Chengfa Li, Guihai Chen, and Jie Wu. 2005. EECS: an Energy Efficient Clustering Scheme in Wireless Sensor Networks. In *IEEE IPCCC*.

[34] Wei Ye, John Heidemann, and Deborah Estrin. 2002. An Energy-Efficient MAC Protocol for Wireless Sensor Networks. In *IEEE INFOCOM*.

[35] Yang Yu, Bhaskar Krishnamachari, and Viktor K Prasanna. 2008. Data Gathering with Tunable Compression in Sensor Networks. *IEEE Transactions on Parallel and Distributed Systems* 19, 2 (2008), 276–287.

[36] Faheem Zafari, Jian Li, Kin K. Leung, Don Towsley, and Aanathram Swami. 2017. Optimal Energy Tradeoff among Communication, Computation and Caching with QoI-Guarantee. *Arxiv preprint arXiv:1712.03565* (2017).

Choice of Aggregation Groups for Layered Performance Model Simplification*

Farhana Islam
Dept. of Systems and Computer
Engineering
Carleton University
Ottawa, Canada
fislam@sce.carleton.ca

Dorina Petriu
Dept. of Systems and Computer
Engineering
Carleton University
Ottawa, Canada
petriu@sce.carleton.ca

Murray Woodside
Dept. of Systems and Computer
Engineering
Carleton University
Ottawa, Canada
cmw@sce.carleton.ca

ABSTRACT

The authors [1] previously showed that a complex layered performance model could be simplified by aggregating the contributions of subsystems, following a few simple principles which give good accuracy in many cases. The question of which subsystems to merge in layered performance models is further examined here, leading to identifying groups of subsystems (corresponding to "tasks" in layered queuing models) which can be safely aggregated. The grouping begins by identifying tasks which should be preserved, not aggregated, including those which are (or might become) bottlenecks. Then the groups are defined by their relationship to these preserved tasks. Aggregation by groups provides adequate accuracy in the vast majority of cases examined.

CCS CONCEPTS

• **Software and its engineering** → Software performance.

KEYWORDS

Performance Models, Layered Queuing Network Models, Model simplification.

ACM Reference format:

F. Islam, D. C. Petriu, C.M. Woodside. 2018. Choice of Aggregation Groups for Layered Performance Model Simplification. In *Proceedings of 9th ACM/SPEC International Conference on Performance Engineering, Berlin, Germany, April 2018 (ICPE 2018)*, 12 pages.
https://doi.org/10.1145/3184407.3184411

1 INTRODUCTION

Analytic performance models are powerful tools to predict the performance and scalability of a system before it is completed

and deployed, and methods have been devised to create such models from software specifications or architectural designs [1], [2]. However these models are often more detailed than really needed, because they include all the design detail when only some details are significant for performance. A simplified model would be more useful, provided it retains the detail of the significant subsystems. This research is focussed on Layered Queueing Network (LQN) models of software systems with distributed and layered operations and resources. LQN models have the useful property that they retain much of the structure of the system, and measures predicted by the model can be traced to software entities. The goal of the research is a process for automatically simplifying a model to an essential core level of detail governed by an accuracy requirement over a range of cases.

The authors previously described a process for aggregating the model elements, which in some cases could reduce a model to just two or three elements with little loss of accuracy [3]. This paper describes a more flexible and robust process.

The paper considers layered queuing (LQ) models of service systems with a single class of users, and with distributed and layered operations and resources.

2 Layered Queueing Network (LQN) Performance Models

The role of performance models is to make predictions for the performance of systems that do not yet exist, either using a model derived from a specification [1], or by studying modifications of an existing system and model [2]. Queueing models are used because they account for the effect of contention for resources, which is important in systems under load, and layered queueing network models (LQNs) are adapted to layered software systems. Fig. 1 shows an example LQN of a three-tiered web application, discussed further below.

An LQN model describes the interaction of system-elements (which may be any kind of software or hardware entity) via requests for service from one entity to another. The entities in the model are called *tasks* (analogous to objects) which accept service requests as *calls* made to *entries* (analogous to methods). Calls may be procedure calls, RPCs, or synchronous or asynchronous messages over a network. Each task is executed by its host (processor) which may be multi-core or a multiprocessor. Tasks may be multi-threaded, with threads sharing a queue, and the threads are scheduled on the host by a host queueing discipline.

Tasks may be used to model software processes and also any system features which generate contention, such as mutexes, buffer pools, or locks.

Entry E is part of a task T(E) and has a host demand parameter d_E (= mean host demand in time units per invocation of E, as determined for a "nominal" host type). The call (E_1, E_2) has a call parameter y_{E_1,E_2} (= mean calls to E_2 per invocation of E_1). We will only consider calls which block the caller (the calling thread waits for the reply after the entry execution is finished), but LQN can also model asynchronous calls and calls which are forwarded along a chain of tasks for service.

Task T has a multiplicity m_T and a host H(T). Host H has a multiplicity m_H and a speed factor S_H (speed relative to the "nominal" host type for which the demand values are found). The actual demand of entry E on host H is d_E/S_H sec. The capacity of the host is the product $c_H = m_H S_H$, with units of seconds of "nominal" execution per second; thus a single-core nominal host has a capacity of 1.0. In general, entries accept calls and also make calls to other tasks, usually at lower layers in a layered system.

A special User task represents the system's user population, with a multiplicity m_{User} equal to the number of users. The User task has a single entry, which may include a thinking time (a pure delay Z_{User}) and one or more calls into the system. One User entry execution corresponds to one user response from the system.

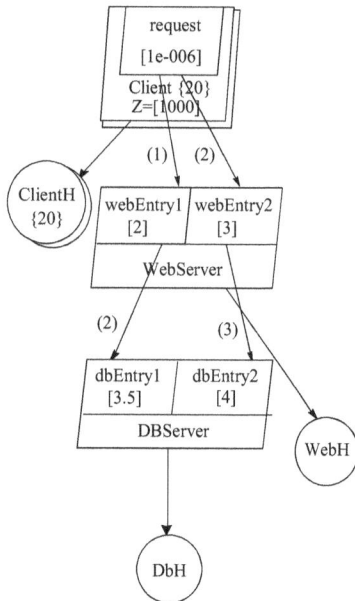

Figure 1: LQN model of a three-tier architecture [3]

Fig. 1 will serve as an example of the LQN notation. In this figure, the LQN model has three tasks - *Client*, *WebServer* and *DBServer*, each of which is deployed on its own host - *ClientH*, *WebH* and *DbH*, respectively. There are 20 users modeled as the 20-multiplicity task *Client* running on the 20-multiplicity host *ClientH*. Each user takes a 1000 ms think time (Z_{User} = 1000)

between requests. Both *WebServer* and *DBServer* are single threaded tasks and each has two entries with host service demands indicated in braces (i.e. *webEntry1* has service demand $D_{webEntry1}$ = *2 ms*). A single user operation includes one request to *webEntry1* and two to *webEntry2*. Storage devices are not shown but they can be modeled by a task representing the storage logic (read, write operations for example) running on a host representing the device.

This paper focuses its attention on LQNs with:

- a single User task (there can in principle be more, representing different classes of user),
- calling patterns with no cycles in the call graph,
- no internal parallelism on execution paths,
- entries that complete execution before replying (there is no "phase-2 execution" in LQN terms).

2.1 Performance Measures

The service time X_E of entry E is the total mean time to complete execution of the entry, including waiting and execution at its host H(T(E)), and waiting for a reply for each call. Each call delay in turn includes waiting for the called task to accept the request, and the entry execution time. Thus X_E is not known before the queueing delays are found; it is this property that makes layered system performance difficult to predict, and drives the use of LQN models.

Some other performance measures predicted by LQN models, that we will use, are

λ_E, λ_T = throughput of entry E and task T in invocations/s.

U_E, U_T, U_H = utilization of entry E, task T, host H,

where in this work utilization is defined as

$U_E = \lambda_E X_E$,

$U_T = \Sigma_E U_E$,

$U_H = \Sigma_{T \text{ deployed on } H} \Sigma_{E \text{ in } T} \lambda_E d_E/S_H$.

With this definition the utilization of a task or host ranges from zero to its multiplicity value. We also use its saturation level which ranges from zero to one, defined as

Saturation level of resource H = U_H / m_H.

Under heavy load the saturation of a bottleneck task or processor approaches one. Under lighter load the most saturated resource can be identified as the bottleneck.

2.2 Expectations for Aggregation

In aggregating LQN tasks and processors, we are aggregating two kinds of things: queueing resources (the tasks and processors) and customer classes (the entries of the tasks that are aggregated).

For queueing resources there is a well-established expectation that overall queueing delays are reduced when resources are aggregated together, which is well-known, for example, if a set of identical servers with separate queues are merged into a multiserver. However there are no comparable results available for layered servers.

For class aggregation the expected tendency is in the opposite direction. An LQN model includes many customer classes, for example, each different operation (entry) of a subsystem (task) is a different class of service. In order to simplify the model it is necessary to aggregate some of these classes, which introduces errors. For certain multi-class queueing models, Dowdy et al showed in [4] that a single-class aggregated model always has lower overall throughput (and thus longer delay). Although their result does not apply to the present models, this result suggests that class aggregation at a server may give worse performance.

Thus the two kinds of aggregation may be expected to produce opposite effects in the performance measures of the simplified LQN.

3 Direct Task and Host Aggregation

We consider an original model M, and methods to aggregate some tasks to produce a final model M'. The previous report [3] described a process we will call Direct Aggregation, which operates directly on the tasks of M. It stated three principles:

- *Capacity limit principle*: preserve the capacity limit of the model by preserving the bottleneck element(s);
- *Total workload principle*: to preserve the total workload (CPU operations) per user response; and
- *Concurrency principle*: to preserve the total concurrency available in software and hardware.

If the host processors are homogeneous, the third principle also preserves the total computing capacity of the system.

In [3] a 4-step procedure was defined to aggregate all the tasks except the User, and any tasks identified as bottlenecks. It was assumed that all operations completed before replying (no second phase operations, in LQN terms) and this assumption is retained here. For our purposes the first two steps of that procedure will be called *Stage 1*, producing a *Stage-1 aggregated model*, and tasks which are not aggregated will be called *preserved tasks*.

Stage 1 aggregates all activities and entries of a task T_i into a single entry as described in [3]. Since each task now has only one entry, we can without confusion label the entry parameters d_E and calls (E1, E2) by the task names, as demand d_T and calls (T1, T2). The aggregated host-demand and call values at Stage 1 are exact; the queueing times in this *Stage-1 model* have some degree of approximation error due to merging of classes, which was however found in [3] to often be small.

Step 3 and 4 in [3] aggregate all the tasks except the bottleneck and the User into a single task. Instead, this work identifies additional possible preserved tasks, and one or more groups of other tasks. It creates an aggregated task for each group, based on the following additional principle:

- *Dependency principle*: the dependency of a preserved task on each original task T will be preserved in M' as a dependency on the aggregated task that includes T.

This work also introduces a different process for aggregating a group of tasks. In [3] this was done incrementally by adding one task at a time; here each group is created in a single step.

4 Defining Groups of Tasks for Aggregation

The tasks that will not be aggregated (the preserved tasks) may include:

1) *Bottleneck tasks*: It was shown in our previous work that aggregating a bottleneck task together with others sometimes gives poor accuracy, and this seems to be generally true. Also the bottleneck is important in defining the saturation properties of a system, so preserving it should preserve those properties.

2) *Other highly saturated tasks*: If we intend to improve the system by mitigating the bottleneck then another task may emerge as a candidate "second bottleneck" and it would then (for the same reasons) be desirable not to have merged that task [3]. In general the candidates for bottlenecks are the highest tasks in an ordering based on task saturation level.

3) *Tasks subject to change*: We may also choose to keep a task out of aggregation if we want to study the effect of major changes in that task,

4) *Tasks with key measures*: We would like to observe the performance measures gathered for that task. In particular the measures for the User task define the user-related performance measures of the system, and it will always be a preserved task.

5) *Tasks deployed on bottleneck processors or highly saturated processor*: Tasks deployed on bottleneck processors also need to be preserved since merging the task (deployed on bottleneck processor) with other non-bottleneck tasks requires merging the bottleneck processor with other non-bottleneck processors. For the same reason as mentioned in item (1) above for tasks, bottleneck processors are preserved in this aggregation. In [3], it has been shown that merging a highly utilized/saturated processor can degrade the accuracy. So, we may preserve a second bottleneck processor as well as the task(s) deployed on it. If there is more than one task deployed on a bottleneck processor and none of them is a bottleneck task, those tasks can be merged into one task and preserved.

Before defining groups for aggregation we define a set **TP** = {TP1, TP2, ...} of tasks to be preserved. We wish the performance measures of these tasks to be well approximated in the aggregated model. Therefore we define the groups to preserve the dependency of the performance of the preserved tasks, on the tasks that are grouped, according to the Dependency Principle above.

4.1 Tasks Grouped by their Dependencies

A task T may affect the performance of a preserved task TP through delay dependency or by processor contention dependency. Delay dependence arises if TP makes a blocking call to T directly, or calls intermediary tasks with delay dependency on T (that is, if there is a path of blocking calls from TP to T). Processor contention dependency arises if T shares a processor with TP. Here we focus on the effect of delay dependency by restricting the original system to provide a separate host, (possibly a virtual machine) for each task, to eliminate processor contention dependency.

A blocking dependency of task T_1 on task T_2 in an LQ model is created by existence of a call path from T_1 to T_2 (that is, there is a direct call from T_1 to T_2 or indirect calls via one or more other tasks). We will define this dependency relative to a set of preserved tasks, as:

Definition: Task T_1 is *Preserved-Task Dependent* (PT-Dependent) on task T_2 if there is a call path from T_1 to T_2 that does not pass through a preserved task.

We will express this PT-dependency as $T_1 \prec T_2$. We assume that the system (and the layered model) does not have cyclical dependencies. If task T_1 has no dependency relation with T_2 we can write $T_1 \| T_2$.

For each task T_i its PT-dependency set $\mathbf{P_i}$ is then defined as

$$\mathbf{P_i} = \{P \mid P \prec T_i\}$$

$\mathbf{P_i}$ is non-empty for every non-preserved task T_i since every task except the User may be called in executing the application, therefore it always contains at least the User task.

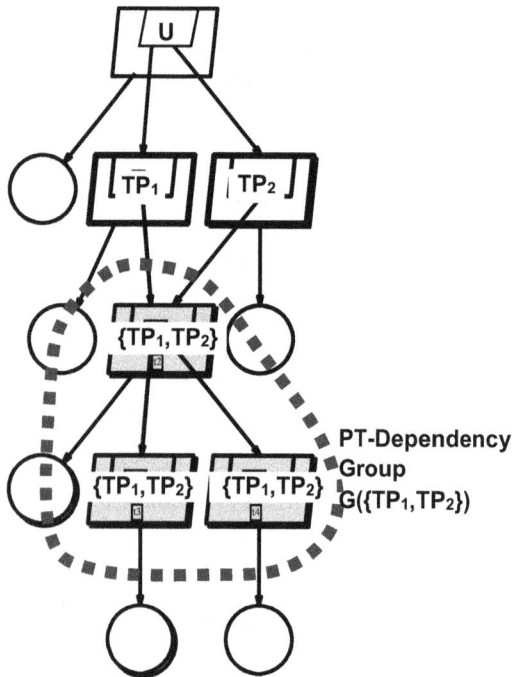

Figure 2: LQN model showing tasks with PT-dependency set {P1, P2}

Fig. 2 shows a model with three preserved tasks in the set $\mathbf{TP}$ = {U, TP_1, TP_2}. The three shaded tasks all have the same PT-dependency set $\mathbf{P}$ = {TP_1, TP_2}. The PT-dependency sets $\mathbf{P}$, one for each non-preserved task, partition the non-preserved tasks into subsets $\mathbf{G(P)}$ which will be a basis for the groups for aggregation. All the tasks in $\mathbf{G(P)}$ have the same PT-dependency set, and all other tasks have different PT-dependency sets. The tasks in a particular $\mathbf{G(P)}$ have an impact (through blocking calls) on just those preserved tasks in subset $\mathbf{P}$, and no others, and in M' all those blocking delay effects are captured approximately by

blocking calls to a single task TA($\mathbf{G(P)}$) created by aggregating the tasks in $\mathbf{G(P)}$.

The groups and the aggregated tasks are illustrated in Fig. 3 by an example "case-A" with three preserved tasks U, TP_1 and TP_2 (shown as parallelograms with bold borders). The tasks have four different dependency sets: {U}, shown as tasks with no shading, {TP_1} as tasks with diagonal stripes, {TP_2} as tasks with grey shading, and {U, TP_2} as the one task with diamond shading. Tasks with the same shading form a group.

To simplify the model, each group is aggregated into a single task running on its own processor, following the method in [3] as modified in the following section. This gives the simplified model in Fig. 4.

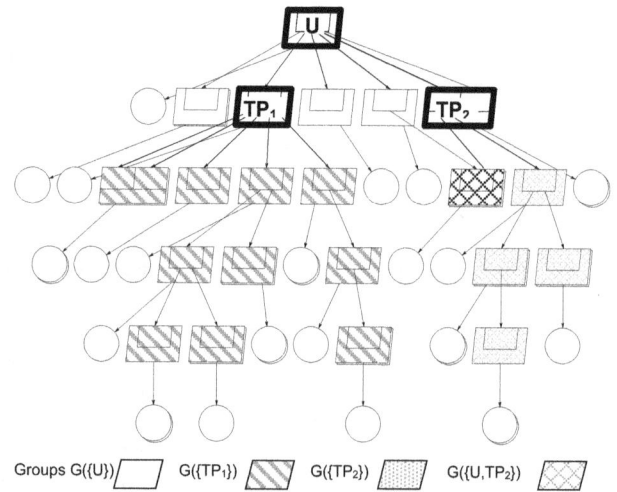

Figure 3: "case-A" showing groups defined by four distinct PT-Dependency sets P = {U}, {TP_1}, {TP_2}, {U, TP_2}

4.2 Desirable properties of the Aggregation Groups

The model simplification described here is motivated by a desire to preserve the essential components of the system, and to make the results traceable back to these components, while merging the elements that contribute less to the performance result. Direct Aggregation as in [3] preserves for each group

- its total workload
- the total processing capacity available to it
- the maximum concurrency of execution threads and cores

What is new here is:

- there can be an arbitrary number of preserved tasks, giving the modeller flexibility
- the dependencies of the preserved tasks are also preserved, in the following sense. For every preserved task P and unpreserved task T:
  o If P depends on T, then in M' P depends on a merged task derived from a group containing T
  o If T depends on P, then a merged task derived from a group containing T depends on P.

Thus, if we can think of each task as contributing a shadow of itself to its merged task, then there is a shadow of every non-persistent task and the dependencies between the persistent tasks and the shadows are preserved in M'.

5 Aggregation of a Group of Tasks

We consider a group or subset G of tasks T, each of which has one entry (as produced by Stage 1 aggregation) and its own processor (as assumed for this paper). T has demand d_T and makes an average of $y_{T,Ti}$ calls to each other task T_i, each time it is invoked.

An aggregated task $TA(G)$ is substituted for G, with CPU demand $DA(G)$, and $y_{Ti,TA(G)}$ calls coming to $TA(G)$ from each task T_i not in G. The calculation of DA and y begins by finding Y_i for each task T_i in M:

$$Y_i = \text{mean invocations of } T_i \text{ per user response, which will be called the "total calls" to } T_i.$$

Total calls Y_i for each task T_i is found by setting $Y_{User} = 1$ (for one user response) and solving these equations for all tasks T_i in M:

$$Y_i = \Sigma_{i,j} (Y_j * y_{Tj,Ti}) \text{ for all tasks } T_j \text{ calls } T_i.$$

From this the invocations of G per user response (or "total calls" to G) is $YA(G)$:

$$YA(G) = \Sigma_{Ti \notin G} \Sigma_{Tj \in G} Y_i * y_{Ti,Tj}$$

Then the demand $DA(G)$ is the total demand of G per user response, divided by the number of calls to G:

$$DA(G) = \Sigma_{Tj \in G} (Y_j * d_{Tj}) / YA(G)$$

The number of calls $y_{TA(G), Tk}$ from $TA(G)$ to target task $T_k \notin G$, per call into group G, is defined by a weighted average of calls from tasks T_j in G, weighted by Y_j:

$$y_{TA(G),Tk} = (\text{total calls from } G \text{ to } T_k)/\text{total calls to } G$$
$$= \Sigma_{Tj \in G} (Y_j * y_{Tj,Tk})/YA(G)$$

If the target tasks are also members of other groups, the number of calls between groups is calculated directly as follows. The number of calls from $TA(G1)$ to a task representing another group, say $TA(G2)$, is $y_{TA(G1),TA(G2)}$, which is the sum of the calls from $TA(G1)$ over tasks T_k in $G2$, thus:

$$y_{TA(G1),TA(G2)} = \Sigma_{Tk \in G2} \Sigma_{Tj \in G1} [(Y_j * y_{Tj,Tk})/YA(G1)]$$

An aggregated host $HA(TA(G))$ is created for the aggregated task $TA(G)$, with processing capacity c and multiplicity m, equal to the total capacity and multiplicity. In M' the host $HA(TA(G))$ has the properties:

$$c_{HA(TA(G))} = \Sigma_{Tj \in G} c(H(T_j))$$
$$m_{HA(TA(G))} = \Sigma_{\{H(T) | T \in G\}} m_{H(T)}$$
$$S_{HA(TA(G))} = c_{HA(TA(G))} / m_{HA(TA(G))}$$

Fig. 4 represents an aggregated model of the original model "case-A" in Fig. 3. The preserved tasks from the original model are shown with bold borders. The aggregated model has 7 tasks and 7 processors whereas the original model in Fig. 3 has 21 tasks and 21 processors.

6 Dependency Grouping vs a Single Group

In [3] a single group of tasks was formed from all the non-bottleneck tasks. This section shows examples which demonstrate the improved accuracy obtained when using the dependency groups proposed in this paper.

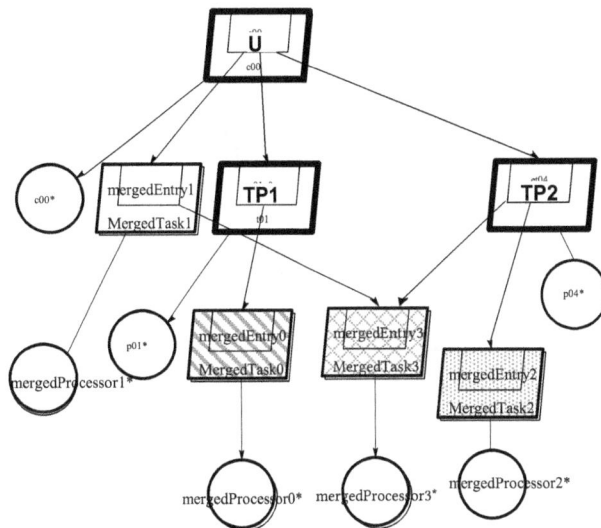

Figure 4: Aggregated model for "case-A" using the dependency groups shown in Fig. 3

First example: Cycle introduced by aggregation

This example shows the value of the dependency groups proposed here. Fig. 5 presents an LQN model called "case-11" with 11 tasks and 11 processors. The bottleneck task is t3 with 89.81% saturation level, shown with a bold outline.

Applying the previous aggregation algorithm [3], we get the model in Fig. 6. In this model, the bottleneck task t3 and its processor p3 are preserved and all other tasks except the user task c0 are merged into one task (with one processor). This produces a cycle in the call graph as seen in Fig. 6.

In comparing with the original model, the aggregated model generates 100% System throughput error and 3.78E+10% System response time error. In fact the calculation did not converge, the solver just stopped. The model is structurally different and the cycle creates a call explosion and an explosive increase in delay, and drop in throughput.

The simplification algorithm of this paper gives the second aggregated model shown in Fig. 7. The bottleneck task t3 is preserved, and there are two groups of tasks in the model in Fig. 5 that are identified by the proposed aggregation algorithm. One group is "below" the bottleneck (and produces the MergedTask0 in Fig. 7) and the other group is "above" the bottleneck (and produces MergedTask1 in Fig. 7).

To summarize the results:

Accuracy: Relative absolute error for "case-11"

Single-group: 100% in throughput,
              3.78E+10% in response time

Dependency groups based on one bottleneck task:
              23.55% in throughput,
              19.06% in response time

Task aggregation based on groups provides a much better aggregated model, although the error is still large.

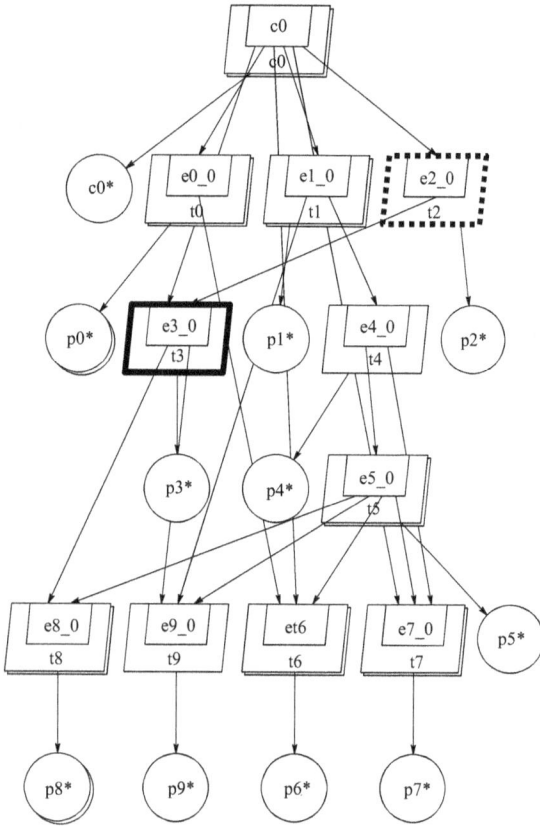

Figure 5: LQN model of "case-11"

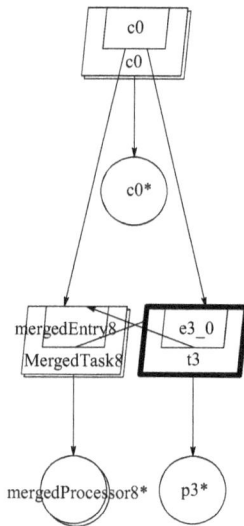

Figure 6: First aggregated model for "case-11" shown in Fig. 5, following the single-group algorithm of [3]

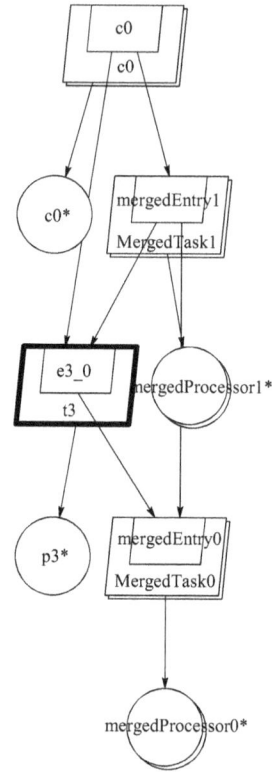

Figure 7: Second aggregated model for "case-11" (shown in Fig. 5) by generating two groups preserving one bottleneck task

Further examination revealed a second highly saturated task t2 (97.26% saturation level) in "case-11" in Fig. 5 shown in dashed outline. Task t2 is a direct caller of the bottleneck task, saturated due to pushback (waiting for service that is delayed by congestion). Preserving both t2 and t3 gives the third aggregated model shown in Fig. 8.

Accuracy: Relative absolute error for "case-11" (continued)
Dependency groups based on two highly saturated tasks:
6.91% in throughput,
6.47% in response time
The saturation level of both of the preserved tasks remain similar to the original model. Task t2's and t3's level of saturation are 97.26% (same as original model) and 87.43% (changed by 2%) respectively.

We can draw two lessons from this example, first that it may be important to preserve more than one highly saturated task, and second that the grouping should avoid aggregations that introduce cyclical calls between aggregated entries. Cyclical calling changes the structure of the system and totally distorts the predictions.

Second Example: Bottleneck Processor
In the following, we discuss another LQN model "case-41" where the model has a bottleneck processor.

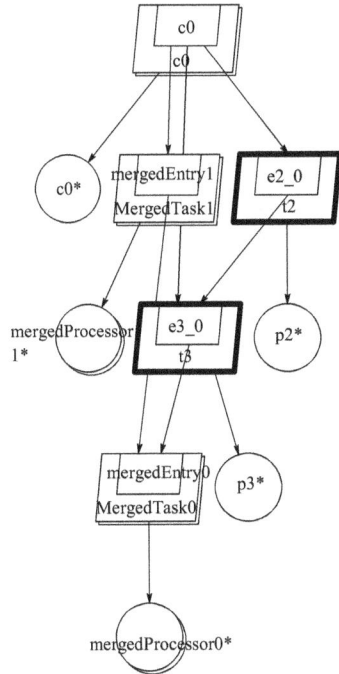

Figure 8: Third aggregated model for "case-11" by generating groups preserving two heavily saturated tasks

We compare the performance results of single group aggregation with dependency grouping. As shown in Fig. 9, the model contains 25 tasks and 25 processors along with a reference task

and its processor. In this model, the bottleneck is the processor p09 with 78.35% saturation (shown in bold outline). The task deployed on p09 is t09 (also shown in bold outline). Both t09 and p09 are preserved in the aggregated model.

Applying the previous single-group aggregation algorithm [3], we get the model presented in Fig. 10, in which the bottleneck processor p09 along with its task t09 are preserved and all other tasks except the user task c00 are merged into one task (and their corresponding processors are merged into one processor).

In the model of Fig. 10 the System throughput error is 27.57% and System response time error is 21.61%, which are substantial. Analysis of "case-41" shows that there is a second bottleneck task t05 (shown in dashed outline) having 98% saturation which is a direct caller of the preserved task t09. Applying the simplification algorithm using task dependency groups which also preserves the second bottleneck, we get the aggregated model as presented in Fig. 11, with 5 tasks and 5 processors along with the reference task and its processor.

The results for the aggregation based on dependency group are much better than those for single-group aggregation:

Accuracy: Relative absolute error for "case-41"

Single-group: 27.57% in throughput,
                  21.61% in response time
                  The saturation level of p09 is changed by 27%

Dependency groups based on two preserved tasks and one bottleneck processor: 1.78% in throughput,
                  1.77% in response time
The saturation of t05 and p09 are 98.33% (changed by 0.34%) and 79.76% (changed by 1.8%) respectively.

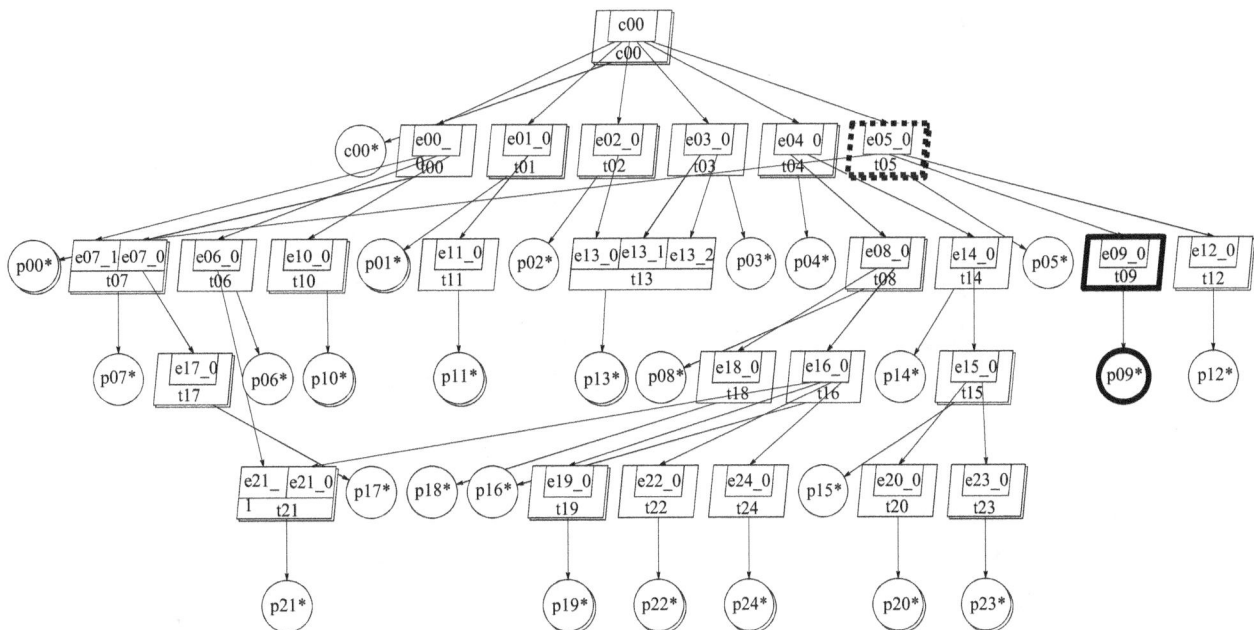

Figure 9: LQN model "case-41" with bottleneck processor p09 and its deployed task t09 in bold outline and second bottleneck task t05 in dashed outline

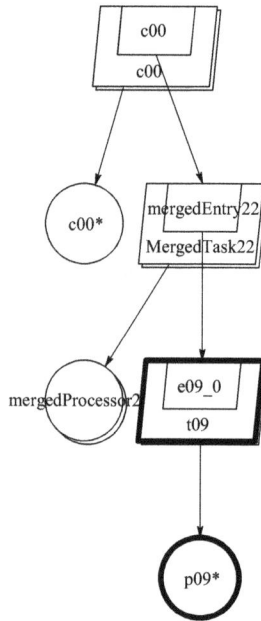

Figure 10: Aggregated LQN model for "case-41" (shown in Fig. 9) following the single-group algorithm of [3]

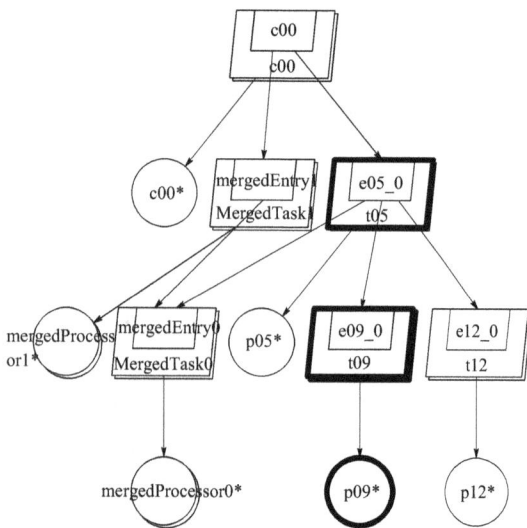

Figure 11: Aggregated model from "case-41" of Fig. 9 by generating groups preserving bottleneck processor and a second bottleneck task

7 Empirical Evaluation of Simplification Accuracy with Groups

This section describes experiments on groups of randomly generated models, to explore the accuracy of the dependency grouping strategy and to identify factors which may degrade the accuracy. Models of different total sizes with random structure and parameters were generated using the tool lqngen [5]. The grouping algorithm was implemented to automatically simplify the models, which were solved with the analytic solver LQNS [5].

Table 1 shows the average absolute errors in system throughput and response time for five groups of models of ten models each. We run all 50 models with random number of users (call it X users).

To investigate how the reduced model could be used for sensitivity studies, the accuracy of predictions for a system with twice as many users was also found, and is reported in the table. During the generation of these models one additional case was created that is treated separately below.

From the table we see that the average throughput error ranges from 3.5% to almost 6% and average response time error ranges from 3.4% to almost 5.5% for X users. There is no apparent relationship between the model sizes and the average error.

For 2X users, the errors are mostly slightly larger, but sometimes smaller, and in every case very little changed.

Table 1: Experiments with average throughput and response time error

Random LQN models	Throughput error (%)		Response time error (%)	
	X users	2X users	X users	2X users
10 models with 10 tasks	4.5	5.47	4.8	5.25
10 models with 15 tasks	3.5	3.45	3.4	3.47
10 models with 20 tasks	5.82	5.95	5.37	5.59
10 models with 25 tasks	3.52	3.56	3.48	3.53
10 models with 30 tasks	5.01	4.33	4.75	4.15

Fig. 12 and 13 show the frequency of absolute System throughput error (%) and absolute System response time error (%) for 50 models and X users, as in Table 1. From the histograms, we see that the frequency of System throughput error ranges mostly from 2% to 4% and System response time ranges mostly from 0 to 3%. They show that in general smaller errors are more frequent than larger errors. From experiments on these models, the maximum throughput error we found is 12.73% and response time error is 11.3%.

The results given so far understate the errors we found because they ignore one outlier. This outlier gives unsatisfactory errors in a case which occurred only rarely; this rare case must be treated by an extended process which is discussed next.

One Difficult Case: Case X

One randomly generated case, which we shall call "case-X", had a much larger error when aggregated following the grouping strategy: over 49% in response time and over 97% in throughput. The initial model and simplification are shown in Fig. 14 and 15. Inspection of the details suggests that the error arises partly through aggregation of very different classes, both moderately

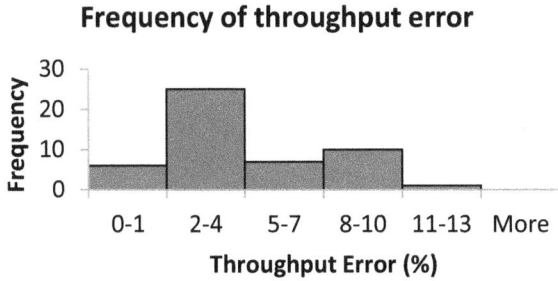

Figure 12: Frequency of absolute System throughput error (%) on the 50 models in Table 1

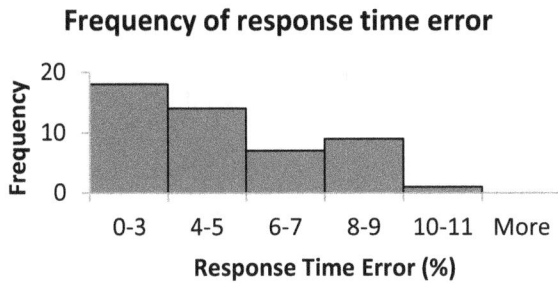

Figure 13: Frequency of absolute System response time error (%) on the 50 models in Table 1

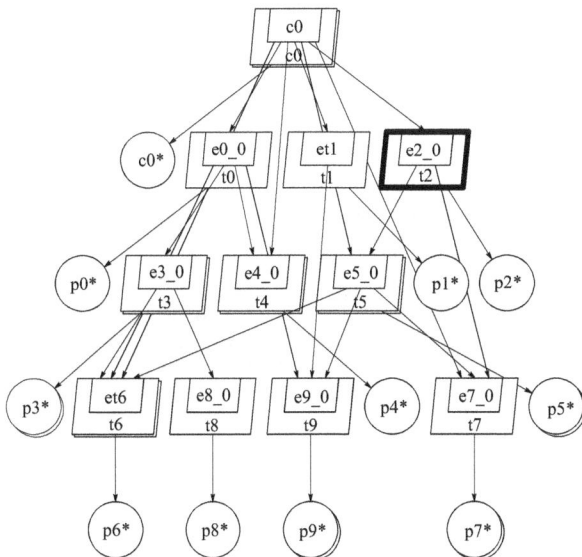

Figure 14: Original LQN model "case-X" with 10 tasks and 10 processors

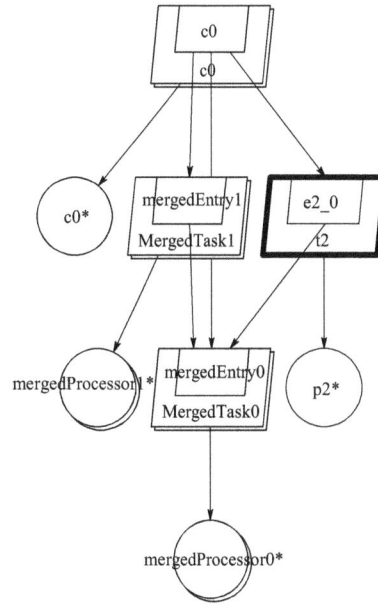

Figure 15: First Aggregated model of "case-X" from Fig. 14 preserving task t2

heavily loaded, in one of the groups. This is an example of the known threat of errors due to class aggregation. To deal with this threat the method must preserve additional tasks. To show that preserving additional tasks is effective, "case-X" was aggregated repeatedly with one task added at each step to the list of preserved tasks, with the results shown in Table 2. At each step, the most saturated non-preserved task or processor was chosen to be preserved. We see that we can obtain as small an error as we wish.

Table 2: Errors of Different Aggregations of "case-X"

Preserved tasks	Throughput error (%)	Response time error (%)
{t2}	97.14	49.25
{t2,t0}	14.29	13.12
{t2,t0,t5}	8.57	6.8
{t2,t0,t5,t6}	0	0.12

8 Scalability

Since our goal is to simplify large models, a much larger and more complex case is included here. Fig. 16 shows a model called "case-50" with 50 tasks and 50 processors that was generated randomly.

Table 3: Errors of Different Aggregations of "case-50"

Figure	Tasks and Processors	Throughput error %	Response time error %
Figure 17	7	12.73	11.3
Figure 18	9	4.85	4.63

The tasks outlined in bold were preserved based on high saturation level. Fig. 17 shows a first aggregated model of "case-50" with 7 tasks and 7 processors based on preserving only the bottleneck task and other highly saturated tasks. If we preserve the next most highly saturated resource which is processor p31 (47.92% saturated) and its deployed task t31 as shown in Fig. 18, the error is reduced as shown in Table 3.

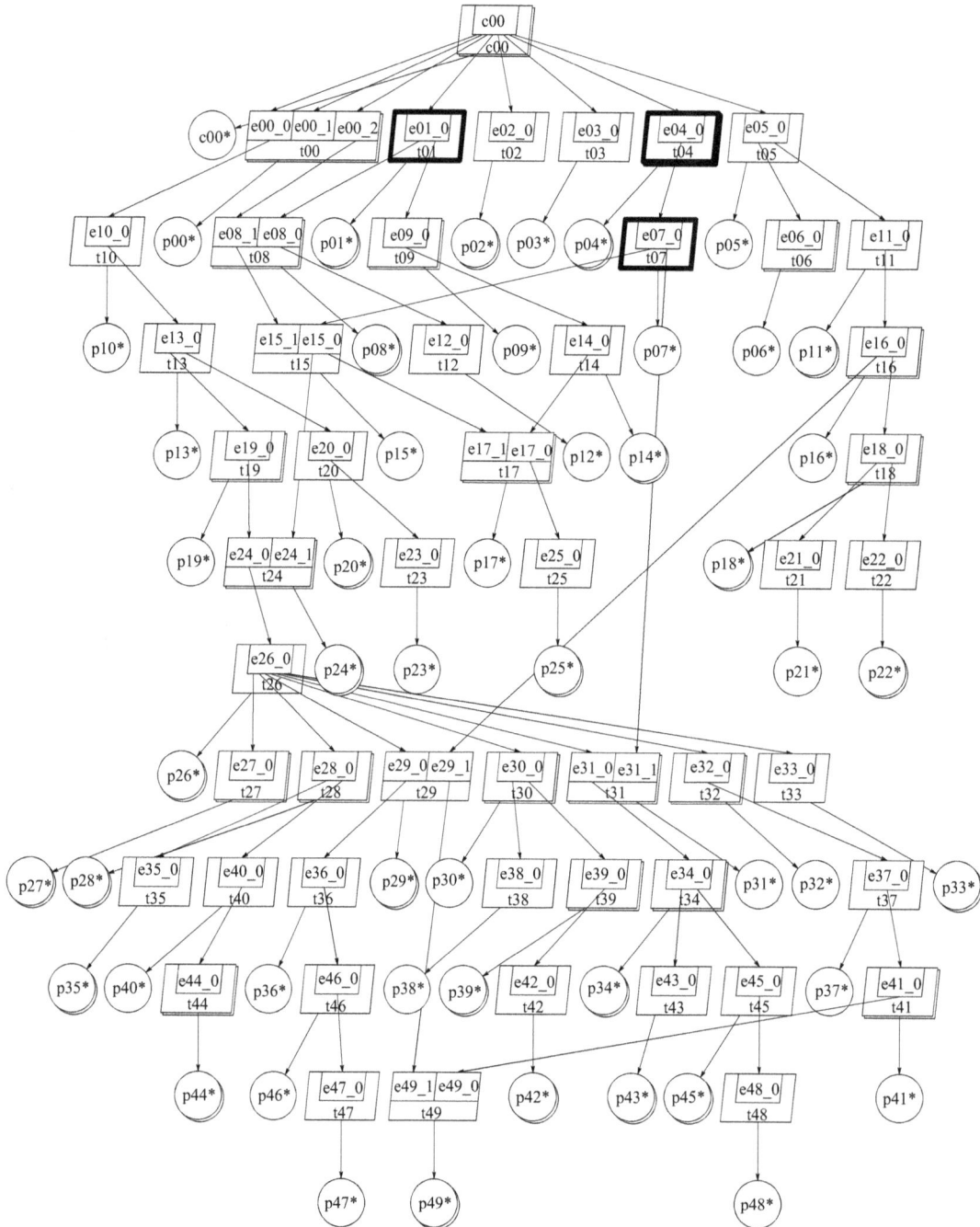

Figure 16: LQN model of "case-50" with 50 tasks and 50 processors

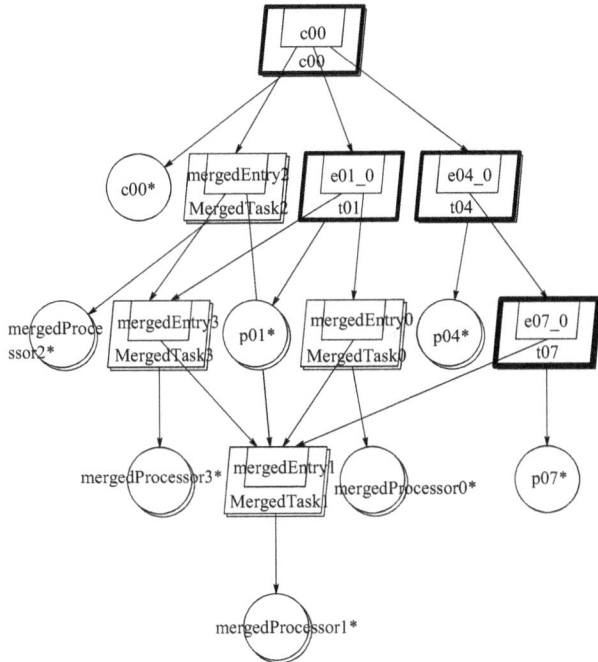

Figure 17: First aggregated model of "case-50" with 7 tasks and 7 processors

The errors under the simplest task-preservation in the first case are barely satisfactory; one improvement step gives a very satisfactory accuracy.

The execution time of the aggregation algorithm was found to be 1.2 second on average, on a commodity PC.

9 Related Work

Various kinds of simplification methods have been used for performance models, particularly for queueing models. There is a powerful and much-used simplification result in the Norton Theorem for Queues [6] which applies to product-form queuing networks. By this theorem any subnetwork of queues can be replaced by a single server with a state-dependent service rate. The replacement is exact in the sense that the throughput and delay at the subnetwork interface is the same for the single server [3]. The original result was for a single class of customers, and it was extended to multiple classes in [7].

A flow-equivalent server (FES) [8] is a generalization of this. When any submodel is replaced by a FES the entire model is smaller and easier to solve, and parameter changes outside the submodel can be studied efficiently. Outside of product-form queueing networks the simplification is approximate. The FES construction method isolates the subnetwork and drives it with a fixed number of customers, cycling endlessly; the mean delay of a customer in the subnetwork is taken as the service time of the FES for that number of customers. This is repeated for every user population that it may experience, which does not scale well to large systems with thousands of customers [3].

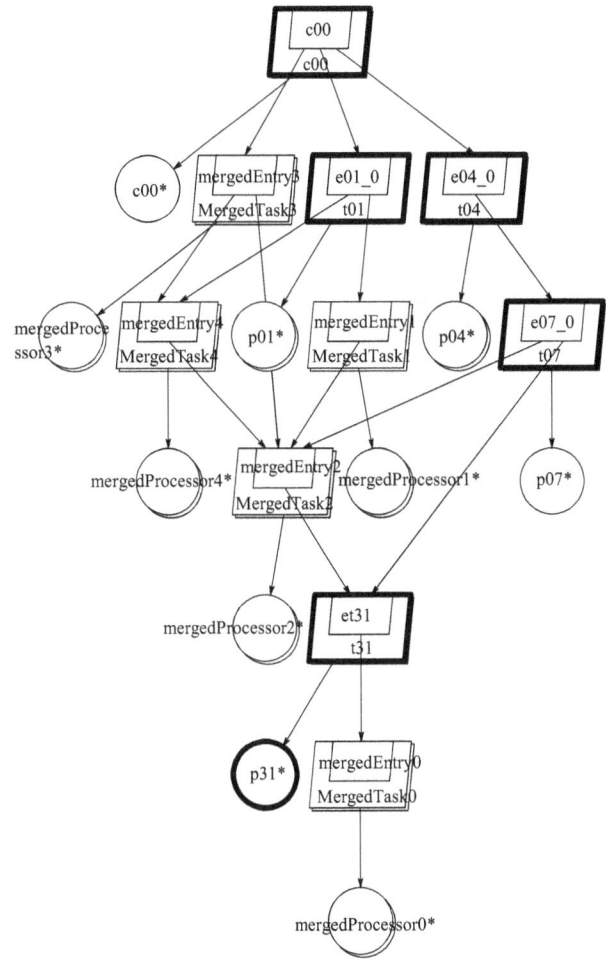

Figure 18: Second aggregated model of "case-50" with 9 tasks and 9 processors

Hierarchical decomposition as described in [8] applies this systematically. In hierarchical decomposition, a large model is partitioned into a number of submodels. Each submodel is then evaluated and individual solutions are combined to get the solution of the original model [8]. In this technique, the system is modeled using multiple levels of models. The highest level (level 0) of the models consists of a number of FESs, each of which represents some portion of the system being modelled. The following level contains a number of models that are more detailed representation of a subsystem represented in the first level as an FES. In general, every level in the hierarchy contains more detailed representation of the submodels from previous level until the final level (Level L) where all models are fully detailed and do not have any FESs. The models in hierarchical decomposition should be evaluated from level L to level 0 so that the performance projections for the system being modeled are obtained from its solution.

Surrogate delay methods (e.g. [8]) replace a subsystem by a delay which is found by solving an auxiliary model. A surrogate delay is somewhat like a FES, but with a fixed delay rather than a state-dependent rate. However the construction method is different and requires an iterative solution which includes the auxiliary model. Surrogate delays are most useful to address problems of simultaneous resource possession, but they can also be used for model simplification.

When performance models are fitted by regression methods as in [9], a choice must be made for the model structure including the level of detail in the model. The modeler can compare the goodness of fit of models with more or less detail. Regression thus automatically raises the question of detail, and can answer it through tests of goodness of fit as discussed in [9]. However this approach cannot be applied to models constructed from a design before a system is built, because it requires operational data for the regression.

In the Shadow Server method, one service node that violates conditions required for efficient, exact analytic solution in queuing network model is replaced by two or more servers that enable efficient analytic solution, such that the performance represents the original server [10]. As an example, a CPU server with a priority queue-scheduling discipline can be replaced with a shadow CPU server for each priority class, with jobs of different priorities being routed to different servers. However, this technique does not generate a simpler and smaller model than the original one.

The authors in [11] proposed an estimation technique for performance parameters in web based software systems. For web based applications, they use a combination of clustering algorithm and tracking filter for effective grouping of classes of services in layered queuing models. Clustering uses the K-means algorithm. The target application is autonomic control of web clusters. They considered the application URLs as first class entities and each URL request as a class. Their proposed tracking approach identifies performance parameters of groups of URLs instead of individual URLs. They proposed an algorithm that finds the appropriate number of clusters with a pre-defined clustering accuracy. For example, if one can accept 17% error, the number of needed clusters for estimation would be dropped from 14 to 9 on average.

Overall, we are unaware of any prior work on deriving a simplified layered queuing model directly from a detailed one, apart from our own paper [3]. In particular, there is a lack of simplification techniques that avoid the scalability problems of calibrating a FES.

10 Conclusion

In this paper, a simplification method for LQN model is presented which is an improved version of previous work of the authors [3]. In this new method, groups of tasks to be aggregated are determined based on the dependency relationships between the tasks in the groups, and a set of "preserved tasks" which should include at least the users and a bottleneck task. The paper defines grouping criteria and shows by experiments on randomly generated models of various sizes that the throughput and response time errors are less than 10% in the vast majority of cases. In every case the error can be reduced by adding

preserved tasks, based on their relative saturation, and can be made as small as desired (at the cost of a larger simplified model and more complex simplification). The best strategy for adding preserved tasks is the subject of current additional research.

This work has considered only systems with a single class of users, and system modules ("tasks") that do not share a host processor. This latter is in line with the practice in cloud deployments of giving each module its own virtual machine. However current work is considering shared hosts. The grouping has also only considered delay dependencies; current work is also considering host dependencies.

The grouping strategies described here address a fundamental problem of the required level of detail in modeling, and could be applied far beyond the domain of LQN performance models, to adjust the detail level of an analysis in real time.

The LQN models used in the cases of this paper can be found at https://github.com/FarhanaIslam/lqnmodels.

ACKNOWLEDGMENTS

This research was supported by grants from NSERC, the Natural Sciences and Engineering Research Council of Canada, through its Discovery Grants program.

REFERENCES

[1]   Murray Woodside, Dorina C. Petriu, José Merseguer, Dorin B. Petriu, Mohammad Alhaj. 2014. Transformation challenges: from software models to performance models. *Software and Systems Modeling*, 13, 4 (Oct 2014), 1529-1552. Published online Oct 2013. DOI: https://doi.org/10.1007/s10270-013-0385-x

[2]   Steffen Becker, Heiko Koziolek, Ralf Reussner. 2009. The Palladio component model for model-driven performance prediction. *Journal of Systems and Software*, 82, 1 (January, 2009), 3–22. DOI: https://doi.org/10.1016/j.jss.2008.03.066

[3]   Farhana Islam, Dorina Petriu, Murray Woodside. 2015. Simplifying Layered Queuing Network Models. In *Computer Performance Engineering: 12th European Performance Engineering Workshop (EPEW 2015)*, Springer LNCS 9272, 65–79. DOI: https://doi.org/10.1007/978-3-319-23267-6_5

[4]   Lawrence W. Dowdy, Brian M. Carlson, Alan T. Krantz, Satish K. Tripathi. 1992. Single-Class Bounds of Multi-Class Queuing Networks, *J.A.C.M*, 39, 1 (Jan 1992), 188-213. DOI: 10.1145/147508.147530

[5]   Layered Queuing Network homepage. Retrieved from http://www.sce.carleton.ca/rads/lqns/.

[6]   K. M. Chandy, U. Herzog, L. Woo. 1975. Parametric analysis of queuing networks. *IBM Journal of Research and Development*, 19, 1 (January 1975), 36-42. DOI: 10.1147/rd.191.0036

[7]   P. S. Kritzinger, S. V. Wyk, A. E. Krzesinski. 1982. A generalization of Norton's theorem for multiclass queueing networks. *Performance Evaluation*, 2, 2 (July, 1982), 98-107. DOI: https://doi.org/10.1016/0166-5316(82)90002-5

[8]   Edward D. Lazowska, John Zahorjan, G. S. Graham, Kenneth C. Sevcik. 1984. *Quantitative System Performance: Computer System Analysis Using Queueing Network Models*. Prentice Hall.

[9]   Murray Woodside. 2008. The Relationship of Performance Models to Data. In *Proc. International Performance Evaluation Workshop (SIPEW)*, Springer, Lecture Notes In Computer Science, 5119, 9 – 28. DOI: https://doi.org/10.1007/978-3-540-69814-2_3

[10]   Connie U. Smith. 1990. *Performance Engineering of Software Systems*. Addison-Wesley Longman Publishing Co., Inc. Boston, MA, USA,.

[11]   Hamoun Ghanbari, Cornel Barna, Marin Litoiu, Murray Woodside, Tao Zheng, Johnny Wong, Gabriel Iszlai. 2011. Tracking adaptive performance models using dynamic clustering of user classes. In *Proc. Int. Conf. on Performance Engineering (ICPE '11)*, Karlsruhe, 179-188. DOI: 10.1145/2160803.2160823

Optimizing Energy-Performance Trade-Offs in Solar-Powered Edge Devices

Peter G. Harrison

Imperial College London

pgh@doc.ic.ac.uk

Naresh M. Patel

NetApp Inc., Sunnyvale, California

naresh@netapp.com

ABSTRACT

Power modes can be used to save energy in electronic devices but a low power level typically degrades performance. This trade-off is addressed in the so-called EP-queue model, which is a queue depth dependent M/G/1 queue augmented with power-down and power-up phases of operation. The ability to change service times by power settings allows us to leverage a Markov Decision Process (MDP). We illustrate this approach by using a simple fully solar-powered case study with finite states representing levels of battery charge and solar intensity.

ACM Reference Format:

Peter G. Harrison and Naresh M. Patel. 2018. Optimizing Energy-Performance Trade-Offs in Solar-Powered Edge Devices. In *ICPE '18: ACM/SPEC International Conference on Performance Engineering, April 9–13, 2018, Berlin, Germany.* ACM, New York, NY, USA, 8 pages. https://doi.org/10.1145/3184407.3184426

1 INTRODUCTION

We consider an edge device that is fully powered by solar energy and connected to a cellular data network for communicating with the core services. Although the energy generated is not under our control and can vary by time of day (and time of year), the energy consumed can be altered by adjusting the processor clock rate which in turn impacts the application response time. This creates a trade-off between the energy consumed and the response time delivered by the cognitive system at the edge. We would like to adjust the clock rates judiciously throughout the day so that acceptable quality of service is delivered without running out of battery power given arrival rates and battery charging rates that depend on the time of day.

To illustrate one particular type of application operating on the edge, consider a camera endpoint that sends a video stream to a compute engine running a deep learning algorithm to identify gender and age of people passing by. The processing needs to be fast enough to classify the video clip and display age/gender-appropriate adverts and information. The inferred output data has some transient value when a person is in the line of sight of the display but that value vanishes as the person walks away. For example, this happens to Tom Cruise in the movie "Minority Report" as he is identified by a retina scan and immediately shown targeted adverts.

An arrival stream of people can often be modeled realistically as a Poisson process, where multiple people walking together at the same time can be modeled as a batch with specified batch-size probability distribution at each arrival instant. The service time will depend on the speed of inference of the learning algorithm, and we assume that the processor clock frequency can be adjusted downward to save energy. In this model, the service times have a general probability distribution but also the service rates vary with the queue depth. The EP-queue provides precisely these features, and more, for example power-up and power-down periods that have their own power demands [6]. In this paper, we derive expressions for the amount of energy consumed as well as standard performance metrics during a non-idle period, and create penalty metrics to make trade-offs at regular periods during the day. The objective is to find the policy or power settings for each period that minimizes the accumulated penalty at the end of the day.

2 ENERGY CONSUMPTION

2.1 Model definition

We extend the generalized $M^B/G/1$ queue defined in [6], with Poisson batch-arrivals and service times that are state-dependent when the queue length i (including the task in service, if any) at the start of a service period is less than some threshold $n \geq 1$; the service time random variable is denoted S_i when $1 \leq i < n$ and S_n when $i \geq n$. The Poisson batch-arrivals have rate λ, the batch size is an integer random variable B with probability generating function $G(z) = \sum_{i=1}^{\infty} b_i z^i$ and the service discipline is first come first served (FCFS). In addition, the server has to be powered-up when an arrival occurs in its idle state (queue length 0) and powered-down when a departure leaves the queue empty. Power-up and power-down times are independent random variables, denoted by U and D respectively. If an arrival occurs during power-down, the power-down continues unaffected and is immediately followed by a power-up period, immediately after which the first task to have arrived commences service. Thus the non-idle, (partially or fully) powered-up period is elongated beyond the regular busy period, which is simply a maximal time period throughout which there is at least one task in the queue. This queue was called an EP_n^G-queue in [6]. It reduces to a standard M/G/1 queue when $U = D = 0$ with probability one, $G(z) = z, n = 1$.

Both power levels and service times are functions of the clock frequency of a device, which we take to be v_i when the queue length is $i > 0$ at the start of service of a task, remaining constant until the end of the task's service period. The power level, or rate of energy consumption, $\omega_i(v_i)$ at queue length $i > 0$ is a function of the clock frequency; to a coarse approximation, $\omega_i \propto v_i^2$, but more accurate functions can be found through profiling. The energy ϵ_i used during a service time S_i that started when the queue length was $i > 0$ may then be approximated by $\epsilon_i = S_i \omega_i(v_i)$, although this too is an approximation due to the fact that a processor is not necessarily running at full power throughout an instruction cycle. Similarly, a common approximation is that the rate at which a task receives service is proportional to the clock frequency, so we may write $S_i = \Delta/v_i$, where the random variable Δ is the number of clock cycles required by a task. Under these approximations, the service times and energy units consumed by a task may be parameterized in terms of the power levels by $S_i \sim \sqrt{\frac{\omega_n}{\omega_i}} S_n$ and $\epsilon_i \sim \omega_i S_i$, where we use the symbol $\sim$ to signify "has the same distribution as". Like the service times, the power levels ω_i have a threshold at $i = n$ so that $\omega_i = \omega_n$ for all $i \geq n$. Thus reducing the power level by a factor of four results in doubling the service times, which may be reasonable when queue depths are low.

Of course, if all power levels ω_i are now replaced by the value 1, *after first resetting the distributions of S_i as above*, ϵ_i is the same as the service time S_i. This is just a mathematical device that conveniently uses one general expression, rather than having to work with multiple expressions: one with energy units and the other, almost identical, with time units. This observation is used to find the moments of the length of the non-idle cycle (either busy, powering up or powering down), required in the next section.

We use the following notation regarding random variables. The cumulative distribution function of a continuous random variable X is denoted by $X(t) = \mathbb{P}(X \leq t)$ and its Laplace-Stieltjes transform (LST) by $X^*(\theta) = \mathbb{E}[e^{-\theta X}]$. The probability density function (PDF) of X is $x(t) = X'(t)$, the derivative of the distribution function. The mth moment of X is written $X_{[m]} = \mathbb{E}[X^m] = (-1)^m X^{*(m)}(0)$, where the parenthesized superscript denotes differentiation m times with respect to θ. Correspondingly, the probability generating function (pgf) of a discrete random variable Y is written $G_Y(z) = \mathbb{E}[z^Y]$ (so that $G(z)$ is an abbreviation for $G_B(z)$).

2.2 Energy usage in non-idle periods

2.2.1 Underlying recurrence formula. Let the energy used between the start of service of a task at queue length i and the first subsequent instant at which the server becomes fully powered down, or idle, be denoted by the random variable W_i, for $i \geq 1$. Further, let W_0 denote the energy used between an instant at which the queue becomes empty and the end of the current non-idle period. The time period associated with W_0 is not just the power-down period D since it may be that new tasks will arrive during this period, starting a busy period after the power-down period has been completed[1]. Then the energy used in the non-idle period, $H = \omega_U U + W_{B+N_U}$, where B is the number of tasks in the batch that started the non-idle period and N_U is the number of task-arrivals during the powering-up period U; N_D is defined similarly with respect to the power-down period D. Let the power levels during power-up and power-down be ω_U and ω_D, respectively. Then, for $j \geq 1$, we have the recurrence $W_j = \omega_j S_j + W_{N_{S_j}+j-1}$, where

$$W_0 = \omega_D D + (\omega_U U + W_{N_U+N_D}) I_{N_D > 0},$$ N_{S_j} is the number of task-arrivals during the service time S_j and $I.$ is the indicator function. For example, when there are no arrivals during the service time that started with j tasks in the queue ($N_{S_j} = 0$), the recurrence is simply the sum of the energies used during that service time and in the non-idle period that starts with $j - 1$ tasks.

2.2.2 Energy PDF in non-idle periods. The LSTs $W_i^*(\theta)$ for $i = 1, 2, \ldots$ are given by the following series of lemmas and propositions, culminating in Theorem 1. The proofs of the lemmas are generalizations to corresponding results in [6] for time delay distributions' LSTs.

LEMMA 1. *For $i \geq n - 1$,*

$$W_i^*(\theta) = (V^*(\omega_n \theta))^{i-n+1} W_{n-1}^*(\theta) \text{ where the function } V^* \text{ is the}$$

fixed point of the equation $v^*(\theta) = S_n^*(\theta + \lambda(1 - G(v^*(\theta))))$. For $1 \leq i < n - 1$, omitting the arguments θ from $W_\cdot^*$ for brevity,

$$W_i^* = \left[S_i^*(\omega_i \theta + \lambda(1 - G(V^*(\omega_n \theta))))(V^*(\omega_n \theta))^{i-n} - \sum_{j=0}^{n-i-1} s_{ij}(\theta)(V^*(\omega_n \theta))^{j+i-n} \right] W_{n-1}^* + \sum_{j=0}^{n-i-1} s_{ij}(\theta) W_{j+i-1}^*$$

where $W_0^*(\theta)$ is to be determined and, for $1 \leq i \leq n, 0 \leq j \leq n$,

$$s_{ij}(\theta) = \frac{1}{j!} \left. \frac{\partial^j S_i^*(\omega_i \theta + \lambda(1 - G(z)))}{\partial z^j} \right|_{z=0}.$$

---

[1] We assume that once started, a power-down period must complete fully before a new startup period can begin. Other modi operandi are possible, e.g., the startup period could begin immediately.

LEMMA 2.

$$W_0^*(\theta) = D^*(\lambda + \omega_D\theta) +$$

$$\sum_{k=1}^{n-2} \left[W_k^*(\theta) - W_{n-1}^*(\theta) V^*(\omega_n\theta)^{k-n+1} \right] \sum_{j=1}^{k} u_{k-j}(\theta) d_j(\theta) +$$

$$W_{n-1}^*(\theta) V^*(\omega_n\theta)^{-n+1} U^*(\omega_U\theta + \lambda(1 - G(V^*(\omega_n\theta)))) \times$$

$$\left[D^*(\omega_D\theta + \lambda(1 - G(V^*(\omega_n\theta)))) - D^*(\lambda + \omega_D\theta) \right]$$

where $u_j(\theta) = \frac{1}{j!} \frac{\partial^j U^*(\omega_U\theta + \lambda(1 - G(z)))}{\partial z^j}\Big|_{z=0}$ and

$d_j(\theta) = \frac{1}{j!} \frac{\partial^j D^*(\omega_D\theta + \lambda(1 - G(z)))}{\partial z^j}\Big|_{z=0}$.

The next result defines an algorithm for the computation of $\{W_i^*(\theta) \mid i \geq 0\}$.

PROPOSITION 1. *For each θ and $i \geq 1$,*
$W_i^*(\theta) = W_0^*(\theta)\tau_i(\theta)/\tau_0(\theta)$, where, omitting the arguments $(\omega_U\theta + \lambda(1 - G(V^*(\omega_n\theta))))$ from U^* and $(\omega_D\theta + \lambda(1 - G(V^*(\omega_n\theta))))$ from D^*,

$$W_0^*(\theta) = D^*(\lambda + \omega_D\theta)\tau_0(\theta) \Big/$$

$$\left[\tau_0(\theta) - V^*(\omega_n\theta)^{-n+1} U^* [D^* - D^*(\lambda + \omega_D\theta)] - \right.$$

$$\left. \sum_{k=1}^{n-2} \left(\tau_k(\theta) - V^*(\omega_n\theta)^{k-n+1} \right) \sum_{j=1}^{k} u_{k-j}(\theta) d_j(\theta) \right]$$

$$\tau_i(\theta) = V^*(\omega_n\theta)^{i-n+1} \quad for \ i \geq n - 1;$$

$$\tau_i(\theta) = \frac{1}{s_{i+1,0}(\theta)} \left[\tau_{i+1}(\theta) - \sum_{j=1}^{n-i-2} s_{i+1,j}(\theta)\tau_{i+j}(\theta) - \right.$$

$$\left(V^*(\omega_n\theta)^{i-n+1} S_{i+1}^*(\omega_{i+1}\theta + \lambda(1 - G(V^*(\omega_n\theta)))) - \right.$$

$$\left. \sum_{j=0}^{n-i-2} s_{i+1,j}(\theta) V^*(\omega_n\theta)^{i+j-n+1} \right) \right] \quad for \ 0 \leq i < n - 1.$$

PROOF. The set of values $\tau_0(\theta), \tau_1(\theta), \ldots$ are proportional to $W_0^*(\theta), W_1^*(\theta), \ldots$ and given by Lemma 1 up to a constant of proportionality, which is chosen to be such that $\tau_{n-1}(\theta) = 1$ for all θ. Thus, for $i > 0$, $W_i^*(\theta) = W_0^*(\theta)\tau_i(\theta)/\tau_0(\theta)$ and the expression for $W_0^*(\theta)$ is obtained by plugging into Lemma 2. □

The required LST of the probability distribution of the energy used in a non-idle period – i.e. a contiguous, partially or fully powered-up period – is given by the following:

THEOREM 1. *The LST of the probability distribution function of the energy used in a non-idle period, H, is:*

$$H^*(\theta) = G(V^*(\omega_n\theta))U^*(\omega_U\theta + \lambda(1 - G(V^*(\omega_n\theta))))$$

$$\times V^*(\omega_n\theta)^{-n+1} W_{n-1}^*(\theta)$$

$$+ \sum_{i=1}^{n-2} b_i \sum_{j=0}^{n-i-2} u_j(\theta) \left(W_{i+j}^*(\theta) - V^*(\omega_n\theta)^{i+j-n+1} W_{n-1}^*(\theta) \right)$$

PROOF.

$$H^*(\theta) = \mathbb{E}[\mathbb{E}[e^{-\theta(\omega_U U + W_{B+N_U})} \mid U]]$$

$$= \mathbb{E}\left[\sum_{i=1}^{\infty} \sum_{j=0}^{\infty} b_i \frac{1}{j!} \frac{\partial^j e^{-\lambda U(1 - G(z))}}{\partial z^j}\Big|_{z=0} e^{-\theta(\omega_U U + W_{i+j})} \right]$$

$$= \mathbb{E}\left[\sum_{i=1}^{\infty} \sum_{j=0}^{\infty} b_i \frac{1}{j!} \frac{\partial^j e^{-U(\omega_U\theta + \lambda(1 - G(z)))}}{\partial z^j}\Big|_{z=0} e^{-\theta W_{i+j}} \right]$$

since $\frac{1}{j!} \frac{\partial^j e^{-\lambda U(1 - G(z))}}{\partial z^j}\Big|_{z=0}$ is the probability that there are j task-arrivals during time U. The rest of the proof is now similar to that of lemma 2. □

Finally, if energy is consumed during the exponentially distributed idle periods, at power level ω_I, the LST of the distribution function of the energy used, C say, in a complete idle-busy cycle is $C^*(\theta) = \lambda H^*(\theta)/(\lambda + \omega_I\theta)$.

The moments of C, H and the W_j depend on the moments of V, which has its Laplace transform defined as a fixed point. When we know *a priori* that only a given number p of moments are required, we only need the function $V^*(\theta) = 1 + \sum_{i=1}^{p} v_i\theta^i$ to order p. The coefficient $v_i = V^{*(i)}(0)/i! = (-1)^i V_{[i]}/i!$ in terms of moments, and it is routine to compute any finite number of these symbolically, using standard mathematical software.

2.3 Energy used in a given time interval

Idle-busy delay-cycles are usually short relative to wall clock times, e.g., energy generation or battery discharge times. We consider the case where a given time period t is many times greater than the mean delay-cycle time c. Suppose that there are n complete cycles that comprise the period t, i.e. $n \simeq \lfloor t/c \rfloor$ to a good approximation at large n. Since cycles are independent and identically distributed (iid), the probability distribution of the combined length of a large number, n, of cycles is well approximated by a Normal distribution with mean nm and variance nv, where m and v are respectively the mean and variance of the length of a single cycle, calculable by the procedure defined in the previous section when all power levels ω_x ($x \in \{U, D, i\}$) are replaced by the value one.

Now, if the random variable N_t is the number of cycles in a given length of time t and T_n is the time elapsed until the end of the nth cycle from the beginning of that time period, then at large n,

$$p_n(t) \stackrel{\text{def}}{=} \mathbb{P}(N_t = n) = \mathbb{P}(T_n \leq t) - \mathbb{P}(T_{n+1} \leq t)$$

$$\simeq \Phi\left(\frac{t - nm}{\sqrt{nv}}\right) - \Phi\left(\frac{t - (n+1)m}{\sqrt{(n+1)v}}\right)$$

Thus, the energy used up to time t has distribution function $F_t(x)$ with Laplace-Stieltjes transform $F_t^*(\theta)$ that can be approximated by (ignoring part-cycles, which are insignificant at large n) $F_t^*(\theta) = \sum_{n=1}^{\infty} p_n(C^*(\theta))^n$, where $C^*(\theta)$ is the LST of the distribution of the energy consumed in a single cycle, as in the previous section. At large n we can also apply the CLT to the energy used over n cycles, X_n, to obtain $C_n(x) = \mathbb{P}(X_n \leq x) \simeq \Phi\left(\frac{x - nm_e}{\sqrt{nv_e}}\right)$, where m_e, v_e are the mean and variance of the energy used in one cycle, simply obtained from $C^*(\theta)$ in the previous section. Thus we arrive at the approximation:

$$F_t(x) = \sum_{n=1}^{\infty} p_n(t) \Phi\left(\frac{x - nm_e}{\sqrt{nv_e}}\right) \tag{1}$$

Notice that when t is small and $[0, t]$ contains few cycles, p_n could be computed exactly (up to numerical approximations) by inverting the Laplace transform $T^*(\theta)^n - T^*(\theta)^{n+1}$ and using $C^*(\theta)$ directly. We would then also have to be concerned with part-cycles. However, as already remarked, such small time periods do not arise in the analysis that follows.

3 ENERGY-LATENCY MANAGEMENT

We seek a control system that sets the device power levels so as to provide the best performance possible, according to a given Quality-of-Service (QoS) metric, throughout the daylight hours, subject to the device remaining powered up through the night, i.e. giving 24-hour availability. We consider a finite horizon, discrete time Markov Decision Process (MDP), which samples the prevailing weather conditions every 15 minutes and sets the power-mode of the device so as to maximize a reward (actually, minimize a certain energy-latency metric) whilst achieving a given minimum battery charge level at the end of the daylight hours [2]. First, therefore, we need to model the charge and discharge rates of the battery under different conditions.

3.1 Battery charge and discharge rates

A brightness intensity function $i(t)$ gives the power harvested by the battery from the lumens of the sun (in watts) at time t (hours) of the day. Observation shows that this function is roughly parabolic. For example, the function $i(t) = \max[0, k_2(1 - k_1(13 - t)^2)]$, where k_1, k_2 are positive constants, gives a peak at 1pm, which is appropriate for the summer time. Setting $k_1 = 0.025$ and $k_2 = 500$ gives a peak output of 500 watts, which is typical for a one meter square PV panel, over a productive day running from about 7am to 7pm. This fits a sunny

climate and simply scaling down the parabolic output represents hazy or cloudy conditions well. We also use a more accurate intensity function obtained from empirical data in section 4.1.2. Changes in the weather may be modeled as a Markov chain, which can be adjusted before running the MDP according to the local weather forecast. However for simplicity, we consider a uniform day with approximately parabolic power input throughout the daylight hours.

Battery discharge rate is determined by the power used by the device, which is approximated by the probability distribution $F_t(x)$, neglecting leakage. We assume that the efficiency of the battery is 100%, so that no more energy is consumed than that required by the application. Obviously we can adapt this to cope with any observed lower efficiency if we take this as constant over output power and charge level. Moreover, we can extend the model to allow efficiency to be a function of the state. We use three battery charge-level states: f, or "full", which means above a (high) threshold, set a little below 100% full; h, or "high", which means below this high threshold but above a low threshold, set a little above 0%; and ℓ, or "low", which means less than the low threshold. Similar to battery charge boundaries used in [7], our model also sets low and high thresholds to 25% and 75% respectively.

3.2 Markov Decision Process

An MDP consists of a finite set of states, a set of actions for each state, transition probabilities for each pair of states dependent on the action taken, an immediate reward for each transition, a goal and, possibly, a discount factor (e.g., to handle infinite time horizons). In our case, we consider the daylight hours of one day with a finite time-horizon, corresponding to the end of the day, with 9 states (3 weather-states × 3 battery states). The state of the system is sampled every 15 minutes to yield a discrete state, discrete time Markov chain that drives the MDP. This Markov chain is defined by the state-transition probabilities $q_{(i_1, j_1),(i_2, j_2)}(t) = q_{i_1 i_2}^w(t) q_{j_1 j_2}^b(t)$, with $i_1, i_2 \in \{s, z, c\}$ (weather states sunny, hazy, or cloudy) and $j_1, j_2 \in \{f, h, \ell\}$ (battery charge states full, high, or low), where (omitting the argument t for brevity where there is no confusion) q^w, q^b are the state-transition probability matrices for the independent weather and battery charge level Markov chains, respectively. The former can be parameterized from the weather forecast, but in our initial model we assume uniform days so the states $\{z, c\}$ do not arise. Hence we only need to estimate the parameters of q^b, giving a three-state model. Clearly it would be straightforward to extend this model to incorporate transitions in the weather, at greater complexity but consequent loss of clarity.

Let $y_s(t) = \int_t^{t+1/4} i_s(u) du$ denote the energy harvested from the sun in the quarter-hour interval beginning at time t hours; in the untruncated parabolic area this would give $y(t) = -3.125t^2 + 81.25t - 403.125$ watt-hours. Let the "low", "high" and "full" battery states have charge-levels in the ranges $[0, b_1), [b_1, b_1 + b_2)$ and $[b_1 + b_2, b_1 + b_2 + b_3]$ respectively; i.e. the low band has width b_1, the half-full band has width b_2

and the high band has width b_3, so that level $b_1 + b_2 + b_3$ represents 100% full. We assume that at the beginning of a quarter hour time slot, the battery charge level random variable is uniformly distributed over the band with which its current state is associated. Then it is straightforward to obtain the parameters listed below, abbreviating the distribution function $F_{0.25}(\cdot)$ for the energy consumed by the device in a quarter-hour interval to $F(\cdot)$. For example, the probability that the state reduces from "full" to "high", given current charge level $x + b_1 + b_2$ with $x \in [0, b_3]$, is the probability that the device consumes more than $y(t) + x$ watt-hours, but less than $y(t) + x + b_2$, which would result in a transition to state "low". Since x is uniformly distributed over $[0, b_3]$, we get the first equation in the following list:

$$q_{fh}^b(t) = \frac{1}{b_3} \int_0^{b_3} [F(y(t) + x + b_2) - F(y(t) + x)]\, dx$$

$$q_{f\ell}^b(t) = 1 - \frac{1}{b_3} \int_0^{b_3} F(y(t) + x + b_2)dx$$

$$q_{hf}^b(t) = \frac{1}{b_2} \int_0^{b_2} F(y(t) - x)dx$$

$$q_{h\ell}^b(t) = 1 - \frac{1}{b_2} \int_0^{b_2} F(y(t) + x)dx$$

$$q_{\ell f}^b(t) = \frac{1}{b_1} \int_0^{b_1} F(y(t) - x - b_2)dx$$

$$q_{\ell h}^b(t) = \frac{1}{b_1} \int_0^{b_1} [F(y(t) - x) - F(y(t) - x - b_2)]\, dx$$

The diagonal entries in the matrix q^b are set so as to make the rows all sum to 1.

4 APPLICATION

The key recurrence, Proposition 1, for computing the LST of the distribution of the energy used during a powered-up cycle with fixed power settings has been implemented in Wolfram's Mathematica, and this LST can be inverted numerically by any of several known algorithms. However, the CLT-based approximations are more applicable for our problem.

4.1 Model Parameters

4.1.1 Foot-traffic arrival rate. In practical applications the arrival rate often varies with the time of day. For our purposes, we use Google Maps data of popularity times for a particular location (Ghirradelli Square in San Francisco), from which we can create a function that gives the instantaneous arrival rate at any time of day using interpolation. We use 15 minute intervals and assume the system has many busy cycles during that interval and reaches steady-state quickly. This gives 96 arrival rates for the 24 hour period. Figure 1 shows Google's "popularity function" over the 24-hour period of December 21, 2016. We normalize this function so that the average rate over 24 hours is one arrival per second, and then use a parameter to scale up the arrival rate as needed to account for batch arrivals. This way the time-dependent arrival rate is modeled by a single parameter λ, the batch-arrival rate of our model.

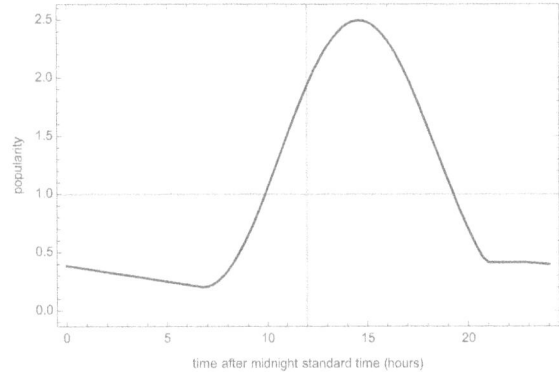

Figure 1: Foot traffic arrival rate at Ghirradelli Square over the 24 hours of the winter solstice, 2016

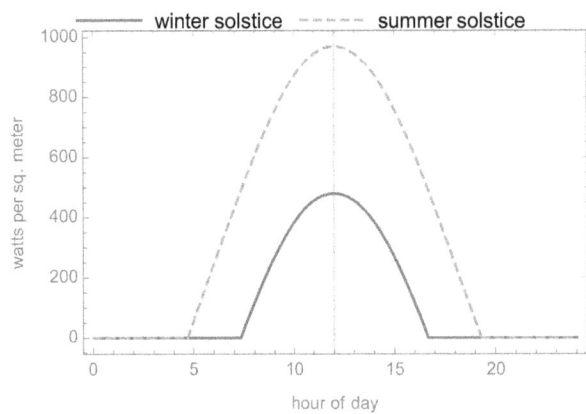

Figure 2: Expected solar intensity at Ghirradelli Square over the 24 hours of the winter and summer solstices

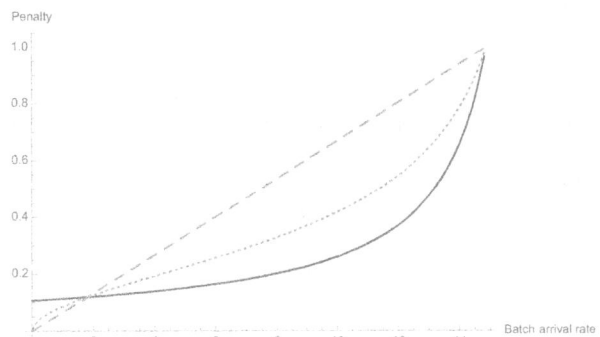

Figure 3: Latency, energy and hybrid penalty functions for the high power level, shown in solid blue, dashed orange and dotted green lines, respectively

4.1.2 Solar power harvesting. The amount of solar power harvested per square meter depends on many factors. We use a simple model that captures the parabola-like shape of the sun's intensity during a particular day – the winter solstice, December 21, which has solar declination angle of -23.5 degrees (due to the tilt of the earth). Ghirradelli Square at 37.8059 degrees North latitude is our chosen location. The solar constant is about 1000 W per square meter but typical solar cells are capable of converting only a fraction of this. Using the equation from [3] the sun insolation at time t hours on a 24 hour clock is the maximum of 0 and $1000(\cos(x)\cos(y)\cos(h(t-12))+\sin(x)\sin(y))$, where x is the latitude (in radians), y is the declination angle (in radians), h is the "hour angle" ($\pi/12$ in radians). Figure 2 shows a chart of the sun insolation equation for the winter solstice and the summer solstice at Ghirradelli Square. In the model we consider in section 4.3, we assume a quarter square meter solar panel.

4.1.3 Device service times. The device may be performing a variety of tasks and service times should be parameterized by fitting to the specific applications being run. Somewhat arbitrarily, we chose to parameterize all our models with respect to a storage system from which we have data; see [6]. Accordingly, service times have gamma distributions with means $(9.808, 7.930, 6.053)$ milliseconds and coefficients of variation $(0.64, 0.401, 0.218)$ for queue lengths of 1, 2 and 3 or more, respectively; i.e. the threshold of the EP-queue is 3 – so the service time distribution is the same for all queue lengths 3 and above. This way the service time is characterized by just 3 service time distributions, each with 2 parameters. Note that the mean service times and variability decrease as the queue depth increases, which is a nice property because it implies the system becomes more efficient with more load.

4.1.4 Penalty function. The goal of the MDP is to identify a policy that chooses power levels for the device over each quarter hour interval so as to minimize a certain aggregated penalty, whilst meeting a goal at the end of a specified finite period. We define the *penalty function* $R_{a,t}(s, s')$ to be a suitable energy-performance metric for the 15-minute slot starting at time t achieved by taking action a when in state s that leads to next state s'. This metric, which is state-dependent, could be the expectation of user-response time, r, (if energy is not a major concern), or the energy used, e, (if this is the only major concern), or of the product of the two if a trade-off is required, as in [6] for example. These metrics are normalized by their values, R and E, obtained at 90% utilization. Our *primary* metric is then the vector $(\frac{r}{R}, \sqrt{\frac{re}{RE}}, \frac{e}{E})$ corresponding to the battery states (f, h, ℓ). Note we used the geometric mean of the first and last value to obtain the middle value. Graphs of these penalty functions are shown in Figure 3 for the model with base power level of 100 watts. To minimize the possibility of a temporarily flat battery and so loss of data, we can instead choose to deter the system from visiting the "low" state. We create this *deterring* metric by setting the penalty in the "low" state to a fixed quantity equal to a multiple of the maximum

power at which the device is run – so that the normalized metric becomes that constant multiple.

4.2 MDP definition

For a given state, actions a_1 or a_2 set the device power to 50 or 100 watts, respectively. The power settings can be changed in the MDP by appropriate choice of action a_1, a_2 at the beginning of a time slot, based on the current state of the system and the predicted energy supply and drain going forward. Once a policy is chosen, the state transition probabilities are fixed and the process is Markovian because the next state only depends on the current state, and not earlier states. Even with binary actions for each state, the number of policies to enumerate is large. Our goal is to find the optimum *policy at the beginning of each quarter-hour time slot t $\pi_t(s) \in \{a_1, a_2\}$*, over states s in the state-space $\mathcal{S} = \{s, z, c\} \times \{f, h, \ell\}$, that yields the minimum penalty over the remainder of a day such that the battery is left full (or above a specified charge level) at the end of the daylight hours: at time T hours, say.

This leads to the following conventional MDP specification: Determine the *value function $V(s, t)$* at discrete time t and policy $\pi(s, t)$ for all $s \in \mathcal{S}$ given by the iteration $V_T(s) = 0$ if $s = f$, $V_T(s) = 1$ if $s \neq f$ and

$$V_t(s) = \min_{a \in \{a_1, a_2\}} \left[\sum_{s' \in \mathcal{S}} P_{a,t}(s, s')\Big(R_{a,t}(s, s') + V_{t+1}(s')\Big) \right],$$

$$\pi_t(s) = \arg\min_{a \in \{a_1, a_2\}} \left[\sum_{s' \in \mathcal{S}} P_{a,t}(s, s')\Big(R_{a,t}(s, s') + V_{t+1}(s')\Big) \right]$$

for $t = T-1, T-2, \ldots, 0$. The terms $P_{a,t}(s, s')$ are the transition probabilities from state s to state s' corresponding to discrete times t and $t + 0.25$ hours, when action a_1 or a_2 is chosen, i.e. when the power mode is set to either ω_1 or ω_2. They are computed as the matrix $q^b(t)$, parameterized with the power level defined by the actions a.

4.3 Numerical experiments

In order to reduce the number of parameters and simplify the results, we assume the weather is fixed at "sunny". This reduces the unexpected variability in power generation from occasional cloudy and hazy states but we retain the variability of the sun intensity during the day. With this simplification we consider two model parameterizations:

(1) The baseline, or "Parabolic" model, which uses the quadratic sun intensity function given in section 3.1 and assumes the arrival rate to be constant at 2 batches per quarter-hour time-slot, with mean batch size 10.
(2) "Ghirradelli" model with arrival rate and sun intensity functions given in sections 4.1.1 and 4.1.2. Mean batch size is again 10.

Both models use the same gamma service time distributions, described in section 4.1.3. For each of these parameterizations, we use either the primary metric or the deterring metric, which gives 4 scenarios for numerical comparison. For each scenario,

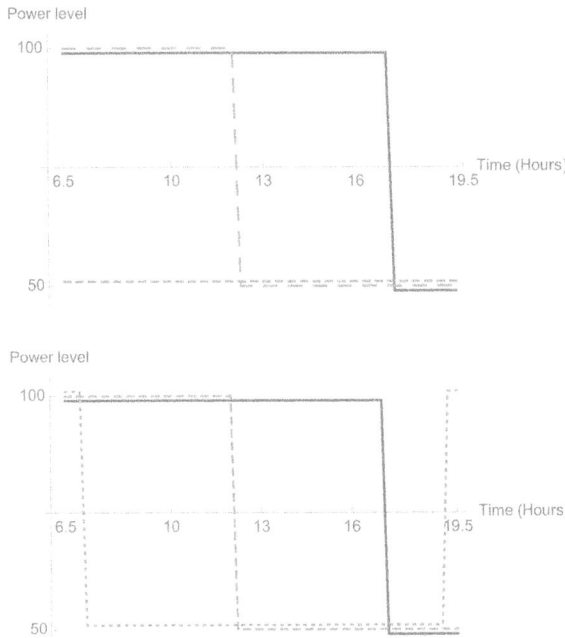

Figure 4: Policy choices made in the MDP for the Parabolic model with the primary (top) and deterring (bottom) metrics. The optimal power levels for states $\{\ell, h, f\}$ are shown in dotted green, dashed orange and solid blue, respectively, at each quarter-hour time point.

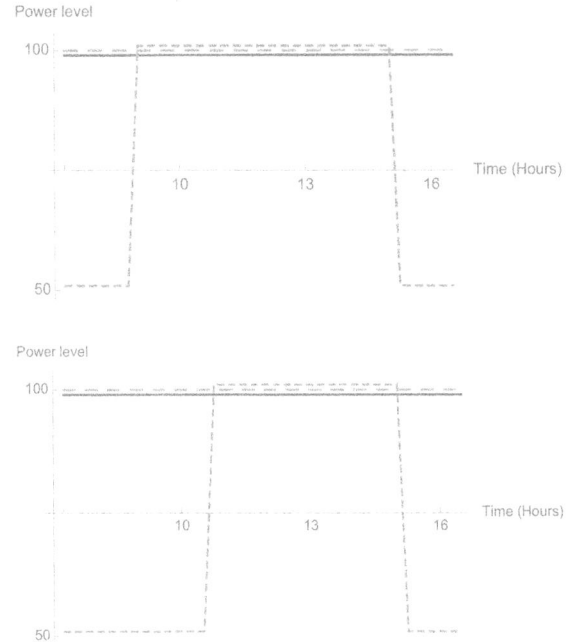

Figure 5: Policy choices made in the MDP for the Ghirradelli model with the primary (top) and deterring (bottom) metrics. The optimal power levels for states $\{\ell, h, f\}$ are shown in dotted green, dashed orange and solid blue, respectively, at each quarter-hour time point.

we want the MDP policy to select the next operating power level (50 or 100 watts) for each battery state in $\{\ell, h, f\}$ at every quarter-hour time point.

4.3.1 Parabolic model.

Figure 4 shows the optimal policy under the primary and deterring (higher penalty in state ℓ) metrics, respectively. In the former case, we see how the high power mode is used in the full battery state for most of the day up to a little after 5pm. Similarly the high battery state can use maximum power until about midday. However, the low battery state ℓ cannot transit to a higher charge level due to insufficient net energy coming from the sun. At a lower arrival rate of work for the device, the sun would supply enough energy to make transition from the low state possible, especially near the middle of the day. Then the ultimate penalty of being in the low state at the end of the day might be avoided.

The situation is similar with the deterring metric under our model parameterization. Notice that the unexpected visits of the low state to the high power mode at the beginning and end of the day are artifacts of equal value functions for each choice of power level: we choose the maximum in the event of such a tie.

4.3.2 Ghirradelli model.

Similarly to the parabolic case, Figure 5 shows the optimal policy under the primary and deterring (higher penalty in state ℓ) metrics, respectfully. These charts are somewhat less interesting since the system is very underloaded for most of the day. However, as solar intensity increases during the day, the low battery state is able to use the high power level and is open to the possibility of transition to a higher charge state. Further experiments allowing for alternate parameterizations and other workloads are in progress.

5　RELATED WORK

The work described in this paper builds on previous research from modeling energy and performance in queues, optimizing energy-performance metrics, and applying MDP for specific domains. Much of the research in energy-performance has been for wireless sensor networks where energy is a scarce resource [1]. Typically, device power can be changed and the focus is about reducing energy consumption so that the batteries last longer. For a survey of energy efficient wireless communication see [9]. Also in the wireless sensor application context, [7] uses MDPs to analyze energy-constrained sensors that can be recharged, and suggests optimal policies for recharging sensors based on battery charge levels and delay times. Energy-performance metrics are optimized for server farms in [4]. MDPs have been used extensively for many applications in other areas, including road maintenance, scheduling policies and reinforcement learning. The idea of adjusting a server's power, with nonlinear impact on the energy used, to increase service rate has been used in discrete-event simulation software to model interference or arbitrary blocking [5, 8]. However, we believe there have been few analytical models in the context of optimizing energy usage to meet some QoS requirement on performance.

6 CONCLUSION

In this paper we have explicitly incorporated energy consumption into the EP-queue model, facilitating a joint investigation of energy and performance. The numerical calculations involved are costly and we have introduced efficient approximations that allow the model's output to be used effectively in a real-time optimizer. This sets the power level at regular time points over the day to achieve optimum aggregated values of a chosen energy-performance metric such that a battery-charge level goal is met at the end of the day. By profiling real-world applications, the task service times at different queue lengths could be obtained accurately and used for finding optimal settings. We developed an MDP framework in a simple example with three sun states (which we reduced to one) and three battery charge levels. The two non-controllable factors are the amount of energy used by arrivals and the amount of energy supplied by the sun. As it stands, the model is highly simplified – in terms of the number of states, use of the power-up and down feature, small number of alternate power levels and efficiency of the implementation. The output of the model shows that the methodology is viable and that the best power setting can be identified and implemented in a timely fashion for dynamic optimization. A significant factor in model-design is always the particular metric that one wants to optimize. We considered two variants of an energy-performance metric – many more are possible, the "best" depending on *what* the application is and *who* is interested in optimizing it. Indeed it is often of most benefit to consider families of metrics; for example, in our case we might consider (in the notation of section 4.1.4) $\{(r^\alpha e^\beta)^{1/(\alpha+\beta)}\}$ for a range of α and β. The geometric mean that we used corresponds to $\alpha = \beta = 1$, and if response time or energy were considered the only relevant metric, we would have $\alpha = 1, \beta = 0$, respectively.

REFERENCES

[1] P. Agrawal, A. Kumar, J. Kuri, M. K. Panda, V. Navda, R. Ramjee, and V. N. Padmanabhan. Analytical models for energy consumption in infrastructure wlan stas carrying tcp traffic. In *Proceedings of the 2Nd International Conference on COMmunication Systems and NETworks*, COMSNETS'10, pages 10–19, Piscataway, NJ, USA, 2010. IEEE Press.

[2] Richard J. Boucherie and Nico van Dijk. *Markov Decision Processes in Practice*. International Series in Operations Research and Management Science. Springer International, 2017.

[3] Ryan Fergerson. *How to Calculate Solar Insolation*, 2017 (accessed January 11, 2018).

[4] Anshul Gandhi, Varun Gupta, Mor Harchol-Balter, and Michael A. Kozuch. Optimality analysis of energy-performance trade-off for server farm management. *Perform. Eval.*, 67(11):1155–1171, November 2010.

[5] Anshul Gandhi, Varun Gupta, Mor Harchol-Balter, and Michael A. Kozuch. Optimality analysis of energy-performance trade-off for server farm management. *Perform. Eval.*, 67(11):1155–1171, November 2010.

[6] Peter G. Harrison, Naresh M. Patel, and William J. Knottenbelt. Energy-performance trade-offs via the ep queue. *ACM Trans. Model. Perform. Eval. Comput. Syst.*, 1(2):6:1–6:31, June 2016.

[7] Sudip Misra, Rashmi Ranjan Rout, T. Raghu Vamsi Krishna, Patel Manish Kumar Manilal, and Mohammad S. Obaidat. Markov decision process-based analysis of rechargeable nodes in wireless sensor networks. In *Proceedings of the 2010 Spring Simulation Multiconference*, SpringSim '10, pages 97:1–97:7, San Diego, CA, USA, 2010. Society for Computer Simulation International.

[8] Priya Sehgal, Vasily Tarasov, and Erez Zadok. Optimizing energy and performance for server-class file system workloads. *Trans. Storage*, 6(3):10:1–10:31, September 2010.

[9] Iñaki Ucar, Carlos Donato, Pablo Serrano, Andres Garcia-Saavedra, Arturo Azcorra, and Albert Banchs. Revisiting 802.11 rate adaptation from energy consumption's perspective. In *Proceedings of the 19th ACM International Conference on Modeling, Analysis and Simulation of Wireless and Mobile Systems*, MSWiM '16, pages 27–34, New York, NY, USA, 2016. ACM.

A Declarative Approach for Performance Tests Execution in Continuous Software Development Environments

Vincenzo Ferme, Cesare Pautasso

Software Institute, Faculty of Informatics, USI Lugano, Switzerland

ABSTRACT

Software performance testing is an important activity to ensure quality in continuous software development environments. Current performance testing approaches are mostly based on scripting languages and framework where users implement, in a procedural way, the performance tests they want to issue to the system under test. However, existing solutions lack support for explicitly declaring the performance test goals and intents. Thus, while it is possible to express how to execute a performance test, its purpose and applicability context remain implicitly described. In this work, we propose a declarative domain specific language (DSL) for software performance testing and a model-driven framework that can be programmed using the mentioned language and drive the end-to-end process of executing performance tests. Users of the DSL and the framework can specify their performance intents by relying on a powerful goal-oriented language, where standard (e.g., load tests) and more advanced (e.g., stability boundary detection, and configuration tests) performance tests can be specified starting from templates. The DSL and the framework have been designed to be integrated into a continuous software development process and validated through extensive use cases that illustrate the expressiveness of the goal-oriented language, and the powerful control it enables on the end-to-end performance test execution to determine how to reach the declared intent.

ACM Reference Format:

Vincenzo Ferme, Cesare Pautasso. 2018. A Declarative Approach for Performance Tests Execution in Continuous Software Development Environments. In *ICPE '18: ACM/SPEC International Conference on Performance Engineering, April 9–13, 2018, Berlin, Germany.* ACM, New York, NY, USA, 12 pages. https://doi.org/10.1145/3184407.3184417

1 INTRODUCTION AND MOTIVATION

The Software is pervasively assembled across different businesses, by professional figures with different skills [22] and

with often-changing technologies [9]. Agile software development is widely used nowadays as a process to conceive, design, develop and operate complex software systems. Agile practices aim at reaching software deployment to production fast and often, to collect feedback from the users to be used in the next release of the same software, enabling continuous software development (CSD) [23].

To guarantee the quality of the software released to production, software development pipelines automation, and pervasive automated testing are vital for succeeding in releasing reliable software [12], so that people involved in the process can get continuous feedback. Performance testing is a kind of testing activity performed within development pipelines and by its complex nature, requires expertise to define performance tests, configure and manage the load infrastructures, the automated deployment of the software in different configurations, and the performance data collection and analysis. Many tools have been proposed to help the professional figures involved in the CSD process to implement performance testing, as for example to specify and execute performance tests (e.g., JMeter[1]), managing the load infrastructure (e.g., Faban[2]), to automate the deployment of the system under test (SUT) (e.g., Docker[3]), and comprehensive solutions to help users in the entire end-to-end performance test execution and results' analysis (e.g., DataMill [14]).

1.1 Context and Motivation

In this paper we focus in particular on CSD lifecycles, where the developed software is represented by (Micro)services, and we look at automating the execution of performance tests issued against the APIs, particularly REST APIs, exposed to the users. The main characteristics of this context are: (1) professional figures having diversified roles and heterogeneous performance knowledge [22], with control and responsibility on part of the developed services throughout their entire lifecycle from development to production; (2) parallel development of different services realizing the developed software, relying on one or more project repositories, and different branches [23] to version code and related artifacts; (3) continuous evolution of the developed software, by leveraging users' feedback and production data about application behavior; (4) automation of release pipelines, including code quality checks, build, test, packaging, delivery and in some cases deployment as well [23].

As argued by us [8], and by other researchers (e.g., [4]), execution of performance tests should be automated, flexible,

---

[1] http://jmeter.apache.org, last visited February 14, 2018
[2] http://faban.org, last visited February 14, 2018
[3] https://www.docker.com, last visited February 14, 2018

context- and business-aware, so that it can cope with the velocity introduced by modern life-cycles and contribute to the validation of the released software quality. Usually in CSD, users define performance tests that they might want to continuously see working, and that they automate in terms of automating the analysis and the process to collect the data for that analysis. Then they define another set of performance tests that is not always continuously executed, based on a model they have (i.e., requirements, design, implementation diagrams, etc.) to explore the system, learn from it and maybe decide to automate other analyses to be able to communicate derived information in a better way.

While for most of the available tools and solutions, users define performance tests using scripts or code, we argue that in this context a declarative model-driven approach [8], exposed to the users by means of a domain specific language (DSL), could help to control the end-to-end process of executing performance tests, by making the purpose and applicability contexts of defined performance tests explicit. Empowered by the DSL, different professional figures can express their performance intents in terms of performance goals, for example, defined by more expert performance people. They can then rely on an extensible framework that can automate and control the end-to-end execution of tests, by following the directives specified in the model behind the DSL definition.

1.2 Requirements

Given the described context, we identified the following requirements the proposed approach embraces:

(1) *declarative* specification of performance tests, performance goals and SUT deployment and configuration;

(2) *automated and model-driven execution* of the end-to-end performance test lifecycle;

(3) *extensibility* of the DSL and the automation infrastructure, to cope with evolving needs in CSD, and custom requirements of different contexts and applications.

We propose two main contributions to enhance the state of the art in this context. The first contribution is a declarative DSL for performance testing (Sect. 3), allowing the users to declare the goal of the specified performance test, as well as control the deployment configuration of the SUT. The second one is a model-driven framework (Sect. 4) that can be programmed using the mentioned DSL, and automate the end-to-end execution of performance tests, by executing all the activities that are needed to answer to the performance intent of the user, declared as a goal of the performance test.

A declarative approach to performance tests execution, implemented in a DSL and a framework, to specify the intent of performance tests, and to describe the SUT deployment and configuration enables the production of shared artifacts that can be exchanged among development team members with different expertise and profiles. We opted for a declarative DSL, so that users can rely on a domain model closer to the performance testing terminology, and the code that defines how to execute the test is actually built into

the framework that represents the runtime of the proposed DSL. We do not want the users to necessarily care about how the actual performance test execution is implemented, but we want them to be able to define performance activities and control the execution of the performance tests. By reducing the needs for the users to write code, the responsibility of translating the business domain into a program shifts from the programmer to the interpreter of the DSL. This has the benefit that the translation is consolidated in one single point (the interpreter of the DSL) and can be verified or even proven to be correct. By abstracting, the expressiveness of the language compared to imperative code is reduced, because only specific concepts are integrated into the DSL. For this reason we made the DSL, and the model-driven framework actually driving the execution of performance tests, open and extensible to new use cases and different needs.

The rest of the paper is structured as follows: in Sect. 2 we present related work on declarative performance testing and DSLs, in Sect. 3 we present the proposed declarative DSL, in Sect. 4 the model-driven framework based on the same and in Sect. 5 use cases in defining and executing performance tests based on the presented DSL and the framework, in Sect. 6 we conclude the paper and briefly present planned future work.

2 RELATED WORK

Declarative Software Performance Testing - Declarative software performance engineering, part of which is also related to performance testing, has been presented as part of the DECLARE project[4] by Walter et al. [20]. The DECLARE project "envisions to reduce the current abstraction gap between the level on which performance-relevant concerns are formulated and the level on which performance evaluations are actually executed", thus dealing with the challenges related to the heterogeneity in performance expertise of software practitioners. The DECLARE project focuses mainly on enabling the possibility of declaratively querying performance knowledge that has been collected and modelled by other systems, while the focus of our work is in applying declarative approaches for performance test specification and automated execution. In this context, Westermann [21] present the concept of goal-driven performance testing, mainly related to smart exploration of the performance spaces for different configurations of software systems (i.e., the space described by all the possible combinations of the configuration variables). This is realized with a DSL, and a runtime framework for automatic performance test execution. The main difference compared to our approach is the context of application, and the focus of the declarative goal-driven definitions, than in our case are related to performance testing of container-packaged (Micro)services

---

[4]http://www.dfg-spp1593.de/declare, last visited February 14, 2018

within CSD lifecycles, and open to answer different performance intents users might have. Other relevant work proposing both a DSL and a framework, are Cloud Work Bench [17], Crawler [5], CloudPerf [13] and Jagger[5], tools for benchmarking the performance of the services offered by cloud providers. The first three tools propose a declarative DSL tailored to Cloud benchmarking, then targeting a different domain than the one proposed in the context of this work. Although Jagger's DSL allows users to declaratively specify success criteria of tests, in our goal-oriented approach we additionally support describing the intent of performance tests.

Other related work propose specific approaches to answer different kinds of performance intents, as for example capacity planning [18], and performance optimization in the presence of constraints [6]. We consider these techniques as declarative approaches to performance testing, because the discussed solutions target specific performance goals to be answered in a (semi)-automated way.

Performance Testing Tools in CSD - Experimentation and continuous automated checking of performance quality criteria, are important activities in CSD environments. Performance experimentation, and experimentation in general, is discussed in different research and industry work as an important activity in continuous development, e.g., by Google with Vizier [11], AutoPerf [1], DataMill [14] and the approaches by Omar et al. [15], Westermann [21] and Cloud Work Bench [17]. They propose languages and framework to help users simplifying exploratory test definition, automating performance test execution, and ensuring rigorous performance data analysis. The solution we propose builds on existing tools, and integrates them to achieve full control over the entire performance testing lifecycle with a declarative DSL.

Different solutions have been proposed for continuous automated checking of performance quality criteria. Blazemeter[6] integrates standard performance testing tools in CSD, by providing the load infrastructure, and a software as a service platform on which automatically schedule and execute performance tests. Other tools rely on performance management platforms[7] to collect performance metrics and validate them over time, others apply live testing [10, 16] for incremental roll-out of new versions of (Micro)service applications according to their performance behaviour. Others continuously check for regressions of different software performance metrics [3, 19] after every set of relevant commits. Overall the plethora of solutions is rich and diversified, and in this work we discuss how to integrate them at a higher level of abstraction with a declarative DSL allowing the user to specify their performance intent, and then automate them in a framework for automating the goal-driven end-to-end process of performance test execution.

3 DECLARATIVE PERFORMANCE DSL

The DSL is used to specify the intent of performance tests and control their entire end-to-end execution process in a declarative manner, and it is particularly tailored to container-packaged (Micro)service systems. In general a DSL for providing the specification of goal-driven performance tests should provide at least the specification of load functions, workloads, simulated users, test data, test bed management and analysis of performance data [2, 21]. Our DSL provides the mentioned features, and adds a goal-oriented, and declarative specification of performance intents as well. The declarative nature of the DSL, enables the users to start from provided templates for defining performance tests. They can then update the tests according to changing requirements, or dispose them in favour of new specifications. This is possible without the need of rebuilding the test or changing code, but by manually or programmatically updating its specification.

3.1 Meta-Model: Overview

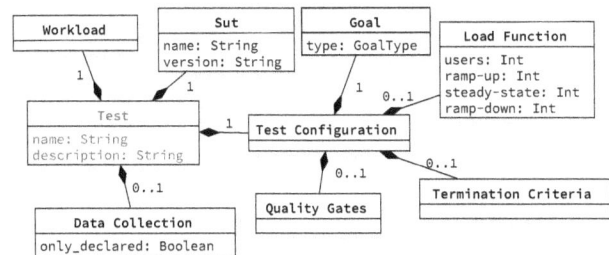

Figure 1: **DSL: The Test Meta-Model**

The main entity in the language is *test*, which as shown in Fig. 1 groups together the *workload*, the *sut*, the *data collection* and the test *configuration*. As part of the configuration, users can indicate the *goal*, the corresponding *load function* as well as the criteria to drive the automated execution of the test needed to achieve the goal: *termination criteria* to control conditions to declare the test completed, and *quality gates* to determine if wanted quality criteria have been achieved or not by the SUT.

Additionally, the user can specify other core performance concepts, such as: 1) the *workload*, in terms of named sets of operations as well as parameters about the way to mix those sets of operations together with the *inter operations timing* specification; 2) details on the *SUT* such as the target endpoint of the test, deployment time configuration settings and specifications about the machines where to deploy the different services realizing the SUT. The actual deployment descriptor of the SUT can be specified using the Docker Cloud and Compose standards[8]; 3) *data collection services* to enable, so that client-side and server-side performance data can be collected.

[5]https://jagger.griddynamics.net, last visited February 14, 2018
[6]Blazemeter - https://www.blazemeter.com, and Taurus - http://gettaurus.org, last visited February 14, 2018
[7]http://rigor.com, last visited February 14, 2018

[8]Docker Cloud - https://docs.docker.com/docker-cloud/apps/stack-yaml-reference/ and Docker Compose - https://docs.docker.com/compose/compose-file/, last visited February 14, 2018

```
name: The test name
description: The test description # Optional
configuration:
    goal:
    load_function:  # Optional IF specified in goal
    termination_criteria:  # Optional
    quality_gates:  # Optional
sut:
workload:
data_collection:  # Optional
```

Listing 1: **DSL: The Test YAML Format Overview**

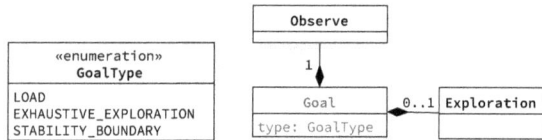

Figure 2: **DSL: The Goal Meta-Model**

In Listing 1 we present the actual format, omitting some details, of the DSL the user is writing to specify a test using the YAML[9] syntax, that is both human and machine readable.

3.2   Meta-Model: Main Entities

Goal - The *goal* is part of the test *configuration* and is used to declaratively specify the users' performance intent by relying on given performance goals (Fig. 2), such as executing a load test or exploring the performance or the stability of the application in a given configuration space.

We defined a taxonomy of goals [8], where we distinguish goals by their different levels of abstractions: meta goals (e.g., comparing the performance of different systems using a benchmark), goals (e.g., capacity planning, stability boundary testing) and base goals (e.g., load test, configuration test). The current main focus of the DSL is to support standard performance tests, such as load test, and exploratory performance testing, thus the goal types currently provided by the language are the `load`, and `exhaustive_exploration` (similar to configuration test) base goals, and the `stability_boundary` goal. We decided to support exploratory testing, because we, and other researchers [10, 11], argue that in CSD, with continuous evolution and feedback, it is very important to be able to explore performance of different system's configuration or alternative solutions at any moment in the development lifecycle, to gain insights on the behaviour of the application.

Depending on the selected goal it might be necessary to specify also other information to automate the test execution, e.g., adding an exploration strategy. The `load` goal is a standard load test and does not require additional configuration. The `exhaustive_exploration` and the `stability_boundary`

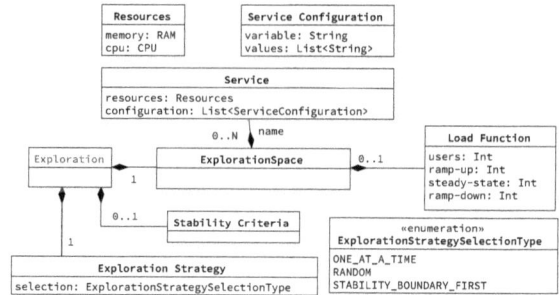

Figure 3: **DSL: The Exploration Meta-Model**

goals execute multiple experiments by exploring the *exploration_space* according to some *exploration_strategy* (e.g., randomly or with a binary search). For the `stability_boundary` it is also required to specify the `stability_criteria`, where the user can define stability conditions using the same semantics of quality gates, presented later in this section.

Exploration Space - The *exploration_space* defines the variables that can be changed between experiments and their possible values (Fig. 3). The currently available variables can be used for varying the load function, and the configuration of one or more services realizing the SUT or the resources allocated to them. The user can directly specify the values to set over different experiments, or specify ranges to navigate with given step functions, that can, for example, apply addition, subtraction, multiplier, division and power for a numeric variable.

We support changes in the load function by number of users, and the ramp-up, steady-state and ramp-down. This is useful when the goal is to explore how the system behaves under different loads. The configuration through environment variables consists of any *variable-values* pair specified by the user. For resources we currently support setting the CPU and RAM allocation, however, these can be extended to other resources supported by the Docker Cloud and Compose standards, e.g., i/o speed as well as other container orchestration and management frameworks (e.g., Kubernetes[10]). The user decides how to traverse the *exploration_space*, by selecting an *exploration_strategy*. Each strategy determines the order in which different experiments are executed to achieve the goal of the test. Currently supported are the `one-at-a-time` strategy, that select the experiment one after the other following the different dimensions of the *exploration_space*, `random` strategy that schedules the experiments in random order, and `stability-boundary-first` strategy that uses a binary search to trace the stability boundary. Other strategies can rely on a statistical sampling approach to reduce the number of experiments required to observe the performance over a representative subset of the exploration space [21].

Termination Criteria - The exploration, and in general a performance test execution might incur into failures, and last for a long amount of time. Thus the *termination_criteria* are

---

[9]http://www.yaml.org, last visited February 14, 2018

[10]https://kubernetes.io, last visited February 14, 2018

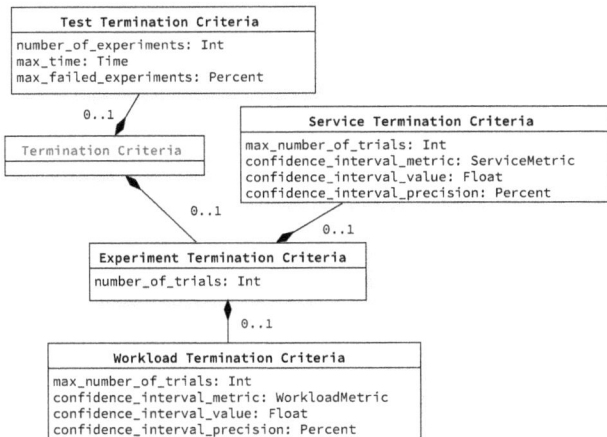

Figure 4: **DSL: The Termination Criteria Meta-Model**

used to determine when the test execution process can be considered to be completed (Fig. 4). The termination criteria apply to different entities, namely: the entire test and the navigation of the exploration space, and the different trials of the experiments, i.e., repeated experiment executions used to collect more precise measurements and to cope with the intrinsic variability of performance, that get executed as part of the test.

The currently supported test termination criteria are: a fixed limit on the number of experiments to be executed, the maximum amount of test running time (`max_time`), and the maximum allowed number of experiments marked as failed (using a percentage of the overall number of experiments to be executed) without providing any result (e.g., in case of unexpected errors in the deployment of the SUT or the impossibility of issuing the workload) or due to failures in passing the *quality gates.*

We support two different experiment termination criteria, which control the number of trials. Thus we support the possibility to statically specify a fixed upper bound on the number of trials to be executed for each experiment, or a target confidence interval (c.i.) to be achieved for one metric of interest on a workload or a service at a given precision, and thus dynamically determine the number of trials to be executed to reach the given c.i. up to the given maximum number of trials. In general, if multiple termination criteria are specified, they are all applied and the test/experiment terminates as soon as one criteria is satisfied.

The final state of the test/experiment depends on whether the termination criteria corresponds to describing a condition under which the goal has been reached or a condition that represents the impossibility of reaching the goal. For example, if the goal is to perform a given number of experiments or trials, reaching the *number_of_experiments, number_of_trials* will result in a successful test or experiment. However, if it was not possible to reach the required confidence interval and instead the upper limit on the number of trials was reached, this results in the failure of the experiment. Likewise, if the duration exceeds the *max_time* or the

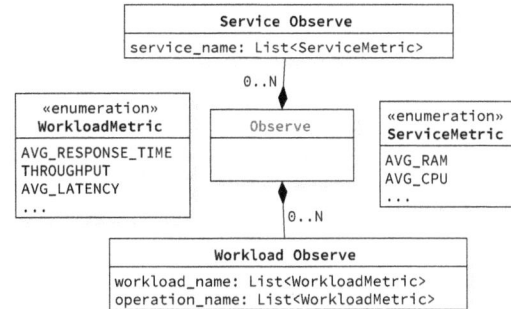

Figure 5: **DSL: The Observe Meta-Model**

number of failures reaches the *max_failed_experiment* limit, the corresponding test will be marked as failed.

Observe - The performance metrics of interest for the test are enumerated within the *observe* entity (Fig. 5). Metrics can be observed on the client-side and the server-side, by relying on the collected performance data.

Client-side metrics can be observed on the entire *workload* and on its operations. Some available metrics are: response time, latency, throughput for each single operation and for the entire workload, for each trial and aggregated at experiment level, as well as time series over the entire load function time. Server-side metrics can be observed on specific services realizing the SUT, and some available metrics are related to: RAM, CPU, IO, network utilization. SUT specific metrics can be defined as well, and integrated in the framework. Other metrics can be computed on top of logs collected from the SUT. On all the metrics we also make available descriptive statistics, and statistical tests to check for the homogeneity of the collected data (e.g., coefficient of variation[11], and Levene's test[12]), that is for example useful to validate whether the collected data over multiple trials of the same experiment exposes the same behaviour. The user can observe specific metric (e.g., throughput) or statistics (e.g., average CPU utilization), or the entire set of metric and statistics computed on an entity (e.g., all the metrics and descriptive statistics of CPU).

Quality Gates - Quality gates help with integrating the tests in CSD, by enabling the possibility to express performance requirements for the SUT, for the current defined test. They declare which are the successful and failure conditions of a test so that these can be checked automatically (Fig. 6).

They currently include success conditions (i.e., conditions that lead to mark a test as successful) on: all the observable metrics, and relative aggregated statistics, on any of the services realizing the SUT, and on the workload issued to the system, to validate that the issued workload satisfied the specified requirements. The conditions (one of $>$, $<$, $>=$, $<=$, $=$) that can be specified on the metrics allow comparing the value of a metric or a statistic with a static value,

---

[11]http://www.ats.ucla.edu/stat/mult_pkg/faq/general/coefficient_of_variation.htm, last visited February 14, 2018
[12]http://www.itl.nist.gov/div898/handbook/eda/section3/eda35a.htm, last visited February 14, 2018

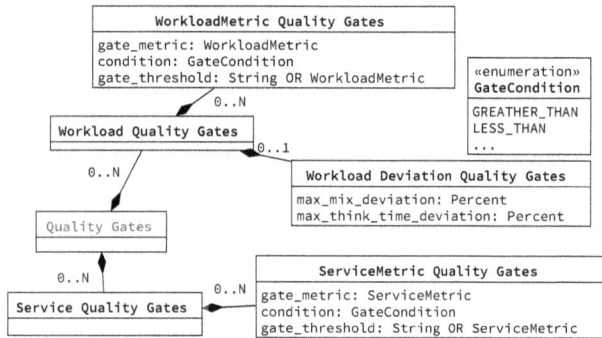

Figure 6: **DSL: The Quality Gates Meta-Model**

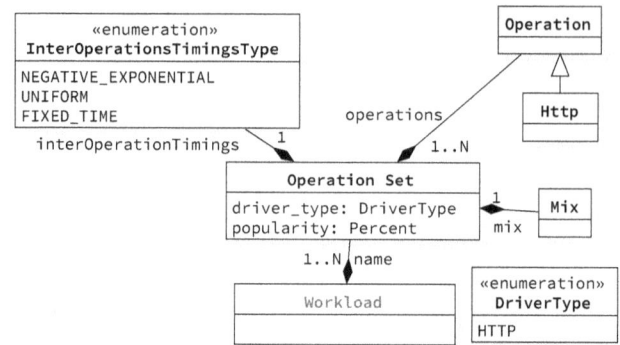

Figure 7: **DSL: The Workload Meta-Model**

or with another metric or statistic. If more than one condition is specified, they are all evaluated and in order for a test to be considered successful, all the conditions have to be satisfied.

The conditions that can be specified on the issued workload, also enable the user to specify the maximum allowed deviation from the defined mix and the maximum allowed deviation from the specified think time for the simulated users. The YAML format depends on the actual mix that is selected by the user. The maximum allowed deviation is relevant to account for possible errors in the interactions with the SUT, because erroneous interactions are not counted as part of the results, thus introducing variations in the specified mix or think time.

Currently all the quality gates are verified after the execution of an experiment, thus are applied to each experiment, and consequently to each test if the gates are defined on a test level metric.

Quality gates complement termination criteria. Quality gates are evaluated after successful executions of experiments to determine whether the test succeeded. Termination criteria instead control and act on the test execution process and determine the final state of execution of experiments as a function of the outcome of the corresponding trials. They are also used to limit the execution time of tests with bounds on the maximum runtime or maximum number of failures.

Workload - The workload entity (Fig. 7) allows the user to specify the different named sets of operations to be executed against the SUT during the performance tests. The user can specify multiple named sets of operations, representing different utilization scenarios of the SUT that have to be executed in parallel. An example for an e-commerce SUT could be a set of operations named "clients" (currently mainly HTTP requests to the SUT) simulating clients browsing the catalogue and buying goods, and a set of operations named "admins" of website admins adding new items to the catalogue. The actual format used to describe them in the DSL is omitted for space reason.

For each set of operations it is possible to specify its popularity, representing the percentage of requests that should be issued to the SUT from the given named workload. Within a single set of operations, it is possible to indicate how to mix

the operations and the `inter_operation_timings`. We rely on Faban[13] and its driver meta-model as performance test execution framework (Sect. 4), and we expose in the DSL all the supported mixes of operations and `inter_operation_timings` Faban supports. These are: `fixed-sequence` defining a fixed order over the operations; `flat-mix` randomly deciding the next operation based on the corresponding probabilities; and `flat-sequence-mix` a combination of `fixed-sequence` and `flat-mix` that allows the user to specify a random selection of fixed sequences, as well as `matrix-mix` that implements a Markov-chain model and select the next operation based on the current operation and the provided probability. More details are available on the Faban documentation, and we omit them here for space reason. The supported `inter_operation_timings` are: `negative-exponential`, `uniform` or `fixed-time`. The `inter_operation_timings` also require configurations, omitted because not central for this work.

Sut - By relying on the integration of the DSL runtime with Docker technologies, the user can also control the SUT configuration and deployment in a declarative way as modeled in Fig. 8. The deployment descriptor of the SUT is currently specified using the Docker Cloud and Compose Standard, and in the DSL is possible to override some resource settings and configurations, and decide which services of the SUT should be deployed on which server (identified using an alias), other than specify a name and a version for the SUT. This way it is possible to reuse the deployment descriptor across different tests.

The user can also decide which service is the target of the defined test and its endpoint, and how to determine that the targeted service is ready to accept requests (currently a regular expression matched against the target service logs). Setting custom configurations and deciding which services to deploy on which server, allow the user to have control on the way the services of the SUT has to be started, for example to rely on stubbing mechanism that might be available in the services, so that to isolate the service from dependent services (e.g., to avoid cyclic dependencies) for the performance test.

---

[13]http://faban.org, last visited February 14, 2018

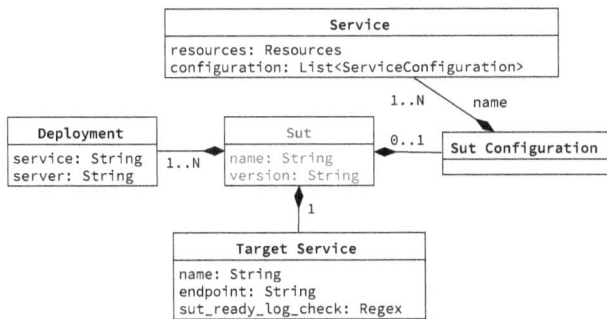

Figure 8: **DSL: The SUT Meta-Model**

Data Collection - In order to compute the metrics to be observed, data collector services need to be available to collect the raw performance data on which the computed metrics are based on. On the client-side we rely on Faban to collect workload performance metrics, thus a Faban collector service can be specified, and optionally configured. On the server-side we provide data collector services for server and service resource utilization, service logs, data on the file system produced by the services, and data stored in databases. The list can be easily extended by integrating new data collector services, according to the user's needs. For many data collector services we provide defaults, for others we require the user to configure the collector so that it can access the data (e.g., the database data collector services require configuration to be able to access the database, and collect the wanted data). To be able to collect all the data required to respond to current and future users need, by default all collector that do not require configurations are enabled on all the services.

3.3 DSL Library and Static Validation

The DSL has been designed to be integrated in CSD, and other than enabling the language with specific entities related to the context, we also make sure that the meta-model behind the DSL can be utilized within those contexts. In CSD different tools are employed to build and control the development and deployment of systems [9], thus being able to access the language features within those tools is fundamental for extensibility. For this reason, we implemented a library exposing the DSL meta-model in a functional way to other programs, so that other systems can parse a DSL definition serialized in YAML, or can rely on a Builder interface to create an instance of the meta-model to be submitted to the framework. By leveraging the meta-model presented in Sect. 3, the library ensures the definition is syntactically and semantically valid, before an instance of a test can be instantiated. This is very important in the context of performance testing and CSD, because performance tests usually require a fair amount of time to be executed. So everything that can be verified statically, must be verified statically, and erroneous test definitions can be spotted early. The meta-model definition supports by design syntactic validation, by ensuring entities can be parsed only if correctly structured

and if using the data types we enforce in the model. For what concern semantic validation, we ensure that the definition of the test is consistent, by verifying that each single entity is defined in a semantically correct way (e.g., data collectors requiring configurations are specified if some metrics computed on top of performance data collected by those collectors are declared as observed by the user), and that the entire definition has not conflicting statements (e.g., we assert that if a test defines an exploration on the load function, then the same is not also defined as part of the configuration).

4 CONTINUOUS, END-TO-END PERFORMANCE TEST AUTOMATION

The DSL, and its library, are paired with a model-driven framework which drives the end-to-end lifecycle of the performance test execution embedded into a continuous software delivery process, presented in this section.

4.1 End-to-end Performance Test Automation

The framework is designed to completely assist the user in all the activities that need to be executed for automating performance tests execution, such as test scheduling, handling of load and SUT deployment infrastructure, issuing the workload, deploying the SUT, collecting client- and server-side data, undeploying the SUT and data analysis. The overall process of end-to-end performance test execution automation as described with the DSL consists of three phases: exploration, execution and analysis.

Exploration - The exploration phase handles the way a performance test is executed in order to reach its goal, and it is the central phase to the lifecycle. Before the test starts, following the test definition described in the DSL, the exploration phase handles the necessary preparations before the performance test is executed in order to reach the goal specified by the user. After the test definition has been statically verified for correctness, based on the goal, one or more experiment definitions are generated together with the corresponding SUT deployment descriptor, and a given number of trials are scheduled for execution.

Given its central role, after the execution of each experiment trial, the exploration phase is also in charge of taking action based on the results of the analysis phase. The exploration phase receives all the metrics declared in the `observe` DSL entity, so that termination criteria and quality gates can be evaluated to decide how to continue the exploration, or failures data about something that went wrong during the execution (Sect. 4.3).

Execution - Deploying and running a performance test is done in the execution phase. The first step of the execution phase concerns the SUT deployment. To deploy the SUT we use Docker[14] containers - a lightweight virtualization platform. The SUT deployment descriptor includes both configuration environment variables and resource constraints, and by altering the specification we are able to automatically define performance tests that involve system and resource

---

[14]Docker - https://www.docker.com, last visited February 14, 2018

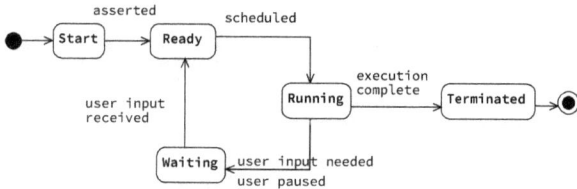

Figure 9: **Test Lifecycle - High-Level States**

configuration. Before starting each trial, a new deployment of the SUT is performed, to ensure that the test starting conditions are always the same for all the trials. After deployment, the experiment execution starts according to the defined workload. The framework takes also care of starting the data collection services needed to collect performance data relevant for the test.

Analysis - In the analysis phase performance data produced by the experiments is collected and analyzed. The computed metrics and statistics are provided to the users for analysis, and fed back in the exploration phase so that decisions on how to continue the exploration can be made.

In this work we mainly focus on the automation of the exploration phase, thus more details are provided on this phase in Sect. 4.2 and Sect. 4.3. For the automation of the execution and the analysis phases, and the overall architecture of the framework, one could refer to our previous work [7].

4.2 Performance Test Exploration Lifecycle

The exploration phase is at the core of declarative goal-driven performance test automation execution. To drive the automated execution, goal exploration, and failures handling of performance tests, we defined a lifecycle implemented through a state machine. The complete lifecycle is realized by a test lifecycle, driving the exploration of the goal, and an experiment lifecycle, driving the execution of the different trials of a single experiment that is scheduled.

Fig. 9 depicts the high-level states of the test lifecycle. The high-level states are inspired by the scheduling of processes in an operating system: start (new), ready, running, waiting and terminated. The start state is reached after the test has been verified as syntactically and semantically correct, and setup the framework to be ready for test execution (i.e., stores relevant data to be accessible in next states). If no errors happen in the start state, the test is moved to the ready state and is available to be scheduled for execution by the framework. If errors are encountered, the stored data are deleted, and the user is alerted that the test can not be scheduled for execution. When there are resource available for execution, the test is moved from the ready state to the running state, where the actual execution of the test exploration and experiment execution happen. The user, or the system, could decide to pause the test. In this case the test is moved to the waiting state, waiting for user input before proceeding. Once the execution of the test is completed, it is moved to the terminated state, that represent a final

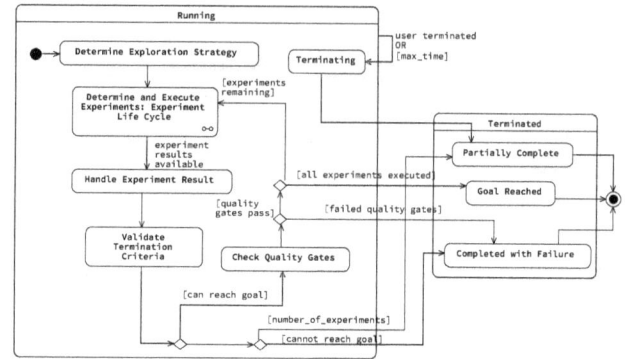

Figure 10: **Test Lifecycle - Running and Terminated States**

test state after which the state of the test can change only if re-started by the user. The running state is the most rich and complex one, thus we define different substates, that are presented in Fig. 10. The same figure also reports the possible final terminated substates a test can end in. The running state is divided into several substates: determine exploration strategy, determine and execute experiments, handle experiment result, validate termination criteria, check quality gates, and terminating. The different states of the state machine, are mapped to the DSL entities, and represent the execution semantics driven by the declarative specification described in Sect. 3. The determine exploration strategy state is used to set a predefined *exploration strategy* for experiment selection in case the user did not specify one in the test. In the determine and execute experiments the experiment to be executed next is determined by the selection strategy. After the selection, the control is handed over to the experiment lifecycle, that we do not show for space reason. The experiment lifecycle handles the execution of trials, and re-execution of the same in case of failures, as described in Sect. 4.3. As per the test lifecycle, also for the experiment lifecycle, termination criteria defined in the test definition are verified, after each trial complete the execution. The possible final sub states for the experiment *terminated* state are: *completed*, when the execution complete as expected, *error* if an error incurs in generating the experiment bundle or in setting up the experiment on Faban for execution, *failure* when some termination criteria can not be reached before the end of the execution (e.g., the expected confidence interval at the wanted precision can not be reached within the defined maximum number of trials) or some unexpected failures happen during the execution (Sect. 4.3), or *aborted* if the execution is aborted due to reaching time based termination criteria in the test lifecycle. Once the experiment has executed, the SUT undeployed, performance data collected and the result, e.g., execution status and metrics, of the execution is available, the handle experiment result state ensures that the result is retrieved and saved for easy access in other parts of the lifecycle, e.g., for use in the check quality gates state. If the data is not received within a given maximum time, e.g., due to errors in data analysis, then the lifecycle is moved to the next state that evaluates the absence of data and ends the test as *partially completed*. After the result is collected, the termination criteria are verified in the `validate termination criteria` state. If the termination criteria verification stops the experiment before the wanted number of experiment is executed, then according to the actual termination criteria the final terminated inner state is *partially complete* or *completed with failure*. The *partially complete* state can also be reached if the user decides to abort the execution or if a time based termination criteria is triggered. If the termination criteria do not stop the execution, then the quality gates are evaluated. If the quality gates pass, then the next experiment, if present, is executed, or the test is moved into the *goal reached* state. If the quality gates fail, the test is moved in the *completed with failure* state and the reason of the failure is embedded as part of the state so that it can be reported to the user.

4.3 Failures Handling

The end-to-end performance test execution can incur in several failures that are unexpected, even though we make sure to statically verify that the test definition in the DSL is syntactically and semantically correct. As performance tests often require a significant amount of execution time, automatic failure handling is crucial in CSD, and failures should therefore be handled as soon as possible. We defined a taxonomy of possible runtime errors that we could encounter during the execution.

The taxonomy covers all the cases we were able to identify, even though it can not yet be considered exhaustive. The taxonomy differentiates between failures that can incur on the three different levels: test level, experiment level and trial level. On the test level a failure happens when the data provided by the results of an experiment are not sufficient to reach the goal (e.g., because the experiments can not be successfully executed), and therefore the test is terminated prematurely. In the cases where a failure on the experiment level does not impact the overall goal, the framework on the other hand continue with the exploration. Experiment level failures are caused by trial failures and stops the execution of additional trials for the given experiment since these are also expected to fail. The trial failures are directly related to the execution of a performance test. It can either be a failure that directly causes an experiment failure since additional executions would likely cause the same behavior (e.g., wrong specified endpoint, or fatal errors in deploying and verifying the SUT as ready), or the trial can be re-executed (if the re-execution does not succeed after a given number or retries, then an experiment failure is triggered) if the failure was more of a random nature. Currently, the presence of failures in verified after each trial completes its execution.

4.4 Open-source Framework as a Service

The framework, as the DSL, has been designed to be integrated in CSD environments. It is open-source[15], extensible

by design and deployed as a service exposing REST APIs. The framework is meant to be used by users for exploratory testing and for automated execution of tests in CSD. Users might want to execute tests at any moment in time, and for this we provide a command line client interacting with the APIs. When tests are automated in CSD, another entry point for test scheduling are other tools in the CSD lifecycle, such as continuous integration systems. These systems can interact with the framework using the same REST APIs as the command line client, and issue pre-defined performance test definitions serialized in YAML, or performance tests built on the fly using the DSL library given the current needs of the CSD process.

The framework is developed to take performance test execution requests, and automate the process of execution up to the point in which users input is required (i.e., when results are ready or failures happen in the process). When executing performance tests, especially in CSD, traceability and reproducibility of what happens is very important, also to improve the process. For this reason the framework logs all the steps and decisions taken during the test execution, such that the process is transparent and inspectable by the users.

5 USE CASES

In this section we present different real-world use cases from our experience in applying the framework in different research contexts. The use cases are meant to show: 1) how the declarative approach implemented in the DSL, and its expressiveness, enables different performance testing activities (use cases: Load Test, Exhaustive Exploration Test, Stability Boundary Test); 2) how the automation framework is configured using the DSL's meta-model, and control the end-to-end lifecycle of test executions (use cases: Termination Criteria, Quality Gates).

We omit final results showing the outcome of the use case execution fro space reason, as the focus of the paper is on the declarative performance test definition using the DSL, and the test execution by the framework.

Load Test - This use case shows how the user can specify a load test using the provided DSL, that for example could be set to be executed continuously as part of nightly builds of the SUT. The SUT we refer to in this use case is realized by two services, one named *catalogue_ws* and a second one named *dbms*. The services are connected and represent a REST Web service handling an items catalogue and the DBMS it relies on. The user's intent is to issue a load test, with the defined load function, and observe some defined metrics, under a given SUT configuration provided using the model presented in Fig. 8, and a given workload where the simulated users interacting with the SUT browse the catalogue, that we omit for space reason. The user is interested in observing the response time metrics for the browse workload, as well as metrics related to the RAM and CPU utilization for both of the services. Listing 2 presents the YAML format for the test specification, with omitted details that are not central to the use case. When the framework executes a load

---
[15]The BenchFlow framework GitHub repository - https://github.com/benchflow, last visited February 14, 2018

```
configuration:
  goal:
    type: load_test
    observe:
      workload:
        browse: [response_time]
      services:
        catalogue_ws: [ram, cpu]
        dbms: [ram, cpu]
    load_function:
      users: 1000
      ramp-up: 2m
      steady-state: 10m
      ramp-down: 2m
```

Listing 2: **Load Test: Metrics and Load Function**

test, only one experiment is executed by the lifecycle presented in Fig. 10, thus after the experiment terminates the execution, the test is concluded. In the case of this example, since no termination criteria nor quality gates are defined, the test ends up in the *goal reached* state, unless failures happen during the execution (for which 3 trials are scheduled by default) or in retrieving the test result, in which cases the final state would be *completed with failure*. The framework implements some default failure handling mechanism, as presented in Sect. 4.3, so that to avoid wasting resources to execute tests that can not reach the final goal. If the test can not reach the final goal its execution is stopped, independently of eventually defined termination criteria or quality gates. After a successful execution, the user is provided with access to the metrics declared in the *observe* section of the test definition and relevant statistical tests to help the user investigate the quality of the obtained results. The user can also optionally access artifacts generated during the automation process, and all the collected raw data, for transparency and reproducibility.

Exhaustive Exploration Test - In this use case we show how a user can define an exploratory test, that performs an exhaustive exploration of the described performance space.

The user's intent could be to learn about the performance of the developed system when setting different configurations and resource allocations. Listing 3 presents the YAML specification responding to this goal, where we omit the specification of the *load function* and the *observed* metrics, that are the same as in Listing 2. By relying on the declarative approach provided in the DSL, the user specifies that she wants to explore the performance in all the 48 configurations in the exploration space defined by the Cartesian product of all the values of the specified exploration variables: *NUM_SERVICE_THREAD* as configuration setting of the catalogue_ws service, *memory*, and CPU as resource settings for the dbms service. As shown in Listing 3 the user can rely on a *step* based definition, as she is doing for exploring the *memory*, to define the way to determine the values

```
configuration:
  goal:
    type: exhaustive_exploration
    exploration:
      exploration_space:
        services:
          catalogue_ws:
            configuration:
              NUM_SERVICE_THREAD: [12, 24]
          dbms:
            resources:
              memory:
                range: [2GB, 24GB]
                step: +2GB
              cpu: [4, 8]
      exploration_strategy:
        selection: one-at-a-time
```

Listing 3: **Exhaustive Exploration Test: Exploration Space**

to explore in the exploration space, that in the case of the example includes all the values between 2GB and 24GB with a step of 2GB.

When the goal declared in Listing 3 is executed by the lifecycle presented in Fig. 10, all the experiments in the exploration space are scheduled one after the other, following the *one-at-a-time* selection strategy that executes the experiments in the order they are defined in the exploration space. In this use case we can see how simple would be to change the way experiments are selected, to explore the space in different ways and getting first results that belongs to other regions of the space. If a user would like to do so, it is a matter of changing the value of the *exploration_strategy.selection* setting to the other strategies that are made available by the framework, or custom strategies added by the user. As in the load test use case, since no termination criteria nor quality gates are specified, if there are no failures the test terminates in the *goal reached* state after all the experiments have been executed, otherwise it terminates in the *terminated with failure* state.

Termination Criteria - Given the expressiveness of the proposed declarative DSL, the user can define tests executing many experiments and potentially lasting a long amount of time to be completed, and that can incur into errors. In this use case we show how a user can have control on the execution lifecycle of the test defined in Listing 3, to set conditions leading to a premature termination of the test execution. This way the users can rely on the automation provided by the framework to continuously execute tests, and she has control on the time allocated to their execution and in deciding when avoiding wasting resources because the test can not be considered valid. In Listing 4 the user decides to define a maximum runtime for the test of 20 hours, with a maximum number of failed experiments set to 5% of the total number of experiments to schedule (48). Each experiment is set to be

```
configuration:
  termination_criteria:
    test:
      max_time: 20h
      max_failed_experiments: 5%
    experiment:
      workload:
        browse:
          confidence_interval_metric:
          ↳ avg_response_time
          confidence_interval_value: 50ms
          confidence_interval_precision: 95%
          max_number_of_trials: 10
```

Listing 4: **Exhaustive Exploration Test: Termination Criteria**

executed multiple times, with a dynamic termination criteria set on the *browse* workload. The termination criteria states that the confidence interval of the *avg_response_time* has to be 50ms at 95% of confidence level, with an upper limit of 10 trials.

When the framework executes the declared goal, each experiment is repeated a variable number of times, and if the wanted confidence interval is achieved within the *max_number_of_trials* its execution is marked as successful. On the contrary, if fatal errors happens, or the confidence interval can not be obtained within 10 trials, the experiment execution is marked as failed. The test is executed for a maximum time of 20 hours, and if it is not completed within the maximum time, it is suspended and moved to the *partially complete* terminated state from where the user could decide to ask the framework to continue its execution by extending the amount of time it can run. If during the execution more than 5% of the experiments fail because of one of the failures presented in Sect. 4.3 or because termination criteria are failing the test, then the test is moved to the *completed with failure* state.

As for the other user cases, the user can access all the metrics and produced data, that in this case would also contain data related to eventual failures that happened.

Quality Gates - The use case presented in Listing 5 is also based on the one presented in Listing 3, and in this case the user's intent during the exploration of the performance of the system in the specified space, is verifying if the system does not exceed a specified $95th$ percentile for the registered response time for the entire browse workload, that the maximum deviation from the specified mix is less or equal to 2%, and that the average CPU utilization of the *catalogue_ws* is less or equal than 70%. By setting quality gates, the user has control on the final result of the test, and can decide to stop the execution as soon as these quality gates are not achieved, marking the test as failed, or continue its execution reaching a successful state. This is important because

```
configuration:
  quality_gates:
    workload:
      browse:
        95thp_response_time: <= 250ms
        max_mix_deviation: 2%
    services:
      catalogue_ws:
        avg_cpu: <= 70%
```

Listing 5: **Exhaustive Exploration Test: Quality Gates**

```
configuration:
  goal:
    type: stability_boundary
    exploration:
      stability_criteria:
        workload:
          browse:
            max_mix_deviation: 5%
        services:
          catalogue_ws:
            avg_cpu: <= 80%
          dbms:
            avg_cpu: <= 90%
      exploration_strategy:
        selection: stability_boundary_first
```

Listing 6: **Stability Boundary Test**

often, in CSD environments, continuous validation of performance benchmarks are executed, to continuously verify that the system keeps achieving specified quality conditions in given configurations.

Stability Boundary Test - In this last use case, we show how the user can specify a more advanced goal, namely a stability boundary goal. We base this use case on the Listing 3, and in Listing 6 we present the changes to be applied to the specification in order to define a stability boundary goal. In the case of stability boundary goal, the *stability_boundary_first* selection strategy has to be specified, and a new section has to be added in the specification, namely *stability_criteria*, to define the stability criteria for the SUT. The *stability_boundary_first* selection strategy is enabled to use the defined stability criteria and decide the order of experiments to be executed in the defined exploration space. In the case of Listing 6 the user is setting stability criteria on the workload and services average CPU utilization.

The framework, by applying the *stability_boundary_first* strategy, determines the order of the experiments such that the first to be executed are the ones were the system is expected to be less stable, and then applies a binary search in the exploration space to trace the stability boundary, if the system is not stable in the first set of mentioned explored points. The current assumption is that the system is expected to be less stable were allocated resources to the service are less, and configuration values are expected to be worst (here the assumption towards the user for the stability boundary goal, is that the values of a configuration variable are provided in the order from expected worst to expected best performance as it is in the case of Listing 3). The idea is that in this way the user can start to collect data about regions of the exploration space were the system is more likely to be not stable, and although the space could be explored completely in case the system is stable in the entire exploration space, she could set termination criteria based on time or on maximum number of failed experiments to decide when to stop the exploration.

6 CONCLUSION AND FUTURE WORK

In this work we presented a declarative DSL for specifying goal-oriented performance tests, mainly focused on container-packaged (Micro)service systems, and a model-driven framework that enables the automated end-to-end execution of the specified tests. As shown with different use cases, the DSL allows developers to explicitly declare the goal of the performance test, as well as precisely control the deployment configuration of the SUT. The framework automates the end-to-end execution of performance tests defined using the DSL, whose execution semantics is defined in terms of state machines controlling the tests execution and allowing to statically checking tests for correctness. The declarative nature of the DSL makes explicit the intent, purpose and applicability context of the defined tests, as well as opening up the possibility to use alternative exploration strategies to achieve a given goal. Both the DSL and the framework have features relevant for CSD environments, such as termination criteria, quality gates, observable metrics and user-defined failure handling mechanisms. As future work we plan to extend the set of goals supported by the DSL, add additional strategies to navigate the exploration space, and integrate statistical model based techniques, to speed up the exploration space exploration [21]. We also plan to collect structured users' feedback on the declarative DSL after applying it to more real-world usage scenarios.

ACKNOWLEDGMENTS

This work is funded by the "BenchFlow" project (DACH Grant Nr. 200021E-145062/1) project.

REFERENCES

[1] Varsha Apte, T V S Viswanath, Devidas Gawali, Akhilesh Kommireddy, and Anshul Gupta. 2017. AutoPerf: Automated load testing and resource usage profiling of multi-tier internet applications. In *Proc. of ICPE*. 115–126.

[2] Maicon Bernardino, Avelino F Zorzo, and Elder M Rodrigues. 2014. Canopus: A Domain-Specific Language for Modeling Performance Testing. In *Proc. of ICSEA*. 157–167.

[3] Andreas Brunnert and Helmut Krcmar. 2017. Continuous performance evaluation and capacity planning using resource profiles for enterprise applications. *Journal of Systems and Software* 123, 1 (2017), 239–262.

[4] Andreas Brunnert, André van Hoorn, Felix Willnecker, et al. 2015. *Performance-oriented DevOps: A Research Agenda*. Technical Report. SPEC RG DevOps.

[5] Matheus Cunha, Nabor C Mendonça, and Américo Sampaio. 2013. A Declarative Environment for Automatic Performance Evaluation in IaaS Clouds. In *Proc. of CLOUD*. 285–292.

[6] Stefano Di Alesio, Shiva Nejati, Arnaud Gotlieb, and Lionel Briand. 2013. Stress testing of task deadlines - A constraint programming approach. In *Proc of. ISSRE*. 158–167.

[7] Vincenzo Ferme, Ana Ivanchikj, and Cesare Pautasso. 2015. A Framework for Benchmarking BPMN 2.0 Workflow Management Systems. In *Proc. of BPM*. 251–259.

[8] Vincenzo Ferme and Cesare Pautasso. 2017. Towards Holistic Continuous Software Performance Assessment. In *Proc. of ICPE Companion*. 159–164.

[9] Brian Fitzgerald and Klaas-Jan Stol. 2017. Continuous software engineering: A roadmap and agenda. *Journal of Systems and Software* 123, 1 (2017), 176–189.

[10] Ilias Gerostathopoulos, Tomas Bures, Sanny Schmid, Vojtech Horký, Christian Prehofer, and Petr Tůma. 2016. Towards Systematic Live Experimentation in Software-Intensive Systems of Systems. In *Proc. of ECSA*. 1–7.

[11] Daniel Golovin, Benjamin Solnik, Subhodeep Moitra, Greg Kochanski, John Karro, and D Sculley. 2017. Google Vizier - A Service for Black-Box Optimization. In *Proc. of KDD*. 1487–1495.

[12] Juha Itkonen, Casper Lassenius, and Eero Laukkanen. 2017. Problems, causes and solutions when adopting continuous delivery - A systematic literature review. *Information and Software Technology* 82, 2 (2017), 55–79.

[13] Nicolas Michael, Nitin Ramannavar, Yixiao Shen, Sheetal Patil, and Jan-Lung Sung. 2017. CloudPerf - A Performance Test Framework for Distributed and Dynamic Multi-Tenant Environments. In *Proc. of ICPE*. 189–200.

[14] Jean Christophe Petkovich, A Oliveira, Y Zhang, Thomas Reidemeister, and Sebastian Fischmeister. 2015. DataMill: a distributed heterogeneous infrastructure for robust experimentation. *Software: Practice and Experience* 46, 10 (2015), 1411–1440.

[15] A Omar Portillo-Dominguez, Miao Wang, John Murphy, Damien Magoni, Nick Mitchell, Peter F Sweeney, and Erik Altman. 2014. Towards an automated approach to use expert systems in the performance testing of distributed systems. In *Proc. of JAMAICA*. 22–27.

[16] Gerald Schermann, Dominik Schöni, Philipp Leitner, and Harald C Gall. 2016. Bifrost - Supporting Continuous Deployment with Automated Enactment of Multi-Phase Live Testing Strategies. In *Proc. of Middleware*. 12:1–12:14.

[17] Joel Scheuner, Philipp Leitner, Jürgen Cito, and Harald C Gall. 2014. Cloud Work Bench - Infrastructure-as-Code Based Cloud Benchmarking.. In *Proc. of CloudCom*. 246–253.

[18] Simon Spinner, Giuliano Casale, Fabian Brosig, and Samuel Kounev. 2015. Evaluating approaches to resource demand estimation. *Performance Evaluation* 92, C (2015), 51–71.

[19] Jan Waller, Nils C Ehmke, and Wilhelm Hasselbring. 2015. Including Performance Benchmarks into Continuous Integration to Enable DevOps. *ACM SIGSOFT Software Engineering Notes* 40, 2 (2015), 1–4.

[20] Jürgen Walter, André van Hoorn, Heiko Koziolek, Dusan Okanovic, and Samuel Kounev. 2016. Asking "What"?, Automating the "How"? - The Vision of Declarative Performance Engineering. In *Proc. of ICPE*. 91–94.

[21] Dennis Westermann. 2014. *Deriving Goal-oriented Performance Models by Systematic Experimentation*. Ph.D. Dissertation. Karlsruhe Institute of Technology.

[22] Johannes Wettinger, Uwe Breitenbücher, Michael Falkenthal, and Frank Leymann. 2016. Collaborative gathering and continuous delivery of DevOps solutions through repositories. *Computer Science - Research and Development* 31, 4 (2016), 1–10.

[23] Liming Zhu, Len Bass, and George Champlin-Scharff. 2016. DevOps and Its Practices. *IEEE Software* 33, 3 (2016), 32–34.

quiho: Automated Performance Regression Testing Using Inferred Resource Utilization Profiles

Ivo Jimenez
UC Santa Cruz
ivo.jimenez@ucsc.edu

Noah Watkins
UC Santa Cruz
nmwatkin@ucsc.edu

Michael Sevilla
UC Santa Cruz
msevilla@ucsc.edu

Jay Lofstead
Sandia National Laboratories
gflofst@sandia.gov

Carlos Maltzahn
UC Santa Cruz
carlosm@ucsc.edu

ABSTRACT

We introduce *quiho*, a framework for profiling application performance that can be used in automated performance regression tests. *quiho* profiles an application by applying sensitivity analysis, in particular statistical regression analysis (SRA), using application-independent performance feature vectors that characterize the performance of machines. The result of the SRA, feature importance specifically, is used as a proxy to identify hardware and low-level system software behavior. The relative importance of these features serve as a performance profile of an application (termed inferred resource utilization profile or IRUP), which is used to automatically validate performance behavior across multiple revisions of an application's code base without having to instrument code or obtain performance counters. We demonstrate that *quiho* can successfully discover performance regressions by showing its effectiveness in profiling application performance for synthetically introduced regressions as well as those found in real-world applications.

CCS CONCEPTS

• **Software and its engineering** → **Software performance**; **Software testing and debugging**; **Acceptance testing**; *Empirical software validation*; • **Social and professional topics** → *Automation*;

KEYWORDS

Software Testing ; Performance Engineering ; Performance Modeling

ACM Reference Format:
Ivo Jimenez, Noah Watkins, Michael Sevilla, Jay Lofstead, and Carlos Maltzahn. 2018. quiho: Automated Performance Regression Testing Using Inferred Resource Utilization Profiles. In *ICPE '18: ACM/SPEC International Conference on Performance Engineering, April 9–13, 2018, Berlin, Germany*. ACM, New York, NY, USA, 12 pages. https://doi.org/10.1145/3184407.3184422

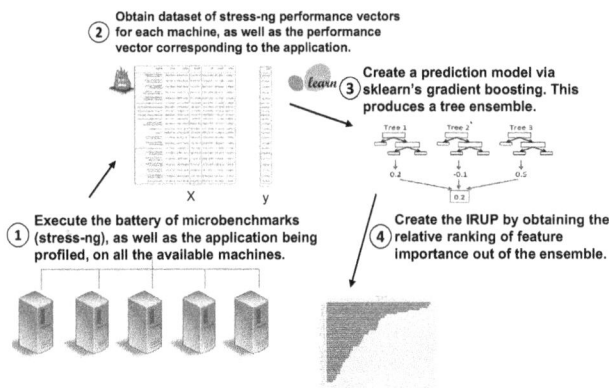

Figure 1: *quiho*'s workflow for generating inferred resource utilization profiles (IRUPs) for an application. An IRUP is used as an alternative for profiling application performance and can complement automated regression testing. For example, after a change in the runtime of an application has been detected across two revisions of the code base, an IRUP can be obtained in order to determine whether this change is significant. IRUPs can also aid in root cause analysis.

1 INTRODUCTION

Quality assurance (QA) is an essential activity in the software engineering process [1–3]. Part of the QA pipeline involves the execution of performance regression tests, where the performance of the application is measured and contrasted against past versions [4–6]. Examples of metrics used in regression testing are throughput, latency, or resource utilization over time. These metrics are captured and compared for multiple versions of an application (usually current and past versions) and, if significant differences are found, this constitutes a regression.

One of the main challenges in automating performance regression tests is defining the criteria to decide whether a change in application performance behavior is significant [7]. Understanding the impact that distinct hardware and low-level system software[1] components have on the performance of applications demands highly-skilled performance engineering [8–10]. Traditionally, this investigation is done by an analyst in charge of looking at changes

---

[1]Throughout this paper, we use "system" to refer to the low-level compute stack composed by hardware, firmware and the operating system (OS).

to the performance metrics captured at runtime, possibly investigating deeply by looking at performance counters, performance profiles, static code analysis, and static/dynamic tracing. One common approach is to find bottlenecks by generating a profile (e.g., using the perf Linux kernel tool) in order to understand which parts of the system an application is hammering on [5]. Profiling involves recording resource utilization for an application over time. In general, this can be done in two ways: timed- and event-based profiles. Timed-based profiling samples the instruction pointer at regular intervals and generates a function call tree with each node having a percentage of time associated with it, which represents the amount of time that the CPU spends within that piece of code. Event-based profiling samples at regular intervals different events at the hardware- and OS-level in order to obtain a distribution of events over time. In either case, the system needs to execute the application in a "profiling" mode in order to enable the instrumentation mechanisms that the OS has available for carrying out this task.

Automated solutions have been proposed in recent years [11–13]. The general approach of these is to analyze runtime logs and/or metrics application in order to build a performance prediction model that can be used to automatically determine whether a regression has occurred. This relies on having accurate predictions and, as with any prediction model, there is the risk of finding false negatives/positives. In addition to striving for highly accurate predictions, one can also use performance modeling as a profiling tool.

In this work we present *quiho*, an approach aimed at complementing automated performance regression testing by using inferred resource utilization profiles (IRUP) associated to an application. *quiho* is an alternative framework for profiling an application where the utilization of one or more subsystems (e.g. virtual memory) is inferred by applying Statistical Regression Analysis[2] (SRA) on a dataset of application-independent performance vectors. The main assumption behind *quiho* is the availability of multiple machines when exercising performance regression testing, a reasonable requirement that is well-aligned with current software engineering practices (performance regression is carried out on multiple architectures and OSs).

When an application is profiled using *quiho* (Fig. 1), the machines available to the performance tests are baselined by executing a battery of microbenchmarks on each. This matrix of performance vectors characterizes the available machines independently from any application and can be used (and re-used) as the foundation for applying statistical learning techniques such as SRA. In order to infer resource utilization, the application under study is executed on the same machines from where the performance vectors where obtained, and SRA is applied. The result of the SRA for an application, in particular feature importance, is used as a proxy to characterize hardware and low-level system utilization behavior. The relative importance of these features constitutes what we refer to as an *inferred resource utilization profile* (IRUP).

In this article, we demonstrate that our approach successfully identifies performance regressions by showing that *quiho* (1) obtains resource utilization profiles for applications that accurately reflect

---

[2]We use the term *Statistical Regression Analysis* (SRA) to differentiate between regression testing in software engineering and regression analysis in statistics.

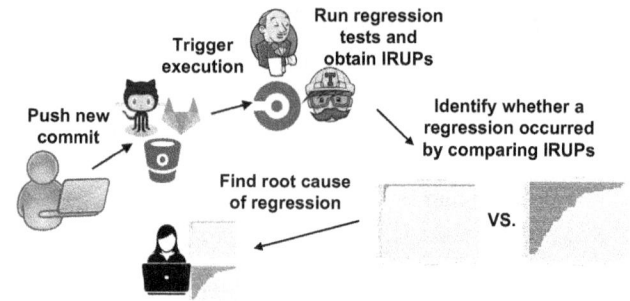

Figure 2: Automated regression testing pipeline integrating inferred resource utilization profiles (IRUP). IRUPs are obtained by *quiho* and can be used both, for identifying regressions, and to aid in the quest for finding the root cause of a regression.

what their code do and (2) effectively uses these profiles to identify induced regressions as well as other regressions found in real-world applications. The contributions of our work are:

- Insight: feature importance in SRA models (trained using application-independent performance vectors) gives us a resource utilization profile (an IRUP) of an application without having to look at the code.
- An automated end-to-end framework (based on the above finding), that aids analysts in identifying significant changes in resource utilization behavior of applications which can also aid in identifying root cause of regressions, and that is resilient to code refactoring.
- Methodology for evaluating automated performance regression. We introduce a set of synthetic benchmarks aimed at evaluating automated regression testing without the need of real bug repositories. These benchmarks take as input parameters that determine their performance behavior, thus simulating different "versions" of an application.

Next section (Section 2) shows the intuition behind *quiho* and how can be used to automate regression tests. We then do a more in-depth description of *quiho* (Section 3), followed by our evaluation of this approach (Section 4). We then discuss different aspects of our work (Section 5), review (Section 6) related work and we lastly close with a brief discussion on challenges and opportunities enabled by *quiho* (Section 7).

2 MOTIVATION AND INTUITION

Fig. 2 shows the workflow of an automated regression testing pipeline and shows how *quiho* fits in this picture. A regression is usually the result of observing a significant change in a performance metric of interest (e.g., runtime). At this point, an analyst will investigate further in order to find the root cause of the problem. One of these activities involves profiling an application to see the resource utilization pattern. Traditionally, coarse-grained profiling (i.e. CPU-, memory- or IO-bound) can be obtained by monitoring an application's resource utilization over time. Fine granularity behavior helps application developers and performance engineers

Variability patterns of an application (zlog), resemble the same variability pattern of one or more performance microbenchmark(s).

machine_id	mmap	crypt	cpu	mremap	shm-sysv	longjmp	zlog
d710.quiho.Schedock.emulab.net-3-1497506400000	0.297225	70.505811	80.725528	6.097482	325.638613	41532.761430	186.0670
d2100.quiho.Schedock.emulab.net-3-1497506400000	0.295866	69.604378	80.590998	6.098675	329.362273	41612.653196	186.3350
c8220.quiho.schedock-PG0.clemson.cloudlab.us-3...	0.696309	106.615614	175.846965	13.698226	442.833765	64387.219967	90.5729
d360.quiho.emulab-net.utahddc.geniracks.net-3...	0.697455	75.883808	191.459620	13.999673	683.060866	60710.313970	126.8800
pc3300.quiho.emulab-net.uky.emulab.net-3-14975...	0.599831	92.132384	123.087463	10.197824	552.422144	66234.210578	112.4690
pc3300.quiho.emulab-net.uky.emulab.net-1-14975...	0.599829	92.819498	122.212472	9.997537	146.649755	65917.974625	116.2350
r720.quiho.schedock-PG0.apt.emulab.net-2-14975...	0.997777	103.150519	123.555510	31.798235	718.593589	79912.927707	72.0655
c6220.quiho.schedock-PG0.apt.emulab.net-2-1497...	0.997847	105.268050	154.967638	31.197037	823.751673	84047.342081	73.0488
c220g1.quiho.schedock-PG0.wisc.cloudlab.us-1-1...	1.099263	156.604364	270.618852	17.498415	479.099150	113802.170174	88.0340
m510.quiho.schedock-PG0.utah.cloudlab.us-3-149...	1.099940	127.926339	218.100286	32.498395	119.077827	88902.232931	121.5200
pc3500.quiho.emulab-net.uky.emulab.net-2-14975...	0.599839	91.964087	123.075853	10.098173	226.481276	66178.014746	115.3070
d430.quiho.Schedock.emulab.net-2-1497506400000	0.296396	70.135194	79.954740	5.996731	85.912807	42465.473596	185.4220
r720.quiho.schedock-PG0.apt.emulab.net-3-14975...	0.997064	104.450324	134.408895	31.797676	692.873106	84677.586680	71.1083

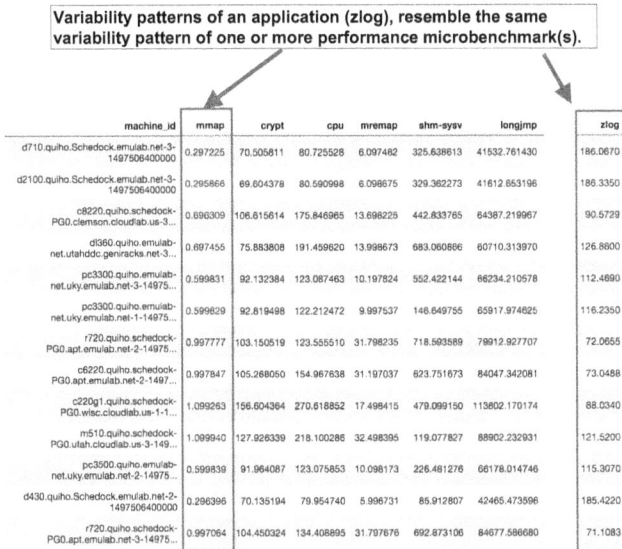

Figure 3: A matrix of performance feature vectors over a colection of CloudLab servers (left), and an array of a performance metric for an application on those same machines (right). Every column in the matrix comes from executing a microbenchmark on that machine. This dataset of microbenchmarks allows us to create a performance prediction model for application. Variability patterns of an application (zlog in the example), resemble the same variability pattern of one or more performance microbenchmark(s). Thus, the system subcomponent exercised by the microbenchmark is likely to be also the cause of why the application exhibits such performance behavior.

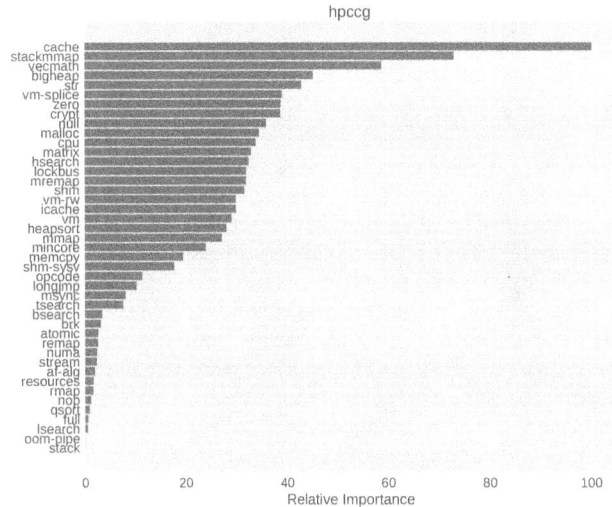

Figure 4: An example profile showing the relative importance of features for an execution of the hpccg miniapp [14]. The x-axis corresponds to the relative performance value, normalized with respect to the most important feature, which corresponds to the first one on the y-axis (from top to bottom). Section 3.2 describes in detail how feature importances are calculated.

quickly understand what they need to focus on while refactoring an application.

Fine granularity performance utilization behavior can better inform the regression testing pipeline. Examples of which resources are included in this type of profiling are the OS memory mapping subsystem, the CPU's cryptographic unit, or the CPU cache. This type of profiling is time-consuming and requires use of more computing resources. This is usually done offline by analysts and involves eyeballing source code, static code analysis, or analyzing hardware/OS performance counters/profiles.

An alternative is to infer resource utilization behavior by comparing the performance of an application on platforms with different performance characteristics. For example, if we know that machine A has higher memory bandwidth than machine B, and an application is memory-bound, then this application will perform better on machine A. There are several challenges with this approach:

1. Consistent Software. We need to ensure that the software stack is the same on all machines where the application runs.
2. Application Testing Overhead. The amount of effort required to run applications on a multitude of platforms is not negligible.
3. Hardware Performance Characterization. It is difficult to obtain the performance characteristics of a machine by just looking at the hardware specs. Therefore, another more practical alternative is required.
4. Correlating Performance. Even if we could solve the above issue (Hardware Performance Characterization) and infer performance characteristics by just looking at the machine hardware specifications, there is still the problem of not being able to correlate baseline performance with application behavior. The problem is that between two platforms, it is rarely the case that the performance change is observed in only one subcomponent of the system. For example, a newer machine doesn't have just faster memory sticks, but also a better CPU and chipset.

The advent of cloud computing allows us to solve (1) using solutions like KVM [15] or software containers [16]. ChameleonCloud [17], CloudLab [18,19] and Grid5000 [20] are examples of bare-metal-as-a-service infrastructure available to researchers that can be used to automate regression testing pipelines for the purposes of investigating new approaches. These solutions to infrastructure automation coupled with DevOps practices [21,22] allows us to address (2), i.e. to reduce the amount of work required to run tests.

Thus, the main challenge to inferring resource utilization patterns lies in quantifying the performance of the platform in a consistent way (3,4). One alternative is to look at the hardware specification and infer performance characteristics from this, a highly inaccurate task due to the lack of correspondence between advertised (or theoretical peak throughput) and actual performance observed in reality. For example, the platform spec might specify that the machine has DDR4 memory sticks with a theoretical peak throughput of 10 GB/s. But the actual memory bandwidth is typically less in practice. How much less is non-deterministic and depends on access patterns.

quiho solves this problem by characterizing machine performance using microbenchmarks. These performance vectors are the "fingerprint" that characterizes the behavior of a machine [23]. These vectors, obtained over a sufficiently large set of machines[3], can serve as the foundation for building a prediction model of the performance of an application when executed on new ("unseen") machines [24]. Thus, a natural next step to take with a dataset like this is to try to build a prediction model.

While building a prediction model is obviously something that can be used to estimate the performance of an application, building one can also serve as a way of identifying resource utilization. If we use these performance vectors to apply SRA and focus on feature importance [25] of the generated models, they can allow us to infer resource utilization patterns. In Fig. 3, we show the intuition behind why this is so. The performance of an application is determined by the performance of the subcomponents that get stressed the most by the application's code. Thus, intuitively, if the performance of an application across multiple machines resembles the performance of a microbenchmark over the same set of machines, then we can say that the application is heavily influenced by that subcomponent. In other words, if the variability of a feature across multiple machines resembles the variability of application performance across those same machines, it is likely due to the application stressing the same subcomponent that the corresponding microbenchmark stresses. While this can be inferred by obtaining correlation coefficients, proper SRA is needed in order to create prediction models, as well as to obtain a relative rank of feature importances.

Relying on SRA as a way of inferring resource utilization behavior has the practical consequence of *quiho* benefiting heavily from an heterogeneous setup. The more the "performance diversity" of machines that are available for testing, the easier that *quiho* can discover an application's resource utilization behavior. Intuitively, this can be explained as follows. If we run a IO-bound application on distinct machines with very different CPU and memory subsystem performance but similar IO throughput, we won't be able to discover that the application's bottleneck is on the IO subsystem. If we create a more heterogeneous mix of machines, with larger IO performance variability, we can discover that this application is IO-intensive since the performance of the application will vary, depending on the capabilities of the underlying IO subsystem of each distinct machine.

Thus, having high performance variability allows *quiho* to infer resource utilization patterns by discovering the underlying correlations between the performance of microbenchmarks and an application's performance. Since SRA results in creating a performance prediction model for an application, we can rank features by sorting them with respect to their relative performance prediction importance. We call this ranking an *Inferred Resource Utilization Profile* (IRUP), as shown in Fig. 4. In the next section we explain how these IRUPs are obtained and how they can be used in automated performance regression tests. Section 4 empirically validates this approach.

---

[3]In Section 5 we briefly sketch how we would apply PAC to find the minimal set of machines needed to obtaining meaningful results from SRA.

3 OUR APPROACH

In this section we describe *quiho*'s approach and the resulting prototype. We first describe how we obtain the performance vectors that characterize system performance. We then show that we can feed these vectors to SRA in order to build a performance model for an application. Lastly, we describe how we obtain feature importance, how this represents an inferred resource utilization profile (IRUP) and the algorithm (and alternative heuristics) to comparing IRUPs.

3.1 Performance Feature Vectors As System Performance Characterization

While the hardware and software specification can serve to describe the performance characteristics of a machine, the real performance characteristics can only feasibly be obtained by executing programs and capturing metrics. One can generate arbitrary performance characteristics by interposing a hardware emulation layer and deterministically associate performance characteristics to each instruction based on specific hardware specs. While possible, this is impractical (we are interested in characterizing "real" performance). The question then boils down to which programs should we use to characterize performance? Ideally, we would like to have many programs that execute every possible opcode mix so that we measure their performance. Since this is an impractical solution, an alternative is to create synthetic microbenchmarks that get as close as possible to exercising all the available features of a system.

stress-ng[26] is a tool that is used to "stress test a computer system in various selectable ways. It was designed to exercise various physical subsystems of a computer as well as the various operating system kernel interfaces". There are multiple stressors for CPU, CPU cache, memory, OS, network and filesystem. Since we focus on system performance bandwidth, we execute 42 stressors for CPU, CPU cache, memory and virtual memory stressors (Tbl. 1 shows the list of stressors used in this paper). A *stressor* (or microbenchmark) is a function that loops for a fixed amount of time, exercising a particular subcomponent of the system. At the end of its execution, stress-ng reports the rate of iterations executed for the specified period of time (referred to as bogo-ops-per-second).

Using this battery of stressors, we can obtain a performance profile of a machine (a performance vector). When this vector is compared against the one corresponding to another machine, we can quantify the difference in performance between the two at a per-stressor level. Fig. 5 shows the variability in these performance vectors. We have significant variability coming from the hardware differences of the underlying nodes. As mentioned in Section 2, in contrast to what one might expect, we prefer higher variability since, as we will show later, the higher the variability among performance between machines, the more information the prediction models have available to identify the underlying system characteristics that affect application performance.

Every stressor (element in the vector) can be mapped to basic features of the underlying platform. For example, bigheap is directly associated to memory bandwidth, zero to memory mapping, qsort to CPU performance (in particular to sorting data), and so on and so forth. However, the performance of a stressor in this set is *not* completely orthogonal to the rest, as implied by the overlapping

Table 1: List of stressors used in this paper, along with the categories assigned to them by stress-ng. Note that some stressors are part of multiple categories.

stressor	CPU	Cache	Mem	VM
af-alg	X			
atomic	X		X	
bigheap				X
brk	X			
bsearch	X	X	X	
cache		X		
cpu	X			
crypt	X			
full			X	
heapsort	X	X	X	
hsearch	X	X	X	
icache			X	
lockbus		X	X	
longjmp	X			
lsearch	X	X	X	
malloc		X	X	X
matrix	X	X	X	
memcpy			X	
mincore			X	
mmap				X
mremap				X
msync				X
nop	X			
numa	X		X	
oom-pipe			X	
qsort	X	X	X	
remap			X	X
resources			X	
rmap			X	
shm				X
shm-sysv				X
stack			X	X
stackmmap			X	X
str	X	X	X	
stream	X		X	
tsearch	X	X	X	
vecmath	X	X		
vm			X	X
vm-rw			X	X
vm-rw				
vm-splice				X
zero			X	

Table 2: Table of machines from CloudLab. The last three entries correspond to computers in our lab.

machine	cpu	num_cpus	cores
c220g2	Intel(R) Xeon(R) CPU E5-2630 v3 @ 2.40GHz	2	8
c8220	Intel(R) Xeon(R) CPU E5-2660 v2 @ 2.20GHz	2	10
dl360	Intel(R) Xeon(R) CPU E5-2450 0 @ 2.10GHz	2	8
m510	Intel(R) Xeon(R) CPU D-1548 @ 2.00GHz	1	8
pc2400	Intel(R) Core(TM)2 Quad CPU Q9550 @ 2.83GHz	1	4
pc3000	Intel(R) Xeon(TM) CPU 3.00GHz	1	1
pc3500	Intel(R) Core(TM)2 Quad CPU Q6600 @ 2.40GHz	1	4
r720	Intel(R) Xeon(R) CPU E5-2450 0 @ 2.10GHz	1	8
scruffy	Intel(R) Xeon(R) CPU E5620 @ 2.40GHz	1	4
dwill	Intel(R) Core(TM) i5-2400 CPU @ 3.10GHz	1	4
issdm-41	Dual-Core AMD Opteron(tm) Processor 2212	2	2

categories in Tbl. 1. Fig. 6 shows a heat-map of Pearson correlation coefficients for performance vectors obtained by executing stress-ng on all the distinct machine configurations available in CloudLab [19] (Tbl. 2 shows a summary of their hardware specs).

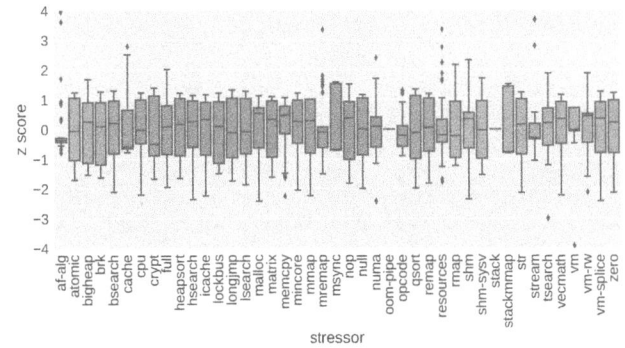

Figure 5: Boxplots illustrating the variability of the performance vector dataset. The data is normalized in order to guard against dimensionality issues. Thus, the y-axis shows variability in terms of the z-score (signed value representing the number of standard deviations by which the value of an observation is below or above the mean). Each stressor was executed five times on each of the machines listed in Tbl. 2.

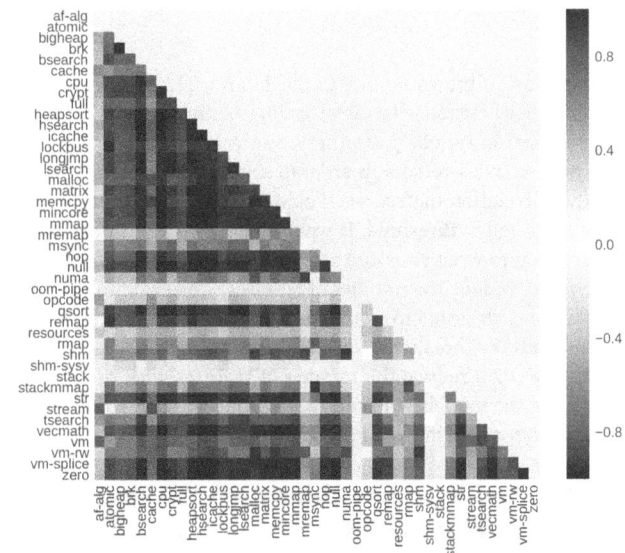

Figure 6: Heat-map of Pearson correlation coefficients for performance vectors obtained by executing stress-ng on all the distinct machine configurations available in CloudLab.

As the figure shows, some stressors are slightly correlated (those near 0) while others show high correlation between them.

In order to analyze this last point further, that is, to try to discern whether there are a few orthogonal features that we could focus on, rather than looking at the totality of the 42 stressors, we applied principal component decomposition (PCA) [27]. Fig. 7 shows the relative (blue) and cumulative (green) explained variance ratio. The explained variance ratio is the amount of variability that a component removes from the dataset. The higher the variance associated to a component, the more the data can be explained by that component. Having 6-8 components would be enough to

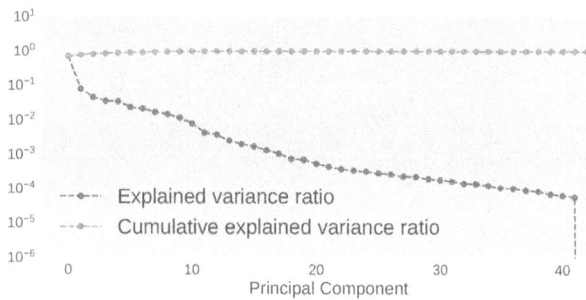

Figure 7: Principal Component Analysis for the performance vector dataset. The y-axis (log-scale) corresponds to the explained variance ratio, while the x-axis denotes the number of components. The blue line denotes the amount of variance reduced by having a particular number of components. The green line corresponds to the cumulative sum of the explained variance. We omit the last point due to space constraints, but we note that the variability at this point, while relatively (in the image), numerically is insignificant (y-axis is in log-scale).

explain most of the variability in the dataset. This confirms what we observe in Fig. 6, in terms of having many stressors that can be explained in function of others. So the reader might wonder, why not remove stressors in order to simplify the analysis? If we use the correlation matrix, we would need to define an arbitrary correlation index threshold. If we use PCA, we lose information with respect to what stressors are explaining a prediction. Instead of trying to reduce the number of features, we decide to leave all the stressors in order to not lose any information or having to define arbitrary thresholds. Part of our future work is to address whether we can reduce the number of features with the goal of improving the models, without having to lose information about which stressors are involved in the prediction.

3.2 System Resource Utilization Via Feature Importance in SRA

SRA is an approach for modeling the relationship between variables, usually corresponding to observed data points [28]. One or more independent variables are used to obtain a *regression function* that explains the values taken by a dependent variable. A common approach is to assume a *linear predictor function* and estimate the unknown parameters of the modeled relationships.

A large number of procedures have been developed for parameter estimation and inference in linear regression. These methods differ in computational simplicity of algorithms, presence of a closed-form solution, robustness with respect to heavy-tailed distributions, and theoretical assumptions needed to validate desirable statistical properties such as consistency and asymptotic efficiency. Some of the more common estimation techniques for linear regression are least-squares, maximum-likelihood estimation, among others.

scikit-learn [29] provides many of the previously mentioned techniques for building regression models. Another technique available in scikit-learn is gradient boosting [30]. Gradient boosting

is a machine learning technique for regression and classification problems, which produces a prediction model in the form of an ensemble of weak prediction models, typically decision trees [31]. It builds the model in a stage-wise fashion like other boosting methods do, and it generalizes them by allowing optimization of an arbitrary differentiable loss function. This function is then optimized over a function space by iteratively choosing a function (weak hypothesis) that points in the negative gradient direction.

Once an ensemble of trees for an application is generated, feature importances are obtained in order to use them as the IRUP for an application. Fig. 1 shows the process applied to obtaining IRUPs for an application. scikit-learn implements the feature importance calculation algorithm introduced in [32] and is sketched in the following pseudo-code algorithm. Given an ensemble of trees:

1. Initialize an f_importance array to hold a score for each feature in the dataset.
2. Take an unseen tree of the ensemble and traverse it using the following steps:
   a. For each node that splits on feature i, compute the error reduction of that node, multiplied by the number of samples that were routed to the node.
   b. Add this quantity to the f_importance array (value corresponding to feature i).
   c. Once all nodes are traversed, pick another unseen tree from the ensemble and go to 2.
3. Assign a score of 100 to the most important feature and normalize the rest of elements in the f_importance array with respect to this one.

For step 2.a, the error reduction is recursively defined by obtaining the difference between the parent node impurity and the weighted sum of the two child node impurities. The impurity criterion depends on whether the problem is a classification or regression one. Gini or MSE (among many others) can be used for classification. For regression, variance impurity is employed and corresponds to the variance of all data points that are routed through that node.

We note that before generating a regression model, we normalize the data by obtaining the z-score of the dataset. Given that the bogo-ops-per-second metric does not quantify work consistently across stressors, we normalize the data in order to prevent some features from dominating in the process of creating the prediction models. In Section 4 we evaluate the effectiveness of IRUPs.

3.3 Using IRUPs in Automated Regression Tests

As shown in Fig. 2 (step 4), when trying to determine whether a performance degradation occurred, IRUPs can be used to compare differences between current and past versions of an application. In order to do so, we apply a simple algorithm. Given two profiles A and B, look at first feature in the ranking (highest in the chart). Then, compare the relative importance value for the feature and importance values for A and B. If relative importance does not have the same value, the importance is considered not equivalent and the algorithm stops. If values are similar, we move to the next, less important factor and the compare again. This is repeated for as many features are present in the dataset.

IRUPs can also be used as a pointer to where to start with an investigation that looks for the root cause of the regression (Fig. 2, step 5). For example, if the *stream* stressor (mimics the STREAM benchmark [33]) ends up being the most important feature, then we can start by looking at any code/libraries that make use of this subcomponent of the system. An analyst could also trace an application by capturing performance counters over time and look at corresponding counters to see which code paths make heavy use of the subcomponent in question.

4 EVALUATION

In this section we answer the following questions:

1. How well can IRUPs accurately capture application performance behavior? (Section 4.1)
2. How well can IRUPs work for identifying simulated regressions? (Section 4.2)
3. How well can IRUPs work for identifying regressions in real world software projects? (Section 4.3)

Note on Replicability of Results: This paper adheres to The Popper Experimentation Protocol and convention[4] [34], so experiments presented here are available in the repository for this article[5]. We note that rather than including all the results in the paper, we instead include representative ones for each section and leave the rest on the paper repository. The dataset associated to this study is open and can be examined in more detail on binder. The dataset can also be re-generated on other platforms by executing the Popper pipeline associated to this experiment. All results presented here are continuously validated and can be replicated easily on Cloudlab (see README on our Github repository for more details).

4.1 Effectiveness of IRUPs to Capture Resource Utilization Behavior

In this subsection we show how IRUPs can effectively describe the fine granularity resource utilization of an application with respect to a set of machines. Our methodology is:

1. Given an application *A*, discover relevant performance features using the *quiho* framework.
2. Do manual performance analysis of *A* to corroborate that discovered features are indeed the cause of performance differences.

Fig. 4 shows the profile of an execution of the hpccg miniapp [14]. This proxy application (or miniapp) [35] is a "conjugate gradient benchmark code for a 3D chimney domain on an arbitrary number of processors [that] generates a 27-point finite difference matrix with a user-prescribed sub-block size on each processor." [14].

Based on the profile, stackmmap and cache are the most important features. In order to corroborate if this matches with what the application does, we profiled this execution with perf. The stacked profile view shows that ~85% of the time the application is running the function HPC_sparsemv(). The code for this function is shown in Lst. 1. As the name implies, this snippet implements a sparse vector multiplication function of the form $y = Ax$ where *A* is a sparse matrix and the *x* and *y* vectors are dense. By looking at this

[4]http://falsifiable.us
[5]http://github.com/ivotron/quiho-popper

Table 3: Table of performance counters for the HPCCG performance test.

counter	HPCCG	stackmmap	cache	bigheap
ins. per cycle	0.78	0.18	0.25	0.39
stalled cycles p/ins.	0.53	2.29	3.52	1.44
stalled cycles (frontend)	13.51%	41.09%	89.70%	18.95%
stalled cycles (backend)	41.19%	9.23%	0.80%	56.53%
branch misses	2.87%	9.24%	0.01%	0.69%
L1-dcache misses	5.62%	5.47%	52.91%	2.75%
LLC misses	1.03%	16.41%	51.88%	5.60%

code, we see that the innermost loop iterates an array, accumulating the sum of a multiplication. This type of code is a potential candidate for manifesting bottlenecks associated with CPU cache locality [36].

Listing 1 Source code for bottleneck function in HPCCG.

```
int HPC_sparsemv(HPC_Sparse_Matrix *A,
                const double * const x,
                double * const y)
{

  const int nrow = (const int) A->local_nrow;

  for (int i=0; i< nrow; i++) {
    double sum = 0.0;
    const double * const cur_vals =
     (const double * const) A->ptr_to_vals_in_row[i];

    const int    * const cur_inds =
     (const int    * const) A->ptr_to_inds_in_row[i];

    const int cur_nnz = (const int) A->nnz_in_row[i];

    for (int j=0; j< cur_nnz; j++)
        sum += cur_vals[j]*x[cur_inds[j]];
    y[i] = sum;
  }

  return(0);
}
```

We analyze the performance of this benchmark further by obtaining performance counters for the application and comparing the counters with those from the top three features (Tbl. 3 shows the summary of hardware-level performance counters). Given that hardware performance counters are architecture-dependent, we can not make generalizations about given that we run an application on a multitude of machines. Having said this, we can try to analyze the counter results for the particular machine where we ran this test. We can see that the performance counters values for the hpccg application correspond to a combination of values for the three most relevant features (stressors). In the case of the stackmmap stressor, similarities between stalled cycle counters are noticeable denoting similarities in stalled cycles, which are associated to application performance [37,38].

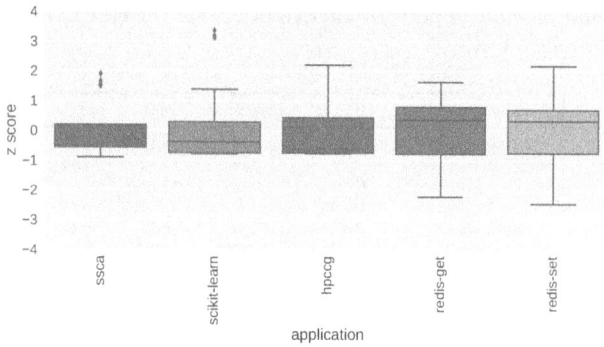

Figure 8: Variability of the four applications presented in this subsection. Y-axis has been normalized.

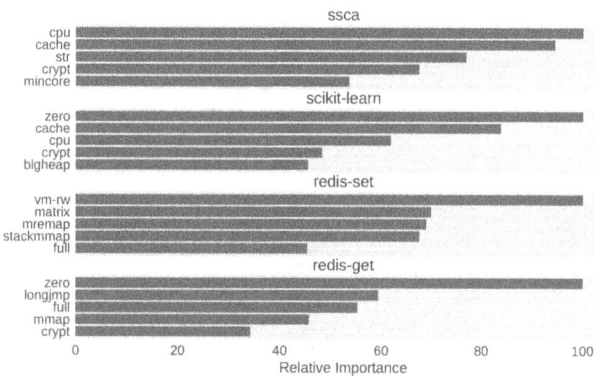

Figure 9: IRUPs for the four tests benchmarked in this section. This and subsequent figures show only the top 5 most important features in order to improve visualization of the plots.

Next, we analyze the IRUPs of other three applications[6]. These applications are Redis [39], Scikit-learn [29], and SSCA [40]. Due to space constraints we omit a similar detailed analysis as the one presented above for hpccg. However, resource utilization characteristics of these code bases is well known and we verify IRUPs using this knowledge. As a way of illustrating the performance variability of these applications on an heterogeneous set of machines, Fig. 8 shows boxplots of their runtime.

In Fig. 9 we show IRUPs for these four applications[7]. The first two on the top correspond to two tests of Redis, a popular open-source in-memory key-value database. These two tests are SET, GET from the redis-benchmark command that test operations that store and retrieve key-value pairs into/from the DB, respectively. The resource utilization profiles suggest that SET and GET are memory intensive operations (first 3 stressors from each test, as shown in Tbl. 1), which is an obvious conclusion.

---

[6]For brevity, we omit other results that corroborate IRUPs can correctly identify resource utilization patterns. All these are available in the Github repository accompanying this article.

[7]In order to enhance the visualization of the IRUPs we only show the top 5 most important features. Complete profiles can be visualized on the Jupyter notebook contained in the github repository.

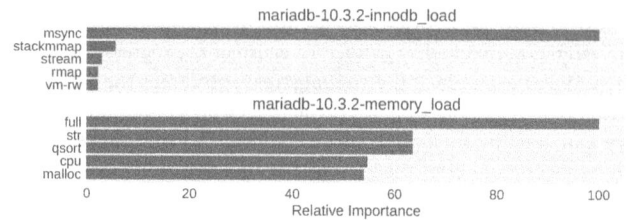

Figure 10: MariaDB with innodb and in-memory backends.

The next two IRUPs (below) correspond to performance tests for Scikit-learn and SSCA. In the case of Scikit-learn, this test runs a comparison of several classifiers in on a synthetic dataset. Scikit-learn uses NumPy [41] internally, which is known to be memory-bound. The profile is aligned to this known behavior since the zero microbenchmark stresses access.

The last application is SSCA, a graph analysis benchmark comprising of a data generator and 4 kernels which operate on the graph. The benchmark is designed to have very little locality, which causes the application to generate a many cache misses. As shown in the profile, the first feature corresponds to the cache stressor, which as it was explained earlier, stresses the CPU cache by generating a non-locality workload.

4.2 Simulating Regressions

In this section we test the effectiveness of *quiho* to detect performance simulations that are artificially induced. We induce regression by having a set of performance tests that take, as input, parameters that determine their performance behavior, thus simulating different "versions" of the same application. In total, we have 10 benchmarks for which we can induce several performance regressions, for a total of 20 performance regressions. For brevity, in this section we present results for two applications, MariaDB [42] and a modified version of the STREAM benchmark.

The MariaDB test is based on the mysqlslap utility for stressing the database engine. In our case we run the data loading test, which populates a database whose schema is specified by the user. We have a fixed set of parameters that load a 10GB database. One of the exposed parameters is the one that selects the backend (storage engine in MySQL terminology). While the workload and test parameters are the same, the code paths are distinct and thus present different performance characteristics. The two engines we use in this case are innodb and memory. Fig. 10 shows the profiles of MariaDB performance for these two engines.

The next test is a modified version of the STREAM benchmark [33], which we refer to as STREAM-NADDS (introduced in [43]). This version of STREAM introduces a NADDS pre-processor parameter that controls the number additions for the Add test of the STREAM benchmark. In terms of the code, when NADDS equals to 1 is equivalent to the "vanilla" STREAM benchmark. For any value greater than 1, the code adds a new term to the sum being executed. Intuitively, since the vanilla version of STREAM is memory bound, so adding more terms to the sum causes the CPU to do more work, eventually moving the bottleneck from memory to being

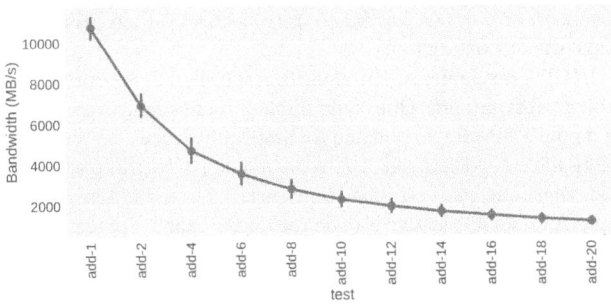

Figure 11: General behavior of the STREAM-NADDS performance test. The y-axis is the throughput of the test in MB/s. The x-axis corresponds to the number of terms in the sum expression of the Add STREAM subtest. The regular ("vanilla") STREAM add test is memory bound, so adding more terms to the Add subtest moves the performance from memory- to cpu-bound; the higher the value of the NADDS parameter, the more CPU-bound the test gets. This test was executed across all available machines (5 times). The bars denote standard deviation.

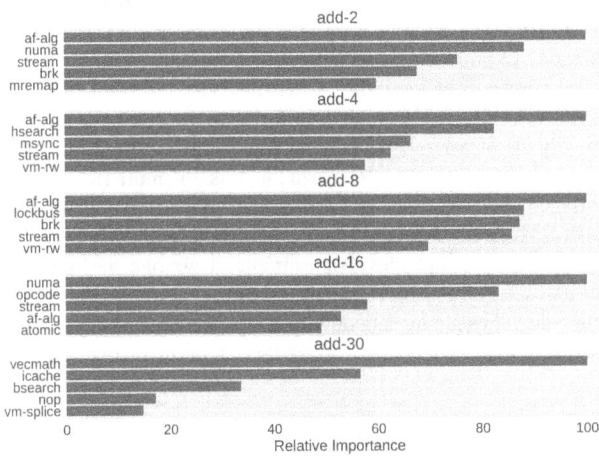

Figure 12: The IRUPs for modified version of STREAM. The parameter of NADDS increases by taking values of 1, 2, 4, ..., 20 and 30. We see that they capture the simulated regression which causes this application to be moving from being memory-bound to being cpu-bound.

cpu-bound; the higher the value of the NADDS parameter, the more cpu-bound the test gets. Fig. 11 shows this behavior.

Fig. 12 shows the IRUPs for the four tests. On the left, we see the resource utilization behavior of the "vanilla" version of STREAM (which corresponds to a value of 1 for the NADDS parameter). As expected, the associated features (stressors) to these are from the memory/VM category, in particular vecmath. As the number of terms for the sum increases, the test moves all the way to being CPU-bound (at NADDS=30), which can be seen by observing the bsearch and hsearch features going up in importance as the number of additions increases.

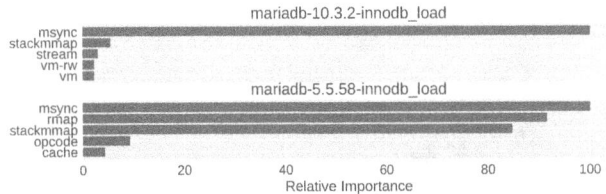

Figure 13: A regression that appears from going in the reversed timeline (from mariadb-10.0.3 to 5.5.38).

4.3 Real world Scenario

In this section we show that *quiho* works with regressions that can be found in real software projects. It is documented that the changes made to the innodb storage engine in version 10.3.2 improves the performance in MariaDB, with respect to previous version 5.5.58. If we take the development timeline and invert it, we can treat 5.5.58 as if it was a "new" revision that introduces a performance regression. To show that this can be captured with IRUPs, we use mysqlslap again and run the load test. Fig. 13 shows the corresponding IRUPs. We can observe that the IRUP generated by *quiho* can identify the difference in performance. For brevity, we omit regressions found in other 4 applications (zlog, postgres, redis, and apache web server).

5 DISCUSSION

In this section we provide a high-level discussion on several aspects of *quiho*.

Application-Independent Performance Characterization. The main advantage of the *quiho* approach is its resiliency. By inferring resource utilization instead of directly instrumenting code to generate profiles, the *quiho* approach is resilient to code refactoring and requires no manual intervention. We used a subset of stress-ng microbenchmarks to quantify machine performance but the approach is not limited to this benchmarking toolkit. Ideally, we would like to extend the amount and type of stressors so that we have more coverage over the distinct subcomponents of a system. An open question is to systematically test whether the current set of stressors is sufficient to cover all subcomponents of a system, and at the same time reduce the number of microbenchmarks.

Falsifiability of IRUPs The reader might have noticed that, regardless of how the performance of an application looks like, SRA will always produce a model with associated feature importances. Thus, one can pose the following question: is there any scenario where an IRUP is *not* correctly associated with what the application is doing? In other words, are IRUPs falsifiable? The answer is yes. An IRUP can be incorrectly representing an application's performance behavior if there is under- or over-fitting when generating the model. Fig. 14 shows the correlation matrix obtained from a dataset containing only 3 data points (generated by selecting two random machines from the set of available ones). Almost all stressors are highly correlated among each other, which suggests (as explained in Section 3) there is little that a prediction model can learn about the underlying resource utilization behavior of an application in this dataset (which contains only a couple of points, coming from two machines with very similar characteristics). This is confirmed by obtaining an IRUP multiple times for an application

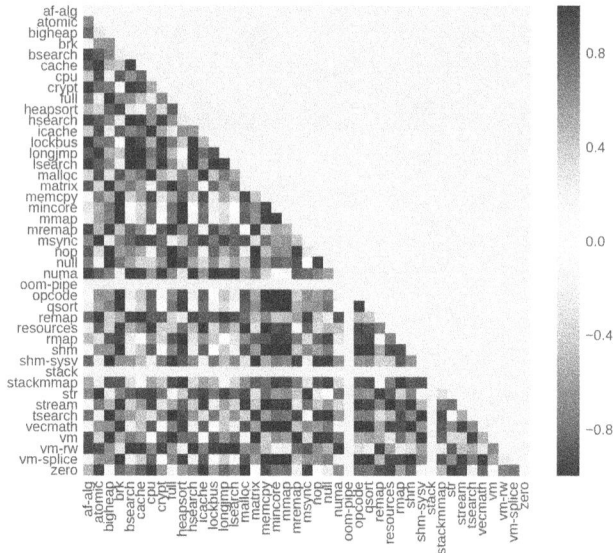

Figure 14: Correlation matrix, obtained from only two randomly selected machines from Tbl. 2.

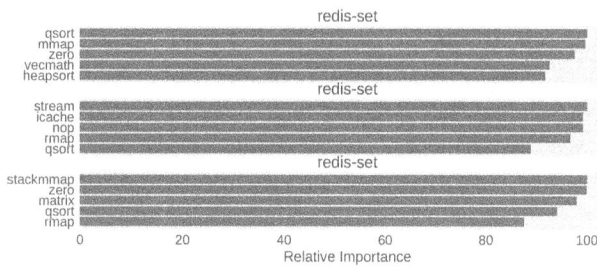

Figure 15: Three IRUPs for the `redis-set` benchmark, obtained sequentialy from the same dataset, which consistes of only two randomly selected machines from Tbl. 2.

contained in this small dataset (Fig. 15). The application in this case is `redis-set`. If we obtain the IRUP 3 times and compare them, we observe that they give completely random and contradictory results (for example, the bottom IRUP ranks CPU stressors as the top important features). This is in contrast to what we observe with well-fitted models, such as the ones in Fig. 9 for which multiple IRUPs show consistent results in their results. The correlation matrix shows why this is so: almost all the features are highly correlated. One way of determining the right amount of machines needed in order to generate good models is to apply probable aproximate correct learning (PAC) [44] to this dataset in order to quantify the probability of obtaining highly accurate estimations.

Quiho vs. other tools. The main advantage of *quiho* over other performance profiling tools is that it is automatic and 100% hands-off. As mentioned before, the main assumption being that there exist performance vectors (or they are obtained as part of the test) for a sufficiently varied set of machines. We see *quiho* as a complement, not a replacement of `perf`, to existing performance engineering

practices: once a test has failed *quiho*'s checks, then proceed to make use of existing tools.

IRUP Comparison. The algorithm specified in Section 3.3 is a straight-forward one. One could think of more sophisticated ways of doing IRUP comparison and finding equivalences. For example, using the categories from Tbl. 1, one could try to group stressors and determine coarse-grained bottlenecks, instead of fine grained ones. Another alternative is to do reduce the number of features by applying PCA, exploratory factor analysis (EFA), or singular value decomposition (SVD), and compare profiles in terms of the mapped factors.

IRUP as a visualization tool. The reader might have noticed that IRUPs can be visually compared by the human eye (and are somewhat similar in this regard to FlameGraphs [45]). Adding a coloring scheme to IRUPs might make it easier to interpret the differences. For example, the categories in Tbl. 1 could be used to define a color palette (by assigning a color to each subset of the powerset of categories).

Reproducibility. Providing performance vectors alongside experimental results allows to preserve information about the performance characteristics of the underlying system that an experiment observed at the time it ran. This is a quantifiable snapshot that provides context and facilitates the interpretation of results. Ideally, this information could be used as input for emulators and virtual machines, in order to recreate original performance characteristics.

Reinforcement Learning. Over the course of its life, an application will be tested on many platforms. If we can have an ever-growing list of machines where an application is tested, the more we run an application in a scenario like this, the more rich the performance vector dataset (and associated application performance history). This can serve as the foundation to applycbecomes we learn about its properties. For example, if we had performance vectors captured as part of executions of the Phoronix benchmark suite (which has public data on https://openbenchmarking.org), we could leverage such a dataset to create rich performance models.

6 RELATED WORK

Automated Regression Testing. Automated regression testing [46] can be broken down in the following three steps. 1) In the case of large software projects, decide which tests to execute [47]. This line of work is complementary to *quiho*. 2) Once a test executes, decide whether a regression has occurred [48]. This can be broken down in mainly two categories, as explained in [12]: pair-wise comparisons and model assisted. *quiho* fits in the latter category, the main difference being that, as opposed to existing solutions, *quiho* does not rely on having accurate prediction models since its goal is to describe resource utilization (obtain IRUPs). 3) If a regression is observed, automatically find the root cause or aid an analyst to find it [13,49]. While *quiho* does not find the root cause of regressions, it complements the information that an analyst has available to investigate further.

Profiling-based Performance Modeling. Modeling performance based on application profiles has been studied before [50–52]. In [50], the MAPS benchmark is used to characterize the performance of machines. These profiles are then convoluted with application traces obtained by the MetaSim tool in order to obtain a prediction on the performance of an application. In [52] the authors use randomized optimization (genetic algorithms) to systematically explore the parameter space of an application in order to create a record of <input, runtime> pairs. *quiho* can be used in this case to augment the available information and have an IRUP associated to the inputs of the application under study.

Performance Profile Visualization. An IRUP can be used to visualize performance and thus have a resemblance with a flame graph [45]. In [53] the authors introduce the concept of differential flame grahps, which can be used to visually compare the changes between two or more flame graphs. A similar approach could be applied to IRUPs in order to visualize the differences between two flame graphs.

Inducing Performance Regressions. In [54], the authors analyzed the code repositories of two open source projects in order to device a way of systematically inducing performance regressions. Our methodology instruments an application in order to parametrize performance and control when changes in performance are triggered, as a way of testing methods that are aimed at detecting these changes.

Decision Trees In Performance Engineering. In [55] the authors use decision trees to detect anomalies and predict performance SLO violations. They validate their approach using a TPC-W workload in a multi-tiered setting. In [12], the authors use performance counters to build a regression model aimed at filtering out irrelevant performance counters. In [56], the approach is similar but statistical process control techniques are employed instead. In the case of *quiho*, the goal is to use decision trees as a way of obtaining feature performance, thus, as opposed to what it's proposed in [12], the leaves of the generated decision trees contain actual performance predictions instead of the name of performance counters

Correlation-based Analysis and Supervised Learning. Correlation and supervised learning approaches have been proposed in the context of software testing, mainly for detecting anomalies in application performance [49]. In the former, runtime performance metrics are correlated to application performance using a variety of distinct metrics. In supervised learning, the goal is the same (build prediction models) but using labeled datasets. Decision trees are a form of supervised learning, however, given that *quiho* applies regression rather than classification techniques, it does not rely on labeled datasets. Lastly, *quiho* is not intended to be used as a way of detecting anomalies, although we have not analyzed its potential use in this scenario.

7 FUTURE WORK

The main limitation in *quiho* is the requirement of having to execute a test on more than one machine in order to obtain IRUPs. On the other hand, we can avoid having to run stress-ng every time the application gets tested by integrating this into the infrastructure (e.g., system administrators can run stress-ng once a day or once a week and make this information for every machine available to users).

We are currently working in adapting this approach to profile distributed and multi-tiered applications. We also plan to analyze the viability of applying *quiho* in multi-tenant configurations and

to profile long-running (multi-stage) applications such as a webservice or big-data applications. In these cases, we would define windows of time and apply *quiho* to each. The main challenge in this scenario is to automatically define the windows in such a way that we can get accurate profiles.

In the era of cloud computing, even the most basic computer systems are complex multi-layered pieces of software, whose performance properties are difficult to comprehend. Having complete understanding of the performance behavior of an application, considering the parameter space (workloads, multi-tenancy, etc.) is challenging. One application of *quiho* we have in mind is to couple it with automated black-box (or even gray-box) testing frameworks to improve our understanding of complex systems.

Acknowledgments: We would like to thank Bernardo Gonzalez for his feedback on a preliminary version of this paper, as well as all the anonymous reviewers. Special thanks go to our ICPE shepherd. This work was partially funded by the Center for Research in Open Source Software[8], Sandia National Laboratories, NSF Award #1450488 and DOE Award #DE-SC0016074. Sandia National Laboratories is a multimission laboratory managed and operated by National Technology and Engineering Solutions of Sandia, LLC, a wholly owned subsidiary of Honeywell International, Inc., for the U.S. Department of Energy's National Nuclear Security Administration under contract DE-NA0003525.

REFERENCES

[1] G.J. Myers, C. Sandler, and T. Badgett, *The Art of Software Testing*, 2011.
[2] A. Bertolino, "Software Testing Research: Achievements, Challenges, Dreams," *2007 Future of Software Engineering*, 2007.
[3] B. Beizer, *Software Testing Techniques*, 1990.
[4] J. Dean and L.A. Barroso, "The tail at scale," *Commun ACM*, vol. 56, Feb. 2013.
[5] B. Gregg, *Systems Performance: Enterprise and the Cloud*, 2013.
[6] F.I. Vokolos and E.J. Weyuker, "Performance Testing of Software Systems," *Proceedings of the 1st International Workshop on Software and Performance*, 1998.
[7] L. Cherkasova, K. Ozonat, N. Mi, J. Symons, and E. Smirni, "Anomaly? Application change? Or workload change? Towards automated detection of application performance anomaly and change," *2008 IEEE International Conference on Dependable Systems and Networks With FTCS and DCC (DSN)*, 2008.
[8] G. Jin, L. Song, X. Shi, J. Scherpelz, and S. Lu, "Understanding and Detecting Real-world Performance Bugs," *Proceedings of the 33rd ACM SIGPLAN Conference on Programming Language Design and Implementation*, 2012.
[9] S. Han, Y. Dang, S. Ge, D. Zhang, and T. Xie, "Performance Debugging in the Large via Mining Millions of Stack Traces," *Proceedings of the 34th International Conference on Software Engineering*, 2012. Available at: http://dl.acm.org/citation.cfm?id=2337223.2337241.
[10] M. Jovic, A. Adamoli, and M. Hauswirth, "Catch Me if You Can: Performance Bug Detection in the Wild," *Proceedings of the 2011 ACM International Conference on Object Oriented Programming Systems Languages and Applications*, 2011.
[11] Z.M. Jiang, "Automated Analysis of Load Testing Results," *Proceedings of the 19th International Symposium on Software Testing and Analysis*, 2010.
[12] W. Shang, A.E. Hassan, M. Nasser, and P. Flora, "Automated Detection of Performance Regressions Using Regression Models on Clustered Performance Counters,"

---

[8]http://cross.ucsc.edu

Proceedings of the 6th ACM/SPEC International Conference on Performance Engineering, 2015.

[13] C. Heger, J. Happe, and R. Farahbod, "Automated Root Cause Isolation of Performance Regressions During Software Development," *Proceedings of the 4th ACM/SPEC International Conference on Performance Engineering*, 2013.

[14] M.A. Heroux, *Hpccg Solver Package*, Sandia National Laboratories, 2007. Available at: https://www.osti.gov/scitech/biblio/1230960.

[15] A. Kivity, Y. Kamay, D. Laor, U. Lublin, and A. Liguori, "Kvm: The Linux virtual machine monitor," *Proceedings of the Linux symposium*, 2007.

[16] D. Merkel, "Docker: Lightweight Linux Containers for Consistent Development and Deployment," *Linux J*, vol. 2014, Mar. 2014. Available at: http://dl.acm.org/citation.cfm?id=2600239.2600241.

[17] J. Mambretti, J. Chen, and F. Yeh, "Next Generation Clouds, the Chameleon Cloud Testbed, and Software Defined Networking (SDN)," *2015 International Conference on Cloud Computing Research and Innovation (ICCCRI)*, 2015.

[18] M. Hibler, R. Ricci, L. Stoller, J. Duerig, S. Guruprasad, T. Stack, K. Webb, and J. Lepreau, "Large-scale Virtualization in the Emulab Network Testbed," *USENIX 2008 Annual Technical Conference*, 2008. Available at: http://dl.acm.org/citation.cfm?id=1404014.1404023.

[19] R. Ricci and E. Eide, "Introducing CloudLab: Scientific Infrastructure for Advancing Cloud Architectures and Applications,";*login:* vol. 39, 2014/December. Available at: http://www.usenix.org/publications/login/dec14/ricci.

[20] R. Bolze, F. Cappello, E. Caron, M. Daydé, F. Desprez, E. Jeannot, Y. Jégou, S. Lanteri, J. Leduc, N. Melab, G. Mornet, R. Namyst, P. Primet, B. Quetier, O. Richard, E.-G. Talbi, and I. Touche, "Grid'5000: A Large Scale And Highly Reconfigurable Experimental Grid Testbed," *Int J High Perform Comput Appl*, vol. 20, Nov. 2006.

[21] A. Wiggins, "The Twelve-Factor App" Available at: http://12factor.net/. Available at: http://12factor.net/.

[22] M. Hüttermann, *DevOps for Developers*, 2012.

[23] I. Jimenez, C. Maltzahn, J. Lofstead, A. Moody, K. Mohror, R. Arpaci-Dusseau, and A. Arpaci-Dusseau, "Characterizing and Reducing Cross-Platform Performance Variability Using OS-Level Virtualization," *2016 IEEE International Parallel and Distributed Processing Symposium Workshops (IPDPSW)*, 2016.

[24] J.W. Boyse and D.R. Warn, "A Straightforward Model for Computer Performance Prediction," *ACM Comput Surv*, vol. 7, Jun. 1975.

[25] K. Kira and L.A. Rendell, "A Practical Approach to Feature Selection," *Proceedings of the Ninth International Workshop on Machine Learning*, 1992. Available at: http://dl.acm.org/citation.cfm?id=645525.656966.

[26] C.I. King, *Stress-ng*, 2017. Available at: https://github.com/ColinIanKing/stress-ng.

[27] S. Wold, K. Esbensen, and P. Geladi, "Principal component analysis," *Chemometrics and Intelligent Laboratory Systems*, vol. 2, Aug. 1987.

[28] D.A. Freedman, *Statistical Models: Theory and Practice*, 2009.

[29] F. Pedregosa, G. Varoquaux, A. Gramfort, V. Michel, B. Thirion, O. Grisel, M. Blondel, P. Prettenhofer, R. Weiss, V. Dubourg, J. Vanderplas, A. Passos, D. Cournapeau, M. Brucher, M. Perrot, and É. Duchesnay, "Scikit-learn: Machine Learning in Python," *J. Mach. Learn. Res.*, vol. 12, 2011. Available at: http://www.jmlr.org/papers/v12/pedregosa11a.html.

[30] P. Prettenhofer and G. Louppe, "Gradient Boosted Regression Trees in Scikit-Learn," Feb. 2014. Available at: http://orbi.ulg.ac.be/handle/2268/163521.

[31] J.H. Friedman, "Greedy Function Approximation: A Gradient Boosting Machine," *Ann. Stat.*, vol. 29, 2001.

[32] L. Breiman, J. Friedman, C.J. Stone, and R.A. Olshen, *Classification and Regression Trees*, 1984.

[33] J.D. McCalpin, "Memory Bandwidth and Machine Balance in Current High Performance Computers," *IEEE Comput. Soc. Tech. Comm. Comput. Archit. TCCA Newsl.*, Dec. 1995.

[34] I. Jimenez, M. Sevilla, N. Watkins, C. Maltzahn, J. Lofstead, K. Mohror, A. Arpaci-Dusseau, and R. Arpaci-Dusseau, "The Popper Convention: Making Reproducible Systems Evaluation Practical," *2017 IEEE International Parallel and Distributed Processing Symposium Workshops (IPDPSW)*, 2017.

[35] M.A. Heroux, D.W. Doerfler, P.S. Crozier, J.M. Willenbring, H.C. Edwards, A. Williams, M. Rajan, E.R. Keiter, H.K. Thornquist, and R.W. Numrich, "Improving

performance via mini-applications," *Sandia Natl. Lab. Tech Rep SAND2009-5574*, vol. 3, 2009.

[36] K. Akbudak, E. Kayaaslan, and C. Aykanat, "Hypergraph Partitioning Based Models and Methods for Exploiting Cache Locality in Sparse Matrix-Vector Multiplication," *SIAM J. Sci. Comput.*, vol. 35, Jan. 2013.

[37] S. Cepeda, "Pipeline Speak, Part 2: The Second Part of the Sandy Bridge Pipeline" Available at: http://intel.ly/2EuwM9J. Available at: http://intel.ly/2EuwM9J.

[38] C. McNairy and D. Soltis, "Itanium 2 processor microarchitecture," *IEEE Micro*, vol. 23, Mar. 2003.

[39] J. Zawodny, "Redis: Lightweight key/value store that goes the extra mile," *Linux Mag.*, vol. 79, 2009.

[40] D.A. Bader and K. Madduri, "Design and Implementation of the HPCS Graph Analysis Benchmark on Symmetric Multiprocessors," *High Performance Computing – HiPC 2005*, 2005.

[41] S. van der Walt, S.C. Colbert, and G. Varoquaux, "The NumPy array: A structure for efficient numerical computation," *Comput. Sci. Eng.*, vol. 13, 2011.

[42] M. Widenius, "MariaDB SQL server project," *Ask Monty* Available at: http://askmonty.org/wiki/index.php/MariaDB. Available at: http://askmonty.org/wiki/index.php/MariaDB.

[43] A. Hutcheson and V. Natoli, "Memory Bound vs. Compute Bound: A Quantitative Study of Cache and Memory Bandwidth in High Performance Applications," 2011.

[44] L.G. Valiant, "A Theory of the Learnable," *Commun ACM*, vol. 27, Nov. 1984.

[45] B. Gregg, "The Flame Graph," *Commun ACM*, vol. 59, May. 2016.

[46] S.E. Perl and W.E. Weihl, "Performance Assertion Checking," *Proceedings of the Fourteenth ACM Symposium on Operating Systems Principles*, 1993.

[47] R. Kazmi, D.N.A. Jawawi, R. Mohamad, and I. Ghani, "Effective Regression Test Case Selection: A Systematic Literature Review," *ACM Comput Surv*, vol. 50, May. 2017.

[48] M.D. Syer, Z.M. Jiang, M. Nagappan, A.E. Hassan, M. Nasser, and P. Flora, "Continuous Validation of Load Test Suites," *Proceedings of the 5th ACM/SPEC International Conference on Performance Engineering*, 2014.

[49] O. Ibidunmoye, F. Hernández-Rodriguez, and E. Elmroth, "Performance Anomaly Detection and Bottleneck Identification," *ACM Comput Surv*, vol. 48, Jul. 2015.

[50] A. Snavely, N. Wolter, and L. Carrington, "Modeling application performance by convolving machine signatures with application profiles," *Proceedings of the Fourth Annual IEEE International Workshop on Workload Characterization. WWC-4 (Cat. No.01EX538)*, 2001.

[51] S. Ghaith, M. Wang, P. Perry, and J. Murphy, "Profile-Based, Load-Independent Anomaly Detection and Analysis in Performance Regression Testing of Software Systems," *2013 17th European Conference on Software Maintenance and Reengineering*, 2013.

[52] D. Shen, Q. Luo, D. Poshyvanyk, and M. Grechanik, "Automating Performance Bottleneck Detection Using Search-based Application Profiling," *Proceedings of the 2015 International Symposium on Software Testing and Analysis*, 2015.

[53] C.P. Bezemer, J. Pouwelse, and B. Gregg, "Understanding software performance regressions using differential flame graphs," *2015 IEEE 22nd International Conference on Software Analysis, Evolution, and Reengineering (SANER)*, 2015.

[54] J. Chen and W. Shang, "An Exploratory Study of Performance Regression Introducing Code Changes," *2017 IEEE International Conference on Software Maintenance and Evolution (ICSME)*, 2017.

[55] G. Jung, G. Swint, J. Parekh, C. Pu, and A. Sahai, "Detecting Bottleneck in n-Tier IT Applications Through Analysis," *Large Scale Management of Distributed Systems*, 2006.

[56] T.H. Nguyen, B. Adams, Z.M. Jiang, A.E. Hassan, M. Nasser, and P. Flora, "Automated Detection of Performance Regressions Using Statistical Process Control Techniques," *Proceedings of the 3rd ACM/SPEC International Conference on Performance Engineering*, 2012.

Characterizing the Performance of Concurrent Virtualized Network Functions with OVS-DPDK, FD.IO VPP and SR-IOV

Nikolai Pitaev

Enterprise Infrastructure and Solutions Group, Cisco Systems

npitaev@cisco.com

Matthias Falkner

Enterprise Infrastructure and Solutions Group, Cisco Systems

mfalkner@cisco.com

Aris Leivadeas

Department of Systems and Computer Engineering, Carleton University

arisleivadeas@sce.carleton.ca

Ioannis Lambadaris

Department of Systems and Computer Engineering, Carleton University

ioannis@sce.carleton.ca

ABSTRACT

The virtualization of network functions is promising significant cost reductions for network operators. Running multiple network functions on a standard x86 server instead of dedicated appliances can increase the utilization of the underlying hardware, while reducing the maintenance and management costs of such functions. However, total cost of ownership calculations are typically a function of the attainable network throughput, which in a virtualized system is highly dependent on the overall system architecture - in particular the input/output (I/O) path. In this paper we investigate the attainable performance of an x86 host running *multiple* virtualized network functions (VNFs) under different I/O architectures: OVS-DPDK, SR-IOV, and FD.io VPP. Running multiple VNFs in parallel on a standard x86 host is a common use-case for cloud-based networking services. We show that the system throughput in a multi-VNF environment differs significantly from deployments where only a single VNF is running on a server.

CCS CONCEPTS

• **Networks** → *Cloud computing*; *Network servers*; *Network experimentation*; *Network performance analysis*; *Network measurement*; • **Hardware** → *Networking hardware*; Buses and high-speed links;

KEYWORDS

NFV; Virtualized System Architectures; VNF Performance; SR-IOV; OVS; OVS-DPDK; FD.io VPP; Hypervisors; KVM

ACM Reference Format:

Nikolai Pitaev, Matthias Falkner, Aris Leivadeas, and Ioannis Lambadaris. 2018. Characterizing the Performance of Concurrent Virtualized Network Functions with OVS-DPDK, FD.IO VPP and SR-IOV. In *ICPE '18: ACM/SPEC International Conference on Performance Engineering, April 9–13, 2018, Berlin, Germany.* ACM, New York, NY, USA, 8 pages. https://doi.org/10.1145/3184407.3184437

1 INTRODUCTION

Service Provider and Infrastructure Provider (e.g. Cloud Provider) networks are increasingly making use of virtualized network functions (VNFs) to reap the benefits of reduced capital expenditures (CAPEX) and operating expenses (OPEX). Running VNFs on standard off-the-shelf server platforms promises to reduce the capital expenditures previously dedicated to hardware appliances. Operators are also expecting a significant reduction in the operating expenses by increasing the level of automation enabled by software defined networking. Total cost of ownership calculations however are typically a function of the attainable network performance, which in a virtualized system is highly dependent on the overall system architecture. For input/output (I/O) intensive workloads such as virtualized network functions (VNFs), the packet path from the physical interface on the server into the virtual machine (VM) is particularly impactful on the overall system throughput. Open vSwitch (OVS) [13, 29], OVS - Data Plane Development Kit [8], Single-Root I/O Virtualization [7], and Fast Data input/output Vector Packet Processing (FD.io VPP) [17] are possible alternative mechanisms to carry network traffic from the physical interface into VNFs.

Also impacting the overall system throughput is the number of concurrent VNFs running on top of the hypervisor. For most use-cases where virtualization is considered, multiple VMs are sharing the hardware resources offered by the underlying x86 host. In some cases, application workloads running in VMs are instantiated alongside VNFs. More commonly, operators separate application workloads from VNFs onto different servers, while still instantiating multiple VMs on each of the systems.

The networking departments of many enterprise or service providers operate their own hardware systems, separate from the IT departments. An example of such a deployment scenario is cloud-based managed services. In this use-case, SP operators offer virtualized networking services to enterprise customers out of their own data centers. VNFs such as virtual routers, virtual firewalls, or virtualized WAN optimization are instantiated on a per-enterprise basis. For basic services, a single VNF can be configured to serve multiple enterprise customers, even with multiple networking features (multi-tenancy combined with multi-feature). For more sophisticated services, dedicated VNFs may be service-chained for each enterprise customer, offering higher per-tenant throughput and customer separation. Multiple VNFs associated with different enterprise customers share the underlying x86 host resources in this case. Sophisticated automation and orchestration environments instantiate such cloud-based networking services within minutes, taking the available hardware resources into account.

Furthermore, multiple VNFs are running in parallel in such a shared server environment, contending for underlying CPU, I/O, memory and storage resources. The overall attainable system throughput may be impacted by various system bottlenecks. In particular, the vSwitch bottleneck is identified as one of the main bottleneck in such a multi-VM configuration. Thus, the performance of different I/O architectures are of utmost importance. In [22], the authors present the performance of running multiple VNFs in parallel while varying the hypervisor's I/O technologies with OVS, SR-IOV and FD.io VPP.

In this paper, we extend the experimental results by replacing OVS with OVS-DPDK, which promises to significantly increase the I/O performance for virtualized network functions. We also use DPDK-enabled VNFs. We show how OVS-DPDK compares from a throughput perspective to SR-IOV and FD.io VPP as the number of VNFs is increased under multiple feature configurations. We demonstrate the system throughput behaviour not just for pure IP forwarding, but also for a realistic virtual router configuration where processing-intensive features like Network Address Translation (NAT), Firewall, Quality-of-Service (QoS) and even deep-packet inspection (DPI) are applied to the packet flows processed by each VNF. Our experiments reveal that OVS-DPDK has comparable performance to FD.io VPP, thus confirming a significant throughput improvement as compared to native OVS. Considering that both OVS-DPDK and FD.io VPP offer richer virtualization functionality with fewer caveats than SR-IOV, network operators looking to deploy VNFs have viable alternatives to trade-off deployment flexibility and overall system throughput.

The remainder of the paper is organized as follows: Section 2 provides an overview of the related work. Section 3 provides insights of the various I/O architectures. Section 4 presents the test methodology followed. The performance evaluation is presented in Section 5. Finally, Section 6 concludes the paper.

2 RELATED WORK

Performance of the I/O path in virtualized system architectures has been widely studied in the literature in recent years. Throughput of FD.io with VPP has been investigated under various system configurations in [19], showing the throughput and latency improvements that can be achieved with FD.io VPP as compared to OVS-DPDK. In [11], the authors perform systematic experiments to investigate various virtual switches, including OVS, Linux bridges and also citing official results for OVS-DPDK. Various traffic flows are tested, going directly into a single VNF, passing through a single VNF, or being service chained through a VNF and terminated in another VNF. A thorough investigation into the system parameters in a similar setup is also reported in [12].

In [20] a user-space virtual switch (SnabbSwitch) is introduced and its performance analyzed against OVS, OVS-DPDK, linux bridges, Virtual Function Input/Output (VFIO), and SR-IOV. The results demonstrate that this implementation performs similar to SR-IOV and VFIO, and out-performing OVS and OVS-DPDK in user-space. The tests are conducted with two VNFs only, generating either uni-directional or bi-directional traffic, following the methodology in [27]. A similar vSwitch development (Lagopus) is described in [23] and its performance studied for both delay and throughput. No comparison to other vSwitches is made, and traffic is not sent to any VNFs.

An elaborate study of SR-IOV performance under multiple VNFs is reported in [10], without making however any comparison to other vSwitches. A similar study for SR-IOV with NAPI optimizations is presented in [15], analyzing CPU utilization and throughput in a multi-VNF scenario, but without comparisons to other I/O techniques. The authors in [24] investigate the switching performance of a virtualized software router with different traffic flows (up to 4) under various packet sizes, and compare the throughput to non-virtualized software routers to show the performance penalty introduced by virtualization, without analyzing different virtual switching technologies. The throughput and latency of OVS and OVS with DPDK with multiple VMs and Docker containers that are service chained is also studied in [2]. The study shows that OVS with DPDK can achieve a 10-fold improvement in the PPS rate for the specified test. However, no comparison to other I/O techniques is made, as the focus of the paper is more on analyzing the number of VMs / containers in a chain. A comparison between physical and VM performance under Intel DPDK is given in [25]. Throughput in terms of Mpps is reported with two VMs and compared to a physical setup. A multi-VNF performance analysis under Openstack is reported in [4], showing also realistic traffic patterns with networking features (DPI, Firewall, routing) applied under Openstack with both a linux bridge and OVS. Newer I/O technologies are not analyzed in the paper.

In comparison with the above presented works, the contribution of this paper is twofold: first, our test study the impact of multiple VNFs running in parallel (not chained) on an x86 host. In such an environment, multiple VNFs place demand for I/O processing and vCPUs on the hypervisor scheduler, thus stressing the latter in a different way to single-VNF tests. This is very common in so-called horizontal-scale use-cases, where multiple VNFs are used in order to fulfil high scale requirements. Our study thus provides insights into a realistic deployment scenario, where there is contention for the servers' hardware resources. In the environment we study, the hypervisor scheduler has to process switch to allocate the available CPU cycles to numerous VNFs as well as to the Linux OS itself. In any of the single-VNF analyses above, such an interaction is not taken into account. Second, we perform our analysis with a commercially available virtual router (the Cisco CSR 1000V® [1]), configured not only for pure IP forwarding, but also showing the impact under a realistic feature processing configuration. Of particular importance in our tests is to avoid any hypervisor tuning steps that may be difficult to operationalize in a production environment. Only those hypervisor or process settings that can be configured at boot time or bring-up are optimized.

3 OVERVIEW OF A VIRTUALIZED SYSTEM ARCHITECTURE

In a basic virtualized system architecture, hardware resources (CPU, Memory, Storage) are being abstracted by a hypervisor layer to present virtual CPU/Memory/Storage to VMs or applications that run on top of the hypervisor. In this paper, we focus on the scenario of networking functions running inside a VM, as opposed to running VNFs in a container (e.g. Docker [6]) or running applications directly on the host OS. For networking VNFs, one or more software processes are running inside the VM to perform packet processing (e.g. firewall, routing, NAT etc.). These software processes are associated with the virtualized CPUs allocated to the VM. In addition to the vCPU threads configured for a VM, numerous VM system threads are also generating processing loads. The aggregate of all vCPU processes from the set of VMs are presented to the hypervisor layer for scheduling onto physical CPU cores.

Unfortunately, a virtualized system architecture may expose various throughput bottlenecks. Specifically, the physical port density and speed of the server may constraint the amount of traffic that can be processed. Another bottleneck may be the hypervisor scheduler itself, in particular if a large number of processes need to be allocated CPU cycles with strict timing. Furthermore, the VNF itself typically has a maximum packet processing capacity that may also limit its throughput. Finally, in an I/O bound networking environment another bottleneck is how the packet path from the physical NIC into the VMs can affect the overall performance. In this paper, we are particularly interested in this final bottleneck and for this reason, we evaluate how different available alternatives such as OVS-DPDK, FD.io VPP, or SR-IOV can contribute to the overall system throughput. Our intent is to share real measurement results, and provide insights on the performance of various I/O techniques.

3.1 Virtualized I/O Architectures

Virtualization of network functions differs from application virtualization. In the former case, the I/O workload generated by packet flows dominates. By definition of a VNF and its purpose being to process networking traffic, packets are continuously arriving into the server and need to be passed to its respective VM for processing. Networking VMs are thus generating high I/O workloads for the hypervisor and thus be referred to as I/O bound. In contrast, many non-networking applications receive only a limited number of external inputs. Their requirement for CPU cycles are predominantly algorithmic computations, possibly also with intensive memory and storage access. Such applications or networking functions consequently become compute-bound.

In general, packets arrive on the physical NIC and are copied into memory via two direct-memory access (DMA) operations. Along with the packet copy, a descriptor specifying the buffer location (memory address and length) is also copied into memory. The pNIC then sends an interrupt to indicate the arrival of the packet (see [10, 24] for details). The packet may then be processed by the virtual switch or a linux bridge process such as OVS-DPDK, FD.io VPP or SR-IOV. The three different system configurations are illustrated in Figures 1a and 1b respectively.

In the case of OVS-DPDK [9], packets are passed to the virtual switch for distribution to the destination VNFs (CSR 1000V® instances), assisted by the data path development kit (DPDK) libraries for fast packet processing. The DPDK libraries offer a poll-mode driver (PMD) that allows packets to pass from the physical interface to the virtual switch directly, thus avoiding the networking

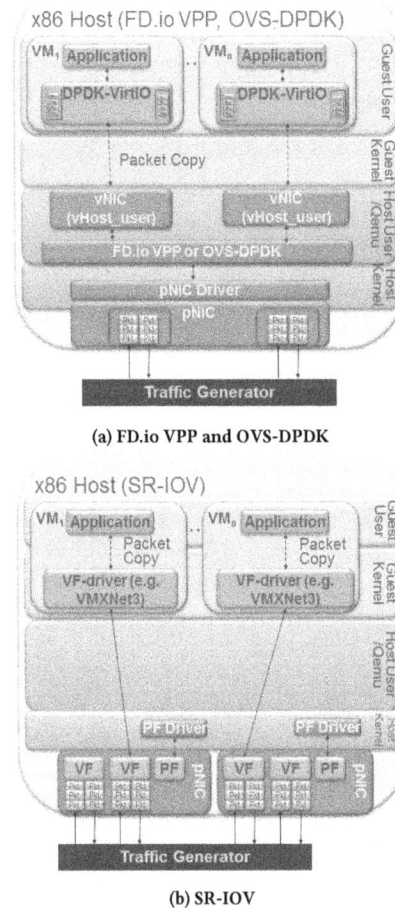

(a) FD.io VPP and OVS-DPDK

(b) SR-IOV

Figure 1: I/O paths of virtualized system architectures

stack of the kernel. OVS-DPDK offers enhanced switching functionality, supporting among others, jumbo-frames, link bonding, native tunnelling support for VXLAN, GRE or Geneve, MPLS, or ingress/egress policing. From a CPU resource perspective, OVS-DPDK is relying on CPU cycles from the host x86 core to switch packets, thus stressing the hypervisor scheduler in a system where multiple VNFs are also contending for the same CPU cycles. Any CPU core associated for switching to OVS-DPDK becomes unavailable to process VNFs. OVS-DPDK can however be configured to use multiple CPU cores for packet switching to increase its throughput towards the VNFs. In our tests below, we have configured 2 cores to be used for switching packets. Note that Figure 1a highlights the pertinent queues in these setups. Such internal queues are setup to pass packets on their path from the virtual switch into the VNFs, and their depths can become a bottleneck with high data rates. For OVS-DPDK the pertinent queues are in the DPDK driver in the guest user space. Note also that the VNFs used in our tests (the Cisco CSR 1000v) are also supporting DPDK to transfer packets efficiently to and from OVS-DPDK, so the entire packet path from the physical interface via the virtual switch into the VNF is supported by DPDK.

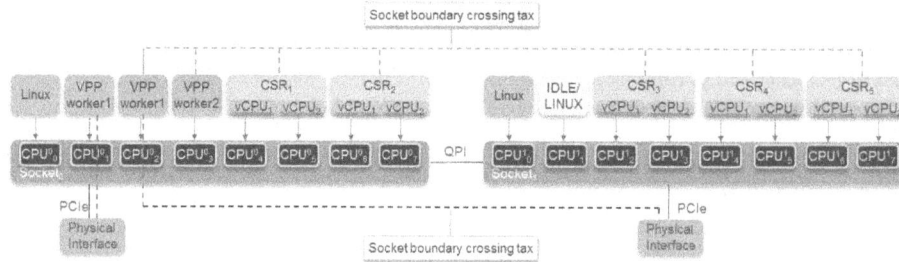

Figure 2: 2-socket x86 NUMA architecture

FD.io VPP [17] is an open-source alternative solution to optimize the I/O path in a virtualized system. Running as a Linux user-space process, the FD.io VPP drivers enable NIC access over PCI. FD.io processes packets in vectors (vector packet processing, VPP). Packets are removed from the receive rings of the interface and are formed into a packet vector, to which a processing graph is then applied [14]. The processing graph represents the features that need to be applied (e.g. IPv4 forwarding, classification, multicast etc.) [17]. This approach minimizes interrupts and traversing a call stack and thus also thrashing of the instruction caches and misses. VPP processes multiple packets at a time, making it a high-performance processing stack that supports even more networking functions than OVS-DPDK. Features such as DHCP, Segment routing, ARP, L2TPv3, VRFs, IPv6, MPLS-over-Ethernet are all supported. Similar to OVS-DPDK, FD.io VPP makes use of Intel's DPDK [8] library to accelerate packet processing, and thus requires CPU cycles to process packets which become unavailable for VNF processing. Again, the number of CPU cores assigned to FD.io VPP can be configured, and is set to 2 in our test to align with the OVS-DPDK setup. FD.io VPP also leverages internal queues in the DPDK driver in the guest user space to pass packets from the virtual switch into the VNFs.

Figure 2 provides a sample illustration of the hypervisor's I/O configuration for FD.io VPP (and can be generalized for OVS-DPDK). The x86 server is shown to offer two sockets with 8 cores each in the diagram. The PCI links of the physical interface are associated with the first socket, which also runs the switching threads (worker-threads) for FD.io VPP. The VNFs are pinned to dedicated cores spread across both sockets. The non-uniform memory access (NUMA) [16] architecture provides separate memory for each processor core and thus enables the cores of hitting their respective memory banks in parallel.

SR-IOV [7] in contrast offers a virtualized PCIe pass-through mechanism that does not rely on the hypervisor to pass packets between the NIC to the individual VNFs. As illustrated in Figure 1b SR-IOV virtualizes PCIe, creating PCIe physical functions (PF) and virtual functions (VF). This allows a physical port to be shared amongst multiple VNFs. The processing of features in a SR-IOV setup is entirely done inside the VNF, requiring the VNF to support the appropriate drivers. Features such as VXLAN, MPLS, policing etc. mentioned above for OVS-DPDK and FD.io VPP now have to be applied to packets inside the VNFs. SR-IOV has some functional limitations [28] due to its dependency on the underlying hardware and software. The server's NIC cards and the BIOS have to support

the technology. Further caveats are for example the number of VFs that can be configured for a physical NIC, currently limiting the number of VFs to 128 on an Intel Fortville NIC - but the practical limit may be as low as 64 [28]. Depending on the hardware and the driver implementation, other caveats may exist such as packet mir-roring, VLAN filtering, multicast addresses or promiscuous unicast [26].

4 TEST METHODOLOGY

To demonstrate the effects of the various I/O options in a multi-VNF system configuration, we apply the following test methodology: A Cisco UCS C240 Series [5] x86 host configured with a Redhat KVM [18] virtualization infrastructure is connected via a NIC with two 10 Gigabit Ethernet (GE) interfaces to a Layer 2 switch (Cisco Nexus 5548), which is in turn connected to an IXIA traffic generator using again 2x10 GE ports. The traffic generator sends IP Traffic with either an IMIX, 128B or 1518B packet size to a variable number of Cisco CSR 1000V® virtual routers hosted on the x86 server. IMIX traffic refers to typical internet traffic with packet sizes distributed within the range of 64 to 1500B. Up to 10 virtual routers are instantiated to ensure that the physical hardware resources are not over-subscribed.

The Cisco 1000V VNFs are configured to either perform basic IPv4 forwarding on the traffic stream (IP Throughput test), or to apply feature processing by executing Network Address Translation (NAT), Firewall, Quality-of-Service (QoS) and Deep-Packet Inspection (DPI) on the traffic stream. The latter feature configuration is representative for the cloud-based managed customer premises equipment (CPE) use-case described in Section 1. The bi-directional traffic is then returned to the traffic generator to measure the attained throughput, packet loss and other statistics, following RFC2544 [3], accepting a packet loss rate of 0.01% over the 1 minute measurement interval[1]. The specifics of the test setup are summarized in Table 1.

The packet path from the physical port in the x86 host to the VNFs is compared for three different system configurations, illustrated in Figures 1a, 1b for SR-IOV and FD.io VPP, and OVS-DPDK respectively, as described in Section 3.

---

[1]In virtualized systems, a non-zero packet loss rate is typically accepted since the Linux scheduler is not designed to accommodate a no drop rate (NDR) for high packet I/O.

Table 1: Details of the Test components

Test Component	Details
x86 Host	Cisco UCS C240 M4 Series: 2 Sockets Intel Xeon E5-2699v3 2.3 GHz with 18 cores each, 262GB RAM
Physical Interfaces	1 NIC with 2 x 10GE ports; Intel X520-DA2 NIC
Hypervisor	Redhat KVM version 7.2; Linux kernel 3.10.0-327.18.2.el7.x86 64; Libvirt 1.2.17; QEMU version 2.3.0
I/O Paths	OVS version 2.4.0
	Cisco FD.io VPP release 16.06, configured for 3 cores
	SR-IOV
Switch	Cisco Nexus 5548 Series, NX-OS 7.0
Traffic Generator	Ixia N2X, IxServer6.80.1100.12 GA
VNFs	Cisco CSR 1000V® virtual Router, IOS XE version 16.3.1a; 2 vCPU, 4GB RAM

5 MULTI-VM PERFORMANCE RESULTS

In this section we present the performance of the different I/O architectures in a multi-VM system. Two separate experiments were carried out. Experiment 1 with the goal to evaluate the performance of the throughput achieved when VNFs are configured to basic IPv4 forwarding (Cisco Express Forwarding - CEF); and Experiment 2 with the goal to evaluate the throughput performance achieved when applying feature processing by executing the feature set (NAT, Firewall, QoS, and DPI) to the VNF.

In our test methodology, the measured results are compared to a benchmark throughput that represents the optimal multi-VM throughput. The benchmark is derived from the measurement of a single VNF test with SR-IOV with either the IP forwarding only (Cisco Express Forwarding - CEF) or the feature set NAT, Firewall, QoS and DPI applied to the VNF. In ideal conditions, each additional VNF would contribute the same throughput to the overall system performance as the first VNF, up to the point where other system bottlenecks (in particular the physical NIC capacity) are reached. The benchmark is thus an additive linear extrapolation of the single-VNF test under SR-IOV. In other words, it is a theoretical optimal increase of the throughput that we would expect to notice as we add VNFs on the server. Details on a similar test setup are reported in [21].

5.1 Experiment 1: IPv4 Forwarding Results

Figures 3 and 4 show the measured performance with multiple VNFs for pure IP forwarding with an IMIX packet size in terms of Gbps and MPPS respectively[2]. SR-IOV shows a near-linear contribution to the overall system throughput for each additional VNF, reaching the physical interface limit of 19.01 Gbps with 3 VNFs under IMIX. The discrepancy between the full interface bandwidth of 20 Gbps and the measured maximum rate is explained by accounting for the inter-frame gap, the preamble and the start-of-frame delimiter in the Ethernet header. The maximum expected packet forwarding rate across both 10GE interfaces is 6.18 MPPS. The observed forwarding rate with SR-IOV of 6.14 is almost matching this rate.

In the case of FD.io VPP and OVS-DPDK, additional VNFs contribute positively to the overall system throughput for the first 2 and 3 VMs respectivey, reaching beyond a system throughput of

[2]Results for a packet size of 1518 bytes are not shown for the IP forwarding traffic profile. Both SR-IOV and FD.io VPP are able to exhaust the physical interface capacity already with a single VNF. OVS-DPDK is able to reach the physical interface capacity with two VNFs.

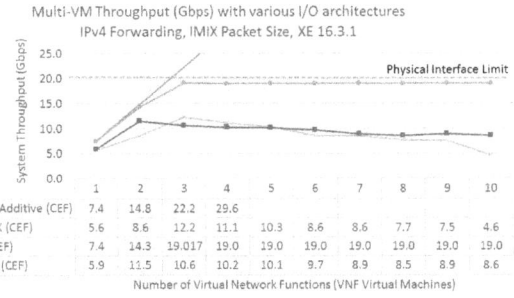

Figure 3: Multi-VM System Throughput with CEF, IMIX Packet Size, Gbps

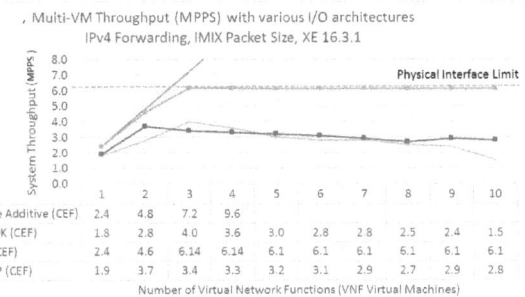

Figure 4: Multi-VM System Throughput with CEF, IMIX Packet Size, MPPS

10 Gbps. However, additional VNFs instantiated thereafter cause the system throughput to decline. This decline is slightly more significant for OVS-DPDK than for FD.io VPP. Such a decline implies a decreasing *average* throughput per VNF as VNFs are added (system throughput divided by number of VNFs), challenging a network operators capacity planning rules. Neither of the latter two I/O techniques reaches the physical interface limit of 20 Gbps in this test. The gradual decline in system throughput is further investigated below.

As expected, the total system throughput is scaled proportionally with a smaller packet size of 128B (see Figures 5 and 6), causing the slope of the benchmark to be shallower. Again, SR-IOV shows a linearity in system throughput as the number of VNFs is increased, up to 8 VNFs. Thereafter however, additional VNFs no longer contribute positively to the overall system throughput, and the maximum interface capacity of 20 Gbps cannot be reached even with 10 instantiated VNFs. Taking the Ethernet overhead (interframe gap, preamble) into account explains the upper limit. To account for the subsequent degradation of system throughput with the 9th and 10th VNF, we examined the packet loss counters of the physical interfaces. We observed packet losses towards the traffic generator, indicating that the NIC buffers are overflowing.

OVS-DPDK and FD.io VPP as I/O mechanisms for 128B packet flows again reach their maximum system throughput with 3 VNFs at around 5 Gbps and 5 Mpps respectively. The total system throughput again tapers off as additional VNFs are added. It is notable that

Multi-VM Throughput (Gbps) with various I/O architectures
IPv4 Forwarding, 128B Packet Size, XE 16.3.1

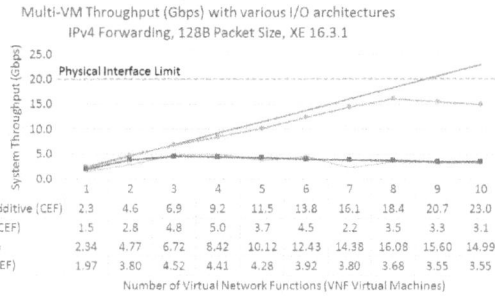

Number of Virtual Network Functions (VNF Virtual Machines)	1	2	3	4	5	6	7	8	9	10
Best Case Additive (CEF)	2.3	4.6	6.9	9.2	11.5	13.8	16.1	18.4	20.7	23.0
OVS-DPDK (CEF)	1.5	2.8	4.8	5.0	3.7	4.5	2.2	3.5	3.3	3.1
SR-IOV (CEF)	2.34	4.77	6.72	8.42	10.12	12.43	14.38	16.08	15.60	14.99
FD.io VPP (CEF)	1.97	3.80	4.52	4.41	4.28	3.92	3.80	3.68	3.55	3.55

Figure 5: Multi-VM System Throughput with CEF, 128B Packet Size, Gbps

Multi-VM Throughput (MPPS) with various I/O architectures
IPv4 Forwarding, 128B Packet Size, XE 16.3.1

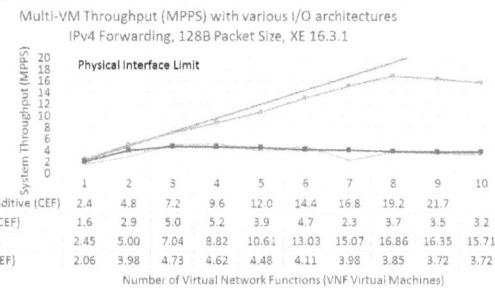

Number of Virtual Network Functions (VNF Virtual Machines)	1	2	3	4	5	6	7	8	9	10
Best case Additive (CEF)	2.4	4.8	7.2	9.6	12.0	14.4	16.8	19.2	21.7	
OVS-DPDK (CEF)	1.6	2.9	5.0	5.2	3.9	4.7	2.3	3.7	3.5	3.2
SR-IOV (CEF)	2.45	5.00	7.04	8.82	10.61	13.03	15.07	16.86	16.35	15.71
FD.io VPP (CEF)	2.06	3.98	4.73	4.62	4.48	4.11	3.98	3.85	3.72	3.72

Figure 6: Multi-VM System Throughput with CEF, 128B Packet Size, MPPS

for small packet sizes of 128B, the attainable system throughput of both FD.io VPP and OVS-DPDK is very comparable.

Next, we examine the impact of varying the switching threads (VPP worker threads for FD.io) on the total system throughput. Figure 7 shows the detailed CPU core configurations with 1, 2 and 4 FD.io VPP switching threads respectively[3]. Multiple VNF instances were again instantiated on the x86 host and subjected to IPv4 traffic with IMIX. Figure 8 shows the corresponding results for this separate experiment. With a single switching thread pinned to a dedicated core, the throughput level reaches 6.31 Gbps with a single VNF, and then again exhibits a slight degradation as VNFs are added to the system. Configuring a second switching thread to the configuration increases the overall system throughput to over 8 Gbps, and then sees the system throughput level off at around 9 Gbps. Configuring further two switching threads (for a total of 4) to the FD.io VPP configuration significantly increases the system throughput. However, in this case the CPU resources are exhausted after instantiating 4 VNFs, demonstrating the trade-off of allocating CPU cores to VNFs or to the I/O path.

A more thorough investigation of the results also shows that the association between the physical interfaces, the switching threads, and the VNFs onto the sockets can impact performance. Instantiating VNFs on the one socket while the physical interface and

the FD.io VPP switching thread are pinned to the other socket (c.f. Figure 2) forces remote memory accesses across sockets (a socket boundary crossing across the QPI link). In a NUMA architecture, this causes a slight performance degradation and is at least a partial explanation for the slight degradation of the system throughput observed in Figures 3 or 5. This socket boundary crossing penalty is more pronounced if the physical interfaces' PCI is associated with different socket to where the FD.io VPP switching threads are processed. Placing VNFs on different sockets to the FD.io VPP switching thread incurs less of a penalty.

5.2 Experiment 2: Throughput with features

The performance profile observed for IP traffic flows changes considerably as features are turned on in the VNFs. More processing cycles are required by the VNFs themselves to manipulate the traffic, in our case applying DPI, NAT, QoS, and Firewall. The overall system throughput that can be achieved in such a configuration is consequently below the IP forwarding throughput, exhibited in Figure 9 by having a significantly smaller gradients as VNFs are added (benchmark comparison between Figures 3 and 9). Interestingly, in this case the system throughput for SR-IOV and FD.io VPP is almost identical as VNFs are added, up to 6 VNFs, and also highly linear, demonstrating the performance of the vector processing approach with FD.io VPP. This linearity is desirable from an operator perspective since it provides the necessary determinism for capacity planning as customers for the networking services are added. Note that for FD.io VPP the system throughput increases up to 6 VNFs and aggregates 9 Gbps. This is below the maximum throughput of 10Gbps observed above for FD.io VPP under IMIX - the feature processing overhead of the VNFs shifts the processing burden to the VNFs instead of the I/O path, and so the switching capacity limits of the FD.io VPP worker threads are not stressed. As observed for the IMIX tests, the system throughput starts to degrade from the 8th VNF onwards. The socket boundary crossing architecture described above offers an explanation for this degradation: for VNFs 7-10 the switching threads are on a different socket, thus forcing a boundary crossing across the QPI link.

For the multi-feature test case, OVS-DPDK exhibits near-linearity until 5 VNFs, but trailing noticeably below SR-IOV and FD.io VPP. However, after the 6th VNF the throughput degradation under OVS-DPDK is significant. Recall that this implies impacts on the already instantiated VNFs as new VNFs are added - the *average* throughput per VNF is 390Mbps for the 10VNFs, so less than half of the throughput achieved for a single VNF (900 Mbps). The NUMA architecture with socket boundary crossings across the QPI link explains part of this degradation. Again, VNFs 7-10 are associated with a different socket than the OVS-DPDK PMD threads, thus forcing cross-socket memory access. However, since the system throughput degradation starts after the 6th VNF, it means that a limit of the OVS-DPDK switching capacity is also reached.

The measurements of the system throughput with large packet sizes (1500B) and with features enabled is shown in Figure 10. In this case, the larger packet size implies that fewer packets are required to fill the physical interface bandwidth, and so no bottlenecks in the I/O path are experienced for the SR-IOV and FD.io VPP cases. The physical interface bandwidth limit of 20Gbps is reached after

---

[3]These test were run on a Cisco UCS C-Series C240M4SX with two Intel E5-2667v3 sockets, 8 cores each, clocked at 3.2 GHZ. Traffic arriving on 4x10GE interfaces, two associated with each socket. The hypervisor details were consistent as in Table 1. The IOS XE version tested was 16.3.0, accounting for some differences in the measured throughput results.

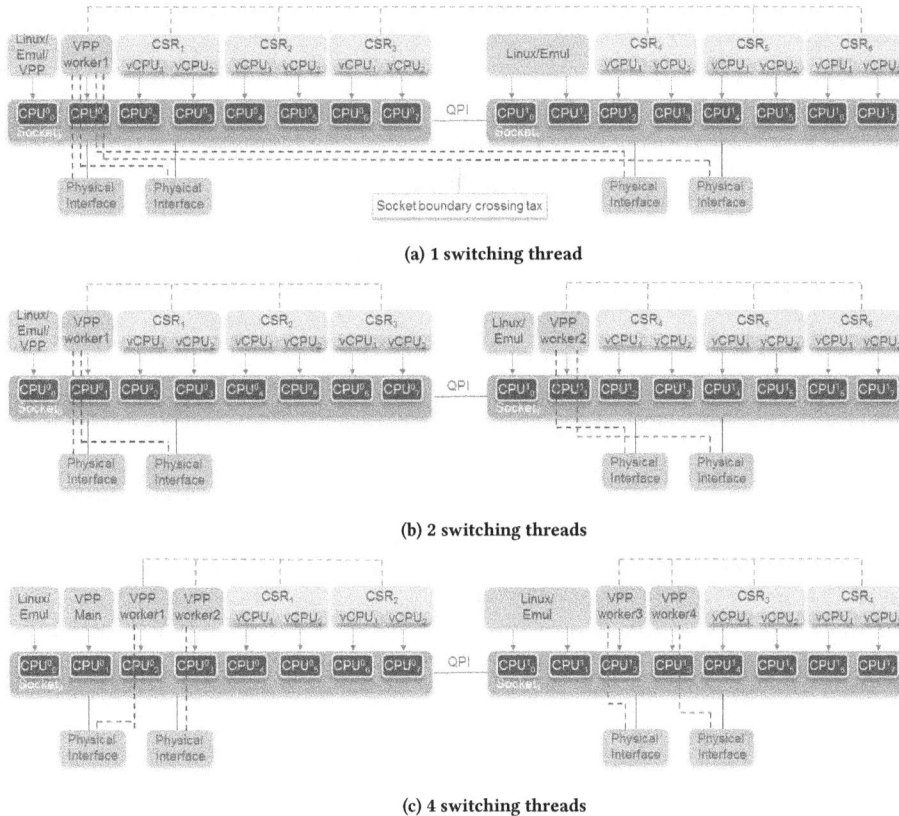

(a) 1 switching thread

(b) 2 switching threads

(c) 4 switching threads

Figure 7: System Architecture for different FD.io VPP switching thread experiments

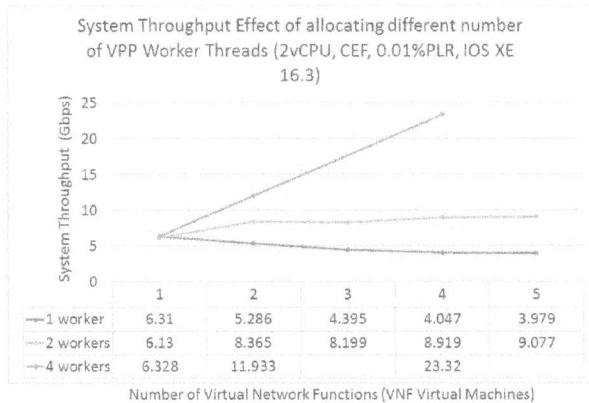

Figure 8: Impact of different worker threads on system throughput

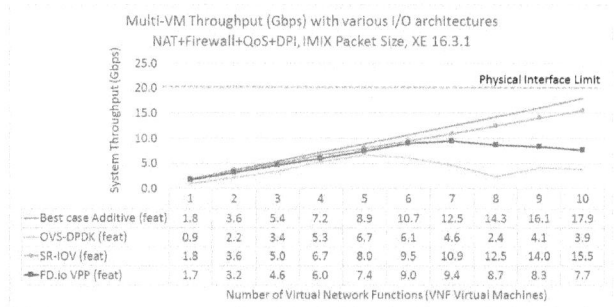

Figure 9: Multi-VM System Throughput with Features, IMIX Packet Size, Gbps

instantiation of the 4th VNF. An I/O path based on OVS-DPDK initially also shows linearity up to the 3rd VNF, reaching 15.2Gbps per server. Thereafter, the total system throughput flattens and starts to decline significantly again after the 4th VNF, pointing again to the less efficient packet processing paradigm of OVS-DPDK

as compared to FD.io VPP. Adding more PMD threads to the OVS-DPDK configuration can improve system throughput at the expense of instantiating fewer VNFs.

6 CONCLUSION AND FUTURE WORK

In this paper we analyzed the performance of running multiple VNFs in parallel under different I/O technologies: SR-IOV, OVS-DPDK and FD.io VPP. Our tests differ from service chained deployments in that each VNF is executing all the functions required for

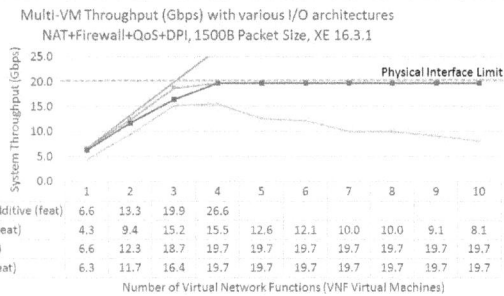

Figure 10: Multi-VM System Throughput with Features, 1500B Packet Size, Gbps

a particular IP traffic flow, instead of service chaining the traffic through multiple VNFs. The hypervisor scheduler thus not only has to fulfil the I/O demands of the VNFs, but also the vCPU demands arising in such a scenario. Our studies show that SR-IOV offers a highly linear contribution to the total system throughput as VNFs are added to a server. However, SR-IOV also comes with some deployment caveats that may restrict a deployment scenario.

FD.IO VPP and OVS-DPDK perform very similar in our test environments, scaling linearly for the initial VNFs, but then reaching a system throughput plateau as further VNFs are added. We show that this plateau is a function of the CPU resources allocated to the virtual switching functions of FD.io VPP and OVS-DPDK. Both FD.io VPP and OVS-DPDK demonstrate a gradual decline in total system throughput as further VNFs are added. We investigated this decline and identified the pinning configuration of the physical interfaces, the virtual switching threads, as well as the VNFs as contributing to this gradual decline. In our tests with demanding features (DPI, NAT, Firewall, QoS), FD.IO VPP outperformed OVS-DPDK, showing the benefits of processing packets in a vector. Both of these I/O techniques are thus viable alternatives to SR-IOV that offer better feature functionality and deployment flexibility if the deployment scenario justifies the resource profiles required.

As further research areas, we are identifying to run similar tests in an oversubscribed setup, where the sum of the offered vCPU resources from the VNFs exceeds the available core count on the x86 host. Such measurements allow a better characterization of the hypervisor scheduler under heavy loads, and are also relevant for SPs and Cloud Providers to further increase the VNF density per server and thus reduce the overall total cost of ownership.

REFERENCES
[1] [n. d.]. Cisco cloud services router 1000v series. ([n. d.]). Retrieved October 13, 2017 from http://www.cisco.com/c/en/us/products/routers/cloud-services-router-1000v-series/index.html
[2] R. Bonafiglia, I. Cerrato, F. Ciaccia, M. Nemirovsky, and F. Risso. 2015. Assessing the Performance of Virtualization Technologies for NFV: a Preliminary Benchmarking. In *Proc. of the 4th IEEE Eur. Wrkshp on Software Defined Networks (EWSDN)*, IEEE (Ed.). 67–72. https://doi.org/10.1109/EWSDN.2015.63
[3] S. Bradner and J. McQuaid. 1999. *Benchmarking Methodology for Network Interconnect Devices*. Technical Report RFC2544. Internet Engineering Task Force (IETF).
[4] F. Callegati, W. Cerroni, and C. Contoli. 2016. Virtual Networking Performance in Openstack Platform for Network Function Virtualization. *J. of Electrical and Computer Engineering* 2016 (March 2016), 1–15. https://doi.org/10.1155/2016/5249421

[5] Cisco. [n. d.]. Cisco ucs c240 m4 rack server. ([n. d.]). Retrieved October 13, 2017 from http://www.cisco.com/c/en/us/products/servers-unified-computing/ucs-c240-m4-rack-server/index.html
[6] Docker Container. [n. d.]. ([n. d.]). Retrieved October 10, 2017 from https://www.docker.com/
[7] Intel Corporation. 2011. Pci-sig SR-IOV Primer: An Introduction to SR-IOV Technology. (2011). Retrieved October 10, 2017 from http://www.intel.com/content/www/us/en/pci-express/pci-sig-sr-iov-primer-sr-iov-technology-paper.html
[8] Intel Corporation. 2014. Intel DPDK vSwitch: Performance Report. (2014). Retrieved October 10, 2017 from https://01.org/sites/default/files/page/intel_dpdk_vswitch_performance_figures_0.10.0_0.pdf
[9] Intel Corporation. 2016. Open vSwitch* with DPDK Overview. (2016). Retrieved October 13, 2017 from https://software.intel.com/en-us/articles/open-vswitch-with-dpdk-overview
[10] Y. Dong, X. Yang, X. Li, J. Li, K. Tian, and H. Guan. 2016. High Performance Network Virtualization with SR-IOV. In *Proc. of the 16th IEEE Int. Symp. on High Performance Computer Architecture (HPCA)*, IEEE (Ed.). 1–10. https://doi.org/10.1109/HPCA.2010.5416637
[11] P. Emmerich, D. Raumer, F. Wohlfart, and G. Carle. 2014. Performance Characteristics of Virtual Switching. In *Proc. of the 3rd IEEE Int. Conf. on Cloud Networking (CloudNet)*, IEEE (Ed.). 120–125. https://doi.org/10.1109/CloudNet.2014.6968979
[12] P. Emmerich, D. Raumer, F. Wohlfart, and G. Carle. 2015. Assessing Soft and Hardware Bottlenecks in Pc-based Packet Forwarding Systems. In *Proc. of the 14th Int. Conf. on Networks (ICN)*. 78–83.
[13] B Pfaff et al. 2015. The Design and Implementation of Open vSwitch. In *In Proc. of the 12th USENIX Symp. on Networked Systems Design and Implementation*, USENIX (Ed.). 117–130.
[14] FD.io. 2016. Fd.io /dev/boot. (2016). Retrieved October 13, 2017 from https://docs.google.com/presentation/d/1JL5O_ZkRUXVaY4ZuKaMj13jEGv90eanOYAB7mHfmPK4/pub?start=false&loop=false&delayms=3000#slide=id.p4
[15] Z. Huang, J. Li, Z. Chang, and H. Guan. 2012. Adaptive and Scalable Optimizations for High Performance SR-IOV. In *Proc. of the IEEE Int. Conf. on Cluster Computing*, IEEE (Ed.). 459–467. https://doi.org/10.1109/CLUSTER.2012.28
[16] C. Kim and K. Park. 2015. Credit-based Runtime Placement of Virtual Machines on a Single NUMA System for QoS of data access performance. *IEEE Trans. on Computers* 64, 6 (June 2015), 1633–1646. https://doi.org/10.1109/TC.2014.2329671
[17] M. Konstantynowicz. [n. d.]. FD.io - How to Push Extreme Limits of Performance and Scale with Vector Packet Processing Technology. ([n. d.]). Retrieved October 10, 2017 from https://www.ietf.org/proceedings/96/slides/slides-96-bmwg-10.pdf
[18] KVM. [n. d.]. Kernel virtual machine. ([n. d.]). Retrieved October 13, 2017 from https://www.linux-kvm.org/
[19] Lightreading Ray Le Maistre. 2015. Validating Cisco's NFV Infrastructure Part 1. (2015). Retrieved October 13, 2017 from http://www.lightreading.com/nfv/nfv-tests-and-trials/validating-ciscos-nfv-infrastructure-pt-1/d/d-id/718684
[20] M. Paolino, N. Nikolaev, J. Fanguede, and D. Raho. 2015. SnabbSwitch User Space Virtual Switch Benchmark and Performance Optimization for NFV. In *Proc. of the IEEE Conf. on Network Function Virtualization and Software Defined Networking (NFV-SDN)*, IEEE (Ed.). 86–92. https://doi.org/10.1109/NFV-SDN.2015.7387411
[21] N. Pitaev. [n. d.]. Cisco CSR 1000v Multi VM / Multi IO Test Report. ([n. d.]). Availableupondemand
[22] N. Pitaev, M. Falkner, A. Leivadeas, and I. Lambadaris. 2017. Multi-VNF Performance Characterization for Virtualized Network Functions. In *Proc. of the IEEE Conf. on Network Softwarization (Netsoft)*, IEEE (Ed.). 1–5. https://doi.org/10.1109/NETSOFT.2017.8004221
[23] R. Rahimi, M. Veeraraghavan, Y. Hakajima, H. Takahashi, S. Okamoto, and N. Yamanaka. 2016. A High-Performance Openflow Software Switch. In *Proc. of the 17th IEEE Int. Conf. on High Performance Switching and Routing (HPSR)*, IEEE (Ed.). 93–99. https://doi.org/10.1109/HPSR.2016.7525645
[24] R. Rojas-Cessa, K. Salehin, and K. Egoh. 2015. Evaluation of Switching Performance of a Virtual Software Router. In *Proc. of the 35th IEEE Sarnoff Symp.*, IEEE (Ed.). 1–5. https://doi.org/10.1109/SARNOF.2012.6222733
[25] V. Sankaran and D. Darde. 2015. Performance Analysis of Intel DPDK on Physical and Virtual Machines. (2015). Retrieved October 13, 2017 from http://www.cs.cornell.edu/courses/cs5413/2014fa/projects/group_of_dsd96_vs444/final_pres.pdf
[26] H. Shimamoto. 2016. SR-IOV ixgbe driver limitations and improvement. (2016). Retrieved October 13, 2017 from http://events.linuxfoundation.org/sites/events/files/slides/20160715_LinuxCon_sriov_final.pdf
[27] M. A. Tahhan and J. M. Morgan. [n. d.]. Vsperf Deep Dive: Virtual Switch Performance in OPNFV. ([n. d.]). Retrieved October 13, 2017 from https://wiki.opnfv.org/display/vsperf/?preview=/2926262/6818343/VSPERF%20Golden.pptx
[28] VMware. [n. d.]. VMware vSphere 5.1 Documentation Center. SR-IOV Support. ([n. d.]). Retrieved October 13, 2017 from https://pubs.vmware.com/vsphere-51/index.jsp?topic=%2Fcom.vmware.vsphere.networking.doc%2FGUID-E8E8D7B2-FE67-4B4F-921F-C3D6D7223869.html
[29] Open vSwitch. [n. d.]. ([n. d.]). Retrieved October 10, 2017 from http://openvswitch.org

Methods for Quantifying Energy Consumption in TPC-H

Meikel Poess
Oracle
Redwood Shores, California
meikel.poess@oracle.com

Da Qi Ren
Futurewei Technologies
Santa Clara, California
Daqi.Ren@huawei.com

Tilmann Rabl
TU Berlin
Berlin, Germany
rabl@tu-berlin.de

Hans-Arno Jacobsen
TU Munich
Munich, Germany
jacobsen@in.tum.de

ABSTRACT

Historically, performance and price-performance of computer systems have been the key purchasing arguments for customers. However, with rising energy costs and increasing power consumption due to the ever-growing demand for compute power (servers, storage, networks), electricity bills have become a significant expense for today's data centers. In order to measure energy consumption in standardized ways, the Standard Performance Evaluation Corporation (SPEC) has developed a benchmark dedicated to measuring the power consumption of single servers (SPECpower_ssj2008), while the Transaction Processing Performance Council (TPC) and the Storage Performance Council (SPC) have developed general specifications that govern how energy is measured for any of its benchmarks. Energy reporting is optional in TPC and SPC results. While there are close to 600 SPECpower_ssj2008 results, there have been only three TPC and no SPC benchmark results published that report energy consumption. In this paper, we argue that the low number of TPC publications is due to the large setups required in TPC benchmarks and the, subsequently, complicated measurement setup. Running on a typical big data setup we evaluate two alternative methods to quantify energy consumption during TPC-H's multi-user runs, namely by taking measurements of on-chip power sensors controlled through Intelligent Platform Management Interface and by estimating power consumption via the nameplate power consumption method. We compare these later two methods with power measurements taken from external power meters as required by SPEC and TPC benchmarks.

CCS CONCEPTS

• **Information systems** → **Database performance evaluation**;

KEYWORDS

Data Warehouse, Benchmarking, Energy Consumption Estimation

ACM Reference Format:
Meikel Poess, Da Qi Ren, Tilmann Rabl, and Hans-Arno Jacobsen. 2018. Methods for Quantifying Energy Consumption in TPC-H. In *ICPE '18: ACM/SPEC International Conference on Performance Engineering, April 9–13, 2018, Berlin, Germany.* ACM, New York, NY, USA, Article 4, 12 pages. https://doi.org/10.1145/3184407.3184429

1 INTRODUCTION

In light of the increasing power consumption of data centers industry standard organizations such as the Transaction Processing Performance Council (TPC) [12], the Standard Performance Evaluation Corporation (SPEC) [10] and the Storage Performance Council (SPC) [9] have developed methodologies to measure energy consumption of computer systems. All of these consortia aim at standardizing power consumption measurement for performance benchmarks to aid IT departments in their purchase decision process. Their approaches, however, differ. Some organizations developed specialized benchmarks (SPEC [11]) while others added energy metrics to existing benchmarks (TPC,SPC [8]).

SPEC has been the front-runner by announcing the first industry standard benchmark, SPECpower_ssj2008, to measure power consumption in relation to performance for server-class computers in 2007. SPECpower_ssj2008 measures the performance of a Java based middle tier emulating client and database tiers. By emulating many components, that would otherwise be painful to setup, SPECpower_ssj2008 can be run on a single server without large hardware installations. It measures processor and memory performance, ignoring disk and network I/O. On the software side it measures the performance of the Java Virtual Machine, just-in-time compilation, garbage collection, user threads and some aspects of the operating system.

SPC, on the other hand, published two optional energy extensions to its existing benchmarks, SPC-1C and SPC-1. They were released in June 2009 and October 2009, respectively. The underlying performance tests for SPC-1C/E and SPC-1/E are identical to those used in their parent benchmarks. The energy extensions focus on defining appropriate enhancements to these core benchmark components, such as approving power meters to measure power consumption, defining disclosure requirements and define appropriate power metrics.

TPC took a similar approach to measuring energy consumption. Since it already has a large suite of benchmarks modeled after real-life scenarios such as TPC-C and TPC-E for online transaction processing, TPC-H for data warehousing, TPC-DS, TPCx-BB, and

TPCx-HS for big data, TPCx-V and TPC-VMS for virtualization, TPC-DI for data integration and TPCx-IoT for the Internet of Things, the TPC developed the *energy specification*. The energy specification is, similar to TPC's pricing specification, a *common* specification. Common specification are intended to supplement existing TPC benchmarks by specifying the amendments necessary to measure and report energy metrics in addition to the other metrics within each of the individual benchmarks. Before the energy specification can be used in conjunction with a benchmark, that benchmark need to define energy specific terms in its specification. These terms are necessary as each TPC benchmark defines its own metric and time measurements. So far only the TPC-E specification has been amended with these terms. The TPC provides a software package, called the TPC-Energy Measurement System (EMS) to aid in implementing the TPC Energy Specification. It includes modules to interface with power instrumentation tools, to log and report power and temperature.

While there are close to 600 SPECpower_ssj2008 results, there have been only three TPC benchmark results published with the optional energy consumption metric and no SPC benchmark results with the optional energy consumption metric. In this paper we argue that the low number of TPC publications is due to the large setups required in TPC benchmarks and the, subsequently, complicated measurement setup.

Using a typical big data setup, an 6 node cluster running Cloudera's Impala engine, we evaluate two alternative methods to quantify energy consumption in large setups, namely by taking measurements of on-chip power sensors controlled through Intelligent Platform Management Interface (IPMI) and by estimating power consumption via the *nameplate* power consumption method[2, 6, 7]. The nameplate value of computing equipment is the rated maximum power consumption of the equipment. It is a conservative power consumption estimate. We compare these later two methods with power measurements taken from external power meters as required by SPEC and TPC benchmarks.

The main contributions of this paper are best summarized as follows:

(1) We amend TPC-H [5] with energy specific terms so that the energy specification can be used with TPC-H;
(2) We apply the nameplate power consumption model to our hardware setup;
(3) We quantify energy consumption of a six node cluster running a 300G TPC-H database with three methodologies: external power meters, IPMI and power estimation using the nameplate power model;
(4) And we analyze the the power results of the above methods.

The remainder of our paper is organized as follows. Section 2 discusses the important characteristics of TPC-H, proposes changes to the TPC-H specification that allows for energy measurements and develops the comparison metrics that will be used to analyze quantitative energy methods compared in this study. We also describe necessary modifications to queries so that they run in Impala. Section 3 describes the hardware and software setup of the system that we are using for our experiments. Section 4 describes the three quantitative methods we use in our paper to determine energy consumption during TPC-H runs: (i) power meters, (ii) IPMI and

(iii) analytical power consumption model using nameplate power consumption. Section 5 we present our findings of measuring power consumption using our three quantitative methods and we conclude in Section 6.

2 WORKLOAD

This section provides an overview of TPC-H including a brief workload characterization that is useful to understand the following sections.

2.1 Workload Characteristics

Generally, analytical workloads can be divided into parallel operations of four distinct types: initial load, queries, incremental load and auxiliary data creation/maintenance operations. These types can be executed in single and multi-user modes. The single-user mode stresses a system's ability to parallelize operations across all available system resources to answer a given request in the least amount of time. The multi-user mode stresses the system's ability to schedule requests from multiple concurrent users to optimally utilize all system resources with the overall aim of increasing system throughput.

TPC-H [5], developed by the Transaction Processing Performance Council, covers both single- and multi-user runs. There are other benchmarks like TPC-DS that also cover both single- and multi-user runs. However, the software stack we are using does not support all queries included in TPC-DS and using the well studied TPC-H benchmark gives the reader an instant understanding of our experiments. TPC-H is based on a relatively simple, yet powerful 3rd NF schema. It allows query execution of various execution paths. The access paths in a 3rd NF analytical workload are often dominated by large hash or sort-merge joins, but conventional index driven joins are also common. Large aggregations, which often include large sort operations, are widespread in TPC-H. This diversity imposes challenges both on hardware and software systems. High sequential I/O-throughput (large I/O operations) is critical to excel in large hash-join operations.

TPC-H's execution rules and main performance metric give equal importance to the single- and multi-user runs, while ignoring load time. The main performance metric (QphH) is calculated as the geometric mean of elapsed times collected during the single- and multi-user tests with concurrent users (see Figure 2) and adjusted using the raw database size specified with the Scale Factor SF. Scale factors allowed for publication are $SF \in \{1, 10, 30, 100, 300, 1000, 3000, 10000, 100000\}$. TPC-H mandates a minimum number of concurrent streams (S), while it defines no upper bound. The number of concurrent query and update streams is identical. Each user in the multi-user executes the 22 queries in a different permutation. The permutations are generated by the query generator *qgen*.

$$S(SF) = \begin{cases} log_{10}(SF) * 2 + 1 & \text{if } SF \in \{10, 100, 1000, 10000, 100000\} \\ (log_{10}(\frac{SF}{3}) + 1) * 2 & \text{otherwise} \end{cases}$$

(1)

Additionally, TPC-H's execution rules allow for the deferral of the update stream until all query streams are finished.

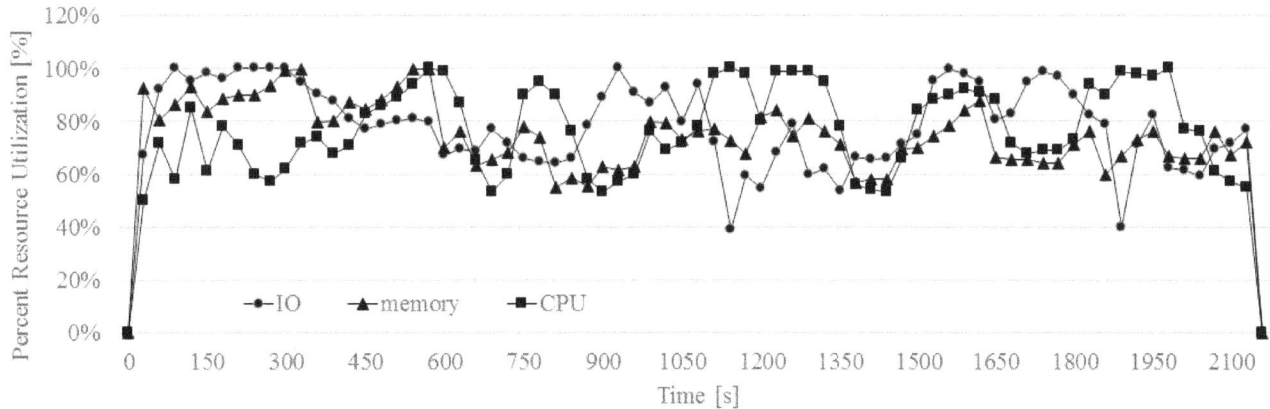

Figure 1: Oscillating resource utilization during a TPC-H throughput run

Each decision support query has its own hardware resource utilization pattern, which is unique to the way it is executed on a particular system. On a symmetrical multi processor (SMP) system the resources that are considered most important, especially when sizing a system for a particular workload, are processor (CPU), reads/writes (I/O) from/to the disk storage subsystem, disks, controllers, and memory. Big data workloads tend to be mostly read-only; however, join operations of large tables, aggregations with a large number of groups and sort operations of large data sets that exceed the internally available amount of memory result in write and read operations to temporary storage.

Except for Query 1 (CPU bound) and Query 6 (I/O bound) TPC-H queries exhibit an oscillating system resource pattern. Many queries join multiple tables and aggregate over a large data set. For an in-depth analysis of TPC-H queries see [1]. Due to their complex nature TPC-H queries do not exhaust all resources of a system during the entire run time of the query. For instance, a hash join is typically CPU bound during the build phase of its hash table and I/O bound during its probe phase. Consequently, a system consumes more power in the storage subsystem during some time of the single-user test and more CPU power during other times of the single-user test. To be able to apply the nameplate power consumption model two key requirements have to be met. Firstly, only workloads that observe steady state can be used. The second requirement is system balance. Depending on the application and system, an optimal component ratio has to be maintained to keep all components (CPU, disks, controllers etc.) utilized during the measurement interval. If a system does not have the optimal ratio between these components, the power consumption model will not produce accurate estimates for the same reason that the system needs to be fully utilized.

The multi-user test alleviates this effect, because the simultaneous execution of different queries cause the overlapping of different query execution phases. Because of many queries being executed at the same time, each query is likely to be in a different execution phase causing the resources of a system to be utilized in a more balanced way. That is, low utilization of resource R_1 in a query execution of one user might overlap with high utilization of R_1 in

another query of another user. Figure 1 shows a multi-user run with 8 users against a SF=1000 TPC-H database. While there are still phases where the system resources drop to 60% the average CPU utilization during this run is 75%, the average IO utilization is 77% and the average memory utilization is 73%.

Traditionally the single-user mode has been mostly used in dedicated batch windows, for example, for data cleansing and the creation of auxiliary data structures. This batch window is becoming less important in today's big data deployments. Big data systems, many of which are based on the Hadoop ecosystem, trade data ownership with flexibility and availability. Traditionally, only one system had control over a given data set, namely the DBMS. This control enabled the DBMS to use techniques and algorithms to implement performance enhancements and to enforce data correctness that rely on persistent auxiliary data structures. Big data systems, on the other hand, follow an open data approach, in which all products in its ecosystem are able to access and modify the same full-fidelity data sets. This approach eliminates the costly process of copying and converting data into different formats and allows for immediate data availability, while rendering traditional DBMS concepts, such as auxiliary data structures, impractical because the big data system is not able to invalidate and, therefore, not able to guarantee correctness.

2.2 Modifications to the TPC-H queries for Impala

In order to run the TPC-H queries on the version of Impala that ships with Cloudera 5, we had to make several modifications to almost all queries. A summary of our changes is listed in Table 1. Most changes were related to the handling of date arithmetic, string and other arithmetic functions. However, we needed to rewrite Query 15, Query 18 and Query 21.

2.2.1 Query 15. The changes to Query 15 are summarized in Listing 2. Impala was not able to execute the original query (see Listing 1) because of the sub-query that returns the maximum total_revenue. Because of this being an uncorrelated sub-query, it only needs to be executed once. Hence, rewriting it as a create table as select statement (CTAS) is a reasonable approach. It does not

Table 1: Modifications to TPC-H queries to run on Impala

Qry	Original	Modifications
1	l_shipdate<=date '1998-12-01' - interval ':1' day	l_shipdate<=date_add(cast('1998-12-01' as timestamp),interval -:1 days)
2	r_name = ':3'	r_name like ':3%'
3	c_mktsegment = ':1'	c_mktsegment like ':1%'
	o_orderdate < date ':2'	o_orderdate < cast(':2' as timestamp)
	l_shipdate > date ':2'	l_shipdate > cast(':2' as timestamp)
4	o_orderdate >= date ':1'	o_orderdate >= cast(':1' as timestamp)
	o_orderdate < date ':1' + interval '3' month	o_orderdate < date_add(cast(':1' as timestamp),interval 3 months)
5	r_name = ':1'	r_name like ':1%'
	o_orderdate >= date ':2'	o_orderdate >= cast(':2' as timestamp)
	o_orderdate < date ':2' + interval '1' year	and o_orderdate < date_add(cast(':2' as timestamp), interval 12 months)
6	l_shipdate >= date ':1'	l_shipdate >= cast(':1' as timestamp)
	l_shipdate < date ':1' + interval '1' year	l_shipdate < date_add(cast(':1' as timestamp),interval 24 months)
7	(n1.n_name = ':1' and n2.n_name = ':2')	(n1.n_name like ':1%' and n2.n_name like ':2%')
	(n1.n_name = ':2' and n2.n_name = ':1')	(n1.n_name like ':2%' and n2.n_name like ':1%')
	l_shipdate between date '1995-01-01' and	l_shipdate between cast('1995-01-01' as timestamp) and
	date '1996-12-31'	cast('1996-12-31' as timestamp)
8	r_name = ':2'	and r_name like ':2%'
	o_orderdate between date '1995-01-01' and	o_orderdate between cast('1995-01-01' as timestamp) and
	date '1996-12-31'	cast('1996-12-31' as timestamp)
	p_type = ':3'	p_type like ':3%'
10	o_orderdate >= date ':1'	o_orderdate >= cast(':1' as timestamp)
	o_orderdate < date ':1' + interval '3' month	o_orderdate < date_add(cast(':1' as timestamp),interval 3 months)
	l_returnflag = 'R'	l_returnflag like 'R%'
11	n_name = ':1'	n_name like ':1%'
12	when o_orderpriority = '1-URGENT'	when o_orderpriority like '1-URGENT%'
	or o_orderpriority = '2-HIGH'	or o_orderpriority like '2-HIGH%'
	when o_orderpriority <> '1-URGENT'	when o_orderpriority not like '1-URGENT%'
	and o_orderpriority <> '2-HIGH'	and o_orderpriority not like '2-HIGH%'
	and l_shipmode in (':1', ':2')	and (l_shipmode like ':1%' or l_shipmode like ':2%')
	and l_receiptdate >= date ':3'	and l_receiptdate >= cast(':3' as timestamp)
	and l_receiptdate < date ':3' + interval '1' year	and l_receiptdate < date_add(cast(':3' as timestamp) , interval 24 months)
13	count(*) as custdist	cast(c_count as int), cast(count(1) as int) as custdist
	count(o_orderkey)	count(o_orderkey) as c_count
	customer left outer join orders on	customer left outer join orders o on
	c_custkey = o_custkey	c.c_custkey = o.o_custkey
	and o_comment not like '%:1%:2%'	and not o.o_comment like '%:1%:2%'
	) as c_orders (c_custkey, c_count)	) c_orders
14	and l_shipdate >= date ':1'	and l_shipdate >= cast(':1' as timestamp)
	and l_shipdate < date ':1' + interval '1' month;	and l_shipdate < date_add(cast(':1' as timestamp),interval 1 months);
15	create view revenue:s (supplier_no, total_revenue) as	create table revenue:s as
	l_shipdate < date ':1' + interval '3' month	l_shipdate < date_add(cast(':1' as timestamp),interval 3 months)
17	and p_brand = ':1'	and p_brand like ':1%'
	and p_container = ':2'	and p_container like ':2%'
19	sum(l_extendedprice* (1 - l_discount)) as revenue	sum(l_extendedprice* (1 - l_discount)) as revenue
	and l_shipdate >= date ':2'	and l_shipdate >= cast(':2' as timestamp
	and l_shipdate < date ':2' + interval '1' year	and l_shipdate < date_add(cast(':2' as timestamp),interval 24 months)
	and n_name = ':3'	and n_name like ':3%'
21	substring(c_phone from 1 for 2) as cntrycode,	substr(c_phone,1,2) as cntrycode,
	substring(c_phone from 1 for 2) in	substr(c_phone,1,2) in
	and substring(c_phone from 1 for 2) in	and substr(c_phone,1,2) in

alter the performance characteristic of the main query. We also rewrote the *revenue* view from the original as CTAS.

Listing 1: Original Query 15

```
create view revenue:s (supplier_no, total_revenue) as
  select l_suppkey, sum(l_extendedprice * (1 - l_discount))
  from lineitem
  where l_shipdate >= date ':1'
    and l_shipdate < date ':1' + interval '3' month
  group by l_suppkey;
select s_suppkey, s_name,s_address, s_phone, total_revenue
from supplier, revenue:s
where s_suppkey = supplier_no
  and total_revenue = (select max(total_revenue)
                         from revenue:s)
order by s_suppkey;
drop view revenue:s;
```

Listing 2: Modified Query 15

```
create table revenue:s as
select l_suppkey as supplier_no,
       sum(l_extendedprice * (1 - l_discount)) as total_revenue
from lineitem
where l_shipdate >= '1996-01-01' and l_shipdate < '1996-04-01'
group by l_suppkey;
create table temp_table_q15:s as
select max(total_revenue) as max_revenue
from revenue:s;
select s_suppkey, s_name, s_address, s_phone, total_revenue
from supplier join revenue:s on
       s_suppkey = supplier_no
     join max_revenue:s on
     table temp_table_q15=max_revenue
order by s_suppkey;
drop table revenue:s;
drop tabletable temp_table_q15:s;
```

2.2.2 Query 18.
The changes to Query 18 are summarized in Listing lst:ModifiedQuery18. Impala was not able to execute the original query (see Listing lst:OriginalQuery18) because of the join condition *o_orderkey IN sub-query*. Similarly to Query 15, the sub-query being uncorrelated, we rewrote it as a CTAS.

Listing 3: Original Query 18

```
select c_name, c_custkey, o_orderkey, o_orderdate,
       o_totalprice, sum(l_quantity)
from customer, orders, lineitem
where o_orderkey in (select l_orderkey
                       from lineitem
                       group by l_orderkey
                       having sum(l_quantity) > :10)
  and c_custkey = o_custkey
  and o_orderkey = l_orderkey
group by c_name, c_custkey, o_orderkey,
       o_orderdate, o_totalprice
order by o_totalprice desc, o_orderdate;
```

Listing 4: Modified Query 18

```
create table temp_table_q18_:s as
select l_orderkey, sum(l_quantity) as temp_sum_of_quantity
from lineitem
group by l_orderkey;
select c_name,c_custkey,o_orderkey,o_orderdate,
     cast(o_totalprice*1000 as int)/1000,sum(l_quantity)
from customer join orders on c_custkey = o_custkey
   join temp_table_q18_:s ttq18 on o_orderkey = ttq18.l_orderkey
       and ttq18.temp_sum_of_quantity > :1
   join lineitem l on o.o_orderkey = l.l_orderkey
group by c_name,c_custkey,o_orderkey,
o_orderdate,cast(o_totalprice*1000 as int)
order by cast(o_totalprice*1000 as int) desc,o_orderdate;
drop table temp_table_q18_:s;
```

Listing 5: Original Query 21

```
select s_name, count(*) as numwait
from supplier, lineitem l1, orders, nation
where s_suppkey = l1.l_suppkey
  and o_orderkey = l1.l_orderkey
  and o_orderstatus = 'F'
  and l1.l_receiptdate > l1.l_commitdate
  and exists (select *
                from lineitem l2
                where l2.l_orderkey = l1.l_orderkey
                  and l2.l_suppkey <> l1.l_suppkey)
     and not exists (select *
              from lineitem l3
              where l3.l_orderkey = l1.l_orderkey
                and l3.l_suppkey <> l1.l_suppkey
                and l3.l_receiptdate > l3.l_commitdate)
       and s_nationkey = n_nationkey
       and n_name = ':1'
group by s_name
order by numwait desc, s_name;
```

2.2.3 Query 21.
The changes to Query 21 are summarized in Listing lst:ModifiedQuery21. Impala was not able to execute the original query (see Listing lst:OriginalQuery21) because of the *exists* and *not exists* join conditions. We rewrote the these join conditions as series of outer joins.

Listing 6: Modified Query 21

```
create table temp_table1_q21:s as
select l_orderkey, cast(count(distinct l_suppkey) as int)
     ,max(l_suppkey) as max_suppkey
from lineitem
group by l_orderkey;
create table table temp_table2_q21:s as
  select l_orderkey, cast(count(distinct l_suppkey) as int)
   , max(l_suppkey) as max_suppkey
from lineitem
where l_receiptdate > l_commitdate
group by l_orderkey;
select s_name, cast(count(1) as int) as numwait
from (select s_name from
       (select s_name, t2.l_orderkey, l_suppkey
           ,count_suppkey, max_suppkey
         from table temp_table2_q21:s t2 right outer join
           (select s_name, l_orderkey, l_suppkey
             from (select s_name, t1.l_orderkey, l_suppkey
                   ,count_suppkey, max_suppkey
                 from table temp_table1_q21:s t1 join
                   (select s_name, l_orderkey, l_suppkey
                     from orders o join
                       (select s_name, l_orderkey, l_suppkey
                         from nation n join supplier s on
                               s.s_nationkey = n.n_nationkey
                             and n.n_name like 'SAUDI_ARABIA%'
                           join lineitem l on
                             s.s_suppkey = l.l_suppkey
                         where l.l_receiptdate > l.l_commitdate
                       ) l1 on o.o_orderkey = l1.l_orderkey
                           and o.o_orderstatus = 'F'
                     ) l2 on l2.l_orderkey = t1.l_orderkey
                 ) a
             where (count_suppkey > 1) or ((count_suppkey=1)
                 and (l_suppkey <> max_suppkey))
           ) l3 on l3.l_orderkey = t2.l_orderkey
       ) b
     where (count_suppkey is null) or ((count_suppkey=1)
                 and (l_suppkey = max_suppkey))
   )c
group by s_name
order by numwait desc, s_name;
drop table table temp_table1_q21;
drop table table temp_table2_q21;
```

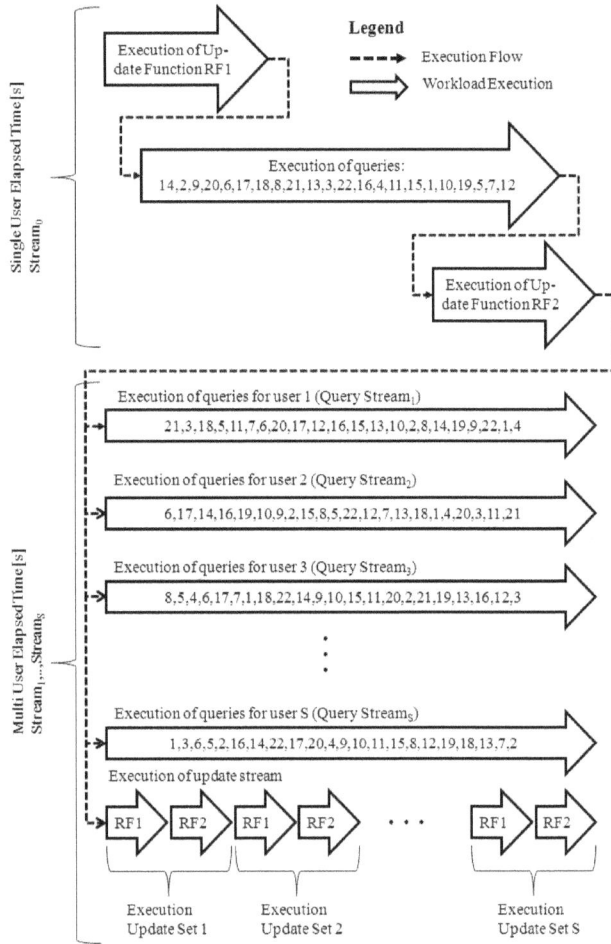

Figure 2: Execution rules of the TPC-H benchmark

2.3 Comparison Metrics

TPC-H defines one main performance metrics, the composite performance, which is calculated as the geometric mean of the single-user metric (*Power@Size*) and the multi-user metric (*Throughput@size*). Size is the scale factor (*SF*), which is a dimensionless quantity. It roughly represents the raw data set size in GB. Power@Size is computed as the geometric mean of the elapsed times for all queries and both refresh functions obtained during the single-user run. Its unit is queries per hour. For a given scale-factor (*SF*), individual query elapsed times (QI_q) $q \in 1..22$ and update functions ($RI_1, RI2$), the single-user metric is computed as:

$$Power@Size = \frac{3600 * SF}{\sqrt[24]{\prod_{q=1}^{22} QI_q \prod_{q=1}^{2} RI_q}} \quad (2)$$

With S being the number of concurrent users during the multi-user run and T_s being the elapsed time multi-user test, the multi-user metric is computed as:

$$Throughput@Size = \frac{3600 * S * 22 * SF}{T_s} \quad (3)$$

The composite performance metric is then calculated as the geometric mean of the single- and multi-user metrics as follows:

$$QphH@Size = \sqrt{Power@Size * Throughput@Size} \quad (4)$$

2.4 Incorporating TPC-Energy into TPC-H

The TPC-Energy specification [13] is designed to augment any TPC benchmark by allowing for the reporting of an energy metric alongside its performance metrics. While a benchmark's performance metrics measures the amount of work completed per unit of time, the TPC-Energy metric measures the energy consumption corresponding to the amount of work completed. TPC-Energy's metric is the ratio of the energy consumed by the entire system *Watt Seconds* [*Ws*] to work completed (number of transactions, queries, transformations) during the benchmark interval $B_{Interval}$ [*s*]. After moving the time element to the denominator, the TPC-Energy metric is plainly represented as *Watts/Performance*.

TPC benchmarks measure the performance of different types of workloads, some of which are time-based, other are task-based. They use different types of metrics and, because they are technology agnostic, the systems being measured are very diverse in terms of type of system components, architecture and number of tiers.

TPC-C and TPC-E follow a time based benchmark model. They report performance as the transaction throughput during steady state condition. TPC-H, on the other hand, follows a static task benchmark model, which is divided into three distinct measurement t tests: (i) *load test*, (ii) *single-user test*, and (iii) *multi-user test*. All three tests exhibit an oscillating system utilization behavior. To deal with such scenarios, the TPC-Energy specification requires measuring power $P_i[W]$ $i \in 1, 2, ..n$ of the entire system for each interval in addition to the performance measurements T_i, and then independently determining the combined value for power $P[W]$ and performance for all intervals using weights corresponding to the duration of each interval:

$$P = \frac{OverallWork}{OverallEnergy} = \frac{\sum_{i=1}^{n} T_i * S_i}{\sum_{i=1}^{n} P_i * S_i} \quad (5)$$

The primary metric, reported by TPC-Energy, is in the form of *Watts per Performance* for the overall System Under Test (SUT) [1] where the performance units are particular to each TPC Benchmark. For TPC-H it would be Watts/QphH. The energy consumption is measured for all subsystems active for the duration of the benchmark run. This includes servers, storage, clients, network switches. The TPC-Energy Specification also defines optional secondary metrics. The purpose of these secondary metrics is to allow more detailed comparisons and analysis of the result for system components such as server chassis, storage system, network gear etc. The secondary metrics are represented in similar units as the primary metric, that is, Watts/Performance, and the summation of all individual secondary metrics equals the primary metric. This is because both the primary and secondary metrics share a common value for the denominator —the performance value. This was done by design when developing the benchmark specification to allow end-users to see the contribution of the subsystems (represented by

---

[1]The system under test is a TPC defined term for system being tested by a benchmark

the secondary metrics) to the overall system results (represented by the primary metric).

In addition to these primary and secondary metrics, the TPC-Energy specification also calls for reporting the *idle power*, which is defined as the energy consumption of the SUT within 30 minutes of the completion of the benchmark run. The intent is to represent the amount of energy consumption of a measured system in a state "ready to accept work". This is useful to customers who have systems that have periods of idle but require the system to respond to a request for work at any time.

In order to enable the reporting of energy numbers in TPC-H the following three clauses need to be amended:

(1) Clause 0.1 has to be amended with the following wording: *To be compliant with the optional TPC-Energy standard, the additional primary metric, expressed as watts-per-QphH, must be reported. The requirements of the TPC-Energy Specification can be found at www.tpc.org.*

(2) Clause 5.4 has to be amended with the following wording: *When the optional TPC-Energy standard is used, the additional primary metric, expressed as $\frac{watts}{QphH}$, must be reported. In addition, the requirements of the TPC-Energy Specification, located at www.tpc.org, must be met.*

(3) Clause 8.3.7 must be amended with *When the optional TPC-Energy standard is used, the additional requirements and formatting of TPC-Energy related items in the executive summary must be reported and used. In addition, the requirements of the TPC- Energy Specification, located at www.tpc.org, must be met.*

3 EXPERIMENTAL SETUP

For our experiments we use six HUAWEI Tecal RH2288 V2 Rack servers, each with 2 Intel Xeon Processor E5-2680 (Sandy Bridge-EP) running at 2.7 GHz. Each processor has 8 cores (16 hyperthreaded) with an 20MB L3 cache. They are connected through two QuickPath (QPI) links, each providing a unidirectional transmission rate of up to 8.0 GB/s. Each server has 24 8GB double data rate 3 (DDR3) at 1066Mhz dimms of main memory with a total ot 192GB. Each server is configured with eight 2.5" SAS HDDs with 7.2TB capacity. One SAS disk hosts the OS and the remaining 7 are configured for HDFS. The server provides four onboard gigabit Ethernet (GE) ports, of which two were bonded to doube bandwidth.

Our system runs Cloudera's CDH 5 on CentOS 6.5. It is configured as one master node and five worker nodes. Each of the nodes has 189.1 GBytes of memory.

4 POWER MEASUREMENT METHODS

This sections gives a brief overview of the measurement methods we are using: (i) Analytical power consumption model (ii) IPMI (iii) Power meter

4.1 Analytical Power Consumption Model

The analytical power consumption models for online transaction processing and analytical workloads, presented in [7], are based on the assumption that the peak power consumption of an entire system can be derived from the aggregate of the nameplate power consumptions of its individual components [2]. Each model

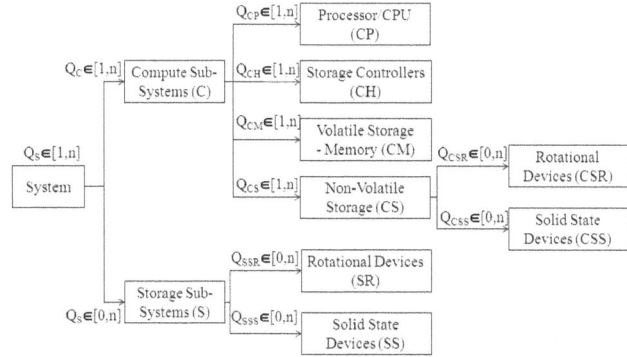

Figure 3: Generalized power consumption model: source [7]

follows the same general approach: The nameplate power information of major system components (see Table 2), such as processor (CPU), volatile storage, internal non-volatile storage devices, that is, rotational disks and solid state memory, and external storage sub-systems, that is, enclosures with non-volatile storage devices, are aggregated discounting the nameplate overhead. Additional power of supporting components, such as motherboards and fans, is calculated with a combination of a fixed overhead and a percentage of the power consumption of the components they support. The models do not account for the power necessary for the air conditioning systems of data centers.

Table 2: Major power consuming components

#	Component	Description
1	Power Supply	2 hot-swappable PSUs
2	Main Board	GIGABYTE GA-EXX58-UD3R
3	CPU	Intel Core i7 920 LA1366
4	Main Memory	24 DDR3 8GB PC3-10600
5	HDD	Seagate, ST91000640NS
4	CPU FAN	4-hot-swappable

Figure 3 shows the hierarchy of the major system components included in our power estimation models. Each component in this hierarchy is abbreviated with up to three capital letters, as indicated in parenthesis. TPC systems may consist of two types of sub-systems, namely compute sub-systems (C) and storage sub-systems (S). In case of a clustered system and systems that have multi-tier architectures, there can be multiple compute sub-systems. We also refer to the compute sub-systems as servers. Each server consists of one or more compute units (CP), that is, processors/CPUs, a number of storage controllers to connect to external storage enclosures (CH), some sort of volatile storage, usually memory DRAM DIMMs (CM), some non-volatile memory (CS), traditionally rotational devices (CSR), but recently also Solid State Devices (CSS) and supporting components, such as the main board and cooling fans. We also refer to the supporting devices of servers as chassis. The storage sub-system (S), which is used to store data persistently, consists of non- volatile storage devices, traditionally rotational devices (*SR*), but recently also Solid State Devices (*SS*). We also refer to the storage sub-systems as storage enclosures.

Each of these components may occur multiple times in a system and each occurrence may have different nameplate characteristics. Hence, we enumerate them with an index on each level. For instance, the second CPU in the first compute sub-system is labeled $CP_{1,2}$. The 5th rotational device in the second supporting component of the first storage sub-system is labeled $SSR_{1,2,5}$. We refer to the quantities and power consumptions of these components with Q and P respectively. For example, the number of CPUs in the first compute sub-system is $Q(CP)$ and the power consumption of the second CPU in the first compute sub-system is $P(CP_{1,2})$.

4.2 Power Meter Setup

For the power consumption measurements of our system we use the industry standard power meter HIOKI 3360. It is a multi-channel meter supporting clamps and voltage probes to measure power on single- to three-phase lines. The 33 Family of power meters is approved by TPC to be used in energy measurements for TPC benchmarks. Power of the entire System was measured.

The Intel CPU is packaged in Intel's LGA775 socket on the main board. We measure the CPU input current and voltage at its 8-pin power plug. The CPU is powered with one 4 pin fan-connector, its measurement is relatively straightforward. A GPU card is plugged into a PCI-Express slot on the main board, it is mainly powered by +12V and +3.3V power from PCI- Express pins, and an additional +12V power directly from the PSU. We measure the current through auxiliary power line with a clamp probe, and measure the PCI power at the main board power inputs. The memory power consumption is dependent on the memory usage of the software running. We make an approximation by measuring power changes on the main board. We use National Instruments USB-6216 BNC data acquisition, Fluke i30s / i310s current probes, and Yokogawa 700925 voltage probe. The room temperature was kept constant at 23 degrees Celsius ± 0.5 degrees Celsius. We use LabView 8.5 as oscilloscopes and analyzer for the results data analysis. By testing the power responses of each component involved in a sample matrix multiplication, we record the real time voltage and current from measurement readings. The product of voltage and current is the instant power at each sampling point during measurement. We aggregate all data into a single power consumption number [W] and plot that data over time.

4.3 Intelligent Platform Management Interface

The Intelligent Platform Management Interface (IPMI) provides management and monitoring capabilities independent of its host system's CPU, firmware (FM) and operating system (OS). It is a powerful framework that has been initiated by Intel in 1998 and has since been adopted by many other system vendors to manage their systems, including power management.

Motherboards that support IPMI 2.0 [4] are able to monitor the power usage of various system components using a baseboard management controller (BMC) and power sensors. The BMC is a specialized microcontroller embedded on the motherboard. It manages the interface between the system management software and the platform hardware.

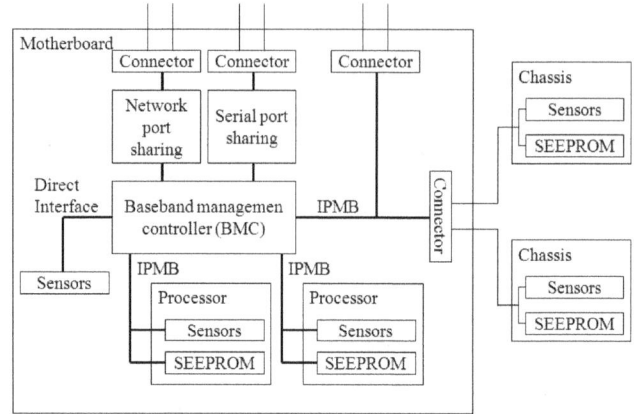

Figure 4: Architecture of IPMI and BMC

In general an IPMI system consists of one BMC and many satellite controllers that are distributed among different system modules, as shown in Figure 4. The satellite controllers within the same chassis connect to the BMC through the IPMI bus or bridge.

The system can be managed with the Remote Management Control Protocol (RMCP). The sensor data record (SDR) repository stores the readings of the individual sensors on the board, which can be temperatures, fan speeds, and voltages.

5 EXPERIMENTAL RESULTS

This section summarizes the power consumption quantities obtained with the three power measurement methods. Firstly, we apply the analytical power consumption model to our hardware setup. The analytical model, being the most conservative, will give us an estimate for the upper bound of the amount of power our system will use during the two types of tests:(i) single-user test, and (ii) multi-user-test. Secondly, we obtain actual power measurements using IPMI and power meters.

5.1 Results Using the Analytical Power Consumption Model

We apply the analytical model to the compute units, the volatile and non-volatile storage units and the supporting components of the compute sub-system.

5.1.1 Power Consumption of Compute Unit. Our system has no separate storage sub-system, hence we only need to consider the compute subsystems without the storage controller, host bus adaptor (HBA), which are usualy Peripheral Component Interconnect (PCI) cards. We obtain the peak power consumption of the compute units (processors/CPUs), which are usually specified as thermal design power (TDP) from the Intel specification [3]. According to it the Intel Xeon E5-2600 series processors's TDP is 130W. Hence, the power consumption of both compute units on each compute sub-system $i \in 1..6$ is:

$$P(CP_i) = 2 * 130W = 260W \qquad (6)$$

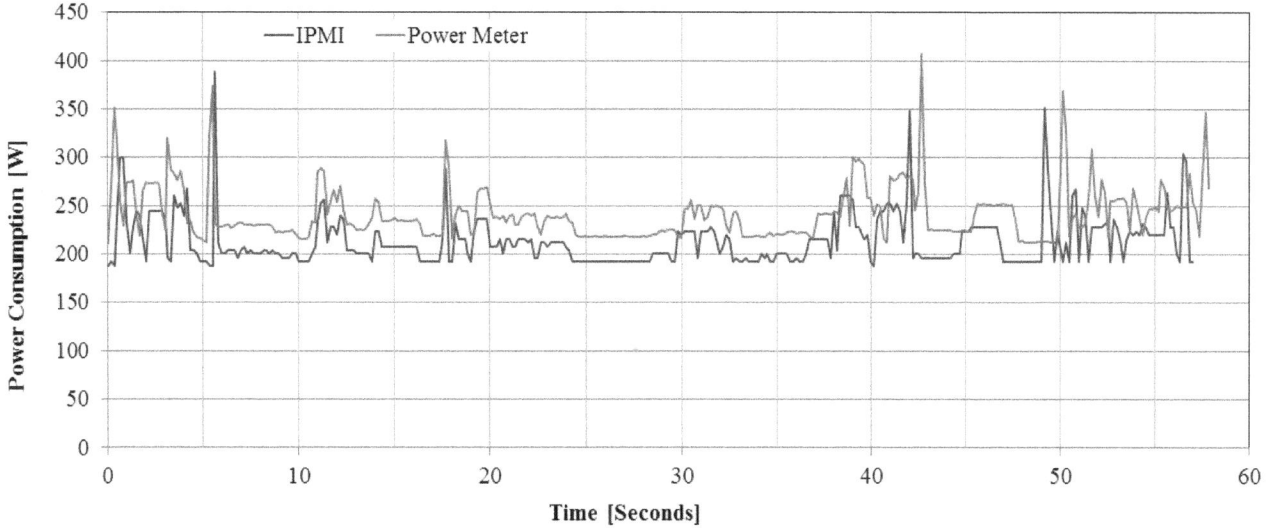

Figure 5: IPMI and power meter readings during the execution of a TPC-H single-user run

5.1.2 Power Consumption of Volatile Storage. Similarly to the compute node nameplate power consumption, we obtain the peak power consumption of our volatile storage (DRAM memory DIMMs) from the manufacturer's website. The power consumption of the entire volatile storage in one compute sub-system i ($i \in 1..8$) can, therefore, be calculated as:

$$P(CM_i) = 24 * 5.21W = 125.0W \tag{7}$$

5.1.3 Power Consumption of Non-Volatile Storage. Each of our compute sub-system contains only rotational storage devices (CSR), that is, disk drives. Peak power consumption levels of disk drives vary widely with the disk's form factor (FF), size, and rotational speed. FF refers to the form factor of the drive. Each of our compute sub-systems holds eight disk drives, each with a peak power consumption of 14.2W. The power consumption of the entire non-volatile storage in each compute sub-system i ($i \in 1..8$) can be estimated with:

$$P(CSR_i) = 8 * 14.2W = 113.6W \tag{8}$$

5.1.4 Power Consumption of Compute Sub-System (servers). In addition to compute units, volatile and non-volatile memory, we need to add the power consumption of the supporting components of the compute sub-system to estimate their total power consumption. Supporting components are the main board, cooling fans, caches, etc. They are also referred to as the server chassis. Studies [7] and [6] suggest that the power consumption of the server chassis can be expressed as a percentage (30%) of the nameplate power consumption of its main components plus a fixed overhead (100W). Hence, we compute the power consumption of one of our compute sub-system $i \in 1..6$ as:

$$P(C_i) = (P(CP_i) + P(CM_i) + P(CSR_i)) * 1.3 + 100 \tag{9}$$

$$P(C_i) = 498.6 * 1.3 + 100 = 748.2W \tag{10}$$

5.1.5 Power Consumption of the Entire System. The power consumption of the entire system is the aggregate of the power consumption of all six nodes: $6 * 748.2 = 4489.1W$. Using the elapsed times for the single- and multi- user runs of 58.3s and 208.8s respectively, the system wide power consumption of our system using the nameplate power consumption estimation model during the single-user run is is $58.3 * 748.2W = 43,620.1Ws = 12.2kWh$. During the multi-user run the system wide power consumption of our system is $208.8 * 748.2W = 156224.2Ws = 43.4kWh$. The power consumption of our system during the entire measured interval as it would be used during a TPC-H publication is $(58.3 + 208.8) * 748.2W = 199,844.2Ws = 55.6kWh$. It is understood that using nameplate power consumption is a very conservative estimate.

5.2 IPMI and Power Meter Measurement Results

With the power consumption estimate from our analytical model we have established an upper bound for the total power consumption. Results from the IPMI and the power meter setups will be more accurate. The following sections summarize results obtained from IPMI and actual power meters. Firstly, we present the results from the single-user run.

5.2.1 Single-User Power Measurement. Figure 5 plots the power consumption of the entire system as measured by IPMI and power meters during a single-user run of TPC-H. We obtained both the IPMI and power meter power consumption readings from the same single-user run. IPMI reports a minimum power consumption of 188.0 W, a maximum power consumption of 388.1 W, and an average power consumption of 241.3 W. The total power consumption during the measurement interval is $12172.0Ws=3.4kWh$.

The power meter reports a minimum power consumption of 211.5 W, a maximum power consumption of 407.1 W and an average power consumption of 241.7 W. The total power consumption

301

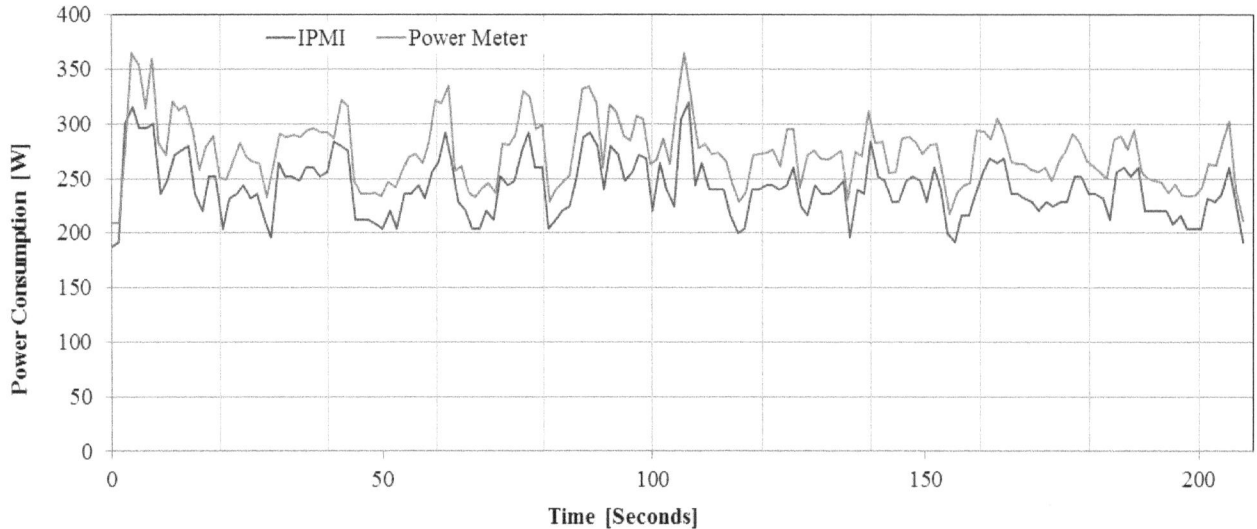

Figure 6: IPMI and power meter readings readings during the execution of a TPC-H multi-user run

during the measurement interval is $13999.8Ws = 3.9kWh$. On average the power meter reports measurement that are 11.7% higher compared to the numbers reported by the IPMI tool. The total power consumption reported by IPMI is 72% lower compared to the estimate of the analytical model and the total power consumption reported by the power meter is 68% compared to the estimate of the analytical model.

The graphs in Figure 5 show that the IPMI readings follow the power meter readings. 30% of the IPMI readings are within 10% of the power meter readings and 88% of the IPMI readings are within 20% of the power meter readings. There are, however, some outliers that are -65% and +52% off from the power meter readings.

5.2.2 Multi-User Power Measurement. Figure 6 shows the power consumption of the entire system as measured by IPMI and power meters during a multi-user run of TPC-H (four concurrent user). As in the single-user case we obtained both the IPMI and power meter power consumption readings from the same multi-user run. IPMI reports a minimum power consumption of 188.0 W, a maximum power consumption of 320.0 W, and an average power consumption of 241.3 W. The total power consumption during the measurement interval is $50264.1Ws = 14.0kWh$.

The power meter reports a minimum power consumption of 208.9 W, a maximum power consumption of 365.0 W and an average power consumption of 274.2 W. The total power consumption during the multi-user run is $55493.0Ws = 15.4kWh$. During the multi-user run the power consumption numbers reported by the power meter 9.4% higher compared to the numbers reported by the IPMI tool. This is slightly lower than during the single-user run (11.7%). The total power consumption during the multi-user run as reported by IPMI is 68% lower compared to the estimate of the analytical model and the total power consumption reported by the power meter is 64% compared to the estimate of the analytical model. These numbers are slightly lower compared to the single-user run (72% and 68%).

Similar to the single-user run the IPMI readings follow the power meter readings very closely. 37% of the IPMI readings are within 10% of the power meter readings and 78% are within 20%. Contrary to the single-user run the outliers in the IPMI readings are smaller. They vary between -20% and +30%.

Figures 7 and 8 graph the percent difference between the IPMI and power meter reading for each sample taken during the single- and multi-user runs. The graphs display the difference in ascending order to show the distribution of the differences.

6 CONCLUSION

With rising energy costs and increasing power consumption due to the ever-growing demand for compute power (servers, storage, networks), energy efficiency is a top priory for system vendors and customers. Measuring energy in a benchmark environment can be very laborious and complicated if the system is very large, which TPC benchmark systems tend to be. As of today, there have been only three TPC benchmark results published that report energy consumption non of which are TPC-H results . In this paper, we have argued that the low number of TPC publications is due to the large setups required in TPC benchmarks and the, subsequently, complicated measurement setup.

We have amended TPC-H to include power measurements and have analyzed three approaches in measuring energy consumption: (i) power meters, (ii) IPMI and (iii) analytical power consumption model using nameplate power consumption.

Analytical power consumption mode using nameplate power consumption delivers an upper bound for energy consumption and is not very accurate. However, our results show that IPMI provides an alternative to gathering power consumption numbers on a system, especially because IPMI is readily available and can be configured very easily.

The following table summarizes the results of the three different quantitative approaches, discussed in this paper.

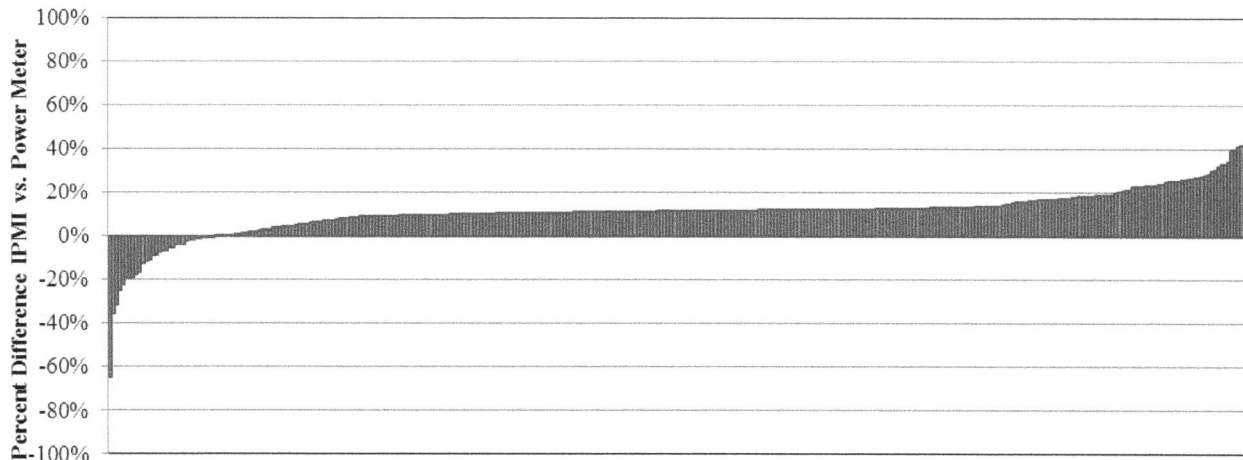

Figure 7: Sorted percent differences of IPMI vs. power meters readings during a single-user run

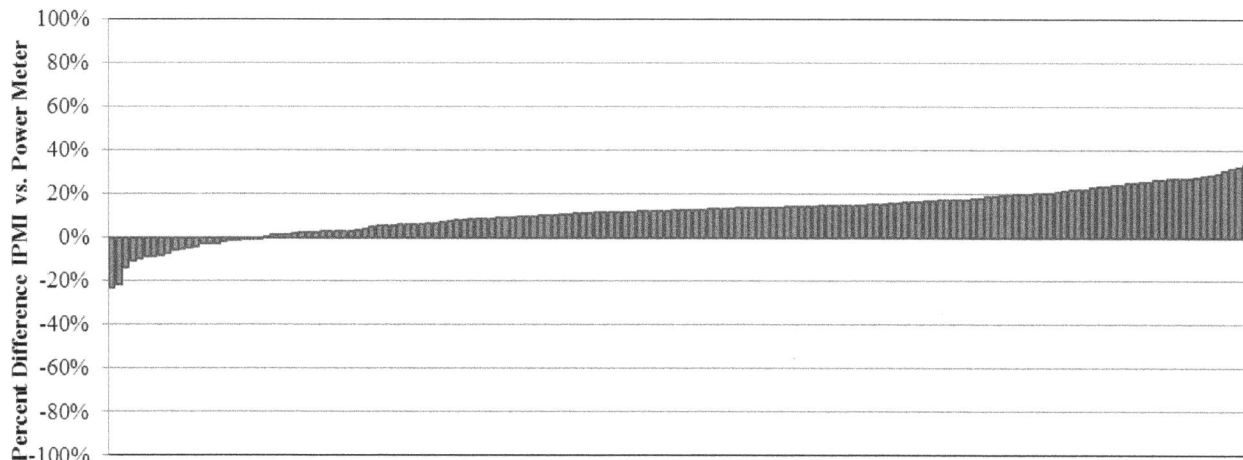

Figure 8: Sorted percent differences of IPMI vs. power meters readings during a multi-user run

Table 3: Power readings using different methods during TPC-H Runs

Test	Nameplate	Power Meter	IPMI
Single-User	12.2 kWh	3.4 kWh	3.9 kWh
Multi-User	43.4 kWh	14.0 kWh	15.4 kWh

The nameplate power consumption model overestimates the power consumption by more than 3x, while the difference between the IPMI and the external power meters is about 10%. It is up to benchmark consortia to allow the use of IPMI as an alternative to traditional power meters in order to increase adaptability of IPMI. It is clearly a trade off between effort/money and accuracy.

ACKNOWLEDGMENTS

This work was partially supported by the German Ministry for Education and Research as BBDC (01IS14013A).

REFERENCES

[1] C. Ballinger. TPC-D: benchmarking for decision support. In *The Benchmark Handbook for Database and Transaction Systems (2nd Edition)*. 1993.
[2] X. Fan, W. Weber, and L. A. Barroso. Power provisioning for a warehouse-sized computer. In D. M. Tullsen and B. Calder, editors, *34th International Symposium on Computer Architecture (ISCA 2007), June 9-13, 2007, San Diego, California, USA*, pages 13–23. ACM, 2007.

[3] Intel. Intel Xeon Processor E5-2680 (20M Cache, 2.70 GHz, 8.00 GT/s Intel QPI), 2013.

[4] Intel. IPMI Specificationv2.0, rev. 1.1: Document, 2013.

[5] M. Poess and C. Floyd. New TPC Benchmarks for Decision Support and Web Commerce. *SIGMOD Record*, 29(4):64–71, 2000.

[6] M. Poess and R. O. Nambiar. A power consumption analysis of decision support systems. In A. Adamson, A. B. Bondi, C. Juiz, and M. S. Squillante, editors, *Proceedings of the first joint WOSP/SIPEW International Conference on Performance Engineering, San Jose, California, USA, January 28-30, 2010*, pages 147–152. ACM, 2010.

[7] M. Poess and R. O. Nambiar. Power based performance and capacity estimation models for enterprise information systems. *IEEE Data Eng. Bull.*, 34(1):34–49, 2011.

[8] M. Poess, R. O. Nambiar, K. Vaid, J. M. Stephens, K. Huppler, and E. Haines. Energy benchmarks: a detailed analysis. In H. de Meer, S. Singh, and T. Braun, editors, *Proceedings of the 1st International Conference on Energy-Efficient Computing and Networking, e-Energy 2010, Passau, Germany, April 13-15, 2010*, pages 131–140. ACM, 2010.

[9] SPC. Storage Performance Council. http://www.storageperformance.org/home/.

[10] SPEC. The Software Performenance Evalution Corporation (SPEC). http://www.businesswire.com/news/home/20070417005047/en/SAS-Smashes-ETL-World-Record-Establishing-New.

[11] SPEC. SPECpower ssj 2008 Specification. https://www.spec.org/power_ssj2008/, 2017.

[12] TPC. Home Page TPC. http://www.tpc.org, 2017.

[13] TPC. The TPC Energy Specification. http://www.tpc.org/TPC_Documents_Current_Versions/pdf/TPC-Energy_v1.5.0.pdf, 2017.

Using the Raspberry Pi and Docker for Replicable Performance Experiments

Experience Paper

Holger Knoche
University of Kiel
hkn@informatik.uni-kiel.de

Holger Eichelberger
University of Hildesheim
eichelberger@sse.uni-hildesheim.de

ABSTRACT

Replicating software performance experiments is difficult. A common obstacle to replication is that recreating the hardware and software environments is often impractical. As researchers usually run their experiments on the hardware and software that happens to be available to them, recreating the experiments would require obtaining identical hardware, which can lead to high costs. Recreating the software environment is also difficult, as software components such as particular library versions might no longer be available.

Cheap, standardized hardware components like the Raspberry Pi and portable software containers like the ones provided by Docker are a potential solution to meet the challenge of replicability. In this paper, we report on experiences from replicating performance experiments on Raspberry Pi devices with and without Docker and show that good replication results can be achieved for microbenchmarks such as JMH. Replication of macrobenchmarks like SPECjEnterprise 2010 proves to be much more difficult, as they are strongly affected by (non-standardized) peripherals. Inspired by previous microbenchmarking experiments on the Pi platform, we furthermore report on a systematic analysis of response time fluctuations, and present lessons learned on dos and don'ts for replicable performance experiments.

ACM Reference Format:
Holger Knoche and Holger Eichelberger. 2018. Using the Raspberry Pi and Docker for Replicable Performance Experiments: Experience Paper. In *ICPE '18: ACM/SPEC International Conference on Performance Engineering, April 9–13, 2018, Berlin, Germany.* ACM, New York, NY, USA, 12 pages. https://doi.org/10.1145/3184407.3184431

1 INTRODUCTION

Replication of scientific work, in particular of experiments, is a prerequisite for good scientific practice, as it allows independent investigation of scientific claims [18]. Replicating experiments with human subjects is inherently difficult as the subjects, their behavior, and their opinions may differ from experiment to experiment. In contrast, due to the different nature of the subjects, technical experiments such as performance benchmarks appear to be better suited

for replication. However, recent work indicates that different obstacles also exist for such experiments. While in some experiments, such as [14], distribution aspects of modern infrastructures were identified as the main inhibitor to replicability, access to similar or identical hardware prevented replication in other experiments [9].

The latter problem could be mitigated by establishing an affordable, common platform for a particular type of experiments. In our previous work, we showed that cheap commodity hardware like the Raspberry Pi allows for good replicability for the MooBench microbenchmark [16]. However, one may also have to accept (so far unexplained) high variances in response time.

The contribution of this paper is a discussion of experiences on using Raspberry Pi devices for replicable performance experiments, in particular, for different forms of benchmarks. Furthermore, we provide an systematic analysis for possible causes of variance in such experiments. We believe that our results and experiences can contribute to a community effort in creating a common platform facilitating replicable performance experiments. We aim at answering the following three research questions:

RQ 1 *Which types of performance experiments can be appropriately replicated using the Raspberry Pi platform?* We perform experiments of different scale on different devices and discuss the effects, e.g., the technical setup and the typical performance drop due to a low-cost compute platform.

RQ 2 *Can component technologies be applied on a Raspberry Pi to facilitate the replicability of performance experiments?* Combining a standardized platform with (technically) packageable experiments as envisioned by Boettiger [2] would facilitate systematic replicability. Therefore, we analyze the performance observations with and without using the Docker container platform.

RQ 3 *Can we identify reasons for the response time fluctuations in microbenchmarks on the Raspberry Pi reported in [16]?* In particular, we wish to investigate whether the fluctuations are caused by the devices themselves, i.e., may affect replication in general, or by (a part of) the software stack.

The paper is structured as follows: In Section 2, we introduce the technical background for the used technologies. The overall approach for setting up our experiments is described in Section 3. In Section 4, we report on the results of different micro- and macrobenchmark experiments on the Raspberry Pi platform. Driven by the experiments, Section 5 investigates causes that may impact performance experiments and their replication, in particular for the fluctuations reported in [16]. Related work is discussed in Section 6, and Section 7 concludes the paper.

2 BACKGROUND

In the following paragraphs, we provide a short technical background on the Raspberry Pi platform as well as Docker. Although there are other single-board computers available, we chose the Raspberry Pi due to its popularity, software support, and widespread availability for purchase.

2.1 Raspberry Pi

The term Raspberry Pi refers to a series of single-board computers, developed by the Raspberry Pi Foundation.[1] Originally conceived as an affordable platform for students to learn programming and computer science, the versatile devices have found many other uses in recent years.

The first models of the Raspberry Pi, the Raspberry Pi 1 Models A and B, were released in 2012. The Model A was designed for a lower retail price, and lacks certain hardware features such as on-board network connectivity. Both models have a single-core 32-bit ARMv6 processor running at 700 MHz, 16KB L1 cache, 128KB L2 cache and originally had 256 MB of RAM shared between the CPU and the GPU. In a later revision, the RAM size was increased to 512 MB. Both models use an SD card reader to host their primary storage device. Peripherals can be attached via one (Model A) or two (Model B) on-board USB 2.0 ports.

In 2015, the second generation of the Model B was released, the Raspberry Pi 2 Model B. This model is based on a quad-core ARMv7 processor running at 900 MHz with 256 KB shared L2 cache. The memory size was increased to 1 GB, and the number of on-board USB ports was increased to 4. Furthermore, the primary storage was changed from SD cards to MicroSDHC cards.

The current generation of the Model B, the Raspberry Pi 3 Model B, was released in 2016. It is equipped with a quad-core 64-bit ARMv8 processor running at up to 1.2 GHz with 512KB shared L2 cache. However, the default firmware configuration currently limits the CPU to running in 32-bit mode, and reports it to the operating system as an ARMv7 CPU. In addition to the new CPU, the Raspberry Pi 3 provides on-board wireless network and Bluetooth connectivity. Shortly after the release of the Raspberry Pi 3, revision 1.2 of the Raspberry Pi 2 was released, which is also based on the new ARMv8 CPU.

In addition to the hardware, the Raspberry Pi foundation also provides an official Linux distribution for all Raspberry Pi models, named *Raspbian*. It is based on the well-known Debian distribution, and offers a large number of software packages for the Raspberry Pi. The Raspberry Pi is also supported by several third-party vendors. In particular, Oracle provides a current Java Virtual Machine for Linux on the ARM platform, and Docker, which is further described below, added support for the Raspberry Pi in 2016 [19]. Furthermore, operating system images from third-party vendors are available, such as Ubuntu and a special edition of Windows 10.

2.2 Docker

Docker[2] is a container-based virtualization solution. In contrast to virtual machines, which use a hypervisor to provide a virtual hardware environment for guest operating systems, containers employ

virtualization capabilities of the host kernel to provide a virtual system environment for applications. Scheduling and resource management for all containers is done by the host kernel, which is also responsible for keeping the containers isolated from each other.

This approach makes containers more „lightweight" than virtual machines in several ways. The absence of a guest kernel avoids the resource consumption due to the additional scheduling and resource management inside the virtual environment. Furthermore, the containers do not have to provide an entire operating system, but only their required programs and libraries, allowing for smaller images. And since no guest operating system needs to be booted or shut down, containers can usually be started and stopped very quickly. Due to these properties, containers have become very popular in the industry, as they allow for rapid resource provisioning for building highly elastic applications.

As discussed in [2], Docker has several features that make it also a promising option for replicable research. The fact that a Docker image contains all its required dependencies (except the underlying operating system) greatly facilitates replicating a software environment, and avoids common pitfalls such as wrong library versions. This enables separating individual experiments as well as running variants of an experiment, e.g., the same experiment on different operating systems or system versions. Although it is possible to build Docker images interactively, it is common practice to create images by means of a so-called Dockerfile. A Dockerfile specifies the necessary steps to build an image using a simple syntax. Thus, it provides a human-readable specification that can, for instance, be used to create variants or other derivations of an experiment.

A particularly interesting property of Docker images is that images are built „on top of" other images, i.e., Docker provides an extension mechanism for images. This mechanism further facilitates variants and extensions of experiments packaged as Docker images. Every Dockerfile must specify its *base image*, i.e., the image it is derived from, with its first instruction [8]. All operations specified by the Dockerfile are then applied on top of the base image, and the resulting image is saved at the end of the build process. To avoid unnecessary data replication, Docker employs a layered file system. Each image only stores the differences to its underlying base image, and all layers are overlaid at runtime to form the complete file system. Moreover, a command can be specified to be executed upon starting a container, i.e., not only the software but also the execution and even the analysis can be packaged in a repeatable manner. By means of environment variables, specific settings can be applied to a container without changing the image itself.

The overlay mechanism is also applied when starting a container off an image. All changes made to the file system by a container are stored in a container-specific layer atop the image, while all other images are immutable. This allows to re-use an image for multiple containers or experiments, at the cost of runtime performance due to the overlay file system.

Docker images can be deployed manually or using a repository. For the latter, Docker provides a mechanism for distributing images over a network. Images can be „pushed" to a registry and „pulled" by the Docker engine on request. By default, Docker interacts with the public *Docker Hub*[3] registry provided by Docker, Inc.

---

[1] http://www.raspberrypi.org
[2] https://www.docker.com/

[3] https://hub.docker.com/

3 APPROACH

In order to assess the viability of the Raspberry Pi platform for replicable performance experiments, we conducted a series of different experiments on multiple Pi devices in different configurations. The general approach is presented below, while the actual experiments are described in Section 4.

Each author bought a Raspberry Pi set from the same supplier within a time frame of two weeks. Each set comprised a Raspberry Pi 3 device by vendor element14, an 8 GB SanDisk class-4 SD card and a power supply capable of delivering 2.5 A at 5 V. These two devices will be referred to as D_1 and D_2 below; the SD cards will be referred to as C_1 and C_2. The intention behind this was to have two devices that were as similar as possible. To evaluate whether a different production lot or a potential minor revision might affect replicability, we bought a third device D_3 with the same specifications at a local electronics shop several months later. This device was from a different vendor (Allied Electronics). All three devices reported to have BCM2835 CPUs (revision a02082) in /proc/cpuinfo.

In a second step, we prepared a master installation images for all three devices[4]. This image is based on Raspbian Stretch Lite, which was released shortly before we conducted our experiments. Raspbian Lite is a minimal variant of the Raspbian distribution without potentially influencing components such as a graphical user interface, a virus scanner, or automated updates. We installed all necessary software to run the experiments, in particular, Oracle JDK 1.8.0_144 for the armhf platform, as the OpenJDK version provided by the distribution does not contain a just-in-time compiler. For investigating performance fluctuations in Section 5, where we needed a direct comparison to our previous Raspberry Pi experiments from [16], we used the same Raspbian Jessie Lite image as for the original experiments.[5]

In order to test the effect of different storage devices, we also used two class-10 SD cards, a Transcend Premium 400x (16 GB, C_3) and a SanDisk Ultra (16 GB, C_4) as well as three commodity USB hard disks, a Toshiba STOR.E ALU 2S (500 GB, H_1), a Hitachi Z7K320 (320 GB, H_2) and a TravelStar Z7K400 (500GB, H_3).

4 EXPERIMENTAL EVALUATION

In order to evaluate the replicability of performance experiments on different Raspberry Pi devices, we ran a selection of experiments, which are described in detail below. Experiments 1 and 2 are based on microbenchmarks and, thus, aim at replicability at a low level, while Experiments 3 and 4 address replicability at higher levels. It should be noted that the experiments are conducted with the aim of assessing replicability, not achieving a particularly high score in any of the benchmarks employed.

4.1 Experiment 1: Microbenchmarks using the Java Microbenchmark Harness

The Java Microbenchmark Harness[6] (JMH) is a test harness for running microbenchmarks on the Java Virtual Machine (JVM), provided by the OpenJDK team. Due to the dynamic compilation performed

```java
public void testMethod(final int depth) {
  if (depth == 0) {
    return;
  } else {
    this.testMethod(depth - 1);
  }
}
```

Listing 1: Test method for JMH microbenchmark

by the JVM, carrying out such benchmarks can be difficult, and subtle errors can happen easily. The JMH facilitates such benchmarks by automatically inserting warmup phases, forking multiple VM instances, measuring execution times, and calculating important statistical figures at the end of a benchmark run. Furthermore, the JMH provides facilities to conveniently influence the behavior of the just-in-time compiler. For instance, methods can be prevented from being inlined or even being compiled at all.

We used the JMH to conduct a total of six microbenchmarks. Each microbenchmark was executed 10 times with a freshly instantiated JVM, with a warmup phase of 20 seconds and a measurement phase of 20 seconds for each run. The first four benchmarks measured the throughput of calling a simple recursive method (see Listing 1) with a recursion depth of 10. This setup is similar to MooBench, the micro-benchmark we evaluated in [16], which is also used in Experiment 2 and in the analysis in Section 5. Benchmark 1 was run with default compilation, Benchmark 2 explicitly requested inlining of the test method, Benchmark 3 explicitly supressed inlining, and Benchmark 4 suppressed any compilation of the test method.

The two remaining microbenchmarks aimed at a rough comparison of the input/output (I/O) behavior of the different devices. Benchmark 5 measured the throughput of a method, which wrote four bytes of data to a file in each invocation, and synced the writes to disk every 100,000 invocations. Four bytes per invocation were chosen as to prevent excessive growth of the test file, so that the benchmarks could also be run on the SD cards. Benchmark 6 was similar, but sent the data to a remote machine via TCP.

Selected results from the microbenchmarks are shown in Table 1. As evident from comparing lines 1 and 4, there is no significant difference between the two devices D_2 and D_3 in Benchmark 1 with the same peripherals, as the confidence intervals overlap. The same is true for Benchmarks 2 and 3 (lines 5 to 8). For Benchmark 4, the confidence intervals do not overlap; however, the gap between the intervals is almost neglegible. As evident from line 2, the benchmark runs slightly slower under Docker, with a slightly higher variance. Although not shown in Table 1, the results for D_1 are rather similar.

As expected, the results from Benchmark 5 vary significantly with the storage devices; none of the peripherals was able to saturate the Pi's storage interface. Again, exchanging only the Pi devices yielded no significant difference in the results (see lines 11 and 17). Surprisingly, hard disk H_1 achieved a considerably higher mean throughput when running under Docker, however, with a much higher variance (see line 12). This behavior seems to be device-specific as it did not occur with disk H_2 (see lines 13 and 14), but was replicable in other runs. Possibly, sync requests are handled differently for the native file system and the overlay file system

---

[4]All (raw) material is available on https://doi.org/10.5281/zenodo.1100975
[5]https://doi.org/10.5281/zenodo.1003075
[6]http://openjdk.java.net/projects/code-tools/jmh/

Line #	Benchmark	Mean Throughput (in invocations / s)	99.9 % CI Throughput (in invocations / s)	σ (in invocations / s)
1	Benchmark 1 ($D_2 - H_1$, native)	12,322,204.022	[12,314,425.859 ; 12,329,982.186]	32,933.231
2	Benchmark 1 ($D_2 - H_1$, Docker)	12,299,546.551	[12,290,438.552 ; 12,308,654.549]	38,563.836
3	Benchmark 1 ($D_2 - H_2$, native)	12,299,680.408	[12,291,599.801 ; 12,307,761.015]	34,213.796
4	Benchmark 1 ($D_3 - H_1$, native)	12,314,181.630	[12,307,645.303 ; 12,320,717.957]	27,675.217
5	Benchmark 2 ($D_2 - H_1$, native)	12,323,493.925	[12,315,117.890 ; 12,331,869.960]	35,464.657
6	Benchmark 2 ($D_3 - H_1$, native)	12,328,094.938	[12,320,806.145 ; 12,335,383.730]	30,861.204
7	Benchmark 3 ($D_2 - H_1$, native)	6,416,150.780	[6,413,796.051 ; 6,418,505.508]	9,970.068
8	Benchmark 3 ($D_3 - H_1$, native)	6,417,104.725	[6,414,305.345, 6,419,904.106]	11,852.753
9	Benchmark 4 ($D_2 - H_1$, native)	410,968.302	[410,577.922 ; 411,358.681]	1,652.890
10	Benchmark 4 ($D_3 - H_1$, native)	411,604.745	[411,525.095 ; 411,684.395]	337.244
11	Benchmark 5 ($D_2 - H_1$, native)	553,927.284	[541,361.418 ; 566,493.149]	53,204.662
12	Benchmark 5 ($D_2 - H_1$, Docker)	882,408.673	[852,324.902 ; 912,492.445]	127,376.572
13	Benchmark 5 ($D_2 - H_2$, native)	773,246.941	[767,199.859 ; 779,294.023]	25,603.722
14	Benchmark 5 ($D_2 - H_2$, Docker)	699,276.759	[692,319.247 ; 706,234.271]	29,458.541
15	Benchmark 5 ($D_2 - C_2$, native)	491,016.010	[421,129.074 ; 560,902.946]	295,905.663
16	Benchmark 5 ($D_2 - C_3$, native)	682,755.400	[659,149.054 ; 706,361.746]	99,950.747
17	Benchmark 5 ($D_3 - H_1$, native)	548,804.364	[536,529.590 ; 561,079.138]	51,972.161
18	Benchmark 6 ($D_2 - H_1$, native)	195,719.580	[192,310.748 ; 199,128.413]	14,433.212
19	Benchmark 6 ($D_2 - H_1$, Docker)	188,548.713	[184,943.513 ; 192,153.912]	15,264.641
20	Benchmark 6 ($D_2 - H_2$, native)	202,397.887	[200,041.480 ; 204,754.293]	9,977.172
21	Benchmark 6 ($D_3 - H_1$, native)	195,727.533	[192,631.759 ; 198,823.306]	13,107.698

Table 1: Selected results from the JMH microbenchmarks (similar for device D_1)

employed by Docker, evoking this maybe even erroneous behavior of the drive.

For Benchmark 6, there were again no signficant differences between the Pi devices (see lines 18 and 21). The throughput under Docker was significantly lower (see line 19), which was to be expected due to the additional network stack of the container.

Summary: *The Raspberry Pi devices show highly replicable behavior in all microbenchmarks. In I/O-related benchmarks, the storage devices had a high influence on replicability, and one even showed highly unexpected behavior when used with Docker.*

4.2 Experiment 2: MooBench

MooBench [23] is a microbenchmark for measuring the runtime overhead of (instrumenting) monitoring frameworks such as Kieker and SPASS-meter, which inject so-called *probes* into an application to collect statistical data at runtime. By default, MooBench executes 2,000,000 calls of a recursive test method (recursion depth 10) and iterates the test 10 times. As baseline, MooBench performs a 'dry' run on the test method without any instrumentation. In [16], we applied MooBench to Kieker and SPASS-meter on a Raspberry Pi 3 platform and concluded that replicating results is possible. Here, we extend these experiments to compare benchmarks running in a Docker container against 'native' runs without Docker. To allow for comparisons of the collected data, we used the specific MooBench setup for Kieker as reported in [16], i.e., a recursion depth of 5 and 1,000,000 calls in 10 iterations.

Table 2 summarizes the collected measurements results, more precisely the data produced during the second half of the runs where the executing JVM is expected to have reached a steady state [23]. As the response time is measured by MooBench in terms of nanoseconds, which is typically rather imprecise on Java (some technical reports state fluctuations of about 400ns for Linux), we report the results here with one significant decimal place Within one type of experiment (a row in Table 2), the confidence intervals are close to the mean and differ only in a range of at maximum 11 μs for all experiments, even for Docker. In our previous work, we achieved similar results for the experiments using the external hard drive and for the corresponding class-4 SD card with a spread of 21 μs for SPASS-meter and 64 μs for Kieker. However, the narrow confidence intervals and partially high deviations also indicate fluctuations, which we will analyze in more detail in Section 5. Regarding the specific variances in Table 2, we observe that the deviations differ between native execution (6 μs for SPASS-meter, 373 μs for Kieker) and Docker (174 μs for SPASS-meter, 491 μs for Kieker). For Kieker, the deviations between native and Docker execution are rather similar. Moreover, in our previous experiment, the differences for SPASS-meter on the external hard drive were around 17 μs and 1,126 μs for Kieker, and even more than 20,000 μs for runs on the SD card. Thus, we classify the deviations for the I/O intensive Kieker experiments to be within the normal range (probably dominated by the hard drive), while for the less I/O-intensive SPASS-meter experiments, the differences may be caused by the Docker virtualization.

Summary: *The Raspberry Pi devices allow for good replication of microbenchmarks for instrumenting monitoring frameworks. This also applies to running inside Docker containers, provided that we accept a certain deviation in response time.*

Experiment	D_1, C_1, H_3			D_2, C_3, H_2			D_3, C_3, H_2		
	mean	95% CI	σ	mean	95% CI	σ	mean	95% CI	σ
Baseline	0.5	[0.5; 0.5]	0.3	0.5	[0.5; 0.5]	0.2	0.5	[0.5; 0.5]	0.4
SPASS-meter native	153.5	[153.5; 153.5]	48.9	145.0	[145.0;145.0]	50.4	151.6	[151.6; 151.7]	44.8
SPASS-meter Docker	152.0	[152.0; 152.0]	43.4	147.7	[147.6;147.8]	186.0	155.2	[155.0; 155.4]	326.5
Kieker native	121.5	[118.8; 124.3]	3,090.6	115.9	[113.6; 118.3]	2,717.2	118.6	[116.2; 121.1]	2,795.2
Kieker Docker	131.4	[128.7; 134.2]	3,142.1	123.3	[120.8; 125.8]	2,872.9	120.5	[118.2;122.8]	2,651.3

Table 2: Summary of MooBench stable state response times in μs with confidence intervals (CI) and standard deviation (σ).

4.3 Experiment 3: JPA RESTful Web Services

In order to evaluate the replicability of macroscopic experiments with multiple interacting Raspberry Pi devices, we created a simple, RESTful web service which interacts with a relational database via the Java Persistence API (JPA). We decided to build this service using Spring Boot,[7] a platform currently popular in the industry for implementing so-called microservices. For the underlying database, we used PostgreSQL 9.6.5, and Spring Data JPA was used to access the data.

The web service provided three operations, which emulated a very simplistic customer database. The first method generated a random customer entry and returned it without accessing the database at all. This method was intended to serve as a baseline to compare the results of the database-enabled operations against. The second method read an existing customer by his customer number, and the third operation changed the first and last name of a given customer in the database.

For this experiment, we used a pair of devices D_2 and D_3 with hard disks H_1 and H_2. Both Pi devices were connected to the same Gigabit ethernet switch, as was the test driver, a notebook with an Intel Core i7-4500U processor, 8 GB of RAM and a Gigabit ethernet interface. The experiment was conducted in six configurations:

(1) Web server running natively on D_2 with hard drive H_1, database running natively on D_3 with hard drive H_2
(2) Same as (1), but both services running in Docker containers
(3) Web server running natively on D_3 with hard drive H_1, database running natively on D_2 with hard drive H_2
(4) Same as (3), but both services running in Docker containers
(5) Web server running natively on D_2 with hard drive H_2, database running natively on D_3 with hard drive H_1
(6) Same as (5), but both services running in Docker containers

The database was pre-loaded with about 1 GB of data (10 million records) to prevent the server from keeping the whole dataset in memory. For the experiment, the test driver then invoked each method 200,000 times using a pool of 16 threads, and measured the response times. The first 100,000 invocations were disregarded as warm-up. Table 3 summarizes the results.

As evident from the table, switching the Raspberry devices only leads to minor changes in response time (e.g., Lines 1 and 3). Although some of the differences (e.g., Lines 7 and 9) are statistically significant, we consider them small enough to speak of good replicability regarding this experiment. The same applies to switching

from running natively to running inside Docker containers. Apparently, the overhead of the virtualization is outweighed by other factors in this experiment.

As expected, swapping the hard drives has a major effect on the results on this benchmark, as the drives are heavily utilized by the database due to the size of the table and the random access pattern. This dependency on the peripherals severely limits the replicability for I/O-heavy experiments. However, we wish to highlight that this is still an improvement to replicating experiments on common PC hardware, as much fewer components are interchangeable. Thus, specifying the execution environment is greatly facilitated.

Summary: *Provided that the peripherals are identical, good replication of macroscopic experiments is possible even for I/O-heavy experiments. Although this can pose a severe limitation to replicability, the limited number of interchangeable components at least facilitates specifying the execution environment of such experiments.*

4.4 Experiment 4: SPECjEnterprise 2010

Our second experiment for assessing the replicability of macroscopic experiments on the Raspberry Pi used SPECjEnterprise 2010,[8] a well-known Java EE benchmark. Similar to our previous experiment, we used one of the Pis as the database server, while the other ran the application server. Deviating from the run rules, we deployed the supplier emulator on the same application server as the actual benchmark application. The test driver was run on the same notebook as before.

Again, we used PostgreSQL 9.6.5 as the underlying RDBMS. Before each run, all tables were dropped, re-created, and loaded with the same data. For the Docker experiments, a new database container was started for each run.

For the application server, we used GlassFish 5.0 (Build 25). Similar to the database, the server was freshly configured and deployed for each run. Due to a connectivity issue, the GlassFish Docker containers had to be run using the host's network stack instead of an own one. Apparently, the application server resolves its own host name locally and transfers the resulting IP address to the client. By default, the host name resolves to a loopback address, and the client fails to connect. The resolution can be corrected by editing the /etc/hosts file, however, the application server also tries to bind to the interface with the resolved IP address. This attempt always fails, as the desired ports are also claimed by the Docker daemon to forward them to the container.

---

[7] https://projects.spring.io/spring-boot/

[8] http://www.spec.org/jEnterprise2010/

Line #	Operation	Configuration	Mean Response Time (in μs)	99% CI Resp. Time (in μs)	σ (in μs)
1		Web: $D_2 + H_1$, DB: $D_3 + H_2$, native	168,914.4	[167,197.2 ; 170,631.7]	210,817.8
2		Web: $D_2 + H_1$, DB: $D_3 + H_2$, Docker	165,467.7	[163,736.3 ; 167,199.1]	212,555.3
3	Read customer	Web: $D_3 + H_1$, DB: $D_2 + H_2$, native	170,284.3	[168,447.3 ; 172,121.3]	225,524.0
4		Web: $D_3 + H_1$, DB: $D_2 + H_2$, Docker	179,067.3	[177,265.1 ; 180,869.4]	221,244.0
5		Web: $D_2 + H_2$, DB: $D_3 + H_1$, native	283,504.3	[280,914.7 ; 286,094.0]	317,924.2
6		Web: $D_2 + H_2$, DB: $D_3 + H_1$, Docker	275,709.3	[272,882.2 ; 278,536.4]	347,072.5
7		Web: $D_2 + H_1$, DB: $D_3 + H_2$, native	11,164.6	[11,081.2 ; 11,248.1]	10,241.8
8		Web: $D_2 + H_1$, DB: $D_3 + H_2$, Docker	12,368.8	[12,276.1 ; 12,461.4]	11,375.3
9	Create random customer	Web: $D_3 + H_1$, DB: $D_2 + H_2$, native	11,832.8	[11,744.1 ; 11,921.6]	10,897.0
10		Web: $D_3 + H_1$, DB: $D_2 + H_2$, Docker	14,136.2	[14,025.4 ; 14,247.0]	13,602.9
11		Web: $D_2 + H_2$, DB: $D_3 + H_1$, native	12,840.9	[12,743.1 ; 12,938.6]	11,999.0
12		Web: $D_2 + H_2$, DB: $D_3 + H_1$, Docker	11,674.5	[11,584.7 ; 11,764.3]	11,024.1
13		Web: $D_2 + H_1$, DB: $D_3 + H_2$, native	356,194.7	[354,663.2 ; 357,726.3]	188,019.6
14		Web: $D_2 + H_1$, DB: $D_3 + H_2$, Docker	354,837.6	[353,323.9 ; 356,351.3]	185,830.1
15	Change customer name	Web: $D_3 + H_1$, DB: $D_2 + H_2$, native	353,910.2	[352,360.9 ; 355,459.6]	190,211.0
16		Web: $D_3 + H_1$, DB: $D_2 + H_2$, Docker	381,395.7	[379,798.5 ; 382,993.0]	196,090.5
17		Web: $D_2 + H_2$, DB: $D_3 + H_1$, native	551,412.8	[549,424.2 ; 553,401.5]	244,138.3
18		Web: $D_2 + H_2$, DB: $D_3 + H_1$, Docker	551,034.6	[548,759.9 ; 553,309.2]	279,250.8

Table 3: Results of the RESTful service experiment

All tests were run with the default configuration, which consists of a 10-minute warmup phase, a measurement phase of 60 minutes, and 5 minutes of cooldown. Table 4 provides information on the response times measured for the five operations performed by the benchmark; the configurations are the same as for the previous experiment (see Section 4.3).

As evident from the table, considerable replicability of the results was achieved only in specific cases. While the response times of the Enterprise Java Beans (EJB)-based operation „Create vehicle" indicate good replicability (Lines 1–6), the response times of the web service (WS)-based variant (Lines 7–12) show substantial differences between the configurations. This also applies to the remaining, web service-based operations. It is particularly remarkable that the response times already differ significantly when swapping the Pi devices, a change which did not have any impact on the previous experiment with RESTful services. As the differences between EJB and web services were much smaller when running the database server on a desktop machine, we assume that the difference is due to different types of database accesses, but are unable to provide an explanation at this point.

Another notable observation is that the response times are considerably lower for the Docker-based Configuration 6 than for the native Configuration 5, while it is the other way around for the other configurations. This may be another occurrence of the disk-related anomaly discussed in Experiment 1, as the respective disk H_1 is used for the database in these configurations.

Besides the unexpected differences in response times, the actual throughput achieved on the Raspberry devices does not meet the requirements of the benchmark. Consequently, all runs are considered as failures by the test driver. We therefore conclude that although running enterprise benchmarks on current Raspberry devices is technically possible, the validity of the results may be questionable. However, this may change with future, more powerful models.

Summary: *Although it is technically possible to run enterprise-oriented benchmarks like SPECjEnterprise on the Raspberry Pi, the results are questionable. The devices are not powerful enough to meet the minimum requirements of the benchmark, although the benchmark is already six years old. Furthermore, the replicability of the results was very limited in our experiments.*

5 FLUCTUATION CAUSE ANALYSIS

While our micro-benchmarking experiments from Section 4.2 and [16] indicate good replicability, even the measures of the baseline show significant deviations (0.2 of 1,6 μs for the base line, factor 3 times for SPASS-meter, factor 25 for Kieker) as well as high maximum values (65 times of the mean for the baseline, 125 times for SPASS-meter, more than 13,160 times for Kieker). The raw data contains massive response time peaks as illustrated for one out of ten experiment runs from [16] in Figure 1.

We may consider these fluctuations as system-immanent, but in the context of evaluating the Raspberry Pi for replicability of experiments, it is worth performing an analysis of potential causes. Moreover, the measurements from [9][9] indicate only some dedicated response time peaks on a server machine rather than a fusillade of peaks as in our Pi experiments. However, the fluctuations that we observed did not exhibit any kind of regular pattern that we could focus on. In order to identify candidates for root causes, we performed a systematic enumeration of potential reasons. Figure 2 illustrates the mind map we obtained from analyzing the system architecture and the involved software stack. For each potential cause, we changed the setup accordingly, re-executed the MooBench experiments for SPASS-meter on D_1 and analyzed the measurements.

[9]https://doi.org/10.5281/zenodo.165513

Line #	Operation	Configuration	Mean Response Time (in s)	99% CI Resp. Time (in s)	σ (in s)
1	Create vehicle (EJB)	Web: $D_2 + H_1$, DB: $D_3 + H_2$, native	0.235	[0.228 ; 0.242]	0.031
2		Web: $D_2 + H_1$, DB: $D_3 + H_2$, Docker	0.243	[0.236 ; 0.251]	0.030
3		Web: $D_3 + H_1$, DB: $D_2 + H_2$, native	0.266	[0.256 ; 0.275]	0.039
4		Web: $D_3 + H_1$, DB: $D_2 + H_2$, Docker	0.259	[0.250 ; 0.267]	0.036
5		Web: $D_2 + H_2$, DB: $D_3 + H_1$, native	0.293	[0.284 ; 0.303]	0.041
6		Web: $D_2 + H_2$, DB: $D_3 + H_1$, Docker	0.310	[0.300 ; 0.319]	0.041
7	Create vehicle (WS)	Web: $D_2 + H_1$, DB: $D_3 + H_2$, native	0.447	[0.411 ; 0.484]	0.156
8		Web: $D_2 + H_1$, DB: $D_3 + H_2$, Docker	0.718	[0.641 ; 0.795]	0.328
9		Web: $D_3 + H_1$, DB: $D_2 + H_2$, native	0.910	[0.807 ; 1.012]	0.436
10		Web: $D_3 + H_1$, DB: $D_2 + H_2$, Docker	1.303	[1.190 ; 1.417]	0.483
11		Web: $D_2 + H_2$, DB: $D_3 + H_1$, native	1.550	[1.457 ; 1.643]	0.396
12		Web: $D_2 + H_2$, DB: $D_3 + H_1$, Docker	0.960	[0.851 ; 1.069]	0.463
13	Purchase	Web: $D_2 + H_1$, DB: $D_3 + H_2$, native	0.750	[0.653 ; 0.847]	0.412
14		Web: $D_2 + H_1$, DB: $D_3 + H_2$, Docker	1.502	[1.273 ; 1.731]	0.972
15		Web: $D_3 + H_1$, DB: $D_2 + H_2$, native	1.991	[1.706 ; 2.276]	1.212
16		Web: $D_3 + H_1$, DB: $D_2 + H_2$, Docker	3.177	[2.844 ; 3.510]	1.417
17		Web: $D_2 + H_2$, DB: $D_3 + H_1$, native	3.830	[3.555 ; 4.106]	1.173
18		Web: $D_2 + H_2$, DB: $D_3 + H_1$, Docker	2.012	[1.708 ; 2.315]	1.289
19	Manage	Web: $D_2 + H_1$, DB: $D_3 + H_2$, native	0.576	[0.522 ; 0.630]	0.229
20		Web: $D_2 + H_1$, DB: $D_3 + H_2$, Docker	0.930	[0.819 ; 1.041]	0.473
21		Web: $D_3 + H_1$, DB: $D_2 + H_2$, native	1.139	[1.004 ; 1.275]	0.576
22		Web: $D_3 + H_1$, DB: $D_2 + H_2$, Docker	1.661	[1.502 ; 1.819]	0.675
23		Web: $D_2 + H_2$, DB: $D_3 + H_1$, native	1.954	[1.817 ; 2.091]	0.582
24		Web: $D_2 + H_2$, DB: $D_3 + H_1$, Docker	1.189	[1.037 ; 1.341]	0.648
25	Browse	Web: $D_2 + H_1$, DB: $D_3 + H_2$, native	1.194	[1.066 ; 1.321]	0.543
26		Web: $D_2 + H_1$, DB: $D_3 + H_2$, Docker	2.231	[1.950 ; 2.513]	1.197
27		Web: $D_3 + H_1$, DB: $D_2 + H_2$, native	2.814	[2.451 ; 3.178]	1.546
28		Web: $D_3 + H_1$, DB: $D_2 + H_2$, Docker	4.425	[4.004 ; 4.847]	1.792
29		Web: $D_2 + H_2$, DB: $D_3 + H_1$, native	5.190	[4.845 ; 5.535]	1.466
30		Web: $D_2 + H_2$, DB: $D_3 + H_1$, Docker	2.823	[2.426 ; 3.220]	1.688

Table 4: Results of the SPECjEnterprise experiment

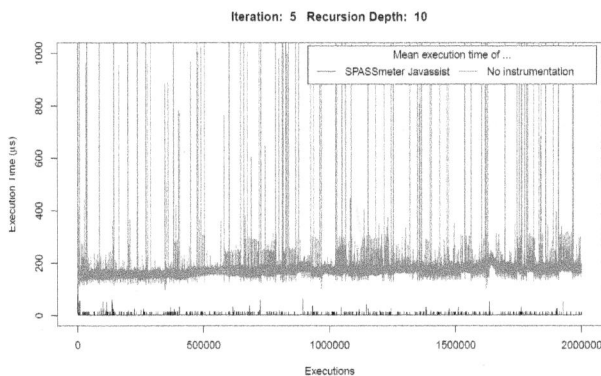

Figure 1: Response time fluctuations observed in [16].

We focused on SPASS-meter, assuming that identified causes will finally also improve the Kieker results.

We discuss now in separate sections the cause categories shown in Figure 2 starting with the 'hardware' category, and then follow a clockwise order. Within each category, we discuss the causes shown in a top-down fashion. We base our discussion on previous experiments from [16][10], but also on the new experiments. For pragmatic reasons, we performed the experiments in a different sequence, focusing first on those experiments that we considered most likely for explaining the peaks. Table 5 details the experiment sequence, the respective (incremental) base cases, descriptive statistics for the baseline and and the SPASS-meter runs, both also indicating the number of peaks. For illustrating our discussion, we count a value as a peak if it is larger than than 5 times the mean value. For the whole data set underlying Figure 1 we identified 1,155 such peaks.

5.1 Hardware

The hardware of the different Raspberry types is rather standardized as detailed in Section 2.1, i.e., the configuration spectrum for a Raspberry Pi is rather restricted compared with desktop, laptop or server machines. This restricted configuration space eases the identification of variation causes.

---

[10] https://doi.org/10.5281/zenodo.1003075

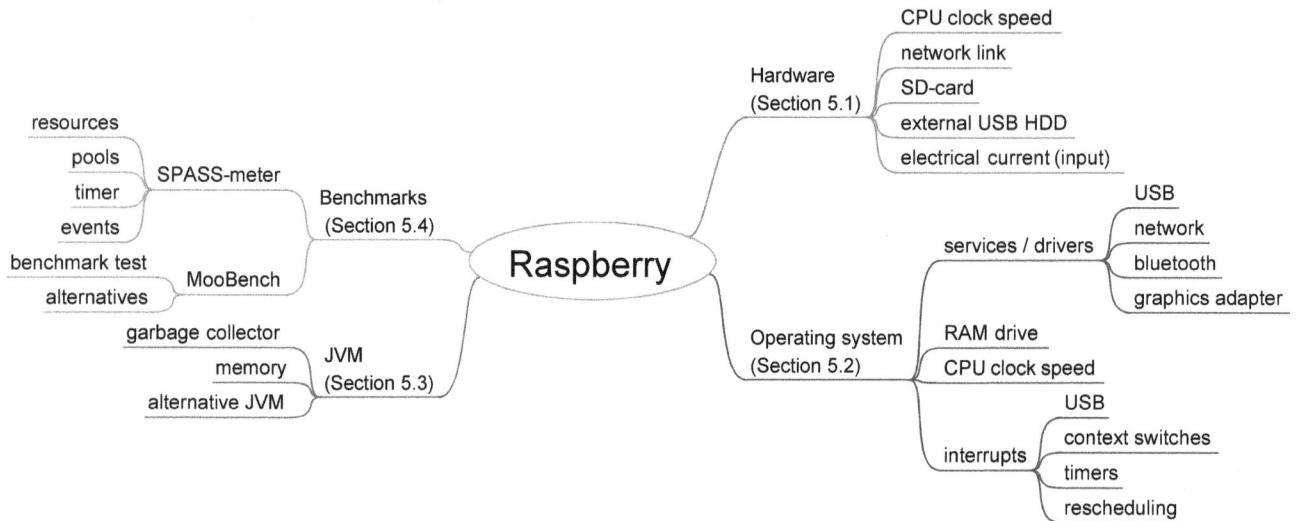

Figure 2: Cause-tree for response time fluctuations.

- The CPU of a Pi allows for changing *clock speeds*, in particular to save energy. On the Raspberry Pi platform, the Raspbian operating system takes active control over the CPU clock speed as we will detail in Section 5.2.
- The *network link* used to control the experiments was active during the experiments and may have caused superfluous interrupts. However, benchmark runs[10] with disconnected network link, background execution of the benchmarks or even an operating network connection during foreground execution showed similar response times and deviations.
- The operating system of a Raspberry device is typically installed on an *exchangeable SD-card*. The Pi sets we obtained contained class-4 SD cards supporting a minimum sequential write speed of 4MByte/s[11]. Previous experiments[10] were also run with a class-10 SD card. For SPASS-meter, the faster card led to an increase of the average response time of 5% as well as an increase of factor 7 of the response time and similar deviations. In contrast, for the I/O intensive Kieker benchmarks, the average response time dropped by 50%, the deviation by factor 2 and the maximum response time by factor 2.6. As a result, a faster SD card can lead to improvements for response time, but may not significantly influence response time peaks (similar to Table 5, Id 1).
- Instead of running the benchmarks on an SD card, we considered a potentially faster *external USB hard disk*. Although Raspberry 3 devices ship only with USB 2.0 ports, previous results [16] show that an external USB hard disk can lead to significant speedup for I/O intensive benchmarks, e.g., for Kieker around factor 4.5, but also to a slowdown, e.g., for

SPASS-meter by roughly 5%. In case of speedups, deviation and maximum response time dropped, e.g., for Kieker by around 95%, but the response time peaks did not disappear (similar to Table 5, Id 1).

- The Raspberry Pi needs at least 700 mA of *electrical current*[12]. Power adapters just fulfilling this specification may affect stability and performance if additional USB devices are connected. We experienced this when replacing the shipped power adapters (2.5 A) with a 2.0 A adapter. For example, in case of the SPEC benchmark in Section 4.4 the results differed significantly. However, we can exclude this cause as the SPASS-meter experiments were conducted with the shipped adapters.

Although the storage device may significantly impact the performance, in particular for I/O intensive benchmarks, the hardware category did not lead to a clear cause for the response time peaks.

5.2 Operating system

Nowadays, an operating system consists of several layers including kernel, drivers and services, whereby each of these layers may cause fluctuations in a benchmark experiment.

- *System services* may allocate resources that cause fluctuations in the measurements. Therefore, unneeded services like window system, virus scanner or automated updates should be disabled. Such services are not included in the Raspbian versions we used for our experiments. For identifying further problematic services, we analyzed the running processes and

---

[11]https://www.sdcard.org/developers/overview/speed_class/

[12]https://www.raspberrypi.org/documentation/hardware/raspberrypi/power/README.md

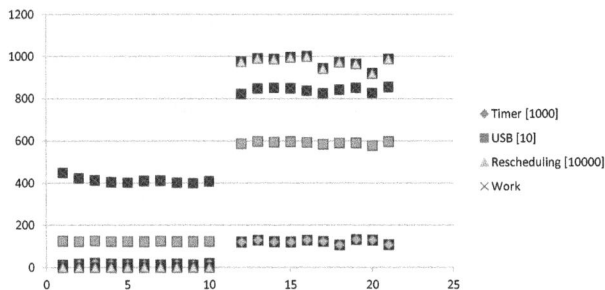

Figure 3: Interrupts during MooBench executions for baseline (left) and SPASS-meter (right).

disabled in subsequent experiments services, such as bluetooth, service discovery (avahi-daemon), extended keyboard handling (triggerhappy), regular task scheduling (cron), or the network service. Table 5, Id 6 is a representative example illustrating that this did not lead to significant changes.

- To reduce the impact of I/O operations during the benchmarks, we created a *RAM drive* with a capacity 100 MBytes so that the JVM could still operate with a 512 MByte heap as described in [16]. However, the RAM drive was too small to store all benchmark results. Therefore, we modified the benchmark script so that the results were moved from the RAM drive to the SD card after completing an individual benchmark step. As shown in Table 5, Id 5, this did not significantly change the results.

- *Swapping* memory pages from/to CPU caches or storage devices may cause response time fluctuations. We disabled swapping for a benchmark run (Table 5, Id 13), but without significant effect on the response time results.

- The Raspbian versions that we used in our experiments adjust the *CPU clock speed* dynamically to the system load. The default mode is ondemand, i.e., for a Pi 3, the operating system switches the CPU clock speed between minimum (600 MHz) and maximum (1.2 GHz) clock speed. Such abrupt frequency changes may cause response time fluctuations. In our experiments, we fixed the CPU frequency either to powersave mode (600 MHz) or performance mode (1.2 GHz). While the powersave mode increased the response time by a factor of 2 and caused an increase of the standard deviation as well as more response time peaks (Table 5, Id 12), the performance mode did not significantly change the results (Table 5, Id 11).

- Hardware and software can cause *interrupts* that suspend normal program execution. A comparison of the system interrupt table before and after a benchmark execution indicated a high number of timer, USB (representing correlated SD-card and direct memory access) and rescheduling interrupts. Figure 3 illustrates the aggregated results for all CPU cores running the baseline and SPASS-meter. The baseline produced fewer interrupts than the SPASS-meter benchmark. This is reasonable as SPASS-meter applies scheduled execution of some probe collections. While we analyze modifications to SPASS-meter in this regard in Section 5.4, we focus here on the rescheduling interrupts To analyze the effects,

we ran the experiments while pinning the benchmarks to specific CPU cores. Utilizing only one core increased the timer and work interrupts by a factor of 2 and avoided more than 98% of the rescheduling interrupts, but also caused a significant performance drop and more response time peaks (Table 5, Id 9). Running the benchmark on two cores reduced the timer interrupts by 37% and led to a similar performance as utilizing all cores (Table 5, Id 10).

Despite some effort and applying typical benchmark preparations such as disabling system services, we did not find a clear root cause for the peaks in the operating system category.

5.3 Java Virtual Machine

The next layer that can influence Java benchmark results is the JVM itself. As described in Section 3, we used an Oracle JVM for ARM in our experiments.

- By default, the Oracle JVM for ARM utilizes a sequential *garbage collector*, while the JVM for Intel processors relies on parallel garbage collection. We forced parallel garbage collection through a command line switch during the benchmark experiments, but this increased the mean response time by 15% as shown in (Table 5, Id 3).

- The fluctuations could be caused by properties of the specific JVM implementation. However, the alternative OpenJDK JVM for ARM does not provide a just-in-time compiler and was, thus, in our trials by orders of magnitude slower, making direct comparisons unfeasible.

Although the JVM or the JVM settings could be a reason for the fluctuations, we were not able to identify a clear root cause.

5.4 Benchmarks

The final layer is the program running within a JVM, in our case MooBench, SPASS-meter, and Kieker. Regarding SPASS-meter, we identified four different potential causes:

- In the original MooBench setup, information on all supported resources is collected. In particular, monitoring the memory usage is a resource-consuming task [10] that stresses the internal event-processing. In this experiment (Table 5, Id 4), we changed the monitoring scope to observe response time as the only resource. This improved the average response time for SPASS-meter by 11% (we classify the change of the average response time of the baseline as an outlier) and reduced the extreme peaks by factor 2.

- As discussed in [9], the initialization of internal object pools for instance reuse may have significant impact on the performance. We re-visited (and adjusted) the object pools of SPASS-meter, which caused only a minor improvement of the mean response time (Table 5, Id 2), while also increasing the maximum (peak) response time and the number of peaks.

- SPASS-meter uses a timer to regularly pull process and system-level resource consumptions. We disabled this timer, which is not relevant for the benchmarking results here. Reconsidering the interrupts discussed Section 5.2, we recorded roughly the same number of USB/SD card interrupts and

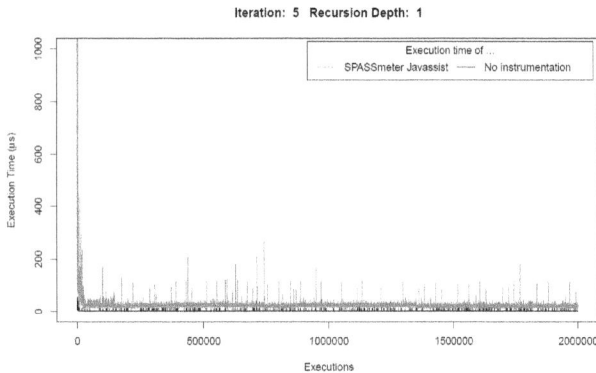

Figure 4: Response time with recursion-depth 1 instead.

work interrupts, while the number of timer interrupts increased by 14% and the number of context switches decreased by 17%. As indicated in (Table 5, Id 7), the mean response time slightly improved by 2.7% and the number of peaks dropped by 39% for most of the following experiments.

- SPASS-meter uses a producer-consumer pattern to asynchronously process collected probe information. For experiments, synchronous event processing can be used [10], which may increase the response time but also reduce threading effects in the timer interrupts. Using this mode, mean and median response time did not change significantly (Table 5, Id 8), the standard deviation increased by factor 4 and the maximum response time by factor 31. As expected, the number of timer interrupts decreased, while the amount of rescheduling and work interrupts did not change.

MooBench itself could also be a cause for the fluctuations. In particular, the parts of the benchmark running during the test could influence the results. We therefore changed the recursion depth in the benchmark from 10 to 1. Although this did not affect the baseline measures (Table 5, Id 14), it did reduce the number of peaks by 67%. Even if smaller peaks remained, the huge peaks disappeared as illustrated by the response time graph in Figure 4. Moreover, the average response time, standard deviation as well as minimum and maximum response time improved significantly.

One important observation is that the *baseline*, i.e., the execution of the benchmark test case without any monitoring, contains a high number of (relative) peaks. This fact remained irrespective of all experiments that we conducted.

5.5 Summary

We identified the recursive benchmark test as a trigger for the massive response time peaks we observed. However, the underlying reason is still unclear. In comparison, the results in [9] (Intel Core i5-2500, 3,3 GHz, 6MB cache, kernel 3.2) only contained few solitary peaks using the same MooBench and SPASS-meter versions without changing the recursion depth. We can imagine that the peaks are caused due to different CPUs/caches, operating systems/kernels or JVMs. As mentioned in Section 5.3, we observed similar fluctuations in the laptop trial (CPU i7-4500U, 1,8 GHz, 4MB cache, kernel 4.8).

Although the cache sizes of the Pi are much smaller (cf. Section 2), we do not believe the CPU/cache to be the reason, as the cache sizes of the non-Pi machines are of roughly the same size. However, the Linux kernel versions and the JDK versions differ between the setup used in [9] (JDK 1.7) and our experiments (all kernel 4.x and JDK 1.8). Therefore, it seems more probable that either the kernel or the JVM apply different scheduling/optimization strategies. Confirming this hypothesis would require more cross-platform experiments, which are out of scope of this paper. Furthermore, we identified some optimizations opportunities regarding the application of SPASS-meter (focusing on the relevant resources to be monitored) as well as its implementation (avoiding unused timers, better initialization of shared instance pools). We also identified potential issues of a benchmark setup that can impact the results such as using the 'wrong' garbage collector, setting the CPU to a fixed frequency, or trying to pin the benchmark to less CPU cores than needed.

6 RELATED WORK

Replicability and reproducibility are well-known problems in empirical software research. However, in particular computational replicability is known to be only episodically aimed at in experimental computer science [3]. A major reason for this are that reproducing experiments from scratch is time-consuming, error-prone, and sometimes just infeasible, typically due to insufficient documentation of the experiment, an experiment setup not running on the target environment, missing libraries, different library versions, or the inability to install the required dependencies [2, 3, 6, 9]. Even in standardized high-performance environments, replicability is difficult to achieve [14].

Several approaches for achieving replicability are discussed in the literature. Similar to our approach, Tso et al. employ Raspberry Pi devices to create an affordable, replicable environments for distributed computing, called the Glasgow PiCloud [22]. This environment consists of about 50 devices, which are used to build a scale model of a data center. The PiCloud also makes use of container-based virtualization. However, the containers are used as a replacement for virtual machines, which are not feasible on the Raspberry Pi due to the limited resources and the lack of hardware support, not for replicating experiments. A similar setup with more than 300 devices is described by Abrahamsson et al. [1].

Instead of replicating performance experiments locally, experiments may also be run in Cloud environments. Although most Cloud providers offer standardized instance types, these types are often not clearly and sufficiently specified [12], and may differ significantly in performance. Furthermore, the provider may move virtual machines to different hosts or even change the underlying hardware or the type specification at its own discretion, posing a threat to replicability.

De Oliveira et al. present an infrastructure called DataMill [7], which allows to run experiments on a pool of different worker machines provided by the DataMill community. This infrastructure aims at producing robust and replicable results by running the experiments on multiple devices with slightly different specifications, thus creating a results less dependent on the specifics of a particular setup. Furthermore, this infrastructure allows researchers to explore how particular changes to the environment (e.g., compiler

Id	Experiment (base)	Baseline						SPASS-meter					
		mean	σ	min	max	95% CI	peaks	mean	σ	min	max	95% CI	peaks
1	from [16]	1.6	0.2	1.5	105.2	[1.6;1.6]	1,667	164.8	44.1	91.9	19,228.7	[164.8;164.8]	1,155
2	object pools (1)	1.6	0.3	1.5	352.2	[1.6;1.6]	1,864	152.3	142.5	89.8	370,604.0	[152.3;152.4]	**818**
3	parallel GC (2)	1.6	0.2	1.5	107.5	[1.6;1.6]	1,632	**194.4**	56.7	110.1	27,715.9	[195.4;194.5]	**6,901**
4	time resources (2)	1.6	0.3	1.5	358.4	[1.6;1.6]	1,729	**146.3**	34.9	88.5	13,034.8	[146.2;146.3]	406
5	ramdrive (2)	1.6	0.2	1.5	132.9	[1.6;1.6]	1,685	146.8	40.0	90.6	19,453.1	[146.7;146.7]	534
6	services (5)	1.6	0.3	1.5	207.2	[1.6;1.6]	1,774	150.5	39.2	91.0	24,952.0	[150.4;150.5]	528
7	SPASS timer(6)	1.6	0.3	1.5	545.9	[1.6;1.6]	1,695	146.1	36.8	91.5	10,972.5	[146.2;146.3]	321
8	SPASS events (7)	1.6	0.2	1.5	108.6	[1.6;1.6]	1,773	146.7	157.7	86.7	349,777.3	[146.6;146.7]	333
9	one CPU core (6)	1.6	0.3	1.5	312.5	[1.6;1.6]	**2,223**	492.8	427.1	86.0	13,560.1	[492.6;493.1]	**37,360**
10	two CPU cores (6)	1.6	0.3	1.5	616.2	[1.6;1.6]	1,818	147.4	46.7	89.7	54,325.9	[147.3;147.4]	348
11	max CPU clock (6)	1.6	0.2	1.5	98.2	[1.6;1.6]	1,628	148.1	41.0	108.5	12,913.6	[148.1;148.2]	359
12	min CPU clock (6)	**3.1**	**0.5**	**3.0**	**945.6**	**[3.1;3.1]**	**3,116**	**294.8**	**80.5**	**177.0**	**120,450.8**	**[294.7;294.8]**	752
13	no swapping (6)	1.6	0.3	1.5	185.1	[1.6;1.6]	1,704	147.4	40.6	88.9	13,771.2	[147.4;147.4]	388
14	no recursion (6)	1.4	0.2	1.3	191.6	[1.4;1.4]	1,534	17.6	1.8	11.35	3,361.3	[17.6;17.6]	53

Table 5: Summary of selected case experiments on response times in μs. Notable changes are shown in bold font.

switches) affect their experiments. A similar goal is pursued by the PerfDiff framework by Zhuang et al. [24].

As previously mentioned, replication of performance experiments also requires replicating the surrounding software environment. We used Docker containers for this purpose, which is recommended by several authors [2, 5]. Chirigati et al. present ReproZip [3, 4], a tool which facilitates creating container images by tracking the accessed files during an experiment by monitoring system calls, and automatically adding them to the image.

Another approach to replicating the software environment is to provide fully configured virtual machines, as suggested by [11]. However, virtual machine images can be very large, and since the entire operating system is included in the image, licensing issues may occur. A third approach relies on using configuration management tools able to automatically set up a machine according to pre-defined rules, such as Ansible,[13] Chef,[14] or Puppet[15] [15].

In order to identify potential root causes for the fluctuations in our previous experiments, we furthermore performed a root cause analysis. Typically, a root cause analysis consists of steps like data collection, causal factor charting, root cause identification and recommendation generation [20]. In our case, performing a complete data collection was not feasible, so we opted for an incremental analysis with interleaved factor charting and progressing based on excluded root causes. Of course, an automated approach to root cause detection would be highly desirable, in particular to reduce the manual effort. Existing automated approaches typically focus on one specific layer of the software stack such regression testing [13], web applications and related services [17], or single programs that can be instrumented to obtain the calling context tree [24]. However, in our situation, we applied an incremental manual process as in statistical debugging [21] or in [9], but here considering a wide range of potential causes across multiple layers of the involved hardware and software stack.

---
[13]https://www.ansible.com/
[14]http://www.chef.io/
[15]http://www.puppet.com/

7 CONCLUSIONS AND FUTURE WORK

In this section, we conclude the paper, present lessons learned from our experiments, and point out directions for future work.

7.1 Conclusions

In this paper, we have presented results and experiences from different experiments to evaluate to what extent the Raspberry Pi and Docker can be used as a platform for replicable performance experiments. Furthermore, we presented a systematic root cause analysis to identify potential sources for variance. Below, we present the answers to the research questions presented in the introduction.

RQ 1: We conclude from the experimental results that the Raspberry Pi appears to be well suited for replicating microbenchmarks, in particular benchmarks that are not very I/O-intensive. Replicating macroscopic experiments may work as well, but depends on the availability of comparable peripherals such as storage devices. The platform is less suited for enterprise-oriented benchmarks, as it may lack the sheer processing power or memory capacity to meet their requirements.

RQ 2: Docker has proven to be a valuable tool for packaging experiments in a replicable way. However, this comes at the cost of slightly increased variance in the results, and a potential performance impact. Furthermore, the virtualization can be a source of additional complexity, such as the connectivity issue observed in Experiment 4.

RQ 3: Despite considerable effort, we identified triggers for the fluctuations observed in the experiments, but, in the end, we were unable to pinpoint root causes. However, our results do not indicate any systematic flaw of the platform itself.

In conclusion, we think that Docker on the Raspberry Pi is indeed a viable option for building replicable performance microbenchmarks.

7.2 Threats to Validity

We see the the greatest threats to the validity of our results in the selection of the experiments and the small number of devices that were available to use. Furthermore, most of our experiments were run on the Java Virtual Machine, so that the results may not be transferable to experiments running in other environments. As discussed in the Future Work section below, we intend to run additional experiments to further increase the validity of our results.

7.3 Lessons Learned

During our experiments, we learned several lessons about running performance experiments with the Raspberry Pi and Docker, which we summarize below:

- *Docker facilitates running benchmarks and fosters experimentation*, especially due to the fact that containers can be easily (re-)created in a defined state.
- *I/O-heavy experiments should be executed only on hard disks.* We broke two SD cards during our experiments due to high write counts.
- *As soon as peripherals are involved, power consumption is an issue.* Common USB power supplies, such as the ones shipped with mobile phones or tablet computers, provide too little electrical current for a Raspberry Pi and a USB hard drive under heavy load.
- *Container networking can be tricky*, as seen in the SPECjEnterprise experiment.
- *Merging and analyzing* experiment results created at different geographical locations as in our case worked pretty well, also in particular to agreements on using the same formats, naming conventions and tools.
- *Legal issues may prevent publication of container images.* Some software components can be used free of charge, but limitations may apply regarding redistribution. For example, it is currently unclear whether distributing Oracle's JDK in a Docker container is compliant with the underlying license.[16]

7.4 Future Work and Directions

In our future work, we intend to extend our analysis to locate potential root causes for the performance fluctuations. We also plan to further evaluate the viability of the Raspberry Pi as well as other single-board computers for additional benchmarks. As we expect the next generation of Raspberry Pi to be equipped with more memory and computing power, executing more demanding benchmarks might become possible in the future. We furthermore intend to conduct experiments on a larger number of Pi devices to reduce the influence of potential device-specific deviations.

Moreover, we envision that the results of different researchers in the direction of replicable performance experiments could foster a community practice, including best practices and default experiment workflows, but also accepted technical means, such as Docker, standardized hardware, or even hardware-benchmark combinations specified and endorsed by benchmark organizations. Further, a public experiment repository containing reference Docker experiment images, but also standardized installation images for the operating system to avoid uncontrolled changes to the host system would be desirable. First steps towards such a community practice are visible as numerous conferences and journals encourage researchers to also submit artifacts, including Docker images.

Future steps might include public experiment repositories or even an accessible science (Pi) cloud. This would facilitate the sharing of experiments between researchers and pave the way for artifact and cross-validation tracks or new publication models, such as, for instance, proposed in [3].

REFERENCES

[1] P. Abrahamsson, S. Helmer, N. Phaphoom, L. Nicolodi, N. Preda, L. Miori, M. Angriman, J. Rikkilä, X. Wang, K. Hamily, and S. Bugoloni. 2013. Affordable and Energy-Efficient Cloud Computing Clusters: The Bolzano Raspberry Pi Cloud Cluster Experiment. In *Intl. Conference on Cloud Computing Technology and Science*.
[2] C. Boettiger. 2015. An Introduction to Docker for Reproducible Research. *SIGOPS Oper. Syst. Rev.* 49, 1 (2015).
[3] F. Chirigati, R. Capone, R. Rampin, J. Freire, and D. Shasha. 2016. A Collaborative Approach to Computational Reproducibility. *Inf. Syst.* 59, C (July 2016), 95–97.
[4] F. Chirigati, D. Shasha, and J. Freire. 2013. Packing Experiments for Sharing and Publication. In *Proc. ACM SIGMOD International Conference on Management of Data*.
[5] J. Cito and H. C. Gall. 2016. Using Docker Containers to Improve Reproducibility in Software Engineering Research. In *Intl. Conference on Software Engineering Companion*. 906–907.
[6] A. Davison. 2012. Automated Capture of Experiment Context for Easier Reproducibility in Computational Research. *Computing in Science & Engineering* 14 (2012), 48–56.
[7] A. B. de Oliveira, J.-C. Petkovich, T. Reidemeister, and S. Fischmeister. 2013. DataMill: Rigorous Performance Evaluation Made Easy. In *Intl. Conference on Performance Engineering*. 137–148.
[8] Docker, Inc. 2017. Dockerfile reference. (2017). https://docs.docker.com/engine/reference/builder/.
[9] H. Eichelberger, A. Sass, and K. Schmid. 2016. From Reproducibility Problems to Improvements: A Journey. In *Symposium on Software Performance*.
[10] H. Eichelberger and K. Schmid. 2014. Flexible Resource Monitoring of Java Programs. *Journal of Systems and Software* 93 (2014).
[11] I. P. Gent and L. Kotthoff. 2014. Recomputation.Org: Experiences of Its First Year and Lessons Learned. In *Proc. of the 2014 IEEE/ACM 7th International Conference on Utility and Cloud Computing*.
[12] Q. He, S. Zhou, B. Kobler, D. Duffy, and T. McGlynn. 2010. Case Study for Running HPC Applications in Public Clouds. In *Intl. Symposium on High Performance Distributed Computing*. 395–401.
[13] C. Heger, J. Happe, and R. Farahbod. 2013. Automated Root Cause Isolation of Performance Regressions During Software Development. In *Intl. Conference on Performance Engineering*. 27–38.
[14] T. Hoefler and R. Belli. 2015. Scientific Benchmarking of Parallel Computing Systems: Twelve ways to tell the masses when reporting performance results. In *Intl. Conference on Supercomputing*.
[15] I. Jimenez, M. Sevilla, N. Watkins, C. Maltzahn, J. Lofstead, K. Mohror, A. Arpaci-Dusseau, and R. Arpaci-Dusseau. 2017. The Popper Convention: Making Reproducible Systems Evaluation Practical. In *Intl. Parallel and Distributed Processing Symposium Workshops*.
[16] H. Knoche and H. Eichelberger. 2017. The Raspberry Pi: A Platform for Replicable Performance Benchmarks?. In *Symposium on Software Performance*. accepted, available on request.
[17] J. P. Magalhães and L. M. Silva. 2011. Root-cause Analysis of Performance Anomalies in Web-based Applications. In *Symposium on Applied Computing*. 209–216.
[18] R. D. Peng. 2011. Reproducible Research in Computational Science. *Science* 334, 6060 (2011).
[19] M. Richardson. 2016. Docker comes to Raspberry Pi. (2016). https://www.raspberrypi.org/blog/docker-comes-to-raspberry-pi.
[20] J.J. Rooney and L.N.V. Heuvel. 2004. Root cause analysis for beginners. *Quality Progress* 37 (2004), 45–53.
[21] L. Song and S. Lu. 2014. Statistical Debugging for Real-world Performance Problems. *SIGPLAN Not.* 49, 10 (2014), 561–578.
[22] F. P. Tso, D. R. White, S. Jouet, J. Singer, and D. P. Pezaros. 2013. The Glasgow Raspberry Pi Cloud: A Scale Model for Cloud Computing Infrastructures. In *Intl. Conference on Distributed Computing Systems Workshops*.
[23] J. Waller, N. C. Ehmke, and W. Hasselbring. 2015. Including Performance Benchmarks into Continuous Integration to Enable DevOps. *Software Engineering Notes* 40, 2 (2015).
[24] C. Zhuang, S. Kim, M. Serrano, and J.-D. Choi. 2008. PerfDiff: A Framework for Performance Difference Analysis in a Virtual Machine Environment. In *Intl. Symposium on Code Generation and Optimization*. 4–13.

---

[16]see http://blog.takipi.com/running-java-on-docker-youre-breaking-the-law/

Author Index